SOUTH AMERICA

Pages 72–73

75

74

AFRICA

Pages 48–49

50–51

47

NORTH AMERICA

Pages 54–55

58–59

56–57

60–61

64–65

68

66

67

62–63

69

70

GENERAL MAPS

AUSTRALASIA

Pages 32–33

34

35

CITY PLANS

San Francisco 91
Los Angeles 91
Chicago 89
Ottawa 89
Toronto 89
Montreal 89
Boston 89
New York 90
Washington 91
Mexico City 92
Copenhagen 83
Amsterdam 81
Brussels 81
London 79
Paris 79
Barcelona 80
Madrid 80
Geneva 82
Milan 82
Rome 80
Stockholm 83
Hamburg 82
Berlin 82
Vienna 81
Athens 83
Istanbul 88
Jerusalem 88
Cairo 88
Moscow 83
Beijing 84
Seoul 85
Tokyo 85
Osaka 85
Shanghai 84
Hong Kong 84
Delhi 87
Bombay 87
Calcutta 87
Bangkok 84
Singapore 87
Nairobi 88
São Paulo 92
Rio de Janeiro 92
Santiago 92
Buenos Aires 92
Perth 86
Melbourne 86
Sydney 86
Auckland 86

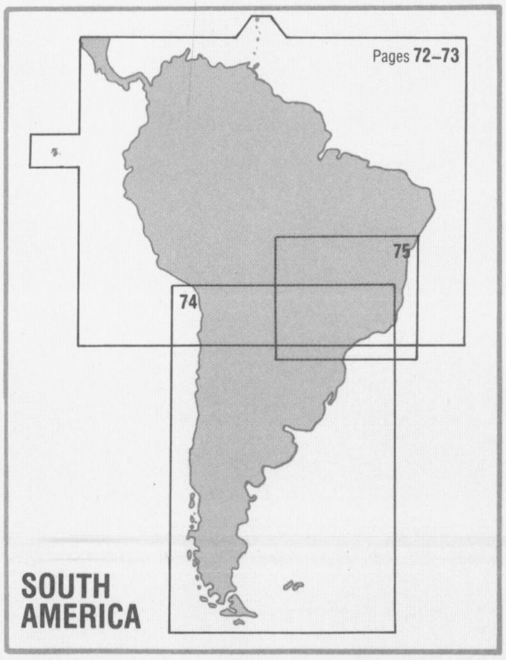

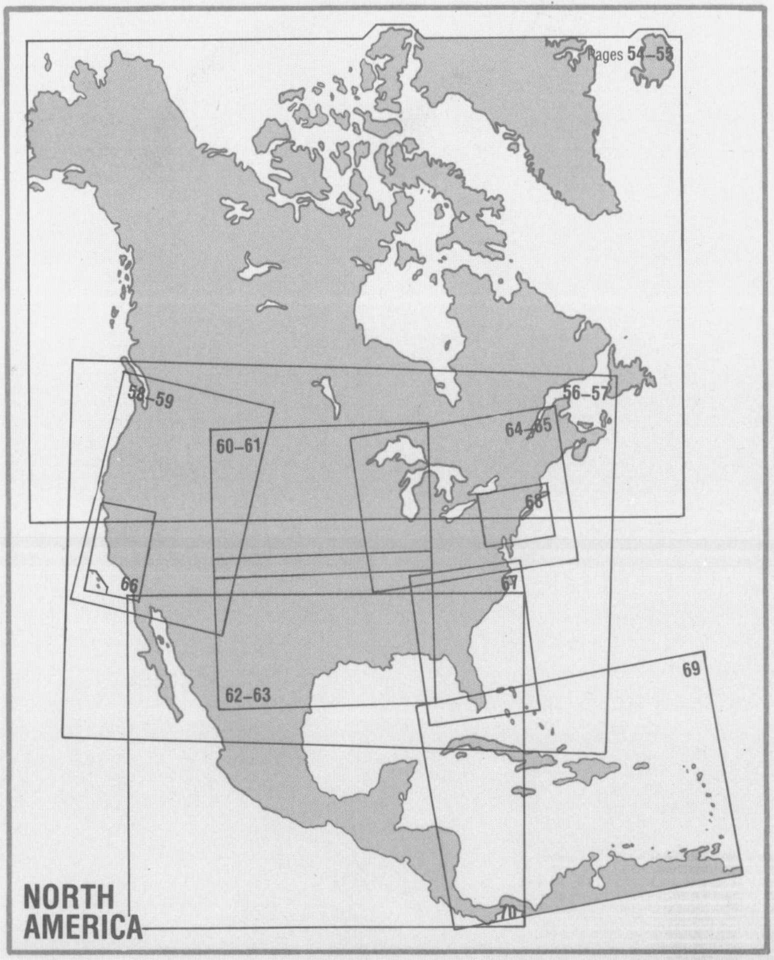

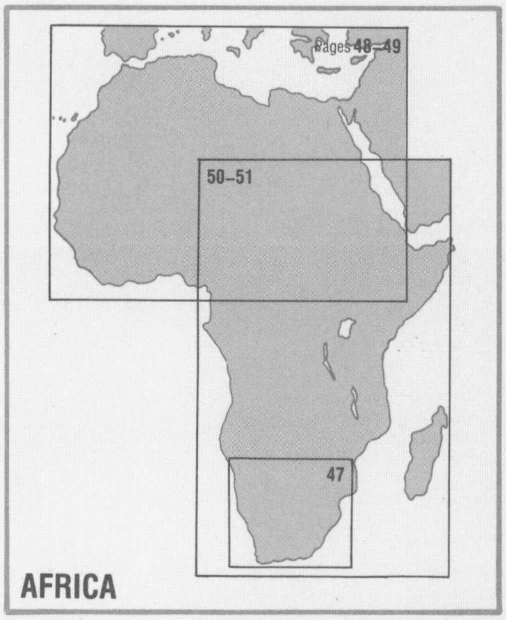

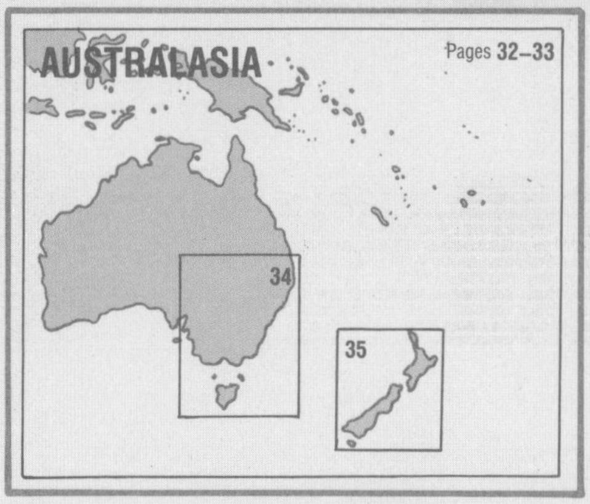

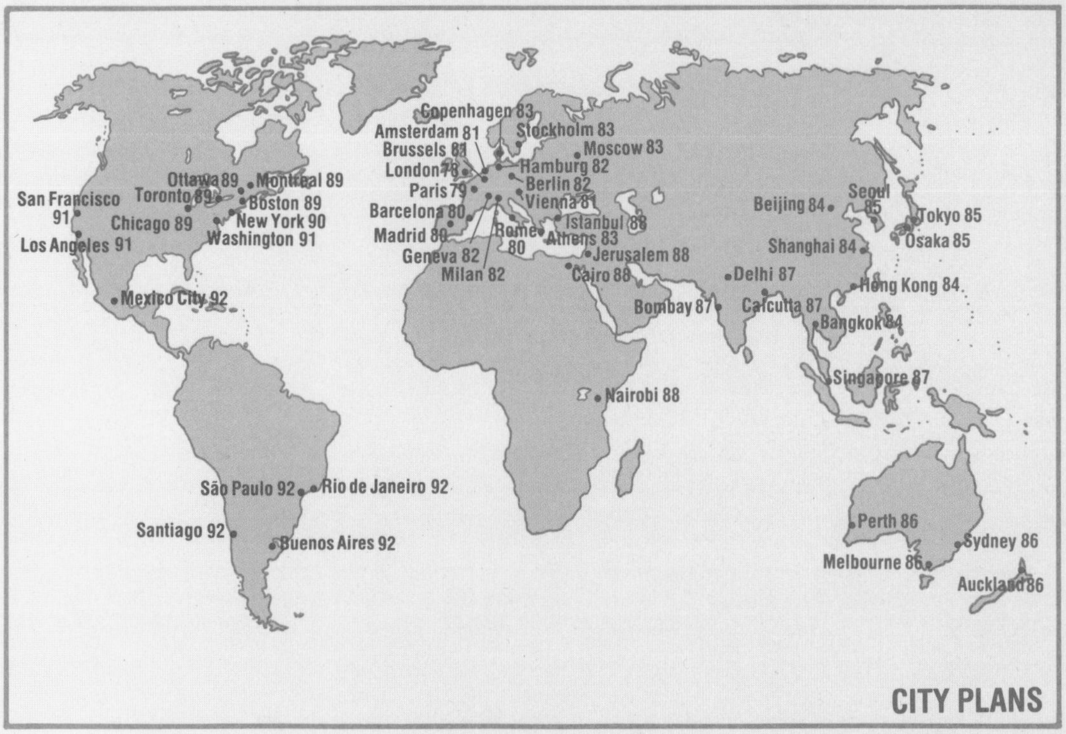

THE TIMES ATLAS OF THE WORLD

FAMILY EDITION

TIMES BOOKS
London

The Times Atlas of the World
Family Edition

Published in 1995 by
Times Books, London
77-85 Fulham Palace Road
Hammersmith
London W6 8JB

First edition published by Times Books 1988
Reprinted 1988
Reprinted with revisions 1989, 1990, 1991
Second edition 1992
Reprinted with revisions 1993 (twice)
Third edition 1995, revised 1995

Printed in Italy

ISBN 0 7230 0809 4

HH8104

Maps and index prepared by
HarperCollins*Cartographic*, Edinburgh

Geographical Dictionary prepared by
Professor B.W. Atkinson

Physical Earth Maps
Duncan Mackay

Design
Ivan Dodd

The publishers would like to extend their grateful thanks to the following:

Mrs J. Candy, Geographical Research Associates, Maidenhead
Flag information provided and authenticated by the Flag Institute, Chester
Mr P.J.M. Geelan, Place-name consultant
Mr Michael Hendrie, Astronomy Correspondent, *The Times*, London
Mr H.A.G. Lewis OBE, Geographical consultant to *The Times*

British Library Cataloguing in Publication Data.
A catalogue record for this book is available from the British Library.

This, *The Times Atlas of the World, Family Edition,* has been extensively revised since it was first published in 1988. This is the third edition of this popular atlas. It is a reference work for use in the home, office or school, for those who travel the world and those, like Francis Bacon, who journey only "in map and chart".

An index of no fewer than 30,000 entries, keyed to the main map plates, will aid those who, whilst familiar with the name of a place, are uncertain of just where it lies on a map.

It is by no means always easy to ascertain the correct title and status of a country as distinct from its everyday name used on maps. The list of states and territories gives in addition to name, title and status, the population and area, the national currency, the major religions and the national flag.

Maps, being an efficient way of storing and displaying information, are used to amplify the list of states and territories and the geographical comparisons of the continents, oceans, lakes and islands. They form the basis of the section on earthquakes, volcanoes, economic minerals, vegetation, temperature, rainfall and population.

Maps are also, by nature, illustrative and a 14-page section shows the world's major physical features in the way they appear from space but with the names of the features added.

Amongst the statistical data contained in the Atlas is a listing of the major metropolitan areas with their populations. For the past several decades there has been, throughout the world, an accelerating flow of people from the land to towns and cities and especially the major cities, some of which now contain the bulk of the national population. Growth in air travel has turned those same cities into centres of tourism. Influx of population and the demands of tourism have enhanced the status of the cities. Generous space has, therefore, been allocated to maps of the major cities and their environs.

Geographical names in this Atlas are given in their anglicized (conventional) form where such a form is in current use. Other names are given in their national Roman alphabet or else converted into English by transliteration (letter to letter) or transcription (sound to sound). Because Roman alphabet letters, sometimes modified, are pronounced in a variety of ways, a brief guide to pronunciation has been included. The whole is supplemented by a dictionary of geographical terms.

In the names, in the portrayal of international boundaries and in the list of states and territories, the aim has been to show the situation as it pertains in the area at the time of going to press. This must not be taken as an endorsement by the publishers of the status of the territories concerned. The aim throughout has been to show things as they are. In that way the Atlas will best serve the reader to whom, it is hoped, it will bring interest, benefit and continuing pleasure.

H.A.G. Lewis, OBE
Geographical Consultant to *The Times*

INTRODUCTORY SECTION

States & Territories of the World *4–43*

Geographical Comparisons: *44–47*
Continents, metropolitan areas, mountain heights, islands, oceans, seas, rivers, drainage basins and lakes.

Physical Earth
North America *48*
Central America *50*
Antarctica & South America *52*
Africa *54*
Europe *56*
Asia *58*
Australasia *60*

Solar System *62*

The Earth *63*

Earthquakes & Volcanoes *64*
Economic Minerals

Temperature: January & July *65*

Annual Rainfall *66*
Natural Vegetation

Population Density *67*
Population Change

Time Zones *68*

Front Endpaper:
Locator guide to World Maps and City Plans

Rear Endpaper:
Table of distances between the major Cities of the World

THE MAPS

Key to Symbols on maps *1*
Nations of the World **1:70M** *2,3*
Nations of Europe **1:15M** *4,5*
England Wales **1:2M** *6,7*
Scotland **1:2M** *8*
Ireland **1:2M** *9*
British Isles & the North Sea **1:5M** *10,11*
Scandinavia & the Baltic **1:7.5M** *12*
Netherlands Belgium **1:2.5M** *13*
France **1:5M** *14*
Spain Portugal **1:5M** *15*
Italy & the Balkans **1:5M** *16,17*
Germany & Central Europe **1:5M** *18,19*
Eastern Europe **1:10M** *20,21*
Nations of Asia & Australasia **1:40M** *22,23*
Northern Asia **1:20M** *24,25*
Eastern Asia **1:20M** *26,27*
Japan Korea **1:5M** *28,29*
South-East Asia, Mainland **1:10M** *30*
Central China **1:10M** *31*
Australia & South West Pacific **1:20M** *32,33*
South-East Australia **1:7.5M** *34*
New Zealand **1:5M** *35*
Indian & Pacific Oceans **1:60M** *36,37*
South Asia & Middle East **1:20M** *38,39*
Turkey Syria Iraq Iran **1:7.5M** *40,41*
Northern India **1:7.5M** *42,43*
The Ganges Plain **1:4M** *43*
Southern India **1:7.5M** *44*
Israel Lebanon Cyprus **1:2.5M** *45*
Nations of Africa **1:40M** *46*
South Africa **1:7.5M** *47*
Northern Africa **1:15M** *48,49*
Central & Southern Africa **1:15M** *50,51*
Atlantic Ocean **1:60M** *52*
Nations of North America **1:35M** *53*
Canada **1:15M** *54,55*
United States of America **1:12.5M** *56,57*
Western USA **1:5M** *58,59*
North Central USA **1:5M** *60,61*
South Central USA **1:5M** *62,63*
USA & Canada: The Great Lakes **1:5M** *64,65*
California & Hawaii **1:2.5M & 1:5M** *66*
Florida & South East USA **1:5M** *67*
USA: Atlantic Seaboard **1:2.5M** *68*
Caribbean **1:10M** *69*
Mexico & Central America **1:15M** *70*
Nations of South America **1:35M** *71*
Northern South America **1:15M** *72,73*
Southern South America **1:15M** *74*
South East Brazil **1:7.5M** *75*
Polar Regions **1:40M** *76*

CITY PLANS

Key to symbols on city plans *77*
London *78*
Paris *79*
Rome Madrid Barcelona *80*
Vienna Amsterdam Brussels *81*
Hamburg Berlin Geneva Milan *82*
Copenhagen Stockholm Athens Moscow *83*
Beijing Shanghai Bangkok Hong Kong *84*
Tokyo Seoul Osaka *85*
Perth Sydney Melbourne Auckland *86*
Delhi Calcutta Bombay Singapore *87*
Jerusalem Istanbul Cairo Nairobi *88*
Montreal Ottawa Toronto Chicago Boston *89*
New York Manhattan *90*
Washington San Francisco Los Angeles *91*
Mexico City São Paulo Santiago Rio de Janeiro Buenos Aires *92*

INDEX

Guide to Pronunciation *93*

Geographical Dictionary *94–99*

Abbreviations used on the maps *100*

Abbreviations used in the Index *101*

Index to the maps *101–156*

Acknowledgements *156*

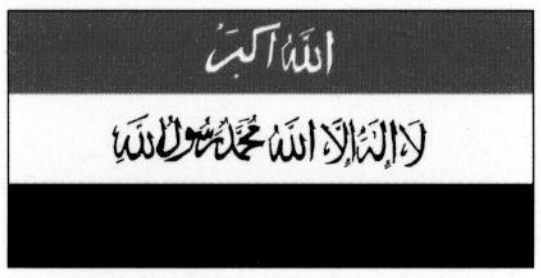

AFGHANISTAN

STATUS: Islamic State
AREA: 652,225 sq km (251,773 sq miles)
POPULATION: 16,433,000
ANNUAL NATURAL INCREASE: 2.5%
CAPITAL: Kabul
LANGUAGE: Pushtu, Dari
RELIGION: 90% Sunni, 9% Shi'a Muslim, Hindu, Sikh and Jewish minorities
CURRENCY: Afghani (AFA)
ORGANIZATIONS: Col. Plan, UN

Afghanistan is a mountainous landlocked country in southwest Asia with a climate of extremes. In summer the lowland southwest reaches a temperature of over 40°C (104°F); in winter this may drop to -26°C (-15°F) in the northern mountains. The country is one of the poorest in the world with barely 10 per cent of the land suitable for agriculture. Main crops are wheat, fruit and vegetables. Sheep and goats are the main livestock. Mineral resources are rich but underdeveloped with natural gas, coal and iron ore deposits predominating. The main industrial area was centred on Kabul, but both Kabul and the rural areas have been devastated by civil war.

ÅLAND

STATUS: Self-governing Island Province of Finland
AREA: 1,505 sq km (581 sq miles)
POPULATION: 24,993
CAPITAL: Mariehamn

ALBANIA

STATUS: Republic
AREA: 28,750 sq km (11,100 sq miles)
POPULATION: 3,363,000
ANNUAL NATURAL INCREASE: 1.7%
CAPITAL: Tirana (Tiranë)
LANGUAGE: Albanian (Gheg, Tosk)
RELIGION: 70% Muslim, 20% Greek Orthodox, 10% Roman Catholic
CURRENCY: lek (ALL)
ORGANIZATIONS: UN

Albania is situated on the eastern seaboard of the Adriatic. With the exception of a coastal strip, most of the territory is mountainous and largely unfit for cultivation. The climate is Mediterranean along the coast, but cooler inland. Average temperatures in July reach 25°C (77°F) and there is 1,400 mm (55 inches) of rainfall annually. The country possesses mineral resources, notably chrome which is a major export, and deposits of coal, oil and natural gas. After decades of self-imposed political and economic isolation Albania shook off its own peculiar variant of communism in 1990. Administrative chaos and a massive fall in production ensued resulting in acute food shortages and widespread emigration. The country is one of the poorest in Europe with a backward rural economy and nearly half the labour force unemployed.

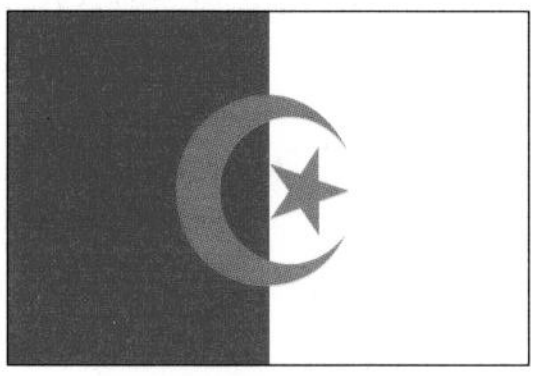

ALGERIA

STATUS: Republic
AREA: 2,381,745 sq km (919,355 sq miles)
POPULATION: 26,600,000
ANNUAL NATURAL INCREASE: 2.7%
CAPITAL: Algiers (Alger, El-Djezaïr)
LANGUAGE: 83% Arabic, French, Berber
RELIGION: Muslim
CURRENCY: Algerian dinar (DZD)
ORGANIZATIONS: Arab League, OAU, OPEC, UN

Physically the country is divided between the coastal Atlas mountain ranges of the north and the Sahara to the south. Algeria is mainly hot, with negligible rainfall, but along the Mediterranean coast temperatures are more moderate, with most rain falling during the mild winters. Arable land occupies small areas of the northern valleys and coastal strip, with wheat, barley and vines the leading crops. Sheep, goats and cattle are the most important livestock. Although oil from the southern deserts dominates the economy, it is now declining and natural gas output has increased dramatically. A virtual civil war has existed between the army and Islamic extremists which has caused the economy to deteriorate.

AMERICAN SAMOA

STATUS: Unincorporated Territory of USA
AREA: 197 sq km (76 sq miles)
POPULATION: 132,726
CAPITAL: Pago Pago

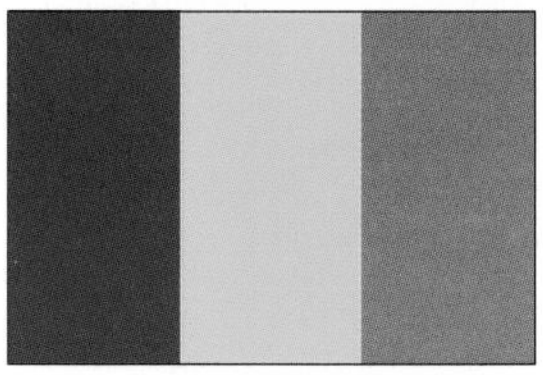

ANDORRA

STATUS: Principality
AREA: 465 sq km (180 sq miles)
POPULATION: 59,000
CAPITAL: Andorra la Vella
LANGUAGE: Catalan, Spanish, French
RELIGION: Roman Catholic majority
CURRENCY: French franc (FRF), Andorran peseta (ADP)
ORGANIZATIONS: UN

Andorra, a tiny state in the Pyrenees between France and Spain, achieved fuller independence from these countries in 1993. The climate is alpine with a long winter, which lasts for six months, a mild spring and a warm summer. Tourism is the main occupation, with Andorra becoming an important skiing centre during the winter. Tobacco and potatoes are the principal crops, sheep and cattle the main livestock. Other important sources of revenue are the sale of hydro-electricity, stamps, duty-free goods and financial services.

ANGOLA

STATUS: Republic
AREA: 1,246,700 sq km (481,225 sq miles)
POPULATION: 10,770,000
ANNUAL NATURAL INCREASE: 2.9%
CAPITAL: Luanda
LANGUAGE: Portuguese, tribal dialects
RELIGION: mainly traditional beliefs, Roman Catholic and Protestant minorities
CURRENCY: new kwanza (AOK)
ORGANIZATIONS: OAU, UN

Independent from the Portuguese since 1975, Angola is a large country south of the equator in southwest Africa. Much of the interior is savannah plateaux with average rainfall varying from 250 mm (10 inches) in the south to 1,270 mm (50 inches) in the north. Most of the population is engaged in agriculture producing cassava, maize and coffee. Most consumer products and textiles are imported. Angola possesses vast wealth in the form of diamonds, oil, iron ore, copper and other minerals. Apart from the production of oil, which is the biggest export, the economy has collapsed as a result of many years of civil war.

ABBREVIATIONS

The following abbreviations have been used. Codes given in brackets following the name of a currency are those issued by the International Standards Organization.

ANZUS	Australia, New Zealand, United States Security Treaty
ASEAN	Association of Southeast Asian Nations
Caricom	Caribbean Community and Common Market
CACM	Central American Common Market
CIS	Commonwealth of Independent States
Col. Plan	Colombo Plan
Comm.	Commonwealth
CSCE	Council for Security and Co-operation in Europe
ECOWAS	Economic Community of West African States
EEA	European Economic Area
EFTA	European Free Trade Association
EU	European Union
G7	Group of seven industrialized nations:– (Canada, France, Germany, Italy, Japan, UK, USA)
Mercosur	Common Market of the Southern Cone
NAFTA	North American Free Trade Agreement
NATO	North Atlantic Treaty Organization
OAS	Organization of American States
OAU	Organization of African Unity
OECD	Organization for Economic Co-operation and Development
OPEC	Organization of Petroleum Exporting Countries
UN	United Nations
WEU	Western European Union

ANGUILLA

STATUS: UK Dependent Territory
AREA: 115 sq km (60 sq miles)
POPULATION: 8,960
CAPITAL: The Valley

ANTIGUA AND BARBUDA

STATUS: Commonwealth State
AREA: 442 sq km (171 sq miles)
POPULATION: 65,962
ANNUAL NATURAL INCREASE: 1.0%
CAPITAL: St John's (on Antigua)
LANGUAGE: English
RELIGION: Anglican Christian majority
CURRENCY: E Caribbean dollar (XCD)
ORGANIZATIONS: Caricom, Comm., OAS, UN

The country consists of two main islands in the Leeward group in the West Indies. Tourism is the main activity. Local agriculture is being encouraged to reduce food imports and the growth of sea island cotton is making a comeback. The production of rum is the main manufacturing industry; there is also an oil refinery.

ARGENTINA

STATUS: Republic
AREA: 2,766,889 sq km (1,068,302 sq miles)
POPULATION: 33,101,000
ANNUAL NATURAL INCREASE: 1.3%
CAPITAL: Buenos Aires
LANGUAGE: Spanish
RELIGION: 90% Roman Catholic, 2% Protestant, Jewish minority
CURRENCY: peso (ARP)
ORGANIZATIONS: Mercosur, OAS, UN

Relief is highest in the west in the Andes mountains, where altitudes exceed 6,000 m (19,500 ft). East of the Andes there are fertile plains known as the Pampas. In the northern scrub forests and grasslands of the Chaco hot tropical conditions exist. Central Argentina lies in temperate latitudes, but the southernmost regions are cold, wet and stormy. The economy of Argentina was long dominated by the produce of the rich soils of the Pampas, beef and grain. Agricultural products still account for some 40 per cent of export revenue, with grain crops predominating, despite a decline due to competition and falling world prices. Beef exports also decreased by over 50 per cent between 1970 and 1983, due to strong competition from western Europe. Industry is now the chief export earner. Industrial activity includes petrochemicals, steel, cars, and food and drink processing. There are oil and gas reserves and an abundant supply of hydroelectric power.

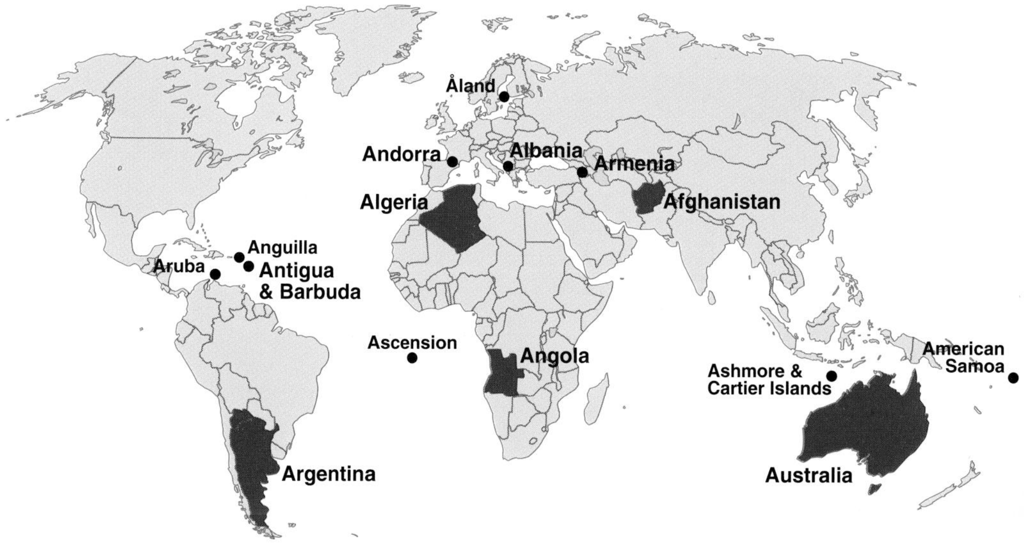

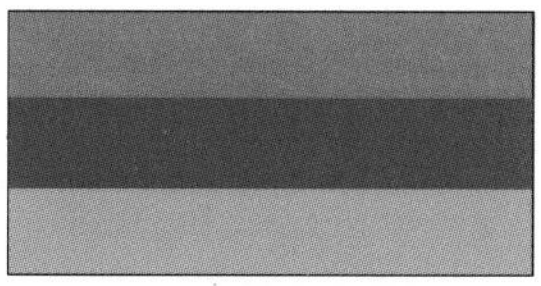

ARMENIA

STATUS: Republic
AREA: 30,000 sq km (11,580 sq miles)
POPULATION: 3,686,000
ANNUAL NATURAL INCREASE: 1.2%
CAPITAL: Yerevan
LANGUAGE: Armenian, Russian
RELIGION: Russian Orthodox, Armenian Catholic
CURRENCY: dram
ORGANIZATIONS: CIS, UN

Armenia is a country of rugged terrain, with most of the land above 1,000 m (3,300 feet). The climate, much influenced by altitude, has continental tendencies. Rainfall, although occurring throughout the year, is heaviest in summer. Agriculture is dependent upon irrigation and the main crops are vegetables, fruit and tobacco. Conflict over the disputed area of Nagornyy Karabakh, an enclave of Armenian Orthodox Christians within the territory of Azerbaijan, is casting a cloud over the immediate future of the country.

ARUBA

STATUS: Self-governing Island of Netherlands Realm
AREA: 193 sq km (75 sq miles)
POPULATION: 68,897
CAPITAL: Oranjestad

ASCENSION

STATUS: Island Dependency of St Helena
AREA: 88 sq km (34 sq miles)
POPULATION: 1,117
CAPITAL: Georgetown

ASHMORE AND CARTIER ISLANDS

STATUS: External Territory of Australia
AREA: 3 sq km (1.2 sq miles)
POPULATION: no permanent population

AUSTRALIA

STATUS: Federal Nation
AREA: 7,682,300 sq km (2,965,370 sq miles)
POPULATION: 17,662,000
ANNUAL NATURAL INCREASE: 1.6%
CAPITAL: Canberra
LANGUAGE: English
RELIGION: 75% Christian, Aboriginal beliefs, Jewish minority
CURRENCY: Australian dollar (AUD)
ORGANIZATIONS: ANZUS, Col. Plan, Comm., OECD, UN

The Commonwealth of Australia was founded in 1901. The British Monarch, as head of state, is represented by a governor-general. It is the sixth largest country in the world in terms of area. The western half of the country is primarily arid plateaux, ridges and vast deserts. The central-eastern area comprises lowlands of river systems draining into Lake Eyre, while to the east is the Great Dividing Range. Climate varies from cool temperate to tropical monsoon. Rainfall is high only in the northeast, where it exceeds 1,000 mm (39 inches) annually, and decreases markedly from the coast to the interior which is hot and dry. Over 50 per cent of the land area comprises desert and scrub with less than 250 mm (10 inches) of rain a year. The majority of the population live in cities concentrated along the southeast coast. Australia is rich in both agricultural and natural resources. It is the world's leading producer of wool, which together with wheat, meat, sugar and dairy products accounts for over 40 per cent of export revenue. There are vast reserves of coal, oil, natural gas, nickel, iron ore, bauxite and uranium ores. Gold, silver, lead, zinc and copper ores are also exploited. Minerals now account for over 30 per cent of Australia's export revenue. New areas of commerce have been created in eastern Asia, particularly in Japan, to counteract the sharp decline of the traditional European markets. Tourism is becoming a large revenue earner and showed a 200 per cent growth between 1983 and 1988. This has slowed recently, although the Olympics Games, due to be held in Sydney in the year 2000, are expected to attract an additional 1.5 million overseas visitors.

AUSTRALIAN CAPITAL TERRITORY
STATUS: Federal Territory
AREA: 2,432 sq km (939 sq miles)
POPULATION: 299,000
CAPITAL: Canberra

NEW SOUTH WALES
STATUS: State
AREA: 801,430 sq km (309,350 sq miles)
POPULATION: 6,009,000
CAPITAL: Sydney

NORTHERN TERRITORY
STATUS: Territory
AREA: 1,346,200 sq km (519,635 sq miles)
POPULATION: 168,000
CAPITAL: Darwin

QUEENSLAND
STATUS: State
AREA: 1,727,000 sq km (666,620 sq miles)
POPULATION: 3,113,000
CAPITAL: Brisbane

SOUTH AUSTRALIA
STATUS: State
AREA: 984,380 sq km (79,970 sq miles)
POPULATION: 1,462,000
CAPITAL: Adelaide

TASMANIA
STATUS: State
AREA: 68,330 sq km (26,375 sq miles)
POPULATION: 472,000
CAPITAL: Hobart

VICTORIA
STATUS: State
AREA: 227,600 sq km (87,855 sq miles)
POPULATION: 4,462,000
CAPITAL: Melbourne

WESTERN AUSTRALIA
STATUS: State
AREA: 2,525,500 sq km (974,845 sq miles)
POPULATION: 1,678,000
CAPITAL: Perth

AUSTRIA

STATUS: Federal Republic
AREA: 83,855 sq km (32,370 sq miles)
POPULATION: 7,910,000
ANNUAL NATURAL INCREASE: 0.6%
CAPITAL: Vienna (Wien)
LANGUAGE: German
RELIGION: 89% Roman Catholic, 6% Protestant
CURRENCY: schilling (ATS)
ORGANIZATIONS: Council of Europe, EEA, EFTA, OECD, UN

Austria is an alpine, landlocked country in central Europe. The mountainous Alps which cover 75 per cent of the land consist of a series of east-west ranges enclosing lowland basins. The climate is continental with temperatures and rainfall varying with altitude. About 25 per cent of the country, in the north and northeast, is lower foreland or flat land containing most of Austria's fertile farmland. Half is arable and the remainder is mainly for root or fodder crops. Manufacturing and heavy industry, however, account for the majority of export revenues, particularly pig-iron, steel, chemicals and vehicles. Over 70 per cent of the country's power is hydro-electric. Tourism and forestry are also important to the economy.

AZERBAIJAN

STATUS: Republic
AREA: 87,000 sq km (33,580 sq miles)
POPULATION: 7,398,000
ANNUAL NATURAL INCREASE: 1.0%
CAPITAL: Baku
LANGUAGE: 83% Azeri, 6% Armenian, 6% Russian
RELIGION: 83% Muslim, Armenian Apostolic, Orthodox
CURRENCY: manat
ORGANIZATIONS: CIS, UN

Azerbaijan gained independence on the breakup of the USSR in 1991. It is a mountainous country that has a continental climate, greatly influenced by altitude. Arable land accounts for less than 10 per cent of the total area, with raw cotton and tobacco the leading products. Major reserves of oil and gas exist beneath and around the Caspian Sea, which are as of yet fully undeveloped. The country includes two autonomous regions: Nakhichevan, which it is cut off by a strip of intervening Armenian territory and the enclave of Nagornyy Karabakh, over which long standing tensions escalated into conflict in 1992.

AZORES
STATUS: Self-governing Island Region of Portugal
AREA: 2,335 sq km (901 sq miles)
POPULATION: 237,100
CAPITAL: Ponta Delgada

BAHAMAS

STATUS: Commonwealth Nation
AREA: 13,865 sq km (5,350 sq miles)
POPULATION: 262,000
ANNUAL NATURAL INCREASE: 1.9%
CAPITAL: Nassau
LANGUAGE: English
RELIGION: Anglican Christian majority, Baptist and Roman Catholic minorities
CURRENCY: Bahamian dollar (BSD)
ORGANIZATIONS: Caricom, Comm., OAS, UN

About 700 islands and over 2,000 coral sand cays (reefs) constitute the sub-tropical Commonwealth of the Bahamas. The island group extends from the coast of Florida to Cuba and Haiti in the south. Only 29 islands are inhabited. Most of the 1,000 mm (39 inches) of rainfall falls in the summer. The tourist industry is the main source of income and, although fluctuating through recession, still employs over 70 per cent of the working population. Recent economic plans have concentrated on reducing imports by developing fishing and domestic agriculture. Other important sources of income are ship registration (the world's fourth largest open-registry fleet), income generated by offshore finance and banking, and export of rum, salt and cement.

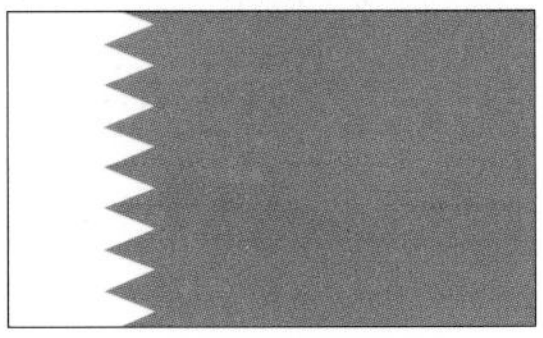

BAHRAIN

STATUS: State
AREA: 661 sq km (225 sq miles)
POPULATION: 539,000
ANNUAL NATURAL INCREASE: 3.2%
CAPITAL: Manama (Al Manāmah)
LANGUAGE: Arabic, English
RELIGION: 60% Shi'a and 40% Sunni Muslim, Christian minority
CURRENCY: Bahraini dinar (BHD)
ORGANIZATIONS: Arab League, UN

The sheikdom is a barren island in the Persian Gulf with less than 80 mm (3 inches) rainfall a year. Summer temperatures average 32°C (89°F). Bahrain was the first country in the Arabian peninsula to strike oil, in 1932. Oil still accounts for 60 per cent of revenue and gas is becoming increasingly important. Lower oil prices and decreased production is now causing the government to diversify the economy with expansion of light and heavy industry and chemical plants, and the subsequent encouragement of trade and foreign investment.

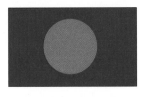

BANGLADESH

STATUS: Republic
AREA: 144,000 sq km (55,585 sq miles)
POPULATION: 118,700,000
ANNUAL NATURAL INCREASE: 2.2%
CAPITAL: Dhaka, (Dhākā, Dacca)
LANGUAGE: Bengali (Bangla), Bihari, Hindi, English
RELIGION: 85% Muslim, Hindu, Buddhist and Christian minorities
CURRENCY: taka (BDT)
ORGANIZATIONS: Col. Plan, Comm., UN

Bangladesh is one of the poorest and most densely populated countries of the world. Most of its territory, except for bamboo-forested hills in the southeast, comprises the vast river systems of the Ganges and Brahmaputra which drain from the Himalayan mountains into the Bay of Bengal, frequently changing course and flooding the flat delta plain. This land is, however, extremely fertile and attracts a high concentration of the population. The climate is tropical, and agriculture is dependent on monsoon rainfall. When the monsoon fails there is drought. Eighty-two per cent of the population are farmers, the main crops being rice and jute. Bangladesh is the world's leading supplier of jute, which accounts for 25 per cent of the country's exports. The main industry and number one export is clothing . Natural gas reserves, under the Bay of Bengal, are beginning to be exploited.

BARBADOS

STATUS: Commonwealth State
AREA: 430 sq km (166 sq miles)
POPULATION: 259,000
ANNUAL NATURAL INCREASE: 0.3%
CAPITAL: Bridgetown
LANGUAGE: English
RELIGION: Anglican Christian majority, Methodist and Roman Catholic minorities
CURRENCY: Barbados dollar (BBD)
ORGANIZATIONS: Caricom, Comm., OAS, UN

The former British colony of Barbados in the Caribbean is the most eastern island of the Antilles chain. The gently rolling landscape of the island is lush and fertile, the temperature ranging from 25–28°C (77–82°F) with 1270–1900 mm (50–75 inches) of rainfall per year. Sugar and its by-products, molasses and rum, are traditional cash crops. These are being overtaken in importance by tourism which provides an occupation for one-third of the population. This is a growth sector, although it has suffered recently from world recession. An oilfield supplies one-third of domestic oil requirements.

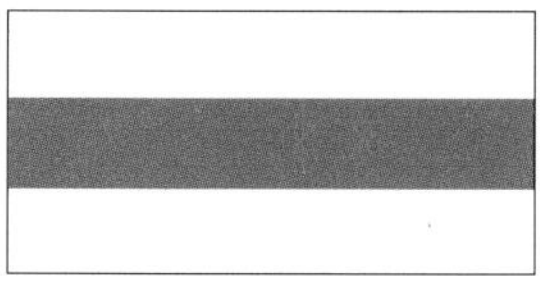

BELARUS

STATUS: Republic
AREA: 208,000 sq km (80,290 sq miles)
POPULATION: 10,280,000
ANNUAL NATURAL INCREASE: 0.5%
CAPITAL: Minsk
LANGUAGE: Belorussian, Russian
RELIGION: Roman Catholic, Uniate
CURRENCY: rouble
ORGANIZATIONS: CIS, UN

Belarus achieved independence in 1991. The country is mainly flat with forests covering more than one-third of the area. Swamps and marshlands cover large areas but, when drained, the soil is very fertile. The climate is continental with fairly cold winters (-7°C or 20°F). Grain, flax, potatoes and sugar beet are the main crops but livestock production accounts for more than half the value of agricultural output. Large areas of Belarus are thinly populated; most people live in the central area. The republic is comparatively poor in mineral resources and suffered terrible devastation during the Second World War. Post-war industrialization has been based on imported raw materials and semi-manufactured goods, concentrating on the production of trucks, tractors, agricultural machinery and other heavy engineering equipment. However, these industries are heavily reliant on imported Russian energy and output has declined since independence.

BELGIUM

STATUS: Kingdom
AREA: 30,520 sq km (11,780 sq miles)
POPULATION: 10,020,000
ANNUAL NATURAL INCREASE: 0.3%
CAPITAL: Brussels (Bruxelles/Brussel)
LANGUAGE: French, Dutch (Flemish), German
RELIGION: Roman Catholic majority, Protestant and Jewish minorities
CURRENCY: Belgium franc (BEF)
ORGANIZATIONS: Council of Europe, EEA, EU, NATO, OECD, UN, WEU

Over two-thirds of Belgium comprises the Flanders plain, a flat plateau covered by fertile wind-blown loess which extends from the North Sea coast down to the forested mountains of the Ardennes in the south. The climate is mild, maritime temperate with 720–1200 mm (28–47 inches) of rainfall a year. Over half the country is intensively farmed – cereals, root crops, vegetables and flax are the main crops and the country is nearly self-sufficient in meat and dairy products. Belgium's tradition as an industrialized nation dates back to the 19th century and Flanders has historically been famed for its textiles. The main industries now are metal-working (including motor vehicle assembly), chemicals, iron and steel, textiles, food and drink processing and diamonds. In recent years many companies have embarked on high-technology specialization including computer software, micro-electronics and telecommunications. Belgium is a trading nation, exporting more than half its national production. Most trade passes through the port of Antwerp, and an efficient communications network links it with the rest of Europe.

BELIZE

STATUS: Commonwealth Nation
AREA: 22,965 sq km (8,865 sq miles)
POPULATION: 230,000
ANNUAL NATURAL INCREASE: 2.6%
CAPITAL: Belmopan
LANGUAGE: English, Spanish, Maya
RELIGION: 60% Roman Catholic, 40% Protestant
CURRENCY: Belizean dollar (BZD)
ORGANIZATIONS: CARICOM, Comm., OAS, UN

Bordering the Caribbean Sea, in Central America, sub-tropical Belize is dominated by its dense forest cover. Principal exports are sugar cane, citrus concentrates and bananas. Since independence from Britain in 1973 the country has developed agriculture to lessen reliance on imported food products. Other commodities produced include tropical fruits, vegetables, fish and timber.

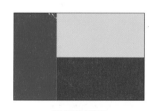

BENIN

STATUS: Republic
AREA: 112,620 sq km (43,470 sq miles)
POPULATION: 5,010,000
ANNUAL NATURAL INCREASE: 3.2%
CAPITAL: Porto Novo
LANGUAGE: French, Fon, Adja
RELIGION: majority traditional beliefs, 15% Roman Catholic, 13% Muslim
CURRENCY: CFA franc (W Africa) (XOF)
ORGANIZATIONS: ECOWAS, OAU, UN

Benin, formerly Dahomey, is a small strip of country descending from the wooded savannah hills of the north to the forested and cultivated lowlands fringing the Bight of Benin. The economy is agricultural, with palm oil, cotton, cocoa, coffee, groundnuts and copra as main exports. The developing offshore oil industry has proven reserves of over 20 million barrels.

BERMUDA

STATUS: Self-governing UK Crown Colony
AREA: 54 sq km (21 sq miles)
POPULATION: 74,837
CAPITAL: Hamilton

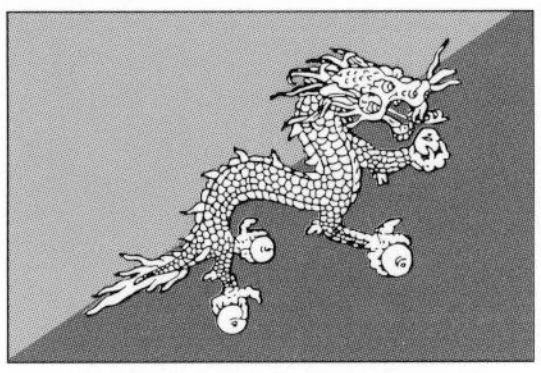

BHUTAN

STATUS: Kingdom
AREA: 46,620 sq km (17,995 sq miles)
POPULATION: 600,000
ANNUAL NATURAL INCREASE: 2.2%
CAPITAL: Thimphu
LANGUAGE: Dzongkha, Nepali, English
RELIGION: Mahayana Buddhist, 30% Hindu
CURRENCY: ngultrum (BTN), Indian rupee (INR)
ORGANIZATIONS: Col. Plan, UN

Bhutan is a small country in the Himalayan foothills between China and India, and to the east of Nepal. Rainfall is high at over 3000 mm (118 inches) a year but temperatures vary between the extreme cold of the northern ranges to a July average of 27°C (81°F) in the southern forests. Long isolated, the economy of Bhutan is dominated by agriculture and small local industries. All manufactured goods are imported.

BOLIVIA

STATUS: Republic
AREA: 1,098,575 sq km (424,050 sq miles)
POPULATION: 7,832,396
ANNUAL NATURAL INCREASE: 2.5%
CAPITAL: La Paz
LANGUAGE: Spanish, Quechua, Aymara
RELIGION: Roman Catholic majority
CURRENCY: Boliviano (BOB)
ORGANIZATIONS: OAS, UN

Bolivia, where the average life expectancy is 51 years, is one of the world's poorest nations. Landlocked and isolated, the country stretches from the eastern Andes across high cool plateaux before dropping to the dense forest of the Amazon basin and the grasslands of the southeast. Bolivia was once rich, its wealth based on minerals (in recent decades tin) but in 1985 world tin prices dropped and the industry collapsed. Oil and gas and agriculture now dominate the economy. Crops include soya, cotton, coca (cocaine shrub), sugar and coffee. Mining is still important, with the emphasis on zinc.

BOSNIA-HERZEGOVINA

STATUS: Republic
AREA: 51,130 sq km (19,736 sq miles)
POPULATION: 2,900,000
ANNUAL NATURAL INCREASE: 0.2%
CAPITAL: Sarajevo
LANGUAGE: Serbo-Croat
RELIGION: Muslim, Christian
CURRENCY: dinar
ORGANIZATIONS: UN

Bosnia-Herzegovina achieved independence in April 1992, but international recognition did not spare the Republic from savage ethnic warfare between Muslims, Serbs and Croats. Partitioning of the country into a new federation acceptable to all warring parties appears to be a necessity for peace. Before the war Bosnia's economy was based predominantly on agriculture – sheep rearing and the cultivation of vines, olives and citrus fruits. The country is mainly mountainous with the Sava valley in the north being the only lowland of consequence. The climate is Mediterranean towards the Adriatic, but continental and cooler inland.

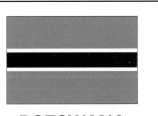

BOTSWANA

STATUS: Republic
AREA: 582,000 sq km (224,652 sq miles)
POPULATION: 1,291,000
ANNUAL NATURAL INCREASE: 3.4%
CAPITAL: Gaborone
LANGUAGE: Setswana, English
RELIGION: traditional beliefs majority, Christian minority
CURRENCY: pula (BWP)
ORGANIZATIONS: Comm., OAU, UN

The arid high plateau of Botswana, with its poor soils and low rainfall, supports little arable agriculture, but over 2.3 million cattle graze the dry grasslands. Diamonds are the chief export, providing 80 per cent of export earnings. Copper, nickel, potash, soda ash, salt and coal are also important. The growth of light industries around the capital has stimulated trade with neighbouring countries.

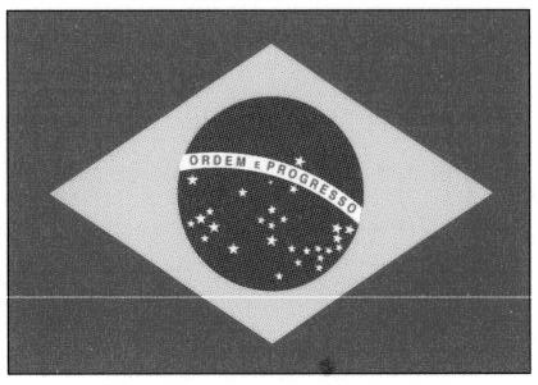

BRAZIL

STATUS: Federal Republic
AREA: 8,511,965 sq km (3,285,620 sq miles)
POPULATION: 156,275,000
ANNUAL NATURAL INCREASE: 2.2%
CAPITAL: Brasília
LANGUAGE: Portuguese
RELIGION: 90% Roman Catholic, Protestant minority
CURRENCY: cruzeiro real (BRC),URV
ORGANIZATIONS: Mercosur, OAS, UN

Brazil is the largest country in South America with the Amazon basin tropical rain forest covers roughly a third of the country. It is one of the world's leading agricultural exporters, with coffee, soya beans, sugar, bananas, cocoa, tobacco, rice and cattle major commodities. Brazil is an industrial power but with development limited to the heavily populated urban areas of the eastern coastal lowlands. Mineral resources, except for iron ore, do not play a significant role in the economy at present, but recent economic policies have concentrated on developing the industrial base – road and rail communications, light and heavy industry and expansion of energy resources, particularly hydro-electric power harnessed from the three great river systems. Unlike other South American countries Brazil still has a serious inflation rate, introducing the 'real', on 1 July 1994 (the fifth new currency in a decade), in an attempt to slow the rate down.

BRITISH ANTARCTIC TERRITORY

STATUS: UK Dependent Territory
AREA: 1,544,000 sq km (599,845 sq miles)
POPULATION: no permanent population

BRITISH INDIAN OCEAN TERRITORY

STATUS: UK Dependency comprising the Chagos Archipelago
AREA: 5,765 sq km (2,225 sq miles)
POPULATION: 266,000

BRUNEI

STATUS: Sultanate
AREA: 5,765 sq km (2,225 sq miles)
POPULATION: 270,000
ANNUAL NATURAL INCREASE: 3.2%
CAPITAL: Bandar Seri Begawan
LANGUAGE: Malay, English, Chinese
RELIGION: 65% Sunni Muslim, Buddhist and Christian minorities
CURRENCY: Brunei dollar (BND)
ORGANIZATIONS: ASEAN, Comm, UN

The Sultanate of Brunei is situated on the northwest coast of Borneo. Its tropical climate is hot and humid with annual rainfall ranging from 2500 mm (98 inches) on the narrow coastal strip to 5000 mm (197 inches) in the mountainous interior. Oil and gas reserves, mostly offshore, are the basis of the Brunei economy. Half the oil and nearly all the natural gas (in liquefied form) are exported to Japan.

BULGARIA

STATUS: Republic
AREA: 110,910 sq km (42,810 sq miles)
POPULATION: 8,467,000
ANNUAL NATURAL INCREASE: 0.0%
CAPITAL: Sofia (Sofiya)
LANGUAGE: Bulgarian, Turkish
RELIGION: Eastern Orthodox majority, Muslim minority
CURRENCY: lev (BGL)
ORGANIZATIONS: Council of Europe, EFTA, OIEC, UN

Bulgaria exhibits great variety in its landscape. In the north, the land from the plains of the Danube slope upwards into the Balkan mountains (Stara Planina), which run east-west through central Bulgaria. The Rhodope mountains dominate the west, with the lowlands of Thrace and the Maritsa valley in the south. Climate is continental with temperatures ranging from -5°C (23°F) in winter to 28°C (82°F) in summer. The economy is based on agricultural products, with cereals, tobacco, cotton, fruits and vines dominating. Wine is a particularly successful export. Nuclear power is the main domestic power source, however the reactors are becoming elderly and other sources of energy are being sought, in particular oil and gas in the Black Sea. The heavy industry sector, which thrived in close association with the former USSR, is declining.

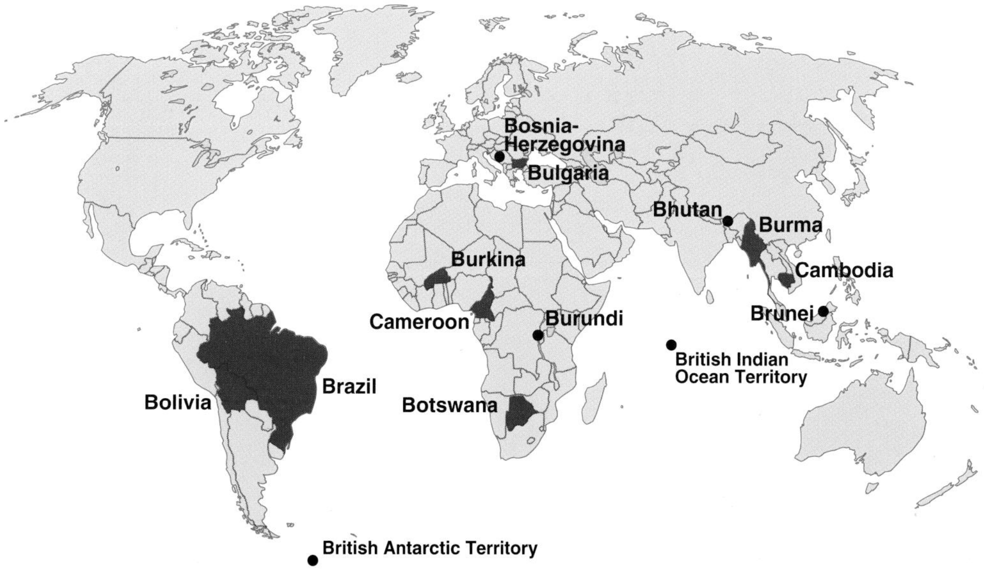

BURKINA

STATUS: Republic
AREA: 274,122 sq km (105,811 sq miles)
POPULATION: 9,490,000
ANNUAL NATURAL INCREASE: 2.8%
CAPITAL: Ouagadougou
LANGUAGE: French, Moré (Mossi), Dyula
RELIGION: 60% animist, 30% Muslim, 10% Roman Catholic
CURRENCY: CFA franc (W Africa) (OXF)
ORGANIZATIONS: ECOWAS, OAU, UN

Situated on the southern edge of the Sahara, Burkina, previously known as Upper Volta, is a poor, landlocked country with thin soils supporting savannah grasslands. Frequent droughts, particularly in the north, seriously affect the economy, which is mainly subsistence agriculture with livestock herding, and the export of groundnuts and cotton. There is virtually no industry. Some minerals are exported and manganese exports began in 1993.

BURMA (MYANMAR)

STATUS: Union of states and divisions
AREA: 678,030 sq km (261,720 sq miles)
POPULATION: 42,330,000
ANNUAL NATURAL INCREASE: 2.2%
CAPITAL: Rangoon (Yangon)
LANGUAGE: Burmese
RELIGION: 85% Buddhist. Animist, Muslim, Hindu and Christian minorities
CURRENCY: kyat (BUK)
ORGANIZATIONS: Col. Plan, UN

Much of Burma (renamed Myanmar by its military leaders in 1989) is covered by tropical rainforest divided by the central valley of the Irrawaddy, the Sittang and the Salween rivers. The western highlands are an extension of the Himalaya mountains; hills to the east and south are a continuation of the Yunnan plateau of China. The economy is based on the export of rice and forestry products. The irrigated central basin and the coastal region to the east of the Irrawaddy delta are the main rice-growing areas. Hardwoods, particularly teak, cover the highlands. There is potential for greater exploitation of tin, copper, gold, oil and natural gas deposits.

BURUNDI

STATUS: Republic
AREA: 27,835 sq km (10,745 sq miles)
POPULATION: 5,786,000
ANNUAL NATURAL INCREASE: 2.9%
CAPITAL: Bujumbura
LANGUAGE: French, Kirundi, Swahili
RELIGION: 60% Roman Catholic, animist minority
CURRENCY: Burundi franc (BIF)
ORGANIZATIONS: OAU, UN

This small central African republic is densely populated and one of the world's poorest nations. Although close to the equator, temperatures are modified because of altitude. Coffee is the main export, followed by tea, cotton and manufactured goods. The country has a history of ethnic fighting between the Hutu farming people, who make up 85 per cent of the population, and the Tutsi, originally pastoralists, who have dominated the army and the running of the country. Massacres of thousands of people in 1993-4 resulted from ethnic war, ignited by a Hutu election victory marking an end to 31 years of Tutsi domination.

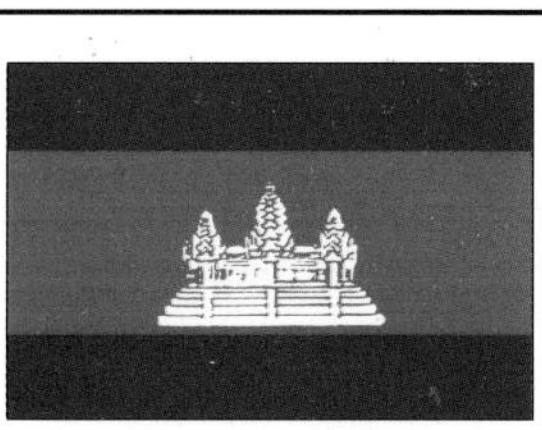

CAMBODIA

STATUS: Kingdom
AREA: 181,000 sq km (69,865 sq miles)
POPULATION: 12,000,000
ANNUAL NATURAL INCREASE: 2.7%
CAPITAL: Phnom Penh
LANGUAGE: Khmer
RELIGION: Buddhist majority, Roman Catholic and Muslim minorities
CURRENCY: reil (KHR)
ORGANIZATIONS: Col. Plan, UN

Cambodia, in southeast Asia, is mostly a lowland basin. Over 70 per cent of the country is covered by the central plain of the Mekong river. The climate is tropical, with average annual temperatures exceeding 25°C (77°F). Monsoon rainfall occurs from May to October. These provide ideal conditions for the country's rice production and fish harvesting. The economy has been damaged since the 1970s by almost constant civil war. Power shortages hamper industrial development, the roads are badly damaged and land mines buried in the countryside make farming hazardous.

CAMEROON

STATUS: Republic
AREA: 475,500 sq km(183,545 sq miles)
POPULATION: 12,198,000
ANNUAL NATURAL INCREASE: 3.0%
CAPITAL: Yaoundé
LANGUAGE: English, French
RELIGION: 40% Christian, 39% traditional beliefs, 21% Muslim
CURRENCY: CRA franc (C Africa) (XAF)
ORGANIZATIONS: OAU, UN

Cameroon, in west Africa, is situated between the Gulf of Guinea in the south and the shores of Lake Chad in the north. In the south, coastal lowlands rise to densely forested plateaux, whereas further northwards savannah takes over, and aridity increases towards the Sahara. Oil products, once the main export, have declined in importance and now agricultural products account for most export revenue. Coffee, cocoa, bananas and avocados are the main cash crops. Mineral resources are underdeveloped but Cameroon is one of Africa's main producers of bauxite (aluminium ore) and aluminium is smelted at Edea.

CANADA

STATUS: Commonwealth Nation
AREA: 9,922,385 sq km (3,830,840 sq miles)
POPULATION: 28,866,000
ANNUAL NATURAL INCREASE: 1.4%
CAPITAL: Ottawa
LANGUAGE: English, French
RELIGION: 46% Roman Catholic, Protestant and Jewish minorities
CURRENCY: Canadian dollar (CAD)
ORGANIZATIONS: Col. Plan, Comm., G7, OAS, OECD, NATO, NAFTA, UN

Canada is the world's second largest country stretching from the great barren islands of the Arctic north to the vast grasslands of the central south, and from the Rocky Mountains in the west to the farmlands of the Great Lakes in the east. This huge area experiences great climatic differences but basically a continental climate prevails with extremes of heat and cold particularly in the central plains. The Arctic tundra of the far north provides summer grazing for caribou. Further south coniferous forests grow on the thin soils of the ancient shield landscape and on the extensive foothills of the Rocky Mountains. In contrast, the rich soils of the central prairies support grasslands and grain crops. The Great Lakes area provides fish, fruit, maize, root crops and dairy products; the prairies produce over 20 per cent of the worlds wheat; and the grasslands of Alberta support a thriving beef industry. Most minerals are mined and exploited in Canada with oil and natural gas, iron ore, bauxite, nickel, zinc, copper, gold and silver the major exports. Recently, diamonds have been discovered in the Northwest Territories. The country's vast rivers provide huge amounts of hydro-electric power but most industry is confined to the Great Lakes and St Lawrence margins. The principal manufactured goods for export are steel products, motor vehicles and paper for newsprint. The USA is Canada's main trading partner, taking 80 per cent of exports. Following a free trade agreement (NAFTA) in 1993 between the USA, Canada and Mexico, even closer economic ties will be made with the USA.

ALBERTA

STATUS: Province
AREA: 661,190 sq km (255,220 sq miles)
POPULATION: 2,672,000
CAPITAL: Edmonton

BRITISH COLUMBIA

STATUS: Province
AREA: 948,565 sq km (366,160 sq miles)
POPULATION: 3,570,000
CAPITAL: Victoria

MANITOBA

STATUS: Province
AREA: 650,090 sq km (250,935 sq miles)
POPULATION: 1,117,000
CAPITAL: Winnipeg

NEW BRUNSWICK

STATUS: Province
AREA: 73,435 sq km (28,345 sq miles)
POPULATION: 751,000
CAPITAL: Fredericton

NEWFOUNDLAND AND LABRADOR

STATUS: Province
AREA: 404,520 sq km (156,145 sq miles)
POPULATION: 581,000
CAPITAL: St John's

NORTHWEST TERRITORIES

STATUS: Territory
AREA: 3,379,685 sq km (1,304,560 sq miles)
POPULATION: 63,000
CAPITAL: Yellowknife

NOVA SCOTIA

STATUS: Province
AREA: 55,490 sq km (21,420 sq miles)
POPULATION: 925,000
CAPITAL: Halifax

ONTARIO

STATUS: Province
AREA: 1,068,630 sq km (412,490 sq miles)
POPULATION: 10,795,000
CAPITAL: Toronto

PRINCE EDWARD ISLAND

STATUS: Province
AREA: 5,655 sq km (2,185 sq miles)
POPULATION: 132,000
CAPITAL: Charlottetown

QUEBEC

STATUS: Province
AREA: 1,540,680 sq km (594,705 sq miles)
POPULATION: 7,226,000
CAPITAL: Quebec

SASKATCHEWAN

STATUS: Province
AREA: 651,900 sq km (251,635 sq miles)
POPULATION: 1,002,000
CAPITAL: Regina

YUKON TERRITORY

STATUS: Province
AREA: 482,515 sq km (186,250 sq miles)
POPULATION: 33,000
CAPITAL: Whitehorse

CANARY ISLANDS

STATUS: Island Provinces of Spain
AREA: 7,275 sq km (2,810 sq miles)
POPULATION: 1,493,784
CAPITAL: Las Palmas (Gran Canaria) and Santa Cruz (Tenerife)

CAPE VERDE

STATUS: Republic
AREA: 4,035 sq km (1,560 sq miles)
POPULATION: 350,000
ANNUAL NATURAL INCREASE: 2.7%
CAPITAL: Praia
LANGUAGE: Portuguese, Creole
RELIGION: 98% Roman Catholic
CURRENCY: Cape Verde escudo (CVE)
ORGANIZATIONS: ECOWAS, OAU, UN

Independent since 1975, the ten inhabited volcanic islands of the republic are situated in the Atlantic 500 km (310 miles) west of Senegal. Rainfall is low but irrigation encourages growth of sugar cane, coffee, coconuts, fruit (mainly bananas) and maize. Fishing accounts for about 70 per cent of export revenue and all consumer goods are imported.

CAYMAN ISLANDS

STATUS: UK Dependent Territory
AREA: 259 sq km (100 sq miles)
POPULATION: 29,000
CAPITAL: George Town

CENTRAL AFRICAN REPUBLIC

STATUS: Republic
AREA: 624,975 sq km (241,240 sq miles)
POPULATION: 3,173,000
ANNUAL NATURAL INCREASE: 2.7%
CAPITAL: Bangui
LANGUAGE: French, Sango (national)
RELIGION: Animist majority, Christian minority
CURRENCY: CFA franc (C Africa) (XAF)
ORGANIZATIONS: OAU, UN

The republic is remote from both east and west Africa. It has a tropical climate with little variation in temperature. Savannah covers the rolling plateaux with rainforest in the southeast. To the north lies the Sahara Desert. Most farming is at subsistence level with a small amount of crops grown for export – cotton, coffee, groundnuts and tobacco. Hardwood forests in the southwest provide timber for export. Diamonds are the major export, accounting for over half of foreign earnings.

CHAD

STATUS: Republic
AREA: 1,284,000 sq km (495,625 sq miles)
POPULATION: 6,288,000
ANNUAL NATURAL INCREASE: 2.5%
CAPITAL: Ndjamena
LANGUAGE: French, Arabic, local languages
RELIGION: 50% Muslim, 45% animist
CURRENCY: CRA franc (C Africa) (XAF)
ORGANIZATIONS: OAU, UN

Chad is a vast state of central Africa stretching deep into the Sahara. The economy is based on agriculture but only the south, with 1,000 mm (39 in) of rainfall, can support crops for export – cotton, rice and groundnuts. Severe droughts, increasing desertification and border disputes have severely restricted development. Life expectancy at birth is still only 43 years. Salt is mined around Lake Chad where the majority of the population live.

CHANNEL ISLANDS

STATUS: British Crown Dependency
AREA: 194 sq km (75 sq miles)
POPULATION: 145,796
CAPITAL: St Hélier (Jersey)
St Peter Port (Guernsey)

CHILE

STATUS: Republic
AREA: 751,625 sq km (290,125 sq miles)
POPULATION: 13,813,000
ANNUAL NATURAL INCREASE: 1.7%
CAPITAL: Santiago
LANGUAGE: Spanish
RELIGION: 85% Roman Catholic, Protestant minority
CURRENCY: Chilean peso (CLP)
ORGANIZATIONS: OAS, UN

Chile is a long narrow country on the west coast of South America, stretching through 38° of latitude from the Atacama desert of the north to the sub-polar islands of Tierra del Fuego. Apart from a coastal strip of lowland, the country is dominated by the Andes mountains. Most energy is provided by hydro-electric power. The economy is based upon the abundance of natural resources with copper (the world's largest reserve), iron ore, nitrates, gold, timber, coal, oil and gas. Light and heavy industries are based around Concepción and Santiago. Traditional major exports are copper, fishmeal and cellulose. In the early 1990s farm production increased dramatically and food products now account for 29 per cent of export earnings.

CHINA

STATUS: People's Republic
AREA: 9,597,000 sq km (3,704,440 sq miles)
POPULATION: 1,154,887,381
ANNUAL NATURAL INCREASE: 1.3%
CAPITAL: Beijing (Peking)
LANGUAGE: Mandarin Chinese, regional languages
RELIGION: Confucianist, Buddhist, Taoist, Christian and Muslim minorities
CURRENCY: yuan (CNY)
ORGANIZATIONS: UN

The land of China is one of the most diverse on Earth and has vast mineral and agricultural resources. The majority of the people live in the east where the economy is dictated by the great drainage basins of the Yellow River (Huang He) and the Yangtze (Chang Jiang). Here, intensively irrigated agriculture produces one-third of the world's rice as well as wheat, maize, sugar, cotton, soya beans and oil seeds. Pigs are reared and fish caught throughout China. The country is basically self-sufficient in foodstuffs.

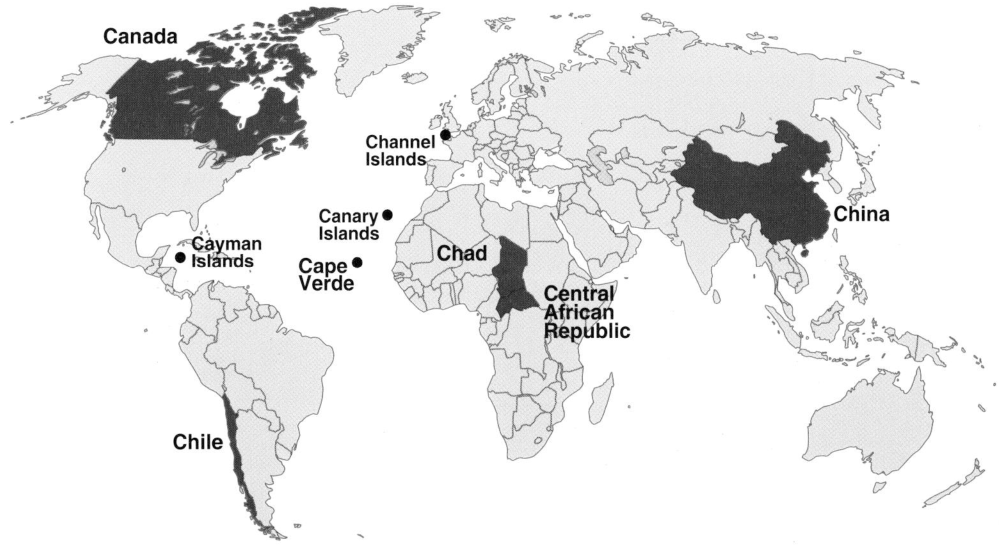

Western and northern China are much less densely populated as cultivation is restricted to oases and sheltered valleys. In the southwest, the Tibetan plateau averages 4,900 m (16,000 ft) and supports scattered sheep herding. To the north are Sinkiang and the desert basins of Tarim (Tarim Pendi) and Dzungaria, and bordering Mongolia the vast dry Gobi desert. In the far north only in Manchuria does a more temperate climate allow extensive arable cultivation, of mainly wheat, barley and maize.

The natural mineral resources of China are immense, varied and under-exploited. The Yunnan plateau of the southeast is rich in tin, copper, and zinc; Manchuria possesses coal and iron ore; and oil is extracted from beneath the Yellow Sea. The main industrial centres concentrate on the production of iron, steel, cement, light engineering and textile manufacturing.

With a population of over one billion, China has made tremendous efforts since the late 1970s to erase the negative economic effects of the collectivization policy implemented from 1955, and the cultural revolution of the late 1960s. In 1978 the Chinese leader, Deng Xiaoping, launched an economic revolution (creating special economic zones and encouraging foreign investment). The country is now experiencing phenomenal economic growth, a new consumer revolution and waves of entrepreneurial activities. A growing inequality in living standards between the rural provinces and the richer urban areas has led to a surge of migrants from the countryside to the cities.

ANHUI (ANHWEI)

STATUS: Province
AREA: 139,900 sq km (54,000 sq miles)
POPULATION: 57,600,000
CAPITAL: Hefei

BEIJING (PEKING)

STATUS: Municipality
AREA: 17,800 sq km (6,870 sq miles)
POPULATION: 10,900,000

FUJIAN (FUKIEN)

STATUS: Province
AREA: 123,000 sq km (47,515 sq miles)
POPULATION: 30,800,000
CAPITAL: Fuzhou

GANSU (KANSU)

STATUS: Province
AREA: 530,000 sq km (204,580 sq miles)
POPULATION: 22,900,000
CAPITAL: Lanzhou

GUANGDONG (KWANGTUNG)

STATUS: Province
AREA: 231,400 sq km (89,320 sq miles)
POPULATION: 64,400,000
CAPITAL: Guangzhou (Canton)

GUANGXI (KWANGSI-CHUANG)

STATUS: Autonomous Region
AREA: 220,400 sq km (85,075 sq miles)
POPULATION: 43,200,000
CAPITAL: Nanning

GUIZHOU (KWEICHOW)

STATUS: Province
AREA: 174,000 sq km (67,165 sq miles)
POPULATION: 33,200,000
CAPITAL: Guiyang

HAINAN

STATUS: Province
AREA: 34,965 sq km (13,500 sq miles)
POPULATION: 6,700,000
CAPITAL: Haikou

HEBEI (HOPEI)

STATUS: Province
AREA: 202,700 sq km (78,240 sq miles)
POPULATION: 62,200,000
CAPITAL: Schijiazhuang

HEILONGJIANG (HEILUNGKIANG)

STATUS: Province
AREA: 710,000 sq km (274,060 sq miles)
POPULATION: 35,800,000
CAPITAL: Harbin

HENAN (HONAN)

STATUS: Province
AREA: 167,000 sq km (64,460 sq miles)
POPULATION: 87,600,000
CAPITAL: Zhengzhou

HUBEI (HUPEH)

STATUS: Province
AREA: 187,500 sq km (72,375 sq miles)
POPULATION: 55,100,000
CAPITAL: Wuhan

HUNAN
STATUS: Province
AREA: 210,500 sq km (81,255 sq miles)
POPULATION: 62,100,000
CAPITAL: Changsha

JIANGSU (KIANGSU)
STATUS: Province
AREA: 102,200 sq km (39,450 miles)
POPULATION: 68,400,000
CAPITAL: Nanjing (Nanking)

JIANGXI (KIANGSI)
STATUS: Province
AREA: 164,800 sq km (63,615 sq miles)
POPULATION: 38,700,000
CAPITAL: Nanchang

JILIN (KIRIN)
STATUS: Province
AREA: 290,000 sq km (111,940 sq miles)
POPULATION: 25,100,000
CAPITAL: Changchun

LIAONING
STATUS: Province
AREA: 230,000 sq km (88,780 sq miles)
POPULATION: 39,900,000
CAPITAL: Shenyang

NEI MONGOL (INNER MONGOLIA)
STATUS: Autonomous Region
AREA: 450,000 sq km (173,700 sq miles)
POPULATION: 21,800,000
CAPITAL: Hohhot

NINGXIA HUI (NINGHSIA HUI)
STATUS: Autonomous Region
AREA: 170,000 sq km (65,620 sq miles)
POPULATION: 4,800,000
CAPITAL: Yinchuan

QINGHAI (CHINGHAI)
STATUS: Province
AREA: 721,000 sq km (278,305 sq miles)
POPULATION: 4,500,000
CAPITAL: Xining

SHAANXI (SHENSI)
STATUS: Province
AREA: 195,800 sq km (75,580 sq miles)
POPULATION: 33,600,000
CAPITAL: Xian (Xi'an)

SHANDONG (SHANTUNG)
STATUS: Province
AREA: 153,300 sq km (59,175 sq miles)
POPULATION: 83,430,000
CAPITAL: Jinan

SHANGHAI
STATUS: Municipality
AREA: 5,800 sq km (2,240 sq miles)
POPULATION: 13,400,000

SHANXI (SHANSI)
STATUS: Province
AREA: 157,100 sq km (60,640 sq miles)
POPULATION: 29,400,000
CAPITAL: Taiyuan

SICHUAN (SZECHWAN)
STATUS: Province
AREA: 569,000 sq km (219,635 sq miles)
POPULATION: 109,000,000
CAPITAL: Chengdu

TIANJIN (TIENTSIN)
STATUS: Municipality
AREA: 4,000 sq km (1,545 sq miles)
POPULATION: 9,100,402

XINJIANG UYGUR (SINKIANG-UIGHUR)
STATUS: Autonomous Region
AREA: 1,646,800 sq km (635,665 sq miles)
POPULATION: 15,600,000
CAPITAL: Urumchi (Ürümqi)

XIZANG (TIBET)
STATUS: Autonomous Region
AREA: 1,221,600 sq km (471,540 sq miles)
POPULATION: 2,300,000
CAPITAL: Lhasa

YUNNAN
STATUS: Province
AREA: 436,200 sq km (168,375 sq miles)
POPULATION: 37,800,000
CAPITAL: Kunming

ZHEJIANG (CHEKIANG)
STATUS: Province
AREA: 101,800 sq km (39,295 sq miles)
POPULATION: 42,000,000
CAPITAL: Hangzhou

CHRISTMAS ISLAND
STATUS: External Territory of Australia
AREA: 135 sq km (52 sq miles)
POPULATION: 1,275

COCOS (KEELING) ISLANDS
STATUS: External Territory of Australia
AREA: 14 sq km (5 sq miles)
POPULATION: 647

COLOMBIA
STATUS: Republic
AREA: 1,138,915 (439,620 sq miles)
POPULATION: 13,813,000
ANNUAL NATURAL INCREASE: 1.8%
CAPITAL: Bogotá
LANGUAGE: Spanish, Indian languages
RELIGION: 95% Roman Catholic, Protestant and Jewish minorities
CURRENCY: Colombian peso (COP)
ORGANIZATIONS: OAS, UN

Colombia is bounded by both the Caribbean Sea and Pacific Ocean. The northernmost peaks of the Andes chain runs from north to south through its western half and the eastern plains, beyond the Andes, contain the headwaters of the Amazon and Orinoco rivers. Almost half of Colombia is covered by the Amazon jungle. Colombia has a tropical climate and temperatures that vary with climate. The fertile river valleys in the uplands produce most of the famous Colombian coffee. Bananas, tobacco, cotton, sugar and rice are grown at lower altitudes. Coffee has always been the major export crop, but manufacturing industry and oil, coal, gold and precious stones are becoming more dominant in the economy. An oil boom is predicted following the discovery of new oil fields at Cusiana and Cupiagua. Immense illegal quantities of cocaine are exported to the US and elsewhere.

COMOROS
STATUS: Federal Islamic Republic
AREA: 1,860 sq km (718 sq miles)
POPULATION: 585,000
ANNUAL NATURAL INCREASE: 3.7%
CAPITAL: Moroni
LANGUAGE: French, Arabic, Comoran
RELIGION: Muslim majority, Christian minority
CURRENCY: Comoro franc (KMF)
ORGANIZATIONS: OAU, UN

The Comoro Islands, comprising Grand Comore, Anjouan, and Móneli, are situated between Madagascar and the east African coast. The climate is tropical and humid all year round, with a moderate average annual rainfall ranging from 1,000–1140 mm (40–45 inches). Less than half the land is cultivated and the country is dependent on imports for food supplies. The island's economy is based on the export of vanilla, copra, cloves and ylang-ylang essence (exported for the French perfume industry). Mangoes, coconuts and bananas are grown around the coastal lowlands. Timber and timber products are important to local development. There is no manufacturing of any importance.

CONGO
STATUS: Republic
AREA: 342,000 sq km (132,010 sq miles)
POPULATION: 2,690,000
ANNUAL NATURAL INCREASE: 3.3%
CAPITAL: Brazzaville
LANGUAGE: French, Kongo, Teke, Sanga
RELIGION: 50% traditional beliefs, 30% Roman Catholic, Protestant and Muslim minorities
CURRENCY: CFA franc (C Africa) (XAF)
ORGANIZATIONS: OAU, UN

The Congo, Africa's first communist state still has strong economic ties with the west, especially France, its former colonial ruler. Situated on the coast of west Africa, it contains over two-thirds swamp and forest, with wooded savannah on the highlands of the Bateké plateau near the Gabon border. Its climate is hot and humid with average rainfall of 1220–1280 mm (48–50 inches). Over 60 per cent of the population is employed in subsistence farming, while sugar, coffee, palm oil and cocoa are all exported. Timber and timber products are major exports but the main source of export revenue is oil from offshore oilfields. Mineral resources are considerable, including industrial diamonds, gold, lead and zinc. Manufacturing industry is concentrated in the major towns and is primarily food processing and textiles.

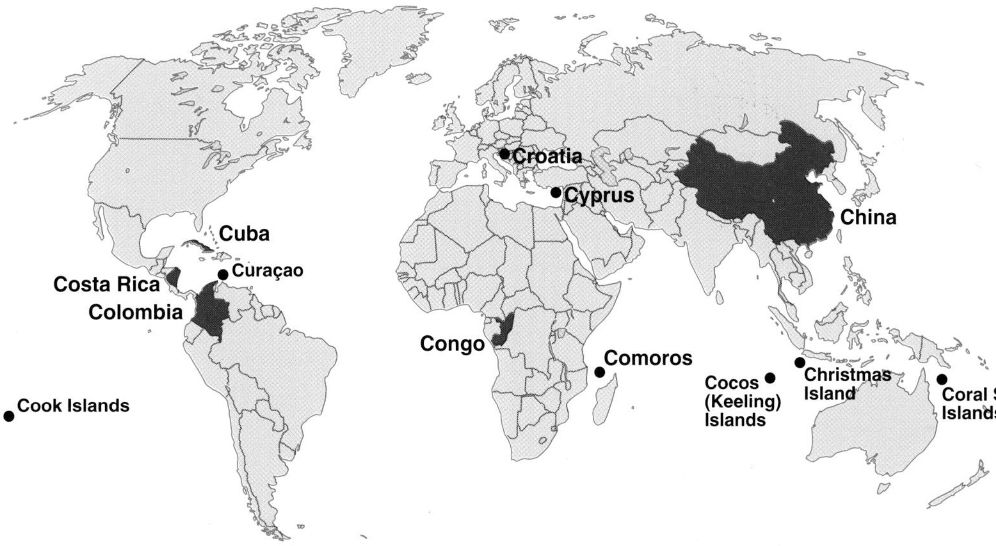

COOK ISLANDS

STATUS: Self-governing Territory Overseas in Free Association with New Zealand
AREA: 233 sq km (90 sq miles)
POPULATION: 18,617
CAPITAL: Avarua on Rarotonga

CORAL SEA ISLANDS

STATUS: External Territory of Australia
AREA: 22 sq km (8.5 sq miles)
POPULATION: no permanent population

COSTA RICA

STATUS: Republic
AREA: 50,900 sq km (19,650 sq miles)
POPULATION: 3,099,000
ANNUAL NATURAL INCREASE: 2.5%
CAPITAL: San José
LANGUAGE: Spanish
RELIGION: 95% Roman Catholic
CURRENCY: Costa Rican colón (CRC)
ORGANIZATIONS: CACM, OAS, UN

Costa Rica is a narrow country, situated between Nicaragua and Panama, with both a Pacific and a Caribbean coastline. Its coastal regions experience hot, humid, tropical conditions, but in upland areas its climate is more equable. The mountain chains that run the length of the country form the fertile uplands where coffee is grown and cattle are kept. Bananas, grown on the Pacific coast, and coffee are the major cash crops for export. Although gold, silver, iron ore and bauxite are mined, the principal industries are food processing and the manufacture of textiles and chemicals, fertilizers and furniture.

CROATIA

STATUS: Republic
AREA: 56,540 sq km (21,825 sq miles)
POPULATION: 4,764,000
ANNUAL NATURAL INCREASE: 0.4%
CAPITAL: Zagreb
LANGUAGE: Serbo-Croat
RELIGION: Roman Catholic majority
CURRENCY: kuna
ORGANIZATIONS: UN

Croatia is an oddly shaped country which runs in a narrow strip along the Adriatic coast and extends inland in a broad curve. Its climate varies from Mediterranean along the coast to continental further inland. Once part of the Yugoslavian Federation, Croatia achieved recognition as an independent nation in 1992 following the 1991 civil war between Serb and Croat factions. The conflict left the country with a damaged economy, disruption of trade, loss of tourist revenue and a huge reconstruction bill. Traditionally the fertile plains of central and eastern Croatia have been intensively farmed, producing surplus crops, meat and dairy products. The mountainous and barren littoral has been developed for tourism. Croatia used to be the most highly developed part of Yugoslavia, concentrating on electrical engineering, metal working, machine building, chemicals and rubber. Economic recovery is dependent upon political stability and an accommodation with the Serbs over the UN-supervised areas still under ethnic Serb control.

CUBA

STATUS: Republic
AREA: 114,525 sq km (44,205 sq miles)
POPULATION: 10,870,000
ANNUAL NATURAL INCREASE: 1.0%
CAPITAL: Havana (Habana)
LANGUAGE: Spanish
RELIGION: Roman Catholic majority
CURRENCY: Cuban peso (CUP)
ORGANIZATIONS: OIEC, UN

Cuba, the largest of the Greater Antilles islands, dominates the entrance to the Gulf of Mexico. It consists of one large and over 1,500 small islands, and is a mixture of fertile plains, mountain ranges and gentle countryside. Temperatures range from 22–28°C (72–82°F) and an there is an average annual rainfall of 1,200 mm (47 inches). Sugar, tobacco and nickel are the main exports. Being a communist state, most of Cuba's trade has been with the former USSR and in the three years following the collapse of the Soviet Union the Cuban economy contracted by over 30 per cent (having lost its principal market for sugar, which it had bartered for oil, food and machinery). The economy was already suffering from US sanctions. Severe shortages of food, fuel and basic necessities were tolerated and in 1993 the government was forced to permit limited private enterprise and the use of American dollars.

CURAÇAO

STATUS: Self-governing Island of the Netherlands Antilles
AREA: 444 sq km (171 sq miles)
POPULATION: 707,000

CYPRUS

STATUS: Republic
(Turkish unilateral declaration of independence in northern area)
AREA: 9,250 sq km (3,570 sq miles)
POPULATION: 725,000
ANNUAL NATURAL INCREASE: 1.1%
CAPITAL: Nicosia
LANGUAGE: Greek, Turkish, English
RELIGION: Greek Orthodox majority, Muslim minority
CURRENCY: Cyprus pound (CYP), Turkish lira (TL)
ORGANIZATIONS: Comm., Council of Europe, UN

Cyprus is a prosperous Mediterranean island. The summers are very hot (38°C or 100°F) and dry, and the winters warm and wet. About two-thirds of the island is under cultivation and citrus fruit, potatoes, barley, wheat and olives are produced. Sheep, goats and pigs are the principal livestock. Copper is mined but the mining industry is declining. The main exports are manufactured goods, clothing and footwear, fruit, wine and vegetables. Tourism is an important source of foreign exchange.

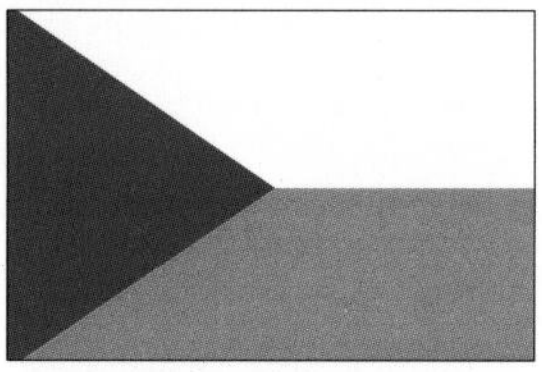

CZECH REPUBLIC

STATUS: Federal Republic
AREA: 127,870 sq km (49,360 sq miles)
POPULATION: 10,330,000
ANNUAL NATURAL INCREASE: 0.3%
CAPITAL: Prague (Praha)
LANGUAGE: Czech
RELIGION: 40% Roman Catholic, 55% no stated religion
CURRENCY: Czech crown or koruna (CSK)
ORGANIZATIONS: Council of Europe, OIEC, UN

Following the break up of Czechoslovakia, the Czech Republic came into being in January 1993. It is a country that lies at the heart of central Europe and has a diversity of landscapes. In Bohemia, to the west of the country, the upper Elbe drainage basin is surrounded by mountains. Moravia, separated from Bohemia by hills and mountains, is a lowland area centred on the town of Brno. The climate is temperate but with continental characteristics. Rain falls mainly in spring and autumn. This is historically one of the most highly industrialized regions of Europe, whose heavy industry once specialized in producing arms for the Soviet Union. Now the main products include cars, aircraft, tramways and locomotive diesel engines. There are raw materials (coal, minerals and timber) and a nuclear power station is being built to replace some polluting coal-fired stations.

DENMARK

STATUS: Kingdom
AREA: 43,075 sq km (16,625 sq miles)
POPULATION: 5,181,000
ANNUAL NATURAL INCREASE: 0.1%
CAPITAL: Copenhagen (København)
LANGUAGE: Danish
RELIGION: 94% Lutheran, Roman Catholic minority
CURRENCY: Danish krone (DKK)
ORGANIZATIONS: Council of Europe, EU, NATO, OECD, UN

Denmark is the smallest of the Scandinavian countries. It consists of the Jutland Peninsula and over 400 islands of which only one quarter are inhabited. The country is low-lying with a mixture of fertile and sandy soils, generally of glacial origin. Climate is temperate, with rainfall all the year round. Denmark's economy stems traditionally from agriculture and dairy products; bacon and sugar are still particularly important. An extensive fishing industry is centred on the shallow lagoons along the western coastline. Danish North Sea oil and gas provide self-sufficiency in energy and gas exports began in 1991. Food processing, beer, pharmaceuticals and specialist biotechnological equipment contribute to the industrial sector which provides 75 per cent of Danish exports.

DJIBOUTI

STATUS: Republic
AREA: 23,000 sq km (8,800 sq miles)
POPULATION: 467,000
ANNUAL NATURAL INCREASE: 2.9%
CAPITAL: Djibouti
LANGUAGE: French, Somali, Dankali, Arabic
RELIGION: Muslim majority, Roman Catholic minority
CURRENCY: Djibouti franc (DJF)
ORGANIZATIONS: Arab League, OAU, UN

Situated at the mouth of the Red Sea, Djibouti consists almost entirely of low-lying desert. There are mountains in the north of which Musa Ālī Terara reaches 2,063 m (6,768 feet). Its climate is very hot all year with annual temperatures between 25–35°C (78–96°F). The annual rainfall is as low as 130 mm (5 inches). The land is barren so Djibouti's economy must rely on activities based on its deep natural port and position along a major shipping route. It therefore acts as a trade outlet for Ethiopia, as well as serving Red Sea shipping. Main exports are cattle and hides.

DOMINICA

STATUS: Commonwealth State
AREA: 751 sq km (290 sq miles)
POPULATION: 72,000
ANNUAL NATURAL INCREASE: -0.3%
CAPITAL: Roseau
LANGUAGE: English, French patois
RELIGION: 80% Roman Catholic
CURRENCY: East Caribbean dollar (XCD)
ORGANIZATIONS: Comm., OAS, UN

Dominica is located in the Windward Islands of the east Caribbean. It is mountainous and forested with a coastline of steep cliffs. Tropical rainforest covers nearly half of the island. The climate is tropical with average temperatures exceeding 25°C (77°F) and has abundant rainfall. Bananas are the major export, followed by citrus fruits, coconuts and timber. Coffee and cocoa production is developing. Tourism is the most rapidly expanding industry.

DOMINICAN REPUBLIC

STATUS: Republic
AREA: 48,440 sq km (18,700 sq miles)
POPULATION: 7,471,000
ANNUAL NATURAL INCREASE: 1.9%
CAPITAL: Santo Domingo
LANGUAGE: Spanish
RELIGION: 90% Roman Catholic, Protestant and Jewish minorities
CURRENCY: Dominican peso (DOP)
ORGANIZATIONS: OAS, UN

The Dominican Republic is situated on the eastern half of the Caribbean island of Hispaniola. The landscape is dominated by a series of mountain ranges, thickly covered with rainforest, reaching up to 3,000 m (9,843 feet). To the south there is a coastal plain where the capital, Santo Domingo, lies. Minerals, in particular nickel, are important but agricultural products account for 70 per cent of export earnings. The traditional dependence on sugar has diminished, with coffee, tobacco and newer products including cocoa, fruit and vegetables gaining importance.

ECUADOR

STATUS: Republic
AREA: 461,475 sq km (178,130 sq miles)
POPULATION: 10,741,000
ANNUAL NATURAL INCREASE: 2.5%
CAPITAL: Quito
LANGUAGE: Spanish, Quechua, other Indian languages
RELIGION: 90% Roman Catholic
CURRENCY: sucre (ECS)
ORGANIZATIONS: OAS, UN

Ecuador falls into two distinctive geographical zones, the coastal lowlands which border the Pacific Ocean and inland, the Andean highlands. The highlands stretch about 400 km (250 miles) north-south, and here limited quantities of maize, wheat and barley are cultivated. Ecuador's main agricultural export, bananas, coffee and cocoa, are all grown on the fertile coastal lowlands. The rapidly growing fishing industry, especially shrimps, is becoming more important. Large resources of crude oil have been found in the thickly-forested lowlands on the eastern border and Ecuador has now become South America's second largest oil producer after Venezuela. Mineral reserves include silver, gold, copper and zinc.

EGYPT

STATUS: Republic
AREA: 1,000,250 sq km (386,095 sq miles)
POPULATION: 55,163,000
ANNUAL NATURAL INCREASE: 2.4%
CAPITAL: Cairo (El Qâhira)
LANGUAGE: Arabic, Berber, Nubian, English, French
RELIGION: 80% Muslim (mainly Sunni), Coptic Christian minority
CURRENCY: Egyptian pound (EGP)
ORGANIZATIONS: Arab league, OAU, UN

The focal point of Egypt, situated on the Mediterranean coast of northeast Africa, is the fertile, irrigated Nile river valley, sandwiched between two deserts. Egypt is virtually dependent on the Nile for water as average rainfall varies between only 200 mm (8 inches) in the north and zero in the deserts. Cotton and Egyptian clover are the two most important crops, with increasing cultivation of cereals, fruits, rice, sugar cane and vegetables. Agriculture is concentrated around the Nile flood plain and delta. In spite of this, however, Egypt has to import over half the food it needs. Buffalo, cattle, sheep, goats and camels are the principal livestock. Tourism is an important source of revenue together with the tolls from the Suez Canal. Major industries include the manufacture of cement, cotton goods, iron and steel, and processed foods. The main mineral deposits are phosphates, iron ore, salt, manganese and chromium. Egypt has sufficient oil and natural gas reserves for its own needs and exports crude oil. Gas is now replacing oil in Egyptian power stations in order to release more crude oil for export.

EL SALVADOR

STATUS: Republic
AREA: 21,395 sq km (8,260 sq miles)
POPULATION: 5,048,000
ANNUAL NATURAL INCREASE: 1.8%
CAPITAL: San Salvador
LANGUAGE: Spanish
RELIGION: 80% Roman Catholic
CURRENCY: El Salvador colón (SVC)
ORGANIZATIONS: CACM, OAS, UN

El Salvador is a small, densely populated country on the Pacific coast of Central America. Most of the population live around the lakes in the central plain. Temperatures range from 24–26°C (75–79°F) with an average annual rainfall of 1,780 mm (70 inches). Coffee provides about 50 per cent of export revenue. Other products include sugar, cotton, bananas and balsam. Industry has expanded considerably with the production of textiles, shoes, cosmetics, cement, processed foods, chemicals and furniture. Geothermal and hydro-electric resources are being developed and there are copper deposits as yet unexploited.

EQUATORIAL GUINEA

STATUS: Republic
AREA: 28,050 sq km (10,825 sq miles)
POPULATION: 369,000
ANNUAL NATURAL INCREASE: 2.3%
CAPITAL: Malabo
LANGUAGE: 85% Fang, Spanish, Bubi, other tribal languages

RELIGION: 96% Roman Catholic, 4% Animist
CURRENCY: CFA franc (C Africa) (XAF)
ORGANIZATIONS: OAU, UN

Independent from Spain since 1968, Equatorial Guinea consists of two separate regions – a mainland area with a tropical, humid climate and dense rainforest but little economic development, and the volcanic island of Bioko. Agriculture is the principal source of revenue. Cocoa and coffee from the island plantations are the main exports with wood products, fish and processed foods manufactured near the coast on the mainland.

ERITREA

STATUS: Republic
AREA: 91,600 sq km (35,370 sq miles)
POPULATION: 3,500,000
CAPITAL: Asmara (Āsmera)
LANGUAGE: Arabic, native languages, English
RELIGION: 50% Christian, 50% Muslim
CURRENCY: Ethiopian birr
ORGANIZATIONS: OAU, UN

Eritrea gained formal recognition of its independence from Ethiopia in 1993. The landscape consists of an arid coastal plain, which borders the Red Sea, and the highlands of the central area, which rise to over 2000 m (6,562 feet). There are few natural resources, with what industry there is being concentrated around Asmara. The consequences of continuing drought and the protracted civil war will affect the population and economy for some time to come.

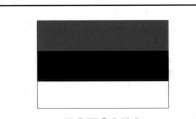

ESTONIA

STATUS: Republic
AREA: 45,100 sq km (17,413 sq miles)
POPULATION: 1,516,000
ANNUAL NATURAL INCREASE: 0.2%
CAPITAL: Tallinn
LANGUAGE: Estonian, Russian
RELIGION: Lutheran, Roman Catholic
CURRENCY: kroon (EKR)
ORGANIZATIONS: Council of Europe, UN

With the mainland situated on the southern coast of the Gulf of Finland and encompassing a large number of islands, Estonia is the smallest and most northerly of the Baltic States. The generally flat and undulating landscape is characterised by extensive forests and many lakes. The climate is temperate. Agriculture, mainly livestock production, woodworking and textiles are also important. The economy is currently undergoing a transformation from central planning and state-ownership to a free market system based on private enterprise. Incorporated into the Soviet Union in 1940, Estonia regained its independence in 1991.

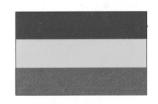

ETHIOPIA

STATUS: Republic
AREA: 1,023,050 sq km (394,895 sq miles)
POPULATION: 51,980,000
ANNUAL NATURAL INCREASE: 3.4%
CAPITAL: Addis Ababa (Ādīs Ābeba)
LANGUAGE: Amharic, English, Arabic
RELIGION: Ethiopian Orthodox, Muslim and animist
CURRENCY: birr (ETB)
ORGANIZATIONS: OAU, UN

Ethiopia's landscape consists of heavily dissected plateaux and plains of arid desert. Rainfall in these latter areas is minimal and unreliable, and drought and starvation are ever-present problems. Farming, in the high rural areas, accounts for 90 per cent of export revenue with coffee as the principal crop and main export together with fruit and vegetables, oil-seeds, hides and skins. Gold is mined on a small scale. The most important industries are cotton textiles, cement, canned foods, construction materials and leather goods. These are concentrated around the capital. In recent years the economy has been devastated by almost constant civil war.

FAEROES

STATUS: Self-governing Island Region of Denmark
AREA: 1,399 sq km (540 sq miles)
POPULATION: 47,000
CAPITAL: Tórshavn

FALKLAND ISLANDS

STATUS: UK Crown Colony
AREA: 12,175 sq km (4,700 sq miles)
POPULATION: 2,121
CAPITAL: Stanley

FIJI

STATUS: Republic
AREA: 18,330 sq km (7,075 sq miles)
POPULATION: 758,275
ANNUAL NATURAL INCREASE: 1.8%
CAPITAL: Suva
LANGUAGE: Fijian, English, Hindi
RELIGION: 51% Methodist Christian, 40% Hindu, 8% Muslim
CURRENCY: Fiji dollar (FJD)
ORGANIZATIONS: Col. Plan, UN

A country of some 320 tropical islands, of which over 100 are inhabited, the Republic of Fiji is located in Melanesia, in the south-central Pacific Ocean. The islands range from tiny coral reefs and atolls to the two largest Vanua Levu and Viti Levu, which are mountainous and of volcanic origin. The climate is tropical with temperatures ranging from 16–33°C (60–90°F) and annual rainfall being 236 mm (60 inches). Fiji's economy is geared to production of sugar cane, which provides 45 per cent of export revenue. Coconuts, bananas and rice are grown and livestock raised. Main industries are sugar processing, gold-mining, copra processing and fish canning. Tourism is also an important revenue earner.

FINLAND

STATUS: Republic
AREA: 337,030 sq km (130,095 sq miles)
POPULATION: 5,076,000
ANNUAL NATURAL INCREASE: 0.4%
CAPITAL: Helsinki
LANGUAGE: Finnish, Swedish
RELIGION: 87% Evangelical Lutheran, Eastern Orthodox minority
CURRENCY: markka (Finnmark) (FIM)
ORGANIZATIONS: Council of Europe, EEA, EFTA, OECD, UN

Finland is a flat land of lakes and forests. Over 70 per cent of the land supports coniferous woodland with a further 10 per cent being water. The Saimaa lake area is Europe's largest inland water system. Its soils are thin and poor on ice-scarred granite plateaux. Most of Finland's population live in towns in the far south because of the harsh northern climate. In the north temperatures can range from -30°C (-22°F) in the winter to 27°C (81°F) in summer. The Baltic Sea can freeze for several miles from the coast during winter months. There is 600 mm (24 inches) of rain per annum throughout the country. Forestry products (timber, pulp and paper) once dominated the economy (80 per cent in 1980) but now account for 40 per cent of the export total and engineering, in particular shipbuilding and forest machinery, is almost equal in importance. Finland is virtually self-sufficient in basic foodstuffs. The country depends heavily on imported energy, producing only 30 per cent of its total consumption (20 per cent by its four nuclear power stations).

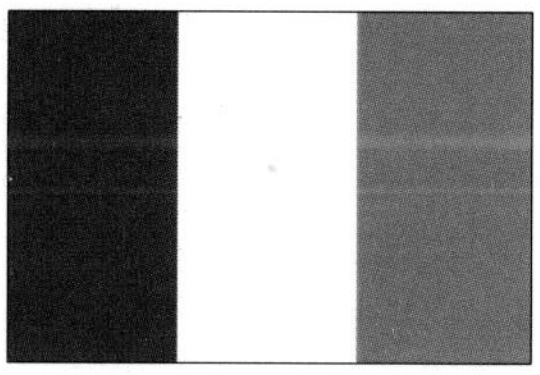

FRANCE

STATUS: Republic
AREA: 543,965 sq km (209,970 sq miles)
POPULATION: 57,800,000
ANNUAL NATURAL INCREASE: 0.6%
CAPITAL: Paris
LANGUAGE: French
RELIGION: 90% Roman Catholic. Protestant, Muslim, Jewish minorities
CURRENCY: French franc (FRF)
ORGANIZATIONS: Council of Europe, EEA, EU, G7, NATO, OECD, UN, WEU

France encompasses a great variety of landscapes, ranging from mountain ranges, high plateaux to lowland plains and river basins. The Pyrenees, in the southwest, form the border with Spain and the Jura mountains, in the west, form a border with Switzerland. The highest mountain range is the Alps, south of the Jura. The Massif Central is the highest of the plateaux, which also include the Vosges bordering the plain of Alsace, and Armorica occupying the granite moors of the Brittany peninsula. The French climate is moderated by proximity to the Atlantic, and is generally mild. The south has a Mediterranean climate with hot dry summers, the rest of the country has rain all year round. (Paris has an average annual rainfall of 600 mm or 24 inches). Much of the French countryside is agricultural and it is estimated that one-third of the population derives an income from the land. France is self-sufficient in cereals, dairy products, meat, fruit and vegetables, and is a leading exporter of wheat, barley and sugar beet. Wine is also a major export. Over the past years there has been a steady drift of labour, mainly of younger people from the countryside to the industrialized areas. France is the fourth industrial power in the world after USA, Japan and Germany. It has reserves of coal, oil and natural gas, and is one of the world's leading producers of iron ore. It has large steel-making and chemical refining industries. Its vehicle, aeronautical and armaments industries are among the world's most important. Leading light industries are fashion, perfumes and luxury goods. Most of its heavy industry is concentrated in the major industrial zone of the northeast. In the past, sources of energy have been provided from its reserves of fossil fuels, however in recent years other sources have increased in importance, such as nuclear power using uranium from French mines, tidal power, and hydroelectricity. Tourism is an important source of income, that will be further encouraged by the opening of the Channel Tunnel.

FRENCH GUIANA

STATUS: Overseas Department of France
AREA: 91,000 sq km (35,125 sq miles)
POPULATION: 114,808
CAPITAL: Cayenne

FRENCH POLYNESIA

STATUS: Overseas Territory of France
AREA: 3,940 sq km (1,520 sq miles)
POPULATION: 199,031
CAPITAL: Papeete

GABON

STATUS: Republic
AREA: 267,665 sq km (103,320 sq miles)
POPULATION: 1,012,000
ANNUAL NATURAL INCREASE: 2.7%
CAPITAL: Libreville
LANGUAGE: French, Bantu dialects, Fang
RELIGION: 60% Roman Catholic.
CURRENCY: CFA franc (C Africa) (XAF)
ORGANIZATIONS: OAU, OPEC, UN,

Gabon, which lies on the equator, consists of the Ogooué river basin covered with tropical rain forest. It is hot and wet all year with average annual temperatures of 25°C (77°F). It is one of the most prosperous states in Africa with valuable timber (mahogany, ebony and walnut) and mineral (manganese and uranium) resources. State-run plantations growing oil palms, bananas, sugar cane and rubber are also important. Gabon's economy, however, is heavily dependent on its oil industry. It is the third largest producer in sub-Saharan Africa after Nigeria and Angola. France supplies nearly half the country's imports and French influence is evident everywhere.

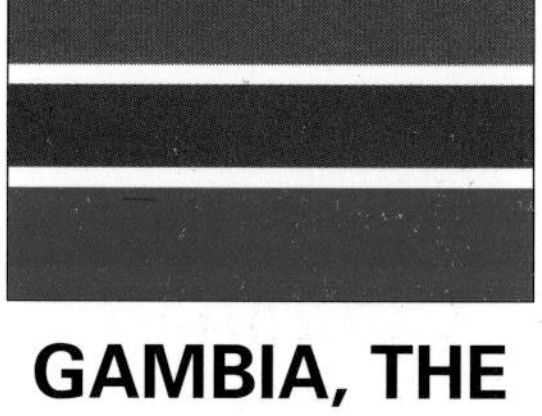

GAMBIA, THE

STATUS: Republic
AREA: 10,690 sq km (4,125 sq miles)
POPULATION: 1,026,000
ANNUAL NATURAL INCREASE: 3.2%
CAPITAL: Banjul
LANGUAGE: English, Madinka, Fula, Wolof

RELIGION: 90% Muslim,
Christian and animist minorities
CURRENCY: dalasi (GMD)
ORGANIZATIONS: Comm., ECOWAS, OAU, UN

The Gambia is the smallest country in Africa. An enclave within Senegal, it is 470 km (292 miles) long, averages 24 km (15 miles) wide and occupies land bordering the Gambia river. The climate has two distinctive seasons. November to May is dry but July to October sees monsoon rainfall of up to 1,300 mm (51 inches). The temperatures average about 23–27°C (73–81°F) throughout the year. Groundnuts and subsidiary products are the mainstay of the economy but tourism is developing rapidly. The production of cotton, livestock, fish and rice is increasing to change the present economic reliance on groundnuts.

GEORGIA

STATUS: Republic
AREA: 69,700 sq km (26,905 sq miles)
POPULATION: 5,471,000
ANNUAL NATURAL INCREASE: 0.5%
CAPITAL: Tbilisi
LANGUAGE: 70% Georgian, 8% Armenian, 6% Russian, 6% Azeri
RELIGION: Orthodox Christian
CURRENCY: coupon
ORGANIZATIONS: CIS

Georgia, covering part of the southern Caucasus, is a mountainous country with forests covering one-third of its area. The climate ranges from sub-tropical on the shores of the Black Sea, to perpetual ice and snow on the Caucasian crests. Rich deposits of coal are mainly unexploited. Cheap oil and gas imports, hydro-electric power and minerals, in particular rich manganese deposits, have led to industrialization successfully concentrated on metallurgy and machine-building. With the exception of the fertile plain to the east, agricultural land is in short supply and difficult to work. This is partly compensated by the cultivation of labour-intensive and profitable crops such as tea, grapes, tobacco and citrus fruit. The break-up of the Soviet Union brought independence for Georgia in 1991. The question of regional autonomy for the Abkhaz, Adzhar and South Ossetian minorities has repeatedly led to violent ethnic conflict in recent years, causing economic collapse.

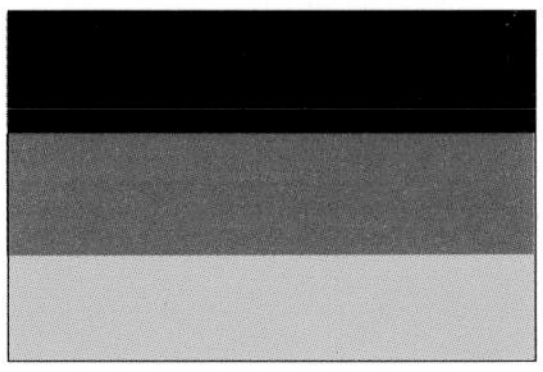

GERMANY

STATUS: Federal Republic
AREA: 356,840 sq km (137,740 sq miles)
POPULATION: 81,051,000
ANNUAL NATURAL INCREASE: 0.6%
CAPITAL: Berlin
(seat of government Berlin/Bonn)
LANGUAGE: German

RELIGION: 45% Protestant
40% Roman Catholic
CURRENCY: Deutsch-mark (DM)
ORGANIZATIONS: Council of Europe, EEA, EU, G7, NATO, OECD, UN, WEU

Germany has three main geographical regions: the Northern plain, stretching from the rivers Oder and Neisse in the east to the Dutch border; the central uplands with elevated plateaux intersected by river valleys and relieved by isolated mountains, gradually rising to peaks of up to nearly 1500 m (5000 feet) in the Black Forest: finally the Bavarian Alps stradling the Austrian border. With exception of the Danube, all German river systems run northwards into the North or the Baltic Seas. The climate is mainly continental with temperatures ranging from -3°–1°C (27–34°F) in January to 16°–19°C (61°–66°F) in July. Only in the north-western corner of the country does the climate become more oceanic in character. Germany on the whole has large stretches of very fertile farmland.

Politically, the division of Germany, a product of the post-1945 Cold War between the victorious Allies against Hitler, was rapidly overcome after the collapse of communism in Eastern Europe, and the unification of the two German states was effected in 1990. Economically, the legacy of 40 years of socialist rule in the East ensures that, in terms of both structure and performance, Germany will encompass two vastly different halves for a long time to come. Having lost its captive markets in what used to be the Soviet Bloc, the eastern economy then all but collapsed under the weight of superior western competition. The task of reconstruction is proving more difficult, more protracted and, most of all, more costly than expected. In the West, the Ruhr basin, historically the industrial heartland of Germany, with its emphasis on coal mining and iron and steel works, has long since been overtaken by more advanced industries elsewhere, notably in the Rhine-Main area and further south in the regions around Stuttgart and Munich. The rapidly expanding services sector apart, the German economy is now dominated by the chemical, pharmaceutical, mechanical engineering, motor and high-tech industries. To lessen the country's dependence on oil imports, an ambitious nuclear energy programme has been adopted. Although poor in minerals and other raw materials with the exception of lignite and potash, Germany has managed to become one of the world's leading manufacturers and exporters of vehicles, machine tools, electrical and electronic products and of consumer goods of various description, in particular textiles. But the massive balance of trade surplus West Germany used to enjoy has now disappeared due to the sucking in of imports by, and the redistribution of output to, the newly acquired territories in the East.

GHANA

STATUS: Republic
AREA: 238,305 sq km (91,985 sq miles)
POPULATION: 15,959,000
ANNUAL NATURAL INCREASE: 3.3%
CAPITAL: Accra
LANGUAGE: English, tribal languages
RELIGION: 42% Christian
CURRENCY: cedi (GHC)
ORGANIZATIONS: Comm., ECOWAS, OAU, UN

Ghana, the west African state once known as the Gold Coast, gained independence from Britain in 1957. The landscape varies from tropical rainforest to dry scrubland, with the terrain becoming hillier to the north, culminating in a plateau averaging some 500 m (1,600 feet). The climate is tropical with the annual rainfall ranging from over 2,000 mm (79 inches) on the coast to less than 1,000 mm (40 inches) inland. The temperature averages 27°C (81°F) all year. Cocoa is the principal crop but although most Ghanaians farm, there is also a thriving industrial base around Tema, where local bauxite is smelted into aluminium. Tema has the largest artificial harbour in Africa. In recent years gold production has surged, Ghana having some of the world's richest gold deposits. Besides gold, Ghana's major exports are cocoa and timber. Principal imports are fuel, food and manufactured goods. Offshore oil has yet to be economically developed.

GIBRALTAR

STATUS: UK Crown Colony
AREA: 6.5 sq km (2.5 sq miles)
POPULATION: 31,000

GREECE

STATUS: Republic
AREA: 131,985 sq km (50,945 sq miles)
POPULATION: 10,269,074
ANNUAL NATURAL INCREASE: 0.4%
CAPITAL: Athens (Athínai)
LANGUAGE: Greek
RELIGION: 97% Greek Orthodox
CURRENCY: drachma (GRD)
ORGANIZATIONS: Council of Europe, EC, NATO, OECD, UN

Greece is a mountainous country and over one-fifth of its area comprises numerous islands, 154 of which are inhabited. The climate is Mediterranean with temperatures averaging 28°C (82°F) in summer. The mountains experience some heavy snowfall during winter. Poor irrigation and drainage mean that much of the agriculture is localized. The main products of olives, fruit and vegetables, cotton, tobacco and wine are exported. The surrounding seas are important, providing two-thirds of Greece's fish requirements and supporting an active merchant fleet. Athens is the main manufacturing base and at least one quarter of the population lives there. Greece is a very popular tourist destination which helps the craft industries – tourism is a prime source of national income.

GREENLAND

STATUS: Self-governing Island Region of Denmark
AREA: 2,175,600 sq km (836,780 sq miles)
POPULATION: 55,558
CAPITAL: Godthåb (Nuuk)

GRENADA

STATUS: Commonwealth State
AREA: 345 sq km (133 sq miles)
POPULATION: 95,343
ANNUAL NATURAL INCREASE: -0.2%
CAPITAL: St George's
LANGUAGE: English, French patois
RELIGION: Roman Catholic majority
CURRENCY: E Caribbean dollar (XCD)
ORGANIZATIONS: Caricom, Comm., OAS, UN

The Caribbean island of Grenada, whose territory includes the southern Grenadines, is the most southern of the Windward Islands. It is mountainous and thickly forested, with a settled warm climate and an average temperature of 27°C (81°F). Rainfall varies with altitude, ranging from 760 mm (30 inches) to 3,560 mm (140 inches) on the higher ground. The island is famous for its spices and nutmeg is the main export. Cocoa and bananas are also important, together with some citrus fruits and vegetables. Tourism is important and continues to expand.

GUADELOUPE

STATUS: Overseas Department of France
AREA: 1,780 sq km (687 sq miles)
POPULATION: 406,000
CAPITAL: Basse-Terre

GUAM

STATUS: External Territory of USA
AREA: 450 sq km (174 sq miles)
POPULATION: 139,000
CAPITAL: Agaña

GUATEMALA

STATUS: Republic
AREA: 108,890 sq km (42,030 sq miles)
POPULATION: 9,745,000
ANNUAL NATURAL INCREASE: 2.9%
CAPITAL: Guatemala City (Guatemala)
LANGUAGE: Spanish, Indian languages
RELIGION: 75% Roman Catholic, 25% Protestant
CURRENCY: quetzal (GTQ)
ORGANIZATIONS: CACM, OAS, UN

The central American country of Guatemala has both a Pacific and a Caribbean coastline. The mountainous interior, with peaks reaching up to 4,000 m (13,120 feet), covers two-thirds of the country while to the north there is the thickly forested area known as the Petén. The northern lowland and the smaller coastal plains have a hot tropical climate, but the central highlands are more temperate. A rainy season lasts from May to October. Annual rainfall reaches up to 5,000 mm (200 inches) in some lowland areas but decreases to an average of 1,150 mm (45 inches) in the mountains. Agricultural products form the bulk of Guatemala's exports, notably coffee, sugar cane, cotton and bananas, but there is also a substantial industrial base. Manufacturing includes textiles, paper and pharmaceuticals. Mineral resources include nickel, antimony, lead, silver and in the north crude oil.

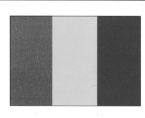

GUINEA

STATUS: Republic
AREA: 245,855 sq km (94,900 sq miles)
POPULATION: 6,116,000
ANNUAL NATURAL INCREASE: 2.8%
CAPITAL: Conakry
LANGUAGE: French, Susu, Manika
RELIGION: 85% Muslim 10% animist, 5% Roman Catholic
CURRENCY: Guinea franc (GNF)
ORGANIZATIONS: ECOWAS, OAU, UN

Guinea, a former French colony, is situated on the west African coast. Its drowned coastline, lined with mangrove swamps, contrasts strongly with its interior highlands containing the headwaters of the Gambia, Niger and Senegal rivers. Agriculture occupies 80 per cent of the workforce, the main exports being coffee, bananas, pineapple and palm products. Guinea has some of the largest resources of bauxite (aluminium ore) in the world as well as gold and diamonds. Bauxite accounts for 80 per cent of export earnings.

GUINEA-BISSAU

STATUS: Republic
AREA: 36,125 sq km (13,945 sq miles)
POPULATION: 1,006,000
ANNUAL NATURAL INCREASE: 1.9%
CAPITAL: Bissau
LANGUAGE: Portuguese, Creole, Guinean dialects
RELIGION: Animist and Muslim majority, Roman Catholic minority
CURRENCY: Guinea-Bissau peso (GWP)
ORGANIZATIONS: ECOWS, OAU, UN

Guinea-Bissau, on the west African coast, was once a centre for the Portuguese slave trade. The coast is swampy and lined with mangroves, and the interior consists of a low-lying plain densely covered with rain forest. The coast is hot and humid with annual rainfall of 2,000–3,000 mm (79–118 inches) a year, although the interior is cooler and drier. Eighty per cent of the country's exports comprise groundnut oil, palm kernels and palm oil. Fish, fish products and coconuts also make an important contribution to trade.

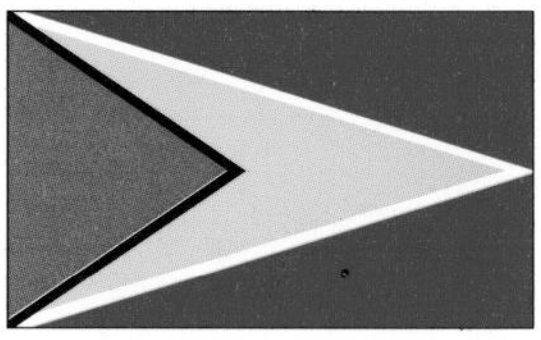

GUYANA

STATUS: Co-operative Republic
AREA: 214,970 sq km (82,980 sq miles)
POPULATION: 808,000
ANNUAL NATURAL INCREASE: 0.3%
CAPITAL: Georgetown
LANGUAGE: English, Hindi, Urdu, Amerindian dialects
RELIGION: Christian majority, Muslim and Hindu minorities
CURRENCY: Guyana dollar (GYD)
ORGANIZATIONS: Caricom, Comm., UN

Guyana, formerly the British colony of British Guiana, borders both Venezuela and Brazil. Its Atlantic coast, the most densely-populated area, is flat and marshy, while towards the interior the landscape gradually rises to the Guiana Highlands – a region densely covered in rainforest. The climate is tropical, with hot, wet and humid conditions, which are modified along the coast by sea breezes. Agriculture, dominated by sugar and rice, is the basis of the economy. Bauxite deposits provide a valuable export and in the mid-1990s gold production increased.

HAITI

STATUS: Republic
AREA: 27,750 sq km (10,710 sq miles)
POPULATION: 6,764,000
ANNUAL NATURAL INCREASE: 2.0%
CAPITAL: Port-au-Prince
LANGUAGE: French, Creole
RELIGION: 80% Roman Catholic, Voodoo folk religion minority
CURRENCY: gourde (HTG)
ORGANIZATIONS: OAS, UN

Haiti occupies the western part of the island of Hispaniola in the Caribbean. It is the poorest country in Central America. The country is mountainous with three main ranges, the highest reaching 2,680 m (8,793 feet). Agriculture is restricted to the plains which divide the ranges. The climate is tropical. Ninety per cent of the workforce are farmers and traditional exports have been coffee, sugar, cotton, and cocoa. In the early to mid-1990s national poverty worsened as a result of UN embargoes imposed against an illegal military regime. Thousands of Haitians fled the country. New sanctions in 1994 threatened to bring an end to all manufacturing and exporting activities.

HEARD AND McDONALD ISLANDS

STATUS: External Territory of Australia
AREA: 412 sq km (159 sq miles)
POPULATION: no permanent population
CAPITAL: Edmonton

HONDURAS

STATUS: Republic
AREA: 112,085 sq km (43,265 sq miles)
POPULATION: 5,462,000
ANNUAL NATURAL INCREASE 3.1%
CAPITAL: Tegucigalpa
LANGUAGE: Spanish, Indian dialects
RELIGION: Roman Catholic majority
CURRENCY: lempira (HNL) or peso
ORGANIZATIONS: CACM, OAS, UN

The central American republic of Honduras is a poor, sparsely populated country which consists substantially of rugged mountains and high plateaux with, on the Caribbean coast, an area of hot and humid plains, densely covered with tropical vegetation. These low-lying plains are subject to high annual rainfall, averaging 2,500 mm (98 inches), and it is in this region that bananas and coffee, accounting for over half the nation's exports, are grown. Other crops include sugar, rice, maize, beans and tobacco. There has been growth in new products such as shrimps, melons and tomatoes. Most industries are concerned with processing local products. Lead and zinc are exported.

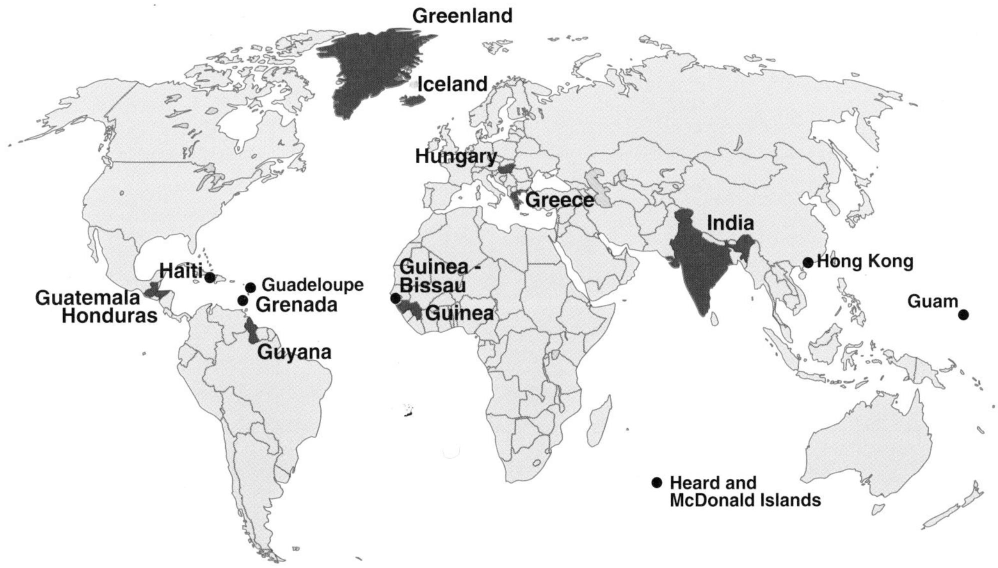

HONG KONG

STATUS: UK Dependent Territory
AREA: 1,067 sq km (412 sq miles)
POPULATION: 5,920,000

HUNGARY

STATUS: Republic
AREA: 93,030 sq km (35,910 sq miles)
POPULATION: 10,289,000
ANNUAL NATURAL INCREASE: -0.6%
CAPITAL: Budapest
LANGUAGE: Hungarian (Magyar)
RELIGION: 60% Roman Catholic, 20% Hungarian Reformed Church, Lutheran and Orthodox minorities
CURRENCY: forint (HUF)
ORGANIZATIONS: Council of Europe,OIEC, UN

Hungary is situated in the heartland of Europe. Its geomorphology consists mainly of undulating fertile plains with the highest terrain in the northeast of the country. The country is bisected north to south by the Danube. It has a humid continental climate, with warm summers that can become very hot on the plains, averaging 20°C (68°F), and cold winters, averaging 0°C (32°F). There is an annual rainfall of 500–750 mm (20–30 inches). Bauxite is Hungary's only substantial mineral resource, and less than 15 per cent of the gross national product is now derived from agriculture. The massive drive for industrialization has fundamentally transformed the structure of the economy since 1945. Both capital and consumer goods industries were developed, and during the 1980s engineering accounted for more than half the total industrial output. After a series of more or less unsuccessful attempts to introduce market elements into what essentially remained a centrally planned and largely state-owned economy, the communist regime finally gave up in 1989/90. However, their democratically elected successors have yet to prove that privatization and free competition will eventually bring general prosperity as well as political stability to what is now a profoundly troubled society.

ICELAND

STATUS: Republic
AREA: 102,820 sq km (39,690 sq miles)
POPULATION: 260,000
ANNUAL NATURAL INCREASE: 1.2%
CAPITAL: Reykjavík
LANGUAGE: Icelandic
RELIGION: 93% Evangelical Lutheran
CURRENCY: Icelandic krona (ISK)
ORGANIZATIONS: Council of Europe, EEA, EFTA, NATO, OECD, UN

One of the most northern islands in Europe, Iceland is 798 km (530 miles) away from Scotland, its nearest neighbour. The landscape is entirely volcanic – compacted volcanic ash has been eroded by the wind and there are substantial ice sheets and lava fields as well as many still active volcanoes, geysers and hot springs. The climate is mild for its latitude, with average summer temperatures of 9–10°C (48–50°F), and vegetation is sparse. Fishing is the traditional mainstay of the economy. An average of some 1,540,000 tonnes of fish are landed each year and 80 per cent of Iceland's exports consist of fish and fish products. Tourism is becoming an increasing source of income.

INDIA

STATUS: Federal Republic
AREA: 3,166,830 sq km (1,222,395 sq miles)
POPULATION: 870,000,000
ANNUAL NATURAL INCREASE: 2.1%
CAPITAL: New Delhi
LANGUAGE: Hindi, English, regional languages
RELIGION: 83% Hindu, 11% Muslim
CURRENCY: Indian rupee (INR)
ORGANIZATIONS: Col. Plan, Comm., UN

Occupying most of the Indian subcontinent, India is second only to China in the size of its population. This vast country contains an extraordinary variety of landscapes, climates and resources. The Himalayas, in the north, are the world's highest mountain range with many peaks reaching over 6,000 km (19,685 feet). The Himalayan foothills, are covered with lush vegetation, water is in abundant supply (rainfall in Assam reaches 10,700 mm or 421 inches in a year) and the climate is hot, making this region a centre for tea cultivation. To the south lies the vast expanse of the Indo-Gangetic plain, 2,500 km (1,550 miles) east-west, divided by the Indus, Ganges and Brahmaputra rivers. This is one of the world's most fertile regions, although it is liable to flooding, and failure of monsoon rainfall (June to September) can result in severe drought. In the pre-monsoon season the heat becomes intense – average temperatures in New Delhi reach 38°C (110°F). Rice, wheat, cotton, jute, tobacco and sugar are the main crops. To the south lies the Deccan plateau, bordered on either side by the Eastern and Western Ghats, and in the northwest lies the barren Thar Desert. India's natural resources are immense – timber, coal, iron ore and nickel – and oil has been discovered in the Indian Ocean. There has been a rapid expansion of light industry, notably in the food processing sector, and the manufacturing of consumer goods. Nevertheless, 70 per cent of the population live by subsistence farming. Main exports by value are precious stones and jewelry, engineering goods, clothing, leather goods, chemicals and cotton. Tourism is a valuable source of revenue.

INDONESIA

STATUS: Republic
AREA: 1,919,445 sq km
(740,905 sq miles)
POPULATION: 187,870,000
ANNUAL NATURAL INCREASE: 1.8%
CAPITAL: Jakarta
LANGUAGE: Bahasa Indonesian, Dutch
RELIGION: 88% Muslim, 9% Christian,
Hindu and Buddhist minorities
CURRENCY: rupiah (IDR)
ORGANIZATIONS: ASEAN, Col. Plan,
OPEC, UN

Indonesia consists of thousands of islands in equatorial southeast Asia which include Kalimantan (the central and southern parts of Borneo), Sumatera, Irian Jaya (the western part of New Guinea), Sulawesi (Celebes) and Java. The climate is tropical: hot (temperatures averaging 24°C or 75°F per year), humid and subject to monsoons. Most of its people live along the coast and river valleys of Java, leaving parts of the other islands virtually uninhabited. It is a Muslim nation and has the fourth largest population in the world. Over three-quarters of the people farm and live in small villages. Oil and gas, manufactured goods and coal are the chief exports. Indonesia is also a leading supplier of forest products, palm oil, rubber, spices, tobacco, tea, coffee and tin. With the use of modern techniques, the country has achieved self-sufficiency in rice.

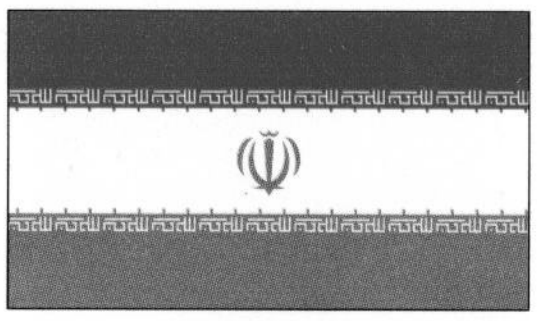

IRAN

STATUS: Republic
AREA: 1,648,000 sq km (636,130 sq miles)
POPULATION: 56,964,000
ANNUAL NATURAL INCREASE: 3.7%
CAPITAL: Tehran
LANGUAGE: Farsi, Kurdish, Arabic,
Baluchi, Turkic
RELIGION: Shi'a Muslim majority, Sunni Muslim
and Armenian Christian minorities
CURRENCY: Iranian rial (IRR)
ORGANIZATIONS: Col. Plan, OPEC, UN

Iran is a large mountainous country north of The Gulf. The climate is one of extremes with temperatures ranging from -20–55°C (-4–131°F) and rainfall varying from 2,000 mm (79 inches) to almost zero. Iran is rich in oil and gas and the revenues have been used to improve communications and social conditions generally. The war with Iraq between 1980 and 1988 seriously restricted economic growth and particularly affected the Iranian oil industry in The Gulf. Oil is the source of 85 per cent of Iran's revenue and thus when world oil prices fall, as in the early–mid 1990s, the economy suffers. Agricultural conditions are poor, except around the Caspian Sea, and wheat is the main crop though fruit (especially dates) and nuts are grown and exported. The main livestock is sheep and goats. Iran has substantial mineral deposits relatively underdeveloped

IRAQ

STATUS: Republic
AREA: 438,317 sq km (169,235 sq miles)
POPULATION: 19,410,000
ANNUAL NATURAL INCREASE: 3.3%
CAPITAL: Baghdad
LANGUAGE: Arabic, Kurdish, Turkoman
RELIGION: 50% Shi'a, 45% Sunni Muslim
CURRENCY: Iraqi dinar (IQD)
ORGANIZATIONS: Arab League, OPEC, UN

Iraq is mostly desert, marsh and mountain, but there are substantial areas of fertile land between the Tigris and the Euphrates. The two great rivers join and become the Shatt al-Arab which flows into The Gulf. The climate is arid with rainfall of less than 500 mm (20 inches) and summers are very hot (averaging 35° or 95°F). Iraq has a short coastline with Basra the only port. Light industry is situated around Baghdad, and there are major petro-chemical complexes around the Basra and Kirkuk oilfields. The war with Iran (1980–8) and the Gulf conflict (1991) wrecked the economy with exports of oil and natural gas, formerly accounting for 95 per cent of export earnings, severely restricted by sanctions. Meanwhile, Arabs living in the Tigris-Euphrates marsh regions are being deprived of their livelihood as the marshes are drained in government reclamation schemes.

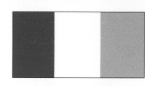

IRELAND (EIRE)

STATUS: Republic
AREA: 68,895 sq km (26,595 sq miles)
POPULATION: 3,548,000
ANNUAL NATURAL INCREASE: -0.1%
CAPITAL: Dublin (Baile Átha Cliath)
LANGUAGE: Irish, English
RELIGION: 95% Roman Catholic, 5% Protestant
CURRENCY: punt or Irish pound (IEP)
ORGANIZATIONS: Council of Europe, EEA, EU,
OECD, UN

The Irish Republic, forming 80 per cent of the island of Ireland, is a lowland country of wide valleys, lakes and marshes, but with some hills of significance, such as the Wicklow Mountains, south of Dublin and Macgillicuddy's Reeks, in the southwest. The Irish climate is maritime and influenced by the Gulf Stream. Temperatures average 5°C (40°F) in winter to 16°C (60°F) in summer, with annual rainfall at about 1,400 mm (55 inches) in the west and half that in the east. There is much rich pastureland and livestock farming predominates. Meat and dairy produce is processed in the small market towns where there are also breweries and mills. Large-scale manufacturing, in which food processing, electronics and textiles have shown recent growth, is centred around Dublin, the capital and main port. The Irish Republic possesses reserves of oil and natural gas, peat and deposits of lead and zinc. A large zinc mine at Galmoy is expected to come into production in 1996.

ISRAEL

STATUS: State
AREA: 20,770 sq km (8,015 sq miles)
POPULATION: 5,287,000
ANNUAL NATURAL INCREASE: 2.7%
CAPITAL: Jerusalem
LANGUAGE: Hebrew, Arabic, Yiddish
RELIGION: 85% Jewish, 13% Muslim
CURRENCY: shekel (ILS)
ORGANIZATIONS: UN

Israel, in the eastern Mediterranean littoral, contains a varied landscape – a coastal plain, interior hills, a deep valley extending from the river Jordan to the Dead Sea, and the Negev semi-desert in the south. Efficient water management is crucial as two-thirds of rainfall, which falls mostly in the mild winters, is lost by evaporation. Fuel needs to be imported (mainly oil from Egypt). Economic development in Israel is the most advanced in the Middle East. Manufacturing, particularly diamond finishing, electronics and science based products are important, although Israel also has flourishing agriculture specializing in exporting fruit, flowers and vegetables to western Europe. The only viable mineral resources are phosphates in the Negev and potash from the Dead Sea.

ITALY

STATUS: Republic
AREA: 301,245 sq km (116,280 sq miles)
POPULATION: 56,767,000
ANNUAL NATURAL INCREASE: 0.2%
CAPITAL: Rome (Roma)
LANGUAGE: Italian, German, French
RELIGION: 90% Roman Catholic
CURRENCY: Italian lira (ITL)
ORGANIZATIONS: Council of Europe, EEA, EU, G7, NATO, OECD, UN, WEU

Italy, separated from the rest of Europe by the great divide of the Alps, thrusts southeastwards into the Mediterranean Sea, in its famous boot-shaped peninsula. Including the large islands of Sicily and Sardinia, over 75 per cent of the landscape is either hill or mountain. The north is dominated by the plain of the river Po rising to the high Alps. Further along the peninsula the Apennine mountains run from north to south. Climate varies with altitude, but generally there is a Mediterranean regime in the south; in the north the climate becomes more temperate. Agriculture flourishes with cereals, vegetables, olives, and cheese the principal products and Italy is the world's largest wine producer. Tourism is a major source of revenue. In spite of the lack of mineral and power resources, Italy has become a trading nation with a sound industrial base. Manufacturing of textiles, cars, machine tools, textile machinery and engineering, mainly in the north, is expanding rapidly and accounts for nearly 50 per cent of the work force. This is increasing the imbalance between the north and south where the average income is far less per head, and where investment is lacking.

IVORY COAST (CÔTE D'IVOIRE)

STATUS: Republic
AREA: 322,465 sq km (124,470 sq miles)
POPULATION: 12,910,000
ANNUAL NATURAL INCREASE: 4.0%
CAPITAL: Yamoussoukro
LANGUAGE: French, tribal languages
RELIGION: 65% traditional beliefs, 23% Muslim, 12% Roman Catholic
CURRENCY: CFA franc (W Africa) (XOF)
ORGANIZATIONS: ECOWAS, OAU, UN,

Independent from the French since 1960, the Ivory Coast rises from low plains in the south to plateaux in the north. The climate is tropical with rainfall in two wet seasons in the south. Much of the population is engaged in subsistence agriculture. The two chief exports are cocoa and coffee. Other products include cotton, timber, fruit and tobacco. Gold mining began in 1990, diamonds are extracted and by 1995 the Ivory Coast is expected to become self-sufficient in oil and gas from the offshore fields.

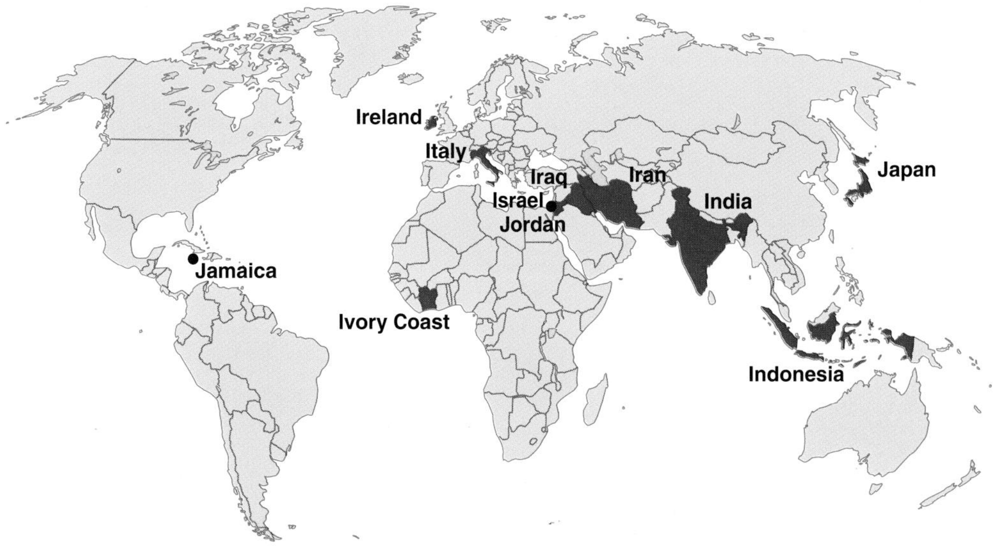

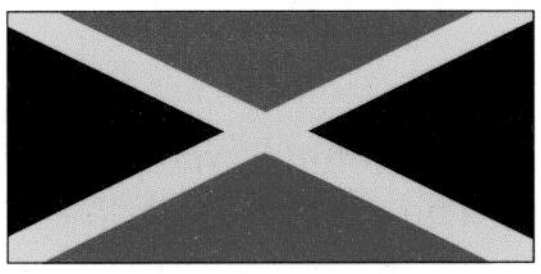

JAMAICA

STATUS: Commonwealth State
AREA: 11,425 sq km (4,410 sq miles)
POPULATION: 2,469,000
ANNUAL NATURAL INCREASE: 0.8%
CAPITAL: Kingston
LANGUAGE: English, local patois
RELIGION: Anglican Christian majority. Rastafarian minority
CURRENCY: Jamaican dollar (JMD)
ORGANIZATIONS: Caricom, Comm., OAS, UN

Jamaica, part of the Greater Antilles chain of islands in the Caribbean, is formed from the peaks of a submerged mountain range. The climate is tropical with an annual rainfall of over 5,000 mm (197 inches) on the high ground. There is a plentiful supply of tropical fruits such as melons, bananas and guavas. Principal crops include sugar cane, bananas, cocoa and coffee. Jamaica is rich in bauxite which, with the refined product alumina, is the main export. Major industries are food processing, textiles, cement and agricultural machinery. Since 1988 tourism has developed rapidly and is now the biggest single source of foreign earnings.

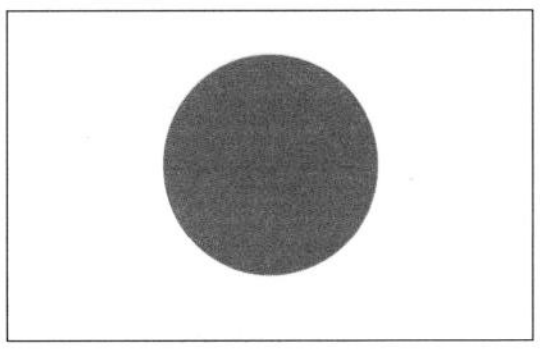

JAPAN

STATUS: Constitutional monarchy
AREA: 369,700 sq km (142,705 sq miles)
POPULATION: 123,653,000
ANNUAL NATURAL INCREASE: 0.4%
CAPITAL: Tokyo (Tōkyō)
LANGUAGE: Japanese
RELIGION: Shintoist, Buddhist, Christian minority
CURRENCY: yen (JPY)
ORGANIZATIONS: Col. Plan, G7, OECD, UN

Japan consists of the main islands of Hokkaido, Honshu, Shikoku and Kyushu which stretch over 1,600 km (995 miles). The land is mountainous and heavily forested with small, fertile patches and a climate ranging from harsh to tropical. The highest mountain is Mt Fuji (Fuji-san) at 3,776 m (12,388 feet). The archipelago is also subject to monsoons, earthquakes, typhoons and tidal waves. Very little of the available land is cultivable. Most food has to be imported but the Japanese both catch and eat a lot of fish. The Japanese fishing fleet is the largest in the world. Japan is a leading economic power. Because of the importance of trade, industry has grown up around the major ports especially Yokohama, Osaka and Tokyo, the capital. The principal exports are motor vehicles, chemicals, iron and steel products and electronic, electric and optical equipment. Japan relies heavily on imported fuel and raw materials and is developing the country's nuclear power resources to reduce this dependence. Production of coal, oil and natural gas is also being increased. In the early–mid 1990s, after four decades of phenomenal growth, industrial output declined as Japan experienced its worst recession for half a century.

JORDAN

STATUS: Kingdom
AREA: 90,650 sq km (35,000 sq miles)
POPULATION: 4,291,000
ANNUAL NATURAL INCREASE: 5.8%
CAPITAL: Amman ('Ammān)
LANGUAGE: Arabic
RELIGION: 90% Sunni Muslim, Christian and Shi'ite Muslim minorities
CURRENCY: Jordanian dinar (JOD)
ORGANIZATIONS: Arab League, UN

Jordan, one of the few kingdoms in the Middle East, is mostly desert, but has fertile pockets. The climate is predominantly arid. Temperatures rise to 49°C (120°F) in the eastern valleys but it is cooler and wetter in the west. Fruit and vegetables account for 20 per cent of Jordan's exports and phosphate, the most valuable mineral, accounts for over 40 per cent of export revenue. Amman is the manufacturing centre, processing bromide and potash from the Dead Sea. Other important industries are food processing and textiles.

KAZAKHSTAN

STATUS: Republic
AREA: 2,717,300 sq km (1,048,880 sq miles)
POPULATION: 17,035,000
ANNUAL NATURAL INCREASE: 1.0%
CAPITAL: Alma-Ata
LANGUAGE: Kazakh, Russian
RELIGION: Muslim majority, Orthodox minority
CURRENCY: tenge
ORGANIZATIONS: CIS, UN

Stretching across central Asia, Kazakhstan is Russia's southern neighbour. Consisting of lowlands, hilly plains and plateaux, with small mountainous areas, the country has a continental climate with hot summers (30°C or 86°F in July) alternating with equally extreme winters. Exceptionally rich in raw materials, extractive industries have played a major role in the country's economy. Vast oil and gas reserves near the Caspian Sea are now being exploited. Rapid industrialization in recent years has focused on iron and steel, cement, chemicals, fertilizers and consumer goods. Although three-quarters of all agricultural land is used for pasture, the nomadic ways of the Kazakh people have all but disappeared. Economic development during the Soviet period brought a massive influx of outside labour which swamped the indigenous population. The proportion of Kazakhs employed in the industrial sector has, until recently, been small, but with the move to towns and better training, the balance is starting to be redressed. Since Kazakhstan's independence in 1991, its economic prospects appear favourable; but the Soviet legacy includes many environmental problems, such as the ruthless exploitation of the Aral Sea for irrigation.

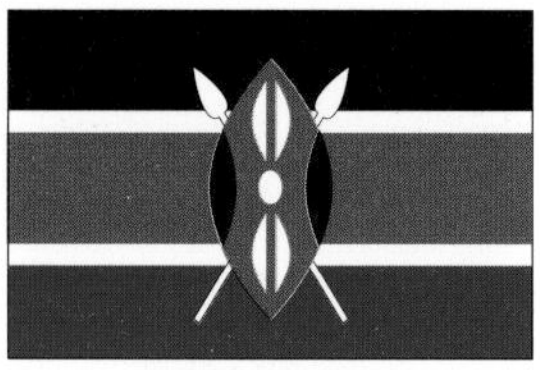

KENYA

STATUS: Republic
AREA: 582,645 sq km (224,900 sq miles)
POPULATION: 25,700,000
ANNUAL NATURAL INCREASE: 3.5%
CAPITAL: Nairobi
LANGUAGE: Kiswahili, English, Kikuyu, Luo
RELIGION: majority traditional beliefs, 25% Christian, 6% Muslim
CURRENCY: Kenya shilling (KES)
ORGANIZATIONS: Comm., OAU, UN

Kenya lies on the equator but as most of the country is on a high plateau the temperatures range from 10–27°C (50–81°F). Rainfall varies from 760–2,500 mm (30–98 inches) depending on aititude. Arable land is scarce but agriculture is the only source of livelihood for over three-quarters of the population. Tea, coffee, flowers and vegetables are the main products for export. Tea, however, has replaced coffee as the chief export and is second only to tourism as a source of foreign revenue. Manufacturing, centred at Nairobi and Mombasa, is dominated by food processing.

KIRGHIZIA (KYRGYZSTAN)

STATUS: Republic
AREA: 198,500 sq km (76,620 sq miles)
POPULATION: 4,502,000
ANNUAL NATURAL INCREASE: 1.7%
CAPITAL: Bishkek
LANGUAGE: Kirghizian, Russian
RELIGION: Muslim
CURRENCY: som
ORGANIZATIONS: CIS, UN

Located in the heart of Asia, to the south of Kazakhstan, Kirghizia is a mountainous country. Traditionally an agrarian-based economy with stock-raising prevalent, the country underwent rapid industrialization during the Soviet period becoming a major producer of machinery and, more recently, producing consumer goods. Valuable mineral deposits include gold, silver, antimony, mercury with the gold deposits believed to be among the world's largest. The cultivation of cotton, sugar beet, tobacco and opium poppies is expanding and provides the basis for a growing processing industry. Independence came unexpectedly in 1991, although Kirghizia had long wanted to control its own affairs.

KIRIBATI

STATUS: Republic
AREA: 717 sq km (277 sq miles)
POPULATION: 72,298
ANNUAL NATURAL INCREASE: 2.1%
CAPITAL: Bairiki (on Tarawa Atoll)
LANGUAGE: I-Kirbati, English
RELIGION: Christian majority
CURRENCY: Australian dollar (AUD)
ORGANIZATIONS: Comm., UN

Kiribati consists of 16 Gilbert Islands, eight Phoenix Islands, three Line Islands and Ocean Island. These four groups are spread over 5 million sq km (1,930,000 miles) in the central and west Pacific. The temperature is a constant 27°–32°C (80–90°F). The islanders grow coconut, breadfruit, bananas and babia (a coarse vegetable). Copra is a major export and fish, particularly tuna, accounts for one-third of total exports. Main imports are machinery and manufactured goods.

KOREA, NORTH

STATUS: Republic
AREA: 122,310 sq km (47,210 sq miles)
POPULATION: 22,618,000
ANNUAL NATURAL INCREASE: 1%
CAPITAL: P'yŏngyang
LANGUAGE: Korean
RELIGION: Chundo Kyo, Buddhism, Confucianism, Daoism
CURRENCY: North Korean won (KPW)
ORGANIZATIONS: OIEC, UN

High, rugged mountains and deep valleys typify North Korea. Climate is extreme with severe winters and warm, sunny summers. Cultivation is limited to the river valley plains where rice, millet, maize and wheat are the principal crops. North Korea, rich in minerals including iron ore and copper, has developed a heavy industrial base. Industry has, however, since the early 1990s, been severely curtailed, firstly by the loss of Soviet aid following the break-up of the Soviet Union and then by losing imports through its isolationist policies and secretive nuclear industries. Its coal supplies, the main energy source for factories, are running out. Complete economic collapse is only salvaged by remittances from Koreans in Japan.

KOREA, SOUTH

STATUS: Republic
AREA: 98,445 sq km (38,000 sq miles)
POPULATION: 44,190,000
ANNUAL NATURAL INCREASE: 1.9%
CAPITAL: Seoul (Sŏul)
LANGUAGE: Korean
RELIGION: 26% Mahayana Buddhism, 22% Christian, Confucianism, Daoism, Chundo Kyo
CURRENCY: won (KPW)
ORGANIZATIONS: Col. Plan, UN

The terrain of South Korea, although mountainous, is less rugged than that of North Korea. The flattest parts lie along the west coast and the extreme south of the peninsula. Its climate is continental, with an average temperature range of -5°C (23°F) in winter to 27°C (81°F) in summer. The majority of the population live in the arable river valleys and along the coastal plain. Agriculture is very primitive, with rice the principal crop. Tungsten, coal and iron ore are the main mineral deposits. Despite having to import oil and industrial materials, the country is a major industrial nation producing iron and steel, textiles, aircraft, chemicals, machinery, vehicles and, in recent years, specializing in electronics and computers. South Korea, with Japan, leads the world in ship-building.

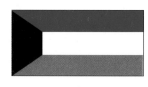

KUWAIT

STATUS: State
AREA: 24,280 sq km (9,370 sq miles)
POPULATION: 1,500,000
ANNUAL NATURAL INCREASE: -2.3%
CAPITAL: Kuwait (Al Kuwayţ)
LANGUAGE: Arabic, English
RELIGION: 95% Muslim, 5% Christian and Hindu

CURRENCY: Kuwaiti dinar (KWD)
ORGANIZATIONS: Arab League, UN

Kuwait comprises low, undulating desert, with summer temperatures as high as 52°C (126°F). Since the discovery of oil, Kuwait has been transformed into one of the world's wealthiest nations, exporting oil to Japan, France, the Netherlands and the UK since 1946. The natural gas fields have also been developed. Other industries include fishing (particularly shrimp), food processing, chemicals and building materials. In agriculture, the aim is to produce half the requirements of domestic vegetable consumption by expanding the irrigated area. The invasion and attempted annexation of Kuwait by Iraq in 1990–1 had severe effects on the country's economy, but by 1994 the oil industry was restored to its pre-Gulf war efficiency.

LAOS

STATUS: Republic
AREA: 236,725 sq km (91,375 sq miles)
POPULATION: 4,469,000
ANNUAL NATURAL INCREASE: 2.9%
CAPITAL: Vientiane (Viangchan)
LANGUAGE: Lao, French, tribal languages
RELIGION: Buddhist majority, Christian and animist minorities
CURRENCY: kip (LAK)
ORGANIZATIONS: Col. Plan, UN

Laos is a landlocked, mostly mountainous and forested country in Indo-China. Temperatures range from 15°C (59°F) in winter, to 32°C (90°F) before the rains, and 26°C (79°F) during the rainy season from May to October. Most of the sparse population are subsistence farmers growing rice, maize, sweet potatoes and tobacco. Mineral resources include tin, iron ore, gold, bauxite and lignite. The major exports are coffee, tin and teak. Almost constant warfare since 1941 has hindered any possible industrial development, and Laos has become one of the world's poorest countries.

LATVIA

STATUS: Republic
AREA: 63,700 sq km (24,590 sq miles)
POPULATION: 2,577,000
ANNUAL NATURAL INCREASE: 0.0%
CAPITAL: Riga
LANGUAGE: Latvian, Lithuanian, Russian
RELIGION: Lutheran, Roman Catholic and Orthodox minorities
CURRENCY: roublis (Latvian rouble), lats
ORGANIZATIONS: UN

Latvia is situated on the shores of the Baltic Sea and the Gulf of Riga. Forests cover more than a third of the total territory, a second third being made up of meadows and marsh, and there are some 4,000 lakes. Farmland supports dairy and meat production and grain crops. The country possesses no mineral resources of any value. Industrial development has been sustained by a massive influx of Russian labour since Latvia's incorporation into the Soviet Union in 1940. Under the Soviets, Latvia was assigned the production of consumer durables such as refrigerators and motorcycles as well as ships, rolling stock and power generators. Latvia regained its independence in 1991. The main industries are now radio engineering, electronics, engineering, instruments and industrial robots.

LEBANON

STATUS: Republic
AREA: 10,400 sq km (4,015 sq miles)
POPULATION: 2,838,000
ANNUAL NATURAL INCREASE: 2.3%
CAPITAL: Beirut (Beyrouth)
LANGUAGE: Arabic, French, English
RELIGION: 62% Shi'a and Sunni Muslim, 38% Roman Catholic and Maronite Christian
CURRENCY: Lebanese pound (LBP)
ORGANIZATIONS: Arab League, UN

Physically, Lebanon can be divided into four main regions: a narrow coastal plain; a narrow, fertile interior plateau; the west Lebanon (Jebel Liban) and the Anti-Lebanon (Jebel esh Sharqi) mountains. It has a Mediterranean climate. Trade and tourism have been severely affected by civil war for 17 years from 1975. Agriculture accounts for nearly half of employment and cement, fertilisers, jewelry, sugar and tobacco products are all manufactured on a small scale.

LESOTHO

STATUS: Kingdom
AREA: 30,345 sq km (11,715 sq miles)
POPULATION: 1,836,000
ANNUAL NATURAL INCREASE: 2.7%
CAPITAL: Maseru
LANGUAGE: Sesotho, English
RELIGION: 80% Christian
CURRENCY: loti (LSL), S African rand (ZAR)
ORGANIZATIONS: Comm., OAU, UN

Lesotho, formerly Basutoland, is completely encircled by South Africa. This small country is rugged and mountainous, with southern Africa's highest mountain, Thabana Ntlenyana (3,482 m or 11,424 feet) to be found in the east of the Drakensberg. From these peaks the land slopes westwards in the form of dissected plateaux. The climate is generally sub-tropical although influenced by altitude; rainfall, sometimes variable, falls mainly in the summer months. Because of the terrain, agriculture is limited to the lowlands and foothills. Sorghum, wheat, barley, maize, oats and legumes are the main crops. Cattle, sheep and goats graze on the highlands.

LIBERIA

STATUS: Republic
AREA: 11,370 sq km (42,990 sq miles)
POPULATION: 2,580,000
ANNUAL NATURAL INCREASE: 3.1%
CAPITAL: Monrovia
LANGUAGE: English, tribal languages
RELIGION: traditional beliefs, Christian, 5% Muslim
CURRENCY: Liberian dollar (LRD)
ORGANIZATIONS: ECOWAS, OAU, UN

The west African republic of Liberia is the only nation in Africa never to have been ruled by a foreign power. The hot and humid coastal plain with its savannah vegetation and mangrove swamps rises gently towards the Guinea Highlands, and the interior is densely covered by tropical rainforest. Until the civil war, which ravaged the country, broke out in 1989 the country enjoyed some prosperity from its rubber plantations, rich iron ore deposits, diamonds and gold. Liberia has the world's largest merchant fleet due to its flag of convenience register and this is the only source of revenue relatively unscathed by the war.

LIBYA

STATUS: Republic
AREA: 1,759,540 sq km (679,180 sq miles)
POPULATION: 4,875,000
ANNUAL NATURAL INCREASE: 3.6%
CAPITAL: Tripoli (Ţarābulus)
LANGUAGE: Arabic, Italian, English
RELIGION: Sunni Muslim
CURRENCY: Libyan dinar (LYD)
ORGANIZATIONS: Arab League, OAU, OPEC, UN

Libya is situated on the lowlands of north Africa which rise southwards from the Mediterranean Sea. Ninety-five per cent of its territory is hot, dry desert or semi-desert with average rainfall of less then 130 mm (5 inches). The coastal plains, however, have a more moist Mediterranean climate with annual rainfall of around 200–610 mm (8–24 inches). In these areas, a wide range of crops are cultivated including grapes, groundnuts, oranges, wheat and barley. Only 30 years ago Libya was classed as one of the world's poorest nations but the exploitation of oil has transformed Libya's economy and now accounts for over 95 per cent of its exports.

LIECHTENSTEIN

STATUS: Principality
AREA: 160 sq km (62 sq miles)
POPULATION: 30,000
ANNUAL NATURAL INCREASE: 1.1%
CAPITAL: Vaduz
LANGUAGE: Alemannish, German
RELIGION: 87% Roman Catholic
CURRENCY: franken (Swiss franc)(CHF)
ORGANIZATIONS Council of Europe, EFTA, UN

Situated in the central Alps between Switzerland and Austria, Liechtenstein is one of the smallest states in Europe. Its territory is divided into two zones – the flood plains of the Rhine to the north and Alpine mountain ranges to the southeast, where cattle are reared. Liechtenstein's other main sources of revenue comprise light industry, chiefly the manufacture of precision instruments, and also textile production, food products, tourism, postage stamps and a fast-growing banking sector.

LITHUANIA

STATUS: Republic
AREA: 65,200 sq km (25,165 sq miles)
POPULATION: 3,742,000
ANNUAL NATURAL INCREASE: 0.7%
CAPITAL: Vilnius
LANGUAGE: Lithuanian, Russian, Polish
RELIGION: 80% Roman Catholic
CURRENCY: litas
ORGANIZATIONS: Council of Europe, UN

Lithuania is one of the three small ex-Soviet states lying on the shores of the Baltic Sea. The country consists of a low-lying plain with many lakes. Its climate is transitional, ranging between the oceanic type of western Europe and continental conditions. Temperatures range between -5–-3°C (24–28°F) in winter to 17–18°C (62–66°F) in summer. There is on average 510 mm–610 mm (20–24 inches) of rainfall per year. Agriculture is dominated by beef and dairy produce; major crops are potatoes and flax. There is a large fishing industry. Industrial products include paper, chemicals, electronics and electrical goods. After almost 50 years' involuntary incorporation into the Soviet Union, Lithuania regained its independence in 1991. The economy is still linked to ex-Soviet countries and the change to a market economy is slow.

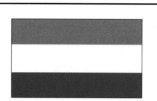

LUXEMBOURG

STATUS: Grand Duchy
AREA: 2,585 sq km (998 sq miles)
POPULATION: 395,200
ANNUAL NATURAL INCREASE: 0.8%
CAPITAL: Luxembourg
LANGUAGE: Letzeburgish, French, German
RELIGION: 95% Roman Catholic
CURRENCY: Luxembourg franc (LUF)
Belgian Franc (BEF)
ORGANIZATIONS: Council of Europe, EEA, EU, NATO, OECD, UN, WEU

The Grand Duchy of Luxembourg is situated between France, Belgium and Germany. The climate is mild and temperate with rainfall ranging from 700–1,000 mm (28–40 inches) a year. Just over half the land is arable, mainly cereals, dairy produce and potatoes. Wine is produced in the Moselle valley. Iron ore is found in the south and is the basis of the thriving steel industry. Other industries are textiles, chemicals and pharmaceutical products. Banking and financial services are growing sectors.

MACAU (MACAO)

STATUS: Chinese Territory under Portuguese Administration
AREA: 16 sq km (6 sq miles)
POPULATION: 374,000
CAPITAL: Macau

MACEDONIA
Former Yugoslav Republic of,

STATUS: Republic
AREA: 25,715 sq km (9,925 sq miles)
POPULATION: 2,066,000
ANNUAL NATURAL INCREASE: 1.1%
CAPITAL: Skopje
LANGUAGE: Macedonian, Albanian
RELIGION: Orthodox
CURRENCY: denar
ORGANIZATIONS: UN,
Council of Europe (non-voting member)

The landlocked Balkan state of the Former Yugoslav Republic of Macedonia is a rugged country crossed from north to south by the Vardar valley. The climate is continental with fine hot summers but bitterly cold winters. The economy is basically agricultural. Cereals, tobacco, fruit and vegetables are grown and livestock raised. Heavy industries include chemicals and textiles, which are the county's major employers. Following a Greek economic blockade in 1994, heavy industry – which had already declined through the loss of markets in other former Yugoslav republics – suffered further collapse.

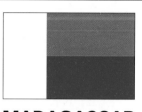

MADAGASCAR

STATUS: Republic
AREA: 594,180 sq km (229,345 sq miles)
POPULATION: 12,827
ANNUAL NATURAL INCREASE: 3.1%
CAPITAL: Antananarivo
LANGUAGE: Malagasy, French, English
RELIGION: 47% animist, 48% Christian, 2% Muslim
CURRENCY: Malagasy franc (MGF)
ORGANIZATIONS: OAU, UN

Madagascar, the world's fourth largest island, is situated 400 km (250 miles) east of the Mozambique coast. The terrain consists largely of a high plateau with steppe and savannah vegetation and desert in the south. Much of the hot humid east coast is covered by tropical rainforest – here rainfall reaches 1,500–2,000 mm (59–79 inches) per annum. Although farming is the occupation of about 85 per cent of the population, only 3 per cent of the land is cultivated. Coffee and vanilla are the major exports, and the shellfish trade is growing rapidly. Much of Madagascar's unique plant and animal life are under increasing threat due to widespread deforestation, caused by the rapid development of forestry and soil erosion.

MADEIRA

STATUS: Self-governing Island Region of Portugal
AREA: 796 sq km (307 sq miles)
POPULATION: 253,400
CAPITAL: Funchal

MALAWI

STATUS: Republic
AREA: 94,080 sq km (35,315 sq miles)
POPULATION: 8,823,000
ANNUAL NATURAL INCREASE: 3.4%

CAPITAL: Lilongwe
LANGUAGE: Chichewa, English
RELIGION: traditional beliefs majority, 10% Roman Catholic, 10% Protestant
CURRENCY: kwacha (MWK)
ORGANIZATIONS: Comm., OAU, UN

Malawi is located at the southern end of the east African Rift Valley. The area around Lake Malawi is tropical and humid with swampy vegetation. In the highlands to the west and south-east conditions are cooler. Malawi has an intensely rural economy – 96 per cent of the population work on the land. Maize is the main subsistence crop, and tea, tobacco, sugar and groundnuts are the main exports. Malawi has deposits of both coal and bauxite, but they are under-exploited at present. Manufacturing industry concentrates on consumer goods and building and construction materials. All energy is produced by hydro-electric power.

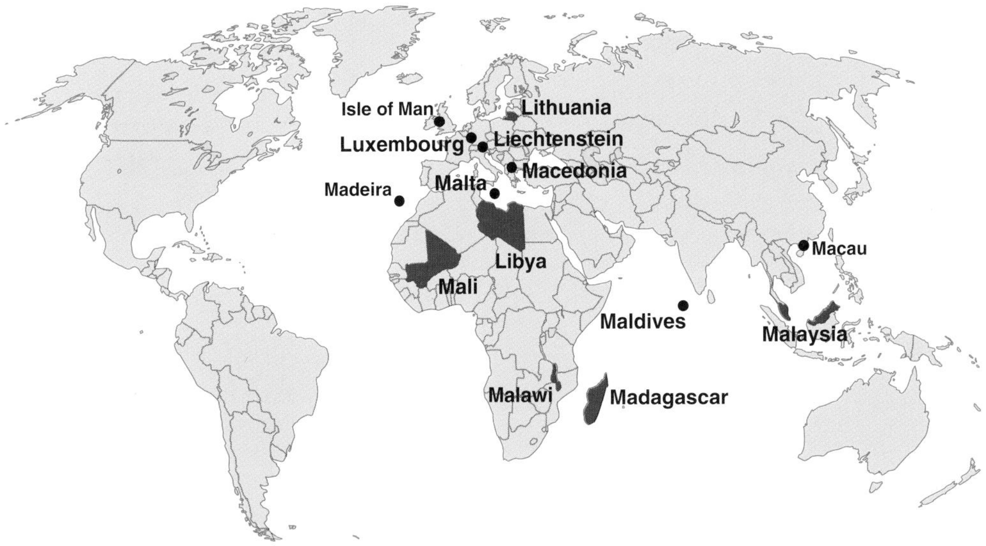

MALAYSIA

STATUS: Federation
AREA: 332,665 sq km (128,405 sq miles)
POPULATION: 18,606,000
ANNUAL NATURAL INCREASE: 2.5%
CAPITAL: Kuala Lumpur
LANGUAGE: 58% Bahasa Malaysian, English, Chinese
RELIGION: 53% Muslim, 25% Buddhist, Hindu, Christian and animist minorities
CURRENCY: Malaysian dollar or ringgit (MYR)
ORGANIZATIONS: ASEAN, Col. Plan, Comm., UN

The Federation of Malaysia consists of two separate parts; west Malaysia is located on the Malay Peninsula, while east Malaysia consists of Sabah and Sarawak on the island of Borneo 700 km (435 miles) across the South China Sea. Despite this distance, both areas share a similar landscape, which is mountainous and covered with lush tropical rainforest. The climate is tropical, hot and humid all the year round, with annual average rainfall of 2,500 mm (98 inches). At one time the economy was dominated by tin, rubber and timber. Now manufactured goods, in particular electronics, account for over two-thirds of the nation's exports in terms of value. Malaysia is rich in natural resources and other major exports include crude oil, timber, palm oil, pepper, rubber and tin. The fast-growing industrial sector demands increased power supplies which are being met by new power stations and hydro-electric power projects.

PENINSULAR MALAYSIA

STATUS: State
AREA: 131,585 sq km (50,790 sq miles)
POPULATION: 15,286,098
CAPITAL: Kuala Lumpur

SABAH

STATUS: State
AREA: 76,115 sq km (29,380 sq miles)
POPULATION: 1,736,902
CAPITAL: Kota Kinabalu

SARAWAK

STATUS: State
AREA: 124,965 sq km (48,235 sq miles)
POPULATION: 1,583,000
CAPITAL: Kuching

MALDIVES

STATUS: Republic
AREA: 298 sq km (115 sq miles)
POPULATION: 238,363
ANNUAL NATURAL INCREASE: 3.3%
CAPITAL: Male
LANGUAGE: Dhivehi
RELIGION: Sunni Muslim majority
CURRENCY: rufiyaa (MVR)
ORGANIZATIONS: Col. Plan, Comm., UN

The Maldives are one of the world's poorest nations. They consist of a series of coral atolls stretching 885 km (550 miles) across the Indian Ocean. Although there are 2,000 islands, only about 215 are inhabited. The main island, Male, is only 1½ miles long. Fishing is the main activity and fish and coconut fibre are both exported. Most staple foods have to be imported but coconuts, millet, cassava, yams and fruit are grown locally. Tourism is developing and this is now the main source of revenue.

MALI

STATUS: Republic
AREA: 1,240,140 sq km (478,695 sq miles)
POPULATION: 9,818,000
ANNUAL NATURAL INCREASE: 2.8%
CAPITAL: Bamako
LANGUAGE: French, native languages
RELIGION: 65% Muslim, 30% traditional beliefs, 1% Christian
CURRENCY: CFA franc (W Africa) (XOF)
ORGANIZATIONS: ECOWAS, OAU, UN

Mali is one of the world's most underdeveloped countries. Over half the area is barren desert. South of Timbuktu (Tombouctou) the savannah-covered plains support a wide variety of wildlife. Most of the population live in the Niger valley and grow cotton, oil seeds and groundnuts. Fishing is important. Mali has few mineral resources, although a gold mine opened in 1994. Droughts have taken their toll of livestock and agriculture. Main exports are cotton, groundnuts and livestock.

MALTA

STATUS: Republic
AREA: 316 sq km (122 sq miles)
POPULATION: 364,593
ANNUAL NATURAL INCREASE: 0.7%
CAPITAL: Valletta
LANGUAGE: Maltese, English, Italian
RELIGION: Roman Catholic majority
CURRENCY: Maltese lira (MTL)
ORGANIZATIONS: Comm., Council of Europe, UN

Malta lies about 96 km (60 miles) south of Sicily, and consists of three islands; Malta, Gozo and Comino. It has a Mediterranean climate with summer temperatures averaging 25°C (77°F). About 40 per cent of the land is under cultivation with wheat, potatoes, tomatoes and vines the main crops. The large natural harbour at Valletta has made it a major transit port, and shipbuilding and repair are traditional industries. Principal exports are machinery, beverages, tobacco, flowers, wine, leather goods and potatoes. Tourism and light manufacturing are booming sectors of the economy.

MAN, ISLE OF

STATUS: British Crown Dependency
AREA: 588 sq km (227 sq miles)
POPULATION: 71,000
CAPITAL: Douglas

MARSHALL ISLANDS

STATUS: Self-governing state in Compact of Free Association with USA
AREA: 605 sq km (234 sq miles)
POPULATION: 48,000
CAPITAL: Majuro
LANGUAGE: English, local languages
RELIGION: Roman Catholic majority
CURRENCY: US dollar (USD)
ORGANIZATIONS: UN

The Marshall Islands, formerly UN Trust Territory under US administration, consist of over 1,000 atolls and islands which in total account for only 181 sq km (70 sq miles) but are spread over a wide area of the Pacific. The climate is hot all year round with a heavy rainfall averaging 4,050 mm (160 inches). Fishing, subsistence farming and tourism provide occupation for most. The economy is heavily dependent on grants from the USA for use of the islands as military bases.

MARTINIQUE

STATUS: Overseas Department of France
AREA: 1,079 sq km (417 sq miles)
POPULATION: 373,000
CAPITAL: Fort-de-France

MAURITANIA

STATUS: Islamic Republic
AREA: 1,030,700 sq km (397,850 sq miles)
POPULATION: 2,143,000
ANNUAL NATURAL INCREASE: 2.7%
CAPITAL: Nouakchott
LANGUAGE: Arabic, French
RELIGION: Muslim
CURRENCY: ouguiya (MRO)
ORGANIZATIONS: Arab League, ECOWAS, OAU, UN

Situated on the west coast of Africa, Mauritania consists of savannah, steppes and vast areas of the Sahara desert. It has high temperatures, low rainfall and frequent droughts. There is very little arable farming except in the Senegal river valley where millet and dates are grown. Most Mauritanians raise cattle, sheep, goats or camels. The country has only one railway which is used to transport the chief export, iron ore, from the mines to the coast at Nouadhibou. Mauritania has substantial copper reserves which are mined at Akjoujt. A severe drought during the last decade decimated the livestock population and forced many nomadic tribesmen into the towns. Coastal fishing contributes nearly 50 per cent of foreign earnings. Exports are almost exclusively confined to iron ore, copper and fish products.

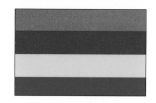

MAURITIUS

STATUS: Republic
AREA: 1,865 sq km (720 sq miles)
POPULATION: 1,098,000
ANNUAL NATURAL INCREASE: 1.1%
CAPITAL: Port Louis
LANGUAGE: English, French Creole, Hindi, Bhojpuri
RELIGION: 51% Hindu, 31% Christian, 17% Muslim
CURRENCY: Mauritian rupee (MUR)
ORGANIZATIONS: Comm., OAU, UN

Mauritius is a mountainous island in the Indian Ocean. It has a varied climate with temperatures ranging from 7–36°C (45–97°F) and annual rainfall of between 1,530–5,080 mm (60–200 inches). The economy of Mauritius once depended wholly on sugar. Although this is still important, with tea as a second crop, earnings from the manufacturing of clothing now surpass those from sugar. Tourism and financial services are also expanding.

MAYOTTE

STATUS: 'Territorial collectivity' of France
AREA: 376 sq km (145 sq miles)
POPULATION: 85,000
CAPITAL: Dzaoudzi

MEXICO

STATUS: Federal Republic
AREA: 1,972,545 sq km (761,400 sq miles)
POPULATION: 89,538,000
ANNUAL NATURAL INCREASE: 1.8%
CAPITAL: Mexico City
LANGUAGE: Spanish
RELIGION: 96% Roman Catholic
CURRENCY: Mexican peso (MXP)
ORGANIZATIONS: NAFTA, OAS, OECD, UN

Mexico consists mainly of mountain ranges and dissected plateaux. The only extensive flat lands are in the Yucatan Peninsula. Temperature and rainfall are modified by altitude – the north is arid but the south is humid and tropical. Mexico has one of the world's fastest growing populations and, with extreme poverty in many rural areas, migration to the cities continues to be prevalent. One-third of the land is used for livestock ranching and only 20 per cent farmed. Communal farms were abolished in 1991 and peasants are encouraged, with private ownership, to vary crops from the traditional corn and beans. Mexico has great mineral wealth, e.g. silver, strontium and gold, but much is still unexploited. There are considerable reserves of oil, natural gas, coal and uranium. Ten years ago petroleum products accounted for 70 per cent of exports. Now oil accounts for 30 per cent and the major exports are manufactured goods from an industrial base of vehicle production, steel, textiles, breweries and food processing. Other exports are coffee, fruit, vegetables and shrimps. Tourism brings in important foreign revenue. Trading should be enhanced by Mexico's decision to join the USA and Canada in the North American Free Trade Association (NAFTA).

MICRONESIA
Federated States of,

STATUS: Self-governing Federation of States in Compact of Free Association with USA
AREA: 702 sq km (271 sq miles)
POPULATION: 109,000
ANNUAL NATURAL INCOME: 2.4%
CAPITAL: Palikir
LANGUAGE: English, eight indigenous languages
RELIGION: Christian majority
CURRENCY: US dollar (USD)
ORGANIZATIONS: UN

Micronesia, a former UN Trust Territory administered by the USA, is a federation of 607 islands and atolls spread over some 3,200 km (2,000 miles) of the Pacific. Being near the equator, the climate is hot and humid all year round with a high annual rainfall of 9,300 mm (194 inches). Subsistence farming and fishing are the traditional occupations while income is derived from the export of phosphates and copper, a growing tourist industry and revenue from foreign fleets fishing within its territorial waters.

MOLDOVA

STATUS: Republic
AREA: 33,700 sq km (13,010 sq miles)
POPULATION: 4,356,000
ANNUAL NATURAL INCREASE: 0.6%
CAPITAL: Kishinev
LANGUAGE: Moldovan, Russian, Romanian
RELIGION: Orthodox
CURRENCY: rouble
ORGANIZATIONS: CIS, UN

A country of hilly plains, Moldova enjoys a warm and dry climate with relatively mild winters. Temperatures range from 5–7°C (23–26°F) during winter , to 20–23°C (68°–72°F) for summer and rainfall averages 305–457mm (12–18 inches) per year. It has very fertile soil, so arable farming dominates agricultural output with viticulture, fruit and vegetables especially important. Sunflower seeds are the main industrial crop; wheat and maize the chief grain crops. Traditionally, food processing has been the major industry but recently light machine building and metal working industries have been expanding. Moldova, part of the Soviet Union between 1939 and 1991, has close ethnic, linguistic and historical ties with neighbouring Romania. Any moves towards re-unification have been fiercely resisted by the Russian minority in the eastern region of Trans-Dniester.

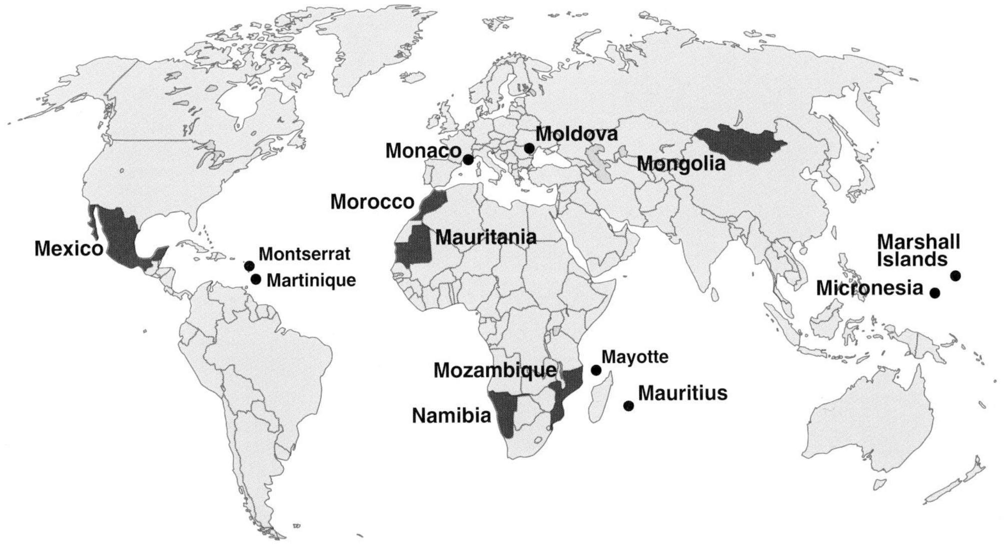

MONACO

STATUS: Principality
AREA: 1.6 sq km (0.6 sq miles)
POPULATION: 28,000
ANNUAL NATURAL INCREASE: 1.4%
CAPITAL: Monaco-ville
LANGUAGE: French, Monegasque, Italian, English
RELIGION: 90% Roman Catholic
CURRENCY: French franc (FRF)
ORGANIZATIONS: UN

The tiny principality is the world's smallest independent state after the Vatican City. It occupies a rocky peninsula on the French Mediterranean coast near the Italian border and is backed by the Maritime Alps. The climate is Mediterranean. It comprises the towns of Monaco, la Condamine, Fontvieille and Monte Carlo. Most revenue comes from tourism, casinos, light industry and financial services. Land has been reclaimed from the sea to extend the area available for commercial development.

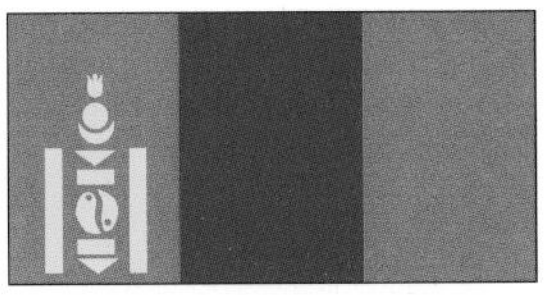

MONGOLIA

STATUS: People's Republic
AREA: 1,565,000 sq km (604,090 sq miles)
POPULATION: 2,310,000
ANNUAL NATURAL INCREASE: 2.8%
CAPITAL: Ulan Bator (Ulaanbaatar)
LANGUAGE: Khalkha Mongolian
RELIGION: some Buddhist Lamaism
CURRENCY: tugrik (MNT)
ORGANIZATIONS: OIEC, UN

Situated between China and the Russian Federation, Mongolia has one of the lowest population densities in the world. Much of the country consists of a high undulating plateau reaching 1,500 m (4,920 feet) covered with grassland. To the north, mountain ranges reaching 4,231 m (13,881 feet) bridge the border with the Russian Federation, and to the south is the vast Gobi desert. The climate is very extreme with January temperatures falling to -34°C (-29°F). Mongolia is predominantly a farming economy, based on rearing cattle and horses. Its natural resources include some oil, rich coal deposits, iron ore, gold , tin and copper. About half the country's exports originate from the Erdanet copper mine. The break-up of the Soviet Union in 1991 brought an end to a partnership whereby Mongolia supplied raw materials in exchange for aid. A year later communism was abandoned. The country is now forced to reform its economy, but is isolated and in need of investment.

MONTSERRAT

STATUS: UK Crown Colony
AREA: 106 sq km (41 sq miles)
POPULATION: 11,000
CAPITAL: Plymouth

MOROCCO

STATUS: Kingdom
AREA: 710,895 sq km
(274,414 sq miles)
POPULATION: 26,318,000
ANNUAL NATURAL INCREASE: 2.5%
CAPITAL: Rabat
LANGUAGE: Arabic, French, Spanish, Berber
RELIGION: Muslim majority, Christian
and Jewish minorities
CURRENCY: Moroccan dirham (MAD)
ORGANIZATIONS: Arab League, UN

One-third of Morocco consists of the Atlas Mountains, reaching 4,165 m (13,665 feet). Beyond the coastal plains and the mountains lies the Sahara. The north of the country has a Mediterranean climate with some winter rainfall, but elsewhere conditions are mostly desert like and arid. Agriculture has diversified in recent years and as well as tomatoes and citrus fruits exports now include a variety of fruit and vegetables. Morocco has considerable phosphate deposits, which in value account for a quarter of total exports. Manufacturing industries include textiles, leather, food processing and chemicals and a growing mechanical and electronic sector. Income from tourism and remittances from Moroccans abroad are the main sources of foreign revenue.

MOZAMBIQUE

STATUS: Republic
AREA: 784,755 sq km
(302,915 sq miles)
POPULATION: 14,872,000
ANNUAL NATURAL INCREASE: 2.7%
CAPITAL: Maputo
LANGUAGE: Portuguese, tribal languages
RELIGION: majority traditional beliefs,
15% Christian, 15% Muslim
CURRENCY: metical (MZM)
ORGANIZATIONS: OAU, UN

The ex-Portuguese colony of Mozambique consists of a large coastal plain, rising towards plateaux and mountain ranges which border Malawi, Zambia and Zimbabwe. The highlands in the north reach 2,436 m (7,992 feet). The climate is tropical on the coastal plain, although high altitudes make it cooler inland. Over 90 per cent of the population are subsistence farmers cultivating coconuts, cashews, cotton, maize and rice. Cashew nuts and shrimps are the main exports. Mozambique also acts as an entrepôt, handling exports from South Africa, and landlocked Zambia and Malawi. Natural resources include large reserves of coal, also iron ore, copper, bauxite, gold and offshore gas, but most are unexploited.

NAMIBIA

STATUS: Republic
AREA: 825,419 sq km
(318,614 sq miles)
POPULATION: 1,534,000
ANNUAL NATURAL INCREASE: 3.1%
CAPITAL: Windhoek
LANGUAGE: Afrikaans, German, English,
regional languages
RELIGION: 90% Christian
CURRENCY: Namibian dollar, SA rand
ORGANIZATIONS: Comm., OAU, UN

The southwest African country of Namibia is one of the driest in the world. The Namib desert, on the coast, has less than 50 mm (2 inches) average rainfall per year, the Kalahari, to the northeast, has 100–250 mm (4–10 inches). The vegetation is sparse. Maize and sorghum are grown in the northern highlands and sheep are reared in the south. Namibia, however, is rich in mineral resources, with large deposits of lead, tin and zinc, and the world's largest uranium mine. The rich coastal waters are the basis of a successful fishing industry.

NAURU

STATUS: Republic
AREA: 21.2 sq km (8 sq miles)
POPULATION: 9,919
ANNUAL NATURAL INCREASE: -0.3%
CAPITAL: Yaren
LANGUAGE: Nauruan, English
RELIGION: Nauruan Protestant majority
CURRENCY: Australian dollar (AUD)
ORGANIZATIONS: Comm. (special member)

Nauru, a small island only 19 km (12 miles) in circumference, is situated in the Pacific, 2,100 km (1,3000 miles) northeast of Australia. The flat coastal lowlands, encircled by coral reefs, rise gently to a central plateau. The country was once rich in phosphates which were exported to Australia and Japan. However these deposits will soon become exhausted.

NEPAL

STATUS: Kingdom
AREA: 141,415 sq km (54,585 sq miles)
POPULATION: 20,577,000
ANNUAL NATURAL INCREASE: 2.6%
CAPITAL: Katmandu (Kathmandu)
LANGUAGE: Nepali, Maithir, Bhojpuri
RELIGION: 90% Hindu, 5% Buddhist, 3% Muslim
CURRENCY: Nepalese rupee (NPR)
ORGANIZATIONS: Col. Plan, UN

Nepal is a Himalayan kingdom sandwiched between China and India. Some of the highest mountains in the world, including Everest, are to be found along its northern borders. The climate changes sharply with altitude from the mountain peaks southwards to the Tarai plain. Central Kathmandu varies between 2–30°C (35–86°F). Most rain falls between June and October and can reach 2,500 mm (100 inches). Agriculture concentrates on rice, maize, cattle, buffaloes, sheep and goats. The small amount of industry processes local products, with carpets and clothing showing particular economic growth.

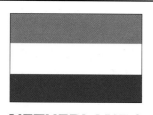

NETHERLANDS

STATUS: Kingdom
AREA: 41,160 sq km (15,890 sq miles)
POPULATION: 15,269,000
ANNUAL NATURAL INCREASE: 0.7%
CAPITAL: Amsterdam
(seat of Government: The Hague)
LANGUAGE: Dutch
RELIGION: 40% Roman Catholic,
30% Protestant, Jewish minority
CURRENCY: gulden (guilder or florin) (NLG)
ORGANIZATIONS: Council of Europe, EEA, EU, NATO, OECD, UN, WEU

The Netherlands is exceptionally low-lying, with about 25 per cent of its territory being reclaimed from the sea. The wide coastal belt consists of flat marshland, mud-flats, sand-dunes and dykes. Further inland, the flat alluvial plain is drained by the Rhine, Maas and Ijssel. A complex network of dykes and canals prevents the area from flooding. To the south and east the land rises. Flat and exposed to strong winds, the Netherlands has a maritime climate with mild winters and cool summers. The Dutch are the leading world producers of dairy goods and also cultivate crops such as cereals, sugar beet and potatoes. Lacking mineral resources, much of the industry of the Netherlands is dependent on natural gas. Most manufacturing industry has developed around Rotterdam, where there are oil refineries, steel-works and chemical and food processing plants.

NETHERLANDS ANTILLES

STATUS: Self-governing Part of Netherlands Realm
AREA: 993 sq km (383 sq miles)
POPULATION: 191,311
CAPITAL: Willemstad

NEW CALEDONIA

STATUS: Overseas Territory of France
AREA: 19,105 sq km (7,375 sq miles)
POPULATION: 164,173
CAPITAL: Nouméa

NEW ZEALAND

STATUS: Commonwealth Nation
AREA: 265,150 sq km (102,350 sq miles)
POPULATION: 3,470,000
ANNUAL NATURAL INCREASE: 0.7%
CAPITAL: Wellington
LANGUAGE: English, Maori
RELIGION: 35% Anglican Christian,
22% Presbyterian, 16% Roman Catholic
CURRENCY: New Zealand dollar (NZD)
ORGANIZATIONS: ANZUS, Col. Plan, Comm., OECD, UN

New Zealand consists of two main and several smaller islands, lying in the south Pacific Ocean. South Island is mountainous, with the Southern Alps running along its length. It has many glaciers and a coast line that is indented by numerous sounds and fjords. On the more heavily populated North Island, mountain ranges, broad fertile valleys and volcanic plateaux predominate. The overall climate is temperate, with an annual average temperature of 9°C (40°F) on South Island and 15°C (59°F) on the North Island. In terms of value the chief exports are meat, dairy produce and forestry products, followed by wood, fruit and vegetables. In the mineral sector there are deposits of coal, iron ore, oil and natural gas. Hydro-electric and geothermal power are well developed. Manufacturing industries are of increasing importance and in the early 1990s tourism expanded rapidly.

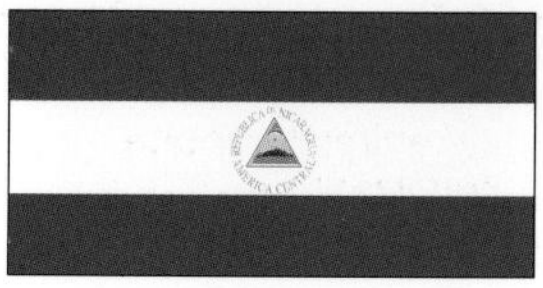

NICARAGUA

STATUS: Republic
AREA: 148,000 sq km (57,130 sq miles)
POPULATION: 4,130,000
ANNUAL NATURAL INCREASE: 2.8%
CAPITAL: Managua
LANGUAGE: Spanish
RELIGION: Roman Catholic
CURRENCY: cordoba (NIO)
ORGANIZATIONS: CACM, OAS, UN

Nicaragua, the largest of the Central American republics, is situated between the Caribbean and the Pacific. Active volcanic mountains run parallel with the western coast. The south is dominated by Lakes Managua and Nicaragua. Climate is tropical, with average daily temperatures in excess of 25°C (77°F) throughout the year. On the west coast wet summer months contrast with a dry period from December to April. Agriculture is the main occupation with cotton, coffee, sugar cane and fruit the main exports. Gold, silver and copper are mined.

NIGER

STATUS: Republic
AREA: 1,186,410 sq km (457,955 sq miles)
POPULATION: 8,252,000
ANNUAL NATURAL INCREASE: 3.2%
CAPITAL: Niamey
LANGUAGE: French, Hausa and other native languages
RELIGION: 85% Muslim, 15% traditional beliefs
CURRENCY: CFA franc (W Africa) (XOF)
ORGANIZATIONS: ECOWAS, OAU, UN

Niger is a vast landlocked southern republic. Apart from savannah in the south and in the Niger valley, most of the vast country lies within the Sahara desert. Rainfall is low, and decreases from 560 mm (22 inches) in the south to near zero in the north. Temperatures are above 35°C (95°F) for much of the year. Most of the population are farmers, particularly of cattle, sheep, and goats. Recent droughts have affected both cereals and livestock. The only significant export is uranium. and phosphates, coal, and tungsten are also mined. The economy depends largely on foreign aid.

NIGERIA

STATUS: Federal Republic
AREA: 923,850 sq km (356,605 sq miles)
POPULATION: 88,515,000
ANNUAL NATURAL INCREASE: 2.9%
CAPITAL: Abuja

LANGUAGE: English, Hausa, Yoruba, Ibo
RELIGION: Muslim majority, 35% Christian, animist minority
CURRENCY: naira (NGN)
ORGANIZATIONS: Comm., ECOWAS, OAU, OPEC, UN

The most populous nation in Africa, Nigeria is bounded to the north by the Sahara and to the west, east and southeast by tropical rainforest. The southern half of the country is dominated by the Niger and its tributaries, the north by the interior plateaux. Temperatures average 32°C (90°F) with high humidity. From a basic agricultural economy, Nigeria is only slowly being transformed by the vast oil discoveries in the Niger delta and coastal regions, which account for 95 per cent of exports. Gas reserves are relatively underdeveloped.

NIUE

STATUS: Self-governing Territory Overseas in Free Association with New Zealand
AREA: 259 sq km (100 sq miles)
POPULATION: 2,267
CAPITAL: Aloli

NORFOLK ISLAND

STATUS: External Territory of Australia
AREA: 36 sq km (14 sq miles)
POPULATION: 1,977
CAPITAL: Kingston

NORTHERN MARIANA ISLANDS

STATUS: Self-governing Commonwealth of USA
AREA: 471 sq km (182 sq miles)
POPULATION: 45,200
CAPITAL: Saipan

NORWAY

STATUS: Kingdom
AREA: 323,895 sq km (125,025 sq miles)
POPULATION: 4,305,000
ANNUAL NATURAL INCREASE: 0.4%
CAPITAL: Oslo
LANGUAGE: Norwegian, Lappish
RELIGION: 92% Evangelical Lutheran Christian
CURRENCY: Norwegian krone (NOK)
ORGANIZATIONS: Council of Europe, EEA, EFTA, NATO, OECD, UN

Norway is a mountainous country stretching from 58° to 72°N. The climate along its indented western coast is modified by the Gulf Stream, with high rainfall and relatively mild winters. Temperatures average -3.9°C (25°F) in January and 17°C (63°F) in July. Rainfall may be as high as 1,960 mm (79 inches). Most settlements are scattered along the fjords, the coast and around Oslo in the south. Norway is rich in natural resources. Oil and natural gas predominate in exports, but are supplemented by metal products, timber, pulp and paper, fish and machinery. The advanced production of hydro-electric power has helped develop industry, particularly chemicals, metal products and paper.

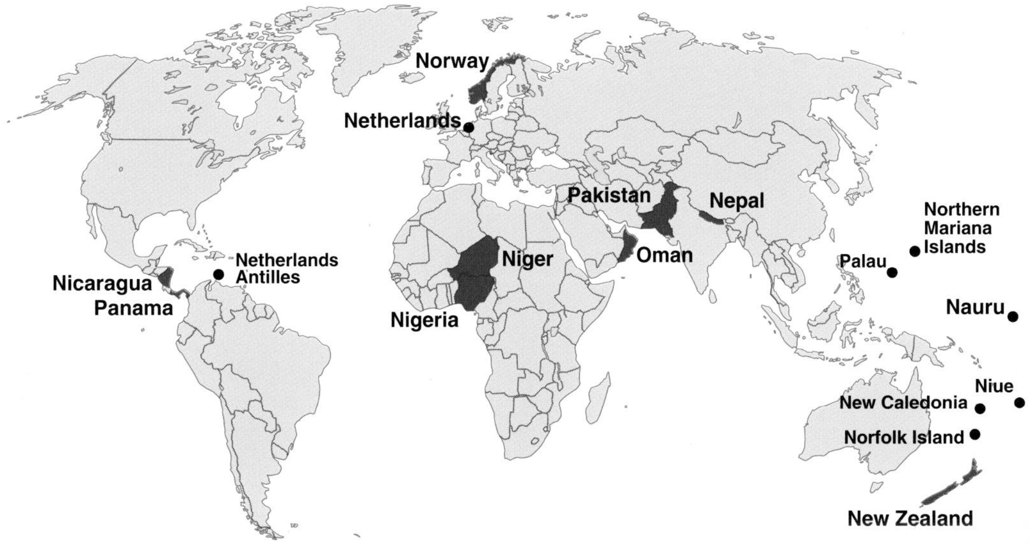

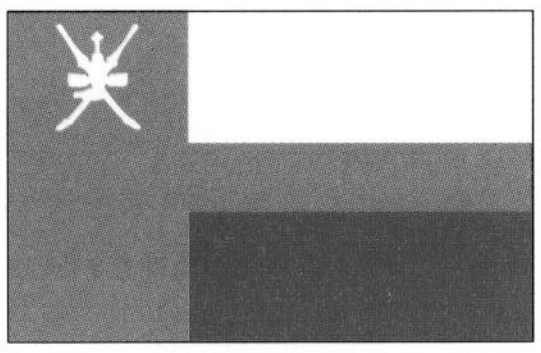

OMAN

STATUS: Sultanate
AREA: 271,950 sq km (104,970 sq miles)
POPULATION: 1,637,000
ANNUAL NATURAL INCREASE: 3.8%
CAPITAL: Muscat (Masqaṭ)
LANGUAGE: Arabic, English
RELIGION: 75% Ibadi Muslim, 25% Sunni Muslim
CURRENCY: rial Omani (OMR)
ORGANIZATIONS: Arab League, UN

The Sultanate of Oman occupies the northeast coast of the Arabian peninsula, with an enclave overlooking the Strait of Hormuz. Its desert landscape consists of a coastal plain and low hills rising to plateau in the interior, and has two fertile areas; Batinah in the north and Dhofar in the south. Copper ores are being mined and exported and oil provides over 95 per cent of export revenue. New discoveries of gas suggest that this will eventually supplant oil in importance.

PAKISTAN

STATUS: Republic
AREA: 803,940 sq km (310,320 sq miles)
POPULATION: 119,107,000
ANNUAL NATURAL INCREASE: 3.1%
CAPITAL: Islamabad
LANGUAGE: Urdu, Punjabi, Sindhi, Pushtu, English
RELIGION: 90% Muslim
CURRENCY: Pakistan rupee (PKR)
ORGANIZATIONS Col. Plan, Comm., UN

The landscape of Pakistan is dominated by the river Indus which flows south through the country flanked by the plateau of Balochistan and the Sulaiman mountains to the west and the Thar desert to the east. The climate is arid with temperatures averaging 27°C (80°F). Rainfall can be less than 127 mm (5 inches) in the southwest and only in the northern mountains does it reach appreciable amounts; 900 mm (36 inches). Over 50 per cent of the population are engaged in agriculture which is confined to the irrigated areas near rivers. Main crops are wheat, cotton, maize, rice and sugar cane. There are many types of low-grade mineral deposits, such as coal and copper, which are little developed. Main industries are textiles, food processing and oil refining but these only contribute about 20 per cent to the economy.

PALAU (BELAU)

STATUS: Republic
AREA: 497 sq km (192 sq miles)
POPULATION: 15,450
CAPITAL: Babelthuap

PANAMA

STATUS: Republic
AREA: 78,515 sq km (30,305 sq miles)
POPULATION: 2,535,000
ANNUAL NATURAL INCREASE: 2.1%
CAPITAL: Panama City (Panamá)
LANGUAGE: Spanish, English
RELIGION: Roman Catholic majority
CURRENCY: balboa (PAB), US dollar (USD)
ORGANIZATIONS: OAS, UN

Panama is situated at the narrowest part of central American isthmus. Mountain ranges, reaching heights exceeding 3,000 m (9,800 feet), run the country's length. Much of its tropical forest has now been cleared, but some remains towards the border with Colombia. Its climate is tropical with little variation throughout the year. The average temperature is around 27°C (80°F). There is a rainy season from April to December. Most of its foreign income is earned from revenues derived from the Panama Canal and from a large merchant fleet that is registered in its name. Petroleum products, bananas and shrimps are the main exports.

PAPUA NEW GUINEA

STATUS: Commonwealth Nation
AREA: 462,840 sq km (178,655 sq miles)
POPULATION: 4,056,000
ANNUAL NATURAL INCREASE: 2.3%
CAPITAL: Port Moresby
LANGUAGE: English, Pidgin English,
RELIGION: Pantheist, Christian minority
CURRENCY: kina (PGK)
ORGANIZATIONS: Col. Plan, Comm., UN

Papua New Guinea (the eastern half of New Guinea and neighbouring islands) is a mountainous country. It has an equatorial climate with temperatures of 21–32°C (70–90°F) and annual rainfall of over 2,000 mm (79 inches). The country is rich in minerals, in particular copper, gold and silver, but development is restricted by rainforest and lack of roads. Exports include coconuts, cocoa, coffee, rubber, tea and sugar. Logging was once dominant but exports are now being reduced in order to preserve forest resources.

PARAGUAY

STATUS: Republic
AREA: 406,750 sq km (157,055 sq miles)
POPULATION: 4,500,000
ANNUAL NATURAL INCREASE: 2.9%
CAPITAL: Asunción
LANGUAGE: Spanish, Guarani
RELIGION: 90% Roman Catholic
CURRENCY: guarani (PYG)
ORGANIZATIONS: OAS, UN

Paraguay is a landlocked country in South America with hot rainy summers, when temperatures reach over 27°C (80°F), and mild winters with an average temperature of 18°C (64°F). Lush, fertile plains and heavily forested plateau east of the River Paraguay contrast with the scrubland of the Chaco to the west. Cassava, cotton, soya beans and maize are the main crops but the rearing of livestock – cattle, horses, pigs and sheep – and food processing, dominate the export trade. The largest hydro-electric power dam in the world is at Itaipú, constructed as a joint project with Brazil, and another massive hydro-electric development is being constructed at Yacyreta in conjunction with Argentina.

PERU

STATUS: Republic
AREA: 1,285,215 sq km (496,095 sq miles)
POPULATION: 22,454,000
ANNUAL NATURAL INCREASE: 2.1%
CAPITAL: Lima
LANGUAGE: Spanish, Quechua, Aymara
RELIGION: Roman Catholic majority
CURRENCY: new sol (PES)
ORGANIZATIONS: OAS, UN

Peru exhibits three geographical regions. The Pacific coastal region is very dry but with fertile oases producing cotton, sugar, fruit and fodder crops. This is the most prosperous and heavily populated area and includes the industrial centres around Lima. In the ranges and plateaux of the Andes and in the Amazon lowlands to the northeast, the soils are thin with the inhabitants depending on cultivation and grazing. Poor communications have hindered the development of Peru and there are great differences between the rich and poor. Peru has rich mineral deposits of copper, gold, lead, zinc and silver and there are oil and gas reserves in the interior.

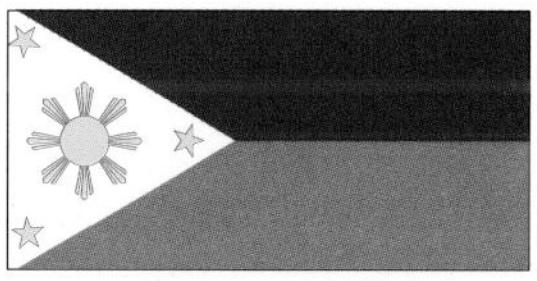

PHILIPPINES

STATUS: Republic
AREA: 300,000 sq km (115,800 sq miles)
POPULATION: 65,650,000
ANNUAL NATURAL INCREASE: 2.3%
CAPITAL: Manila
LANGUAGE: Filipino (Tagalog), English, Spanish, Cebuano
RELIGION: 90% Christian, 7% Muslim
CURRENCY: Philippine peso (PHP)
ORGANIZATIONS: ASEAN, Col. Plan, UN

The Philippine archipelago consists of some 7,000 islands and is subject to earthquakes and typhoons. It has a monsoonal climate, with up to 6,350 mm (250 inches) of rainfall per annum in some areas. This once supported tropical rain forest but, apart from Palawan island, this has now been destroyed. Fishing is important but small farms dominate the economy, producing rice and copra for domestic consumption and other coconut and sugar products for export. Main exports are textiles, fruit and electronic products. Remittances from Filipinos working overseas are important to the economy. There is high unemployment and the extent of poverty is widespread.

PITCAIRN ISLAND

STATUS: UK Dependent Territory
AREA: 45 sq km (17.25 sq miles)
POPULATION: 71
CAPITAL: Adamstown

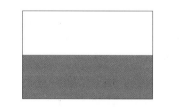

POLAND

STATUS: Republic
AREA: 312,685 sq km (120,695 sq miles)
POPULATION: 38,310,000
ANNUAL NATURAL INCREASE: 0.4%
CAPITAL: Warsaw (Warszawa)
LANGUAGE: Polish
RELIGION: 90% Roman Catholic
CURRENCY: zloty (PLZ)
ORGANIZATIONS: Council of Europe, OIEC, UN,

Much of Poland lies in the north European plain, south of the Baltic Sea. It is a land of woods and lakes, gently rising southwards from the coast towards the Tartry mountains in the south and Sudety mountains in Silesia. The climate is continental with short, warm summers and long severe winters, when average temperatures can drop below freezing point (32°F). Rainfall occurs mainly in the summer months and averages between 520 and 730 mm (21–29 inches). Both agriculture and natural resources play an important part in the economy and Poland is nearly self-sufficient in cereals, sugar beet and potatoes. There are large reserves of coal, copper, sulphur and natural gas. Its major industries are ship-building in the north and the production of machinery, transport equipment, metals and chemicals in the major mining centres of the south. Manufacturing industries in both the private and public sectors are expanding rapidly and the government is committed to a programme of economic reforms and privatization.

PORTUGAL

STATUS: Republic
AREA: 91,630 sq km (35,370 sq miles)
POPULATION: 9,846,000
ANNUAL NATURAL INCREASE: -0.7%
CAPITAL: Lisbon (Lisboa)
LANGUAGE: Portuguese
RELIGION: Roman Catholic majority
CURRENCY: escudo (PTE)
ORGANIZATIONS: Council of Europe, EEA, EU, NATO, OECD, UN, WEU

Portugal occupies the western Atlantic coast of the Iberian Peninsula. The river Tagus, on whose estuary is Lisbon, divides the country physically. In the north the land lies mainly above 4,000 m (1,220 feet) with plateaux cut by westward flowing rivers. Here, the climate is modified by westerly winds and the Gulf Stream. This is reflected in the lush mixed deciduous/coniferous forests. Land to the south is generally less than 300 m (1,000 feet) and the climate becomes progressively more arid further south, with Mediterranean scrub predominating in the far south. A quarter of the population are farmers growing vines, olives, wheat and maize. Wines, cork and fruit are important exports. In industry the chief exports are textiles, clothing, footwear and wood products. Mineral deposits include coal, copper, kaolinite and uranium. Tourism is an important source of revenue, with many visitors coming to the Algarve region in the far south of the country.

PUERTO RICO

STATUS: Self-governing Commonwealth of USA
AREA: 8,960 sq km (3,460 sq miles)
POPULATION: 3,580,000
CAPITAL: San Juan

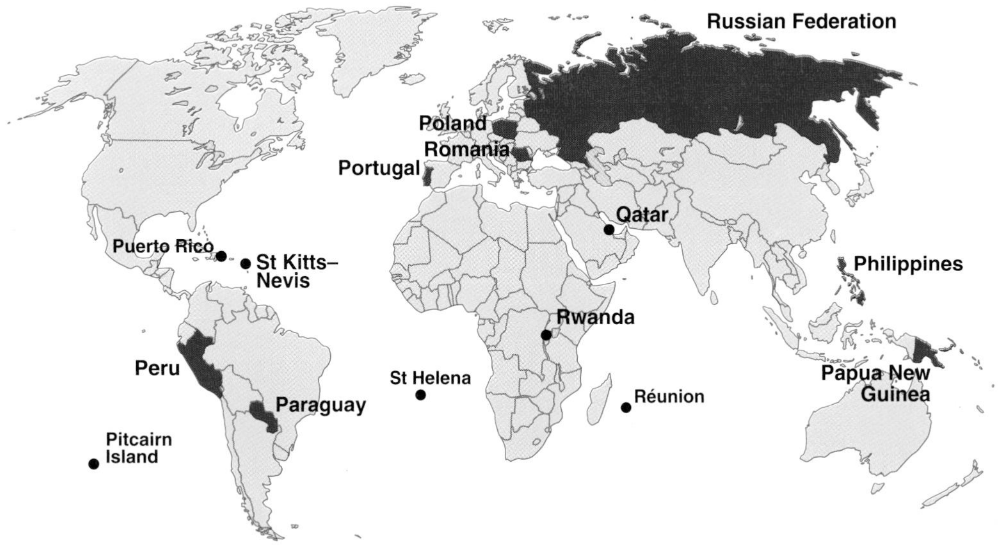

QATAR

STATUS: State
AREA: 11,435 sq km (4,415 sq miles)
POPULATION: 453,000
ANNUAL NATURAL INCREASE: 6%
CAPITAL: Doha (Ad Dawḩah)
LANGUAGE: Arabic, English
RELIGION: Muslim
CURRENCY: Qatari riyal (QAR)
ORGANIZATIONS: Arab League, OPEC, UN

The country occupies all of the Qatar peninsula in the Gulf and is a land of flat, arid desert. July temperatures average 37°C (98°F) and annual rainfall averages 62mm (2.5 inches). The main source of revenue is from the exploitation of oil and gas reserves. The North Field gas reserves are the world's largest single field and the development of these has a high priority.

RÉUNION

STATUS: Overseas Department of France
AREA: 2,510 sq km (969 sq miles)
POPULATION: 624,000
CAPITAL: Saint-Denis

ROMANIA

STATUS: Republic
AREA: 237,500 sq km (91,699 sq miles)
POPULATION: 22,767,000
ANNUAL NATURAL INCREASE: 0.1%
CAPITAL: Bucharest (Bucureşti)
LANGUAGE: Romanian, Magyar
RELIGION: 85% Romanian Orthodox,
CURRENCY: leu (ROL)
ORGANIZATIONS: Council of Europe, OIEC, UN

Romania is dominated by the great curve of the Carpathians, flanked by rich agricultural lowlands and has a continental climate. Forced industrialization has taken the economy from one based on agriculture to one dependent on heavy industry, notably chemicals, metal processing and machine-building. Since the fall of the communist dictatorship in 1989, most land has been privatized and there has been a re-emergence of Romania's traditional agriculture, with exports of cereals, fruit and wine. There are natural resources including oil, gas and minerals but industrial reform is slow and the economy is sluggish. Living standards are among the lowest in Europe.

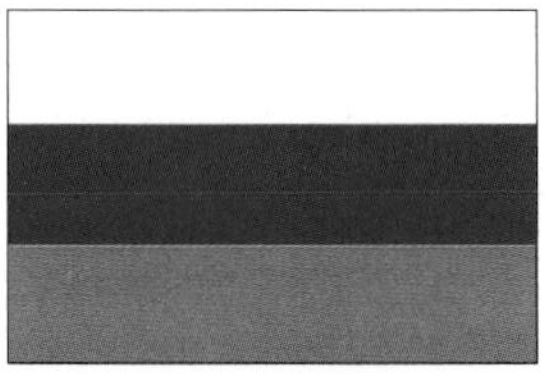

RUSSIAN FEDERATION

STATUS: Federation
AREA: 17,078,005 sq km (6,592,110 sq miles)
POPULATION: 148,673,000
ANNUAL NATURAL INCREASE: 0.5%
CAPITAL: Moscow (Moskva)
LANGUAGE: Russian
RELIGION: Russian Orthodox, Jewish and Muslim minorities
CURRENCY: rouble
ORGANIZATIONS: CIS, UN

Covering much of east and northeast Europe and all of north Asia, the Russian Federation (Russia) displays an enormous variety of landforms and climates. The Arctic deserts of the north give way to tundra wastes and taiga which cover two-thirds of the country. In the far south, beyond the steppes, some areas assume subtropical and semi-desert landscapes. The majority of the population live west of the north-south spine of the Urals but in recent decades there has been a substantial migration eastwards to the Siberian basin in order to exploit its vast natural resources. Massive oil fields off the east coast of Sakhalin north of Japan and also in the Russian Arctic (Timan Pechora basin) are now to be developed. Russia's extraordinary wealth of natural resources was a key factor in the country's speedy industrialization during the Soviet period. Heavy industry still plays a decisive role in the economy, while light and consumer industries have remained relatively under-developed. Agricultural land covers one-sixth of Russia's territory but there remains great potential for increase through drainage and clearance. By the mid-1980s the Soviet system was finally acknowledged to have reached an impasse, and the failure of the *perestroika* programme for reform precipitated the disintegration of the Soviet Union, which finally broke up in 1991. A transition from a state-run Communist economy to a market economy is taking place. Between 1992 and 1994 70 per cent of state-owned enterprises were privatized and farms are also starting to be re-organized.

RWANDA

STATUS: Republic
AREA: 26,330 sq km (10,165 sq miles)
POPULATION: 7,526,000
ANNUAL NATURAL INCREASE: 3%
CAPITAL: Kigali
LANGUAGE: French, Kinyarwanda (Bantu), tribal languages
RELIGION: 50% animist, 50% Christian (mostly Roman Catholic)
CURRENCY: Rwanda franc (RWF)
ORGANIZATIONS: OAU, UN

Small and isolated, Rwanda supports a high density of population on the mountains and plateaux east of the Rift Valley. It has a tropical climate with a dry season between June and August. Agriculture is basically subsistence with coffee the major export. Tin is mined and there are major natural gas reserves. Since 1990 a civil war has raged between the Tutsi and Hutu tribes, creating many thousands of casualties and well over one million refugees. The country has become reliant on foreign aid, and will require a massive international relief effort to avert disease and famine.

ST HELENA

STATUS: UK Dependent Territory
AREA: 122 sq km (47 sq miles)
POPULATION: 5,564
CAPITAL: Jamestown

ST KITTS-NEVIS

STATUS: Commonwealth State
AREA: 262 sq km (101 sq miles)
POPULATION: 40,618
ANNUAL NATURAL INCREASE: -0.4%
CAPITAL: Basseterre
LANGUAGE: English
RELIGION: Christian (mostly Protestant)
CURRENCY: E Caribbean dollar (XCD)
ORGANIZATIONS: CARICOM, Comm., OAS, UN

St Kitts-Nevis, in the Leeward Islands, comprises two volcanic islands: St Kitts and Nevis. The climate is tropical with temperatures of 16–33°C (61–91°F) and an average annual rainfall of 1,400 mm (55 inches). Main exports are sugar, molasses and cotton. Tourism is an important industry.

ST LUCIA

STATUS: Commonwealth State
AREA: 616 sq km (238 sq miles)
POPULATION: 136,000
ANNUAL NATURAL INCREASE: 1.9%
CAPITAL: Castries
LANGUAGE: English, French patois
RELIGION: 82% Roman Catholic
CURRENCY: E. Caribbean dollar (XCD)
ORGANIZATIONS: Caricom, Comm., OAS, UN

Independent since 1979 this small tropical Caribbean island in the Lesser Antilles grows coconuts, cocoa and fruit. Bananas account for over 40 per cent of export earnings. Main industries are food and drink processing and all consumer goods are imported. Tourism is a major growth sector.

ST PIERRE AND MIQUELON

STATUS: Territorial Collectivity of France
AREA: 241 sq km (93 sq miles)
POPULATION: 6,392
CAPITAL: St Pierre

ST VINCENT AND THE GRENADINES

STATUS: Commonwealth State
AREA: 389 sq km (150 sq miles)
POPULATION: 107,598
ANNUAL NATURAL INCREASE: 0.9%
CAPITAL: Kingstown
LANGUAGE: English
RELIGION: Christian
CURRENCY: E. Caribbean dollar (XCD)
ORGANIZATIONS: Caricom, Comm., OAS, UN

St Vincent in the Lesser Antilles comprises a forested main island and the northern part of the Grenadines. It has a tropical climate. Most exports are foodstuffs: arrowroot, sweet potatoes, coconut products and yams, but the principal crop is bananas. Some sugar cane is grown for the production of rum and other drinks. Tourism is well-established.

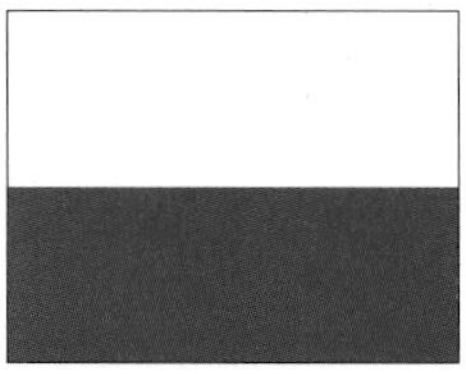

SAN MARINO

STATUS: Republic
AREA: 61 sq km (24 sq miles)
POPULATION: 24,003
ANNUAL NATURAL INCREASE: 1.2%
CAPITAL: San Marino
LANGUAGE: Italian
RELIGION: Roman Catholic
CURRENCY: Italian lira (ITL), San Marino coinage
ORGANIZATIONS: Council of Europe, UN

An independent state within Italy, San Marino straddles a limestone peak in the Apennines south of Rimini. The economy is centred around tourism and the sale of postage stamps. Most of the population are farmers growing cereals, olives and vines and tending herds of sheep and goats.

SÃO TOMÉ AND PRÍNCIPE

STATUS: Republic
AREA: 964 sq km (372 sq miles)
POPULATION: 124,000
ANNUAL NATURAL INCREASE: 2.3%
CAPITAL: São Tomé
LANGUAGE: Portuguese, Fang
RELIGION: Roman Catholic majority
CURRENCY: dobra (STD)
ORGANIZATIONS: OAU, UN

This tiny state, independent from Portugal since 1975, comprises two large and several small islands near the equator, 200 km (125 miles) off west Africa. The climate is tropical with temperatures averaging 25°C (77°F) and rainfall of between 1,000–5,000 mm (40–197 inches). Cocoa (which provides 90 per cent of revenue), coconuts and palm oil are the main crops grown on the rich volcanic soil. Other foods and consumer goods are imported.

SAUDI ARABIA

STATUS: Kingdom
AREA: 2,400,900 sq km (926,745 sq miles)
POPULATION: 16,900,000
ANNUAL NATURAL INCREASE: 3.5%
CAPITAL: Riyadh (Ar Riyāḍ)
LANGUAGE: Arabic
RELIGION: 90% Sunni Muslim, 5% Roman Catholic
CURRENCY: Saudi riyal (SAR)
ORGANIZATIONS: Arab League, OPEC, UN

Saudi Arabia occupies the heart of the vast arid Arabian Peninsula. The country is mostly desert and there are no rivers which flow all year round. To the west, the Hejaz and Asir mountains fringe the Red Sea but even here rainfall rarely exceeds 380 mm (15 inches). Temperatures rise beyond 44°C (111°F) in the summer. The interior plateau slopes gently eastwards down to the Gulf and supports little vegetation. The southeast of the country is well named as the 'Empty Quarter'; it is almost devoid of population. Only in the coastal strips and oases are cereals and date palms grown. Oil is the most important resource – Saudi Arabia has a quarter of the world's known oil reserves – and export commodity and economic development is dependent on its revenue.

SENEGAL

STATUS: Republic
AREA: 196,720 sq km (75,935 sq miles)
POPULATION: 7,970,000
ANNUAL NATURAL INCREASE: 3.0%
CAPITAL: Dakar
LANGUAGE: French, native languages
RELIGION: 94% Sunni Muslim, animist minority
CURRENCY: CFA franc (W Africa) (XOF)
ORGANIZATIONS: ECOWAS, OAU, UN

Senegal is a flat, dry country cut through by the Gambia, Casamance and Senegal rivers. Rainfall rarely exceeds 580 mm (23 inches) on the wetter coast. The interior savannah supports varied wildlife but little agriculture. Cultivation is mainly confined to the south where groundnuts account for nearly half of the agricultural output. Cotton and millet are also grown, but frequent droughts have reduced their value as cash crops. Phosphate mining, ship-repairing, textiles, petroleum products and food processing are the major industries. Both tourism and fishing are becoming increasingly important.

SEYCHELLES

STATUS: Republic
AREA: 404 sq km (156 sq miles)
POPULATION: 72,000
ANNUAL NATURAL INCREASE: 0.8%
CAPITAL: Victoria
LANGUAGE: English, French, Creole
RELIGION: 92% Roman Catholic
CURRENCY: Seychelles rupee (SCR)
ORGANIZATIONS: Comm., OAU, UN

This archipelago in the Indian Ocean comprises over 100 granite or coral islands. Main exports are copra, coconuts and cinnamon and in recent years tea and tuna. All domestic requirements, including most foodstuffs, have to be imported. Tourism has developed rapidly in the 1990s and is now the dominant sector in the economy.

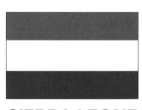

SIERRA LEONE

STATUS: Republic
AREA: 72,325 sq km (27,920 sq miles)
POPULATION: 4,376,000
ANNUAL NATURAL INCREASE: 2.4%
CAPITAL: Freetown
LANGUAGE: English, Krio Temne, Mende
RELIGION: 52% animist, 39% Muslim and 8% Christian

CURRENCY: leone (SLL)
ORGANIZATIONS: Comm., ECOWAS, OAS, UN

Sierra Leone, a former British colony, has a coast dominated by swamps but is essentially a flat plain some 70 miles wide which extends to interior plateaux and mountains. Three-quarters of the population are employed in subsistence farming. Cash crops include cocoa and coffee but the main source of revenue is from minerals. Diamonds, gold, bauxite and iron ore are mined but the most important export is now rutile (titanium ore). Manufacturing in the form of processing local products has developed around Freetown.

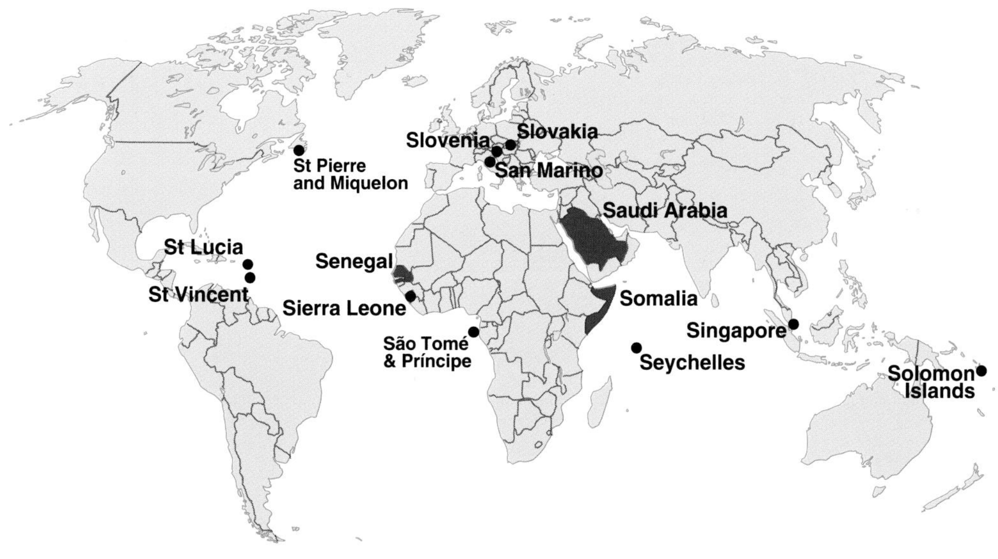

SINGAPORE

STATUS: Republic
AREA: 616 sq km (238 sq miles)
POPULATION: 2,874,000
ANNUAL NATURAL INCREASE: 1.2%
CAPITAL: Singapore
LANGUAGE: Malay, Chinese (Mandarin), Tamil, English
RELIGION: Daoist, Buddist, Muslim, Christian and Hindu
CURRENCY: Singapore dollar (SGD)
ORGANIZATIONS: ASEAN, Col. Plan, Comm., UN

The republic of Singapore, independent from Britain since 1959, has been transformed from an island of mangrove swamps into one of the world's major entrepreneurial centres. The island, connected to Peninsular Malaysia by a manmade causeway, has a tropical, humid climate with 2,240 mm (96 inches) of rain per year. With few natural resources, Singapore depends on manufacturing precision goods, electronic products, financial services and activities associated with its port, which is one of the world's largest.

SLOVAKIA

STATUS: Republic
AREA: 49,035 sq km (18,932 sq miles)
POPULATION: 5,320,000
ANNUAL NATURAL INCREASE: 0.4%
CAPITAL: Bratislava
LANGUAGE: Slovak, ~~Hungarian~~
RELIGION: Roman Catholic
CURRENCY: Slovak crown or koruna
ORGANIZATIONS: Council of Europe, UN

On 1 January 1993 Czechoslovakia ceased to exist and Slovakia and the Czech Republic came into being. Slovakia's geomorphology is dominated by the Tatry mountains in the north. Bratislava, the capital, lies in the extreme southwest, on the north bank of the Danube. Natural resources include iron ore, copper, antimony, mercury, magnesite and oil. Under Communism large manufacturing complexes developed, many of which specialized in arms and tanks. The end of the Cold War in 1989 brought a collapse in demand for these products. This, and a decline in trade with the Czech Republic, has forced Slovakia to restructure existing industry and look to new developments such as aluminium smelting and car assembly.

SLOVENIA

STATUS: Republic
AREA: 20,250 sq km (7,815 sq miles)
POPULATION: 1,990,000
ANNUAL NATURAL INCREASE: 0.7%
CAPITAL: Ljubljana
LANGUAGE: Slovene
RELIGION: Roman Catholic
CURRENCY: Slovenian tolar (SLT)
ORGANIZATIONS: Council of Europe, UN

The northernmost republic of the former Yugoslav federation, Slovenia, has always been one of the key gateways from the Balkans to central and western Europe. Much of the country is mountainous, its heartland and main centre of population being the Ljubljana basin. The climate generally shows continental tendencies, with warm summers and cold winters, when snow is plentiful on the ground. The small coastal region has a Mediterranean regime. Extensive mountain pastures provide profitable dairy-farming, but the amount of cultivable land is restricted. There are large mercury mines in the northwest and, in recent decades, this area has also developed a broad range of light industries. Combined with tourism, this has given the country a well-balanced economy. After a brief military conflict Slovenia won its independence in 1991.

SOLOMON ISLANDS

STATUS: Commonwealth Nation
AREA: 29,790 sq km (11,500 sq miles)
POPULATION: 349,500
ANNUAL NATURAL INCREASE: 2.9%
CAPITAL: Honiara
LANGUAGE: English, Pidgin English, native languages
RELIGION: 95% Christian
CURRENCY: Solomon Islands dollar (SBD)
ORGANIZATIONS: Comm., UN

Situated in the South Pacific Ocean the Solomon Islands consist of a 1400 km (870 miles) archipelago of six main and many smaller islands. The mountainous large islands are covered by tropical rain forest reflecting the high temperatures, on average 22–34°C (72–95°F) and heavy rainfall, about 3,050 mm (120 inches). The main crops are coconuts, cocoa and rice, with copra, timber and palm oil being the main exports. Mineral deposits include reserves of bauxite, gold and phosphate, mined on the small island of Bellona south of Guadalcanal. Once a British protectorate, the Solomons became independent in 1978.

SOMALIA

STATUS: Republic
AREA: 6300,000sq km (243,180 sq miles)
POPULATION: 7,497,000
ANNUAL NATURAL INCREASE: 3.0%
CAPITAL: Mogadishu (Muqdisho)
LANGUAGE: Somali, Arabic, English, Italian
RELIGION: Muslim, Roman Catholic minority
CURRENCY: Somali shilling (SOS)
ORGANIZATIONS: UN, Arab League, OAU

Independent since 1960, Somalia is a hot and arid country in northeast Africa. The semi-desert of the northern mountains contrasts with the plains of the south where the bush country is particularly rich in wildlife. Most of the population are nomadic, following herds of camels, sheep, goats and cattle. Little land is cultivated but cotton, maize, millet and sugar cane are grown. Bananas are a major export. Iron ore, gypsum and uranium deposits are as yet unexploited. Five years of inter-clan warfare and a lack of coherent government have led to the collapse of the economy.

SOUTH AFRICA

STATUS: Republic
AREA: 1,220,845 sq km (471,369 sq miles)
POPULATION: 37,600,000
ANNUAL NATURAL INCREASE: 2.4%
CAPITAL: Pretoria (administrative)
Cape Town (legislative)
LANGUAGE: Afrikaans, English,
various African languages
RELIGION: mainly Christian, Hindu,
Jewish and Muslim minorities
CURRENCY: rand (ZAR)
ORGANIZATIONS: Comm., OAU, UN

The interior of South Africa consists of a plateau of over 900 m (2,955 feet) drained by the Orange and Limpopo rivers. Surrounding the plateau is a pronounced escarpment below which the land descends by steps to the sea. Rainfall in most areas is less than 500 mm (20 inches) and the land is increasingly drier towards the west. Agriculture is limited by poor soils but sheep and cattle are extensively grazed. Main crops are maize, wheat, sugar cane, vegetables, cotton and vines. Wine is an important export commodity. South Africa abounds in minerals. Diamonds, gold, platinum, silver, uranium, copper, manganese and asbestos are mined and nearly 80 per cent of the continent's coal reserves are in South Africa. Manufacturing and engineering is concentrated in the southern Transvaal area and around the ports. In 1994 the first ever multiracial elections were held resulting in Nelson Mandela coming to power. In a post-apartheid era, economic sanctions have been lifted, boosting exports, but the country faces adaptation, beginning with a rush of complicated land-ownership claims.

EASTERN CAPE

STATUS: Province
AREA: 174,405 sq km (67,338 sq miles)
POPULATION: 5,900,000
CAPITAL: East London

EASTERN TRANSVAAL

STATUS: Province
AREA: 73,377 sq km (28,311 sq miles)
POPULATION: 2,600,000
CAPITAL Nelspruit

KWAZULU-NATAL

STATUS: Province
AREA: 90,925 sq km (35,106 sq miles)
POPULATION: 8,000,000
CAPITAL: Durban

NORTHERN CAPE

STATUS: Province
AREA: 369,552 sq km (142,684 sq miles)
POPULATION: 700,000
CAPITAL: Kimberley

NORTHERN TRANSVAAL

STATUS: Province
AREA: 121,766 sq km (47,014 sq miles)
POPULATION: 4,700,000
CAPITAL: Pietersburg

NORTH WEST

STATUS: Province
AREA: 120,170 sq km (46,398 sq miles)
POPULATION: 3,300,000
CAPITAL: Klerksdorp

ORANGE FREE STATE

STATUS: Province
AREA: 123,893 sq km (47,835 sq miles)
POPULATION: 2,500,000
CAPITAL: Bloemfontein

PRETORIA-WITWATERSRAND-VEREENIGING (PWV)

STATUS: Province
AREA: 18,078 sq km (6,980 sq miles)
POPULATION: 6,500,000
CAPITAL: Johannesburg

WESTERN CAPE

STATUS: Province
AREA: 128,679 sq km
(49,683 sq miles)
POPULATION: 3,400,000
CAPITAL: Cape Town

SOUTHERN AND ANTARCTIC TERRITORIES

STATUS: Overseas Territory of France
AREA: 439,580 sq km (169,680 sq miles)
POPULATION: 180

SOUTH GEORGIA AND THE SOUTH SANDWICH ISLANDS

STATUS: UK Dependent Territory
AREA: 3,755 sq km (1,450 sq miles)
POPULATION: no permanent population

SPAIN

STATUS: Kingdom
AREA: 504,880 sq km (194,885 sq miles)
POPULATION: 39,166,000
ANNUAL NATURAL INCREASE: 0.5%
CAPITAL: Madrid
LANGUAGE: Spanish (Castilian), Catalan,
Basque, Galician
RELIGION: Roman Catholic
CURRENCY: Spanish peseta (ESP)
ORGANIZATIONS: Council of Europe, EEA, EU,
NATO, OECD, UN, WEU

Spain occupies most of the Iberian Peninsula, from the Bay of Biscay and the Pyrenees mountains in the north, to the Strait of Gibraltar in the south. It includes in its territory the Balearic Islands in the Mediterranean Sea, and the Canary Islands in the Atlantic. The mainland of Spain is mostly plateaux, often forested in the north, but becoming more arid and open further south. Climate is affected regionally by latitude and proximity to the Atlantic Ocean and Mediterranean Sea. Although the climate and terrain are not always favourable, agriculture is important to the Spanish economy. Wheat and other cereals such as maize, barley and rice are cultivated while grapes, citrus fruits and olives are important cash crops. Textile manufacturing in the northeast and steel, chemicals, consumer goods and vehicle manufacturing in the towns and cities have proved a magnet for great numbers of the rural population. The main minerals found are coal, iron ore, uranium and zinc. Tourism is of vital importance to the economy.

SRI LANKA

STATUS: Republic
AREA: 65,610 sq km (25,325 sq miles)
POPULATION: 17,405,000
ANNUAL NATURAL INCREASE: 1.5%
CAPITAL: Colombo
LANGUAGE: Sinhala, Tamil, English
RELIGION: 70% Buddhist, 15% Hindu, Roman
Catholic and Muslim minorities
CURRENCY: Sri Lanka rupee (LKR)
ORGANIZATIONS: Col. Plan, Comm., UN

The island of Sri Lanka is situated only 19 km (12 miles) from mainland India. The climate is tropical along the coastal plain and temperate in the central highlands. Annual rainfall averages only 1,000 mm (39 inches) in the north and east while the south and west receive over 2,000 mm (79 inches). The traditional economy of Sri Lanka is based on agriculture in which rubber, coffee, coconuts and particularly tea are dominant. The nation is also self-sufficient in rice. In recent years, however, manufacturing, especially of clothing and textiles, has become the main export earner. Gemstones and tourism are also important, but the tourist industry has suffered because of the activities of Tamil separatists.

SUDAN

STATUS: Republic
AREA: 2,505,815 sq km (967,245 sq miles)
POPULATION: 24,941,000
ANNUAL NATURAL INCREASE: 3.0%
CAPITAL: Khartoum
LANGUAGE: Arabic, tribal languages
RELIGION: 60% Sunni Muslim,
animist and Christian
CURRENCY: Sudanese pound (SDP)
ORGANIZATIONS: Arab League, OAU, UN

Sudan, in the upper Nile basin, is Africa's largest country. The land is mostly flat and infertile with a hot, arid climate. The White and Blue Niles are invaluable, serving not only to irrigate cultivated land but also as a potential source of hydro-electric power. Subsistence farming accounts for 80 per cent of Sudan's total production. Major exports include cotton, groundnuts, sugar cane and sesame seed. The principal activity is nomadic herding with over 40 million cattle and sheep and 14 million goats. However, economic activity has been damaged by the effects of drought and civil war.

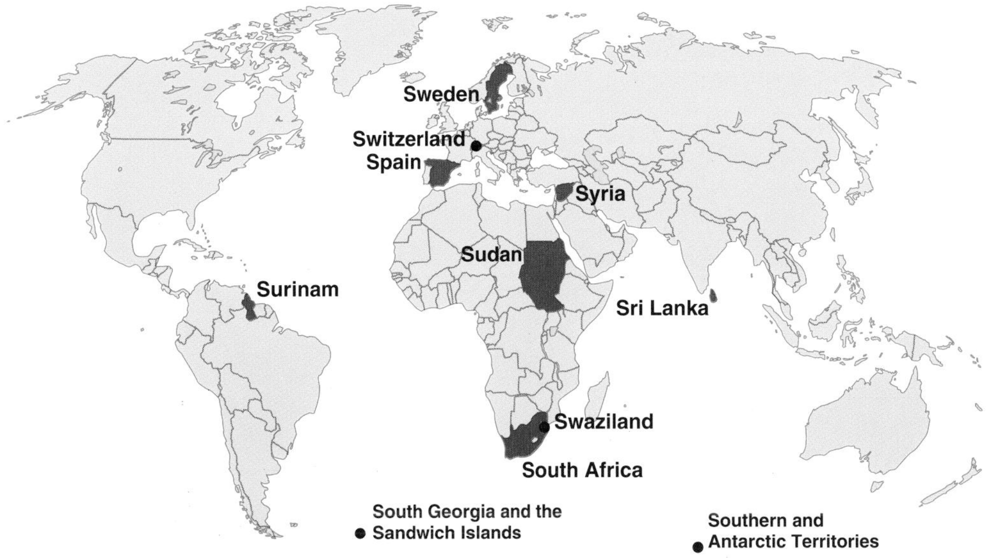

SURINAM

STATUS: Republic
AREA: 163,820 sq km (63,235 sq miles)
POPULATION: 438,000
ANNUAL NATURAL INCREASE: 2.5%
CAPITAL: Paramaribo
LANGUAGE: Dutch, English, Spanish, Surinamese (Sranang Tongo), Hindi
RELIGION: 45% Christian, 28% Hindu, 20% Muslim
CURRENCY: Surinam guilder (SRG)
ORGANIZATIONS: OAS, UN

Independent from the Dutch since 1976, Surinam is a small state lying on the northeast coast in the tropics of South America. Physically, there are three main regions: a low-lying, marshy coastal strip; undulating savannah; densely forested highlands. Rice growing takes up 75 per cent of all cultivated land; sugar and pineapples are also grown, while cattle rearing for both meat and dairy products has been introduced. Bauxite accounts for 90 per cent of Surinam's foreign earnings. Timber resources offer great potential but as yet are largely untapped.

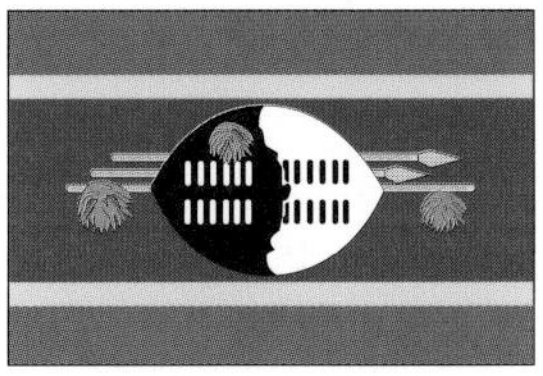

SWAZILAND

STATUS: Kingdom
AREA: 17,365 sq km (6,705 sq miles)
POPULATION: 823,000
ANNUAL NATURAL INCREASE: 3.4%
CAPITAL: Mbabane
LANGUAGE: English, Siswati
RELIGION: 60% Christian, 40% traditional beliefs
CURRENCY: lilangeni (SZL), South African rand (ZAR)
ORGANIZATIONS: Comm., OAU, UN

Landlocked Swaziland in southern Africa, is a sub-tropical, savannah country. It is divided into four main regions: the High, Middle and Low Velds and the Lebombo Mountains. Rainfall is abundant, promoting good pastureland for the many cattle and sheep. Major exports include sugar, meat, citrus fruits, textiles, wood products and asbestos.

SWEDEN

STATUS: Kingdom
AREA: 449,790 sq km (173,620 sq miles)
POPULATION: 8,721,000
ANNUAL NATURAL INCREASE: 0.2%
CAPITAL: Stockholm
LANGUAGE: Swedish, Finnish, Lappish
RELIGION: 95% Evangelical Lutheran
CURRENCY: Swedish krona (SED)
ORGANIZATIONS: Council of Europe, EEA, EFTA, OECD, UN

Glacial debris, glacier-eroded valleys and thick glacial clay are all dominant features of Sweden. Physically, Sweden comprises four main regions: Norrland, the northern forested mountains; the Lake District of the centre south; the southern uplands of Jönköping; the extremely fertile Scania plain of the far south. Summers are short and hot with long, cold winters. Temperatures vary with latitude; in the south from -3–18°C (27–64°F) and in the north from -14–14°C (7–57°F). Annual rainfall varies between 2,000 mm (79 inches) in the southwest, to 500 mm (20 inches) in the east. Over half the land area is forested resulting in a thriving timber industry, but manufacturing industry, particularly cars and trucks, metal products and machine tools, is well established. Mineral resources are also rich and plentiful – iron ore production alone exceeds 17 million tons a year. There are also deposits of copper, lead and zinc.

SWITZERLAND

STATUS: Federation
AREA: 41,285 sq km (15,935 sq miles)
POPULATION: 6,908,000
ANNUAL NATURAL INCREASE: 0.3%
CAPITAL: Bern (Berne)
LANGUAGE: German, French, Italian, Romansch
RELIGION: 48% Roman Catholic, 44% Protestant, Jewish minority
CURRENCY: Swiss franc (CHF)
ORGANIZATIONS: Council of Europe, EFTA, OECD

Switzerland is a landlocked, mountainous country of great scenic beauty, situated in western Europe. The Alps traverse the southern half of the country, in which are to be found some of Europe's highest peaks. In the north the Jura mountains form a natural border with France. Winters are cold with heavy snowfall in the highest regions. Summers are mild with an average July temperature of 18–19°C (64–66°F). Most rain falls in the summer months. Agriculture is based mainly on dairy farming. Major crops include hay, wheat, barley and potatoes. Industry plays a major role in Switzerland's economy, centred on metal engineering, watchmaking, food processing, textiles and chemicals. The high standard of living enjoyed by the Swiss owes much to the tourist industry. The financial services sector, especially banking, is also of great importance. Switzerland's history of neutrality has made it an attractive location for the headquarters of several international organizations.

SYRIA

STATUS: Republic
AREA: 185,680 sq km (71,675 sq miles)
POPULATION: 13,400,000
ANNUAL NATURAL INCREASE: 3.6%
CAPITAL: Damascus, (Dimashq, Esh Sham)
LANGUAGE: Arabic
RELIGION: 65% Sunni Muslim, Shi'a Muslim and Christian minorities
CURRENCY: Syrian pound (SYP)
ORGANIZATIONS: Arab League, UN

Syria is situated in the heart of the Middle East. Its most fertile areas lie along the coastal strip on the Mediterranean Sea which supports the bulk of its population, and in the depressions and plateaux of the northeast which are cut through by the rivers Orontes and Euphrates. In the south the Anti-Lebanon mountains (Jebel esh Sharqi) is bordered to the east by the Syrian desert. While the coast has a Mediterranean climate with dry hot summers and mild winters, the interior becomes increasingly hot and arid – average summer temperatures in the desert reach 43°C (109°F). Rainfall varies between 220–400 mm (9–16 inches). Cotton is Syria's main export crop, and wheat and barley are also grown. Cattle, sheep and goats are the main livestock. Although traditionally an agriculturally-based economy, the country is rapidly becoming industrialized as oil, natural gas, salt, gypsum and phosphate are being exploited.

TAHITI

STATUS: Main Island of French Polynesia
AREA: 1,042 sq km (402 sq miles)
POPULATION: 199,031

TAIWAN

STATUS: Island 'Republic of China'
AREA: 35,990 sq km
(13,890 sq miles)
POPULATION: 20,600,000
ANNUAL NATURAL INCREASE: 1.5%
CAPITAL: Taipei (T'ai-pei)
LANGUAGE: Mandarin Chinese, Taiwanese
RELIGION: Buddhist majority, Muslim,
Daoist and Christian minorities
CURRENCY: New Taiwan dollar (TWD), yuan (CNY)
ORGANIZATIONS: none listed

Taiwan is separated from mainland China by the Taiwan Strait (the former Formosa Channel) in which lie the Pescadores. Two-thirds of Taiwan is mountainous, the highest point is 3,950 m (12,959 feet). The flat to rolling coastal plain in the western part of the island accommodates the bulk of the population and the national commerce, industry and agriculture. The climate is tropical marine, with persistent cloudy conditions. The monsoon rains fall in June to August, with an annual average of 2,600 mm (102 inches). Main crops are rice, tea, fruit, sugar cane and sweet potatoes. Industry has been founded on textiles but in recent years electronic products have gained in importance. The Taiwanese economy is inevitably influenced by its large neighbour and is likely to benefit from improving Chinese performance.

TAJIKISTAN

STATUS: Republic
AREA: 143,100 sq km (55,235 sq miles)
POPULATION: 5,465,000
ANNUAL NATURAL INCREASE: 3.0%
CAPITAL: Dushanbe
LANGUAGE: Tajik, Uzbek, Russian
RELIGION: Sunni Muslim
CURRENCY: Russian rouble
ORGANIZATIONS: CIS, UN

Situated in the mountainous heart of Asia, more than half the territory of Tajikistan lies above 3,000 m (10,000 feet). The major settlement areas lie within the Fergana valley in the west. The climate varies from continental to subtropical according to elevation and shelter. Extensive irrigation, without which agriculture would be severely limited, has made it possible for cotton growing to develop into the leading branch of agriculture, and on that basis textiles have become the largest industry in the country. Tajikistan is rich in mineral and fuel deposits, the exploitation of which became a feature of economic development during the Soviet era. Preceding full independence in 1991 there was an upsurge of sometimes violent Tajik nationalism as a result of which many Russians and Uzbeks have left the country.

TANZANIA

STATUS: Republic
AREA: 939,760 sq km (362,750 sq miles)
POPULATION: 27,829,000
ANNUAL NATURAL INCREASE: 3.5%
CAPITAL: Dodoma
LANGUAGE: Swahili, English
RELIGION: 40% Christian, 35% Muslim
CURRENCY: Tanzanian shilling
ORGANIZATIONS: Comm., OAU, UN

Much of this east African country consists of high interior plateaux covered by scrub and grassland, bordered to the north by the volcanic Kilimanjaro region and Lake Victoria, to the west by Lake Tanganyika, by highlands to the south and by the Indian Ocean in the east. Despite its proximity to the equator, the altitude of much of Tanzania means that temperatures are reduced, and only on the narrow coastal plain is the climate truly tropical. Average temperatures vary between 19–28°C (67–82°F), and annual rainfall is around 570–1,060 mm (23–43 inches). The economy is heavily based on agriculture and subsistence farming is the main way of life for most of the population, although coffee, cotton, sisal, cashew nuts and tea are exported. Industry is limited, but gradually growing in importance, and involves textiles, food processing and tobacco. Tourism could be a future growth area.

THAILAND

STATUS: Kingdom
AREA: 514,000 sq km (198,405 sq miles)
POPULATION: 57,800,000
ANNUAL NATURAL INCREASE: 1.9%
CAPITAL: Bangkok (Krung Thep)
LANGUAGE: Thai
RELIGION: Buddhist, 4% Muslim
CURRENCY: baht (THB)
ORGANIZATIONS: ASEAN, Col. Plan, UN

Thailand is a land of flat undulating plains and mountains, consisting of the plains of the Chao Phraya and Mae Nam Mun river systems, fringed by mountains, a plateau in the northeast drained by the tributaries of the Mekong river, and the northern half of the Malay peninsula. From May to October, monsoon rains are heavy with an annual average rainfall of 1,500 mm (59 inches). The climate is tropical with temperatures reaching 36°C (97°F) and much of the country is forested. The central plain is well-served with irrigation canals which supply the paddy fields for rice cultivation; Thailand is the world's leading exporter of this crop. Maize, cassava, sugar and rubber also contribute to the economy. Tin production has declined in importance in recent years and has, in part, been replaced by a small scale petro-chemical industry. Other industries of importance include textiles and clothing. Tourism, which grew at a record rate during the 1980s, has since levelled out after the military coup of 1991.

TOGO

STATUS: Kingdom
AREA: 699 sq km (270 sq miles)
POPULATION: 130,000
ANNUAL NATURAL INCREASE: 3.5%
CAPITAL: Lomé
LANGUAGE: French, Kabre, Ewe
RELIGION: Christian
CURRENCY: pa'anga (TOP)
ORGANIZATIONS: Comm.

Togo, formerly a German protectorate and French colony, is situated between Ghana and Benin in west Africa. A long narrow country, it has only 65 km (40 miles) of coast. The interior consists of mountains and high infertile tableland. The climate is tropical with an average temperature of 27°C (81°F). Most of Togo's farmers grow maize, cassava, yams, groundnuts and plantains, and the country is virtually self-sufficient in food stuffs. Phosphates account for half of export revenue. Cotton, cocoa and coffee are also exported.

TOKELAU ISLANDS

STATUS: Overseas Territory of New Zealand
AREA: 10 sq km (4 sq miles)
POPULATION: 1,577
CAPITAL: none, each island has its own
administration centre

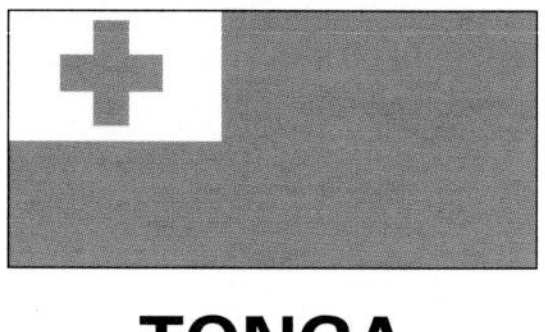

TONGA

STATUS: Kingdom
AREA: 699 sq km (270 sq miles)
POPULATION: 103,000
ANNUAL NATURAL INCREASE: 0.4%
CAPITAL: Nuku'alofa
LANGUAGE: Tongan, English
RELIGION: Christian
CURRENCY: pa'anga (TOP)
ORGANIZATIONS: Comm.

Tonga consists of an archipelago of 169 islands in the Pacific 180 km (112 miles) north of New Zealand. There are seven groups of islands, but the most important are Tongatapu, Ha'apai and Vava'u. All the islands are covered with dense tropical vegetation, and temperatures range from 11–29°C (52–84°F). Main exports are coconut products and bananas.

TRINIDAD & TOBAGO

STATUS: Republic
AREA: 5,130 sq km (1,980 sq miles)
POPULATION: 1,265,000
ANNUAL NATURAL INCREASE: 1.7%
CAPITAL: Port of Spain
LANGUAGE: English, Hindi, French, Spanish
RELIGION: 60% Christian, 25% Hindu, 6% Muslim
CURRENCY: Trinidad and Tobago dollar (TTD)
ORGANIZATIONS: Caricom, Comm., OAS, UN

Trinidad and Tobago, the southernmost Caribbean islands of the Lesser Antilles lie only 11 and 30 km (7 and 19 miles) respectively from the Venezuelan coast. Both islands are mountainous, the Northern Range of Trinidad reaching 940 m (3,084 feet) with its highest parts retaining tropical forest cover. The country has a humid, tropical climate with temperatures averaging 25°C (76°F) per annum. Rain falls mostly between June and December and varies between 1,300–3,000 mm (51–118 inches) annually. Sugar was once the mainstay of the economy but oil is now the leading source of revenue accounting for over 70 per cent of export revenue. There is also a petro-chemical industry based on significant gas reserves.

TRISTAN DA CUNHA

STATUS: Dependency of St Helena
AREA: 98 sq km (38 sq miles)
POPULATION: 295

TUNISIA

STATUS: Republic
AREA: 164,150 sq km (63,360 sq miles)
POPULATION: 8,401,000
ANNUAL NATURAL INCREASE: 2.0%
CAPITAL: Tunis
LANGUAGE: Arabic, French
RELIGION: Muslim
CURRENCY: Tunisian dinar (TND)
ORGANIZATIONS: Arab League, OAU, UN

Tunisia, on the southern shores of the Mediterranean is largely an arid, desert country of northern Africa. The eastern limits of the Atlas mountain range extend into northern parts of the country, which are separated from the Sahara desert to the south by a lowland belt of salt pans, called the Chott El Jerid. Average annual temperatures are in the range 10–27°C (50–81°F) and rainfall averages 380–500 mm (15–20 inches) in the north, but drops to virtually nothing in the south. The majority of the population live along the northeast coast. Wheat, barley, olives and citrus fruit are the main crops and oil, natural gas and sugar refining are the main industries. The tourist industry is expanding and is becoming increasingly important to the economy.

TURKEY

STATUS: Republic
AREA: 779,450 sq km (300,870 sq miles)
POPULATION: 59,869,000
ANNUAL NATURAL INCREASE: 2.2%
CAPITAL: Ankara
LANGUAGE: Turkish, Kurdish
RELIGION: 98% Sunni Muslim, Christian minority
CURRENCY: Turkish lira (TRL)
ORGANIZATIONS: Council of Europe, NATO, OECD, UN

Turkey has always occupied a strategically important position linking Europe and Asia. It is a rugged, mountainous country particularly in the east. The central Anatolian plateau is bordered in the north by the Pontine mountains (Anadolu Dağlari) and in the south by the Taurus mountains (Toros Dağlari) which converge in the east, crowned by Mt Ararat (Büyük Ağri). Thrace, in European Turkey is flatter with rolling hills. Coastal regions exhibit Mediterranean conditions with short mild winters with some rainfall and long hot, dry summers. The interior is relatively arid with average rainfall in some places less than 250 mm (10 inches). The main crops are wheat and barley, but tobacco, olives, sugar beet, tea and fruit are also grown, and sheep, goats and cattle are raised. Turkey is becoming increasingly industrialized; textiles account for a third of exports and the car industry is developing. The nation now leads the Middle East in the production of iron, steel, chrome, coal and lignite. Tourism is a rapidly growing industry.

TURKMENISTAN

STATUS: Republic
AREA: 488,100 sq km (188,405 sq miles)
POPULATION: 3,714,000
ANNUAL NATURAL INCREASE: 2.5%
CAPITAL: Ashkhabad
LANGUAGE: Turkmen, Russian, Uzbek
RELIGION: Muslim
CURRENCY: manat
ORGANIZATIONS: CIS, UN

Situated in the far south of the former Soviet Union, Turkmenistan is a desert land except for the lowlands in the west along the Caspian shore, the mountains along its southern borders and the valley of Amudar'ya river in the north. The continental climate is responsible for great fluctuations in temperature, both during the day and throughout the year. Traditionally nomads, the Turkmen tribes under the Soviet regime, turned from pastoral farming to cotton-growing, made possible by extensive irrigation. Turkmenistan enjoys substantial natural resources, principally oil and gas but also potassium, sulphur and salt.

TURKS & CAICOS ISLANDS

STATUS: UK Dependent Territory
AREA: 430 sq km (166 sq miles)
POPULATION: 11,696
CAPITAL: Cockburn Town

TUVALU

STATUS: Special membership of the Commonwealth
AREA: 24.6 sq km (9.5 sq miles)
POPULATION: 10,090
ANNUAL NATURAL INCREASE: 1.5%
CAPITAL: Funafuti
LANGUAGE: Tuvaluan, English
RELIGION: 98% Protestant
CURRENCY: Australian dollar (AUD), Tuvaluan coinage
ORGANIZATIONS: Comm., (special member)

Tuvalu consists of nine dispersed coral atolls, north of Fiji, in the Pacific Ocean. The climate is tropical; hot, with heavy annual rainfall exceeding 3,000 mm (118 inches). Fish is the staple food but coconuts and bread-fruit are cultivated. The sale of postage stamps abroad is, however, the largest source of revenue.

UGANDA

STATUS: Republic
AREA: 236,580 sq km
(91,320 sq miles)
POPULATION: 18,674,000
ANNUAL NATURAL INCREASE: 3.1%
CAPITAL: Kampala
LANGUAGE: English, tribal languages
RELIGION: 62% Christian, 6% Muslim
CURRENCY: Uganda shilling (UGS)
ORGANIZATIONS: Comm., OAU, UN

Uganda is bordered in the west by the great Rift Valley and the Ruwenzori mountain range which reaches 5,220 m (16,765 feet). In the east it is bordered by Kenya and Lake Victoria, from which the Nile flows northwards. Most of the country is high plateau with savannah vegetation although the lands around Lake Victoria have been cleared for cultivation and have become the most populated and developed areas. The climate is warm (21–24°C or 70–75°F), and rainfall ranges from 750–1,500 mm (30–59 inches) per annum. The Ugandan economy is firmly based on agriculture with a heavy dependence on coffee, the dominant export crop, and cotton. Fishing, from the waters of Lake Victoria is also important for local consumption.

UKRAINE

STATUS: Republic
AREA: 603,700 sq km (233,030 sq miles)
POPULATION: 52,194,000
ANNUAL NATURAL INCREASE: 0.3%
CAPITAL: Kiev (Kiyev)
LANGUAGE: Ukrainian, Russian
RELIGION: Russian Orthodox,
Roman Catholic (Uniate)
CURRENCY: karbovanets (coupon)
ORGANIZATIONS: CIS, UN

Ukraine consists mainly of level plains and mountainous border areas. The landscape is, however, diverse, with marshes, forests, wooded and treeless steppe. Deposits of 'black earth', among the most fertile soils, cover about 65 per cent of Ukraine. Grain, potatoes, vegetables and fruits, industrial crops (notably sugar beets and sunflower seeds) and fodder crops are grown. Food processing is important to the economy, and southern regions are renowned for wines. Ukraine is rich in mineral resources, such as iron ore, coal and lignite, and has large reserves of petroleum and gas. Extensive mining, metal production, machine-building, engineering and chemicals dominate Ukrainian industry, most of it located in the Donetsk basin and the Dneiper lowland. These two regions account for four-fifths of the urban population. Despite its natural wealth and industrial development, Ukraine has failed to respond to the economic needs of its independent status and has experienced sharp declines in agricultural and industrial output.

UNITED ARAB EMIRATES (UAE)

STATUS: Federation of seven Emirates
AREA: 75,150 sq km (29,010 sq miles)
POPULATION: 2,083,000
ANNUAL NATURAL INCREASE: 3.1%
CAPITAL: Abu Dhabi (Abū Ẓabī)
LANGUAGE: Arabic, English
RELIGION: Sunni Muslim
CURRENCY: UAE dirham (AED)
ORGANIZATIONS: Arab League, OPEC, UN

The United Arab Emirates (UAE), comprising seven separate emirates, are stretched along the southeastern coast of the Gulf. It is a country covered mostly by flat deserts with the highest land in the Hajar mountains of the Musandam Peninsula. Summer temperatures reach 40°C (104°F); meagre rains of 130 mm (5 inches) fall mainly in the winter. Only the desert oases are fertile, producing fruit and vegetables. The economic wealth of the UAE is founded on its huge reserves of hydrocarbons, mainly within the largest Emirate, Abu Dhabi, with smaller supplies in three others – Dubai, Sharjah and Ras al Khaimah. Natural gas and oil are the major exports for which Japan and the Far East are the major markets. Revenue gained from these has allowed the economy to grow rapidly, with there being huge investment in the service industries. It has a population that is overwhelmingly made up of foreign immigrants.

ABU DHABI

STATUS: Emirate
AREA: 64,750 sq km (24,995 sq miles)
POPULATION: 670,175

AJMAN

STATUS: Emirate
AREA: 260 sq km (100 sq miles)
POPULATION: 64,318

DUBAI

STATUS: Emirate
AREA: 3,900 sq km (1,505 sq miles)
POPULATION: 419,104

FUJAIRAH

STATUS: Emirate
AREA: 1,170 sq km (452 sq miles)
POPULATION: 54,425

RAS AL KHAIMAH

STATUS: Emirate
AREA: 1,690 sq km (625 sq miles)
POPULATION: 116,470

SHARJAH

STATUS: Emirate
AREA: 2,600 sq km (1,005 sq miles)
POPULATION: 268,722

UMM AL QAIWAIN

STATUS: Emirate
AREA: 780 sq km (300 sq miles)
POPULATION: 29,229

UNITED KINGDOM OF GREAT BRITAIN & NORTHERN IRELAND (UK)

STATUS: Kingdom
AREA: 244,755 sq km
(94,475 sq miles)
POPULATION: 57,998,400
ANNUAL NATURAL INCREASE: 0.3%
CAPITAL: London
LANGUAGE: English, Welsh, Gaelic
RELIGION: Protestant majority, Roman Catholic,
Jewish, Muslim, Hindu minorities
CURRENCY: pound sterling (GBP)
ORGANIZATIONS: Col. Plan, Comm.,
Council of Europe, EEA, EU, G7, NATO,
OECD, UN, WEU

The United Kingdom, part of the British Isles, is situated off the northwest European coast, separated from France by the English Channel. It includes the countries of England and Scotland, the principality of Wales, and the region of Northern Ireland in the north of the island of Ireland.

In broad terms Britain can be divided into the upland regions of Wales, Northern England and Scotland, characterized by ancient dissected and glaciated mountain regions, and the lowland areas of southern and eastern England where low ranges of chalk, limestone and sandstone hills are interspersed with wide clay vales. The highest point in the United Kingdom is Ben Nevis in the Grampians of Scotland at 1,344 m (4,409 feet).

The climate of the British Isles is mild, wet and variable. Summer temperatures average 13–17°C (55–63°F) and winter temperatures 5–7°C (41–45°F). Annual rainfall varies between 640–5,000 mm (26–200 inches) with the highest rainfall in the Lake District and the lowest in East Anglia.

Although only a tiny percentage of the nation's workforce is employed in agriculture, farm produce is important to both home and export markets. Seventy-six per cent of the total UK land area is farmland. The main cereal crops are wheat, barley and oats. Potatoes, sugar beet and green vegetable crops are widespread.

About 20 per cent of the land is permanent pasture for raising dairy and beef stock and 28 per cent, mainly hill and mountain areas, is used for rough grazing of sheep. The best fruit-growing areas are the southeast, especially Kent, East Anglia and the central Vale of Evesham. Fishing supplies two-thirds of the nation's requirements but overfishing and encroachment into territorial waters by other countries have created problems.

The major mineral resources of the UK are coal, oil and natural gas. Over two-thirds of deep-mined coal came from the Yorkshire and East Midlands fields and substantial reserves remain. However, the coal industry, which had already been in slow decline for some 30 years, collapsed rapidly in 1993–4 when many of the remaining pits were closed. The number of employees fell from 208,000 in 1983 to 18,000 in early 1994 and by mid-1994 only 16 deep coal mines remained in operation, compared with 50 pits two years earlier.

Before the 1970s Britain relied on imports from the Middle East for its oil supplies, but in 1975 supplies of oil and gas from the vast North Sea oil fields began to provide both self-sufficiency and enough to export. Some of the older fields are now nearly worked out and operating costs for these are rising. The major Scott Field came on-stream in 1993 and in 1994 approval was granted for the development of the Fife and Birch oil fields and the Armada gas fields.

Wind farms as a source of energy, often the subject of controversy with environmentalists, contribute less than 1 per cent of Britain's electricity.

Although the UK is an industrialized nation, the traditional mainstays of heavy industry such as coal, iron and steel and shipbuilding no longer figure prominently in the economy. Concurrent with the decline of heavy industry, there has been a substantial growth of light industries. High technology and electronic products predominate, as well as pharmaceuticals, motor parts and food processing. Tourism is an essential part of the economy, especially in London, and in five years up to 1993 the number of visitors to the UK rose by 22 per cent. Financial services is another expanding sector, the 'City' of London having the greatest concentration of banks in the world.

The UK is a trading nation. The balance of trade has changed during the last 30 years because of increasingly closer economic ties with Europe and the move towards a Single European Market. Consequently, trading with Commonwealth nations, particularly Australia, has assumed lower priority. In terms of value, the most important exports from the UK are machinery, chemicals and transport equipment, followed by food, beverages and tobacco, petroleum products, iron and steel.

The transport network in the UK is highly developed. Out of 362,357 km (225,164 miles) of public roads, 9 per cent are motorways and 13 per cent are other major roads. The railway network covers over 16,730 km (10,395 miles) and carries over 150 million tonnes of freight annually. The opening of the Channel Tunnel in 1994 has connected the motorway and rail networks of Britain with those of northern France and southern Belgium. The inland waterway system totals only 563 navigable kilometres (350 miles) but has potential to carry more than its present 4 million tonnes of goods annually.

ENGLAND

STATUS: Constituent Country
AREA: 130,360 sq km (50,320 sq miles)
POPULATION: 48,208,100
CAPITAL: London

NORTHERN IRELAND

STATUS: Constituent Region
AREA: 14,150 sq km (5,460 sq miles)
POPULATION: 1,573,282
CAPITAL: Belfast

SCOTLAND

STATUS: Constituent Country
AREA: 78,750 sq km (30,400 sq miles)
POPULATION: 4,998,567
CAPITAL: Edinburgh

WALES

STATUS: Principality
AREA: 20,760 sq km (8,015 sq miles)
POPULATION: 2,891,500
CAPITAL: Cardiff

UNITED STATES OF AMERICA (USA)

STATUS: Federal Republic
AREA: 9,363,130 sq km (3,614,170 sq miles)
POPULATION: 255,020,000
ANNUAL NATURAL INCREASE: 0.9%
CAPITAL: Washington D.C.
LANGUAGE: English, Spanish
RELIGION: Christian majority, Jewish minority
CURRENCY: US dollar (USD)
ORGANIZATIONS: ANZUS, Col. Plan, G7, NAFTA, NATO, OAS, OECD, UN

The United States of America is the world's fourth largest country after Canada, China and Russia with the world's fourth largest population. The 19th and 20th centuries have brought 42 million immigrants to its shores, and the population of the USA now has the highest living standard of any country in the world. The large land area covers a huge spectrum of different landscapes, environments and climates. The eastern coast of New England, where the European settlers first landed, is rocky, mountainous and richly wooded. South of New England is the Atlantic coastal plain, rising to the west towards the Appalachian mountain system. Beyond the Appalachians lie the central lowlands, a large undulating plain cut through by the Mississippi and Ohio rivers. Further west lie the Great Plains crossed by the Missouri, Red and Arkansas rivers and rising gently towards the mighty Rocky Mountains, a spine of mountains running south from Alaska. Beyond these lie the Great Valley of California, the coastal ranges and the Pacific coast.

Climatic variety within the United States is enormous, ranging from the Arctic conditions of Alaska to the desert of the southwest – winter temperatures in Alaska plummet to -28°C (-19°F); in Florida they maintain a steady 19°C (66°F). The centre of the continent is dry, but both the northwest Pacific and the New England Atlantic coast are humid with heavy rainfall. Many areas of the USA fall prey to exceptional, often disastrous, weather conditions: the northeastern seaboard is susceptible to heavy blizzards, the southern lowlands are vulnerable to spring thaw flooding and the Mississippi valley is prone to tornadoes.

The natural vegetation of the USA reflects its climatic diversity. The northwest coast is rich in coniferous forest, while the Appalachian mountain region is well endowed with hardwoods. In the arid southwest, vegetation is limited to desert scrub whereas the Gulf and South Atlantic coast are fringed with swampy wetlands. The central lowlands are endowed with rich black-earth soils (the agricultural heartland), gradually supplanted, towards the Rockies, by tall-grass prairie. The northeastern states of Illinois, Iowa, Indiana and Nebraska form the 'corn belt', which produces 45 per cent of the world's corn. Further west wheat supplements corn as the main crop. The northeastern states are predominantly dairy country, and the south is famous for cotton and tobacco. Rice is grown in Texas, California and Louisiana, and fruit and vegetables in Florida.

The USA consumes 25 per cent of all the world's energy resources but is well endowed with energy reserves. There are substantial coal resources, particularly in the Appalachians. The great rivers have been harnessed extensively for hydro-electric power. Oil and natural gas fields are found in Texas, Alaska, Louisiana and California and new deep-sea exploratory drilling is underway in the Gulf of Mexico. Oil production, however, has declined steadily since 1983.

The industrial base is diverse, the main industries being steel, motor vehicles, aerospace, chemicals, computers, electronics, telecommunications and consumer goods. The service industries (encompassing tourism and finance) are by far the biggest source of employment in the United States.

ALABAMA

STATUS: State
AREA: 131,485 sq km (50,755 sq miles)
POPULATION: 4,136,000
CAPITAL: Montgomery

ALASKA

STATUS: State
AREA: 1,478,450 sq km (570,680 sq miles)
POPULATION: 587,000
CAPITAL: Juneau

ARIZONA

STATUS: State
AREA: 293,985 sq km (113,480 sq miles)
POPULATION: 3,832,000
CAPITAL: Phoenix

ARKANSAS
STATUS: State
AREA: 134,880 sq km (52,065 sq miles)
POPULATION: 2,399,000
CAPITAL: Little Rock

CALIFORNIA
STATUS: State
AREA: 404,815 sq km (156,260 sq miles)
POPULATION: 30,867,000
CAPITAL: Sacramento

COLORADO
STATUS: State
AREA: 268,310 sq km (103,570 sq miles)
POPULATION: 3,470,000
CAPITAL: Denver

CONNECTICUT
STATUS: State
AREA: 12,620 sq km (4,870 sq miles)
POPULATION: 3,281,000
CAPITAL: Hartford

DELAWARE
STATUS: State
AREA: 5,005 sq km (1,930 sq miles)
POPULATION: 689,000
CAPITAL: Dover

DISTRICT OF COLUMBIA
STATUS: Federal District
AREA: 163 sq km (63 sq miles)
POPULATION: 589,000
CAPITAL: Washington D.C.

FLORIDA
STATUS: State
AREA: 140,255 sq km (54,1405 sq miles)
POPULATION: 13,488,000
CAPITAL: Tallahassee

GEORGIA
STATUS: State
AREA: 150,365 sq km (58,040 sq miles)
POPULATION: 6,751,000
CAPITAL: Atlanta

HAWAII
STATUS: State
AREA: 16,640 sq km (6,425 sq miles)
POPULATION: 1,160,000
CAPITAL: Honolulu

IDAHO
STATUS: State
AREA: 213,445 sq km (82,390 sq miles)
POPULATION: 1,067,000
CAPITAL: Boise

ILLINOIS
STATUS: State
AREA: 144,120 sq km (55,630 sq miles)
POPULATION: 11,631,000
CAPITAL: Springfield

INDIANA
STATUS: State
AREA: 93,065 sq km (35,925 sq miles)
POPULATION: 5,662,000
CAPITAL: Indianapolis

IOWA
STATUS: State
AREA: 144,950 sq km (55,950 sq miles)
POPULATION: 2,812,000
CAPITAL: Des Moines

KANSAS
STATUS: State
AREA: 211,805 sq km (81,755 sq miles)
POPULATION: 2,523,000
CAPITAL: Topeka

KENTUCKY
STATUS: State
AREA: 102,740 sq km (39,660 sq miles)
POPULATION: 3,755,000
CAPITAL: Frankfort

LOUISIANA
STATUS: State
AREA: 115,310 sq km (44,510 sq miles)
POPULATION: 4,287,000
CAPITAL: Baton Rouge

MAINE
STATUS: State
AREA: 80,275 sq km (30,985 sq miles)
POPULATION: 1,235,000
CAPITAL: Augusta

MARYLAND
STATUS: State
AREA: 25,480 sq km (9,835 sq miles)
POPULATION: 4,908,000
CAPITAL: Annapolis

MASSACHUSETTS
STATUS: State
AREA: 20,265 sq km (7,820 sq miles)
POPULATION: 5,998,000
CAPITAL: Boston

MICHIGAN
STATUS: State
AREA: 147,510 sq km (56,940 sq miles)
POPULATION: 9,437,000
CAPITAL: Lansing

MINNESOTA
STATUS: State
AREA: 206,030 sq km (79,530 sq miles)
POPULATION: 4,480,000
CAPITAL: St Paul

MISSISSIPPI
STATUS: State
AREA: 122,335 sq km (47,220 sq miles)
POPULATION: 2,614,000
CAPITAL: Jackson

MISSOURI
STATUS: State
AREA: 178,565 sq km (68,925 sq miles)
POPULATION: 5,193,000
CAPITAL: Jefferson City

MONTANA
STATUS: State
AREA: 376,555 sq km (145,350 sq miles)
POPULATION: 824,000
CAPITAL: Helena

NEBRASKA
STATUS: State
AREA: 198,505 sq km (76,625 sq miles)
POPULATION: 1,606,000
CAPITAL: Lincoln

NEVADA
STATUS: State
AREA: 284,625 sq km (109,865 sq miles)
POPULATION: 1,327,000
CAPITAL: Carson City

NEW HAMPSHIRE
STATUS: State
AREA: 23,290 sq km (8,990 sq miles)
POPULATION: 1,111,000
CAPITAL: Concord

NEW JERSEY
STATUS: State
AREA: 19,340 sq km (7,465 sq miles)
POPULATION: 7,789,000
CAPITAL: Trenton

NEW MEXICO
STATUS: State
AREA: 314,255 sq km (121,300 sq miles)
POPULATION: 1,581,000
CAPITAL: Sante Fe

NEW YORK
STATUS: State
AREA: 122,705 sq km (47,365 sq miles)
POPULATION: 18,119,000
CAPITAL: Albany

NORTH CAROLINA
STATUS: State
AREA: 126,505 sq km (48,830 sq miles)
POPULATION: 6,843,000
CAPITAL: Raleigh

NORTH DAKOTA
STATUS: State
AREA: 179,485 sq km (69,280 sq miles)
POPULATION: 636,000
CAPITAL: Bismarck

OHIO
STATUS: State
AREA: 106,200 sq km (40,995 sq miles)
POPULATION: 11,016,000
CAPITAL: Columbus

OKLAHOMA
STATUS: State
AREA: 177,815 sq km (68,635 sq miles)
POPULATION: 3,212,00
CAPITAL: Oklahoma City

OREGON
STATUS: State
AREA: 249,115 sq km (96,160 sq miles)
POPULATION: 2,977,000
CAPITAL: Salem

PENNSYLVANIA
STATUS: State
AREA: 116,260 sq km (44,875 sq miles)
POPULATION: 12,009,000
CAPITAL: Harrisburg

RHODE ISLAND
STATUS: State
AREA: 2,730 sq km (1,055 sq miles)
POPULATION: 1,005,000
CAPITAL: Providence

SOUTH CAROLINA
STATUS: State
AREA: 78,225 sq km (30,195 sq miles)
POPULATION: 3,603,000
CAPITAL: Columbia

SOUTH DAKOTA
STATUS: State
AREA: 196,715 sq km (75,930 sq miles)
POPULATION: 711,000
CAPITAL: Pierre

TENNESSEE
STATUS: State
AREA: 106,590 sq km (41,145 sq miles)
POPULATION: 5,024,000
CAPITAL: Nashville

TEXAS
STATUS: State
AREA: 678,620 sq km (261,950 sq miles)
POPULATION: 17,656,000
CAPITAL: Austin

UTAH
STATUS: State
AREA: 212,570 sq km (82,050 sq miles)
POPULATION: 1,813,000
CAPITAL: Salt Lake City

VERMONT
STATUS: State
AREA: 24,015 sq km (9,270 sq miles)
POPULATION: 570,000
CAPITAL: Montpelier

VIRGINIA
STATUS: State
AREA: 102,835 sq km (39,695 sq miles)
POPULATION: 6,377,000
CAPITAL: Richmond

WASHINGTON
STATUS: State
AREA: 172,265 sq km (66,495 sq miles)
POPULATION: 5,136,000
CAPITAL: Olympia

WEST VIRGINIA
STATUS: State
AREA: 62,470 sq km (24,115 sq miles)
POPULATION: 1,812,000
CAPITAL: Charleston

WISCONSIN
STATUS: State
AREA: 140,965 sq km (54,415 sq miles)
POPULATION: 5,007,000
CAPITAL: Madison

WYOMING
STATUS: State
AREA: 251,200 sq km (96,965 sq miles)
POPULATION: 466,000
CAPITAL: Cheyenne

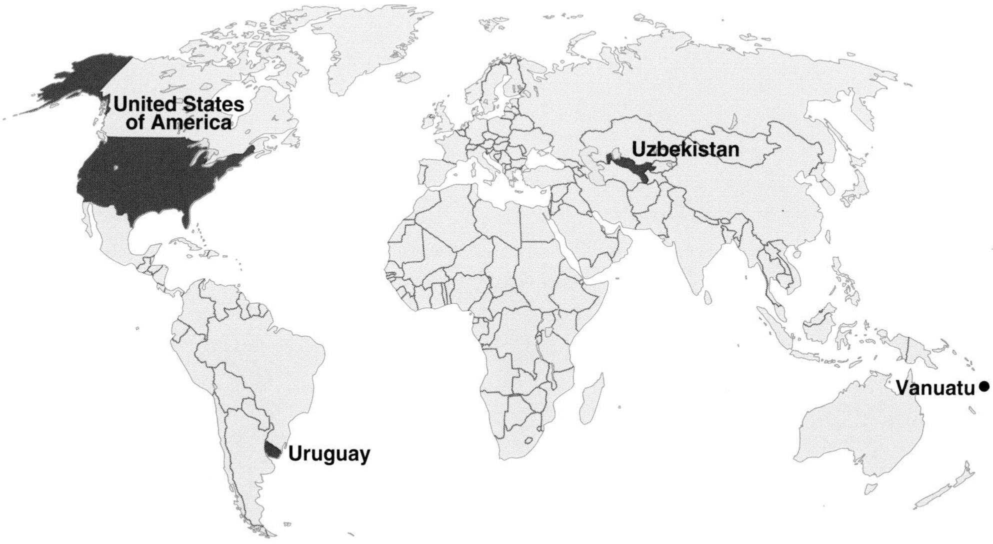

URUGUAY
STATUS: Republic
AREA: 186,925 sq km (72,155 sq miles)
POPULATION: 3,131,000
ANNUAL NATURAL INCREASE: 0.6%
CAPITAL: Montevideo
LANGUAGE: Spanish
RELIGION: Roman Catholic
CURRENCY: Uruguayan peso (UYP)
ORGANIZATIONS: Mercosur, OAS, UN

Uruguay is a small country on the southeast coast of south America. Geographically it consists firstly of a narrow plain, fringed with lagoons and dunes, skirting along the coast and the estuary of the river Plate. Further inland, rolling grassland hills are broken by minor ridges of the Brazilian highlands, which reach heights of no more than 500 m (1,600 feet). The climate is temperate and rainfall is spread evenly throughout the year at about 100 mm (4 inches) per month. Monthly temperatures average in the range of 10–22°C (50–72°F). The land has good agricultural potential, however most is given over to the grazing of sheep and cattle. The economy relies heavily on the production of meat and wool with 87 per cent of the area devoted to farming. Uruguay has no oil or gas reserves, and most of its energy requirements are obtained from hydro-electricity.

UZBEKISTAN
STATUS: Republic
AREA: 447,400 sq km (172,695 sq miles)
POPULATION: 20,708,000
ANNUAL NATURAL INCREASE: 2.4%
CAPITAL: Tashkent
LANGUAGE: Uzbek, Russian, Turkish
RELIGION: Muslim
CURRENCY: som
ORGANIZATIONS: CIS, UN

Established in 1924 as a constituent republic of the Soviet Union, Uzbekistan became an independent state in 1991. The majority of the country consists of flat, sun-baked lowlands with mountains in the south and east. The climate is markedly continental and very dry with an abundance of sunshine and mild, short winters. The southern mountains are of great economic importance, providing ample supplies of water for hydro-electric plants and irrigation schemes. The mountain regions also contain substantial reserves of natural gas, oil, coal, iron and other metals. With its fertile soils (when irrigated) and good pastures, Uzbekistan is well situated for cattle raising and the production of cotton. It is also the largest producer of machines and heavy equipment in central Asia, and has been specializing mainly in machinery for cotton cultivation and harvesting, for irrigation projects, for road-building and textile processing. During the Soviet period the urban employment market became increasingly dominated by Russians and other outsiders. The gradual emergence of better educated and better trained Uzbeks has generated fiercely nationalist sentiments.

VANUATU
STATUS: Republic
AREA: 14,765 sq km (5,700 sq miles)
POPULATION: 154,000
ANNUAL NATURAL INCREASE: 2.4%
CAPITAL: Port-Vila
LANGUAGE: Bislama (national), English, French, Melanesian languages
RELIGION: Christian
CURRENCY: vatu (VUV)
ORGANIZATIONS: Comm., UN

Vanuatu is a chain of some 80 densely forested, mountainous, volcanic islands, situated in the Melanesian south Pacific. Its climate is tropical, with a high rainfall and a continuous threat of cyclones. Copra, cocoa and coffee are grown mainly for export, with fish, pigs and sheep as well as yams, taro, manioc and bananas important only for home consumption. Manganese is the only mineral with deposits of economic value. Tourism is becoming important, particularly with Australian and Japanese visitors.

VATICAN CITY

STATUS: Ecclesiastical State
AREA: 0.44 sq km (0.17 sq miles)
POPULATION: 1,000
LANGUAGE: Italian, Latin
RELIGION: Roman Catholic
CURRENCY: Italian lira (ITL), Papal coinage
ORGANIZATIONS: none

The Vatican City, the headquarters of the Roman Catholic Church, is the world's smallest independent state. It is entirely surrounded by the city of Rome, occupying a hill to the west of the river Tiber. It has been the papal residence since the 5th century and a destination for pilgrims and tourists from all over the world. Most income is derived from voluntary contributions (Peter's Pence), tourism and interest on investments. The only industries are those connected with the Church.

VENEZUELA

STATUS: Republic
AREA: 912,045 sq km (352,050 sq miles)
POPULATION: 20,410,000
ANNUAL NATURAL INCREASE: 2.5%
CAPITAL: Caracas
LANGUAGE: Spanish
RELIGION: Roman Catholic
CURRENCY: bolivar (VEB)
ORGANIZATIONS: OAS, OPEC, UN

Venezuela, one of the richest countries of Latin America, is divided into four topographical regions: the continuation of the Andes in the west; the humid lowlands around Lake Maracaibo in the north; the savannah-covered central plains (Llanos), and the extension of the Guiana Highlands covering almost half the country. The climate varies between tropical in the south to warm temperate along the northern coasts. The majority of the population live along the north coast. Venezuela's economy is built around oil production in the Maracaibo region; over three-quarters of export revenue comes from oil. Bauxite and iron ore are also important. The majority of employment is provided by industrial and manufacturing sectors of the economy.

VIETNAM

STATUS: Republic
AREA: 329,566 sq km (127,246 sq miles)
POPULATION: 69,306,000
ANNUAL NATURAL INCREASE: 2.3%
CAPITAL: Hanoi
LANGUAGE: Vietnamese, French, Chinese
RELIGION: Buddhist
CURRENCY: dong (VND)
ORGANIZATIONS: OIEC, UN

Situated on the eastern coast of the Indo-Chinese peninsula of southeastern Asia, Vietnam is predominantly a rugged, mountainous country. The north-south oriented mountainous spine separates two major river deltas: the Red River (Hong river) in the north and the Mekong in the south. Monsoons bring 1,500 mm (59 inches) of rain every year and temperatures average 15°C (59°F) annually. Rainforest still covers some of the central mountainous areas, but most has been cleared for agriculture and habitation. Rice is grown extensively throughout the north (Vietnam is the world's third largest exporter after the USA and Thailand) along with coffee and rubber in other parts of the country. Vietnam possesses a wide range of minerals including coal, lignite, anthracite, iron ore and tin. Industry is expanding rapidly, but decades of warfare and internal strife have impeded development. The US government has lifted its 20-year-old trade embargo, which will further help strengthen Vietnam's trade position.

VIRGIN ISLANDS (UK)

STATUS: UK Dependent Territory
AREA: 153 sq km (59 sq miles)
POPULATION: 16,749
CAPITAL: Road Town

VIRGIN ISLANDS (USA)

STATUS: External Territory of USA
AREA: 345 sq km (133 sq miles)
POPULATION: 101,809
CAPITAL: Charlotte Amalie

WALLIS & FUTUNA ISLANDS

STATUS: Self-governing Overseas Territory of France
AREA: 274 sq km (106 sq miles)
POPULATION: 14,100
CAPITAL: Mata-Uta

WESTERN SAHARA

STATUS: Territory in dispute, administered by Morocco
AREA: 266,000 sq km (102,675 sq miles)
POPULATION: 250,000
CAPITAL: Laayoune

WESTERN SAMOA

STATUS: Commonwealth State
AREA: 2,840 sq km (1,095 sq miles)
POPULATION: 170,000
ANNUAL NATURAL INCREASE: 0.5%
CAPITAL: Apia
LANGUAGE: English, Samoan
RELIGION: Christian
CURRENCY: tala (dollar) (WST)
ORGANIZATIONS: Comm., UN

Western Samoa constitutes a 160 km (100 mile) chain of nine south Pacific islands. The two largest islands, Savaii and Upolu, are mountainous and volcanic. Annual rainfall averages 2,500 mm (100 inches) per year and temperatures average 26°C (79°F) for most months. Only four of the islands are populated – Savaii, Upolu, Manono and Apolima. Main exports are copra, timber, coffee, cocoa and fruit. Western Samoa has some light industries, such as food processing, textiles and cigarette manufacture and a tourist trade is developing. Remittances from citizens abroad are, however, also very important to the economy.

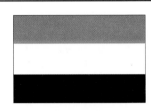

YEMEN

STATUS: Republic
AREA: 527,970 sq km (328,065 sq miles)
POPULATION: 11,092,084
ANNUAL NATURAL INCREASE: 4.4%
CAPITAL: San'a (Şan'ā')
LANGUAGE: Arabic
RELIGION: Sunni and Shi'a Muslim
CURRENCY: Yemeni dinar and rial
ORGANIZATIONS: Arab League, UN

The Yemen Arab Republic and the People's Democratic Republic of Yemen were unified in 1990 to form a single state with its capital at San'a. Situated in the southern part of the Arabian Peninsula the country comprises several contrasting physical landscapes. The north is mainly mountainous and relatively wet with rainfall reaching 890 mm (35 inches) in inland areas which helps to irrigate the cereals, cotton, fruits and vegetables grown on the windward mountain sides and along the coast. The south coast stretches for 1,100 km (685 miles) from the mouth of the Red Sea to Oman. These southern regions are generally arid except along the coastal plain where irrigation schemes support some agriculture and away from the coast in the Hadhramaut valley where sufficient rainfall occurs for cereal cultivation. To the north of the Hadhramaut lies the uninhabited Arabian Desert. The population, most of whom are subsistence farmers or nomadic herders of sheep and goats, are concentrated in western regions. Until recently the only mineral exploited commercially was salt but since the discovery of oil in 1984 and 1991, that commodity is making an important contribution to the economy. Otherwise, industrial activity is limited to small scale manufacturing.

YUGOSLAVIA
Federal Republic of,

STATUS: Federation of former Yugoslav Republics of Serbia and Montenegro

AREA: 102,170 sq km (39,435 sq miles)
POPULATION: 10,479,000
ANNUAL NATURAL INCREASE: 0.8%
CAPITAL: Belgrade (Beograd)
LANGUAGE: Serbo-Croat, Albanian and Hungarian
RELIGION: Orthodox Christian, 10% Muslim
CURRENCY: new Yugoslav dinar (YUD)
ORGANIZATIONS: UN (suspended)

Serbia and Montenegro are the last remaining elements of the Federal Republic of Yugoslavia. Until 1918, they were separate kingdoms. Union of the two, including Vojvodina, followed by unification with lands freed from the Turkish and Austro-Hungarian Empires, resulted in the creation of the Kingdom of Serbs, Croats and Slovenes, a name which was changed to the Kingdom of Yugoslavia in 1929. Yugoslavia became a Socialist Federal Republic in 1945. Economic difficulties from 1980 onwards, combined with regional and ethnic factors, culminated in the secession of Slovenia and Croatia in 1992. International recognition of their sovereignty did not deter Serbia, with the Serb-dominated army at its disposal, from armed incursion to secure areas inhabited by Serbians. Macedonia's claim for recognition was not so well received internationally because of Greek objection to the name Macedonia. Yet, it has ceased to be a part of Yugoslavia. No such impediment stood in the way of recognizing the independence of Bosnia-Herzegovina. Armed conflict intensified in this ethnically complex republic as rival factions fought to support their kinsfolk.

The climate is essentially continental with hot summers and cold winters. Agriculture, which is largely in private hands, features cotton and cereal cultivation on the fertile plains of Vojvodina in the north, livestock production in central Serbia and fruit and tobacco growing in Kosovo in the south. Industry, however, which had accounted for 80 per cent of economic wealth, has suffered severely from the effects of civil war and United Nations sanctions. Inflation is rife and only the black market flourishes.

MONTENEGRO

STATUS: Constituent Republic
AREA: 13,810 sq km (5,330 sq miles)
POPULATION: 664,000
CAPITAL: Podgorica

SERBIA

STATUS: Constituent Republic
AREA: 88,360 sq km (34,105 sq miles)
POPULATION: 9,815,000
CAPITAL: Belgrade (Beograd)

ZAIRE

STATUS: Republic
AREA: 2,345,410 sq km (905,330 sq miles)
POPULATION: 39,882,000
ANNUAL NATURAL INCREASE: 3.3%
CAPITAL: Kinshasa
LANGUAGE: French, Lingala, Kiswahili, Tshiluba, Kikongo

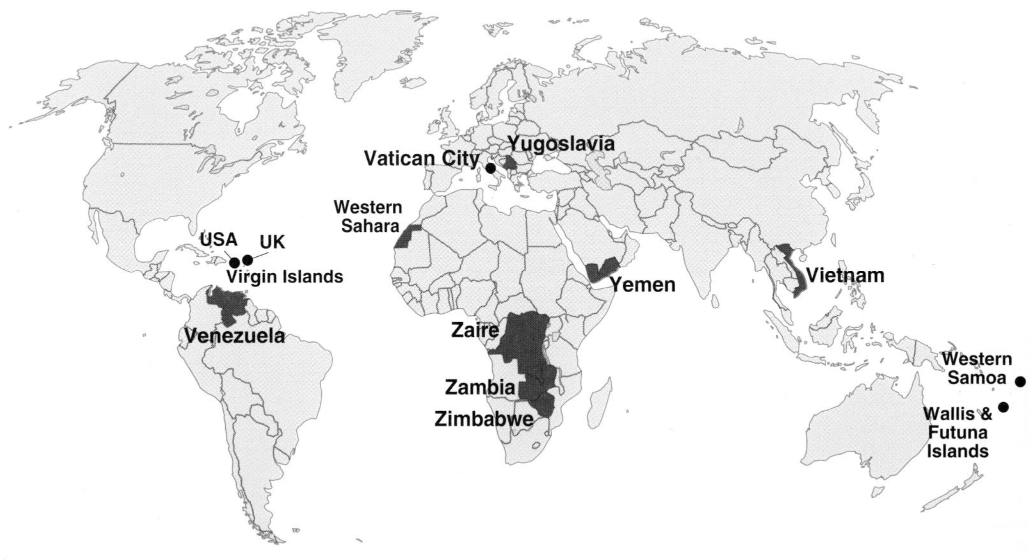

RELIGION: 46% Roman Catholic, 28% Protestant, traditional beliefs
CURRENCY: zaire (ZRZ)
ORGANIZATIONS: OAU, UN

Zaire, formerly the Belgian Congo, lies astride the Equator and is Africa's third largest country after Sudan and Algeria. It is dominated by the drainage basin of the Zaire, Kasai, and Oubangui rivers, which join to flow into the Atlantic. The land gradually rises from these basins to the south and east, culminating in the Chaine des Mitumba or Mitumbar mountains. On its eastern border the great Rift Valley forms a natural boundary with Uganda and Tanzania. Tropical rainforest covers most of the basin. Zaire's climate is equatorial with both high temperatures, averaging 27°C (80°F) throughout the year, and high rainfall of about 1,500–2,000 (59–79 inches). The majority of the population is engaged in shifting agriculture. Cassava, cocoa, coffee, cotton, millet, rubber and sugar cane are grown. Although the nation possesses mineral wealth, particularly copper which alone has provided 40 per cent of foreign earnings, political turmoil has reduced the country to bankruptcy. The copper mines are closed and diamonds are the only source of income. Zaire faces expulsion from the IMF because of debt arrears.

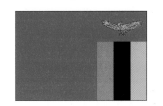

ZAMBIA

STATUS: Republic
AREA: 752,615 sq km (290,510 sq miles)
POPULATION: 8,638,000
ANNUAL NATURAL INCREASE: 3.5%
CAPITAL: Lusaka
LANGUAGE: English, African languages
RELIGION: 75% Christian, animist minority
CURRENCY: kwacha (ZMK)
ORGANIZATIONS: Comm., OAU, UN

Mineral-rich Zambia, is situated in the interior of southern central Africa. Its geography consists mainly of high rolling plateaux, with mountains to the north and northeast. In the south is the Zambezi river basin and the man-made reservoir of Lake Kariba, which forms Zambia's border with Zimbabwe. Altitude moderates the potentially tropical climate so that the summer temperature averages only 13–27°C (55–81°F). The north receives over 1,250 mm (49 inches) of rain per annum, the south less. Most of the country is grassland with some forest in the north. Farming is now mainly at subsistence level, as droughts have had an adverse effect on many crops, but some cattle rearing still takes on importance in the east. Copper remains the mainstay of the country's economy although reserves are fast running out. Lead, zinc, cobalt, cotton, groundnuts and tobacco are also exported. Wildlife is diverse and abundant and contributes to expanding tourism.

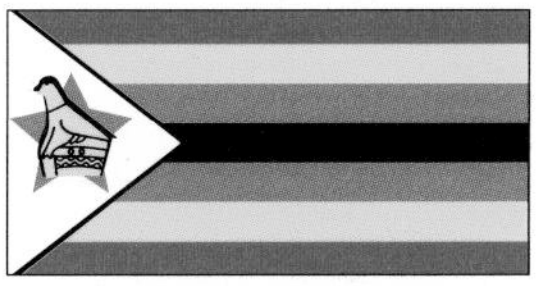

ZIMBABWE

STATUS: Republic
AREA: 390,310 sq km (150,660 sq miles)
POPULATION: 10,402,000
ANNUAL NATURAL INCREASE: 3.0%
CAPITAL: Harare
LANGUAGE: English, native languages
RELIGION: 58% Christian, traditional beliefs
CURRENCY: Zimbabwe dollar (ZWD)
ORGANIZATIONS: Comm., OAU, UN

Landlocked Zimbabwe (formerly southern Rhodesia) in south central Africa consists predominantly of rolling plateaux and valleys. A broad ridge of upland plateaux (the high veld) crosses east-west over the greater part of the country reaching heights of 1,200–1,500 m (3,940–4,920 feet). There are lowland areas (the low veld) formed by the valleys of the Zambezi and Limpopo rivers, in the north and south respectively. The climate varies with altitude and distance from the ocean. Rainfall across the country averages between 600-1,000 mm (24-39 inches). The exploitation of mineral deposits have traditionally supported the economy although recent years have seen a shift in the decline of chrome and coal and a rise in the importance of platinum, nickel and asbestos. Maize is the most important crop as it is the staple food of a large proportion of the population. Tobacco, tea, sugar cane and fruit are also grown. Manufacturing industry is slowly developing and now provides a wide range of consumer products.

North and Central America
25 349 000
9 785 000

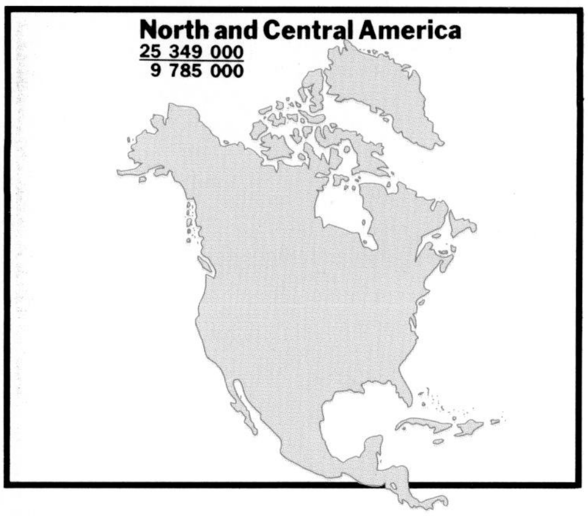

CONTINENTS

land area ▧ = **1 000 000** sq kms / **386 000** sq miles

Europe
10 498 000
4 052 000

Asia
43 608 000
16 833 000

Europe

Asia

Africa
30 335 000
11 709 000

South America
17 611 000
6 798 000

Antarctica
13 340 000
5 149 240

Australasia
8 923 000
3 444 278

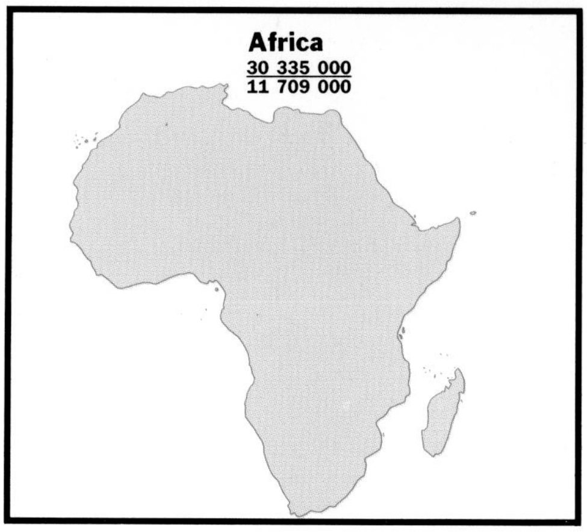

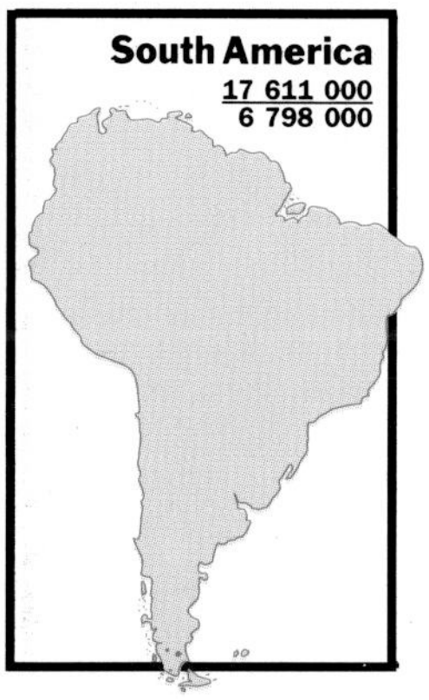

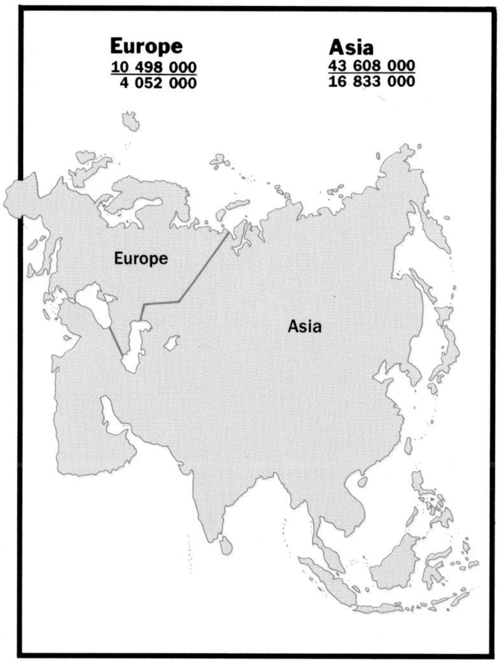

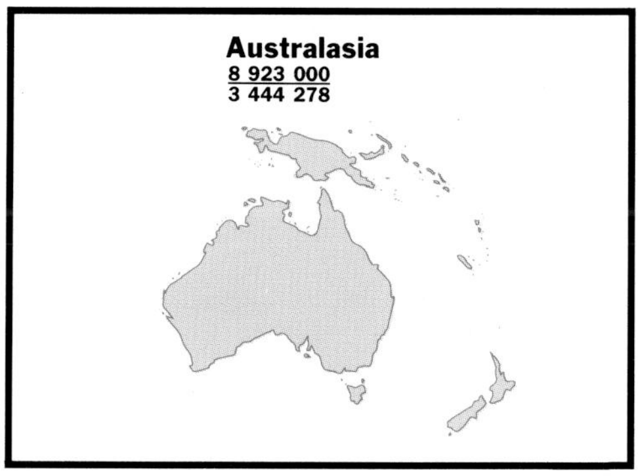

METROPOLITAN AREAS

Population	City	Country
2,500,000	**Adibjan**	Ivory Coast
1,891,000	**Addis Ababa**	Ethiopia
3,297,655	**Ahmadabad**	India
3,380,000	**Alexandria**	Egypt
3,033,000	**Algiers**	Algeria
1,151,300	**Alma-Ata**	Kazakhstan
1,091,338	**Amsterdam**	Netherlands
3,022,236	**Ankara**	Turkey
1,390,000	**Anshan**	China
3,096,775	**Athens**	Greece
3,051,000	**Atlanta**	USA
896,700	**Auckland**	New Zealand
4,044,000	**Baghdad**	Iraq
1,779,500	**Baku**	Azerbaijan
2,414,000	**Baltimore**	USA
4,086,548	**Bangalore**	India
5,876,000	**Bangkok**	Thailand
1,625,542	**Barcelona**	Spain
10,900,000	**Beijing (Peking)**	China
1,500,000	**Beirut**	Lebanon
1,168,454	**Belgrade**	Yugoslavia
3,461,905	**Belo Horizonte**	Brazil
3,446,000	**Berlin**	Germany
2,310,900	**Birmingham**	UK
5,025,989	**Bogotá**	Colombia
12,571,720	**Bombay**	India
4,497,000	**Boston**	USA
1,803,478	**Brasília**	Brazil
950,339	**Brussels**	Belgium
2,350,984	**Bucharest**	Romania
2,992,000	**Budapest**	Hungary
12,200,000	**Buenos Aires**	Argentina
13,300,000	**Cairo**	Egypt
10,916,000	**Calcutta**	India
320,000	**Canberra**	Australia
2,350,157	**Cape Town**	South Africa
4,092,000	**Caracas**	Venezuela
3,210,000	**Casablanca**	Morocco
2,214,000	**Changchun**	China
1,362,000	**Changsha**	China
1,148,000	**Chelyabinsk**	Russian Federation
3,004,000	**Chengdu**	China
7,498,000	**Chicago**	USA
3,010,000	**Chongqing**	China
1,342,679	**Copenhagen**	Denmark
2,543,000	**Dalian**	China
4,135,000	**Dallas – Fort Worth**	USA
2,913,000	**Damascus**	Syria
1,657,000	**Dar-es-Salaam**	Tanzania
8,375,000	**Delhi**	India
4,285,000	**Detroit**	USA
6,105,160	**Dhaka**	Bangladesh
915,516	**Dublin**	Republic of Ireland
2,720,400	**Essen – Dortmund**	Germany
1,420,000	**Fushun**	China
383,900	**Geneva**	Switzerland
2,846,720	**Guadalajara**	Mexico
3,620,000	**Guangzhou (Canton)**	China
1,669,000	**Hamburg**	Germany

Population	City	Country
1,412,000	**Hangzhou**	China
3,056,146	**Hanoi**	Vietnam
2,840,000	**Harbin**	China
2,099,000	**Havana**	Cuba
3,924,435	**Ho Chi Minh (Saigon)**	Vietnam
5,812,000	**Hong Kong**	UK colony
3,437,000	**Houston**	USA
4,280,000	**Hyderabad**	India
6,407,215	**Istanbul**	Turkey
9,000,000	**Jakarta**	Indonesia
608,000	**Jerusalem**	Israel
1,327,000	**Jilin**	China
2,415,000	**Jinan**	China
1,916,063	**Johannesburg**	South Africa
1,300,000	**Kābul**	Afghanistan
7,702,000	**Karachi**	Pakistan
1,947,000	**Khartoum**	Sudan
2,616,000	**Kiev**	Ukraine
3,505,000	**Kinshasa**	Zaire
1,711,000	**Kuala Lumpur**	Malaysia
5,689,000	**Lagos**	Nigeria
4,092,000	**Lahore**	Pakistan
1,566,000	**Lanzhou**	China
6,483,901	**Lima**	Peru
1,742,000	**Lisbon**	Portugal
9,277,687	**London**	UK
11,420,000	**Los Angeles**	USA
5,361,468	**Madras**	India
2,909,792	**Madrid**	Spain
2,578,900	**Manchester**	UK
8,475,000	**Manila – Quezon City**	Philippines
1,594,967	**Medellín**	Colombia
3,178,000	**Melbourne**	Australia
20,200,000	**Mexico City**	Mexico
1,814,000	**Miami**	USA
2,583,000	**Minneapolis – St Paul**	USA
1,633,000	**Minsk**	Belarus
2,521,697	**Monterrey**	Mexico
1,383,660	**Montevideo**	Uruguay
3,127,100	**Montréal**	Canada
8,957,000	**Moscow**	Russian Federation
1,236,000	**Munich**	Germany
2,095,000	**Nagoya**	Japan
1,503,000	**Nairobi**	Kenya
1,415,000	**Nanchang**	China
2,265,000	**Nanjing**	China
16,972,000	**New York**	USA
1,442,000	**Novosibirsk**	Russian Federation
1,106,000	**Odessa**	Ukraine
8,520,000	**Osaka-Kobe**	Japan
473,344	**Oslo**	Norway
921,000	**Ottawa**	Canada

Population	City	Country
9,318,000	**Paris**	France
4,941,000	**Philadelphia**	USA
2,287,000	**Phoenix**	USA
2,404,000	**Pittsburgh**	USA
3,015,960	**Pôrto Alegre**	Brazil
1,214,174	**Prague**	Czech Republic
3,797,566	**Pusan**	South Korea
2,230,000	**Pyôngyang**	North Korea
645,000	**Quebec**	Canada
2,060,000	**Qingdao**	China
1,281,849	**Quito**	Ecuador
3,295,000	**Rangoon**	Burma
2,859,469	**Recife**	Brazil
910,200	**Riga**	Latvia
9,871,165	**Rio de Janeiro**	Brazil
1,500,000	**Riyadh**	Saudi Arabia
2,723,327	**Rome**	Italy
1,388,000	**Sacramento**	USA
2,472,131	**Salvador**	Brazil
2,549,000	**San Deigo**	USA
5,240,000	**San Francisco**	USA
1,390,000	**San Juan**	Puerto Rico
4,628,000	**Santiago**	Chile
2,055,000	**Santo Domingo**	Dominican Republic
15,199,423	**São Paulo**	Brazil
10,627,000	**Seoul**	South Korea
13,341,896	**Shanghai**	China
4,763,000	**Shenyang**	China
2,874,000	**Singapore**	Singapore
1,221,000	**Sofia**	Bulgaria
2,507,000	**St Louis**	USA
5,004,000	**St Petersburg**	Russian Federation
1,669,840	**Stockholm**	Sweden
2,473,272	**Surabaya**	Indonesia
3,700,000	**Sydney**	Australia
2,228,000	**Taegu**	South Korea
2,720,000	**Taipei**	Taiwan
2,199,000	**Taiyuan**	China
452,000	**Tallinn**	Estonia
2,094,000	**Tashkent**	Uzbekistan
1,400,000	**Tbilisi**	Georgia
6,773,000	**Tehran**	Iran
1,135,800	**Tel Aviv**	Israel
9,100,000	**Tianjin**	China
11,609,735	**Tokyo**	Japan
3,893,400	**Toronto**	Canada
2,062,000	**Tripoli**	Libya
1,603,600	**Vancouver**	Canada
1,565,000	**Vienna**	Austria
593,000	**Vilnius**	Lithuania
1,655,700	**Warsaw**	Poland
4,293,000	**Washington DC**	USA
325,700	**Wellington**	New Zealand
652,000	**Winnipeg**	Canada
3,921,000	**Wuhan**	China
2,859,000	**Xian**	China
1,202,000	**Yerevan**	Armenia
726,770	**Zagreb**	Croatia
2,460,000	**Zibo**	China

MOUNTAIN HEIGHTS

metres	feet		
8,848	29,028	**Everest (Qomolangma Feng)**	*China–Nepal*
8,611	28,250	**K2 (Qogir Feng) (Godwin Austen)**	*India – China*
8,598	28,170	**Kangchenjunga**	*India–Nepal*
8,481	27,824	**Makalu**	*China–Nepal*
8,217	26,958	**Cho Oyu**	*China–Nepal*
8,167	26,795	**Dhaulagiri**	*Nepal*
8,156	26,758	**Manaslu**	*Nepal*
8,126	26,660	**Nanga Parbat**	*India*
8,078	26,502	**Annapurna**	*Nepal*
8,088	26,470	**Gasherbrum**	*India–China*
8,027	26,335	**Xixabangma Feng (Gosainthan)**	*China*
7,885	25,869	**Distaghil Sar**	*Kashmir, India*
7,820	25,656	**Masherbrum**	*India*
7,817	25,646	**Nanda Devi**	*India*
7,788	25,550	**Rakaposhi**	*India*
7,756	25,446	**Kamet**	*China–India*
7,756	25,447	**Namjagbarwa Feng**	*China*
7,728	25,355	**Gurla Mandhata**	*China*
7,723	25,338	**Muztag**	*China*
7,719	25,325	**Kongur Shan (Kungur)**	*China*
7,690	25,230	**Tirich Mir**	*Pakistan*
7,556	24,790	**Gongga Shan**	*China*
7,546	24,757	**Muztagata**	*China*
7,495	24,590	**Pik Kommunizma**	*Tajikistan*
7,439	24,406	**Pik Pobedy (Tomur Feng)**	*Kirghizia–China*
7,313	23,993	**Chomo Lhari**	*Bhutan–Tibet*
7,134	23,406	**Pik Lenina**	*Kirghizia*
6,960	22,834	**Aconcagua**	*Argentina*
6,908	22,664	**Ojos del Salado**	*Argentina–Chile*
6,872	22,546	**Bonete**	*Argentina*
6,800	22,310	**Tupungato**	*Argentina–Chile*
6,770	22,221	**Mercedario**	*Argentina*

metres	feet		
6,768	22,205	**Huascarán**	*Peru*
6,723	22,057	**Llullaillaco**	*Argentina–Chile*
6,714	22,027	**Kangrinboqê Feng (Kailas)**	*Tibet, China*
6,634	21,765	**Yerupaja**	*Peru*
6,542	21,463	**Sajama**	*Bolivia*
6,485	21,276	**Illampu**	*Bolivia*
6,425	21,079	**Coropuna**	*Peru*
6,402	21,004	**Illimani**	*Bolivia*
6,310	20,702	**Chimborazo**	*Ecuador*
6,194	20,320	**McKinley**	*USA*
5,959	19,551	**Logan**	*Canada*
5,896	19,344	**Cotopaxi**	*Ecuador*
5,895	19,340	**Kilimanjaro**	*Tanzania*
5,800	19,023	**Sa. Nevada de Sta. Marta (Cristobal Colon)**	*Columbia*
5,775	18,947	**Bolivar**	*Venezuela*
5,699	18,697	**Citlaltépetl (Orizaba)**	*Mexico*
5,642	18,510	**El'brus**	*Russian Federation*
5,601	18,376	**Damāvand**	*Iran*
5,489	18,008	**Mt St. Elias**	*Canada*
5,227	17,149	**Mt Lucania**	*Canada*
5,199	17,057	**Kenya (Kirinyaga)**	*Kenya*
5,165	16,945	**Ararat (Büyük Ağri Daği)**	*Turkey*
5,140	16,860	**Vinson Massif**	*Antarctica*
5,110	16,763	**Stanley (Margherita)**	*Uganda–Zaire*
5,029	16,499	**Jaya (Carstensz)**	*Indonesia*
5,005	16,421	**Mt Bona**	*USA*
4,949	16,237	**Sandford**	*USA*

metres	feet		
4,936	16,194	**Mt Blackburn**	*Canada*
4,808	15,774	**Mont Blanc**	*France–Italy*
4,750	15,584	**Klyuchevskaya Sopka**	*Russian Federation*
4,634	15,203	**Monte Rosa (Dufour)**	*Italy–Switzerland*
4,565	14,979	**Meru**	*Tanzania*
4,545	14,910	**Dom (Mischabel group)**	*Switzerland*
4,533	14,872	**Ras Dashen**	*Ethiopia*
4,528	14,855	**Kirkpatrick**	*Antarctica*
4,508	14,790	**Wilhelm**	*Papua, New Guinea*
4,507	14,786	**Karisimbi**	*Rwanda–Zaire*
4,477	14,688	**Matterhorn**	*Italy–Switzerland*
4,418	14,495	**Whitney**	*USA*
4,398	14,431	**Elbert**	*USA*
4,392	14,410	**Rainier**	*USA*
4,351	14,275	**Markham**	*Antarctica*
4,321	14,178	**Elgon**	*Kenya–Uganda*
4,307	14,131	**Batu**	*Ethiopia*
4,169	13,677	**Mauna Loa**	*USA, Hawaii*
4,165	13,644	**Toubkal**	*Morocco*
4,095	13,435	**Cameroon (Caméroun)**	*Cameroon*
4,094	13,431	**Kinabalu**	*Malaysia*
3,794	12,447	**Erebus**	*Antarctica*
3,776	12,388	**Fuji**	*Japan*
3,754	12,316	**Cook**	*New Zealand*
3,718	12,198	**Teide**	*Canary Is*
3,482	11,424	**Thabana Ntlenyana**	*Lesotho*
3,482	11,424	**Mulhacén**	*Spain*
3,415	11,204	**Emi Koussi**	*Chad*
3,323	10,902	**Etna**	*Italy, Sicily*
2,743	9,000	**Mt Balbi**	*Bougainville, Papua New Guinea*
2,655	8,708	**Gerlachovsky stit (Tatra)**	*Czech Republic*
2,230	7,316	**Kosciusko**	*Australia*

ISLANDS

land area □ = 10 000 sq kms / 3 860 sq miles

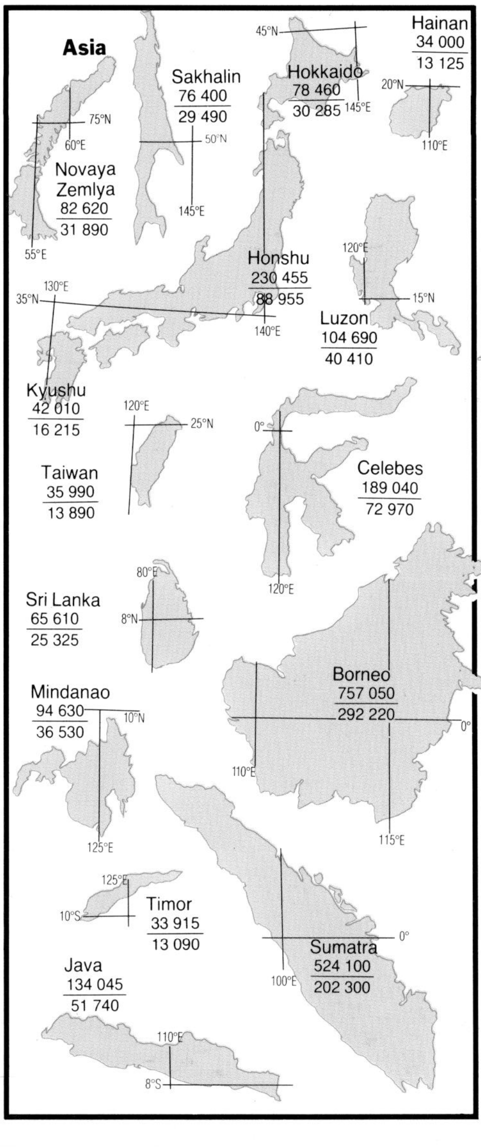

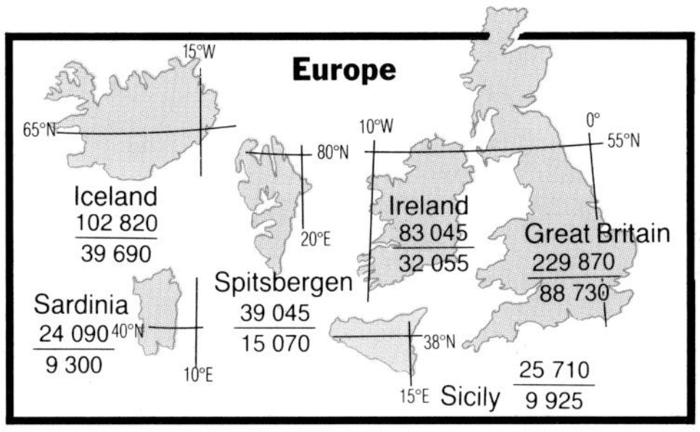

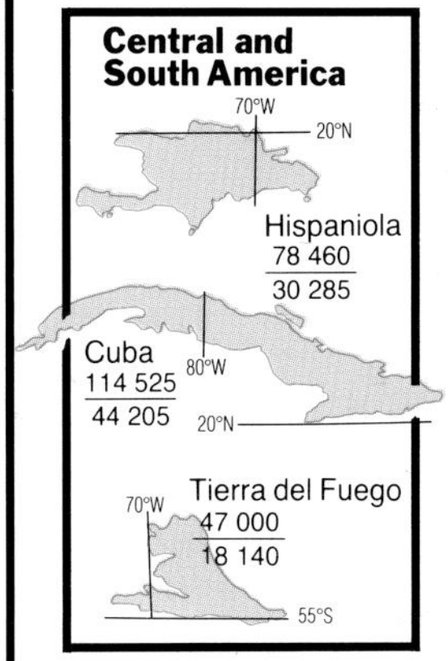

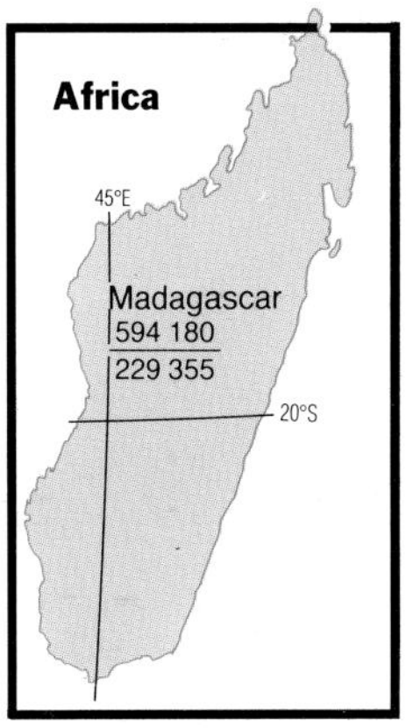

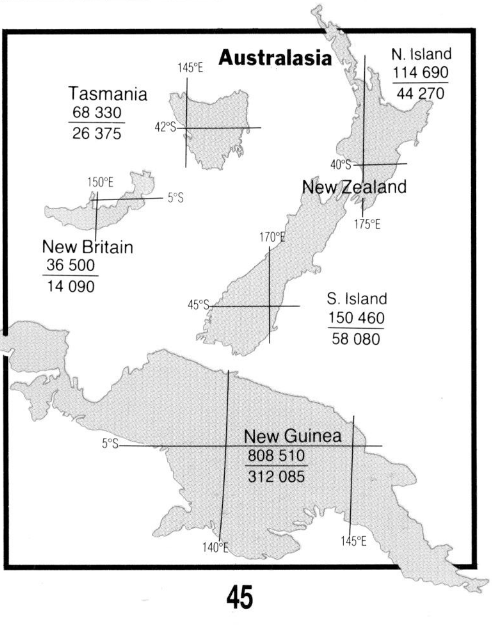

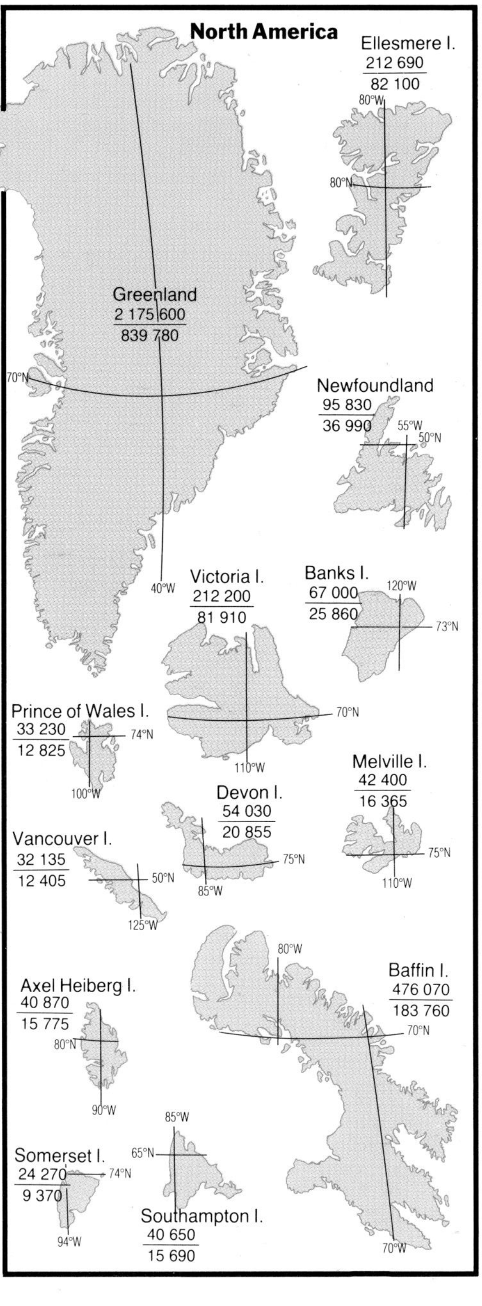

OCEANS AND SEAS

water area = $\dfrac{1\,000\,000}{386\,000}$ sq km / sq miles

OCEAN FACTS AND FIGURES

The area of the Earth covered by sea is estimated to be 361,740,000 sq km (139,670,000 sq miles), or 70.92% of the total surface. The mean depth is estimated to be 3554 m (11,660 ft), and the volume of the oceans to be 1,285,600,000 cu. km (308,400,000 cu. miles).

INDIAN OCEAN

Mainly confined to the southern hemisphere, and at its greatest breadth (Tasmania to Cape Agulhas) 9600 km. Average depth is 4000 m; greatest depth is the Amirante Trench (9000 m).

ATLANTIC OCEAN

Commonly divided into North Atlantic (36,000,000 sq km) and South Atlantic (26,000,000 sq km). The greatest breadth in the North is 7200 km (Morocco to Florida) and in the South 9600 km (Guinea to Brazil). Average depth is 3600 m; the greatest depths are the Puerto Rico Trench 9220 m, S. Sandwich Trench 8264 m, and Romansh Trench 7728 m.

PACIFIC OCEAN

Covers nearly 40% of the world's total sea area, and is the largest of the oceans. The greatest breadth (E/W) is 16,000 km and the greatest length (N/S) 11,000 km. Average depth is 4200 m; also the deepest ocean. Generally the west is deeper than the east and the north deeper than the south. Greatest depths occur near island groups and include Mindanao Trench 11,524 m, Mariana Trench 11,022 m, Tonga Trench 10,882 m, Kuril-Kamchatka Trench 10,542 m, Philippine Trench 10,497 m, and Kermadec Trench 10,047 m.

Comparisons (where applicable)	greatest distance N/S (km)	greatest distance E/W (km)	maximum depth (m)
Indian Ocean	—	9600	9000
Atlantic Ocean	—	9600	9220
Pacific Ocean	11,000	16,000	11,524
Arctic Ocean	—	—	5450
Mediterranean Sea	960	3700	4846
S. China Sea	2100	1750	5514
Bering Sea	1800	2100	5121
Caribbean Sea	1600	2000	7100
Gulf of Mexico	1200	1700	4377
Sea of Okhotsk	2200	1400	3475
E. China Sea	1100	750	2999
Yellow Sea	800	1000	91
Hudson Bay	1250	1050	259
Sea of Japan	1500	1100	3743
North Sea	1200	550	661
Red Sea	1932	360	2246
Black Sea	600	1100	2245
Baltic Sea	1500	650	460

EARTH'S SURFACE WATERS

Total volume	c.1400 million cu. km
Oceans and seas	1370 million cu. km
Ice	24 million cu. km
Interstitial water (in rocks and sediments)	4 million cu. km
Lakes and rivers	230 thousand cu. km
Atmosphere (vapour)	c.140 thousand cu. km

to convert metric to imperial measurements:
1 m = 3.281 feet
1 km = 0.621 miles
1 sq km = 0.386 sq miles

Red Sea
438 000
169 000

Indian Ocean
73 481 000
28 364 000

Arctic Ocean
14 056 000
5 426 000

Baltic Sea
422 000
163 000

Hudson Bay
1 233 000
476 000

North Sea
575 000
222 000

Black Sea
461 000
178 000

Gulf of Mexico
1 544 000
596 000

Mediterranean Sea
2 505 000
967 000

Caribbean Sea
1 943 000
750 000

Atlantic Ocean
82 217 000
31 736 000

Sea of Japan
1 008 000
389 000

Sea of Okhotsk
1 528 000
590 000

Yellow Sea
404 000
156 000

Bering Sea
2 269 000
876 000

East China Sea
1 248 000
482 000

South China Sea
2 318 000
895 000

Pacific Ocean
165 384 000
63 838 000

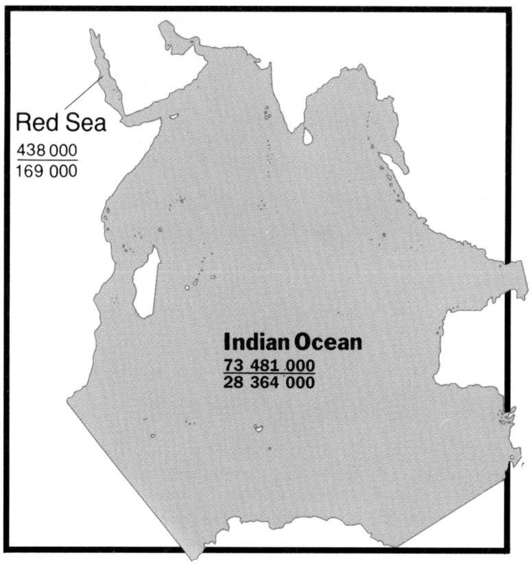

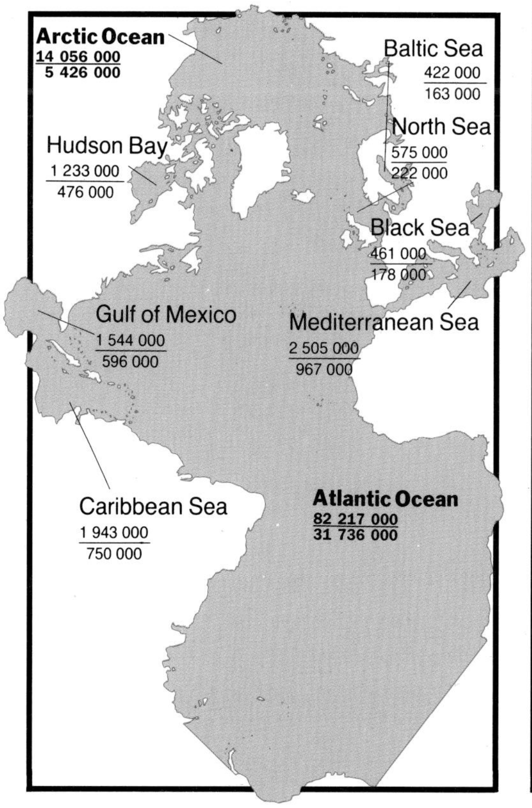

FEATURES OF THE OCEAN BASIN

The majority of land drainage occurs in the Atlantic, yet this is the most saline ocean due to interchange of waters with its marginal seas. The continental margins (21% of ocean floors) are the most important economic areas.

	PACIFIC	ATLANTIC	INDIAN	WORLD
AVERAGE OCEAN DEPTH (metres)				
3000				
3500				
4000				
OCEAN AREA (million sq km)	180	107	74	361
LAND AREA DRAINED (million sq km)	19	69	13	101
AREA AS PERCENTAGE OF TOTAL				
Continental margin	15.8	27.9	14.8	20.6
Ridges, rises and fracture zones	38.4	33.3	35.6	35.8
Deep ocean floor	42.9	38.1	49.3	41.9
Island arcs and trenches	2.9	0.7	0.3	1.7

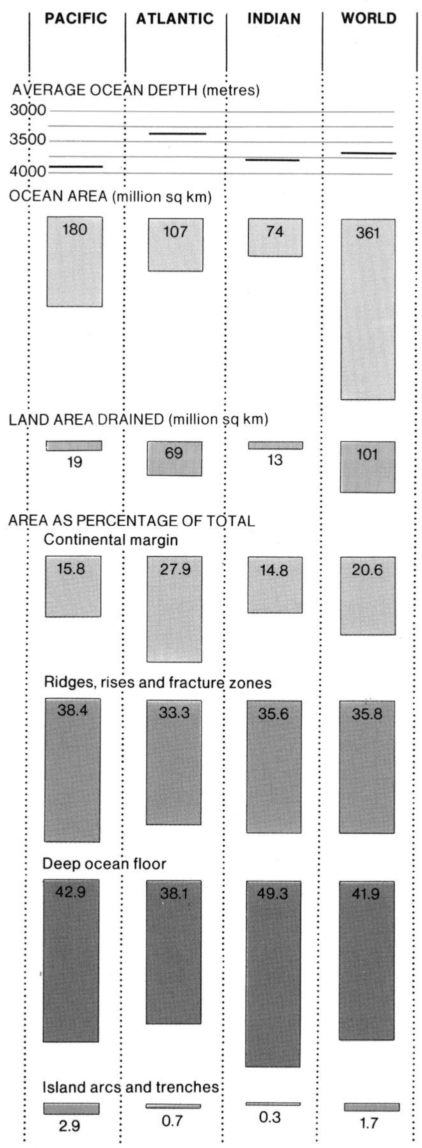

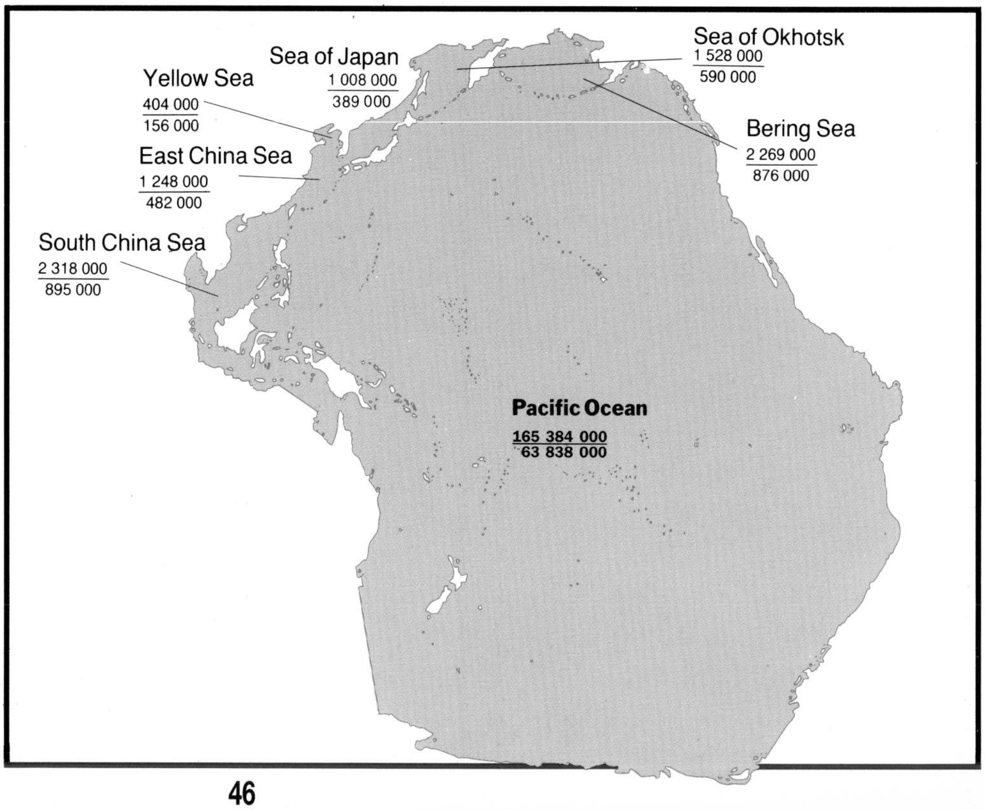

RIVER LENGTHS

km	miles		
6,695	4,160	**Nile**	*Africa*
6,515	4,050	**Amazon**	*South America*
6,380	3,965	**Yangtze (Chang Jiang)**	*Asia*
6,019	3,740	**Mississippi-Missouri**	*North America*
5,570	3,460	**Ob'-Irtysh**	*Asia*
5,550	3,450	**Yenisei-Angara**	*Asia*
5,464	3,395	**Yellow River (Huang He)**	*Asia*
4,667	2,900	**Congo (Zaire)**	*Africa*
4,500	2,800	**Paraná**	*South America*
4,440	2,775	**Irtysh**	*Asia*
4,425	2,750	**Mekong**	*Asia*
4,416	2,744	**Amur**	*Asia*
4,400	2,730	**Lena**	*Asia*
4,250	2,640	**Mackenzie**	*North America*
4,090	2,556	**Yenisei**	*Asia*
4,030	2,505	**Niger**	*Africa*
3,969	2,466	**Missouri**	*North America*
3,779	2,348	**Mississippi**	*North America*
3,750	2,330	**Murray-Darling**	*Australasia*
3,688	2,290	**Volga**	*Europe*
3,218	2,011	**Purus**	*South America*
3,200	1,990	**Madeira**	*South America*
3,185	1,980	**Yukon**	*North America*
3,180	1,975	**Indus**	*Asia*
3,078	1,913	**Syrdar'ya**	*Asia*
3,060	1,901	**Salween**	*Asia*
3,058	1,900	**St Lawrence**	*North America*
2,900	1,800	**São Francisco**	*South America*
2,870	1,785	**Rio Grande**	*North America*
2,850	1,770	**Danube**	*Europe*
2,840	1,765	**Brahmaputra**	*Asia*
2,815	1,750	**Euphrates**	*Asia*
2,750	1,710	**Pará-Tocantins**	*South America*
2,750	1,718	**Tarim**	*Asia*
2,650	1,650	**Zambezi**	*Africa*
2,620	1,630	**Amudar'ya**	*Asia*
2,620	1,630	**Araguaia**	*South America*
2,600	1,615	**Paraguay**	*South America*
2,570	1,600	**Nelson-Saskatchewan**	*North America*

km	miles		
2,534	1,575	**Ural**	*Asia*
2,513	1,562	**Kolyma**	*Asia*
2,510	1,560	**Ganges (Ganga)**	*Asia*
2,500	1,555	**Orinoco**	*South America*
2,490	1,550	**Shabeelle**	*Africa*
2,490	1,550	**Pilcomayo**	*South America*
2,348	1,459	**Arkansas**	*North America*
2,333	1,450	**Colorado**	*North America*
2,285	1,420	**Dneper**	*Europe*
2,250	1,400	**Columbia**	*North America*
2,150	1,335	**Irrawaddy**	*Asia*
2,129	1,323	**Pearl River (Xi Jiang)**	*Asia*
2,032	1,270	**Kama**	*Europe*
2,000	1,240	**Negro**	*South America*
1,923	1,195	**Peace**	*North America*
1,899	1,186	**Tigris**	*Asia*
1,870	1,162	**Don**	*Europe*
1,860	1,155	**Orange**	*Africa*
1,809	1,124	**Pechora**	*Europe*
1,800	1,125	**Okavango**	*Africa*
1,609	1,000	**Marañón**	*South America*
1,609	1,095	**Uruguay**	*South America*
1,600	1,000	**Volta**	*Africa*
1,600	1,000	**Limpopo**	*Africa*
1,550	963	**Magdalena**	*South America*
1,515	946	**Kura**	*Asia*
1,480	925	**Oka**	*Europe*
1,480	925	**Belaya**	*Europe*
1,445	903	**Godavari**	*Asia*
1,430	893	**Senegal**	*Africa*
1,410	876	**Dnester**	*Europe*
1,400	875	**Chari**	*Africa*
1,368	850	**Fraser**	*North America*
1,320	820	**Rhine**	*Europe*
1,314	821	**Vyatka**	*Europe*
1,183	735	**Donets**	*Europe*
1,159	720	**Elbe**	*Europe*
1,151	719	**Kizilirmak**	*Asia*

RIVER LENGTHS & DRAINAGE BASINS

km	miles		
1,130	706	**Desna**	*Europe*
1,094	680	**Gambia**	*Africa*
1,080	675	**Yellowstone**	*North America*
1,049	652	**Tennessee**	*North America*
1,024	640	**Zelenga**	*Asia*
1,020	637	**Duena**	*Europe*
1,014	630	**Vistula (Wisła)**	*Europe*
1,012	629	**Loire**	*Europe*
1,006	625	**Tagus (Tejo)**	*Europe*
977	607	**Tisza**	*Europe*
925	575	**Meuse (Maas)**	*Europe*
909	565	**Oder**	*Europe*
761	473	**Seine**	*Europe*
354	220	**Severn**	*Europe*
346	215	**Thames**	*Europe*
300	186	**Trent**	*Europe*

DRAINAGE BASINS

sq km	sq miles		
7,050,000	2,721,000	**Amazon**	*South America*
3,700,000	1,428,000	**Congo**	*Africa*
3,250,000	1,255,000	**Mississippi-Missouri**	*North America*
3,100,000	1,197,000	**Paraná**	*South America*
2,700,000	1,042,000	**Yenisei**	*Asia*
2,430,000	938,000	**Ob'**	*Asia*
2,420,000	934,000	**Lena**	*Asia*
1,900,000	733,400	**Nile**	*Africa*
1,840,000	710,000	**Amur**	*Asia*
1,765,000	681,000	**Mackenzie**	*North America*
1,730,000	668,000	**Ganges-Brahmaputra**	*Asia*
1,380,000	533,000	**Volga**	*Europe*
1,330,000	513,000	**Zambezi**	*Africa*
1,200,000	463,000	**Niger**	*Africa*
1,175,000	454,000	**Yangtze**	*Asia*
1,020,000	394,000	**Orange**	*Africa*
980,000	378,000	**Yellow River**	*Asia*
960,000	371,000	**Indus**	*Asia*
945,000	365,000	**Orinoco**	*South America*
910,000	351,000	**Murray-Darling**	*Australasia*
855,000	330,000	**Yukon**	*North America*
815,000	315,000	**Danube**	*Europe*
810,000	313,000	**Mekong**	*Asia*
225,000	86,900	**Rhine**	*Europe*

North and Central America

L.Superior 83270 *393* / 32140 *1289*

L.Huron 60700 *229* / 23430 *751*

L.Ontario 19230 *237* / 7425 *778*

L.Michigan 58020 *281* / 22395 *922*

L.Erie 25680 *64* / 9915 *210*

L.de Nicaragua 8270 *70* / 3190 *230*

Great Bear Lake 31790 *319* / 12270 *1047*

L.Athabasca 8080 *91* / 3120 *299*

Great Slave Lake 28440 *140* / 10980 *459*

Nettilling Lake 5250 / 2030

L.Winnipeg 24510 *21* / 9460 *69*

Reindeer Lake 6390 / 2470

INLAND WATERS

water surface area ☐ = 1 000 sq km / 386 sq miles

deepest point 229 metres / 751 feet

Africa

L.Victoria 68800 *100* / 26560 *328*

L.Tanganyika 32900 *1435* / 13860 *4708*

L.Nyasa (Malawi) 22490 *706* / 8680 *2316*

L.Turkana (Rudolf) 4250 *73* / 1640 *240*

L.Chad 10-26000 *4-7* / 4-10000 *13-23*

L.Albert 6410 *48* / 2475 *158*

L.Mweru 4920 *14* / 1900 *46*

South America

L.Titicaca 8340 *304* / 3220 *997*

Australasia

L.Eyre (salt) 0-8900 *0-20* / 0-3435 *0-66*

L.Torrens 5780 (salt) / 2230

Europe

L.Onega 9600 *124* / 3705 *407*

L.Vänern 5580 *98* / 2155 *322*

L.Ladoga 18390 *230* / 7100 *755*

Asia

L.Balkhash 17 400 *26* / 6 715 *85*

Caspian Sea (salt) 371 000 *980* / 143 205 *3215*

L.Baikal 30 500 *1741* / 11 775 *5712*

D.-ye Orūmīyeh 5900 *15* / 2280 *49*

Issyk-Kul' 6200 *702* / 2395 *2303*

Qinghai Hu 2300 *38* / 890 *125*

Poyang Hu 5000 / 1930

47

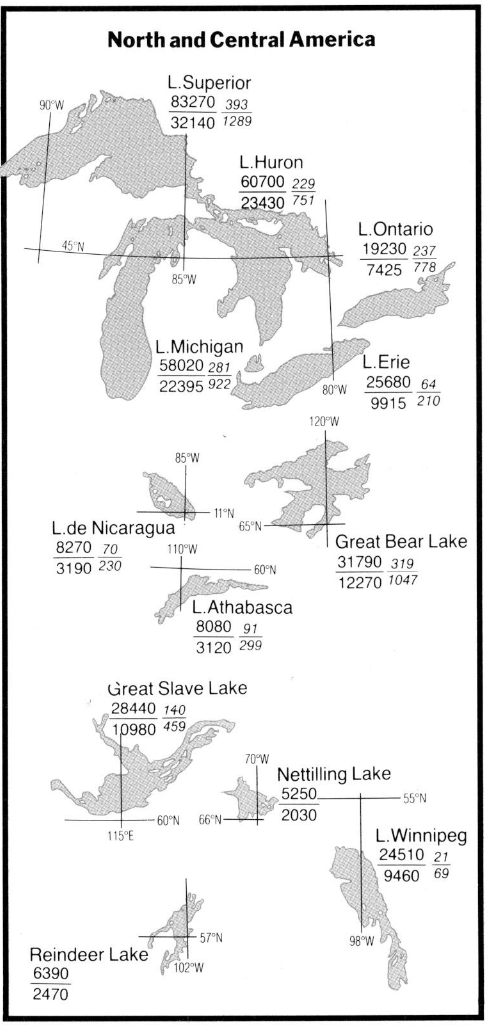

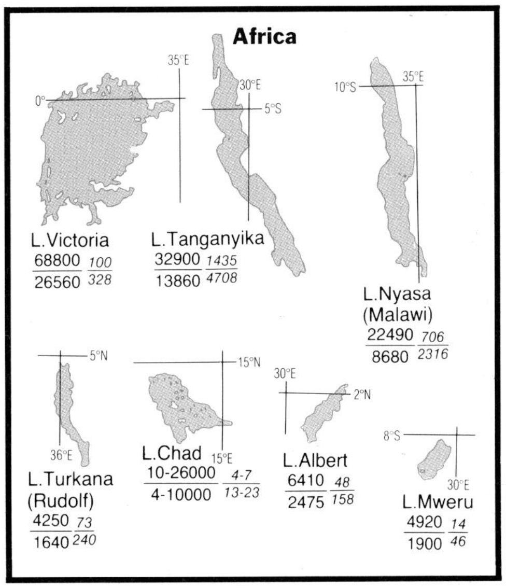

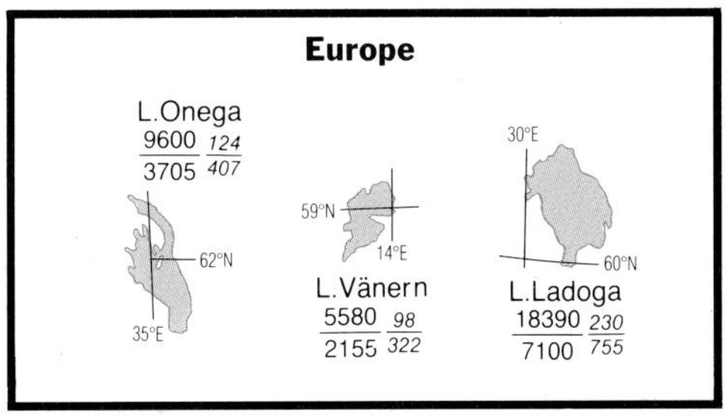

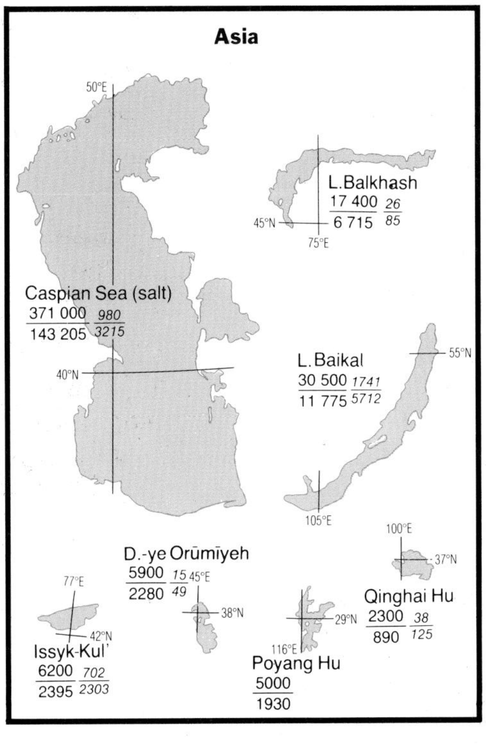

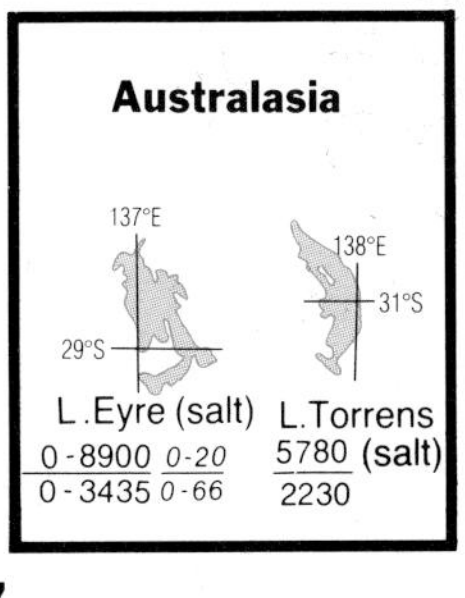

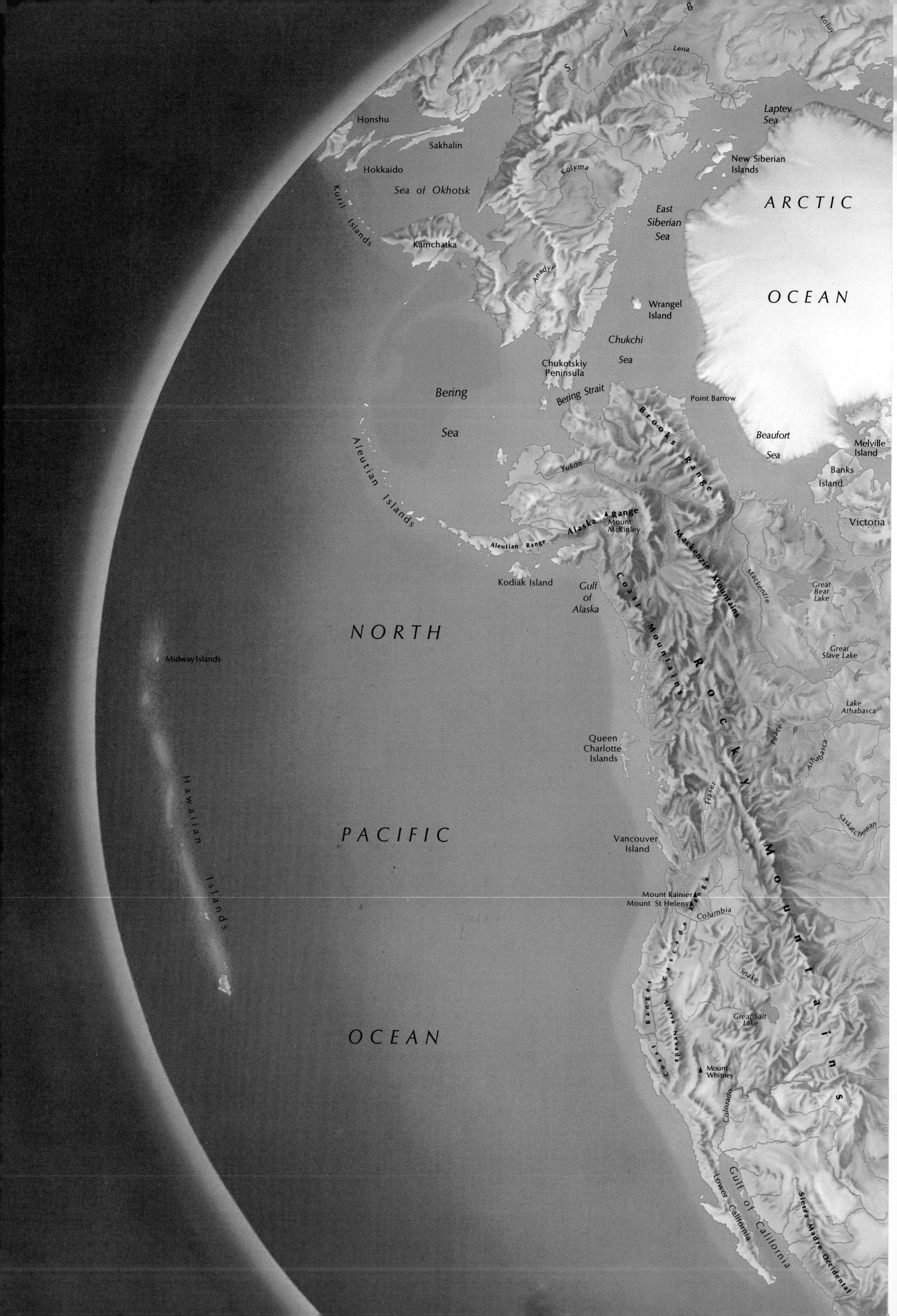
S I B
Lena
Kolyma
Laptev Sea
Honshu
Sakhalin
New Siberian Islands
Hokkaido
Kolyma
Sea of Okhotsk
ARCTIC
Kuril Islands
East Siberian Sea
Kamchatka
Anadyr
OCEAN
Wrangel Island
Chukchi Sea
Chukotskiy Peninsula
Bering Sea
Bering Strait
Point Barrow
Brooks Range
Aleutian Islands
Beaufort Sea
Melville Island
Yukon
Banks Island
Victoria
Alaska Range
Mount McKinley
Aleutian Range
Kodiak Island
Gulf of Alaska
Mackenzie Mountains
Mackenzie
Great Bear Lake
Coast Mountains
NORTH
Midway Islands
Great Slave Lake
ROCKY MOUNTAINS
Lake Athabasca
Queen Charlotte Islands
Peace
Athabasca
Hawaiian Islands
Fraser
PACIFIC
Saskatchewan
Vancouver Island
Mount Rainier
Mount St Helens
Cascade Range
Columbia
Snake
Coast Ranges
Sierra Nevada
Great Salt Lake
OCEAN
Mount Whitney
Colorado
Lower California
Gulf of California
Sierra Madre Occidental

Yenisey
Ob'
Urals
Novaya Zemlya
Kara Sea
Barents Sea
Black Sea
Severnaya Zemlya
North Cape
S C A N D I N A V I A
Baltic Sea
Franz Josef Land
Limit of permanent pack ice
Bear Island
Svalbard
Norwegian Sea
Mediterranean Sea
NORTH POLE
Wandell Sea
North Sea
Jan Mayen
Greenland Sea
Lincoln Sea
BRITISH ISLES
Bay of Biscay
Greenland
Denmark Strait
Iceland
Ellesmere Island
Axel Heiburg Island
Queen Elizabeth Islands
NORTH AFRICA
Parry Islands
Devon Island
Baffin Bay
Prince of Wales Island
Somerset Island
Davis Strait
Island
Cape Farewell
Baffin Island
Madeira
Nettiling Lake
NORTH
Canary Islands
Foxe Basin
Labrador Sea
Southampton Island
Hudson Strait
Cape Chidley
Azores
Labrador
Hudson Bay
Churchill
Reindeer Lake
Churchill
Southern Indian Lake
Nelson
La Grande Rivière
Laurentian Highlands
Newfoundland
Cape Race
ATLANTIC
James Bay
Rupert
Lake Winnipeg
Nova Scotia
Lake Manitoba
St Lawrence
Lake of the Woods
Lake Superior
Lake Huron
Lake Ontario
Cape Cod
Missouri
Mississippi
Lake Michigan
Lake Erie
Great Plains
Platte
Mountains
Ohio
Bermuda
OCEAN
Appalachian
Tennessee
Cape Hatteras
Ozark Plateaus
Arkansas
Mississippi
Savannah
Red River
Florida
The Bahamas
West Indies
Rio Grande
Gulf of Mexico
Sierra Madre Oriental
Sea
Yucatan
Caribbean
Orinoco

Florida
Rio Grande
Sierra Madre Occidental
Gulf of California
Lower California
Sierra Madre Oriental
GULF OF MEXICO
Gulf of Campeche
Yucatan
Popocatépetl
Sierra Madre del Sur
Islas Revillagigedo
Gulf of Honduras
Lake Nicaragua
Clipperton Island
Isthmus of
Gulf of Panama
PACIFIC
Isla del Coco
Isla de Malpelo
Galapagos Islands
Cotopaxi
Chimborazo
OCEAN

Bermuda
NORTH ATLANTIC OCEAN
BAHAMAS
Sargasso Sea
INDIES
Hispaniola
Jamaica
ANTILLES
Puerto Rico
CARIBBEAN SEA
LESSER ANTILLES
Trinidad
Lake Maracaibo
Gulf of Darien
Panama
Orinoco
LLANOS
Cauca
Magdalena
Cordillera Occidental
Cordillera Oriental
Roraima
Guiana Highlands
Branco
Mouths of the Amazon
Negro
Japurá
Putumayo
Amazon
Juruá
Marañón
Purus
Madeira
Tapajós
Xingu
Tocantins
Ucayali
Parnaíba
Huascarán
Araguaia
São Francisco
Madre de Dios
MATO GROSSO
Brazilian Highlands
Lake Titicaca
Ancohuma
Lake Poopó
Salar de Uyuni
Atacama Desert
GRAN CHACO
Paraguay
Pilcomayo
Paraná

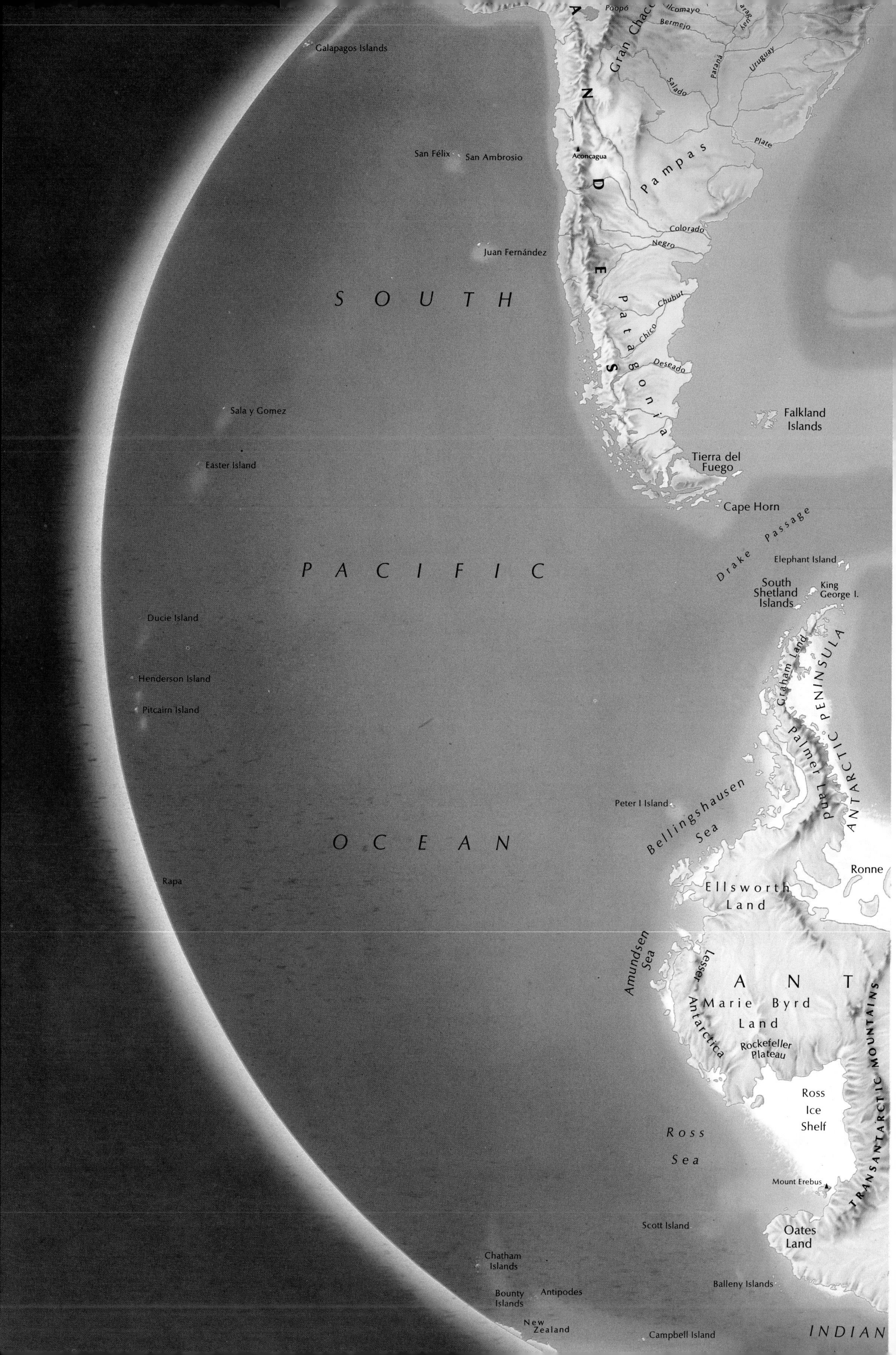
Galapagos Islands
Poopó
Bermejo
Gran Chaco
Salado
Paraná
Uruguay
Plate
San Félix
San Ambrosio
Aconcagua
A N D E S
Pampas
Colorado
Negro
Juan Fernández
S O U T H
Chubut
Chico
Patagonia
Deseado
Sala y Gomez
Falkland Islands
Easter Island
Tierra del Fuego
Cape Horn
Drake Passage
Elephant Island
P A C I F I C
South Shetland Islands
King George I.
Ducie Island
Graham Land
Henderson Island
Pitcairn Island
ANTARCTIC PENINSULA
Palmer Land
Peter I Island
Bellingshausen Sea
O C E A N
Ronne
Rapa
Ellsworth Land
Amundsen Sea
Lesser Antarctica
A N T
Marie Byrd Land
Rockefeller Plateau
TRANSANTARCTIC MOUNTAINS
Ross Ice Shelf
Ross Sea
Mount Erebus
Scott Island
Oates Land
Chatham Islands
Balleny Islands
Bounty Islands
Antipodes
New Zealand
Campbell Island
INDIAN

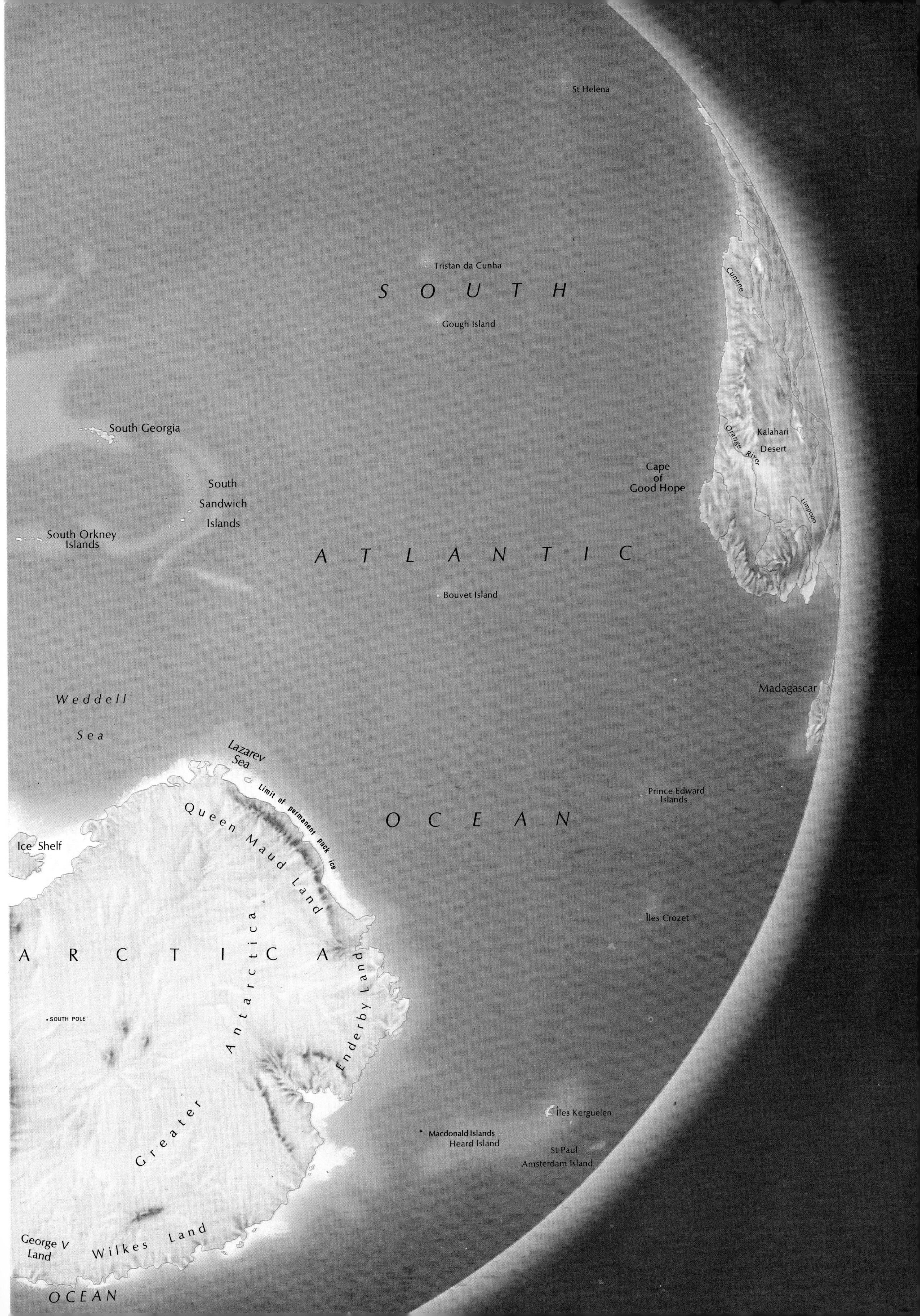

St Helena
Tristan da Cunha
SOUTH
Gough Island
Cunene
Kalahari
Desert
Orange River
South Georgia
Cape
of
Good Hope
South
Sandwich
Islands
Limpopo
South Orkney
Islands
ATLANTIC
Bouvet Island
Madagascar
Weddell
Sea
Lazarev
Sea
Limit of permanent pack ice
Prince Edward
Islands
Queen Maud Land
OCEAN
Ice Shelf
Îles Crozet
ARCTICA
Antarctica
Enderby Land
SOUTH POLE
Greater
Îles Kerguelen
Macdonald Islands
Heard Island
St Paul
Amsterdam Island
George V
Land
Wilkes Land
OCEAN

Azores
Strait of Gibraltar
Chott Melrhir
El Jerid
Mediterra
Gulf of Sirte
Madeira
ATLAS MOUNTAINS
Canary Islands
Libyan
NORTH ATLANTIC OCEAN
Hoggar
Tibesti
S A H A R A
Lac Faguibine
Jebel Marra
Cape Verde Islands
Sénégal
Niger
Lake Chad
Cape Verde
S A H E L
Gambia
Benue
Lake Volta
Adamawa Highlands
Grain Coast
Ivory Coast
Gold Coast
Slave Coast
Bight of Benin
Mouths of the Niger
Ubangi
Sanaga
Uele
Bioko
Gulf of Guinea
Zaire
Príncipe
St Paul Rocks
São Tomé
Pagalu
Lac Mai-Ndombe
Congo
Kasai
Cuango
SOUTH AMERICA
Ascension
S O U T H
Bié Plateau
St Helena
Cubango
Cunene
Okavango
Etosha Pan
A T L A N T I C
Okavango
Lake Ngami
Namib Desert
Walvis Bay
Kalahari Desert
O C E A N
Orange River
Great Karoo
Cape of Good Hope

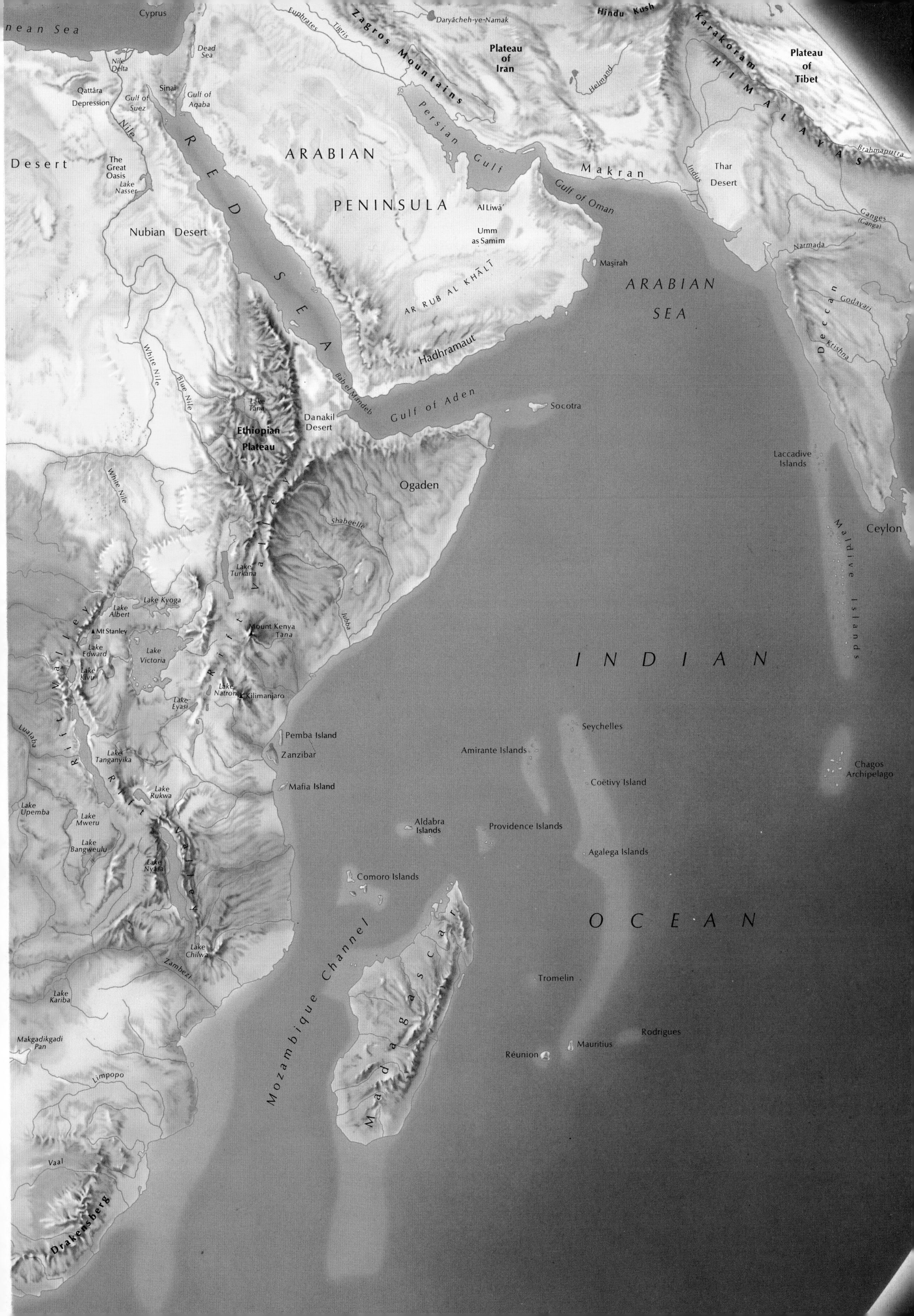

Cyprus
nean Sea
Euphrates
Tigris
Zagros Mountains
Daryācheh-ye-Namak
Hindu Kush
Karakoram
HIMALAYAS
Plateau of Iran
Plateau of Tibet
Dead Sea
Nile Delta
Qattâra Depression
Sinai
Gulf of Suez
Gulf of Aqaba
Nile
Helmand
Persian Gulf
Brahmaputra
Desert
The Great Oasis
Lake Nasser
RED SEA
ARABIAN PENINSULA
Makran
Gulf of Oman
Indus
Thar Desert
Al Liwā'
Umm as Samim
Ganges (Ganga)
Nubian Desert
Narmada
Maṣīrah
AR RUB AL KHĀLĪ
ARABIAN SEA
Godavari
Deccan
Krishna
White Nile
Blue Nile
Hadhramaut
Bab el Mandeb
Lake Tana
Danakil Desert
Gulf of Aden
Socotra
Ethiopian Plateau
Laccadive Islands
Ogaden
Shabeelle
Ceylon
Maldive Islands
Lake Turkana
Rift Valley
Lake Kyoga
Lake Albert
Mt Stanley
Mount Kenya
Tana
Jubba
Lake Edward
Lake Victoria
Lake Kivu
INDIAN
Lake Natron
Kilimanjaro
Lake Eyasi
Lualaba
Pemba Island
Seychelles
Zanzibar
Amirante Islands
Lake Tanganyika
Chagos Archipelago
Mafia Island
Coëtivy Island
Lake Rukwa
Lake Upemba
Lake Mweru
Aldabra Islands
Providence Islands
Lake Bangweulu
Agalega Islands
Lake Nyasa
Comoro Islands
Mozambique Channel
Madagascar
OCEAN
Lake Chilwa
Zambezi
Tromelin
Lake Kariba
Makgadikgadi Pan
Rodrigues
Mauritius
Réunion
Limpopo
Vaal
Drakensberg

NORTH POLE
ARCTIC
Ellesmere Island
Hudson Bay
Baffin Island
Davis Strait
Greenland
LABRADOR
Greenland Sea
Svalbard
Bear Island
Jan Mayen
Denmark Strait
Norwegian Sea
Iceland
Cape Farewell
Faeroe Islands
NORTH
Shetland
Orkney
Rockall
British Isles
Grampians
North Sea
Lake Vänern
Lake Vättern
Irish Sea
Bal
ATLANTIC
Severn
Thames
Elbe
Oder
Neisse
English Channel
Rhine
NOR
Seine
Loire
Danube
Bay of Biscay
OCEAN
Massif Central
Mt. Blanc
ALPS
Azores
Cantabrian Mts
Garonne
Rhône
Po
Dinaric
Pyrenees
Adriatic Sea
Apennines
Ebro
Corsica
Tagus
Balearic Islands
Sardinia
Guadalquivir
MEDITERR
Strait of Gibraltar
Sicily
Madeira
Malta
ATLAS MOUNTAINS
Chott Melrhir
El Jerid
Canary Islands

OCEAN
Severnaya Zemlya
Limit of permanent pack ice
Franz Josef Land
Spitsbergen
Kara Sea
Novaya Zemlya
Barents Sea
North Cape
White Sea
Gulf of Bothnia
Lake Onega
Lake Ladoga
Gulf of Finland
Pechora
Severnaya Dvina
URAL MOUNTAINS
Lena
CENTRAL SIBERIAN PLATEAU
Nizhnyaya Tunguska
Yenisey
Angara
Lake Baikal
WEST SIBERIAN PLAIN
Ob'
Irtysh
EUROPEAN PLAIN
Volga
Dvina
Central Russian Uplands
Vistula
KIRGHIZ STEPPE
Lake Balkhash
Ural
Aral Sea
Syrdar'ya
Kyzylkum
Amudar'ya
Karakumy
Caspian Sea
Dnieper
Dniester
Don
CARPATHIANS
Hungarian Plain
Tisza
Sea of Azov
Caucasus
Black Sea
Danube
Balkan Mountains
Alps
Rhodope
Thrace
Bosporus
Sea of Marmara
Araxes
Lake Van
Lake Urmia
Elbruz Mts
Daryācheh-ye-Namak
ASIA MINOR
Kizil Irmak
Dardanelles
Pindus
Aegean Sea
Tuz Gölü
Taurus
Zagros Mountains
Plateau of Iran
Mesopotamia
Tigris
Euphrates
Cyprus
Crete
ANEAN SEA
Jordan
Dead Sea
Syrian Desert
Persian Gulf
Gulf of Oman

Baltic Sea
Lake Ladoga
Lake Onega
Pechora
Kheta
NORTH EUROPEAN PLAIN
CENTRAL SIBERIAN PLATEAU
Ural Mountains
Ob
Yenisey
Nizhnyaya Tunguska
WEST SIBERIAN PLAIN
Dnieper
Volga
Tobol
Angara
Lena
Ural
Don
Ishim
Ozero Tengiz
Black Sea
Caucasus
Caspian Sea
Kirghiz Steppe
Ustyurt Plateau
Aral Sea
Syrdar'ya
Amudar'ya
Kyzylkum
Karakumy
Irtysh
Lake Baikal
Yablonovyy
Hövsgöl Nuur
Selenga
Kerulen
ALTAI
Ozero Zaysan
Lake Balkhash
Ozero Alakol'
Ebi Nor
Ili
Dzungaria
MONGOLI
Issyk Kul
Tian Shan
Bosten Hu
GOBI
Pik Kommunizma
Tarim
Pamirs
Lop Nur
Yellow River (Huang He)
Plateau of Iran
Hindu Kush
Takla Makan
Ordos
Karakoram
K2
Kunlun Shan
Altun Shan
Qaidam Pendi
Helmand
Qinghai Hu
Plateau of Tibet
Moron Us He (Chang Jiang)
Yellow River (Huang He)
HIMALAYA
Chenab
Sutlej
Indus
Yalong He
Tongtian He
Qin Ling
Indo-Gangetic Plain
Salween
Lancang Jiang
Red Basin
Thar Desert
Brahmaputra
Everest
Kangchenjunga
Dongting Hu
Yangtze Kiang (Chang Jiang)
Ganges (Ganga)
Naga Hills
Narmada
Khasi Hills
Nan Ling
Arabian Sea
Mahanadi
Arakan
Pearl River (Xi Jiang)
Mouths of the Ganges
Red River (Song Hong)
Godavari
Irrawaddy
Salween
Gulf of Tongking
Western Ghats
Deccan
Krishna
Eastern Ghats
Bay of Bengal
INDOCHINA
Hainan
Laccadive Islands
Gulf of Martaban
Chao Phraya
Paracel Islands
Cauvery
Andaman Islands
Andaman Sea
Mekong
Palk Strait
Kra Isthmus
Gulf of Thailand
Maldive Islands
Ceylon
Nicobar Islands
Mouths of the Mekong
Malay Peninsula
INDIAN OCEAN

Nunivak Island
Anadyr
Kolyma
Yana
Indigirka
Verkhoyanskiy Khrebet
Lena
Vilyuy
A
I
R
Aldan
Khr. Dzhungdzhur
Bering Sea
Aleutian Islands
Komandorskiye Ostrova
Kamchatka
Sea of Okhotsk
Kuril Islands
Sakhalin
Tatarskiy Proliv
Khrebet
Shilka
Greater Khingan Range
Hulun Nur
Manchuria
A
Amur
Ussuri
Sikhote Alin
Songhua
Oz Khanka
Hokkaido
NORTH PACIFIC OCEAN
Midway Islands
Sea of Japan
Changbai Shan
Honshu
Korea
Bo Hai
Yellow River (Huang He)
Great Plain of China
Yellow Sea
Korea Strait
Shikoku
Kyushu
Yangtze Kiang (Chang Jiang)
Poyang Hu
East China Sea
Bonin Islands
Volcano Islands
Ryukyu Islands
Taiwan Strait
Taiwan
Marianas
Marshall Islands
Guam
Kiribati
South China Sea
PHILIPPINES
Luzon
Caroline Islands
Mindoro
Samar
Panay
Palawan
Negros
Sulu Sea
Spratly Islands
Mindanao
New Ireland

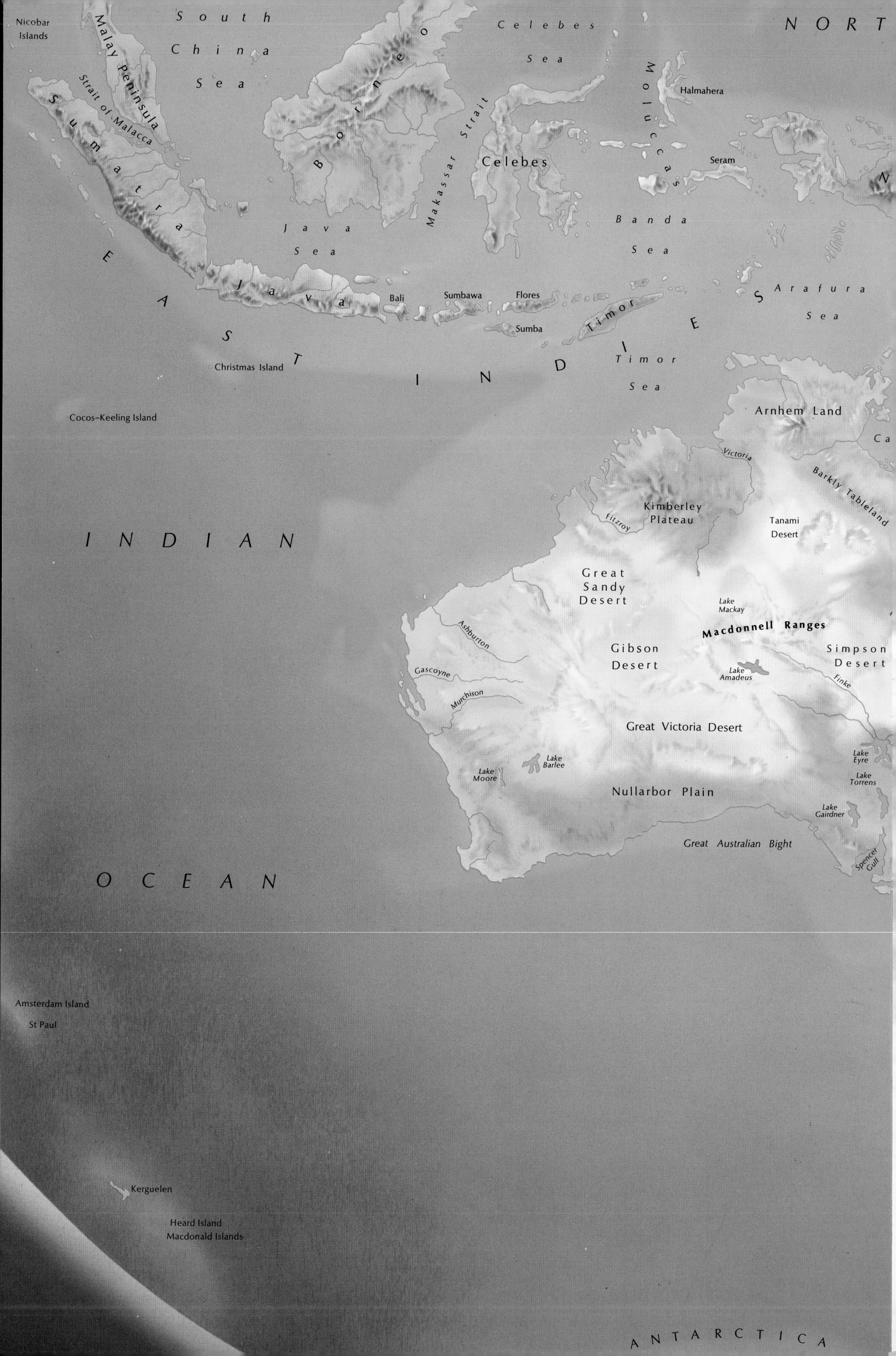
Nicobar Islands
South China Sea
Malay Peninsula
Strait of Malacca
Sumatra
Borneo
Celebes Sea
Makassar Strait
Celebes
Moluccas
Halmahera
Seram
NORT
Java Sea
Banda Sea
Java
Bali
Sumbawa
Flores
Sumba
Timor
Arafura Sea
Timor Sea
EAST INDIES
Christmas Island
Cocos-Keeling Island
Arnhem Land
Ca
Victoria
Barkly Tableland
Kimberley Plateau
Fitzroy
Tanami Desert
INDIAN
Great Sandy Desert
Lake Mackay
Macdonnell Ranges
Ashburton
Gibson Desert
Simpson Desert
Gascoyne
Lake Amadeus
Finke
Murchison
Great Victoria Desert
Lake Eyre
Lake Barlee
Lake Moore
Lake Torrens
Nullarbor Plain
Lake Gairdner
Great Australian Bight
Spencer Gulf
OCEAN
Amsterdam Island
St Paul
Kerguelen
Heard Island
Macdonald Islands
ANTARCTICA

CRONESIA
SOUTH
POLYNESIA
MELANESIA
Admiralty Islands
New Ireland
Bismarck Sea
ew Guinea
New Britain
Bougainville
Solomon Islands
Nauru
Banaba
Kiribati
Tokelau Islands
Tuvalu
Santa Cruz Islands
PACIFIC
OCEAN
Torres Strait
Cape York Peninsula
Gulf of
rpentaria
Coral Sea
Great Barrier Reef
Vanuatu
Samoan Islands
Fiji
Tahiti
Tonga
New Caledonia
Flinders
Georgina
Great Dividing Range
Diamantina
Cooper Creek
Fraser Island
Warrego
Culgoa
Barwon
Lake Frome
Darling
Lachlan
Murray
Murrumbidgee
Mount Kosciusko
Australian Alps
Norfolk Island
Lord Howe Island
Kermadec Islands
Tasman Sea
King Island
Bass Strait
Flinders Island
Tasmania
New Zealand
Cook Strait
Chatham Islands
Foveaux Strait
Stewart Island
Bounty Islands
Antipodes Islands
Auckland Islands
Campbell Island
Macquarie Island

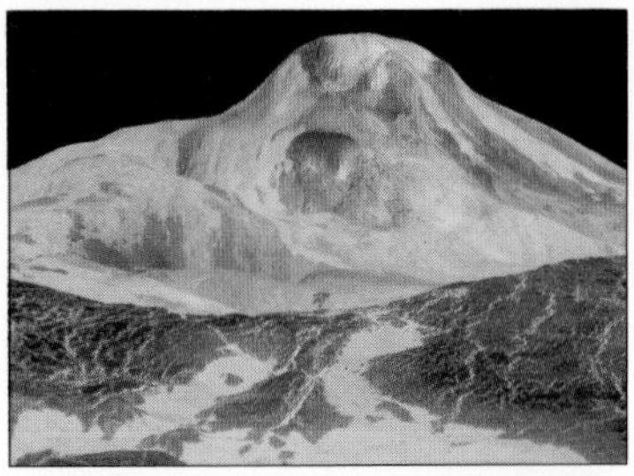

Far left The Caloris basin of Mercury is the largest impact feature on the planet.

Left Radar mapping of Venus has provided this computer-generated image of the volcano, Maat Mons.

Top right Io (left) and Europa are clearly visible as they cross the face of Jupiter.

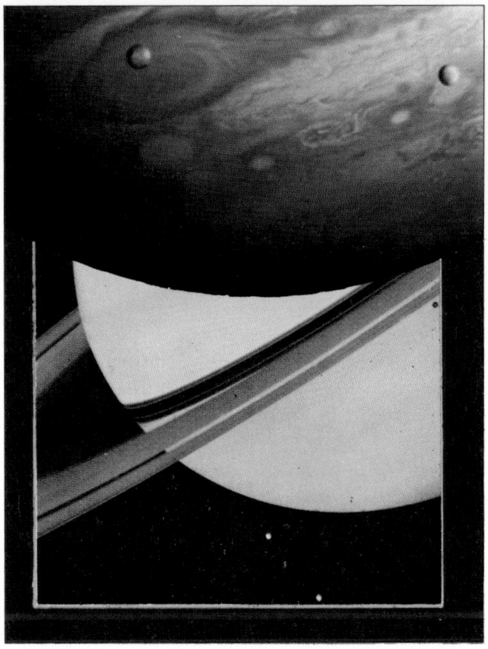

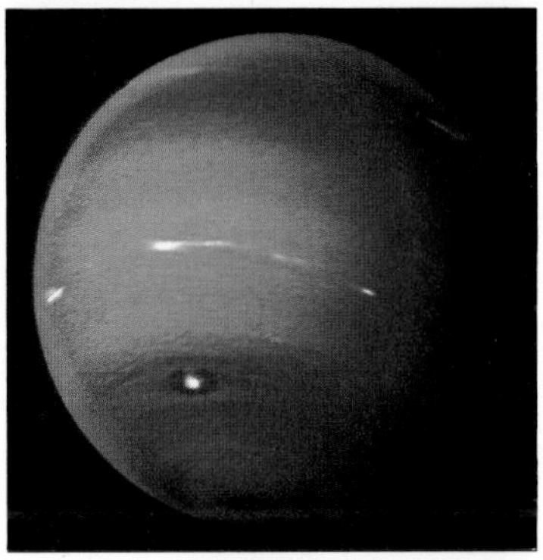

Far left Olympus Mons on Mars is the largest known volcano in the solar system. It is 550 km across at the base and more than 26 km high.

Right The rings of Saturn lie in the equatorial plane and consist of countless ice-covered particles, perhaps up to several metres across.

Left Voyager 2 produced this false-colour image of Neptune in August 1989. A planet-wide haze (red) and white clouds are visible.

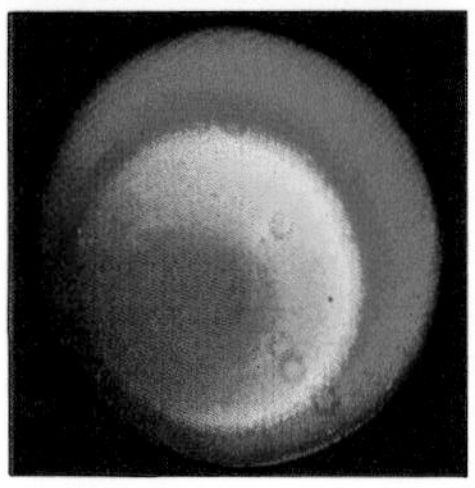

Left This image of Uranus in false-colour was taken from 9.1 million km by Voyager 2. The atmosphere is deep, cold and remarkably clear, but the false colours enhance the polar region. Here, the suggestion is that a brownish haze of smog is concentrated over the pole.

Current theory suggests that the solar system condensed from a primitive solar nebula of gas and dust during an interval of a few tens of millions of years about 4600 million years ago. Gravity caused this nebula to contract, drawing most of its mass into the centre. Turbulence gave the original cloud a tendency to rotate faster and faster, forcing the remainder of the cloud into a disc shape.

The centre of the cloud heated up as it compressed, and so eventually became hot enough for the Sun to begin to shine, through nuclear energy released at its core. Meanwhile the surrounding disc of cloud cooled, allowing material to condense into solid form. Particles stuck together as they collided and progressively larger bodies were built up. These swept up most of the debris to form the planets, which now orbit the Sun.

EARTHLIKE PLANETS

Mercury is the nearest planet to the Sun, spinning three times for every two orbits around the Sun. It has an exceptionally large metallic core which may be responsible for Mercury's weak magnetic field. Mercury is an airless world subject to vast extremes of temperature, from −180°C (−292°F) at night to 430°C (806°F) near the middle of its long day. The Mariner 10 space probe, during the mid-1970s, revealed the surface to be dominated by heavily cratered areas.

Venus has a dense atmosphere with a surface pressure 90 times that of the Earth. Made up of 96% carbon dioxide, the lower layers are rich in sulphur dioxide while sulphuric acid droplets populate the higher clouds. The clouds maintain a mean surface temperature of about 480°C (896°F). The hidden surface has been mapped by radar from orbiting probes and shows a rugged surface with some volcanoes, possibly still active.

Mars has a thin atmosphere of about 96% carbon dioxide mixed with other minor gasses. The polar caps consist of semi-permanent water-ice and solid carbon dioxide. Day and night surface temperatures vary between about −120°C (−184°F) and −20°C (−4°F). Mars has two small satellites, Phobos and Deimos, each less than about 25km (15.5 miles) across, probably captured asteroids.

Mars also shows evidence of erosional processes. The effect of winds is seen in the form of the deposition of sand dunes. Dust storms frequently obscure the surface. The large channels, such as the 5000km (3107 miles) long Valles Marineris, may have been cut by flowing water. Water is abundant in the polar caps and may be widespread, held in as permafrost.

GAS GIANTS

Jupiter has at least 16 satellites and a debris ring system about 50,000km (31,070 miles) above the cloud tops. The outer atmosphere is all that can be directly observed of the planet itself. It is mostly hydrogen with lesser amounts of helium, ammonia, methane and water vapour. Jupiter's rapid rotation causes it to be flattened towards the poles. This rotation and heat flow from the interior cause complex weather patterns. Where cloud systems interact vast storms can occur in the form of vortices. Some last only a few days, but the most persistent of these, the Great Red Spot, has been present since it was first detected in the 17th century.

Saturn is the least dense of the planets. It has a stormy atmosphere situated above a 30,000km (18,640 miles) layer of liquid hydrogen and helium distorted by rotation.

The rings of Saturn are thought to be mostly made of icy debris, from 10m (33 ft) down to a few microns in size, derived from the break-up of a satellite. The rings are less than 1km thick.

Uranus, consisting mainly of hydrogen, was little known until Voyager 2 flew by it in 1986. The probe discovered ten new satellites and provided images of the planet's eleven icy rings of debris.

Neptune was visited by Voyager 2 in 1989. Six new satellites were discovered, one larger than Nereid, the smaller of the two known satellites. Triton, the largest satellite, was found to be smaller than previous estimates. The turbulent atmosphere is a mixture of hydrogen, helium and methane.

Pluto is now 4500 million km from the Sun, closer than Neptune until 1999, but its eccentric orbit will take it to 7500 million km by 2113. A tenuous atmosphere has been found above a surface of frozen methane. Charon, the satellite, is half Pluto's diameter.

	SUN	MERCURY	VENUS	EARTH	(MOON)	MARS	JUPITER	SATURN	URANUS	NEPTUNE	PLUTO
Mass (Earth = 1)	333 400	0.055	0.815	1 (5.97 10^{24}kg)	0.012	0.107	317.8	95.2	14.5	17.2	0.003
Volume (Earth = 1)	1 306 000	0.06	0.88	1	0.020	0.150	1 323	752	64	54	0.007
Density (water = 1)	1.41	5.43	5.24	5.52	3.34	3.94	1.33	0.70	1.30	1.64	2.0
Equatorial diameter (km)	1 392 000	4 878	12 104	12 756	3 476	6 794	142 800	120 000	52 000	48 400	2 302
Polar flattening	0	0	0	0.003	0	0.005	0.065	0.108	0.060	0.021	0
'Surface' gravity (Earth = 1)	27.9	0.37	0.88	1	0.16	0.38	2.69	1.19	0.93	1.22	0.05
Number of satellites greater than 100 km diameter	—	0	0	1	—	0	7	13	7	6	1
Total number of satellites	—	0	0	1	—	2	16	17	15	8	1
Period of rotation (in Earth days)	25.38	58.65	−243 (retrograde)	23hr 56m 4 secs	27.32	1.03	0.414	0.426	−0.74 (retrograde)	0.67	−6.39 (retrograde)
Length of year (in Earth days and years)	—	88 days	224.7 days	365.26 days	—	687 days	11.86 years	29.46 years	84.01 years	164.8 years	247.7 years
Distance from Sun (mean) Mkm	—	57.9	108.9	149.6	—	227.9	778.3	1 427	2 870	4 497	5 900

EARTH STRUCTURE

Internally, the Earth may be divided broadly into crust, mantle and core (*see right*).

The crust is a thin shell constituting only 0.2% of the mass of the Earth. The continental crust varies in thickness from 20 to 90km (12 to 56 miles) and is less dense than ocean crust. Two-thirds of the continents are overlain by sedimentary rocks of average thickness less than 2km (1.2 miles). Ocean crust is on average 7km (4.4 miles) thick. It is composed of igneous rocks, basalts and gabbros.

Crust and mantle are separated by the Mohorovičić Discontinuity (Moho). The mantle differs from the crust. It is largely igneous. The upper mantle extends to 350km (218 miles). The lower mantle has a more uniform composition. A sharp discontinuity defines the meeting of mantle and core. The inability of the outer core to transmit seismic waves suggests it is liquid. It is probably of metallic iron with other elements – sulphur, silicon, oxygen, potassium and hydrogen have all been suggested. The inner core is solid and probably of nickel-iron. Temperature at the core-mantle boundary is about 3700°C (5430°F) and 4000°–4500°C (7230°–8130°F) in the inner core.

THE ATMOSPHERE

The ancient atmosphere lacked free oxygen. Plant life added oxygen to the atmosphere and transferred carbon dioxide to the crustal rocks and the hydrosphere. The composition of air today at 79% nitrogen and 20% oxygen remains stable by the same mechanism.

Solar energy is distributed around the Earth by the atmosphere. Most of the weather and climate processes occur in the troposphere at the lowest level. The atmosphere also shields the Earth. Ozone exists to the extent of 2 parts per million and is at its maximum at 30km (19 miles). It is the only gas which absorbs ultra-violet radiation. Water-vapour and CO_2 keep out infra-red radiation.

Above 80km (50 miles) nitrogen and oxygen tend to separate into atoms which become ionized (an ion is an atom lacking one or more of its electrons). The ionosphere is a zone of ionized belts which reflect radio waves back to Earth. These electrification belts change their position dependent on light and darkness and external factors.

Beyond the ionosphere, the magnetosphere extends to outer space. Ionized particles form a plasma (a fourth state of matter, ie. other than solid, liquid, gas) held in by the Earth's magnetic field.

ORIGIN AND DEVELOPMENT OF LIFE

Primitive life-forms (blue-green algae) are found in rocks as old as 3500Ma (million years) and, although it cannot yet be proved, the origin of life on Earth probably dates back to about 4000Ma. It seems likely that the oxygen levels in the atmosphere increased only slowly at first, probably to about 1% of the present amount by 2000Ma. As the atmospheric oxygen built up so the protective ozone layer developed to allow organisms to live in shallower waters. More highly developed photosynthesising organisms led to the development of oxygen breathing animals. The first traces of multicellular life occur about 1000Ma; by 700Ma complex animals, such as jellyfish, worms and primitive molluscs, had developed.

Organisms developed hard parts that allowed their preservation as abundant fossils at about 570Ma. This coincided with a period of explosive evolution of marine life. Fishes appeared about 475Ma and by 400Ma land plants had developed. Between 340 and 305Ma dense vegetation covered the land, amphibians emerged from the sea, and by about 250Ma had given rise to reptiles and the first mammals. These expanded hugely about 65Ma.

EARTHQUAKES

Earthquakes are the manifestation of a slippage at a geological fault. The majority occur at tectonic plate boundaries. The interior of a plate tends to be stable and less subject to earthquakes. When plates slide past each other strain energy is suddenly released. Even though the amount of movement is very small the energy released is colossal. It

THE EARTH'S SHELLS

Lithosphere

oceanic crust — continental crust

Moho

depth (km) 350 — transition zone

upper mantle

900

seismic discontinuities

lower mantle

2900 — core-mantle discontinuity

outer core

4700 — transition zone

5150

inner core

6370

SEISMIC WAVES

Earthquake focus

S

surface waves

S waves

Mantle

Core

P waves

Shadow zone

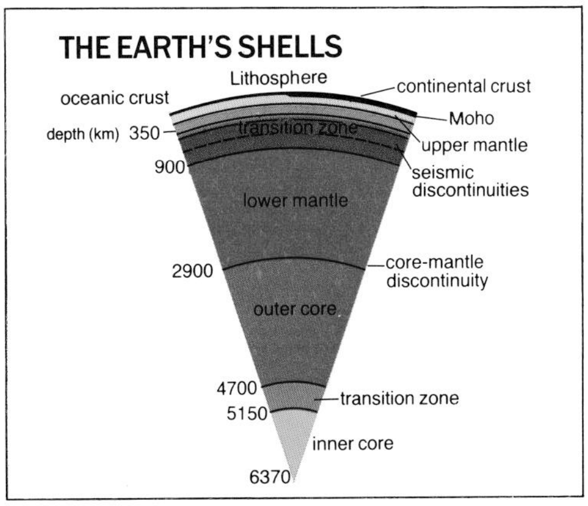

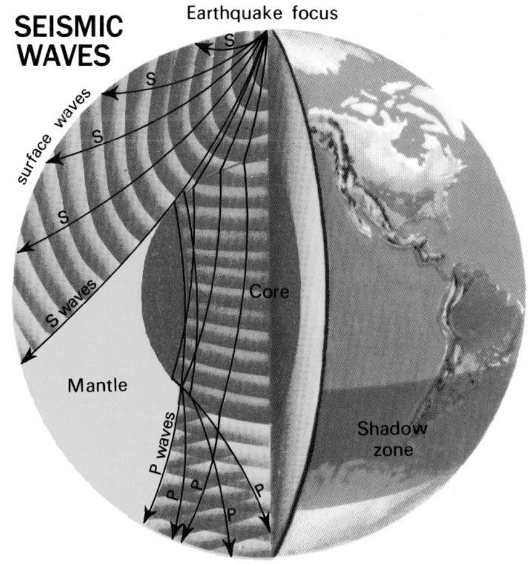

Above In an earthquake the shock generates vibrations, or seismic waves, which radiate in all directions from the focus. The slowest waves are Surface waves which transmit the bulk of the energy in shallow earthquakes.

Other waves known as body waves pass through the body of the Earth. Primary (P) waves are compressional. They are able to travel through solids and fluids and cause the particles of the Earth to vibrate in the direction of travel. Secondary (S) waves are transverse, or shear, waves. They can only pass through solids and do not penetrate the Earth's outer core.

is transferred in shock waves.

Some earthquakes originate at depths as shallow as 5km (3 miles) below the surface. Others, however, may be as deep as 700km (435 miles). The precise cause of these very deep earthquakes is not known. The point from which the earthquake is generated is the focus and the point on the surface immediately above the focus is the epicentre.

The Richter Scale is used to define the magnitude of earthquakes. Each unit represents an increase in the amount of energy released by a factor of around 30 over the preceding point on the Scale. There is no upper limit, but the greatest magnitude yet recorded is 8.9.

VOLCANOES

Almost all the world's active volcanoes, numbering 500–600 are located at convergent plate boundaries. Those are the volcanoes which give spectacular demonstrations of volcanic activity. Yet far greater volcanic activity continues unnoticed and without cessation at mid-ocean ridges where magma from the upper mantle is quietly being extruded on to the ocean floor to create new crustal material.

Chemical composition of magmas and the amount of gas they contain determine the nature of a volcanic eruption. Gas-charged basalts produce cinder cones. Violent eruptions usually occur when large clouds of lava come into contact with water to produce fine-grained ash. When andesites are charged with gas they erupt with explosive violence.

Nuées ardentes (burning clouds) are extremely destructive. They are produced by magmas which erupt explosively sending molten lava fragments and gas at great speeds down the mountain sides.

In spite of the destructiveness of many volcanoes people still live in their vicinity because of the fertile volcanic soils. Geothermal energy in regions of volcanic activity is another source of attraction.

GRAVITY AND MAGNETISM

The Earth is spheroidal in form because it is a rotating body. Were it not so it would take the form of a sphere. The shape is determined by the mass of the Earth and its rate of rotation. Centrifugal force acting outwards reduces the pull of gravity acting inwards so that gravity at the equator is less than at the poles. Uneven distribution of matter within the Earth distorts the shape taken up by the mean sea-level surface (the geoid). Today the belief is that electric currents generated in the semi-molten outer core are responsible for the magnetic field. The Earth's magnetic poles have experienced a number of reversals, the north pole becoming the south and vice-versa.

ROCK AND HYDROLOGICAL CYCLES

Right In the most familiar cycle rain falls onto the land, drains to the sea, evaporates, condenses into cloud and is precipitated onto the land again. Water is also released and recirculated. In the rock cycle rocks are weathered and eroded, forming sediments which are compacted into rocks that are eventually exposed and then weathered again.

radiation from the Sun — interplanetary space

escape of hydrogen

ozone layer

clouds

circulation through atmosphere

precipitation

condensation

volcanic gases

photosynthesis

evaporation and transpiration

snow

evaporation from oceans

effusion

glacial ice

mid-ocean ridge

volcanic rocks

sediments

surface run-off

weathering of rocks

hydrothermal circulation

plutonic rocks

rock – gas reactions

magma

conduction

magma

convection

gas – magma devolatilisation of minerals

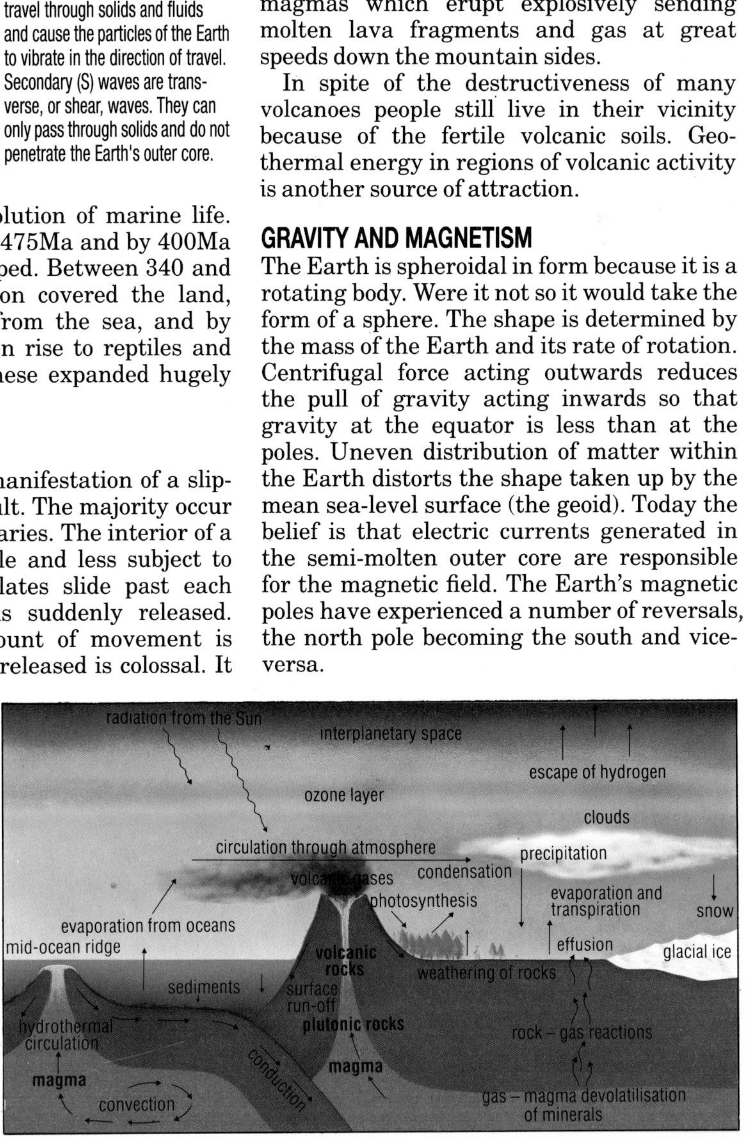

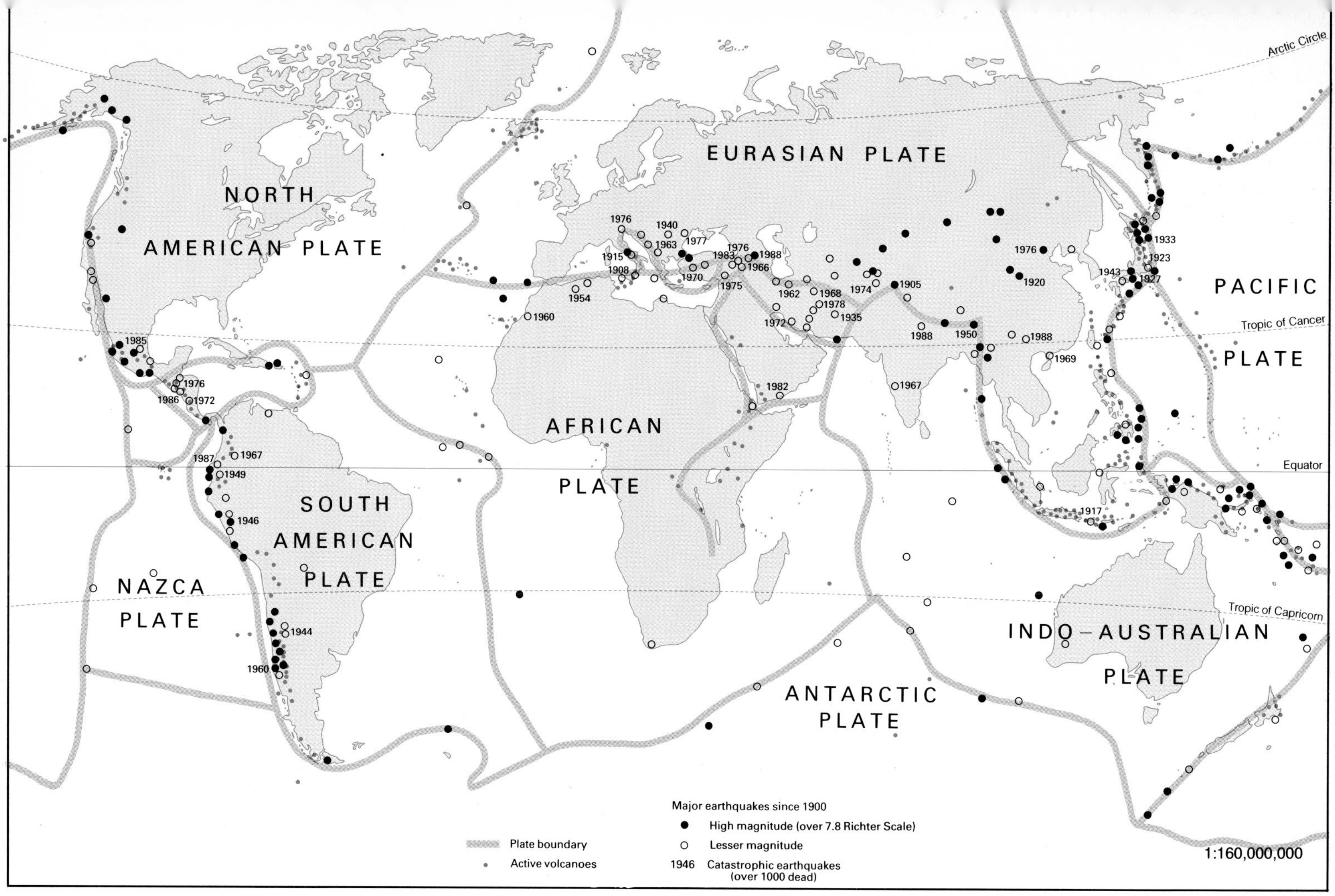

ECONOMIC MINERALS

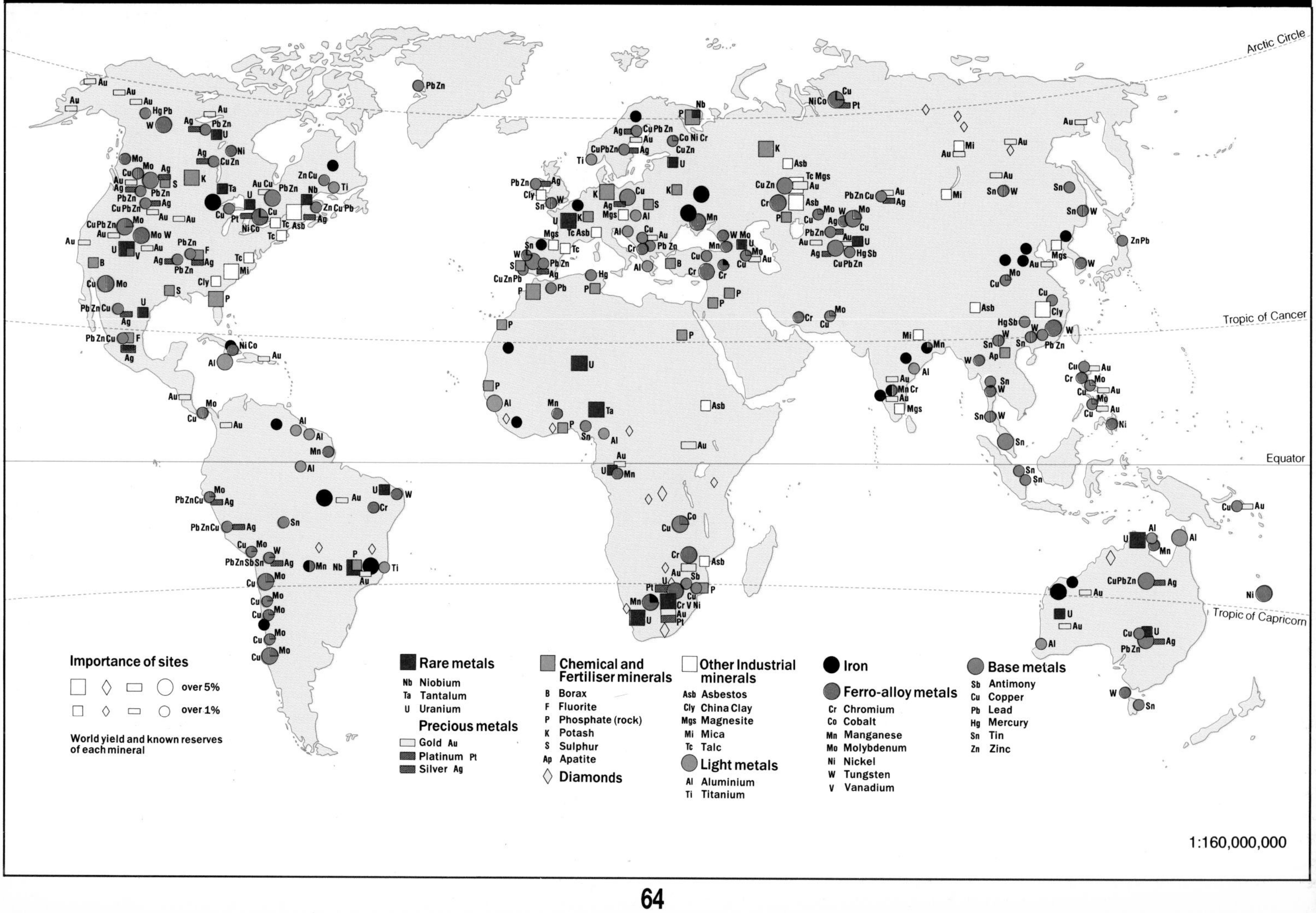

EURASIAN PLATE

NORTH
AMERICAN PLATE

PACIFIC
PLATE

1976 1940
1963 1977
1915 1983 1988
1908 1976 1966
1970 1975
1954 1905
1960 1962
1968 1974
1978
1972 1935

1933
1923
1943 1927
1920
1976

Tropic of Cancer

1985

1976
1986 1972

AFRICAN

PLATE

1987 1967
1949

1946

SOUTH
AMERICAN
PLATE

NAZCA
PLATE

1982

1988 1950

1988

1969

1967

Equator

1917

INDO–AUSTRALIAN

PLATE

1944

Tropic of Capricorn

1960

ANTARCTIC
PLATE

Major earthquakes since 1900

● High magnitude (over 7.8 Richter Scale)

○ Lesser magnitude

1946 Catastrophic earthquakes
(over 1000 dead)

Plate boundary

· Active volcanoes

1:160,000,000

Arctic Circle

Tropic of Cancer

Equator

Tropic of Capricorn

Importance of sites

▢ ◇ ▭ ◯ over 5%

▫ ◇ ▭ ◯ over 1%

World yield and known reserves
of each mineral

Rare metals
Nb Niobium
Ta Tantalum
U Uranium

Precious metals
Gold Au
Platinum Pt
Silver Ag

**Chemical and
Fertiliser minerals**
B Borax
F Fluorite
P Phosphate (rock)
K Potash
S Sulphur
Ap Apatite

◇ Diamonds

**Other Industrial
minerals**
Asb Asbestos
Cly China Clay
Mgs Magnesite
Mi Mica
Tc Talc

Light metals
Al Aluminium
Ti Titanium

● **Iron**

● **Ferro-alloy metals**
Cr Chromium
Co Cobalt
Mn Manganese
Mo Molybdenum
Ni Nickel
W Tungsten
V Vanadium

● **Base metals**
Sb Antimony
Cu Copper
Pb Lead
Hg Mercury
Sn Tin
Zn Zinc

1:160,000,000

64

Westerlies

N.E.
Trades

N.E. Trades

Doldrums

S.E. Trades

S.E. Trades

N.E. Monsoon

Inter-tropical Convergence Zone

N.E. Trades

S.E. Trades

Equator

Tropic of Capricorn

Arctic Circle

Tropic of Cancer

Westerlies

Roaring Forties

Roaring Forties

| | -40 | -30 | -20 | -10 | 0 | 10 | 20 | 30 | 40 | 50 | 60 | 70 | 80 | 90 | °F |
| | -40 | | -30 | | -20 | | -10 | | 0 | | 10 | | 20 | | 30 | °C |

⟶ Prevailing Surface Wind

1:160,000,000

TEMPERATURE: JULY

Arctic Circle

Westerlies

Tropic of Cancer

N.E. Trades

S.W. Monsoon

Inter-tropical Convergence Zone

Doldrums

S.E. Trades

S.E. Trades

Equator

S.E. Monsoon

Tropic of Capricorn

Roaring Forties

S.E. Trades

Roaring Forties

| | -40 | -30 | -20 | -10 | 0 | 10 | 20 | 30 | 40 | 50 | 60 | 70 | 80 | 90 | °F |
| | -40 | | -30 | | -20 | | -10 | | 0 | | 10 | | 20 | | 30 | °C |

⟶ Prevailing Surface Wind

1:160,000,000

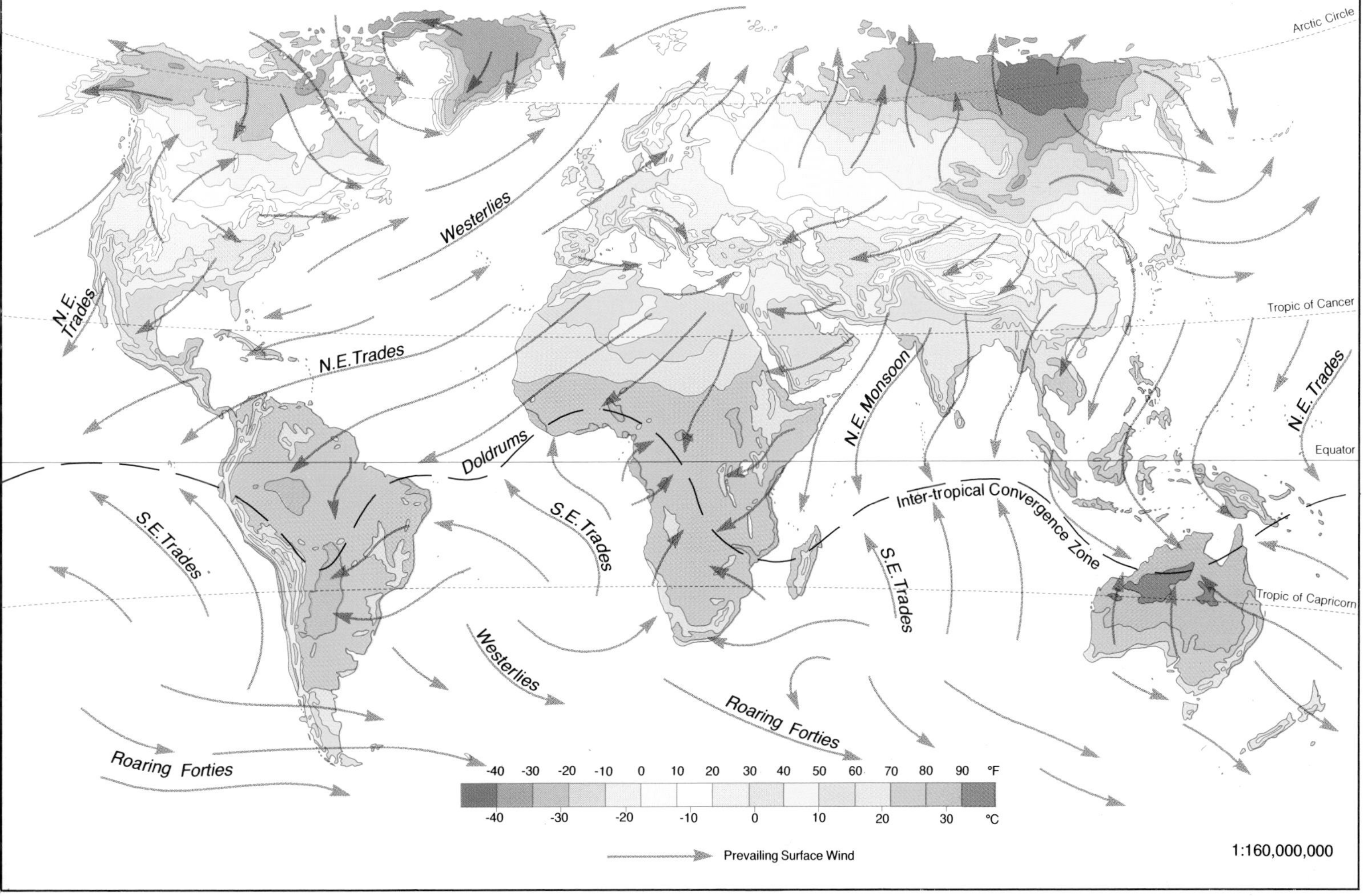

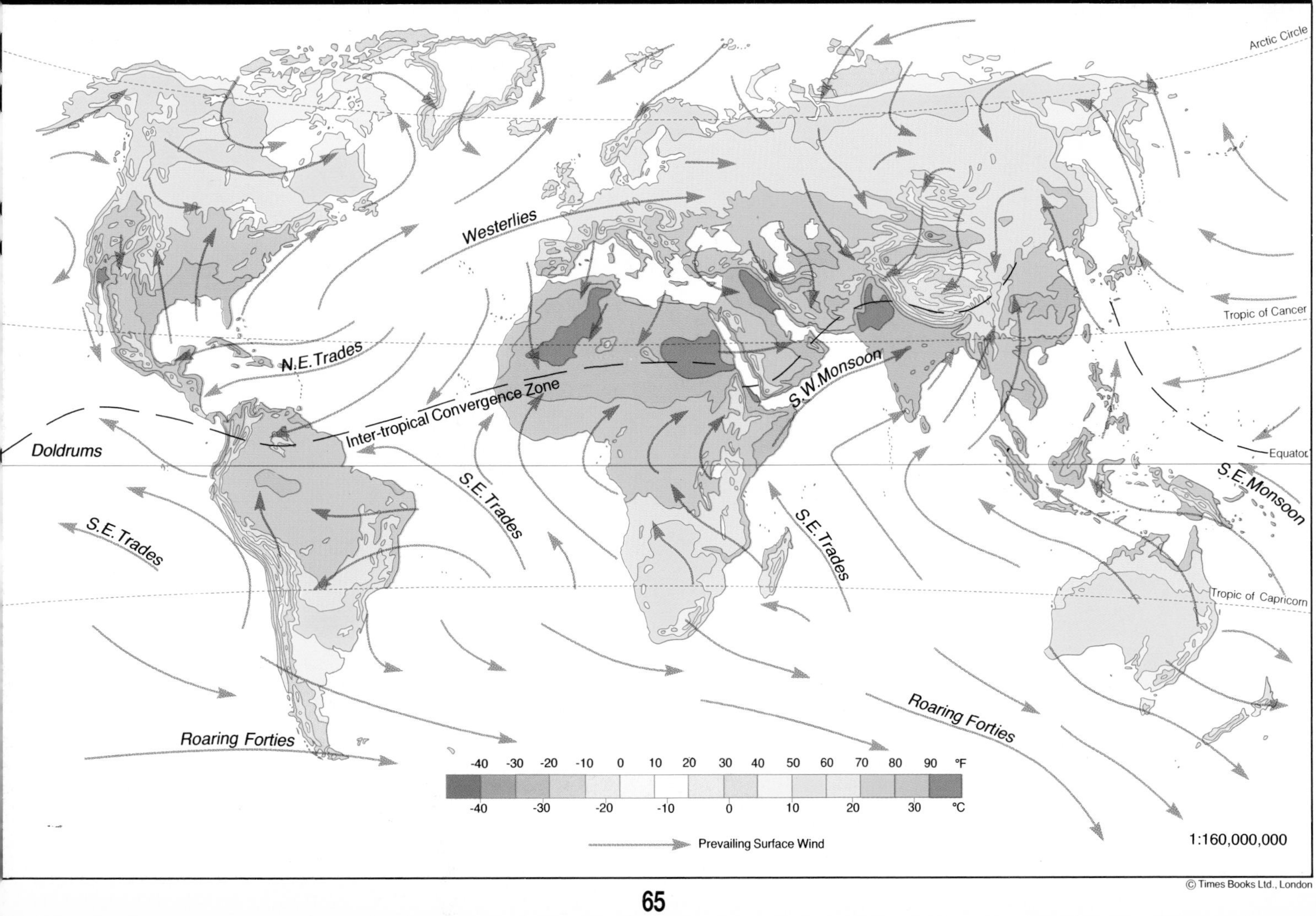

Mean Annual Precipitation

0	100	200	400	600	1000	2000	4000 millimetres
0	3·9	7·9	15·7	23·6	39·4	78·7	157·5 inches

1:160,000,000

NATURAL VEGETATION

Types of Natural Vegetation

Tundra and Mountain Vegetation	Mediterranean Scrub	Monsoon Forest
Coniferous Forest	Prairie and Steppe	Dry Tropical Forest
Mixed Forest	Savannah	Sub-Tropical Forest
Broadleaf Forest	Tropical Rain Forest	Desert

1:160,000,000

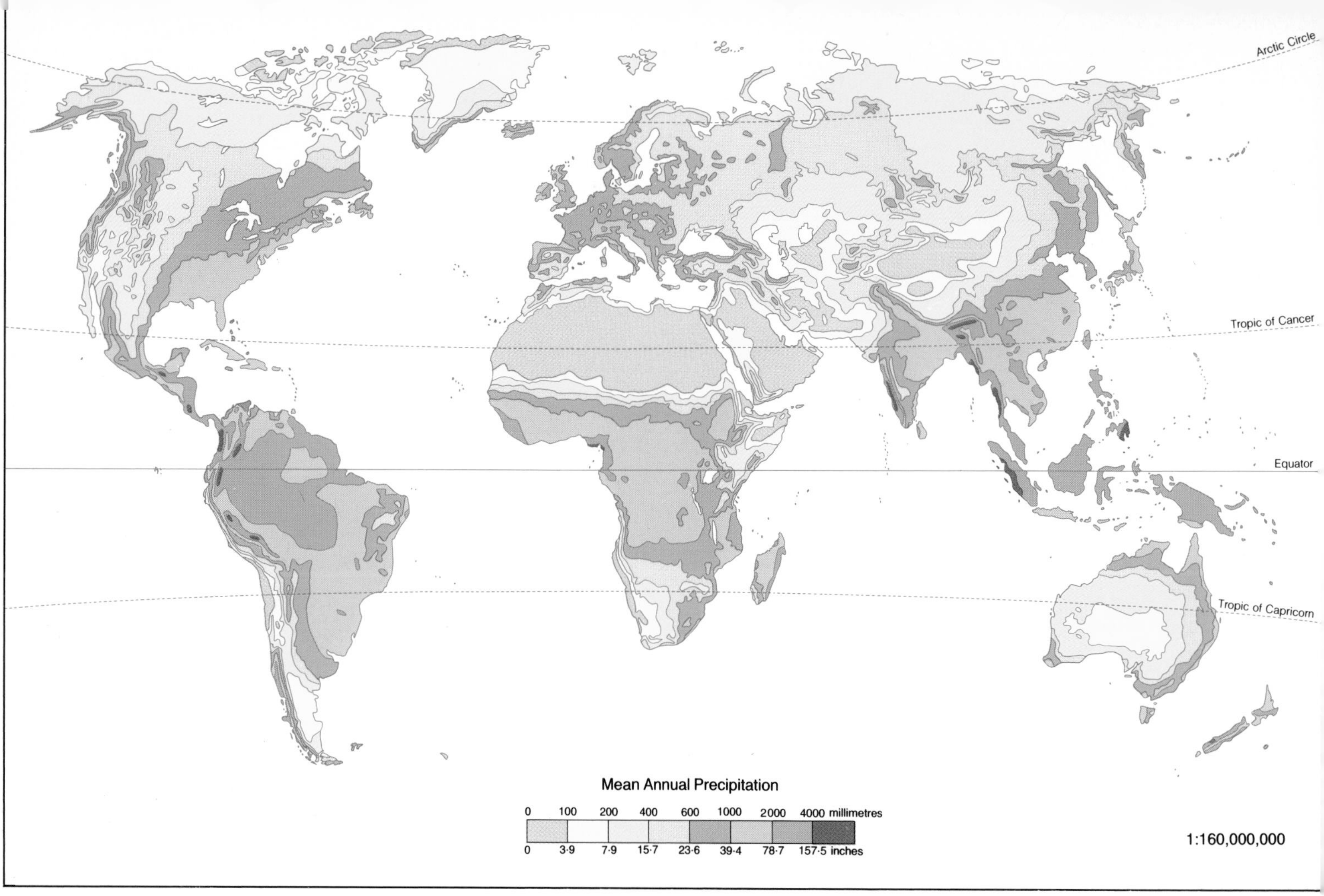

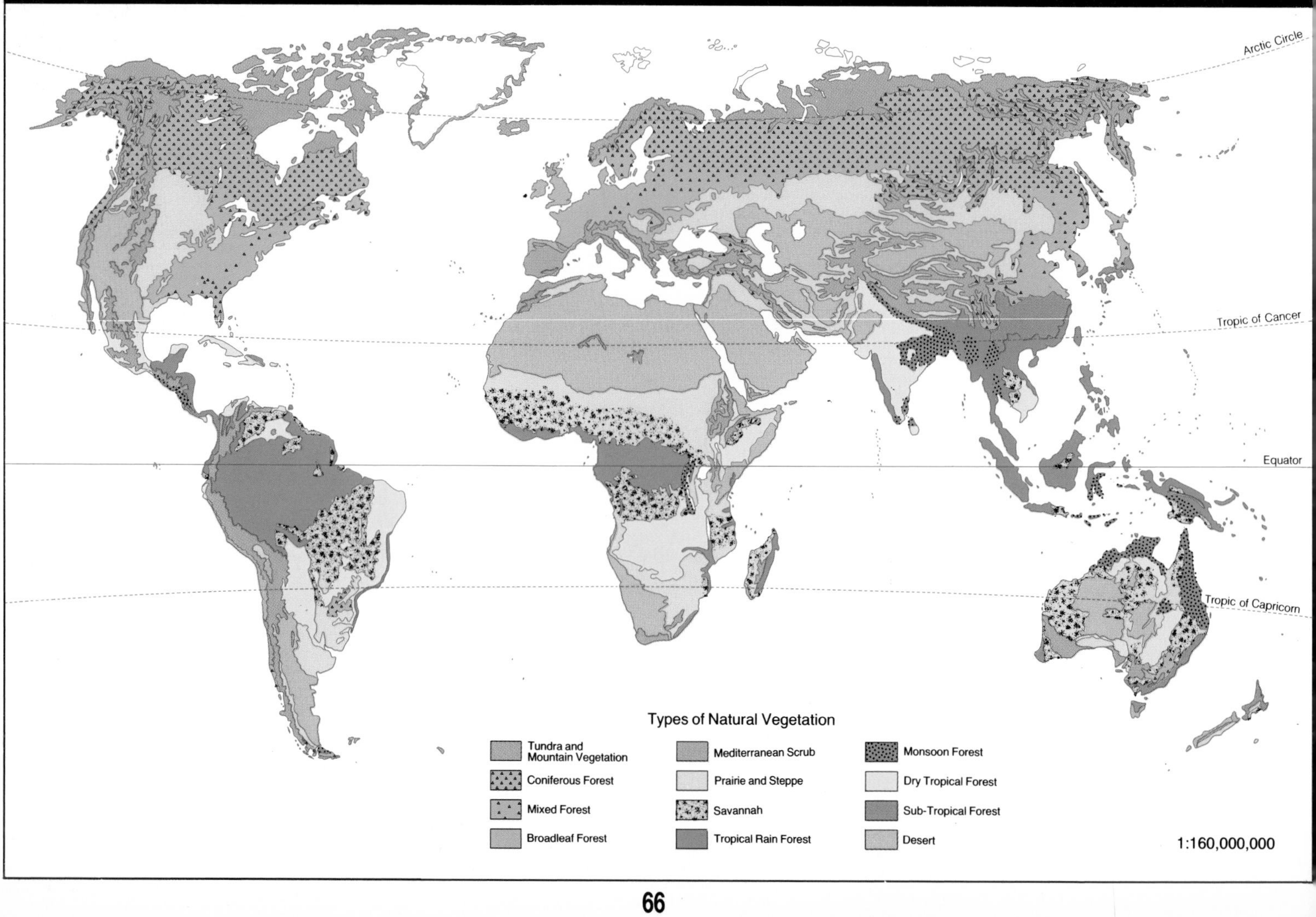

Metropolitan Areas

- ■ Population over 10 million
- ● Population over 5 million
- ○ Population over 1 million

| 0 | 1 | 5 | 25 | 100 | 250 | 500 | Persons per square mile |
| 0 | 0·4 | 2 | 10 | 40 | 100 | 200 | Persons per square kilometre |

1:160,000,000

POPULATION CHANGE

Percentage Change

- 4
- 3
- 2
- 0

INCREASE

DECREASE

WORLD POPULATION GROWTH

Estimated (x 1000 millions)

Rest of Asia
China
Africa
C. & S. America
N. America
U.S.S.R.*
Europe
Oceania

1950 60 70 80 90 2000

1:160,000,000

* USSR – Former USSR including Estonia, Latvia and Lithuania

© Times Books Ltd., London

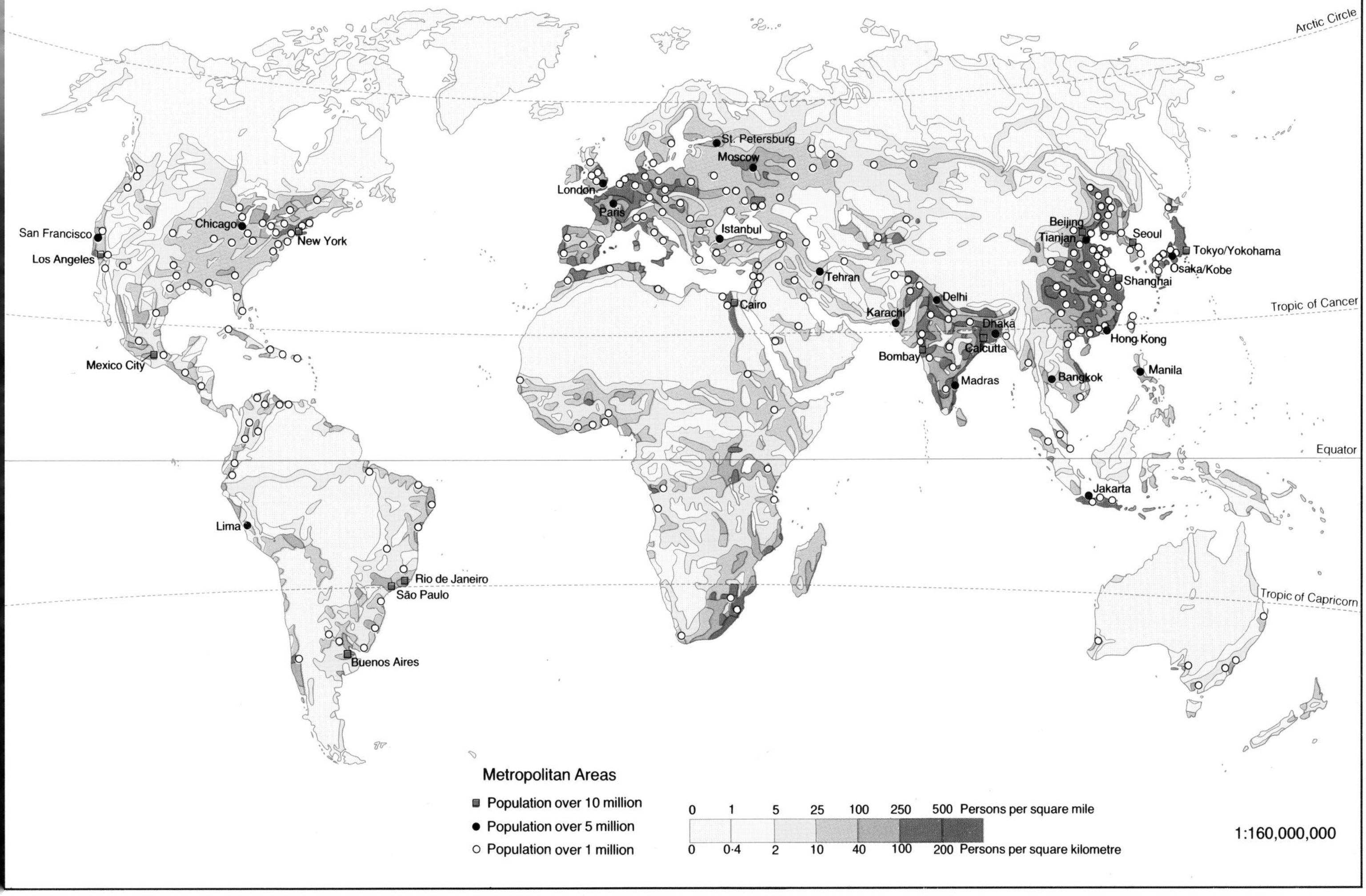

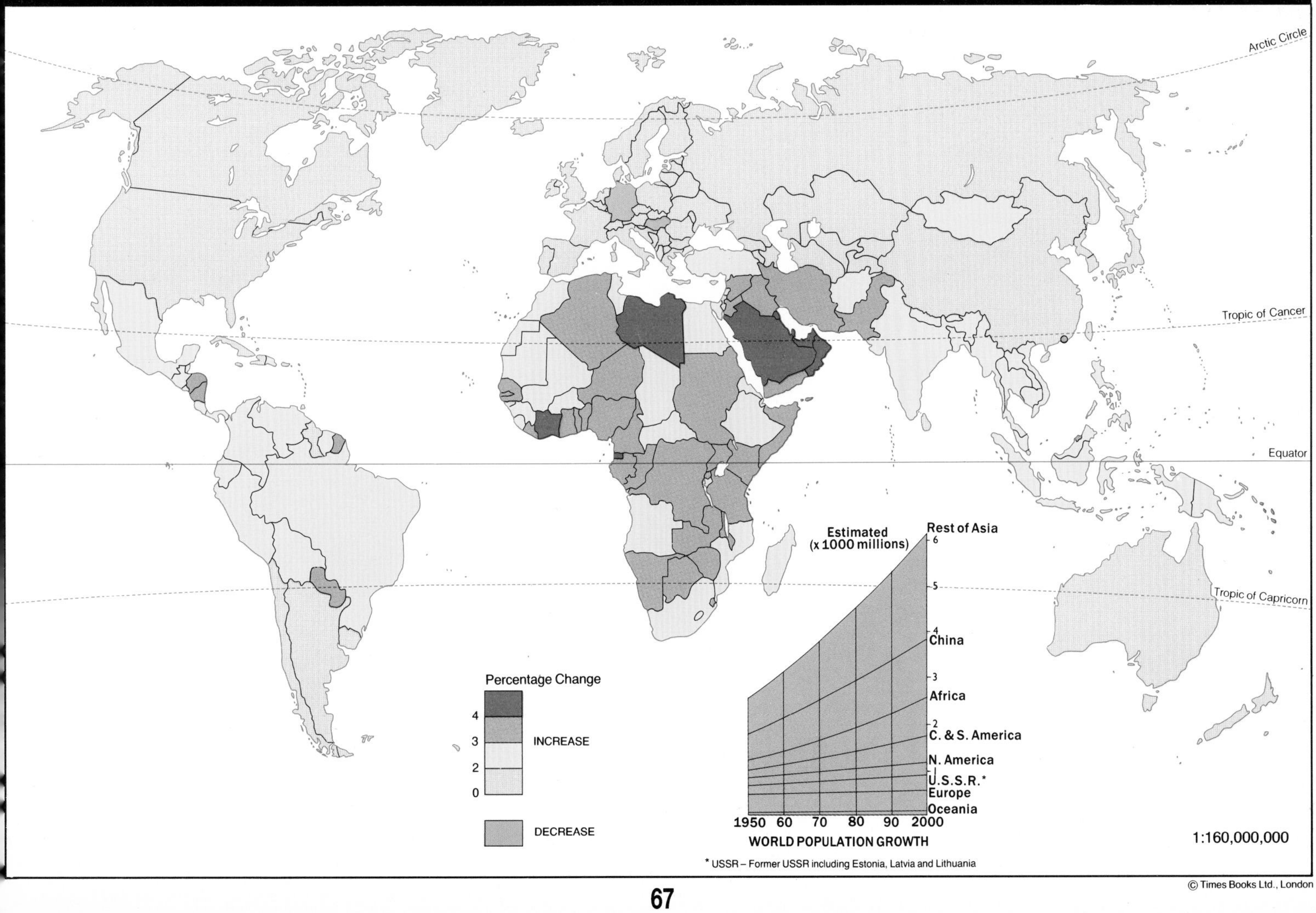

TIME ZONES

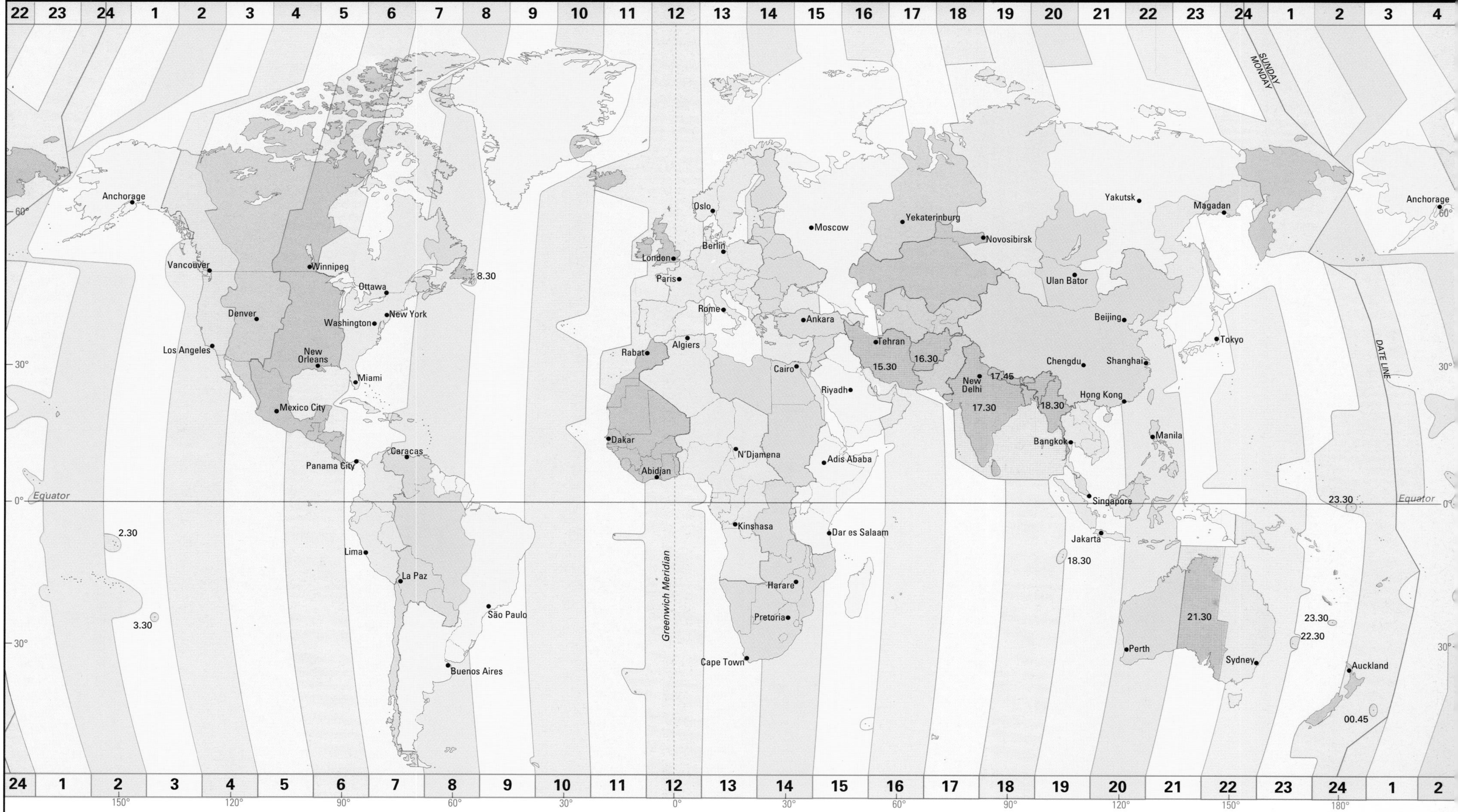

Zone times (given in bold figures at the top and bottom of map) are the Standard Times kept on land and sea compared with 12 hours (noon) Greenwich Mean Time. Daylight Saving Time (normally one hour in advance of local Standard time), which is observed by certain countries for part of the year, is not shown on the map.

1:105 000 000

This page explains the main symbols, lettering style and height/depth colours used on the reference maps on pages 2 to 76. The scale of each map is indicated at the foot of each page. Abbreviations used on the maps appear at the beginning of the index.

BOUNDARIES

- International
- International under Dispute
- Cease Fire Line
- Autonomous or State
- Administrative
- Maritime (National)
- International Date Line

COMMUNICATIONS

- Motorway/Express Highway
- Under Construction
- Major Highway
- Other Roads
- Under Construction
- Track
- Road Tunnel
- Car Ferry
- Main Railway
- Other Railway
- Under Construction
- Rail Tunnel
- Rail Ferry
- Canal
- International Airport
- Other Airport

LAKE FEATURES

- Freshwater
- Saltwater
- Seasonal
- Salt Pan

LANDSCAPE FEATURES

- Glacier, Ice Cap
- Marsh, Swamp
- Sand Desert, Dunes

OTHER FEATURES

- River
- Seasonal River
- Pass, Gorge
- Dam, Barrage
- Waterfall, Rapid
- Aqueduct
- Reef
- 4231 Summit, Peak
- 217 Spot Height, Depth
- Well
- Oil Field
- Gas Field
- Gas / Oil Oil/Natural Gas Pipeline
- Gemsbok Nat. Pk National Park
- UR Historic Site

LETTERING STYLES

CANADA	Independent Nation
FLORIDA	State, Province or Autonomous Region
Gibraltar (U.K.)	Sovereignty of Dependent Territory
Lothian	Administrative Area
LANGUEDOC	Historic Region
Loire *Vosges*	Physical Feature or Physical Region

TOWNS AND CITIES

Square symbols denote capital cities. Each settlement is given a symbol according to its relative importance, with type size to match.

New York	Major City
Montréal	City
Ottawa	Small City
Québec	Large Town
St John's	Town
Yorkton	Small Town
Jasper	Village
	Built-up-area

Height

6000m
5000m
4000m
3000m
2000m
1000m
500m
200m
0 Sea Level

0
200m
2000m
4000m
6000m
8000m

Depth

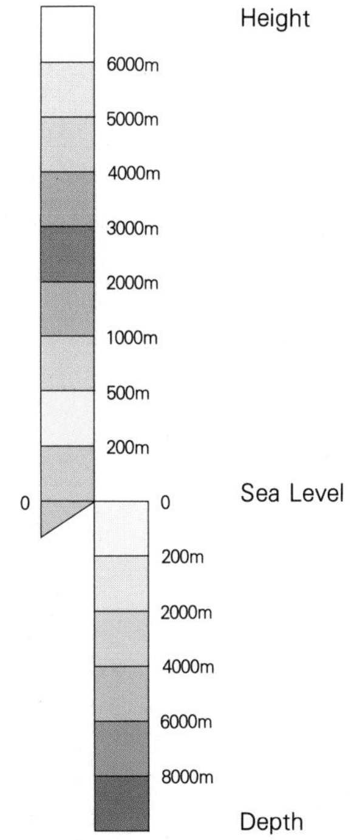

For more information about each country refer to the States and Territories section (page number in bold type). For large scale map refer to map section (page number in italic).

Burma **9** *30*
Cambodia **9** *30*
China **11-12** *31*
Georgia **17** *21*
India **19-20** *42-44*
Indonesia **20** *27*
Iran **20** *41*
Iraq **20** *40-41*
Israel **20** *45*
Japan **21** *28-29*
Jordan **21** *40*
Kazakhstan **22** *24*
Kirghizia **22** *24*
Korea, North **22** *28*
Korea, South **22** *28*
Kuwait **22-23** *41*
Laos **23** *30*
Lebanon **23** *45*
Malaysia **25** *30*
Maldives **25** *44*
Mongolia **27** *26*

Nepal **28** *43*
Oman **29** *38*
Pakistan **29** *42*
Philippines **30** *27*
Qatar **31** *41*
Russian Federation **31** *24-25*
Saudi Arabia **32** *40-41*
Singapore **33** *30*
Sri Lanka **34** *44*
Syria **35** *40*
Taiwan **36** *31*
Tajikistan **36** *39*
Thailand **36** *30*
Turkey **37** *40*
Turkmenistan **37** *38*
United Arab Emirates **38** *41*
Uzbekistan **41** *38*
Vietnam **42** *30*
Yemen **42** *38*
AUSTRALASIA
Australia **5-6** *32-34*

Fiji **16** *33*
Kiribati **22** *33*
Marshall Islands **26** *37*
Micronesia,
Federated States of **26** *36*
Nauru **28** *33*
New Zealand **28** *35*
Papua New Guinea **30** *32*
Solomon Islands **33** *33*
Tonga **36** *33*
Tuvalu **37** *33*
Vanuatu **41** *33*
Western Samoa **42** *33*
EUROPE
Albania **4** *17*
Andorra **4** *15*
Austria **6** *18*
Belarus **7** *19*
Belgium **7** *13*
Bosnia-Herzegovina **8** *16-17*
Bulgaria **8-9** *17*

Croatia **13** *16*
Cyprus **13** *45*
Czech Republic **14** *18-19*
Denmark **14** *11*
Estonia **15** *20*
Finland **16** *12*
France **16** *14*
Germany **17** *18*
Greece **18** *17*
Hungary **19** *18-19*
Iceland **19** *12*
Ireland **20** *9*
Italy **21** *16*
Latvia **23** *19*
Liechtenstein **24** *16*
Lithuania **24** *19*
Luxembourg **24** *13*
Macedonia **24** *17*
Malta **25** *16*
Moldova **26** *19*
Monaco **27** *14*

Netherlands **28** *13*
Norway **29** *12*
Poland **30** *18-19*
Portugal **30** *15*
Romania **31** *17*
Russian Federation **31** *20-21*
San Marino **32** *16*
Slovakia **33** *18-19*
Slovenia **33** *16*
Spain **34** *15*
Sweden **35** *12*
Switzerland **35** *16*
Ukraine **38** *21*
United Kingdom **38-39** *6-9*
Vatican City **42**
Yugoslavia **42-43** *17*

NATIONS OF EUROPE

1:15M 0 200 400 600 km; 0 100 200 300 mls

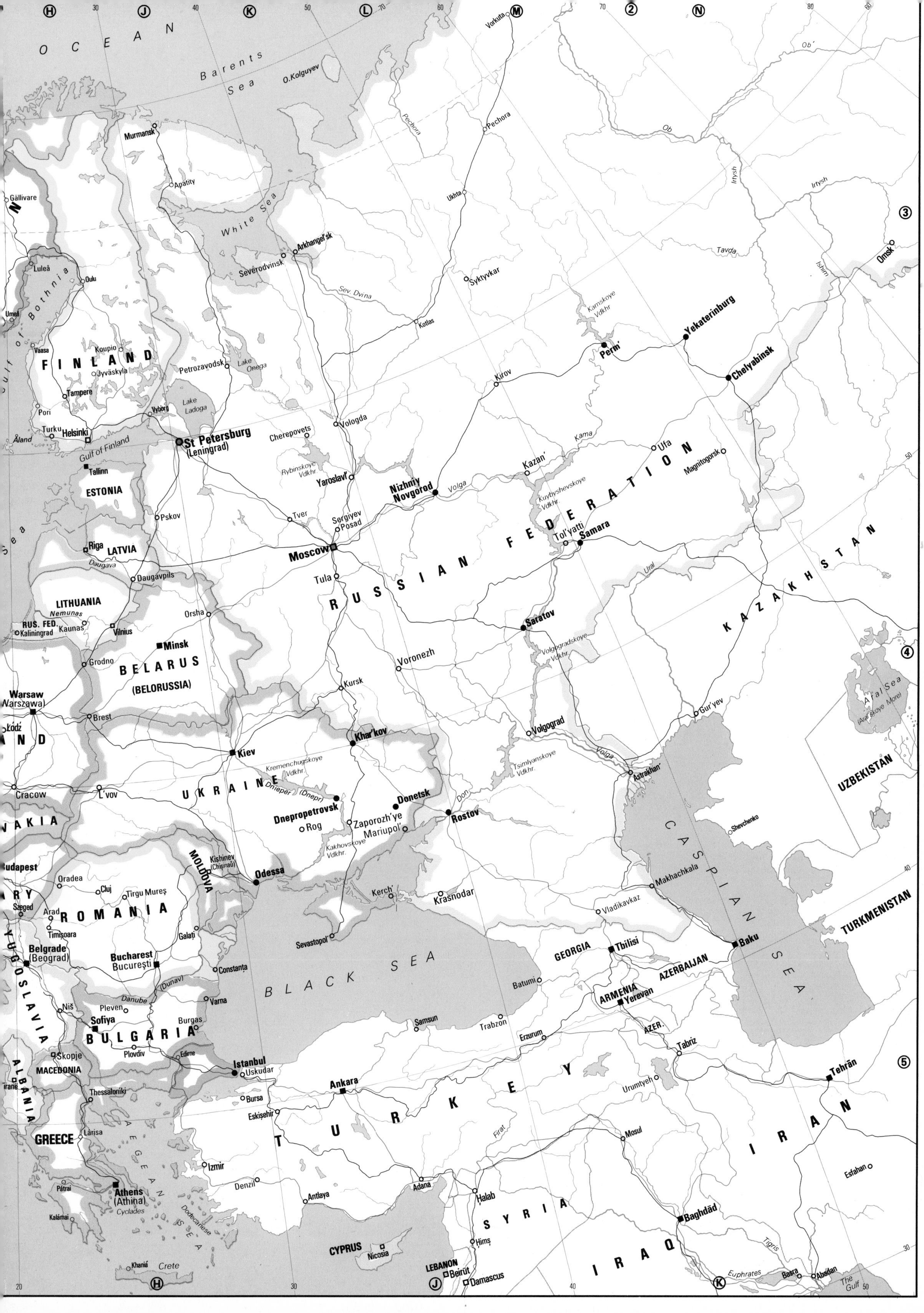

H
J
K
L
M
N
2
3
4
5
20
30
40
50
60
70
80
O C E A N
Barents Sea
O.Kolguyev
Vorkuta
Ob'
Pechora
Ob
Murmansk
Apatity
Gällivare
White Sea
Ukhta
Irtysh
Arkhangel'sk
Severodvinsk
Tavda
Omsk
Ishim
Luleå
Oulu
Gulf of Bothnia
Syktyvkar
Sev. Dvina
Umeå
Karnskoye Vdkhr
Kotlas
Yekaterinburg
Vaasa
Koupio
FINLAND
Jyväskylä
Petrozavodsk
Lake Onega
Perm'
Chelyabinsk
Tampere
Kirov
Pori
Lake Ladoga
Vyborg
Vologda
Turku
Helsinki
Åland
St Petersburg
(Leningrad)
Cherepovets
Gulf of Finland
Kama
Ufa
Magnitogorsk
Tallinn
Rybinskoye Vdkhr.
Kazan'
ESTONIA
Yaroslavl'
Nizhniy Novgorod
Volga
Kuybyshevskoye Vdkhr.
RUSSIAN FEDERATION
Pskov
Tver
Sergiyev Posad
Tol'yatti
Samara
Riga
LATVIA
Moscow
Daugava
Daugavpils
Tula
Ural
KAZAKHSTAN
LITHUANIA
Nemunas
Orsha
RUS. FED.
Kaliningrad
Kaunas
Vilnius
Saratov
Minsk
Grodno
BELARUS
(BELORUSSIA)
Voronezh
Volgogradskoye Vdkhr.
Aral Sea
(Aral'skoye More)
Warsaw
(Warszawa)
Kursk
Brest
Gur'yev
Łódź
Volgograd
Khar'kov
Kiev
Kremenchugskoye Vdkhr.
Tsimlyanskoye Vdkhr.
Volga
Astrakhan'
UZBEKISTAN
Cracow
L'vov
UKRAINE
Dnieper
(Dnepr)
Donetsk
Don
Dnepropetrovsk
Zaporozh'ye
Rostov
Rog
Mariupol'
Kakhovskoye Vdkhr.
Shevchenko
MOLDOVA
Kishinev
(Chişinău)
CASPIAN SEA
Budapest
Odessa
Oradea
Cluj
Tirgu Mureş
Makhachkala
Szeged
Kerch'
Krasnodar
Arad
ROMANIA
Vladikavkaz
TURKMENISTAN
Timişoara
Galaţi
Sevastopol'
Baku
Belgrade
(Beograd)
Bucharest
Bucureşti
GEORGIA
Tbilisi
AZERBAIJAN
YUGOSLAVIA
Constanţa
BLACK SEA
(Dunav)
Batumi
Danube
ARMENIA
Yerevan
Niš
Pleven
Varna
Sofiya
Burgas
Samsun
Trabzon
AZER.
BULGARIA
Erzurum
Tabriz
Skopje
Plovdiv
Edirne
ALBANIA
MACEDONIA
Istanbul
Uskudar
Tehrān
Thessaloniki
Ankara
Urumtyeh
TURKEY
Bursa
Eskişehir
IRAN
Mosul
GREECE
Larisa
AEGEAN SEA
Firat
Izmir
Esfahan
Denizli
Adana
Athens
(Athina)
Pátrai
Antlaya
Halab
SYRIA
Cyclades
Kalámai
Dodecanese
Baghdād
CYPRUS
Nicosia
Hims
IRAQ
Tigris
Khaniá
Crete
LEBANON
Beirūt
Damascus
Euphrates
Basra
Abadan
The Gulf

NORTH SEA
SCOTLAND
Grampian
Grampian Mountains
Tayside
Central
Fife
Lothian
Borders
Strathclyde
Dumfries and Galloway
Northumberland
Cumbria
Durham
Tyne and Wear
Cleveland
N. Yorkshire
Humberside
Lancashire
W. Yorkshire
Pennines
Cheviot Hills
NORTHERN IRELAND
Antrim
Down
Armagh
Louth
IRISH SEA
North Channel
Isle of Man
Isle of Skye
Rum
Eigg
Mull
Jura
Islay
Colonsay
Arran
Kintyre
Aberdeen
Dundee
Perth
Edinburgh
Glasgow
Stirling
Inverness
Oban
Fort William
Fort Augustus
Ben Nevis 1344
Ben Macdui 1310
Cairngorms
Monadhliath Mts
Dumfries
Carlisle
Newcastle upon Tyne
Sunderland
Sth Shields
Tynemouth
Middlesbrough
Darlington
Durham
York
Leeds
Bradford
Harrogate
Scarborough
Kingston upon Hull
Blackpool
Preston
Lancaster
Kendal
Belfast
Douglas
Long Forties
Devil's Hole
Farne Deep
Buchan Deep
Bergen - Stavanger
Lomond
Clyde
Fulmar
Auk
Ravenspurn
West Sole
Rough
Cleeton
Nat. Gas
100 km
50 mls

1:2M

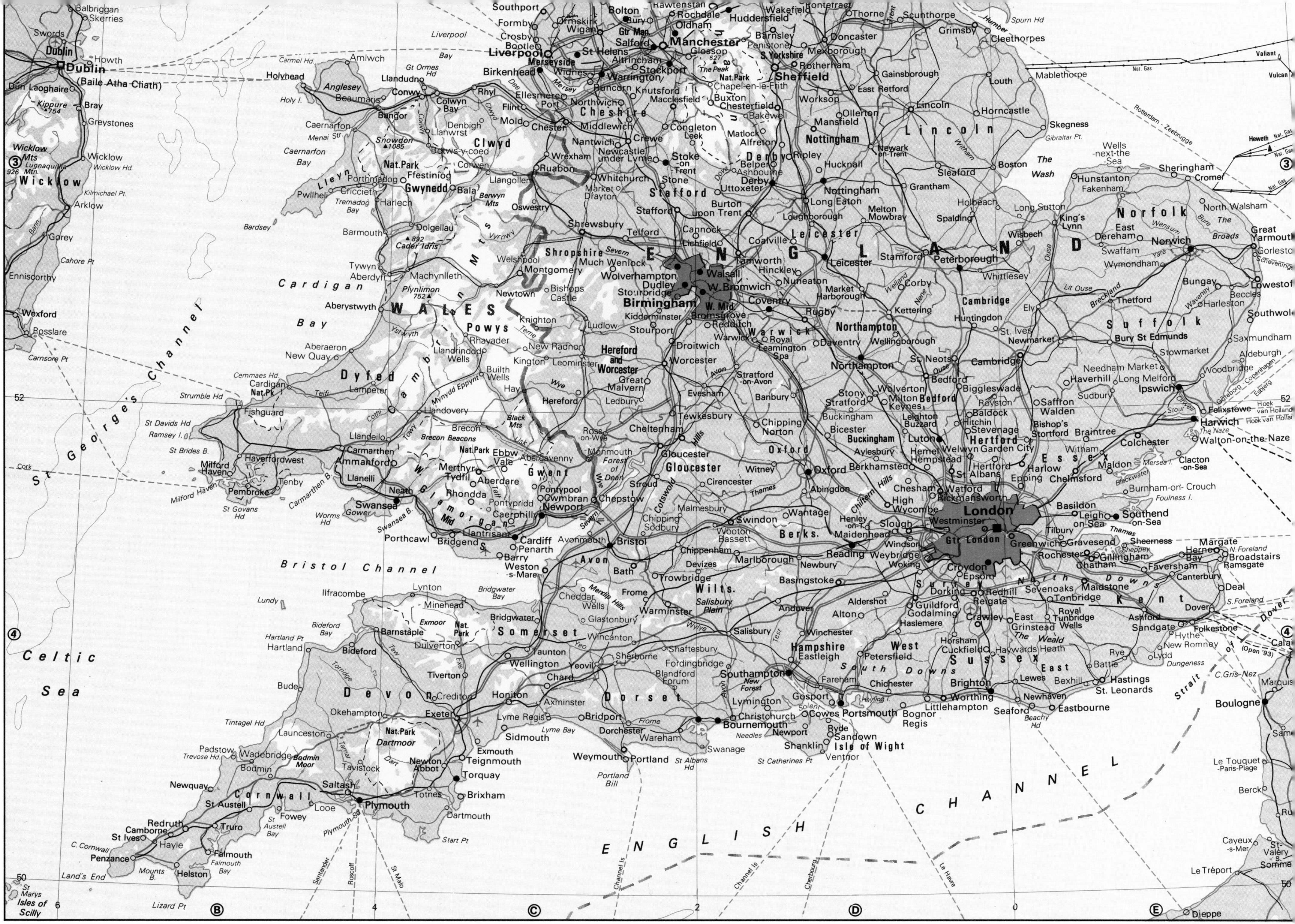
ENGLAND
WALES
ENGLISH CHANNEL
Bristol Channel
St George's Channel
Celtic Sea
Cardigan Bay
The Wash
Strait of Dover
London
Gt London
Westminster
Birmingham
Manchester
Liverpool
Sheffield
Bristol
Cardiff
Dublin
(Baile Atha Cliath)
Swords
Howth
Balbriggan
Skerries
Dun Laoghaire
Bray
Greystones
Wicklow
Arklow
Gorey
Enniscorthy
Wexford
Rosslare
Wicklow Mts
Lugnaquilla Mtn. 926
Kippure 754
Southport
Formby
Crosby
Bootle
Birkenhead
Merseyside
St Helens
Wigan
Ormskirk
Bolton
Bury
Rochdale
Oldham
Salford
Gtr Man.
Warrington
Widnes
Runcorn
Altrincham
Stockport
Huddersfield
Wakefield
Pontefract
Barnsley
Penistone
Doncaster
Thorne
Scunthorpe
Grimsby
Cleethorpes
Rotherham
Mexborough
S. Yorkshire
Glossop
The Peak
Nat.Park
Chapel-en-le-Frith
Buxton
Chesterfield
Bakewell
Matlock
Alfreton
Ripley
Derby
Belper
Ashbourne
Nottingham
Mansfield
Ollerton
Worksop
East Retford
Gainsborough
Lincoln
Horncastle
Louth
Mablethorpe
Skegness
Boston
Sleaford
Grantham
Newark on-Trent
Hucknall
Long Eaton
Loughborough
Melton Mowbray
Leicester
Coalville
Hinckley
Nuneaton
Tamworth
Lichfield
Cannock
Burton upon Trent
Uttoxeter
Stafford
Stoke -on -Trent
Leek
Congleton
Macclesfield
Knutsford
Northwich
Middlewich
Crewe
Nantwich
Newcastle under Lyme
Cheshire
Chester
Ellesmere Port
Wrexham
Ruabon
Whitchurch
Market Drayton
Stone
Shrewsbury
Shropshire
Telford
Much Wenlock
Wolverhampton
Walsall
W. Bromwich
Dudley
Stourbridge
W. Mid
Kidderminster
Bromsgrove
Redditch
Stourport
Droitwich
Worcester
Hereford and Worcester
Great Malvern
Ledbury
Hereford
Leominster
Ludlow
Coventry
Warwick
Royal Leamington Spa
Stratford -on-Avon
Rugby
Daventry
Northampton
Wellingborough
Kettering
Corby
Market Harborough
Stamford
Peterborough
Spalding
Holbeach
Long Sutton
Wisbech
King's Lynn
Hunstanton
Wells -next-the -Sea
Fakenham
Sheringham
Cromer
North Walsham
Norfolk
East Dereham
Swaffam
Wymondham
Norwich
Great Yarmouth
Gorleston
Lowestoft
Beccles
Bungay
Harleston
Thetford
Breckland
Southwold
Saxmundham
Aldeburgh
Woodbridge
Ipswich
Felixstowe
Harwich
Walton-on-the-Naze
Stowmarket
Bury St Edmunds
Suffolk
Needham Market
Haverhill
Long Melford
Sudbury
Cambridge
Ely
Huntingdon
St. Ives
Newmarket
St Neots
Bedford
Biggleswade
Royston
Baldock
Hitchin
Stevenage
Hertford
Welwyn Garden City
Luton
Leighton Buzzard
Milton Keynes
Wolverton
Stony Stratford
Buckingham
Bicester
Aylesbury
Hemel Hempstead
Berkhamsted
St Albans
Watford
Rickmansworth
Chesham
High Wycombe
Slough
Windsor
Maidenhead
Reading
Henley -on-T.
Oxford
Abingdon
Wantage
Witney
Chipping Norton
Banbury
Evesham
Tewkesbury
Cheltenham
Gloucester
Cirencester
Stroud
Chepstow
Newport
Cwmbran
Pontypool
Abergavenny
Monmouth
Forest of Dean
Ross -on-Wye
Caerphilly
Pontypridd
Rhondda
Aberdare
Merthyr Tydfil
Ebbw Vale
Gwent
Llantrisant
Bridgend
Porthcawl
Penarth
Barry
Neath
Swansea
Gower
Llanelli
Ammanford
Carmarthen
Llandeilo
Llandovery
Brecon
Brecon Beacons
Builth Wells
Llandrindod Wells
Rhayader
Powys
Knighton
New Radnor
Kington
Hay
Bishops Castle
Montgomery
Welshpool
Newtown
Machynlleth
Aberdyfi
Tywyn
Aberystwyth
Aberaeron
New Quay
Cardigan
Lampeter
Dyfed
Fishguard
Haverfordwest
Milford Haven
Pembroke
Tenby
St Davids Hd
Strumble Hd
Ramsey I.
St Brides B.
St Govans Hd
Worms Hd
Carmarthen B.
Swansea B.
Barmouth
Dolgellau
Cader Idris 892
Plynlimon 752
Harlech
Porthmadog
Criccieth
Pwllheli
Lleyn
Ffestiniog
Bala
Gwynedd
Snowdon 1085
Nat.Park
Betws-y-coed
Corwen
Llangollen
Oswestry
Clwyd
Denbigh
Llanrwst
Mold
Flint
Rhyl
Colwyn Bay
Conwy
Llandudno
Bangor
Caernarfon
Beaumaris
Anglesey
Amlwch
Holyhead
Holy I.
Caernarfon Bay
Bardsey
Liverpool Bay
Gt Ormes Hd
Carmel Hd.
Avon
Bath
Avonmouth
Weston -s-Mare
Chippenham
Malmesbury
Chipping Sodbury
Swindon
Wootton Bassett
Marlborough
Devizes
Trowbridge
Wilts.
Salisbury Plain
Salisbury
Warminster
Frome
Newbury
Berks.
Basingstoke
Andover
Winchester
Hampshire
Eastleigh
Southampton
New Forest
Lymington
Christchurch
Bournemouth
Poole
Swanage
Wareham
Dorchester
Weymouth
Portland
Portland Bill
Bridport
Lyme Regis
Axminster
Chard
Dorset
Blandford Forum
Fordingbridge
Shaftesbury
Sherborne
Yeovil
Wincanton
Glastonbury
Wells
Cheddar
Mendip Hills
Somerset
Bridgwater
Taunton
Wellington
Minehead
Exmoor
Dulverton
Lynton
Ilfracombe
Barnstaple
Bideford
Hartland
Lundy
Tiverton
Crediton
Honiton
Exeter
Exmouth
Sidmouth
Teignmouth
Newton Abbot
Torquay
Brixham
Dartmouth
Totnes
Dartmoor
Devon
Okehampton
Tavistock
Plymouth
Saltash
Looe
Fowey
Launceston
Bude
Bodmin
Bodmin Moor
Wadebridge
Padstow
Newquay
St Austell
Cornwall
Truro
Falmouth
Redruth
Camborne
Hayle
St Ives
Penzance
Helston
Land's End
Lizard Pt
Isles of Scilly
St Marys
Start Pt
Portsmouth
Gosport
Fareham
Cowes
Ryde
Newport
Sandown
Shanklin
Ventnor
Isle of Wight
St Catherines Pt
Needles
Chichester
Bognor Regis
Littlehampton
Worthing
Brighton
Seaford
Newhaven
Eastbourne
Beachy Hd
Lewes
Bexhill
Hastings
St. Leonards
Battle
Rye
Dungeness
New Romney
Hythe
Folkestone
Dover
Deal
Sandwich
Ramsgate
Broadstairs
Margate
Herne Bay
Canterbury
Faversham
Ashford
Kent
Maidstone
Tonbridge
Royal Tunbridge Wells
Sevenoaks
Crawley
East Grinstead
Horsham
Haywards Heath
Cuckfield
Sussex
West
East
The Weald
South Downs
North Downs
Guildford
Godalming
Haslemere
Dorking
Reigate
Redhill
Epsom
Croydon
Surrey
Woking
Weybridge
Aldershot
Alton
Petersfield
Gravesend
Rochester
Chatham
Gillingham
Sheerness
Southend -on-Sea
Leigh -on-Sea
Basildon
Tilbury
Greenwich
Chelmsford
Essex
Harlow
Epping
Bishop's Stortford
Saffron Walden
Braintree
Witham
Maldon
Colchester
Clacton -on-Sea
Burnham-on- Crouch
Foulness I.
Boulogne
Le Touquet -Paris-Plage
Berck
Cayeux -s-Mer
St- Valery -s- Somme
Le Tréport
Dieppe
Calais
Marquise
C.Gris-Nez
(Open '93)
Le Havre
Cherbourg
Channel Is
St Malo
Roscoff
Santander
Cork
Rotterdam - Zeebrugge
Hoek van Holland
Valiant
Vulcan
Nat. Gas
50
52
6
4
2
0
B
C
D
E
3
4

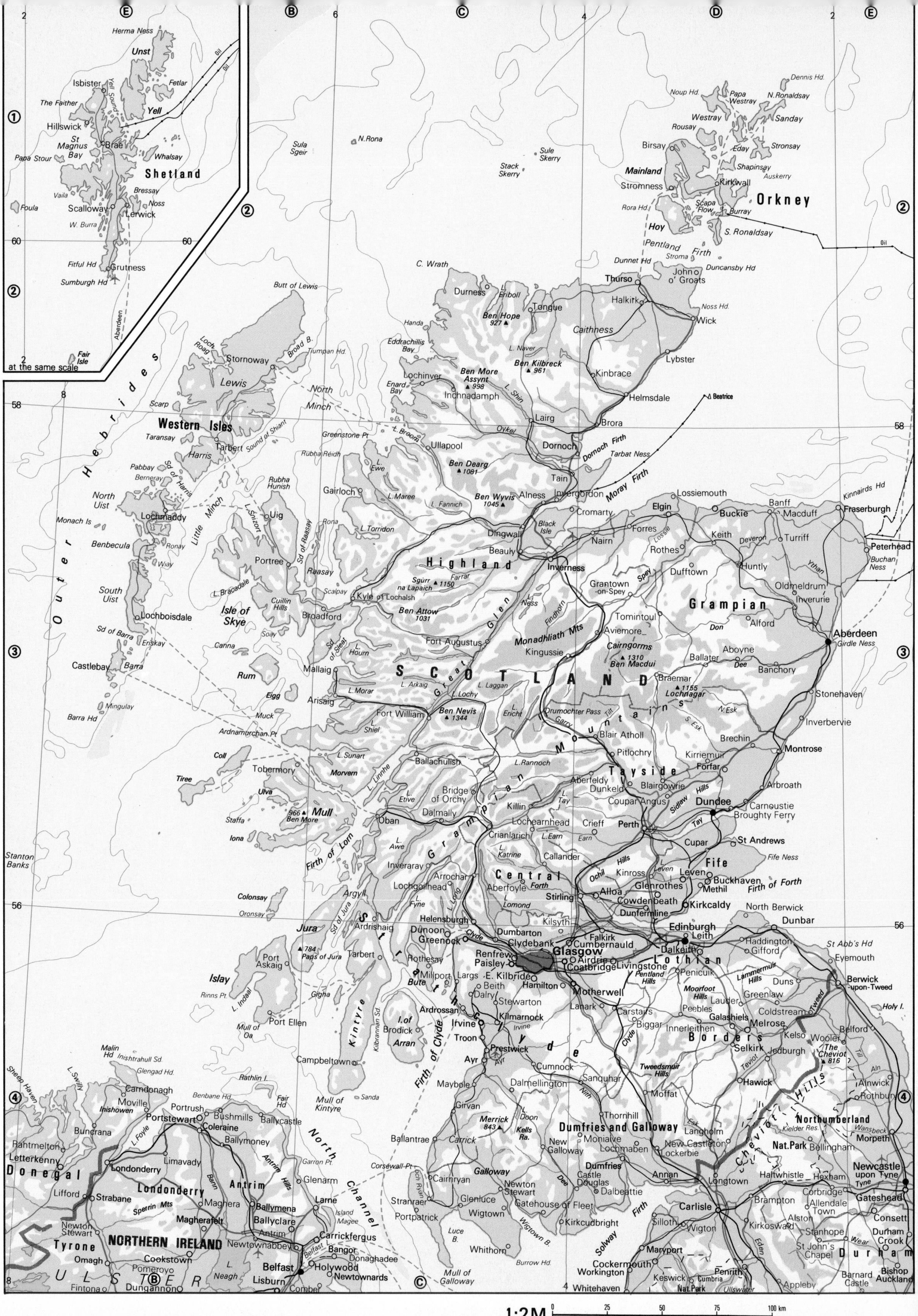

Herma Ness
Unst
Fetlar
Isbister
Yell Sound
The Faither
Yell
Hillswick
St Magnus Bay
Brae
Papa Stour
Whalsay
Shetland
Bressay
Vaila
Noss
Foula
Scalloway
Lerwick
W. Burra
Fitful Hd
Grutness
Sumburgh Hd
Aberdeen
Fair Isle
at the same scale
Oil
Dennis Hd.
Noup Hd.
Papa Westray
N. Ronaldsay
Westray
Sanday
Rousay
Birsay
Eday
Stronsay
Shapinsay
Auskerry
Mainland
Stromness
Kirkwall
Orkney
Rora Hd.
Scapa Flow
Burray
Hoy
S. Ronaldsay
Pentland Firth
Stroma
Dunnet Hd
John o' Groats
Duncansby Hd
Thurso
Halkirk
Noss Hd.
Wick
Caithness
Lybster
Kinbrace
Helmsdale
Beatrice
N. Rona
Sula Sgeir
Sule Skerry
Stack Skerry
C. Wrath
Butt of Lewis
Durness
L. Eriboll
Tongue
Ben Hope 927
Handa
Eddrachillis Bay
L. Naver
Ben Kilbreck 961
Tiumpan Hd.
Broad B.
Loch Roag
Stornoway
Lewis
Outer Hebrides
Lochinver
Enard Bay
Ben More Assynt 998
Inchnadamph
L. Shin
North Minch
Scarp
Western Isles
Lairg
Brora
Taransay
Tarbert
Sound of Shiant
Greenstone Pt
L. Broom
Ullapool
Oykel
Dornoch
Dornoch Firth
Tarbat Ness
Harris
Rubha Reidh
Ben Dearg 1081
Pabbay
Berneray
Sd of Harris
Rubha Hunish
L. Ewe
Tain
North Uist
Lochmaddy
Little Minch
L. Snizort
Uig
Gairloch
L. Maree
Ben Wyvis 1045
L. Fannich
Alness
Invergordon
Moray Firth
Lossiemouth
Cromarty
Monach Is
Rona
L. Torridon
Black Isle
Elgin
Buckie
Banff
Macduff
Kinnairds Hd
Fraserburgh
Benbecula
Ronay
Sd of Raasay
Dingwall
Forres
Lossie
Keith
Deveron
Turriff
Peterhead
Wiay
Portree
Beauly
Nairn
Rothes
Highland
Inverness
Huntly
Buchan Ness
Ythan
Raasay
Sgùrr na Lapaich 1150
Farrar
Spey
Dufftown
Grantown-on-Spey
Oldmeldrum
L. Bracadale
South Uist
Scalpay
Kyle of Lochalsh
L. Ness
Findhorn
Inverurie
Grampian
Cuillin Hills
Isle of Skye
Broadford
Ben Attow 1031
Lochboisdale
Tomintoul
Alford
Don
Sd of Barra
Eriskay
Soay
Canna
Sd of Sleat
Fort Augustus
Monadhliath Mts
Aviemore
Cairngorms
Aberdeen
Girdle Ness
L. Hourn
Great Glen
Kingussie
Ben Macdui 1310
Aboyne
Castlebay
Barra
Rum
Mallaig
SCOTLAND
Ballater
Dee
Banchory
Braemar
L. Morar
L. Arkaig
L. Laggan
Lochnagar 1155
Eigg
Arisaig
L. Lochy
Stonehaven
Mingulay
Fort William
Ben Nevis 1344
L. Ericht
Drumochter Pass
Tilt
Mountains
S. Esk
N. Esk
Barra Hd
Muck
L. Shiel
Garry
Inverbervie
Ardnamurchan Pt
Blair Atholl
Brechin
Pitlochry
Coll
L. Sunart
Montrose
Kirriemuir
Tobermory
Morvern
Ballachulish
L. Rannoch
Tayside
Forfar
Tiree
Grampian
L. Linnhe
Aberfeldy
Dunkeld
Blairgowrie
Arbroath
Ulva
Etive
Bridge of Orchy
Sidlaw Hills
Carnoustie
Coupar Angus
Dundee
Broughty Ferry
Mull
Ben More 966
Dalmally
Killin
L. Tay
Staffa
Oban
Lochearnhead
Crieff
Perth
Tay
Iona
L. Awe
Crianlarich
L. Earn
Earn
Cupar
St Andrews
Stanton Banks
Firth of Lorn
L. Katrine
Callander
Fife
Fife Ness
Inveraray
Arrochar
Ochil Hills
Kinross
Leven
Buckhaven
Methil
Central
Glenrothes
Firth of Forth
Lochgoilhead
Aberfoyle
Forth
Argyll
Alloa
Stirling
Cowdenbeath
Colonsay
L. Fyne
Long
L. Lomond
Dunfermline
Kirkcaldy
North Berwick
Oronsay
Sd of Jura
Kilsyth
Dunbar
Helensburgh
Edinburgh
Leith
Jura
Ardrishaig
Dunoon
Dumbarton
Falkirk
Haddington
Greenock
Clyde
Clydebank
Cumbernauld
Dalkeith
Gifford
St Abb's Hd
Paps of Jura 784
Tarbert
Rothesay
Renfrew
Glasgow
Lothian
Eyemouth
Port Askaig
Paisley
Airdrie
Livingstone
Strathclyde
Coatbridge
Pentland Hills
Penicuik
Lammermuir Hills
Duns
Berwick-upon-Tweed
Islay
Bute
Millport
Largs
E. Kilbride
Beith
Hamilton
Moorfoot Hills
Greenlaw
Rinns Pt.
L. Indaal
Gigha
Dalry
Stewarton
Motherwell
Lanark
Lauder
Holy I.
Peebles
Galashiels
Coldstream
Tweed
Ardrossan
Kilmarnock
Carstairs
Port Ellen
Kintyre
I. of Arran
Brodick
Irvine
Biggar
Innerleithen
Melrose
Kelso
Wooler
Belford
Mull of Oa
Kilbrannan Sd.
Troon
Clyde
Borders
Selkirk
The Cheviot 816
Firth of Clyde
Prestwick
Jedburgh
Teviot
Till
Malin Hd
Inishtrahull Sd.
Ayr
Cumnock
Tweedsmuir Hills
Campbeltown
Aln
Glengad Hd.
Rathlin I.
Sanquhar
Hawick
Cheviot Hills
Alnwick
Sheep Haven
L. Swilly
Carndonagh
Maybole
Dalmellington
Nith
Rothbury
Moville
Benbane Hd
Fair Hd
Mull of Kintyre
Inishowen
Portrush
Bushmills
Moffat
Portstewart
Ballycastle
Girvan
Thornhill
Northumberland
Coleraine
North Channel
Merrick 843
Kells Ra.
Dumfries and Galloway
Kielder Res
Buncrana
Ballymoney
Ballantrae
Carrick
Doon
Langholm
Wansbeck
Morpeth
Rathmelton
L. Foyle
Monaive
Esk
New Galloway
Lochmaben
New Castleton
Nat. Park
Bellingham
Letterkenny
Londonderry
Limavady
Antrim Hills
Garron Pt.
Corsewall Pt
Lockerbie
Dumfries
Donegal
Antrim
Glenarm
Cairnryan
Galloway
Castle Douglas
Annan
Longtown
Haltwhistle
Hexham
Newcastle upon Tyne
Tyne
Lifford
Strabane
Londonderry
Bann
Maghera
Loch Ryan
Newton Stewart
Dee
Dalbeattie
Corbridge
Gateshead
Sperrin Mts
Ballymena
Larne
Stranraer
Glenluce
Carlisle
Brampton
Allendale Town
Newton Stewart
Magherafelt
Ballyclare
Island Magee
Gatehouse of Fleet
Consett
Portpatrick
Wigtown
Solway Firth
Silloth
Wigton
Alston
Tyrone
NORTHERN IRELAND
Antrim
Carrickfergus
Luce B.
Kirkcudbright
Kirkoswald
Stanhope
Durham
Newtownabbey
Bangor
Wigtown B.
Eden
Wear
Crook
Omagh
Cookstown
Belfast
Donaghadee
Whithorn
Maryport
St John's Chapel
Durham
Pomeroy
L. Neagh
Holywood
Burrow Hd.
Cockermouth
Bishop Auckland
ULSTER
Newtownards
Mull of Galloway
Workington
Penrith
Lisburn
Keswick
Cumbria
Barnard Castle
Fintona
Dungannon
Comber
Whitehaven
Nat. Park
Ullswater
Appleby
1:2M
0 25 50 75 100 km
0 25 50 mls

Stanton Banks
Firth of Lorn
Colonsay
Oronsay
Jura
Sd of Jura
Paps of Jura
Islay
Rinns Pt.
L. Indaal
Port Askaig
Gigha
Port Ellen
Mull of Oa
Kintyre
Kilbrannon Sd
Campbeltown
Mull of Kintyre
Sanda
Inveraray
Arrochar
Lochgoilhead
Argyll
L. Fyne
L. Long
Helensburgh
Ardrishaig
Dunoon
Greenock
Clyde
Tarbert
Rothesay
Bute
Largs
Millport
Ardrossan
Irvine
I. of Arran
Brodick
Troon
Prestwick
Ayr
Firth of Clyde
Maybole
Girvan
Strathclyde
Ballantrae
Carrick
Corsewall Pt.
Cairnryan
Stranraer
Glenluce
Portpatrick
Luce B.
Mull of Galloway
Malin Hd
Inishtrahull Sd.
Glengad Hd.
Tory I.
Tory Sound
Sheep Haven
L. Swilly
Carndonagh
Moville
Inishowen
Bloody Foreland
Gola
Errigal 752
Rathmelton
Buncrana
Aran I.
Letterkenny
Donegal
Donegal Mts
Gweebarra B.
Finn
Lifford
Strabane
Glenties
Blue Stack 676
Rossan Pt
Killybegs
Donegal
L. Derg
Muckros Hd.
Donegal Bay
Inishmurray
Bundoran
Ballyshannon
Rathlin I.
Benbane Hd.
Fair Hd
Portrush
Bushmills
Ballycastle
Portstewart
Coleraine
L. Foyle
Ballymoney
Limavady
Londonderry
Bann
Antrim Hills
Garron Pt.
Glenarm
Antrim
Larne
Island Magee
Londonderry
Sperrin Mts
Maghera
Ballymena
Magherafelt
Ballyclare
Newton Stewart
Tyrone
NORTHERN IRELAND
Antrim
Carrickfergus
Belfast
Newtownabbey
Cookstown
Pomeroy
Omagh
Bangor
Donaghadee
Holywood
Belfast
Newtownards
Neagh
Fintona
ULSTER
Dungannon
Lisburn
Comber
Lurgan
Craigavon
Portadown
Strangford Lough
Ballynahinch
Killyleagh
Portaferry
Down
L. Melvin
L. Erne
Enniskillen
Aughnacloy
Fermanagh
Armagh
Banbridge
Downpatrick
Monaghan
Armagh
Keady
Newcastle
Rathfriland
Mourne Mts
Newry
Clones
St. John's Pt.
Dundrum B.
Upper L. Erne
Castleblayney
Monaghan
Warrenpoint
Kilkeel
Carlingford L.
Isle of Man
Peel
Port Erin
Calf of Man
North Channel
Benwee Hd.
Broad Haven
Killala B.
Erris Hd.
The Mullet
Belmullet
Ballycastle
Carrowmore L.
Inishkea
Ballina
Ox Mts
Sligo Bay
Sligo
Leitrim
Sligo
Blacksod B.
Mts of Mayo
Nephin 807
L. Conn
Moy
L. Allen
Achill Hd
Achill
Corraun Pen.
L. Oughter
Cootehill
Clare I.
Clew Bay
Swinford
Boyle
Carrick on Shannon
Cavan
Cavan
Carrickmacross
Dundalk
Dundalk Bay
Castlebar
L. Gara
Mayo
Westport
Ballaghaderreen
L. Boderg
Louth
Ardee
Inishturk
Ballyhaunis
Roscommon
L. Sheelin
Dunany Pt.
Inishbofin
Claremorris
Castlerea
REPUBLIC
Clogher Hd.
Inishshark
Partry Mts.
L. Mask
CONNAUGHT
L. Bowna
Longford
L. Derravaragh
Kells
Boyne
Drogheda
Ballinrobe
Roscommon
Longford
An Uaimh
IRISH SEA
Mts of Connemara
Clifden
L. Ree
Tuam
Meath
Balbriggan
Skerries
Slyne Hd
L. Corrib
Suck
Mullingar
OF
Trim
Swords
Galway
Westmeath
Royal Canal
Dublin
Bertraghboy B.
Athlone
Moate
Clara
L. Ennell
Howth
Galway
Athenry
Ballinasloe
Edenderry
Kildare
Liffey
Dublin (Baile Atha Cliath)
Holyhead
Kilkieran B.
Tullamore
IRELAND
Dún Laoghaire
Black Hd.
Galway B.
Loughrea
Offaly
Holy I.
Inishmore
Aran Is
Slieve Aughty Mts.
Shannon
Drohead Nua
Portarlington
Naas
Kippure 754
Bray
Inishmaan
Portumna
Banagher
Birr
Mountmellick
Gort
Ballyvaghan
Kildare
Greystones
LEINSTER
Slieve Bloom Mts.
Hags Hd
Ennistimon
Lough Derg
Port Laoise
Athy
Barrow
Wicklow Mts
Caernarfon Bay
Scarriff
Roscrea
Wicklow
Wicklow Hd.
Liscannor B.
Clare
Laois
926
Lugnaquillia Mtn
Mutton I.
Milltown Malbay
Ennis
Killaloe
Nenagh
Templemore
Carlow
Wicklow
Donegal Pt.
Kilmichael Pt.
Kilkee
Tullow
Arklow
Kilrush
Shannon
Carlow
Thurles
Limerick
Loop Hd
Muine Bheag
Foynes
Kilkenny
Bardsey
Mouth of the Shannon
Rathkeale
Tipperary
Gorey
Kerry Hd.
Limerick
Kilkenny
Slaney
Cashel
Cahore Pt
Listowel
Newcastle W.
Thomastown
MUNSTER
Tipperary
Fethard
Enniscorthy
Abbeyfeale
Nore
Tralee Bay
Tralee
Rath Luirc
Carrick on-Suir
Wexford
Castleisland
Kilmallock
Galty Mts.
Cahir
Sybil Pt.
New Ross
Dingle
Mitchelstown
Clonmel
Wexford
Blasket Sd
Newmarket
Knockmealdown Mts.
Comeragh Mts
Rosslare
Kanturk
Waterford
Gt. Blasket
Kerry
Fermoy
Dingle B.
Killorglin
Lismore
Waterford
Tramore
Ballyteige Bay
Carnsore Pt
Killarney
Mallow
Blackwater
Cappoquin
Hook Hd
Waterford Harb.
Saltee
Valencia
1041
MacGillycuddy's Reeks
Millstreet
Boggeragh Mts
Cork
Dungarvan
Cahersiveen
Helvick Hd.
Cardigan
Mine Hd
Nat. Pk
Sneem
Kenmare
Macroom
Lee
Cork
Youghal
Strumble Hd
Fishguard
Bolus Hd
Passage West
Midleton
Youghal Harb.
Ballinskelligs B.
Kenmare River
Cobh
Ballycotton Bay
St Davids Hd
St. Davids
Ramsey I.
Caha Mts
Bandon
St George's Channel
Castletown Bere
Bantry
Dunmanway
Kinsale
Cork
St Brides B.
Haverfordwest
Dursey I.
Bantry Bay
Clonakilty
Skomer
Milford Haven
Dunmanus Bay
Schull
Clonakilty Bay
Old Head of Kinsale
Tenby
Pembroke
Milford Haven
Caldy
Mizen Hd
Roaringwater B.
Skibbereen
Baltimore
St Govans Hd
C. Clear
Fastnet Rock
Kinsale
Lundy
Taf
A
B
C
D
1
2
3
4
56
54
52
8
6
1:2M
0 25 50 75 100 km
0 25 50 mls

A
B
1
C
D
Shetland
Fetlar
Yell
St Magnus B.
Whalsay
Foula
Lerwick
Sumburgh Hd
Nordhordland
Viking Bank
Bergen
Sotra
Sunnhordland
Leirvik
Bømlo
Skjold
Haugesund
Karmøy
Fair Isle
Westray
Rousay
Sanday
Stronsay
Sula Sgeir
N.Rona
Sule Skerry
Stromness
Stack Skerry
Kirkwall
Hoy
Scapa Flow
Orkney
Butt of Lewis
C.Wrath
Thurso
Duncansby Hd
Flannan Is
Stornoway
Lewis
Ben Hope 927
Wick
St Kilda
Outer Hebrides
The Minch
Ben More Assynt 998
Helmsdale
2
Harris
Ullapool
Dornoch
Dornoch Firth
N.Uist
Moray Firth
Dingwall
Elgin
Banff
Fraserburgh
Portree
Inverness
Peterhead
Buchan Ness
S.Uist
Skye
Kyle of Lochalsh
L.Ness
Spey
Barra
Fort Augustus
Don
Rum
Mallaig
Ben Macdui 1309
Dee
Aberdeen
Long Forties
Fort William
SCOTLAND
Coll
Ben Nevis 1344
Braemar
Stonehaven
Tiree
Ben Lawers 1214
Grampian Mts
Pitlochry
Montrose
Mull
Oban
Dundee
Arbroath
Great Fisher Bank
F.of Lorn
L.Awe
Perth
F.of Tay
St Andrews
Colonsay
Jura
L.Lomond
Stirling
Kirkcaldy
Greenock
F.of Forth
NORTH SEA
Islay
Glasgow
Paisley
Edinburgh
St Abbs Hd
Motherwell
Malin Hd
Tory I.
Campbeltown
Arran
Irvine
Clyde
Berwick-upon-Tweed
Rathlin I.
Kilmarnock
White Coomb 822
Galashiels
Holy I.
Aran I.
Errigal 752
L.Foyle
Coleraine
F.of Clyde
Ayr
Moffat
Alnwick
Londonderry
Girvan
Merrick 843
Hawick
Rossan Pt
N.IRELAND
Ballymena
Dumfries
Nith
Cheviots
Stranraer
Morpeth
Blyth
Donegal
Larne
Donegal B.
L.Neagh
Erris Hd
Sligo B.
L.Erne
Omagh
Belfast
Bangor
Kirkcudbright
Carlisle
Newcastle upon Tyne
Gateshead
S.Shields
Solway Firth
Luce B.
Enniskillen
Sunderland
Sligo
Portadown
Penrith
Durham
Achill I.
L.Conn
Ballina
Armagh
Hartlepool
Monaghan
Pennines
Clew B.
Castlebar
L.Allen
Scafell Pike 977
Darlington
Dogger Bank
Boyle
Newry
Douglas
Isle of Man
Middlesbrough
L.Mask
Cavan
Kendal
Roscommon
Dundalk
Barrow-in-Furness
Yorkshire Moors
Scarborough
Longford
Morecambe
L.Corrib
IRISH SEA
Lancaster
Slyne Hd
L.Ree
Drogheda
Harrogate
Flamborough Hd
Galway
Athlone
Mullingar
Blackpool
Ouse
York
Preston
Galway B.
Bradford
Leeds
Aran Is
Shannon
Dublin
(Baile Atha Cliath)
Huddersfield
Hull
3
Monastereven
Holyhead
Liverpool
Manchester
Spurn Hd
Dun Laoghaire
Birkenhead
Bolton
Trent
Humber
REP. OF IRELAND
Ennis
L.Derg
Bray
Anglesey
Doncaster
Grimsby
Port Laoise
Wicklow Mts
Mouth of the Shannon
Kilrush
Carlow
Wicklow
Bangor
Warrington
Sheffield
Snowdon 1085
Chester
Terschelling
Limerick
Kilkenny
Pwllheli
Dee
Crewe
Stoke on-Trent
Lincoln
Dingle
Tralee
Suir
Arklow
Vlieland
Tipperary
Harlingen
Cambrian Mts
The Wash
Nottingham
Texel
Dingle B.
Clonmel
Cardigan Bay
Derby
Barrow
Shrewsbury
King's Lynn
Den Helder
Waterford
Carrauntoohill 1041
Killarney
Blackwater
Wexford
Aberystwyth
Wolverhampton
Leicester
Norwich
Great Yarmouth
St George's Channel
Nene
Rosslare
WALES
Birmingham
Coventry
Cork
Peterborough
Hoorn
Dungarvan
Alkmaar
Zaanstad
ENGLAND
Youghal
Bantry B.
Bantry
Lowestoft
Haarlem
St David's Hd
Builth Wells
Worcester
Amsterdam
Newmarket
Old Hd of Kinsale
Fishguard
Wye
Northampton
Bedford
Hilversum
Cambridge
Leiden
Carmarthen
Amersfoort
C.Clear
Brecon
Severn
Milton Keynes
Ipswich
The Hague ('s-Gravenhage)
Gloucester
Felixstowe
Pembroke
Utrecht
Luton
Colchester
Harwich
Oxford
Rotterdam
Swansea
Newport
Swindon
Lek
Dordrecht
London
Cardiff
Chelmsford
Maas
Bristol
Windsor
Southend-on-Sea
Lundy I.
Bristol Chan.
Bath
's-Hertogenbosch
Thames
Weston-super-Mare
Reading
Breda
Barnstaple
Tilburg
Vlissingen
Eindhoven
Maidstone
Canterbury
Zeebrugge
Taunton
Salisbury
Guildford
Antwerp (Antwerpen)
Oostende
Bude
Winchester
Dover
Bruges
Crawley
Mechelen
Exeter
Folkestone
Southampton
Hastings
Str. of Dover
Hasselt
Bournemouth
Dunkirk
Gent
Dartmoor
Brighton
Calais
Brussels (Bruxelles)
Newquay
Portsmouth
Leuven
Weymouth
Eastbourne
St-Omer
Kortrijk
Tourcoing
Plymouth
Torquay
Isle of Wight
Boulogne
Lille
Roubaix
Truro
Tournai
Soignies
Penzance
Béthune
Land's End
Mons
Namur
Falmouth
Montreuil
Lens
Valenciennes
Isles of Scilly
Prawle Pt
Douai
Arras
Charleroi
English Channel
Lizard Pt
Denain
Maubeuge
Cambrai
Le Tréport
C.de la Hague
Abbeville
Dieppe
Alderney
Pte de Barfleur
Fourmies
Amiens
Fécamp
Guernsey
Cherbourg
Neufchâtel
Montdidier
St-Quentin
Charleville-Mézières
Sark
Le Havre
Bolbec
Channel Is (To U.K.)
Valognes
Deauville
Seine
Beauvais
Sedan
Jersey
Bayeux
Rouen
Oise
Laon
St Helier
St-Lô
Caen
Compiègne
Lisieux
Elbeuf
Aisne
Golfe de St-Malo
Louviers
Soissons
Coutances
Senlis
Reims
Roscoff
Granville
Mantes
Cergy-Pontoise
Château-Thierry
Verdun
Morlaix
NORMANDIE
Evreux
Épernay
I.d'Ouessant
Brest
St-Malo
Argentan
ÎLE-DE-FRANCE
Châlons-s.-M.
St-Brieuc
Orne
Eure
Paris
Meaux
BRITTANY
Dinan
Mont-St-Michel
Domfront
Dreux
Versailles
Vitry-le-F.
Carhaix-Plouguer
Sézanne
Rambouillet
Provins
St-Dizier
Châteaulin
Alençon
Chartres
Étampes
Loudéac
Fougères
Melun
Romilly-s.-S.
Pontivy
Mayenne
Fontainebleau
Quimper
Rennes
Vitré
MAINE
Troyes
Concarneau
FRANCE
CHAMPAGNE
Quimperlé
Laval
Bar-s.-A.
Lorient
Ploërmel
Châteaudun
Sens
Le Mans
Chaumont
4
1:5M
0 50 100 150 200 km
0 50 100 mls

E
F
G
H
1
2
3
4
NORWAY
SWEDEN
DENMARK
GERMANY
POLAND
CZECH REP.
SLOVAKIA
ESTONIA
LATVIA
LITHUANIA
RUS. FED.
BALTIC SEA
Skagerrak
Kattegat
Ålands Hav
Gulf of Riga
(Rīgas Jūras Līcis)
Gulf of Gdańsk
(Z. Gdańska)
Myrdal
Hallingdal
Dale
Voss
Geilo
Hårteigen 1691
Odda
Hamar
Glåma
Kongsvinger
Hønefoss
Klöfta
Oslo
Lillestrøm
Rjukan
Drammen
Kongsberg
Mysen
Sauda
Notodden
Dalen
Horten
Moss
Sarpsborg
Fredrikstad
Halden
Skien
Porsgrunn
Larvik
Oslofjord
Jørpeland
Stavanger
Sandnes
Kragerø
Bygland
Risør
Tvedestrand
Evje
Arendal
Grimstad
Flekkefjord
Kristiansand
Lindesnes
Mandal
Säter
Hedemora
Östhammar
Ludvika
Avesta
Uppsala
Norrtälje
Kapellskär
Rimbo
Sala
Enköping
Västerås
Mälaren
Arvika
Köping
Solna
Stockholm
Karlstad
Karlskoga
Eskilstuna
Strängnäs
Årjäng
Kristinehamn
Örebro
Kumla
Hjälmaren
Södertälje
Katrineholm
Nynäshamn
Säffle
Åmål
Askersund
Nyköping
Oxelösund
Vänern
Mariestad
Finspång
Motala
Lidköping
Skövde
Vättern
Linköping
Vänersborg
Skara
Mjölby
Åtvidaberg
Uddevalla
Trollhättan
Falköping
Tranås
Göteborg
Jönköping
Huskvarna
Borås
Eksjö
Nässjö
Västervik
Hultsfred
Mölndal
Kungsbacka
Vetlanda
Oskarshamn
Värnamo
Mönsterås
Varberg
Falkenberg
Växjö
Ljungby
Nybro
Kalmar
Borgholm
Öland
Älem
Halmstad
Laholm
Lagan
Älmhult
Båstad
Markaryd
Ronneby
Karlskrona
Ängelholm
Hässleholm
Karlshamn
Kristianstad
Helsingborg
Landskrona
Hanöbukten
Lund
Simrishamn
Malmö
Ystad
Trelleborg
Bornholm
Rønne
Gotska Sandön
Fårö
Visby
Gotland
Klintehamn
Hemse
Burgsvik
Hiiumaa
Haapsalu
Saaremaa
(Riia Laht)
Kuressaare
Roja
Ventspils
Venta
Kuldīga
Sakasleja
Saldus
Liepāja
Mazeikiai
Telšiai
Klaipėda
Priekule
Šilute
Courland Lagoon
Sovetsk
Svetlogorsk
Chernyakhovsk
Talpaki
Pregolya
Kaliningrad
(Königsberg)
Hirtshals
Skagen
Hjørring
Frederikshavn
Læsø
Åby
Ålborg
Thisted
Limfjorden
Nykøbing
Hadsund
Anholt
Skive
Hobro
Randers
Grenå
Holstebro
Viborg
Herning
Silkeborg
Århus
Skjern
Jylland
(Jutland)
Horsens
Samsø
Helsingør
Hillerød
Copenhagen
(København)
Øresund
Roskilde
Kalundborg
Vejle
Varde
Kolding
Fredericia
Sjælland
Køge
Esbjerg
Odense
Korsør
Næstved
Haderslev
Assens
Nyborg
Fyn
Svendborg
Vordingborg
Møn
Rømø
Åbenrå
Als
Sylt
Westerland
Sønderborg
Nakskov
Lolland
Falster
Flensburg
Rødbyhavn
Nykøbing
Gedser
Sassnitz
Rügen
Husum
Schleswig
Puttgarden
Fehmarn
Kiel
Oldenburg
Stralsund
Greifswald
Rendsburg
Mecklenburger Bucht
Warnemünde
Heide
Neumünster
Neustadt
Travemünde
Rostock
Świnoujście
Z. Szczeciński
SCHLESWIG-HOLSTEIN
Itzehoe
Lübeck
Wismar
Malchin
Anklam
Cuxhaven
Elmshorn
Ostfriesische Ins.
Schwerin
Neubrandenburg
Hamburg
Stade
Wilhelmshaven
Bremerhaven
MECKLENBURG-VORPOMMERN
Neustrelitz
Prenzlau
Emden
Lauenburg
Ludwigslust
Pritzwalk
Groningen
Leer
Lüneburg
Elbe
Leeuwarden
Oldenburg
Rotenburg
Wittenberge
Neuruppin
Eberswalde
Sneek
Bremen
Uelzen
Oranienburg
Heerenveen
Assen
NIEDERSACHSEN
Salzwedel
Rathenow
Berlin
Emmen
Meppen
Nienburg
Celle
Stendal
Nauen
Fürstenwalde
Ems
Diepholz
Brandenburg
Potsdam
Kampen
Zwolle
Lingen
Langenhagen
Wolfsburg
Genthin
BRANDENBURG
Frankfurt an-der-O.
Słubice
Deventer
Hengelo
Minden
Hannover
Braunschweig
Magdeburg
Burg
Luckenwalde
Spree
Apeldoorn
Enschede
Rheine
Osnabrück
Hildesheim
Salzgitter
Wittenberg
Cottbus
Coesfeld
Münster
Bielefeld
SACHSEN-ANHALT
Dessau
Arnhem
Bocholt
NORDRHEIN-
Gütersloh
Aschersleben
Bernburg
Bitterfeld
Torgau
Finsterwalde
Nijmegen
Wesel
Haltern
Hamm
Lippe
Paderborn
Saale
Mulde
Göttingen
Nordhausen
Halle
Riesa
Elsterwerda
Rhein
Duisburg
Dortmund
Heiligenstadt
Leipzig
Wurzen
Bautzen
Görlitz
Venlo
Essen
Hagen
Münden
Kassel
Weissenfels
Meissen
Krefeld
Wuppertal
Ruhr
Dresden
Elbe
Zittau
Düsseldorf
Korbach
Mühlhausen
Naumburg
Zeitz
SACHSEN
Mönchen-gladbach
WESTFALEN
Erfurt
Chemnitz
Ústí
Liberec
Maastricht
Cologne
(Köln)
Siegen
Bad Hersfeld
Eisenach
Jena
Gera
Teplice
Marburg
Werra
THÜRINGEN
Zwickau
Aachen
Bonn
Bad Godesberg
Alsfeld
Fulda
Thüringer Wald
Most
Chomutov
Liège
Euskirchen
Giessen
Plauen
Erzgebirge
Ohře
HESSEN
Andernach
Koblenz
Limburg
Hof
Karlovy Vary
Kladno
Mosel
Coburg
Cheb
Frankfurt
Offenbach
Schweinfurt
Prague
(Praha)
Bastogne
Bitburg
Wiesbaden
Mainz
Aschaffenburg
Bayreuth
Berounka
Bingen
Bamberg
Plzeň
Brdy
Benešov
Bad-Kreuznach
Darmstadt
Weiden
LUXEMBOURG
Trier
RHEINLAND-PFALZ
Würzburg
Erlangen
Worms
Kitzingen
Luxembourg
Ludwigshafen
Mannheim
Amberg
Klatovy
Písek
Tábor
Longwy
SAARLAND
Fürth
Nürnberg
Kaiserslautern
Heidelberg
Ansbach
Cham
Thionville
Saarlouis
Saarbrücken
Speyer
Parsberg
Rachel 1452
České Budějovice
Pirmasens
Crailsheim
Fränkische Alb
BAYERN
Metz
Sarreguemines
Karlsruhe
Heilbronn
Regensburg
Böhmerwald
Donau
Kaplice
Pforzheim
BADEN-
Ludwigsburg
Rastatt
Stuttgart
Donauwörth
Ingolstadt
Passau
Freistadt
Sarrebourg
Nancy
Baden-Baden
Esslingen
Heidenheim
Schärding
Strasbourg
Tübingen
Landshut
Linz
Offenburg
Reutlingen
Ulm
Augsburg
Mühldorf
Inn
Wels
Épinal
St Dié
Biberach
Dachau
Munich
(München)
Vöcklabruck
Gmunden
Steyr
Colmar
Freiburg
WÜRTTEMBERG
Landsberg
Starnberg
Rosenheim
Salzburg
Enns
Mariazell
Tuttlingen
Memmingen
LORRAINE
ALSACE
Władysławowo
Łeba
Gdynia
Ustka
Lębork
Sopot
Gdańsk
(Danzig)
Elbląg
Braniewo
Bartoszyce
Słupsk
Sławno
Tczew
Malbork
Kętrzyn
Koszalin
Kościerzyna
Starogard Gdański
Olsztyn
Kołobrzeg
Karlino
Białogard
Bory Tucholskie
Kwidzyn
Ostróda
Szczytno
Świdwin
Chojnice
Grudziądz
Nidzica
Szczecinek
Świecie
Chełmno
Brodnica
Mława
Goleniów
Jastrowie
Szczecin
Stargard Szczeciński
Wałcz
Piła
Bydgoszcz
Toruń
Sierpc
Ciechanów
Choszczno
Pułtusk
Oder (Odra)
Krzyż
Noteć
Znin
Inowrocław
Płock
Nowy Dwór Maz.
Myślibórz
Włocławek
Wisła (Vistula)
Warsaw
(Warszawa)
Gorzów Wlkp.
Oborniki
Gniezno
Gostynin
Pruszków
Kostrzyn
Skwierzyna
Poznań
Września
Kutno
Sochaczew
Żyrardów
Pniewy
Konin
Koło
Łowicz
Skierniewice
Świebodzin
Środa Wlk.
Łódź
Zgierz
Jarocin
Pleszew
Tomaszów Maz.
Zielona Góra
Kalisz
Pabianice
Gubin
Nowa Sól
Leszno
Ostrów Wlkp.
Głogów
Rawicz
Zduńska Wola
Piotrków Tryb.
Pilica
Końskie
Żary
Szprotawa
Wieluń
Radomsko
Wołów
Kępno
Warta
Bolesławiec
Legnica
Wrocław
(Breslau)
Kluczbork
Częstochowa
Jędrzejów
Zawiercie
Jelenia Góra
Świdnica
Brzeg
Opole
Wałbrzych
Dzierżoniów
Bielawa
Odra
Bytom
Dąbrowa-Górn
Jablonec n.N.
Sněžka 1603
Kłodzko
Nysa
Gliwice
Zabrze
Sosnowiec
Katowice
Cracow
Chorzów
Rybnik
Oświęcim
Mladá Boleslav
Labe
Hradec Králové
Praděd 1490
Jeseníky
Karviná
Bielsko-Biała
Myślenice
Brandýs n.L.
Pardubice
Opava
Zabreh
Ostrava
Cieszyn
Żywiec
Kolín
Kutná Hora
Sázava
Svitavy
Hranice
Čadca
Zakopane
Českomoravská Vysočina
Olomouc
Přerov
Žilina
Tatry
Havlíčkův Brod
Prostějov
Zlín
Ružomberok
Jihlava
Vyškov
Třebíč
Bílé Karpaty
Martin
Brno
Banská Bystrica
Vltava
Třeboň
Hodonín
Trenčín
Znojmo
Mikulov
Gmünd
Břeclav
Piešťany
Hron
Zvolen
Horn
Hollabrunn
Malé Karpaty
Nitra
Lučenec
Trnava
Levice
Stockerau
Klosterneuburg
Váh
Vienna
(Wien)
Bratislava
Nové Zámky
Váč
Mödling
Komárno
Hatvan
St Pölten
Hainfeld
Esztergom
Wr. Neustadt
M'óvár
Győr
Budapest
Sopron
Tatabánya
Neunkirchen
Rába

ICELAND
Arctic Circle
Grimsey
Bolungarvik
Ísafjörður
Dranga-jökull
Siglufjörður
Olafsfjörður
Dalvik
Húsavik
Húna-flói
Sauðárkrókur
Bakkaflói
Gláma 845
Biargtangar
Blönduós
Akureyri
Njarðvik
Seyðisfjörður
Breiðafjörður
Stykkishólmur
Neskaupstaður
Eskifjörður
Langjökull
Hofsjökull
Ódáðahraun
Tungnafellsjökull
Snæfell 1833
Vatnajökull
Faxaflói
Akranes
Reykjavik
Kópavogur
Hafnarfjörður
Keflavik
Grindavik
Selfoss
Hjórsá
Öræfajökull 2119
Mýrdalsjökull
Ingólfshöfði
Vestmannaeyjar
Surtsey
at the same scale
Faeroes (Færøerne) (Den.)
Streymoy
Vágar
Tórshavn
Sandoy
Suduroy
at the same scale
ARCTIC OCEAN
BARENTS SEA
NORWEGIAN SEA
Arctic Circle
Nordkapp
Honningsvåg
Hammerfest
Sørøya
Porsanger
Laksefj.
Tanafj.
Varanger halvøya
Vardø
Rustefjelbma
Vadsø
Varangerfj.
Pov Rybachiy
Lakselv
Kirkenes
Alta
Tana
Utsjoki
Pechenga
Tromsø
Sørkjosen
Karasjok
Nikel
Polyarnyy
Murmansk
Halti 1328
Kol'skiy Poluostrov
Finnsnes
Andenes
Salangen
Kautokeino
Inarijärvi
Inari
Ivalo
Kola
Pulozero
Lotta
Olenegorsk
Lovozero
Harstad
Hinnøya
Stokmarknes
Lofoten-Vesterålen
Narvik
Karesuando
Pallastunturi 807
Porttipahdan tekojärvi
Lokan tekojärvi
Monchegorsk
Oz. Imandra
Apatity
Svolvær
Vestfjorden
Torneträsk
Kebnekaise 2111
Kiruna
Muonio
Kittilä
Sodankylä
Savukoski
Sorsatunturi 626
Kovdor
Nivskiy
Kandalaksha
Umba
Kandalakshskaya Guba
Bodø
Fauske
Sarektjåkkå 2090
Malmberget
Gällivare
Pajala
Salla
Alakurtti
Oz. Kovdozero
Sulitjelma
Kvikkjokk
Porjus
Pello
Rovaniemi
Kemijärvi
Glomfjord
Svartisen 1599
Jokkmokk
Övertorneå
Ylitornio
Kemi
Yli Kitka
Oz. Pyaozero
Loukhi
Dønna
Mo i Rana
Vuollerim
Kuusamo
Kestenga
Sandnessjøen
Hornavan
Uddjaur
Boden
Tornio
Oz. Topozero
Vega
Mosjøen
N. Storfjället
Vindel
Storavan
Älvsbyn
Haparanda
Luleå
Pudasjärvi
Taivalkoski
Kalevala
Kem'
Brønnøysund
Kvigtind 1703
Sorsele
Arvidsjaur
Piteå
Hailuoto
Oulu
Oz. Kuyto
Yushkozero
Vikna
Rørvik
Storuman
Jörn
Muhos
Ammänsaari
Hyrynsalmi
Karelian R.
Kolvereid
Namsos
Vilhelmina
Lycksele
Skellefteå
Raahe
Oulujärvi
Kuhmo
Muyezerskiy
Hartkjølen 1390
Ströms Vattudal
Dorotea
Burträsk
Robertsfors
Kalajoki
Oulainen
Ylivieska
Kajaani
Reboly
Lendery
Åfjord
Malm
Steinkjer
Asele
Vännäs
Umeå
Haapajärvi
Kokkola
Iisalmi
Nurmes
Smøla
Hitra
Levanger
Strömsund
Jakobstad
Pielinen
Sukkozero
Kristiansund
Trondheim
Trondheimfj.
Stjørdal
Hammerdal
Bredbyn
Holmsund
Nykarleby
FINLAND
Molde
Trollheimen 1667
Støren
Järpen
Örnsköldsvik
Vaasa
Lapua
Kuopio
Outokumpu
Ilomantsi
Porosozero
Ålesund
Åndalsnes
Sylarna 1710
Storsjön
Östersund
Sollefteå
Seinäjoki
Karstula
Kallavesi
Joensuu
Pyhäselkä
Spjelkavik
Ørsta
Stranda
Snøhetta 2286
Oppdal
Ljungan
Bräcke
Indals
Kramfors
Härnösand
Laihia
Äänekoski
Suonenjoki
Varkaus
Orivesi
Vyartsilya
Suojarvi
Måløy
Nordfj.
Florø
Jostedalsbreen 1953
Dombås
Røros
Tynset
Hede
Ånge
Kaskinen
Kurikka
Kristiinankaupunki
Jyväskylä
Pieksämäki
Savonlinna
Pitkyaranta
Femund
Sundsvall
Mänttä
Jämsä
Puulavesi
Mikkeli
Sortavala
Salmi
Førde
Glittertind 2470
Otta
Österdalen
Sveg
Ljusnan
Ljusdal
Hudiksvall
Päijänne
Elisenvaara
Høyanger
Sognefjorden
Årdal
Lillehammer
Särna
Arbrå
Iggesund
Kankaanpää
Tampere
Heinola
Saimaa
Imatra
Priozersk
Lake Ladoga
Myrdal
Sälen
Söderhamn
Pori
Valkeakoski
Hämeenlinna
Lappeenranta
Svetogorsk
Bergen
Voss
Hallingdal
Gjøvik
Hamar
Rena
Älvdalen
Bollnäs
Yammala
Kokemäki
Forssa
Lahti
Kouvola
Vyborg
Hardangerfj.
Hårteigen 1691
Glåma
Vorma
Mora
Rättvik
Norrsundet
Rauma
Uusikaupunki
Riihimäki
Salpausselkä
Hamina
Primorsk
Odda
Malung
Sandviken
Gävle
Loimaa
Hyvinkää
Porvoo
Kotka
Zelenogorsk
Leirvik
Hønefoss
Falun
Borlänge
Åland
Turku
Salo
Kerava
Helsinki (Helsingfors)
St Petersburg (Leningrad)
Sauda
Rjukan
Oslo
Kongsvinger
Säter
Hedemora
Tierp
Öregrund
Naantali
Lohja
Karis
Kronshtadt
Lomonosov
Pushkin
Haugesund
Kongsberg
Notodden
Drammen
Lillestrøm
Ludvika
Avesta
Östhammar
Mariehamn
Gulf of Finland
Hangö
Gatchina
Tosno
Boknafj.
Dalen
Horten
Moss
Arvika
Sala
Uppsala
Kapellskär
Tallinn
Kunda
Narva
Jørpeland
Stavanger
Sandnes
Skien
Porsgrunn
Fredrikstad
Sarpsborg
Karlstad
Säffle
Karlskoga
Köping
Västerås
Enköping
Mälaren
Norrtälje
Paldiski
Tapa
Kohtla-Järve
Luga
Bygland
Larvik
Halden
Kristinehamn
Eskilstuna
Örebro
Strängnäs
Stockholm
Södertälje
Haapsalu
Türi
Lake Peipus
Gdov
Novgorod
Egersund
Evje
Kragerø
Risør
Arendal
Grimstad
Åmål
Vänern
Askersund
Kumla
Katrineholm
Nyköping
Nynäshamn
Hiiumaa
ESTONIA
Pärnu
Viljandi
Peipsi Järv
Tartu
Flekkefjord
Lindesnes
Mandal
Kristiansand
Uddevalla
Vänersborg
Lidköping
Mariestad
Skövde
Finspång
Motala
Norrköping
Oxelösund
Saaremaa
Kuressaare
Pskov
Dno
Trollhättan
Skara
Vättern
Linköping
Mjölby
Gotska Sandön
Skagerrak
Skagen
Hirtshals
Falköping
Tranås
Åtvidaberg
Fårö
Võru
Valga
Ostrov
Hjørring
Kungsbacka
Frederikshavn
Göteborg
Jönköping
Huskvarna
Västervik
Borås
Kinna
Nässjö
Eksjö
Vetlanda
Visby
Gotland
Gulf of Riga
Cēsis
Thisted
Ålborg
Varberg
Värnamo
Oskarshamn
Ventspils
Jūrmala
Riga
LATVIA
Opochka
Nykøbing
Kattegat
Falkenberg
Lammhult
Hemse
Kuldīga
Skive
Hadsund
Halmstad
Växjö
Borgholm
Saldus
Jelgava
Daugava
Rezekne
Velikiye Luki
Holstebro
Viborg
Randers
Grenå
Båstad
Ljungby
Nybro
Kalmar
Öland
Liepāja
Krustpils
Idritsa
Nevel
North Sea
Herning
Silkeborg
Århus
Ängelholm
Olofström
Venta
Mazeikiai
Biržai
Daugavpils
Ringkøbing
DENMARK
Helsingborg
Hässleholm
Karlskrona
Grobina
Varde
Horsens
Vejle
Helsingør
Kristianstad
Karlshamn
Ronneby
Šiauliai
Panevežys
Zap. Dvina
Polotsk
Esbjerg
Fredericia
Copenhagen
Roskilde
Landskrona
Åhus
Hanöbukten
Klaipėda
Vitebsk
Kolding
Odense
Slagelse
Kalundborg
Køge
Malmö
Lund
Simrishamn
BALTIC SEA
LITHUANIA
Haderslev
Åbenrå
Fåborg
Korsør
Nyborg
Næstved
Svendborg
Ystad
Trelleborg
Glubokoye
Flensburg
Sønderborg
Nakskov
Rønne
Bornholm (Den.)
Courland Lag.
Nemunas
Sovetsk
Ukmerge
Lepel'
Harwich
Nordfriesische Is.
Gelting
Rødbyhavn
Nykøbing
Gedser
Schleswig
Gulf of Gdańsk
RUS. FED.
Kaliningrad
Kaunas
Vilnius
Vileyka
Borisov
Kiel
Neumünster
Puttgarden
Travemünde
Sassnitz
Rügen
Stralsund
Słupsk
Gdynia
Sopot
Chernyakhovsk
Marijampole
Alytus
Molodechno
Cuxhaven
Elbe
Wilhelmshaven
Lübeck
Wismar
Rostock
Kołobrzeg
Koszalin
Gdańsk (Danzig)
Elbląg
Braniewo
Kętrzyn
Suwałki
Augustów
Minsk
Chervenʼ
Emden
Bremerhaven
Hamburg
Schwerin
Świnoujście
Szczecinek
Malbork
Ełk
Olsztyn
J. Śniardwy
Grodno
BELARUS
Stolbtsy
Oldenburg
Bremen
Pasewalk
Szczecin
Chojnice
Wisła
Kwidzyn
Ostróda
Bobruysk
Delmenhorst
Soltau
Neustrelitz
Oder
Stargard Szczeciński
POLAND
Narew
Łomża
Volkovysk
Baranovichi
Slutsk
Soligorsk
Emmen
GERMANY
Wittenberge
Piła
Bydgoszcz
Mława
Białystok
(BELORUSSIA)
Rheine
Hannover
Celle
Neuruppin
Eberswalde
Noteć
Toruń
Ostrów Mazowiecka
Gantsevichi
Enschede
Osnabrück
Braunschweig
Stendal
Berlin
Gorzów Wielkopolski
Włocławek
Płońsk
Pinsk
Pripyat'
Mozyr
Frankfurt
Słubice
Poznań
Warsaw
Bug
Brest
Kobrin
RUSSIAN FEDERATION
1:7.5M
0 100 200 300 km
0 50 100 150 mls

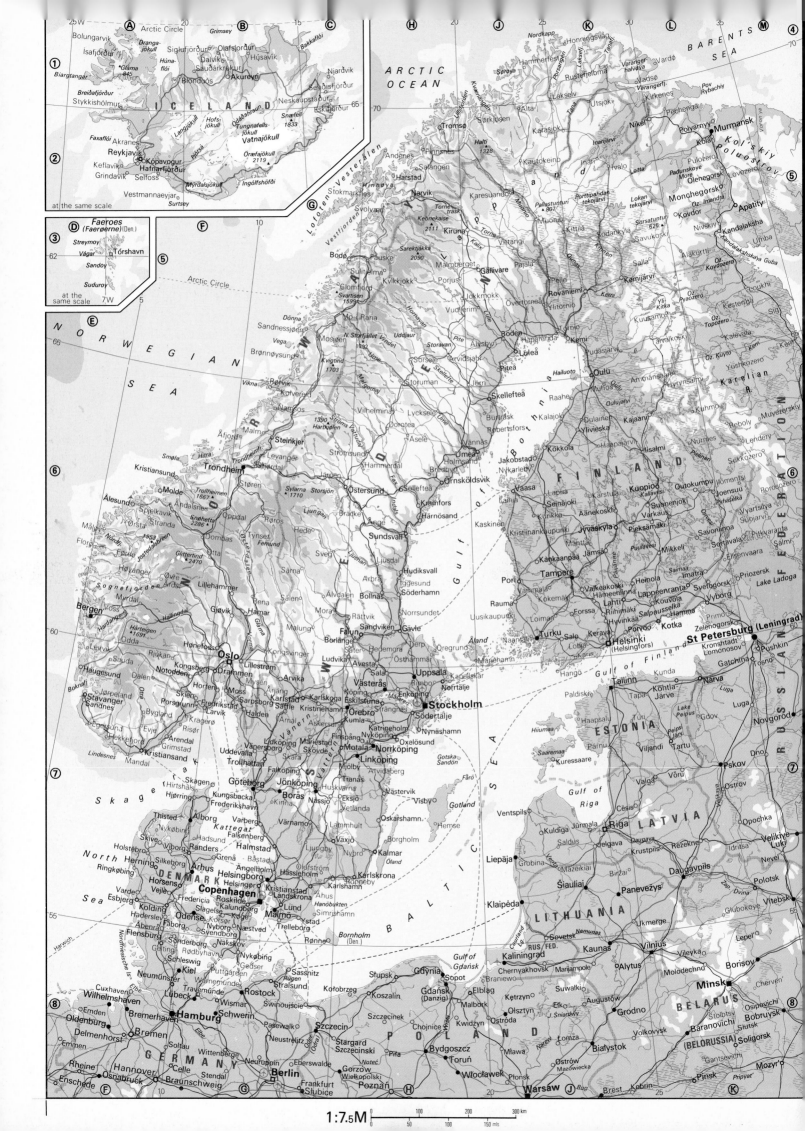

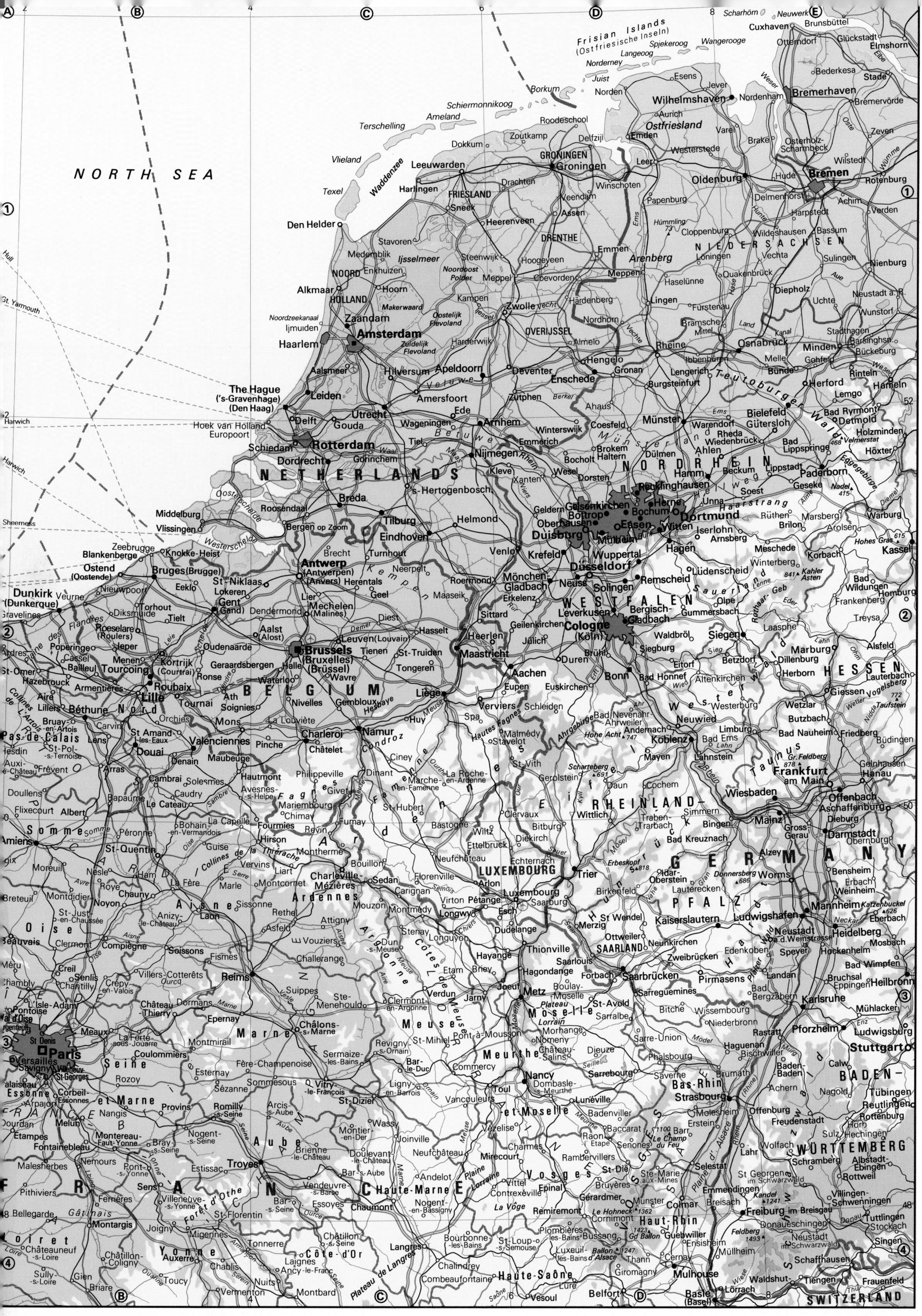
NORTH SEA
Frisian Islands
(Ostfriesische Inseln)
Borkum
Juist
Norderney
Langeoog
Spiekeroog
Wangerooge
Scharhörn
Neuwerk
Cuxhaven
Brunsbüttel
Glückstadt
Elmshorn
Otterndorf
Bederkesa
Stade
Bremerhaven
Bremervörde
Wilhelmshaven
Nordenham
Norden
Aurich
Ostfriesland
Emden
Jever
Esens
Schiermonnikoog
Ameland
Terschelling
Vlieland
Texel
Waddenzee
Dokkum
Zoutkamp
Roodeschool
Delfzijl
GRONINGEN
Groningen
Leeuwarden
Harlingen
FRIESLAND
Sneek
Drachten
Leer
Westerstede
Varel
Brake
Zeven
Osterholz-Scharmbeck
Wilstedt
Oldenburg
Bremen
Delmenhorst
Rotenburg
Achim
Verden
Winschoten
Veendam
Assen
Papenburg
Den Helder
Heerenveen
DRENTHE
Harpstedt
Wildeshausen
Bassum
Cloppenburg
NIEDERSACHSEN
Stavoren
Medemblik
Ijsselmeer
Steenwijk
Hoogeveen
Emmen
Arenberg
Löningen
Vechta
Sulingen
Nienburg
NOORD HOLLAND
Enkhuizen
Noordoost Polder
Meppel
Coevorden
Meppen
Haselünne
Quakenbrück
Diepholz
Alkmaar
Hoorn
Makerwaard
Kampen
Zwolle
Hardenberg
Lingen
Uchte
Neustadt a. R.
Noordzeekanaal
Ijmuiden
Zaandam
Amsterdam
Oostelijk Flevoland
Zuidelijk Flevoland
OVERIJSSEL
Nordhorn
Fürstenau
Bramsche
Wunstorf
Haarlem
Harderwijk
Almelo
Rheine
Osnabrück
Minden
Stadthagen
Bückeburg
Aalsmeer
Hilversum
Apeldoorn
Deventer
Hengelo
Enschede
Gronau
Ibbenbüren
Lengerich
Melle
Bünde
Herford
Rinteln
Hameln
The Hague
('s-Gravenhage)
(Den Haag)
Leiden
Amersfoort
Zutphen
Burgsteinfurt
Teutoburger Wald
Lemgo
Harwich
Hoek van Holland
Europoort
Delft
Utrecht
Gouda
Ede
Arnhem
Wageningen
Ahaus
Coesfeld
Münster
Warendorf
Bielefeld
Gütersloh
Rheda
Wiedenbrück
Bad Pyrmont
Detmold
Holzminden
Schiedam
Rotterdam
Tiel
Winterswijk
Emmerich
Ahlen
Bad Lippspringe
Höxter
Dordrecht
Gorinchem
Nijmegen
Bocholt
Brokem
Haltern
Dülmen
NETHERLANDS
's-Hertogenbosch
Kleve
Xanten
Wesel
Dorsten
Recklinghausen
Hamm
Beckum
Lippstadt
Paderborn
Geseke
NORDRHEIN
Oosterschelde
Breda
Roosendaal
Middelburg
Vlissingen
Westerschelde
Bergen op Zoom
Tilburg
Eindhoven
Helmond
Gelsenkirchen
Bottrop
Oberhausen
Duisburg
Mülheim
Essen
Bochum
Herne
Dortmund
Unna
Soest
Witten
Haarstrang
Rüthen
Marsberg
Warburg
Brilon
Arolsen
Iserlohn
Arnsberg
Sheerness
Zeebrugge
Blankenberge
Knokke-Heist
Ostend
(Oostende)
Brecht
Turnhout
Antwerp
(Antwerpen)
(Anvers)
Herentals
Neerpelt
Kempen
Venlo
Krefeld
Wuppertal
Düsseldorf
Hagen
Meschede
Korbach
Kassel
Dunkirk
(Dunkerque)
Veurne
Nieuwpoort
Bruges (Brugge)
Eeklo
St-Niklaas
Lokeren
Gent
(Gand)
Lier
Mechelen
(Malines)
Geel
Roermond
Mönchengladbach
Neuss
Solingen
Remscheid
Lüdenscheid
Winterberg
Bad Wildungen
Homberg
Frankenberg
Gravelines
Torhout
Diksmuide
Tielt
Dendermond
Maaseik
Erkelenz
WESTFALEN
Leverkusen
Bergisch-Gladbach
Olpe
Gummersbach
Rothaar-Geb
Treysa
Roeselare
(Roulers)
Poperinge
Ieper
Menen
Kortrijk
(Courtrai)
Aalst
(Alost)
Oudenaarde
Diest
Hasselt
Sittard
Geilenkirchen
Cologne
(Köln)
Waldbröl
Siegen
Laasphe
Brussels
(Bruxelles)
(Brüssel)
Leuven (Louvain)
Tienen
St-Truiden
Heerlen
Jülich
Maastricht
Brühl
Siegburg
Marburg
Alsfeld
St-Omer
Cassel
Bailleul
Tourcoing
Geraardsbergen
Halle
Tongeren
Aachen
Düren
Bonn
Eitorf
Betzdorf
Dillenburg
Herborn
HESSEN
Hazebrouck
Armentières
Roubaix
Lille
Ronse
Waterloo
Wavre
Eupen
Euskirchen
Bad Honnef
Altenkirchen
Lauterbach
Vogelsberg
BELGIUM
Liège
Verviers
Schleiden
Westerburg
Giessen
Béthune
Tournai
Ath
Soignies
Nivelles
Gembloux
Hesbaye
Huy
Spa
Hautes Fagnes
Malmédy
Stavelot
Bad Neuenahr-Ahrweiler
Andernach
Neuwied
Wetzlar
Butzbach
Pas-de-Calais
Lens
Carvin
Orchies
Mons
La Louvière
Charleroi
Namur
Condroz
Koblenz
Bad Ems
Limburg
Bad Nauheim
Friedberg
Büdingen
St Amand-les-Eaux
Douai
Valenciennes
Pinche
Châtelet
Ciney
Hohe Acht
Mayen
Lahnstein
Taunus
Gr. Feldberg
Frankfurt am Main
Hanau
Gelnhausen
Hesdin
St-Pol-s-Ternoise
Arras
Denain
Maubeuge
Philippeville
Dinant
Marche-en-Famenne
La Roche-en-Ardenne
St-Vith
Gerolstein
Daun
Cochem
Wiesbaden
Offenbach
Aschaffenburg
Doullens
Cambrai
Solesmes
Hautmont
Avesnes-s-Helpe
Givet
Famenne
Mariembourg
Chimay
St-Hubert
Eifel
RHEINLAND-
Wittlich
Traben-Trarbach
Simmern
Bingen
Mainz
Dieburg
Flixecourt
Albert
Bapaume
Le Cateau
Caudry
Bohain-en-Vermandois
La Capelle
Fourmies
Fumay
Revin
Bastogne
Clervaux
Bitburg
Diekirch
Wiltz
Bad Kreuznach
Gross-Gerau
Darmstadt
Amiens
Somme
Péronne
Hirson
Ardennes
Ettelbruck
Echternach
Hunsrück
Alzey
Oberburg
GERMANY
St-Quentin
Guise
Collines de la Thiérache
Monthermé
Neufchâteau
Bouillon
LUXEMBOURG
Trier
Erbeskopf
Idar-Oberstein
Donnersberg
Worms
Bensheim
Erbach
Moreuil
Nesle
Ham
Vervins
Liart
Charleville-Mézières
Florenville
Sedan
Arlon
Luxembourg
Birkenfeld
Lauterecken
Weinheim
Breteuil
Montdidier
Roye
Chauny
La Fère
Marle
Montcornet
Carignan
Virton
Pétange
Saarburg
PFALZ
Mannheim
Katzenbuckel
Noyon
Aisne
Sissonne
Rethel
Montmédy
Longwy
Esch
Merzig
St Wendel
Kaiserslautern
Ludwigshafen
Eberbach
St-Just-en-Chaussée
Anizy-le-Château
Laon
Attigny
Stenay
Longuyon
Dudelange
Ottweiler
Neunkirchen
Neustadt a.d. Weinstrasse
Heidelberg
Mosbach
Beauvais
Clermont
Compiègne
Soissons
Asfeld
Vouziers
Argonne
Côtes de Meuse
Thionville
Saarlouis
SAARLAND
Zweibrücken
Edenkoben
Speyer
Hockenheim
Oise
Fismes
Challerange
Dun-s-Meuse
Hayange
Briey
Hagondange
Forbach
Saarbrücken
Pirmasens
Landau
Bruchsal
Bad Wimpfen
Méru
Creil
Senlis
Chantilly
Villers-Cotterêts
Crépy-en-Valois
Reims
Suippes
Ste-Menehould
Etain
Verdun
Jarny
Metz
Boulay-Moselle
Sarreguemines
Bad Bergzabern
Eppingen
Heilbronn
Chambly
L'Isle-Adam
Pontoise
Château-Thierry
Dormans
Clermont-en-Argonne
Jœuf
Plateau Lorrain
St-Avold
Sarralbe
Bitche
Wissembourg
Niederbronn
Karlsruhe
Mühlacker
Val d'Oise
Argenteuil
St Denis
Paris
Versailles
Savigny
Villeneuve-St-Georges
Meaux
La Ferté-sous-Jouarre
Montmirail
Epernay
Marne
Châlons-s-Marne
Meuse
Revigny-s-Ornain
St-Mihiel
Pont-à-Mousson
Moselle
Morhange
Nomeny
Château-Salins
Sarre-Union
Dieuze
Phalsbourg
Sarrebourg
Saverne
Haguenau
Bischwiller
Rastatt
Baden-Baden
Pforzheim
Ludwigsburg
Stuttgart
Coulommiers
Fère-Champenoise
Sermaize-les-Bains
Bar-le-Duc
Commercy
Meurthe
Nancy
Dombasle-s-Meurthe
Lunéville
Bas-Rhin
Brumath
Calw
BADEN-
Essonne
Corbeil-Essonnes
Seine
Rozoy
Esternay
Sézanne
Sommesous
Vitry-le-François
St-Dizier
Ligny-en-Barrois
Vaucouleurs
Toul
Meurthe-et-Moselle
Badenviller
Strasbourg
Achern
Nagold
Tübingen
Reutlingen
Arpajon
Seine-et-Marne
Provins
Romilly-s-Seine
Arcis-s-Aube
Wassy
Montier-en-Der
Joinville
Vézelise
Baccarat
Raon-l'Etape
Senones
Le Champ du Feu
Molsheim
Offenburg
Freudenstadt
Rottenburg
Horb
Herrenberg
Dourdan
Etampes
Melun
Nangis
Montereau-Faut-Yonne
Bray-s-Seine
Nogent-s-Seine
Fontainebleau
Aube
Brienne-le-Château
Doulevant-le-Château
Neufchâteau
Mirecourt
Charmes
Rambervillers
St-Dié
Ste-Marie-aux-Mines
Sélestat
Erstein
Lahr
Wolfach
Schramberg
WÜRTTEMBERG
Albstadt-Ebingen
Rottweil
Malesherbes
Nemours
Pont-s-Yonne
Estissac
Troyes
Bar-s-Aube
Andelot
Plaine Lorraine
Vittel
Contrexéville
Vosges
Epinal
Bruyères
Gérardmer
Colmar
Emmendingen
St Georgen im Schwarzwald
Villingen-Schwenningen
Pithiviers
Sens
Villeneuve-s-Yonne
Forêt d'Othe
Vendeuvre-s-Barse
Haute-Marne
Chaumont
Nogent-en-Bassigny
La Vôge
Remiremont
Le Hohneck
Munster
Breisach
Kandel
Freiburg im Breisgau
Bellegarde
Gâtinais
Montargis
Ferrières
Joigny
St-Florentin
Essoyes
Mignennes
Bourbonne-les-Bains
Plombières-les-Bains
Cornimont
Haut-Rhin
Gd Ballon
Guebwiller
Ensisheim
Feldberg
Donaueschingen
Tuttlingen
Stockach
Loiret
Châteauneuf-s-Loire
Châtillon-Coligny
Yonne
Auxerre
Tonnerre
Châtillon-s-Seine
Langres
Côte-d'Or
Laignes
Ancy-le-Franc
St-Loup-s-Semouse
Luxeuil-les-Bains
Bussang
Ballon d'Alsace
Thann
Cernay
Mülheim
Neustadt im Schwarzwald
Singen
Schaffhausen
Sully-s-Loire
Gien
Briare
Toucy
Chablis
Nuits
Vermenton
Montbard
Plateau de Langres
Chalindrey
Combeaufontaine
Haute-Saône
Lure
Giromagny
Mulhouse
Belfort
Vesoul
Basle (Basel)
Lörrach
Waldshut-Tiengen
Frauenfeld
SWITZERLAND
1:2.5M
0 25 50 75 100 km
0 25 50 mls

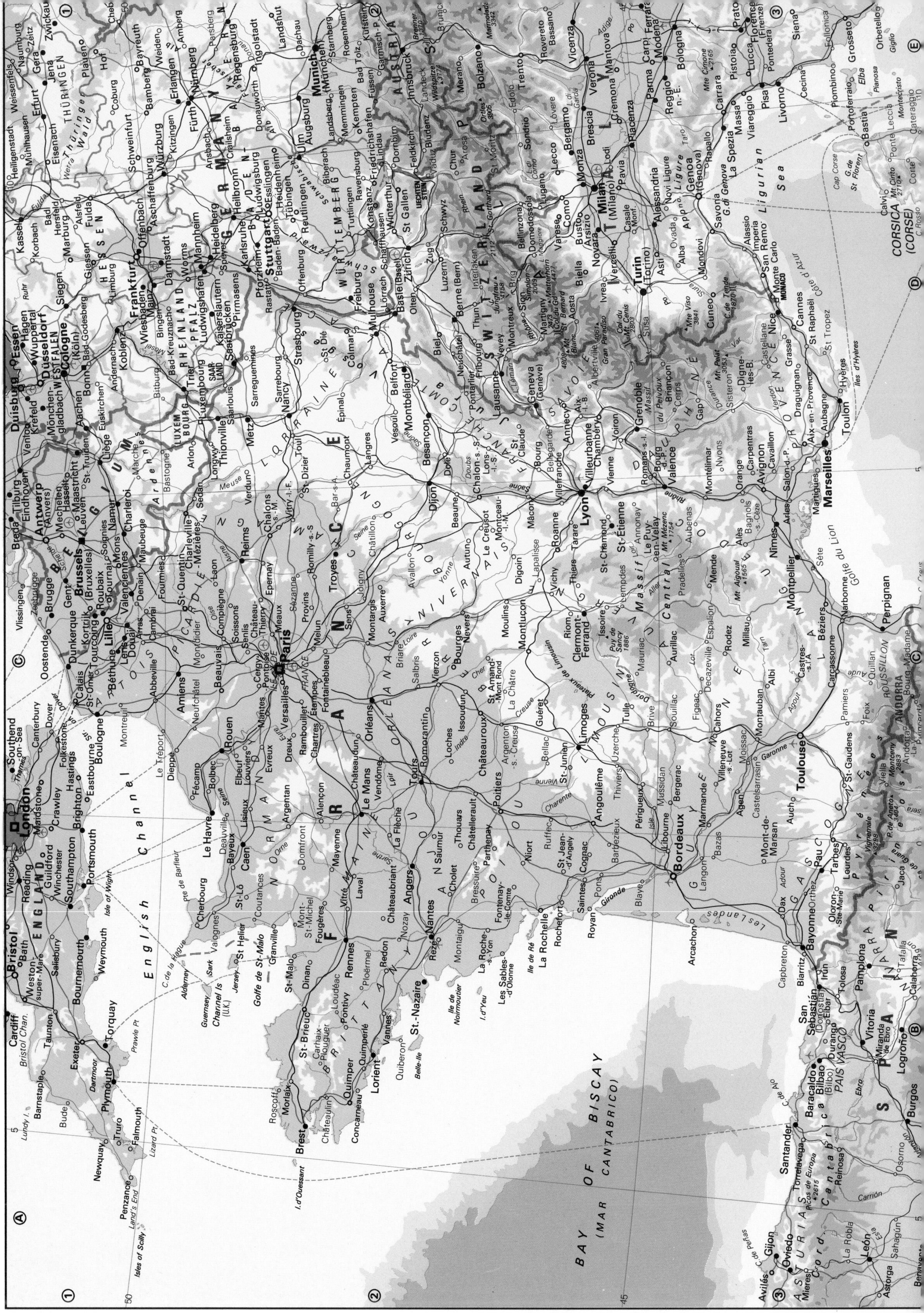

1:5M
0 50 100 150 200 km
0 50 100 mls
ENGLAND
London
Bristol
Cardiff
Southampton
Portsmouth
Brighton
Plymouth
English Channel
Channel Is (U.K.)
BAY OF BISCAY
(MAR CANTABRICO)
FRANCE
Paris
Lille
Rouen
Le Havre
Brest
Rennes
Nantes
Le Mans
Orléans
Tours
Poitiers
Limoges
Bordeaux
Toulouse
Montpellier
Marseilles
Toulon
Nice
Lyon
Grenoble
St-Étienne
Clermont-Ferrand
Dijon
Besançon
Strasbourg
Nancy
Metz
Reims
Amiens
BRITTANY
NORMANDY
PICARDIE
LORRAINE
BOURGOGNE
PROVENCE
LANGUEDOC
GASCOGNE
Massif Central
BELGIUM
Brussels (Bruxelles)
Antwerp (Anvers)
Liège
LUXEMBOURG
GERMANY
Cologne (Köln)
Düsseldorf
Frankfurt
Stuttgart
Munich (München)
Nürnberg
SWITZERLAND
Zürich
Berne (Bern)
Geneva (Genève)
Basle (Basel)
AUSTRIA
Innsbruck
ITALY
Milan (Milano)
Turin (Torino)
Genoa (Genova)
Ligurian Sea
CORSICA (CORSE)
SPAIN
Bilbao (Bilbo)
San Sebastián
Pamplona
Pyrénées
ANDORRA
Perpignan
Golfe du Lion

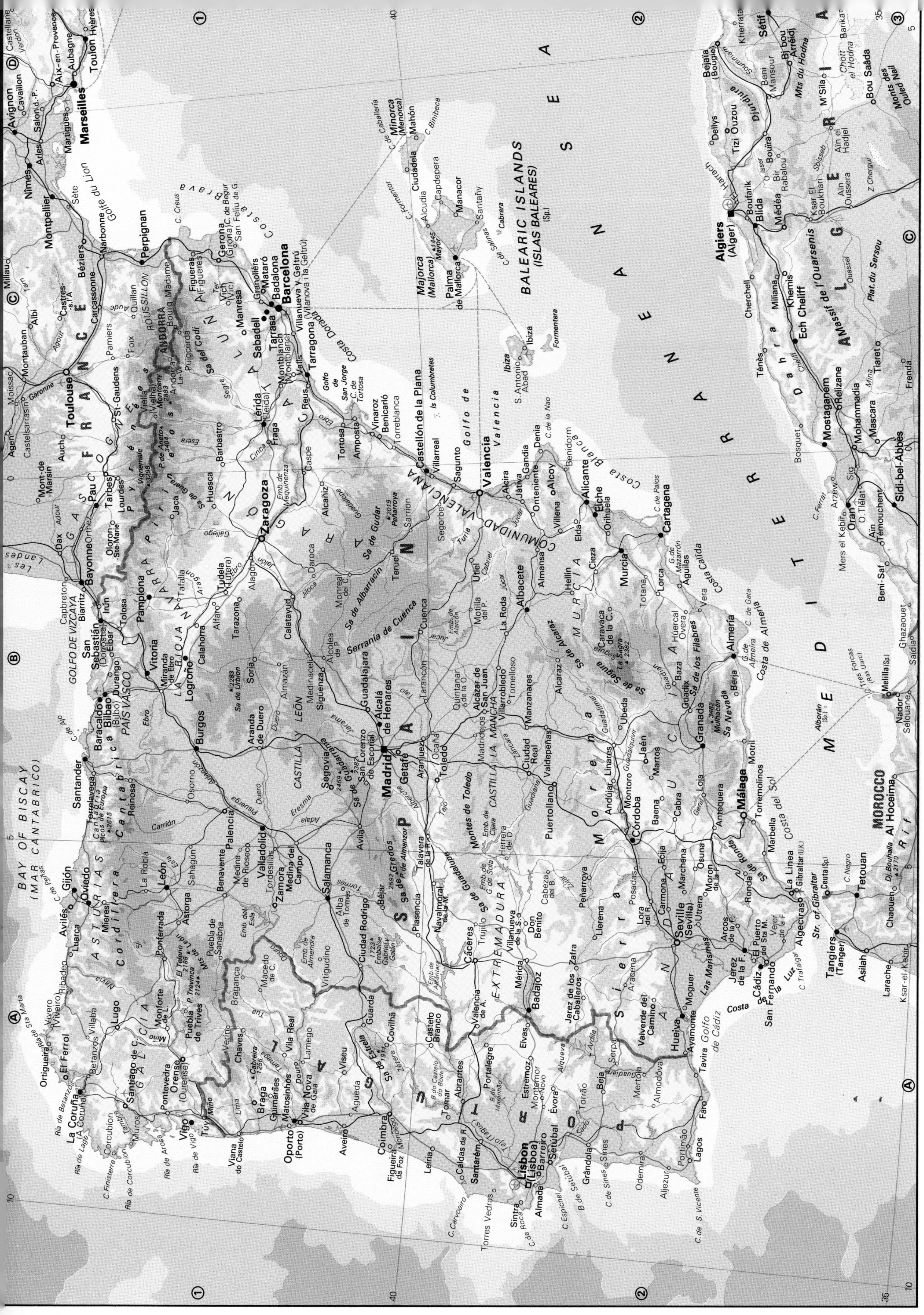
BAY OF BISCAY
(MAR CANTABRICO)
GOLFO DE VIZCAYA
Golfe du Lion
FRANCE
GASCOGNE
ROUSSILLON
ANDORRA
Pyrénées
PAÍS VASCO
NAVARRA
LA RIOJA
ARAGÓN
CATALUÑA
ASTURIAS
Cordillera Cantabrica
GALICIA
CASTILLA Y LEÓN
CASTILLA LA MANCHA
EXTREMADURA
COMUNIDAD VALENCIANA
MURCIA
ANDALUCIA
Sierra Morena
Sa Nevada
SPAIN
PORTUGAL
BALEARIC ISLANDS
(ISLAS BALEARES)
(Sp.)
Majorca
(Mallorca)
Minorca
(Menorca)
Ibiza
Formentera
Golfo de Valencia
Costa Brava
Costa Dorada
Costa Blanca
Costa del Sol
Costa de Almería
Costa Calida
Golfo de Cádiz
MEDITERRANEAN SEA
Str. of Gibraltar
Alborán
MOROCCO
Rif
ALGERIA
Massif de l'Ouarsenis
Madrid
Barcelona
Valencia
Zaragoza
Seville
(Sevilla)
Málaga
Bilbao
Lisbon
(Lisboa)
Oporto
(Porto)
Algiers
(Alger)
Oran
Toulouse
Marseilles
Montpellier
Perpignan
Bayonne
Palma de Mallorca
Gibraltar (U.K.)
Ceuta (Sp.)
Melilla (Sp.)
Tangiers
(Tanger)
1:5M
0 50 100 150 200 km
0 50 100 mls

Avallon
Vesoul
Belfort
Mulhouse
Freiburg
Biberach
Tuttlingen
Landsberg
Memmingen
Munich
Starnberg
Rosenheim
Vöcklabruck
Wels
St Pölten
Vienna
Mödling
Bratislava
Hainfeld
Lörrach
Konstanz
Ravensburg
Kempten
GERMANY
Salzburg
Gmunden
Steyr
Schaffhausen
Friedrichshafen
Bad Tölz
Bad Ischl
Mariazell
Wr. Neustadt
M'ovar
Basle (Basel)
Winterthur
Lindau
Füssen
Enns
Neunkirchen
Sopron
Dijon
Besançon
Montbéliard
Olten
Zürich
Dornbirn
Garmisch-P.
Kufstein
Dachstein 2996
Liezen
Eisenerz
St Gallen
Beaune
Dôle
Autun
Biel
Feldkirch
Kitzbühel
Hochkönig 2938
Radstad
Leoben
Bruck an der Mur
Le Creusot
Chalon-s.-S.
Neuchâtel
Zug
LIECHTENSTEIN
Vaduz
Bludenz
Innsbruck
AUSTRIA
Digoin
Montceau-l.-M.
Pontarlier
Lons-l.-S.
Berne (Bern)
Luzern
Schwyz
Landeck
Brenner 1375
Grossglockner 3798
Badgastein
Mur
Judenburg
Graz
Gleisdorf
Szombathely
Fribourg
Thun
Interlaken
Rhein
Chur
Wildspitze 3774
Mâcon
Lausanne
SWITZERLAND
Jungfrau 4158
Arosa
Brunico
Lienz
Spittal
Wolfsberg
Leibnitz
Zalaegerszeg
St Claude
Vevey
Montreux
St Gotthard 2112
Merano
Bourg
Sion
Brig
Villach
Klagenfurt
Maribor
Roanne
Geneva (Genève)
Bellegarde
Villefranche
Bellinzona
St Moritz
Ortles 3905
Bolzano
Cortina d'A.
Tarvisio
Drava
Nagykanizsa
Tarare
Martigny
Simplon 2009
Domodossola
Marmolada 3342
Jesenice
Velenje
Lyon
Annecy
Col du Gd St Bernard 2473
Matterhorn 4477
L. Maggiore
Edolo
Dolomitiche
Gemona
Kranj
Celje
Varazdin
Villeurbanne
Mt Blanc 4808
Lugano
L. di Como
Sondrio
Trento
Belluno
St-Chamond
Aix-l.-B.
Chambéry
Aosta
Varese
Lecco
Alpi
Udine
Ljubljana
Koprivnica
St-Étienne
Vienne
Albertville
Biella
Como
SLOVENIA
Bjelovar
Annonay
FRANCE
Voiron
4061 Gran Paradiso
Busto Arsizio
Bergamo
Lóvere
Rovereto
Bassano
Piave
Gorizia
Monfalcone
Brežice
Zagreb
Virovitica
Romans-s.-I.
Grenoble
Ivrea
Novara
Monza
L. di Garda
Treviso
Trieste
Postojna
Novo Mesto
Daruvar
Mt Mézenc 1754
Bourg-d'O.
Col du Mt Cenis 2083
Vercelli
Milan (Milano)
Brescia
Vicenza
Mestre
Koper
Karlovac
Pakrac
Valence
Massif du Pelvoux
Susa
Turin (Torino)
Lodi
Verona
Padova
Venice (Venezia)
Sisak
Aubenas
Briançon
Casale Monf.
Pavia
Cremona
Mantova
G. di Venezia
Poreč
Rijeka (Fiume)
Vrbovsko
CROATIA
Corps
Asti
Piacenza
Adige
Rovigo
Chioggia
Istra
Ogulin
Una
Montélimar
Gap
Mte Viso 3841
Alessandria
Po
Rovinj
Krk
Senj
Nyons
Alba
Ovada
Novi Ligure
Parma
Carpi
Ferrara
Pula
Cres
Bihać
Banja Luka
Bagnols-s.-Cèze
Orange
Durance
Mt Pelat 3053
Cuneo
Stura
Mondovi
App. Ligure
Taro
Reggio n.-E.
Modena
Reno
Argenta
Rab
Velebit
Perušić
Vrtoče
Carpentras
Sisteron
Genoa (Genova)
Bologna
Lošinj
Karlobag
Gospić
Ključ
Nîmes
Avignon
Digne
C. de Tende 1870
Savona
Rapallo
Mte Cimone 2165
Imola
Ravenna
Cavaillon
Var
G. di Genova
Faenza
Forlì
Pag
Arles
Salon-d.-P.
Verdon
Castellane
Alassio
Imperia
La Spezia
Carrara
Cesena
Zadar
Jajce
PROVENCE
Nice
San Remo
Massa
Pistoia
Rimini
SAN MARINO
Dugi O.
Knin
Draguignan
Grasse
MONACO
Monte Carlo
Ligurian Sea
Viareggio
Lucca
Prato
Pesaro
Fano
Martigues
Aix-en-Provence
Cannes
Pisa
Florence (Firenze)
Urbino
Senigallia
Šibenik
Cincer 2004
Marseilles
Aubagne
St-Raphaël
Côte d'Azur
Pontedera
Livorno
Kornat
ADRIATIC SEA
Toulon
Hyères
St-Tropez
Cecina
Siena
Arezzo
Città di Castello
Ancona
Split (Spalato)
Iles d'Hyères
Cap Corse
G. de St Florent
Macerata
Fabriano
Brač
Makarska
Piombino
Follonica
Perugia
Hvar
Portoferraio
Bastia
Elba
Mte Amiata 1738
Grosseto
Foligno
Ascoli Piceno
Vis
Korčula
Calvi
Mt Cinto 2710
Pianosa
L. di Bolsena
Terni
Teramo
Lastovo
Ponte Leccia
Orbetello
Mte Corno 2912
C. Rosso
Corte
Montecristo
Giglio
Viterbo
Rieti
L'Aquila
Pescara
Chieti
Palagruža
Cateraggio
L. di Bracciano
Pianosa
Ajaccio
L'Incudine 2136
CORSICA (CORSE)
Civitavecchia
Tevere (Tiber)
Sulmona
Vasto
Termoli
I. Tremiti
G. d'Ajaccio
Porticcio
Città del Vaticano
Tivoli
Avezzano
Atessa
Rodi Garganico
Vieste
Sartène
Porto Vecchio
Rome (Roma)
Lido di Ostia
Ostia
Sora
Biferno
S. Severo
Prom. del Gargano
Manfredonia
Bonifacio
Strait of Bonifacio
Frosinone
Isernia
Campobasso
Sta Teresa di G.
Anzio
Latina
Cassino
Mte Miletto 2050
Foggia
Barletta
Molfetta
Asinara
Terracina
Gaeta
Formia
Cerignola
Andria
Bari
Porto Torres
Olbia
Caserta
Benevento
Ofanto
Sassari
L. del Coghinas
I. Ponziane
Naples (Napoli)
Pozzuoli
Vesuvio 1277
Avellino
Altamura
Le Murge
Alghero
Siniscola
Tirso
Ischia
Torre del G.
Salerno
Potenza
Matera
Taranto
Macomer
Capri
Sorrento
Eboli
Basento
Nuoro
SARDINIA (SARDEGNA)
Agropoli
Metaponto
L. Omodeo
Mti del Gennargentu 1835
TYRRHENIAN SEA
Agri
Oristano
Pta Licosa
Appno. Lucano
G. di Oristano
Arbatax
Sapri
Mte Pollino 2248
G. di Policastro
Sanluri
Castrovillari
Corigliano Calabro
Rossano
Iglesias
Muravera
S. Pietro
Carbonia
Cagliari
Paola
La Sila
Botte Donato 1929
S. Antioco
San Antioco
G. di Cagliari
C. Carbonara
Cosenza
Crotone
C. Teulada
Nicastro
Catanzaro
Stromboli
G. di Squillace
Ustica
Vibo Valentia
Alicudi
Salina
Filicudi
Lipari
Pecoraro 1423
MEDITERRANEAN SEA
SICILY (SICILIA)
Isole Lipari
Vulcano
Palmi
C. San Vito
Palermo
Barcellona
Messina
Montallo 1956
Locri
Trapani
Partinico
Cefalù
Reggio di Calabria
I. Egadi
Alcamo
Mti Nebrodi
Str. de Messina
C. Spartivento
Marsala
Castelvetrano
Etna 3323
Giarre
La Galite
Mazara del Vallo
Acireale
C. Bougaroun
Ras El Hadid
C. Serrat
C. Blanc
Sciacca
Enna
Paterno
Catania
Bizerte
Caltanissetta
Jijel
Skikda
Annaba (Bône)
El Kala
Mateur
Menzel
G. de Tunis
C. Bon
Sicilian Channel
Agrigento
Canicatti
Lentini
Petite Kabylie
El Milia
Azzaba
Tabarka
Licata
Gela
Syracuse (Siracusa)
Béja
Tunis
Halq el Qued
Kelibia
Pantelleria (It.)
Ragusa
Constantine
Guelma
Mts de la Medjerda
Medjerda
Vittoria
Modica
Noto
El Eulma
El Kroub
Souk Ahras
Jendouba
Téboursouk
Nabeul
C. I. d. Correnti
ALGERIA
1295 Dj Zaghouan
Hammamet
Malta Channel
Le Kef
Mellègue
TUNISIA
Enfida
Golfe de Hammamet
Oumel Bouaghi
Aïn Beïda
Gozo
Mts de Belezma
Batna
Makthar
MALTA
Valletta
Khenchela
Kalaat Khasba
Sousse
Mf de l'Aures
2328 Dj Chélia
Tébessa
Mts de Tébessa
M'saken
Monastir
Kairouan
Moknine
Mts des Nementcha

1:5M — 0 50 100 150 200 km; 0 50 100 mls

Nové Zámky
Salgótarján
Miskolc
Nyíregyháza
Mátészalka
Satu Mare
Baia Mare
Borşa
Suceava
Orgeyev
Kalarash
Dubossary
Zhovten'
Berezovka
Komárno
Esztergom
Vác
Gyöngyös
Eger
Hatvan
Hajdúböszörmény
Debrecen
Újfehértó
Carei
Mtii Rodnei
Vatra Dornei
Fălticeni
Paşcani
Iaşi
MOLDOVA
Kishinev
(Chişinău)
Tiraspol'
Razdel'naya
Győr
Tatabánya
Budapest
Marghita
Bistriţa
Pietrosu 2303
Roman
Bendery
Kotovsk
(MOLDAVIA)
Odessa
Székesfehérvár
Szolnok
Karcag
Berettyóújfalu
Oradea
Zalău
Dej
Mtii Călimani
Bicaz
Piatra-Neamţ
Huşi
Dniester (Dnestr)
Belgorod Dnestrovskiy
Veszprém
Dunaújváros
Cegléd
Nagykőrös
Kecskemét
Siófok
Balaton
Salonta
Vlădeasa 1836
Cluj-Napoca
Reghin
Gheorgheni
Bacău
Vaslui
Komrat
HUNGARY
Turda
Luduş
Tîrgu Mureş
Miercurea-Ciuc
Oneşti
Bîrlad
Sarata
Fonyód
Paks
K'félegyháza
Békéscsaba
Orosháza
Bihor 1849
Mtii Apuseni
Tîrnăveni
Sighişoara
Nemira 1649
Adjud
Kagul
Artsiz
Dombóvár
Kaposvár
Kiskunhalas
Szekszárd
Baja
Hódmezővásárhely
Sîntana
Mediaş
Sfîntu Gheorghe
Tecuci
Prut (Prutul)
UKRAINE
Bolgrad
Kiliya
Vilkovo
Pécs
Szeged
Makó
Arad
Mtii Zarandului
Alba Iulia
Sebeş
Rupea
Făgăraş
Focşani
Reni
Izmail
Subotica
Senta
Lipova
Mureş
Deva
Orăştie
Sibiu
Moldoveanu 2543
Braşov
Galaţi
Sulina
Sombor
Kikinda
Timişoara
Lugoj
Hunedoara
ROMANIA
Cindrelu 2245
Carpaţii Meridionali
Rîmnicu Sărat
Brăila
Tulcea
Apatin
Vrbas
Bečej
Caransebeş
Peleaga 2509
Mtii
(Transylvanian Alps)
Buzău
Babadag
L. Razim
Našice
Osijek
Zrenjanin
Deta
Reşiţa
Rîmnicu Vîlcea
Cîmpina
Mizil
Hîrşova
Dakovo
Vukovar
Danube (Dunav)
Novi Sad
Vojvodina
Vršac
Vinkovci
Ruma
Oraviţa
Tîrgu Jiu
Piteşti
Tîrgovişte
Ploieşti
Urziceni
Slobozia
Ialomiţa
Bosanski Brod
Pancevo
Belgrade (Beograd)
Dobreta-Turnu-Severin
Jiu
Olt
Buftea
Bucharest (Bucureşti)
Argeş
Calarasi
Feteşti
Danube (Dunărea)
Medgidia
Constanţa
Doboj
Bijeljina
Šabac
Sava
Smederevo
Filiaşi
Slatina
Videle
Silistra
Negru Vodă
Mangalia
Tuzla
Loznica
Smed. Palanka
Craiova
Caracal
Roşiori de Vede
Tutrakan
Alfatar
Bosna
Zvornik
Valjevo
YUGOSLAVIA
Bor
Băileşti
Alexandria
Giurgiu
Ruse
Ludogorie
Dobrich
Zenica
Drina
Kragujevac
Svetozarevo
Ćuprija
Vidin
Calafat
Corabia
Turnu Măgurele
Balchik
N. Kaliakra
Sarajevo
Užice
Zaječar
Lom
Danube (Dunav)
Razgrad
Novi Pazar
Višegrad
Čačak
Paracin
Byala Slatina
Pleven
Levski
Byala
Popovo
Shumen
Varna
Goražde
Kraljevo
Mikhaylovgrad
Iskur
Tŭrgovishte
Konjic
Lelija 2032
Kruševac
Berkovitsa
Vratsa
Lovech
Sevlievo
Gorna Orjahovica
Veliko Tŭrnovo
Byala
BLACK SEA
Pljevlja
SERBIA
Niš
2169 Midžor
Morava
Pirot
Kom 2016
Troyan
Gabrovo
Aytos
N. Emine
Mostar
Avtovac
Lim
Leskovac
Botevgrad
Stara Planina
Sliven
Karnobat
Burgas
2522 Durmitor
Tara
Novi Pazar
Kazanlŭk
Tundzha
Ploče
Neretva
MONTENEGRO
Ibar
Kosovska Mitrovica
Sofia (Sofiya)
Karlovo
Panagyurishte
Stara Zagora
Nova Zagora
Yambol
Michurin
Pelješac
Bileća
Nikšić
Ivangrad
Priština
Pernik
BULGARIA
Mljet
CRO.
Trebinje
Peć
Kosovo
Vranje
Ikhtiman
Elkhovo
Malko Tŭrnovo
Dubrovnik
Podgorica
Kotor
2692 Jezerce
Dakovica
Uroševac
Kyustendil
Stanke Dimitrov
Chirpan
Dimitrovgrad
Demirköy
Budva
Prizren
Rujen 2252
Musala 2925
Pazardzhik
Plovdiv
Khaskovo
Kharmanli
Yıldız Dağları
Karadeniz Boğazı (Bosporus)
Drin
Kumanovo
Blagoevgrad
Asenovgrad
Svilengrad
Kırklareli
Edirne
Havsa
Bar
Shkodër (Scutari)
Kukës
Rudoka Pl. 2702
Skopje
Kočani
Struma
Vikhren 2915
Mesta
Rodopi
Smolyan
Kŭrdzhali
Arda
Babaeski
Lüleburgaz
Ulcinj
Gostivar
Titov Veles
Sadanski
Ergene
Uzunköprü
Çorlu
Üsküdar
Kartal
Lezhe
Peshkopi
MACEDONIA
Strumica
Kulata
Néstos (Mesta)
İstanbul
Krujë
Kicevo
Kavadarci
Prilep
Dráma
Xánthi
Komotiní
Sápai
Ipsala
Malkara
Tekirdağ
Sea of Marmara
Yalova
İznik G.
SEA
Durrës
Tiranë
Gevgelija
Sérrai
Keşan
Tekir D.
Marmara Adasi
Gemlik
Kavajë
ALBANIA
Ohrid
Bitola
Kilkís
Kavála
Alexandroúpolis
Bursa
Elbasan
Ohridsko Jez.
Prispansko Jezero
Nigríta
Thásos
Saros Körfezi
Gelibolu (Gallipoli)
Bandırma
Karacabey
Monopoli
Lushnjë
Tomorrit 2480
Yiannitsá
Edhessa
Thessaloníki (Salonica)
K. Strimonikós
Samothráki
Biga
Mustafa-Kemalpasa
Fier
Berat
Devoll
Flórina
Véroia
Khalkidhikí
Gökçeada
Eceabat
Çanakkale
Gönen
Kus G.
Orhaneli
Brindisi
Ballsh
Korçë
Kastoria
Ptolemaís
Kozaní
Kateríni
Políyiros
Áthos 2033
Vlorë
Grámmos 2503
Aliákmon
K. Singitikós
Manduria
Lecce
Strait of Otranto
Vjosë
Ólimbos (Olympus) 2917
K. Toronaíos
Límnos
Kástron
Bozca Ada
Ezine
Edremit
Balıkesir
Simav
Dursunbey
Tavşanlı
Gjirokastër
Smólikas 2633
Thermaïkós Kólpos
Ayvacık
Bigadiç
Akdağ 2089
Maglie
Otranto
Gallipoli
Sarandë
Kalabáka
Tírnavos
Lárisa
Áyios Evstrátios
Edremit K.
Burhaniye
Ayvalık
Sındırgı
Soma
Simav
Corfu (Kérkira)
Ioánnina
GREECE
Pindhos
Pinios
Vólos
Kallonís K.
Mitilíni
Bergama
Kırkağaç
Akhisar
C. Sta Maria di Leuca
Corfu (Kérkira)
Igoumenítsa
Tzoumérka 2469
Kardhítsa
Fársala
Almirós
Skíathos
Iliodhrómia
Lésvos
TURKEY
Pta Alice
Árta
Dhomokós
Óthris 1726
Skópelos
Skíros
Çandarlı K.
Manisa
Turgutlu
Kula
Gediz
IONIAN ISLANDS (Iónioi Nísoi)
Timfristós 2316
Istiáia
Euboea (Évvoia)
AEGEAN SEA
Menemen
Bornova
Salihli
Alaşehir
Préveza
Lamía
Amfilokhía
Livanátais
Kími
Psará
Khíos
İzmir (Smyrna)
Boz Dağları
Ödemiş
Levkás
Levkás
2510 Gióna
Amfissa
Khalkis
Urla
Çeşme
Torbalı
Tire
Buldan
C. Rizzuto
Agrinion
Návpaktos
Levádhia
Thívai
Akr. Kafirévs
Selçuk
Aydın
Nazilli
Denizli
Kefallinía
Mesolóngion
Pátrai
Gulf of Corinth
Akharnai
Athens (Athína)
Káristos
Kuşadası K.
Sámos
Argostólion
Aíyion
Sikionia
Killini 2376
Mégara
Piraiévs
Ándros
Ikaría
Pagondhas
Söke
Çine
IONIAN SEA
Corinth (Kórinthos)
Saronikós K.
Tínos
Fournoi
Milas
Muğla
Zákinthos
Amaliás
Peloponnese
Aíyna
Kéa
Míkonos
Pátmos
Güllük K.
Pirgos
Árgos
Návplion
Síros
Léros
Bodrum
Zákinthos (Zante)
Trípolis
Kíthnos
CYCLADES (Kikládhes)
DODECANESE (Dhodhekánisos)
Kálimnos
Gökova K.
Marmaris
Kiparissiakós Kólpos
Alfiós
Argolikós K.
Ídhra
Sérifos
Páros
Náxos
Kos
Kiparissía
Megalópolis
1935 Párnon Ó.
Sífnos
Mirtoan Sea
Amorgós
Sími
Rhodes (Ródhos)
Filiatrá
Kalámai
Spartí
Messíni
Mílos
Síkinos
Íos
Astipálaia
Tílos
Alimniá
Rhodes (Ródhos)
Pílos
Yíthion
Moláoi
Messiniakós Kólpos
Lakonikós Kólpos
Neápolis
Akr. Maléa
Thíra
Anáfi
Khálki
Líndos
Akr. Taínaron
Kíthira
Sea of Crete
Kárpathos
Andikíthira
Akr. Spátha
Crete (Kríti)
Khaniá
Réthimnon
Iráklion
Merabéllou K.
Akr. Sídheros
Kásos
Kastéli
Lévka Óri 2452
Ídhi Óros 2456
Dhíkti Óri 2148
Sitía
Timbákion
Ierápetra
Akr. Líthinon
Gávdhos
45
40
35
20
25
30
D
E
F
G
A
①
②
③
④

NORTH SEA
DENMARK
Jylland (Jutland)
Kattegat
SWEDEN
BALTIC
Göteborg
Skagen
Hirtshals
Hjørring
Frederikshavn
Ålborg
Thisted
Nykøbing
Skive
Hobro
Hadsund
Holstebro
Viborg
Randers
Grenå
Herning
Silkeborg
Århus
Skjern
Horsens
Samsø
Varde
Vejle
Kolding
Esbjerg
Fredericia
Kalundborg
Odense
Fyn
Sjælland
Copenhagen (København)
Roskilde
Køge
Haderslev
Åbenrå
Assens
Nyborg
Korsør
Næstved
Svendborg
Vordingborg
Sønderborg
Flensburg
Nakskov
Lolland
Rødbyhavn
Nykøbing
Falster
Gedser
Møn
Bornholm
Rønne
Helsingør
Hillerød
Helsingborg
Landskrona
Lund
Malmö
Trelleborg
Ystad
Simrishamn
Hanöbukten
Kristianstad
Karlshamn
Ronneby
Karlskrona
Kalmar
Öland
Borgholm
Nybro
Växjö
Älmhult
Markaryd
Hässleholm
Ängelholm
Båstad
Halmstad
Laholm
Falkenberg
Varberg
Ljungby
Värnamo
Kungsbacka
Mölndal
Borås
Jönköping
Huskvarna
Nässjö
Eksjö
Vetlanda
Hultsfred
Västervik
Oskarshamn
Mönsterås
Emån
Ålem
Anholt
Læsø
Limfjorden
Sylt
Westerland
Rømø
Als
SCHLESWIG-HOLSTEIN
Husum
Schleswig
Kiel
Kieler Bucht
Heide
Rendsburg
Neumünster
Oldenburg
Puttgarden
Fehmarn
Mecklenburger Bucht
Itzehoe
Neustadt
Travemünde
Lübeck
Warnemünde
Rostock
Stralsund
Rügen
Sassnitz
Greifswald
Wismar
Cuxhaven
Ostfriesische Ins.
Wilhelmshaven
Elmshorn
Stade
Bremerhaven
Hamburg
Elbe
Lauenburg
Schwerin
MECKLENBURG-VORPOMMERN
Malchin
Anklam
Neubrandenburg
Świnoujście
Szczecin
Ustka
Kołobrzeg
Koszalin
Karlino
Białogard
Świdwin
Szczecinek
Goleniów
Stargard Szczeciński
Choszczno
Wałcz
Piła
Jastrowie
Myślibórz
Krzyż
Noteć
Gorzów Wlkp.
Kostrzyn
Skwierzyna
Pniewy
Oborniki
Poznań
Słubice
Świebodzin
Środa Wlk.
Zielona Góra
Nowa Sól
Leszno
Jarocin
Gubin
Żary
Głogów
Szprotawa
Rawicz
Wołow
Bolesławiec
Legnica
Wrocław (Breslau)
Jelenia Góra
Świdnica
Wałbrzych
Dzierżoniów
Śnieżka 1603
Jablonec n.N.
Bielawa
Kłodzko
Nysa
Terschelling
Ameland
Vlieland
Texel
Den Helder
Leeuwarden
Harlingen
Groningen
Emden
Leer
Sneek
Heerenveen
Assen
Emmen
Meppen
Alkmaar
Hoorn
Zaanstad
Haarlem
Amsterdam
Kampen
Zwolle
Lingen
The Hague ('s-Gravenhage) (Den Haag)
Leiden
Hilversum
Deventer
Hengelo
Apeldoorn
Enschede
Amersfoort
Utrecht
Rotterdam
Dordrecht
Nijmegen
Arnhem
Coesfeld
Vlissingen
Breda
Tilburg
's-Hertogenbosch
Eindhoven
Venlo
Bocholt
Haltern
Oostende
Zeebrugge
Bruges
Gent
Antwerp (Antwerpen) (Anvers)
Mechelen
Kortrijk
Brussels (Bruxelles) (Brussel)
Hasselt
Leuven
Maastricht
Tourcoing
Roubaix
Lille
Tournai
Soignies
Mons
Namur
Liège
St-Truiden
Béthune
Valenciennes
Douai
Arras
Cambrai
Denain
Charleroi
Maubeuge
Fourmies
BELGIUM
Marche
Ardennes
Bastogne
St-Quentin
Charleville-Mézières
Sedan
Arlon
LUXEMBOURG
Luxembourg
Compiègne
Laon
Soissons
Aisne
Oise
Château-Thierry
Reims
Epernay
Longwy
Thionville
Verdun
Metz
Châlons-s.-M.
Sézanne
Provins
Vitry-l.-F.
St-Dizier
Romilly-s.-S
Toul
Nancy
Troyes
Sens
Joigny
Bar-s.-A.
Chaumont
Épinal
St Dié
Auxerre
Châtillon
Langres
Colmar
Vosges
Avallon
Vesoul
Belfort
Mulhouse
Montbéliard
Dijon
Besançon
Dôle
Beaune
Autun
Chalon-s.-S
Lons-l.-S.
Le Creusot
Montceau-l.-M.
Digoin
Mâcon
Roanne
Bourg
Tarare
Villefranche
Lyon
Villeurbanne
St-Chamond
St-Étienne
Vienne
Annonay
Romans-s.-I.
Valence
Grenoble
Aubenas
Montélimar
Gap
Briançon
FRANCE
CHAMPAGNE
LORRAINE
BOURGOGNE
FRANCHE-COMTÉ
Jura
SAVOIE
DAUPHINÉ
Saarlouis
Saarbrücken
Sarreguemines
Sarrebourg
Strasbourg
Offenburg
Kaiserslautern
Pirmasens
Trier
SAARLAND
RHEINLAND-PFALZ
Bad-Kreuznach
Bingen
Mainz
Wiesbaden
Worms
Ludwigshafen
Mannheim
Heidelberg
Speyer
Karlsruhe
Rastatt
Baden-Baden
Pforzheim
Stuttgart
Esslingen
Ludwigsburg
Heilbronn
Crailsheim
Reutlingen
Tübingen
Heidenheim
Ulm
Augsburg
Freiburg
Schwarzwald
Lörrach
Basle (Basel)
BADEN-WÜRTTEMBERG
Tuttlingen
Konstanz
Schaffhausen
Ravensburg
Friedrichshafen
Biberach
Kempten
Memmingen
Landsberg
Füssen
Lindau
Münster
NORDRHEIN-WESTFALEN
Hamm
Gütersloh
Bielefeld
Osnabrück
Rheine
Duisburg
Essen
Dortmund
Krefeld
Wuppertal
Hagen
Mönchengladbach
Düsseldorf
Cologne (Köln)
Aachen
Bonn
Bad-Godesberg
Euskirchen
Siegen
Andernach
Koblenz
Limburg
Bitburg
Frankfurt am Main
Offenbach
Darmstadt
Aschaffenburg
Giessen
Marburg
HESSEN
Fulda
Alsfeld
Bad Hersfeld
Kassel
Paderborn
Ruhr
Korbach
Göttingen
Münden
Heiligenstadt
Mühlhausen
Eisenach
Erfurt
Jena
Gera
Weimar
THÜRINGEN
Thüringer Wald
Zwickau
Plauen
Hof
Coburg
Schweinfurt
Würzburg
Bamberg
Bayreuth
Kitzingen
Erlangen
Fürth
Nürnberg
Ansbach
Amberg
Weiden
Cham
Regensburg
Ingolstadt
Donauwörth
Landshut
Dachau
Munich (München)
Mühldorf
Starnberg
Rosenheim
Garmisch-P.
BAYERN
Passau
Donau
Oldenburg
Bremen
NIEDERSACHSEN
Nienburg
Diepholz
Minden
Hannover
Hildesheim
Celle
Langenhagen
Wolfsburg
Braunschweig
Salzgitter
Lüneburg
Rotenburg
Uelzen
Salzwedel
Stendal
Magdeburg
SACHSEN-ANHALT
Aschersleben
Bernburg
Dessau
Bitterfeld
Halle
Nordhausen
Leipzig
Weissenfels
Naumburg
Zeitz
Wittenberg
Torgau
Riesa
Meissen
Dresden
SACHSEN
Chemnitz
Bautzen
Görlitz
Zittau
Erzgebirge
Cottbus
Finsterwalde
Elsterwerda
Luckenwalde
Potsdam
Berlin
Brandenburg
BRANDENBURG
Rathenow
Nauen
Oranienburg
Eberswalde
Fürstenwalde
Frankfurt an-der-Oder
Neuruppin
Wittenberge
Pritzwalk
Ludwigslust
Neustrelitz
Prenzlau
GERMANY
CZECH REP.
Ústí n.L.
Teplice
Most
Chomutov
Liberec
Mladá Boleslav
Hradec Králové
Kladno
Karlovy Vary
Cheb
Prague (Praha)
Brandýs-nad-L.
Kolín
Pardubice
Kutná Hora
Plzeň
Beroun
Benešov
Klatovy
Písek
Tábor
Havlíčkův Brod
Svitavy
Jihlava
Třebíč
Brno
Olomouc
Prostějov
Přerov
Vyškov
Zábřeh
Českomoravská Vysočina
České Budějovice
Kaplice
Znojmo
Mikulov
Hodonín
Břeclav
Šumava
Böhmerwald
Rachel 1452
AUSTRIA
Schärding
Linz
Freistadt
Wels
Steyr
Gmünd
Horn
Hollabrunn
Stockerau
Klosterneuburg
Vienna (Wien)
St Pölten
Mödling
Hainfeld
Wr. Neustadt
Bratislava
Vöcklabruck
Gmunden
Salzburg
Bad Ischl
Mariazell
Neunkirchen
Sopron
Eisenerz
Leoben
Bruck an der Mur
Radstad
Liezen
Dachstein 2996
Hochkönig 2938
Kufstein
Kitzbühel
Innsbruck
Landeck
Wildspitze 3774
Brenner 1370
Grossglockner 3798
Badgastein
Lienz
Spittal
Villach
Klagenfurt
Wolfsberg
Judenburg
Graz
Leibnitz
Gleisdorf
Szombathely
Zalaegerszeg
Nagykanizsa
Varazdin
Maribor
Celje
Velenje
Ljubljana
SLOVENIA
Kranj
Jesenice
Tarvisio
Gorizia
Postojna
Koper
Trieste
Rijeka (Fiume)
Istra
Rovinj
Poreč
Karlovac
Novo Mesto
Zagreb
Sisak
CROATIA
Vrbovsko
Ogulin
Koprivnica
Bjelovar
Virovitica
Daruvar
Pakrac
SWITZERLAND
Zürich
Winterthur
St Gallen
Olten
Biel
Neuchâtel
Berne (Bern)
Luzern
Zug
Schwyz
Thun
Interlaken
Fribourg
Pontarlier
Lausanne
Vevey
Montreux
Jungfrau 4158
St Gotthard 2112
Chur
Arosa
Davos
St Moritz
Vaduz
Bludenz
Feldkirch
Dornbirn
LIECHTENSTEIN
Sion
Brig
Simplon 2005
Martigny
Col du Gd St Bernard 2469
Matterhorn 4477
Bellinzona
Domodossola
Lugano
Geneva (Genève)
Annecy
Chambéry
Aix-l.-B.
Albertville
Mont Blanc 4808
Gran Paradiso 4061
Col du Mt Cenis 2083
Massif du Pelvoux
Mte Viso 3841
ITALY
Aosta
Ivrea
Biella
Novara
Vercelli
Turin (Torino)
Asti
Alessandria
Casale Monf.
Pavia
Milan (Milano)
Monza
Varese
Como
Busto Arsizio
Lecco
Bergamo
Brescia
Cremona
Piacenza
Lodi
Mantova
Verona
Vicenza
Padova
Rovigo
Venice (Venezia)
Mestre
Chioggia
G. di Venezia
Treviso
Bassano
Belluno
Rovereto
Trento
Bolzano
Merano
Brunico
Cortina d'A
Marmolada 3342
Alpi Dolomitiche
Ortles 3899
Sondrio
Edolo
Udine
Monfalcone
Gemona
Adige
Po
Piave
Pisek
1:5M
0 50 100 150 200 km
0 50 100 mls

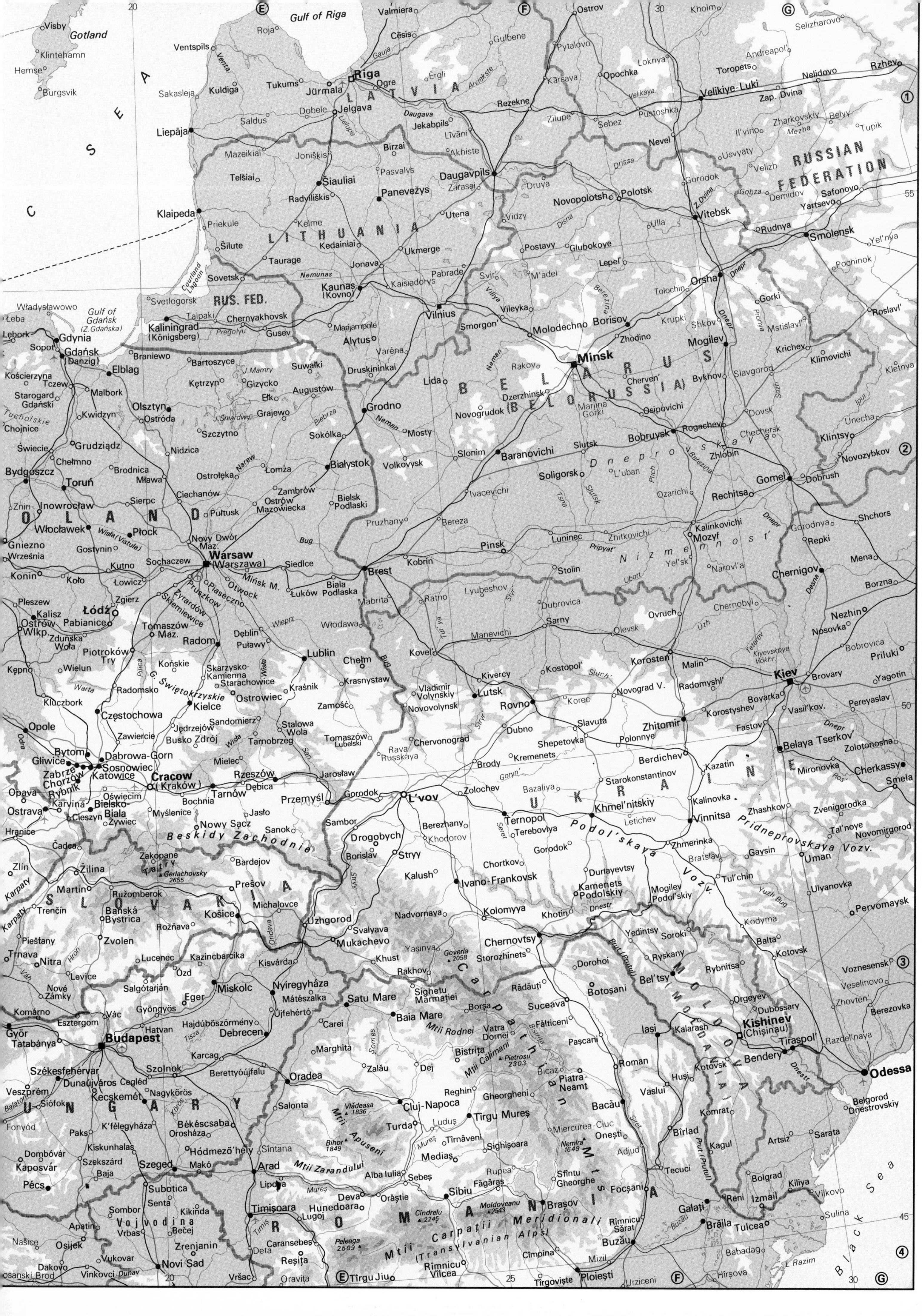

Gulf of Riga
Visby
Gotland
Klintehamn
Hemse
Burgsvik
SEA
Ventspils
Roja
Valmiera
Cēsis
Gauja
Ostrov
Pytalovo
Kholm
Selizharovo
Andreapol'
Toropets
Rzhev
Nelidovo
Gulbene
Kuldiga
Sakasleja
Tukums
Jūrmala
Riga
Ogre
Ergli
Aiviekste
Kārsava
Opochka
Loknya
LATVIA
Velikiye-Luki
Zap. Dvina
Dobele
Jelgava
Saldus
Daugava
Jekabpils
Līvāni
Rezekne
Zilupe
Sebez
Pustoshka
Liepāja
Birzai
Akhiste
Nevel
Il'yino
Zharkovskiy
Belyy
Tupik
Mezha
Mazeikiai
Joniškis
Usvyaty
Velizh
RUSSIAN FEDERATION
Telšiai
Šiauliai
Pasvalys
Daugavpils
Druya
Drissa
Gorodok
Radviliškis
Panevežys
Zarasai
Novopolotsk
Polotsk
Gobza
Demidov
Safonovo
Yartsevo
Klaipeda
Priekule
Kelme
Utena
Vidzy
Disna
Ulla
Vitebsk
Rudnya
Smolensk
Yel'nya
Šilute
LITHUANIA
Kedainiai
Ukmerge
Postavy
Glubokoye
Lepel'
Taurage
Jonava
Pochinok
Courland Lagoon
Sovetsk
Nemunas
Pabrade
Svir'
M'adel
Tolochin
Orsha
Dnepr
Kaunas (Kovno)
Kaisiadorys
Viliya
Berezina
Gorki
Roslavl'
Władysławowo
Gulf of Gdańsk (Z. Gdańska)
Svetlogorsk
RUS. FED.
Vileyka
Łeba
Talpaki
Chernyakhovsk
Vilnius
Smorgon'
Molodechno
Borisov
Krupki
Shkov
Mstislavl'
Lebork
Gdynia
Kaliningrad (Königsberg)
Pregolya
Gusev
Marijampolė
Zhodino
Mogilev
Krichev
Sopot
Gdańsk (Danzig)
Braniewo
Alytus
Varėna
Minsk
Klimovichi
Kletnya
Kościerzyna
Tczew
Elblag
Bartoszyce
Suwałki
Druskininkai
Rakov
Lida
BELARUS (BELORUSSIA)
Cherven'
Bykhov
Slavgorod
Starogard Gdański
Malbork
Kętrzyn
J. Mamry
Gizycko
Augustów
Ełk
Dzerzhinsk
Unecha
Olsztyn
Grajewo
Grodno
Novogrudok
Marjina Gorki
Osipovichi
Dovsk
Iput
Chojnice
Kwidzyn
Ostróda
J. Śniardwy
Biebrza
Neman
Mosty
Bobruysk
Rogachev
Chechersk
Klintsy
Świecie
Grudziądz
Szczytno
Sokółka
Slonim
Slutsk
Zhlobin
Novozybkov
Chełmno
Nidzica
Baranovichi
Dnepro
Bydgoszcz
Brodnica
Ostrołęka
Narew
Łomża
Białystok
Volkovysk
Soligorsk
L'uban
Gomel
Dobrush
Toruń
Mława
Ciechanów
Zambrów
Ostrów Mazowiecka
Bielsk Podlaski
Ivacevichi
Ptich
Ozarichi
Rechitsa
Znin
Inowrocław
Sierpc
Pułtusk
Shchors
POLAND
Włocławek
Płock
Wisła (Vistula)
Pruzhany
Bereza
Kalinkovichi
Mozyr
Gorodnya
Repki
Gniezno
Września
Gostynin
Nowy Dwór Maz.
Bug
Pinsk
Luninec
Zhitkovichi
Pripyat'
Nizmennost'
Warsaw (Warszawa)
Siedlce
Brest
Kobrin
Stolin
Yel'sk
Narovl'a
Chernigov
Mena
Konin
Koło
Kutno
Sochaczew
Łowicz
Mińsk M.
Biala Podlaska
Łuków
Ubort
Desna
Borzna
Pleszew
Łódź
Zgierz
Otwock
Piaseczno
Mabrita
Ratno
Lyubeshov
Styr'
Dubrovica
Chernobyl'
Nezhin
Kalisz
Ostrów Wlkp.
Pabianice
Żyrardów
Pruszków
Skierniewice
Sarny
Ovruch
Uzh
Nosovka
Zduńska Wola
Tomaszów Maz.
Dęblin
Puławy
Wieprz
Włodawa
Manevichi
Olevsk
Bobrovica
Priluki
Piotrków Try
Radom
Lublin
Chełm
Kovel'
Teterev
Kievskoye Vodkhr.
Kępno
Wieluń
Końskie
Skarzysko-Kamienna
Starachowice
Krasnystaw
Korosten'
Malin
Kiev
Brovary
Yagotin
Warta
Radomsko
G. Świętokrzyskie
Kraśnik
Ostrowiec
Vladimir Volynskiy
Kivercy
Kostopol'
Sluch'
Novograd V.
Radomyshl'
Kluczbork
Częstochowa
Kielce
Zamość
Lutsk
Novovolynsk
Rovno
Korec
Boyarka
Pereyaslav
Opole
Sandomierz
Jedrzejów
Busko Zdrój
Stalowa Wola
Zhitomir
Korostyshev
Vasil'kov.
Odra
Zawiercie
Tomaszów Lubelski
Chervonograd
Dubno
Slavuta
Fastov
Bytom
Dąbrowa-Gorn
Tarnobrzeg
San
Rava Russkaya
Shepetovka
Polonnye
Belaya Tserkov'
Zolotonosha
Gliwice
Zabrze
Chorzów
Sosnowiec
Katowice
Mielec
Kremenets
Berdichev
Kazatin
Cherkassy
Rybnik
Cracow (Kraków)
Rzeszów
Dębica
Jarosław
Brody
Goryn'
Starokonstantinov
UKRAINE
Mironovka
Smela
Opava
Oświęcim
Bochnia
Tarnów
Przemyśl
Gorodok
L'vov
Zolochev
Bazaliya
Kalinovka
Zvenigorodka
Ostrava
Karviná
Bielsko-Biala
Cieszyn
Myślenice
Jasło
Sambor
Ternopol
Khmel'nitskiy
Vinnitsa
Zhashkov
Żywiec
Nowy Sącz
Berezhany
Letichev
Tal'noye
Novomirgorod
Hranice
Beskidy Zachodnie
Sanok
Drogobych
Khodorov
Terebovlya
Podol'skaya Vozv.
Pridneprovskaya Vozv.
Čadca
Zakopane
Tatry
Gerlachovsky 2655
Bardejov
Borislav
Stryy
Seret
Gorodok
Zhmerinka
Gaysin
Uman
Zlín
Žilina
Kalush
Chortkov
Dunayevtsy
Bratslav
Tul'chin
Karpaty
Martin
Ružomberok
Prešov
Ivano-Frankovsk
Kamenets Podolskiy
Mogilev Podol'skiy
Yuzh Bug
Ulyanovka
Trenčín
SLOVAKIA
Banská Bystrica
Košice
Michalovce
Uzhgorod
Nadvornaya
Kolomyya
Khotin
Dnestr
Kodyma
Pervomaysk
Rožňava
Ondava
Svalyava
Piešťany
Zvolen
Mukachevo
Yasinya
Goverla 2058
Chernovtsy
Yedintsy
Soroki
Balta
Trnava
Nitra
Hron
Lučenec
Kazincbarcika
Kisvárda
Khust
Storozhinets
Ryskany
Kotovsk
Váh
Levice
Ózd
Rakhov
Dorohoi
Prut (Prutul)
Bel'tsy
Rybnitsa
Voznesensk
Nové Zámky
Salgótarján
Miskolc
Nyíregyháza
Carpathian Mts
MOLDOVA (MOLDAVIA)
Veselinovo
Eger
Mátészalka
Satu Mare
Sighetu Marmaţiei
Rădăuţi
Botoşani
Orgeyev
Zhovten'
Komárno
Vác
Gyöngyös
Újfehértó
Baia Mare
Borsa
Suceava
Dubossary
Berezovka
Esztergom
Hajdúböszörmény
Mtii Rodnei
Kishinev (Chişinau)
Győr
Tatabánya
Budapest
Hatvan
Tisza
Debrecen
Carei
Vatra Dornei
Bistriţa
Fălticeni
Iaşi
Kalarash
Tiraspol'
Razdel'naya
Someş
Marghita
Bistriţa
Mtii Călimani
Pietrosu 2303
Paşcani
Bendery
Székesfehérvár
Dunaújváros
Cegléd
Szolnok
Karcag
Berettyóújfalu
Oradea
Zalău
Dej
Bicaz
Roman
Kotovsk
Odessa
Veszprém
Balaton
Siófok
Kecskemét
Nagykőrös
Körös
Reghin
Gheorgheni
Piatra-Neamţ
Huşi
Vaslui
Belgorod Dnestrovskiy
HUNGARY
Salonta
Vlădeasa 1836
Mtii Apuseni
Cluj-Napoca
Tirgu Mureş
Bacău
Komrat
Fonyód
Paks
K'félegyháza
Békéscsaba
Orosháza
Turda
Luduş
Miercurea-Ciuc
Oneşti
Birlad
Sarata
Kiskunhalas
Hódmezővásárhely
Sîntana
Bihor 1849
Mureş
Tîrnăveni
Sighişoara
Nemira 1649
Kagul
Artsiz
Dombóvár
Kaposvár
Szekszárd
Baja
Szeged
Makó
Arad
Mtii Zarandului
Mediaş
Adjud
Tecuci
Pécs
Alba Iulia
Sebeş
Făgăraş
Rupea
Sfîntu Gheorghe
Focşani
Bolgrad
Izmail
Kiliya
Vilkovo
Black Sea
Subotica
Lipova
Deva
Orăştie
Sibiu
Reni
Galaţi
Sulina
Sombor
Senta
Kikinda
Timişoara
Hunedoara
Lugoj
Cindrelu 2245
Moldoveanu 2543
Braşov
Brăila
Tulcea
Apatin
Vojvodina
Vrbas
Bečej
Timiş
ROMANIA
Mtii Carpatii Meridionali (Transylvanian Alps)
Rîmnicu Sărat
Buzău
Našice
Osijek
Zrenjanin
Caransebeş
Peleaga 2509
Cîmpina
Babadag
L. Razim
Dakovo
Vukovar
Novi Sad
Deta
Reşiţa
Mizil
Bosanski Brod
Vinkovci
Dunav
Vršac
Oravita
Tîrgu Jiu
Rîmnicu Vîlcea
Tirgovişte
Ploieşti
Urziceni
Hîrşova
20
25
30
45
50
55
E
F
G
1
2
3
4

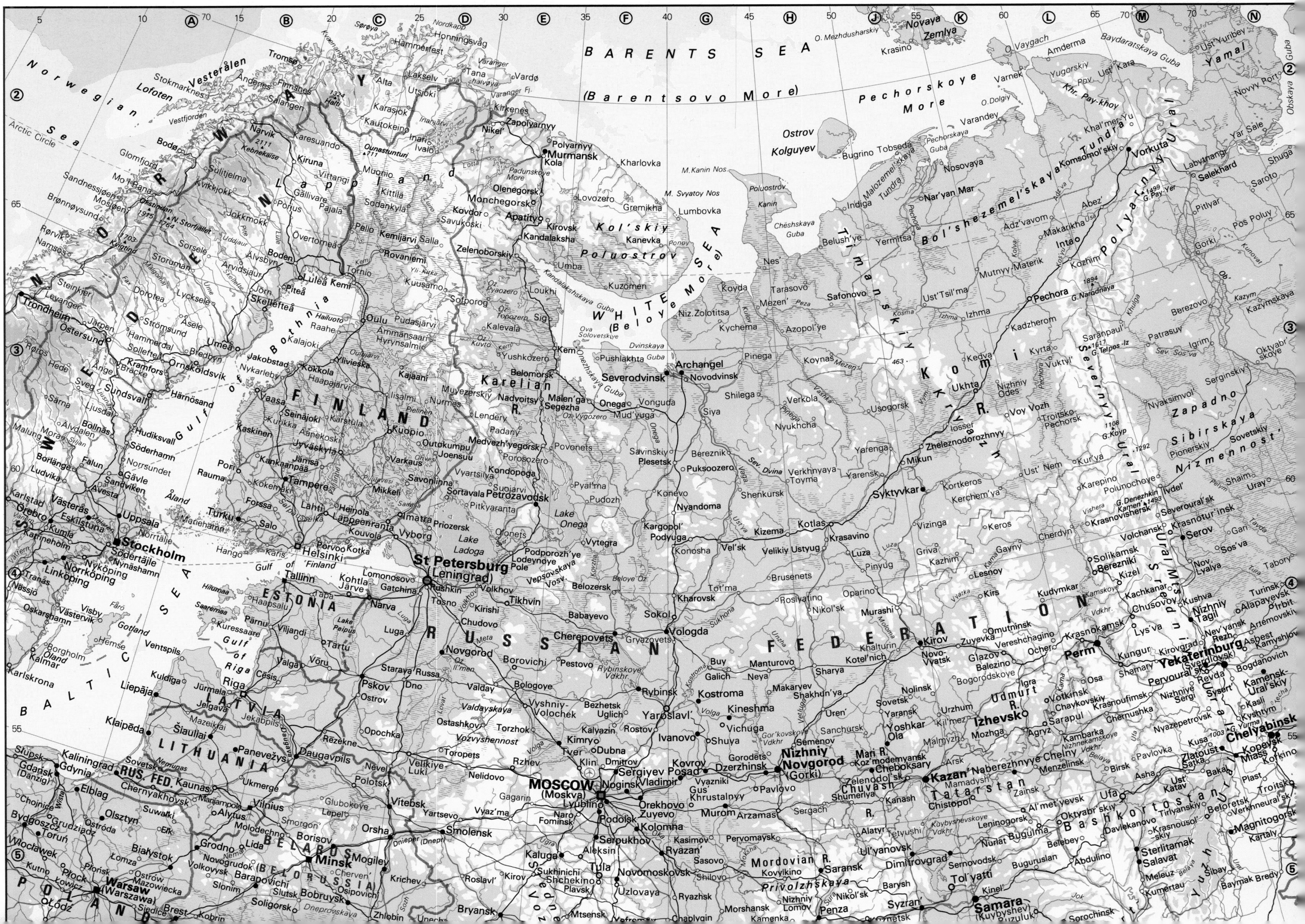
BARENTS SEA
(Barentsovo More)
Norwegian Sea
WHITE SEA (Beloye More)
Pechorskoye More
BALTIC SEA
Gulf of Bothnia
Gulf of Finland
Gulf of Riga
NORWAY
SWEDEN
FINLAND
ESTONIA
LATVIA
LITHUANIA
BELARUS (BELORUSSIA)
POLAND
RUSSIAN FEDERATION
RUS. FED.
Lapland
Kol'skiy Poluostrov
Karelian R.
Komi R.
Timanskiy Kryazh
Ural Mts
Severnyy Ural
Polyarnyy Ural
Zapadno Sibirskaya Nizmennost'
Tatarstan
Bashkortostan
Udmurt R.
Mari R.
Chuvash R.
Mordovian R.
Privolzhskaya
Yamal
Novaya Zemlya
Ostrov Kolguyev
MOSCOW (Moskva)
St Petersburg (Leningrad)
Helsinki
Stockholm
Tallinn
Riga
Vilnius
Minsk
Warsaw (Warszawa)
Murmansk
Archangel
Severodvinsk
Petrozavodsk
Vorkuta
Syktyvkar
Perm
Yekaterinburg
Chelyabinsk
Kazan'
Izhevsk
Samara (Kuybyshev)
Nizhniy Novgorod (Gorki)
Yaroslavl'
Vologda
Novgorod
Pskov
Smolensk
Kaliningrad
Gdańsk (Danzig)
Trondheim
Turku
Tampere
Oulu
Kuopio
Arctic Circle
1:10M
0 100 200 300 400 km
0 100 200 mls

1 North Ossetia R.
2 Adzhar R.
3 Ingush R.
4 Kabardin-Balkar R.
5 Nakhichevan R. (to Azerbaijan)
BLACK SEA
CASPIAN SEA
Sea of Azov
Mediterranean Sea
Sea of Crete
Aegean Sea
Sea of Marmara
UZBEKISTAN
TURKMENISTAN
KAZAKHSTAN
UKRAINE
MOLDOVA
ROMANIA
BULGARIA
HUNGARY
SLOVAKIA
GREECE
TURKEY
SYRIA
IRAQ
IRAN
CYPRUS
GEORGIA
ARMENIA
AZERBAIJAN
CRIMEA (Krym)
Kalmyk R.
Daghestan R.
Caucasus
Lesser Caucasus
Anadolu Dağlari
Taurus Mts
Reshteh-ye Alborz (Elburz Mts)
Ustyurt Plateau
Mugodzhary
Kiev (Kiyev)
Khar'kov
Volgograd (Stalingrad)
Saratov
Astrakhan'
Baku
Tbilisi
Yerevan
Ankara
Istanbul
Bucharest (Bucureşti)
Sofia (Sofiya)
Athens (Athína)
Tehran
Odessa
Dnepropetrovsk
Donetsk
Rostov na-Donu
Krasnodar
Halab (Aleppo)
Mosul
Nicosia

NATIONS OF ASIA & AUSTRALASIA

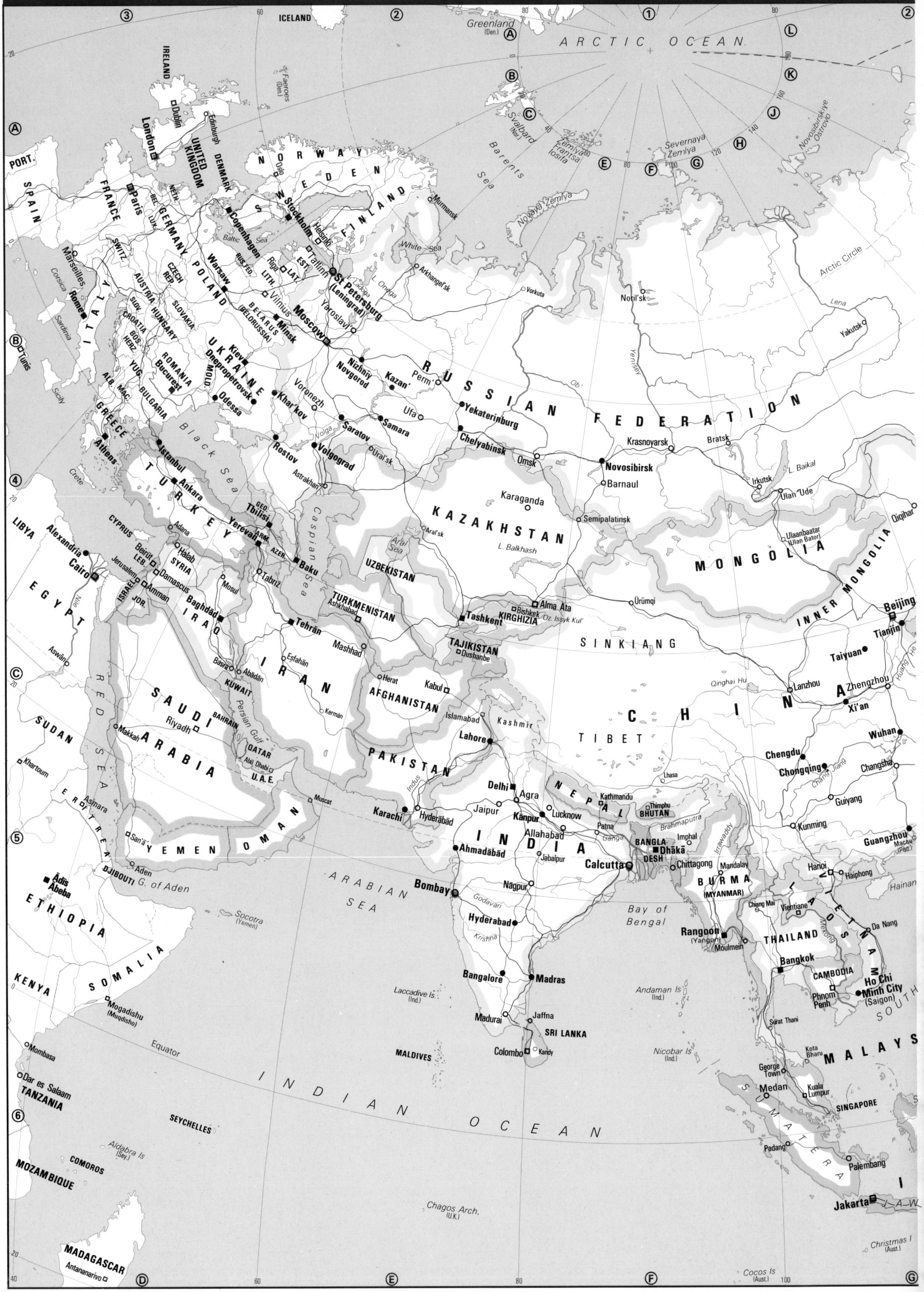

1:40M — 0 400 800 1200 1600 km; 0 400 800 mls

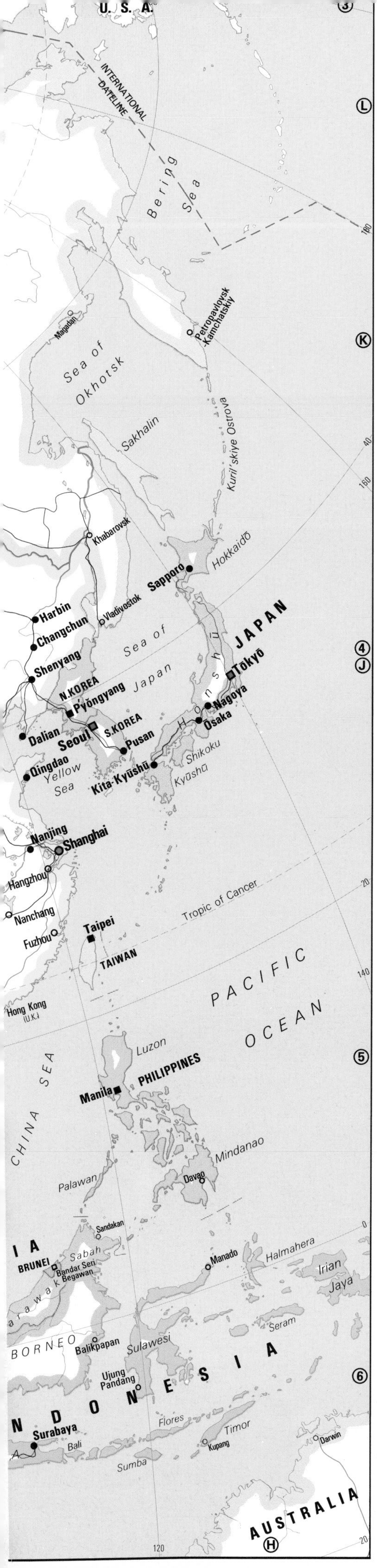
U.S.A.
INTERNATIONAL DATELINE
Bering Sea
Magadan
Petropavlovsk-Kamchatsky
Sea of Okhotsk
Sakhalin
Kuril'skiye Ostrova
Khabarovsk
Hokkaidō
Sapporo
Harbin
Vladivostok
Changchun
Sea of Japan
JAPAN
Shenyang
Honshu
Tokyo
N.KOREA
Pyongyang
Nagoya
Osaka
Dalian
Seoul
S.KOREA
Pusan
Qingdao
Yellow Sea
Kita-Kyushu
Shikoku
Kyūshū
Nanjing
Shanghai
Hangzhou
Tropic of Cancer
Nanchang
Taipei
Fuzhou
TAIWAN
PACIFIC OCEAN
Hong Kong (U.K.)
CHINA SEA
Luzon
PHILIPPINES
Manila
Mindanao
Davao
Palawan
Sandakan
Sabah
BRUNEI
Bandar Seri Begawan
Manado
Halmahera
Irian Jaya
Seram
BORNEO
Balikpapan
Sulawesi
Ujung Pandang
INDONESIA
Surabaya
Bali
Flores
Timor
Kupang
Sumba
Darwin
AUSTRALIA

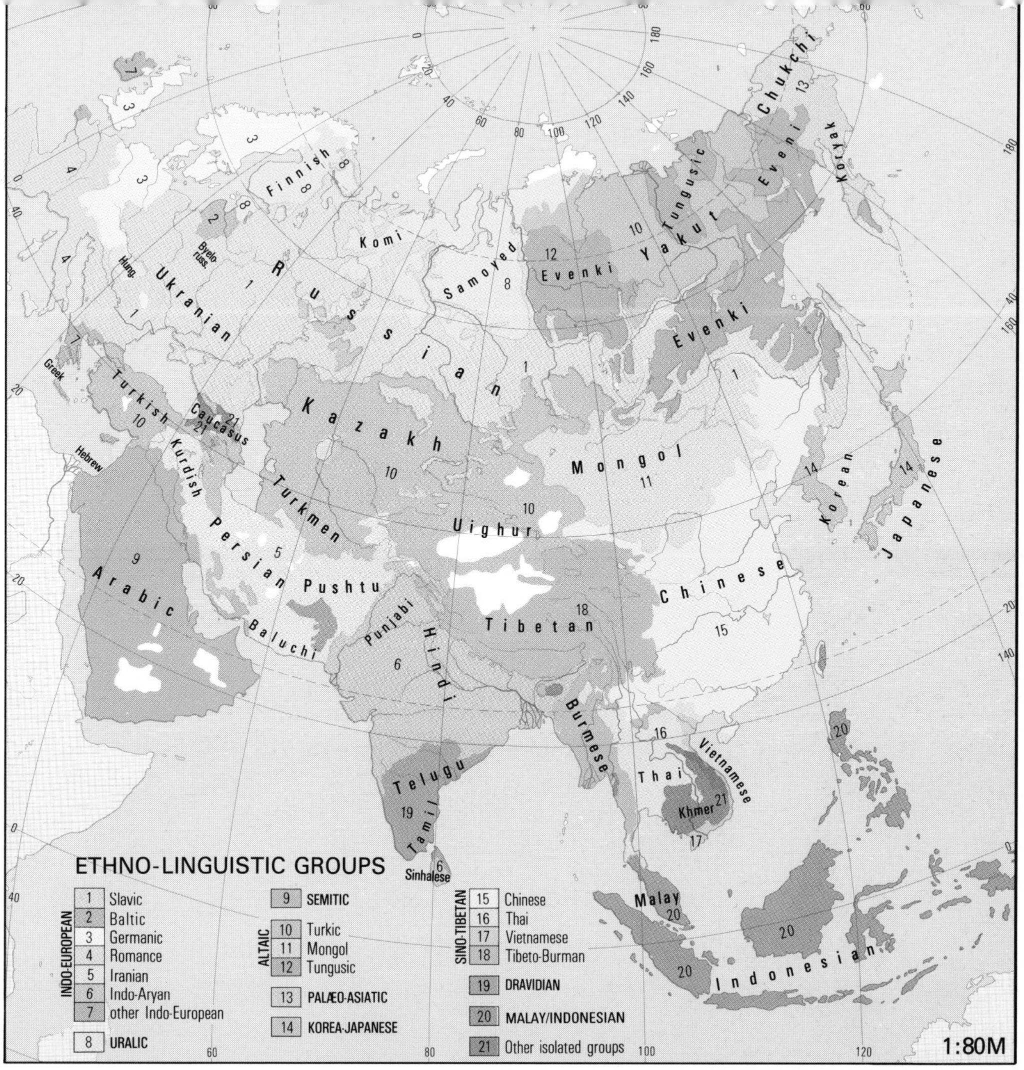
Chukchi
Koryak
Evenki
Tungusic
Yakut
Finnish
Komi
Samoyed
Russian
Ukranian
Byelo russ.
Hung.
Greek
Turkish
Caucasus
Kurdish
Hebrew
Kazakh
Turkmen
Mongol
Uighur
Korean
Japanese
Persian
Pushtu
Arabic
Baluchi
Punjabi
Hindi
Tibetan
Chinese
Burmese
Telugu
Tamil
Sinhalese
Thai
Vietnamese
Khmer
Malay
Indonesian
ETHNO-LINGUISTIC GROUPS
INDO-EUROPEAN
1 Slavic
2 Baltic
3 Germanic
4 Romance
5 Iranian
6 Indo-Aryan
7 other Indo-European
8 URALIC
9 SEMITIC
ALTAIC
10 Turkic
11 Mongol
12 Tungusic
13 PALÆO-ASIATIC
14 KOREA-JAPANESE
SINO-TIBETAN
15 Chinese
16 Thai
17 Vietnamese
18 Tibeto-Burman
19 DRAVIDIAN
20 MALAY/INDONESIAN
21 Other isolated groups
1:80M

Manila
PHILIPPINES
PACIFIC OCEAN
Guam (U.S.A.)
Northern Mariana Islands (U.S.A.)
MARSHALL ISLANDS
MALAYSIA
Sandakan
Davao
PALAU (BELAU)
FEDERATED STATES OF MICRONESIA
BRUNEI
Bandar Seri Begawan
Caroline Islands
Halmahera
Equator
Borneo
Balikpapan
Sulawesi (Celebes)
Jayapura
Irian Jaya
PAPUA NEW GUINEA
NAURU
KIRIBATI
Ujung Pandang
Seram
New Guinea
INDONESIA
Port Moresby
SOLOMON ISLANDS
TUVALU
Sumba
Timor
Arafura Sea
Timor Sea
Darwin
Wrn SAMOA
Is Wallis (Fr.)
G. of Carpentaria
Coral Sea
VANUATU
FIJI
TONGA
Cairns
Townsville
Suva
New Caledonia (Fr.)
Rockhampton
Alice Springs
Tropic of Capricorn
AUSTRALIA
Brisbane
L. Eyre
L. Torrens
Darling
INTERNATIONAL DATELINE
Kalgoorlie
Perth
Fremantle
Murray
Wollongong
Sydney
Canberra
Adelaide
Melbourne
Geelong
Bass Strait
NEW ZEALAND
North I.
Auckland
Launceston
Tasmania
Hobart
Tasman Sea
Wellington
South I.
Christchurch
Dunedin
Stewart I.
Chatham I. (N.Z.)
AUSTRALASIA
1:60M

RUSSIAN FEDERATION
1 Ingush R.
2 Chechen R.
3 North Ossetia R.
4 Kabardin- Balkar R.
GEORGIA
5 Abkhaz R.
6 Adzhar R.
AZERBAIJAN
7 Nakhichevan R.

1:20M

200   400   600   800 km
200   400 mls

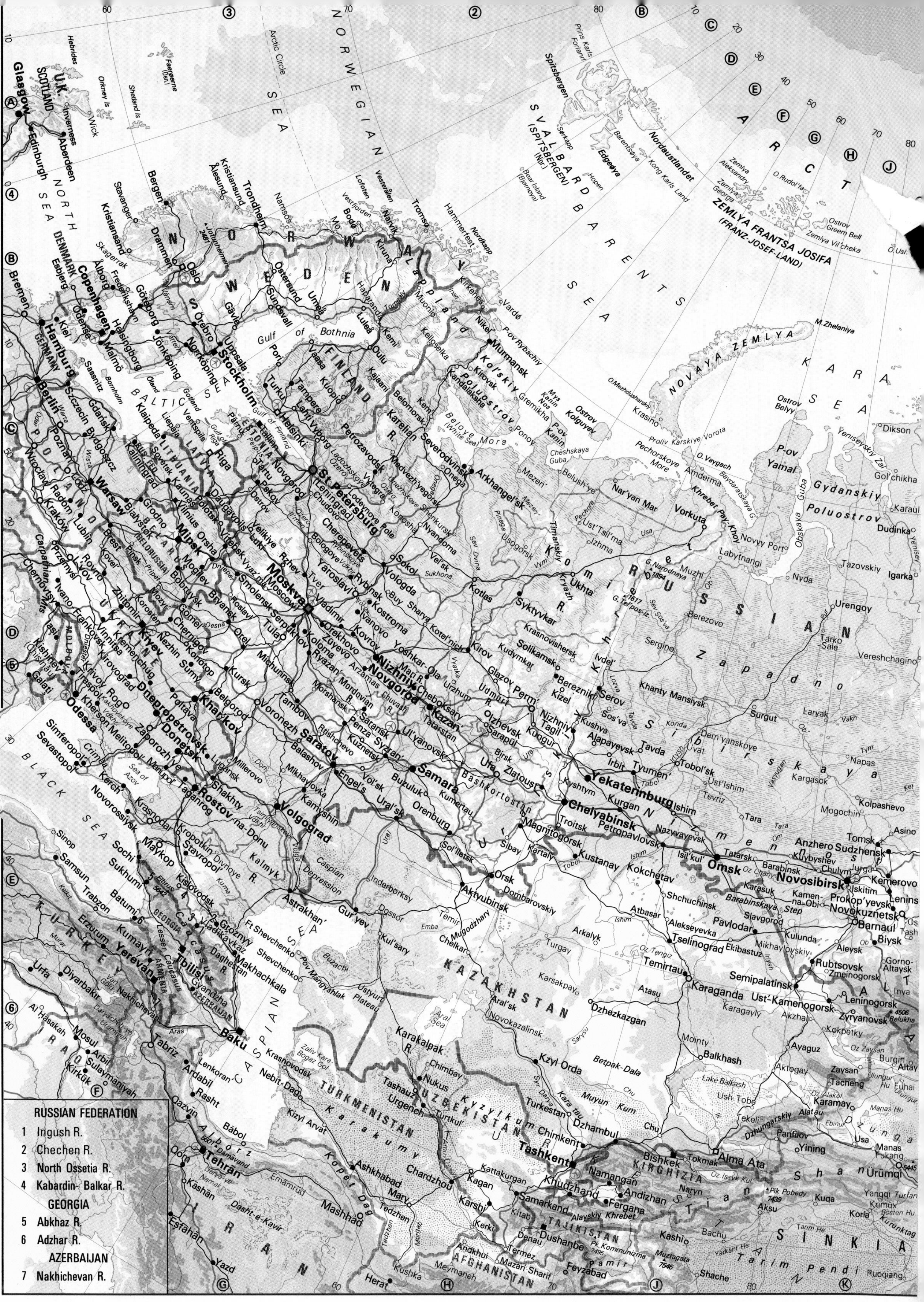

OCEAN
EAST SIBERIAN SEA
LAPTEV SEA
CHUKCHI SEA
BERING SEA
SEA OF OKHOTSK
SEA OF JAPAN
YELLOW SEA
Korea Bay
Bo Hai
SEVERNAYA ZEMLYA (NORTH LAND)
Ostrov Komsomolets
Ostrov Bol'shevik
O. Oktyabrskoy Revolyutsii
O. Shmidta
O. Pioner
Mys Chelyusin
Proliv Vilkitskogo
Arkipelag Nordenshelda
NOVOSIBIRSKYE OSTROVA (NEW SIBERIAN ISLANDS)
Ostrova De-Longa
Ostrov Faddeyevskiy
O. Novaya Sibir
Ostrov Kotel'nyy
O. Bol'shoy Lyakhovskiy
O. Malyy Lyakhovskiy
Proliv Dmitriya Lapteva
Medvezh'i Ova
O. Ayon
Wrangel I.
Proliv Longa
Mys Shelagskiy
Chukotskiy Poluostrov
Chukotskiy Khrebet
Anadyrskiy Zaliv
Anadyrskoye Ploskogor'ye
Kolymskoye Nagor'ye
Koryakskoye Nagor'ye
Mys Navarin
Mys Olyutorskiy
St Lawrence (U.S.A.)
St Matthew (U.S.A.)
Uelen
Provideniya
Pevek
Bilibino
Anadyr'
Beringovskiy
Markovo
Egvekinot
Ambarchik
Cherskiy
Srednekolymsk
Zyryanka
Ust'Nera
Oymyakon
Magadan
Okhotsk
Ayan
Gory Byrranga
Poluostrov Taymyr
Ozero Taymyr
Khatanga
Nordvik
Saskylakh
Tiksi
Kazach'ye
Deputatskiy
Chokurdakh
Polyarnyy
Khrebet Cherskogo
Khrebet Orulgan
Verkhoyanskiy Khrebet
Verkhoyansk
Zhigansk
Sangar
Yakutsk
Pokrovsk
Olenek
Aykhal
Mirnyy
Vilyuysk
Noril'sk
Gory Putorana
Turukhansk
Tura
Sredne Sibirskoye Ploskogor'ye
SIBERIA
RUSSIAN FEDERATION
Kamchatka
Sredinnyy Khrebet
Petropavlovsk-Kamchatskiy
Ust'Kamchatsk
Komandorskiye Ostrova
Mys Lopatka
Paramushir
Kuril Islands (Kuril'skiye Ostrova)
SAKHALIN
Okha
Poronaysk
Yuzhno-Sakhalinsk
Aleksandrovsk-Sakhalinskiy
Tatarskiy Proliv
La Pérouse Strait
Zaliv Shelikhova
Penzhinskaya Guba
Aldan
Aldanskoye Nagor'ye
Stanovoy Khrebet
Dzhugdzhur
Patomskoye Nagor'ye
Olekminsk
Lensk
Bodaybo
Kirensk
Ust'-Kut
Bratsk
Tynda
Skovorodino
Zeya
Svobodnyy
Blagoveshchensk
Komsomol'sk-na-Amure
Khabarovsk
Birobidzhan
Sikhote Alin'
Vladivostok
Nakhodka
Ussuriysk
Severo Baykal'skoye Nagor'ye
Ozero Baykal
Irkutsk
Angarsk
Ulan Ude
Chita
Krasnoyarsk
Kansk
Achinsk
Abakan
Minusinsk
Kyzyl
Tuva
Yeniseysk
Yeniseyskiy Kryazh
Zapadnyy Sayan
Vostochnyy Sayan
MONGOLIA
Ulaanbaatar
Darhan
Erdenet
Choybalsan
Hovd
Uliastay
Tsetserleg
Mandalgovi
Saynshand
Dalandzadgad
Altay
Gobi
Khentiyn Nuruu
Mongol Altay
CHINA
INNER MONGOLIA
MANCHURIA
Harbin
Qiqihar
Changchun
Jilin
Shenyang
Dalian
Beijing (Peking)
Tianjin (Tientsin)
Shijiazhuang
Jinan
Qingdao
Taiyuan
Baotou
Hohhot
Yinchuan
Datong
Zhangjiakou
Erenhot
Hailar
Manzhouli
Da Hinggan Ling
Xiao Hinggan Ling
Hami
Turpan
Yumen
Gobi
Ordos
NORTH KOREA
P'yŏngyang
Wŏnsan
SOUTH KOREA
Seoul (Sŏul)
Inch'ŏn
Taegu
Pusan
Kwangju
Cheju Do
JAPAN
HOKKAIDO
Sapporo
Asahikawa
Wakkanai
Hakodate
HONSHU
Aomori
Sendai
Tokyo
Yokohama
Nagoya
Kyoto
Osaka
Kobe
Hiroshima
Niigata
KYUSHU
Fukuoka
Kita-Kyushu
Nagasaki
Kagoshima
Shikoku
Osumi-shoto

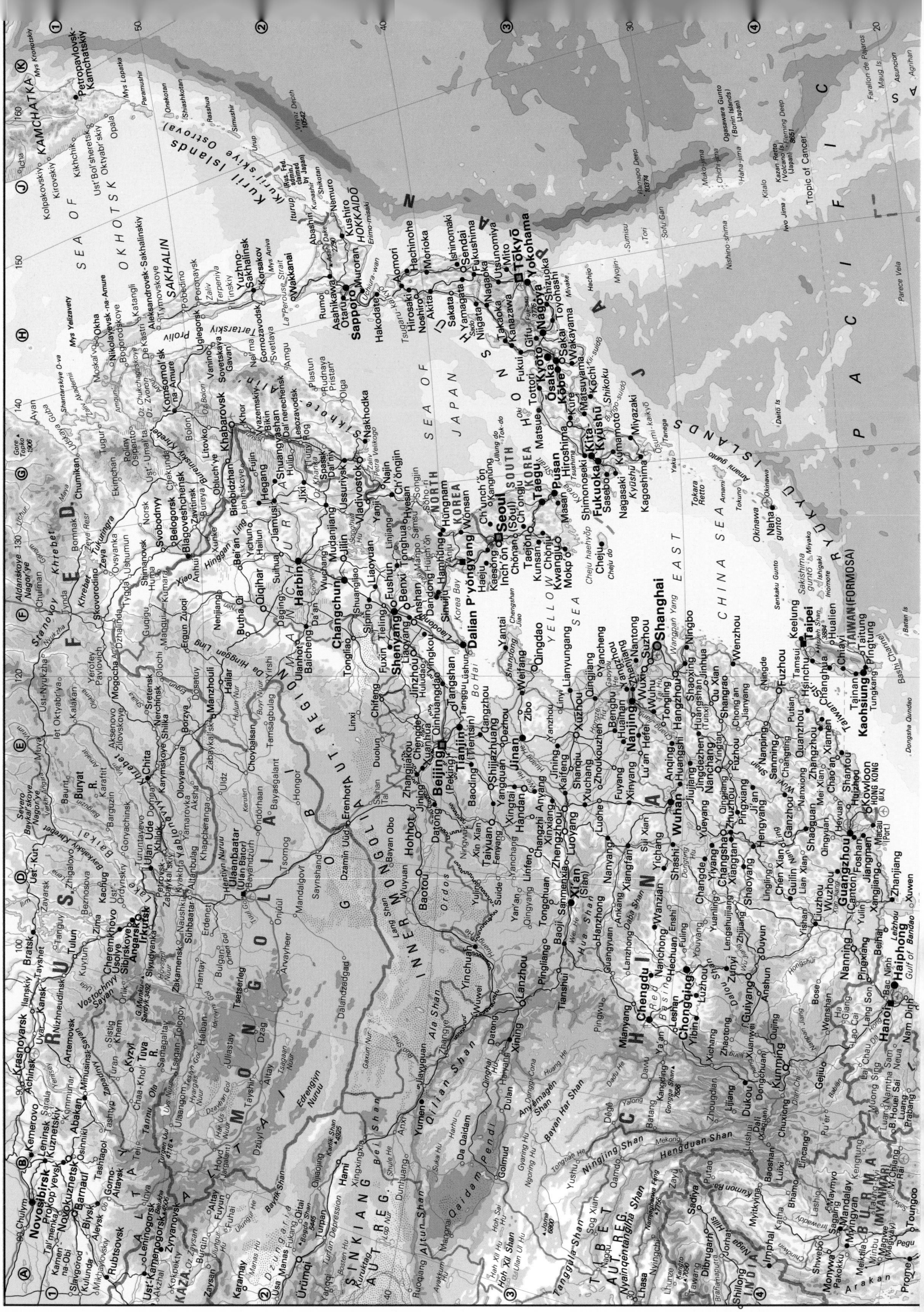
1:20M
0 200 400 600 800 km
0 200 400 mls
SEA OF OKHOTSK
KAMCHATKA
Petropavlovsk-Kamchatskiy
SAKHALIN
Kuril Islands (Kuril'skiye Ostrova)
HOKKAIDŌ
Sapporo
Hakodate
SEA OF JAPAN
HONSHŪ
JAPAN
Tōkyō
Yokohama
Nagoya
Kyōto
Ōsaka
Kōbe
Hiroshima
Kita-Kyūshū
Fukuoka
Kyūshū
Shikoku
PACIFIC
RYŪKYŪ ISLANDS
Okinawa
Tropic of Cancer
NORTH KOREA
P'yŏngyang
SOUTH KOREA
Seoul (Sŏul)
Pusan
Taegu
YELLOW SEA
EAST CHINA SEA
Korea Bay
Bo Hai
TAIWAN (FORMOSA)
Taipei
Kaohsiung
HONG KONG (U.K.)
Kowloon
Macau (Port.)
CHINA
Beijing (Peking)
Tianjin (Tientsin)
Shanghai
Nanjing
Wuhan
Chongqing
Chengdu
Xi'an (Sian)
Guangzhou (Canton)
Shenyang
Harbin
Changchun
Dalian
Kunming
Lanzhou
MANCHURIA
INNER MONGOLIA AUT. REGION
GOBI
MONGOLIA
Ulaanbaatar (Ulan Bator)
SINKIANG AUT. REG.
Ürümqi
TIBET AUT. REG.
Lhasa
RUS. FED.
Novosibirsk
Irkutsk
Lake Baikal
Chita
Khabarovsk
Vladivostok
Krasnoyarsk
BURMA (MYANMAR)
Mandalay
INDIA
Hanoi
Haiphong
Gulf of Bandao

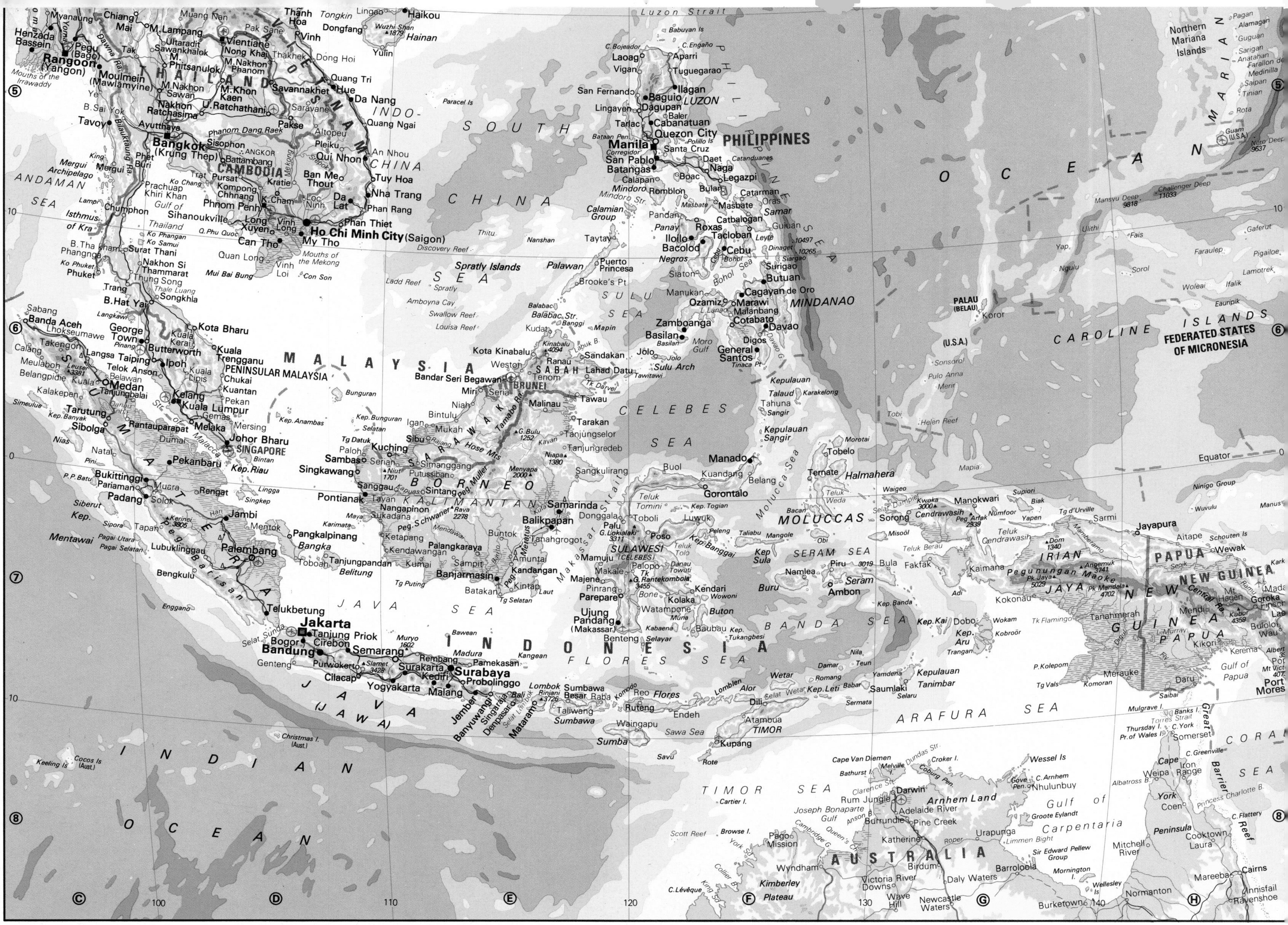

PHILIPPINES
LUZON
MINDANAO
MALAYSIA
PENINSULAR MALAYSIA
SINGAPORE
BRUNEI
SABAH
SARAWAK
BORNEO
KALIMANTAN
SULAWESI (CELEBES)
INDONESIA
THAILAND
CAMBODIA
VIETNAM
MOLUCCAS
IRIAN JAYA
PAPUA NEW GUINEA
AUSTRALIA
PALAU (BELAU)
FEDERATED STATES OF MICRONESIA
CAROLINE ISLANDS
Northern Mariana Islands
SOUTH CHINA SEA
SULU SEA
CELEBES SEA
JAVA SEA
FLORES SEA
BANDA SEA
SERAM SEA
ARAFURA SEA
TIMOR SEA
ANDAMAN SEA
INDIAN OCEAN
CORAL SEA
Gulf of Carpentaria
Gulf of Thailand
Luzon Strait
Equator
Rangoon (Yangon)
Bangkok (Krung Thep)
Phnom Penh
Ho Chi Minh City (Saigon)
Vientiane
Hue
Da Nang
Haikou
Hainan
Manila
Quezon City
Cebu
Davao
Zamboanga
Kota Kinabalu
Bandar Seri Begawan
Kuching
Kuala Lumpur
Johor Bharu
Medan
Padang
Palembang
Jakarta
Bandung
Semarang
Surabaya
Yogyakarta
Pontianak
Banjarmasin
Balikpapan
Samarinda
Ujung Pandang (Makassar)
Manado
Ambon
Kupang
Dili
Jayapura
Darwin
Cairns
Port Moresby
Gulf of Papua
Great Barrier Reef
Cape York Peninsula
Arnhem Land
100
110
120
130
140
10
0

A
B
C
130
125
40
35
2
3
4
Changchun
Jilin
Kailu
Tongliao
Huaidezhen
Yongji
Chaluhe
Shuangyang
Xinzhan
Jiaohe
Emu
Dongning
Mikhaylovka
Ussuriysk
Razdol'noye
Baixingt
Wafang
Bag Tai
Haisgai
Shuangliao
Sanjiangkou
Huaide
Yitong
Yantongshan
Badaohe
Huangnihe
Dunhua
Guandi
Chunyang
Tianqiaoling
Uglovoye
Artem
Sergeyevka
Horqin Zuoyi Houqi
Naiman Qi
Hure Qi
Liaoyangwopu
Siping
CHINA
Liaoyuan
Panshi
Huinan
Huadian
Jilin
Liangbingtai
Wangqing
Chunhua
Vladivostok
Barabash
Bol'shoy Kamen
Partizansk
Dunay
Nakhodka
Zaliv Petra Velikogo
Kangping
Changtu
Xifeng
Kaiyuan
Dongfeng
Hailong
Yanji
Tumen
Hunchun
Kraskino
Pos'yet
Hartao
Zhangwu
Faku
Tieling
Shansonggang
Narhong
Longjing
Helong
Kaishantun
Antu
Erdaobaihe
Fuxin
Xinlitun
Xinmin
Gaotaishan
Xinchengzi
Qingyuan
Liuhe
Caoshi
Jingyu
Fusong
Hoeryŏng
Khasan
Unggi
Fuxin
Dahonggi
Fushun
Sanyuanpu
Nanping
Musan
Najin
Beipiao
Heishan
Shenyang
Nanzamu
Gangou
Yi Xian
Beizhen
Dahushan
Liaozhong
Tonghua
Hunjiang
Linjiang
Puryŏng
Ch'ŏngjin
Nanam
Kyŏngsŏng
Goubangzi
Tai'an
Benxi
Xinbin
Changbai
Paegam
Jin Xian
Panshan
Liaoyang
Laoling
Chasong
Hyesan
Orang
Ŏdaejin
Jinzhou
Nu'erhe
Dawa
Anshan
Huanren
Hwapyong
Huch'ang
Sinpa
Samsu
Mantap-san 2205
Kwanmo-bong 2540
Niuzhuang
Haicheng
Ji'an
Manp'o
Nangnim
Kapsan
Myonggan
Myongchon
Yingkou
Yingkou
Tongyuanpu
Kuandian
Kanggye
Songgan
Pungso
Pungsan
Kilchu
Liaodong Wan
Linjiatai
Chosan
Hwadae
Musu-dan
Gai Xian
Shagang
Pyŏktong
Chonchon
Pujŏn Resr
Hochon
Kimch'aek
Xiongyuecheng
Fengcheng
Lagusha
Koin
Changjin Resr
Pujŏn
Xujiatun
Xiuyan
Dandong
Okkang-dong
Tongchang
Pukchin
Changjin
Pukch'ŏng
Tanch'ŏn
Riwon
Ch'aho
Wanjialing
Sinŭiju
Hŭich'ŏn
Sinhŭng
Fuzhoucheng
Qingduizi
Donggou
Unsan
Taehung
Oro
Sinp'o
Hongwon
NORTH KOREA
SEA
Pihyŏn
Fu Xian
Taedasa-do
Kusŏng
T'aech'ŏn
Kujang
Hamhŭng
Gushan
Wudao
Zhuanghe
Sŏnch'ŏn
Chŏngju
Kaechon
Nyongwon
Hamju
Hŭngnam
Xinjin
Chengzitan
Anju
Maengsan
Chongpyong
Tongjosŏn-man
Changhai
Yŏnghŭng
Sunch'ŏn
Sukch'ŏn
Kowŏn
Taegang-got
Jin Xian
Korea
Sunan
Munchŏn
Yŏnghŭng-man
Dalian
Chŭngsan
Sŏngch'ŏn
Wŏnsan
Amnyong-dan
Lüshun
P'yŏngyang
Samdŭng
Anbyŏn
Bay
Namp'o
Chungwa
Sinp'yong
Suan
Koksan
Kosan
Hoeyang
Kosŏng
Changnyŏn
Sin'gye
Sep'o
Kumgang
Sariwŏn
J
A
Chaeryŏng
Pyonggang
Changdo
Changyŏn
P'yŏngsan
Kimwha
Kansŏng
Kŭmch'ŏn
Kumwha
Haeju
Ch'ŏrwŏn
Sokcho
Ongjin
Yŏnan
Kaesŏng
Yanggu
Yangyang
P'anmunjom
Munsan
Ch'unch'ŏn
Yantai
Weihai
Haeju-man
Uijŏngbu
Kapyŏng
Kangnŭng
Muping
Kanghwa
Seoul
(Sŏul)
Hongchŏn
Wendeng
Inch'ŏn
Hoengsŏng
Rongcheng
Suwŏn
Ryoju
Wŏnju
Samch'ŏk
Ullung-do
Todong
Tok-do (Take-shima) (Liancourt Rocks)
Rushan
Kopo-ri
Chŏngsŏn
Shidao
Asan-man
Changhowan
Chech'ŏn
Nyongwol
SOUTH KOREA
P'yŏngt'aek
Ch'unyang
Ulchin
Tangjin
Ch'ungju
Tanyang
Sŏsan
Onyang
Ch'ŏnan
Yŏngju
Anhŭng
Hongsong
Ch'ŏngju
Chŏmch'ŏn
Yŏngyang
Chochi'wŏn
Andong
Pyŏnggok-dong
Taech'ŏn
Kongju
Sanju
Uisŏng
Taejŏn
Yŏngdŏk
YELLOW SEA
Sŏch'ŏn
Changhang
Nonsan
Kimch'ŏn
Sinnyong
Oki-shotō
Yŏngil-man
Nishino-shima
Dōzen
Kunsan
Iri
Waegwan
Yŏngch'ŏn
P'ohang
Chiburi-jima
Kimje
Puan
Ch'ŏnju
Koryong
Taegu
Kyŏngju
(HUANG HAI)
Insil
Kŏch'ang
H
Anui
Chongdo
Ulsan
Kochang
Chŏngŭp
Hapch'ŏn
Miryang
Matsue
Yŏnggwang
Sagŏ-ri
Namwŏn
Ŭiryŏng
Taisha
Songjŏng
Koksong
Yangsan
Izumo
Naju
Kwangju
Hadong
Chinju
Masan
Kimhae
Tongnae
Oda
Mokp'o
Yŏngsanp'o
Sunch'ŏn
Kwangyang
Sach'ŏn
Chinhae
Pusan
Gōtsu
Yongam
Samch'ŏnp'o
Kohyon
Hamada
Shobara
Changhŭng
Posŏng
Yŏsu
Ch'ungmu
Kŏje-do
Nishi-suidō
Miyoshi
Usŭng
Haenam
Kohŭng
Tolsan-do
Sasuna
Masuda
Chindo
Kŭmo-do
Mi-shima
Susa
Kake
KOREA STRAIT (TSUSHIMA-KAIKYŌ)
Tsushima
Hiroshima
Wando
Ch'o-do
Nagato
Hagi
Mihara
Soan kundo
Izuhara
Yamaguchi
Iwakuni
Kure
Higashi-suidō
Hōfu
Shimonoseki
Ube
Tokuyama
Imabari
Cheju haehyŏp
Kita-Kyūshū
Hōjō
Matsuyama
Saijo
Iki
Nakama
Suō-nada
Iyo
Cheju
Kŭmnyŏng
Nōgata
Iyo-nada
KYŪSHŪ
Fukuoka
Iizuka
Nakatsu
Naganama
Halla-san 1950
Sŏngsan-ni
Hirado-shima
Karatsu
Tosu
Usa
Kitsuki
Yawatahama
Cheju do
Uku-jima
Hirado
Beppu
Ōita
Sŏgwi-ri
Imari
Saga
Kurume
Uwajima
Sasebo
Yanagawa
Kuju-san 1791
Usuki
Bungo-suidō
Gotō-rettō
Nakadori-jima
Kashima
Takeo
Ōmuta
Nakamura
Isahaya
Ōmura
Arao
Aso
Taketa
Saiki
Sukumo
Kumamoto
Tosashimizu
Fukue
Fukue
Nagasaki
Shimabara
Nobeoka
Ashizuri-misaki
Tomie
Nomo-saki
Yatsushiro
Hyūga
Hitoyoshi
Minamata
Takanabe
Akune
Kobayashi
Sendai
Miyazaki
Kajiki
Kushikino
Miyakonojō
Kagoshima
Fukuyama
Makurazaki
Kanoya
Yamagawa
1:5M
0 50 100 150 200 km
0 50 100 mls

RUS. FED.
Arkhipovka
Ol'ga
Vangou
Lazo
Margaritovo
continued on inset
135
140
145
40
35
D
E
F
2
3
4
Asahikawa
Takikawa
Fukagawa
Akabira
Ashibetsu
Sunagawa
Asahi dake 2290
Kutcharo-ko
Teshikaga
1503 Me-akan dake
Nemuro
Shakotan-misaki
Furubira
Ishikari-wan
Bibai
Iwamizawa
Furano
Yūbari
Otaru
Sapporo
Ebetsu
Kushiro
Ikeda
Obihiro
Hidaka-sammyaku
Iwanai
Kutchan
Eniwa
Chitose
Tomakomai
Mukawa
Suttsu
Shikotsu-ko
Tokachi
HOKKAIDŌ
Oshamambe
Toya-ko
Date
Monbetsu
Taiki
Setana
Noboribetsu
Uchiura-wan
Muroran
Hiroo
Yakumo
Urakawa
Samani
Mori
Komaga take 1133
Erimo-misaki
Okushiri-tō
Esashi
Esan-misaki
Hakodate
Kikonai
Ōma-saki
Ōhata
Shiriya-saki
Matsumae
Mutsu
Tsugaru-kaikyō
Ominato
Kodomari-misaki
Mimmaya
Mutsu-wan
Goshogawara
Noheji
Ajigasawa
Aomori
Iwaki-san 1625
Towada
Kuroishi
Hirosaki
Hachinohe
Henashi-zaki
Towada-ko
Odate
Noshiro
Kuji
Mi-zaki
O
F
Oga
Koma
Tazawa-ko
Morioka
Miyako
Akita
Tazawako
Yamada
Hanamaki
Yokote
Honjō
Tono
Kamaishi
Kitakami
Yuzawa
Mizusawa
Ofunato
Tobi-shima
Chokai-san 2230
Rikuzen
Yokobori
Tanaka
Ichinoseki
Kesennuma
Sakata
Shinjō
Naruko
Tsuruoka
H
Furukawa
Obanazawa
Ishinomaki
P
A
N
Murayama
Higashine
Sendai
Tendo
Awa-shima
Shiogama
Hajiki-saki
Yamagata
Natori
Murakami
Arato
Sado-shima
Nagai
Kaminoyama
Kakuda
Ryōtsu
Sōma
Aikawa
Yonezawa
Niigata
Shibata
Fukushima
Mano-wan
Iide san 2105
Niitsu
Haramachi
Hegura-jima
S
Teradomari
Sanjō
Aizu-Wakamatsu
Kitakata
Nihommatsu
Nanatsu-jima
Suzu-misaki
Inawashiro-ko
Nagaoka
Kōriyama
Kashiwazaki
Wajima
Suzu
Ojiya
Koide
Sukagawa
Mikuni-sammyaku
Shirakawa
Taira
Iwaki
Noto-hantō
Itoigawa
Naoetsu
Takada
Tokamachi
Kuroiso
Otawara
Nanao
N
Arai
Shinano
Toyama-wan
Shirane-san 2368
Nikko
Yaita
Hakui
Kurabe
Himi
Shinminato
Nakano
Imaichi
Hitachi
Takaoka
Toyama
Numata
Hitachi-Ota
Tsubame
Suzaka
Utsonomiya
Kanazawa
Nagano
Shibukawa
Kiryū
Mito
Katsuta
Omachi
Maebashi
Isesaki
Ashikaga
Komatsu
Tsurugi
Yariga-take 3180
Ueda
Oyama
Nakaminato
Ōta
Ishioka
Kaga
Komoro
Takasaki
Hok
Dōgo
O
Haku-san 2702
Matsumoto
Kumagaya
Koga
Saigō
Tsuchiura
Katsuyama
Kōnosu
Nakano-shima
Okaya
Suwa
Takayama
Omiya
Sawara
Fukui
Chichibu
Urawa
Chōshi
Ono
3063 Ontake-san
Kawagoe
Tokyo
Narita
Sabae
Takefu
Osaka
Chino
Inubo-saki
Kawaguchi
Funabashi
Shirotori
Kanayama
Wakasa-wan
Agematsu
Enzan
Hachiman
Hachiōji
Ina
Kofu
Chiba
Kasumi
Amino
Tsuruga
3192 Shirani-san
Fuji
Yokohama
Kawasaki
Bōsō-hantō
Sakaiminato
Toyooka
Nakatsugawa
Kurayoshi
Obama
Kinomoto
Gifu
Iida
Yoshida
Mobara
Miyazu
Maizuru
Yonago
Ogaki
Ichinomiya
Fujisawa
Kisarazu
Katsuura
Tottori
Biwa-ko
Akaishi-sanchi
Fuji-san 3776
Yokosuka
Yasugi
Fukuchiyama
Ayabe
Hikone
Kasugai
Seto
Fujinomiya
Odawara
Miura
Kamogawa
Chizu
Toyota
Numazu
Tsuyama
Kyōto
Nagoya
Shimizu
Tateyama
Otsu
Kuwana
Shizuoka
Nishiwaki
Tsushima
Sagami-nada
Nojima-zaki
Niimi
Tatsuno
Himeji
Uji
Yokkaichi
Okazaki
Shimada
Yaizu
Ito
Ō-shima
Takahashi
Aioi
Toyonaka
Handa
Suruga-wan
Okayama
Kakogawa
Kōbe
Nara
Tsu
Toyohashi
Kurashiki
Akashi
Suzuka
Hamamatsu
Shimoda
To-shima
Sakai
Ōsaka
Nabari
Ise-wan
Omae-zaki
Iro-zaki
Fukuyama
Harima-nada
Matsusaka
Ise
Nii-jima
Onomichi
Awaji-shima
Kishiwada
Toba
J
A
P
A
N
Kōzu-shima
Tamano
Sumoto
Izumi-Sano
Miyake-jima
Sakaide
Takamatsu
Hashimoto
Hiuchi-nada
Marugame
Naruto
Wakayama
Ōnohara-jima
Mikura-jima
Tokushima
Kainan
Owase
Nagashima
Niihama
Komatsushima
Kii-sanchi
Kumano
Shikoku-sanchi
Anan
Gobo
Hiwasa
Kii-suidō
Tanabe
Shingū
Inamba-jima
Kōchi
Nankoku
Hikigawa
Aki
Kushimoto
Shiono-misaki
Tosa
Susaki
Tosa-wan
Muroto
Muroto-zaki
SHIKOKU
C
I
F
I
C
A
P
O
C
E
A
N
Wakkanai
Sōya-misaki
145 at the same scale
Rebun-tō
Rishiri-tō
Hama-Tombetsu
Kitami-Esashi
Otoineppu
Teshio
Ōmu
Okoppe
Yagishiri-tō
Teuri-tō
Nayoro
Mombetsu
M. Dokuchayevo
Shiretoko-misaki
Rudnaya
Uryū-ko
Takinoue
Engaru
Saroma-ko
Abashiri-wan
O. Kunashir (Rus. Fed. admin./ claimed by Japan)
Shibetsu
Abashiri
Rausu
Rumoi
Teshio dake 1558
Kitami
Shari
Golovnino
Nemuro-kaikyō

1:10M
0 100 200 300 400 km
0 100 200 mls

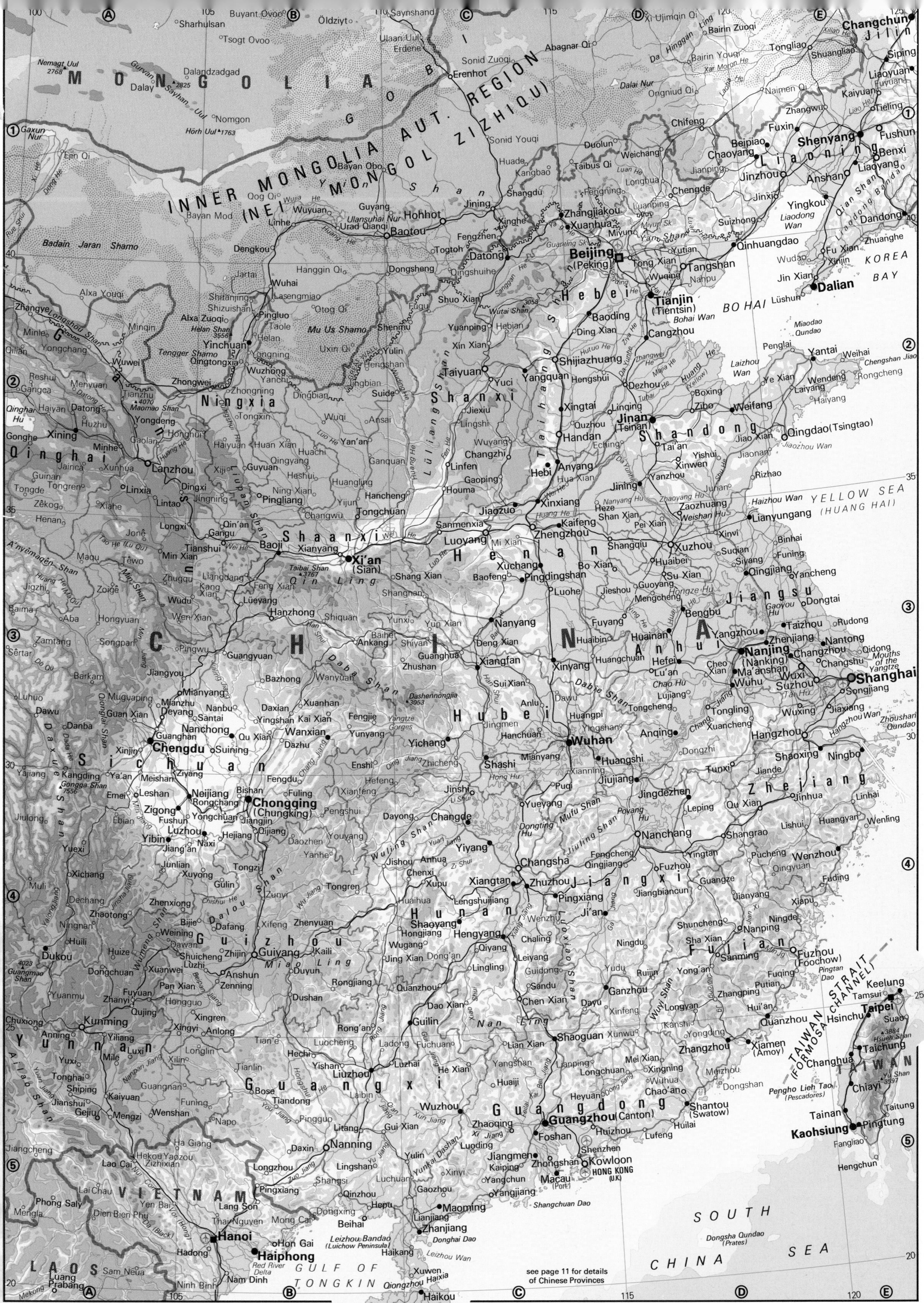

MONGOLIA
G O B I
INNER MONGOLIA AUT. REGION
(NEI MONGOL ZIZHIQU)
CHINA
Sharhulsan
Buyant Ovoo
Öldziyt
Saynshand
Tsogt Ovoo
Nemagt Uul 2768
Dalandzadgad
Dalay
Gurvan Sayhan Uul 2825
Nomgon
Hörh Uul 1763
Gaxun Nur
Ulaan Uul
Erdene
Sonid Zuoqi
Erenhot
Abagnar Qi
Xi Ujimqin Qi
Bairin Zuoqi
Bairin Youqi
Da Hinggan Ling
Tongliao
Changchun
Jilin
Shuangliao
Siping
Liaoyuan
Kaiyuan
Tieling
Zhangwu
Naimen Qi
Ongniud Qi
Dalai Nur
Sonid Youqi
Chifeng
Fuxin
Shenyang
Fushun
Benxi
Liaoyang
Anshan
Beipiao
Chaoyang
Jinzhou
Liaoning
Duolun
Weichang
Taibus Qi
Huade
Kangbao
Ejin Qi
Bayan Obo
Yin Shan
Qog Qi
Wuyuan
Guyang
Hohhot
Bayan Mod
Linhe
Ulansuhai Nur
Urad Qianqi
Baotou
Jining
Xinghe
Shangdu
Fengning
Chengde
Zhangjiakou
Xuanhua
Luanping
Miyun
Miyun Sk.
Suizhong
Jinxi
Yingkou
Liaodong Wan
Dandong
Zhuanghe
Qinhuangdao
Badain Jaran Shamo
Dengkou
Togtoh
Fengzhen
Datong
Beijing (Peking)
Tong Xian
Tangshan
Yutian
Wudao
Fu Xian
Xinjin
KOREA BAY
Jin Xian
Dalian
Lüshun
Hanggin Qi
Dongsheng
Jartai
Wuhai
Lasengmiao
Alxa Youqi
Shitanjing
Shizuishan
Pingluo
Otog Qi
Shuo Xian
Wutai Shan 3058
Hebei
Baoding
Tianjin (Tientsin)
BO HAI
Bohai Wan
Zhangye
Minle
Qilian
Yongchang
Alxa Zuoqi
Helan Shan 3556
Yinchuan
Taole
Helan
Mu Us Shamo
Shenmu
Yuanping
Hebian
Ding Xian
Cangzhou
Miaodao Qundao
Penglai
Yantai
Weihai
Wuwei
Tengger Shamo
Qingtongxia
Lingwu
Uxin Qi
Yulin
Hengshan
Xin Xian
Shijiazhuang
Laizhou Wan
Wendeng
Rongcheng
Zhongwei
Wuzhong
Yanchi
Taiyuan
Yuci
Yangquan
Hengshui
Dezhou
Ye Xian
Laiyang
Haiyang
Qinghai Hu
Haiyan
Datong
Tianzhu
Maomao Shan 4070
Zhongning
Dingbian
Suide
Shanxi
Lüliang Shan
Taihang Shan
Xingtai
Linqing
Jinan (Tsinan)
Zibo
Weifang
Qingdao (Tsingtao)
Xining
Huzhu
Yongdeng
Ningxia
Tongxin
Wuqi
Ansai
Jiexiu
Lingshi
Handan
Shandong
Jiaozhou Wan
Gonghe
Minhe
Gaolan
Honghui
Haiyuan
Huan Xian
Yan'an
Wuyang
Changzhi
Qingyang
Huachi
Linfen
Anyang
Hebi
Tai'an
Yishui
Xinwen
Jiaonan
Rizhao
Qinghai
Jainca
Xunhua
Lanzhou
Guinan
Tongren
Linxia
Xiji
Guyuan
Heshui
Ganquan
Gaoping
Houma
Yanzhou
Jining
Haizhou Wan
YELLOW SEA (HUANG HAI)
Tongde
Zêkog
Henan
Dingxi
Lintao
Pingliang
Ning Xian
Huangling
Yijun
Hancheng
Tongchuan
Jiaozuo
Xinxiang
Heze
Shan Xian
Zaozhuang
Lianyungang
Longxi
Qin'an
Gangu
Tianshui
Shaanxi
Baoji
Xianyang
Xi'an (Sian)
Sanmenxia
Luoyang
Zhengzhou
Kaifeng
Shangqiu
Xuzhou
Pei Xian
Xinyi
Binhai
A'nyêmaqên Shan
Maqu
Têwo
Min Xian
Taibai Shan 3767
Qin Ling
Henan
Xuchang
Bo Xian
Huaibei
Suqian
Siyang
Funing
Zhugqu
Zoigê
Min Shan
Liangdang
Kang Xian
Feng Xian
Shang Xian
Baofeng
Pingdingshan
Su Xian
Qingjiang
Yancheng
Jigzhi
Baima
Wudu
Lüeyang
Shangnan
Luohe
Jieshou
Guoyang
Mengcheng
Jiangsu
Dongtai
Aba
Hongyuan
Wen Xian
Hanzhong
Shiquan
Nanyang
Fuyang
Bengbu
Gaoyou Hu
Taizhou
Rudong
Zamtang
Songpan
Pingwu
Ankang
Yunxi
Yun Xian
Deng Xian
Huaibin
Huainan
Yangzhou
Zhenjiang
Nantong
Sêrtar
Guangyuan
Shiyan
Guanghua
Xiangfan
Xinyang
Huangchuan
Hefei
Nanjing (Nanking)
Changzhou
Qidong
Mouths of the Yangtze
Barkam
Jiangyou
Bazhong
Wanyuan
Daba Shan
Zhushan
Dashennongjia 3053
Sui Xian
Anhui
Chao Hu
Lu'an
Ma'anshan
Wuhu
Wuxi
Suzhou
Shanghai
Changshu
Luhuo
Mianyang
Xuanhan
Anlu
Dabie Shan
Songjiang
Dawu
Muguaping
Mianzhu
Deyang
Nanbu
Daxian
Kai Xian
Fengjie
Yangtze Gorges
Hubei
Huangpi
Tongcheng
Lujiang
Tongling
Jiaxing
Hangzhou Wan
Zhoushan Qundao
Danba
Guan Xian
Santai
Yingshan
Jingmen
Xiaogan
Anqing
Xuancheng
Guanghan
Nanchong
Qu Xian
Wanxian
Yunyang
Hanchuan
Hangzhou
Chengdu
Suining
Dazhu
Yichang
Wuhan
Dongzhi
Shaoxing
Ningbo
Xinjin
Sichuan
Enshi
Zhicheng
Shashi
Mianyang
Huangshi
Tunxi
Jiande
Yajiang
Kangding
Ya'an
Meishan
Ziyang
Fengdu
Hefeng
Jinshi
Pugi
Jiujiang
Jingdezhen
Zhejiang
Jinhua
Linhai
Gongga Shan 7556
Emei
Leshan
Neijiang
Rongchang
Bishan
Chongqing (Chungking)
Xianfeng
Yueyang
Qu Xian
Leping
Jiulong
Zigong
Fushun
Yongchuan
Jiangjin
Pengshui
Dayong
Changde
Mufu Shan
Poyang Hu
Huangyan
Wenling
Ebian
Luzhou
Qijiang
Dongting Hu
Nanchang
Shangrao
Lishui
Yuexi
Yibin
Naxi
Hejiang
Daozhen
Youyang
Yanhe
Yiyang
Jiuling Shan
Yingtan
Pucheng
Wenzhou
Jiang'an
Junlian
Xuyong
Tongzi
Wuling Shan
Jishou
Anhua
Changsha
Fengcheng
Qingjiang
Fuzhou
Qingyuan
Xichang
Gulin
Chenxi
Xupu
Xiangtan
Zhuzhou
Jiangxi
Guangze
Fuding
Muli
Zunyi
Tongren
Pingxiang
Jiangbiancun
Jianyang
Dechang
Zhenxiong
Huaihua
Lengshuijiang
Xiapu
Zhaotong
Bijie
Dalou Shan
Xifeng
Zhenyuan
Hunan
Wenzhu
Ji'an
Ningde
Ningnan
Weining
Dafang
Shaoyang
Hengyang
Shuncheng
Nanping
Huili
Dawan
Guizhou
Hongjiang
Chaling
Ningdu
Sha Xian
Fujian
Fuzhou (Foochow)
Dukou
Huize
Shuicheng
Zhijin
Guiyang
Kaili
Wugang
Qiyang
Sanming
Pingtan Dao
Xuanwei
Lüzhi
Miao Ling
Fuling
Jing Xian
Dong'an
Leiyang
Yudu
Fuqing
4023 Gongwang Shan
Dongchuan
Anshun
Duyun
Lingling
Guidong
Ruijin
Yong'an
Putian
TAIWAN STRAIT (FORMOSA CHANNEL)
Pan Xian
Zenning
Rongjiang
Quanzhou
Sandu
Ganzhou
Zhangping
Keelung
Yuanmu
Zhanyi
Fuyuan
Dushan
Dao Xian
Chen Xian
Wuyi Shan
Hui'an
Tamsui
Taipei
Chuxiong
Kunming
Qujing
Hongguo
Xingren
Guilin
Nan Ling
Xinfeng
Longyan
Quanzhou
Hsinchu
Suao
Anning
Yiliang
Xingyi
Anlong
Rong'an
Kanshi
Yongding
Hsueh Shan 3884
Yunnan
Luxi
Tian'e
Luocheng
Ladong
Fuchuan
Shaoguan
Xunwu
Zhangzhou
Xiamen (Amoy)
Taichung
Mile
Longlin
Xilin
Hechi
Yishan
Liuzhou
Luzhai
He Xian
Lian Xian
Mei Xian
Xingning
Changhua
TAIWAN
Yuxi
Tonghai
Tianlin
Yangshan
Lianping
Longchuan
Wuhua
Pengho Lieh Tao (Pescadores)
Chiayi
Yü Shan 3997
Shiping
Guangnan
Guangxi
Bose
Laibin
Huaiji
Heyuan
Chao'an
Dongshan
Jianshui
Kaiyuan
Tiandong
Wuzhou
Guangdong
Shantou (Swatow)
Taitung
Gejiu
Mengzi
Wenshan
Funing
Napo
Pingguo
Zhaoqing
Guangzhou (Canton)
Huilai
Tainan
Pingtung
Kaohsiung
Ha Giang
Litang
Gui Xian
Foshan
Huizhou
Lufeng
Fangliao
Jiangcheng
Hekou Yaozu Zizhixian
Daxin
Nanning
Yulin
Luoding
Shenzhen
Hengchun
Lao Cai
Longzhou
Lingshan
Jiangmen
Zhongshan
Kowloon
HONG KONG (U.K.)
Lai Chau
VIETNAM
Pingxiang
Shangsi
Luchuan
Xinyi
Kaiping
Yangchun
Macau (Port.)
Phong Saly
Yen Bai
Lang Son
Qinzhou
Gaozhou
Yangjiang
Mengla
Dien Bien Phu
Thai Nguyen
Mong Cai
Dongxing
Hepu
Maoming
Shangchuan Dao
SOUTH
Beihai
Lianjiang
Zhanjiang
Hanoi
Hon Gai
Haiphong
Leizhou Bandao (Luichow Peninsula)
Donghai Dao
Dongsha Qundao (Pratas)
Hadong
Haikang
Leizhou Wan
SEA
LAOS
Sam Neua
Red River Delta
GULF OF TONGKIN
Xuwen
CHINA
Luang Prabang
Ninh Binh
Nam Dinh
Qiongzhou Haixia
Haikou
HAINAN
see page 11 for details of Chinese Provinces
1:10M
0 100 200 300 400 km
0 100 200 mls

120
130
C
140
D
150
Tajungselor
Tanjungredeb
Kelolokan
BORNEO
Samarinda
Balikpapan
Tanjung
Banjarmasin
Kintap
Laut
Tg Selatan
Manado
Minahassa Peninsula
Tolitoli
Gorontalo
Belang
Ternate
Halmahera
Teluk Tomini
Kep. Togian
Luwuk
Peleng
Donggala
Toboli
Palu
Poso
Teluk Tolo
Kep. Banggai
SULAWESI (CELEBES)
Palopo
Kendari
Majene
Parepare
Teluk Bone
Watampone
Buton
Baubau
Kabaena
Ujung Pandang (Makassar)
Bonthain
Selayar
Kep. Takabonerate
Makassar Strait
Molucca Sea
MOLUCCAS
Taliabu
Obi
Kep. Sula
Seram
Seram Sea
Buru
Namlea
Piru
Bula
Ambon (Amboina)
Kep. Gorong
Kep. Watubela
Kep. Banda
Kep. Kai
Kep. Tukangbesi
INDONESIA
Banda Sea
Kep. Asia
Kep. Ayu
Mapia
Waigeo
Weda
Teluk Weda
Selat Dampier
Salawati
Sorong
Cendrawasih
Misool
Teluk Berau
Babo
Fakfak
IRIAN
Kaimana
Manokwari
Biak
Numfoor
Yapen
Teluk Cendrawasih
JAYA
Pegunungan Maoke
Pk Jaya 5029
Mamberamo
Sarmi
Jayapura
Aitape
Wewak
Sepik
Central Ra.
NEW GUINEA
Kokonau
Tanahmerah
Digul
Fly
Dobo
Kep. Aru
Dolak
Merauke
Tg Vals
Kep. Tanimbar
Kep. Babar
Kep. Damar
Wetar
Roma
Alor
Dili
Timor
Kep. Leti
Sermata
Kangean
Bali
Flores Sea
Flores
Reo
Ruteng
Ende
Lomblen
Raba
Denpasar
Mataram
Lombok
Sumbawa
Memboroo
Sumba
Waingapu
Savu
Kupang
Rote
Ninigo Is
Hermit Is
Admiralty Is
Manus
Mussau
Saint Matthias Group
New Hanover
Kavieng
Bismarck Archipelago
Schouten Is
Manam
Bismarck Sea
New Ireland
Rabaul
PAPUA
Madang
Long
Umboi
Talasea
New Britain
Ramu
Bismarck Ra.
Mt Wilhelm 4508
Mt Hagen
Mendi
Goroka
Lae
Bulolo
Morobe
Kikori
Kerema
Mt St Mary 3664
Popondetta
Gulf of Papua
Kokoda
Owen Stanley Ra.
Trobriand Is
D'Entrecasteaux Islands
Daru
Saibai I.
Port Moresby
Kupiano
Alotau
Samarai
Arafura Sea
Torres Strait
Pr. of Wales I.
C. York
Somerset
Great Barrier Reef
Wessel Is
Melville I.
Cobourg Pen
Croker I.
Bathurst I.
Van Diemen G.
Clarence Str.
Darwin
Rum Jungle
C. Arnhem
Nhulunbuy
Arnhem Land
Groote Eylandt
Gulf of Carpentaria
Timor Sea
Cartier I.
Adelaide River
Batchelor
Burrundie
Pine Creek
Katherine
Daly
Roper
Limmen Bight
Sir Edward Pellew Group
Java Trench
INDIAN OCEAN
C. Londonderry
Joseph Bonaparte Gulf
Pago Mission
Scott Reef
Wyndham
L. Argyle
Victoria
Victoria River Downs
Birdum
Daly Waters
Borroloola
Mornington
Wellesley Is
Collier B.
King Sound
C. Lévêque
Mt Ord 936
King Leopold Ra
Kimberley Plateau
Ord
Derby
Fitzroy Crossing
Hall's Creek
Fitzroy
Sturt Ck
Wave Hill
Newcastle Waters
Powell Creek
Barkly Tableland
NORTHERN TERRITORY
Burketown
Leichhardt
Normanton
Croydon
Flinders
Gregory Ra.
Gilbert
Mitchell
Mitchell River
Laura
Cooktown
Weipa
Cape York Peninsula
Iron Range
Coen
C. Grenville
Princess Charlotte B.
Mt Bartle Frere 1612
Cairns
Innisfail
Ravenshoe
Forsayth
Ingham
Palm Is
Townsville
Charters Towers
Ayr
Bowen
Proserpine
Collinsville
Mackay
Northumberland Is
Sarina
Coral Sea
Coral Island Ter
Willis Group
Coringa Is
Rowley Shoals
Broome
Lagrange
Eighty Mile Beach
Great Sandy Desert
Tennant Creek
Camooweal
Cloncurry
Richmond
Hughenden
Mount Isa
Dajarra
Georgina
Selwyn
Winton
QUEENSLAND
Great Dividing Range
Barrow Creek
Port Hedland
Shay Gap
De Grey
Marble Bar
Nullagine
Dampier
Roebourne
Monte Bello Is
Barrow I.
Fortescue
Wittenoom
Hamersley Ra.
Mt Bruce 1226
North West C.
Onslow
Paraburdoo
Newman
Ashburton
L. Mackay
L. Disappointment
Macdonnell Ranges
Mt Ziel 1510
Alice Springs
AUSTRALIA
Simpson Desert
Finke
Eyre Ck
Birdsville
Diamantina
Thomson
Barcoo
Longreach
Barcaldine
Blackall
Windorah
Clermont
Emerald
Rockhampton
Mount Morgan
Gladstone
Dawson
Theodore
Taroom
Marlborough
Charleville
Quilpie
Roma
Miles
Dalby
Toowoomba
Goondiwindi
Stanthorpe
St George
Cunnamulla
Warrego
Paroo
Grey Range
Gibson Desert
Petermann Ra
Mt Aloysius 987
Tomkinson Ra
Musgrave Ra.
Mt Woodroffe 1440
Lake Eyre Basin
Oodnadatta
L. Eyre
Cooper Ck
Barlee Ra.
Mt Augustus 1106
L. McLeod
Lyons
Gascoyne
Carnarvon
WESTERN AUSTRALIA
L. Carnegie
L. Wells
Wiluna
Great Victoria Desert
Coober Pedy
SOUTH AUSTRALIA
Marree
Milparinka
Bourke
Walgett
Moree
Glen Innes
Narrabri
Armidale
Tamworth
Gwydir
Shark B.
Dirk Hartog I.
Murchison
Meekatharra
Cue
Sandstone
Mt Magnet
Leonora
Northampton
Mullewa
L. Barlee
L. Torrens
Woomera
Leigh Ck
L. Frome
Flinders Ra.
Mt St Mary Pk 1189
Wilcannia
Darling
Cobar
Nyngan
NEW SOUTH WALES
Broken Hill
Menindee
Ivanhoe
Dubbo
Mt Barrington 1585
Maitland
Cessnock
Newcastle
Orange
Lithgow
Bathurst
Sydney
Wollongong
Houtman Abrolhos
Geraldton
Dongara
L. Moore
Kalgoorlie
Coolgardie
Rawlinna
Forrest
Nullarbor Plain
Ooldea
Tarcoola
L. Everard
L. Gairdner
Penong
Gawler Ranges
Iron Knob
Whyalla
Quorn
Port Augusta
Peterborough
Port Pirie
Ceduna
Eyre
Great Australian Bight
Flinders I.
Eyre Pen.
Spencer Gulf
Wallaroo
Condobolin
Lachlan
Hay
Griffith
Cootamundra
Goulburn
Canberra
A.C.T.
Moora
Bencubbin
Bullfinch
Southern Cross
Goomalling
Merredin
Northam
Corrigin
Norseman
Perth
Fremantle
Pinjarra
Narrogin
Collie
Wagin
Katanning
Bunbury
Esperance
C. Pasley
Arch. of the Recherche
Bluff Knoll 1110
C. Knob
Albany
C. Naturaliste
Busselton
Augusta
C. Leeuwin
Manjimup
Port Lincoln
Elizabeth
Adelaide
Murray Bridge
Investigator Str.
Victor Harbour
Kangaroo I.
Renmark
Mildura
Murray
Balranald
Riverina
Wagga Wagga
Deniliquin
Albury
Junee
Mt Kosciusko 2230
Shepparton
Australian Alps
VICTORIA
Bendigo
Kingston
Horsham
Naracoorte
Ararat
Ballarat
Melbourne
Hamilton
Mount Gambier
Portland
Geelong
Colac
Port Fairy
Warrnambool
Wonthaggi
Morwell
Sale
Bairnsdale
Bombala
Orbost
C. Howe
Wilson's Prom.
King I.
Bass Strait
Flinders
Furneaux Group
C. Barren
C. Grim
Smithton
Burnie
Devonport
Launceston
Queenstown
Mt Ossa 1617
St Mary's
Hobart
Geeveston
TASMANIA
South West C.
South East C.
10
20
30
40
1
2
3
4
5
110
A
120
B
130
C
140
D
150
1:20M
0
200
400
600
800 km
0
200
400 mls

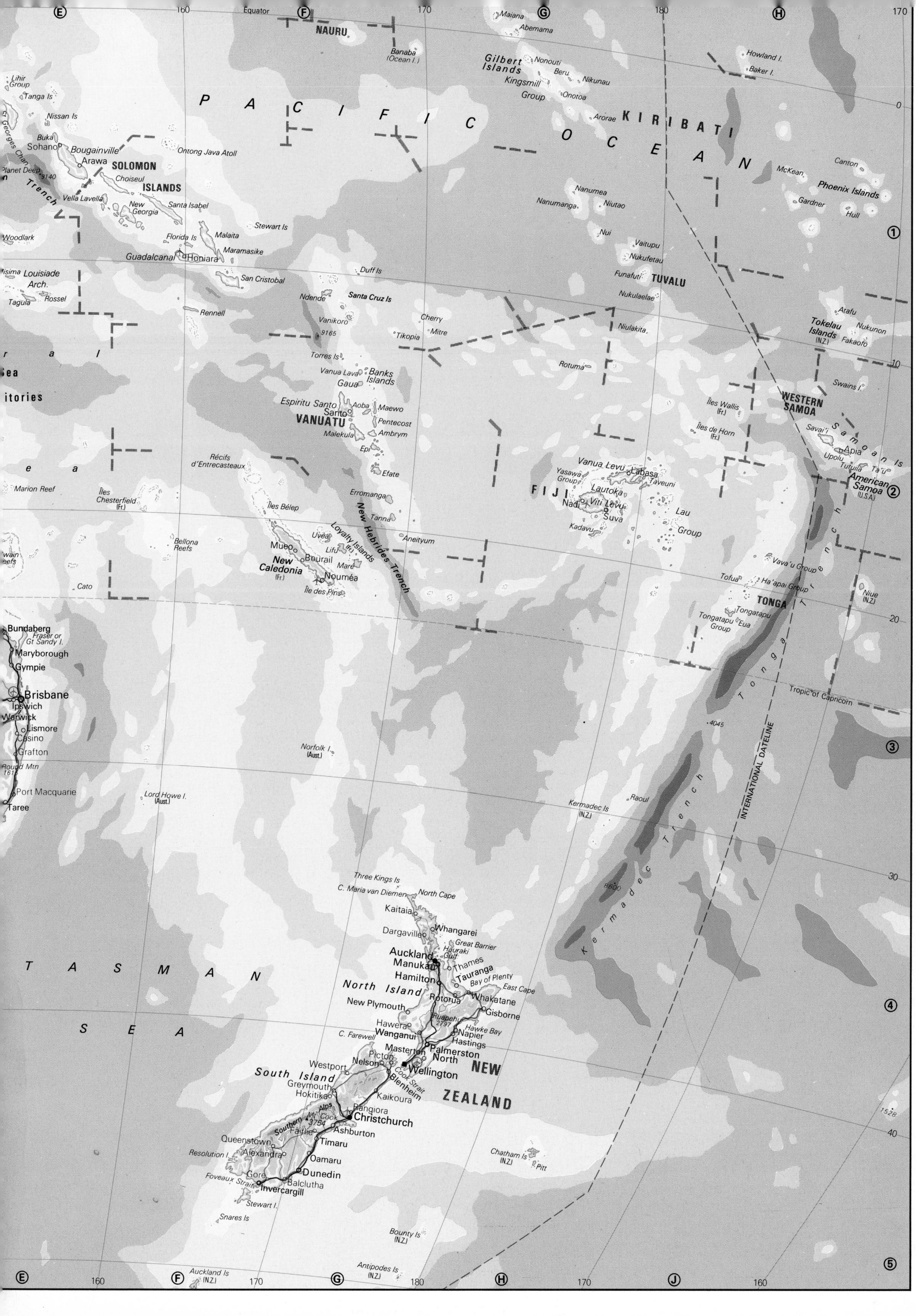

Equator
NAURU
Banaba (Ocean I.)
Maiana
Abemama
Gilbert Islands
Nonouti
Beru
Nikunau
Kingsmill Group
Onotoa
Arorae
KIRIBATI
Howland I.
Baker I.
P A C I F I C O C E A N
Lihir Group
Tanga Is
Nissan Is
Buka
Sohano
Bougainville
Arawa
Ontong Java Atoll
SOLOMON ISLANDS
Choiseul
Planet Deep 9140
Vella Lavella
New Georgia
Santa Isabel
Stewart Is
Florida Is
Malaita
Maramasike
Guadalcanal
Honiara
San Cristobal
Woodlark
Louisiade Arch.
Rossel
Tagula
Rennell
Duff Is
Santa Cruz Is
Ndende
Vanikoro
9165
Cherry
Mitre
Tikopia
Torres Is
Vanua Lava
Banks Islands
Gaua
Espiritu Santo
Santo
Aoba
Maewo
VANUATU
Pentecost
Malekula
Ambrym
Epi
Efate
Erromanga
Tanna
Aneityum
Récifs d'Entrecasteaux
Îles Bélep
Marion Reef
Îles Chesterfield (Fr.)
Bellona Reefs
Cato
Uvéa
Lifu
Loyalty Islands (Fr.)
Maré
New Hebrides Trench
Mueo
Bourail
New Caledonia (Fr.)
Nouméa
Île des Pins
Canton
McKean
Phoenix Islands
Gardner
Hull
Nanumea
Nanumanga
Niutao
Nui
Vaitupu
Nukufetau
Funafuti
TUVALU
Nukulaelae
Niulakita
Rotuma
Atafu
Tokelau Islands (N.Z.)
Nukunon
Fakaofo
Swains I.
WESTERN SAMOA
Îles Wallis (Fr.)
Îles de Horn (Fr.)
Savai'i
Apia
Upolu
Samoan Is
Tutuila
Ta'u
American Samoa (U.S.A.)
Vanua Levu
Labasa
Taveuni
Yasawa Group
FIJI
Lautoka
Viti Levu
Nadi
Suva
Kadavu
Lau Group
Vava'u Group
Tofua
Ha'apai Group
TONGA
Tongatapu
'Eua
Tongatapu Group
Niue (N.Z.)
Tonga Trench
Tropic of Capricorn
4045
INTERNATIONAL DATELINE
Bundaberg
Fraser or Gt Sandy I.
Maryborough
Gympie
Brisbane
Ipswich
Warwick
Lismore
Casino
Grafton
Round Mtn 1615
Port Macquarie
Taree
Norfolk I. (Aust.)
Lord Howe I. (Aust.)
Kermadec Is (N.Z.)
Raoul
Kermadec Trench
8600
Three Kings Is
C. Maria van Diemen
North Cape
Kaitaia
Dargaville
Whangarei
Great Barrier
Hauraki Gulf
Auckland
Manukau
Thames
Hamilton
Tauranga
Bay of Plenty
East Cape
North Island
Rotorua
Whakatane
New Plymouth
Gisborne
Ruapehu 2797
Hawera
Hawke Bay
Wanganui
Napier
Hastings
C. Farewell
Masterton
Palmerston North
Picton
Nelson
Westport
Wellington
NEW ZEALAND
Cook Strait
South Island
Greymouth
Blenheim
Hokitika
Kaikoura
Rangiora
Southern Alps
Mt Cook 3754
Christchurch
Fairlie
Ashburton
Queenstown
Timaru
Resolution I.
Alexandra
Oamaru
Gore
Dunedin
Balclutha
Foveaux Strait
Invercargill
Stewart I.
Snares Is
Chatham Is (N.Z.)
Pitt
Bounty Is (N.Z.)
Antipodes Is (N.Z.)
Auckland Is (N.Z.)
T A S M A N S E A
1528
E F G H J
160 170 180 170 160
0 10 20 30 40
1 2 3 4 5

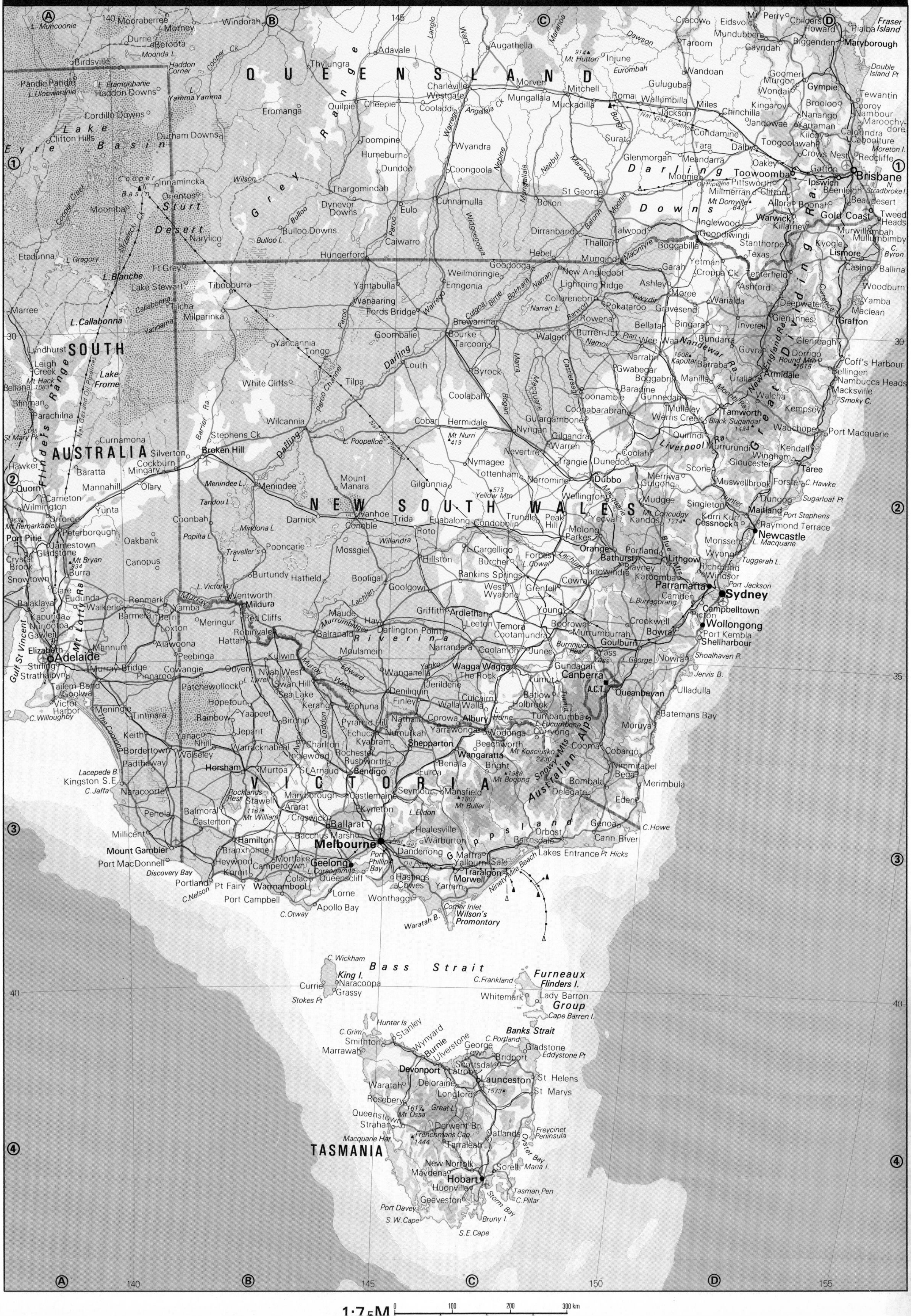
QUEENSLAND
NEW SOUTH WALES
SOUTH AUSTRALIA
VICTORIA
TASMANIA
A.C.T.
Brisbane
Sydney
Canberra
Melbourne
Adelaide
Hobart
Newcastle
Wollongong
Geelong
Launceston
Broken Hill
Mildura
Dubbo
Orange
Bathurst
Wagga Wagga
Albury
Bendigo
Ballarat
Toowoomba
Mount Gambier
Devonport
Burnie
Lake Eyre Basin
Sturt Desert
Grey Range
Darling Downs
Great Dividing Ra.
Australian Alps
Snowy Mts
Flinders Ranges
Riverina
Gippsland
Bass Strait
Furneaux Group
Flinders I.
King I.
Banks Strait
Wilson's Promontory
Port Phillip Bay
Murray
Darling
Murrumbidgee
Lachlan
Mt Kosciusko 2230
Fraser Island
Moreton I.
Port Jackson
Botany
Port Macquarie
Coff's Harbour
Grafton
Lismore
Tamworth
Armidale
Maitland
Parramatta
Queanbeyan
Goulburn
Cooma
Shepparton
Wangaratta
Warrnambool
Portland
Horsham
Port Pirie
Gulf St Vincent
Tweed Heads
Gold Coast
Maryborough
Gympie
Bundaberg
1:7.5M
0 100 200 300 km
140
145
150
155
30
35
40
A B C D
1 2 3 4

170
175
North Cape
van Diemen
Ninety Mile Beach
Rangaunu B.
Doubtless B.
Ahipara B.
Tauroa Pt
Kaitaia
Bay of Islands
C.Brett
Russell
Kaikohe
Kawakawa
Hokianga Har.
Hikurangi
Whangarei
Hen & Chickens Is
Bream B.
Dargaville
Little Barrier I.
Great Barrier I.
Wellsford
Kaipara Har.
Hauraki Gulf
C.Colville
Manly
Mercury Is
Takapuna
Auckland
Mercury Bay
Coromandel Ra.
Papatoetoe
Manukau
Coromandel Peninsula
Papakura
Pukekohe
Thames
Waiuku
Mayor I.
NORTH
Paeroa
Waihi
Huntly
Te Aroha
Matakana I.
White I.
Glen Afton
Tauranga Har.
C. Runaway
Hicks Bay
Ngaruawahia
Morrinsville
Tauranga
East C.
TASMAN SEA
Hamilton
Cambridge
Te Puke
Bay of Plenty
ISLAND
Te Awamutu
Whakatane
Opotiki
Raukumara Ra.
Kawhia
Putaruru
L. Rotorua
Taneatua
Otorohanga
Kawerau
Rotorua
Tokomaru Bay
Waitomo
Waikato
Te Kuiti
Mangakino
Murupara
Tolaga Bay
Whakatane
Rangitaiki
Huiarau Ra.
Hauhungaroa Ra.
N.Taranaki Bight
Mokau
Taupo
L. Taupo
Gisborne
Ohura
Waitara
Poverty Bay
New Plymouth
Taumarunui
L. Waikaremoana
Mt Ngauruhoe 2291
Kaimanawa Mts
Mt Makorako 1727
Mt Egmont (Mt Taranaki) 2518
Inglewood
Tarawera
Wairoa
C. Egmont
Stratford
Mt Ruapehu 2797
Mohaka
Mahia Peninsula
Hawke Bay
Opunake
Eltham
Raetihi
Ohakune
Portland I.
Patea
Whanganui
Eskdale
Taradale
Waiouru
Napier
Hawera
Ngaruroro
Taihape
C. Kidnappers
S.Taranaki Bight
Patea
Hastings
Havelock North
Wanganui
Rangitikei
Ruahine Ra.
40
Marton
Waipukurau
Feilding
Dannevirke
Palmerston N.
C. Farewell
Farewell Spit
COOK STRAIT
Foxton
Woodville
Pahiatua
Golden Bay
C.Stephens
Levin
C.Turnagain
Collingwood
Separation Pt
Herbertville
Eketahuna
Rocks Pt
D'Urville I.
Otaki
Takaka
Tasman Bay
Paraparaumu
Tararua Ra.
Tasman Mts
C.Jackson
Mt Hector 1529
Masterton
Motueka
Porirua
Carterton
The Twins 1826
Tawa
Upper Hutt
Karamea
Karamea Bight
Nelson
Picton
Lower Hutt
Wairarapa
Richmond
Wellington
Martinborough
Motueka
Richmond Ra.
Wairau
Blenheim
Palliser Bay
Mt Ross 983
Seddonville
Awatere
C. Campbell
C. Palliser
Westport
Murchison
C. Foulwind
L. Rotoroa
L. Rotoiti
Buller
Kaikoura Ra.
Tapuaenuku 2885
Mt Travers 2338
Reefton
Victoria Ra.
Spenser Mts
Clarence
Runanga
Grey
Kaikoura
Greymouth
Lewis Pass
Hanmer Springs
Kaikoura Pen.
L. Brunner
Waiau
Waiau
Hokitika
L. Sumner
Culverden
Ross
Hurunui
Cheviot
SOUTH
Arthurs Pass
Puketeraki Ra.
Waipara
Abut Hd
Pegasus Bay
SOUTHERN ALPS
Rangiora
Kaiapoi
Franz Josef Gl.
L. Coleridge
Waimakariri
Rakaia
Hornby
Christchurch
ISLAND
3754 Mt Cook
Methven
Lyttelton
Mt Sefton 3157
Lincoln
Banks Peninsula
Hermitage
Rangitata
Canterbury Plains
Akaroa
L. Tekapo
Ashburton
L. Ellesmere
Jackson Hd
Geraldine
Cascade Pt
Pollux 2542
Young Ra.
L. Pukaki
Lake Pukaki
Fairlie
Canterbury Bight
Ohau
Temuka
Awarua Pt
L. Benmore
Timaru
Mt Aspiring 3027
Wanaka
L. Hawea
Omarama
Milford Sd
L. Aviemore
Milford Sd
Hawkdun Ra.
Kurow
Waimate
Homer Tunnel
Wanaka
Mt Pyramid 2326
Waitaki
PACIFIC
George Sd
Arrowtown
Dunstan Mts
Caswell Sd
Queenstown
Cromwell
Ranfurly
Oamaru
45
Secretary I.
Fiordland
L. Te Anau
Wakatipu
Clyde
Alexandra
Doubtful Sd
Nat. Park
Te Anau
Kingston
Hampden
Manapouri
Roxburgh
Palmerston
Breaksea Sd
OCEAN
L. Manapouri
Waiau
Taieri
Waikouaiti
Mt Ward 1718
Port Chalmers
Resolution I.
Lumsden
Heriot
Otago Peninsula
Dusky Sd
Riversdale
Mosgiel
Dunedin
Oreti
Clutha
Ohai
L. Hauroko
Tapanui
Lawrence
Cameron Mts
Tuatapere
Winton
Gore
Milton
Mataura
Balclutha
Puysegur Pt
Te Waewae Bay
Edendale
Kaitangata
Riverton
Invercargill
Owaka
Foveaux Strait
Solander I.
Bluff
Codfish I.
Oban
Paterson Inlet
Stewart Island
Mt Allen 730
Shelter Pt
Port Pegasus
1:5M
0 50 100 150 200 km
0 50 100 mls

Barents Sea

Norwegian Basin

ICELAND

North Sea

EUROPE

Mediterranean Sea

Black Sea

Caspian Sea

Aral Sea

ASIA

Arctic Circle

Sea of Okhotsk

Sakhalin

Vityaz Depth 10542

Sea of Japan

JAPAN

Kuril Trench

Red Sea

Persian Gulf

Arabian Sea

Ganga

Bay of Bengal

Huang He

Chang Jiang

TAIWAN

S. Honshu Ridge

Japan Trench

AFRICA

Raas Caseyr

Arabian Basin

Carlsberg Ridge

MALDIVES

Maldives Ridge

SRI LANKA (CEYLON)

Andaman Is.

Nicobar Is

Mekong

Hainan

South China Sea

PHILIPPINES

Kyushu-Palau Ridge

Northern Mariana Is.

Guam

Philippine Trench

Challenger Depth

NORTHERN

MARIANA

ISLANDS

MICRON

Mariana Trench

11022

C. Johnson Depth 10497

Somali Basin

SEYCHELLES

Mascarene Ridge

Chagos Arch.

Mid Indian Basin

Ninety-East Ridge

Sumatra

Celebes Sea

Borneo

Celebes

INDONESIA

Java

PALAU (BELAU)

Caroline Is

FEDERATED STATES OF MICRONESIA

6920

MELA

New Guinea

Planet Deep 9140

COMOROS

INDIAN

Java Trench

7450

Cocos Is

West Australian Basin

Christmas I.

Timor

Arafura Sea

Coral Sea Basin

MADAGASCAR

Réunion

MAURITIUS

OCEAN

1737

1924

Tropic of Capricorn

AUSTRALIA

Great Barrier Reef

Mozambique Channel

S. Madagascar Ridge

Madagascar Basin

2067

W. Australian Ridge

7102

South Australia Basin

Tas ma

Natal Basin

C.Agulhas

Agulhas Plateau

South West Indian Ridge

Crozet Basin

I.Amsterdam

I.St Paul

Indian-Antarctic Ridge

Tasmania Sea

Agulhas Basin

Ìs Crozet

Pr.Edward Is

Kerguelen Ridge

Ìs Kerguelen

1922

Macquarie Is

Atlantic-Indian Ridge

Heard I.

Atlantic-Indian Antarctic Basin

Banzare Seamount 186

Indian-Antarctic Basin

ANTARCTICA

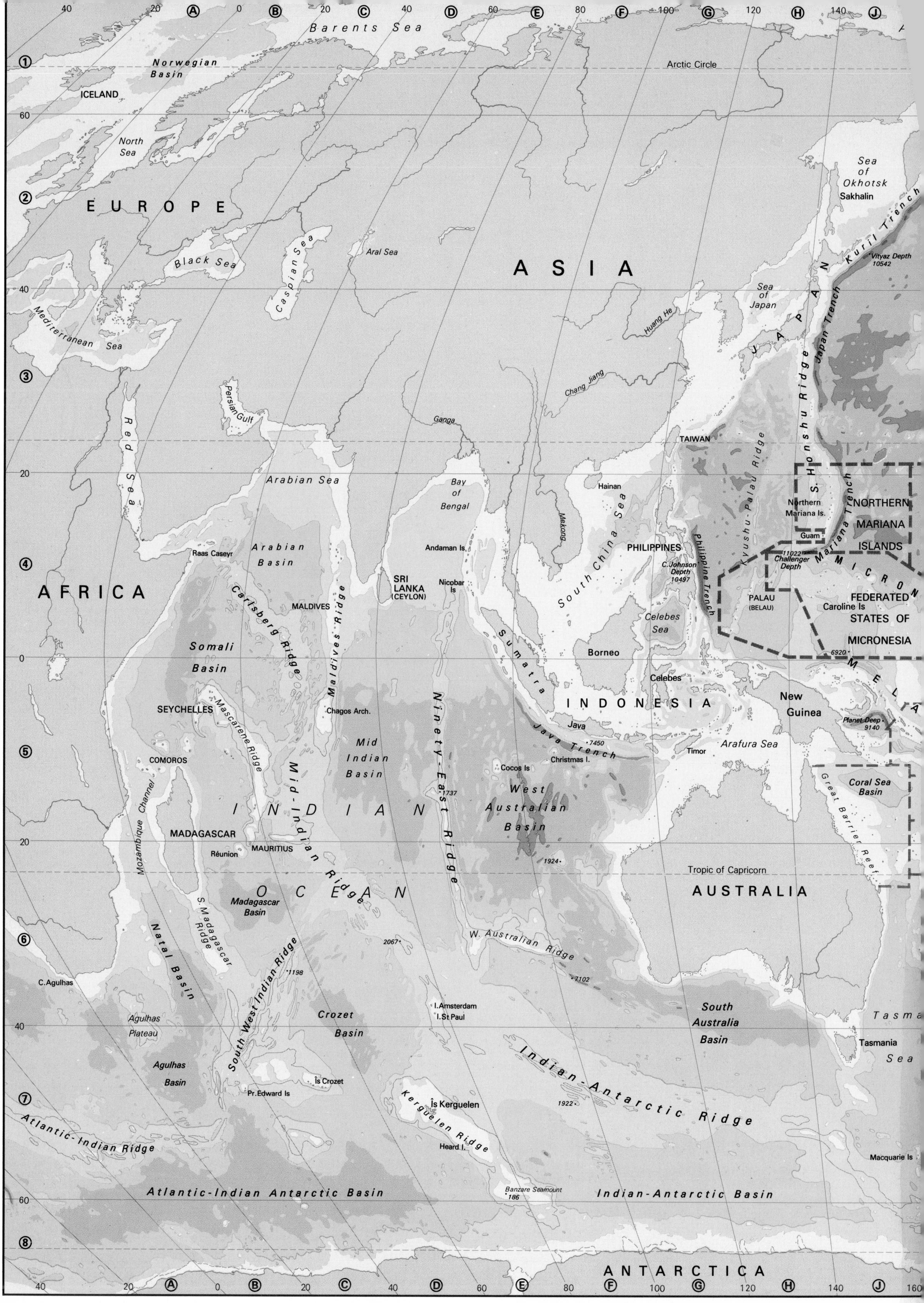

1:60M

0   600   1200   1800   2400 km

0   600   1200 mls

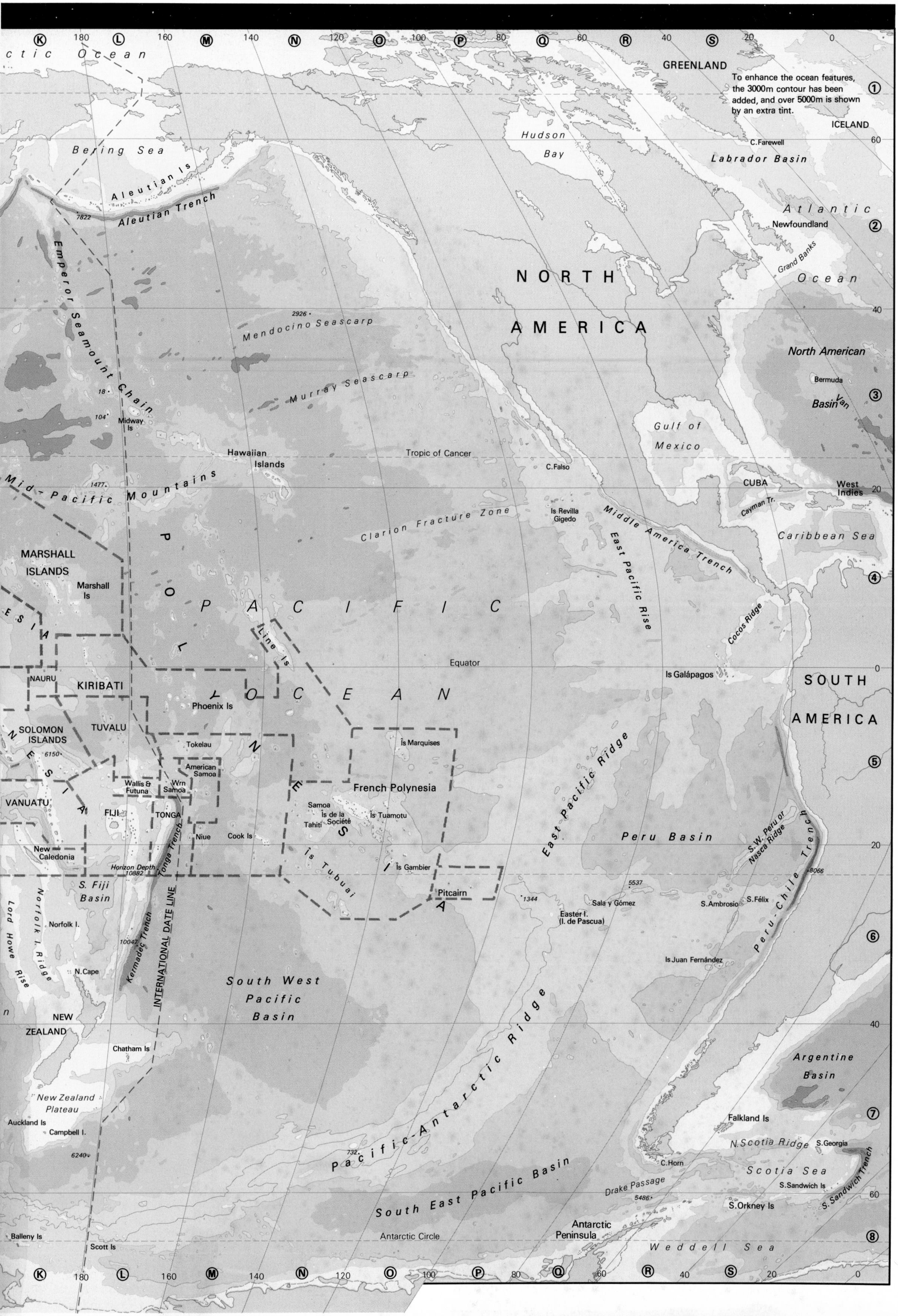

To enhance the ocean features, the 3000m contour has been added, and over 5000m is shown by an extra tint.
K
L
M
N
O
P
Q
R
S
180
160
140
120
100
80
60
40
20
0
ctic Ocean
GREENLAND
ICELAND
C.Farewell
Labrador Basin
Hudson Bay
Bering Sea
Aleutian Is
Aleutian Trench
7822
Atlantic Ocean
Newfoundland
Grand Banks
NORTH AMERICA
Emperor Seamount Chain
2926
Mendocino Seascarp
Murray Seascarp
North American Basin
Bermuda
18
104
Midway Is
Hawaiian Islands
Tropic of Cancer
Gulf of Mexico
C.Falso
CUBA
West Indies
Cayman Tr.
1477
Mid-Pacific Mountains
Clarion Fracture Zone
Is Revilla Gigedo
Middle America Trench
East Pacific Rise
Caribbean Sea
MARSHALL ISLANDS
Marshall Is
PACIFIC OCEAN
POLYNESIA
Line Is
Cocos Ridge
Equator
Is Galápagos
NAURU
KIRIBATI
Phoenix Is
SOUTH AMERICA
SOLOMON ISLANDS
TUVALU
Tokelau
Îs Marquises
6150
American Samoa
Wallis & Futuna
Wrn Samoa
French Polynesia
East Pacific Ridge
VANUATU
FIJI
TONGA
Samoa
Îs de la Société
Tahiti
Îs Tuamotu
New Caledonia
Niue
Cook Is
Peru Basin
S.W. Peru or Nasca Ridge
Îs Tubuai
Îs Gambier
Horizon Depth 10882
Tonga Trench
8066
S. Fiji Basin
Pitcairn
5537
1344
Sala y Gómez
Easter I. (I. de Pascua)
S.Ambrosio
S.Félix
Peru-Chile Trench
Norfolk I.
Norfolk I. Ridge
Lord Howe Rise
10047
Kermadec Trench
INTERNATIONAL DATE LINE
Is Juan Fernández
N.Cape
South West Pacific Basin
NEW ZEALAND
Chatham Is
Pacific-Antarctic Ridge
Argentine Basin
New Zealand Plateau
Auckland Is
Campbell I.
6240
Falkland Is
N.Scotia Ridge
S.Georgia
732
C.Horn
Scotia Sea
South East Pacific Basin
Drake Passage
S.Sandwich Is
S.Sandwich Trench
5486
S.Orkney Is
Antarctic Peninsula
Balleny Is
Antarctic Circle
Scott Is
Weddell Sea
1
2
3
4
5
6
7
8

SOUTH ASIA & MIDDLE EAST

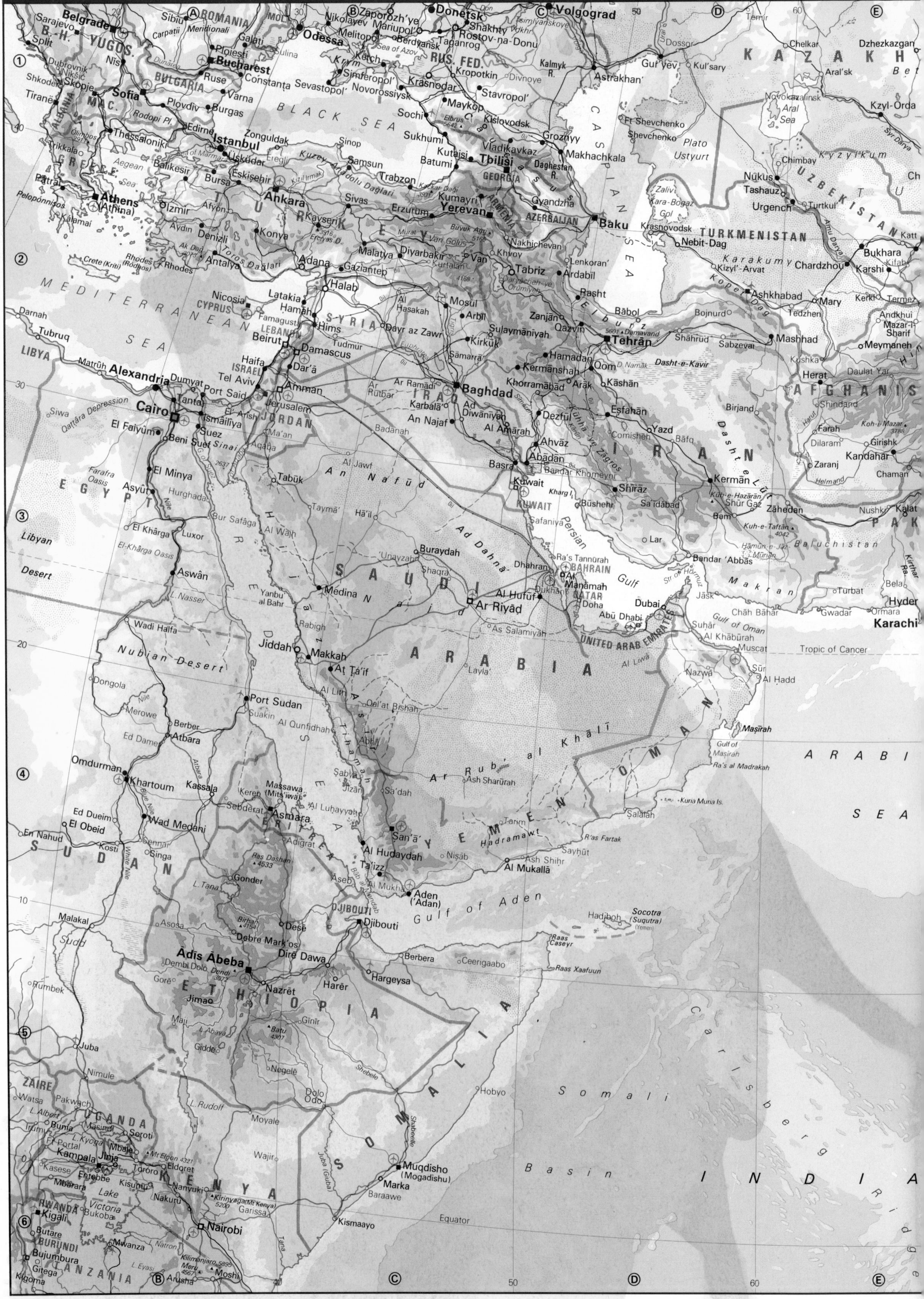

1:20M

0 200 400 600 800 km

0 200 400 mls

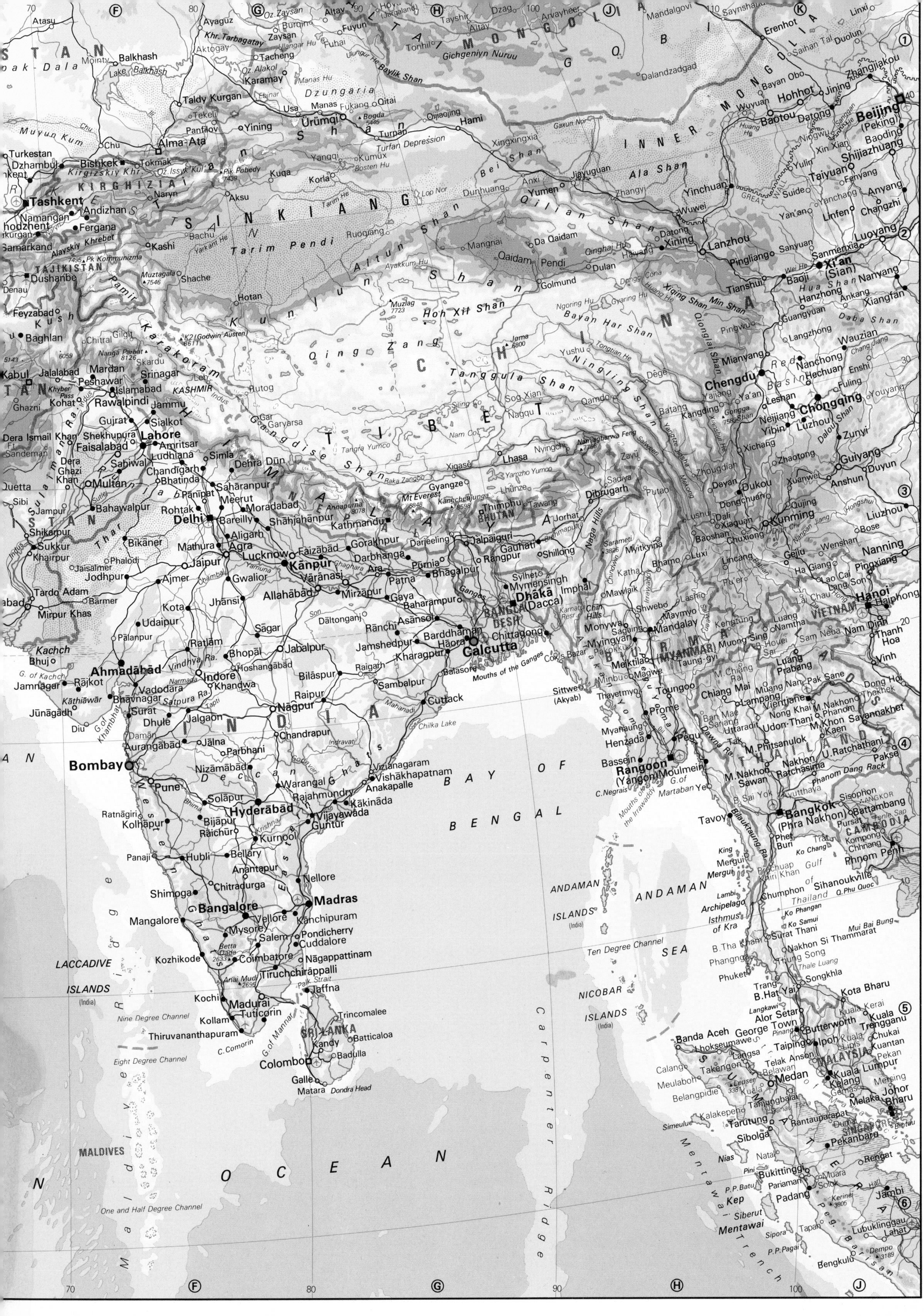

MONGOLIA
GOBI
INNER MONGOLIA
Altai
Gichgeniyn Nuruu
Dzungaria
Tarim Pendi
SINKIANG
Tien Shan
Kunlun Shan
Altun Shan
Qaidam Pendi
Qilian Shan
Bei Shan
Ala Shan
Hoh Xil Shan
Qing Zang
Tanggula Shan
Bayan Har Shan
TIBET
CHINA
Gangdise Shan
HIMALAYA
Karakoram
KASHMIR
Red Basin
Daba Shan
Min Shan
Qionglai Shan
Ningjing Shan
Xiqing Shan
Hua Shan
Turfan Depression
Lop Nor
Bosten Hu
Nam Co
Tangra Yumco
Yamzho Yumco
Qinghai Hu
Mt Everest 8848
Annapurna 8078
K2 (Godwin Austen) 8611
Nanga Parbat 8126
Muztagata 7546
Pk Kommunizma 7495
Pik Pobedy 7439
Muztag 7723
Gongga Shan 7589
Namjagbarwa Feng 7756
Jomo 6800
Bogda 5445
KIRGHIZIA
TAJIKISTAN
Alma-Ata
Bishkek
Tashkent
Dushanbe
Fergana
Andizhan
Namangan
Samarkand
Balkhash
Lake Balkhash
Taldy Kurgan
Yining
Ürümqi
Turpan
Hami
Karamay
Kashi
Hotan
Aksu
Kuqa
Korla
Dunhuang
Golmud
Xining
Lanzhou
Yinchuan
Baotou
Hohhot
Datong
Beijing (Peking)
Baoding
Shijiazhuang
Taiyuan
Luoyang
Xi'an (Sian)
Baoji
Tianshui
Hanzhong
Chengdu
Chongqing
Nanchong
Guiyang
Kunming
Dali
Lhasa
Xigazê
Qamdo
Nagqu
Nanning
Hanoi
Haiphong
Kabul
Jalalabad
Peshawar
Islamabad
Rawalpindi
Srinagar
Jammu
Lahore
Faisalabad
Multan
Bahawalpur
Sukkur
Quetta
Amritsar
Ludhiana
Simla
Chandigarh
Delhi
Meerut
Agra
Jaipur
Jodhpur
Bikaner
Ajmer
Gwalior
Lucknow
Kanpur
Allahabad
Varanasi
Patna
Kathmandu
Thimphu
BHUTAN
Darjeeling
Gauhati
Shillong
Dibrugarh
Imphal
Dhaka (Dacca)
BANGLADESH
Chittagong
Calcutta
Asansol
Ranchi
Jamshedpur
Cuttack
Bhopal
Indore
Jabalpur
Nagpur
Ahmadabad
Vadodara
Rajkot
Bhavnagar
Surat
Jalgaon
Aurangabad
Bombay
Pune
Solapur
Hyderabad
Warangal
Vishakhapatnam
Vijayawada
Guntur
Kurnool
Bellary
Hubli
Panaji
Bangalore
Mysore
Mangalore
Madras
Pondicherry
Coimbatore
Kozhikode
Tiruchchirappalli
Madurai
Kochi
Kollam
Thiruvananthapuram
C. Comorin
Jaffna
Trincomalee
SRI LANKA
Kandy
Colombo
Galle
INDIA
Deccan
Western Ghats
Eastern Ghats
Thar
Vindhya Ra.
Satpura Ra.
Mouths of the Ganges
Chilka Lake
Palk Strait
G. of Mannar
G. of Kachch
G. of Khambhat
BURMA (MYANMAR)
Mandalay
Myitkyina
Bhamo
Lashio
Monywa
Sittwe (Akyab)
Prome
Pegu
Rangoon (Yangon)
Moulmein
Bassein
Mouths of the Irrawaddy
G. of Martaban
Tavoy
Mergui
Arakan Yoma
Pegu Yoma
Chiang Mai
Vientiane
Luang Prabang
LAOS
THAILAND
Bangkok (Phra Nakhon)
Nakhon Ratchasima
CAMBODIA
Phnom Penh
Battambang
Tonle Sap
VIETNAM
Gulf of Thailand
Isthmus of Kra
Phuket
Songkhla
Surat Thani
Nakhon Si Thammarat
Kota Bharu
Alor Setar
George Town
Ipoh
Kuala Lumpur
MALAYSIA
Melaka
Johor Bharu
SINGAPORE
Banda Aceh
Medan
SUMATRA
Padang
Pekanbaru
Jambi
Bengkulu
Mentawai
Siberut
Nias
Simeulue
BAY OF BENGAL
ANDAMAN ISLANDS (India)
ANDAMAN SEA
Ten Degree Channel
NICOBAR ISLANDS (India)
LACCADIVE ISLANDS (India)
Nine Degree Channel
Eight Degree Channel
One and Half Degree Channel
MALDIVES
Maldive Ridge
Carpenter Ridge
Mentawai Trench
INDIAN OCEAN
70
80
90
100
F
G
H
J
K

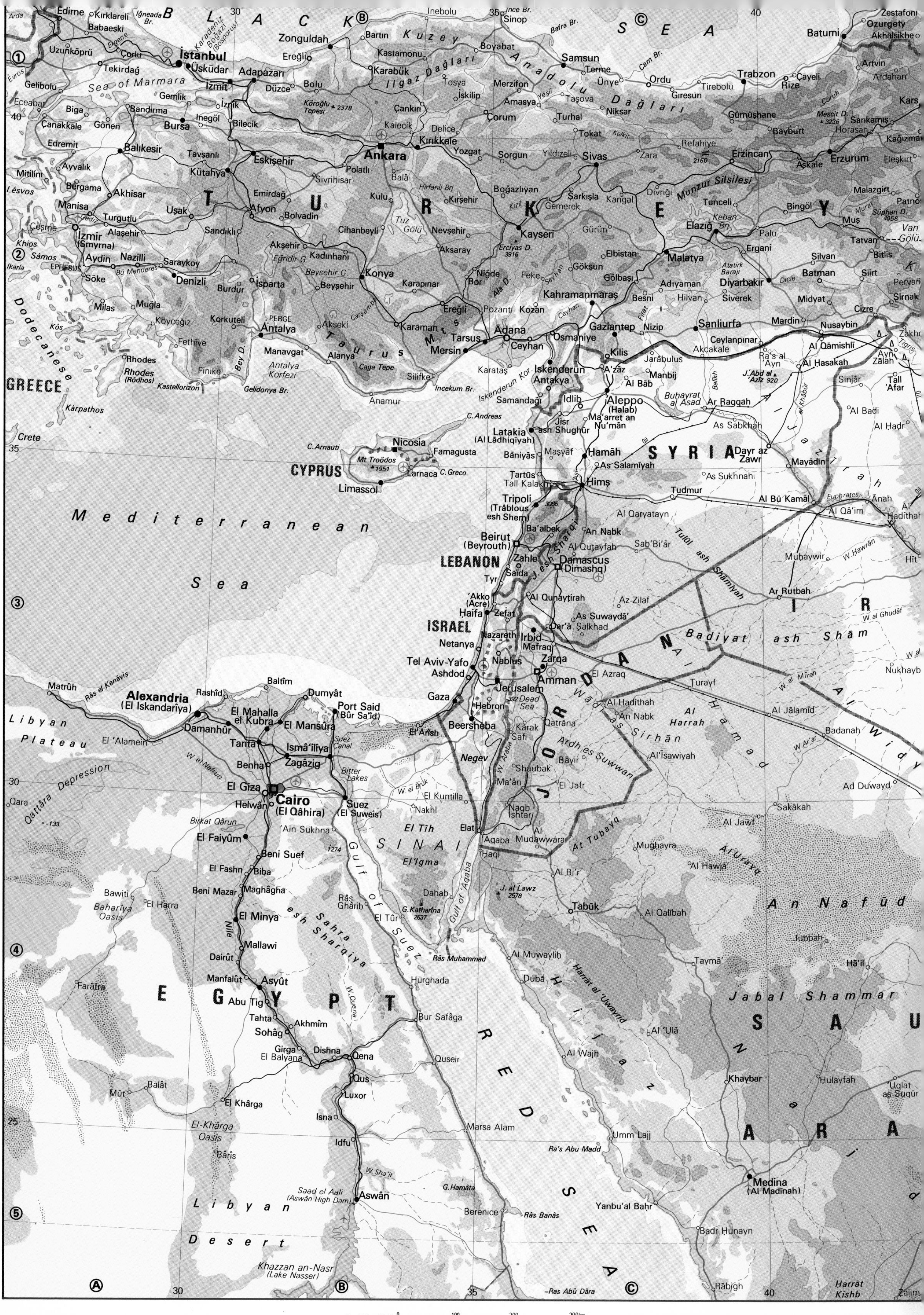

B L A C K
S E A
Edirne
Kırklareli
Babaeski
Uzunköprü
Çorlu
İstanbul
Üsküdar
Tekirdağ
Gelibolu
Sea of Marmara
İzmit
Adapazarı
Gemlik
İznik
Bursa
Bandırma
İnegöl
Bilecik
Çanakkale
Biga
Gönen
Edremit
Balıkesir
Ayvalık
Mitilini
Lésvos
Bergama
Akhisar
Manisa
Turgutlu
Çeşme
İzmir
(Smyrna)
Alaşehir
Sámos
Ikaría
Aydın
Nazilli
Söke
Denizli
Saraykoy
Milas
Muğla
Köyceğiz
Fethiye
Dodecanese
Kós
Rhodes
Kastellorizon
Kárpathos
GREECE
Crete
Zonguldak
Bartın
Ereğli
Kastamonu
Karabük
Düzce
Bolu
Çankırı
Tosya
Köroğlu Tepesi 2378
Inebolu
Sinop
Boyabat
Kuzey Anadolu Dağları
Ilgaz Dağları
Samsun
Terme
Ünye
Ordu
Giresun
Tirebolu
Trabzon
Rize
Çayeli
Batumi
Ozurgety
Zestafoni
Akhalsikhe
Artvin
Ardahan
Kars
Sarıkamış
Horasan
Kağızman
Gümüşhane
Bayburt
Erzurum
Eleşkirt
Erzincan
Aşkale
Merzifon
Amasya
İskilip
Çorum
Taşova
Niksar
Turhal
Tokat
Kelkit
Refahiye
Zara
Sivas
Yıldızeli
Kırıkkale
Kalecik
Delice
Yozgat
Sorgun
Ankara
Polatlı
Eskişehir
Tavşanlı
Kütahya
Sivrihisar
Emirdağ
Afyon
Uşak
Bolvadin
Sandıklı
Kulu
Tuz Gölü
Kırşehir
Nevşehir
Aksaray
Cihanbeyli
Akşehir
Kadınhanı
Eğirdir G.
Beyşehir G.
Beyşehir
Konya
Isparta
Burdur
Karapınar
Niğde
Bor
Ereğli
Karaman
Akseki
Antalya
Manavgat
Alanya
Antalya Korfezi
Finike
Gelidonya Br.
Anamur
Silifke
Taurus Mts
Tarsus
Mersin
Adana
Ceyhan
Osmaniye
Kozan
Pozantı
Kahramanmaraş
Göksun
Gürün
Elbistan
Kayseri
Erciyas D. 3916
Boğazlıyan
Şarkışla
Gemerek
Kangal
Divriği
Munzur Silsilesi
Tunceli
Bingöl
Malazgirt
Patnos
Muş
Tatvan
Van Gölü
Bitlis
Siirt
Şırnak
Pervari
Batman
Silvan
Ergani
Palu
Elazığ
Keban
Malatya
Gölbaşı
Adıyaman
Diyarbakır
Dicle
Siverek
Hilvan
Besni
Gaziantep
Nizip
Sanliurfa
Mardin
Midyat
Cizre
Nusaybin
Ceylanpınar
Akçakale
Kilis
A'zaz
Iskenderun
Antakya
Karataş
Samandağı
Idlib
Aleppo
(Halab)
Al Bāb
Manbij
Jarābulus
Buhayrat al Asad
Ar Raqqah
Al Qāmishlī
Al Ḩasakah
Ra's al 'Ayn
Sinjār
Tall 'Afar
Zakho
Al Jazirah
Jisr ash Shughūr
Ma'arret an Nu'mān
Latakia
(Al Lādhiqīyah)
Bāniyās
Maşyāf
Ḩamāh
As Salamīyah
As Sabkhah
Dayr az Zawr
Mayādīn
SYRIA
Ţarţūs
Tall Kalakh
Ḩimş
As Sukhnah
Tudmur
Al Bū Kamāl
Euphrates
'Ānah
Al Qā'im
Al Ḩadīthah
Tripoli
(Trâblous esh Shem)
3086
Ba'albek
An Nabk
Al Qaryatayn
Sab'Bi'ār
Al Quţayfah
Beirut
(Beyrouth)
LEBANON
Zahle
Saida
Damascus
(Dimashq)
Tyr
'Akko
(Acre)
Ḩaifa
Zefat
Al Qunayţirah
Az Zilaf
As Suwaydā'
Şalkhad
ISRAEL
Netanya
Nazareth
Irbid
Dar'ā
Mafraq
Tel Aviv-Yafo
Ashdod
Nablus
Zarqa
Amman
Al Azraq
Jerusalem
392 Dead Sea
Gaza
Hebron
Beersheba
Karak
Qaţrāna
Negev
Shaubak
Ma'ān
El Jafr
Bāyir
Al Ḩadīthah
Wādī as Sirḩān
Ardh es Şuwwan
Al 'Isāwiyah
Naqb Ishtar
Al Mudawwara
At Tubayq
Elat
Aqaba
Ḩaql
JORDAN
Ar Rutbah
Muḩaywir
Badiyat ash Shām
Nukhayb
Turayf
Al Jalāmīd
Badanah
Al Ḩarrah
Al Ḩamad
Ad Duwayd
Sakākah
Al Jawf
Mughayra
Al Hawjā
An Nafūd
Jubbah
Tabūk
Al Qalībah
Taymā'
Ḩā'il
Jabal Shammar
Al Muwayliḩ
Dubā
Ḩarrāt al 'Uwayrid
Ḩijāz
Al 'Ulā
Al Wajh
Khaybar
Ḩulayfah
'Uqlat as Şuqūr
Umm Lajj
Medina
(Al Madīnah)
Yanbu'al Baḩr
Badr Ḩunayn
Rābigh
Ḩarrāt Kishb
Ẓalim
SAUDI ARABIA
Mediterranean Sea
C. Andreas
C. Arnauti
Nicosia
Famagusta
Mt Troödos 1951
CYPRUS
Larnaca
C. Greco
Limassol
Matrûh
Râs el Kenâyis
Alexandria
(El Iskandarîya)
Rashîd
Baltîm
Dumyât
Port Said
(Bûr Sa'îd)
El Mahalla el Kubra
El Mansûra
Damanhûr
Tanta
Ismâ'ilîya
Suez Canal
Zagâzig
Benha
Bitter Lakes
El 'Arîsh
El 'Alamein
Libyan Plateau
Qattâra Depression
Qara
-133
El Gîza
Cairo
(El Qâhira)
Helwân
Suez
(El Suweis)
Birkat Qârûn
El Faiyûm
'Ain Sukhna
Beni Suef
El Fashn
Biba
Beni Mazar
Maghâgha
Bawiti
Baharîya Oasis
El Harra
El Minya
Mallawi
Dairût
Manfalût
Asyût
Abu Tig
Tahta
Sohâg
Akhmîm
Girga
El Balyana
Dishna
Qena
Qus
Luxor
Isna
Idfu
Aswân
Saad el Aali
(Aswân High Dam)
Khazzan an-Nasr
(Lake Nasser)
Farâfra
Mût
Balât
El Khârga
El-Khârga Oasis
Bâris
Libyan Desert
EGYPT
Nile
Sahra esh Sharqiya
SINAI
El Tîh
El 'Igma
El Kuntilla
Nakhl
Gulf of Suez
Gulf of 'Aqaba
Dahab
G. Katharîna 2637
El Tûr
Râs Ghârib
Râs Muhammad
Hurghada
Bur Safâga
Quseir
Marsa Alam
G. Hamâta
Berenice
Râs Banâs
Ras Abû Dâra
Ra's Abu Madd
RED SEA
1:7.5M
0 100 200 300km
0 50 100 150 mls

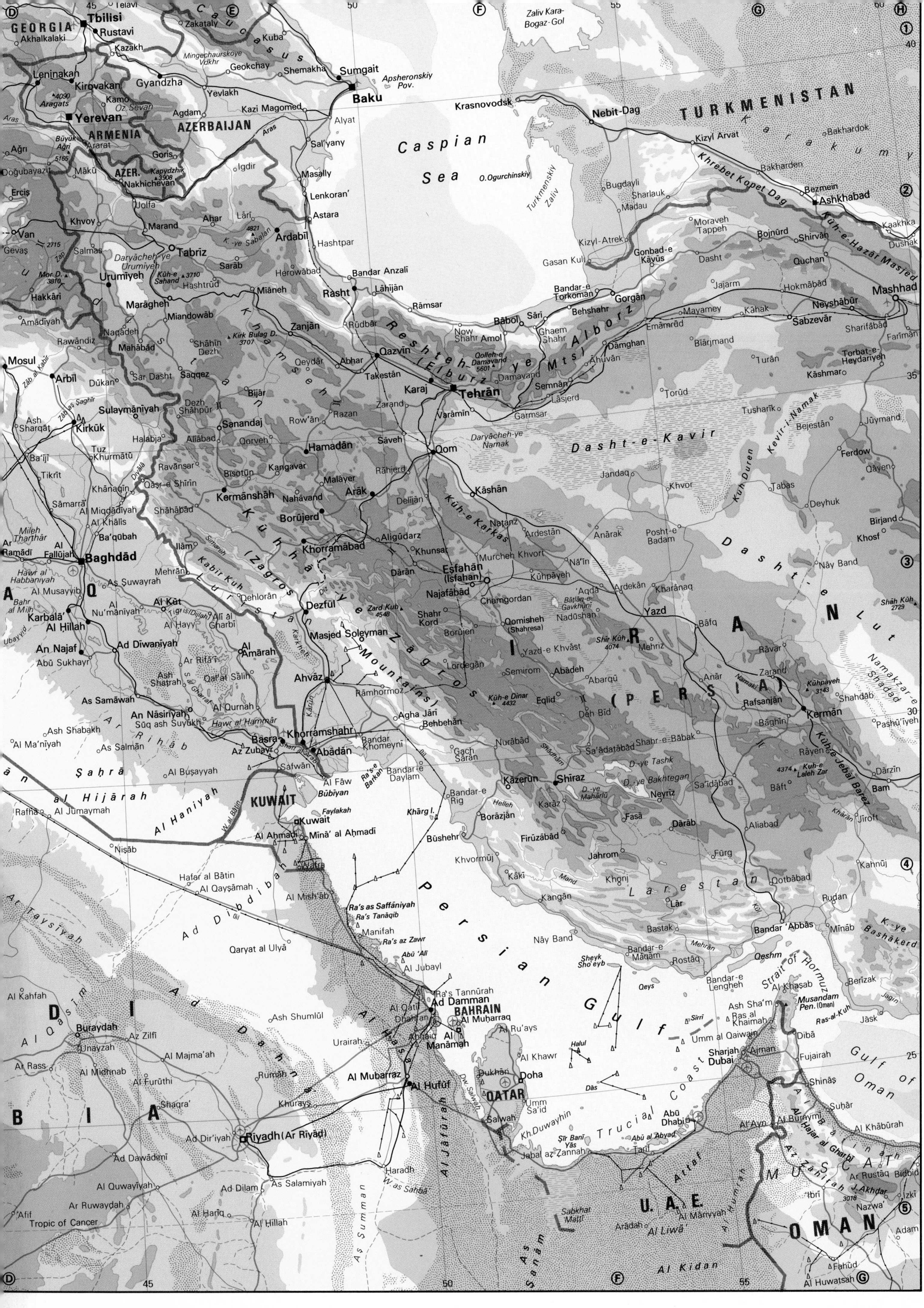

GEORGIA
Tbilisi
Rustavi
Akhalkalaki
Kazakh
Zakataly
Kuba
Caucasus
Mingechaurskoye Vdkhr
Geokchay
Shemakha
Sumgait
Baku
Apsheronskiy Pov.
Leninakan
Kirovakan
Gyandzha
Kamo
Oz. Sevan
Aragats
Yerevan
ARMENIA
AZERBAIJAN
Yevlakh
Kazi Magomed
Agdam
Alyat
Sal'yany
Aras
Ağrı
Büyük Ağri
Ararat
Doğubayazıt
Goris
AZER.
Kapydzhik
Nakhichevan
Igdir
Masally
Lenkoran'
Astara
Caspian Sea
O. Ogurchinskiy
Turkmenskiy Zaliv
Zaliv Kara-Bogaz-Gol
Krasnovodsk
Nebit-Dag
TURKMENISTAN
Karakumy
Kizyl Arvat
Bakhardok
Bakharden
Khrebet Kopet Dag
Bezmein
Ashkhabad
Bugdayli
Sharlauk
Madau
Erciş
Khvoy
Jolfa
Marand
Ahar
Lārī
Ardabīl
Hashtpar
Van
Gevaş
Salmas
Daryācheh-ye Urumīyeh
Tabrīz
Sarāb
Kūh-e Sahand
Hashtrūd
Urumīyeh
Mor D.
Hakkâri
Herowābād
Rasht
Bandar Anzalī
Lāhījān
Mīāneh
Rāmsar
Marāgheh
Miandowāb
Zanjān
Rūdbār
Amādīyah
Naqadeh
Mahābād
Rawāndiz
Shāhīn Dezh
Kirk Bulag D.
Reshteh-ye Alborz (Elburz Mts)
Now Shahr
Amol
Bābol
Sārī
Ghaem Shahr
Behshahr
Gorgān
Bandar-e Torkoman
Gasan Kuli
Kizyl-Atrek
Gonbad-e Kāvūs
Moraveh Tappeh
Bojnūrd
Shīrvān
Dasht
Quchan
Kūh-e Hazār Masjed
Kaakhka
Dushak
Jajarm
Mashhad
Hokmābād
Neyshābūr
Sabzevār
Kahak
Mayamey
Emāmrūd
Dāmghan
Biārjmand
Sharifābād
Farīmān
Torbat-e Heydarīyeh
Turān
Kāshmar
Mosul
Arbīl
Dūkān
Sar Dasht
Saqqez
Qeydār
Abhar
Qazvīn
Takestān
Karaj
Tehrān
Qolleh-ye Damāvand
Damāvand
Semnān
Āhuvān
Lāsjerd
Garmsar
Torūd
Tusharīk
Kevīr-i-Namak
Bejestān
Jūymand
Ash Sharqāt
Kirkūk
Sulaymānīyah
Dezh Shāhpūr
Bījār
Sanandaj
Halabja
Zarand
Row'ān
Razan
Varāmīn
Alīābād
Qorveh
Hamadān
Sāveh
Qom
Daryācheh-ye Namak
Dasht-e-Kavir
Ba'ījī
Tuz Khurmātū
Tikrīt
Ravānsar
Bīsotūn
Kangāvar
Malāyer
Rāhjerd
Kāshān
Jandaq
Khvor
Kūh Duren
Ferdow
Qāyen
Tabas
Deyhuk
Khānaqīn
Qaşr-e Shīrīn
Kermānshāh
Nahāvand
Arāk
Delījān
Kūh-e Karkas
Sāmarrā'
Al Miqdādīyah
Shāhābād
Borūjerd
Naţanz
Bīrjand
Khosf
Al Khālis
Ba'qūbah
Mileh Tharthār
Ar Ramādī
Al Fallūjah
Baghdād
Hawr al Habbānīyah
Īlām
Saimareh
Khorramābād
Alīgūdarz
Khunsar
Ardestān
Anārak
Posht-e Badam
Dasht-e Lut
Murcheh Khvort
Nā'īn
Kabir Kuh
Mehrān
Aş Şuwayrah
Kūhhā-ye Zāgros (Zagros Mountains)
Luristan
Dārān
Eşfahān (Isfahan)
Kūhpāyeh
Nāy Band
Al Musayyib
Dehlorān
Dez
Najafābād
Chamgordan
'Aqda
Ardekān
Kharānaq
Bahr al Milh
Karbalā'
Al Ḩillah
Al Kūt
Nu'mānīyah
Tigris (Dijlah)
Alī al Gharbī
Al Ḩayy
Dezfūl
Zard Kuh
Shahr Kord
Bātlāq-e Gavkhūnī
Nadūshan
Yazd
Shāh Kūh
Ubayyid
An Najaf
Abū Sukhayr
Ad Dīwanīyah
Ar Rifā'ī
Al 'Amārah
Masjed Soleyman
Borūjen
Qomisheh (Shahresa)
IRAN
Bāfq
Mehrīz
Shīr Kūh
Yazd-e Khvāst
Rāvar
Namakzar-e Shahdad
Ash Shaţrah
Qal'at Şālih
Karkheh
Ahvāz
Kārūn
Lordegān
Semirom
Ābādeh
Abarqū
Anār
Zarand
Kūhpāyeh
As Samāwah
An Nāşirīyah
Sūq ash Suyūkh
Al Qurnah
Hawr al Hammār
Rāmhormoz
Kūh-e Dīnār
Eqlīd
(PERSIA)
Rafsanjān
Namakī
Shahdāb
Kermān
Pashū'īyeh
Ash Shabakh
Ar Rihāb
Al Ma'nīyah
As Salmān
Basra
Khorramshahr
Abādān
Az Zubayr
Shaţţ al 'Arab
Agha Jārī
Behbehān
Bandar Khomeynī
Deh Bīd
Bāghīn
Gach Sārān
Nūrābād
Shādhām
Sa'ādatābād
Shahr-e Bābak
Kūh-e Jebāl Bārez
Rāyen
Dārzīn
Şahrā al Hijārah
Al Buşayyah
Şafwān
Al Fāw
Ra's-e Barkan
Bandar-e Daylam
Kāzerūn
Shīrāz
D-ye Tashk
D-ye Bakhtegān
Sa'īdābād
Laleh Zar
Bāft
Bam
KUWAIT
Būbīyan
Faylakah
Bandar-e Rīg
Helleh
D-ye Mahārlū
Neyrīz
Rafhā
Al Jumaymah
Al Haniyah
W. al Bāţin
Kuwait
Khārg I.
Borāzjān
Karāz
Fasā
Dārāb
Aliabad
Kharān
Jīroft
Al Aḩmadī
Mīnā' al Aḩmadī
Būshehr
Fīrūzābād
Nişāb
Wafra
Jahrom
Fūrg
Khvormūj
Kahnūj
Hafar al Bāţin
Al Qayşūmah
Kākī
Mand
Khonj
Larestan
Qotbābād
Ar Taysiyah
Al Mish'āb
Ad Dibdibah
Oil
Ra's as Saffānīyah
Ra's Tanāqib
Kangān
Lār
Rudan
Persian Gulf
Manīfah
Ra's az Zawr
Bastak
Bandar 'Abbās
Mīnāb
K.-ye Bashākerd
Nāy Band
Mehrān
Qaryat al Ulyā
Abū 'Alī
Bandar-e Māqām
Qeshm
Al Jubayl
Sheyk Sho'eyb
Rostāq
Strait of Hormuz
Ra's Tannūrah
Qeys
Bandar-e Lengheh
Al Khaşab
Berīzak
Al Kahfah
Ad Dahnā
Al Qaţīf
Ad Damman
Dhahran
BAHRAIN
Al Muḩarraq
Musandam Pen. (Oman)
Jagīn
Ash Shumlūl
Abqaiq
Al Manāmah
Al Ru'ays
Sirrī
Ash Sha'm
Ras al Khaimah
Ras-al-Kuh
Jāsk
Al Qaşīm
Buraydah
Az Zilfī
Al Ḩasā
Uraīrah
Halul
Umm al Qaiwain
Dibā
'Unayzah
Al Majma'ah
Al Khawr
Ajman
Sharjah
Dubai
Fujairah
Gulf of Oman
Ar Rass
Al Midhnab
Al Mubarraz
Dukhān
Doha
Dās
Trucial Coast
Al Furūthī
Rumāh
Al Hufūf
Dw. Salwah
QATAR
Umm Sa'īd
Shinās
Şuḩār
Shaqra'
Khurayş
Salwah
Kh. Duwayhin
Abū Dhabi
Al 'Ayn
Al Buraymī
Al Khābūrah
SAUDI ARABIA
Ad Dir'iyah
Riyadh (Ar Riyāḑ)
Şīr Banī Yās
Abū al Abyad
Al Batinah
Al Hajar al Gharbī
Ad Dawādimī
Jabal az Zannah
Ţarīf
Attaf
MUSCAT
Haradh
Al Jāfūrah
Az Zāhirah
Ar Rustāq
Bidbid
Al Quwayīyah
Ad Dilam
As Salamiyah
W. as Sahbā
'Ibrī
J. Akhdar
Izkī
Nazwā
Ar Ruwaydah
Aş Şummān
Sabkhat Maţţī
U.A.E.
Al Humrah
Al Māriyyah
'Afīf
Tropic of Cancer
Al Ḩarīq
Al Ḩillah
Arādah
Al Liwā
OMAN
Adam
As Şanām
Al Kidan
Fahūd
Al Huwatsah
D E F G H
45 50 55 60
40 35 30 25
1 2 3 4 5

TURKMENISTAN
UZBEK.
TAJIKIST.
TAJIKISTAN
CHINA
AFGHANISTAN
PAKISTAN
BALOCHISTĀN
N.W. FRONTIER PROV.
JAMMU AND KASHMĪR
HIMĀCHAL PRADESH
PUNJAB
HARYĀNA
RĀJASTHĀN
SINDH
KHAIRPUR
BAHAWALPUR
GUJARĀT
MADHYA PRADESH
MAHĀRĀSHTRA
UTTAR PRADESH
ANDRA PRADESH
TIBET
HINDU KUSH
KARAKORAM
Ladākh Range
Zāskār Mountains
Pir Panjāl Range
Salt Ra.
Sulaiman Range
Toba and Kakar Ranges
Sinkai Hills
Koh-i-Baba
Safed Koh
Siah Koh
Hazarajat
Registan
Central Makran Ra.
Makran Coast Range
Kirthar Range
THAR DESERT
INDIAN DESERT
Arāvalli Range
Malwa Plateau
Vindhya Range
Sātpura Range
Mahadeo Hills
Rann of Kachchh
Kāthiāwār
Gir Hills
Mouths of the Indus
Gulf of Khambhat
G. of Kachchh
Sonmiani Bay
Tropic of Cancer
ARABIAN SEA
Aksai Chin
Deosai Plain
Nuristan
Tirich Mir
Nanga Parbat 8126
K2 8611
Nunkun 7135
Nanda Devi 7817
Kamat 7756
Muztag 7282
Khunjerab Pass
Karakoram Pass 5575
Khyber Pass
Indus
Chenab
Jhelum
Ravi
Sutlej
Ganga (Ganges)
Yamuna
Chambal
Narmada
Tapi
Godāvari
Kabul
Kandahar
Ghazni
Herat
Mazar-i-Sharif
Kunduz
Baghlan
Charikar
Jalalabad
Islamabad
Rawalpindi
Peshawar
Lahore
Faisalabad
Multan
Quetta
Sukkur
Hyderabad
Karachi
Srīnagar
Jammu
Amritsar
Ludhiana
Chandīgarh
Simla
Dehra Dūn
Delhi
New Delhi
Meerut
Agra
Jaipur
Ajmer
Jodhpur
Bīkāner
Udaipur
Kota
Gwalior
Jhānsi
Kānpur
Bareilly
Aligarh
Ahmadābād
Vadodara
Rājkot
Jāmnagar
Bhāvnagar
Sūrat
Indore
Ujjain
Bhopāl
Jabalpur
Nāgpur
Amrāvati
Akola
Aurangābād
Nāsik
Bombay
Pune (Poona)
Ahmadnagar
Nānded
Diu (Goa, Daman & Diu)
Damān (G.D. & D.)
Silvassa

1:7.5M
0 100 200 300 km
0 50 100 150 mls

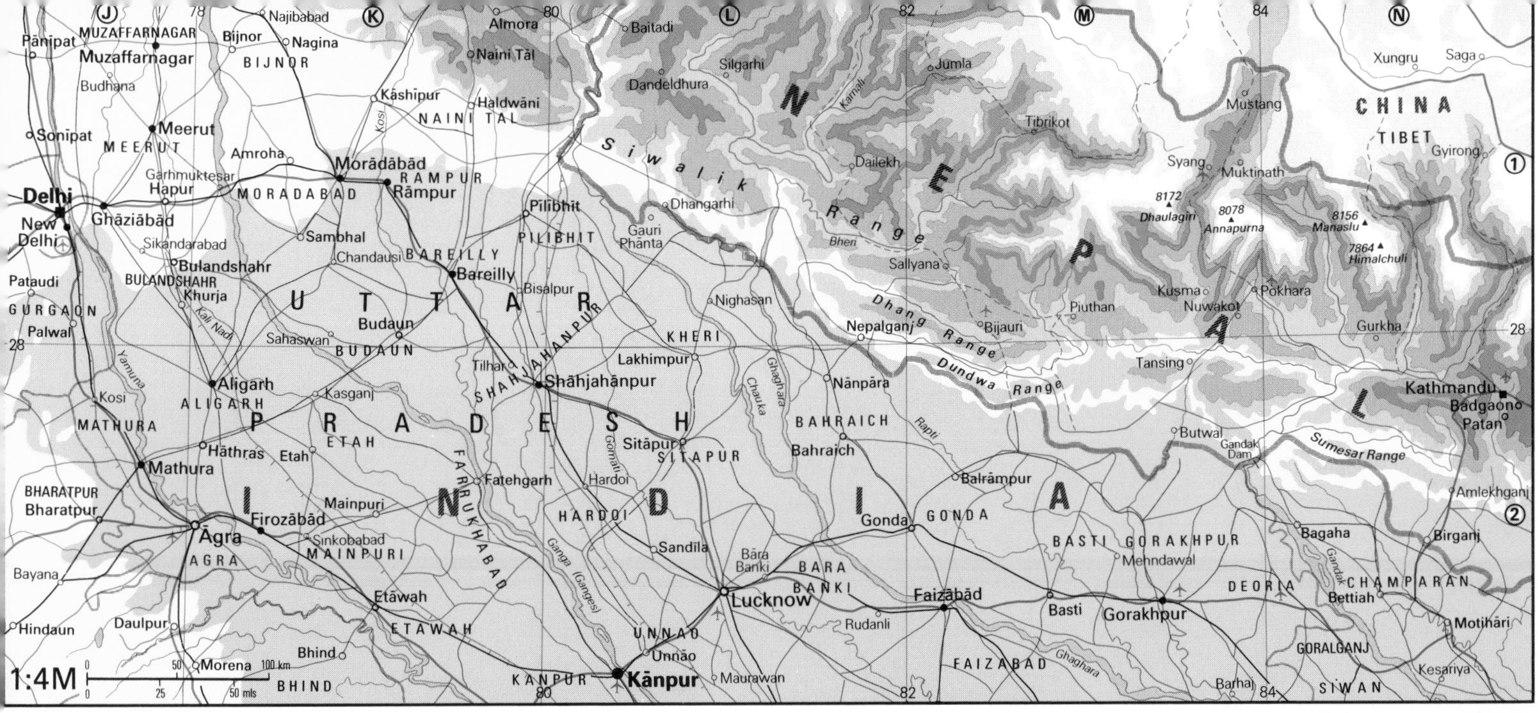
NEPAL
CHINA
TIBET
UTTAR PRADESH
INDIA
1:4M
Delhi
New Delhi
Ghāziābād
Meerut
Muzaffarnagar
Moradābād
Rāmpur
Bareilly
Pilibhit
Shāhjahānpur
Aligarh
Mathura
Āgra
Firozābād
Etāwah
Lucknow
Kānpur
Unnāo
Faizābād
Gorakhpur
Basti
Gonda
Bahraich
Sitāpur
Hardoi
Lakhimpur
Nānpāra
Balrāmpur
Bettiah
Motihāri
Birganj
Kathmandu
Badgaon
Patan
Pokhara
Nepalganj
Dhangarhi
Siwalik Range
Dhang Range
Dundwa Range
Sumesar Range
Dhaulagiri
Annapurna
Manaslu
Himalchuli
Almora
Naini Tāl
Haldwāni
Kāshipur
Bijnor
Najibabad
Nagina
Jumla
Mustang
Muktinath
Tansing
Butwal
Saga
Xungru
Gyirong
Mainpuri
Bharatpur
Hindaun
Daulpur
Morena
Bhind
Bulandshahr
Khurja
Budaun
Sambhal
Chandausi
Amroha
Hāpur
Sonipat
Pānipat
Pataudi
Palwal
Kosi
Hāthras
Etah
Fatehgarh
Sandīla
Bāra Banki
Bahraich
Rudanli
Maurawan
Barhaj
Kesariya
Bagaha
Gandak Dam
Amlekhganj

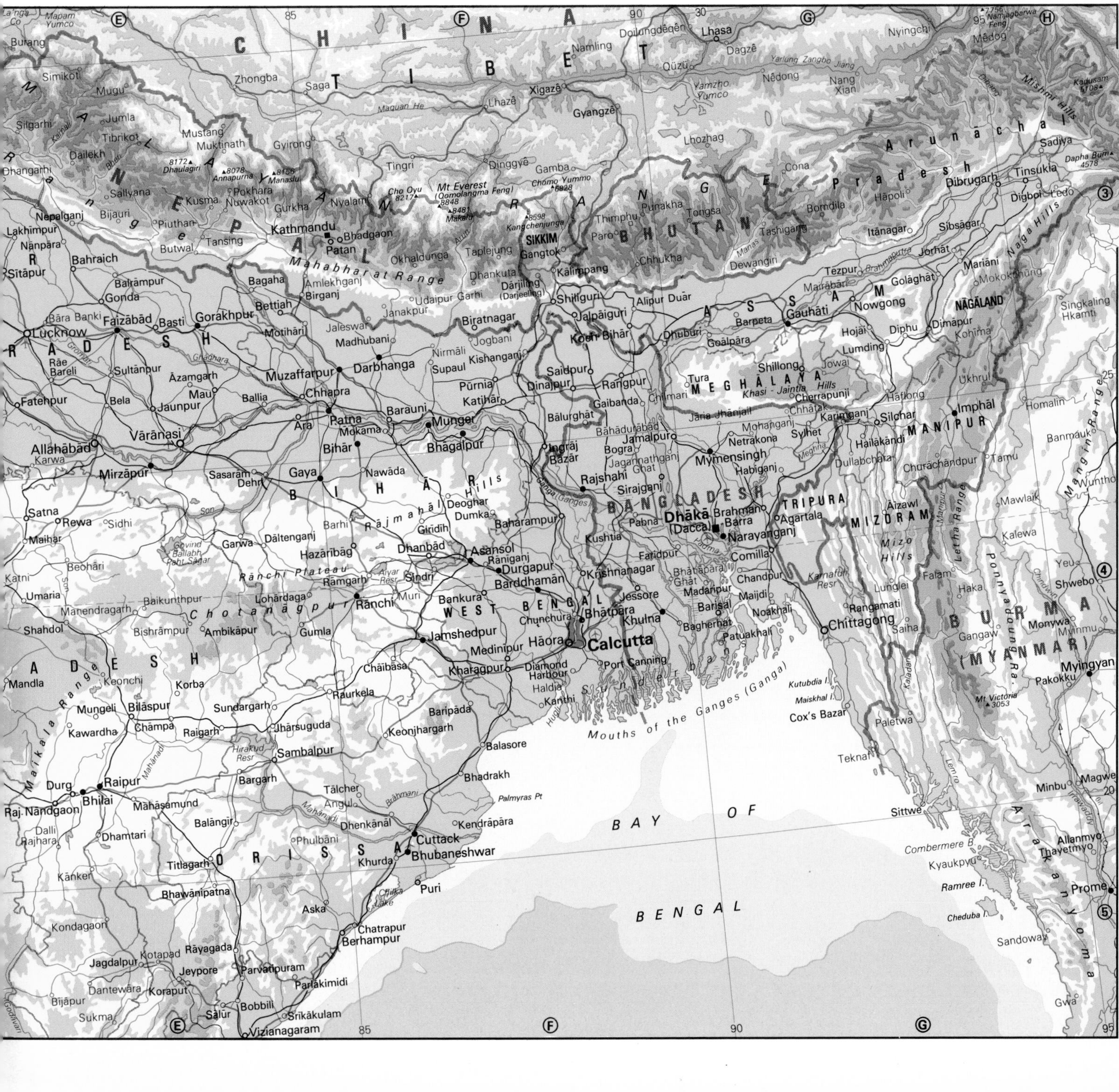
CHINA
TIBET
NEPAL
BHUTAN
SIKKIM
BANGLADESH
BURMA (MYANMAR)
ASSAM
MEGHĀLAYA
NĀGĀLAND
MANIPUR
TRIPURA
MIZORAM
Arunāchal Pradesh
WEST BENGAL
BIHĀR
ORISSA
BAY OF BENGAL
Mouths of the Ganges (Ganga)
Lhasa
Xigazê
Gyangzê
Mt Everest (Qomolangma Feng) 8848
Kanchenjunga 8598
Makalu 8481
Cho Oyu 8217
Kathmandu
Patan
Bhadgaon
Gangtok
Dārjiling (Darjeeling)
Thimphu
Punakha
Paro
Lucknow
Allahābād
Vārānasi
Patna
Gaya
Muzaffarpur
Darbhanga
Bhāgalpur
Munger
Rānchi
Jamshedpur
Asansol
Durgapur
Barddhamān
Calcutta
Hāora
Kharagpur
Cuttack
Bhubaneshwar
Puri
Berhampur
Sambalpur
Raipur
Bhilai
Durg
Bilāspur
Dhākā (Dacca)
Narayanganj
Chittagong
Khulna
Rajshahi
Mymensingh
Sylhet
Comilla
Gauhāti
Shillong
Imphāl
Kohima
Dibrugarh
Tinsukia
Sadiya
Aizawl
Agartala
Sittwe
Prome
Myingyan
Cox's Bazar
Mahābhārat Range
Rājmahāl Hills
Rānchi Plateau
Chotanāgpur
Khasi - Jaintia Hills
Naga Hills
Mishmi Hills
Patkai Range
Arakan Yoma
Mizo Hills
Ganga (Ganges)
Brahmaputra
Yarlung Zangbo Jiang
Satna
Rewa
Mirzāpur
Kodagaon
Jagdalpur
Vizianagaram
Srīkākulam
Balasore
Kendrāpāra
Palmyras Pt
Sundarbans
Ramree I.
Cheduba I.
Combermere B.
Kyaukpyu
Sandoway
Gwa
Minbu
Magwe
Allanmyo
Thayetmyo

GUJARĀT
Ahmadābād
Vadodara
Bhāvnagar
Sūrat
Gulf of Khambhat
Bombay
Thāne
Pune (Poona)
Nāsik
MADHYA PRADESH
Indore
Bhopāl
Ujjain
Jabalpur
Tropic of Cancer
Vindhya Range
Sātpura Range
Mahadeo Hills
Maikala Range
Chotanāgpur
Rānchi
Jamshedpur
Nāgpur
Raipur
Bhilai
Durg
Bilāspur
Sambalpur
Amrāvati
Akola
Jalgaon
Dhule
Malegaon
Aurangābād
MAHĀRĀSHTRA
Ahmadnagar
Nānded
Chandrapur
ORISSA
Cuttack
Bhubaneshwar
Puri
Chilka Lake
Berhampur
Eastern Ghats
Western Ghats
Solāpur
Gulbarga
Bījāpur
Kolhāpur
Sāngli
Hyderābād
ANDHRA PRADESH
Warangal
Nizāmābād
Vishākhapatnam
Vizianagaram
Rājahmundry
Kākināda
Vijayawada
Guntūr
Machilīpatnam
Nellore
Kurnool
Nallamala Range
BAY OF BENGAL
Belgaum
Hubli
KARNĀTAKA
Goa, Daman & Diu
Panaji
Bellary
Dāvangere
Shimoga
Mangalore
Bangalore
Mysore
Madras
Kānchipuram
Vellore
Pondicherry
Cuddalore
Coromandel Coast
ARABIAN SEA
Lakshadweep
(Laccadive Islands)
(India)
Kozhikode
Cannanore
Malabar Coast
KERALA
Coimbatore
Tiruppur
Salem
TAMIL NĀDU
Tiruchchirāppalli
Thanjāvūr
Madurai
Kochi
Alleppey
Kollam
Thiruvananthapuram
Nāgercoil
Kanniyākumari
C.Comorin
Tirunelveli
Tuticorin
Palk Strait
Gulf of Mannār
Adam's Bridge
Jaffna
SRI LANKA
CEYLON
Trincomalee
Anurādhapura
Kandy
Colombo
Dehiwala-Mt Lavinia
Moratuwa
Galle
Matara
Batticaloa
Nine Degree Channel
Eight Degree Channel
Minicoy
MALDIVES
Preparis I.
Preparis South Channel
Gt Coco I.
(Burma)
Coco Channel
North Andaman
Middle Andaman
South Andaman
ANDAMAN ISLANDS
(India)
Port Blair
Duncan Passage
Little Andaman
Ten Degree Channel
Car Nicobar
NICOBAR ISLANDS
(India)
Sombrero Channel
Little Nicobar
Great Nicobar
at the same scale

1:7 M

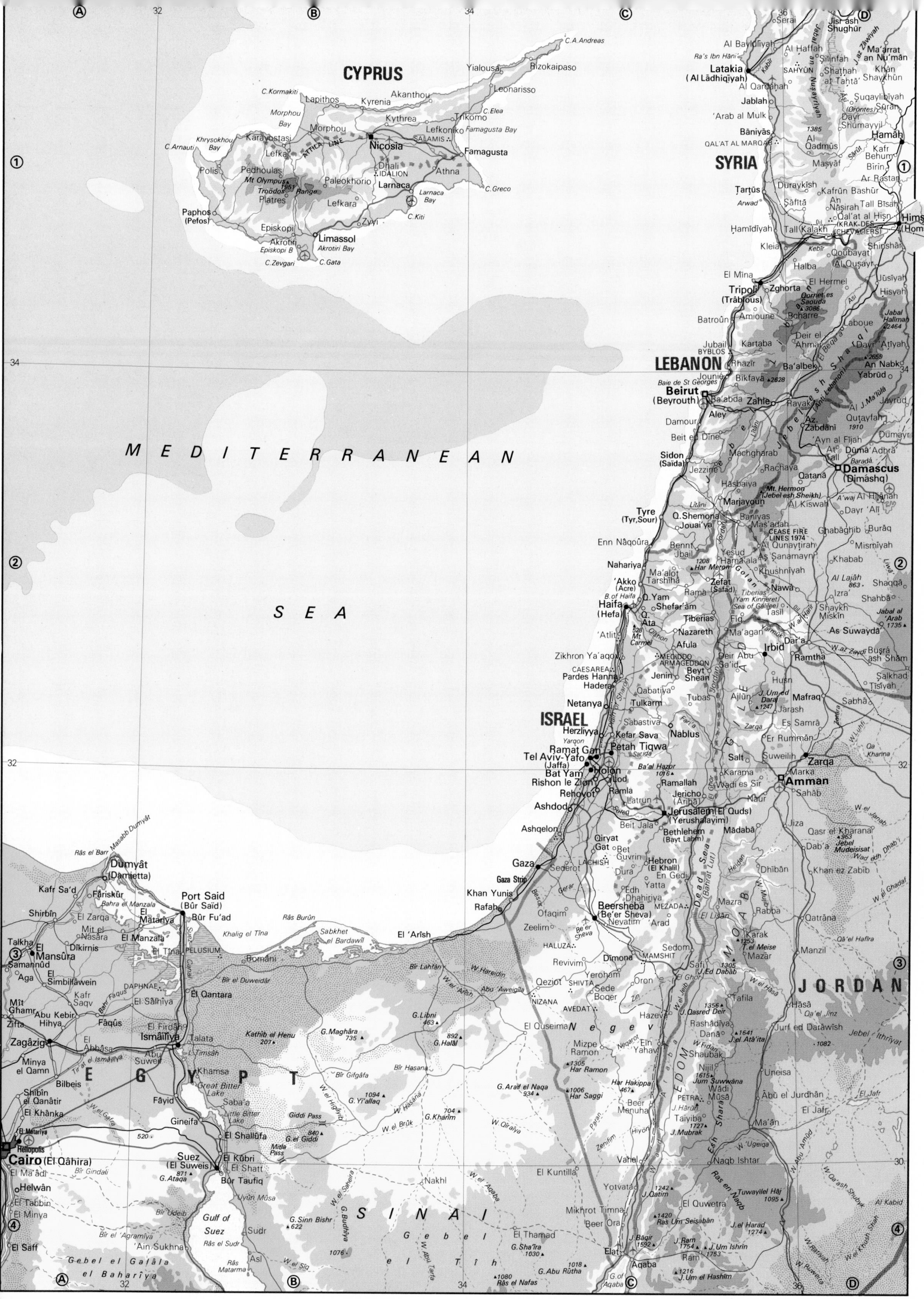
CYPRUS
C.A. Andreas
Yialousa
Rizokaipaso
C. Kormakiti
Lapithos
Kyrenia
Akanthou
Leonarisso
Morphou Bay
Kythrea
C. Elea
Trikomo
Morphou
Lefkoniko
Famagusta Bay
Khrysokhou Bay
Karavostasi
ATTILA LINE
Nicosia
SALAMIS
C. Arnauti
Lefka
Famagusta
Polis
Pedhoulas
Dhali
IDALION
Athna
Mt Olympus 1951
Troodos Range
Paleokhorio
Larnaca
C. Greco
Platres
Lefkara
Larnaca Bay
Paphos (Pefos)
Zyyi
C. Kiti
Episkopi
Limassol
Akrotiri
Episkopi B
Akrotiri Bay
C. Zevgari
C. Gata
M E D I T E R R A N E A N
S E A
SYRIA
Serai
Jisr ash Shughur
Al Bayḑiyah
Al Haffah
Ma'arrat an Nu'man
Ras Ibn Hani
Latakia (Al Lādhiqīyah)
Slinfah
SAHYŪN
Shaṭhah
Khān Shaykhūn
Al Qardaḩah
Jablah
Suqaylibīyah
'Arab al Mulk
Bāniyās
QAL'AT AL MARQAB
Hamāh
Al Qadmūs
Kafr Behum
Maşyāf
Birin
Ar Rastan
Ţarţūs
Durayklsh
Arwad
Şāfītā
Kafrūn Bashūr
Tall Bīsah
Ḩamīdīyah
Tall Kalakh
KRAK DES CHEVALIERS
Hims (Homs)
Kleiat
Qoubayat
Shinshār
Al Quşayr
Halba
El Mina
Tripoli (Trâblous)
Zghorta
El Hermel
Qornet es Saouda 3086
Bcharre
Batroûn
Amioune
Jabal Halimah 2464
Laboue
Jubail
BYBLOS
Kartaba
Deir el Ahmar
LEBANON
Rhazir
Ba'albek
An Nabk
Jouniė
Bikfaya 2628
Yabrūd
Baie de St Georges
Beirut (Beyrouth)
Ba'abda
Zahle
Rayak
Aley
Az Zabdani 1910
Damour
Beit ed Dine
Sidon (Saïda)
Jezzine
Rachaya
Qatana
Damascus (Dimashq)
Hasbaiya
Mt. Hermon (Jebel esh Sheikh)
Marjayoun
Litani
Tyre (Tyr, Sour)
Q. Shemona
Baniyas
Jouai'ya
CEASE FIRE LINES 1974
Enn Nâqoura
Nahariya
Yesud Hama'ala
As Sanamayn
1208 Har Meron
'Akko (Acre)
Zefat (Safad)
Nawa
B. of Haifa
Haifa (Hefa)
Q. Yam
Shefar'am
Tiberias (Yam Kinneret) (Sea of Galilee)
Q. Ata
Nazareth
Ma'agan
'Atlit
528 Mt Carmel
Afula
Irbid
Dar'a
Zikhron Ya'aqov
MEGIDDO ARMAGEDDON
Deir Abu Sa'id
Ramtha
Buşrá ash Shām
CAESAREA
Pardes Hanna
Hadera
Jenin
Beyt Shean
Qabatiya
Mafraq
Netanya
Tulkarm
Tubas
Ajlun
ISRAEL
Herzliyya
Sabastiya
Kefar Sava
Nablus
Jarash
Ramat Gan
Petah Tiqwa
Tel Aviv-Yafo (Jaffa)
Salt
Zarqa
Bat Yam
Holon
Lod
Karama
Rishon le Zion
Ramallah
Amman
Rehovot
Ramla
Jericho (Ariha)
Ashdod
Latrun
Jerusalem (El Quds) (Yerushalayim)
Ashqelon
Beit Jala
Bethlehem (Bayt Lahm)
Mādabā
Qiryat Gat
Gaza
Gaza Strip
LACHISH
Hebron (El Khalil)
En Gedi
Dead Sea (Bahrat Lut)
Dhībān
Khan Yunis
Rafah
Beersheba (Be'er Sheva)
Nevatim
Ofaqim
Arad
Zeelim
MEZADA
Karak
Sedom
HALUZA
Dimona
MAMSHIT
Revivim
J. Ed Dabab
Qeziot
SHIVTA
Yeroham
Oron
NIZANA
AVEDAT
Sede Boqer
JORDAN
Tafila
Hasa
El Quseima
N e g e v
Hazeva
Rashadiya
Mizpe Ramon
1305 Har Ramon
EDOM
Shaubak
Jurf ed Darawīsh
1006 Har Saggi
Har Hakippa
Jum Suwwāna
Wādī Mūsā
PETRA
Beer Menuha
Ābū el Jurdhān
Taiyiba
J. Mubrak
Ma'ān
Naqb Ishtar
Vahel
El Kuntilla
Yotvata
J. Qatim
El Quweira
Ras en Naqb
Tuwayilel Hāj 1095
Mikhrot Timna
Beer Ora
Ras Um Seisaban
J. el Harad 1274
Elat
Aqaba
J. Um Ishrin
Rum
J. Um el Hashim
G. of Aqaba
Râs el Barr
Dumyât (Damietta)
Kafr Sa'd
Fâriskûr
Bahra el Manzala
Port Said (Bûr Saîd)
Bûr Fu'ad
Shirbîn
El Zarqa
El Matarîya
Râs Burûn
Khalig el Tîna
Sabkhet el Bardawîl
El 'Arîsh
Talkha
El Mansûra
Dikirnis
El Manzala
El Tîna
PELUSIUM
Samannûd
Români
Aga
El Simbillâwein
Bîr el Duweidâr
DAPHNAE
El Qantara
Mît Ghamr
Abu Kebîr
El Sâlhîya
Zifta
Hihya
Fâqûs
El Firdân
Zagâzig
Ismâilîya
Talata
Minya el Qamn
Abu Suweir
Khamsa
E G Y P T
Bilbeis
Great Bitter Lake
Shibîn el Qanâtir
Fâyid
El Khânka
Little Bitter Lake
Gineifa
El Shallûfa
El Matarîya
Heliopolis
Cairo (El Qâhira)
Suez (El Suweis)
El Kûbri
El Shatt
Bûr Taufiq
Helwân
El Tabbîn
Gulf of Suez
Nakhl
S I N A I
G e b e l   e l   T î h
El Saff
'Ain Sukhna
Râs el Sudr
Sudr
Asl
Gebel el Galâla el Baharîya
El Thamad
G. Sha'îra 1030
G. Abu Rûtha
Râs el Nafas
Bîr Lahfân
G. Libni 463
G. Maghâra 735
Kathîb el Henu 207
G. Halâl 892
Bîr Hasana
Bîr Gifgâfa
G. Yi'allaq 1094
Giddi Pass
G. Kharîm 704
Mitla Pass
G. el Giddi 840
G. Sinn Bishr 622
1 2 3 4
A B C D
32 34 36 30

1:2.5M 0 25 50 75 100 km 0 25 50 mls

NATIONS OF AFRICA

NORTH ATLANTIC OCEAN
Azores (Port.)
Madeira (Port.)
Canary Is. (Sp.)
NORWAY
SWEDEN
FINLAND
UNITED KINGDOM
IRELAND
Dublin
Edinburgh
London
North Sea
DENMARK
Copenhagen
Oslo
Stockholm
Göteborg
Helsinki
Tallinn
St Petersburg (Leningrad)
EST.
LAT.
Riga
LITH.
Vilnius
Baltic Sea
Nizhniy Novgorod
RUSSIAN FEDERATION
Samara
Magnitogorsk
KAZAKHSTAN
Lake Balkhash
Moscow
Minsk
BELARUS (BELORUSSIA)
RUS. FED.
Gdansk
Hamburg
NETH.
The Hague
Brussels
BELG.
LUX.
Bonn
GERMANY
Berlin
Warsaw
POLAND
Prague
CZECH REP.
Cracow
SLOVAKIA
Bratislava
Vienna
AUSTRIA
Munich
Budapest
HUNGARY
Kiev
UKRAINE
Dnieper
Khar'kov
Volgograd
Volga
Ural
Syr Darya
Aral Sea
UZBEKISTAN
Tashkent
KIR.
TAJ.
Amu Darya
Rostov
Don
MOLD.
Odessa
Paris
Seine
FRANCE
Bay of Biscay
Berne
SWITZ.
Milan
SL.
CR.
B.-H.
Belgrade
YUG.
Sarajevo
ROMANIA
Bucharest
Danube
Black Sea
Sofia
BULGARIA
Skopje
MAC.
ALB.
Tiranë
Istanbul
Ankara
TURKEY
GEO.
Tbilisi
AZER.
Baku
ARM.
Caspian Sea
TURKMENISTAN
Ashkhabad
Mashhad
Tabriz
Tehran
AFGHANISTAN
IRAN
PAK.
Bordeaux
Rhône
Marseilles
Corsica
Oporto
PORTUGAL
Lisbon
Madrid
SPAIN
Tajo
Ebro
Barcelona
Sardinia
Balearic Is.
Rome
ITALY
Adriatic Sea
Naples
Sicily
GREECE
Athens
Crete
Mediterranean Sea
CYPRUS
Nicosia
SYRIA
LEB.
Beirut
Damascus
IRAQ
Baghdad
Tigris
Euphrates
Shiraz
Jerusalem
Amman
ISR.
JORDAN
Basra
KUWAIT
Kuwait
Persian Gulf
BAHRAIN
Doha
QATAR
Abu Dhabi
UNITED ARAB EMIRATES
Muscat
OMAN
Kuria Muria Is
Tangiers
Rabat
Fes
Oran
Algiers
Skikda
Annaba
Tunis
Constantine
TUNISIA
Sfax
Safi
Casablanca
Marrakesh
Oujda
Agadir
MOROCCO
Tarfaya
La'youn
Béchar
Touggourt
Ouargla
Tripoli
Misratah
Benghazi
Tobruk
Alexandria
Port Said
Suez
Cairo
El Faiyûm
El Minya
Asyût
Nile
Tindouf
Timimoun
ALGERIA
Ghudamis
Reggane
In Salah
LIBYA
Sabhā
Ghāt
EGYPT
Aswân
L. Nasser
Tabuk
SAUDI ARABIA
Medina
Riyadh
Mecca (Makkah)
Jiddah
Red Sea
Western Sahara
Bir Moghrein
Zouerate
F'dérik
Tropic of Cancer
Nouadhibou
Atar
MAURITANIA
Nouakchott
SAHARA
Tamanrasset
Wadi Halfa
Port Sudan
St-Louis
Sénégal
Dakar
Tombouctou
MALI
Niger
NIGER
Agadez
Atbara
Kassala
ERITREA
Asmara
Omdurman
Khartoum
Wad Medani
Blue Nile
El Obeid
San'a
YEMEN
Ta'izz
Aden
Gulf of Aden
Socotra (Yemen)
SENEGAL
THE GAMBIA
Banjul
Kayes
Tambacounda
GUINEA BISSAU
Bissau
Bamako
Niamey
Zinder
L. Chad
CHAD
DJIBOUTI
Djibouti
GUINEA
Mamou
Kankan
BURKINA
Ouagadougou
Bobo Dioulasso
Kano
Maiduguri
Ndjamena
Hargeysa
Dire Dawa
Conakry
SIERRA LEONE
Freetown
Bo
IVORY COAST
Tamale
BENIN
Kaduna
Jos
NIGERIA
SUDAN
White Nile
Ādīs Ābeba
ETHIOPIA
Monrovia
LIBERIA
Buchanan
Bouaké
Yamoussoukro
GHANA
Volta
TOGO
Ilorin
Abuja
Ogbomosho
Ibadan
Porto Novo
Lomé
Lagos
Enugu
Onitsha
Port Harcourt
Aba
Ngaoundéré
CENTRAL AFRICAN REPUBLIC
Bambari
Wau
Juba
Jimma
SOMALIA
Abidjan
Kumasi
Accra
CAMEROON
Douala
Garoua Boulai
Bangui
Bangassou
L. Turkana
Mogadishu (Muqdisho)
Marka
Gulf of Guinea
Bioco
Malabo
Yaoundé
EQUAT. GUINEA
Bata
Principe
SÃO TOMÉ & PRINCIPE
São Tomé
Libreville
Zaire (Congo)
Gulu
L. Albert
UGANDA
Kampala
KENYA
Equator
Kisangani
Entebbe
Annobon (Eq.G)
GABON
Lambaréné
CONGO
Mbandaka
L. Edward
Goma
Lake Victoria
Nairobi
Kismaayo
RWANDA
Kigali
Kindu
ZAIRE
Bujumbura
BURUNDI
Mwanza
Arusha
Mombasa
INDIAN OCEAN
Seychelles Arch.
Amirante Is.
SEYCHELLES
Brazzaville
Pointe Noire
Kinshasa
Bandundu
Kikwit
Ilebo
Kananga
Mbuji-Mayi
Kigoma
Lake Tanganyika
Kalémié
Dodoma
Zanzibar
Dar es Salaam
TANZANIA
Cabinda (Ang.)
Matadi
Kwango
Kasai
Lualaba
Ascension (U.K.)
SOUTH ATLANTIC OCEAN
Luanda
Malanje
Kamina
L. Mweru
Mbala
Mbeya
Aldabra Is
Farquhar Is
Kolwezi
Likasi
L. Bangweulu
Ruvuma
Lobito
Kuito
Huambo
ANGOLA
Lubumbashi
Ndola
ZAMBIA
MALAWI
Lake Nyasa
Lichinga
COMOROS
Pemba
Mayotte (Fr.)
Antseranana
Tromelin (Fr.)
Namibe
Lubango
Cubango
Lusaka
Lilongwe
Blantyre
Zomba
Nampula
Moçambique
Mozambique Channel
Mahajanga
St Helena (U.K.)
Kunene
Zambezi
Livingstone
L. Kariba
Harare
MOZAMBIQUE
Quelimane
Tsumeb
Hwange
ZIMBABWE
Mutare
Gweru
Sofala (Beira)
Antananarivo
Toamasina
MADAGASCAR
Otjiwarongo
Francistown
Bulawayo
BOTSWANA
Serowe
Walvis Bay
Windhoek
NAMIBIA
Limpopo
MAURITIUS
Réunion (Fr.)
Fianarantsoa
Toliara
Inhambane
Tropic of Capricorn
Gaborone
Pietersburg
Pretoria
Xai Xai
Maputo
Mbabane
SWAZILAND
Lüderitz
Keetmanshoop
Johannesburg
Grunau
SOUTH AFRICA
Welkom
Kimberley
Bloemfontein
Maseru
LESOTHO
Pietermaritzburg
Durban
Orange
Bitterfontein
Worcester
Paarl
Cape Town
Port Elizabeth
East London
Mossel Bay
Tristan da Cunha (U.K.)
0 400 800 1200 1600 km

ZIMBABWE
MOZAMBIQUE
BOTSWANA
NAMIBIA
SOUTH AFRICA
LESOTHO
SWAZILAND
ATLANTIC
OCEAN
INDIAN
OCEAN
Kalahari
Desert
Makgadikgadi
Central Kalahari Game Reserve
Gemsbok National Park
Kalahari Gemsbok Nat. Park
Kruger National Park
Tropic of Capricorn
NORTHERN TRANSVAAL
EASTERN TRANSVAAL
GAUTENG
NORTH WEST
ORANGE FREE STATE
KWAZULU NATAL
NORTHERN CAPE
WESTERN CAPE
EASTERN CAPE
Ciskei
Windhoek
Walvis Bay
Swakopmund
Lüderitz
Keetmanshoop
Gaborone
Francistown
Pretoria
Johannesburg
Soweto
Maputo
Mbabane
Maseru
Bloemfontein
Kimberley
Durban
Pietermaritzburg
East London
Port Elizabeth
Cape Town
Orange
Limpopo
Vaal
Great Karoo
Little Karoo
Drakensberg
C. Agulhas
Cape of Good Hope
1:7.5M
0 100 200 300 km
0 50 100 150 mls

Azores
(Açores)
(Portugal)
Flores
São Jorge
Angra Do Heroismo
Terceira
Faial
Pico
São Miguel
Ponta Delgada
Formigas
Santa Maria
at the same scale
Madeira
(Portugal)
Porto Santo
Funchal
Deserta Grande
Canary Islands
(Islas Canarias)
(Spain)
Ilhas Selvagens
(Port.)
Santa Cruz De La Palma
La Palma
Santa Cruz De Tenerife
Tenerife
Gomera
Hierro
Gran Canaria
Las Palmas De Gran Canaria
Lanzarote
Arrecife
Pto Del Rosario
Fuerteventura
C. Yubi
PORTUGAL
SPAIN
Beja
Badajoz
Sierra Morena
Ciudad Real
Albacete
Murcia
Alicante
Ibiza
BALEARIC ISLANDS
(Islas Baleares)
Sardinia
(Sardegna)
Cagliari
Faro
Huelva
C.de S. Vincente
Córdoba
Seville
(Sevilla)
Linares
Granada
Cartagena
Cádiz
Málaga
Almería
Str. of Gibraltar
Gibraltar (U.K.)
Tangier
(Tanger)
Ceuta (Sp.)
Tetouan
Larache
Ksar-El-Kebir
Melilla (SP.)
Al Hoceima
Kenitra
Rabat
Casablanca
(Dar-el-Beida)
El Jadida
Settat
Oued Zem
Ouezzane
Sidi Kacem
Meknès
Fès
Azrou
Khenifra
Taza
Taourirt
Oujda
Safi
Essaouira
Marrakech
Beni Mellal
Midelt
Missour
Haut Atlas
Moyen Atlas
Toubkal 4165
Ouarzazate
Taroudannt
Agadir
Anti Atlas
Jbel Sarhro
Zagora
Er Rachidia
Figuig
Bouârfa
Béchar
Abadla
Beni Abbès
Tiznit
Tata
Bou Izakarn
Tan-Tan
Tarfaya
Laâyoune
Hamada du Dra
Jbel Ouarkziz
Tinfouchy
Tindouf
MOROCCO
Algiers
(Alger)
Tizi Ouzou
Bejaïa
(Bougie)
Skikda
(Philippeville)
Annaba
(Bône)
Bizerte
Tunis
Cherchell
Blida
Ech Cheliff
Mostaganem
Oran
Mascara
Ighil-Izane
Sidi-bel-Abbès
Saïda
Tlemcen
Tiaret
Ksar El Boukhari
M'sila
Sétif
Constantine
Batna
Souk Ahras
Tébessa
Kairouan
Sousse
Mahdia
Sfax
Bou Saâda
Djelfa
Aflou
Chott ech Chergui
Hauts Plateaux
Mts des Ouled Nail
Biskra
Kasserine
Gafsa
Gabès
Tozeur
Kebili
Medenine
Zarzis
Tataouine
Dehibat
Nalut
Chott Melrhir
El Oued
Touggourt
Laghouat
Berriane
Ghardaïa
Ouargla
Atlas Saharien
Mecheria
Ain Sefra
Ksour
Ft Lallemand
El Golea
El Gassi
Grand Erg Oriental
Ghadamis
Daraj
Grand Erg Occidental
Tabelbala
Kerzaz
Timimoun
Hassi Inifel
Plateau du Tademait
Adrar
In Belbel
Reggane
Aoulef
In Salah
Plaine du Tidikelt
Bordj Omar Driss
Ohanet
In Amenas
Hamada de Tinrhert
Hammadah
Idehan
ALGERIA
TUNISIA
MEDITERRANEAN
Hamada Tounassine
Hassi Mdakane
Bj Flye Ste Marie
Erg Iguidi
Erg Mcherrah
El Eglab
Chenachèn
Chegga
Aioun Abd el Malek
El Mzereb
Saguia el Hamra
Smara
El Farsia
C. Bojador
Western Sahara
Guelta Zemmur
Bir Moghrein
Dakhla
B. de Rio de Oro
Tiris
Ausert
Aguenit
Adrar Soutouf
Tichla
Zouerate
Fdérik
Tourine
Karet
El Mreiti
Bir Zreigat
El Hank
Erg Chech
Asedjirad
Ouallen
Tanezrouft
Tropic of Cancer
Bidon 5
(Ruins)
Arak
Mts du Mouydir
Tassili N'Ajjer
Illizi
Tarat
Sardalas
Ghat
Adrar
Zaouatallaz
Djanet
In Ecker
Idelès
Hoggar
(Ahaggar)
Tahat 2918
Tamanrasset
In Ebeggi
Abalessa
Silet
In Afaleleh
In Ezzane
Nouadhibou
Ras Nouadhibou
Azeffal
Akchar
Adrar
Ouarane
Ouadâne
Chinguetti
Atar
Troudenni
El Harricha
In Dagouber
El Guettara
Oguilet Khenachich
El Khenachich
Taguenout Hagguerete
Djouf
MAURITANIA
I. Tidra
C. Mirik
Akjoult
Nouakchott
Trarza
Tidjikja
Tichitt
Tagant
Aouker
Tamchaket
Boutilimit
Brakna
Aleg
Kiffa
Kaédi
Rosso
Aioun El Atrouss
Hodh
Affolé
Akle Aouana
Dhar Oualata
Néma
El Mreyé
Araouane
Azaouad
Guir
Foum el Alba
Timetrine Monts
Ardar des Iforas
Tessalit
Aguelhok
Kidal
Anéfis
Tin Zaouaten
Tassili du Hoggar
In Guezzam
Ténéré du Tafassasset
Mt Gréboun 1944
Aïr
Iférouane
Timia
Talak
Fachi
Agadez
Erg du Ténéré
Ingal
NIGER
Zegueren
Vallée de l'Azaouak
Ménaka
Tillia
Tchin Tabaradene
Aderbissinat
Tasker
L. Faguibine
Tombouctou
Goundam
Gourma Rharous
Bourem
Gao
Ansongo
MALI
Niafounké
Timbédra
St-Louis
Dagana
Louga
Matam
Linguère
Mbout
C. Vert
(C. Verde)
Thiès
Dakar
Rufisque
Diourbel
Kébémer
Touba
Joal
Kaolack
Kaffrine
SENEGAL
Bakel
Kidira
Kayes
Tambacounda
THE GAMBIA
Banjul
Georgetown
Dioulouloù
Bignona
Ziguinchor
Sédhiou
Kolda
Vélingara
Kédougou
Bafoulabé
Kéniéba
Nioro du Sahel
Diéma
Nara
Nampala
Goumbou
Sokolo
Massina
Mopti
Bandiagara
Douentza
Ke Macina
Djenné
Kolokani
Banamba
Ségou
Kita
Bamako
Koulikoro
San
Tougan
Nouna
Dédougou
Koudougou
Ouahigouya
Djibo
Aribinda
Dori
Téra
Tillabéri
Bani Bangou
Abala
Tahoua
Illéla
Keita
Dakoro
Madaoua
Tanout
Birnin N'Konni
Mayahi
Zinder
Gouré
Goudoumaria
Tessaoua
Niamey
Ouallam
Say
Dogondoutchi
Maradi
Daura
Matameye
Katsina
Kaura Namoda
Gumel
Hadejia
Kano
Gaya
Gusau
Funtua
Zaria
Azare
Potiskum
Kaduna
Bauchi
Jos
Gombe
Dosso
Sokoto
Birnin-Kebbi
BURKINA
Ouagadougou
Kaya
Kantchari
Koupéla
Fada N'Gourma
Tenkodogo
Bogandé
Pama
Malanville
Kandi
Bissau
Bafatá
Gabú
Bolama
GUINEA-BISSAU
Arquipélago dos Bijagós
Catió
Boké
Gaoual
Labé
Tougué
Dinguiraye
Siguiri
Kangaba
Bougouni
Sikasso
Bobo Dioulasso
Boromo
Po
Bolgatanga
Bawku
GUINEA
Dalaba
Dabola
Kouroussa
Kankan
Mamou
Fria
Kindia
Boffa
C. Verga
Conakry
Forécariah
Kambia
Faranah
Kabala
Loma Mts
Kissidougou
SIERRA LEONE
C. Sierra Leone
Port Loko
Makeni
Freetown
Moyamba
Mano
Bo
Kenema
Sherbro
Bonthe
Manikan
Tingrela
Korhogo
Ferkessédougou
Odienné
Boundiali
Diébougou
Gaoua
Batié
Tumu
Wa
Gambaga
Yendi
Tamale
Bole
Bouna
Kanté
Bassar
Sokodé
Kouandé
Djougou
Natitingou
Parakou
Bassila
Savalou
Nikki
Bembéréké
Kainji Resr
Kontagora
Zungeru
Bida
Minna
Abuja
NIGERIA
Kafanchan
Wamba
Lafia
Shendam
Keffi
Nasarawa
Jebba
Yashikera
Lafiagi
Shaki
Ilorin
Ogbomosho
Oshogbo
Iwo
Ife
Ibadan
Abeokuta
Ondo
Owo
Okene
Okoja
Makurdi
Lagos
Ijebu Ode
Benin City
Sapele
Warri
Enugu
Onitsha
Abakaliki
Owerri
Aba
Port Harcourt
Calabar
Bonny
Forcados
Mouths of the R. Niger
Kumba
Mt Cameroun 4095
Buéa
Douala
Limbe
Edéa
Yaoundé
CAMEROON
Bamenda
Mamfé
Foumban
Bafoussam
Nkongsamba
Jalingo
Shebshi Mts 2042
Yola
Gashaka
Wukari
Takum
Gotel Mts
Ogoja
Ikom
Afikpo
Beyla
Macenta
Voinjama
Nzérékoré
Zotzor
Mankono
Séguéla
Katiola
Bouaké
Dabakala
Touba
Niakaramandougou
IVORY COAST
(CÔTE D'IVOIRE)
Man
Danané
Duékoué
Daloa
Yamoussoukro
Dimbokro
Bondoukou
Agnibilékrou
Abengourou
Adzopé
Agboville
Abidjan
Grand Bassam
Dabou
Lakota
Sassandra
San Pédro
Tabou
Harper
C. Palmas
Bomi Hills
Gbarnga
Sanniquellie
Robertsport
LIBERIA
Monrovia
Buchanan
River Cess
Greenville
Chiehn
Mt Niete
Guiglo
Soubré
Gagnoa
GHANA
Wenchi
Berekum
Sunyani
Kumasi
Mampong
Bibiani
Obuasi
Dunkwa
Winneba
Cape Coast
Sekondi Takoradi
C. Three Points
Accra
Nsawam
Koforidua
Jasikan
Volta
Kpalimé
Notsé
TOGO
Atakpamé
BENIN
Abomey
Pobé
Sakété
Porto Novo
Cotonou
Ouidah
Lomé
Aného
Tsévié
Kéta
Bight of Benin
Bight of Biafra
GULF OF GUINEA
EQUATORIAL GUINEA
Bata
Ebebiyin
Mbini
Rio Benito
Evinayong
Cocobeach
S.TOME & PRINCIPE
Principe
São Tomé
Pagalu
(Equat. Guinea)
Libreville
Pte Pongara
Medouneu
Kango
Mitzic
Ndjolé
GABON
Ebolowa
Kribi
Campo
Ambam
Sangmélima
Bitam
Oyem
Mbalmayo
Eséka
Nyong
Malabo
1:15M
0 200 400 600 km
0 100 200 300 mls
40N
30W
30
20
10
0
10
25W
15N
A
B
C
1
2
3
4
Sto Antão
Sta Luzia
S Vincente
S Nicolau
Sal
Boa Vista
CAPE VERDE
S Tiago
Maio
Fogo
Brava
Praia
at the same scale

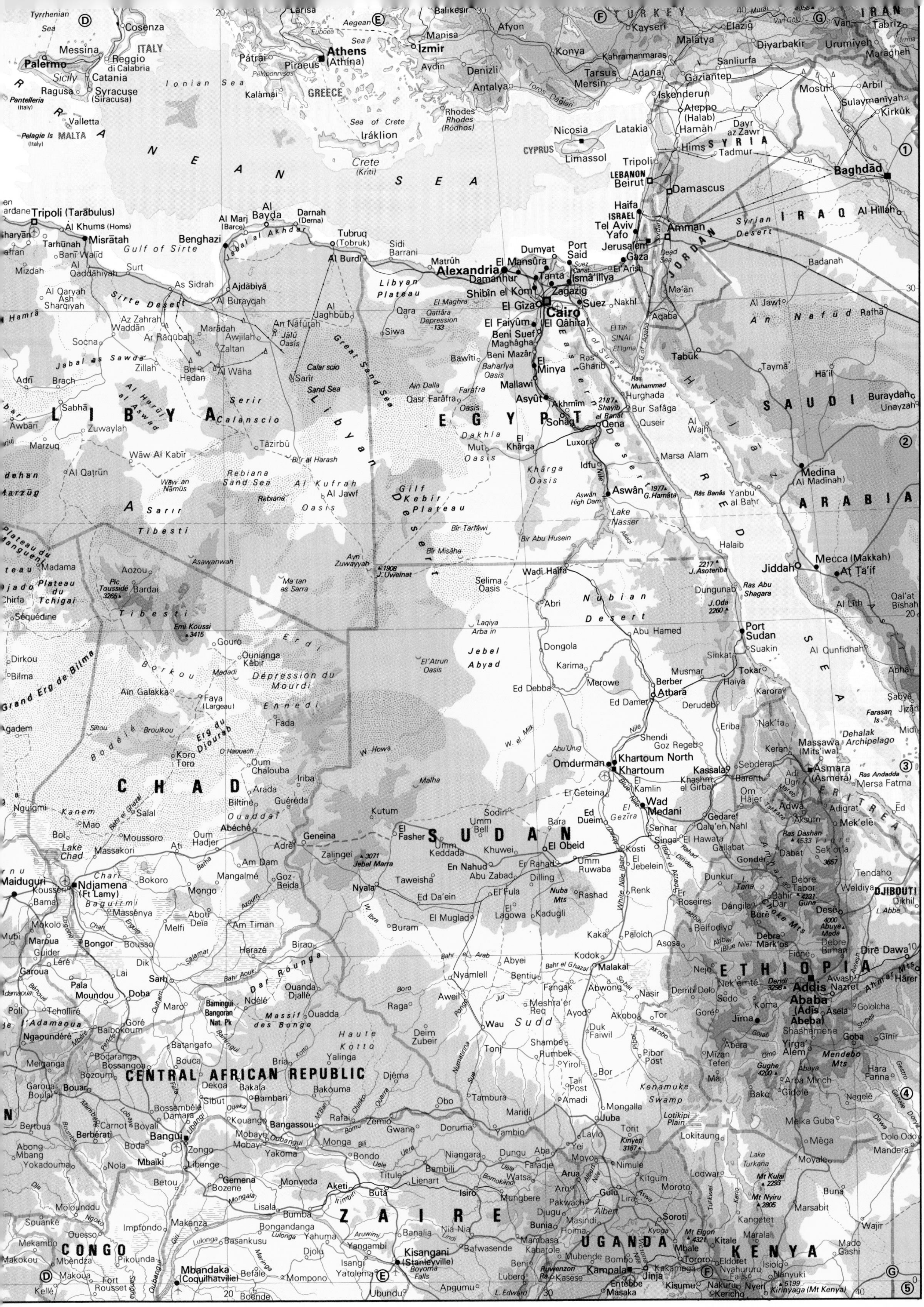

TURKEY
IRAN
Tyrrhenian Sea
Cosenza
Messina
ITALY
Palermo
Reggio di Calabria
Sicily
Catania
Ragusa
Syracuse (Siracusa)
Pantelleria (Italy)
Valletta
Pelagie Is (Italy)
MALTA
Larisa
Euboea
Aegean Sea
Balikesir
Manisa
Izmir
Aydin
Afyon
Kayseri
Elazig
Van
Tabriz
Malatya
Diyarbakir
Urumiyeh
Maragheh
Athens (Athína)
Pátrai
Piraeus
Peloponnisos
GREECE
Kalámai
Ionian Sea
Konya
Kahramanmaras
Sanliurfa
Denizli
Antalya
Tarsus
Mersin
Adana
Gaziantep
Toros Daglari
Mosul
Arbil
Sulaymaniyah
Kirkuk
Iskenderun
Aleppo (Halab)
Hamah
Dayr az Zawr
Rhodes (Ródhos)
Sea of Crete
Iráklion
Crete (Kriti)
Nicosia
CYPRUS
Limassol
Latakia
Hims
SYRIA
Tadmur
Tripoli
LEBANON
Beirut
Damascus
Baghdad
MEDITERRANEAN SEA
Tripoli (Tarabulus)
Al Khums (Homs)
Misratah
Tarhunah
Bani Walid
Mizdah
Al Qaddahiyah
Gulf of Sirte
Al Marj (Barce)
Al Bayda
Darnah (Derna)
Benghazi
Jabal al Akhdar
Tubruq (Tobruk)
Sidi Barrani
Al Burdi
Surt
As Sidrah
Ajdabiya
Al Burayqah
Sirte Desert
Al Qaryah Ash Sharqiyah
Hamra
Az Zahrah
Waddan
Ar Raqubah
Maradah
Awjilah
An Nafurah
Jalu Oasis
Al Jaghbub
Zaltan
Socna
Jabal as Sawda
Zillah
Bel Hedan
Al Waha
Calanscio Sand Sea
Great Sand Sea
Adri
Brach
Al Haruj al Aswad
Serir Calanscio
Sabha
LIBYA
Awbari
Zuwaylah
Marzuq
Tazirbu
Bi'r al Harash
Waw Al Kabir
Al Qatrun
Rebiana Sand Sea
Waw an Namus
Rebiana
Al Kufrah
Al Jawf
Oasis
Sarir Tibesti
Libyan Desert
Haifa
ISRAEL
Tel Aviv Yafo
Jerusalem
Amman
JORDAN
IRAQ
Syrian Desert
Al Hillah
Gaza
Dead Sea
El Arish
Port Said
Suez Canal
Dumyat
El Mansura
Alexandria
Damanhur
Tanta
Ismailiya
Zagazig
Shibin el Kom
Matruh
Libyan Plateau
El Maghra
Qattara Depression -133
Qara
Siwa
El Giza
Cairo (El Qahira)
Suez
Nakhl
El Tih
SINAI
El Faiyum
Beni Suef
Maghagha
Beni Mazar
El Minya
Bawiti
Bahariya Oasis
Mallawi
Asyut
Akhmim
Sohag
Qena
Luxor
Farafra Oasis
Ain Dalla
Qasr Farafra
EGYPT
Dakhla Oasis
Mut
El Kharga
Kharga Oasis
Eastern Desert
Ras Gharib
Ras Muhammad
Hurghada
2187 Shayib el Banat
Bur Safaga
Quseir
Marsa Alam
Idfu
Nile
Aswan
Aswan High Dam
1977 G. Hamata
Lake Nasser
Gilf Kebir Plateau
Bir Tarfawi
Bir Abu Husein
Bir Misaha
Ayn Zuwayyah
1908 J. Uweinat
Wadi Halfa
Selima Oasis
Halaib
2217 J. Asoteriba
Ras Abu Shagara
Dungunab
J. Oda 2260
Aqaba
G. of Aqaba
G. of Suez
Al Jawf
Nafud
Rafha
Tabuk
Tayma
Ha'il
Buraydah
Unayzah
SAUDI ARABIA
Al Wajh
Medina (Al Madinah)
Ras Banas
Yanbu al Bahr
Jiddah
Mecca (Makkah)
At Ta'if
Al Lith
Qal'at Bishah
Al Qunfidhah
Abha
Sabya
Jizan
Farasan Is
RED SEA
Hijaz
Badanah
Ma'an
Madama
Aozou
Pic Toussidé 3265
Bardai
Plateau du Mangueni
Plateau du Tchigai
Séguédine
Tibesti
Emi Koussi 3415
Asawanwah
Ma'tan as Sarra
Chirfa
Djado
Dirkou
Bilma
Grand Erg de Bilma
Gouro
Ounianga Kebir
Borkou
Madadi
Dépression du Mourdi
Erdi
Ennedi
Ain Galakka
Faya (Largeau)
Fada
Agadem
Siltou
Broulkou
Bodélé
Erg du Djourab
O. Haouach
Koro Toro
Oum Chalouba
CHAD
Arada
Biltine
Guéréda
Iriba
Ouaddai
Abéché
Nguigmi
Kanem
Mao
Salal
Bahr el Ghazal
Bol
Lake Chad
Moussoro
Massakori
Oum Hadjer
Ati
Adré
Geneina
Chari
Maiduguri
Ndjamena (Ft Lamy)
Kousseri
Bama
Baguirmi
Massenya
Mokolo
Marroua
Guider
Garoua
Bongor
Bousso
Lai
Am Dam
Mangalmé
Goz Beida
Mongo
Bokoro
Abou Deia
Melfi
Am Timan
Harazé
Birao
Dik
Sarh
Pala
Moundou
Doba
Maro
Laï
Léré
Tchollire
Poli
l'Adamaoua
Ngaoundéré
Goré
Baibokoum
Bamingui Bangoran Nat. Pk
Ndélé
Dar Rounga
Ouanda Djallé
Massif des Bongo
Ouadda
Bria
Haute Kotto
Yalinga
Djéma
Batangafo
Bouca
Bossangoa
Bozoum
Bouar
Bodaranga
Meiganga
Garoua Boulai
CENTRAL AFRICAN REPUBLIC
Dekoa
Bakala
Bambari
Bakouma
Sibut
Bossembélé
Damara
Bangui
Berbérati
Carnot
Boyali
Bertoua
Abong Mbang
Yokadouma
Boda
Mbaiki
Zongo
Libenge
Nola
Mobaye
Kouango
Bangassou
Rafai
Zemio
Obo
Gwane
Monga
Bondo
Yakoma
Gemena
Bozene
Betou
Titule
Bambili
Lienart
Buta
Aketi
Monveda
Lisala
Bumba
Moloundou
Souanké
Impfondo
Makanza
Ouesso
Mekambo
Makokou
Mbendza
CONGO
Pikounda
Makoua
Fort Rousset
Kellé
Boende
Mbandaka (Coquilhatville)
Basankusu
Lulonga
Befale
Mompono
Djolu
Yahuma
Yangambi
Isangi
Yatolema
Bongandanga
ZAIRE
Kisangani (Stanleyville)
Boyoma Falls
Ubundu
Angumu
Banalia
Nia Nia
Bafwasende
Isiro
Mungbere
Watsa
Dungu
Niangara
Doruma
Faradje
Aba
Bunia
Djugu
Mambasa
Mahagi
Masindi
Hoima
Ruwenzori
Kasese
Beni
Lubero
L. Edward
L. Albert
UGANDA
Mubende
Bombo
Kampala
Entebbe
Masaka
Jinja
Kakamega
Kisumu
Nakuru
Nyeri
Kericho
Mt Elgon 4321
Mbale
Tororo
Eldoret
Kitale
Nyahururu Falls
Nanyuki
Isiolo
5199 Kirinyaga (Mt Kenya)
KENYA
Maralal
Mado Gashi
Kangetet
Wajir
Mt Nyiru 2805
Mt Kulal 2293
Marsabit
Buna
Lake Turkana
Lodwar
Moyale
Lokitaung
Kitgum
Moroto
Soroti
Lira
Gulu
Arua
Pakwach
Nimule
Moyo
Yei
Kinyeti 3187
Torit
Lotikipi Plain
Kenamuke Swamp
Juba
Mongalla
Amadi
Tali Post
Yirol
Bor
Pibor Post
Akobo
Rumbek
Shambe
Tonj
Wau
Sudd
Meshra'er Req
Ayod
Duk Faiwil
Aweil
Nyamlell
Raga
Deim Zubeir
Tambura
Yambio
Maridi
Malakal
Fangak
Abwong
Nasir
Bentiu
Abyei
Kodok
Kaka
Paloich
Renk
Kadugli
Nuba Mts
Talodi
Rashad
Dilling
El Lagowa
El Fula
Muglad
En Nahud
Abu Zabad
Khuwei
El Obeid
Er Rahad
Umm Ruwaba
Kosti
El Jebelein
Dinder
Rahad
Sennar
Singa
Er Roseires
Ed Dueim
Wad Medani
El Geteina
Gezira
El Kamlin
Omdurman
Khartoum North
Khartoum
Blue Nile
White Nile
Shendi
Goz Regeb
Kassala
Khashm el Girba
Gedaref
Qala'en Nahl
Gallabat
Sodiri
Umm Bell
Bara
SUDAN
El Fasher
Umm Keddada
Kutum
Malha
W. Howa
Zalingei
3071 Jebel Marra
Nyala
Taweisha
Ed Da'ein
Buram
Bahr el Arab
Bahr el Ghazal
Abu 'Urug
W. el Milk
Jebel Abyad
El'Atrun Oasis
Laqiya Arba in
Dongola
Karima
Merowe
Ed Debba
Abri
Nubian Desert
Abu Hamed
Berber
Atbara
Ed Damer
Musmar
Derudeb
Port Sudan
Suakin
Sinkat
Tokar
Haiya
Eriba
Karora
Nak'fa
Keren
Massawa (Mits'iwa)
Dehalak Archipelago
Asmara (Asmera)
ERITREA
Ras Andadda
Mersa Fatma
Sebderat
Barentu
Om Hajer
Adi Ugri
Adwa
Aksum
Adigrat
Mek'ele
Ras Dashan 4533
Tigre
Sek'ot'a
Dabat
Gonder
Tendaho
L. Tana
Debre Tabor
Bahir Dar
Weldiya
DJIBOUTI
Dikhil
L. Abbe
4231 Gune
Bure
Choke Mts
Dese
4000 Abuye Meda
Debre Mark'os
Debre Birhan
Dangila
Belfodiyo
Dunkur
Asosa
Abbai (Blue Nile)
Fiche
Dire Dawa
Harer
Nejo
Dembi Dolo
ETHIOPIA
Nek'emte
Denti 3298
Addis Ababa (Adis Abeba)
Awash
Nazret
Ahmar Mts
Sodo
Koma
Gololcha
Gore
Jima
Shashemene
Goba
Ginir
Mendebo Mts
Gojab
Abera
Omo
Yirga Alem
Mizan Teferi
Guge 4200
Hara Fanna
Maji
Arba Minch
Gidole
Bako
Negele
Melka Guba
Mega
Dolo Odo
Mandera
Dawa
Genale Doria
20
30
40
10
0
D
E
F
G
1
2
3
4
5

1:15M
100
200
300 mls
200
400
600 km
LIBYA
SAUDI ARABIA
YEMEN
NIGER
CHAD
SUDAN
ETHIOPIA
ERITREA
DJIBOUTI
SOMALIA
KENYA
UGANDA
RWANDA
BURUNDI
TANZANIA
ZAIRE
CONGO
GABON
CAMEROON
NIGERIA
CENTRAL AFRICAN REPUBLIC
RED SEA
Gulf of Aden
INDIAN
Nubian Desert
Lake Victoria
Lake Chad
Khartoum
Omdurman
Addis Ababa
Nairobi
Mogadishu
Kinshasa
Brazzaville
Djibouti
Asmara
Kampala
Bangui
Ndjamena
Mecca (Makkah)
Jiddah
San'ā
Adan
Equator

ATLANTIC
OCEAN
OCEAN
ANGOLA
ZAMBIA
ZIMBABWE
MOZAMBIQUE
MALAWI
NAMIBIA
BOTSWANA
SOUTH AFRICA
LESOTHO
SWAZI-LAND
MADAGASCAR
(MALAGASY REP.)
COMOROS
SEYCHELLES
MAURITIUS
Mozambique Channel
Kalahari Desert
Namib Desert
Kaokoveld
Ovamboland
Great Namaland
Namaqualand
Great Karoo
Okavango Delta
Tropic of Capricorn
Luanda
Lobito
Benguela
Huambo (Nova Lisboa)
Namibe (Moçâmedes)
Tombua (Porto Alexandre)
Lusaka
Kitwe
Ndola
Lubumbashi (Elisabethville)
Likasi (Jadotville)
Lilongwe
Blantyre
Harare
Bulawayo
Windhoek
Walvis Bay
Gaborone
Francistown
Pretoria
Johannesburg
Maputo (Lourenço Marques)
Mbabane
Maseru
Bloemfontein
Kimberley
Durban
Pietermaritzburg
East London
Port Elizabeth
Cape Town
Cape of Good Hope
C. Agulhas
Sofala (Beira)
Quelimane
Nampula
Dar es Salaam
Antananarivo (Tananarive)
Toamasina (Tamatave)
Mahajanga (Majunga)
Fianarantsoa
Toliara
Moroni
Port Louis
St Denis
Réunion (Fr.)
at the same scale

A · 140 · 60 · B · 120 · ① · C · 100 · D · 80 · E · F · 40 · G · H · 0 · J · 20 · K · 40 · L · ① · 60 · M · N · 80

NORTH AMERICA

Baffin Bay

GREENLAND

Greenland Basin
Bear Island
Barents Sea
N.Cape
Arctic Circle

Hudson Bay

Denmark Strait
Norwegian Basin

ICELAND

Faeroes
Shetland Is

EUROPE

Labrador Sea

C.Farewell

Rockall

North Sea

Land's End

Black Sea

Newfoundland

Grand Banks

Newfoundland Basin

Mid-Atlantic Ridge

N. E. Atlantic Basin

Mediterranean Sea

Azores

North American Basin

Bermuda

Madeira

Canary Basin

Canary Is

Nile

Tropic of Cancer

Gulf of Mexico

Mississippi

West Indies

Cayman Tr.

Puerto Rico Trench
·9220

Caribbean Sea

Cape Verde Is

C.Vert

Cape Verde Basin

AFRICA

Cocos Ridge

Guyana Basin

Equator

Guinea Basin

Bioco
Principe

Galapagos Is

Amazon

Romanche Gap
7856

São Tomé

Zaire

Rocas · Fernando de Noronha

SOUTH AMERICA

Mid-Atlantic Ridge

Ascension

Angola Basin

Peru-Chile Trench

S.W. Peru or Nazca Ridge

·8066
·7635

I.San Ambrosia
I.San Felix

Brazil Basin

St Helena

Martin Vaz
Trindade

Walvis Ridge

·6081

Rio Grande Rise
·637

Tropic of Capricorn

Is Juan Fernandez

Tristan da Cunha

Cape Basin

C.Agulhas

Gough I.

Discovery Tablemount
411

Agulhas Plateau

Argentine Basin

Crozet Plateau

Pacific-Antarctic Ridge

Falkland Is

S.Georgia

Prince Edward Is

Is Crozet

N.Scotia Ridge

S.Sandwich Tr.
8264

Atlantic-Indian Ridge

C.Horn

Scotia Sea

S.Sandwich Is

Bouvet I.

Drake Passage

S.Orkney Is

Atlantic-Indian Antarctic Basin

Is Kerguelen

South East Pacific Basin

Antarctic Penin.

Weddell Sea

Maud Seamount
1199

Antarctic Circle

Peter 1st I.

ANTARCTICA

A · 140 · B · 120 · C · 100 · D · 80 · E · F · 40 · G · 20 · H · J · 20 · K · 40 · L · 60 · M · N · 80

To enhance the ocean features, the 3000m contour has been added, and over 5000m is shown by an extra tint.

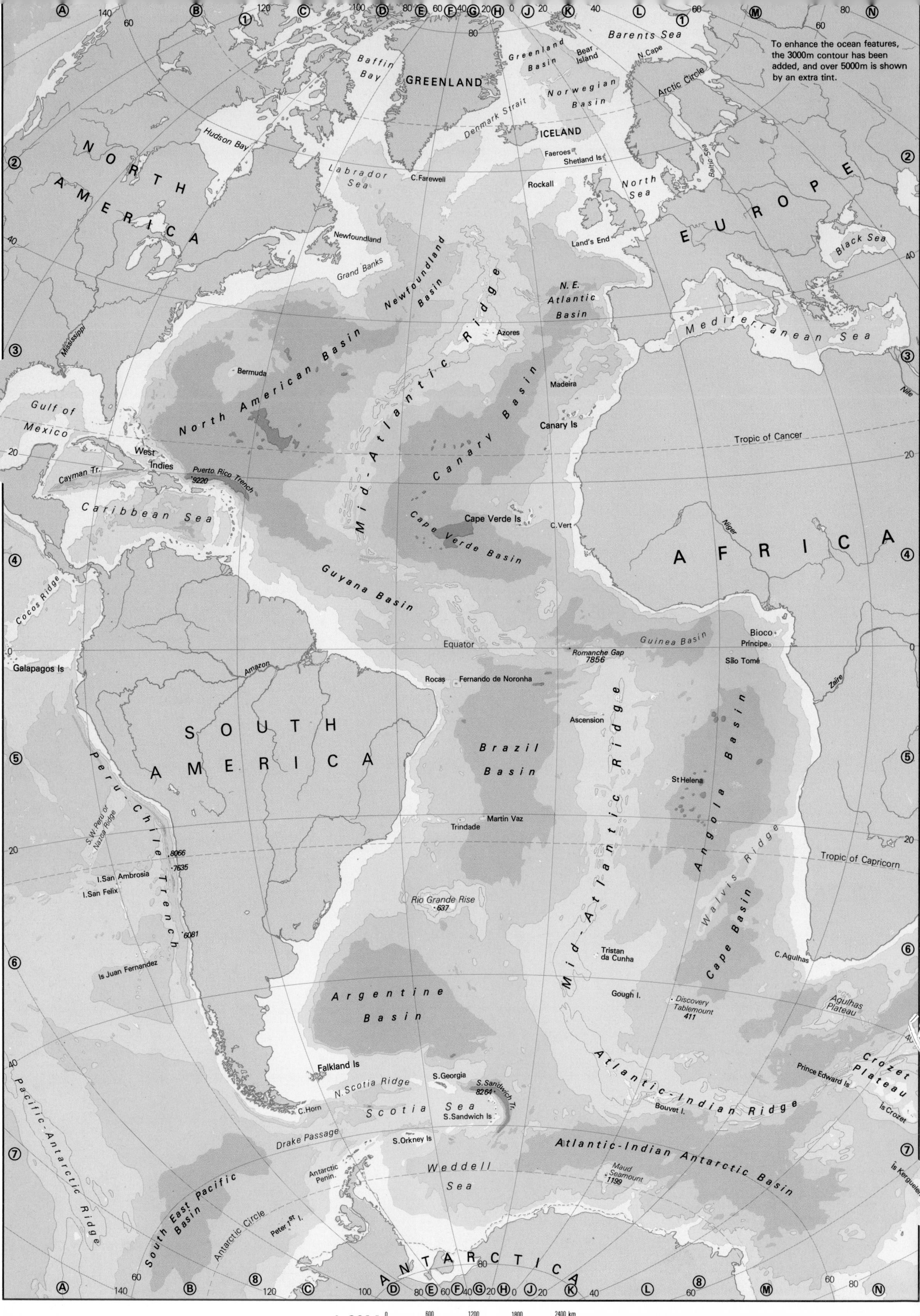

1:60M
0 · 600 · 1200 · 1800 · 2400 km
0 · 600 · 1200 mls

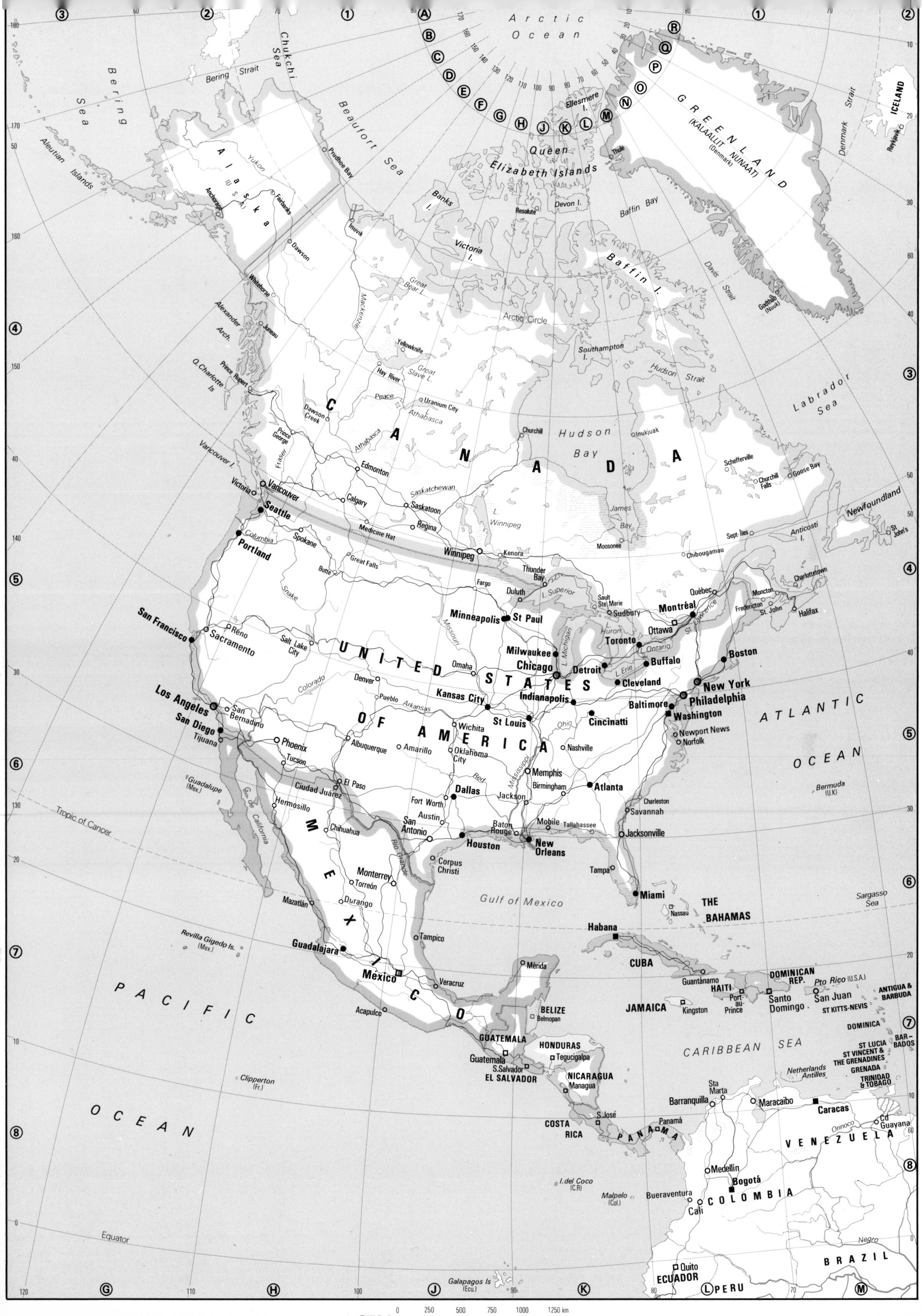

Arctic Ocean
Chukchi Sea
Bering Strait
Bering Sea
Aleutian Islands
Beaufort Sea
Alaska (U.S.A.)
Yukon
Prudhoe Bay
Fairbanks
Anchorage
Dawson
Whitehorse
Juneau
Alexander Arch.
Q.Charlotte Is
Prince Rupert
Vancouver I.
Victoria
Vancouver
Seattle
Portland
Columbia
Spokane
Banks I.
Victoria I.
Inuvik
Mackenzie
Great Bear L.
Yellowknife
Great Slave L.
Hay River
Peace
Uranium City
Athabasca
Dawson Creek
Prince George
Fraser
Edmonton
Calgary
Saskatchewan
Saskatoon
Regina
Medicine Hat
Ellesmere I.
Queen Elizabeth Islands
Resolute
Devon I.
Thule
Baffin Bay
Baffin I.
Arctic Circle
Southampton I.
Hudson Strait
Hudson Bay
Churchill
Inukjuak
James Bay
L. Winnipeg
Winnipeg
Kenora
Moosonee
Chibougamau
Schefferville
Churchill Falls
Goose Bay
Labrador Sea
Sept-Iles
Anticosti I.
Newfoundland
St John's
GREENLAND (KALAALLIT NUNAAT) (Denmark)
Davis Strait
Godthåb (Nuuk)
Denmark Strait
ICELAND
Reykjavik
CANADA
Great Falls
Butte
Snake
Fargo
Duluth
Thunder Bay
L. Superior
Sault Ste Marie
Sudbury
Québec
Montréal
Ottawa
St Lawrence
Toronto
L. Ontario
L. Huron
L. Michigan
Moncton
Fredericton
St John
Charlottetown
Halifax
Minneapolis
St Paul
Missouri
Milwaukee
Chicago
Detroit
L. Erie
Buffalo
Cleveland
Boston
New York
Philadelphia
Baltimore
Washington
Newport News
Norfolk
San Francisco
Reno
Sacramento
Salt Lake City
Omaha
Denver
Colorado
Pueblo
Arkansas
Kansas City
Indianapolis
Cincinnati
Ohio
St Louis
Wichita
UNITED STATES OF AMERICA
Los Angeles
San Bernadino
San Diego
Tijuana
Phoenix
Tucson
Albuquerque
Amarillo
Oklahoma City
Nashville
Memphis
Mississippi
Red
Atlanta
Birmingham
El Paso
Ciudad Juárez
Dallas
Fort Worth
Jackson
Charleston
Savannah
Austin
San Antonio
Houston
Baton Rouge
Mobile
Tallahassee
New Orleans
Jacksonville
Corpus Christi
Tampa
Miami
Rio Grande
Guadalupe (Mex.)
G. de California
Hermosillo
Chihuahua
Monterrey
Torreón
Durango
Mazatlán
Tampico
Guadalajara
México
Veracruz
Acapulco
Mérida
MEXICO
Tropic of Cancer
Revilla Gigedo Is. (Mex.)
Gulf of Mexico
ATLANTIC OCEAN
Bermuda (U.K.)
Sargasso Sea
Nassau
THE BAHAMAS
Habana
CUBA
Guantánamo
HAITI
Port-au-Prince
DOMINICAN REP.
Santo Domingo
Pto Rico (U.S.A.)
San Juan
ANTIGUA & BARBUDA
ST KITTS-NEVIS
DOMINICA
ST LUCIA
ST VINCENT & THE GRENADINES
BAR-BADOS
GRENADA
TRINIDAD & TOBAGO
JAMAICA
Kingston
CARIBBEAN SEA
Netherlands Antilles
BELIZE
Belmopan
GUATEMALA
Guatemala
S.Salvador
EL SALVADOR
HONDURAS
Tegucigalpa
NICARAGUA
Managua
COSTA RICA
S.José
PANAMA
Panamá
Sta Marta
Barranquilla
Maracaibo
Caracas
Orinoco
Cd Guayana
VENEZUELA
Medellín
Bogotá
COLOMBIA
Bueraventura
Cali
Quito
ECUADOR
PERU
BRAZIL
Negro
PACIFIC OCEAN
Clipperton (Fr.)
I.del Coco (C.R.)
Malpelo (Col.)
Galapagos Is (Ecu.)
Equator
1:35M
0 250 500 750 1000 1250 km
0 250 500 750 mls

1:15M 0 200 400 600 km

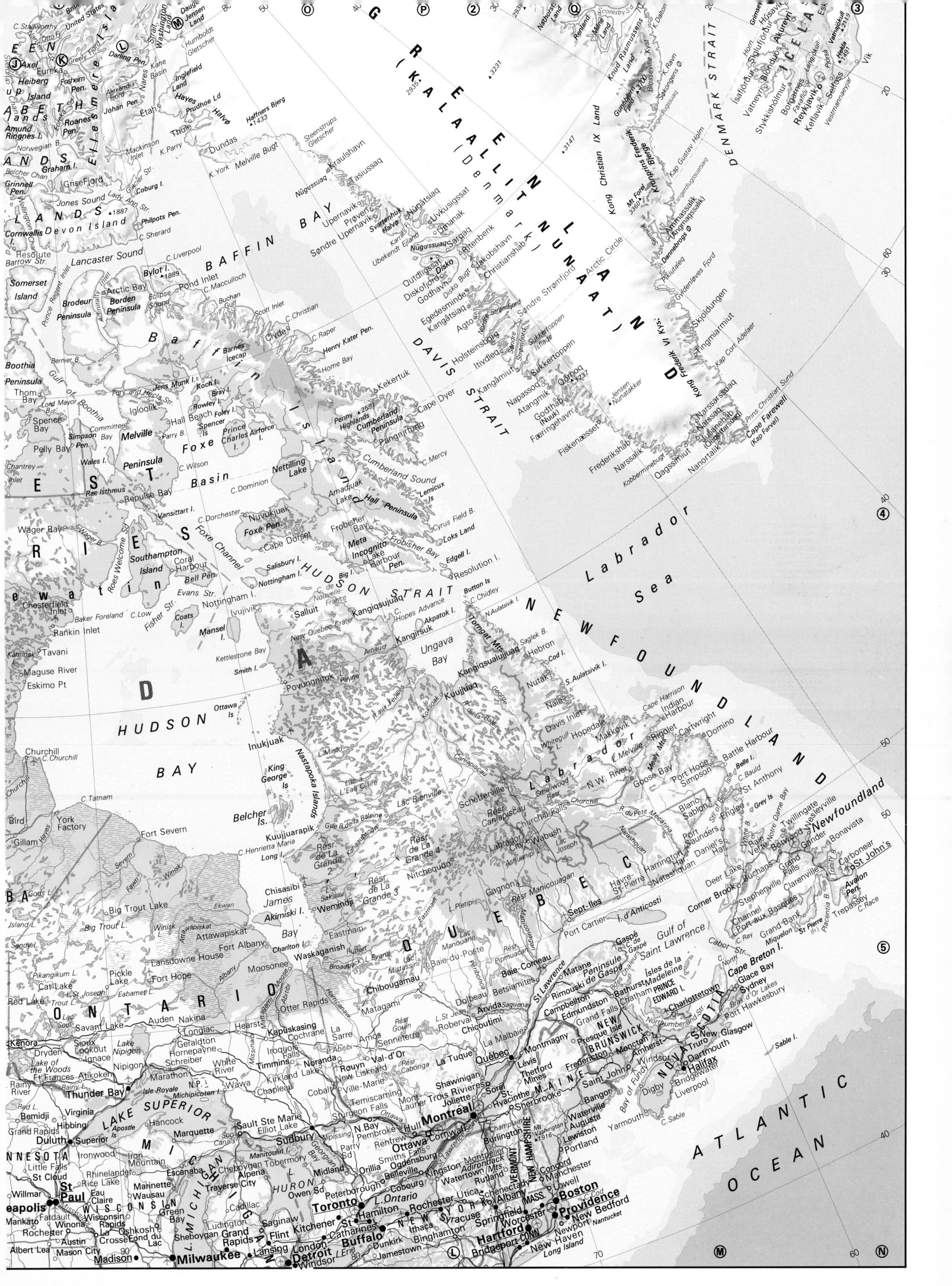

GREENLAND
(KALAALLIT NUNAAT)
(Denmark)
ICELAND
Reykjavík
Keflavík
Selfoss
Vík
Hekla
Akureyri
Húsavík
Ísafjörður
Blönduós
Borgarnes
Stykkishólmur
DENMARK STRAIT
BAFFIN BAY
Baffin Island
DAVIS STRAIT
Labrador Sea
HUDSON STRAIT
HUDSON BAY
James Bay
Ungava Bay
Foxe Basin
Foxe Channel
Gulf of Boothia
Lancaster Sound
Jones Sound
Cumberland Sound
Frobisher Bay
Devon Island
Ellesmere Island
Axel Heiberg Island
Somerset Island
Southampton Island
Coats I.
Mansel I.
Nottingham I.
Salisbury I.
Resolution I.
Akimiski I.
Belcher Is.
Melville Peninsula
Brodeur Peninsula
Borden Peninsula
Boothia Peninsula
Cumberland Peninsula
Hall Peninsula
Meta Incognito Pen.
Foxe Pen.
Thule
Dundas
Upernavik
Qutdligssat
Disko
Jakobshavn
Christianshåb
Egedesminde
Holsteinsborg
Sukkertoppen
Godthåb (Nuuk)
Frederikshåb
Julianehåb
Nanortalik
Cape Farewell (Kap Farvel)
Angmagssalik
Scoresby Sd
Kong Christian IX Land
Kong Frederik VI Kyst
Knud Rasmussens Land
Arctic Circle
Resolute
Arctic Bay
Pond Inlet
Clyde
Igloolik
Hall Beach
Repulse Bay
Coral Harbour
Cape Dorset
Frobisher Bay
Pangnirtung
Cape Dyer
Chesterfield Inlet
Rankin Inlet
Eskimo Pt
Churchill
York Factory
Fort Severn
NEWFOUNDLAND
Labrador
QUEBEC
ONTARIO
Nain
Hopedale
Makkovik
Cartwright
Goose Bay
N.W. River
Labrador City
Wabush
Churchill Falls
Schefferville
Kuujjuaq
Kangiqsualujjuaq
Kangirsuk
Kangiqsujuaq
Salluit
Ivujivik
Povungnituk
Inukjuak
Kuujjuarapik
Chisasibi
Eastmain
Waskaganish
Chibougamau
Moosonee
Fort Albany
Attawapiskat
Sept-Îles
Baie-Comeau
Gaspé
Gulf of Saint Lawrence
Î. d'Anticosti
Corner Brook
St John's
Gander
Grand Falls
Stephenville
Channel Port aux Basques
Cape Race
Avalon Pen.
Sydney
Cape Breton I.
Halifax
NOVA SCOTIA
NEW BRUNSWICK
PRINCE EDWARD I.
Charlottetown
Fredericton
Moncton
Saint John
Bay of Fundy
Sable I.
ATLANTIC OCEAN
Québec
Montréal
Ottawa
Trois Rivières
Sherbrooke
MAINE
Bangor
Augusta
Portland
NEW HAMPSHIRE
VERMONT
MASS.
Boston
Providence
Hartford
New Haven
Albany
Syracuse
Rochester
Buffalo
Toronto
Hamilton
L. Ontario
Kingston
Sudbury
North Bay
Sault Ste Marie
Timmins
Thunder Bay
LAKE SUPERIOR
L. HURON
L. MICHIGAN
MICHIGAN
WISCONSIN
MINNESOTA
Duluth
St Paul
Minneapolis
Milwaukee
Madison
Detroit
Windsor
London
Lansing
Flint
Grand Rapids
Kenora
Dryden
Lake of the Woods
Lake Nipigon
Long Island

BRITISH COLUMBIA
ALBERTA
SASKATCHEWAN
MANITOBA
CANADA
WASHINGTON
OREGON
IDAHO
MONTANA
WYOMING
NORTH DAKOTA
SOUTH DAKOTA
NEBRASKA
NEVADA
UTAH
COLORADO
KANSAS
CALIFORNIA
ARIZONA
NEW MEXICO
OKLAHOMA
TEXAS
UNITED STATES
MEXICO
BAJA CALIFORNIA
PACIFIC OCEAN
Golfo de California
Vancouver Island
Channel Islands
Tropic of Cancer
ROCKY MOUNTAINS
SIERRA NEVADA
CASCADE RANGE
Coast Ranges
SIERRA MADRE OCCIDENTAL
Sierra Madre Oriental
Colorado Plateau
Great Basin
Sonoran Desert
Llano Estacado
Edwards Plateau
Bolson de Mapimí
Great Salt L.
Edmonton
Calgary
Vancouver
Victoria
Seattle
Tacoma
Portland
Spokane
Boise
Salt Lake City
Reno
Sacramento
San Francisco
Oakland
San Jose
Fresno
Los Angeles
San Diego
Las Vegas
Phoenix
Tucson
Albuquerque
Santa Fe
Denver
Cheyenne
Helena
Billings
Regina
Saskatoon
Winnipeg
Bismarck
Pierre
Lincoln
Omaha
Topeka
Wichita
Oklahoma City
Tulsa
Dallas
Fort Worth
Austin
San Antonio
El Paso
Cd Juárez
Chihuahua
Hermosillo
Monterrey
Saltillo
Torreón
Durango
Culiacán
Mazatlán
La Paz
Tijuana
Mexicali
Laredo
Nuevo Laredo
Corpus Christi
Brownsville
Matamoros
Names underlined indicate Province/State capitals
1:12.5M
0 100 200 300 400 500 km
0 100 200 300 mls

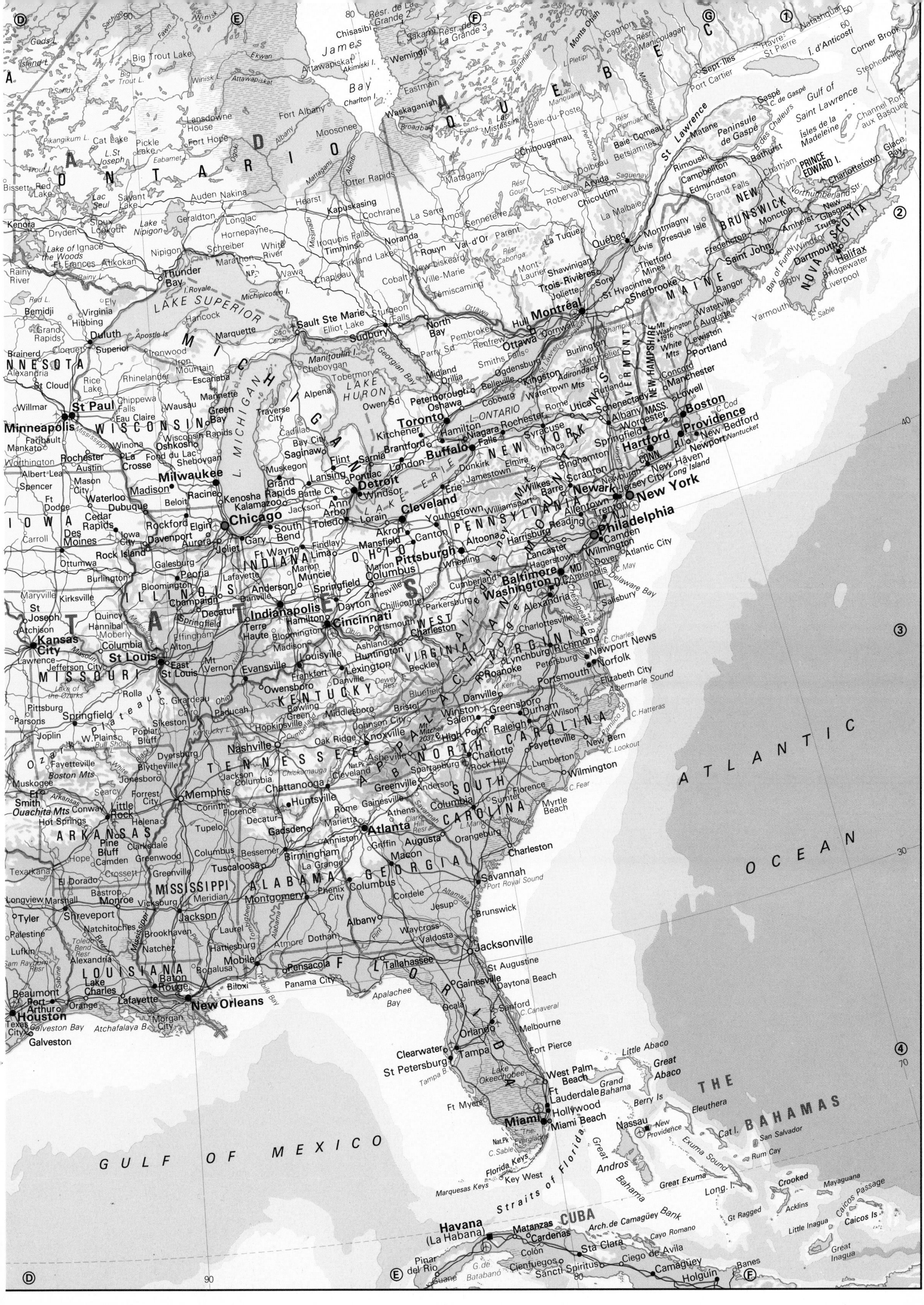
ONTARIO
QUEBEC
James Bay
Gulf of Saint Lawrence
NEW BRUNSWICK
NOVA SCOTIA
PRINCE EDWARD I.
LAKE SUPERIOR
LAKE HURON
L. ONTARIO
LAKE ERIE
L. MICHIGAN
MICHIGAN
MINNESOTA
WISCONSIN
IOWA
ILLINOIS
INDIANA
OHIO
PENNSYLVANIA
NEW YORK
VERMONT
NEW HAMPSHIRE
MAINE
MASS.
CONN.
R.I.
N.J.
MD.
DEL.
D.C.
WEST VIRGINIA
VIRGINIA
KENTUCKY
MISSOURI
TENNESSEE
NORTH CAROLINA
SOUTH CAROLINA
GEORGIA
ALABAMA
MISSISSIPPI
ARKANSAS
LOUISIANA
FLORIDA
UNITED STATES
APPALACHIAN MTS
Ozark Plateau
ATLANTIC OCEAN
GULF OF MEXICO
THE BAHAMAS
CUBA
Straits of Florida
Great Bahama Bank
Minneapolis
St Paul
Duluth
Milwaukee
Chicago
Detroit
Toronto
Montréal
Québec
Ottawa
Buffalo
Cleveland
Pittsburgh
Boston
Providence
Hartford
New York
Newark
Philadelphia
Baltimore
Washington
Richmond
Norfolk
Newport News
Indianapolis
Cincinnati
Columbus
St Louis
Kansas City
Louisville
Nashville
Memphis
Atlanta
Charlotte
Raleigh
Charleston
Savannah
Jacksonville
Tallahassee
Orlando
Tampa
St Petersburg
Miami
Miami Beach
Ft Lauderdale
West Palm Beach
Key West
Florida Keys
New Orleans
Baton Rouge
Houston
Galveston
Jackson
Birmingham
Montgomery
Mobile
Pensacola
Shreveport
Little Rock
Halifax
Saint John
Fredericton
Charlottetown
Havana (La Habana)
Matanzas
Cienfuegos
Camagüey
Holguin
Nassau
New Providence
Andros
Eleuthera
Great Abaco
Grand Bahama
Cat I.
San Salvador
Long I.
Great Exuma
Crooked
Acklins
Mayaguana
Great Inagua
Little Inagua
Caicos Is
Caicos Passage
C. Hatteras
C. Cod
C. Fear
C. May
C. Lookout
C. Canaveral
C. Sable
Lake Okeechobee
Long Island
Nantucket
Mt Mitchell 2037
Mt Washington 1916
Adirondack Mts
White Mts
Boston Mts
Ouachita Mts
Apalachee Bay
Mobile Bay
Tampa B.
Delaware Bay
Chesapeake B.
Pamlico Sd
Albemarle Sound
Port Royal Sound
Galveston Bay
Atchafalaya B.
Bay of Fundy
Northumberland Str.
Îles de la Madeleine
Î. d'Anticosti
Péninsule de Gaspé
St Lawrence
Cabot Strait

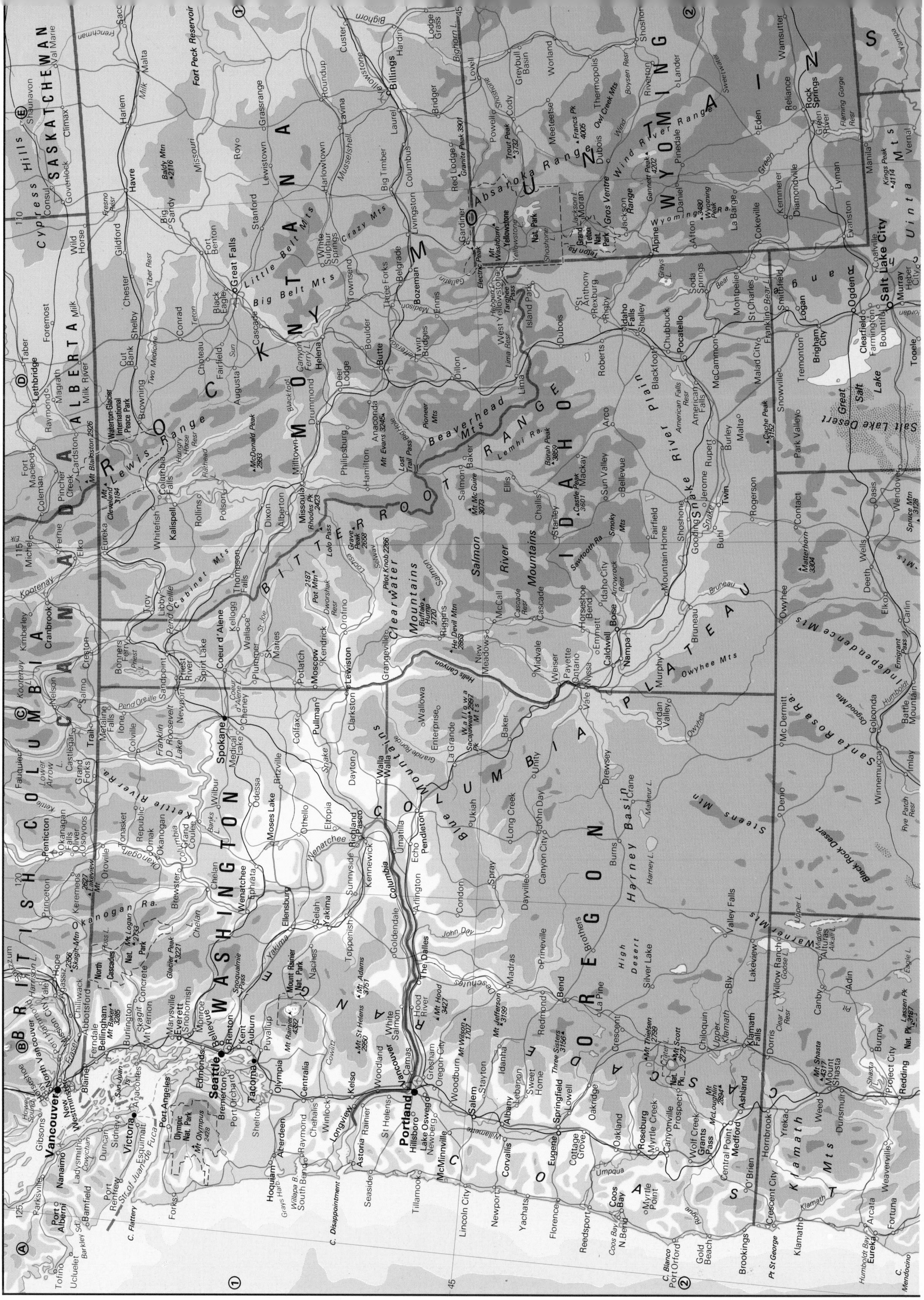

BRITISH COLUMBIA
CANADA
ALBERTA
SASKATCHEWAN
Cypress Hills
WASHINGTON
OREGON
IDAHO
MONTANA
WYOMING
ROCKY MOUNTAINS
BITTERROOT RANGE
CASCADE RANGE
COLUMBIA PLATEAU
Blue Mountains
Clearwater Mountains
Salmon River Mountains
Beaverhead Mts
Lemhi Ra.
Sawtooth Ra.
Lewis Range
Absaroka Range
Wind River Range
Gros Ventre Range
Wyoming Ra.
Big Belt Mts
Little Belt Mts
Crazy Mts
Cabinet Mts
Okanogan Ra.
Kettle River Ra.
Klamath Mts
Owyhee Mts
Warner Mts
Independence Mts
Santa Rosa Ra.
Osgood Mts
Uinta Mts
Harney Basin
High Desert
Snake River Plain
Great Salt Lake
Salt Lake Desert
Black Rock Desert
Steens Mtn
Hells Canyon
Fort Peck Reservoir
Yellowstone Nat. Park
Grand Teton Nat. Park
Olympic Nat. Park
Mount Rainier Nat. Park
North Cascades Nat. Park
Waterton-Glacier International Peace Park
Mt Rainier 4392
Mt Adams 3751
Mt Hood 3427
Mt St Helens 2950
Mt Olympus 2428
Mt Baker 3285
Mt Jefferson 3199
Three Sisters 3156
Mt Shasta 4317
Lassen Pk 3187
Granite Peak 3901
Gannett Peak 4202
Borah Peak 3859
Kings Peak 4114
Vancouver
Victoria
Seattle
Tacoma
Olympia
Spokane
Portland
Salem
Eugene
Boise
Pocatello
Idaho Falls
Missoula
Helena
Butte
Great Falls
Billings
Bozeman
Salt Lake City
Ogden
Medford
Klamath Falls
Bend
Yakima
Walla Walla
Lewiston
Coeur d'Alene
Kalispell
Lethbridge
Redding
Eureka
C. Flattery
C. Disappointment
C. Blanco
Pt St George
C. Mendocino
Columbia
Snake
Missouri
Yellowstone
Bighorn
1
2
A
B
C
D
E
125
120
115
110
45

1:5M 0 50 100 150 200 km
0 50 100 mls

PACIFIC OCEAN
CALIFORNIA
SIERRA NEVADA
NEVADA
GREAT BASIN
UTAH
ARIZONA
COLORADO PLATEAU
MEXICO
SONORA
BAJA CALIFORNIA
Sacramento Valley
San Joaquin Valley
Diablo Range
Santa Lucia Range
Mojave Desert
Death Valley
Painted Desert
Grand Canyon
Lake Powell
Lake Mead
Channel Islands
San Francisco
Oakland
Sacramento
San Jose
Stockton
Fresno
Reno
Las Vegas
Los Angeles
San Diego
Tijuana
Mexicali
Phoenix
Tucson
Flagstaff
Bakersfield
Monterey
Santa Barbara
Long Beach
Anaheim
Riverside
San Bernardino
Pasadena
Yosemite Nat. Park
Sequoia Nat. Park
Kings Canyon Nat. Park
Grand Canyon Nat. Park
Zion Nat. Pk
Bryce Canyon N.P.
Capitol Reef Nat. Pk
Canyonlands Nat. Pk
Arches N.P.
Petrified Forest Nat. Park
Mt Whitney 4418
G. de California

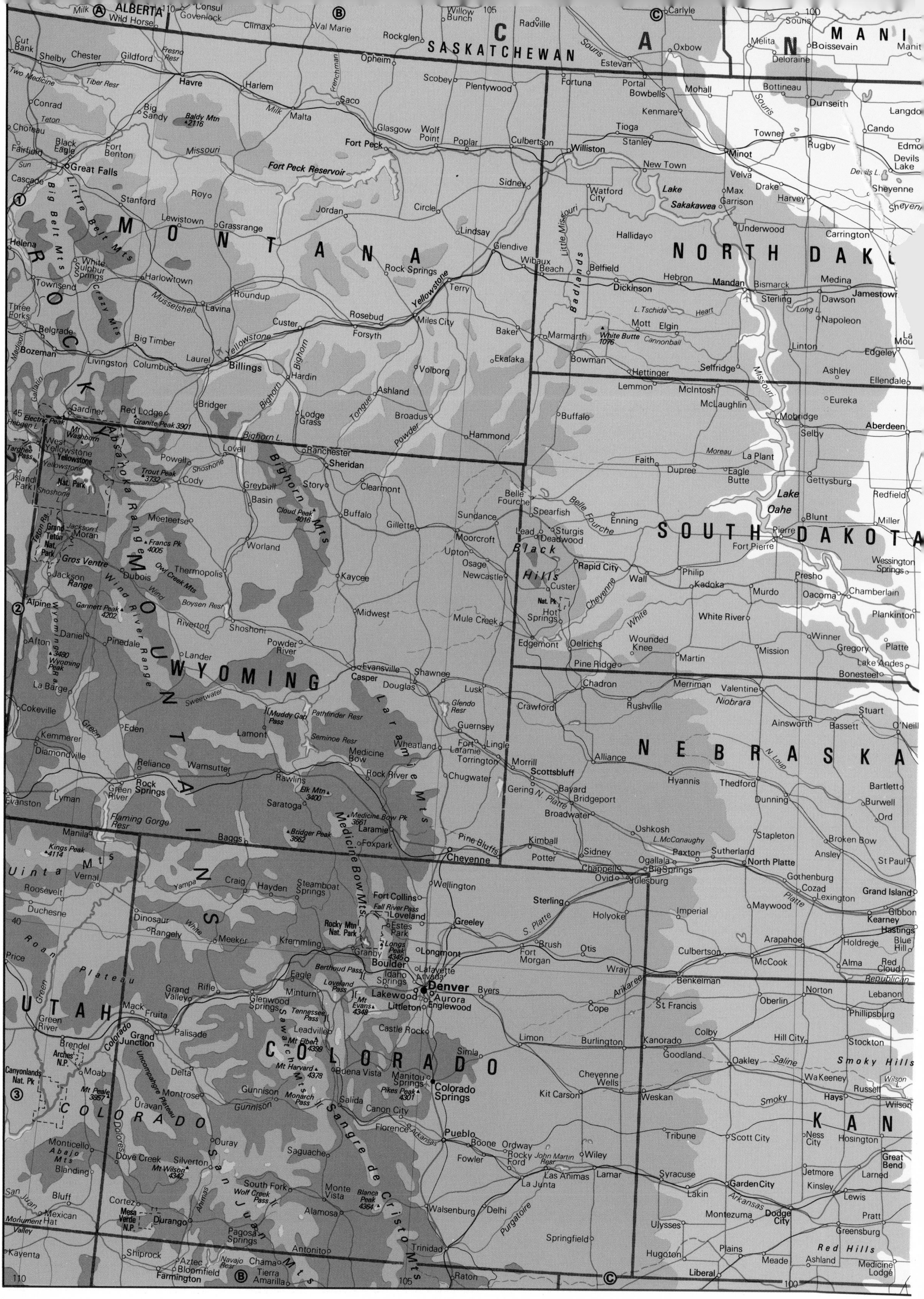

1:5M 0 50 100 150 200 km
0 50 100 mls

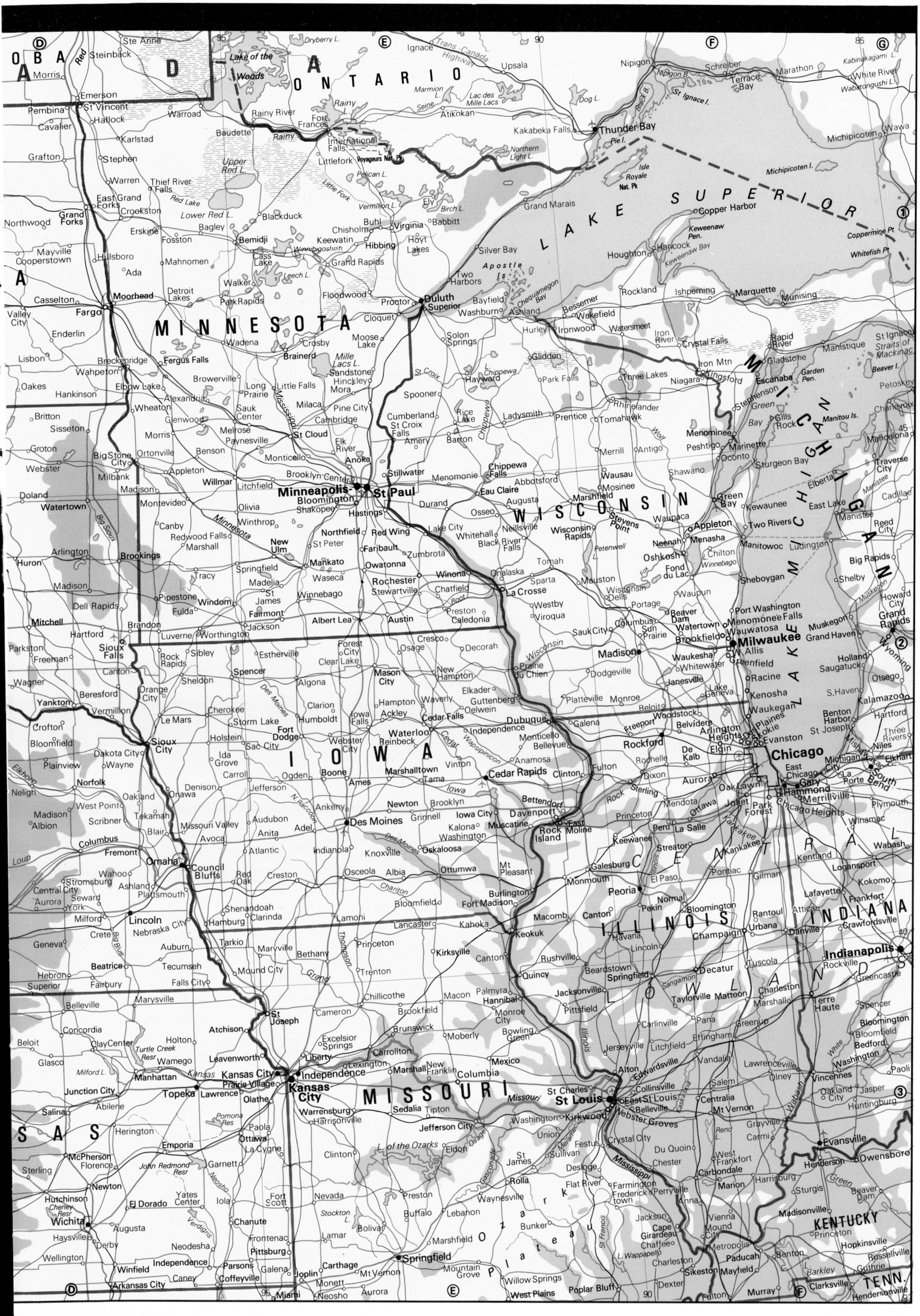
ONTARIO
Lake of the Woods
Ste Anne
Steinbach
Morris
Emerson
St Vincent
Pembina
Cavalier
Hallock
Karlstad
Warroad
Rainy River
Baudette
Fort Frances
International Falls
Littlefork
Voyageurs Nat. Pk
Upper Red L.
Lower Red L.
Red Lake
Thief River Falls
Stephen
Warren
Grafton
East Grand Forks
Grand Forks
Crookston
Northwood
Erskine
Fosston
Bagley
Blackduck
Bemidji
Mahnomen
Hillsboro
Mayville
Cooperstown
Ada
Cass Lake
Winnibigoshish
Leech L.
Walker
Park Rapids
Detroit Lakes
Moorhead
Fargo
Casselton
Valley City
Enderlin
Lisbon
Oakes
Hankinson
Wahpeton
Breckenridge
Fergus Falls
Elbow Lake
Wadena
Brainerd
Crosby
Mille Lacs L.
Long Prairie
Little Falls
Alexandria
Wheaton
Glenwood
Morris
Sauk Centre
Melrose
Paynesville
St Cloud
Milaca
Mora
Pine City
Hinckley
Sandstone
Cambridge
Elk River
Monticello
Anoka
Brooklyn Centers
Minneapolis
St Paul
Bloomington
Shakopee
Hastings
Stillwater
Benson
Willmar
Litchfield
Montevideo
Madison
Appleton
Ortonville
Big Stone City
Milbank
Britton
Sisseton
Groton
Webster
Doland
Watertown
Clark
Brookings
Arlington
Huron
Madison
Canby
Marshall
Redwood Falls
Olivia
Winthrop
New Ulm
St Peter
Mankato
Northfield
Faribault
Owatonna
Red Wing
Zumbrota
Rochester
Stewartville
Winona
Waseca
Springfield
Tracy
Pipestone
Windom
Madelia
St James
Fairmont
Winnebago
Albert Lea
Austin
Chatfield
Preston
Caledonia
Fulda
Jackson
Worthington
Luverne
Brandon
Dell Rapids
Sioux Falls
Mitchell
Hartford
Parkston
Freeman
Canton
Wagner
Beresford
Yankton
Vermillion
Crofton
Bloomfield
Plainview
Norfolk
Neligh
Wayne
Dakota City
Sioux City
Madison
Albion
West Point
Scribner
Columbus
Fremont
Blair
Tekamah
Oakland
Onawa
Wahoo
Omaha
Council Bluffs
Central City
Stromsburg
Aurora
Seward
York
Ashland
Plattsmouth
Lincoln
Milford
Crete
Nebraska City
Geneva
Beatrice
Hebron
Superior
Fairbury
Tecumseh
Auburn
Falls City
Belleville
Marysville
Concordia
Clay Center
Beloit
Glasco
Turtle Creek Resr
Milford L.
Wamego
Manhattan
Junction City
Topeka
Lawrence
Salina
Abilene
Herington
Emporia
McPherson
Florence
Sterling
Hutchinson
Cheney Resr
Newton
Wichita
Haysville
Derby
Augusta
El Dorado
Wellington
Winfield
Arkansas City
Independence
Caney
Coffeyville
Parsons
Neodesha
Chanute
Iola
Yates Center
John Redmond Resr
Garnett
Ottawa
Paola
La Cygne
Olathe
Prairie Village
Kansas City
Independence
Leavenworth
Atchison
St Joseph
Holton
Pomona Res
Fort Scott
Nevada
Lamar
Pittsburg
Frontenac
Galena
Joplin
Carthage
Neosho
Monett
Miami
Aurora
Mt Vernon
Springfield
Bolivar
Stockton L.
Buffalo
Lebanon
Marshfield
Mountain Grove
Willow Springs
West Plains
Poplar Bluff
Clinton
Warrensburg
Harrisonville
Sedalia
Tipton
L. of the Ozarks
Eldon
Jefferson City
Columbia
Mexico
Marshall
New Franklin
Lexington
Carrollton
Excelsior Springs
Liberty
Cameron
Chillicothe
Brookfield
Brunswick
Moberly
Macon
Kirksville
Hannibal
Palmyra
Monroe City
Bowling Green
Canton
Princeton
Trenton
Bethany
Maryville
Tarkio
Mound City
Hamburg
Shenandoah
Clarinda
Red Oak
Lamoni
Lancaster
Bloomfield
MISSOURI
Ozark Plateau
Rolla
St James
Waynesville
Sullivan
Union
Washington
St Charles
St Louis
Kirkwood
Webster Groves
Festus
Crystal City
Desloge
Flat River
Farmington
Fredericktown
Perryville
Bunker
Jackson
Cape Girardeau
Chaffee
L. Wappapello
Charleston
Sikeston
Dexter
Fulton
Mayfield
Paducah
Murray
Benton
Metropolis
Vienna
Mound City
Anna
Marion
Carbondale
Harrisburg
West Frankfort
Du Quoin
Chester
Mt Vernon
Centralia
Salem
Vandalia
Effingham
Olney
Lawrenceville
Carmi
Grayville
Belleville
East St Louis
Collinsville
Edwardsville
Alton
Jerseyville
Litchfield
Carlinville
Taylorville
Pana
Mattoon
Charleston
Greenup
Marshall
Decatur
Springfield
Jacksonville
Pittsfield
Beardstown
Rushville
Quincy
Keokuk
Kahoka
Macomb
Canton
Havana
Lincoln
Peoria
Pekin
Normal
Bloomington
El Paso
Galesburg
Monmouth
Burlington
Fort Madison
Mt Pleasant
Ottumwa
Albia
Oskaloosa
Knoxville
Osceola
Creston
Indianola
Des Moines
Ankeny
Adel
Anita
Atlantic
Audubon
Avoca
Missouri Valley
Denison
Carroll
Jefferson
Ogden
Boone
Ames
Marshalltown
Tama
Newton
Grinnell
Brooklyn
Iowa City
Kalona
Washington
Muscatine
Davenport
Bettendorf
Rock Island
Moline
East Moline
Clinton
Fulton
Cedar Rapids
Anamosa
Vinton
Monticello
Bellevue
Dubuque
Galena
Independence
Waterloo
Cedar Falls
Reinbeck
Webster City
Fort Dodge
Sac City
Ida Grove
Holstein
Storm Lake
Cherokee
Le Mars
Orange City
Sheldon
Rock Rapids
Sibley
Spencer
Estherville
Algona
Humboldt
Clarion
Iowa Falls
Hampton
Ackley
Mason City
Clear Lake
Forest City
Osage
Cresco
Decorah
New Hampton
Waverly
Oelwein
Elkader
Guttenberg
Prairie du Chien
IOWA
MINNESOTA
WISCONSIN
ILLINOIS
INDIANA
KENTUCKY
TENN.
LAKE SUPERIOR
LAKE MICHIGAN
CENTRAL LOWLAND
Duluth
Superior
Proctor
Cloquet
Floodwood
Moose Lake
Two Harbors
Silver Bay
Grand Marais
Chisholm
Hibbing
Virginia
Keewatin
Grand Rapids
Buhl
Ely
Babbitt
Hoyt Lakes
Thunder Bay
Kakabeka Falls
Upsala
Ignace
Atikokan
Nipigon
Schreiber
Terrace Bay
Marathon
White River
Wawa
Michipicoten
Isle Royale Nat. Pk
Copper Harbor
Keweenaw Pen.
Houghton
Hancock
Apostle Is
Bayfield
Washburn
Ashland
Hurley
Ironwood
Bessemer
Wakefield
Watersmeet
Rockland
Ishpeming
Marquette
Munising
Iron River
Crystal Falls
Iron Mtn
Kingsford
Niagara
Escanaba
Gladstone
Rapid River
Manistique
St Ignace
Straits of Mackinac
Petoskey
Charlevoix
Solon Springs
Spooner
Hayward
Glidden
Park Falls
Three Lakes
Rhinelander
Tomahawk
Prentice
Ladysmith
Rice Lake
Cumberland
St Croix Falls
Amery
Barron
Menomonie
Chippewa Falls
Eau Claire
Durand
Osseo
Augusta
Abbotsford
Marshfield
Wausau
Mosinee
Merrill
Antigo
Shawano
Stevens Point
Wisconsin Rapids
Neillsville
Whitehall
Black River Falls
Lake City
La Crosse
Onalaska
Sparta
Tomah
Mauston
Westby
Viroqua
Wisconsin Dells
Portage
Sauk City
Madison
Dodgeville
Platteville
Monroe
Janesville
Beloit
Waukesha
Whitewater
Watertown
Beaver Dam
Columbus
Sun Prairie
Brookfield
Milwaukee
Wauwatosa
Menomonee Falls
Port Washington
Sheboygan
Fond du Lac
Waupun
Oshkosh
Neenah
Menasha
Appleton
Waupaca
Green Bay
Kewaunee
Two Rivers
Manitowoc
Oconto
Peshtigo
Marinette
Menominee
Sturgeon Bay
Racine
Kenosha
Waukegan
Lake Geneva
Woodstock
Freeport
Rockford
Belvidere
Elgin
De Kalb
Rochelle
Dixon
Sterling
Aurora
Oak Lawn
Joliet
Park Forest
Chicago Heights
Chicago
Evanston
Des Plaines
Skokie
Arlington Heights
East Chicago
Gary
Hammond
Merrillville
Michigan City
La Porte
South Bend
Elkhart
Niles
Plymouth
Winamac
Kankakee
Streator
Ottawa
La Salle
Peru
Mendota
Princeton
Kewanee
Pontiac
Gilman
Rantoul
Champaign
Urbana
Danville
Tuscola
Kentland
Wabash
Logansport
Kokomo
Lafayette
Frankfort
Crawfordsville
Attica
Indianapolis
Rockville
Greencastle
Terre Haute
Spencer
Bloomington
Bloomfield
Bedford
Washington
Vincennes
Jasper
Oakland City
Huntingburg
Paoli
Evansville
Henderson
Owensboro
Sturgis
Beaver Dam
Madisonville
Princeton
Hopkinsville
Russellville
Guthrie
Clarksville
Hendersonville
Manistee
Ludington
Big Rapids
Shelby
Muskegon
Grand Haven
Holland
Saugatuck
Grand Rapids
Benton Harbor
St Joseph
Kalamazoo
Hartford
Three Rivers
South Haven
Otsego
Howard City
Reed City
Cadillac
Traverse City
Mancelona
Elberta
Frankfort
Gills Rock
Garden Pen.
Manitou Is.
Beaver I.
Keweenaw Bay
Chequamegon Bay
Nipigon B.
St Ignace I.
Black B.
Pie I.
Dog L.
Northern Light L.
Marmion L.
Lac des Mille Lacs
Rainy L.
Pelican L.
Little Fork
Vermilion L.
Birch L.
Kabinakagami L.
Wabatongushi L.
Michipicoten I.
Coppermine Pt
Whitefish Pt
Trans-Canada Highway
Dryberry L.
Mississippi
Missouri
Minnesota
Des Moines
Cedar
Iowa
Wapsipinicon
Wisconsin
Chippewa
St Croix
Rock
Illinois
Sangamon
Kankakee
Wabash
White
Green
Kaskaskia
Big Muddy
Ohio
Meramec
Gasconade
Osage
Grand
Thompson
Chariton
Kansas
Big Blue
Neosho
Verdigris
Elkhorn
Loup
Big Sioux
James
Platte
Wolf
Red
95
90
85
45
40
D
E
F
G
1
2
3

COLORADO
KANS
NEW MEXICO
OK
TEXAS
CHIHUAHUA
COAHUILA
MEXICO
DURANGO
SINALOA
NUEVO LEON

Plateau
Llano Estacado
Edwards Plateau
San Juan Mts
Sangre de Cristo Mts
Sacramento Mts
San Andres Mts
Zuni Mts
Wichita Mts
Red Hills
Sierra Madre Occidental
Sierra Madre Oriental
Sa del Burro
Bolson de Mapimi
Sa de los Alamitos

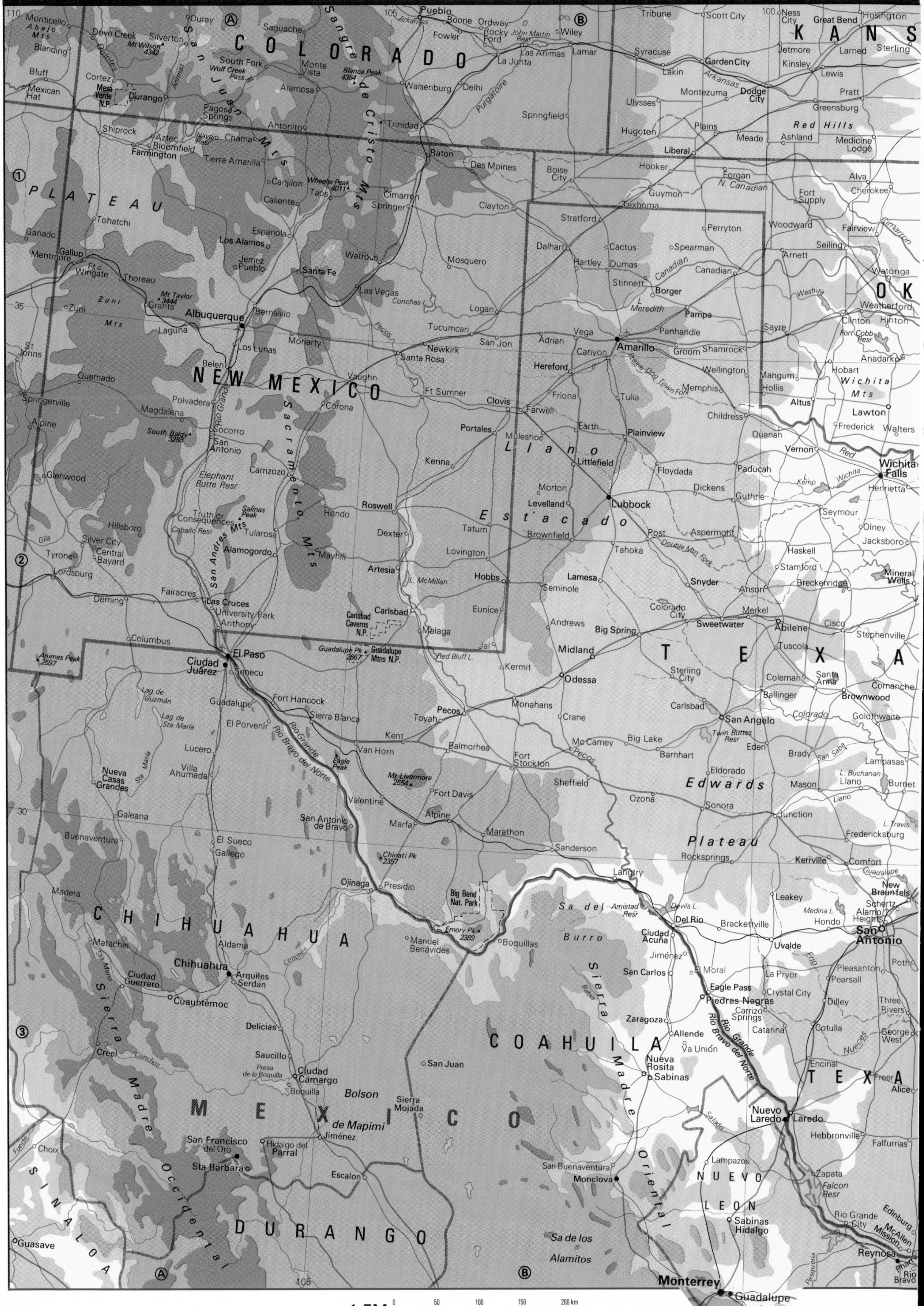

1:5M
0 50 100 150 200 km
0 50 100 mls

KENTUCKY
TENNESSEE
ARKANSAS
LOUISIANA
MISSISSIPPI
ALABAMA
LAHOMA
GULF OF MEXICO
Ozark Plateau
Boston Mts
Ouachita Mts
Springfield
Memphis
Nashville
Little Rock
North Little Rock
Oklahoma City
Tulsa
Wichita
Dallas
Fort Worth
Houston
Galveston
New Orleans
Baton Rouge
Shreveport
Jackson
Vicksburg
Mobile
Birmingham
Evansville
Paducah
Fort Smith
Corpus Christi
Brownsville
Matamoros
Austin
Waco
Beaumont
Port Arthur
Lake Charles
Lafayette
Alexandria
Monroe
Natchez
Hattiesburg
Meridian
Tuscaloosa
Pensacola
Biloxi
Gulfport
Pascagoula
Texarkana
Hot Springs
Pine Bluff
Jonesboro
Fayetteville
Springdale
Joplin
Muskogee
McAlester
Tyler
Longview
Marshall
Nacogdoches
Lufkin
Victoria
Port Lavaca
Kingsville
Harlingen
San Benito
Weslaco
Raymondville
Robstown
Mississippi Delta
Breton Sound
Chandeleur Is
Atchafalaya Bay
Terre Bonne Bay
Timbalier Bay
Matagorda I.
St Joseph I.
Baffin Bay
Laguna Madre
Galveston Bay
L. Pontchartrain
Toledo Bend Resr
Sam Rayburn Resr
Lake Texoma
Ross Barnett Resr
Mississippi
Arkansas
Red
Ouachita
Sabine
Neches
Trinity
Brazos
Colorado
Tombigbee
Pearl
Yazoo
Big Black
White
Black
Tennessee
30
35
90
95

1:5M
0 50 100 150 200 km
0 50 100 mls

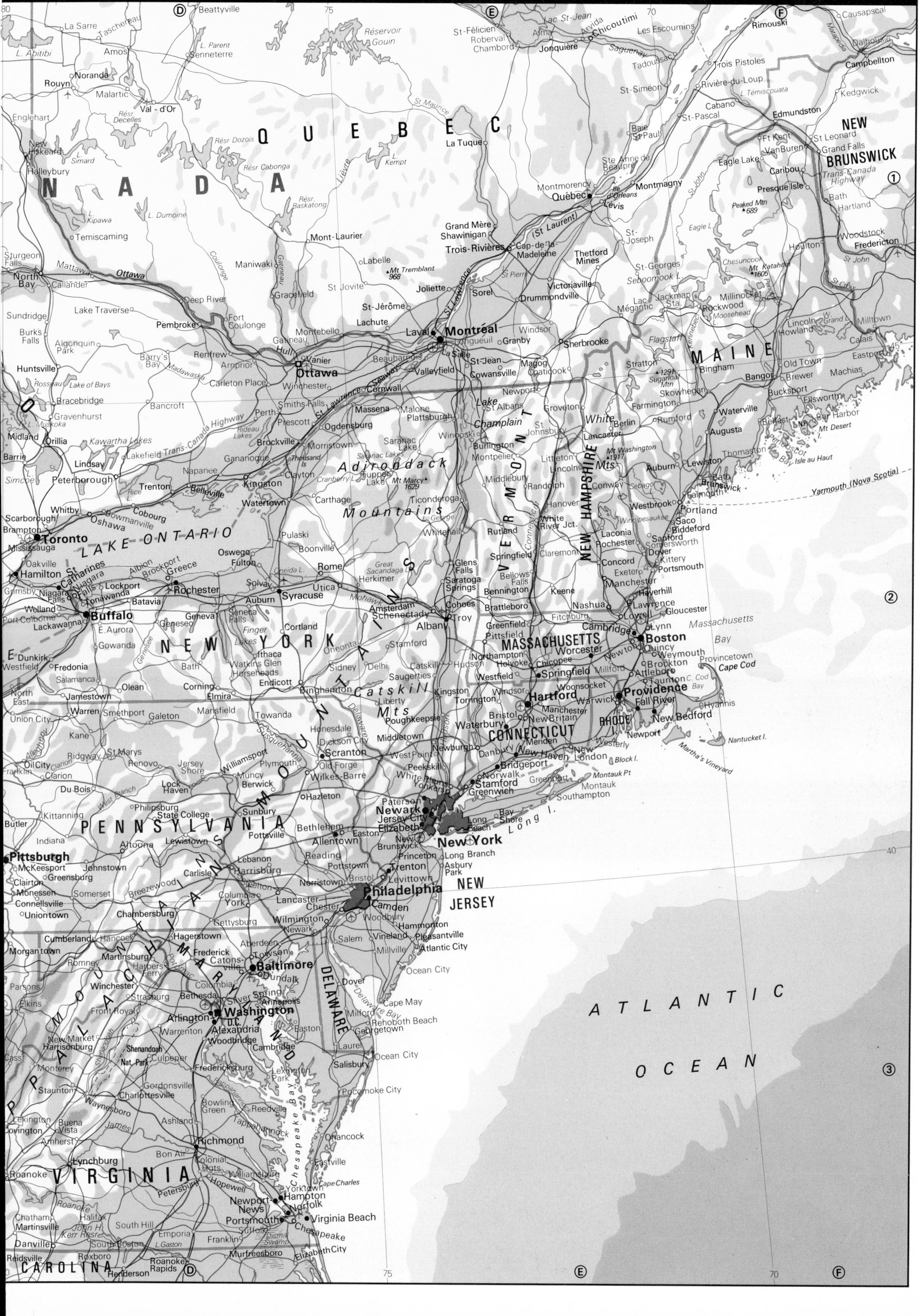
QUEBEC
NADA
LAKE ONTARIO
NEW YORK
PENNSYLVANIA
VIRGINIA
CAROLINA
MARYLAND
DELAWARE
NEW JERSEY
CONNECTICUT
RHODE
MASSACHUSETTS
VERMONT
NEW HAMPSHIRE
MAINE
NEW BRUNSWICK
ATLANTIC OCEAN
Adirondack Mountains
Catskill Mts
APPALACHIAN MOUNTAINS
White Mts
Lake Champlain
Finger Lakes
Long I.
Cape Cod
Cape Cod Bay
Massachusetts Bay
Nantucket I.
Martha's Vineyard
Block I.
Montauk Pt
Delaware Bay
Chesapeake Bay
Cape Charles
Cape May
Yarmouth (Nova Scotia)
Trans-Canada Highway
Mt Washington 1917
Mt Marcy 1629
Mt Katahdin 1605
Mt Tremblant 968
Peaked Mtn 689
Sugarloaf Mtn 1291
Mt Desert
Isle au Haut
Lac St-Jean
Saguenay
St Laurent
St Lawrence
St Lawrence Seaway
Ottawa
Mattawa
St Maurice
Réservoir Gouin
Résr Dozois
Résr Cabonga
Résr Baskatong
Résr Decelles
L. Abitibi
L. Parent
L. Simard
L. Kipawa
L. Dumoine
L. Kempt
L. Témiscouata
Chesuncook L.
Moosehead L.
Sebago L.
Winnipesaukee L.
Kawartha Lakes
Rideau Lakes
L. Muskoka
L. Simcoe
Lake of Bays
Thousand Is
Cranberry L.
Saranac Lakes
Great Sacandaga L.
Oneida L.
Mohawk
Hudson
Connecticut
Delaware
Susquehanna
West Branch
Potomac
Shenandoah
James
Rappahannock
Roanoke
Kennebec
Penobscot
St John
St Croix
Allegheny
Genesee
Coulonge
Gatineau
Lièvre
Madawaska
Clarion
Kerr Resr
John H.
Dismal Swamp
L. Gaston
Taschereau
La Sarre
Amos
Senneterre
Beattyville
Rouyn
Noranda
Malartic
Val-d'Or
Englehart
New Liskeard
Haileybury
Temiscaming
Sturgeon Falls
North Bay
Callander
Sundridge
Burk's Falls
Algonquin Park
Huntsville
Bracebridge
Gravenhurst
Midland
Orillia
Barrie
Lindsay
Peterborough
Lakefield
Trenton
Belleville
Napanee
Kingston
Gananoque
Brockville
Prescott
Smiths Falls
Perth
Bancroft
Barry's Bay
Carleton Place
Arnprior
Renfrew
Pembroke
Deep River
Fort Coulonge
Lake Traverse
Maniwaki
Mont-Laurier
Gracefield
Gatineau
Hull
Vanier
Ottawa
Winchester
Cornwall
Valleyfield
Beauharnois
Montebello
Lachute
St-Jérôme
St Jovite
Labelle
Joliette
Laval
Montréal
Longueuil
La Salle
St-Jean
Cowansville
Granby
Windsor
Sherbrooke
Magog
Coaticook
Sorel
Drummondville
Victoriaville
Thetford Mines
Trois-Rivières
Cap-de-la-Madeleine
Grand Mère
Shawinigan
La Tuque
Québec
Lévis
Montmorency
Ile d'Orléans
Montmagny
Ste Anne de Beaupré
Baie St Paul
St-Félicien
Roberval
Chambord
Alma
Jonquière
Arvida
Chicoutimi
Les Escoumins
Tadoussac
St-Siméon
Rimouski
Trois Pistoles
Rivière-du-Loup
Cabano
St-Pascal
St-Joseph
St-Georges
Lac Mégantic
Jackman Sta
Causapscal
Dalhousie
Campbellton
Kedgwick
Edmundston
Ft Kent
St Leonard
Grand Falls
Van Buren
Eagle Lake
Caribou
Presque Isle
Bath
Hartland
Woodstock
Fredericton
Houlton
Millinocket
Rockwood
Lincoln
Howland
Milltown
Calais
Eastport
Machias
Old Town
Bangor
Brewer
Bucksport
Ellsworth
Bar Harbor
Belfast
Waterville
Augusta
Skowhegan
Bingham
Farmington
Stratton
Flagstaff
Rumford
Berlin
Lewiston
Auburn
Brunswick
Bath
Falmouth
Portland
Thomaston
Westbrook
Saco
Biddeford
Sanford
Somersworth
Dover
Kittery
Portsmouth
Rochester
Laconia
Concord
Exeter
Manchester
Haverhill
Lawrence
Lowell
Gloucester
Lynn
Cambridge
Boston
Quincy
Weymouth
Brockton
Provincetown
Newton
Attleboro
Taunton
Providence
Warwick
Fall River
New Bedford
Hyannis
Newport
Westerly
New London
Norwich
Woonsocket
Worcester
Fitchburg
Milford
Springfield
Chicopee
Holyoke
Northampton
Westfield
Pittsfield
Greenfield
Brattleboro
Keene
Nashua
Claremont
Hanover
White River Jct.
Lebanon
Littleton
Lincoln
Conway
Groveton
Lancaster
St Johnsbury
Newport
St Albans
Burlington
Winooski
Montpelier
Middlebury
Randolph
Rutland
Springfield
Bellows Falls
Bennington
Troy
Albany
Cohoes
Schenectady
Amsterdam
Saratoga Springs
Glens Falls
Whitehall
L. George
Ticonderoga
Plattsburgh
Malone
Massena
Ogdensburg
Morristown
Saranac Lake
Lake Placid
Clayton
Watertown
Carthage
Pulaski
Boonville
Oswego
Fulton
Rome
Utica
Herkimer
Syracuse
Solvay
Auburn
Seneca Falls
Geneva
Cortland
Ithaca
Watkins Glen
Horseheads
Elmira
Corning
Bath
Binghamton
Endicott
Oneonta
Sidney
Delhi
Stamford
Catskill
Saugerties
Kingston
Liberty
Poughkeepsie
Middletown
Newburgh
West Point
Peekskill
White Plains
Yonkers
Rochester
Greece
Brockport
Albion
Lockport
Batavia
Geneseo
Niagara Falls
St Catharines
Tonawanda
Buffalo
Lackawanna
E. Aurora
Gowanda
Dunkirk
Fredonia
Westfield
Jamestown
Salamanca
Olean
Toronto
Mississauga
Brampton
Scarborough
Whitby
Oshawa
Bowmanville
Cobourg
Oakville
Hamilton
Grimsby
Welland
Port Colborne
North East
Warren
Smethport
Galeton
Mansfield
Towanda
Honesdale
Carbondale
Dickson City
Scranton
Old Forge
Wilkes-Barre
Plymouth
Berwick
Hazleton
Williamsport
Jersey Shore
Lock Haven
Muncy
Sunbury
State College
Philipsburg
Renovo
St Marys
Ridgway
Kane
Union City
Oil City
Franklin
Clarion
Du Bois
Kittanning
Butler
Indiana
Altoona
Lewistown
Pittsburgh
McKeesport
Johnstown
Greensburg
Clairton
Monessen
Connellsville
Uniontown
Somerset
Breezewood
Carlisle
Harrisburg
Lebanon
Pottsville
Reading
Pottstown
Allentown
Bethlehem
Easton
Lancaster
York
Columbia
Chambersburg
Gettysburg
Hanover
Norristown
Bristol
Philadelphia
Chester
Camden
Wilmington
Newark
Trenton
Levittown
Princeton
New Brunswick
Long Branch
Asbury Park
Paterson
Newark
Jersey City
Elizabeth
New York
Long Beach
Bay Shore
Southampton
Montauk
Greenport
Stamford
Norwalk
Greenwich
Bridgeport
New Haven
Meriden
Waterbury
Danbury
Bristol
New Britain
Torrington
Hartford
Manchester
Windsor
Woodbury
Hammonton
Pleasantville
Atlantic City
Vineland
Millville
Salem
Ocean City
Dover
Milford
Rehoboth Beach
Georgetown
Laurel
Salisbury
Easton
Cambridge
Aberdeen
Towson
Baltimore
Dundalk
Columbia
Annapolis
Silver Spring
Bethesda
Washington
D.C.
Arlington
Alexandria
Woodbridge
Frederick
Catonsville
Hagerstown
Cumberland
Hancock
Martinsburg
Harpers Ferry
Morgantown
Romney
Winchester
Strasburg
Front Royal
Parsons
Elkins
Harrisonburg
New Market
Shenandoah Nat. Park
Culpeper
Warrenton
Fredericksburg
Lexington Park
Gordonsville
Charlottesville
Waynesboro
Staunton
Monterey
Lexington
Covington
Buena Vista
Amherst
Lynchburg
Roanoke
Bowling Green
Ashland
Reedville
Tappahannock
Richmond
Bon Air
Colonial Hgts
Hopewell
Petersburg
Williamsburg
Yorktown
Hampton
Newport News
Norfolk
Portsmouth
Virginia Beach
Chesapeake
Suffolk
Franklin
Emporia
South Hill
South Boston
Halifax
Chatham
Martinsville
Danville
Reidsville
Roxboro
Henderson
Roanoke Rapids
Murfreesboro
Elizabeth City
Onancock
Eastville
Pocomoke City
Crisfield
Lewes
80
75
70
40
D
E
F
1
2
3

Sacramento
Stockton
San Francisco
Oakland
Berkeley
San Jose
Fresno
Bakersfield
Los Angeles
San Diego
Santa Barbara
Riverside
Long Beach
Santa Ana
Pasadena
Monterey
Salinas
Modesto
Merced
Visalia
Tulare
Hanford
San Luis Obispo
Santa Maria
Ventura
Oxnard
Lancaster
Palmdale
Mojave
San Bernardino
Oceanside
Tonopah
Goldfield
Bishop
Lone Pine
Yosemite National Park
Kings Canyon National Park
Sequoia National Park
Death Valley National Monument
SIERRA NEVADA
COAST RANGES
San Joaquin Valley
Diablo Range
Santa Lucia Range
Santa Cruz Mts
Temblor Range
Sierra Madre Mts
San Rafael Mts
Santa Ynez Mts
San Gabriel Mts
White Mts
Inyo Mts
Panamint Ra.
Mojave Desert
N E V A D A
Mt Whitney 4418
Mt Lyell 3997
Mt Dana 3978
P A C I F I C
O C E A N
Santa Barbara Channel
Channel Islands
San Miguel
Santa Rosa
Santa Cruz
Santa Catalina
San Clemente
San Pedro Channel
Gulf of Santa Catalina
Outer Santa Barbara Channel
Monterey Bay
Santa Monica Bay
Kauai
Niihau
Oahu
Honolulu
Molokai
Lanai
Maui
Kahoolawe
Hawaii
Mauna Kea 4201
Mauna Loa 4169
Hilo
Kailua
Hawaii Volcanoes Nat. Park
Kauai Channel
Alenuihaha Channel
PACIFIC
OCEAN
USA, HAWAII
1:5M
1:2.5M

KENTUCKY
VIRGINIA
TENNESSEE
NORTH CAROLINA
SOUTH CAROLINA
GEORGIA
ALABAMA
FLORIDA
CUMBERLAND PLATEAU
APPALACHIAN MTS
BLUE RIDGE
Great Smoky Mts
Clinch Mountains
ATLANTIC OCEAN
GULF OF MEXICO
THE BAHAMAS
Straits of Florida
Great Bahama Bank
Little Bahama Bank
Hopkinsville
Bowling Green
Corbin
Harlan
Big Stone Gap
Middlesboro
Albany
Glasgow
Russellville
Guthrie
Clarksville
Springfield
Gallatin
Hendersonville
Nashville
Dickson
Lebanon
Livingston
Cookeville
Center Hill L.
Dale Hollow L.
Oak Ridge
Crossville
Harriman
Knoxville
Morristown
Greeneville
Kingsport
Bristol
Elizabethton
Johnson City
Abingdon
Mt Rogers 1743
Galax
Hillsville
Martinsville
Danville
Chatham
South Boston
Halifax
Kerr Resr
South Hill
Emporia
L. Gaston
Franklin
Suffolk
Portsmouth
Chesapeake
Dismal Swamp
Murfreesboro
Elizabeth City
Kitty Hawk
Albemarle Sd
Manteo
Ahoskie
Roanoke Rapids
Roxboro
Henderson
Enfield
Windsor
Rocky Mt
Tarboro
Williamston
Phelps Lake
Washington
Englehard
Pamlico Sound
Cape Hatteras
Greenville
Wilson
Raleigh
Durham
Chapel Hill
Cary
Burlington
Greensboro
Winston-Salem
High Point
Thomasville
Lexington
Statesville
Salisbury
Asheboro
Sanford
Smithfield
Goldsboro
La Grange
Kinston
Dunn
New Bern
Havelock
Morehead City
Cape Lookout
Jacksonville
Onslow Bay
Wilmington
Carolina Beach
Cape Fear
Whiteville
Lumberton
Elizabethtown
Burgaw
Clinton
Fayetteville
Pinehurst
Southern Pines
Laurinburg
Rockingham
Albemarle
Concord
Kannapolis
Charlotte
Gastonia
Shelby
L. Norman
Hickory
Morganton
Mt Mitchell 2037
Boone
Lenoir
Mt Airy
Reidsville
Asheville
Hendersonville
Waynesville
Great Smoky Mts Nat. Park
Gatlinburg
Maryville
Athens
Cleveland
Chattanooga
East Ridge
Chickamauga Lake
Dayton
Manchester
Tullahoma
Shelbyville
McMinnville
Murfreesboro
Franklin
Columbia
Pulaski
Fayetteville
Tims Ford L.
Duck
Bridgeport
Huntsville
Athens
Decatur
Hartselle
Tennessee
Scottsboro
Guntersville L.
Guntersville
Arab
Cullman
Attalla
Gadsden
Weiss L.
Lewis Smith L.
Jasper
Center Point
Birmingham
Mountain Brook
Homewood
Bessemer
Talladega
Anniston
Sylacauga
Alabaster
Centreville
Clanton
Cahaba
Alexander City
Roanoke
Lanett
L. Martin
Auburn
Opelika
Prattville
Montgomery
Selma
Phenix City
Columbus
Union Springs
Fort Deposit
Greenville
Eufaula
Walter F. George Resr
Troy
Evergreen
Andalusia
Conecuh
Enterprise
Ozark
Daleville
Opp
Dothan
Florala
Brewton
Crestview
Milton
De Funiak Springs
Marianna
Valparaiso
Fort Walton Beach
Lynn Haven
Panama City
St Andrew Bay
Port St Joe
C. San Blas
Apalachicola
St George I.
Apalachicola Bay
Apalachee Bay
Carrabelle
Crawfordville
Tallahassee
Chattahoochee
Seminole
Bainbridge
Thomasville
Perry
Live Oak
Greenville
Jasper
Valdosta
Lake City
Baldwin
Jacksonville
Jacksonville Beach
Orange Park
St Augustine
Fernandina Beach
Okefenokee Swamp
Folkston
Kingsland
St Marys
Homerville
Waycross
Satilla
Brunswick
St Simons I.
St Andrew Sound
Darien
Jesup
Ludowici
Baxley
Douglas
Fitzgerald
Ashburn
Tifton
Moultrie
Albany
Camilla
Blakely
Flint
Cordele
Americus
Dawson
Cuthbert
Ocmulgee
McRae
Lyons
Vidalia
Altamaha
Eastman
Dublin
Warner Robins
Perry
Macon
Thomaston
La Grange
Barnesville
Griffin
Newnan
Carrollton
Bremen
Cedartown
Rome
Calhoun
Dalton
Mt Oglethorpe
Dahlonega
Trion
Ft Payne
Blue Ridge
Murphy
Franklin
Brevard
Toccoa
Gainesville
L. Sidney Lanier
Buford
Marietta
Smyrna
Roswell
Decatur
Atlanta
E. Point
College Park
Forest Park
Covington
Eatonton
Milledgeville
L. Sinclair
Louisville
Oconee
Wrightsville
Swainsboro
Statesboro
Pembroke
Savannah
Windsor Forest
St Catherines I.
Waynesboro
Augusta
N. Augusta
Thomson
Washington
Athens
Elberton
Abbeville
Hartwell Resr
Anderson
Easley
Westminster
Greenville
Spartanburg
Gaffney
Landrum
Union
Laurens
Newberry
Greenwood
Saluda
L. Murray
Calhoun Falls
Clark Hill Resr
Johnston
Aiken
Batesburg
Columbia
Cayce
Sumter
Camden
Kershaw
Lancaster
Chester
Rock Hill
Whitmire
Winnsboro
Cheraw
Darlington
Florence
Marion
Lake City
Conway
Myrtle Beach
Long Bay
Georgetown
Manning
L. Marion
Santee
Moultrie
St Stephen
St George
Goose Creek
Bamberg
Orangeburg
Edisto
Allendale
Varnville
Estill
Walterboro
Charleston
Cape Romain
Beaufort
Ridgeland
St Helena Sound
Port Royal Sound
Savannah
Gainesville
High Springs
Palatka
Bunnell
Chiefland
Williston
Suwannee
Ocala
Ormond Beach
Daytona Beach
New Smyrna Beach
Waccasassa Bay
Leesburg
Wildwood
Sanford
Winter Park
Titusville
Apopka
Orlando
Winter Garden
Pine Hills
Disney World
Dade City
Brooksville
Hudson
Cape Canaveral
Merritt Island
Cocoa
Rockledge
Melbourne
Palm Bay
Lakeland
Plant City
Dunedin
Clearwater
Largo
Pinellas Park
Tampa
St Petersburg
Tampa Bay
Ruskin
Palmetto
Bradenton
Sarasota
Wauchula
Lake Wales
Avon Park
L. Kissimmee
Sebring
Istokpoga
Okeechobee
Lake Okeechobee
Arcadia
Peace
Port Charlotte
Punta Gorda
Charlotte Harb.
Pine I.
Caloosahatchee
Fort Myers
La Belle
Bonita Springs
Naples
The Everglades
Big Cypress Swamp
Marco
C. Romano
Ten Thousand Islands
Gifford
Vero Beach
Fort Pierce
Stuart
Pahokee
Belle Glade
South Bay
Riviera Beach
W. Palm Beach
Palm Beach
Lake Worth
Boynton Beach
Delray Beach
Boca Raton
Pompano Beach
Ft Lauderdale
Plantation
Hollywood
Carol City
N. Miami Beach
Hialeah
N. Miami
Miami
Miami Beach
South Miami
Coral Gables
Cutler Ridge
Biscayne Bay
Homestead
National Park
Florida City
Ponce de Leon Bay
Cape Sable
Florida Bay
Key Largo
Islamorada
Florida Keys
Marathon
Big Pine Key
Boca Chica Key
Key West
Marquesas Keys
Little Abaco
Cooper's Town
Marsh Harbour
Great Abaco
West End
Freeport City
Lucaya
Grand Bahama
Bimini Is.
Berry Is.
Nassau
Adelaide
New Providence
Nicholl's Town
Andros Town
Andros
Kemp's Bay
A
B
C
1
2
3
4
85
80
35
30
25

1:5M
0 50 100 150 200 km
0 50 100 mls

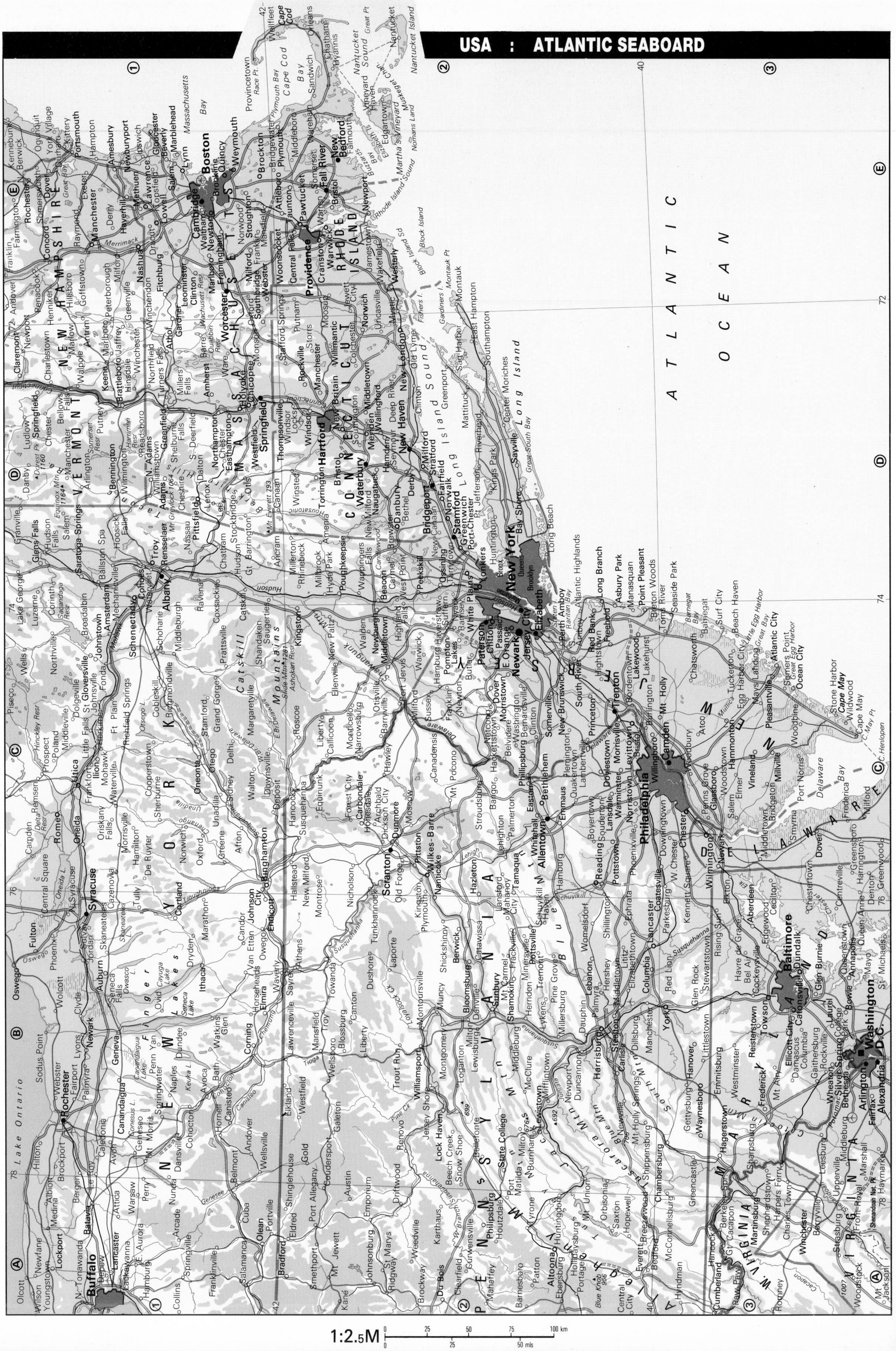
ATLANTIC OCEAN
NEW YORK
PENNSYLVANIA
NEW HAMPSHIRE
VERMONT
MASSACHUSETTS
CONNECTICUT
RHODE ISLAND
NEW JERSEY
DELAWARE
MARYLAND
VIRGINIA
W. VIRGINIA
Lake Ontario
Long Island
Long Island Sound
Cape Cod
Cape Cod Bay
Massachusetts Bay
Delaware Bay
Nantucket Sound
Martha's Vineyard
Nantucket Island
Catskill Mountains
Finger Lakes
Blue Mtn
Boston
Providence
Hartford
New Haven
New York
Newark
Jersey City
Philadelphia
Trenton
Baltimore
Washington D.C.
Harrisburg
Albany
Syracuse
Rochester
Buffalo
Springfield
Worcester
Allentown
Scranton
Wilkes-Barre
Wilmington
Camden
Atlantic City
Cape May
1:2.5M
0 25 50 75 100 km
0 25 50 mls

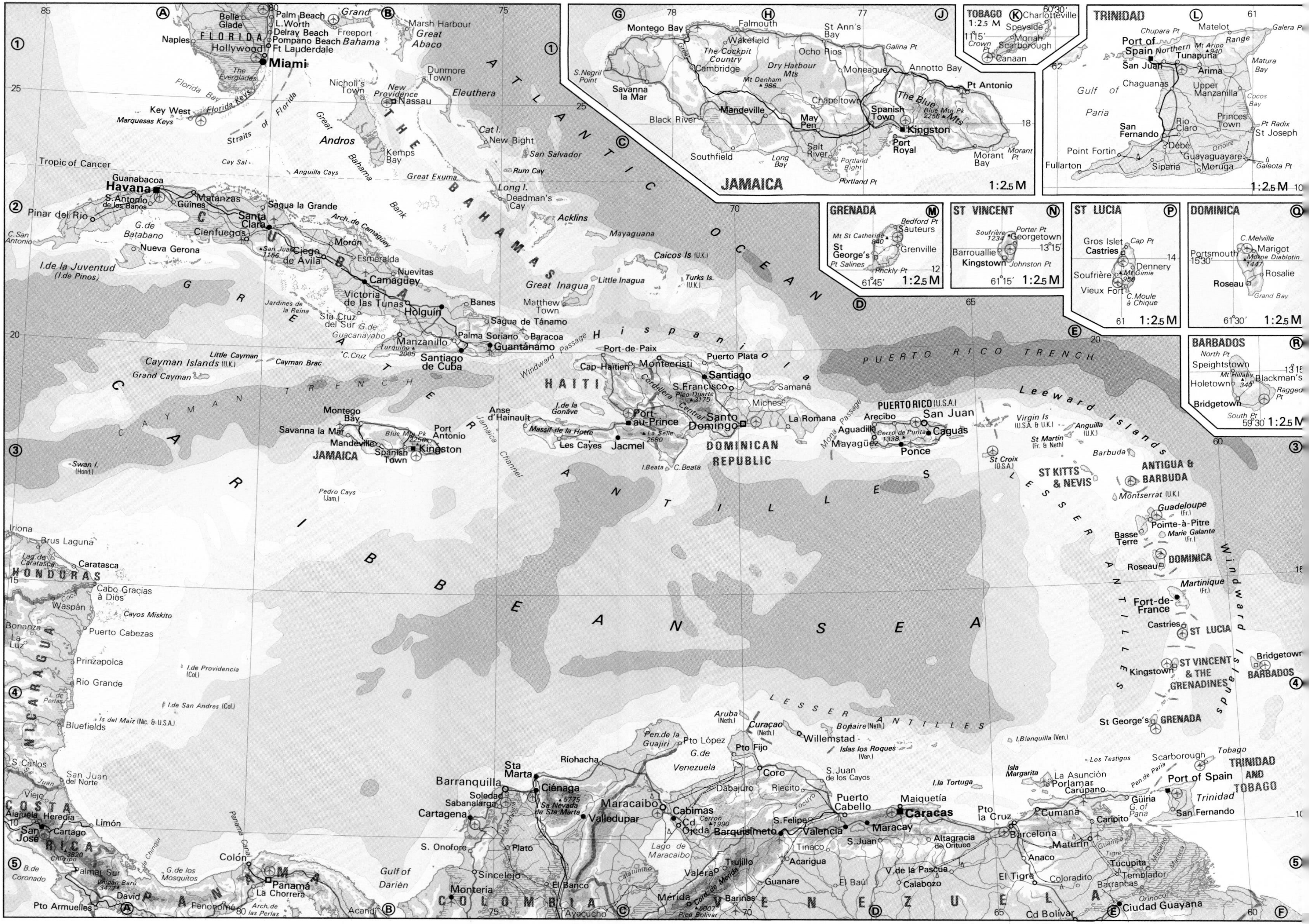

1:10M
0 100 200 300 400 km
0 100 200 mls

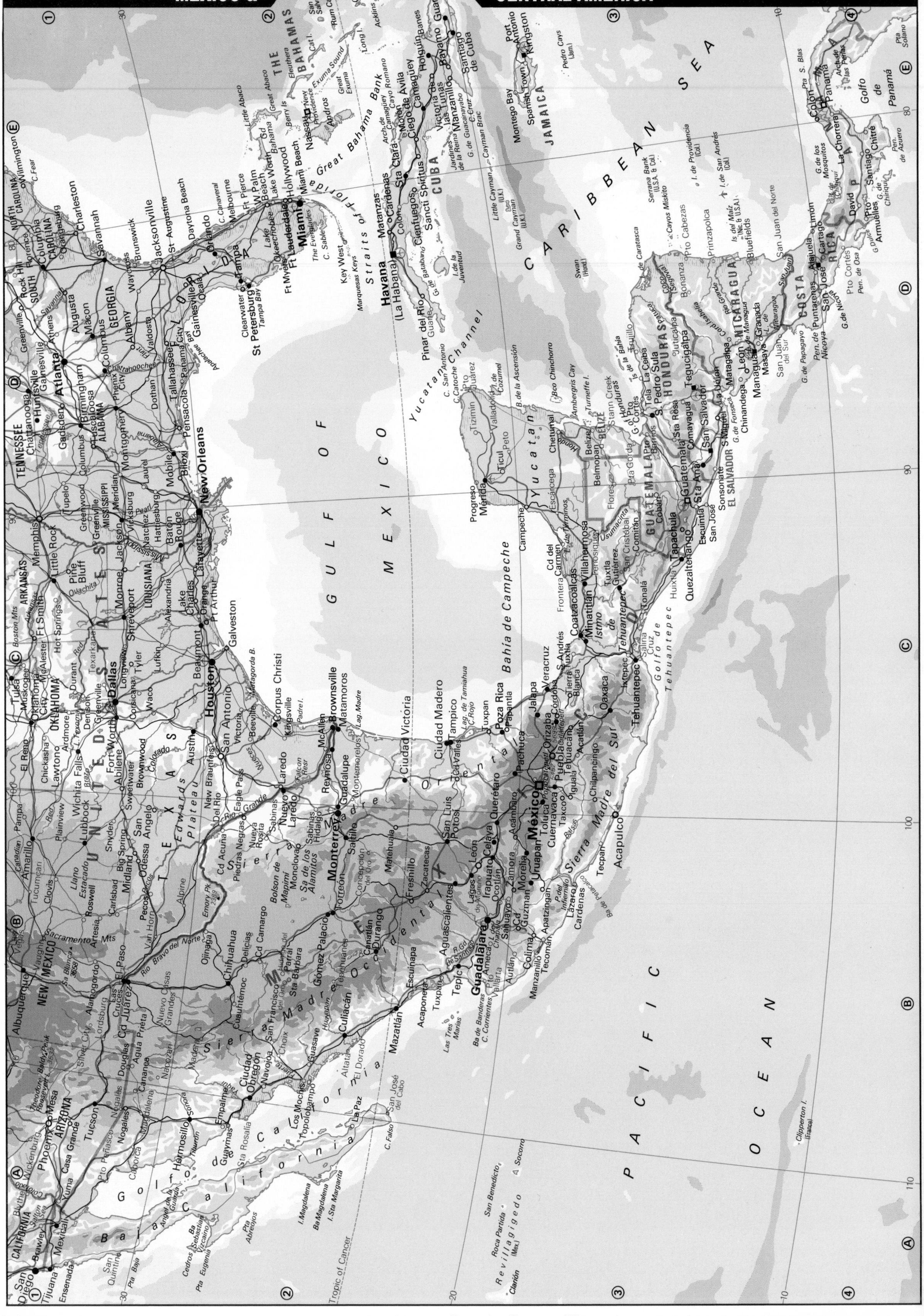

GULF OF MEXICO
CARIBBEAN SEA
PACIFIC OCEAN
UNITED STATES
MEXICO
CUBA
JAMAICA
THE BAHAMAS
BELIZE
GUATEMALA
HONDURAS
EL SALVADOR
NICARAGUA
COSTA RICA
PANAMA
TEXAS
NEW MEXICO
ARIZONA
CALIFORNIA
OKLAHOMA
ARKANSAS
LOUISIANA
MISSISSIPPI
ALABAMA
GEORGIA
FLORIDA
TENNESSEE
SOUTH CAROLINA
NORTH CAROLINA
Sierra Madre Occidental
Sierra Madre Oriental
Sierra Madre del Sur
Golfo de California
Baja California
Bahía de Campeche
Yucatan
Yucatan Channel
Istmo de Tehuantepec
Golfo de Tehuantepec
Golfo de Panamá
Straits of Florida
Great Bahama Bank
Edwards Plateau
Tropic of Cancer
Mexico
Guadalajara
Monterrey
Houston
Dallas
New Orleans
Miami
Havana (La Habana)
Acapulco
Veracruz
Mérida
Puebla
Oaxaca
Chihuahua
Ciudad Juárez
El Paso
San Antonio
Tampico
Torreón
Culiacán
Mazatlán
Hermosillo
Tucson
Phoenix
Atlanta
Jacksonville
Tampa
Guatemala
Tegucigalpa
San Salvador
Managua
San José
Panamá
Kingston
Belize
Santiago de Cuba
0 200 400 600 km

U.S.A.
Miami
THE BAHAMAS
Gulf of Mexico
Tropic of Cancer
Habana
Mérida
CUBA
Guantanamo
Santiago de Cuba
MEXICO
BELIZE
Belmopan
DOMINICAN REP.
Santiago
HAITI
JAMAICA
Kingston
Port-au-Prince
Santo Domingo
Pto Rico (U.S.A.)
San Juan
ANTIGUA & BARBUDA
ST KITTS-NEVIS
Guadeloupe (Fr.)
DOMINICA
Martinique (Fr.)
GUATEMALA
Guatemala
HONDURAS
Tegucigalpa
S.Salvador
EL SALVADOR
NICARAGUA
Managua
CARIBBEAN SEA
ST LUCIA
ST VINCENT & THE GRENADINES
BARBADOS
GRENADA
Neth. Antilles
Curaçao
COSTA RICA
S.José
Barranquilla
Sta Marta
Cartagena
Maracaibo
Caracas
Barcelona
Port of Spain
TRINIDAD & TOBAGO
Colón
Panamá
PANAMA
Barquisimeto
Cd. Bolivar
Cd. Guayana
Orinoco
S.Cristóbal
VENEZUELA
Georgetown
GUYANA
I. del Coco (C.R.)
Medellín
Manizales
Bogotá
Paramaribo
Cayenne
SURINAM
FR. GUIANA
Malpelo (Col.)
Buenaventura
Cali
COLOMBIA
Popayán
Pasto
Boa Vista
Branco
S.Lorenzo
Quito
ECUADOR
Guayaquil
Galapagos Is (Ecu.)
Putumayo
Negro
Macapá
I. de Marajó
S.Pedro e S.Paulo (Braz.)
Equator
Belém
Amazon
Manaus
Santarém
Iquitos
Juruá
Purus
Madeira
Tapajós
Xingu
Tocantins
São Luís
Codó
Teresina
Sobral
Fortaleza
Rocas
I. Fernando de Noronha (Braz.)
Piura
Chiclayo
Marañón
Ucayali
Natal
João Pessoa
Recife
Trujillo
Chimbote
PERU
Pto Velho
Rio Branco
Araguaia
Juazeiro
Maceió
Aracajú
Alagoinhas
Salvador
BRAZIL
Callao
Lima
Huancayo
Pto Maldonado
Cuzco
Arequipa
La Paz
Cáceres
Cuiabá
Goiânia
Brasília
São Francisco
Ilhéus
SOUTH PACIFIC OCEAN
BOLIVIA
Oruro
Cochabamba
Sucre
Sta Cruz
Montes Claros
Corinto
Belo Horizonte
Arica
Corumbá
Iquique
Campo Grande
Dourados
Ribeirão Prêto
Juiz de Fora
Vitória
Campos
Campinas
PARAGUAY
Concepción
Paraná
Rio de Janeiro
São Paulo
Santos
Trindade (Braz.)
Antofagasta
Asunción
Foz do Iguacu
Ponta Grossa
Curitiba
Salta
Tropic of Capricorn
S.Félix (Chile)
S.Miguel de Tucumán
Salado
Resistencia
Posadas
Florianópolis
Uruguay
CHILE
Córdoba
Sante Fe
Paraná
Rivera
Paysandu
Pelotas
Pto Alegre
Rio Grande
URUGUAY
Viña del Mar
Valparaiso
Mendoza
Santiago
Rosario
Buenos Aires
Montevideo
SOUTH ATLANTIC OCEAN
Juan Fernández Is. (Chile)
R. de la Plata
Talca
Concepción
Mar del Plata
Colorado
Bahía Blanca
Temuco
Valdivia
Negro
Pto Montt
ARGENTINA
Chico
Cmd. Rivadavia
G.San Jorge
Deseado
Falkland Is (U.K.)
Stanley
Río Gallegos
Pto Natales
Punta Arenas
Tierra del Fuego
Cape Horn
S.Georgia (U.K.)
S.Shetland Is (U.K.)
S.Orkney Is (U.K.)
S.Sandwich Is (U.K.)
ANTARCTICA
1:35M
0 250 500 750 1000 1250 km
0 250 500 750 mls

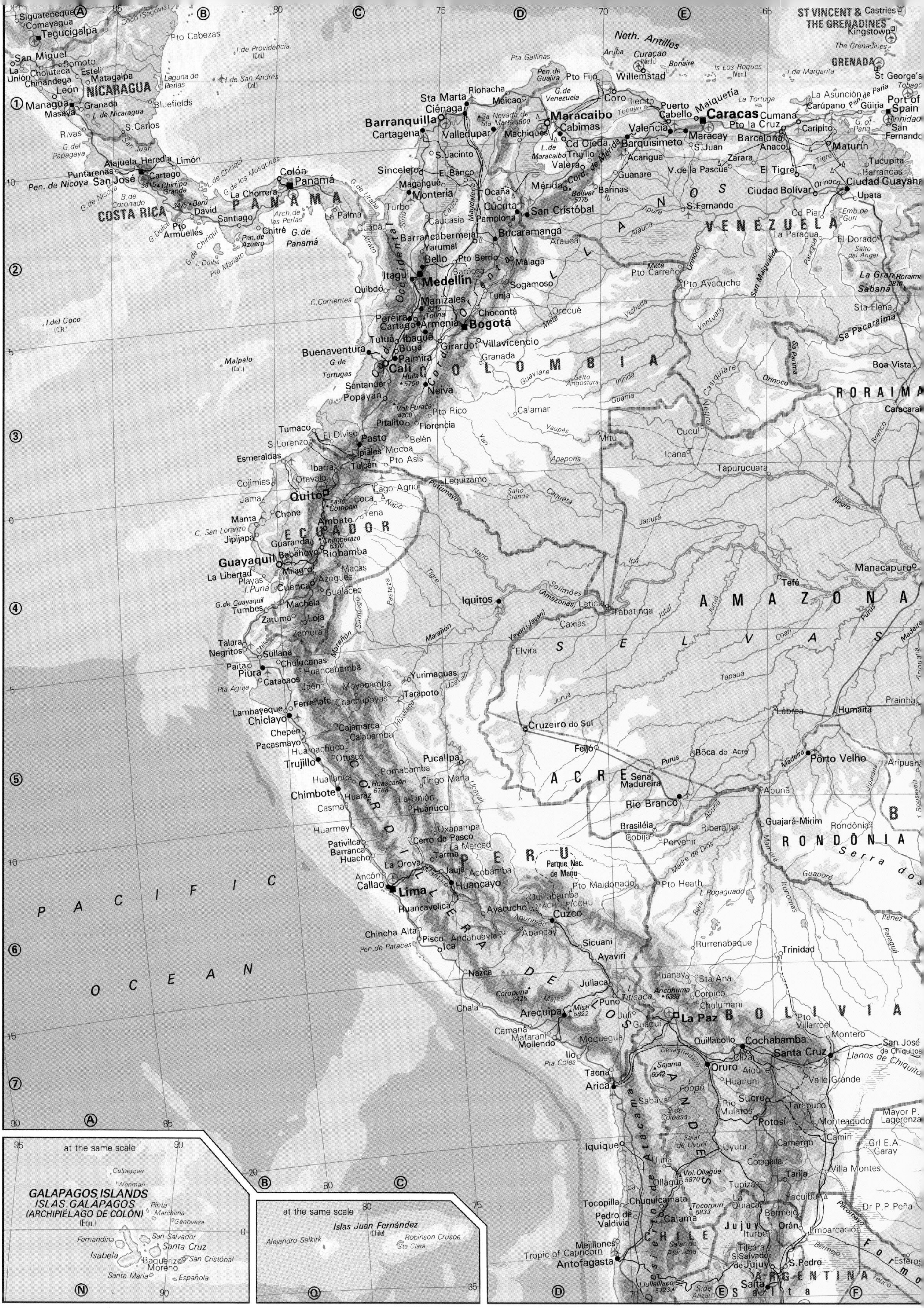

1:15M

0 200 400 600 km

0 100 200 300 mls

ST VINCENT & Castries
THE GRENADINES
Kingstown
The Grenadines
GRENADA
St George's

PACIFIC

OCEAN

NICARAGUA

COSTA RICA

PANAMA

COLOMBIA

ECUADOR

PERU

VENEZUELA

RORAIMA

AMAZONAS
SELVAS

ACRE

RONDÔNIA

BOLIVIA

CHILE

ARGENTINA

Siguatepeque
Comayagua
Tegucigalpa
San Miguel
La Choluteca
Unión Chinandega Esteli
León Matagalpa
Managua Granada
Masaya
Rivas
S. Carlos
Alajuela Heredia Limón
Puntarenas San José Cartago
Pen. de Nicoya

Pto Cabezas
I. de Providencia
(Col.)
I. de San Andrés
(Col.)
Laguna de
Perlas
Bluefields
L. de Nicaragua
Puerto Cabezas
San Juan
L. de los Mosquitos
Colón
Panamá
La Chorrera
La Palma
Arch. de
las Perlas
Santiago
Chitré
David
Pto Armuelles

Riohacha
Sta Marta
Ciénaga
Maicao
Barranquilla
Cartagena
Valledupar
Sincelejo
Magangué
Montería
S. Jacinto
El Banco
Caucasia
Turbo
Barrancabermeja
Yarumal
Bello Pto Berrío
Itagüí
Medellín
Quibdó
Manizales
Pereira
Cartago Armenia
Tuluá Ibagué
Buenaventura
Buga
Cali Palmira
Santander
Popayán
Neiva

Maracaibo
Cabimas
Coro
Valencia
Caracas
Barquisimeto Maracay
San Cristóbal
Bucaramanga
Cúcuta
Pamplona
Málaga
Sogamoso
Tunja
Chocontá
Bogotá
Girardot
Villavicencio
Granada

Tumaco
El Diviso
Pasto
Esmeraldas
S. Lorenzo
Ibarra
Otavalo
Cojimíes
Jama
Quito
Manta
Chone
Cotopaxi
Guaranda
Jipijapa
Ambato
Riobamba
Guayaquil
Babahoyo
Milagro
La Libertad
Playas
Cuenca
Machala
Tumbes
Zaruma
Loja
Zamora
Talara
Negritos
Sullana
Paita
Piura
Catacaos
Chulucanas
Lambayeque
Chiclayo
Chepén
Pacasmayo
Trujillo
Chimbote
Casma
Huarmey

Galápagos

1:15M

GALAPAGOS ISLANDS
ISLAS GALÁPAGOS
(ARCHIPIÉLAGO DE COLÓN)
(Equ.)
at the same scale
Culpepper
Wenman
Pinta
Marchena
Genovesa
Fernandina
Isabela
San Salvador
Santa Cruz
Baquerizo
Moreno San Cristóbal
Santa María
Española

Islas Juan Fernández
(Chile)
at the same scale
Alejandro Selkirk
Robinson Crusoe
Sta Clara
Mayor

BARBADOS
Bridgetown
TRINIDAD AND TOBAGO
ATLANTIC OCEAN
GUYANA
SURINAM
FRENCH GUIANA
AMAPÁ
PARÁ
MARANHÃO
CEARÁ
RIO GRANDE DO NORTE
PARAÍBA
PERNAMBUCO
ALAGOAS
SERGIPE
PIAUÍ
BAHIA
TOCANTINS
GOIÁS
MATO GROSSO
MATO GROSSO DO SUL
MINAS GERAIS
ESPÍRITO SANTO
SÃO PAULO
PARANÁ
PARAGUAY
BRAZIL
Mabaruma
Charity
Suddie
Leguan I.
Georgetown
New Amsterdam
Nieuw Amsterdam
V.en Hoop
Bartica
Linden
Paramaribo
Nieuw Nickerie
Totness
Marienburg
Albina
Sinnamary
I. du Diable (Devil's I.)
Kourou
Cayenne
Cabo Orange
Apoera
Witagron
Blommestemmeer
Kaieteur Falls
Julianatop 1280
Bonfim
Lethem
Oiapoque
Serra Tumucumaque
Amapá
Ilha de Maracá
Sa do Navio
Macapá
Pto Santana
C. Maguarinho
I. de Marajó
B. de Marajó
Salinópolis
Bragança
Capanema
Belém
Abaetetuba
Cametá
Oriximiná
Obidos
Amazonas
Monte Alegre
Santarém
Manaus
Careiro
Itacoatiara
Altamira
Aveiro
Itaituba
Parque Nacional Amazonia
Pimenta
Tucuruí
Alcântara
Pinheiro
B. de São Marcos
São Luís
Rosário
Parnaíba
Camocim
Acaraú
Monção
Chapadinha
Bacabal
Coroatá
Codó
Caxias
Sobral
Itapipoca
Caucaia
Fortaleza (Ceará)
Piripiri
Sta Quitéria
Canindé
Aracati
Campo Maior
Nova Russas
Quixadá
Teresina
Castelo
Crateús
Morada N.
Areia Branca
Macau
Pta do Calcanhar
I. Fernando de Noronha
Rocas
Marabá
Imperatriz
Grajaú
Pto Franco
Mombaça
Tauá
Acopiara
Mossoró
Natal
Iguatu
Patu
Caicó
Carolina
Araguaína
Balsas
Floriano
Oeiras
Picos
J. do Norte
Crato
Sousa
Patos
Cabedelo
João Pessoa
Campina Grande
Jacareacanga
S. Félix
Serra do Cachimbo
Cachimbo
C. do Araguaia
Paulistana
Salgueiro
Ouricuri
Sa Talhada
Limoeiro
Caruaru
Olinda
Recife (Pernambuco)
S. Raimundo Nonato
Petrolina
Juazeiro
Garanhuns
Palmares
Palmeira dos Índ.
Jaboatão
Barreiros
Maceió
Cach. de P. Afonso
Barragem de Sobradinho
Barra
Sen. do Bonfim
Propriá
Arapiraca
Penedo
Jacobina
Lagarto
Aracajú
Estância
Vilhena
Sa dos Caiabis
Sa Formosa
Pto Artur
São Félix
Ilha do Bananal
Barreiras
Ibotirama
R. de Jacuípe
Serrinha
Chapada Diamantina
Feira de S.
Alagoinhas
Iaçu
Cachoeira
Bom Jesus da Lapa
Castro Alves
Salvador (Bahia)
B. de T. os Santos
Valença
Jequié
Caetité
Mato Grosso
Uruaçu
Aruanã
Cuiabá
Planalto de Mato Grosso
Fatima du Sul
Ceres
Formosa
Jaraguá
Brasília
Goiás
Vitória da Conquista
Itabuna
Ilhéus
Ipiaú
San Matías
Cáceres
Aragarças
Pirenópolis
Anápolis
São Francisco
Januária
Porteirinha
Itapetinga
Rondonópolis
Iporá
Goiânia
Salinas
Canavieiras
Montes Claros
Belmonte
Caldas Novas
Paracatu
Araçuaí
Pôrto Seguro
Mineiros
Rio Verde
Jataí
Pirapora
Sa do Chifre
Itamaraju
Coxim
Itumbiara
Goiandira
João Pinheiro
Teófilo Otôni
Nanuque
Catalão
Diamantina
Corumbá
Pto Suárez
Araguari
Patos de Minas
Corinto
Curvelo
Gov. Valadares
Uberlândia
Barragem de São Simão
Iturama
Barragem Água Vermelha
Araxá
Sete Lagoas
Itabira
São Mateus
Uberaba
Belo Horizonte
Cnl Fabriciano
Linhares
Campo Grande
Ilha Solteira Dam
Rubinéia
Fernandópolis
Caratinga
Colatina
Aquidauana
Três Lagoas
S. José do R. Prêto
Barretos
Franca
Divinópolis
Manhuaçu
Cariacica
Fte Olimpo
Araçatuba
Passos
S. João del Rei
Con. Lafaiete
Ponte Nova
Vitória
Vila Velha
Jardim
Panorama
Catanduva
Ribeirão Prêto
Lavras
Carangola
Pto Murtinho
Pres. Epitácio
Represa Pôrto Primavera
Tupã
Poços de Caldas
Barbacena
Cachoeiro de Itapemirim
Filadelfia
Pedro J. Caballero
Dourados
Pres. Prudente
Araraquara
Marília
São Carlos
Juiz de Fora
Itaperuna
Ponta Porã
Pto E. Cunha
Assis
Bauru
Limeira
Volta Redonda
S. João da Barra
Campos
Pozo Colorado
Concepción
Horqueta
Represa Ilha Grande
Paranavaí
Ourinhos
Piracicaba
Sa de Mantiqueira
Nova Friburgo
Petrópolis
Maringá
Londrina
Umuarama
Campinas
Jundiaí
Barra Mansa
Magé
Niterói
San Pedro
Apucarana
Jacarézinho
Sorocaba
C. Mourão
Itapeva
Itapetininga
São Paulo
Rio de Janeiro
Mts de Aracanguy
Guaíra
Goio-Erê
Itararé
Juquiá
Santos
São Vicente
Asunción
Luque
Toledo
Cascavel
Castro
Itanhaém
Iguape
Equator
Tocantins
Xingu
Tapajós
Araguaia
Parnaíba
São Francisco
Paraná
Paraguay
Grande
Paranaíba
Teles Pires
Juruena
Iriri
Jari
Paru
Maroni
Litani
Corantijn
Essequibo
Gurupi
Capim
Pindaré
Jequitinhonha
Doce
Serra do Espinhaço
Velhas
Taquari
Aporé
Arinos
Parecis
Mortes
55
50
45
40
35
30
10
5
0
15
20
H
J
K
L
M
1
2
3
4
5
6
7
8

BOLIVIA
BRAZIL
MATO GROSSO DO SUL
MINAS GERAIS
SÃO PAULO
PARANÁ
SANTA CATARINA
RIO GRANDE DO SUL
PARAGUAY
URUGUAY
ARGENTINA
CHILE
GRAN CHACO
ATLANTIC OCEAN
FALKLAND ISLANDS (ISLAS MALVINAS) (U.K.)
West Falkland
East Falkland
Stanley
South Georgia (U.K.)
Grytviken
Shag Rocks
Tropic of Capricorn
Desierto de Atacama
Cordillera de los Andes
Arica
Tacna
Iquique
Tocopilla
Antofagasta
Calama
Taltal
Chañaral
Copiapó
Vallenar
La Serena
Coquimbo
Ovalle
Valparaíso
Viña del Mar
Santiago
Rancagua
Curicó
Talca
Chillán
Concepción
Talcahuano
Los Angeles
Temuco
Valdivia
Osorno
Puerto Montt
Castro
Coihaique
Punta Arenas
Puerto Natales
Oruro
Sucre
Potosí
Tarija
Corumbá
Campo Grande
Asunción
Encarnación
Foz do Iguaçu
Curitiba
São Paulo
Rio de Janeiro
Belo Horizonte
Santos
Florianópolis
Pôrto Alegre
Pelotas
Rio Grande
Montevideo
Punta del Este
Buenos Aires
La Plata
Mar del Plata
Bahía Blanca
Rosario
Santa Fe
Paraná
Córdoba
Mendoza
San Juan
La Rioja
Catamarca
Tucumán
Salta
Jujuy
Santiago del Estero
Resistencia
Corrientes
Posadas
Formosa
Neuquén
Viedma
Carmen de Patagones
Trelew
Rawson
Comodoro Rivadavia
Caleta Olivia
Puerto Deseado
San Julián
Río Gallegos
Ushuaia
Tierra del Fuego
C. de Hornos (C. Horn)
Río de la Plata
Golfo San Matías
Golfo San Jorge
La Pampa
Río Negro
Chubut
Santa Cruz

1:15M 0 200 400 600 km 0 100 200 300 mls

B R A Z I L
BOLIVIA
PARAGUAY
ARGENTINA
ARG.
ATLANTIC OCEAN
Tropic of Capricorn
MATO GROSSO
GOIÁS
BAHIA
MINAS GERAIS
MATO GROSSO DO SUL
SÃO PAULO
PARANÁ
ESPÍRITO SANTO
RIO DE JANEIRO
DISTRITO FEDERAL
Brasília
Salvador (Bahia)
Rio de Janeiro
São Paulo
Belo Horizonte
Goiânia
Anápolis
Campo Grande
Curitiba
Vitória
Niterói
Santos
Campinas
Uberlândia
Uberaba
Ribeirão Prêto
Londrina
Cuiabá
Corumbá
Cáceres
Asunción
Montes Claros
Teófilo Otôni
Gov. Valadares
Juiz de Fora
Campos
Ilhéus
Vitória da Conquista
Jequié
Dourados
Foz do Iguaçu
Ponta Grossa
Maringá
Cascavel
Sa Geral de Goiás
Serra do Espinhaço
Planalto do Mato Grosso
Pantanal
Paranaíba
São Francisco
Araguaia
Paraguay
1:7.5M
0 100 200 300 km
0 50 100 150 mls

Portland
Seattle
Vancouver I.
Vancouver
U.S.A.
Anchorage
Mt McKinley
6194
Yukon
Teller
Bering Str.
Prince Rupert
Juneau
ROCKY MTS
Fairbanks
Dawson
Alaska (U.S.A.)
Chukchi Sea
Vankarem
Pevek
Ambarchik
Wrangel I. (O. Vrangel'ya)
East Siberian Sea
Prudhoe Bay
Barrow
Calgary
Edmonton
Inuvik
Norman Wells
Mackenzie
Beaufort Sea
Gt Bear L.
Gt Slave L.
Yellowknife
Saskatoon
L. Athabasca
CANADA
Coppermine
Banks I.
Victoria I.
McClure Str.
Flin Fon
L. Winnipeg
Churchill
Queen Elizabeth Islands
N. Magnetic Pole (1990)
Resolute
G. of Boothia
Eureka
Ellesmere I.
Alert
North Pole
Hudson Bay
Southampton I.
Foxe Basin
Baffin I.
Pond Inlet
Nares Str.
Thule
Lincoln Sea
James B.
Fort George
Inukjuak
Tree Limit
Hudson Str.
Baffin Bay
Upernavik
Davis Str.
Greenland (Kalaallit Nunaat) (Den.)
Godhavn (Qeqertarsuaq)
Søndre Strømfjord
Godthåb (Nuuk)
Schefferville
Hebron
Nain
Labrador Sea
Gulf of St Lawrence
Newfoundland
Gander
Julianehåb (Qaqortoq)
K. Farvel
Ammassalik (Angmagssalik)
Watkins Bjerge 3700
Scoresbysund
Denmark Strait
ICELAND
Reykjavik
ATLANTIC OCEAN
Nord
Svalbard (Spitsbergen) (Nor.)
Greenland Sea
Bjørnøya (Bear I.) (Nor.)
Jan Mayen (Nor.)
Norwegian Sea
Arctic Circle
Nordkapp
Tromsø
Narvik
NORWAY
SWEDEN
FINLAND
Umeå
Oulu
Murmansk
White Sea
Arkhangel'sk
St Petersburg (Leningrad)
Yaroslavl'
Nizhniy Novgorod
Kotlas
Sev. Dvina
Kirov
Kazan'
Samara
Perm'
Ufa
Magnitogorsk
Orsk
Aktyubinsk
Yekaterinburg
Syktyvkar
Mezen'
Serov
Ural'skiy Khrebet
Barents Sea
Kara Sea
Novaya Zemlya
Zemlya Frantsa Iosifa
average minimum extent of sea ice
Severnaya Zemlya
Laptev Sea
Novosibirskiye Ostrova
Vorkuta
Salekhard
Berezovo
Nadym
Tobol'sk
Tselinograd
Omsk
Novosibirsk
Barnaul
Krasnoyarsk
Yenisey
Turukhansk
Noril'sk
Dudinka
Dikson
Khatanga
Nordvik
Tiksi
Lena
Zhigansk
Kazach'ye
Verkhoyansk
Polyarnyy
Indigirka
Kolyma
Ust'Nera
Yakutsk
Aldan
Ayan
Blagoveshchensk
Skovorodino
Chul'man
Amur
Chita
Ulan-Ude
Oz. Baykal
Irkutsk
Ust'Kut
RUSSIAN FEDERATION
CHINA
ATLANTIC OCEAN
Antarctic Circle
Orcadas (Arg.)
S. Orkney Is (U.K.)
Signy (U.K.)
Falkland Is (U.K.)
Scotia Sea
S. Shetland Is (U.K.)
King George I.
ARGENTINA
Tierra del Fuego
CHILE
Drake Passage
Graham Land
Palmer Arch.
Antarctic Peninsula
Palmer Land
Alexander I.
Charcot I.
Bellingshausen Sea
Weddell Sea
C. Norvegia
Sanae (S.A.)
Maitri (India)
Georg Forster (Germany)
Novolozarevskaya (Former USSR)
Asuka (Japan)
Prinsesse Astrid Kyst
Prinsesse Ragnhild Kyst
Georg Von Neumayer (Germany)
Syowa (Jap.)
Molodezhnaya (Former USSR)
Enderby Land
Dronning Maud Land
Coats Land
Halley (U.K.)
General Belgrano II (Arg.)
Ronne Ice Shelf
Berkner I.
Pensacola Mts
Mawson (Aust.)
Mac. Robertson Land
3355
Pr. Charles Mts
C. Darnley
Amery Ice Shelf
Lambert Gl.
Zhongshan (China)
Davis (Aust.)
Heard I. (Aust.)
GREATER ANTARCTICA
American Highland
INDIAN OCEAN
Ellsworth Land
Siple (U.S.)
4897
Vinson Massif
South Pole
Amundsen-Scott (U.S.)
Transantarctic Mts
LESSER ANTARCTICA
3022
Mt Seelig
Peter I Øy (Nor.)
Thurston I.
Walgreen Coast
Queen Mary Land
Mirnyy (Former USSR)
Shackleton Ice Shelf
Vostok (Former USSR)
Q. Maud Mts
Mt Kirkpatrick
4528
Mt Markham
4351
PACIFIC OCEAN
Amundsen Sea
Mt Sidley 4181
Marie Byrd Land
Ross Ice Shelf
Roosevelt I.
Siple I.
Knox Coast
Wilkes Land
Casey (Aust.)
C. Poinsett
Scott (N.Z.)
McMurdo (U.S.)
Victoria Land
C. Colbeck
Cape Evans (Greenpeace)
Ross Sea
average minimum extent of sea ice
C. Adare
Oates Land
George V Land
Terre Adélie
Dumont d'Urville (Fr.)
S. Magnetic Pole (1990)
Leningradskaya (Former USSR)
Sturge I.
Scott I.
Balleny Is
King George Island
62°S
58°30'W
0 10 20 30km
Antarctic Research Stations
1 Commandante Ferraz (Brazil)
2 Henryk Arctowski (Poland)
3 Teniente Jubany (Argentina)
4 King Sejong (Korea)
5 Artigas (Uruguay)
6 Teniente Rodolfo Marsh (Chile)
7 Bellingshausen (Former USSR)
8 Great Wall (China)
9 Captain Arturo Prat (Chile)
10 Esperanza (Argentina)
11 General Bernardo O'Higgins (Chile)
12 Marambio (Argentina)
13 Palmer (USA)
14 Faraday (UK)
15 General San Martin (Argentina)
16 Rothera (UK)
1:40M
0 400 800 1200 1600 km
0 400 800 mls

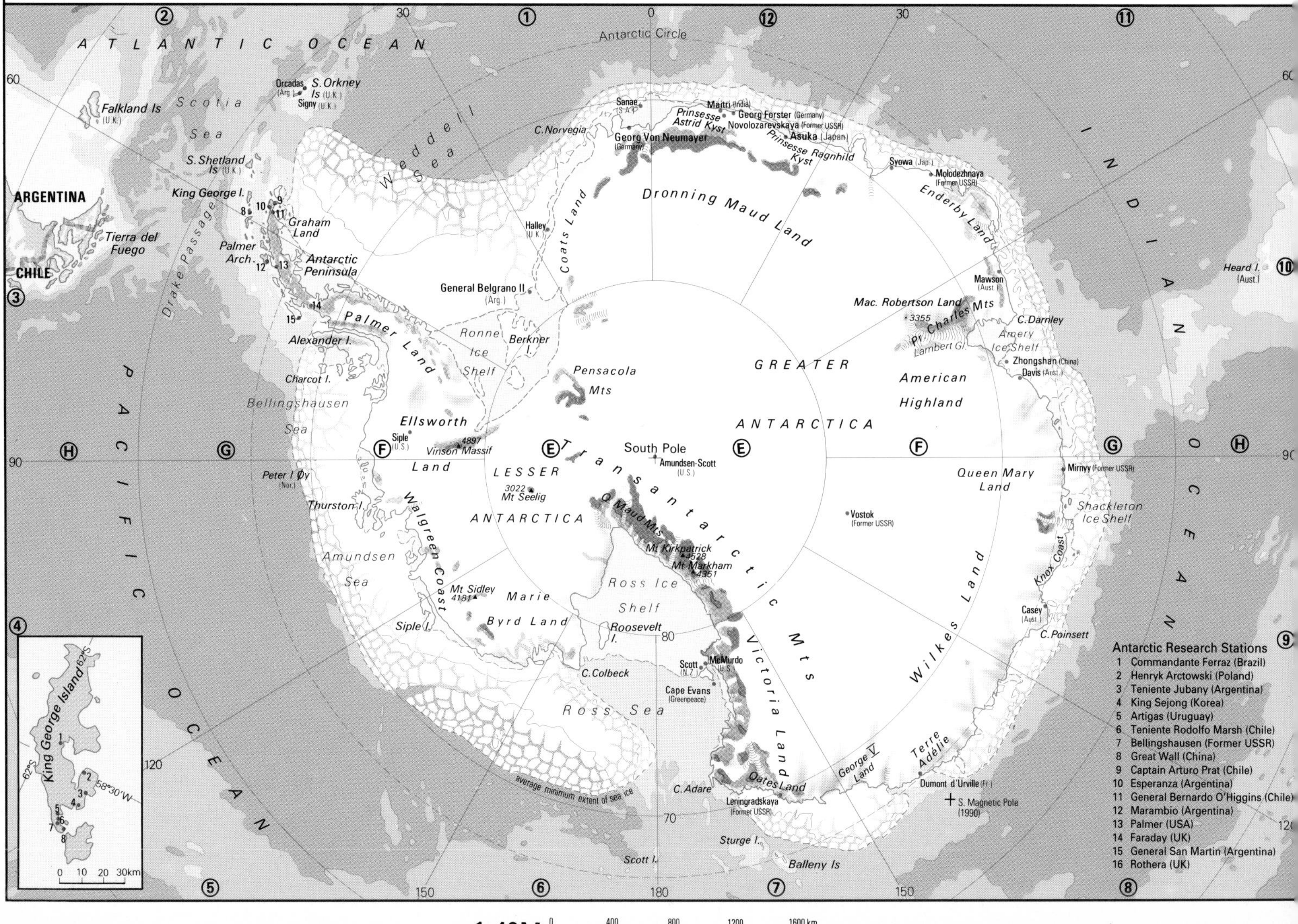

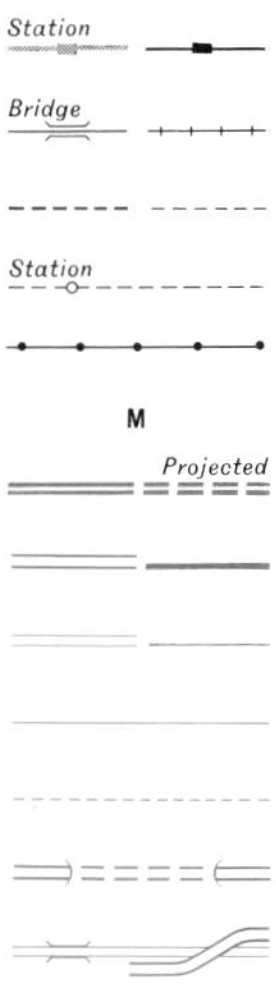

International Boundary
State Boundary
Department Boundary
City Limits
Borough, District Boundary
Military Zones
Armistice, Ceasefire Line
Demilitarised Zone
Main Railways
Other Railways
Projected Railways
Underground Railway
Aerial Cableway, Funicular
Metro Stations
Special Highway
Main Road
Secondary Road
Other Road, Street
Track
Road Tunnel
Bridge, Flyover

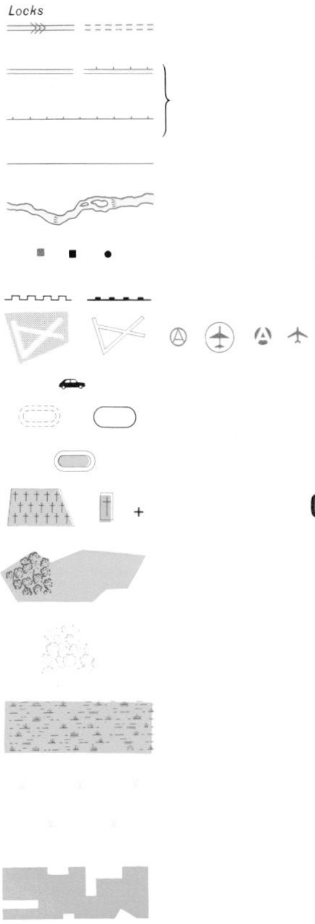

Seaway
Canals
Drainage Canal
Waterfalls, Rapids
Important Buildings
Historic Walls
Airports
Car Ferry
Racecourses
Stadium
Cemetery, Churches
Woodland, Park
Jungle
Mangrove Swamp
Farmland
Built-up Area

Amsterdam 81
Athens 83
Auckland 86
Bangkok 84
Barcelona 80
Beijing 84
Berlin 82
Bombay 87
Boston 89
Brussels 81
Buenos Aires 92
Cairo 88
Calcutta 87
Chicago 89
Copenhagen 83
Delhi 87
Geneva 82
Hamburg 82
Hong Kong 84
Istanbul 88
Jerusalem 88
London 78
Los Angeles 91
Madrid 80
Manhattan 90
Melbourne 86
Mexico City 92
Milan 82
Montreal 89
Moscow 83
Nairobi 88
New York 90
Osaka 85
Ottawa 89
Paris 79
Perth 86
Rio de Janeiro 92
Rome 80
San Francisco 91
Santiago 92
São Paulo 92
Seoul 85
Shanghai 84
Singapore 87
Stockholm 83
Sydney 86
Tokyo 85
Toronto 89
Vienna 81
Washington 91

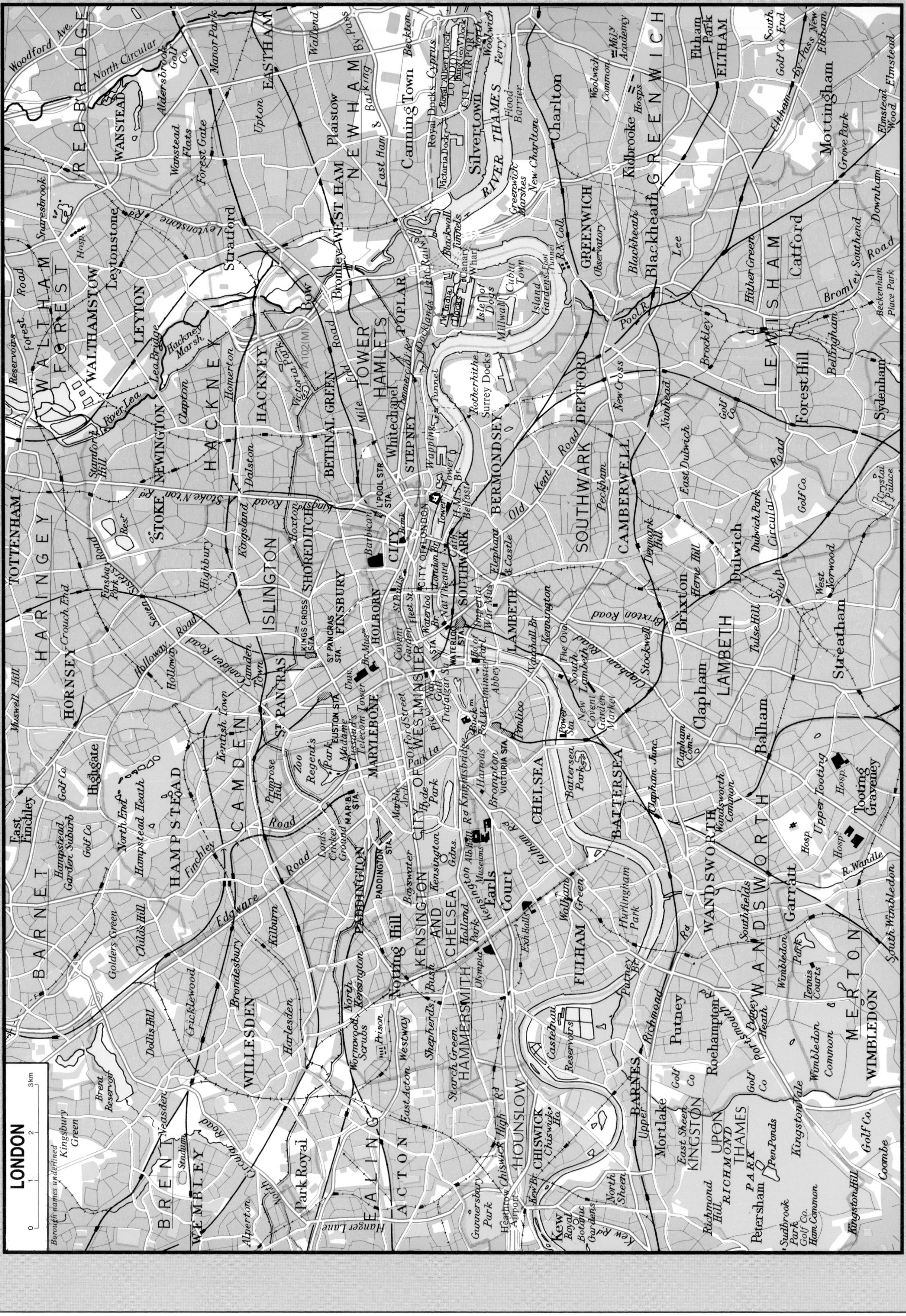
LONDON
Borough names underlined
0 1 2 3km
BARNET
HARINGEY
REDBRIDGE
WALTHAM FOREST
NEWHAM
GREENWICH
LEWISHAM
HACKNEY
TOWER HAMLETS
ISLINGTON
CAMDEN
CITY OF WESTMINSTER
KENSINGTON AND CHELSEA
HAMMERSMITH
SOUTHWARK
LAMBETH
WANDSWORTH
MERTON
BRENT
EALING
HOUNSLOW
KINGSTON UPON THAMES
RICHMOND
RIVER THAMES
TOTTENHAM
WALTHAMSTOW
LEYTON
STOKE NEWINGTON
HORNSEY
HAMPSTEAD
WILLESDEN
WEMBLEY
ACTON
CHISWICK
FULHAM
CHELSEA
BATTERSEA
BERMONDSEY
DEPTFORD
CAMBERWELL
WIMBLEDON
WANSTEAD
EAST HAM
WEST HAM
POPLAR
STEPNEY
SHOREDITCH
FINSBURY
HOLBORN
MARYLEBONE
ST PANCRAS
PADDINGTON
BARNES
ELTHAM
CITY AIRPORT
Canning Town
Silvertown
Charlton
Stratford
Leytonstone
Plaistow
Blackheath
Catford
Forest Hill
Sydenham
Mottingham
Brixton
Dulwich
Streatham
Clapham
Balham
Tooting
Putney
Roehampton
Mortlake
Kew
Park Royal
Notting Hill
Whitechapel
Isle of Dogs
Surrey Docks
Peckham
Earls Court
Hyde Park
Regent's Park
Wimbledon Common

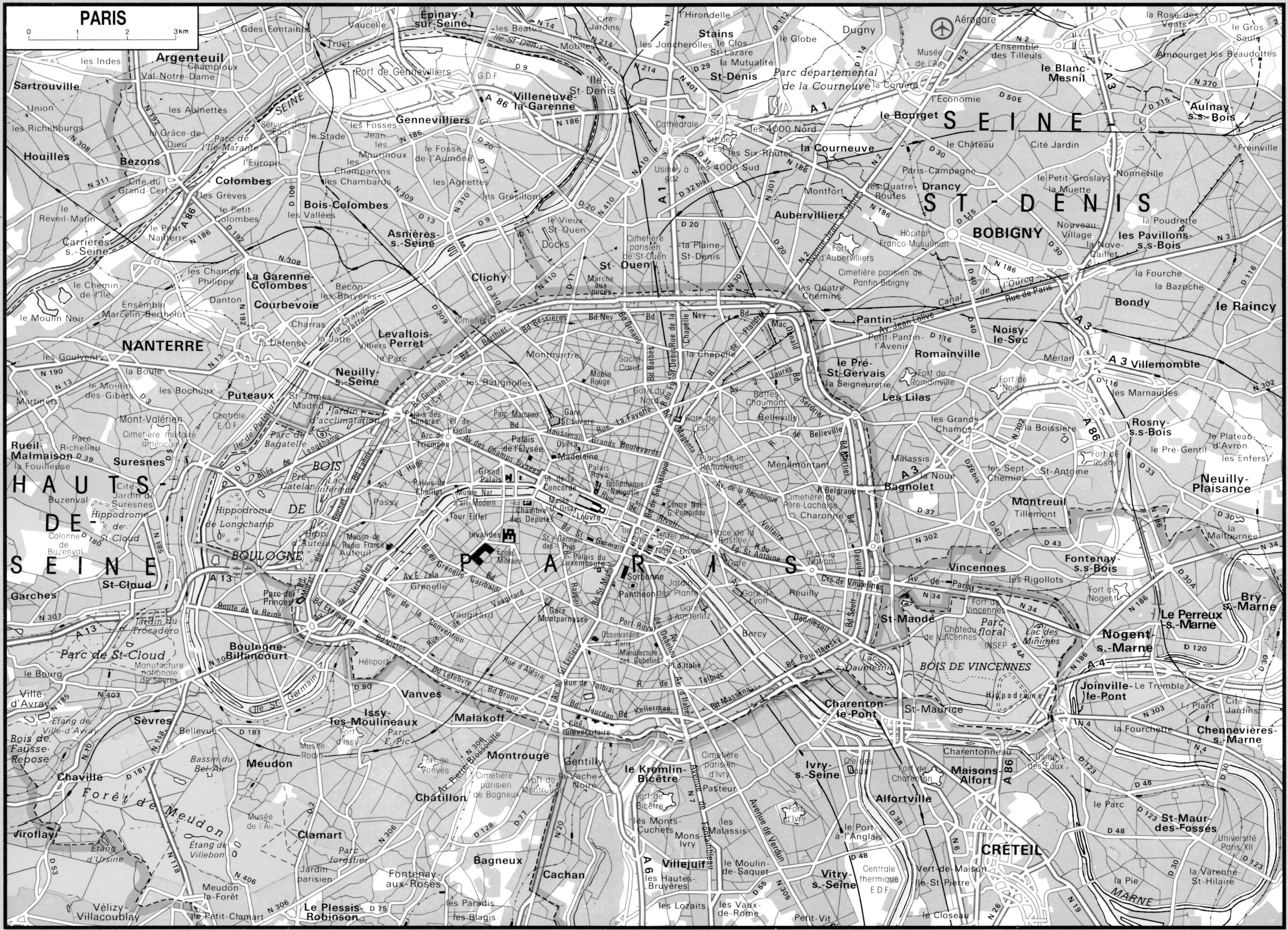

PARIS
0 1 2 3km
SEINE-ST-DENIS
HAUTS-DE-SEINE
PARIS
Argenteuil
Sartrouville
Houilles
Bezons
Colombes
Bois-Colombes
Gennevilliers
Villeneuve-la-Garenne
Epinay-sur-Seine
Asnières-s.-Seine
Clichy
Levallois-Perret
Neuilly-s.-Seine
Courbevoie
La Garenne-Colombes
Puteaux
NANTERRE
Rueil-Malmaison
Suresnes
St-Cloud
Garches
Boulogne-Billancourt
Sèvres
Chaville
Meudon
Issy-les-Moulineaux
Vanves
Malakoff
Montrouge
Châtillon
Clamart
Bagneux
Cachan
Fontenay-aux-Roses
Le Plessis-Robinson
Vélizy-Villacoublay
Viroflay
Gentilly
le Kremlin-Bicêtre
Villejuif
Ivry-s.-Seine
Vitry-s.-Seine
Alfortville
Maisons-Alfort
CRÉTEIL
Charenton-le-Pont
St-Maurice
St-Maur-des-Fossés
Joinville-le-Pont
Chennevières-s.-Marne
Nogent-s.-Marne
Le Perreux-s.-Marne
Bry-s.-Marne
Fontenay-s.s-Bois
Vincennes
St-Mandé
Montreuil
Bagnolet
Les Lilas
Romainville
Noisy-le-Sec
le Pré-St-Gervais
Pantin
Rosny-s.s-Bois
Neuilly-Plaisance
Villemomble
le Raincy
Bondy
les Pavillons-s.s-Bois
BOBIGNY
Drancy
Aubervilliers
la Courneuve
le Bourget
Dugny
Stains
St-Denis
le Blanc-Mesnil
Aulnay-s.s-Bois
St-Ouen
BOIS DE BOULOGNE
BOIS DE VINCENNES
Forêt de Meudon
Parc de St-Cloud
Parc départemental de la Courneuve
SEINE
MARNE
A 1
A 3
A 4
A 6
A 13
A 86

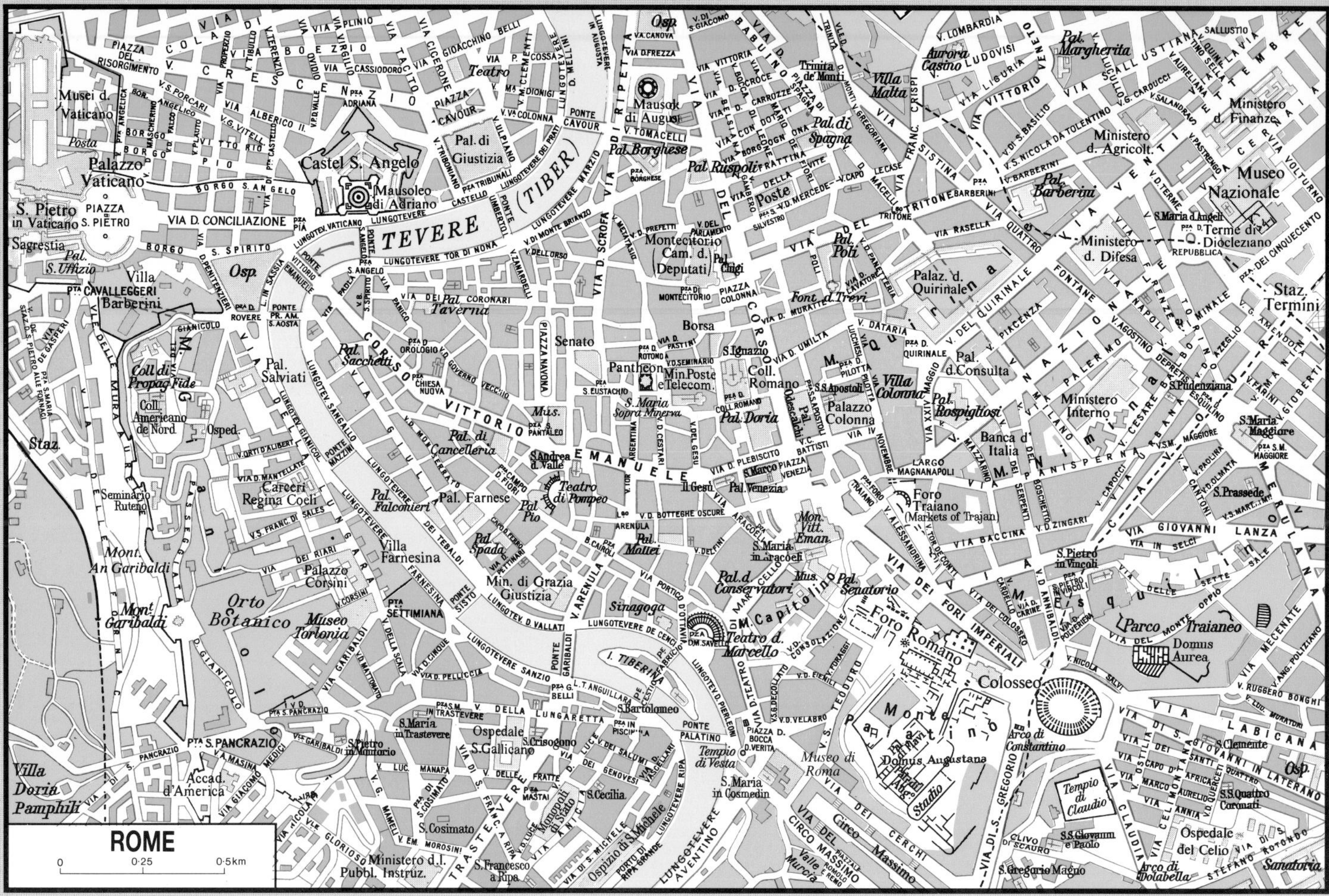
ROME
0
0·25
0·5km
TEVERE
(TIBER)
Castel S. Angelo
Mausoleo di Adriano
Palazzo Vaticano
Musei d. Vaticano
S. Pietro in Vaticano
VIA D. CONCILIAZIONE
Pal. di Giustizia
Mausoleo di Augusto
Pal. Borghese
Pal. Ruspoli
Trinità de Monti
Villa Malta
Pal. di Spagna
Pal. Margherita
Pal. Barberini
Ministero d. Agricolt.
Ministero d. Finanze
Museo Nazionale
Terme di Diocleziano
Ministero d. Difesa
Staz. Termini
Montecitorio Cam. d. Deputati
Pal. Chigi
Font. d. Trevi
Palaz. d. Quirinale
Pal. d. Consulta
Pantheon
Senato
PIAZZA NAVONA
Pal. Sacchetti
Pal. Salviati
Pal. Farnese
Pal. di Cancelleria
Teatro di Pompeo
Pal. Falconieri
Villa Farnesina
Palazzo Corsini
Orto Botanico
Museo Torlonia
Min. di Grazia Giustizia
Sinagoga
Teatro d. Marcello
M. Capitolino
Pal. Senatorio
Foro Romano
Foro Traiano (Markets of Trajan)
Colosseo
Parco Traianeo
Domus Aurea
Arco di Costantino
Domus Augustana
Stadio
Circo Massimo
Tempio di Claudio
Ospedale del Celio
Pal. Venezia
Coll. Romano
Palazzo Colonna
Villa Colonna
Pal. Rospigliosi
Banca d'Italia
Ministero Interno
S. Maria Maggiore
S. Prassede
S. Pietro in Vincoli
VIA GIOVANNI LANZA
VIA LABICANA
S. Clemente
SS. Quattro Coronati
S. Maria in Cosmedin
Tempio di Vesta
S. Maria in Trastevere
Ospedale S. Gallicano
S. Cecilia
S. Cosimato
Ministero d. I. Pubbl. Instruz.
Villa Doria Pamphili
Accad. d'America
Mont. Garibaldi
Seminario Ruteno
Carceri Regina Coeli
Coll. Americano de Nord
Coll. di Propag. Fide
Villa Barberini
Mus. Vitt. Eman.
Pal. d. Conservatori
S. Gregorio Magno
Arco di Dolabella
Sanatoria
Osp.

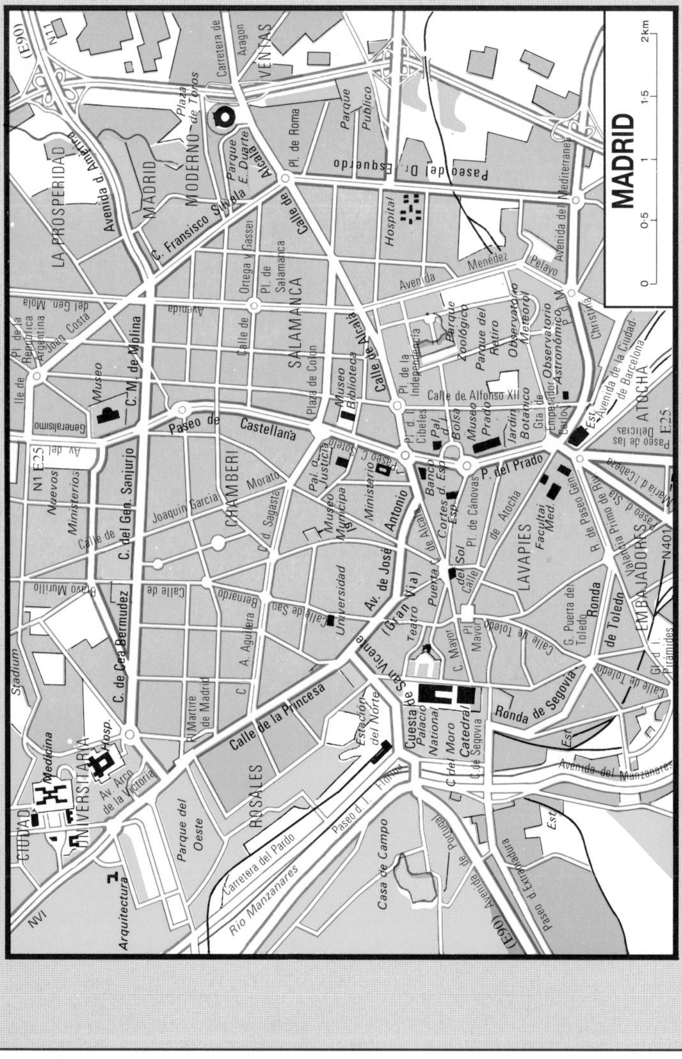
MADRID
0
0·5
1
1·5
2km
Paseo de la Castellana
Calle de Alcalá
Parque del Retiro
Gran Via
Calle de la Princesa
Palacio Nacional
Catedral
P. del Prado
SALAMANCA
CHAMBERI
LAVAPIES
ROSALES
LA PROSPERIDAD
VENTAS
ATOCHA
EMBAJADORES
CIUDAD UNIVERSITARIA
Parque del Oeste
Casa de Campo
Rio Manzanares
Ronda de Segovia
Ronda de Toledo
Puerta del Sol
Plaza de Colón
Plaza de Toros
Museo del Prado
Jardín Botánico
Observatorio Astronómico
Estación del Norte
Hospital
N401
E25
N1
NVI
E90

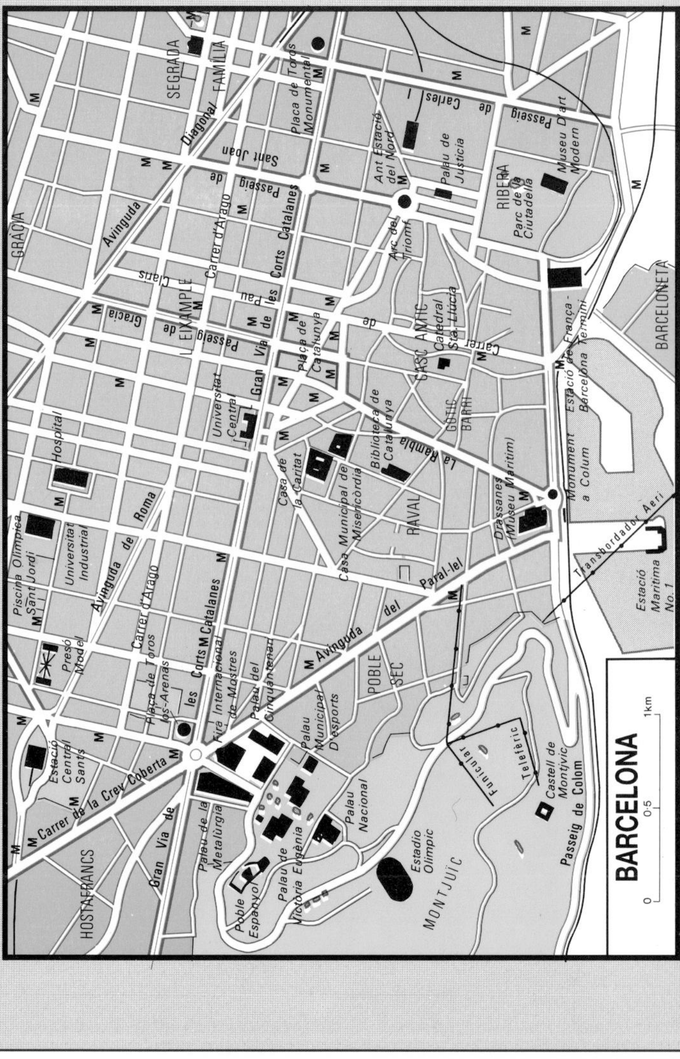
BARCELONA
0
0·5
1km
Diagonal
Gran Via de les Corts Catalanes
Passeig de Gracia
Avinguda del Paral·lel
La Rambla
Plaça de Catalunya
Plaça d'Espanya
SAGRADA FAMILIA
GRACIA
L'EIXAMPLE
RIBERA
BARCELONETA
GOTIC
RAVAL
POBLE SEC
MONTJUIC
HOSTAFRANCS
SANTS
Parc de la Ciutadella
Museu d'Art Modern
Palau de Justicia
Arc de Triomf
Estació del Nord
Estació de França
Catedral
Drassanes (Museu Marítim)
Monument a Colom
Estació Marítima No. 1
Transbordador Aeri
Castell de Montjuïc
Estadi Olímpic
Palau Nacional
Poble Espanyol
Palau dels Esports
Estació Central Sants
Plaça de Toros Monumental
Plaça de Toros les Arenas
Universitat Industrial
Passeig de Colom
Funicular
Teleferic

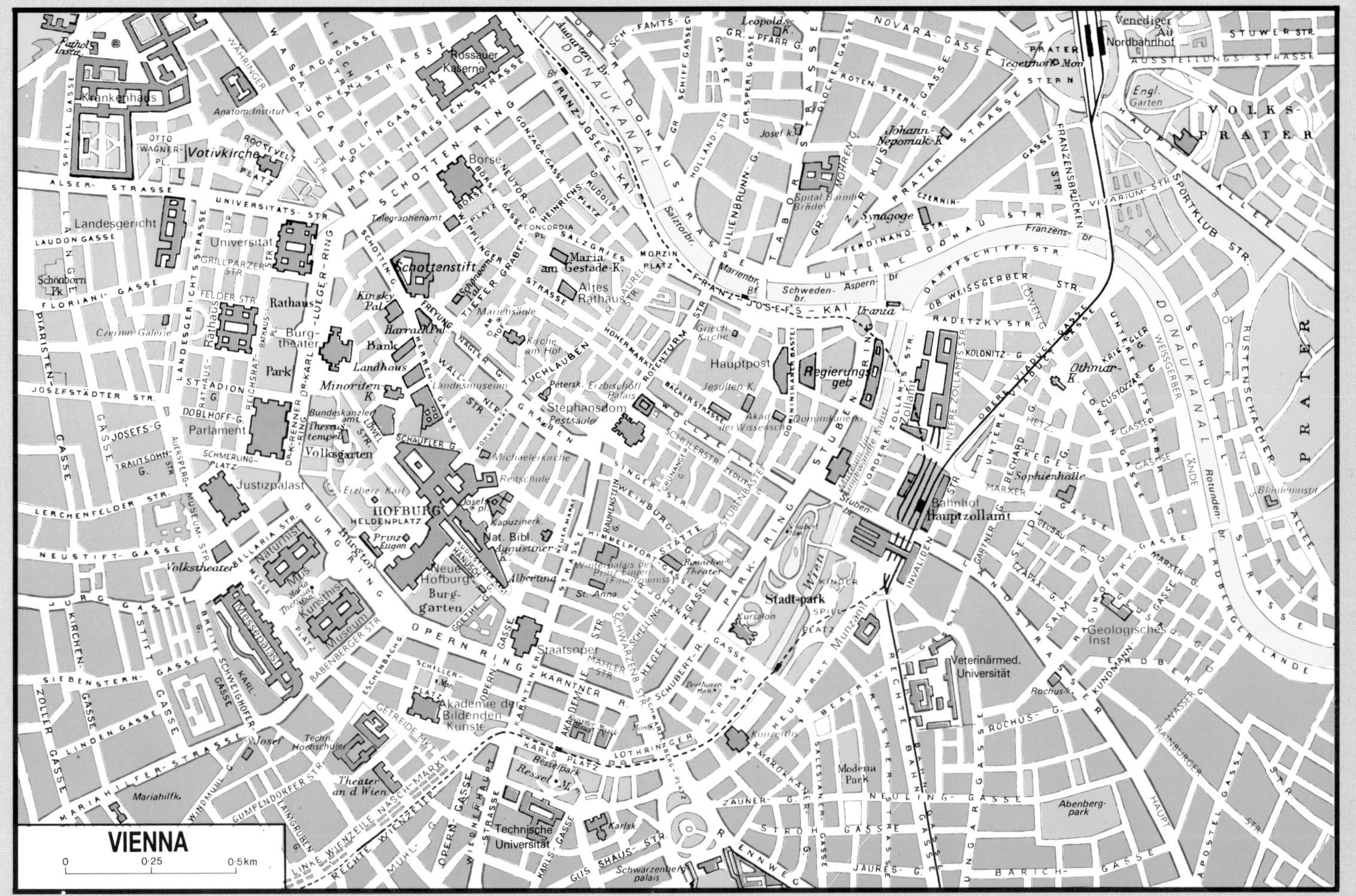
VIENNA
0
0·25
0·5km
Rossauer Kaserne
Krankenhaus
Votivkirche
Börse
Landesgericht
Universität
Schottenstift
Rathaus
Burg-theater
Parlament
Volksgarten
Justizpalast
HOFBURG
HELDENPLATZ
Nat. Bibl.
Neue Hofburg
Burg-garten
Staatsoper
Akademie der Bildenden Künste
Technische Universität
Karlsk.
Schwarzenberg palais
Stadt-park
Hauptpost
Regierungs geb
Bahnhof Hauptzollamt
Veterinärmed. Universität
Geologische Inst
Modena Park
Abenberg-park
Stephansdom
Maria am Gestade K.
Altes Rathaus
Nordbahnhof
VOLKS-PRATER
PRATER
DONAUKANAL
SCHOTTEN RING
OPERN RING
BURG RING
PARK RING
STUBEN RING
ALSER STRASSE
MARIAHILFER STRASSE

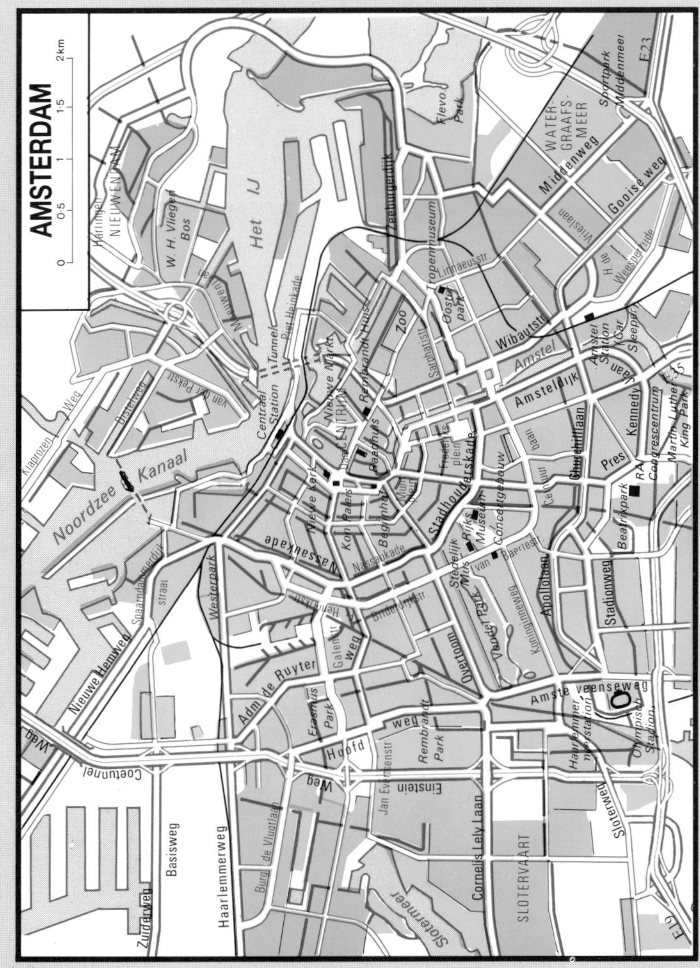
AMSTERDAM
0
0.5
1
1.5
2km
Het IJ
Noordzee Kanaal
Centraal Station
Zoo
Tropenmuseum
Amstel
Rijks Museum
Concertgebouw
Vondel Park
Stadionweg
Olympisch Stadion
Rembrandt Park
Erasmus Park
Westerpark
Nieuwe Hemweg
Haarlemmerweg
Basisweg
Einstein
Cornelis Lely Laan
SLOTERVAART
Sloterweg
Sloterweer
Amstelveenseweg
Adm. de Ruyter
Amstelkade
Wibautstr.
Gooise weg
Flevo Park
WATER-GRAAFS-MEER
Middenweg
NIEUWENDAM
W. H. Vliegen Bos

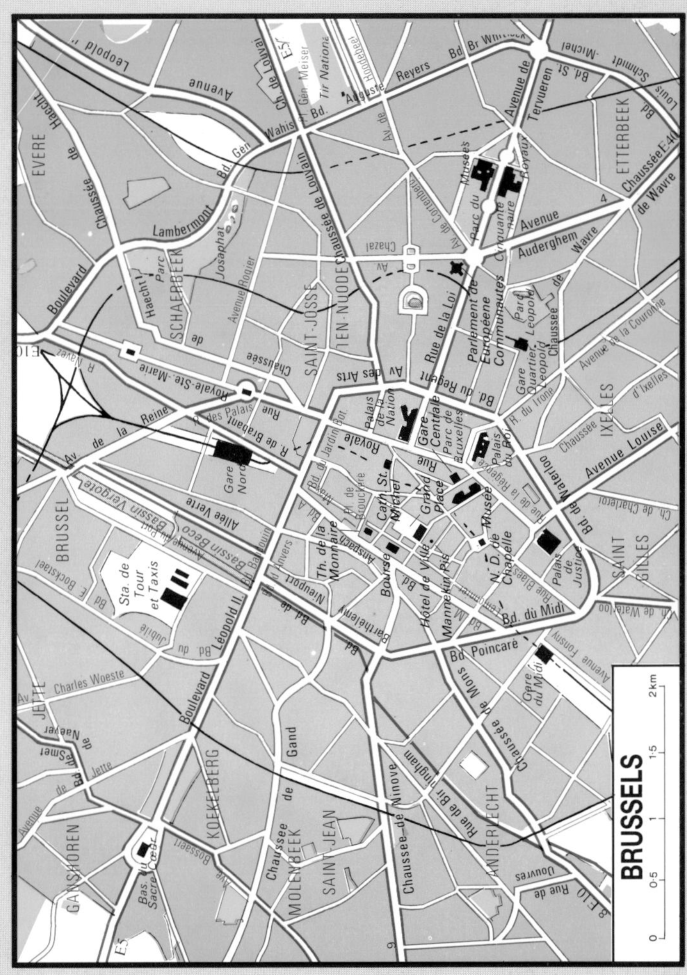
BRUSSELS
0
0.5
1
1.5
2km
EVERE
SCHAERBEEK
SAINT-JOSSE
ETTERBEEK
IXELLES
SAINT GILLES
ANDERLECHT
MOLENBEEK SAINT JEAN
KOEKELBERG
GANSHOREN
JETTE
BRUSSEL
Gare du Nord
Gare Centrale
Gare du Midi
Gare Quartier Léopold
Grand' Place
Bourse
Palais de Justice
Palais de la Nation
Parlement Européen
Parc de Bruxelles
Avenue Louise
Bd du Midi
Bd Poincaré
Chaussée de Ninove
Chaussée de Mons
Chaussée de Gand
Boulevard Léopold II
Bassin Vergote
Bd du Régent
Rue de la Loi
Chaussée de Louvain
Avenue de Tervueren
Chaussée de Wavre

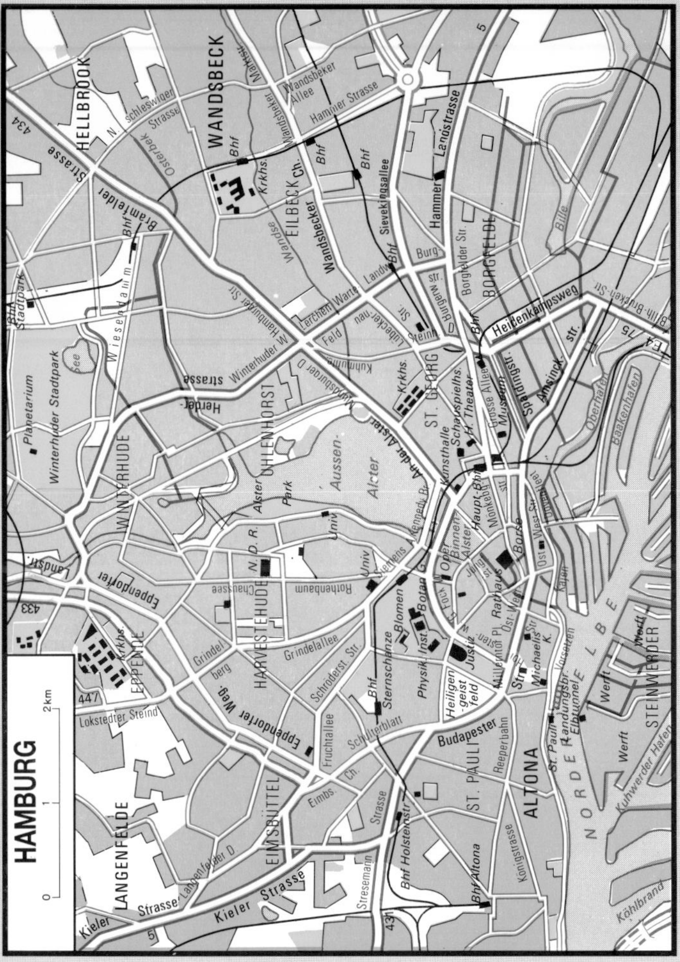
HAMBURG
0 1 2km
WANDSBECK
HELLBROOK
EILBECK
BORGFELDE
ST. GEORG
UHLENHORST
WINTERHUDE
HARVESTEHUDE
EPPENDORF
EIMSBÜTTEL
LANGENFELDE
ST. PAULI
ALTONA
STEINWERDER
Aussen Alster
Binnen Alster
NORDERELBE

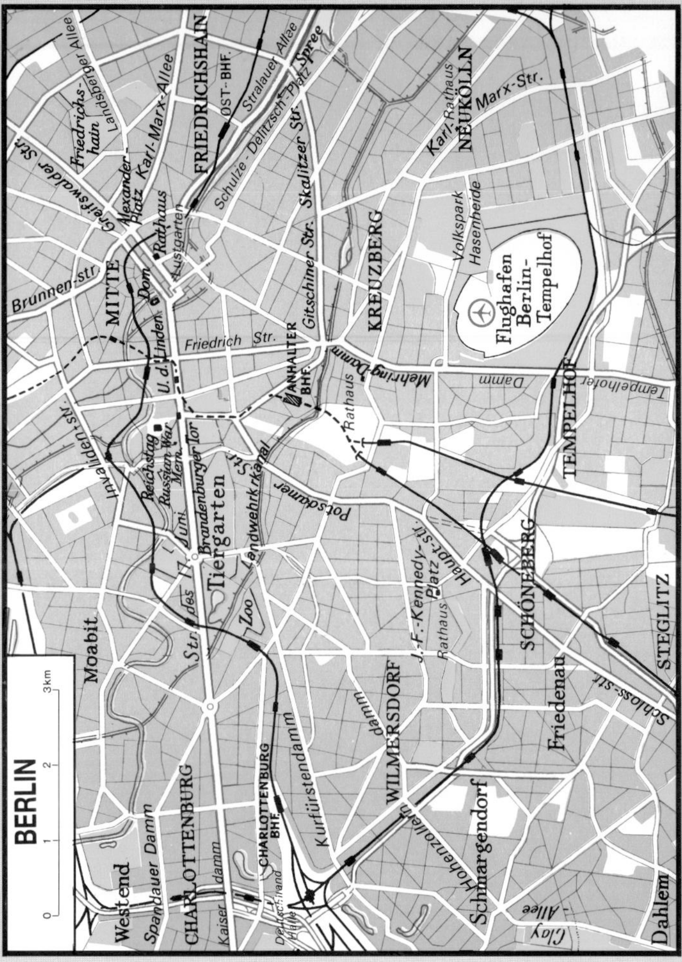
BERLIN
0 1 2 3km
FRIEDRICHSHAIN
MITTE
KREUZBERG
NEUKÖLLN
Flughafen Berlin-Tempelhof
TEMPELHOF
Tiergarten
Moabit
CHARLOTTENBURG
WILMERSDORF
SCHÖNEBERG
STEGLITZ
Friedenau
Schmargendorf
Westend
Dahlem

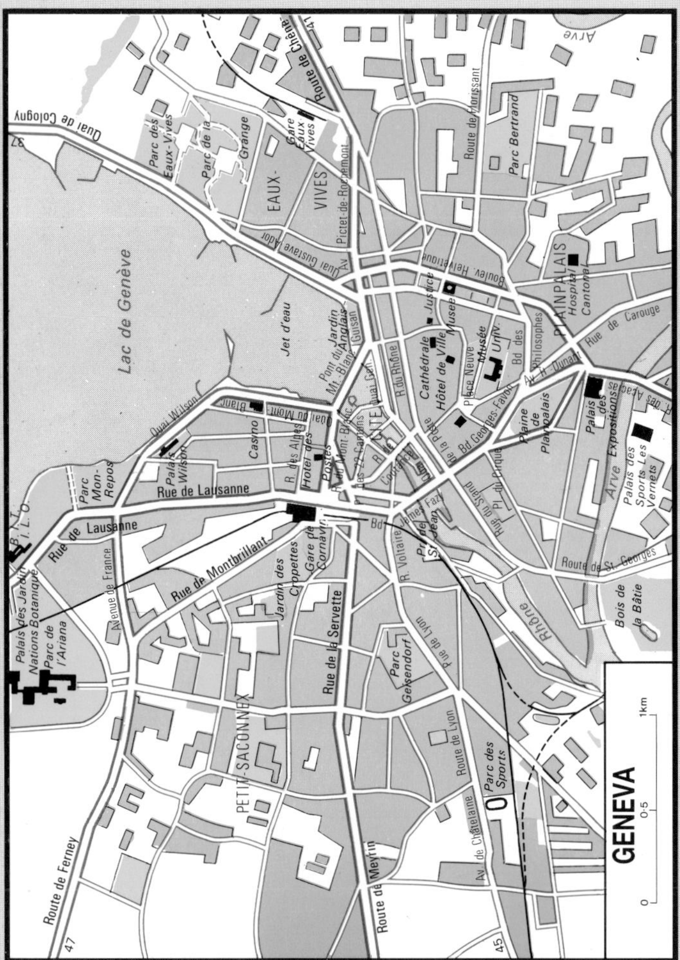
GENEVA
0 0·5 1km
Lac de Genève
EAUX-VIVES
PLAINPALAIS
PETIT-SACONNEX
Jet d'eau
Rhône
Arve
Palais des Nations
Rue de Lausanne
Route de Ferney
Quai de Cologny

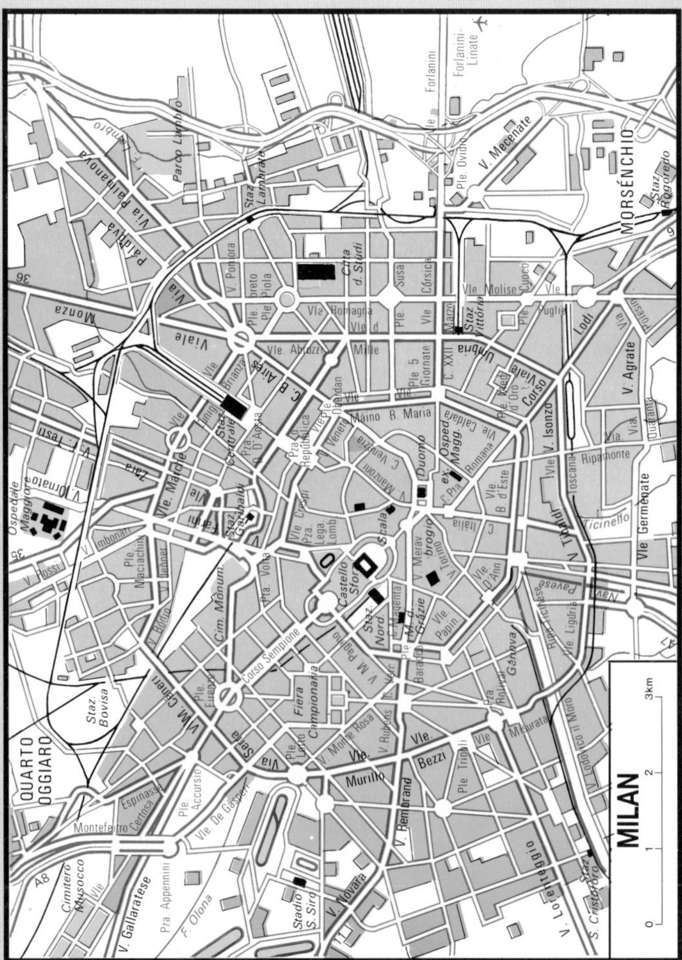
MILAN
0 1 2 3km
QUARTO OGGIARO
MORSÈNCHIO
Duomo
Scala
Castello Sforzesco
Staz. Centrale
Città d. Studi
Ospedale Maggiore
Fiera Campionaria
Stadio S. Siro
Cimitero Musocco

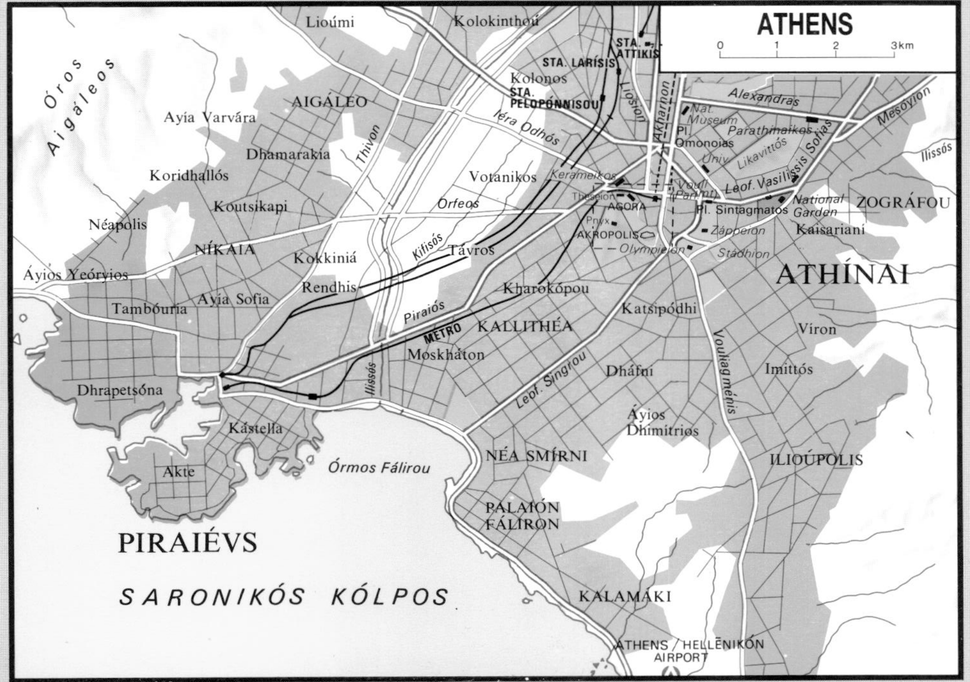
ATHENS
0 1 2 3km
ATHÍNAI
PIRAIÉVS
SARONIKÓS KÓLPOS
Órmos Fálirou
AIGÁLEO
NÍKAIA
KALLITHÉA
NÉA SMÍRNI
PALAIÓN FÁLIRON
ILIOÚPOLIS
ZOGRÁFOU
KALAMÁKI
ATHENS / HELLENIKÓN AIRPORT
Óros Aigáleos
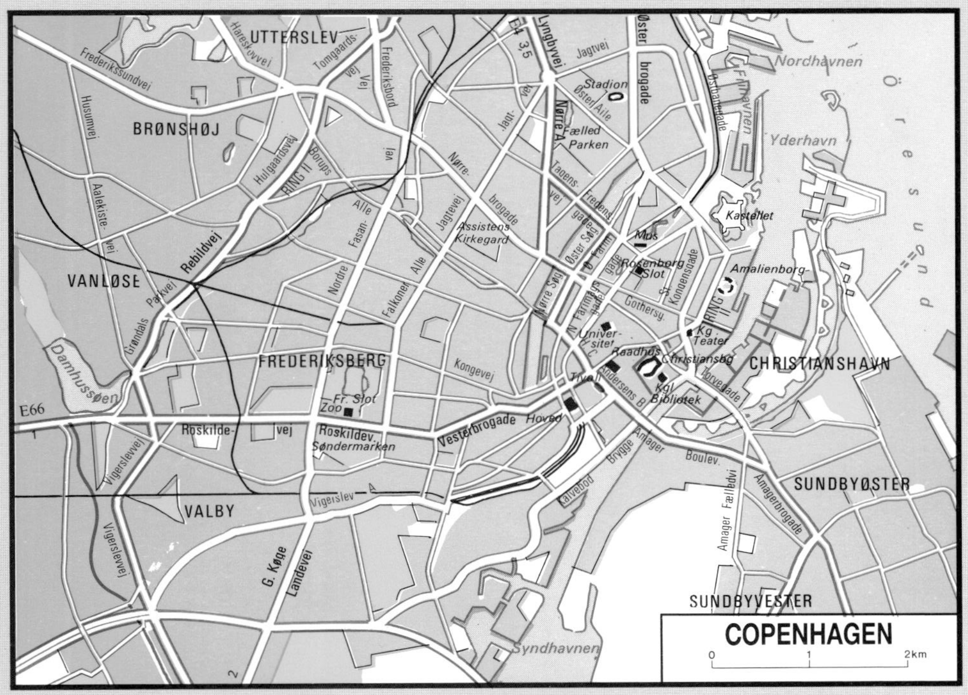
COPENHAGEN
0 1 2km
UTTERSLEV
BRØNSHØJ
VANLØSE
FREDERIKSBERG
VALBY
CHRISTIANSHAVN
SUNDBYØSTER
SUNDBYVESTER
Öresund
Nordhavnen
Yderhavn
Kastellet
Amalienborg
Rosenborg Slot
Vesterbrogade
Roskildevej
Syndhavnen
Damhussøen
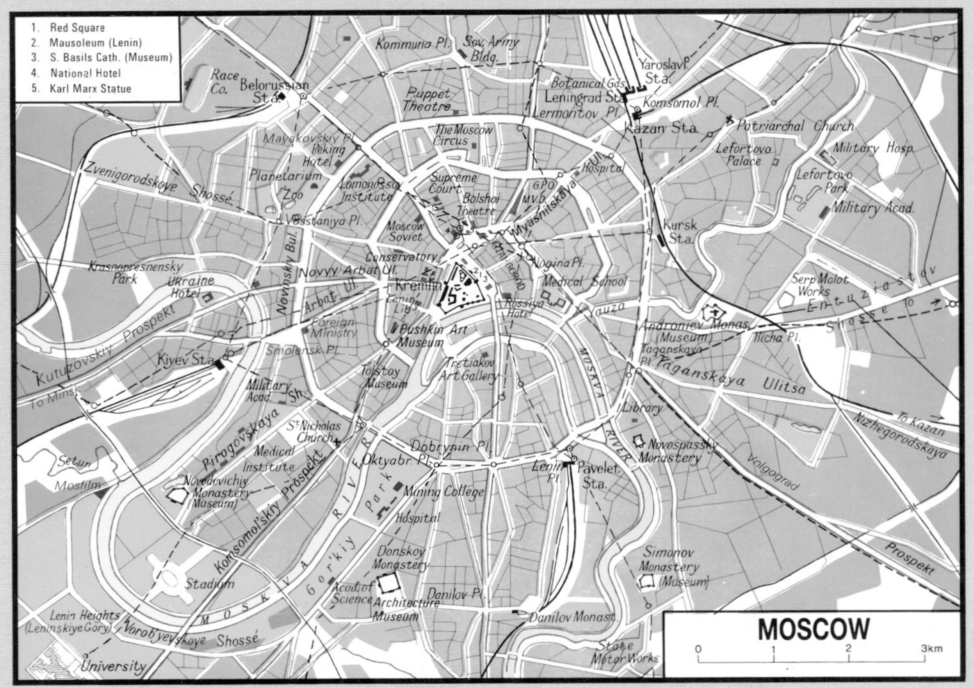
1. Red Square
2. Mausoleum (Lenin)
3. S. Basils Cath. (Museum)
4. National Hotel
5. Karl Marx Statue
MOSCOW
0 1 2 3km
Kremlin
Kursk Sta.
Kazan Sta.
Yaroslavl Sta.
Leningrad Sta.
Belorussian Sta.
Kiyev Sta.
Pavelet. Sta.
MOSKVA RIVER
Gorkiy Park
Stadium
University
Novodevichiy Monastery (Museum)
Novospassky Monastery
Danilov Monast.
Simonov Monastery (Museum)
Taganskaya Ulitsa
Kutuzovskiy Prospekt
Komsomol'skiy Prospekt
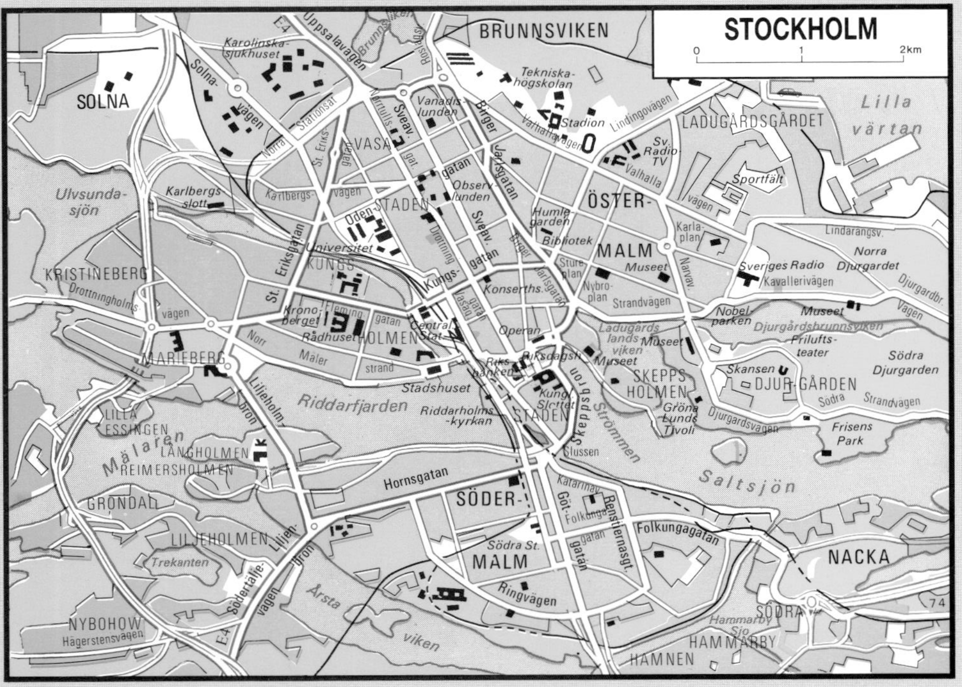
STOCKHOLM
0 1 2km
BRUNNSVIKEN
SOLNA
LADUGÅRDSGÄRDET
Lilla värtan
ÖSTER-MALM
VASA-STADEN
KUNGS-HOLMEN
KRISTINEBERG
MARIEBERG
STADEN
SKEPPS-HOLMEN
DJURGÅRDEN
SÖDER-MALM
NACKA
Saltsjön
Riddarfjärden
Mälaren
Ulvsundasjön
Strömmen
Årsta viken
LILJEHOLMEN
LÅNGHOLMEN
REIMERSHOLMEN
GRÖNDAL
NYBOHOW
HAMMARBY HAMNEN
Skansen
Stadshuset

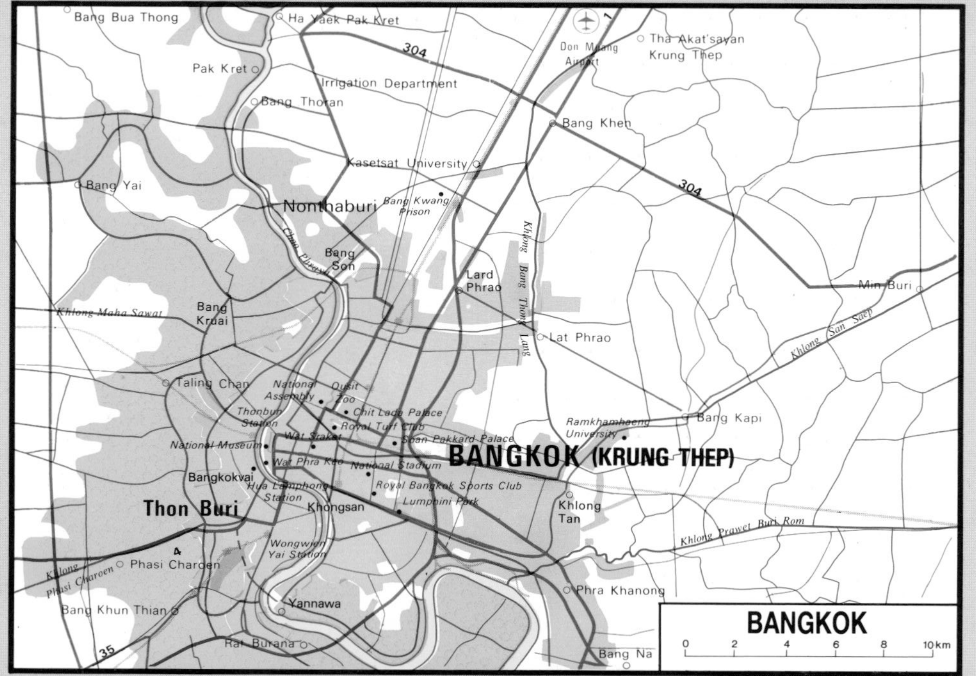
BANGKOK
0 2 4 6 8 10km
BANGKOK (KRUNG THEP)
Thon Buri
Nonthaburi
Bang Bua Thong
Pak Kret
Bang Yai
Bang Khen
Lat Phrao
Min Buri
Bang Kapi
Phra Khanong
Bang Na
Khlong Tan
Khongsan
Yannawa
Bang Khun Thian
Phasi Charoen
Rat Burana
Irrigation Department
Kasetsat University
Don Muang Airport
Tha Akat'sayan Krung Thep

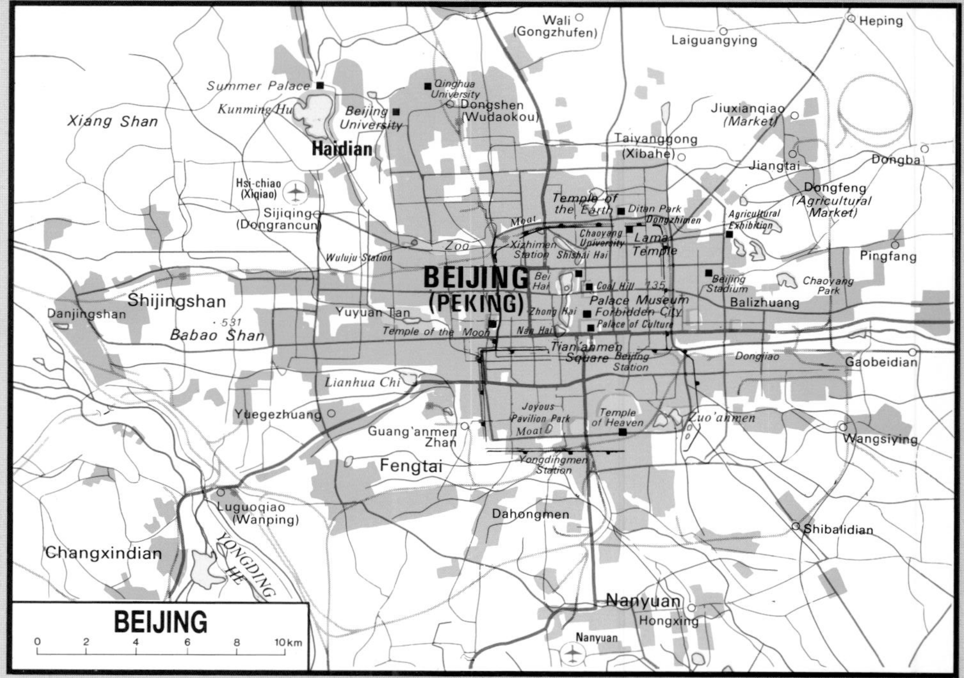
BEIJING
0 2 4 6 8 10km
BEIJING (PEKING)
Haidian
Fengtai
Shijingshan
Changxindian
Nanyuan
Summer Palace
Beijing University
Qinghua University
Temple of Heaven
Palace Museum Forbidden City
Tian'anmen Square
Lama Temple
Temple of the Earth
Yongding He
Xiang Shan
Babao Shan
Heping
Wangsiying
Gaobeidian
Pingfang
Dongba
Balizhuang
Dahongmen
Shibalidian

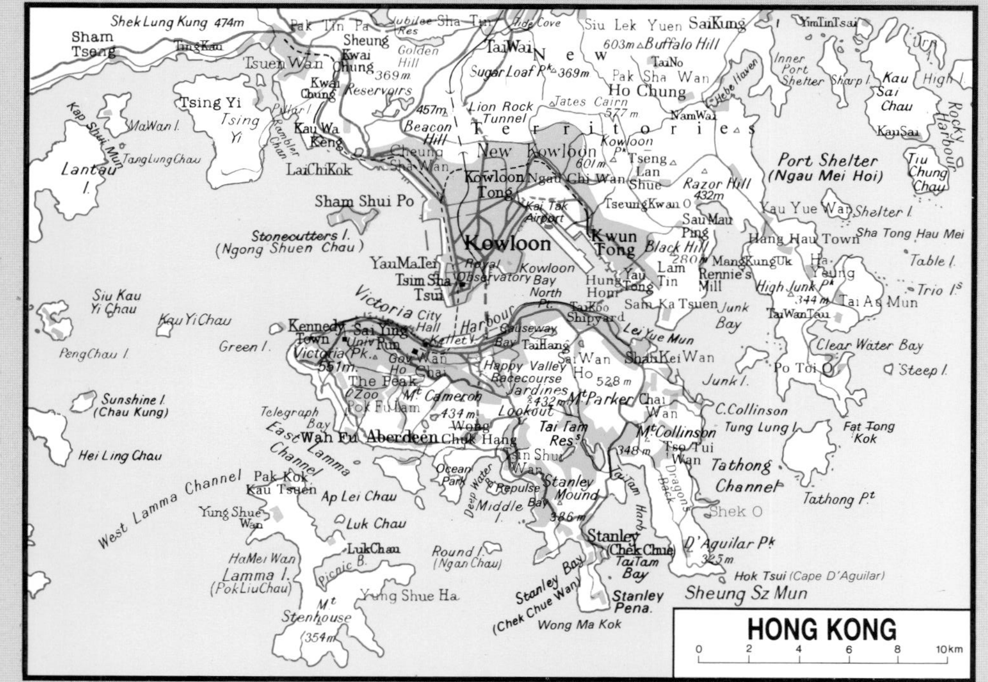
HONG KONG
0 2 4 6 8 10km
Kowloon
Victoria City
Victoria Harbour
New Territories
Kwun Tong
Sha Tin
Tsuen Wan
Aberdeen
Stanley
Lantau I.
Lamma I.
Tsing Yi
Sham Shui Po
Port Shelter (Ngau Mei Hoi)
Clear Water Bay
Stonecutters I. (Ngong Shuen Chau)
West Lamma Channel
East Lamma Channel
Tathong Channel
Sheung Sz Mun
Kai Tak Airport
The Peak

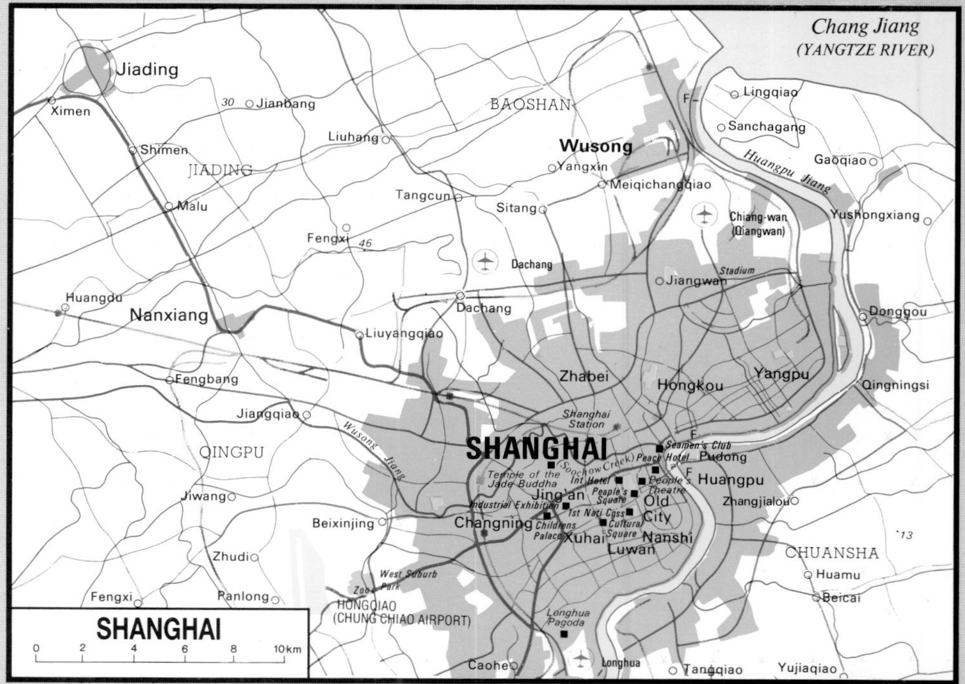
SHANGHAI
0 2 4 6 8 10km
SHANGHAI
Chang Jiang (YANGTZE RIVER)
Huangpu Jiang
Wusong
Jiading
Nanxiang
BAOSHAN
JIADING
QINGPU
CHUANSHA
Zhabei
Hongkou
Yangpu
Huangpu
Nanshi
Luwan
Xuhai
Jing'an
Changning
Old City
Pudong
Dachang
HONGQIAO (CHUNG CHIAO AIRPORT)
Longhua Pagoda
Shanghai Station

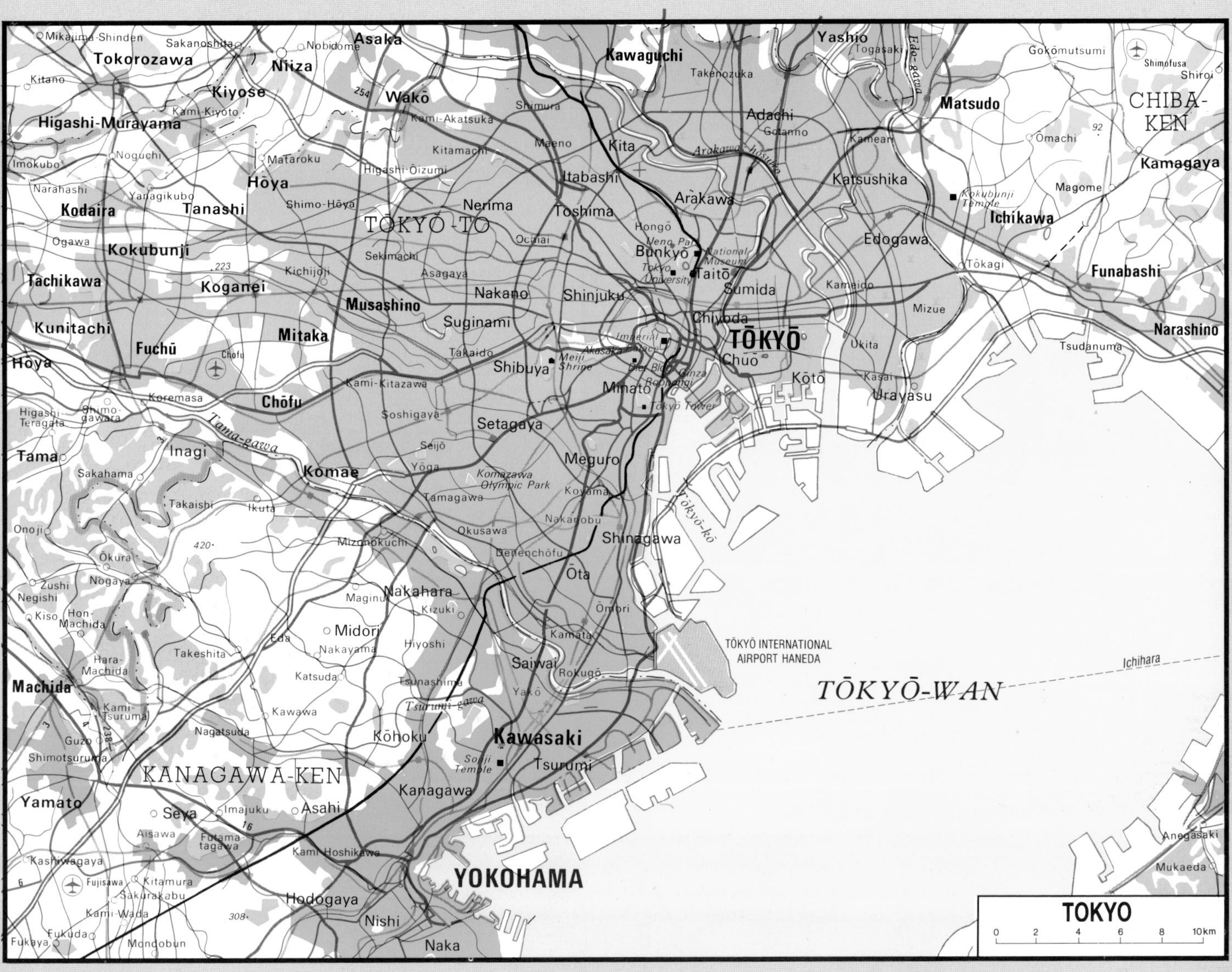
TOKYO
0 2 4 6 8 10km
TŌKYŌ
TŌKYŌ-TO
TŌKYŌ-WAN
CHIBA-KEN
KANAGAWA-KEN
YOKOHAMA
Kawasaki
Tokorozawa
Niiza
Asaka
Kiyose
Wakō
Kawaguchi
Yashio
Matsudo
Higashi-Murayama
Hōya
Tanashi
Kodaira
Kokubunji
Koganei
Tachikawa
Musashino
Kunitachi
Fuchū
Mitaka
Chōfu
Komae
Inagi
Tama
Machida
Yamato
Nerima
Itabashi
Kita
Adachi
Arakawa
Toshima
Katsushika
Edogawa
Ichikawa
Funabashi
Narashino
Kamagaya
Bunkyō
Taitō
Sumida
Nakano
Shinjuku
Suginami
Shibuya
Chiyoda
Chūō
Minato
Kōtō
Urayasu
Setagaya
Meguro
Shinagawa
Ōta
Saiwai
Nakahara
Midori
Kōhoku
Tsurumi
Kanagawa
Seya
Asahi
Hodogaya
Nishi
Naka
TŌKYŌ INTERNATIONAL
AIRPORT HANEDA
Ichihara
Anegasaki
Mukaeda

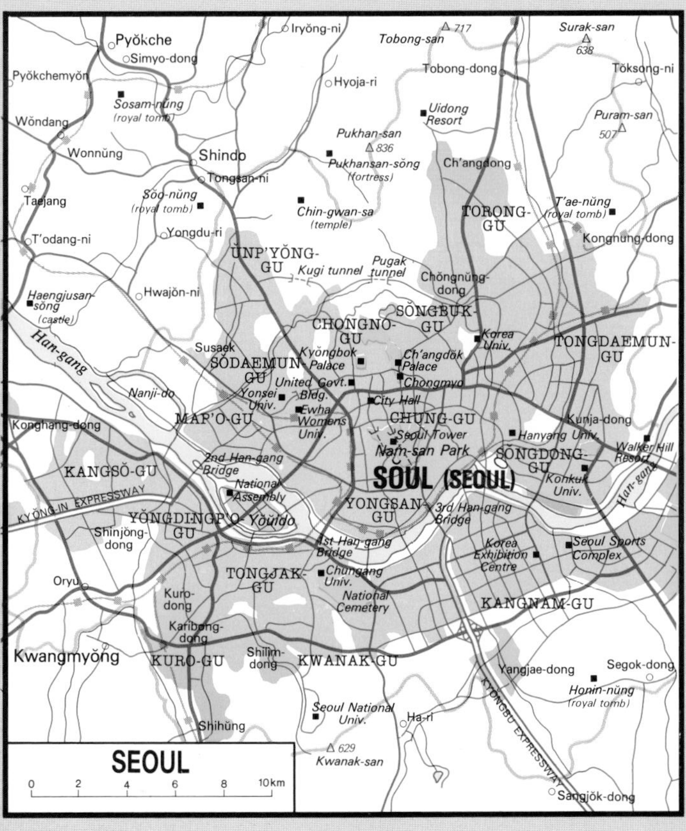
SEOUL
0 2 4 6 8 10km
SŎUL (SEOUL)
ŬNP'YŎNG-GU
TORONG-GU
SŎNGBUK-GU
CHONGNO-GU
TONGDAEMUN-GU
SŎDAEMUN-GU
MAP'O-GU
CHUNG-GU
SŎNGDONG-GU
KANGSŎ-GU
YONGSAN-GU
YŎNGDINGP'O-GU
TONGJAK-GU
KANGNAM-GU
KURO-GU
KWANAK-GU
Han-gang
Kwangmyŏng
Pyŏkche
Shindo
Ch'angdong
Yŏido

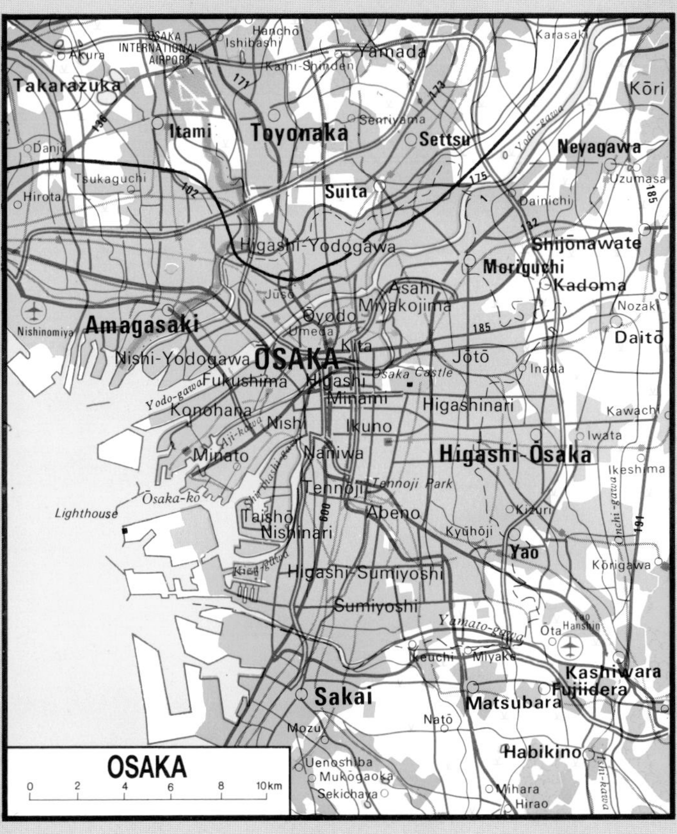
OSAKA
0 2 4 6 8 10km
ŌSAKA
Takarazuka
Itami
Toyonaka
Settsu
Neyagawa
Suita
Kōri
Higashi-Yodogawa
Shijōnawate
Moriguchi
Kadoma
Amagasaki
Daitō
Nishi-Yodogawa
Jōtō
Fukushima
Konohana
Higashinari
Minato
Ikuno
Naniwa
Higashi-Ōsaka
Taishō
Nishinari
Abeno
Tennoji
Yao
Higashi-Sumiyoshi
Sumiyoshi
Sakai
Matsubara
Kashiwara
Fujiidera
Habikino
Lighthouse

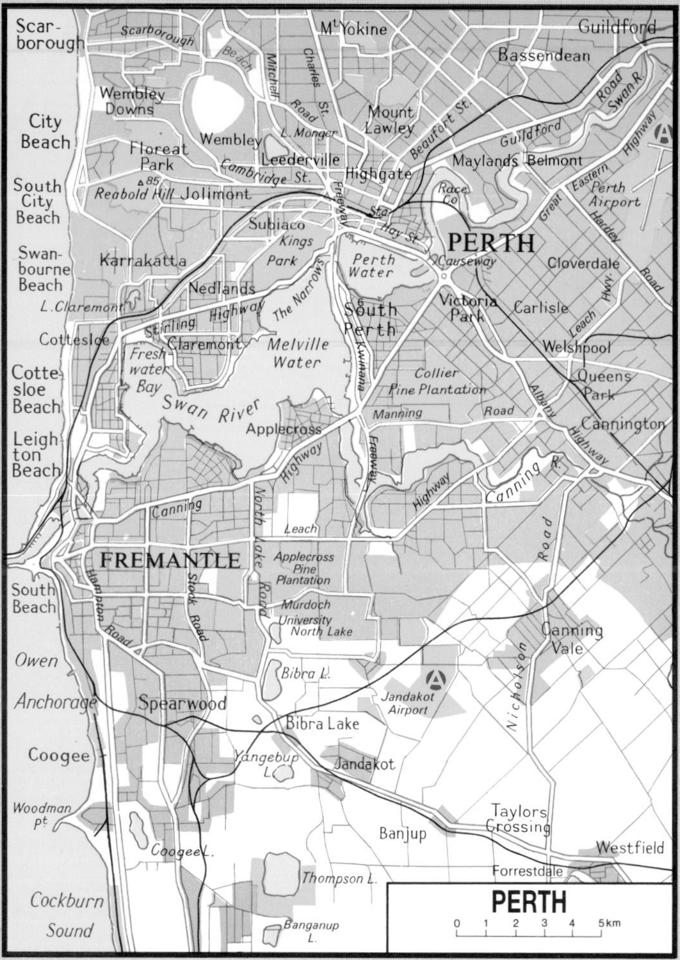
PERTH
0 1 2 3 4 5 km
Scarborough
Mt Yokine
Guildford
Bassendean
Wembley Downs
Mount Lawley
City Beach
Floreat Park
Wembley
Leederville
Maylands
Belmont
South City Beach
Reabold Hill
Jolimont
Highgate
Perth Airport
Swanbourne Beach
Karrakatta
Subiaco
Kings Park
PERTH
Causeway
Cloverdale
Perth Water
Nedlands
South Perth
Victoria Park
Carlisle
L. Claremont
Cottesloe
Claremont
Melville Water
Welshpool
Cottesloe Beach
Freshwater Bay
Queens Park
Swan River
Collier Pine Plantation
Leighton Beach
Applecross
Manning
Cannington
Canning
FREMANTLE
Leach
Applecross Pine Plantation
South Beach
Murdoch University
North Lake
Canning Vale
Owen Anchorage
Bibra L.
Jandakot Airport
Spearwood
Bibra Lake
Coogee
Yangebup L.
Jandakot
Woodman Pt
Taylors Crossing
Banjup
Westfield
Coogee L.
Forrestdale
Thompson L.
Cockburn Sound
Banganup L.

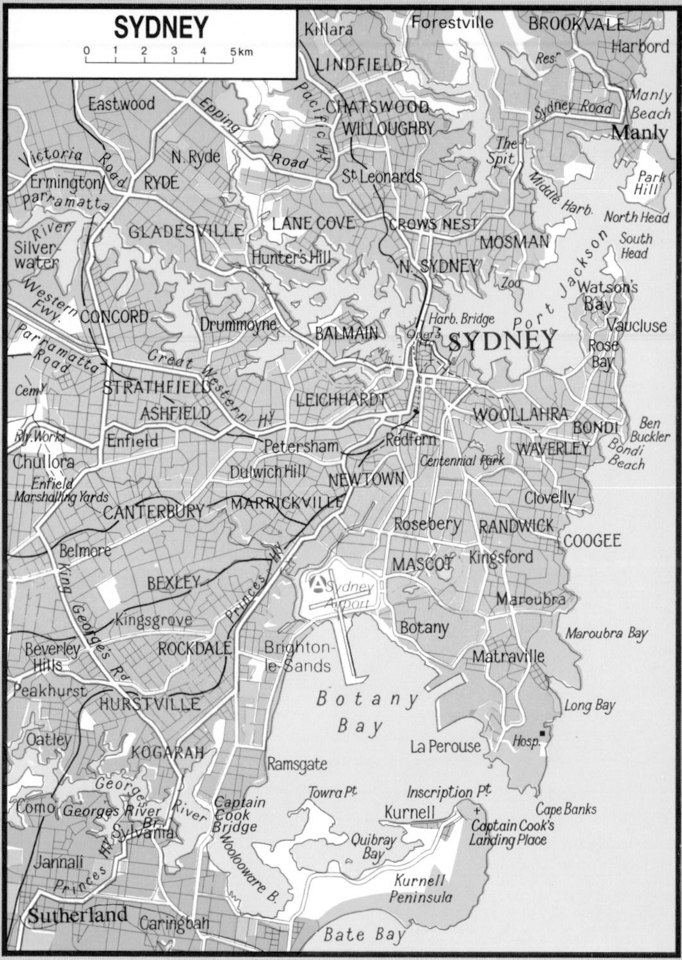
SYDNEY
0 1 2 3 4 5 km
Killara
Forestville
BROOKVALE
Harbord
LINDFIELD
Eastwood
CHATSWOOD
WILLOUGHBY
Manly Beach
Manly
Ermington
N. Ryde
RYDE
St Leonards
The Spit
Park Hill
GLADESVILLE
LANE COVE
CROWS NEST
MOSMAN
North Head
South Head
Silverwater
Hunters Hill
N. SYDNEY
Zoo
Watson's Bay
Vaucluse
CONCORD
Drummoyne
BALMAIN
Harb. Bridge
SYDNEY
Rose Bay
Cemy
STRATHFIELD
LEICHHARDT
ASHFIELD
WOOLLAHRA
BONDI
Ben Buckler
Bondi Beach
Rly. Works
Chullora
Enfield
Petersham
Redfern
Centennial Park
WAVERLEY
Enfield Marshalling Yards
Dulwich Hill
NEWTOWN
Clovelly
CANTERBURY
MARRICKVILLE
Rosebery
RANDWICK
COOGEE
Belmore
MASCOT
Kingsford
BEXLEY
Sydney Airport
Maroubra
Kingsgrove
Botany
Maroubra Bay
Beverley Hills
ROCKDALE
Brighton-le-Sands
Matraville
Peakhurst
HURSTVILLE
Botany Bay
Long Bay
Oatley
KOGARAH
La Perouse
Hosp.
Ramsgate
Towra Pt
Inscription Pt
Cape Banks
Como
Georges River
Sylvania
Captain Cook Bridge
Kurnell
Captain Cook's Landing Place
Quibray Bay
Jannali
Woolooware B.
Kurnell Peninsula
Sutherland
Caringbah
Bate Bay

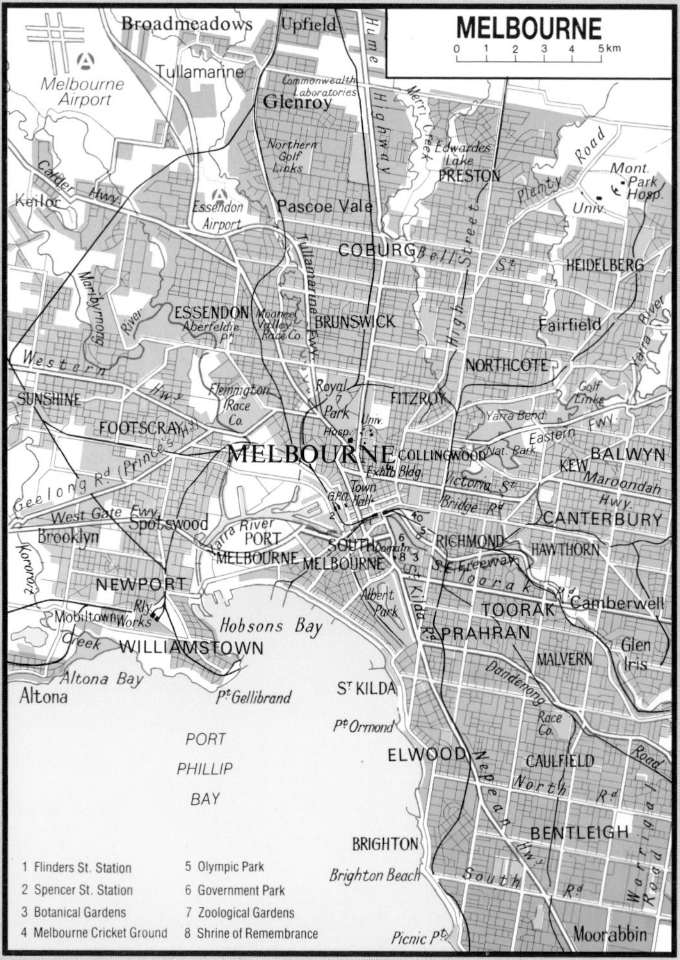
MELBOURNE
0 1 2 3 4 5 km
Broadmeadows
Upfield
Melbourne Airport
Tullamarine
Commonwealth Laboratories
Glenroy
Edwardes Lake
PRESTON
Mont. Park Hosp.
Northern Golf Links
Keilor
Essendon Airport
Pascoe Vale
Univ.
COBURG
HEIDELBERG
ESSENDON
Aberfeldie
Moonee Valley Race Co.
BRUNSWICK
Fairfield
NORTHCOTE
SUNSHINE
Flemington Race Co.
Royal Park
FITZROY
FOOTSCRAY
Yarra Bend
Golf Links
MELBOURNE
COLLINGWOOD
KEW
BALWYN
Exhib Bldg.
Town Hall
CANTERBURY
West Gate Fwy.
Spotswood
PORT MELBOURNE
SOUTH MELBOURNE
RICHMOND
HAWTHORN
Brooklyn
NEWPORT
TOORAK
Camberwell
Mobiltown Works
Hobsons Bay
PRAHRAN
Glen Iris
WILLIAMSTOWN
MALVERN
Altona Bay
Altona
Pt Gellibrand
St KILDA
Pt Ormond
Race Co.
PORT PHILLIP BAY
ELWOOD
CAULFIELD
BRIGHTON
BENTLEIGH
Brighton Beach
Picnic Pt
Moorabbin
1 Flinders St. Station
2 Spencer St. Station
3 Botanical Gardens
4 Melbourne Cricket Ground
5 Olympic Park
6 Government Park
7 Zoological Gardens
8 Shrine of Remembrance

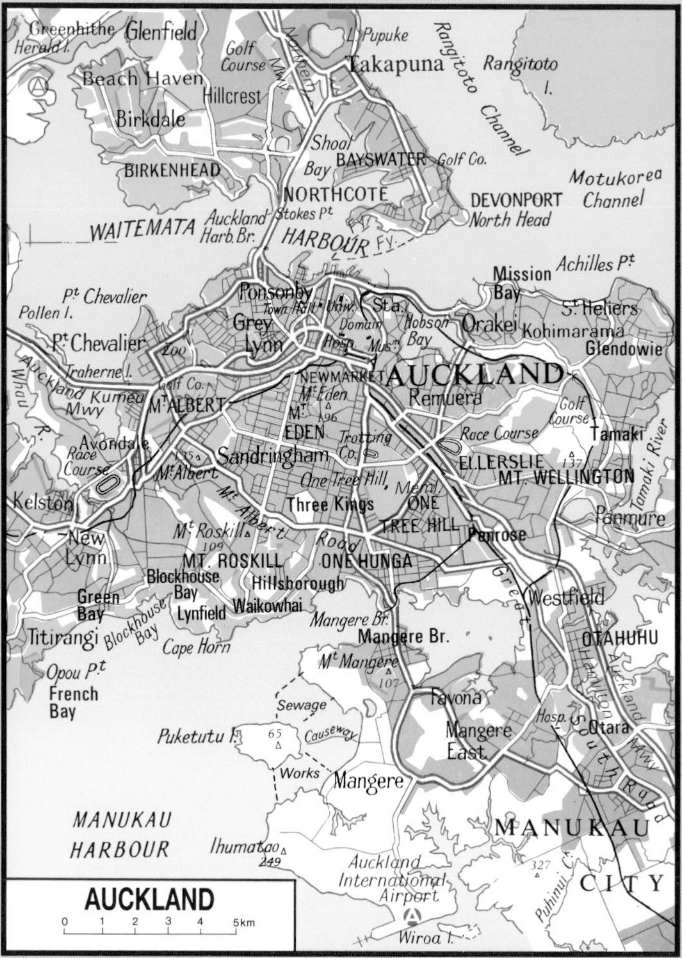
Greenhithe
Glenfield
L. Pupuke
Takapuna
Rangitoto
Rangitoto I.
Beach Haven
Golf Course
Hillcrest
Birkdale
Rangitoto Channel
Shoal Bay
BAYSWATER
Golf Co.
BIRKENHEAD
NORTHCOTE
Motukorea Channel
DEVONPORT
North Head
WAITEMATA
Auckland Harb. Br.
Stokes Pt
HARBOUR
Achilles Pt
Mission Bay
Pt Chevalier
Ponsonby
St Heliers
Pollen I.
Grey Lynn
Domain
Hobson Bay
Orakei
Kohimarama
Glendowie
Pt Chevalier
Traherne I.
Zoo
NEWMARKET
AUCKLAND
Mt Eden
Remuera
Mt ALBERT
EDEN
Race Course
Tamaki
Avondale
Sandringham
Trotting Co.
ELLERSLIE
Race Course
One Tree Hill
MT. WELLINGTON
Kelston
ONE TREE HILL
Three Kings
Panmure
New Lynn
Mt Roskill
MT. ROSKILL
ONEHUNGA
Penrose
Green Bay
Blockhouse Bay
Hillsborough
Westfield
Lynfield
Waikowhai
Titirangi
Mangere Br.
OTAHUHU
Cape Horn
Opou Pt
French Bay
Mt Mangere
Favona
Sewage
Hosp.
Otara
Puketutu I.
Causeway
Mangere East
Works
Mangere
MANUKAU HARBOUR
MANUKAU CITY
Ihumatao
Auckland International Airport
Wiroa I.
AUCKLAND
0 1 2 3 4 5 km

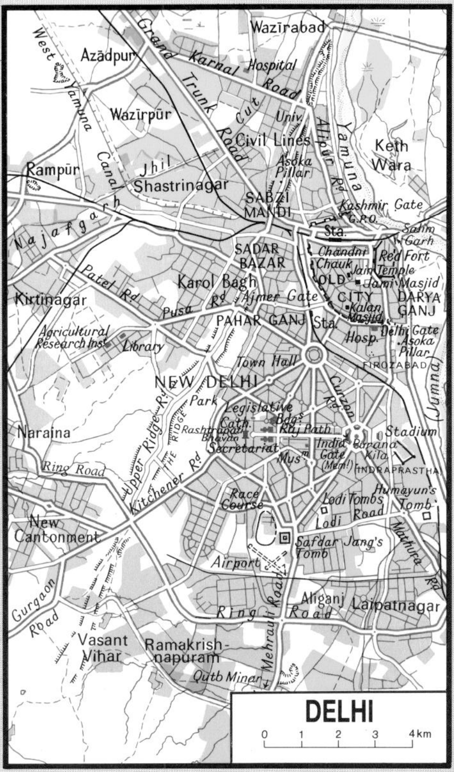

DELHI

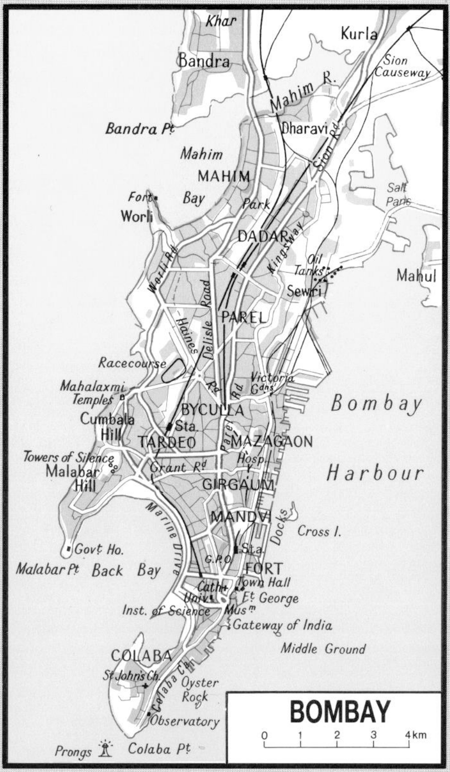

BOMBAY

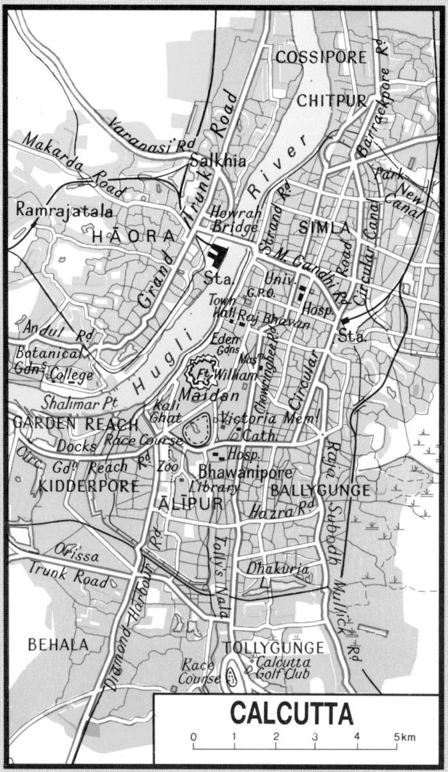

CALCUTTA

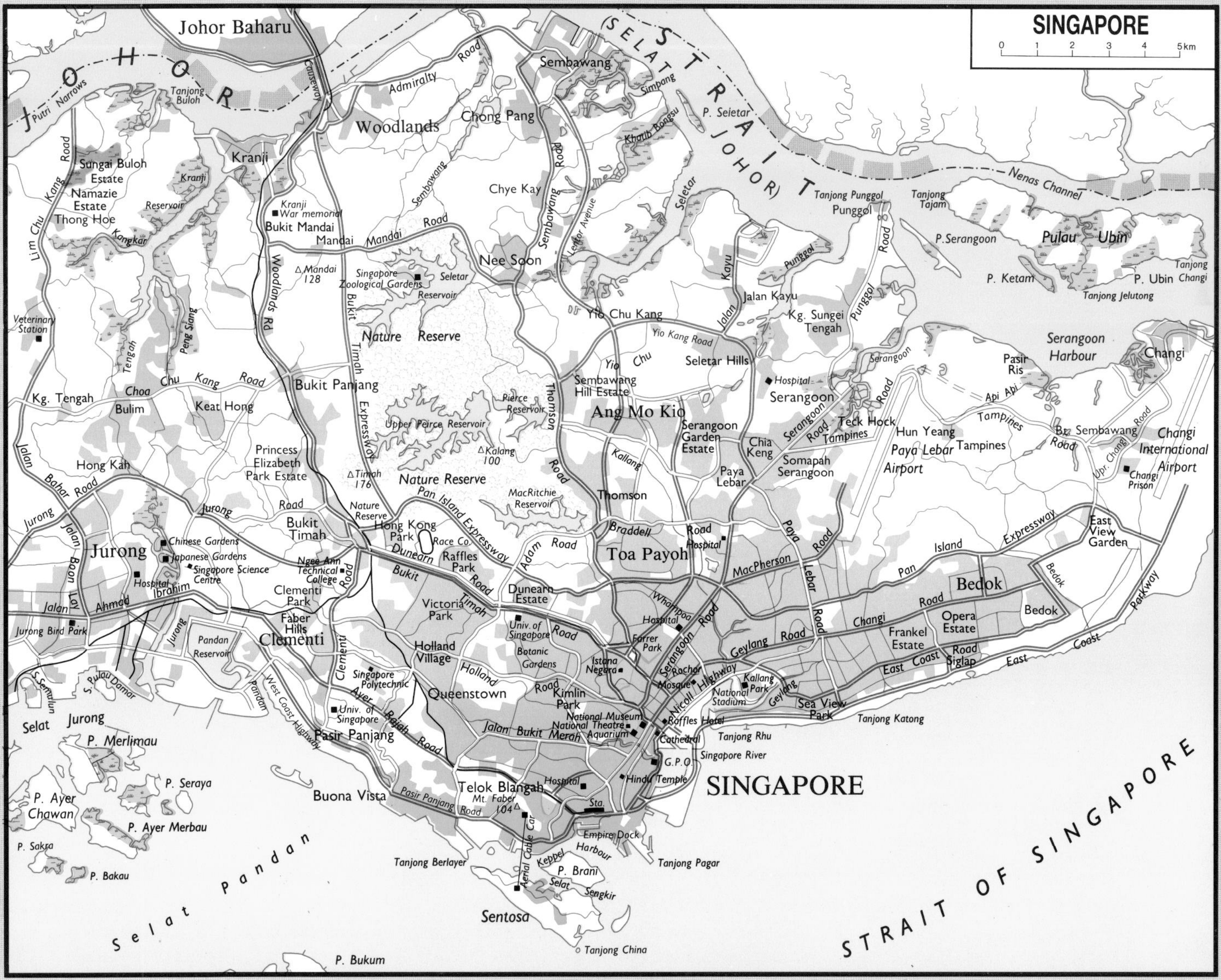

SINGAPORE

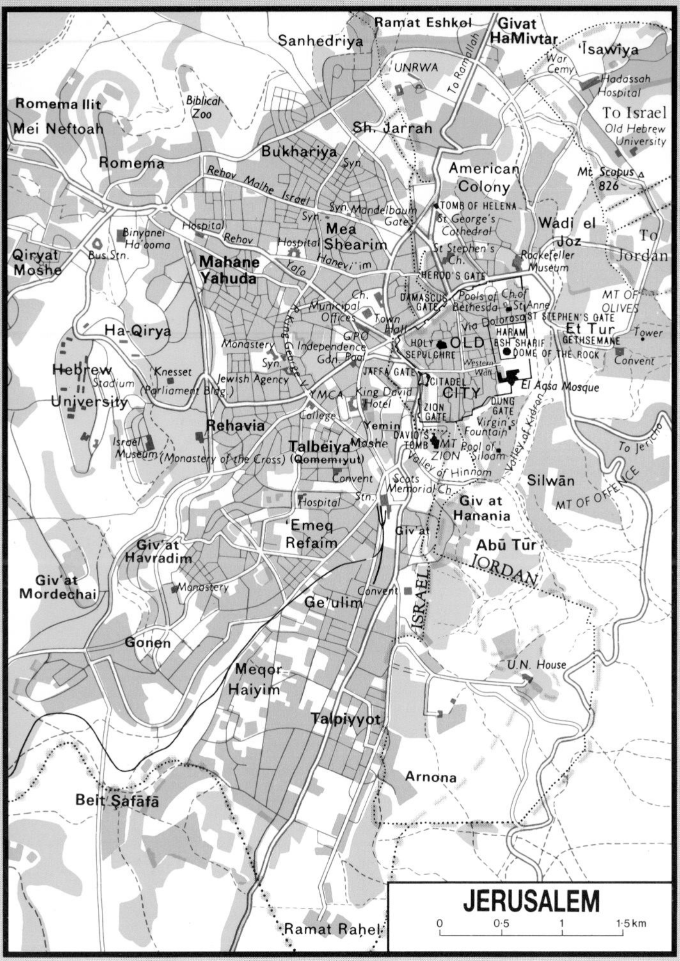
JERUSALEM
0 0·5 1 1·5km
Ramat Eshkol
Givat HaMivtar
Sanhedriya
UNRWA
To Ramallah
War Cemy
'Isawiya
Hadassah Hospital
To Israel
Old Hebrew University
Romema Ilit
Mei Neftoah
Biblical Zoo
Sh. Jarrah
Bukhariya
Romema
Syn
American Colony
Mt. Scopus 826
Rehov Malhe Israel
Syn
Mandelbaum Gate
TOMB OF HELENA
St George's Cathedral
Wadi el Joz
Binyanei Ha'ooma
Hospital
Rehov
Hospital
Mea Shearim
St Stephen's Ch.
Rockefeller Museum
To Jordan
Qiryat Moshe
Bus Stn.
Mahane Yahuda
HEROD'S GATE
Ch.
DAMASCUS GATE
Pools of Bethesda
St Anne
MT OF OLIVES
Municipal Offices
Via Dolorosa
ST STEPHEN'S GATE
Ha-Qirya
Town Hall
HOLY SEPULCHRE
OLD
HARAM ESH SHARIF
DOME OF THE ROCK
Et Tur
GETHSEMANE
Tower
Monastery
Independence Gdn.
GPO
Syn
Convent
Hebrew University
Knesset
Stadium
(Parliament Bldg.)
Jewish Agency
JAFFA GATE
CITADEL
Western Wall
El Aqsa Mosque
YMCA
King David Hotel
CITY
ZION GATE
DUNG GATE
Rehavia
College
Yemin Moshe
DAVID'S TOMB
Virgin's Fountain
Valley of Kedron
Israel Museum
(Monastery of the Cross)
Talbeiya (Qomemiyut)
MT ZION
Pool of Siloam
To Jericho
Valley of Hinnom
Convent
Scots Memorial Ch.
Silwān
Hospital
Stn.
Giv at Hanania
MT OF OFFENCE
'Emeq Refaim
Giv'at
Abū Tūr
Giv'at Havradim
JORDAN
Giv'at Mordechai
Monastery
Convent
ISRAEL
Ge'ulim
Gonen
U.N. House
Meqor Haiyim
Talpiyyot
Arnona
Beit Şafāfā
Ramat Raḥel

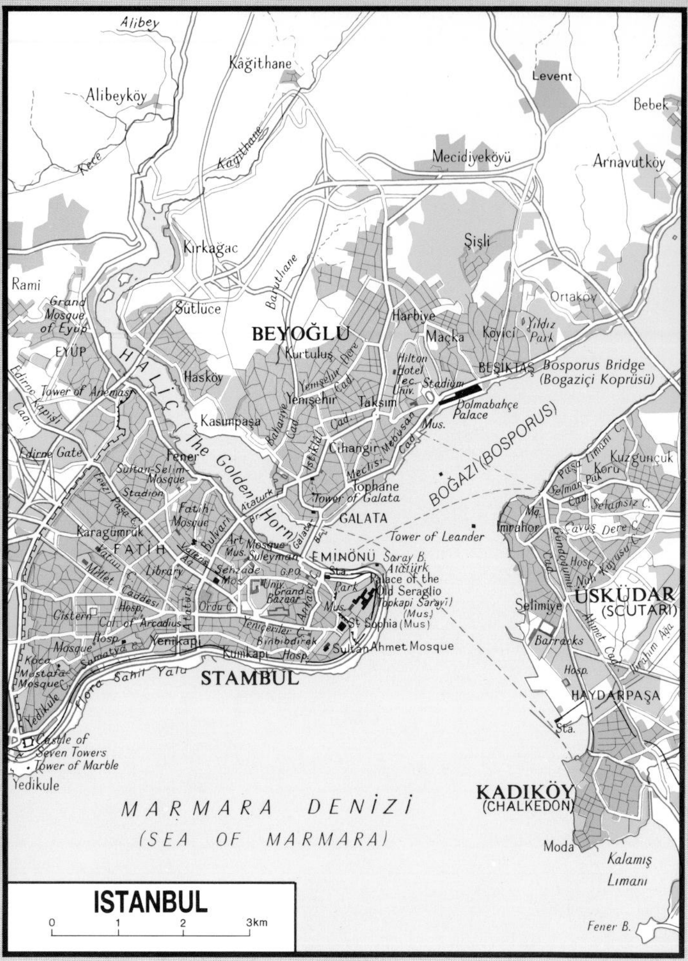
ISTANBUL
0 1 2 3km
Alibey
Kâğıthane
Levent
Bebek
Alibeyköy
Kâğıthane
Mecidiyeköyü
Arnavutköy
Kirkagac
Şişli
Rami
Ortaköy
Grand Mosque of Eyüp
Sütlüce
BEYOĞLU
Harbiye
Yıldız Park
EYÜP
Kurtuluş
Maçka
Köyiçi
Hasköy
Hilton Hotel
Tec. Univ.
BEŞİKTAŞ
Bosporus Bridge (Bogaziçi Koprüsü)
Tower of Anemas
Stadium
Dolmabahçe Palace
Edirne Kapısı
Yenişehir
Taksim
Kasımpaşa
BOĞAZI (BOSPORUS)
HALIÇ (The Golden Horn)
Edirne Gate
Fener
Cihangir
Kuzguncuk
Sultan Selim Mosque
Tophane
Tower of Galata
Stadion
Fatih Mosque
GALATA
Karagümrük
Tower of Leander
FATIH
Library
EMINÖNÜ
Sta.
Saray B.
Atatürk
Park
Palace of the Old Seraglio (Topkapı Sarayı) (Mus)
Şehzade Mosque
Süleyman Mosque
Univ.
Grand Bazaar
G.P.O.
Mus.
St Sophia (Mus)
Cistern
Col. of Arcadius
Hosp.
Yenikapı
Kumkapı
Ordu C.
Binbirdirek
Sultan Ahmet Mosque
ÜSKÜDAR (SCUTARI)
Selimiye
Barracks
Hosp.
HAYDARPAŞA
Sta.
Mosque
Mustafa Mosque
Flora Sahil Yolu
STAMBUL
Castle of Seven Towers
Tower of Marble
Yedikule
MARMARA DENİZİ
(SEA OF MARMARA)
KADIKÖY (CHALKEDON)
Moda
Kalamış Limanı
Fener B.

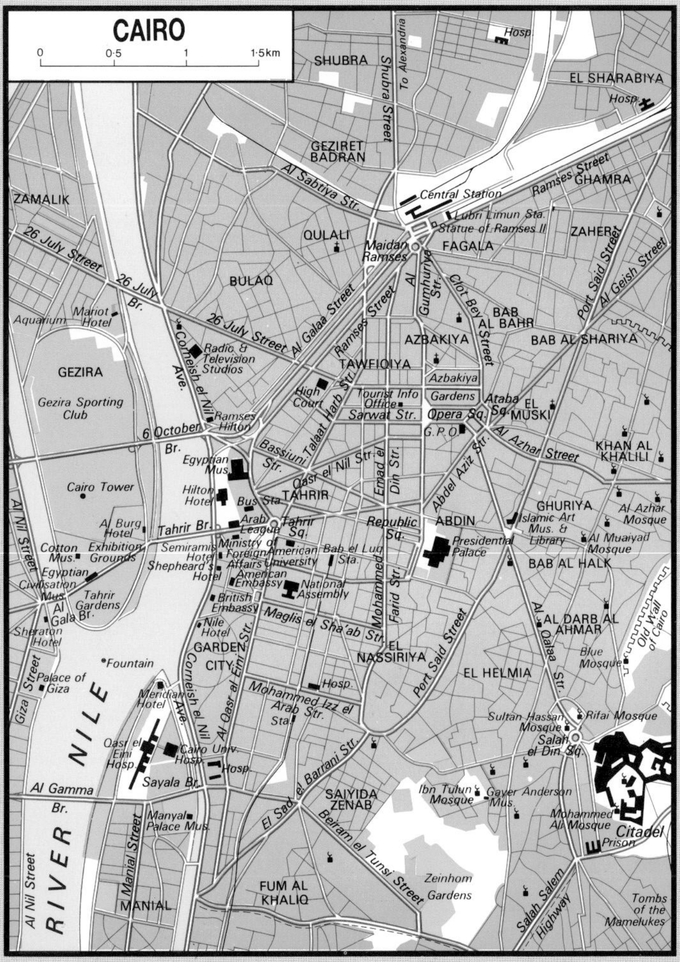
CAIRO
0 0·5 1 1·5km
Hosp.
SHUBRA
Shubra Street
To Alexandria
EL SHARABIYA
Hosp.
GEZIRET BADRAN
Al Sabtiya Str.
Ramses Street
GHAMRA
ZAMALIK
Central Station
Lubri Limun Sta.
Statue of Ramses II
ZAHER
QULALI
Maidan Ramses
FAGALA
26 July Street
26 July Br.
BULAQ
Clot Bey Str.
Port Said Street
Al Geish Street
Gumhuriya Str.
Mariot Hotel
Aquarium
Ramses Street
BAB AL BAHR
26 July Street
Al Galaa Street
AZBAKIYA
BAB AL SHARIYA
Radio & Television Studios
GEZIRA
TAWFIQIYA
Azbakiya Gardens
High Court
Tourist Info. Office
Gezira Sporting Club
Talaat Harb Str.
Ataba Sq.
EL MUSKI
Sarwat Str.
Opera Sq.
Ramses Hilton
G.P.O.
Al Azhar Street
6 October Br.
Bassiuni Str.
KHAN AL KHALILI
Egyptian Mus.
Qasr el Nil Str.
Emad el Din Str.
Abdel Aziz Str.
Cairo Tower
Hilton Hotel
TAHRIR
GHURIYA
Bus Sta.
Al Azhar Mosque
Al Burg Hotel
Tahrir Br.
Arab League
Tahrir Sq.
Republic Sq.
ABDIN
Islamic Art Mus. & Library
Cotton Exhibition Grounds
Semiramis Hotel
Ministry of Foreign Affairs
American University
Bab el Luq Sta.
Presidential Palace
Al Muaiyad Mosque
Egyptian Civilisation Mus.
Shepheard's Hotel
American Embassy
BAB AL HALK
Tahrir Gardens
National Assembly
Mohammed Farid Str.
Gala Br.
British Embassy
Sheraton Hotel
Maglis el Sha'ab Str.
AL DARB AL AHMAR
Nile Hotel
Old Wall of Cairo
Fountain
GARDEN CITY
EL NASSIRIYA
Blue Mosque
Palace of Giza
Corniche el Nil
Qasr el Aini Str.
Port Said Street
Al Qalaa Str.
Giza Street
Meridien Hotel
Mohammed Izz el Arab Str.
Hosp.
EL HELMIA
Sultan Hassan Mosque
Rifai Mosque
Qasr el Aini Hosp.
Cairo Univ. Hosp.
Salah el Din Sq.
Hosp.
Sayala Br.
Al Gamma Br.
El Sadd el Barrani Str.
SAIYIDA ZENAB
Ibn Tulun Mosque
Gayer Anderson Mus.
Mohammed Ali Mosque
Citadel
Manyal Palace Mus.
Beiram el Tunsi Street
Prison
RIVER NILE
Al Nil Street
Manial Street
Zeinhom Gardens
FUM AL KHALIG
MANIAL
Salah Salem Highway
Tombs of the Mamelukes

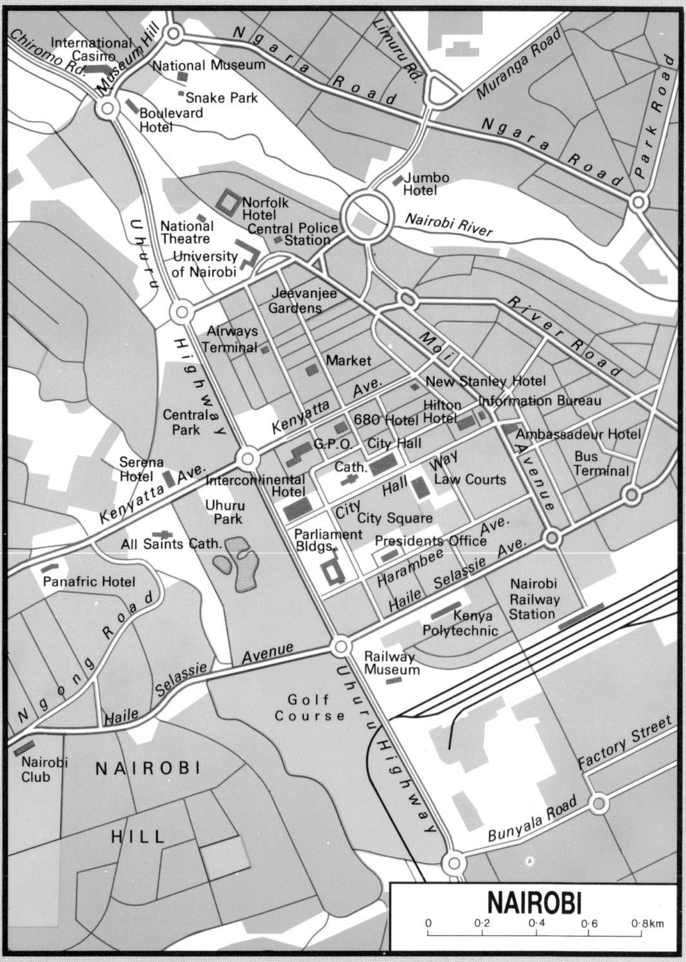
International Casino
Chiromo Rd.
Museum Hill
Ngara Road
Limuru Rd.
Muranga Road
National Museum
Snake Park
Boulevard Hotel
Park Road
Ngara Road
Jumbo Hotel
Norfolk Hotel
Central Police Station
Nairobi River
National Theatre
University of Nairobi
Uhuru Highway
Jeevanjee Gardens
River Road
Airways Terminal
Moi
Market
New Stanley Hotel
Kenyatta Ave.
Information Bureau
Central Park
680 Hotel
Hilton Hotel
Ambassadeur Hotel
G.P.O.
City Hall
Serena Hotel
Cath.
Way
Bus Terminal
Kenyatta Ave.
Intercontinental Hotel
City Hall
Law Courts
Avenue
Uhuru Park
City Square
Parliament Bldgs.
Presidents Office
All Saints Cath.
Ave.
Harambee Ave.
Panafric Hotel
Haile Selassie Ave.
Nairobi Railway Station
Ngong Road
Kenya Polytechnic
Haile Selassie Avenue
Railway Museum
Golf Course
Uhuru Highway
Nairobi Club
NAIROBI
HILL
Factory Street
Bunyala Road
NAIROBI
0 0·2 0·4 0·6 0·8km

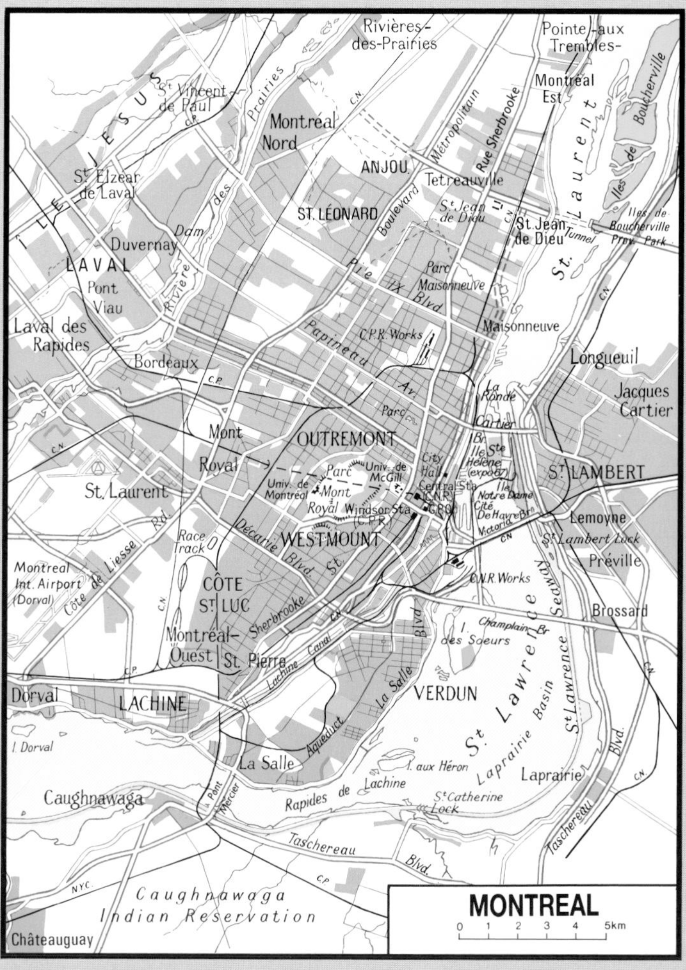
MONTREAL
0 1 2 3 4 5km
Rivières-des-Prairies
Pointe-aux-Trembles
Montreal Est
St. Vincent de Paul
Montreal Nord
ANJOU
Tetreauville
St. Elzear de Laval
ST. LÉONARD
St. Jean de Dieu
Duvernay
LAVAL
Pont Viau
Laval des Rapides
Bordeaux
Maisonneuve
Longueuil
Jacques Cartier
OUTREMONT
Mont Royal
St. Laurent
ST. LAMBERT
WESTMOUNT
Lemoyne
Préville
CÔTE ST. LUC
Montreal Int. Airport (Dorval)
Montréal-Ouest
St. Pierre
Brossard
Dorval
LACHINE
VERDUN
La Salle
Laprairie
Caughnawaga
St. Lawrence
Lachine Canal
Rapides de Lachine
Caughnawaga Indian Reservation
Châteauguay
Taschereau Blvd.

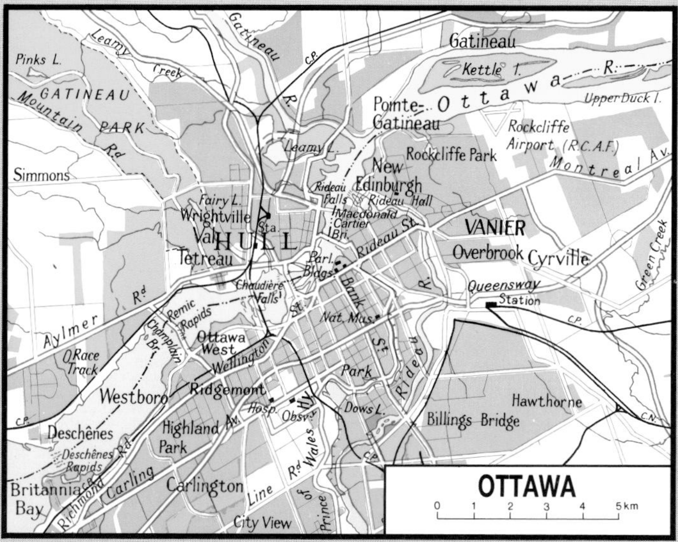
OTTAWA
0 1 2 3 4 5km
Gatineau
Kettle I.
Ottawa R.
Pinks L.
GATINEAU PARK
Pointe-Gatineau
Rockcliffe Airport (R.C.A.F.)
Rockcliffe Park
Simmons
New Edinburgh
Wrightville
HULL
VANIER
Overbrook
Cyrville
Tetreau
Queensway Station
Aylmer Rd
Ottawa West
Westboro
Ridgemont
Hawthorne
Deschênes
Highland Park
Billings Bridge
Britannia Bay
Carlington
City View

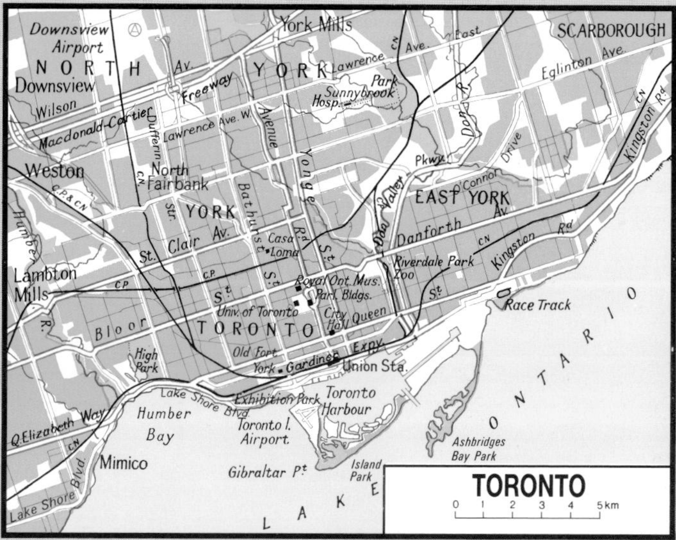
TORONTO
0 1 2 3 4 5km
Downsview Airport
York Mills
SCARBOROUGH
NORTH YORK
Downsview
Wilson
Eglinton Ave
Sunnybrook Hosp.
Weston
North Fairbank
YORK
EAST YORK
St. Clair Av.
Danforth Av.
Casa Loma
Lambton Mills
Riverdale Park Zoo
Race Track
Bloor St.
TORONTO
Univ. of Toronto
High Park
Union Sta.
Humber Bay
Toronto Harbour
Toronto I. Airport
Mimico
Gibraltar Pt.
Ashbridges Bay Park
LAKE ONTARIO

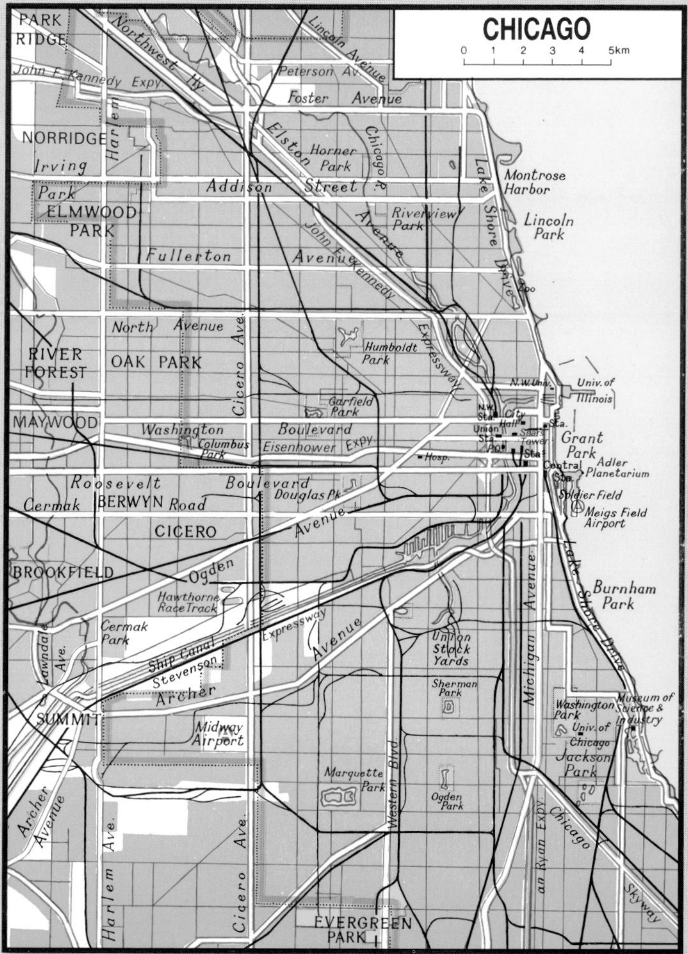
CHICAGO
0 1 2 3 4 5km
PARK RIDGE
John F. Kennedy Expy
Peterson Av.
Foster Avenue
NORRIDGE
Irving Park
Horner Park
Addison Street
Montrose Harbor
ELMWOOD PARK
Riverview Park
Lincoln Park
Fullerton Avenue
North Avenue
RIVER FOREST
OAK PARK
Humboldt Park
MAYWOOD
Garfield Park
Grant Park
Roosevelt Road
BERWYN
Cermak
CICERO
Soldier Field
Meigs Field Airport
BROOKFIELD
Hawthorne Race Track
Burnham Park
Cermak Park
Union Stock Yards
SUMMIT
Midway Airport
Sherman Park
Washington Park
Univ. of Chicago
Jackson Park
Marquette Park
Ogden Park
EVERGREEN PARK
Harlem Ave.
Cicero Ave.
Skyway

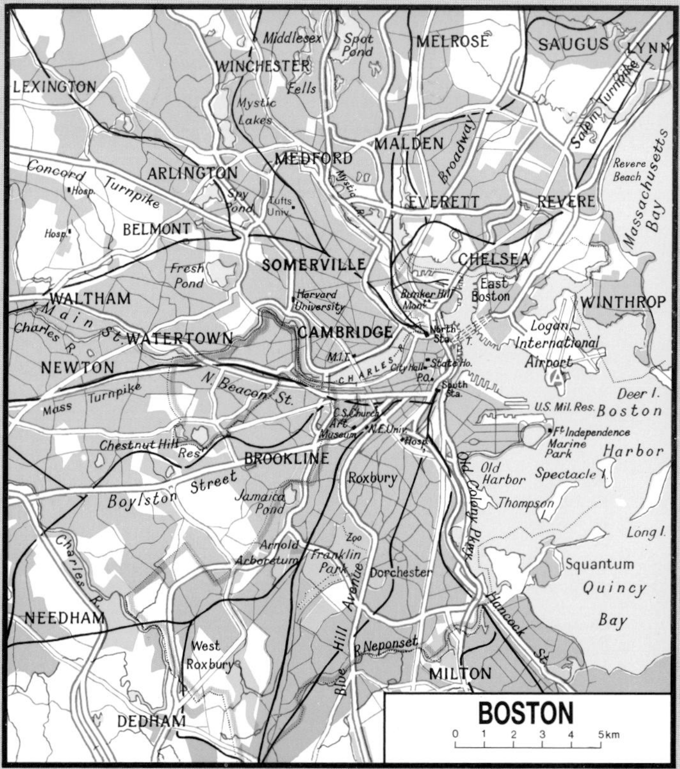
BOSTON
0 1 2 3 4 5km
MELROSE
SAUGUS
LYNN
LEXINGTON
WINCHESTER
Middlesex Fells
Spot Pond
Mystic Lakes
MALDEN
ARLINGTON
MEDFORD
EVERETT
REVERE
Concord Turnpike
BELMONT
SOMERVILLE
CHELSEA
Massachusetts Bay
WALTHAM
Harvard University
CAMBRIDGE
East Boston
WINTHROP
WATERTOWN
Logan International Airport
NEWTON
Boston Harbor
Chestnut Hill Res.
BROOKLINE
Roxbury
Boylston Street
Jamaica Pond
Arnold Arboretum
Franklin Park
Dorchester
Squantum
Quincy Bay
NEEDHAM
West Roxbury
MILTON
DEDHAM

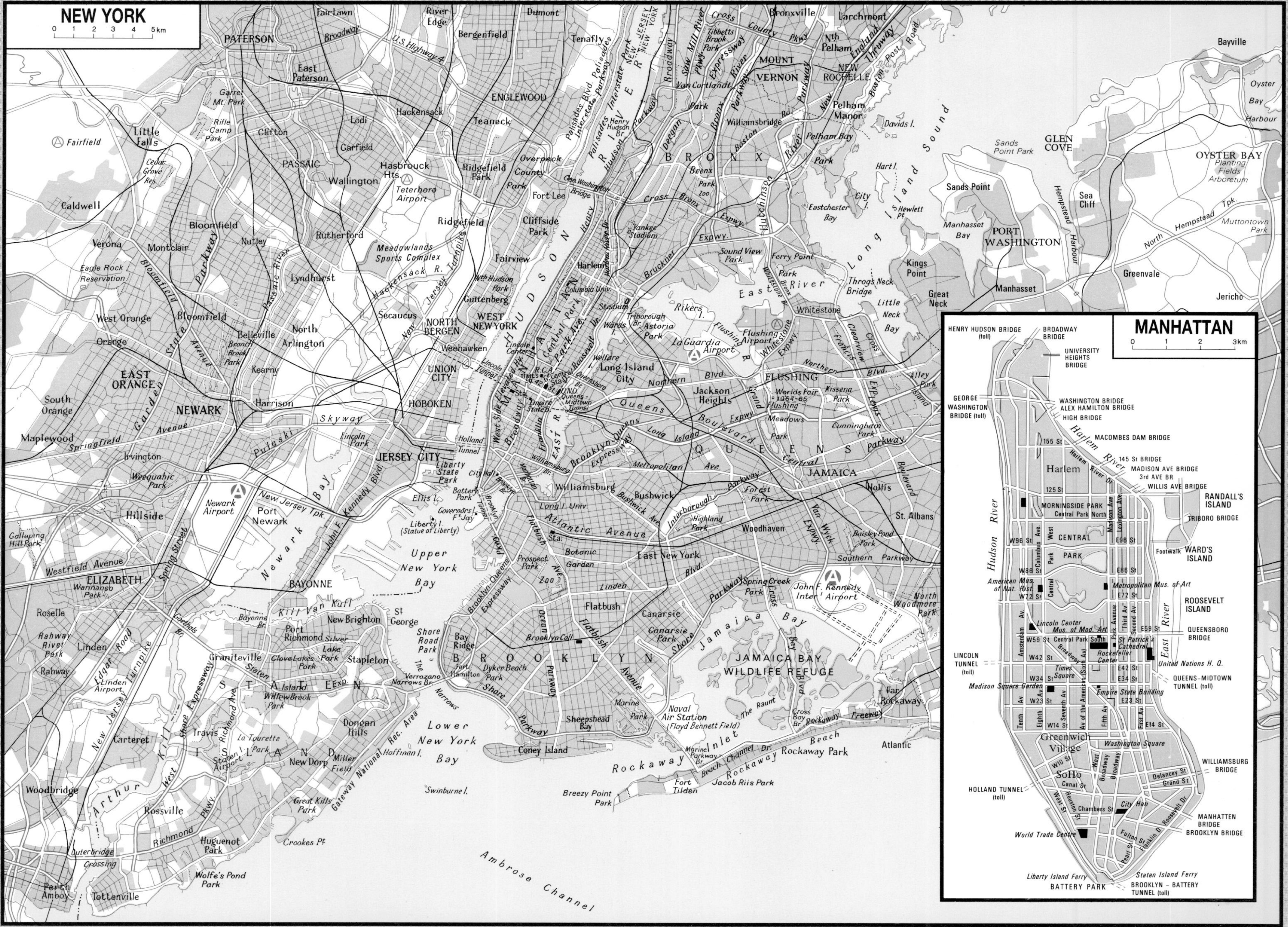
NEW YORK
0 1 2 3 4 5km
MANHATTAN
0 1 2 3km
PATERSON
East Paterson
Fair Lawn
River Edge
Bergenfield
Dumont
Tenafly
ENGLEWOOD
Teaneck
Hackensack
Lodi
Clifton
PASSAIC
Garfield
Wallington
Hasbrouck Hts
Teterboro Airport
Ridgefield Park
Ridgefield
Rutherford
Meadowlands Sports Complex
Lyndhurst
Nutley
Bloomfield
Montclair
Verona
Caldwell
Fairfield
Little Falls
West Orange
Orange
EAST ORANGE
South Orange
Maplewood
NEWARK
Harrison
Kearny
Belleville
North Arlington
Irvington
Hillside
Newark Airport
Port Newark
ELIZABETH
Roselle
Linden
Rahway
Carteret
Woodbridge
Perth Amboy
Tottenville
Secaucus
NORTH BERGEN
Weehawken
UNION CITY
HOBOKEN
JERSEY CITY
Liberty State Park
BAYONNE
WEST NEW YORK
Guttenberg
Fairview
Cliffside Park
Fort Lee
HUDSON
MANHATTAN
BRONX
Harlem
Yankee Stadium
MOUNT VERNON
Bronxville
Larchmont
NEW ROCHELLE
Pelham Manor
Long Island Sound
QUEENS
FLUSHING
La Guardia Airport
Jackson Heights
Long Island City
JAMAICA
Hollis
St. Albans
Woodhaven
Williamsburg
Bushwick
East New York
Flatbush
Canarsie
BROOKLYN
Bay Ridge
Sheepshead Bay
Coney Island
John F. Kennedy Intern'l Airport
JAMAICA BAY WILDLIFE REFUGE
Rockaway Park
Far Rockaway
Atlantic
Upper New York Bay
Lower New York Bay
Ambrose Channel
STATEN ISLAND
St George
New Brighton
Stapleton
Port Richmond
Dongan Hills
New Dorp
Rossville
Huguenot Park
Great Kills Park
Liberty I. (Statue of Liberty)
Ellis I.
Governors I.
GLEN COVE
Sands Point
PORT WASHINGTON
Manhasset
Great Neck
Kings Point
OYSTER BAY
Bayville
Greenvale
Jericho
HENRY HUDSON BRIDGE (toll)
BROADWAY BRIDGE
UNIVERSITY HEIGHTS BRIDGE
GEORGE WASHINGTON BRIDGE (toll)
WASHINGTON BRIDGE
ALEX HAMILTON BRIDGE
HIGH BRIDGE
MACOMBES DAM BRIDGE
145 St BRIDGE
MADISON AVE BRIDGE
3rd AVE BR
WILLIS AVE BRIDGE
RANDALL'S ISLAND
TRIBORO BRIDGE
WARD'S ISLAND
ROOSEVELT ISLAND
QUEENSBORO BRIDGE
United Nations H. Q.
QUEENS-MIDTOWN TUNNEL (toll)
WILLIAMSBURG BRIDGE
MANHATTEN BRIDGE
BROOKLYN BRIDGE
BROOKLYN - BATTERY TUNNEL (toll)
Staten Island Ferry
BATTERY PARK
Liberty Island Ferry
World Trade Centre
HOLLAND TUNNEL (toll)
LINCOLN TUNNEL (toll)
Madison Square Garden
Empire State Building
Times Square
Rockefeller Center
St Patrick's Cathedral
Lincoln Center
Mus. of Mod. Art
Metropolitan Mus. of Art
American Mus. of Nat. Hist.
CENTRAL PARK
MORNINGSIDE PARK
Harlem
Greenwich Village
SoHo
City Hall
Washington Square
Hudson River
Harlem River
East River

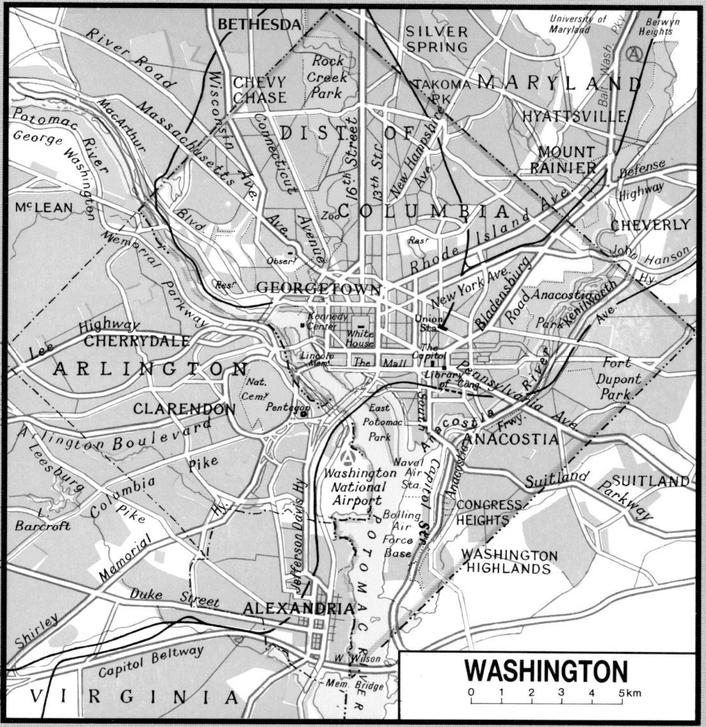

WASHINGTON

BETHESDA
SILVER SPRING
River Road
University of Maryland
Berwin Heights
Nash Pk.
ROCK CREEK PARK
CHEVY CHASE
MARYLAND
TAKOMA PK.
HYATTSVILLE
MOUNT RAINIER
DIST. OF COLUMBIA
16th Street
13th Str.
Rhode Island Ave.
Defense Highway
John Hanson Hy.
CHEVERLY
GEORGETOWN
Potomac River
George Washington
McLean
MacArthur Blvd.
Massachusetts Ave.
Wisconsin Ave.
Connecticut Ave.
New York Ave.
Bladensburg Road
Anacostia River
Kenilworth Ave.
Fort Dupont Park
CHERRYDALE
Highway
CLARENDON
ARLINGTON
Lee Highway
Memorial Bridge
The Mall
White House
Capitol
Union Sta.
Lincoln Mem.
Nat. Cem'
Pentagon
East Potomac Park
Anacostia
CONGRESS HEIGHTS
ANACOSTIA
Columbia Pike
Arlington Boulevard
Leesburg Pike
Shirley Highway
Barcroft
Jefferson Davis Hy.
Washington National Airport
Naval Air Sta.
Bolling Air Force Base
Suitland Fwy.
Pennsylvania Ave.
SUITLAND PARKWAY
WASHINGTON HIGHLANDS
Duke Street
ALEXANDRIA
Capitol Beltway
W. Wilson Mem. Bridge
VIRGINIA
POTOMAC RIVER
0 1 2 3 4 5km

SAN FRANCISCO

Anselmo
San Rafael
San Pablo
El Sobrante
Concord
Ross
Kentfield
RICHMOND–SAN RAFAEL BRIDGE
Richmond
San Pablo Res.
Pleasant Hill
Cowell
Larkspur
San Quentin
Richmond
Briones Res.
Mill Valley
Corte Madera
El Cerrito
Charles Lee Tilden Regional Park
Orinda Village
Walnut Creek
Muir Woods Nat. Monument
Tiburon
Belvedere
Albany
University of California
Orinda
CALDECOTT TUNNEL
Lafayette
Lafayette Reservoir
Alamo
Sausalito
Angel Island State Park
Berkeley
Piedmont
Danville
GOLDEN GATE BRIDGE
Alcatraz I.
Treasure Island
Oakland
San Ramon
Golden Gate
Gate
SAN FRANCISCO
Golden Gate Park
Richmond
Univ. of San Francisco
OAKLAND BAY BRIDGE
Redwood Regional Park
Sunset
Mt. Davidson 929
Mission
Alameda N.A.S.
Alameda
San Leandro
Lake Chabot
State Univ
Zoological Gardens
Naval Shipyard
Oakland International Airport
Castro Valley
Lake Merced
Daly City
Brisbane
San Lorenzo
Hayward
Pacifica
South San Francisco
San Francisco Bay
Mt. Eden
Shelter Cove
San Bruno
San Francisco International Airport
Point San Pedro
Pedro Valley
San Andreas Lake
Millbrae
SAN MATEO BRIDGE
Union City
Burlingame
Hillsborough
Alameda Cr.
Niles
Montara
San Francisco State Fish and Game Refuge
Foster City
Coyote Hills Reg. Park
Fremont
Moss Beach
San Mateo
Bair Island
Newark
El Granada
Crystal Springs Res.
Belmont
Greco Is.
San Carlos
DUMBARTON BRIDGE
Redwood City
Menlo Park
land
0 5 10 15km

LOS ANGELES

Van Norman Lakes
Sylmar
San Gabriel Mountains
Mt. San Antonio 10,064
San Fernando
Chatsworth
Sunland
La Crescenta
Cogswell Reservoir
Northridge
Sepulveda
Sun Valley
Verdugo Mountains
Montrose
San Gabriel Peak 6161
Mt. Wilson Observatory
San Gabriel Reservoir
LOS
ANGELES
Winnetka
San Fernando Valley
Burbank
La Cañada
Altadena
Morris Reservoir
Canoga Park
Tarzana
North Hollywood
San Rafael Hills
Rose Bowl
Sierra Madre
Woodland Hills
Encino
Sherman Oaks
Glendale
Griffith Park
Eagle Rock
Pasadena
Monrovia
Duarte
Azusa
Glendora
Cucamonga
Santa Monica Mts.
West Hollywood
Hollywood Bowl
South Pasadena
Arcadia
San Marino
Temple City
Puddingstone Reservoir
San Dimas
Claremont
La Verne
Upland
Beverly Hills
Hollywood
Dodgers Stad.
Elysian Park
Arroyo Seco Park
Alhambra
Baldwin Park
Covina
Pomona
Ontario
University of California
20th Century Fox Studios
LOS ANGELES
San Gabriel
Rosemead
El Monte
West Covina
SAN
Pacific Palisades
Culver City
Boyle Heights
Monterey Park
South San Gabriel
La Puente
Chino
Topanga Beach
Santa Monica
Venice
Maywood
East Los Angeles
Montebello
North Whittier Hts.
Diamond Bar
Los Serranos
BERNARDINO
Marina del Rey
Commerce
Pico Rivera
Hacienda Hts.
Rowland Heights
Cal Inst for men
Los Angeles International Airport
Florence
Huntington Park
Whittier
La Habra Heights
Chino Hills
Santa Monica Bay
Inglewood
Watts
South Gate
Bell Gardens
Downey
La Habra
Cal Inst for women
El Segundo
Lennox
Hawthorne
Lynwood
Hollydale
South Whittier
Brea
Prado Flood Control Basin
Manhattan Beach
Willow Brook
Paramount
Norwalk
La Mirada
Movieland Wax Mus.
Corona
Lawndale
Compton
Bellflower
Buena Park
Fullerton
Yorba Linda
Prado Dam
Gardena
Dominguez Hills
Artesia
Cerritos
Hermosa Beach
North Long Beach
La Palma
Cypress
Redondo Beach
Carson
Lakewood
Anaheim
Palos Verdes Estates
Lomita
Wilmington
Signal Hill
Los Alamitos
Race Track
Disneyland
Stanton
Orange
Santiago Res.
PACIFIC
OCEAN
Palos Verdes Pt.
Palos Verdes Hills
Rossmoor
Garden Grove
4007
Rancho Palos Verdes
San Pedro
Long Beach
Westminster
Santa Ana
Cowan Heights
Lemon Heights
CLEVELAND NATIONAL FOREST
Marineland of the Pacific
San Pedro Bay
Seal Beach
Sunset Bay
Tustin
San Pedro Channel
Point Fermin
Passenger Ferry to Santa Catalina Island
Sunset Beach
ORANGE
Como
Fountain Valley
Huntington Beach
Irvine
Costa Mesa
0 1 2 3 4 5km

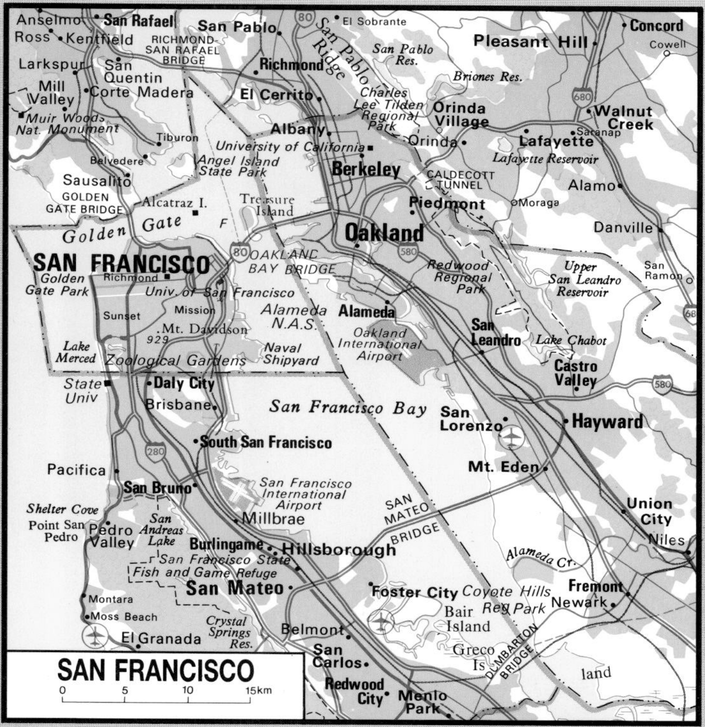

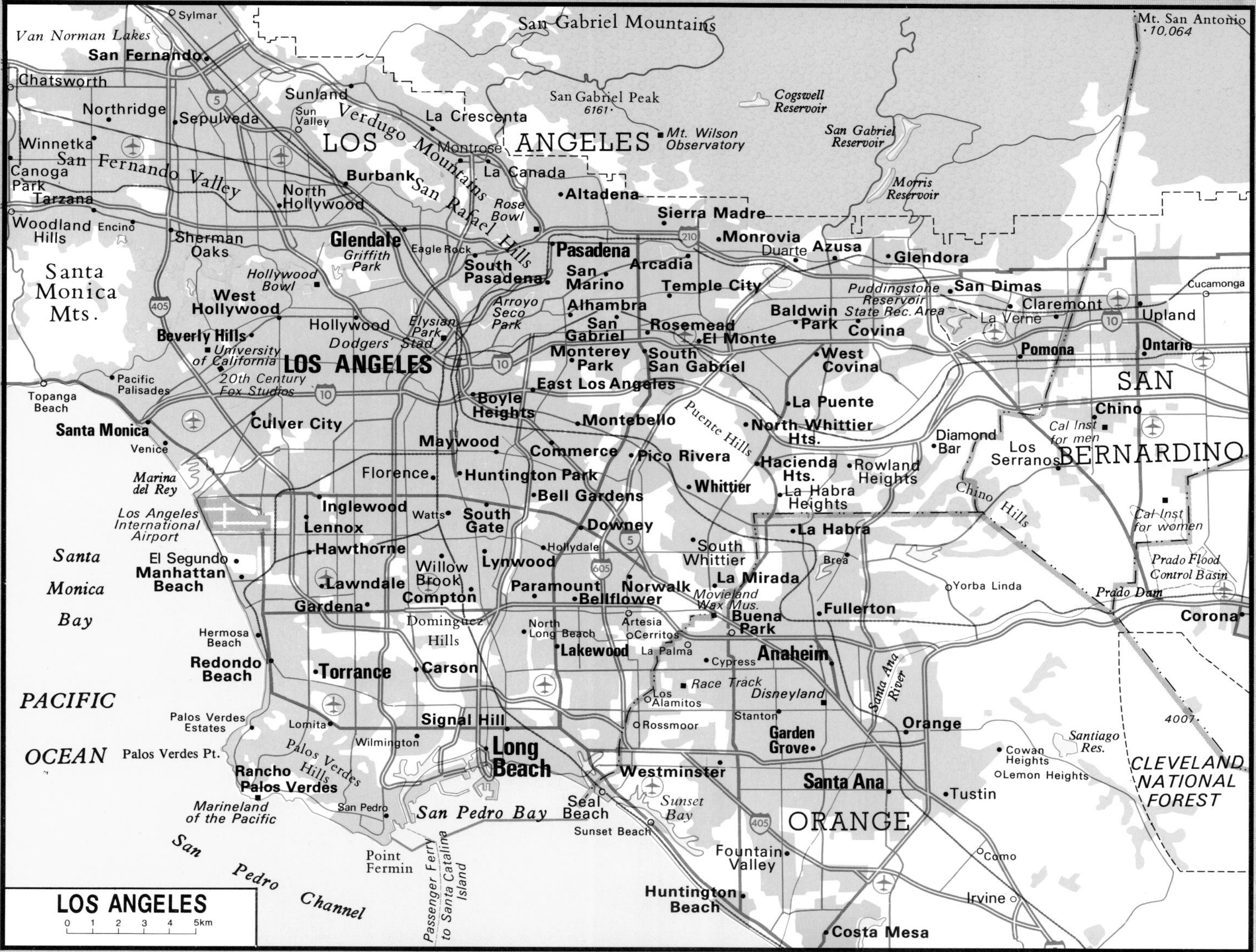

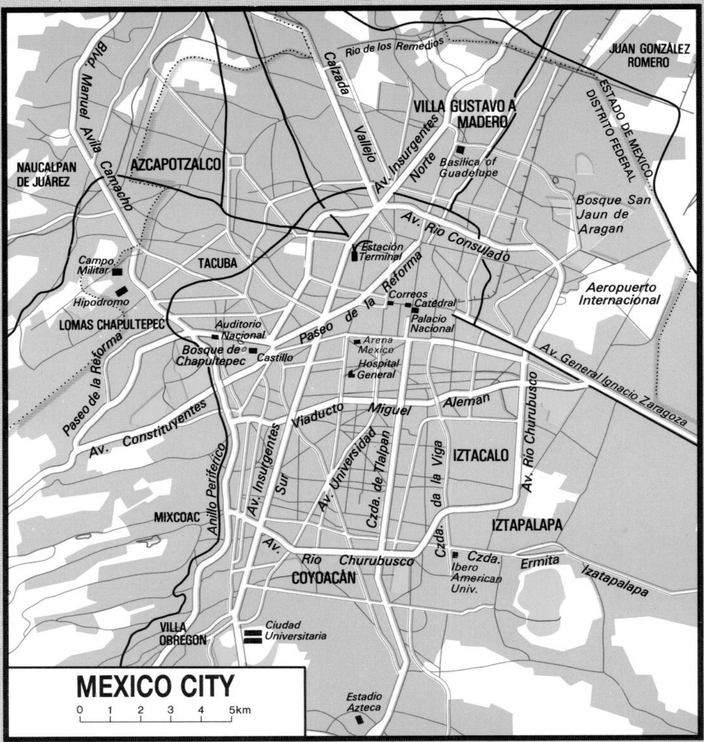
MEXICO CITY
0 1 2 3 4 5km
Rio de los Remedios
JUAN GONZÁLEZ ROMERO
Blvd. Manuel Avila Camacho
Calzada Vallejo
Av. Insurgentes Norte
VILLA GUSTAVO A MADERO
ESTADO DE MEXICO
DISTRITO FEDERAL
NAUCALPAN DE JUÁREZ
AZCAPOTZALCO
Basilica of Guadelupe
Bosque San Jaun de Aragan
Av. Rio Consulado
Estación Terminal
Campo Militar
TACUBA
Hipodromo
Correos
Catedral
Palacio Nacional
Aeropuerto Internacional
LOMAS CHAPULTEPEC
Auditorio Nacional
Paseo de la Reforma
Bosque de Chapultepec
Castillo
Arena Mexico
Hospital General
Av. General Ignacio Zaragoza
Av. Constituyentes
Viaducto
Miguel
Aleman
Av. Rio Churubusco
Av. Insurgentes Sur
Av. Universidad
Czda. de Tlalpan
Czda. de la Viga
IZTACALO
MIXCOAC
Anillo Periferico
IZTAPALAPA
Av. Rio Churubusco
COYOACÁN
Czda. Ermita Izatapalapa
Ibero American Univ.
VILLA OBREGON
Ciudad Universitaria
Estadio Azteca

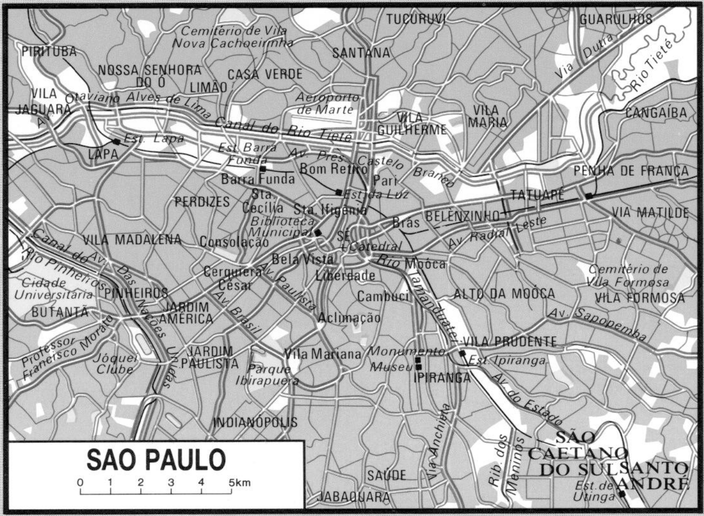
SAO PAULO
0 1 2 3 4 5km
TUCURUVI
GUARULHOS
PIRITUBA
Cemitério de Vila Nova Cachoeirinha
SANTANA
NOSSA SENHORA DO Ó
CASA VERDE
LIMÃO
Via Dutra
Rio Tietê
VILA JAGUARA
Otaviano Alves de Lima
Canal do Rio Tietê
Aeroporto de Marte
VILA GUILHERME
VILA MARIA
CANGAÍBA
LAPA
Est. Lapa
Est. Barra Funda
Av. Pres. Castelo Branco
Barra Funda
Bom Retiro
Pari
Est. da Luz
PENHA DE FRANÇA
TATUAPÉ
PERDIZES
Sta. Cecília
Sta. Ifigenia
Biblioteca Municipal
Brás
BELENZINHO
Av. Radial Leste
VIA MATILDE
VILA MADALENA
Consolação
Sé
Catedral
Bela Vista
Liberdade
Rio Mooca
Canal do Av. Rio Pinheiros
Cidade Universitária
PINHEIROS
Cerqueira César
Av. Paulista
JARDIM AMÉRICA
Av. Brasil
Cambuci
ALTO DA MOOCA
Cemitério de Vila Formosa
VILA FORMOSA
BUTANTÃ
Aclimação
Av. Sapopemba
Professor Francisco Morato
Jóquei Clube
JARDIM PAULISTA
Parque Ibirapuera
Vila Mariana
Monumento
Museu
IPIRANGA
VILA PRUDENTE
Est. Ipiranga
Av. do Estado
Via Anchieta
INDIANÓPOLIS
SAÚDE
JABAQUARA
Rib. dos Meninos
SÃO CAETANO DO SUL
SANTO ANDRÉ
Est. de Utinga

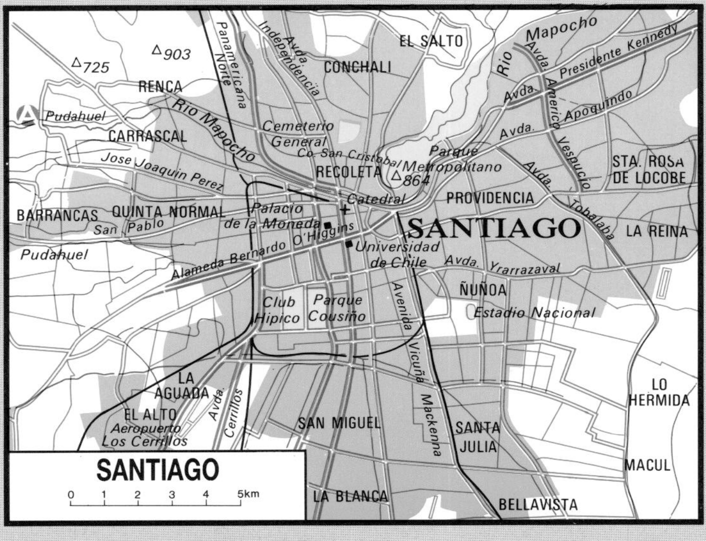
SANTIAGO
0 1 2 3 4 5km
△725
△903
Panamericana Norte
Avda. Independencia
EL SALTO
Rio Mapocho
Avda. Presidente Kennedy
CONCHALI
RENCA
Pudahuel
Rio Mapocho
CARRASCAL
Cemeterio General
Co. San Cristobal
Parque Metropolitano
△864
Avda. Americo Vespucio
Avda. Apoquindo
Jose Joaquin Perez
RECOLETA
STA. ROSA DE LOCOBE
Tobalaba
BARRANCAS
QUINTA NORMAL
San Pablo
Palacio de la Moneda
Catedral
PROVIDENCIA
SANTIAGO
LA REINA
Pudahuel
Alameda Bernardo O'Higgins
Universidad de Chile
Avda. Yrrarazaval
ÑUÑOA
Club Hipico
Parque Cousiño
Avenida Vicuña Mackenna
Estadio Nacional
LA AGUADA
Avda. Cerrillos
EL ALTO
Aeropuerto Los Cerrillos
SAN MIGUEL
SANTA JULIA
LO HERMIDA
MACUL
LA BLANCA
BELLAVISTA

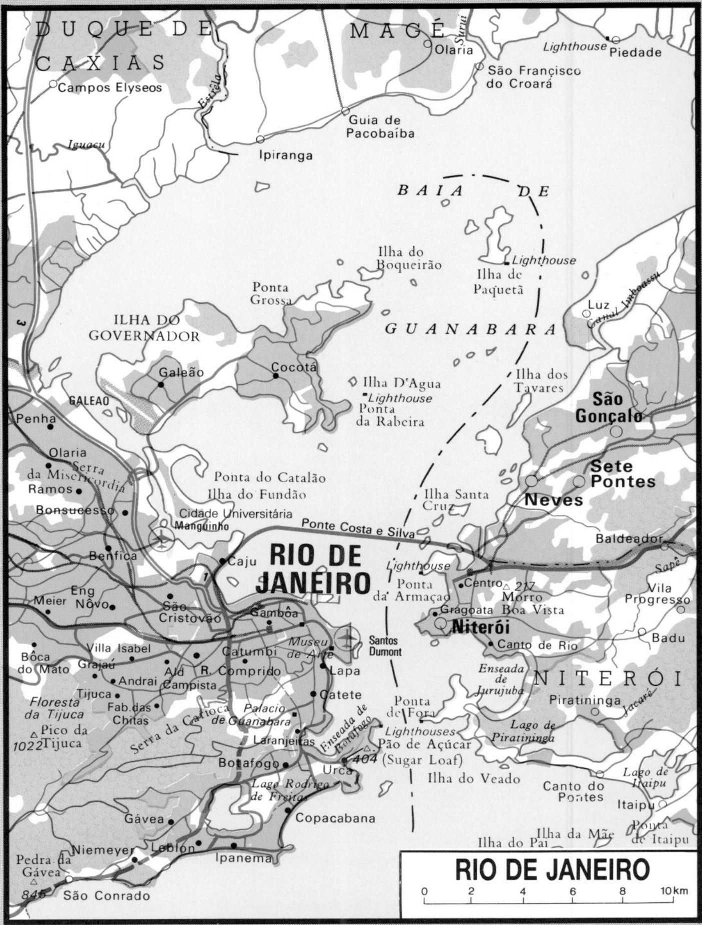
RIO DE JANEIRO
0 2 4 6 8 10km
DUQUE DE CAXIAS
Campos Elyseos
MAGÉ
Olaria
Lighthouse
Piedade
São Francisco do Croará
Guia de Pacobaíba
Iguaçu
Ipiranga
BAIA DE GUANABARA
Ilha do Boqueirão
Lighthouse
Ilha de Paquetá
Ponta Grossa
ILHA DO GOVERNADOR
Luz
Galeão
Cocotá
Ilha D'Agua
Lighthouse
Ponta da Rabeira
Ilha dos Tavares
São Gonçalo
GALEAO
Penha
Olaria
Serra da Misericórdia
Ramos
Ponta do Catalão
Ilha do Fundão
Ilha Santa Cruz
Sete Pontes
Neves
Bonsucesso
Cidade Universitária
Manguinho
Ponte Costa e Silva
Baldeador
Benfica
Caju
RIO DE JANEIRO
Lighthouse
Ponta da Armação
Centro
217
Morro Boa Vista
Vila Progresso
Meier
Eng. Novo
São Cristovão
Gamboa
Gragoatá
Niterói
Santos Dumont
Museu de Arte
Badu
Canto de Rio
Boca do Mato
Villa Isabel
Grajaú
Andrai
Ald. Campista
Catumbi
R. Comprido
Lapa
Enseada de Jurujuba
NITERÓI
Floresta da Tijuca
Tijuca
Fab. das Chitas
Catete
Ponta do Fora
Piratininga
Pico da Tijuca
1022
Serra da Carioca
Palacio de Guanabara
Laranjeiras
Enseada de Botafogo
Lighthouses
Pão de Açúcar
404 (Sugar Loaf)
Lago de Piratininga
Botafogo
Urca
Lage Rodrigo de Freitas
Ilha do Veado
Canto do Pontes
Lago de Itaipu
Itaipu
Gávea
Copacabana
Ilha da Mãe
Ponta de Itaipu
Ilha do Pai
Pedra da Gávea
845
Niemeyer
Leblon
Ipanema
São Conrado

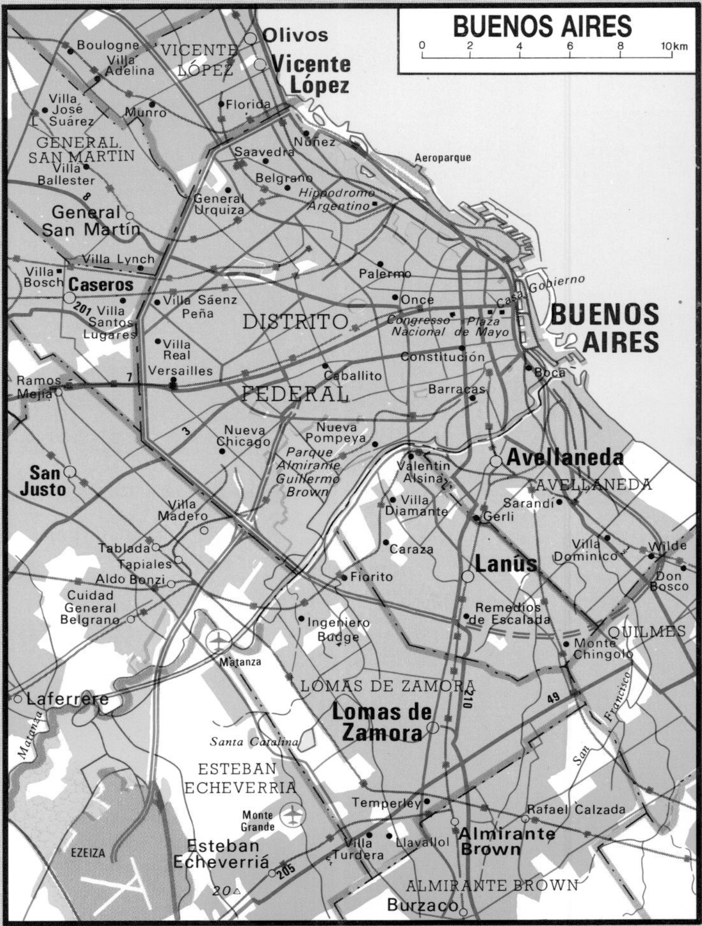
BUENOS AIRES
0 2 4 6 8 10km
Boulogne
Villa Adelina
VICENTE LÓPEZ
Olivos
Vicente López
Florida
Villa José Suárez
Munro
Núñez
GENERAL SAN MARTIN
Saavedra
Aeroparque
Villa Ballester
Belgrano
General Urquiza
Hipódromo Argentino
General San Martin
Villa Lynch
Palermo
Villa Bosch
Caseros
Villa Sáenz Peña
Once
Casa Gobierno
BUENOS AIRES
Villa Santos Lugares
DISTRITO FEDERAL
Congreso Nacional
Plaza de Mayo
Villa Real
Versailles
Constitución
Caballito
Barracas
Ramos Mejía
Boca
Nueva Chicago
Nueva Pompeya
Parque Almirante Guillermo Brown
Avellaneda
AVELLANEDA
San Justo
Valentin Alsina
Villa Diamante
Sarandí
Gerli
Villa Madero
Villa Dominico
Wilde
Tablada
Tapiales
Caraza
Lanús
Aldo Bonzi
Fiorito
Don Bosco
Cuidad General Belgrano
Ingeniero Budge
Remedios de Escalada
QUILMES
Monte Chingolo
Matanza
Laferrere
LOMAS DE ZAMORA
Lomas de Zamora
Santa Catalina
ESTEBAN ECHEVERRIA
Monte Grande
Temperley
Rafael Calzada
EZEIZA
Esteban Echeverriá
Villa Turdera
Llavallol
Almirante Brown
20△
ALMIRANTE BROWN
Burzaco

The roman alphabet is used world-wide. Yet the sounds of Latin from which it was inherited were far too few to allow the alphabet to be applied unaltered to the languages of the world. As a result numerous modifications have been made by adding supplementary letters, by changing the original letters or by adding accents or other diacritical signs.

This brief guide is intended to give no more than an indication of the English language equivalents of the more important letters or combinations of letters in the various alphabets used in the Atlas. An English word is added in brackets to illustrate the sound intended.

FRENCH
There are four nasal vowels:
am an aen em en aon ã
aim ain en eim ein im in ẽ
om on õ
um un e͠u
ã ẽ õ e͠u are like a in hart; e in met; o in corn; oo in book pronounced nasally.
au, eau = o (no); é = ay (lay); è, ê, = e (met);
oi oî = wa (wand)
c + a = k; c + e or i = ç = s (sit)
ch = sh (fresh); g + a, o or u = g (got)
g + e or i = j = zh†; gn = ni (onion)
gu = g (got); gü = gw (iguana)
ll = l or y; qu = k; th = t
u = between e in few and oo in too

SPANISH
c + a, o or u = k; c + e or i = th (thin) or s (sit)
ch = ch (cheese); g + a, o or u = g (got)
g + e or i = kh*; gu + a, o or u = gw (iguana)
gu + e or i = g (got); j = kh*; ñ = ny (canyon);
ll = y (yes)
qu + a, o or u = kw (quick); qu + e or i = k (kite)
y = y (yes); z = th (thin) or z depending on dialect

ITALIAN
c + a, o or u = k; c + e or i = ch (cheese)
ch = k
g + a, o or u = g (got); g + e or i = j (jet)
gh = g (got); gli = lli (million)
qu = kw (quick); z = ts or dz

ROMANIAN
ă = a in relative
â = i in ravine
c + a, o or u = k
c + e or i = ch (cheese); ch = k
g + a, o or u = g (got); g + e or i = j (jet)
ş = sh (fresh); ţ = ts (sits)

PORTUGUESE
ã, ãe = French ẽ
õa, õe = French õ
c + a, o or u = k; c + e or i = s
ç = s; ch = sh (fresh)
ih = lli (million)
x = sh (fresh); z = z but = zh when final

GERMAN
ä = e (met); au = ow (down)
äu = oy (boy); c = ts (sits)
ch = kh*; ei, ey = eye (= y in why)
eu = oy (boy); g = g (got)
ie = ie (retrieve); j = y (yes)
ö = oo (book); s = z but s when final
sch = sh (fresh); sp, st = shp, sht
ü = French u; v = f; w = v; z = ts (sits)

DUTCH
aa ee are long vowels
c + e or i or z = s, otherwise k
ij = eye (= y in why)

SCANDINAVIAN
å = aw (law); ä = e (met)
ø = oo (book); øj = oy (boy)
j = y (yes)

ICELANDIC
ð = dh = th (then)
hv = kw; ll = tl; þ = th

FINNISH
ay = eye (= y in why)
j = y; y = French u; w = v

HUNGARIAN
a = aw (law); cs = ch (cheese); ccs = chch;
gy = d + y (dew)
j = y; ny = ny (canyon)
s = sh (fresh); ss = shsh
sz = s (sit); ty = t + y (yes)

ai = e (met); av = au or av
dh = th (then); th = th (thin)
kh = kh*; oi = i (ravine)
ou = oo (too)

TURKISH
c = j (jet); ç = ch (cheese)
ö = oo (book); ş = sh
ü = French u
ı and i = i (ravine)

RUSSIAN
ay = a + y (yes)
e = e or ye
ë = yaw; ëy = yoy
ch = ch (cheese); sh = sh (fresh)
sh ch = sh ch (fresh cheese)
ts = ts (sits)
ya = ya (yam); z = z (zoo)
zh = zh (measure)
' = sound of y (yes)
" = silent

OTHER SLAVONIC

§S-C	Pol	Cz		
c	c	c	=	ts (sits)
	ć		=	ts + y (yes)
č	cz	č	=	ch (cheese)
ć			=	t + y (yes)
đ		ď	=	d + y (yes)
		ě	=	e (mother)
h	ch	ch	=	kh*
j	j	j	=	y (yes)
	l		=	w (wood)
nj	ń	ň	=	ny (canyon)
		ř	=	rzh*
š	sz	š	=	sh (fresh)
		ť	=	t + y (yes)
ž	z̊, rz, ź	ž	=	zh*

ARABIC
long vowels have a macron (bar), ā
dh = th (then)
h = h (hat); j = (jet)
gh = French r, pronounce as g (got)
kh = kh* q = g (got)
' and ' are best treated as glottal stops
ḍ ḥ ṣ ṭ ẓ = d, h, s, t, z
Note: 1. in Egypt and Sudan g = g (got)
2. in NW Africa Dj = j (jet)
ou = w (wadi)

FARSI (IRAN)
Can be read as Arabic above. Stress is on the last syllable.

SOMALI
long vowels are aa, ee, ii, oo, uu
c is silent = glottal stop
dh = th (then)
g = g (got); q = k (kite)
sh = sh (fresh); w = w (wadi)
x = kh*

MALAY – INDONESIAN
As English except
c = ch (cheese)

CHINESE (PINYIN)
q = ch (church); c = ts (sits)
x = hs = h + s

†zh = s in measure;
*kh = ch in Scottish loch
= German ch in achtung

§**S-C** = Serbo-Croat
Pol = Polish
Cz = Czech

A

ABLATION The loss of water from ice and snow surfaces, by melting and run-off, calving of icebergs, evaporation and snow-blowing.

ABRASION The wearing down or away of rocks by friction.

ABSOLUTE HUMIDITY The amount of water vapour in a specified amount of air, frequently expressed as grams of water vapour per kilogram of dry air containing the vapour.

ABYSSAL Usually applied to the very deep parts of the oceans, over 3km below the surface.

ACCRETION The growth of objects by collection of additional material, usually of smaller size. Ice particles in the atmosphere can grow by this process.

ACID PRECIPITATION Rain and snow with a pH of less than 5.6.

ADVECTION Movement of a property in air and water by their motion. Usually applied to horizontal rather than vertical motion.

AEOLIAN Related to winds. Thus aeolian geomorphology is concerned with the processes whereby wind removes, distributes and deposits materials of the earth's surface.

AGGLOMERATE A rock made of small pieces of lava that have been fused by heat.

AGGRADATION The building up of a land surface by deposition of material by wind, water or ice.

AGGREGATE A loose collection of rock fragments.

ALLUVIAL PLAIN A plain, usually at low altitude, made of alluvium.

ANTICYCLONE An extensive region of relatively high atmospheric pressure, usually a few thousand kilometres across, in which the low level winds spiral outwards, clockwise in the northern hemisphere and anticlockwise in the southern hemisphere.

ARCHIPELAGO A sea or lake containing numerous islands, such as the area between Sumatra and the Philippines.

ARTESIAN WELL A well which taps water held under pressure in rocks below the surface. The pressure results in a well water level higher than the highest part of the water-bearing rocks.

ATOLL A coral reef surrounding a lagoon found in the tropical oceans.

AURORA BOREALIS (Northern Lights) Flashing lights in the atmosphere some 400km above polar regions caused by solar particles being trapped in the earth's magnetic field.

AVALANCHE The sudden and rapid movement of ice, snow, earth and rock down a slope.

AZIMUTH Horizontal angle between two directions.

B

BADLANDS Highly dissected landscapes, usually associated with poorly consolidated materials and sparse vegetation cover.

BAR A usually sandy feature, lying parallel to the coast and frequently underwater.

BARCHAN A crescentic sand dune whose horns point in the direction of dune movement.

BAROGRAPH An instrument for recording atmospheric pressure. The output is a graph of pressure changes through time.

BAROMETER An instrument for measuring atmospheric pressure. The reading is either by measuring the height of a column of mercury or by the compression or expansion of a series of vacuum chambers.

BARRIER REEF A coral reef characterized by the presence of a lagoon or body of water between it and the associated coastline.

BASALT A fine-grained and dark coloured igneous rock.

BASE LEVEL The lower limit to the operation of erosional processes generating on land – usually defined with reference to the role of running water. Sea level is the most general form of base level.

BASIN An area of land encompassing the water flow into any specific river channel – hence usually known as a drainage basin.

BATHOLITH A large mass of intrusive igneous rock.

BATHYMETRY Measurement of water depth.

BAUXITE The main ore of aluminium.

BEACH A coastal accumulation of various types of sediment, usually sands and pebbles.

BEAUFORT SCALE A scale of wind speed devised by Admiral Sir Francis Beaufort based on effects of winds on ships. Later modified to include land-based phenomena.

BENCH MARK A reference point used in the measurement of land height in topographic surveying.

BENTHIC Relating to plants, animals and other organisms that inhabit the floors of lakes, seas and oceans.

BERGSCHRUND The crevasse existing at the head of a glacier because of the movement of glacier ice away from the rock wall.

BIGHT A bend in a coast forming an open bay, or the bay itself.

BIOMASS The mass of biological material present per plant or animal, per community or per unit area.

BIOME A mixed community of plants and animals occupying a large area of continental size.

BIOSPHERE The zone at the interface of the earth's surface, ocean and atmosphere where life is found.

BIOTA The entire collection of species or organisms, plants and animals found in a given region.

BISE A cold, dry northerly to north-easterly wind occurring in the mountains of Central Europe in winter.

BLACK EARTH A black soil rich in humus, found extensively in temperate grasslands such as the Russian Steppes.

BLOW HOLE Vertical shaft leading from a sea cave to the surface. Air and water are frequently forced through it by advancing seas.

BORE A large solitary wave which moves up funnel-shaped rivers and estuaries.

BOREAL A descriptive term, usually of climate and forest, to characterize conditions in middle to high latitudes.

BOURNE A river channel on chalk terrain that flows after heavy rain.

BUTTE A small, flat-topped and often steep-sided hill standing isolated on a flat plain. *(see picture below)*

C

CALDERA A depression, usually several kilometres across.

CALVING The breaking away of a mass of ice from a floating glacier or ice shelf to form an iceberg.

CANYON A steep sided valley, usually found in semi-arid and arid areas.

CAPE An area of land jutting out into water, frequently as a peninsula or promontory.

CARDINAL POINTS The four principal compass points, north, east, south and west.

CATARACT A large waterfall over a precipice.

CHINOOK A warm, dry wind that blows down the eastern slopes of the Rocky Mountains of North America.

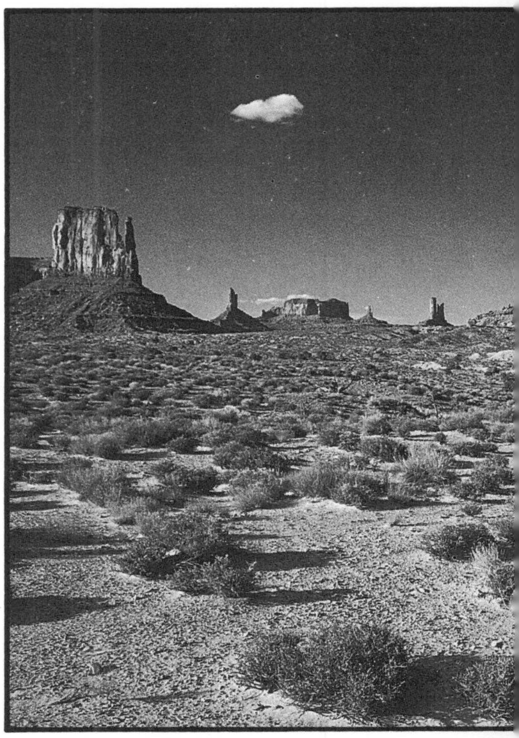

Above Butte, Monument Valley, Arizona USA. This type of flat-topped, steep sided hill is characteristic of the arid plateau region of the western United States.

CIRQUE OR CORRIE A hollow, open downstream but bounded upstream by a curved, steep headwall, with a gently sloping floor. Found in areas that have been glaciated.

CLIMATE The long-term atmospheric characteristics of a specified area.

CLOUD A collection of a vast number of small water droplets or ice crystals or both in the atmosphere.

COL A pass or saddle between two mountain peaks.

COLD FRONT A zone of strong horizontal temperature gradient in the atmosphere moving such that, for the surface observer, cold air replaces warm.

CONDENSATION The process of formation of liquid water from water vapour.

CONFLUENCE The 'coming together' of material

flows, most usually used in fluids such as the atmosphere and oceans.

CONGLOMERATE A rock which comprises or contains rounded pebbles more than about 2mm in diameter.

CONTINENTAL DRIFT The movement of continents relative to each other. (See *Plate Tectonics*)

CONTINENTAL SHELF A portion of the continental crust below sea level that slopes gently seaward forming an extension of the adjacent coastal plain separated from the deep ocean by the steeply sloping continental slope.

CONTINENTAL SLOPE Lies on the seaward edge of the continental shelf and slopes steeply to the ocean floor.

CONTOUR A line on a map that joins points of equal height or equal depth.

CONVECTION CURRENT A current resulting from convection which is a mode of mass transport within a fluid (especially heat) resulting in movement and mixing of properties of that fluid.

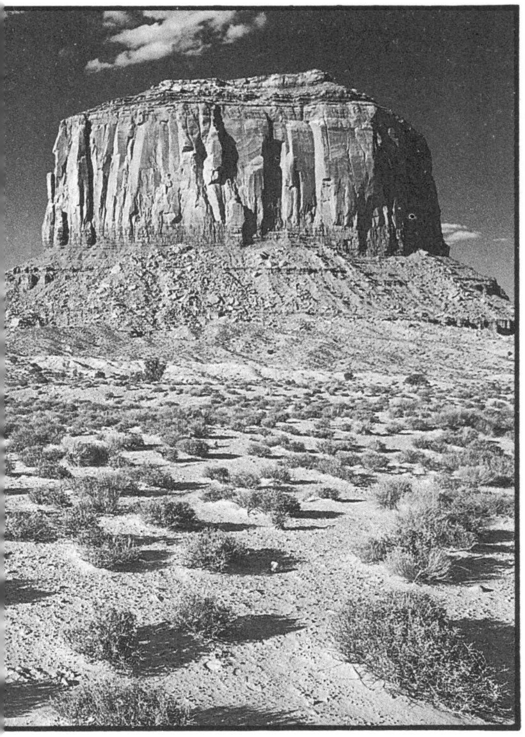

CONVERGENCE The opposite of divergence which is the outflowing mass of fluid. Hence convergence is the inflowing of such mass.

CORAL REEF Large structures fringing islands and coastlines consisting mostly of corals and algae.

CORDILLERA A system of mountain ranges consisting of a number of more or less parallel chains of mountain peaks – such as in the Rocky Mountains.

CRATER A depression at the top of a volcano where a vent carrying lava and gasses reaches the surface.

CRATON A continental area that has experienced little internal deformation in the last 600 million years.

CREVASSE A deep fissure in the surface of a body of ice.

CYCLONE A region of relatively low atmospheric pressure about 2000 km across around which air rotates anticlockwise in the northern hemisphere and clockwise in the southern.

D

DATUM LEVEL Something (such as a fixed point or assumed value) used as a basis for calculating or measuring. Frequently a height of ground relative to which other heights are assessed.

DECLINATION Angular distance north or south from the equator measured along a line of longitude.

DECIDUOUS FOREST Forest in which the trees shed their leaves at a particular time, season or growth stage. The most common manifestation is the shedding in winter.

DEFLATION The process whereby the wind removes fine materials from the surface of a beach or desert.

DEGRADATION The lowering and often flattening of a land surface by erosion.

DELTA Accumulations of sediment deposited at the mouths of rivers. The Nile and Mississippi deltas are two famous examples.

DENUDATION The laying bare of underlying rocks or strata by the removal of overlying material.

DEPOSITION The laying down of material, which, in geomorphological terms, was previously carried by wind, liquid water or ice.

DEPRESSION See *cyclone*

DESALINIZATION To take out the salt content of a material. Usually applied to the extraction of salt from sea water to give fresh water.

DESERT An area in which vegetation cover is sparse or absent and precipitation is low in amount. Deserts can be hot or cold.

DISCHARGE The volume of flow of fluid in a given time period.

DISSECTED PLATEAU A relatively flat, high level area of land which has been cut by streams.

DIURNAL Occurring everyday or having a daily cycle.

DIVERGENCE A spreading of material. Frequently found in high pressure areas (anticyclones) in the atmosphere where air spirals outwards from the centre.

DOLDRUMS A zone of light, variable winds and low atmospheric pressure near or slightly north of the equator.

DRAINAGE The flow of material (usually a fluid) over the earth's surface due to the force of gravity. Most familiarly seen as rivers.

DRIFT ICE Ice bodies drifting in ocean currents.

DROUGHT Dryness caused by lack of precipitation, most easily seen in the hot, dry desert areas of the world.

DROWNED VALLEY A valley which has been filled with water due to a rise of sea level relative to the level with which the river mouth was previously in accord.

DRUMLIN A depositional landform, usually made of glacially-derived material, which has been streamlined by the passage of overlying ice.

DRY VALLEY A valley which is seldom, if ever, occupied by a stream channel.

DUNE An accumulation of sand deposited and shaped by wind.

DUST Solid particles carried in suspension by the atmosphere.

DYKE A sheet-like intrusion of igneous rock, usually oriented vertically, which cuts across the structural planes of the host rocks.

E

EARTH PILLAR A pinnacle of soil or other unconsolidated material that is protected from erosion by the presence of a stone at the top.

EARTHQUAKE A series of shocks and tremors resulting from the sudden release of pressure along active faults and in areas of volcanic activity.

EBB TIDE Tide receding to or at its lowest point.

ECLIPSE, LUNAR The total or partial obscuring of the Moon by the Earth lying on a line between the Moon and the Sun.

ECLIPSE, SOLAR The total or partial obscuring of the Sun by the Moon lying on a line between the Sun and the Earth.

ECOLOGY A branch of science that studies the relations of plants and animals with each other and with their non-living environment.

ECOSYSTEM An entity within which ecological relations operate.

EPICENTRE The point on the earth's surface which lies directly above the focus of an earthquake.

EQUINOX The time of year when the sun is directly overhead at noon at the equator.

ERG A sand desert.

EROSION The group of processes whereby debris is loosened or dissolved and removed from any part of the earth's surface.

ERRATIC A rock that has been carried to its present location by a glacier.

ESCARPMENT A linear land form with one steep side (scarp slope) and one less steep side (dip slope).

ESKER A sinuous ridge of coarse gravel which has been deposited by a meltwater stream normally flowing underneath a glacier.

ESTUARY The sections of a river which flow into the sea and are influenced by tidal currents.

EVAPORATION The diffusion of water vapour into the atmosphere from freely exposed water surfaces.

EXFOLIATION The weathering of a rock by the peeling off of surface layers.

F

FATHOM A unit of length equal to six feet, most usually used in measuring depth of water.

FAULT A crack or fissure in rock, resulting from tectonic movement.

FAUNA Animals or animal life of an area.

FEN A low lying area partially covered by water which is characterized by accumulations of peat.

FJORD A glacially eroded valley whose floor is occupied by the sea.

FIRTH A sea inlet, particularly in Scotland.

FLORA Plants or plant life in an area.

FLUVIOGLACIAL The activity of rivers which are fed by water melted from glaciers.

FOG An accumulation of water droplets or ice crystals in the atmosphere such that visibility is reduced to 1km or less.

FÖHN WIND A strong, gusty, warm, down-slope wind which occurs on the lee side of a mountain range.

FOLD A bend in rock strata resulting from movement of the crustal rocks.

FOOD CHAIN The transfer of food from one type of organism to another in a sequence.

FORD A shallow part of a river that allows easy crossing.

FRACTURE The splitting of material into parts: usually concerned with geological materials.

FRAZIL ICE Fine spikes of ice in suspension in water, usually associated with the freezing of sea water.

FRONT A transition zone between air of different density, temperature and humidity.

FROST A situation resulting from air temperatures falling to 0°C – either in the air (air frost) or at the ground (ground frost).

FUMAROLE A small, volcanic vent through which hot gasses are emitted.

G

GABBRO A basic igneous rock, usually coarse grained and dark grey to black in colour.

GEEST Ancient alluvial sediments which still cover the land surfaces on which they were originally deposited.

GEODESY The determination of the size and shape of the earth by survey and calculation.

GEOID The shape of the earth at mean sea level.

GEOLOGY Science that deals with the nature and origin of the earth's rocks and sediments.

GEOMORPHOLOGY Science that deals with the nature and origin of landforms of the earth's surface.

GEOSYNCLINE A very large depression, tens or hundreds of kilometres across and up to ten kilometres deep, the floor of which is built up by sedimentation.

GEYSER A spring of geothermally heated water that erupts intermittently due to pressures beneath the surface. Old Faithful in Yellowstone National Park, USA, is the most famous example.

GLACIATION The incursion of ice into (or over) a landscape resulting in a whole suite of glacial processes operating thereupon.

GLACIER A large body of ice, in a valley or covering a much larger area. The largest are found in polar regions.

GLEN Valley. Term especially used in Scotland.

GNEISS A coarse-grained igneous rock that has been metamorphosed.

GONDWANALAND A large continent which it is thought was split very early in geological time to form parts of Africa, Australia, Antarctica, South America and India.

GORGE A deep and narrow section of a river valley, usually with very steep sides.

GRAVEL Loose, rounded fragments of rock.

GREAT CIRCLE A circle formed on the surface of the earth by the intersection of a plane through the centre of the earth with the surface. Lines of longitude and the Equator are great circles.

GROUND FROST See *frost*

GROUND WATER All water (gaseous, liquid or solid) lying below the earth's surface and not chemically combined with the minerals present.

GROYNE A man-made barrier running across a beach and into the sea; constructed to reduce erosion of the beach by longshore currents.

GULF A part of the sea that is partly or almost completely enclosed by land.

GULLY A linear depression worn in the earth by running water after rains.

GUYOT A flat-topped mountain on the sea floor which does not reach the sea surface.

GYRE Large circulations of water in the world's oceans, involving the major currents.

H

HAFF A coastal lagoon separated from the open seas by a sand spit.

HAIL Solid precipitation which falls as ice particles from cumulonimbus clouds. Contrasts markedly with snow.

HEMISPHERE Half of the earth, usually thought of in terms of its surface. The most familiar are the northern and southern hemispheres, bounded by the Equator.

HORIZON Apparent junction of earth and sky.

HORSE LATITUDE The latitude belts over the oceans at latitudes of 30–35° where winds are predominantly calm or light and weather is often hot and dry.

HOT SPOT A small area of the earth's crust where an unusually high heat flow is associated with volcanic activity.

HOT SPRING An emission of hot water at the land surface.

HURRICANE A severe cyclone occurring in the tropics, characterized by high wind speeds and heavy precipitation.

HYDROLOGICAL CYCLE The continuous movement of all forms of water (vapour, liquid and solid) on, in and above the earth.

HYDROSPHERE The earth's water – saline, fresh, gaseous, liquid and solid.

HYGROMETER A device for measuring the relative humidity of the atmosphere.

HYPSOGRAPHIC CURVE A generalized profile of the earth and ocean floors which represents the proportions of the area of the surface at various altitudes above or below a datum.

I

ICEBERG A large floating mass of ice detached from a glacier, usually tens of metres deep and can be several kilometres across.

ICE-CAP A dome-shaped glacier with a generally outward flow of ice.

ICE FLOE A piece of floating ice which is not attached to the land and is usually 2–3 metres thick.

ICE SHELF A floating sheet of ice attached to an embayment in the coast.

IGNEOUS ROCK Rock formed when molten material solidifies, either within the earth's crust or at the surface.

INSELBERG A large, residual hill which overlooks a surrounding eroded plain.

INSOLATION The amount of solar radiation received over a specified area and a specified time.

INTERNATIONAL DATE LINE An arbitary line, roughly along the 180° longitude line, east and west of which the date differs by one day.

INVERSION (temperature)
An increase of temperature with height.

IRRIGATION The supply of water to land by artificial means. Usually to improve agricultural productivity.

ISLAND ARC A chain of islands with an arcuate plan form. The islands are usually volcanic in origin.

ISOBAR A line drawn on diagrams joining equal values of atmospheric pressure. A particular kind of isopleth.

ISOPLETH A line drawn on diagrams joining equal values of the plotted element.

ISOSTASY The condition of balance between the rigid crustal elements of the earth's surface and the underlying, denser and more mobile material.

Above Limestone towers in the world's most spectacular karst region – Li River near Guilin, Guangxi Province, China. The towers are the result of erosional processes.

ISTHMUS A narrow strip of land which connects two islands or two large land masses.

J

JOINT A fracture or crack in a rock.

JUNGLE An area of land overgrown with dense vegetation, usually in the tropics.

K

KAME An irregular mound of stratified sediment deposited by, in association with stagnant ice.

KARST Limestone areas which have distinctive landforms such as caves, sinks and frequently a lack of surface water. *(see picture above)*

KELP A mass of large brown seaweeds.

KETTLE HOLE An enclosed depression resulting from the melting of buried ice.

KNOT A measure of speed – one nautical mile per hour (1.15 mi hr^{-1}; 0.85 km hr^{-1}).

KOPJE A small hill or rock outcrop; term used particularly in South Africa.

KRILL Small marine animals, resembling shrimps.

L

LACCOLITH A mass of intrusive rock, usually with a horizontal base and causing the doming of overlying strata.

LAGOON A shallow pool separated from a larger body of water by a bar or reef.

LANDSAT An unmanned satellite that carries sensors to record the resources of the earth.

LANDSLIDE The movement downward under the influence of gravity of a mass of rock debris.

LATERITE A red clay formed by the weathering of rock that consists especially of compounds of iron and aluminium.

LAURASIA The northern part of Pangaea, a super-continent thought to have been broken up by continental drift.

LAVA Molten rock material that emerges from volcanoes and volcanic fissures.

LEACHING The downward movement of water through soil resulting in the removal of water-soluble materials from upper layers and their accumulation in lower layers.

LEEWARD To the lee (downwind, downstream) of an obstacle lying in a flow.

LEVEE A broad, long ridge running parallel and adjacent to a river on its flood-plain.

LIGNITE A brownish black coal in which the texture of the original wood is distinct.

LITHOSPHERE The earth's crust and a portion of the upper mantle that together comprise a layer of strength relative to the more easily deformable layer below.

LITTORAL A coastal region.

LLANOS An open grassy plain in S. America.

LOAM A crumbly soil consisting of a mixture of clay, silt and sand.

LOCH A lake or narrow sea inlet in Scotland.

LOESS Unconsolidated and frequently unstratified material deposited after transport by wind.

LONGSHORE CURRENT A current that runs along a coast. It may result in longshore drift, the transport of beach material along the coast.

LOW See *cyclone*

LUNAR MONTH The period of time between two successive new moons, being about 29½ days.

M

MAGMA Fused, molten rock material beneath the earth's crust from which igneous rocks are formed.

MAGNETIC ANOMALIES Areas with local surface variations in the earth's magnetic field relative to large-scale values.

MAGNETIC FIELD The field of force exerted by the earth by virtue of its being like a giant magnet. Its most familiar manifestation is in the behaviour of a compass.

MAGNETIC REVERSAL The reversal of the earth's magnetic field, such that a north-seeking compass points toward the South Pole. Such reversals have occurred in geological time.

MANTLE The zone within the earth's interior extending from 25 to 70km below the surface to a depth of 2900km.

MAP PROJECTION A mathematical device for representing a portion of all of the earth's curved surface on a flat surface.

MAP SCALE A measure of the ratio of distances represented on a map to their true value.

MAQUIS Scrub vegetation of evergreen shrubs characteristic of the western Mediterranean.

MARL A fine grained mixture of clay and silt with a high proportion of calcium carbonate.

MASSIF A large mountainous area, often quite distinct, containing several individual substantial mountains.

MEANDER A sinuously winding portion of a river channel; also applied to similar forms within larger flows, such as the atmosphere and oceans.

MEAN SEA LEVEL The level of the sea determined from a mean of the tidal ranges over periods of several months to several years.

METAMORPHIC ROCKS Rocks in which their composition, structure and texture have been significantly altered by the action of heat and pressure greater than that produced normally by burial.

METEOROLOGY The study of the workings of the atmosphere.

MILLIBAR A unit of pressure, most widely used in meteorology. The average pressure exerted by the atmosphere on the surface of the earth is just over 1013 millibars.

MISTRAL A cold, dry, north or northwest wind affecting the Rhone Valley.

MONSOON A wind regime with marked seasonal reversal in direction, most famously found in the Indian sub-continent.

MORAINE A landform resulting from the deposition of till by glaciers, taking on several distinctive forms depending upon the location and mode of deposition.

N

NADIR A point that is vertically below the observer.

NASA National Aeronautics and Space Administration (USA).

NEAP TIDE A tide of minimum height occurring at the first and third quarter of the moon.

NÉVÉ Snow that is being compacted into ice, as found in the birth place of glaciers.

NUNATAK A mountain completely surrounded by an ice cap or ice sheet.

O

OASIS An area within a desert region where there is sufficient water to sustain animal and plant life throughout the year.

OCEAN BASIN A large depression in the ocean floor analogous to basins on land.

OCEANIC CRUST The portion of the earth's surface crust comprising largely sima (silica-magnesia rich rocks) about 5km thick. Underlies most of the world's oceans.

OCEAN RIDGE A ridge in the ocean floor, sometimes 150 to 1500 km wide and hundreds of metres high.

OCCLUSION The coming together of warm and cold fronts in cyclones in the latest stages of its evolution.

OROGENESIS The formation of mountains, such as the Andes and Rocky Mountains. The mechanism is still uncertain but is probably related to plate tectonics.

OUTWASH PLAIN Stratified material deposited by glacio-fluvial waters beyond the ice margin.

OXBOW LAKE A lake, usually curved in plan, occupying an abandoned section of meandering river.

P

PACK ICE Ice formed on sea surface when water temperatures fall to about −2°C and floating free under the influence of currents and wind.

PAMPAS An extensive, generally grass-covered plain of temperate South America east of the Andes.

PANGAEA The name given to a postulated continental landmass which split up to produce most of the present northern hemisphere continents.

PASS A narrow passage over relatively low ground in a mountain range.

PEDIMENT A smooth, erosional land surface typically sloping from the foot of a high-land area to a local base level.

PELAGIC The part of an aquatic system that excludes its margins and substrate; it is essentially the main part of the water body.

PENEPLAIN The supposed end land form resulting from erosional processes wearing down an initially uplifted block.

PENUMBRA A region of partial darkness in a shadow surrounding the region of total darkness (umbra), such as seen in an eclipse.

PERIHELION The point in its orbit about the sun that a planet is closest to the sun.

PIEDMONT GLACIER A glacier which spreads out into a lobe as it flows onto a lowland.

PILLOW LAVA Lava that has solidified, probably under water, in rounded masses.

PLACER DEPOSIT A sediment, such as in the bed of a stream, which contains particles of valuable minerals.

PLAIN Extensive area of level or rolling treeless country.

PLANKTON Small freshwater and marine organisms that tend to move with water currents and comprise the food of larger and higher order organisms.

PLATE TECTONICS A theory which holds that the earth's surface is divided into several major rigid plates which are in motion with respect to each other and the underlying mantle. Continental drift results from plate motion and earthquakes, volcanoes and mountain-building tend to occur at the plate boundaries.

PLUTONIC ROCK Rock material that has formed at depth where cooling and crystallization have occurred slowly.

POLAR WANDERING The movements of the North and South Poles throughout geological time relative to the positions of the continents.

POLDER A low lying area of land that has been reclaimed from the sea or a lake by artificial means and is kept free of water by pumping.

PRECIPITATION The deposition of water from the atmosphere in liquid and solid form. Rain, snow, hail and dew are the most familiar forms.

PRAIRIE An extensive area of level or rolling, almost treeless grassland in North America.

PRESSURE GRADIENT The change per unit distance of pressure, perhaps most frequently met in atmospheric studies. The cause of winds.

Q

QUARTZ A crystalline mineral consisting of silicon dioxide that is a major constituent of many rocks.

QUICKSAND Water-saturated sand that is semi-liquid and cannot bear the weight of heavy objects.

R

RADAR A device that transmits radio waves and locates objects in the vicinity by analysis of the waves reflected back from them (radio detection and ranging).

RADIATION The transmission of energy in the form of electromagnetic waves and requiring no intervening medium.

RAIN SHADOW An area experiencing relatively low rainfall because of its position on the leeward side of a hill.

RAISED BEACH An emerged shoreline represented by stranded marine deposits and wave cut platforms, usually backed by former cliffs.

RANGE An open region over which livestock may roam and feed, particularly in North America.

RAVINE A narrow, steep sided valley usually formed by running water.

REEF A rocky construction found at or near sea-level; coral reefs are perhaps the most familiar type.

RELATIVE HUMIDITY The amount of water vapour in an air sample relative to the amount the sample could hold if it were saturated at the same temperature; expressed as a percentage.

REMOTE SENSING The observation and measurement of an object without touching it.

RHUMB LINE An imaginary line on the surface of the earth which makes equal oblique angles with all lines of longitude so that it forms a spiral coiling round the poles but never reaching them. This would be the course sailed by a ship following a single compass direction.

RIA An inlet of the sea formed by the flooding of river valleys by rising sea or sinking land. Contrast to fjords which are drowned glacial valleys.

RIFT VALLEY A valley formed when the area between two parallel faults sinks.

RIVER TERRACE A step like land form in the flood plain of rivers due to the river incising further into the plain and leaving remnants of its former flood plain at levels higher than the present level of the river channel.

ROARING FORTIES The area between 40° and 50°S, so called because of the high speeds of the winds occurring there. Sometimes applied to the winds themselves.

RUN-OFF The section of the hydrological cycle connecting precipitation to channel flow.

S

SALINITY The presence of salts in the waters and soils of arid, semi-arid and coastal areas.

SALT-MARSH Vegetated mud-flats found commonly on many low-lying coasts in a wide range of temperate environments.

SANDBANK A large deposit of sand, usually in a river or coastal waters.

SANDSTORM A wind storm driving clouds of sand, most usually in hot, dry deserts.

SAVANNAH A grassland region of the tropics and sub-tropics.

SCHIST Medium to coarse-grained crystalline metamorphic rock.

SEA-FLOOR SPREADING The phenomenon when tectonic plates move apart.

SEAMOUNT A mountain or other area of high relief on the sea-floor which does not reach the surface.

SEASAT A satellite especially designed to sense remotely wind and sea conditions on the oceans.

SEDIMENTARY ROCK Rock composed of the fragments of older rocks which have been eroded and the debris deposited by wind and water, often as distinct strata.

SEISMIC WAVE Wave resulting from the movements of materials in earthquakes.

SEISMOLOGY Science that deals with earthquakes and other vibrations of the earth.

SHALE A compacted sedimentary rock, usually with fine-grained particles.

SHALLOW-FOCUS EARTHQUAKE An earthquake with a focus (or centre) at a shallow level relative to the earth's surface.

SIAL The part of the earth's crust with a composition dominated by minerals rich in silicon and aluminium.

SIDEREAL DAY A period of complete rotation of the earth on its axis, about 23 hours 56 minutes.

SILL A tabular sheet of igneous rock injected along the bedding planes of sedimentary and volcanic formations.

SILT An unconsolidated material of small particles ranging in size from about 2 to 60 micrometres.

SIMA The part of the earth's crust with a composition dominated by minerals rich in silicon and magnesium.

SOIL CREEP The slow movement downslope of soil, usually resulting in thinning of soils on the upper reaches and accumulations on the lower.

SOLIFLUCTION The slow movement downslope of water saturated, seasonally thawed materials.

SOLSTICE The days of maximum declination of the sun measured relative to the equator. When the midday sun is overhead at 23½°N it gives the longest day in the northern hemisphere and the shortest day in the southern. The reverse applies when the sun is overhead at 23½°S.

Above On May 18 1980, Mt St Helens demonstrated a plinian eruption (a kind first described by Pliny the Elder). The apparent smoke cloud is pulverised ash.

SPIT Usually linear deposits of beach material attached at one end to land and free at the other.

SPRING TIDE A tide of greater than average range occurring at or around the times of the new and full moon.

SQUALL A sudden, violent wind, often associated with rain or hail; frequently occurs under cumulonimbus clouds.

STALACTITE A deposit of calcium carbonate, rather like an icicle, hanging from the roof of a cave.

STALAGMITE A deposit of calcium carbonate growing up from the floor of a cave due to the constant drip of water from the roof.

STANDARD TIME The officially established time, with reference to Greenwich Mean Time, of a region or country.

STEPPE Mid-latitude grasslands with few trees, most typically found in USSR.

STORM SURGE Changes in sea level caused by extreme weather events, notably the winds in storms.

STRAIT A narrow passage joining two large bodies of water.

STRIAE Scratches of a rock surface due to the passage over it of another rock of equal or greater hardness.

SUBDUCTION ZONE An area where the rocks comprising the sea floor are forced beneath continental rocks at a plate margin to be reincorporated in the magma beneath the earth's crust.

SUBSEQUENT RIVER A stream which follows a course determined by the structure of the local bedrock.

SUBSIDENCE Usually applied to the sinking of air in the atmosphere or the downward movement of the earth's surface.

SUBSOIL The layer of weathered material that underlies the surface soil.

SUDD Floating vegetable matter that forms obstructive masses in the upper White Nile.

SUNSPOT Relatively dark regions on the disk of the sun with surface temperature of about 4500K compared to the more normal 6000K of the rest of the surface.

SURGE A sudden excess over the normal value, usually of a flow of material (soil, ice, water).

SWELL A long, perturbation (usually wavelike) of a water surface that continues beyond its cause (eg a strong wind).

T

TAIGA The most northerly coniferous forest of cold temperature regions found in Canada, Alaska and Eurasia.

TECTONIC Concerned with the broad structures of the earth's rocks and the processes of faulting, folding and warping that form them.

TETHYS OCEAN An ocean formed in the Palaeozoic Era which extended from what is now the Mediterranean Sea eastwards as far as South-east Asia.

THERMOCLINE A layer of water or a lake or sea that separates an upper, warmer, oxygen-rich zone from a lower, colder, oxygen-poor zone and in which temperature decreases by 1°C for every metre of increased depth.

THRUST FAULT A low-angle reverse fault.

THUNDERSTORM A cloud in which thunder and lightning occur, usually associated with heavy precipitation and strong winds.

TIDAL BORE A large solitary wave that moves up funnel-shaped rivers and estuaries with the rising tide, especially spring tides.

TIDAL CURRENT The periodic horizontal motions of the sea, generated by the gravitational attraction of the moon and sun, typically of 1ms^{-1} on continental shelves.

TIDE The regular movements of the seas due to the gravitational attraction of the moon and sun, most easily observed as changes in coastal sea levels.

TOPOGRAPHY The configuration of a land surface, including its relief and the position of its natural and man-made features.

TOR An exposure of bedrock usually as blocks and boulders, forming an abrupt, steep sided culmination of a more gentle rise to the summits of hills. Famous tors exist on Dartmoor.

TORNADO A violent, localized rotating storm with winds of 100ms^{-1} circulating round a funnel cloud some 100m in diameter. Frequent in mid-western USA.

TRADE WIND Winds with an easterly component which blow from the subtropic high pressure areas around 30° toward the equator.

TROPICAL CYCLONE See *hurricane*

TROPOSPHERE The portion of the earth's atmosphere between the earth's surface and a height about 15–20km. This layer contains virtually all the world's weather. Mean temperatures decrease and mean wind speeds increase with height in the troposphere.

TSUNAMI Sea-surface waves caused by submarine earthquakes and volcanic activity. Popularly called tidal waves.

TURBULENCE Chaotic and apparently random fluctuations in fluid flow, familiarly seen in the behaviour of smoke, either from a cigarette, a chimney or a volcano.

TUNDRA Extensive, level, treeless and marshy regions lying polewards of the taiga.

TYPHOON A term used in the Far East to describe tropical cyclones or hurricanes.

U

UMBRA A region of total shadow, especially in an eclipse.

UPWELLING The upward movement of deeper water towards the sea surface.

V

VARVE A sediment bed deposited in a body of water within the course of one year.

VOE An inlet or narrow bay of the Orkney or Shetland Islands.

VOLCANIC ASH Ash emitted from a volcano.

VOLCANO An opening through which magma, molten rock ash or volatiles erupts onto the earth's surface. Also used to describe the landform produced by the erupted material. *(see picture below left)*

W

WADI An ephemeral river channel in deserts.

WARM FRONT An atmospheric front whereby, as it passes over an individual on the ground, warm air replaces cold.

WATERFALL A vertical or very steep descent of water in a stream.

WATERSHED A boundary dividing and separating the areas drained by different rivers.

WATERSPOUT A funnel-shaped, rotating cloud that forms occasionally over water when the atmosphere is very unstable. Akin to tornadoes which occur over land.

WATER TABLE The level below which the ground is wholly and permanently saturated with water.

WAVE HEIGHT The vertical extent of a wave.

WAVE LENGTH The horizontal extent of a wave, most easily seen as the distance along the direction of wave movement between crests or troughs.

WAVE PERIOD The time taken for a complete cycle of the oscillation occurring within a wave.

WAVE VELOCITY The velocity of a wave form, best seen by concentrating on one part of the wave such as its crest or trough.

WEATHERING The alteration by physical, chemical and biological processes of rocks and sediments in the top metres of the earth's crust. So called because this material is exposed to the effects of atmospheric and atmospherically related conditions.

WEATHER ROUTEING Choosing a route for a ship or aeroplane to minimise the deleterious effects of weather.

WESTERLIES Winds with a westerly component occurring between latitudes of about 35° and 60°. The whole regime forms a 'vortex' around each of the poles and forms a major element in world climate.

WHIRLWIND A general term to describe rotating winds of scales up to that of a tornado, usually a result of intense convection over small areas.

WILLY-WILLY Australasian term for a tropical cyclone or hurricane.

WINDSHEAR The variation of speed or direction or both of wind over a distance.

Y

YARDANG A desert landform, usually but not always, of unconsolidated material, shaped by and lying roughly along the direction of the wind.

Z

ZENITH A point that is vertically above the observer: the opposite of nadir.

ZOOPLANKTON One of the three kinds of plankton, including mature representatives of many animal groups such as Protozoa and Crustacea.

ABBREVIATIONS	FULL FORM	ENGLISH FORM
A		
a.d.	an der	on the
Akr.	Ákra, Akrotírion	cape
Appno	Appennino	mountain range
Arch.	Archipelago	
	Archipiélago	archipelago
B		
B.	1. Bahía, Baía, Baie, Bay, Bucht, Bukhta, Bugt	bay
	2. Ban	village
	3. Barrage,	dam
	4. Bir, Bîr, Bi'r	well
Bol.	Bol'sh, -oy	big
Br.	1. Branch	branch
	2. Bridge, Brücke	bridge
	3. Burun	cape
Brj	Baraj, -i	dam
C		
C.	Cabo, Cap, Cape	cape
Can.	Canal	canal
Cd	Ciudad	town
Chan.	Channel	channel
Ck	Creek	creek
Co., Cord.	Cordillera	mountain chain
D		
D.	1. Dağ, Dagh, Dağı, Dagları	mountain, range
	2. Daryācheh	lake
Dj.	Djebel	mountain
Dr.	doctor	doctor
E		
E.	East	east
Emb.	Embalse	reservoir
Escarp.	Escarpment	escarpment
Estr.	Estrecho	strait
F		
F.	Firth	estuary
Fj.	Fjord, Fjörður	fjord
Ft	Fort	fort
G		
G.	1. Gebel	mountain
	2. Göl, Gölü	lake
	3. Golfe, Golfo, Gulf	Gulf
	4. Gora, -gory	mountain, range
	5. Gunung	mountain
Gd, Gde	Grand, Grande	grand
Geb.	Gebirge	mountain range
Gl.	Glacier	glacier
Grl	General	general
Gt, Gtr	Great, Groot, -e, Greater	greater
H		
Har.	Harbour, Harbor	harbour
Hd	Head	head
I		
I.	Ile, Ilha, Insel, Isla, Island, Isle Isola, Isole	island / islands
In.	1. Inner	inner
	2. Inlet	inlet
Is	Iles, Ilhas, Islands, Isles, Islas	islands
Isth.	Isthmus	isthmus
J		
J.	Jabal, Jebel,	mountain
K		
K.	1. Kaap, Kap, Kapp	cape
	2. Kūh(hā)	mountain(s)
	3. Kólpos	gulf
Kep.	Kepulauan	islands
Khr.	Khrebet	mountain range
Kör.	Körfez, -i	gulf, bay
L		
L.	Lac, Lago, Lagoa, Lake, Liman, Limni, Loch, Lough	lake
Lag.	Lagoon, Laguna, Lagune, Lagoa	lagoon
Ld.	Land	land
Lit.	Little	little

ABBREVIATIONS	FULL FORM	ENGLISH FORM
M		
M.	1. Muang	town
	2. Mys	cape
m	metre, -s	metre(s)
Mal.	Malyy	small
Mf	Massif	mountain group
Mgne	Montagne(s)	mountain(s)
Mt	Mont, Mount	mountain
Mte	Monte	mountain
Mti	Monti	mountains, range
Mtn	Mountain	mountain
Mts	Monts, Mountains, Montañas, Montes	mountains
N		
N.	1. Neu-, Ny-	new
	2. Noord, Nord, Norte, North, Norra, Nørre	north
	3. Nos	cape
Nat.	National	national
Nat. Pk	National Park	national park
Ndr	Nieder	lower
N.E.	North East	north east
N.M.	National Monument	national monument
N.P.	National Park	national park
N.W.	North West	north west
O		
O.	1. Oost, Ost	east
	2. Ostrov	island
Ø	-øy	island
Oz.	Ozero, Ozera	lake(s)
P		
P.	1. Pass, Passo	pass
	2. Pic, Pico, Pizzo	peak
	3. Pulau	island
Pass.	Passage	passage
Peg.	Pegunungan	mountains
Pen.	Peninsula, Penisola	peninsula
Pk	1. Park	park
	2. Peak, Pik	peak
Plat.	Plateau, Planalto	plateau
Pov	Poluostrov	peninsula
Pr.	Prince	prince
P.P.	Pulau-pulau	islands
Pres.	Presidente	president
Promy	Promontory	promontory
Pt	Point	point
Pta	1. Ponta, Punta	point
	2. Puerta	pass
Pte	Pointe	point
Pto	Porto, Puerto	port
R		
R.	Rio, Río, River, Rivière	river
Ra.	Range	range
Rap.	Rapids	rapids
Res.	Reserve, Reservation	reserve, reservation
Resp.	Respublika	Republic
Resr	Reservoir	reservoir
S		
S.	1. Salar, Salina	salt marsh
	2. San, São	saint
	3. See	sea, lake
	4. South, Sud	south
s.	sur	on
Sa	Serra, Sierra	mountain range
Sd	Sound, Sund	sound
S.E.	South East	south east
Sev.	Severo-, Severnaya, -nyy	north
Sp.	Spitze	peak
St	Saint	saint
Sta	Santa	saint
Ste	Sainte	saint
Sto	Santo	saint
Str.	Strait	strait
S.W.	South West	south west
T		
T.	Tall, Tell	hill, mountain
Tg	Tanjung	cape
Tk	Teluk	bay
Tr.	Trench, Trough	trench, trough
U		
U.	Uad	wadi
Ug	Ujung	cape
Upr	Upper	upper

ABBREVIATIONS	FULL FORM	ENGLISH FORM
V		
V.	1. Val, Valle	valley
	2. Ville	town
Va	Villa	town
Vdkhr.	Vodokhranilishche	reservoir
Vol.	Volcán, Volcano, Vulkan	volcano
Vozv.	Vozvyshennost'	upland
W		
W.	1. Wadi	wadi
	2. Water	water
	3. Well	well
	4. West	west
Y		
Yuzh.	Yuzhno-, Yuzhnyy	south
Z		
Z	1. Zaliv	gulf, bay
	2. Zatoka	
Zap.	Zapad-naya, Zapadno-, Zapadnyy	western
Zem.	Zemlya	country, land

Introduction to the index

In the index, the first number refers to the page, and the following letter and number to the section of the map in which the index entry can be found.
For example, 14C2 **Paris** means that Paris can be found on page 14 where column C and row 2 meet.

Abbreviations used in the index

Arch	Archipelago
B	Bay
C	Cape
Chan	Channel
Gl	Glacier
I(s)	Island(s)
Lg	Lagoon
L	Lake
Mt(s)	Mountain(s)
P	Pass
Pass	Passage
Pen	Peninsula
Plat	Plateau
Pt	Point
Res	Reservoir
R	River
S	Sea
Sd	Sound
Str	Strait
UAE	United Arab Emirates
UK	United Kingdom
USA	United States of America
V	Valley

A

18B2 **Aachen** Germany
13C1 **Aalsmeer** Netherlands
13C2 **Aalst** Belgium
12K6 **Äänekoski** Finland
31A3 **Aba** China
48C4 **Aba** Nigeria
50D3 **Aba** Zaïre
41E3 **Abādān** Iran
41F3 **Abādeh** Iran
48B1 **Abadla** Algeria
75C2 **Abaeté** Brazil
75C2 **Abaeté** *R* Brazil
73J4 **Abaetetuba** Brazil
31D1 **Abagnar Qi** China
59E3 **Abajo Mts** USA
48C4 **Abakaliki** Nigeria
25L4 **Abakan** Russian Federation
48C3 **Abala** Niger
48C2 **Abalessa** Algeria
72D6 **Abancay** Peru
41F3 **Abarqū** Iran
29E2 **Abashiri** Japan
29E2 **Abashiri-wan** *B* Japan
27H7 **Abau** Papua New Guinea
50D3 **Abaya, L** Ethiopia
50D2 **Abbai** *R* Ethiopia/Sudan
50E2 **Abbe, L** Djibouti/Ethiopia
14C1 **Abbeville** France
63D3 **Abbeville** Louisiana, USA
67B2 **Abbeville** S Carolina, USA
58B1 **Abbotsford** Canada
64A2 **Abbotsford** USA
42C2 **Abbottabad** Pakistan
40D2 **'Abd al 'Azīz, Jebel** *Mt* Syria
20J5 **Abdulino** Russian Federation
50C2 **Abéché** Chad
48B4 **Abengourou** Ivory Coast
18B1 **Åbenrå** Denmark
48C4 **Abeokuta** Nigeria
50D3 **Abera** Ethiopia
7B3 **Aberaeron** Wales
7C4 **Aberdare** Wales
66C2 **Aberdeen** California, USA
65D3 **Aberdeen** Maryland, USA
63E2 **Aberdeen** Mississippi, USA
47C3 **Aberdeen** South Africa
8D3 **Aberdeen** Scotland
56D2 **Aberdeen** S Dakota, USA
56A2 **Aberdeen** Washington, USA
54J3 **Aberdeen L** Canada
7B3 **Aberdyfi** Wales
8D3 **Aberfeldy** Scotland
8C3 **Aberfoyle** Scotland
7C4 **Abergavenny** Wales
7B3 **Aberystwyth** Wales
20L2 **Abez'** Russian Federation
50E2 **Abhā** Saudi Arabia
41E2 **Abhar** Iran
48B4 **Abidjan** Ivory Coast
61D3 **Abilene** Kansas, USA
62C2 **Abilene** Texas, USA
7D4 **Abingdon** England
64C3 **Abingdon** USA
55K4 **Abitibi** *R* Canada
55L5 **Abitibi,L** Canada
21G7 **Abkhazian Republic** Georgia
42C2 **Abohar** India
48C4 **Abomey** Benin
50B3 **Abong Mbang** Cameroon
50B2 **Abou Deïa** Chad
8D3 **Aboyne** Scotland
41E4 **Abqaiq** Saudi Arabia
15A2 **Abrantes** Portugal
70A2 **Abreojos, Punta** *Pt* Mexico
50D1 **'Abri** Sudan
32A3 **Abrolhos** *I* Australia
75E2 **Abrolhos, Arquipélago dos** *Is* Brazil
56B2 **Absaroka Range** *Mts* USA
41F5 **Abū al Abyaḍ** *I* UAE
41E4 **Abū 'Alī** *I* Saudi Arabia
45D3 **Abu 'Amūd, Wadi** Jordan
45C3 **Abu 'Aweigîla** *Well* Egypt
41F5 **Abū Dhabi** UAE
45C3 **Ābū el Jurdhān** Jordan
50D2 **Abu Hamed** Sudan
48C4 **Abuja** Nigeria
45A3 **Abu Kebir Hihya** Egypt
72E5 **Abunã** Brazil
72E6 **Abunã** *R* Bolivia/Brazil
45C4 **Abu Rûtha, Gebel** *Mt* Egypt
41D3 **Abú Sukhayr** Iraq
45B3 **Abu Suweir** Egypt
45B4 **Abu Tarfa, Wadi** Egypt
35B2 **Abut Head** *C* New Zealand
40B4 **Abu Tig** Egypt
50D2 **Abu'Urug** *Well* Sudan
50D2 **Abuye Meda** *Mt* Ethiopia
50C2 **Abu Zabad** Sudan
50D3 **Abwong** Sudan
18B1 **Åby** Denmark
50C3 **Abyei** Sudan
65F2 **Acadia Nat Pk** USA
70B2 **Acámbaro** Mexico
69B5 **Acandí** Colombia
70B2 **Acaponeta** Mexico
70B3 **Acapulco** Mexico
73L4 **Acaraú** Brazil
72E2 **Acarigua** Venezuela
70C3 **Acatlán** Mexico
48B4 **Accra** Ghana
6C3 **Accrington** England
42D4 **Achalpur** India
74B6 **Achao** Chile
13E3 **Achern** Germany
9A3 **Achill Hd** *Pt* Irish Republic
10A3 **Achill I** Irish Republic
13E1 **Achim** Germany
25L4 **Achinsk** Russian Federation
16D3 **Acireale** Sicily, Italy
61E2 **Ackley** USA
69C2 **Acklins** *I* The Bahamas
72D6 **Acobamba** Peru
74B4 **Aconcagua** *Mt* Chile
73L5 **Acopiara** Brazil
Açores *Is* = **Azores**
A Coruña = La Coruña
Acre = 'Akko
72D5 **Acre** *State* Brazil
66C3 **Acton** USA
63C2 **Ada** USA
15B1 **Adaja** *R* Spain
41G5 **Adam** Oman
50D3 **Adama** Ethiopia
75B3 **Adamantina** Brazil
50B3 **Adamaoua** *Region* Cameroon/Nigeria
50B3 **Adamaoua, Massif de l'** *Mts* Cameroon
68D1 **Adams** USA
44B4 **Adam's Bridge** India/Sri Lanka
56A2 **Adams,Mt** USA
44C4 **Adam's Peak** *Mt* Sri Lanka
'Adan = Aden
21F8 **Adana** Turkey
21E7 **Adapazarı** Turkey
76F7 **Adare,C** Antarctica
34B1 **Adavale** Australia
41E4 **Ad Dahnā'** *Region* Saudi Arabia
41F4 **Ad Damman** Saudi Arabia
41D5 **Ad Dawādimī** Saudi Arabia
41E4 **Ad Dibdibah** *Region* Saudi Arabia
41E5 **Ad Dilam** Saudi Arabia
41E5 **Ad Dir'iyah** Saudi Arabia
50D3 **Addis Ababa** Ethiopia
41D3 **Ad Dīwanīyah** Iraq
40D3 **Ad Duwayd** Saudi Arabia
61E2 **Adel** USA
32C4 **Adelaide** Australia
67C4 **Adelaide** Bahamas
76G3 **Adelaide** *Base* Antarctica
54J3 **Adelaide Pen** Canada
27G8 **Adelaide River** Australia
66D3 **Adelanto** USA
38C4 **Aden** Yemen
38C4 **Aden,G of** Somalia/Yemen
48C3 **Aderbissinat** Niger
45D2 **Adhrā'** Syria
27G7 **Adi** *I* Indonesia
16C1 **Adige** *R* Italy
50D2 **Adigrat** Ethiopia
42D5 **Adilābād** India
58B2 **Adin** USA
65E2 **Adirondack Mts** USA
50D2 **Adī Ugrī** Eritrea
40C2 **Adıyaman** Turkey
17F1 **Adjud** Romania
54E4 **Admiralty I** USA
55K2 **Admiralty Inlet** *B* Canada
32D1 **Admiralty Is** Papua New Guinea
44B2 **Ādoni** India
14B3 **Adour** *R* France
48B2 **Adrar** Algeria
48C2 **Adrar** *Mts* Algeria
48A2 **Adrar** *Region* Mauritius
48A2 **Adrar Soutouf** *Region* Morocco
50C2 **Adré** Chad
49D2 **Adri** Libya
64C2 **Adrian** Michigan, USA
62B1 **Adrian** Texas, USA
16C2 **Adriatic S** Italy/Yugoslavia
50D2 **Adwa** Ethiopia
25P3 **Adycha** *R* Russian Federation
48B4 **Adzopé** Ivory Coast
20K2 **Adz'va** *R* Russian Federation
20K2 **Adz'vavom** Russian Federation
17E3 **Aegean Sea** Greece
38E2 **Afghanistan** *Republic* Asia
50E3 **Afgooye** Somalia
41D5 **'Afif** Saudi Arabia
48C4 **Afikpo** Nigeria
12G6 **Åfjord** Norway
48C1 **Aflou** Algeria
50E3 **Afmado** Somalia
48A3 **Afollé** *Region* Mauritius
68C1 **Afton** New York, USA
58D2 **Afton** Wyoming, USA
45C2 **Afula** Israel
21E8 **Afyon** Turkey
45A3 **Aga** Egypt
50B2 **Agadem** Niger
48C3 **Agadez** Niger
48B1 **Agadir** Morocco
42D4 **Agar** India
43G4 **Agartala** India
58B1 **Agassiz** Canada
48B4 **Agboville** Ivory Coast
40E1 **Agdam** Azerbaijan
29C3 **Agematsu** Japan
14C3 **Agen** France
41E3 **Agha Jārī** Iran
48B4 **Agnibilékrou** Ivory Coast
14C3 **Agout** *R* France
42D3 **Āgra** India
41D2 **Ağrı** Turkey
16D2 **Agri** *R* Italy
16C3 **Agrigento** Sicily, Italy
26H5 **Agrihan** *I* Marianas
17E3 **Agrínion** Greece
16C2 **Agropoli** Italy
20J4 **Agryz** Russian Federation
55N3 **Agto** Greenland
75B3 **Agua Clara** Brazil
69D3 **Aguadilla** Puerto Rico
70B1 **Agua Prieta** Mexico
75A3 **Aguaray Guazú** Paraguay
70B2 **Aguascalientes** Mexico
75D2 **Aguas Formosas** Brazil
75C2 **Agua Vermelha, Barragem** Brazil
15A1 **Agueda** Portugal
48C3 **Aguelhok** Mali
48A2 **Agüenit** *Well* Morocco
15B2 **Águilas** Spain
72B5 **Aguja, Puerta** Peru
36C7 **Agulhas Basin** Indian Ocean
51C7 **Agulhas,C** South Africa
36C6 **Agulhas Plat** Indian Ocean
Ahaggar = Hoggar
21H8 **Ahar** Iran
13D1 **Ahaus** Germany
35B1 **Ahipara B** New Zealand
13D2 **Ahlen** Germany
42C4 **Ahmadābād** India
44A2 **Ahmadnagar** India
50E3 **Ahmar Mts** Ethiopia
67C1 **Ahoskie** USA
13D2 **Ahr** *R* Germany
13D2 **Ahrgebirge** *Mts* Germany
12G7 **Åhus** Sweden
41F2 **Āhuvān** Iran
41E3 **Ahvāz** Iran
69A4 **Aiajuela** Costa Rica
14C3 **Aigoual, Mount** France
29C3 **Aikawa** Japan
67B2 **Aiken** USA
31A5 **Ailao Shan** *Upland* China
75D2 **Aimorés** Brazil
16B3 **Aïn Beïda** Algeria
48B1 **Ain Beni Mathar** Morocco
49E2 **Ain Dalla** *Well* Egypt
15C2 **Aïn el Hadjel** Algeria
50B2 **Aïn Galakka** Chad
15C2 **Aïn Oussera** Algeria
48B1 **Aïn Sefra** Algeria
40B4 **'Ain Sukhna** Egypt
60D2 **Ainsworth** USA
15B2 **Aïn Témouchent** Algeria
29B4 **Aioi** Japan
48B2 **Aïoun Abd el Malek** *Well* Mauritius
48B3 **Aïoun El Atrouss** Mauritius
72E7 **Aiquile** Bolivia
48C3 **Aïr** *Desert Region* Niger
8D4 **Airdrie** Scotland
13B2 **Aire** France
6D3 **Aire** *R* England
13C3 **Aire** *R* France
55L3 **Airforce I** Canada
54E3 **Aishihik** Canada
13B3 **Aisne** *Department* France
14C2 **Aisne** *R* France
27H7 **Aitape** Papua New Guinea
19F1 **Aiviekste** *R* Latvia
14D3 **Aix-en-Provence** France
14D2 **Aix-les-Bains** France
43F4 **Aiyar Res** India
17E3 **Aíyion** Greece
17E3 **Aíyna** *I* Greece
43G4 **Āīzawl** India
51B6 **Aizeb** *R* Namibia
29D3 **Aizu-Wakamatsu** Japan
16B2 **Ajaccio** Corsica, Italy
16B2 **Ajaccio, G d'** Corsica, Italy
49E1 **Ajdābiyā** Libya
29E2 **Ajigasawa** Japan
45C2 **Ajlūn** Jordan
41G4 **Ajman** UAE
42C3 **Ajmer** India
59D4 **Ajo** USA
15B1 **Ajo, Cabo de** *C* Spain
17F3 **Ak** *R* Turkey
29D2 **Akabira** Japan
29C3 **Akaishi-sanchi** *Mts* Japan
44B2 **Akalkot** India
45B1 **Akanthou** Cyprus
35B2 **Akaroa** New Zealand
29B4 **Akashi** Japan
21K5 **Akbulak** Russian Federation
40C2 **Akçakale** Turkey
48A2 **Akchar** *Watercourse* Mauritius
50C3 **Aketi** Zaïre
41D1 **Akhalkalaki** Georgia
40D1 **Akhalsikhe** Georgia
17E3 **Akharnái** Greece
49E1 **Akhdar, Jabal al** *Mts* Libya
41G5 **Akhdar, Jebel** *Mt* Oman
40A2 **Akhisar** Turkey
19F1 **Akhiste** Latvia
49F2 **Akhmîm** Egypt
21H6 **Akhtubinsk** Russian Federation
21E5 **Akhtyrka** Ukraine
29B4 **Aki** Japan
55K4 **Akimiski I** Canada
29E3 **Akita** Japan
48A3 **Akjoujt** Mauritius
45C2 **'Akko** Israel
54E3 **Aklavik** Canada
48B3 **Aklé Aouana** *Desert Region* Mauritius
50D3 **Akobo** Ethiopia
50D3 **Akobo** *R* Ethiopia/Sudan
42B1 **Akoha** Afghanistan
42D4 **Akola** India
42D4 **Akot** India
55M3 **Akpatok I** Canada
17E3 **Ákra Kafirévs** *C* Greece
17E4 **Ákra Líthinon** *C* Greece
17E3 **Ákra Maléa** *C* Greece
12A2 **Akranes** Iceland
17F3 **Ákra Sídheros** *C* Greece
17E3 **Ákra Spátha** *C* Greece
17E3 **Ákra Taínaron** *C* Greece
57E2 **Akron** USA
45B1 **Akrotiri** Cyprus
45B1 **Akrotiri B** Cyprus
42D1 **Aksai Chin** *Mts* China
21E8 **Aksaray** Turkey
21J5 **Aksay** Kazakhstan
42D1 **Aksayquin Hu** *L* China
40B2 **Akşehir** Turkey
40B2 **Akseki** Turkey
25N4 **Aksenovo Zilovskoye** Russian Federation
26E1 **Aksha** Russian Federation
39G1 **Aksu** China
50D2 **Aksum** Ethiopia
24J5 **Aktogay** Kazakhstan
21K6 **Aktumsyk** Kazakhstan
21K5 **Aktyubinsk** Kazakhstan
12B1 **Akureyri** Iceland
Akyab = Sittwe
24K5 **Akzhal** Kazakhstan
63E2 **Alabama** *R* USA
57E3 **Alabama** *State* USA
67A2 **Alabaster** USA
40C2 **Ala Dağları** *Mts* Turkey
21G7 **Alagir** Russian Federation
73L5 **Alagoas** *State* Brazil
73L6 **Alagoinhas** Brazil
15B1 **Alagón** Spain
41E4 **Al Ahmadi** Kuwait
70D3 **Alajuela** Costa Rica
54B3 **Alakanuk** USA
24K5 **Alakol, Ozero** *L* Kazakhstan/Russian Federation
12L5 **Alakurtti** Russian Federation
27H5 **Alamagan** *I* Pacific Ocean
41E3 **Al Amārah** Iraq
59B3 **Alameda** USA
59C3 **Alamo** USA
62A2 **Alamogordo** USA
62C3 **Alamo Heights** USA
62A1 **Alamosa** USA
12H6 **Åland** *I* Finland
21E8 **Alanya** Turkey
67B2 **Alapaha** *R* USA
42L4 **Alapayevsk** Russian Federation
15B2 **Alarcón, Embalse de** *Res* Spain
40A2 **Alaşehir** Turkey
26D3 **Ala Shan** *Mts* China
54C3 **Alaska** *State* USA
54D4 **Alaska,G of** USA
54C3 **Alaska Range** *Mts* USA
16B2 **Alassio** Italy
20H5 **Alatyr'** Russian Federation
34B2 **Alawoona** Australia
41G5 **Al'Ayn** UAE
39F2 **Alayskiy Khrebet** *Mts* Tajikistan
25R3 **Alazeya** *R* Russian Federation
14D3 **Alba** Italy
15B2 **Albacete** Spain
15A1 **Alba de Tormes** Spain
40D2 **Al Badi** Iraq
17E1 **Alba Iulia** Romania
17D2 **Albania** *Republic* Europe
32A4 **Albany** Australia
67B2 **Albany** Georgia, USA
64B3 **Albany** Kentucky, USA
65E2 **Albany** New York, USA
56A2 **Albany** Oregon, USA
55K4 **Albany** *R* Canada
15B1 **Albarracin, Sierra de** *Mts* Spain
41G5 **Al Bātinah** *Region* Oman
27H8 **Albatross B** Australia
49E1 **Al Bayḍa** Libya
45C1 **Al Baylūlīyah** Syria
67B1 **Albemarle** USA
67C1 **Albemarle Sd** USA
15B1 **Alberche** *R* Spain
13B2 **Albert** France
54G4 **Alberta** *Province* Canada
27H7 **Albert Edward** *Mt* Papua New Guinea
47C3 **Albertinia** South Africa
50D3 **Albert,L** Uganda/Zaïre
57D2 **Albert Lea** USA
50D3 **Albert Nile** *R* Uganda
58D1 **Alberton** USA
14D2 **Albertville** France
14C3 **Albi** France
61E2 **Albia** USA
73H2 **Albina** Surinam
64C2 **Albion** Michigan, USA
61D2 **Albion** Nebraska, USA
65D2 **Albion** New York, USA
40C4 **Al Bi'r** Saudi Arabia
15B2 **Alborán** *I* Spain
12G7 **Ålborg** Denmark
13E3 **Albstadt-Ebingen** Germany
40D3 **Al Bū Kamāl** Syria
56C3 **Albuquerque** USA
41G5 **Al Buraymī** Oman
49D1 **Al Burayqah** Libya
49E1 **Al Burdī** Libya
32D4 **Albury** Australia
41E3 **Al Buşayyah** Iraq
15B1 **Alcalá de Henares** Spain
16C3 **Alcamo** Sicily, Italy
15B1 **Alcañiz** Spain
73K4 **Alcântara** Brazil
15A2 **Alcántara, Embalse de** *Res* Spain
15B2 **Alcaraz** Spain

15B2 Alcaraz, Sierra de Mts Spain
15B2 Alcázar de San Juan Spain
15B2 Alcira Spain
75E2 Alcobaça Brazil
15B1 Alcolea de Pinar Spain
15B2 Alcoy Spain
15C2 Alcudia Spain
46J8 Aldabra Is Indian Ocean
62A3 Aldama Mexico
25O4 Aldan Russian Federation
25P4 Aldan R Russian Federation
25O4 Aldanskoye Nagor'ye Upland Russian Federation
7E3 Aldeburgh England
14B2 Alderney I Channel Islands
7D4 Aldershot England
48A3 Aleg Mauritius
75A2 Alegre R Brazil
74E3 Alegrete Brazil
25Q4 Aleksandrovsk Sakhalinskiy Russian Federation
24J4 Alekseyevka Kazakhstan
20F5 Aleksin Russian Federation
18D1 Ålem Sweden
75D3 Além Paraíba Brazil
14C2 Alençon France
66E5 Alenuihaha Chan Hawaiian Islands
21F8 Aleppo Syria
55M1 Alert Canada
14C3 Alès France
16B2 Alessandria Italy
24B3 Ålesund Norway
54C4 Aleutian Ra Mts USA
37L2 Aleutian Trench Pacific Ocean
54E4 Alexander Arch USA
47B2 Alexander Bay South Africa
67A2 Alexander City USA
76G3 Alexander I Antarctica
35A3 Alexandra New Zealand
74J8 Alexandra,C South Georgia
55L2 Alexandra Fjord Canada
49E1 Alexandria Egypt
57D3 Alexandria Louisiana, USA
57D2 Alexandria Minnesota, USA
57F3 Alexandria Virginia, USA
17F2 Alexandroúpolis Greece
45C2 Aley Lebanon
24K4 Aleysk Russian Federation
41D3 Al Fallūjah Iraq
15B1 Alfaro Spain
17F2 Alfatar Bulgaria
41E4 Al Fāw Iraq
75C3 Alfensas Brazil
17E3 Alfiós R Greece
75D3 Alfonso Cláudio Brazil
8D3 Alford Scotland
75D3 Alfredo Chaves Brazil
7D3 Alfreton England
41E4 Al Furūthi Saudi Arabia
21K6 Alga Kazakhstan
15A2 Algeciras Spain
Alger = Algiers
48B2 Algeria Republic Africa
16B2 Alghero Sardinia, Italy
15C2 Algiers Algeria
61E2 Algona USA
65D1 Algonquin Park Canada
38D3 Al Ḩadd Oman
40D3 Al Hadīthah Iraq
40C3 Al Hadīthah Saudi Arabia
40D2 Al Ḩaḑr Iraq
45D1 Al Haffah Syria
41G5 Al Ḩajar al Gharbī Mts Oman
40C3 Al Hamad Desert Region Jordan/Saudi Arabia
41E4 Al Haniyah Desert Region Iraq
41E5 Al Ḩarīq Saudi Arabia
40C3 Al Harrah Desert Region Saudi Arabia
49D2 Al Harūj al Aswad Upland Libya
41E4 Al Hasa Region Saudi Arabia
40D2 Al Ḩasakah Syria
40C4 Al Hawjā' Saudi Arabia
41E3 Al Hayy Iraq
45D2 Al Hījānah Syria
41D3 Al Ḩillah Iraq
41E5 Al Ḩillah Saudi Arabia
15B2 Al Hoceima Morocco
50E2 Al Ḩudaydah Yemen
41E4 Al Hufūf Saudi Arabia
41F5 Al Humrah Region UAE
41G5 Al Huwatsah Oman
41E2 Alīābad Iran
41G4 Aliabad Iran
17E2 Aliákmon R Greece
41E3 Alī al Gharbī Iraq
44A2 Alībāg India
15B2 Alicante Spain
56D4 Alice USA
16D3 Alice, Punta Pt Italy
32C3 Alice Springs Australia
16C3 Alicudi I Italy
42D3 Aligarh India
41E3 Aligūdarz Iran
42B2 Ali-Khel Afghanistan
17F3 Alimniá I Greece
43F3 Alīpur Duār India
64C2 Aliquippa USA
40C3 Al' Isawiyah Saudi Arabia
47D3 Aliwal North South Africa
49E2 Al Jaghbūb Libya
40D3 Al Jālamīd Saudi Arabia
49E2 Al Jawf Libya
40C4 Al Jawf Saudi Arabia
40D2 Al Jazīrah Desert Region Iraq/Syria
15A2 Aljezur Portugal
41E4 Al Jubayl Saudi Arabia
41D4 Al Jumaymah Saudi Arabia
45D4 Al Kabid Desert Jordan
41D4 Al Kahfah Saudi Arabia
41E4 Al Kāmil Oman
40D2 Al Khābūr R Syria
41G5 Al Khābūrah Oman
41D3 Al Khālis Iraq
41G4 Al Khaşab Oman
41F4 Al Khawr Qatar
49D1 Al Khums Libya
41F5 Al Kidan Region Saudi Arabia
45D2 Al Kiswah Syria
18A2 Alkmaar Netherlands
49E2 Al Kufrah Oasis Libya
41E3 Al Kūt Iraq
Al Lādhiqīyah = Latakia
43E3 Allahābād India
45D2 Al Lajāh Mt Syria
54C3 Allakaket USA
30B2 Allanmyo Burma
67B2 Allatoona L USA
47D1 Alldays South Africa
65D2 Allegheny R USA
57F3 Allegheny Mts USA
67B2 Allendale USA
6C2 Allendale Town England
9B2 Allen, Lough L Irish Republic
35A3 Allen,Mt New Zealand
65D2 Allentown USA
44B4 Alleppey India
14C2 Aller R France
60C2 Alliance USA
50E1 Al Līth Saudi Arabia
41F5 Al Liwā' Region UAE
8D3 Alloa Scotland
34D1 Allora Australia
65E1 Alma Canada
64C2 Alma Michigan, USA
60D2 Alma Nebraska, USA
39F1 Alma Ata Kazakhstan
15A2 Almada Portugal
41E4 Al Majma'ah Saudi Arabia
41F4 Al Manāmah Bahrain
41D3 Al Ma'nīyah Iraq
59B2 Almanor,L USA
15B2 Almansa Spain
41F5 Al Māriyyah UAE
49E1 Al Marj Libya
75C2 Almas R Brazil
15B1 Almazán Spain
13E2 Alme R Germany
13D1 Almelo Netherlands
75D2 Almenara Brazil
15A1 Almendra, Embalse de Res Spain
15B2 Almería Spain
15B2 Almería, Golfo de Spain
20J5 Al'met'yevsk Russian Federation
18C1 Älmhult Sweden
41D4 Al Midhnab Saudi Arabia
41E3 Al Miqdādīyah Iraq
17E3 Almirós Greece
41E4 Al Mish'āb Saudi Arabia
15A2 Almodôvar Portugal
42D3 Almora India
41E4 Al Mubarraz Saudi Arabia
40C4 Al Mudawwara Jordan
41F4 Al Muḩarraq Bahrain
38C4 Al Mukallā Yemen
50E2 Al Mukhā Yemen
41D3 Al Musayyib Iraq
40C4 Al Muwaylih Saudi Arabia
8C3 Alness Scotland
6D2 Aln, R England
41E3 Al Nu'mānīyah Iraq
6D2 Alnwick England
27F7 Alor I Indonesia
30C4 Alor Setar Malaysia
Alost = Aalst
32E2 Alotau Papua New Guinea
32B3 Aloysius,Mt Australia
64C1 Alpena USA
16C1 Alpi Dolomitiche Mts Italy
59E4 Alpine Arizona, USA
62B2 Alpine Texas, USA
58D2 Alpine Wyoming, USA
16B1 Alps Mts Europe
49D1 Al Qaddāhiyah Libya
45D1 Al Qadmūs Syria
40D3 Al Qā'im Iraq
40C4 Al Qalībah Saudi Arabia
40D2 Al Qāmishlī Syria
45D1 Al Qardāḩah Syria
49D1 Al Qaryah Ash Sharqiyah Libya
40C3 Al Qaryatayn Syria
41D4 Al Qasim Region Saudi Arabia
41E4 Al Qatīf Saudi Arabia
49D2 Al Qatrūn Libya
41E4 Al Qayşūmah Saudi Arabia
15A2 Alquera Res Portugal/Spain
40C3 Al Qunayţirah Syria
50E2 Al Qunfidhah Saudi Arabia
41E3 Al Qurnah Iraq
45D1 Al Quşayr Syria
45D2 Al Quţayfah Syria
41E5 Al Quwayīyah Saudi Arabia
18B1 Als I Denmark
14D2 Alsace Region France
13D3 Alsace, Plaine d' France
18B2 Alsfeld Germany
6C2 Alston England
12J5 Alta Norway
74D4 Alta Gracia Argentina
69D5 Altagracia de Orituco Venezuela
26B2 Altai Mts Mongolia
67B2 Altamaha R USA
73H4 Altamira Brazil
16D2 Altamura Italy
26D1 Altanbulag Mongolia
70B2 Altata Mexico
24K5 Altay China
25L5 Altay Mongolia
24K4 Altay Mts Russian Federation
13D2 Altenkirchen Germany
75B2 Alto Araguaia Brazil
51D5 Alto Molócue Mozambique
7D4 Alton England
64A3 Alton USA
65D2 Altoona USA
75B2 Alto Sucuriú Brazil
7C3 Altrincham England
39G2 Altun Shan Mts China
58B2 Alturas USA
62C2 Altus USA
40C4 Al'Ulā Saudi Arabia
40C4 Al Urayq Desert Region Saudi Arabia
62C1 Alva USA
63C2 Alvarado USA
12G6 Älvdalen Sweden
63C3 Alvin USA
12J5 Älvsbyn Sweden
49D2 Al Wāha Libya
40C4 Al Wajh Saudi Arabia
42D3 Alwar India
40D3 Al Widyān Desert Region Iraq/Saudi Arabia
31A2 Alxa Youqi China
31B2 Alxa Zuoqi China
41E2 Alyat Azerbaijan
12J8 Alytus Lithuania
13E3 Alzey Germany
50D3 Amadi Sudan
41D2 Amādīyah Iraq
55L3 Amadjuak L Canada
12G7 Åmål Sweden
25N4 Amalat R Russian Federation
17E3 Amaliás Greece
42C4 Amalner India
75A3 Amambaí Brazil
75B3 Amambaí R Brazil
75A3 Amamba, Serra Mts Brazil/Paraguay
26F4 Amami I Japan
26F4 Amami gunto Arch Japan
73H3 Amapá Brazil
73H3 Amapá State Brazil
62B1 Amarillo USA
21F7 Amasya Turkey
73H4 Amazonas R Brazil
72E4 Amazonas State Brazil
42D2 Ambāla India
44C4 Ambalangoda Sri Lanka
51E6 Ambalavao Madagascar
50B3 Ambam Cameroon
51E5 Ambanja Madagascar
25S3 Ambarchik Russian Federation
72C4 Ambato Ecuador
51E5 Ambato-Boeny Madagascar
51E5 Ambatolampy Madagascar
51E5 Ambatondrazaka Madagascar
18C3 Amberg Germany
70D3 Ambergris Cay I Belize
43E4 Ambikāpur India
51E5 Ambilobe Madagascar
6C2 Ambleside England
51E6 Amboasary Madagascar
51E5 Ambodifototra Madagascar
51E6 Ambohimahasoa Madagascar
Amboina = Ambon
27F7 Ambon Indonesia
51E6 Ambositra Madagascar
51E6 Ambovombe Madagascar
27E6 Amboyna Cay I S China Sea
51E5 Ambre, Montagne d' Mt Madagascar
51B4 Ambriz Angola
33F2 Ambrym I Vanuatu
50C2 Am Dam Chad
20L2 Amderma Russian Federation
70B2 Ameca Mexico
18B2 Ameland I Netherlands
68D2 Amenia USA
58D2 American Falls USA
58D2 American Falls Res USA
59D2 American Fork USA
76F10 American Highland Upland Antarctica
37L5 American Samoa Is Pacific Ocean
67B2 Americus USA
18B2 Amersfoort Netherlands
47D2 Amersfoort South Africa
61E1 Amery USA
76G10 Amery Ice Shelf Antarctica
61E2 Ames USA
68E1 Amesbury USA
17E3 Amfilokhía Greece
17E3 Amfissa Greece
25P3 Amga Russian Federation
25P3 Amgal R Russian Federation
26G2 Amgu Russian Federation
26G1 Amgun' R Russian Federation
50D2 Amhara Region Ethiopia
55M5 Amherst Canada
68D1 Amherst Massachusetts, USA
65D3 Amherst Virginia, USA
44B3 Amhūr India
16C2 Amiata, Monte Mt Italy
14C2 Amiens France
29C3 Amino Japan
45C1 Amioune Lebanon
46K8 Amirante Is Indian Ocean
62B3 Amistad Res Mexico
43F3 Amlekhganj Nepal
7B3 Amlwch Wales
40C3 Amman Jordan
7C4 Ammanford Wales
12K6 Ämmänsaari Finland
55P3 Ammassalik Greenland
28A3 Amnyong-dan C N Korea
41F2 Amol Iran
17F3 Amorgós I Greece
55L5 Amos Canada
Amoy = Xiamen
51E6 Ampanihy Madagascar
75C3 Amparo Brazil
51E5 Ampasimanolotra Madagascar
15C1 Amposta Spain
42D4 Amrāvati India
42C4 Amreli India
42C2 Amritsar India
43K1 Amroha India
36E6 Amsterdam I Indian Ocean
18A2 Amsterdam Netherlands
47E2 Amsterdam South Africa
65E2 Amsterdam USA
50C2 Am Timan Chad
24H5 Amu Darya R Uzbekistan
55J2 Amund Ringnes I Canada
54F2 Amundsen G Canada
76E Amundsen-Scott Base Antarctica
76F4 Amundsen Sea Antarctica
27E7 Amuntai Indonesia
26F1 Amur R Russian Federation
25N2 Anabar R Russian Federation
66C4 Anacapa Is USA
72F2 Anaco Venezuela
56B2 Anaconda USA
58B1 Anacortes USA
62C1 Anadarko USA
25T3 Anadyr' Russian Federation
25T3 Anadyr' R Russian Federation
25U3 Anadyrskiy Zaliv S Russian Federation
25T3 Anadyrskoye Ploskogor'ye Plat Russian Federation
17F3 Anáfi I Greece
75D1 Anagé Brazil
40D3 'Ānah Iraq
59C4 Anaheim USA
44B3 Anaimalai Hills India
44C2 Anakāpalle India
51E5 Analalava Madagascar
27D6 Anambas, Kepulauan Is Indonesia
64A2 Anamosa USA
21E8 Anamur Turkey
29B4 Anan Japan
44B3 Anantapur India
42D2 Anantnag India
73J7 Anápolis Brazil
41G3 Anār Iran
41F3 Anārak Iran
27H5 Anatahan I Pacific Ocean
74D3 Añatuya Argentina
28B3 Anbyŏn N Korea
54D3 Anchorage USA
72E7 Ancohuma Mt Bolivia
72C6 Ancón Peru
16C2 Ancona Italy
68D1 Ancram USA
74B6 Ancud Chile
74B6 Ancud, Golfo de G Chile
13C4 Ancy-le-Franc France
72D6 Andahuaylas Peru
12F6 Åndalsnes Norway
15A2 Andalucia Region Spain
67A2 Andalusia USA
39H4 Andaman Is India
75D1 Andaraí Brazil
13C3 Andelot France
12H5 Andenes Norway
18B2 Andernach Germany
64B2 Anderson Indiana, USA
63D1 Anderson Missouri, USA
67B2 Anderson S Carolina, USA
54F3 Anderson R Canada
72C5 Andes, Cordillera de los Mts Peru
44B2 Andhra Pradesh State India
17E3 Andikíthira I Greece
24J5 Andizhan Uzbekistan
24H6 Andkhui Afghanistan
28B3 Andong S Korea
15C1 Andorra Principality SW Europe
15C1 Andorra-La-Vella Andorra
7D4 Andover England
68E1 Andover New Hampshire, USA
68B1 Andover New York, USA
75B3 Andradina Brazil
19G1 Andreapol' Russian Federation
40B2 Andreas,C Cyprus
62B2 Andrews USA
16D2 Andria Italy
17E3 Ándros I Greece
57F4 Andros I The Bahamas
67C4 Andros Town Bahamas
44A3 Androth I India
15B2 Andújar Spain
51B5 Andulo Angola
48C3 Anéfis Mali
48C4 Anécho Togo
33F3 Aneityum I Vanuatu
25M4 Angarsk Russian Federation
20A3 Ånge Sweden
70A2 Angel de la Guarda I Mexico
12G7 Ängelholm Sweden
34C1 Angellala Creek R Australia
66B1 Angels Camp USA
27G7 Angemuk Mt Indonesia
14B2 Angers France
13B3 Angerville France
30C3 Angkor Hist Site Cambodia
10C3 Anglesey I Wales
63C3 Angleton USA
Angmagssalik = Ammassalik
51E5 Angoche Mozambique
74B5 Angol Chile
64C2 Angola Indiana, USA
51B5 Angola Republic Africa
52J5 Angola Basin Atlantic Ocean
14C2 Angoulême France
48A1 Angra do Heroismo Azores
75D3 Angra dos Reis Brazil
69E3 Anguilla I Caribbean Sea
69B2 Anguilla Cays Is Caribbean Sea
43F4 Angul India
50C4 Angumu Zaïre
18C1 Anholt I Denmark
31C4 Anhua China
26F2 Anhui China
31D3 Anhui Province China
75B2 Anhumas Brazil
28A3 Anhŭng S Korea
54C3 Aniak USA
75C2 Anicuns Brazil
62A1 Animas R USA
62A2 Animas Peak Mt USA

61E2 **Anita** USA
26H2 **Aniva, Mys** *C* Russian Federation
13B3 **Anizy-le-Château** France
14B2 **Anjou** *Region* France
51E5 **Anjouan** *I* Comoros
51E5 **Anjozorobe** Madagascar
28B3 **Anju** N Korea
31B3 **Ankang** China
21E8 **Ankara** Turkey
51E5 **Ankaratra** *Mt* Madagascar
51E6 **Ankazoabo** Madagascar
51E5 **Ankazobe** Madagascar
61E2 **Ankeny** USA
18C2 **Anklam** Germany
30D3 **An Loc** Vietnam
31B4 **Anlong** China
31C3 **Anlu** China
64B3 **Anna** USA
16B3 **'Annaba** Algeria
40C3 **An Nabk** Saudi Arabia
40C3 **An Nabk** Syria
40D4 **An Nafūd** *Desert* Saudi Arabia
49E2 **An Nāfūrah** Libya
41D3 **An Najaf** Iraq
8D4 **Annan** Scotland
65D3 **Annapolis** USA
43E3 **Annapurna** *Mt* Nepal
64C2 **Ann Arbor** USA
45D1 **An Nāsirah** Syria
41E3 **An Nāsirīyah** Iraq
14D2 **Annecy** France
30D3 **An Nhon** Vietnam
31A5 **Anning** China
67A2 **Anniston** USA
48C4 **Annobon** *I* Equatorial Guinea
14C2 **Annonay** France
69J1 **Annotto Bay** Jamaica
31D3 **Anqing** China
31B2 **Ansai** China
18C3 **Ansbach** Germany
69C3 **Anse d'Hainault** Haiti
31E1 **Anshan** China
31B4 **Anshun** China
60D2 **Ansley** USA
62C2 **Anson** USA
27F8 **Anson B** Australia
48C3 **Ansongo** Mali
64C1 **Ansonville** Canada
64C3 **Ansted** USA
21F8 **Antakya** Turkey
51F5 **Antalaha** Madagascar
21E8 **Antalya** Turkey
21E8 **Antalya Körfezi** *B* Turkey
51E5 **Antananarivo** Madagascar
76G1 **Antarctic Circle** Antarctica
76G3 **Antarctic Pen** Antarctica
15B2 **Antequera** Spain
62A2 **Anthony** USA
48B1 **Anti-Atlas** *Mts* Morocco
55M5 **Anticosti, Ī. de** Canada
64B1 **Antigo** USA
69E3 **Antigua** *I* Caribbean Sea
Anti Lebanon = Sharqi, Jebel esh
59B3 **Antioch** USA
33G5 **Antipodes Is** New Zealand
63C2 **Antlers** USA
72B2 **Antofagasta** Chile
75C4 **Antonina** Brazil
62A1 **Antonito** USA
9C2 **Antrim** Northern Ireland
68E1 **Antrim** USA
9C2 **Antrim** *County* Northern Ireland
9C2 **Antrim Hills** Northern Ireland
51E5 **Antsirabe** Madagascar
51E5 **Antsirañana** Madagascar
51E5 **Antsohiny** Madagascar
28B2 **Antu** China
30D3 **An Tuc** Vietnam
13C2 **Antwerp** Belgium
Antwerpen = Antwerp
9C3 **An Uaimh** Irish Republic
28A3 **Anui** S Korea
42C3 **Anūpgarh** India
44C4 **Anuradhapura** Sri Lanka
Anvers = Antwerp
54B3 **Anvik** USA
25L5 **Anxi** China
31C2 **Anyang** China
31A3 **A'nyêmaqên Shan** *Mts* China
25S3 **Anyuysk** Russian Federation
24K4 **Anzhero-Sudzhensk** Russian Federation
16C2 **Anzio** Italy
33F2 **Aoba** *I* Vanuatu
29E2 **Aomori** Japan
16B1 **Aosta** Italy
48B3 **Aouker** *Desert Region* Mauritius
48C2 **Aoulef** Algeria
50B1 **Aozou** Chad
74E2 **Apa** *R* Brazil/Paraguay
57E4 **Apalachee B** USA
67B3 **Apalachicola** USA
67A3 **Apalachicola B** USA
72D3 **Apaporis** *R* Brazil/Colombia
75B3 **Aparecida do Taboado** Brazil
27F5 **Aparri** Philippines
17D1 **Apatin** Croatia
20E2 **Apatity** Russian Federation
70B3 **Apatzingan** Mexico
18B2 **Apeldoorn** Netherlands
33H2 **Apia** Western Samoa
75C3 **Apiaí** Brazil
73G2 **Apoera** Surinam
34B3 **Apollo Bay** Australia
67B3 **Apopka,L** USA
73H7 **Aporé** *R* Brazil
64A1 **Apostle Is** USA
57E3 **Appalachian Mts** USA
16C2 **Appennino Abruzzese** *Mts* Italy
16B2 **Appennino Ligure** *Mts* Italy
16D2 **Appennino Lucano** *Mts* Italy
16D2 **Appennino Napoletano** *Mts* Italy
16C2 **Appennino Tosco-Emilliano** *Mts* Italy
16C2 **Appennino Umbro-Marchigiano** *Mts* Italy
6C2 **Appleby** England
61D1 **Appleton** Minnesota, USA
64B2 **Appleton** Wisconsin, USA
21J7 **Apsheronskiy Poluostrov** *Pen* Azerbaijan
74F2 **Apucarana** Brazil
72E2 **Apure** *R* Venezuela
72D6 **Apurimac** *R* Peru
40C4 **'Aqaba** Jordan
40B4 **'Aqaba,G of** Egypt/Saudi Arabia
45C4 **'Aqaba, Wadi el** Egypt
41F3 **'Aqdā** Iran
73G8 **Aqidauana** Brazil
75A3 **Aquidabán** *R* Paraguay
74E2 **Aquidauana** Brazil
75A2 **Aquidauana** *R* Brazil
43E3 **Ara** India
67A2 **Arab** USA
45C1 **'Arab al Mulk** Syria
45C3 **'Araba, Wadi** Israel
36E4 **Arabian Basin** Indian Ocean
38E4 **Arabian Sea** SW Asia
45D2 **'Arab, Jabal al** *Mt* Syria
73L6 **Aracajú** Brazil
75A3 **Aracanguy,Mts de** Paraguay
73L4 **Aracati** Brazil
75D1 **Aracatu** Brazil
73H8 **Araçatuba** Brazil
15A2 **Aracena** Spain
73K7 **Araçuaí** Brazil
45C3 **'Arad** Israel
21C6 **Arad** Romania
50C2 **Arada** Chad
41F5 **'Arādah** UAE
32C1 **Arafura S** Indonesia/Australia
73H7 **Aragarças** Brazil
21G7 **Aragats** *Mt* Armenia
15B1 **Aragon** *R* Spain
15B1 **Aragón** *Region* Spain
75C1 **Araguaçu** Brazil
73H6 **Araguaia** *R* Brazil
73J5 **Araguaína** Brazil
73J7 **Araguari** Brazil
75C2 **Araguari** *R* Brazil
29C3 **Arai** Japan
45C3 **Araif el Naqa, Gebel** *Mt* Egypt
48C2 **Arak** Algeria
41E3 **Arāk** Iran
30A2 **Arakan Yoma** *Mts* Burma
44B3 **Arakkonam** India
24G5 **Aral S** Kazakhstan
24H5 **Aral'sk** Kazakhstan
15B1 **Aranda de Duero** Spain
10B2 **Aran I** Irish Republic
10B3 **Aran Is** Irish Republic
15B1 **Aranjuez** Spain
47B1 **Aranos** Namibia
63C3 **Aransas Pass** USA
28B4 **Arao** Japan
48B3 **Araouane** Mali
60D2 **Arapahoe** USA
74E4 **Arapey** *R* Uruguay
73L5 **Arapiraca** Brazil
75B3 **Araporgas** Brazil
74G3 **Ararangua** Brazil
73J8 **Araraquara** Brazil
75C3 **Araras** Brazil
32D4 **Ararat** Australia
41D2 **Ararat** Armenia
Ararat, Mt = Büyük Ağri Daği
75D3 **Araruama, Lagoa de** Brazil
40D3 **Ar'ar, Wadi** *Watercourse* Saudi Arabia
41D1 **Aras** *R* Turkey
41E2 **Aras** *R* Azerbaijan/Iran
29D3 **Arato** Japan
72E2 **Arauca** *R* Venezuela
72D2 **Arauea** Colombia
42C3 **Arāvalli Range** *Mts* India
33E1 **Arawa** Papua New Guinea
73J7 **Araxá** Brazil
21G8 **Araxes** *R* Iran
50D3 **Arba Minch** Ethiopia
16B3 **Arbatax** Sardinia, Italy
21G8 **Arbīl** Iraq
12H6 **Arbrå** Sweden
8D3 **Arbroath** Scotland
14B3 **Arcachon** France
68A1 **Arcade** USA
67B3 **Arcadia** USA
58B2 **Arcata** USA
66D1 **Arc Dome** *Mt* USA
20G3 **Archangel** Russian Federation
68C2 **Archbald** USA
59E3 **Arches Nat Pk** USA
13C3 **Arcis-sur-Aube** France
58D2 **Arco** USA
75C3 **Arcos** Brazil
15A2 **Arcos de la Frontera** Spain
55K2 **Arctic Bay** Canada
76C1 **Arctic Circle**
54E3 **Arctic Red** *R* Canada
54E3 **Arctic Red River** Canada
54D3 **Arctic Village** USA
76G2 **Arctowski** *Base* Antarctica
17F2 **Arda** *R* Bulgaria
21H8 **Ardabīl** Iran
21G7 **Ardahan** Turkey
12F6 **Årdal** Norway
48C2 **Ardar des Iforas** *Upland* Algeria/Mali
9C3 **Ardee** Irish Republic
41F3 **Ardekān** Iran
13C3 **Ardennes** *Department* France
18B2 **Ardennes** *Region* Belgium
41F3 **Ardestāh** Iran
40C3 **Ardh es Suwwan** *Desert Region* Jordan
15A2 **Ardila** *R* Portugal
34C2 **Ardlethan** Australia
56D3 **Ardmore** USA
8B3 **Ardnamurchan Pt** Scotland
13A2 **Ardres** France
8C3 **Ardrishaig** Scotland
8C4 **Ardrossan** Scotland
69D3 **Arecibo** Puerto Rico
73L4 **Areia Branca** Brazil
59B3 **Arena,Pt** USA
13D1 **Arenberg** *Region* Germany
12F7 **Arendal** Norway
72D7 **Arequipa** Peru
16C2 **Arezzo** Italy
16C2 **Argenta** Italy
14C2 **Argentan** France
13B3 **Argenteuil** France
71D7 **Argentina** *Republic* S America
52F7 **Argentine Basin** Atlantic Ocean
74B8 **Argentino, Lago** Argentina
14C2 **Argenton-sur-Creuse** France
17F2 **Argeș** *R* Romania
42B2 **Arghardab** *R* Afghanistan
17E3 **Argolikós Kólpos** *G* Greece
13C3 **Argonne** *Region* France
17E3 **Árgos** Greece
17E3 **Argostólion** Greece
66B3 **Arguello,Pt** USA
66D3 **Argus Range** *Mts* USA
32B2 **Argyle,L** Australia
8C3 **Argyll** Scotland
18C1 **Århus** Denmark
51C6 **Ariamsvlei** Namibia
48B3 **Aribinda** Burkina
74B1 **Arica** Chile
42C2 **Arifwala** Pakistan
Arihā = Jericho
60C3 **Arikaree** *R* USA
69L1 **Arima** Trinidad
75C2 **Arinos** Brazil
73G6 **Arinos** *R* Brazil
69L1 **Aripo,Mt** Trinidad
72F5 **Aripuanã** Brazil
72F5 **Aripuanã** *R* Brazil
8C3 **Arisaig** Scotland
45B3 **'Arîsh, Wadi el** *Watercourse* Egypt
56B3 **Arizona** *State* USA
12G7 **Årjäng** Sweden
25Q4 **Arka** Russian Federation
21G5 **Arkadak** Russian Federation
63D2 **Arkadelphia** USA
8C3 **Arkaig, L** Scotland
24H4 **Arkalyk** Kazakhstan
57D3 **Arkansas** *R* USA
57D3 **Arkansas** *State* USA
63C1 **Arkansas City** USA
29C2 **Arkhipovka** Russian Federation
25K2 **Arkipelag Nordenshelda** *Arch* Russian Federation
10B3 **Arklow** Irish Republic
15B1 **Arlanzón** *R* Spain
14C3 **Arles** France
61D2 **Arlington** S Dakota, USA
63C2 **Arlington** Texas, USA
65D3 **Arlington** Virginia, USA
58B1 **Arlington** Washington, USA
64B2 **Arlington Heights** USA
18B3 **Arlon** Belgium
Armageddon = Megiddo
9C2 **Armagh** Northern Ireland
9C2 **Armagh** *County* Northern Ireland
13B4 **Armançon** *R* France
21G7 **Armavir** Russian Federation
72C3 **Armenia** Colombia
21G7 **Armenia** *Republic* Europe
13B2 **Armentières** Belgium
32E4 **Armidale** Australia
55L3 **Arnaud** *R* Canada
40B2 **Arnauti** *C* Cyprus
62C1 **Arnett** USA
18B2 **Arnhem** Netherlands
32C2 **Arnhem,C** Australia
32C2 **Arnhem Land** Australia
66B1 **Arnold** USA
65D1 **Arnprior** Canada
13E2 **Arnsberg** Germany
47B2 **Aroab** Namibia
13E2 **Arolsen** Germany
33G1 **Arorae** *I* Kiribati
16B1 **Arosa** Switzerland
13B3 **Arpajon** France
75C1 **Arraias** Brazil
75C1 **Arraias, Serra de** *Mts* Brazil
41D3 **Ar Ramādī** Iraq
8C4 **Arran, I of** Scotland
40C2 **Ar Raqqah** Syria
49D2 **Ar Rāqūbah** Libya
14C1 **Arras** France
41D4 **Ar Rass** Saudi Arabia
45D1 **Ar Rastan** Syria
48A2 **Arrecife** Canary Islands
41E3 **Ar Rifā'ī** Iraq
41E3 **Ar Rihāb** *Desert Region* Iraq
Ar Rīyād = Riyadh
8C3 **Arrochar** Scotland
75C1 **Arrojado** *R* Brazil
58C2 **Arrowrock Res** USA
35A2 **Arrowtown** New Zealand
66B3 **Arroyo Grande** USA
41F4 **Ar Ru'ays** Qatar
41G5 **Ar Rustāq** Oman
40D3 **Ar Rutbah** Iraq
41D5 **Ar Ruwayḍah** Saudi Arabia
44B3 **Arsikere** India
20H4 **Arsk** Russian Federation
17E3 **Árta** Greece
28C2 **Artem** Russian Federation
25L4 **Artemovsk** Russian Federation
25N4 **Artemovskiy** Russian Federation
56C3 **Artesia** USA
35B2 **Arthurs P** New Zealand
74E4 **Artigas** Uruguay
54H3 **Artillery L** Canada
14C1 **Artois** *Region* France
19F3 **Artsiz** Ukraine
76G2 **Arturo Prat** *Base* Antarctica
21G7 **Artvin** Turkey
50D3 **Aru** Zaïre
73H6 **Aruanã** Brazil
69C4 **Aruba** *I* Caribbean Sea
27G7 **Aru, Kepulauan** *Arch* Indonesia
43F3 **Arun** *R* Nepal
43G3 **Arunāchal Pradesh** *Union Territory* India
44B4 **Aruppukkottai** India
50D4 **Arusha** Tanzania
50C3 **Aruwimi** *R* Zaïre
60B3 **Arvada** USA
26D2 **Arvayheer** Mongolia
55L5 **Arvida** Canada
12H5 **Arvidsjaur** Sweden
12G7 **Arvika** Sweden
59C3 **Arvin** USA
45C1 **Arwad** *I* Syria
20G4 **Arzamas** Russian Federation
15B2 **Arzew** Algeria
42C2 **Asadabad** Afghanistan
29B4 **Asahi** *R* Japan
29E2 **Asahi dake** *Mt* Japan
29E2 **Asahikawa** Japan
28A3 **Asan-man** *B* S Korea
43F4 **Asansol** India
49D2 **Asawanwah** *Well* Libya
20L4 **Asbest** Russian Federation
47C2 **Asbestos Mts** South Africa
65E2 **Asbury Park** USA
52H5 **Ascension** *I* Atlantic Ocean
70D3 **Ascensión, B de la** Mexico
18B3 **Aschaffenburg** Germany
18C2 **Aschersleben** Germany
16C2 **Ascoli Piceno** Italy
50E2 **Āseb** Eritrea
48C2 **Asedjrad** *Upland* Algeria
50D3 **Asela** Ethiopia
12H6 **Åsele** Sweden
17E2 **Asenovgrad** Bulgaria
13C3 **Asfeld** France
20K4 **Asha** Russian Federation
7D3 **Ashbourne** England
67B2 **Ashburn** USA
33G5 **Ashburton** New Zealand
32A3 **Ashburton** *R* Australia
40B3 **Ashdod** Israel
63D2 **Ashdown** USA
67A1 **Asheboro** USA
57E3 **Asheville** USA
34D1 **Ashford** Australia
7E4 **Ashford** England
59D3 **Ash Fork** USA
29D2 **Ashibetsu** Japan
29D3 **Ashikaga** Japan
28B4 **Ashizuri-misaki** *Pt* Japan
24G6 **Ashkhabad** Turkmenistan
62C1 **Ashland** Kansas, USA
57E3 **Ashland** Kentucky, USA
60B1 **Ashland** Montana, USA
61D2 **Ashland** Nebraska, USA
64C2 **Ashland** Ohio, USA
56A2 **Ashland** Oregon, USA
65D3 **Ashland** Virginia, USA
61E1 **Ashland** Wisconsin, USA
34C1 **Ashley** Australia
60D1 **Ashley** USA
68C2 **Ashokan Res** USA
45C3 **Ashqelon** Israel
41D3 **Ash Shabakh** Iraq
41G4 **Ash Sha'm** UAE
41D2 **Ash Sharqāṭ** Iraq
41E3 **Ash Shaṭrah** Iraq
38C4 **Ash Shiḥr** Yemen
41E4 **Ash Shumlūl** Saudi Arabia
64C2 **Ashtabula** USA
55M4 **Ashuanipi L** Canada
21F8 **Asi** *R* Syria
15A2 **Asilah** Morocco
16B2 **Asinara** *I* Sardinia, Italy
24K4 **Asino** Russian Federation
50E1 **Asīr** *Region* Saudi Arabia
43E5 **Aska** India
40D2 **Aşkale** Turkey
12G7 **Askersund** Sweden
45B4 **Asl** Egypt
42C1 **Asmar** Afghanistan
50D2 **Asmara** Eritrea
Āsmera = Asmara
28B4 **Aso** Japan
50D2 **Asosa** Ethiopia
50D1 **Asoteriba, Jebel** *Mt* Sudan
62B2 **Aspermont** USA
35A2 **Aspiring,Mt** New Zealand
40C2 **As Sabkhah** Syria
41E5 **As Salamiyah** Saudi Arabia
40C2 **As Salamīyah** Syria
41D3 **As Salmān** Iraq
43G3 **Assam** *State* India
41E3 **As Samāwah** Iraq
41F5 **Aş Şanām** *Region* Saudi Arabia
45D2 **Aş Şanamayn** Syria
18B2 **Assen** Netherlands
18C1 **Assens** Denmark
49D1 **As Sidrah** Libya
54H5 **Assiniboia** Canada
54G4 **Assiniboine,Mt** Canada
73H8 **Assis** Brazil
40C3 **As Sukhnah** Syria
41E5 **Aş Şumman** *Region* Saudi Arabia
51E4 **Assumption** *I* Seychelles
40C3 **As Suwaydā'** Syria
41D3 **Aş Şuwayrah** Iraq
41E2 **Astara** Azerbaijan
16B2 **Asti** Italy
17F3 **Astipálaia** *I* Greece
15A1 **Astorga** Spain
56A2 **Astoria** USA
21H6 **Astrakhan'** Russian Federation
15A1 **Asturias** *Region* Spain
76F12 **Asuka** *Base* Antarctica
74E3 **Asunción** Paraguay
26H5 **Asuncion** *I* Marianas
50D3 **Aswa** *R* Uganda
40B5 **Aswân** Egypt
49F2 **Aswân High Dam** Egypt
49F2 **Asyût** Egypt
74C2 **Atacama, Desierto de** *Desert* Chile
33H1 **Atafu** *I* Tokelau Islands

45C3 **Atā'ita, Jebel el** *Mt* Jordan
48C4 **Atakpamé** Togo
27F7 **Atambua** Indonesia
55N3 **Atangmik** Greenland
45B4 **Ataqa, Gebel** *Mt* Egypt
48A2 **Atar** Mauritius
40C2 **Atatirk Baraji** *Res* Turkey
66B3 **Atascadero** USA
24J5 **Atasu** Kazakhstan
50D2 **Atbara** Sudan
24H4 **Atbasar** Kazakhstan
57D4 **Atchafalaya B** USA
57D3 **Atchison** USA
68C3 **Atco** USA
16C2 **Atessa** Italy
13B2 **Ath** Belgium
54G4 **Athabasca** Canada
54G4 **Athabasca** *R* Canada
54H4 **Athabasca,L** Canada
67A2 **Athens** Alabama, USA
57E3 **Athens** Georgia, USA
17E3 **Athens** Greece
64C3 **Athens** Ohio, USA
68B2 **Athens** Pennsylvania, USA
67B1 **Athens** Tennessee, USA
63C2 **Athens** Texas, USA
Athína = Athens
10B3 **Athlone** Irish Republic
45B1 **Athna** Cyprus
68D1 **Athol** USA
17E2 **Áthos** *Mt* Greece
9C3 **Athy** Irish Republic
50B2 **Ati** Chad
55J5 **Atikoken** Canada
25R3 **Atka** Russian Federation
21G5 **Atkarsk** Russian Federation
63D1 **Atkins** USA
57E3 **Atlanta** Georgia, USA
64C2 **Atlanta** Michigan, USA
61D2 **Atlantic** USA
57F3 **Atlantic City** USA
68C2 **Atlantic Highlands** USA
52H8 **Atlantic-Indian Antarctic Basin** Atlantic Ocean
52H7 **Atlantic Indian Ridge** Atlantic Ocean
Atlas Mts = Haut Atlas, Moyen Atlas
48C1 **Atlas Saharien** *Mts* Algeria
54E4 **Atlin** Canada
54E4 **Atlin L** Canada
45C2 **'Atlit** Israel
57E3 **Atmore** USA
51E6 **Atofinandrahana** Madagascar
63C2 **Atoka** USA
72C2 **Atrato** *R* Colombia
41F5 **Attaf** *Region* UAE
50E1 **Aṭ Ṭā'if** Saudi Arabia
45D2 **At Tall** Syria
67A2 **Attalla** USA
55K4 **Attawapiskat** Canada
55K4 **Attawapiskat** *R* Canada
41D3 **At Taysīyah** *Desert Region* Saudi Arabia
64B2 **Attica** Indiana, USA
68A1 **Attica** New York, USA
13C3 **Attigny** France
45B1 **Attila Line** Cyprus
65E2 **Attleboro** Massachusetts, USA
30D3 **Attopeu** Laos
40C4 **At Tubayq** *Upland* Saudi Arabia
12H7 **Atvidaberg** Sweden
66B2 **Atwater** USA
14D3 **Aubagne** France
13C3 **Aube** *Department* France
13C3 **Aube** *R* France
14C3 **Aubenas** France
67A2 **Auburn** Alabama, USA
59B3 **Auburn** California, USA
64B2 **Auburn** Indiana, USA
65E2 **Auburn** Maine, USA
61D2 **Auburn** Nebraska, USA
65D2 **Auburn** New York, USA
58B1 **Auburn** Washington, USA
14C3 **Auch** France
33G4 **Auckland** New Zealand
37K7 **Auckland Is** New Zealand
14C3 **Aude** *R* France
55K4 **Auden** Canada
61E2 **Audubon** USA
34C1 **Augathella** Australia
9C2 **Aughnacloy** Northern Ireland
47B2 **Aughrabies Falls** South Africa
18C3 **Augsburg** Germany
32A4 **Augusta** Australia
57E3 **Augusta** Georgia, USA
63C1 **Augusta** Kansas, USA
57G2 **Augusta** Maine, USA
58D1 **Augusta** Montana, USA
64A2 **Augusta** Wisconsin, USA
19E2 **Augustów** Poland
32A3 **Augustus,Mt** Australia
47B1 **Auob** *R* Namibia
42D3 **Auraiya** India
42D5 **Aurangābād** India
48C1 **Aurès** *Mts* Algeria
16B3 **Aurès, Mt de l'** Algeria
13D1 **Aurich** Germany
14C3 **Aurillac** France
56C3 **Aurora** Colorado, USA
64B2 **Aurora** Illinois, USA
64C3 **Aurora** Indiana, USA
63D1 **Aurora** Mississippi, USA
61D2 **Aurora** Nebraska, USA
47B2 **Aus** Namibia
64C2 **Au Sable** USA
48A2 **Ausert** *Well* Morocco
8D2 **Auskerry, I** Scotland
57D2 **Austin** Minnesota, USA
59C3 **Austin** Nevada, USA
68A2 **Austin** Pennsylvania, USA
56D3 **Austin** Texas, USA
32D4 **Australian Alps** *Mts* Australia
18C3 **Austria** *Federal Republic* Europe
70B3 **Autlán** Mexico
14C2 **Autun** France
14C2 **Auvergne** *Region* France
14C2 **Auxerre** France
13A2 **Auxi-le-Château** France
14C2 **Avallon** France
66C4 **Avalon** USA
55N5 **Avalon Pen** Canada
75C3 **Avaré** Brazil
13E1 **Ave** *R* Germany
45C3 **Avedat** *Hist Site* Israel
73G4 **Aveíro** Brazil
15A1 **Aveiro** Portugal
74E4 **Avellaneda** Argentina
16C2 **Avellino** Italy
66B3 **Avenal** USA
13B2 **Avesnes-sur-Helpe** France
12H6 **Avesta** Sweden
16C2 **Avezzano** Italy
8D3 **Aviemore** Scotland
35B2 **Aviemore,L** New Zealand
14C3 **Avignon** France
15B1 **Avila** Spain
15A1 **Avilés** Spain
61D2 **Avoca** Iowa, USA
68B1 **Avoca** New York, USA
34B3 **Avoca** *R* Australia
68B1 **Avon** USA
7C4 **Avon** *County* England
7D4 **Avon** *R* Dorset, England
7D3 **Avon** *R* Warwick, England
59D4 **Avondale** USA
7C4 **Avonmouth** Wales
67B3 **Avon Park** USA
13B3 **Avre** *R* France
17D2 **Avtovac** Bosnia-Herzegovina
45D2 **A'waj** *R* Syria
29D4 **Awaji-shima** *I* Japan
50E3 **Awarē** Ethiopia
35A2 **Awarua Pt** New Zealand
50E3 **Awash** Ethiopia
50E3 **Awash** *R* Ethiopia
29C3 **Awa-shima** *I* Japan
35B2 **Awatere** *R* New Zealand
49D2 **Awbārī** Libya
50C3 **Aweil** Sudan
8C3 **Awe, Loch** *L* Scotland
49E2 **Awjilah** Libya
55J1 **Axel Heiberg I** Canada
7C4 **Axminster** England
29C3 **Ayabe** Japan
74E5 **Ayacucho** Argentina
69C5 **Ayacucho** Colombia
72D6 **Ayacucho** Peru
24K5 **Ayaguz** Kazakhstan
39G2 **Ayakkum Hu** *L* China
15A2 **Ayamonte** Spain
25P4 **Ayan** Russian Federation
72D6 **Ayaviri** Peru
21D8 **Aydin** Turkey
17F3 **Áyios Evstrátios** *I* Greece
25N3 **Aykhal** Russian Federation
7D4 **Aylesbury** England
45D2 **'Ayn al Fījah** Syria
40D2 **Ayn Zālah** Iraq
49E2 **Ayn Zuwayyah** *Well* Libya
50D3 **Ayod** Sudan
32D2 **Ayr** Australia
8C4 **Ayr** Scotland
8C4 **Ayr** *R* Scotland
6B2 **Ayre,Pt of** Isle of Man, British Islands
17F2 **Aytos** Bulgaria
30C3 **Ayutthaya** Thailand
17F3 **Ayvacık** Turkey
17F3 **Ayvalık** Turkey
43E3 **Āzamgarh** India
48B3 **Azaouad** *Desert Region* Mali
48C3 **Azaouak, Vallée de l'** Niger
48D3 **Azare** Nigeria
40C2 **A'zāz** Syria
Azbine = Aïr
48A2 **Azeffal** *Watercourse* Mauritius
21H7 **Azerbaijan** *Republic* Europe
72C4 **Azogues** Ecuador
20H2 **Azopol'ye** Russian Federation
46B4 **Azores** *Is* Atlantic Ocean
50C2 **Azoum** *R* Chad
21F6 **Azov, S of** Russian Federation/Ukraine
48B1 **Azrou** Morocco
62A1 **Aztec** USA
72B2 **Azuero,Pen de** Panama
74E5 **Azul** Argentina
75B1 **Azul, Serra** *Mts* Brazil
16B3 **Azzaba** Algeria
45D2 **Az-Zabdānī** Syria
41G5 **Az Ẕāhirah** *Mts* Oman
49D2 **Az Zahrah** Libya
40C3 **Az Zilaf** Syria
41D4 **Az Zilfī** Saudi Arabia
41E3 **Az Zubayr** Iraq

B

45C2 **Ba'abda** Lebanon
40C3 **Ba'albek** Lebanon
45C3 **Ba'al Hazor** *Mt* Israel
50E3 **Baardheere** Somalia
17F2 **Babadag** Romania
40A1 **Babaeski** Turkey
72C4 **Babahoyo** Ecuador
50E2 **Bāb al Mandab** *Str* Djibouti/Yemen
32B1 **Babar, Kepulauan** *I* Indonesia
50D4 **Babati** Tanzania
20F4 **Babayevo** Russian Federation
61E1 **Babbitt** USA
64C2 **Baberton** USA
54F4 **Babine L** Canada
32C1 **Babo** Indonesia
41F2 **Bābol** Iran
27F5 **Babuyan Is** Philippines
73J4 **Bacabal** Brazil
27F7 **Bacan** *I* Indonesia
21D6 **Bacău** Romania
30D1 **Bac Can** Vietnam
13D3 **Baccarat** France
34B3 **Bacchus Marsh** Australia
39F2 **Bachu** China
54J3 **Back** *R* Canada
30D1 **Bac Ninh** Vietnam
27F5 **Bacolod** Philippines
6C3 **Bacup** England
44B3 **Badagara** India
31A1 **Badain Jaran Shamo** *Desert* China
15A2 **Badajoz** Spain
15C1 **Badalona** Spain
40D3 **Badanah** Saudi Arabia
28B2 **Badaohe** China
13E3 **Bad Bergzabern** Germany
13D2 **Bad Ems** Germany
18B3 **Baden-Baden** Germany
13D3 **Badenviller** France
18B3 **Baden-Württemberg** *State* Germany
18C3 **Badgastein** Austria
66C2 **Badger** USA
18B2 **Bad-Godesberg** Germany
18B2 **Bad Hersfeld** Germany
13D2 **Bad Honnef** Germany
42B4 **Badin** Pakistan
16C1 **Bad Ischl** Austria
40C3 **Badiyat ash Sham** *Desert Region* Iraq/Jordan
18B3 **Bad-Kreuznach** Germany
60C1 **Badlands** *Region* USA
13E2 **Bad Lippspringe** Germany
13E2 **Bad Nauheim** Germany
13D2 **Bad Nevenahr-Ahrweiler** Germany
40C5 **Badr Ḩunayn** Saudi Arabia
13E2 **Bad Ryrmont** Germany
18C3 **Bad Tolz** Germany
44C4 **Badulla** Sri Lanka
13E2 **Bad Wildungen** Germany
13E3 **Bad Wimpfen** Germany
15B2 **Baena** Spain
48A3 **Bafatá** Guinea-Bissau
55L2 **Baffin B** Canada/Greenland
63C3 **Baffin B** USA
55L2 **Baffin I** Canada
50B3 **Bafia** Cameroon
48A3 **Bafing** *R* Mali
48A3 **Bafoulabé** Mali
50B3 **Bafoussam** Cameroon
41G3 **Bāfq** Iran
21F7 **Bafra Burun** *Pt* Turkey
41G4 **Bāft** Iran
50C3 **Bafwasende** Zaïre
43E3 **Bagaha** India
44B2 **Bāgalkot** India
51D4 **Bagamoyo** Tanzania
59D4 **Bagdad** USA
74F4 **Bagé** Brazil
60B2 **Baggs** USA
41D3 **Baghdād** Iraq
43F4 **Bagherhat** Bangladesh
41G3 **Bāghīn** Iran
42B1 **Baghlan** Afghanistan
61D1 **Bagley** USA
48B4 **Bagnoa** Ivory Coast
14C3 **Bagnols-sur-Cèze** France
Bago = Pegu
48B3 **Bagoé** *R* Mali
28A2 **Bag Tai** China
27F5 **Baguio** Philippines
43F3 **Bāhādurābād** Bangladesh
57F4 **Bahamas,The** *Is* Caribbean Sea
43F4 **Baharampur** India
40A4 **Baharîya Oasis** Egypt
42C3 **Bahawalnagar** Pakistan
42C3 **Bahawalpur** Pakistan
42C3 **Bahawalpur** *Division* Pakistan
Bahia = Salvador
73K6 **Bahia** *State* Brazil
74D5 **Bahía Blanca** Argentina
70D3 **Bahía, Islas de la** Honduras
56B4 **Bahia Kino** Mexico
74C6 **Bahias, Cabo dos** Argentina
50D2 **Bahir Dar** Ethiopia
45A3 **Bahra el Manzala** *L* Egypt
43E3 **Bahraich** India
38D3 **Bahrain** *Sheikhdom* Arabian Pen
41D3 **Bahr al Milh** *L* Iraq
50C3 **Bahr Aouk** *R* Chad/Central African Republic
Bahrat Lut = Dead Sea
Bahr el Abiad = White Nile
50C3 **Bahr el Arab** *Watercourse* Sudan
Bahr el Azraq = Blue Nile
50D3 **Bahr el Ghazal** *R* Sudan
50B2 **Bahr el Ghazal** *Watercourse* Chad
45A3 **Bahr Fâqûs** *R* Egypt
15A2 **Baia de Setúbal** *B* Portugal
51B5 **Baia dos Tigres** Angola
21C6 **Baia Mare** Romania
50B3 **Baïbokoum** Chad
26F2 **Baicheng** China
55M5 **Baie-Comeau** Canada
45C2 **Baie de St Georges** *B* Lebanon
55L4 **Baie-du-Poste** Canada
65E1 **Baie St Paul** Canada
55N5 **Baie-Verte** Canada
31B3 **Baihe** China
31C3 **Bai He** *R* China
41D3 **Ba'ījī** Iraq
25M4 **Baikal, L** Russian Federation
43E4 **Baikunthpur** India
Baile Atha Cliath = Dublin
17E2 **Băileşti** Romania
13B2 **Bailleul** France
31A3 **Baima** China
67B2 **Bainbridge** USA
54B3 **Baird Mts** USA
31D1 **Bairin Youqi** China
31D1 **Bairin Zuoqi** China
32D4 **Bairnsdale** Australia
43E3 **Baitadi** Nepal
28A2 **Baixingt** China
17D1 **Baja** Hungary
70A1 **Baja California** *Pen* Mexico
59C4 **Baja California** *State* Mexico
70A2 **Baja, Punta** *Pt* Mexico
20K5 **Bakal** Russian Federation
50C3 **Bakala** Central African Republic
48A3 **Bakel** Senegal
59C3 **Baker** California, USA
56C2 **Baker** Montana, USA
56B2 **Baker** Oregon, USA
55J3 **Baker Foreland** *Pt* Canada
54J3 **Baker L** Canada
54J3 **Baker Lake** Canada
56A2 **Baker,Mt** USA
56B3 **Bakersfield** USA
7D3 **Bakewell** England
41G2 **Bakharden** Turkmenistan
41G2 **Bakhardok** Turkmenistan
21E5 **Bakhmach** Ukraine
12C1 **Bakkaflói** *B* Iceland
50D3 **Bako** Ethiopia
50C3 **Bakouma** Central African Republic
21H7 **Baku** Azerbaijan
40B2 **Balâ** Turkey
7C3 **Bala** Wales
27E6 **Balabac** *I* Philippines
27E6 **Balabac Str** Malaysia/Philippines
43E4 **Bālaghāt** India
34A2 **Balaklava** Australia
21H5 **Balakovo** Russian Federation
43E4 **Balāngīr** India
21G5 **Balashov** Russian Federation
43F4 **Balasore** India
17D1 **Balaton** *L* Hungary
9C3 **Balbriggan** Irish Republic
74E5 **Balcarce** Argentina
17F2 **Balchik** Bulgaria
33F5 **Balclutha** New Zealand
63D1 **Bald Knob** USA
7D4 **Baldock** England
67B2 **Baldwin** USA
58E1 **Baldy Mt** USA
56C3 **Baldy Peak** *Mt* USA
15C2 **Balearic Is** Spain
75E2 **Baleia, Ponta da** *Pt* Brazil
55M4 **Baleine, Rivière de la** *R* Canada
27F5 **Baler** Philippines
20J4 **Balezino** Russian Federation
32A1 **Bali** *I* Indonesia
40A2 **Balıkesir** Turkey
40C2 **Balīkh** *R* Syria/Turkey
27E7 **Balikpapan** Indonesia
75B2 **Baliza** Brazil
42B1 **Balkh** Afghanistan
24J5 **Balkhash** Kazakhstan
24J5 **Balkhash, L** Kazakhstan
8C3 **Ballachulish** Scotland
8C4 **Ballantrae** Scotland
54G2 **Ballantyne Str** Canada
44B3 **Ballāpur** India
32D4 **Ballarat** Australia
8D3 **Ballater** Scotland
6B2 **Ballaugh** England
76G7 **Balleny Is** Antarctica
43E3 **Ballia** India
34D1 **Ballina** Australia
10B3 **Ballina** Irish Republic
62C2 **Ballinger** USA
9A4 **Ballinskelligis B** Irish Republic
13D4 **Ballon d'Alsace** *Mt* France
17D2 **Ballsh** Albania
68D1 **Ballston Spa** USA
9C2 **Ballycastle** Northern Ireland
9D2 **Ballyclare** Northern Ireland
9C4 **Ballycotton B** Irish Republic
9B3 **Ballyhaunis** Northern Ireland
9C2 **Ballymena** Northern Ireland
9C2 **Ballymoney** Northern Ireland
9C2 **Ballynahinch** Northern Ireland
9B2 **Ballyshannon** Irish Republic
9C3 **Ballyteige B** Irish Republic
34B3 **Balmoral** Australia
62B2 **Balmorhea** USA
42B3 **Balochistān** *Region* Pakistan
51B5 **Balombo** Angola
34C1 **Balonn** *R* Australia
42C3 **Bālotra** India
43E3 **Balrāmpur** India
32D4 **Balranald** Australia
73J5 **Balsas** Brazil
70B3 **Balsas** *R* Mexico
21D6 **Balta** Ukraine
12H7 **Baltic S** N Europe
40B3 **Baltîm** Egypt
57F3 **Baltimore** USA
43F3 **Bālurghāt** India
21J6 **Balykshi** Kazakhstan
41G4 **Bam** Iran
50B2 **Bama** Nigeria
48B3 **Bamako** Mali
50C3 **Bambari** Central African Republic
67B2 **Bamberg** USA
18C3 **Bamberg** Germany
50C3 **Bambili** Zaïre
75C3 **Bambuí** Brazil
50B3 **Bamenda** Cameroon
28A2 **Bamiancheng** China
50B3 **Bamingui** *R* Central African Republic
50B3 **Bamingui Bangoran National Park** Central African Republic
42B2 **Bamiyan** Afghanistan
33F1 **Banaba** *I* Kiribati
50C3 **Banalia** Zaïre
48B3 **Banamba** Mali
44E4 **Bananga** Nicobar Is, Indian Ocean
30C3 **Ban Aranyaprathet** Thailand
30C2 **Ban Ban** Laos
30C4 **Ban Betong** Thailand
9C2 **Banbridge** Northern Ireland
7D3 **Banbury** England
8D3 **Banchory** Scotland
70D3 **Banco Chinchorro** *Is* Mexico
65D1 **Bancroft** Canada
43E3 **Bānda** India
27C6 **Banda Aceh** Indonesia

27G7 **Banda, Kepulauan** *Arch* Indonesia
48B4 **Bandama** *R* Ivory Coast
41G4 **Bandar 'Abbās** Iran
21H8 **Bandar Anzalī** Iran
41F4 **Bandar-e Daylam** Iran
41F4 **Bandar-e Lengheh** Iran
41F4 **Bandar-e Māqām** Iran
41F4 **Bandar-e Rig** Iran
21J8 **Bandar-e Torkoman** Iran
41E3 **Bandar Khomeynī** Iran
27E6 **Bandar Seri Begawan** Brunei
27F7 **Banda S** Indonesia
75D3 **Bandeira** *Mt* Brazil
75B1 **Bandeirantes** Brazil
70B2 **Banderas, B de** Mexico
48B3 **Bandiagara** Mali
21D7 **Bandırma** Turkey
47D1 **Bandolier Kop** South Africa
50B4 **Bandundu** Zaïre
27D7 **Bandung** Indonesia
21H8 **Baneh** Iran
70E2 **Banes** Cuba
8D3 **Banff** Scotland
54G4 **Banff** *R* Canada
44B3 **Bangalore** India
50C3 **Bangassou** Central African Republic
32B1 **Banggai, Kepulauan** *I* Indonesia
27E6 **Banggi** *I* Malaysia
30D2 **Bang Hieng** *R* Laos
27D7 **Bangka** *I* Indonesia
30C3 **Bangkok** Thailand
30C3 **Bangkok, Bight of** *B* Thailand
39G3 **Bangladesh** *Republic* Asia
42D2 **Bangong Co** *L* China
57G2 **Bangor** Maine, USA
9D2 **Bangor** Northern Ireland
68C2 **Bangor** Pennsylvania, USA
7B3 **Bangor** Wales
30B3 **Bang Saphan Yai** Thailand
50B3 **Bangui** Central African Republic
51D5 **Bangweulu, L** Zambia
30C4 **Ban Hat Yai** Thailand
30C2 **Ban Hin Heup** Laos
30C1 **Ban Houei Sai** Laos
30B3 **Ban Hua Hin** Thailand
48B3 **Bani** *R* Mali
48C3 **Bani Bangou** Niger
49D1 **Banī Walīd** Libya
40C2 **Bāniyās** Syria
16D2 **Banja Luka** Bosnia-Herzegovina
27E7 **Banjarmasin** Indonesia
48A3 **Banjul** The Gambia
30B4 **Ban Kantang** Thailand
30D2 **Ban Khemmarat** Laos
30B4 **Ban Khok Kloi** Thailand
27H8 **Banks I** Australia
54E4 **Banks I** British Columbia, Canada
54F2 **Banks I** Northwest Territories, Canada
33F2 **Banks Is** Vanuatu
58C1 **Banks L** USA
35B2 **Banks Pen** New Zealand
34C4 **Banks Str** Australia
43F4 **Bankura** India
30B2 **Ban Mae Sariang** Thailand
30B2 **Ban Mae Sot** Thailand
43H4 **Banmauk** Burma
30D3 **Ban Me Thuot** Vietnam
9C3 **Bann** *R* Irish Republic
9C2 **Bann** *R* Northern Ireland
30B4 **Ban Na San** Thailand
42C2 **Bannu** Pakistan
30C2 **Ban Pak Neun** Laos
30C4 **Ban Pak Phanang** Thailand
30D3 **Ban Pu Kroy** Cambodia
30B3 **Ban Sai Yok** Thailand
30C3 **Ban Sattahip** Thailand
19D3 **Banská Bystrica** Slovakia
42C4 **Bānswāra** India
30B4 **Ban Tha Kham** Thailand
30D2 **Ban Thateng** Laos
30C2 **Ban Tha Tum** Thailand
10B3 **Bantry** Irish Republic
10A3 **Bantry** *B* Irish Republic
27C6 **Banyak, Kepulauan** *Is* Indonesia
30D3 **Ban Ya Soup** Vietnam
27E7 **Banyuwangi** Indonesia
36E7 **Banzare Seamount** Indian Ocean
31D2 **Baoding** China
31C3 **Baofeng** China
30C1 **Bao Ha** Vietnam
31B3 **Baoji** China
30D3 **Bao Loc** Vietnam
26C4 **Baoshan** China
31C1 **Baotou** China
44C2 **Bāpatla** India
13B2 **Bapaume** France
45C4 **Bāqir, Jebel** *Mt* Jordan
41D3 **Ba'qūbah** Iraq
17D2 **Bar** Montenegro, Yugoslavia
50D2 **Bara** Sudan
50E3 **Baraawe** Somalia
43E3 **Bāra Banki** India
28C2 **Barabash** Russian Federation
24J4 **Barabinsk** Kazakhstan/Russian Federation
24J4 **Barabinskaya Step** *Steppe* Kazakhstan/Russian Federation
15B1 **Baracaldo** Spain
69C2 **Baracoa** Cuba
45D2 **Baradá** *R* Syria
34C2 **Baradine** Australia
44A2 **Bārāmati** India
42C2 **Baramula** Pakistan
42D3 **Bārān** India
54E4 **Baranof I** USA
20D5 **Baranovichi** Belarus
34A2 **Baratta** Australia
43F3 **Barauni** India
73K8 **Barbacena** Brazil
69F4 **Barbados** *I* Caribbean Sea
15C1 **Barbastro** Spain
47E2 **Barberton** South Africa
14B2 **Barbezieux** France
72D2 **Barbosa** Colombia
69E3 **Barbuda** *I* Caribbean Sea
32D3 **Barcaldine** Australia
Barce = Al Marj
16D3 **Barcellona** Sicily, Italy
15C1 **Barcelona** Spain
72F1 **Barcelona** Venezuela
32D3 **Barcoo** *R* Australia
50B1 **Bardai** Chad
74C5 **Bardas Blancas** Argentina
43F4 **Barddhamān** India
19E3 **Bardejov** Slovakia
7B3 **Bardsey** *I* Wales
64B3 **Bardstown** USA
42D3 **Bareilly** India
Barentsovo More *S* = **Barents Sea**
24D2 **Barentsøya** *I* Svalbard
20F1 **Barents S** Russian Federation
50D2 **Barentu** Eritrea
14B2 **Barfleur, Pointe de** France
43E4 **Bargarh** India
25M4 **Barguzin** Russian Federation
25N4 **Barguzin** *R* Russian Federation
65F2 **Bar Harbor** USA
43F4 **Barhi** India
16D2 **Bari** Italy
15D2 **Barika** Algeria
72D2 **Barinas** Venezuela
43F4 **Baripāda** India
40B5 **Bârîs** Egypt
42C4 **Bari Sādri** India
43G4 **Barisal** Bangladesh
27D7 **Barisan, Pegunungan** *Mts* Indonesia
27E7 **Barito** *R* Indonesia
49D2 **Barjuj** *Watercourse* Libya
31A3 **Barkam** China
64B3 **Barkley,L** USA
47D3 **Barkly East** South Africa
32C2 **Barkly Tableland** *Mts* Australia
13C3 **Bar-le-Duc** France
32A3 **Barlee,L** Australia
32A3 **Barlee Range** *Mts* Australia
16D2 **Barletta** Italy
42C3 **Bārmer** India
34B2 **Barmera** Australia
7B3 **Barmouth** Wales
6D2 **Barnard Castle** England
24K4 **Barnaul** Russian Federation
68C3 **Barnegat** USA
68C3 **Barnegat B** USA
68A2 **Barnesboro** USA
55L2 **Barnes Icecap** Canada
67B2 **Barnesville** Georgia, USA
64C3 **Barnesville** Ohio, USA
62B2 **Barnhart** USA
7D3 **Barnsley** England
7B4 **Barnstaple** England
48C4 **Baro** Nigeria
43G3 **Barpeta** India
72E1 **Barquisimeto** Venezuela
13D3 **Barr** France
73K6 **Barra** Brazil
8B3 **Barra** *I* Scotland
34D2 **Barraba** Australia
75D1 **Barra da Estiva** Brazil
75A2 **Barra do Bugres** Brazil
75B2 **Barra do Garças** Brazil
75D3 **Barra do Piraí** Brazil
51D6 **Barra Falsa, Punta de** *Pt* Mozambique
73K6 **Barragem de Sobradinho** *Res* Brazil
15A2 **Barragem do Castelo do Bode** *Res* Portugal
15A2 **Barragem do Maranhão** *Res* Portugal
8B3 **Barra Head** *Pt* Scotland
73K8 **Barra Mansa** Brazil
72C6 **Barranca** Peru
72D2 **Barrancabermeja** Colombia
72F2 **Barrancas** Venezuela
74E3 **Barranqueras** Argentina
72D1 **Barranquilla** Colombia
8B3 **Barra,Sound of** *Chan* Scotland
68D1 **Barre** USA
73J6 **Barreiras** Brazil
15A2 **Barreiro** Portugal
73L5 **Barreiros** Brazil
32D5 **Barren,C** Australia
73J8 **Barretos** Brazil
65D2 **Barrie** Canada
34B2 **Barrier Range** *Mts* Australia
32E4 **Barrington,Mt** Australia
75C2 **Barro Alto** Brazil
27G8 **Barroloola** Australia
64A1 **Barron** USA
69N2 **Barrouallie** St Vincent
54C2 **Barrow** USA
9C3 **Barrow** *R* Irish Republic
32C3 **Barrow Creek** Australia
32A3 **Barrow I** Australia
6C2 **Barrow-in-Furness** England
54C2 **Barrow,Pt** USA
55J2 **Barrow Str** Canada
7C4 **Barry** Wales
65D1 **Barry's Bay** Canada
68C2 **Barryville** USA
44B2 **Barsi** India
13E1 **Barsinghausen** Germany
56B3 **Barstow** USA
14C2 **Bar-sur-Aube** France
13C3 **Bar-sur-Seine** France
73G2 **Bartica** Guyana
40B1 **Bartın** Turkey
32D2 **Bartle Frere,Mt** Australia
56D3 **Bartlesville** USA
60D2 **Bartlett** USA
51D6 **Bartolomeu Dias** Mozambique
6D3 **Barton-upon-Humber** England
19E2 **Bartoszyce** Poland
72B2 **Barú** *Mt* Panama
42D4 **Barwāh** India
42C4 **Barwāni** India
34C1 **Barwon** *R* Australia
20H5 **Barysh** Russian Federation
66C1 **Basalt** USA
50B3 **Basankusu** Zaïre
Basel = Basle
16D2 **Basento** *R* Italy
26F4 **Bashi Chan** Philippines/Taiwan
20J5 **Bashkortostan** *Republic* Russian Federation
27F6 **Basilan** Philippines
27F6 **Basilan** *I* Philippines
7E4 **Basildon** England
58E2 **Basin** USA
7D4 **Basingstoke** England
56B2 **Basin Region** USA
65D1 **Baskatong, Réservoir** Canada
16B1 **Basle** Switzerland
41E3 **Basra** Iraq
13D3 **Bas-Rhin** *Department* France
30D3 **Bassac** *R* Cambodia
16C1 **Bassano** Italy
48C4 **Bassar** Togo
51D6 **Bassas da India** *I* Mozambique Channel
30A2 **Bassein** Burma
69E3 **Basse Terre** Guadeloupe
60D2 **Bassett** USA
48C4 **Bassila** Benin
66C2 **Bass Lake** USA
32D5 **Bass Str** Australia
13E1 **Bassum** Germany
12G7 **Båstad** Sweden
41F4 **Bastak** Iran
43E3 **Basti** India
16B2 **Bastia** Corsica, Italy
18B3 **Bastogne** Belgium
63D2 **Bastrop** Louisiana, USA
63C2 **Bastrop** Texas, USA
48C4 **Bata** Equatorial Guinea
27F5 **Bataan Pen** Philippines
69A2 **Batabanó, G de** Cuba
27E7 **Batakan** Indonesia
42D2 **Batāla** India
26C3 **Batang** China
50B3 **Batangafo** Central African Republic
27F5 **Batangas** Philippines
26F4 **Batan Is** Philippines
75C3 **Batatais** Brazil
65D2 **Batavia** USA
34D3 **Batemans Bay** Australia
67B2 **Batesburg** USA
63D1 **Batesville** Arkansas, USA
63E2 **Batesville** Mississippi, USA
65F1 **Bath** Canada
7C4 **Bath** England
65F2 **Bath** Maine, USA
65D2 **Bath** New York, USA
50B2 **Batha** *R* Chad
64C1 **Bathawana Mt** Canada
32D4 **Bathurst** Australia
55M5 **Bathurst** Canada
54F2 **Bathurst,C** Canada
32C2 **Bathurst I** Australia
54H2 **Bathurst I** Canada
54H3 **Bathurst Inlet** *B* Canada
48B4 **Batié** Burkina
41E4 **Bāţin, Wadi al** *Watercourse* Iraq
41F3 **Bāţlāq-e-Gavkhūnī** *Salt Flat* Iran
34C3 **Batlow** Australia
40D2 **Batman** Turkey
16B3 **Batna** Algeria
57D3 **Baton Rouge** USA
45C1 **Batroûn** Lebanon
30C3 **Battambang** Cambodia
44C4 **Batticaloa** Sri Lanka
44E4 **Batti Malv** *I* Nicobar Is, Indian Ocean
7E4 **Battle** England
57E2 **Battle Creek** USA
55N4 **Battle Harbour** Canada
58C2 **Battle Mountain** USA
21G7 **Batumi** Georgia
30C5 **Batu Pahat** Malaysia
45C2 **Bat Yam** Israel
32B1 **Baubau** Indonesia
48C3 **Bauchi** Nigeria
61E1 **Baudette** USA
55N4 **Bauld,C** Canada
25N4 **Baunt** Russian Federation
73J8 **Bauru** Brazil
75B2 **Baús** Brazil
18C2 **Bautzen** Germany
27E7 **Bawean** *I* Indonesia
49E2 **Bawîti** Egypt
48B3 **Bawku** Ghana
30B2 **Bawlake** Burma
34A2 **Bawlen** Australia
67B2 **Baxley** USA
70E2 **Bayamo** Cuba
43J2 **Bayana** India
26D2 **Bayandzürh** Mongolia
26C3 **Bayan Har Shan** *Mts* China
31A1 **Bayan Mod** China
31B1 **Bayan Obo** China
60C2 **Bayard** Nebraska, USA
62A2 **Bayard** New Mexico, USA
25N2 **Bayasgalant** Mongolia
40D1 **Bayburt** Turkey
57E2 **Bay City** Michigan, USA
63C3 **Bay City** Texas, USA
20M2 **Baydaratskaya Guba** *B* Russian Federation
50E3 **Baydhabo** Somalia
18C3 **Bayern** *State* Germany
14B2 **Bayeux** France
64A1 **Bayfield** USA
40C3 **Bāyir** Jordan
Baykal, Ozero *L* = **Baikal, L**
26D1 **Baykalskiy Khrebet** *Mts* Russian Federation
25L3 **Baykit** Russian Federation
25L5 **Baylik Shan** *Mts* China/Mongolia
20K5 **Baymak** Russian Federation
63E2 **Bay Minette** USA
14B3 **Bayonne** France
18C3 **Bayreuth** Germany
63E2 **Bay St Louis** USA
65E2 **Bay Shore** USA
65D1 **Bays,L of** Canada
26B2 **Baytik Shan** *Mts* China
Bayt Lahm = Bethlehem
63D3 **Baytown** USA
15B2 **Baza** Spain
19F3 **Bazaliya** Ukraine
21H7 **Bazar-Dyuzi** *Mt* Azerbaijan
51D6 **Bazaruto, Ilha** Mozambique
14B3 **Bazas** France
31B3 **Bazhong** China
45D1 **Bcharre** Lebanon
60C1 **Beach** USA
68C3 **Beach Haven** USA
7E4 **Beachy Head** England
68D2 **Beacon** USA
51E5 **Bealanana** Madagascar
58D2 **Bear** *R* USA
64A2 **Beardstown** USA
24C2 **Bear I** Barents Sea
58D2 **Bear L** USA
66B1 **Bear Valley** USA
69C3 **Beata, Cabo** *C* Dominican Republic
69C3 **Beata, Isla** Dominican Republic
56D2 **Beatrice** USA
8D2 **Beatrice** *Oilfield* N Sea
54F4 **Beatton River** Canada
56B3 **Beatty** USA
65D1 **Beattyville** Canada
74E8 **Beauchene Is** Falkland Islands
34D1 **Beaudesert** Australia
67B2 **Beaufort** USA
54D2 **Beaufort S** Canada/USA
47C3 **Beaufort West** South Africa
65E1 **Beauharnois** Canada
8C3 **Beauly** Scotland
7B3 **Beaumaris** Wales
59C4 **Beaumont** California, USA
57D3 **Beaumont** Texas, USA
14C2 **Beaune** France
14C2 **Beauvais** France
54D3 **Beaver** USA
59D3 **Beaver** Utah, USA
54G4 **Beaver** *R* Canada
54D3 **Beaver Creek** Canada
64B3 **Beaver Dam** Kentucky, USA
64B2 **Beaver Dam** Wisconsin, USA
58D1 **Beaverhead Mts** USA
64B1 **Beaver I** USA
63D1 **Beaver L** USA
42C3 **Beāwar** India
75C3 **Bebedouro** Brazil
7E3 **Beccles** England
17E1 **Bečej** Serbia, Yugoslavia
48B1 **Béchar** Algeria
57E3 **Beckley** USA
13E2 **Beckum** Germany
6D2 **Bedale** England
13E1 **Bederkesa** Germany
7D3 **Bedford** England
64B3 **Bedford** Indiana, USA
68A3 **Bedford** Pennsylvania, USA
7D3 **Bedford** *County* England
69M2 **Bedford Pt** Grenada
68B2 **Beech Creek** USA
54D2 **Beechey Pt** USA
34C3 **Beechworth** Australia
34D1 **Beenleigh** Australia
45C3 **Beer Menuha** Israel
45C4 **Beer Ora** Israel
40B3 **Beersheba** Israel
Be'er Sheva = Beersheba
45C3 **Be'er Sheva** *R* Israel
56D4 **Beeville** USA
50C3 **Befale** Zaïre
51E5 **Befandriana** Madagascar
34C3 **Bega** Australia
Begicheva, Ostrov *I* = **Bol'shoy Begichev, Ostrov**
15C1 **Begur, C de** Spain
41F3 **Behbehān** Iran
41F2 **Behshahr** Iran
42B2 **Behsud** Afghanistan
26F2 **Bei'an** China
31B5 **Beihai** China
31D2 **Beijing** China
30E1 **Beiliu** China
31B4 **Beipan Jiang** *R* China
31E1 **Beipiao** China
Beira = Sofala
40C3 **Beirut** Lebanon
26C2 **Bei Shan** *Mts* China
47E1 **Beitbridge** Zimbabwe
45C2 **Beit ed Dīne** Lebanon
8C4 **Beith** Scotland
45C3 **Beit Jala** Israel
28A2 **Beizhen** China
15A2 **Beja** Portugal
16B3 **Béja** Tunisia
15C2 **Bejaïa** Algeria
15A1 **Béjar** Spain
41G3 **Bejestān** Iran
19E3 **Békéscsaba** Hungary
51E6 **Bekily** Madagascar
43E3 **Bela** India
42B3 **Bela** Pakistan
68B3 **Bel Air** USA
44B2 **Belampalli** India
27F6 **Belang** Indonesia
27C6 **Belangpidie** Indonesia
20D5 **Belarus** *Republic* Europe
Belau = Palau
75A3 **Béla Vista** Brazil/Paraguay
47E2 **Bela Vista** Mozambique
27C6 **Belawan** Indonesia
20K4 **Belaya** *R* Russian Federation
19G3 **Belaya Tserkov'** Ukraine
55J2 **Belcher Chan** Canada
55L4 **Belcher Is** Canada
42B1 **Belchiragh** Afghanistan
20J5 **Belebey** Russian Federation
50E3 **Beledweyne** Somalia
73J4 **Belém** Brazil
72C3 **Belén** Colombia
75A3 **Belén** Paraguay
56C3 **Belen** USA
33F2 **Bélep, Îles** Nouvelle Calédonie
16B3 **Belezma, Mts de** Algeria
9C2 **Belfast** Northern Ireland

47E2 **Belfast** South Africa
9C2 **Belfast Lough** *Estuary* Northern Ireland
60C1 **Belfield** USA
50D2 **Bēlfodiyo** Ethiopia
6D2 **Belford** England
14D2 **Belfort** France
44A2 **Belgaum** India
18A2 **Belgium** *Kingdom* NW Europe
21F5 **Belgorod** Russian Federation
21E6 **Belgorod Dnestrovskiy** Ukraine
58D1 **Belgrade** USA
17E2 **Belgrade** Serbia, Yugoslavia
49D2 **Bel Hedan** Libya
27D7 **Belitung** *I* Indonesia
70D3 **Belize** Belize
70D3 **Belize** *Republic* Central America
25P2 **Bel'kovskiy, Ostrov** *I* Russian Federation
14C2 **Bellac** France
54F4 **Bella Coola** Canada
63C3 **Bellaire** USA
44B2 **Bellary** India
34C1 **Bellata** Australia
68B2 **Bellefonte** USA
56C2 **Belle Fourche** USA
60C2 **Belle Fourche** *R* USA
14D2 **Bellegarde** France
13B4 **Bellegarde** France
67B3 **Belle Glade** USA
55N4 **Belle I** Canada
14B2 **Belle-Ile** *I* France
55N4 **Belle Isle,Str of** Canada
55L5 **Belleville** Canada
64B3 **Belleville** Illinois, USA
61D3 **Belleville** Kansas, USA
58D2 **Bellevue** Idaho, USA
64A2 **Bellevue** Iowa, USA
58B1 **Bellevue** Washington, USA
34D2 **Bellingen** Australia
6C2 **Bellingham** England
56A2 **Bellingham** USA
76G2 **Bellingshausen** *Base* Antarctica
76G3 **Bellingshausen S** Antarctica
16B1 **Bellinzona** Switzerland
72C2 **Bello** Colombia
33E3 **Bellona Reefs** Nouvelle Calédonie
66B1 **Bellota** USA
65E2 **Bellows Falls** USA
55K3 **Bell Pen** Canada
16C1 **Belluno** Italy
74D4 **Bell Ville** Argentina
68B1 **Belmont** USA
73L7 **Belmonte** Brazil
70D3 **Belmopan** Belize
26F1 **Belogorsk** Russian Federation
51E6 **Beloha** Madagascar
73K7 **Belo Horizonte** Brazil
61D3 **Beloit** Kansas, USA
57E2 **Beloit** Wisconsin, USA
20E3 **Belomorsk** Russian Federation
20K5 **Beloretsk** Russian Federation
Belorussia = Belarus
51E5 **Belo-Tsiribihina** Madagascar
Beloye More *S* **= White Sea**
20F3 **Beloye Ozero** *L* Russian Federation
20F3 **Belozersk** Russian Federation
7D3 **Belper** England
64C3 **Belpre** USA
34A2 **Beltana** Australia
63C2 **Belton** USA
19F3 **Bel'tsy** Moldavia
24K5 **Belukha** *Mt* Russian Federation
20H2 **Belush'ye** Russian Federation
64B2 **Belvidere** Illinois, USA
68C2 **Belvidere** New Jersey, USA
24J2 **Belyy, Ostrov** *I* Russian Federation
51B4 **Bembe** Angola
48C3 **Bembéréké** Benin
57D2 **Bemidji** USA
63E1 **Bemis** USA
50C4 **Bena Dibele** Zaïre
34C3 **Benalla** Australia
8C3 **Ben Attow** *Mt* Scotland
15A1 **Benavente** Spain
8B3 **Benbecula** *I* Scotland
32A4 **Bencubbin** Australia
56A2 **Bend** USA
8C3 **Ben Dearg** *Mt* Scotland
50E3 **Bendarbeyla** Somalia
19F3 **Bendery** Moldavia
32D4 **Bendigo** Australia
18C3 **Benešov** Czech Republic
16C2 **Benevento** Italy
39G4 **Bengal,B of** Asia
49D1 **Ben Gardane** Tunisia
31D3 **Bengbu** China
49E1 **Benghazi** Libya
27D7 **Bengkulu** Indonesia
51B5 **Benguela** Angola
40B3 **Benha** Egypt
8C2 **Ben Hope** *Mt* Scotland
50C3 **Beni** Zaïre
72E6 **Béni** *R* Bolivia
48B1 **Beni Abbès** Algeria
15C1 **Benicarló** Spain
15B2 **Benidorm** Spain
15C2 **Beni Mansour** Algeria
49F2 **Beni Mazâr** Egypt
48B1 **Beni Mellal** Morocco
48C4 **Benin** *Republic* Africa
48C4 **Benin City** Nigeria
15B2 **Beni-Saf** Algeria
49F2 **Beni Suef** Egypt
60C3 **Benkelman** USA
8C2 **Ben Kilbreck** *Mt* Scotland
10C2 **Ben Lawers** *Mt* Scotland
8D3 **Ben Macdui** *Mt* Scotland
8B3 **Ben More** Scotland
8C2 **Ben More Assynt** *Mt* Scotland
35B2 **Benmore,L** New Zealand
25R2 **Bennetta, Ostrov** *I* Russian Federation
8C3 **Ben Nevis** *Mt* Scotland
65E2 **Bennington** USA
45C2 **Bennt Jbail** Lebanon
50B3 **Bénoué** *R* Cameroon
13E3 **Bensheim** Germany
56B3 **Benson** Arizona, USA
61D1 **Benson** Minnesota, USA
27F7 **Benteng** Indonesia
50C3 **Bentiu** Sudan
75A2 **Bento Gomes** *R* Brazil
63D2 **Benton** Arkansas, USA
66C2 **Benton** California, USA
64B3 **Benton** Kentucky, USA
64B2 **Benton Harbor** USA
48C4 **Benue** *R* Nigeria
8C3 **Ben Wyvis** *Mt* Scotland
31E1 **Benxi** China
Beograd = Belgrade
43E4 **Beohāri** India
28C4 **Beppu** Japan
17D2 **Berat** Albania
27G7 **Berau, Teluk** *B* Indonesia
50D2 **Berber** Sudan
50E2 **Berbera** Somalia
50B3 **Berbérati** Central African Republic
19F3 **Berdichev** Ukraine
21F6 **Berdyansk** Ukraine
64C3 **Berea** USA
48B4 **Berekum** Ghana
66B2 **Berenda** USA
40C5 **Berenice** Egypt
54J4 **Berens** *R* Canada
54J4 **Berens River** Canada
61D2 **Beresford** USA
19E3 **Berettyóújfalu** Hungary
19E2 **Bereza** Belarus
19E3 **Berezhany** Ukraine
19F2 **Berezina** *R* Belarus
20G3 **Bereznik** Russian Federation
20K4 **Berezniki** Russian Federation
21E6 **Berezovka** Ukraine
20L3 **Berezovo** Russian Federation
40A2 **Bergama** Turkey
16B1 **Bergamo** Italy
12F6 **Bergen** Norway
68B1 **Bergen** USA
13C2 **Bergen op Zoom** Netherlands
14C3 **Bergerac** France
13D2 **Bergisch-Gladbach** Germany
44C2 **Berhampur** India
25S4 **Beringa, Ostrov** *I* Russian Federation
25T3 **Beringovskiy** Russian Federation
37K2 **Bering S** Russian Federation/USA
76C6 **Bering Str** Russian Federation/USA
41G4 **Berīzak** Iran
15B2 **Berja** Spain
13D1 **Berkel** *R* Germany/Netherlands
56A3 **Berkeley** USA
68A3 **Berkeley Spring** USA
7D4 **Berkhamsted** England
76F2 **Berkner I** Antarctica
17E2 **Berkovitsa** Bulgaria
7D4 **Berkshire** *County* England
68D1 **Berkshire Hills** USA
18C2 **Berlin** Germany
18C2 **Berlin** *State* Germany
65E2 **Berlin** New Hampshire, USA
72F8 **Bermejo** Bolivia
74E3 **Bermejo** *R* Argentina
53M5 **Bermuda** *I* Atlantic Ocean
Bern = Berne
62A1 **Bernalillo** USA
75B4 **Bernardo de Irigoyen** Argentina
68C2 **Bernardsville** USA
18C2 **Bernburg** Germany
16B1 **Berne** Switzerland
8B3 **Berneray, I** Scotland
55K2 **Bernier B** Canada
18C3 **Berounka** *R* Czech Republic
34B2 **Berri** Australia
48C1 **Berriane** Algeria
14C2 **Berry** *Region* France
66A1 **Berryessa,L** USA
57F4 **Berry Is** The Bahamas
68B3 **Berryville** USA
47B2 **Berseba** Namibia
60B3 **Berthoud P** USA
50B3 **Bertoua** Cameroon
33G1 **Beru** *I* Kiribati
65D2 **Berwick** USA
6C2 **Berwick-upon-Tweed** England
7C3 **Berwyn Mts** Wales
51E5 **Besalampy** Madagascar
14D2 **Besançon** France
19E3 **Beskidy Zachodnie** *Mts* Poland
40C2 **Besni** Turkey
45C3 **Besor** *R* Israel
67A2 **Bessemer** Alabama, USA
64B1 **Bessemer** Michigan, USA
51E5 **Betafo** Madagascar
15A1 **Betanzos** Spain
45C3 **Bet Guvrin** Israel
47D2 **Bethal** South Africa
47B2 **Bethanie** Namibia
61E2 **Bethany** Missouri, USA
63C1 **Bethany** Oklahoma, USA
54B3 **Bethel** Alaska, USA
68D2 **Bethel** Connecticut, USA
64C2 **Bethel Park** USA
65D3 **Bethesda** USA
45C3 **Bethlehem** Israel
47D2 **Bethlehem** South Africa
65D2 **Bethlehem** USA
47D3 **Bethulie** South Africa
14C1 **Béthune** France
51E6 **Betioky** Madagascar
34B1 **Betoota** Australia
50B3 **Betou** Congo
39E1 **Betpak Dala** *Steppe* Kazakhstan
51E6 **Betroka** Madagascar
55M5 **Betsiamites** Canada
64A2 **Bettendorf** USA
43E3 **Bettiah** India
42D4 **Betūl** India
13C2 **Betuwe** *Region* Netherlands
42D3 **Betwa** *R* India
7C3 **Betws-y-coed** Wales
13D2 **Betzdorf** Germany
7D3 **Beverley** England
68E1 **Beverly** USA
66C3 **Beverly Hills** USA
7E4 **Bexhill** England
40B2 **Bey Dağları** Turkey
48B4 **Beyla** Guinea
44B3 **Beypore** India
Beyrouth = Beirut
40B2 **Beyşehir** Turkey
21E8 **Beyşehir Gölü** *L* Turkey
45C2 **Beyt Shean** Israel
20F4 **Bezhetsk** Russian Federation
14C3 **Béziers** France
41G2 **Bezmein** Turkmenistan
26D1 **Beznosova** Russian Federation
43F3 **Bhadgaon** Nepal
44C2 **Bhadrāchalam** India
43F4 **Bhadrakh** India
44B3 **Bhadra Res** India
44B3 **Bhadrāvati** India
42B3 **Bhag** Pakistan
43F3 **Bhāgalpur** India
42C2 **Bhakkar** Pakistan
42D4 **Bhandāra** India
42D3 **Bharatpur** India
42C4 **Bharūch** India
43F4 **Bhātiāpāra Ghat** Bangladesh
42C2 **Bhatinda** India
44A3 **Bhatkal** India
43F4 **Bhātpāra** India
42C4 **Bhāvnagar** India
43E5 **Bhawānipatna** India
42C2 **Bhera** Pakistan
43E3 **Bheri** *R* Nepal
43E4 **Bhilai** India
42C3 **Bhīlwāra** India
44C2 **Bhīmavaram** India
42D3 **Bhind** India
42D3 **Bhiwāni** India
44B2 **Bhongir** India
42D4 **Bhopāl** India
43F4 **Bhubaneshwar** India
42B4 **Bhuj** India
42D4 **Bhusāwal** India
39H3 **Bhutan** *Kingdom* Asia
27G7 **Biak** *I* Indonesia
19E2 **Biala Podlaska** Poland
18D2 **Białogard** Poland
19E2 **Bialystok** Poland
12A1 **Biargtangar** *C* Iceland
41G2 **Biārjmand** Iran
14B3 **Biarritz** France
40B4 **Biba** Egypt
29E2 **Bibai** Japan
51B5 **Bibala** Angola
18B3 **Biberach** Germany
48B4 **Bibiani** Ghana
17F1 **Bicaz** Romania
7D4 **Bicester** England
59D3 **Bicknell** USA
48C4 **Bida** Nigeria
44B2 **Bīdar** India
41G5 **Bidbid** Oman
65E2 **Biddeford** USA
7C6 **Bideford** England
7B4 **Bideford B** England
48C2 **Bidon 5** Algeria
19E2 **Biebrza** *R* Poland
16B1 **Biel** Switzerland
18D2 **Bielawa** Poland
18B2 **Bielefeld** Germany
16B1 **Biella** Italy
19E2 **Bielsk Podlaski** Poland
30D3 **Bien Hoa** Vietnam
55L4 **Bienville, Lac** Canada
16C2 **Biferno** *R* Italy
40A1 **Biga** Turkey
17F3 **Bigadiç** Turkey
58D1 **Big Belt Mts** USA
62B3 **Big Bend Nat Pk** USA
63E2 **Big Black** *R* USA
61D2 **Big Blue** *R* USA
67B3 **Big Cypress Swamp** USA
54D3 **Big Delta** USA
8D4 **Biggar** Scotland
54H4 **Biggar Kindersley** Canada
34D1 **Biggenden** Australia
7D3 **Biggleswade** England
58D1 **Big Hole** *R* USA
60B1 **Bighorn** *R* USA
60B1 **Bighorn L** USA
60B2 **Bighorn Mts** USA
48C4 **Bight of Benin** *B* W Africa
48C4 **Bight of Biafra** *B* Cameroon
55L3 **Big I** Canada
62B2 **Big Lake** USA
48A3 **Bignona** Senegal
59C3 **Big Pine** USA
67B4 **Big Pine Key** USA
66C3 **Big Pine Mt** USA
64B2 **Big Rapids** USA
54H4 **Big River** Canada
58D1 **Big Sandy** USA
61D2 **Big Sioux** *R* USA
66D1 **Big Smokey V** USA
56C3 **Big Spring** USA
60C2 **Big Springs** USA
61D1 **Big Stone City** USA
64C3 **Big Stone Gap** USA
66B2 **Big Sur** USA
58E1 **Big Timber** USA
55J4 **Big Trout L** Canada
55K4 **Big Trout Lake** Canada
16D2 **Bihać** Bosnia-Herzegovina
43F3 **Bihār** India
43F4 **Bihār** *State* India
50D4 **Biharamulo** Tanzania
21C6 **Bihor** *Mt* Romania
48A3 **Bijagós, Arquipélago dos** *Is* Guinea-Bissau
44B2 **Bijāpur** India
44C2 **Bījāpur** India
41E2 **Bījār** Iran
43E3 **Bijauri** Nepal
17D2 **Bijeljina** Bosnia-Herzegovina
31B4 **Bijie** China
42D3 **Bijnor** India
42C3 **Bijnot** Pakistan
42C3 **Bīkāner** India
45C2 **Bikfaya** Lebanon
26G2 **Bikin** Russian Federation
50B4 **Bikoro** Zaïre
Bilbo = Bilbao
42C3 **Bilāra** India
42D2 **Bilāspur** India
43E4 **Bilāspur** India
30B3 **Bilauktaung Range** *Mts* Burma/Thailand
15B1 **Bilbao** Spain
45A3 **Bilbeis** Egypt
18D3 **Bílé** *R* Czech Republic/Slovakia
17D2 **Bileća** Bosnia-Herzegovina
40B1 **Bilecik** Turkey
50C3 **Bili** *R* Zaïre
25S3 **Bilibino** Russian Federation
56C2 **Billings** USA
50B2 **Bilma** Niger
57E3 **Biloxi** USA
50C2 **Biltine** Chad
67C3 **Bimini Is** Bahamas
42D4 **Bīna-Etawa** India
51D5 **Bindura** Zimbabwe
51C5 **Binga** Zimbabwe
51D5 **Binga, Mt** Mozambique/Zimbabwe
34D1 **Bingara** Australia
18B3 **Bingen** Germany
65F1 **Bingham** USA
57F2 **Binghamton** USA
40D2 **Bingöl** Turkey
31D3 **Binhai** China
15C2 **Binibeca, Cabo** *C* Spain
27D6 **Bintan** *I* Indonesia
27E6 **Bintulu** Malaysia
74B5 **Bió Bió** *R* Chile
48C4 **Bioco** *I* Equatorial Guinea
44B2 **Bīr** India
49E2 **Bîr Abu Husein** *Well* Egypt
49E2 **Bi'r al Harash** *Well* Libya
50C2 **Birao** Central African Republic
43F3 **Biratnagar** Nepal
34B3 **Birchip** Australia
61E1 **Birch L** USA
54G4 **Birch Mts** Canada
55J4 **Bird** Canada
32C3 **Birdsville** Australia
32C2 **Birdum** Australia
45A4 **Bîr el 'Agramîya** *Well* Egypt
45B3 **Bîr el Duweidâr** *Well* Egypt
43E3 **Birganj** Nepal
45B3 **Bîr Gifgâfa** *Well* Egypt
45A4 **Bîr Gindali** *Well* Egypt
45B3 **Bîr Hasana** *Well* Egypt
75B3 **Birigui** Brazil
45D1 **Bīrīn** Syria
41G3 **Bīrjand** Iran
40B4 **Birkat Qârun** *L* Egypt
13D3 **Birkenfeld** Germany
7C3 **Birkenhead** England
21D6 **Bîrlad** Romania
45B3 **Bîr Lahfân** *Well* Egypt
7C3 **Birmingham** England
57E3 **Birmingham** USA
49E2 **Bîr Misâha** *Well* Egypt
48A2 **Bir Moghrein** Mauritius
48C3 **Birnin-Kebbi** Nigeria
26G2 **Birobidzhan** Russian Federation
9C3 **Birr** Irish Republic
15C2 **Bir Rabalou** Algeria
34C1 **Birrie** *R* Australia
8D2 **Birsay** Scotland
20K4 **Birsk** Russian Federation
49E2 **Bîr Tarfâwi** *Well* Egypt
45B4 **Bîr Udelb** *Well* Egypt
25L4 **Biryusa** *R* Russian Federation
12J7 **Biržai** Lithuania
48B2 **Bir Zreigat** *Well* Mauritius
43K1 **Bisalpur** India
59E4 **Bisbee** USA
14A2 **Biscay,B of** France/Spain
67B3 **Biscayne B** USA
13D3 **Bischwiller** France
64C1 **Biscotasi L** Canada
31B4 **Bishan** China
39F1 **Bishkek** Kirgizia
56B3 **Bishop** USA
6D2 **Bishop Auckland** England
7C3 **Bishops Castle** England
7E4 **Bishop's Stortford** England
43E4 **Bishrāmpur** India
48C1 **Biskra** Algeria
56C2 **Bismarck** USA
32D1 **Bismarck Arch** Papua New Guinea
32D1 **Bismarck Range** *Mts* Papua New Guinea
32D1 **Bismarck S** Papua New Guinea
41E3 **Bīsotūn** Iran
48A3 **Bissau** Guinea-Bissau
57D1 **Bissett** Canada
54G4 **Bistcho L** Canada
17F1 **Bistrita** *R* Romania
50B3 **Bitam** Gabon
18B3 **Bitburg** Germany
13D3 **Bitche** France
40D2 **Bitlis** Turkey
17E2 **Bitola** Macedonia, Yugoslavia
18C2 **Bitterfeld** Germany
47B3 **Bitterfontein** South Africa
40B3 **Bitter Lakes** Egypt
56B2 **Bitteroot Range** *Mts* USA
48D3 **Biu** Nigeria
29D3 **Biwa-ko** *L* Japan
50E2 **Biyo Kaboba** Ethiopia
24K4 **Biysk** Russian Federation
16B3 **Bizerte** Tunisia
16D1 **Bjelovar** Croatia
48B2 **Bj Flye Ste Marie** Algeria
Bjørnøya *I* **= Bear I**
63D1 **Black** *R* USA

32D3 **Blackall** Australia
64B1 **Black B** Canada
6C3 **Blackburn** England
54D3 **Blackburn, Mt** USA
59D4 **Black Canyon City** USA
61E1 **Blackduck** USA
58D1 **Black Eagle** USA
58D2 **Blackfoot** USA
58D1 **Blackfoot** *R* USA
9B3 **Black Hd** *Pt* Irish Republic
54H5 **Black Hills** USA
8C3 **Black Isle** *Pen* Scotland
69Q2 **Blackman's** Barbados
59D3 **Black Mts** USA
7C4 **Black Mts** Wales
47B1 **Black Nosob** *R* Namibia
6C3 **Blackpool** England
69H1 **Black River** Jamaica
64A2 **Black River Falls** USA
56B2 **Black Rock Desert** USA
21D7 **Black S** Asia/Europe
64C3 **Blacksburg** USA
34D2 **Black Sugarloaf** *Mt* Australia
48B4 **Black Volta** *R* W Africa
63E2 **Black Warrior** *R* USA
7E4 **Blackwater** *R* England
10B3 **Blackwater** *R* Irish Republic
63C1 **Blackwell** USA
17E2 **Blagoevgrad** Bulgaria
25O4 **Blagoveshchensk** Russian Federation
58D1 **Blaikiston,Mt** Canada
58B1 **Blaine** USA
61D2 **Blair** USA
8D3 **Blair Atholl** Scotland
8D3 **Blairgowrie** Scotland
67C2 **Blakely** USA
74D5 **Blanca, Bahía** *B* Argentina
62A1 **Blanca Peak** *Mt* USA
16B3 **Blanc, C** Tunisia
34A1 **Blanche** *L* Australia
16B1 **Blanc, Mont** *Mt* France/Italy
56A2 **Blanco,C** USA
55N4 **Blanc Sablon** Canada
7C4 **Blandford Forum** England
59E3 **Blanding** USA
13B2 **Blankenberge** Belgium
69E4 **Blanquilla, Isla** Venezuela
51D5 **Blantyre** Malawi
9A3 **Blasket Sd** Irish Republic
14B2 **Blaye** France
34C2 **Blayney** Australia
33G5 **Blenheim** New Zealand
15C2 **Blida** Algeria
64C1 **Blind River** Canada
34A2 **Blinman** Australia
65E2 **Block I** USA
68E2 **Block Island Sd** USA
47D2 **Bloemfontein** South Africa
47D2 **Bloemhof** South Africa
47D2 **Bloemhof Dam** *Res* South Africa
73G3 **Blommesteinmeer** *L* Surinam
12A1 **Blönduós** Iceland
64B3 **Bloomfield** Indiana, USA
61E2 **Bloomfield** Iowa, USA
61D2 **Bloomfield** Nebraska,USA
62A1 **Bloomfield** New Mexico, USA
64B2 **Bloomington** Illinois, USA
64B3 **Bloomington** Indiana, USA
61E2 **Bloomington** Minnesota, USA
68B2 **Bloomsburg** USA
68B2 **Blossburg** USA
55Q3 **Blosseville Kyst** *Mts* Greenland
47D1 **Blouberg** *Mt* South Africa
18B3 **Bludenz** Austria
57E3 **Bluefield** USA
72B1 **Bluefields** Nicaragua
60D2 **Blue Hill** USA
68A2 **Blue Knob** *Mt* USA
69J1 **Blue Mountain Peak** *Mt* Jamaica
68B2 **Blue Mt** USA
34D2 **Blue Mts** Australia
56A2 **Blue Mts** USA
69J1 **Blue Mts, The** Jamaica
50D2 **Blue Nile** *R* Sudan
54G3 **Bluenose L** Canada
67C2 **Blue Ridge** USA
57E3 **Blue Ridge Mts** USA
9C2 **Blue Stack** *Mt* Irish Republic
35A3 **Bluff** New Zealand
59E3 **Bluff** USA
32A4 **Bluff Knoll** *Mt* Australia
74G3 **Blumenau** Brazil
60D2 **Blunt** USA
58B2 **Bly** USA
6D2 **Blyth** England
56B3 **Blythe** USA
57E3 **Blytheville** USA
48A4 **Bo** Sierra Leone
27F5 **Boac** Philippines
75D1 **Boa Nova** Brazil
64C2 **Boardman** USA
72F3 **Boa Vista** Brazil
48A4 **Boa Vista** *I* Cape Verde
30E1 **Bobai** China
44C2 **Bobbili** India
48B3 **Bobo Dioulasso** Burkina
19G2 **Bobrovica** Ukraine
20D5 **Bobruysk** Belarus
67B4 **Boca Chica Key** *I* USA
72E5 **Bôca do Acre** Brazil
75D2 **Bocaiúva** Brazil
50B3 **Bocaranga** Central African Republic
67B3 **Boca Raton** USA
19E3 **Bochnia** Poland
18B2 **Bocholt** Germany
13D2 **Bochum** Germany
51B5 **Bocoio** Angola
50B3 **Boda** Central African Republic
25N4 **Bodaybo** Russian Federation
59B3 **Bodega Head** *Pt* USA
50B2 **Bodélé** *Desert Region* Chad
12J5 **Boden** Sweden
9C3 **Boderg, L** Irish Republic
44B2 **Bodhan** India
44B3 **Bodināyakkanūr** India
7B4 **Bodmin** England
7B4 **Bodmin Moor** *Upland* England
12G5 **Bodø** Norway
17F3 **Bodrum** Turkey
50C4 **Boende** Zaïre
48A3 **Boffa** Guinea
30B2 **Bogale** Burma
63E2 **Bogalusa** USA
34C2 **Bogan** *R* Australia
48B3 **Bogande** Burkina
40C2 **Boğazlıyan** Turkey
20L4 **Bogdanovich** Russian Federation
26B2 **Bogda Shan** *Mt* China
47B2 **Bogenfels** Namibia
34D1 **Boggabilla** Australia
34C2 **Boggabri** Australia
7D4 **Bognor Regis** England
34C3 **Bogong** *Mt* Australia
27D7 **Bogor** Indonesia
25Q4 **Bogorodskoye** Russian Federation
20J4 **Bogorodskoye** Russian Federation
72D3 **Bogotá** Colombia
25K4 **Bogotol** Russian Federation
43F4 **Bogra** Bangladesh
31D2 **Bo Hai** *B* China
13B3 **Bohain-en-Vermandois** France
31D2 **Bohai Wan** *B* China
18C3 **Bohmer-wald** *Upland* Germany
27F6 **Bohol** *I* Philippines
27F6 **Bohol S** Philippines
75E1 **Boipeba, Ilha de** Brazil
75B2 **Bois** *R* Brazil
64C1 **Bois Blanc I** USA
56B2 **Boise** USA
62B1 **Boise City** USA
54F3 **Bois, Lac des** Canada
60C1 **Boissevain** Canada
48A2 **Bojador,C** Morocco
27F5 **Bojeador, C** Philippines
41G2 **Bojnūrd** Iran
48A3 **Boké** Guinea
34C1 **Bokhara** *R* Australia
12F7 **Boknafjord** *Inlet* Norway
50B4 **Boko** Congo
30C3 **Bokor** Cambodia
50B2 **Bokoro** Chad
50C4 **Bokungu** Zaïre
50B2 **Bol** Chad
48A3 **Bolama** Guinea-Bissau
14C2 **Bolbec** France
48B4 **Bole** Ghana
18D2 **Bolesławiec** Poland
48B3 **Bolgatanga** Ghana
21D6 **Bolgrad** Ukraine
63D1 **Bolivar** Missouri, USA
63E1 **Bolivar** Tennessee, USA
72D2 **Bolívar** *Mt* Venezuela
72E7 **Bolivia** *Republic* S America
12H6 **Bollnäs** Sweden
34C1 **Bollon** Australia
50B4 **Bolobo** Zaïre
16C2 **Bologna** Italy
20E4 **Bologoye** Russian Federation
26G1 **Bolon'** Russian Federation
26G2 **Bolon', Oz** *L* Russian Federation
16C2 **Bolsena, L di** Italy
25M2 **Bol'shevik, Ostrov** *I* Russian Federation
20J2 **Bol'shezemel'skaya Tundra** *Plain* Russian Federation
25S3 **Bol'shoy Anyuy** *R* Russian Federation
25N2 **Bol'shoy Begichev, Ostrov** *I* Russian Federation
21H5 **Bol'shoy Irgiz** *R* Russian Federation
28C2 **Bol'shoy Kamen** Russian Federation
25Q2 **Bol'shoy Lyakhovskiy, Ostrov** *I* Russian Federation
21H6 **Bol'shoy Uzen** *R* Kazakhstan
56C4 **Bolson de Mapimí** *Desert* Mexico
7C3 **Bolton** England
40B1 **Bolu** Turkey
12A1 **Bolungarvik** Iceland
9A4 **Bolus Hd** *Pt* Irish Republic
40B2 **Bolvadin** Turkey
16C1 **Bolzano** Italy
50B4 **Boma** Zaïre
32D4 **Bombala** Australia
44A2 **Bombay** India
51E5 **Bombetoka, Baie de** *B* Madagascar
50D3 **Bombo** Uganda
75C2 **Bom Despacho** Brazil
43G3 **Bomdila** India
48A4 **Bomi Hills** Liberia
73K6 **Bom Jesus da Lapa** Brazil
25O4 **Bomnak** Russian Federation
50C3 **Bomokāndi** *R* Zaïre
50C3 **Bomu** *R* Central African Republic/Zaïre
65D3 **Bon Air** USA
69D4 **Bonaire** *I* Caribbean Sea
70D3 **Bonanza** Nicaragua
55N5 **Bonavista** Canada
16C3 **Bon, C** Tunisia
50C3 **Bondo** Zaïre
48B4 **Bondoukou** Ivory Coast
Bône = 'Annaba
60D2 **Bonesteel** USA
73G3 **Bonfim** Guyana
50C3 **Bongandanga** Zaïre
50C3 **Bongo, Massif des** *Upland* Central African Republic
50B2 **Bongor** Chad
63C2 **Bonham** USA
16B2 **Bonifacio** Corsica, France
16B2 **Bonifacio,Str of** *Chan* Corsica, France/Sardinia, Italy
Bonin Is = Ogasawara Gunto
67B3 **Bonita Springs** USA
75A3 **Bonito** Brazil
18B2 **Bonn** Germany
58C1 **Bonners Ferry** USA
48C4 **Bonny** Nigeria
32A1 **Bonthain** Indonesia
48A4 **Bonthe** Sierra Leone
50E2 **Booaaso** Somalia
34B2 **Booligal** Australia
34D1 **Boonah** Australia
62B1 **Boone** Colorado, USA
61E2 **Boone** Iowa, USA
67B1 **Boone** North Carolina, USA
65D2 **Boonville** USA
34C2 **Boorowa** Australia
55J2 **Boothia,G of** Canada
55J2 **Boothia Pen** Canada
7C3 **Bootle** England
50B4 **Booué** Gabon
62B3 **Boquillas** Mexico
50D3 **Bor** Sudan
40B2 **Bor** Turkey
17E2 **Bor** Serbia, Yugoslavia
56B2 **Borah Peak** *Mt* USA
12G7 **Borås** Sweden
41F4 **Borāzjān** Iran
14B3 **Bordeaux** France
54G2 **Borden I** Canada
55K2 **Borden Pen** Canada
68C2 **Bordentown** USA
8D4 **Borders** *Region* Scotland
34B3 **Bordertown** Australia
15C2 **Bordj bou Arréidj** Algeria
48C2 **Bordj Omar Driss** Algeria
Borgå = Porvoo
55Q3 **Borgarnes** Iceland
56C3 **Borger** USA
12H7 **Borgholm** Sweden
19E3 **Borislav** Ukraine
21G5 **Borisoglebsk** Russian Federation
20D5 **Borisov** Belarus
21F5 **Borisovka** Russian Federation
75A4 **Borja** Paraguay
50B2 **Borkou** *Desert Region* Chad
13D1 **Borkum** *I* Germany
12H6 **Borlänge** Sweden
27E6 **Borneo** *I* Indonesia/Malaysia
12H7 **Bornholm** *I* Denmark
17F3 **Bornova** Turkey
48D3 **Bornu** *Region* Nigeria
50C3 **Boro** *R* Sudan
25P3 **Borogontsy** Russian Federation
48B3 **Boromo** Burkina
66D3 **Boron** USA
20E4 **Borovichi** Russian Federation
32C2 **Borroloola** Australia
17E1 **Borsa** Romania
41F3 **Borūjen** Iran
41E3 **Borūjerd** Iran
18D2 **Bory Tucholskie** *Region* Poland
19G2 **Borzna** Ukraine
25N4 **Borzya** Russian Federation
31B5 **Bose** China
47D2 **Boshof** South Africa
17D2 **Bosna** *R* Bosnia-Herzegovina
17D2 **Bosnia-Herzegovina** *Republic* Europe
29D3 **Bōsō-hantō** *B* Japan
Bosporus = Karadeniz Boğazi
15C2 **Bosquet** Algeria
50B3 **Bossangoa** Central African Republic
50B3 **Bossèmbélé** Central African Republic
63D2 **Bossier City** USA
24K5 **Bosten Hu** *L* China
7D3 **Boston** England
57F2 **Boston** USA
57D3 **Boston Mts** USA
42C4 **Botād** India
17E2 **Botevgrad** Bulgaria
47D2 **Bothaville** South Africa
20B3 **Bothnia,G of** Finland/Sweden
51C6 **Botletli** *R* Botswana
21D6 **Botoşani** Romania
51C6 **Botswana** *Republic* Africa
16D3 **Botte Donato** *Mt* Italy
60C1 **Bottineau** USA
13D2 **Bottrop** Germany
75C3 **Botucatu** Brazil
75D1 **Botuporã** Brazil
55N5 **Botwood** Canada
48B4 **Bouaké** Ivory Coast
50B3 **Bouar** Central African Republic
48B1 **Bouârfa** Morocco
50B3 **Bouca** Central African Republic
15C2 **Boufarik** Algeria
33E1 **Bougainville** *I* Papua New Guinea
16B3 **Bougaroun, C** Algeria
Bougie = Bejaïa
48B3 **Bougouni** Mali
15A2 **Bouhalla, Djebel** *Mt* Morocco
13C3 **Bouillon** France
15C2 **Bouïra** Algeria
48B2 **Bou Izakarn** Morocco
13D3 **Boulay-Moselle** France
56C2 **Boulder** Colorado, USA
58D1 **Boulder** Montana, USA
56B3 **Boulder City** USA
66A2 **Boulder Creek** USA
14C1 **Boulogne** France
50B3 **Boumba** *R* Cameroon/Central African Republic
48B4 **Bouna** Ivory Coast
56B3 **Boundary Peak** *Mt* USA
48B4 **Boundiali** Ivory Coast
58D2 **Bountiful** USA
33G5 **Bounty Is** New Zealand
33F3 **Bourail** New Caledonia
13C4 **Bourbonne-les-Bains** France
48B3 **Bourem** Mali
14D2 **Bourg** France
14D2 **Bourg de Péage** France
14C2 **Bourges** France
14C3 **Bourg-Madame** France
14C2 **Bourgogne** *Region* France
34C2 **Bourke** Australia
7D4 **Bournemouth** England
15C2 **Bou Saâda** Algeria
50B2 **Bousso** Chad
48A3 **Boutilimit** Mauritius
52J7 **Bouvet I** Atlantic Ocean
60C1 **Bowbells** USA
32D2 **Bowen** Australia
59E4 **Bowie** Arizona, USA
63C2 **Bowie** Texas, USA
6C3 **Bowland Fells** England
57E3 **Bowling Green** Kentucky, USA
63D1 **Bowling Green** Missouri, USA
64C2 **Bowling Green** Ohio, USA
65D3 **Bowling Green** Virginia, USA
60C1 **Bowman** USA
65D2 **Bowmanville** Canada
9C3 **Bowna, L** Irish Republic
34D2 **Bowral** Australia
31D3 **Bo Xian** China
31D2 **Boxing** China
40B1 **Boyabat** Turkey
50B3 **Boyali** Central African Republic
19G2 **Boyarka** Ukraine
54J4 **Boyd** Canada
68C2 **Boyertown** USA
10B3 **Boyle** Irish Republic
9C3 **Boyne** *R* Irish Republic
67B3 **Boynton Beach** USA
50C3 **Boyoma Falls** Zaïre
58E2 **Boysen Res** USA
17D1 **Bozanski Brod** Bosnia-Herzegovina/Croatia
17F3 **Bozca Ada** *I* Turkey
17F3 **Boz Dağları** *Mts* Turkey
56B2 **Bozeman** USA
Bozen = Bolzano
50B3 **Bozene** Zaïre
50B3 **Bozoum** Central African Republic
16D2 **Brač** *I* Croatia
8B3 **Bracadale, Loch** *Inlet* Scotland
16C2 **Bracciano, L di** Italy
65D1 **Bracebridge** Canada
49D2 **Brach** Libya
12H6 **Bräcke** Sweden
62B3 **Brackettville** USA
67B3 **Bradenton** USA
6D3 **Bradford** England
68A2 **Bradford** USA
66B3 **Bradley** USA
62C2 **Brady** USA
8E1 **Brae** Scotland
8D3 **Braemar** Scotland
15A1 **Braga** Portugal
73J4 **Bragança** Brazil
15A1 **Bragança** Portugal
75C3 **Bragança Paulista** Brazil
43G4 **Brahman-Baria** Bangladesh
43F4 **Brāhmani** *R* India
43G3 **Brahmaputra** *R* Bangladesh/India
21D6 **Brăila** Romania
57D2 **Brainerd** USA
7E4 **Braintree** England
47C3 **Brak** *R* South Africa
47D1 **Brak** *R* South Africa
13E1 **Brake** Germany
48A3 **Brakna** *Region* Mauritius
54F4 **Bralorne** Canada
65D2 **Brampton** Canada
6C2 **Brampton** England
13D1 **Bramsche** Germany
72F3 **Branco** *R* Brazil
51B6 **Brandberg** *Mt* Namibia
18C2 **Brandenburg** Germany
18C2 **Brandenburg** *State* Germany
47D2 **Brandfort** South Africa
56D2 **Brandon** Canada
61D2 **Brandon** USA
47C3 **Brandvlei** South Africa
18C2 **Brandýs-nad-Laben** Czech Republic
19D2 **Braniewo** Poland
57E2 **Brantford** Canada
34B3 **Branxholme** Australia
55M5 **Bras d'Or Lakes** Canada
72E6 **Brasiléia** Brazil
73J7 **Brasília** Brazil
75D2 **Brasília de Minas** Brazil
17F1 **Braşov** Romania
18D3 **Bratislava** Slovakia
25M4 **Bratsk** Russian Federation
19F3 **Bratslav** Ukraine
65E2 **Brattleboro** USA
18C2 **Braunschweig** Germany
48A4 **Brava** *I* Cape Verde
56B3 **Brawley** USA
9C3 **Bray** Irish Republic
55L3 **Bray I** Canada
13B3 **Bray-sur-Seine** France
71E5 **Brazil** *Republic* S America
52G5 **Brazil Basin** Atlantic Ocean
56D3 **Brazos** *R* USA
50B4 **Brazzaville** Congo
18C3 **Brdy** *Upland* Czech Republic
35A3 **Breaksea Sd** New Zealand
35B1 **Bream B** New Zealand
8D3 **Brechin** Scotland
13C2 **Brecht** Belgium
61D1 **Breckenridge** Minnesota, USA
62C2 **Breckenridge** Texas, USA
7E3 **Breckland** England
18D3 **Břeclav** Czech Republic
7C4 **Brecon** Wales
7C4 **Brecon Beacons** *Mts* Wales
7B3 **Brecon Beacons Nat Pk** Wales
18A2 **Breda** Netherlands

47C3 **Bredasdorp** South Africa
12H6 **Bredbyn** Sweden
20K5 **Bredy** Russian Federation
47B3 **Breede** *R* South Africa
65D2 **Breezewood** USA
12A1 **Breiethafjörethur** *B* Iceland
13D3 **Breisach** Germany
67A2 **Bremen** USA
18B2 **Bremen** Germany
18B2 **Bremerhaven** Germany
58B1 **Bremerton** USA
13E1 **Bremervörde** Germany
59E3 **Brendel** USA
63C2 **Brenham** USA
18C3 **Brenner** *P* Austria/Italy
66B2 **Brentwood** USA
16C1 **Brescia** Italy
Breslau = Wrocław
8E1 **Bressay** *I* Scotland
14B2 **Bressuire** France
14B2 **Brest** France
19E2 **Brest** Belarus
14B2 **Bretagne** *Region* France
13B3 **Breteuil** France
63E3 **Breton Sd** USA
68C2 **Breton Woods** USA
35B1 **Brett,C** New Zealand
67B1 **Brevard** USA
34C1 **Brewarrina** Australia
65F2 **Brewer** USA
68D2 **Brewster** New York, USA
58C1 **Brewster** Washington, USA
67A2 **Brewton** USA
47D2 **Breyten** South Africa
16D1 **Brežice** Slovenia
50C3 **Bria** Central African Republic
14D3 **Briançon** France
14C2 **Briare** France
7C4 **Bridgend** Wales
8C3 **Bridge of Orchy** Scotland
67A2 **Bridgeport** Alabama, USA
59C3 **Bridgeport** California, USA
65E2 **Bridgeport** Connecticut, USA
60C2 **Bridgeport** Nebraska, USA
63C2 **Bridgeport** Texas, USA
66C1 **Bridgeport Res** USA
58E1 **Bridger** USA
60B2 **Bridger Peak** USA
68C3 **Bridgeton** USA
69R3 **Bridgetown** Barbados
55M5 **Bridgewater** Canada
68E2 **Bridgewater** USA
7C4 **Bridgwater** England
7C4 **Bridgwater B** England
6D2 **Bridlington** England
6E3 **Bridlington Bay** England
34C4 **Bridport** Australia
7C4 **Bridport** England
13C3 **Brienne-le-Château** France
13C3 **Briey** France
16B1 **Brig** Switzerland
56B2 **Brigham City** USA
34C3 **Bright** Australia
7D4 **Brighton** England
75A3 **Brilhante** *R* Brazil
13E2 **Brilon** Germany
17D2 **Brindisi** Italy
63D2 **Brinkley** USA
33E3 **Brisbane** Australia
65E2 **Bristol** Connecticut, USA
7C4 **Bristol** England
65E2 **Bristol** Pennsylvania, USA
68E2 **Bristol** Rhode Island, USA
57E3 **Bristol** Tennessee, USA
64C3 **Bristol** USA
7B4 **Bristol Chan** England/ Wales
54F4 **British Columbia** *Province* Canada
55K1 **British Empire Range** *Mts* Canada
54E3 **British Mts** Canada
47D2 **Brits** South Africa
47C3 **Britstown** South Africa
61D1 **Britton** USA
14C2 **Brive** France
7C4 **Brixham** England
18D3 **Brno** Czech Republic
67B2 **Broad** *R* USA
68C1 **Broadalbin** USA
55L4 **Broadback** *R* Canada
8B2 **Broad Bay** *Inlet* Scotland
8C3 **Broadford** Scotland
9B2 **Broad Haven, B** Irish Republic
7E4 **Broadstairs** England
60B1 **Broadus** USA
60C2 **Broadwater** USA
54H4 **Brochet** Canada
54G2 **Brock I** Canada
65D2 **Brockport** USA
68E1 **Brockton** USA
65D2 **Brockville** Canada
68A2 **Brockway** USA
55K2 **Brodeur Pen** Canada
8C4 **Brodick** Scotland
19D2 **Brodnica** Poland
21D5 **Brody** Ukraine
13D2 **Brokem Haltern** Germany
60D2 **Broken Bow** Nebraska, USA
63D2 **Broken Bow** Oklahoma, USA
63D2 **Broken Bow L** USA
32D4 **Broken Hill** Australia
7C3 **Bromsgrove** England
12G5 **Brønnøysund** Norway
68D2 **Bronx** *Borough* New York, USA
27E6 **Brooke's Pt** Philippines
61E3 **Brookfield** Missouri, USA
64B2 **Brookfield** Wisconsin, USA
57D3 **Brookhaven** USA
58B2 **Brookings** Oregon, USA
56D2 **Brookings** South Dakota, USA
68E1 **Brookline** USA
61E2 **Brooklyn** USA
68D2 **Brooklyn** *Borough* New York, USA
61E1 **Brooklyn Center** USA
54G4 **Brooks** Canada
54C3 **Brooks Range** *Mts* USA
67B3 **Brooksville** USA
34D1 **Brooloo** Australia
32B2 **Broome** Australia
8C3 **Broom, Loch** *Estuary* Scotland
8D2 **Brora** Scotland
58B2 **Brothers** USA
6C2 **Broughton** England
8D3 **Broughty Ferry** Scotland
50B2 **Broulkou** *Well* Chad
19G2 **Brovary** Ukraine
61E1 **Browerville** USA
62B2 **Brownfield** USA
56D4 **Brownsville** USA
56D3 **Brownwood** USA
27F8 **Browse I** Australia
13B2 **Bruay-en-Artois** France
32A3 **Bruce,Mt** Australia
64C1 **Bruce Pen** Canada
13E3 **Bruchsal** Germany
18D3 **Bruck an der Mur** Austria
Bruges = Brugge
13B2 **Brugge** Belgium
13D2 **Brühl** Germany
45B3 **Brûk, Wadi el** Egypt
75D1 **Brumado** Brazil
13D3 **Brumath** France
58C2 **Bruneau** USA
58C2 **Bruneau** *R* USA
27E6 **Brunei** *State* Borneo
16C1 **Brunico** Italy
35B2 **Brunner,L** New Zealand
13E1 **Brunsbüttel** Germany
57E3 **Brunswick** Georgia, USA
65F2 **Brunswick** Maine, USA
61E3 **Brunswick** Mississippi, USA
74B8 **Brunswick,Pen de** Chile
34C4 **Bruny I** Australia
20G3 **Brusenets** Russian Federation
60C2 **Brush** USA
69A3 **Brus Laguna** Honduras
Brüssel = Brussels
18A2 **Brussels** Belgium
Bruxelles = Brussels
13D3 **Bruyères** France
56D3 **Bryan** USA
34A2 **Bryan,Mt** Australia
20E5 **Bryansk** Russian Federation
63D2 **Bryant** USA
59D3 **Bryce Canyon Nat Pk** USA
18D2 **Brzeg** Poland
41E4 **Būbīyan** *I* Kuwait
50D4 **Bubu** *R* Tanzania
47E1 **Bubye** *R* Zimbabwe
72D2 **Bucaramanga** Colombia
8E3 **Buchan** *Oilfield* N Sea
48A4 **Buchanan** Liberia
62C2 **Buchanan,L** USA
8E3 **Buchan Deep** N Sea
55L2 **Buchan G** Canada
10C2 **Buchan Ness** *Pen* Scotland
55N5 **Buchans** Canada
17F2 **Bucharest** Romania
66B3 **Buchon,Pt** USA
13E1 **Bückeburg** Germany
59D4 **Buckeye** USA
8D3 **Buckhaven** Scotland
8D3 **Buckie** Scotland
7D3 **Buckingham** England
65F2 **Bucksport** USA
50B4 **Buco Zau** Congo
București = Bucharest
19D3 **Budapest** Hungary
42D3 **Budaun** India
7B4 **Bude** England
63D2 **Bude** USA
21G7 **Budennovsk** Russian Federation
43J1 **Budhana** India
45B4 **Budhîya, Gebel** Egypt
13E2 **Büdingen** Germany
17D2 **Budva** Montenegro, Yugoslavia
48C4 **Buéa** Cameroon
66B3 **Buellton** USA
72C3 **Buenaventura** Colombia
62A3 **Buenaventura** Mexico
60B3 **Buena Vista** Colorado, USA
65D3 **Buena Vista** Virginia, USA
66C3 **Buena Vista L** USA
74E4 **Buenos Aires** Argentina
74E5 **Buenos Aires** *State* Argentina
74B7 **Buenos Aires, Lago** Argentina
63D1 **Buffalo** Mississipi, USA
57F2 **Buffalo** New York, USA
60C1 **Buffalo** S Dakota, USA
63C2 **Buffalo** Texas, USA
56C2 **Buffalo** Wyoming, USA
47E2 **Buffalo** *R* South Africa
58C1 **Buffalo Hump** *Mt* USA
54G3 **Buffalo L** Canada
54H4 **Buffalo Narrows** Canada
67B2 **Buford** USA
17F2 **Buftea** Romania
19E2 **Bug** *R* Poland/Ukraine
72C3 **Buga** Colombia
41F2 **Bugdayli** Turkmenistan
20H2 **Bugrino** Russian Federation
20J5 **Bugulma** Russian Federation
20J5 **Buguruslan** Russian Federation
40C2 **Buḩayrat al Asad** *Res* Syria
58D2 **Buhl** Idaho, USA
61E1 **Buhl** Minnesota, USA
7C3 **Builth Wells** Wales
50C4 **Bujumbura** Burundi
33E1 **Buka** *I* Papua New Guinea
51C4 **Bukama** Zaïre
50C4 **Bukavu** Zaïre
38E2 **Bukhara** Uzbekistan
27D7 **Bukittinggi** Indonesia
50D4 **Bukoba** Tanzania
27G7 **Bula** Indonesia
27F5 **Bulan** Philippines
42D3 **Bulandshahr** India
51C6 **Bulawayo** Zimbabwe
17F3 **Buldan** Turkey
42D4 **Buldāna** India
26D2 **Bulgan** Mongolia
17E2 **Bulgaria** *Republic* Europe
35B2 **Buller** *R* New Zealand
34C3 **Buller,Mt** Australia
32A4 **Bullfinch** Australia
34B1 **Bulloo** *R* Australia
34B1 **Bulloo Downs** Australia
34B1 **Bulloo L** Australia
63D1 **Bull Shoals Res** USA
32D1 **Bulolo** Papua New Guinea
47D2 **Bultfontein** South Africa
27E6 **Bulu, Gunung** *Mt* Indonesia
50C3 **Bumba** Zaïre
21D8 **Bu Menderes** *R* Turkey
30B2 **Bumphal Dam** Thailand
50D3 **Buna** Kenya
32A4 **Bunbury** Australia
9C2 **Buncrana** Irish Republic
33E3 **Bundaberg** Australia
34D2 **Bundarra** Australia
13E1 **Bünde** Germany
42D3 **Būndi** India
7E3 **Bungay** England
34C1 **Bungil** *R* Australia
51B4 **Bungo** Angola
28B4 **Bungo-suidō** *Str* Japan
27D6 **Bunguran** *I* Indonesia
27D6 **Bunguran, Kepulauan** *I* Indonesia
50D3 **Bunia** Zaïre
63D1 **Bunker** USA
63D2 **Bunkie** USA
67B3 **Bunnell** USA
27E7 **Buntok** Indonesia
27F6 **Buol** Indonesia
50C2 **Buram** Sudan
43E2 **Burang** China
50E3 **Burao** Somalia
45D2 **Burāq** Syria
41D4 **Buraydah** Saudi Arabia
59C4 **Burbank** USA
34C2 **Burcher** Australia
21E8 **Burdur** Turkey
50D2 **Burē** Ethiopia
7E3 **Bure** *R* England
26G1 **Bureinskiy Khrebet** *Mts* Russian Federation
26F2 **Bureya** Russian Federation
45B3 **Bûr Fu'ad** Egypt
18C2 **Burg** Germany
17F2 **Burgas** Bulgaria
67C2 **Burgaw** USA
47D3 **Burgersdorp** South Africa
15B1 **Burgos** Spain
13D1 **Burgsteinfurt** Germany
19D1 **Burgsvik** Sweden
17F3 **Burhaniye** Turkey
42D4 **Burhānpur** India
30C2 **Buriram** Thailand
75C2 **Buritis** Brazil
32C2 **Burketown** Australia
48B3 **Burkina** *Republic* W Africa
65D1 **Burk's Falls** Canada
56B2 **Burley** USA
60C3 **Burlington** Colorado, USA
57D2 **Burlington** Iowa, USA
68C2 **Burlington** New Jersey, USA
67C1 **Burlington** North Carolina, USA
57F2 **Burlington** Vermont, USA
58B1 **Burlington** Washington, USA
39H3 **Burma** *Republic* Asia
62C2 **Burnet** USA
58B2 **Burney** USA
68B2 **Burnham** USA
7E4 **Burnham-on-Crouch** England
32D5 **Burnie** Australia
6C3 **Burnley** England
58C2 **Burns** USA
54F4 **Burns Lake** Canada
24K5 **Burqin** China
34A2 **Burra** Australia
34D2 **Burragorang,L** Australia
8D2 **Burray** *I* Scotland
34C2 **Burren Junction** Australia
34C2 **Burrinjuck Res** Australia
62B3 **Burro, Serranías del** *Mts* Mexico
8C4 **Burrow Head** *Pt* Scotland
27G8 **Burrundie** Australia
21D7 **Bursa** Turkey
40B4 **Bur Safâga** Egypt
Bûr Saîd = Port Said
45B4 **Bûr Taufiq** Egypt
64C2 **Burton** USA
7D3 **Burton upon Trent** England
12J6 **Burtrask** Sweden
34B2 **Burtundy** Australia
27F7 **Buru** *I* Indonesia
50C4 **Burundi** *Republic* Africa
60D2 **Burwell** USA
7C3 **Bury** England
25N4 **Buryat Republic** Russian Federation
21J6 **Burynshik** Kazakhstan
7E3 **Bury St Edmunds** England
28A3 **Bushan** China
41F4 **Būshehr** Iran
9C2 **Bushmills** Northern Ireland
50B4 **Busira** *R* Zaïre
19E2 **Busko Zdrój** Poland
45D2 **Buṣrá ash Shām** Syria
13D4 **Bussang** France
32A4 **Busselton** Australia
16B1 **Busto Arsizio** Italy
50C3 **Buta** Zaïre
50C4 **Butare** Rwanda
8C4 **Bute** *I* Scotland
26F2 **Butha Qi** China
65D2 **Butler** USA
32B1 **Buton** *I* Indonesia
48C4 **Butta** Togo
56B2 **Butte** USA
30C4 **Butterworth** Malaysia
47D3 **Butterworth** South Africa
10B2 **Butt of Lewis** *C* Scotland
55M3 **Button Is** Canada
66C3 **Buttonwillow** USA
27F6 **Butuan** Philippines
21G5 **Buturlinovka** Russian Federation
43E3 **Butwal** Nepal
13E2 **Butzbach** Germany
50E3 **Buulobarde** Somalia
50E3 **Buurhakaba** Somalia
7D3 **Buxton** England
20G4 **Buy** Russian Federation
31B1 **Buyant Ovoo** Mongolia
21H7 **Buynaksk** Russian Federation
25N5 **Buyr Nuur** *L* Mongolia
21G8 **Büyük Ağri Daği** *Mt* Turkey
40A2 **Büyük Menderes** *R* Turkey
17F1 **Buzău** Romania
17F1 **Buzău** *R* Romania
75D3 **Búzios, Ponta dos** *Pt* Brazil
20J5 **Buzuluk** Russian Federation
68E2 **Buzzards B** USA
17F2 **Byala** Bulgaria
17E2 **Byala Slatina** Bulgaria
54H2 **Byam Martin Channel** Canada
54H2 **Byam Martin I** Canada
45C1 **Byblos** *Hist site* Lebanon
19D2 **Bydgoszcz** Poland
60C3 **Byers** USA
12F7 **Bygland** Norway
19G2 **Bykhov** Belarus
55L2 **Bylot I** Canada
34C2 **Byrock** Australia
66B2 **Byron** USA
34D1 **Byron** *C* Australia
25P3 **Bytantay** *R* Russian Federation
19D2 **Bytom** Poland

C

74E3 **Caacupú** Paraguay
75A4 **Caaguazú** Paraguay
51B5 **Caála** Angola
75A4 **Caapucú** Paraguay
75B3 **Caarapó** Brazil
74E3 **Caazapá** Paraguay
15C1 **Caballería, Cabo de** *C* Spain
62A2 **Caballo Res** USA
27F5 **Cabanatuan** Philippines
65F1 **Cabano** Canada
73M5 **Cabedelo** Brazil
15A2 **Cabeza del Buey** Spain
72D1 **Cabimas** Venezuela
50B4 **Cabinda** Angola
50B4 **Cabinda** *Province* Angola
58C1 **Cabinet Mts** USA
75D3 **Cabo Frio** Brazil
55L5 **Cabonga,Réservoire** Canada
34D1 **Caboolture** Australia
51D5 **Cabora Bassa Dam** Mozambique
70A1 **Caborca** Mexico
55M5 **Cabot Str** Canada
15B2 **Cabra** Spain
75D2 **Cabral, Serra do** *Mts* Brazil
15A1 **Cabreira** *Mt* Portugal
15C2 **Cabrera** *I* Spain
15B2 **Cabriel** *R* Spain
17E2 **Čačak** Serbia, Yugoslavia
68A3 **Cacapon** *R* USA
73G7 **Cáceres** Brazil
15A2 **Cáceres** Spain
63D1 **Cache** *R* USA
66A1 **Cache Creek** *R* USA
58D2 **Cache Peak** *Mt* USA
74C3 **Cachi** Argentina
73G5 **Cachimbo** Brazil
73G5 **Cachimbo, Serra do** *Mts* Brazil
73L6 **Cachoeira** Brazil
75B2 **Cachoeira Alta** Brazil
73L5 **Cachoeira de Paulo Afonso** *Waterfall* Brazil
74F4 **Cachoeira do Sul** Brazil
73K8 **Cachoeiro de Itapemirim** Brazil
66C3 **Cachuma,L** USA
51B5 **Cacolo** Angola
51B5 **Caconda** Angola
62B1 **Cactus** USA
75B2 **Caçu** Brazil
75D1 **Caculé** Brazil
51B5 **Caculuvar** *R* Angola
19D3 **Čadca** Slovakia
7C3 **Cader Idris** *Mt* Wales
57E2 **Cadillac** USA
15A2 **Cádiz** Spain
15A2 **Cádiz, Golfo de** *G* Spain
14B2 **Caen** France
7B3 **Caernarfon** Wales
7B3 **Caernarfon B** Wales
7C4 **Caerphilly** Wales
45C2 **Caesarea** *Hist Site* Israel
75D1 **Caetité** Brazil
74C3 **Cafayate** Argentina
40B2 **Caga Tepe** *Mt* Turkey
27F6 **Cagayan de Oro** Philippines
16B3 **Cagliari** Sardinia, Italy
16B3 **Cagliari, G di** Sardinia, Italy
69D3 **Caguas** Puerto Rico
67A2 **Cahaba** *R* USA
9C3 **Cahir** Irish Republic
9C3 **Cahore Pt** Irish Republic
14C3 **Cahors** France
51D5 **Caia** Mozambique
73G6 **Caiabis, Serra dos** *Mts* Brazil
51C5 **Caianda** Angola
75B2 **Caiapó** *R* Brazil
75B2 **Caiapônia** Brazil
75B2 **Caiapó, Serra do** *Mts* Brazil
73L5 **Caicó** Brazil
69C2 **Caicos Is** Caribbean Sea
57F4 **Caicos Pass** The Bahamas
8D3 **Cairngorms** *Mts* Scotland
8C4 **Cairnryan** Scotland
32D2 **Cairns** Australia
40B3 **Cairo** Egypt
57E3 **Cairo** USA
8D2 **Caithness** Scotland
34B1 **Caiwarro** Australia
72C5 **Cajabamba** Peru
72C5 **Cajamarca** Peru
48C4 **Calabar** Nigeria
69D5 **Calabozo** Venezuela

17E2 **Calafat** Romania
74B8 **Calafate** Argentina
15B1 **Calahorra** Spain
14C1 **Calais** France
65F1 **Calais** USA
74C2 **Calama** Chile
72D3 **Calamar** Colombia
27E5 **Calamian Group** *Is* Philippines
51B4 **Calandula** Angola
27C6 **Calang** Indonesia
49E2 **Calanscio Sand Sea** Libya
27F5 **Calapan** Philippines
17F2 **Calarasi** Romania
15B1 **Calatayud** Spain
66B2 **Calaveras Res** USA
63D3 **Calcasieu L** USA
43F4 **Calcutta** India
15A2 **Caldas da Rainha** Portugal
73J7 **Caldas Novas** Brazil
74B3 **Caldera** Chile
56B2 **Caldwell** USA
47B3 **Caledon** South Africa
47D3 **Caledon** *R* South Africa
64A2 **Caledonia** Minnesota, USA
68B1 **Caledonia** New York, USA
74C7 **Caleta Olivia** Argentina
56B3 **Calexico** USA
54G4 **Calgary** Canada
67B2 **Calhoun** USA
67B2 **Calhoun Falls** USA
72C3 **Cali** Colombia
66C3 **Caliente** California, USA
56B3 **Caliente** Nevada, USA
62A1 **Caliente** New Mexico, USA
56A3 **California** *State* USA
66C3 **California Aqueduct** USA
70A1 **California, G de** Mexico
44B3 **Calimera,Pt** India
59C4 **Calipatria** USA
47C3 **Calitzdorp** South Africa
34B1 **Callabonna** *R* Australia
34A1 **Callabonna,L** Australia
65D1 **Callander** Canada
8C3 **Callander** Scotland
72C6 **Callao** Peru
68C2 **Callicoon** USA
67B3 **Caloosahatchee** *R* USA
34D1 **Caloundra** Australia
16C3 **Caltanissetta** Sicily, Italy
51B4 **Caluango** Angola
51B5 **Calulo** Angola
51B5 **Caluquembe** Angola
50F2 **Caluula** Somalia
16B2 **Calvi** Corsica, France
47B3 **Calvinia** South Africa
13E3 **Calw** Germany
75E1 **Camacari** Brazil
70E2 **Camagüey** Cuba
70E2 **Camagüey,Arch de** *Is* Cuba
75E1 **Camamu** Brazil
72D7 **Camaná** Peru
75B2 **Camapuã** Brazil
72E8 **Camargo** Bolivia
66C3 **Camarillo** USA
74C6 **Camarones** Argentina
58B1 **Camas** USA
51B4 **Camaxilo** Angola
51B4 **Cambatela** Angola
30C3 **Cambodia** *Republic* SE Asia
7B4 **Camborne** England
14C1 **Cambrai** France
66B3 **Cambria** USA
7C3 **Cambrian Mts** Wales
64C2 **Cambridge** Canada
7E3 **Cambridge** England
69H1 **Cambridge** Jamaica
65D3 **Cambridge** Maryland, USA
65E2 **Cambridge** Massachussets, USA
61E1 **Cambridge** Minnesota, USA
35C1 **Cambridge** New Zealand
64C2 **Cambridge** Ohio, USA
7D3 **Cambridge** *County* England
54H3 **Cambridge Bay** Canada
27F8 **Cambridge G** Australia
21F7 **Cam Burun** *Pt* Turkey
57D3 **Camden** Arkansas, USA
34D2 **Camden** Australia
65E3 **Camden** New Jersey, USA
68C1 **Camden** New York, USA
67B2 **Camden** South Carolina, USA
61E3 **Cameron** Missouri, USA
63C2 **Cameron** Texas, USA
54H2 **Cameron I** Canada
35A3 **Cameron Mts** New Zealand
50B3 **Cameroon** *Federal Republic* Africa
48C4 **Cameroun, Mt** Cameroon
73J4 **Cametá** Brazil
67B2 **Camilla** USA
66B1 **Camino** USA
72F8 **Camiri** Bolivia
51C4 **Camissombo** Angola
73K4 **Camocim** Brazil
32C2 **Camooweal** Australia
44E4 **Camorta** *I* Nicobar Is, Indian Ocean
74A7 **Campana** *I* Chile
47C2 **Campbell** South Africa
35B2 **Campbell,C** New Zealand
37K7 **Campbell I** New Zealand
54E3 **Campbell,Mt** Canada
42C2 **Campbellpore** Pakistan
54F5 **Campbell River** Canada
64B3 **Campbellsville** USA
55M5 **Campbellton** Canada
34D2 **Campbelltown** Australia
8C4 **Campbeltown** Scotland
70C3 **Campeche** Mexico
70C2 **Campeche, B de** Mexico
34B3 **Camperdown** Australia
73L5 **Campina Grande** Brazil
73J8 **Campinas** Brazil
75C2 **Campina Verde** Brazil
66C2 **Camp Nelson** USA
48C4 **Campo** Cameroon
16C2 **Campobasso** Italy
75C3 **Campo Belo** Brazil
75C2 **Campo Florido** Brazil
74D3 **Campo Gallo** Argentina
74F2 **Campo Grande** Brazil
73K4 **Campo Maior** Brazil
74F2 **Campo Mourão** Brazil
75D3 **Campos** Brazil
75C2 **Campos Altos** Brazil
59D4 **Camp Verde** USA
30D3 **Cam Ranh** Vietnam
54G4 **Camrose** Canada
51B5 **Camucuio** Angola
69K1 **Canaan** Tobago
68D1 **Canaan** USA
51B5 **Canacupa** Angola
53F3 **Canada** *Dominion* N America
74D4 **Cañada de Gómez** Argentina
68C2 **Canadensis** USA
62B1 **Canadian** USA
56C3 **Canadian** *R* USA
21D7 **Çanakkale** Turkey
68B1 **Canandaigua** USA
68B1 **Canandaigua L** USA
70A1 **Cananea** Mexico
75C4 **Cananeia** Brazil
Canarias, Islas = Canary Islands
52G3 **Canary Basin** Atlantic Ocean
48A2 **Canary Is** *Atlantic Ocean*
75C3 **Canastra, Serra da** *Mts* Brazil
70B2 **Canatlán** Mexico
57E4 **Canaveral,C** USA
73L7 **Canavieiras** Brazil
32D4 **Canberra** Australia
58B2 **Canby** California, USA
61D2 **Canby** Minnesota, USA
17F3 **Çandarlı Körfezi** *B* Turkey
68D2 **Candlewood,L** USA
60D1 **Cando** USA
68B1 **Candor** USA
74E4 **Canelones** Uruguay
63C1 **Caney** USA
51C5 **Cangamba** Angola
51C5 **Cangombe** Angola
31D2 **Cangzhou** China
55M4 **Caniapiscau** *R* Canada
55M4 **Caniapiscau, Réservoir** *Res* Canada
16C3 **Canicatti** Sicily, Italy
73L4 **Canindé** Brazil
68B1 **Canisteo** USA
68B1 **Canisteo** *R* USA
62A1 **Canjilon** USA
40B1 **Çankırı** Turkey
8B3 **Canna** *I* Scotland
44B3 **Cannanore** India
14D3 **Cannes** France
7C3 **Cannock** England
60C1 **Cannonball** *R* USA
34C3 **Cann River** Australia
74F3 **Canōas** Brazil
75B4 **Canoinhas** Brazil
60B3 **Canon City** USA
34B2 **Canopus** Australia
54H4 **Canora** Canada
34C2 **Canowindra** Australia
15B1 **Cantabria** *Region* Spain
14A3 **Cantabrica, Cord** *Mts* Spain
7E4 **Canterbury** England
35B2 **Canterbury Bight** *B* New Zealand
35B2 **Canterbury Plains** New Zealand
30D4 **Can Tho** Vietnam
66D3 **Cantil** USA
Canton = Guangzhou
63E2 **Canton** Mississippi, USA
64A2 **Canton** Missouri, USA
57E2 **Canton** Ohio, USA
68B2 **Canton** Pensylvania, USA
61D2 **Canton** S Dakota, USA
33H1 **Canton** *I* Phoenix Islands
75B3 **Cantu, Serra do** *Mts* Brazil
62B2 **Canyon** USA
58C2 **Canyon City** USA
58D1 **Canyon Ferry L** USA
59E3 **Canyonlands Nat Pk** USA
58B2 **Canyonville** USA
51C4 **Canzar** Angola
30D1 **Cao Bang** Vietnam
28B2 **Caoshi** China
73J4 **Capanema** Brazil
75C3 **Capão Bonito** Brazil
75D3 **Caparaó, Serra do** *Mts* Brazil
14B3 **Capbreton** France
16B2 **Cap Corse** *C* Corsica, France
14B2 **Cap de la Hague** *C* France
65E1 **Cap-de-la-Madeleine** Canada
15C2 **Capdepera** Spain
34C4 **Cape Barren I** Australia
52J6 **Cape Basin** Atlantic Ocean
55N5 **Cape Breton I** Canada
Cape, Cabo etc: see also individual cape names
48B4 **Cape Coast** Ghana
65E2 **Cape Cod B** USA
55M3 **Cape Dyer** Canada
76F7 **Cape Evans** *Base* Antarctica
67C2 **Cape Fear** *R* USA
63E1 **Cape Girardeau** USA
74C8 **Cape Horn** Chile
36H4 **Cape Johnson Depth** Pacific Ocean
75D2 **Capelinha** Brazil
54B3 **Cape Lisburne** USA
51B5 **Capelongo** Angola
65E3 **Cape May** USA
54F5 **Cape Mendocino** USA
51B4 **Capenda Camulemba** Angola
54F2 **Cape Parry** Canada
47B3 **Cape Town** South Africa
52G4 **Cape Verde** *Is* Atlantic Ocean
52G4 **Cape Verde Basin** Atlantic Ocean
32D2 **Cape York Pen** Australia
69C3 **Cap-Haïtien** Haiti
73J4 **Capim** *R* Brazil
75A3 **Capitán Bado** Paraguay
59E3 **Capitol Reef Nat Pk** USA
75A2 **Capivari** *R* Brazil
9C3 **Cappoquin** Irish Republic
69P2 **Cap Pt** St Lucia
16C2 **Capri** *I* Italy
51C5 **Caprivi Strip** *Region* Namibia
72D4 **Caquetá** *R* Colombia
17E2 **Caracal** Romania
72F3 **Caracaraí** Brazil
72E1 **Caracas** Venezuela
75A3 **Caracol** Brazil
75C3 **Caraguatatuba** Brazil
74B5 **Carahue** Chile
75D2 **Caraí** Brazil
75D3 **Carandaí** Brazil
75A2 **Carandazal** Brazil
73K8 **Carangola** Brazil
17E1 **Caransebeş** Romania
69A3 **Caratasca** Honduras
70D3 **Caratasca, L de** *Lg* Honduras
75D2 **Caratinga** Brazil
15B2 **Caravaca de la Cruz** Spain
75E2 **Caravelas** Brazil
16B3 **Carbonara, C** Sardinia, Italy
64B3 **Carbondale** Illinois, USA
68C2 **Carbondale** Pennsylvania, USA
55N5 **Carbonear** Canada
16B3 **Carbonia** Sardinia, Italy
54G4 **Carcajou** Canada
50E2 **Carcar Mts** Somalia
14C3 **Carcassonne** France
54E3 **Carcross** Canada
30C3 **Cardamomes, Chaîne des** *Mts* Cambodia
70D2 **Cardenas** Cuba
7C4 **Cardiff** Wales
7B3 **Cardigan** Wales
7B3 **Cardigan B** Wales
75C4 **Cardoso, Ilha do** Brazil
17E1 **Carei** Romania
73G4 **Careiro** Brazil
64C2 **Carey** USA
14B2 **Carhaix-Plouguer** France
74D5 **Carhué** Argentina
73K8 **Cariacíca** Brazil
71C2 **Caribbean S** Central America
54J4 **Caribou** Canada
65F1 **Caribou** USA
54G4 **Caribou Mts** Alberta, Canada
54F4 **Caribou Mts** British Columbia, Canada
13C3 **Carignan** France
75D1 **Carinhanha** Brazil
75D1 **Carinhanha** *R* Brazil
72F1 **Caripito** Venezuela
65D1 **Carleton Place** Canada
47D2 **Carletonville** South Africa
58C2 **Carlin** USA
9C2 **Carlingford, L** Northern Ireland
64B3 **Carlinville** USA
6C2 **Carlisle** England
65D2 **Carlisle** USA
75D2 **Carlos Chagas** Brazil
9C3 **Carlow** Irish Republic
9C3 **Carlow** *County* Irish Republic
59C4 **Carlsbad** California, USA
56C3 **Carlsbad** New Mexico, USA
62B2 **Carlsbad Caverns Nat Pk** USA
36E4 **Carlsberg Ridge** Indian Ocean
54H5 **Carlyle** Canada
54E3 **Carmacks** Canada
7B4 **Carmarthen** Wales
7B4 **Carmarthen B** Wales
66B2 **Carmel** California, USA
68D2 **Carmel** New York, USA
7B3 **Carmel Hd** *Pt* Wales
45C2 **Carmel,Mt** Israel
66B2 **Carmel Valley** USA
56B4 **Carmen** *I* Mexico
74D6 **Carmen de Patagones** Argentina
64B3 **Carmi** USA
59B3 **Carmichael** USA
75C2 **Carmo do Paranaiba** Brazil
15A2 **Carmona** Spain
75E2 **Carnacá** Brazil
32A3 **Carnarvon** Australia
47C3 **Carnarvon** South Africa
9C2 **Carndonagh** Irish Republic
32B3 **Carnegie,L** Australia
44E4 **Car Nicobar** *I* Nicobar Is, Indian Ocean
50B3 **Carnot** Central African Republic
8D3 **Carnoustie** Scotland
9C3 **Carnsore Pt** Irish Republic
67B3 **Carol City** USA
73J5 **Carolina** Brazil
47E2 **Carolina** South Africa
67C2 **Carolina Beach** USA
27H6 **Caroline Is** Pacific Ocean
19F3 **Carpathian Mts** Romania
21C6 **Carpathians** *Mts* E Europe
32C2 **Carpentaria,G of** Australia
39H5 **Carpenter Ridge** Indian Ocean
14D3 **Carpentras** France
16C2 **Carpi** Italy
66C3 **Carpinteria** USA
67B3 **Carrabelle** USA
16C2 **Carrara** Italy
10B3 **Carrauntoohill** *Mt* Irish Republic
8C4 **Carrick** Scotland
9D2 **Carrickfergus** Northern Ireland
9C3 **Carrickmacross** Irish Republic
9C3 **Carrick-on-Suir** Irish Republic
34A2 **Carrieton** Australia
54J5 **Carrington** USA
15B1 **Carrión** *R* Spain
62C3 **Carrizo Springs** USA
62A2 **Carrizozo** USA
57D2 **Carroll** USA
67A2 **Carrollton** Georgia, USA
64B3 **Carrollton** Kentucky, USA
61E3 **Carrollton** Missouri, USA
9B2 **Carrowmore,L** *Irish Republic*
63E1 **Carruthersville** USA
21F7 **Carşamba** Turkey
21E8 **Carşamba** *R* Turkey
56B3 **Carson City** USA
64C2 **Carsonville** USA
8D4 **Carstairs** Scotland
69B4 **Cartagena** Colombia
15B2 **Cartagena** Spain
72C3 **Cartago** Colombia
70D4 **Cartago** Costa Rica
66C2 **Cartago** USA
35C2 **Carterton** New Zealand
63D1 **Carthage** Missouri, USA
65D2 **Carthage** New York, USA
63D2 **Carthage** Texas, USA
32B2 **Cartier I** Timor Sea
55N4 **Cartwright** Canada
73L5 **Caruaru** Brazil
72F1 **Carúpano** Venezuela
13B2 **Carvin** France
15A2 **Carvoeiro, Cabo** *C* Portugal
67C1 **Cary** USA
48B1 **Casablanca** Morocco
75C3 **Casa Branca** Brazil
56B3 **Casa Grande** USA
16B1 **Casale Monferrato** Italy
58D1 **Cascade** USA
35A2 **Cascade Pt** New Zealand
56A2 **Cascade Range** *Mts* USA
58C2 **Cascade Res** USA
74F2 **Cascavel** Brazil
16C2 **Caserta** Italy
76G9 **Casey** *Base* Antarctica
9C3 **Cashel** Irish Republic
33E3 **Casino** Australia
72C5 **Casma** Peru
66B3 **Casmalia** USA
15C1 **Caspe** Spain
56C2 **Casper** USA
21H6 **Caspian Depression** *Region* Kazakhstan
21H7 **Caspian S** Asia/Europe
65D3 **Cass** USA
51C5 **Cassamba** Angola
13B2 **Cassel** France
61D1 **Casselton** USA
54E3 **Cassiar Mts** Canada
75B2 **Cassilândia** Brazil
16C2 **Cassino** Italy
61E1 **Cass Lake** USA
66C3 **Castaic** USA
14D3 **Castellane** France
16C2 **Castello, Città di** Italy
15C1 **Castellón de la Plana** Spain
73K5 **Castelo** Brazil
15A2 **Castelo Branco** Portugal
14C3 **Castelsarrasin** France
16C3 **Castelvetrano** Sicily, Italy
34B3 **Casterton** Australia
15B2 **Castilla la Mancha** *Region* Spain
15B1 **Castilla y León** *Region* Spain
10B3 **Castlebar** Irish Republic
8B3 **Castlebay** Scotland
9C2 **Castleblayney** Irish Republic
59D3 **Castle Dale** USA
8D4 **Castle Douglas** Scotland
6D3 **Castleford** England
58C1 **Castlegar** Canada
34B3 **Castlemaine** Australia
66B3 **Castle Mt** USA
58D2 **Castle Peak** *Mt* USA
34C2 **Castlereagh** *R* Australia
60C3 **Castle Rock** USA
6B2 **Castletown** England
9B4 **Castletown Bere** Irish Republic
14C3 **Castres-sur-l'Agout** France
69P2 **Castries** St Lucia
74B6 **Castro** Argentina
74F2 **Castro** Brazil
73L6 **Castro Alves** Brazil
16D3 **Castrovillari** Italy
66B2 **Castroville** USA
35A2 **Caswell Sd** New Zealand
70E2 **Cat** *I* The Bahamas
72B5 **Catacaos** Peru
75D3 **Cataguases** Brazil
63D2 **Catahoula L** USA
75C2 **Catalão** Brazil
15C1 **Cataluña** *Region* Spain
74C3 **Catamarca** Argentina
74C3 **Catamarca** *State* Argentina
51D5 **Catandica** Mozambique
27F5 **Catanduanes** *I* Philippines
74G2 **Catanduva** Brazil
75B4 **Catanduvas** Brazil
16D3 **Catania** Sicily, Italy
16D3 **Catanzaro** Italy
62C3 **Catarina** USA
27F5 **Catarman** Philippines
69C5 **Catatumbo** *R* Venezuela
68B2 **Catawissa** USA
27F5 **Catbalogan** Philippines
16B2 **Cateraggio** Corsica, France
51B4 **Catete** Angola
47D3 **Cathcart** South Africa
48A3 **Catio** Guinea-Bissau
55J4 **Cat Lake** Canada
33E3 **Cato** *I* Australia
70D2 **Catoche,C** Mexico
68B3 **Catoctin Mt** USA
65D3 **Catonsville** USA
65E2 **Catskill** USA
65E2 **Catskill Mts** USA
72D2 **Cauca** *R* Colombia
73L4 **Caucaia** Brazil
72C2 **Caucasia** Colombia
21G7 **Caucasus** *Mts* Georgia
13B2 **Caudry** France
51B4 **Caungula** Angola
74B5 **Cauquenes** Chile
65F1 **Causapscal** Canada
44B3 **Cauvery** *R* India
14D3 **Cavaillon** France
75C1 **Cavalcante** Brazil
61D1 **Cavalier** USA
48B4 **Cavally** *R* Liberia
9C3 **Cavan** Irish Republic
9C3 **Cavan** *County* Irish Republic
72D4 **Caxias** Brazil

73K4 **Caxias** Brazil
74F3 **Caxias do Sul** Brazil
51B4 **Caxito** Angola
67B2 **Cayce** USA
40D1 **Çayeli** Turkey
73H3 **Cayenne** French Guiana
70E3 **Cayman Brac** *I* Cayman Is, Caribbean Sea
69A3 **Cayman Is** Caribbean Sea
69A3 **Cayman Trench** Caribbean Sea
50E3 **Caynabo** Somalia
70E2 **Cayo Romano** *I* Cuba
70D3 **Cayos Miskito** *Is* Nicaragua
69A2 **Cay Sal** *I* Caribbean Sea
66B3 **Cayucos** USA
68B1 **Cayuga L** USA
68C1 **Cazenovia** USA
51C5 **Cazombo** Angola
Ceará = Fortaleza
73K5 **Ceará** *State* Brazil
27F5 **Cebu** Philippines
27F5 **Cebu** *I* Philippines
68C3 **Cecilton** USA
16C2 **Cecina** Italy
61E2 **Cedar** *R* USA
56B3 **Cedar City** USA
63C2 **Cedar Creek Res** USA
61E2 **Cedar Falls** USA
54H4 **Cedar L** Canada
66D1 **Cedar Mts** USA
57D2 **Cedar Rapids** USA
67A2 **Cedartown** USA
70A2 **Cedros** *I* Mexico
56B4 **Cedros, Isla de** Mexico
32C4 **Ceduna** Australia
50E3 **Ceelbuur** Somalia
50E2 **Ceerigaabo** Somalia
16C3 **Cefalù** Sicily, Italy
19D3 **Cegléd** Hungary
51B5 **Cela** Angola
70B2 **Celaya** Mexico
Celebes = Sulawesi
27F6 **Celebes S** SE Asia
64C2 **Celina** USA
16D1 **Celje** Slovenia
18C2 **Celle** Germany
7A4 **Celtic S** British Islands
7B3 **Cemmaes Hd** *Pt* Wales
27G7 **Cendrawasih** *Pen* Indonesia
63D2 **Center** USA
67A1 **Center Hill L** USA
68D2 **Center Moriches** USA
67A2 **Center Point** USA
62A2 **Central** USA
8C3 **Central** *Region* Scotland
50B3 **Central African Republic** Africa
61D2 **Central City** Nebraska, USA
68A2 **Central City** Pennsylvania, USA
68E2 **Central Falls** USA
64B3 **Centralia** Illinois, USA
56A2 **Centralia** Washington, USA
47C1 **Central Kalahari Game Res** Botswana
42A3 **Central Makran Ra** *Mts* Pakistan
58B2 **Central Point** USA
27H7 **Central Range** *Mts* Papua New Guinea
68B1 **Central Square** USA
67A2 **Centreville** Alabama, USA
68B3 **Centreville** Maryland, USA
Ceram = Seram
Ceram Sea = Seram Sea
73J7 **Ceres** Brazil
47B3 **Ceres** South Africa
66B2 **Ceres** USA
14C2 **Cergy-Pontoise** France
16D2 **Cerignola** Italy
21D7 **Cernavodă** Romania
13D4 **Cernay** France
56C4 **Cerralvo** *I* Mexico
72C6 **Cerro de Pasco** Peru
69D3 **Cerro de Punta** *Mt* Puerto Rico
69C4 **Cerron** *Mt* Venezuela
74C5 **Cerros Colorados, Embalse** *Res* Argentina
16C2 **Cesena** Italy
20D4 **Cēsis** Latvia
18C3 **České Budějovice** Czech Republic
18D3 **Českomoravská Vyosina** *Region* Czech Republic
17F3 **Çeşme** Turkey
32E4 **Cessnock** Australia
16D2 **Cetina** *R* Croatia
15A2 **Ceuta** NW Africa
40C2 **Ceyhan** Turkey
40C2 **Ceyhan** *R* Turkey
40C2 **Ceylanpınar** Turkey
44C4 **Ceylon** *I* Indian Oc
Ceylon *Republic* **= Sri Lanka**
25L4 **Chaa-Khol** Russian Federation
14C2 **Chaâteaudun** France
13B4 **Chablis** France
72C5 **Chachapoyas** Peru
42C3 **Chachran** Pakistan
42C3 **Chachro** Pakistan
74D3 **Chaco** *State* Argentina
50B2 **Chad** *Republic* Africa
50B2 **Chad, L** C Africa
56C2 **Chadron** USA
28B3 **Chaeryŏng** N Korea
63E1 **Chaffee** USA
42A3 **Chagai** Pakistan
25P4 **Chagda** Russian Federation
42B2 **Chaghcharan** Afghanistan
36E5 **Chagos Arch** Indian Ocean
69L1 **Chaguanas** Trinidad
38E3 **Chāh Bahār** Iran
28A2 **Ch'aho** N Korea
30C2 **Chai Badan** Thailand
43F4 **Chāībāsa** India
30C2 **Chaiyaphum** Thailand
42C2 **Chakwal** Pakistan
72D7 **Chala** Peru
51D5 **Chalabesa** Zambia
42A2 **Chalap Dalam** *Mts* Afghanistan
57G2 **Chaleurs, B des** Canada
13C4 **Chalindrey** France
31C4 **Chaling** China
42D4 **Chālisgaon** India
27H5 **Challenger Deep** Pacific Ocean
13C3 **Challerange** France
58D2 **Challis** USA
13C3 **Châlons-sur-Marne** France
14C2 **Chalon sur Saône** France
28B2 **Chaluhe** China
18C3 **Cham** Germany
62A1 **Chama** USA
42B2 **Chaman** Pakistan
42D2 **Chamba** India
42D3 **Chambal** *R* India
60D2 **Chamberlain** USA
65D3 **Chambersburg** USA
14D2 **Chambéry** France
13B3 **Chambly** France
65E1 **Chambord** Canada
42A3 **Chambor Kalat** Pakistan
41F3 **Chamgordan** Iran
43E4 **Chāmpa** India
14C2 **Champagne** *Region* France
47D2 **Champagne Castle** *Mt* Lesotho
57E2 **Champaign** USA
43N2 **Champaran** *District* India
30D3 **Champassak** Laos
57F2 **Champlain,L** USA
44B3 **Chāmrājnagar** India
74B3 **Chañaral** Chile
54D3 **Chandalar** USA
54D3 **Chandalar** *R* USA
63E3 **Chandeleur Is** USA
42D2 **Chandīgarh** India
59D4 **Chandler** USA
43G4 **Chandpur** Bangladesh
42D5 **Chandrapur** India
47E1 **Changane** *R* Mozambique
51D5 **Changara** Mozambique
28B2 **Changbai** China
28B2 **Changbai Shan** *Mts* China
28B2 **Changchun** China
31C4 **Changde** China
28A3 **Changdo** N Korea
28A3 **Changhai** China
28A3 **Changhang** S Korea
28A3 **Changhowan** S Korea
26E4 **Changhua** Taiwan
28A4 **Changhŭng** S Korea
30D2 **Changjiang** China
31D3 **Chang Jiang** *R* China
28B2 **Changjin** N Korea
28A2 **Changjin** *R* N Korea
28A2 **Changjin Res** N Korea
28B3 **Changnyŏn** N Korea
31C4 **Changsha** China
31E3 **Changshu** China
31B2 **Changwu** China
28A3 **Changyŏn** N Korea
31C2 **Changzhi** China
31E3 **Changzhou** China
14B2 **Channel Is** British Isles
56B3 **Channel Is** USA
55N5 **Channel Port-aux-Basques** Canada
30C3 **Chanthaburi** Thailand
13B3 **Chantilly** France
55J3 **Chantrey Inlet** *B* Canada
63C1 **Chanute** USA
24J4 **Chany, Ozero** *L* Russian Federation
31D5 **Chao'an** China
31D3 **Chao Hu** *L* China
30C3 **Chao Phraya** *R* Thailand
15A2 **Chaouen** Morocco
31E1 **Chaoyang** China
73K6 **Chapada Diamantina** *Mts* Brazil
73K4 **Chapadinha** Brazil
70B2 **Chapala, L de** Mexico
21J5 **Chapayevo** Kazakhstan
74F3 **Chapecó** Brazil
7D3 **Chapel-en-le-Frith** England
67C1 **Chapel Hill** USA
69H1 **Chapeltown** Jamaica
55K5 **Chapleau** Canada
25U3 **Chaplino, Mys** *C* Russian Federation
20G5 **Chaplygin** Russian Federation
60C2 **Chappell** USA
76G3 **Charcot I** Antarctica
7C4 **Chard** England
38E2 **Chardzhou** Turkmenistan
14C2 **Charente** *R* France
50B2 **Chari** *R* Chad
50B2 **Chari Baguirmi** *Region* Chad
42B1 **Charikar** Afghanistan
61E2 **Chariton** *R* USA
73G2 **Charity** Guyana
42D3 **Charkhāri** India
13C2 **Charleroi** Belgium
57F3 **Charles,C** USA
64B3 **Charleston** Illinois, USA
63E1 **Charleston** Missouri, USA
57F3 **Charleston** S Carolina, USA
57E3 **Charleston** W Virginia, USA
59C3 **Charleston Peak** *Mt* USA
68B3 **Charles Town** USA
68D1 **Charlestown** USA
50C4 **Charlesville** Zaïre
32D3 **Charleville** Australia
14C2 **Charleville-Mézières** France
64B1 **Charlevoix** USA
64C2 **Charlotte** Michigan, USA
57E3 **Charlotte** N Carolina, USA
67B3 **Charlotte Harbor** *B* USA
57F3 **Charlottesville** USA
55M5 **Charlottetown** Canada
69K1 **Charlotteville** Tobago
34B3 **Charlton** Australia
57F1 **Charlton I** Canada
13D3 **Charmes** France
42C2 **Charsadda** Pakistan
32D3 **Charters Towers** Australia
14C2 **Chartres** France
74E5 **Chascomús** Argentina
28B2 **Chasong** N Korea
14B2 **Châteaubriant** France
14B2 **Châteaulin** France
13B4 **Châteauneuf-sur-Loire** France
14C2 **Châteauroux** France
13D3 **Château-Salins** France
14C2 **Château-Thierry** France
13C2 **Châtelet** Belgium
14C2 **Châtellerault** France
61E2 **Chatfield** USA
7F6 **Chatham** England
68E2 **Chatham** Massachusetts, USA
55M5 **Chatham** New Brunswick, Canada
68D1 **Chatham** New York, USA
64C2 **Chatham** Ontario, Canada
65D3 **Chatham** Virginia, USA
33H5 **Chatham Is** New Zealand
54E4 **Chatham Str** USA
14C2 **Châtillon** France
13B4 **Châtillon-Coligny** France
13C4 **Châtillon-sur-Seine** France
43E5 **Chatrapur** India
68C3 **Chatsworth** USA
67B2 **Chattahoochee** USA
67A2 **Chattahoochee** *R* USA
57E3 **Chattanooga** USA
30A1 **Chauk** Burma
43L2 **Chauka** *R* India
14D2 **Chaumont** France
13B3 **Chauny** France
30D3 **Chau Phu** Vietnam
44E4 **Chaura** *I* Nicobar Is, Indian Ocean
15A1 **Chaves** Portugal
20J4 **Chaykovskiy** Russian Federation
18C2 **Cheb** Czech Republic
20H4 **Cheboksary** Russian Federation
57E2 **Cheboygan** USA
19G2 **Chechersk** Belarus
28B3 **Chech'on** S Korea
63C1 **Checotah** USA
7C4 **Cheddar** England
30A2 **Cheduba I** Burma
34B1 **Cheepie** Australia
48B2 **Chegga** Mauritius
51D5 **Chegutu** Zimbabwe
58B1 **Chehalis** USA
28B4 **Cheju** S Korea
28B4 **Cheju Do** *I* S Korea
28B4 **Cheju Haehyŏp** *Str* S Korea
25P4 **Chekunda** Russian Federation
58B1 **Chelan,L** USA
21J8 **Cheleken** Turkmenistan
16B3 **Chélia, Dj** *Mt* Algeria
15C2 **Cheliff** *R* Algeria
38D1 **Chelkar** Kazakhstan
19E2 **Chełm** Poland
19D2 **Chełmno** Poland
7E4 **Chelmsford** England
7C4 **Cheltenham** England
20L4 **Chelyabinsk** Russian Federation
25M2 **Chelyuskin, Mys** *C* Russian Federation
51D5 **Chemba** Mozambique
18C2 **Chemnitz** Germ
68B1 **Chemung** *R* USA
42D2 **Chenab** *R* India/Pakistan
48B2 **Chenachen** Algeria
68C1 **Chenango** *R* USA
58C1 **Cheney** USA
63C1 **Cheney Res** USA
31D1 **Chengde** China
31A3 **Chengdu** China
31E2 **Chengshan Jiao** *Pt* China
28A3 **Chengzitan** China
31C4 **Chenxi** China
31C4 **Chen Xian** China
31D3 **Cheo Xian** China
72C5 **Chepén** Peru
7C4 **Chepstow** Wales
64A1 **Chequamegon B** USA
14C2 **Cher** *R* France
67C2 **Cheraw** USA
14B2 **Cherbourg** France
15C2 **Cherchell** Algeria
20K3 **Cherdyn** Russian Federation
25M4 **Cheremkhovo** Russian Federation
20F4 **Cherepovets** Russian Federation
21E6 **Cherkassy** Ukraine
21G7 **Cherkessk** Russian Federation
21E5 **Chernigov** Ukraine
19G2 **Chernobyl** Ukraine
21D6 **Chernovtsy** Ukraine
20K4 **Chernushka** Russian Federation
20C5 **Chernyakhovsk** Russian Federation
21H6 **Chernyye Zemli** *Region* Russian Federation
61D2 **Cherokee** Iowa, USA
62C1 **Cherokee** Oklahoma, USA
63D1 **Cherokees,L o'the** USA
43G3 **Cherrapunji** India
33F2 **Cherry** *I* Solomon Islands
25S3 **Cherskiy** Russian Federation
25Q3 **Cherskogo, Khrebet** *Mts* Russian Federation
20D5 **Cherven'** Belarus
19E2 **Chervonograd** Ukraine
65D3 **Chesapeake** USA
65D3 **Chesapeake B** USA
7D4 **Chesham** England
68D1 **Cheshire** USA
7C3 **Cheshire** *County* England
20H2 **Chëshskaya Guba** *B* Russian Federation
59B2 **Chester** California, USA
7C3 **Chester** England
64B3 **Chester** Illinois, USA
68D1 **Chester** Massachusets, USA
58D1 **Chester** Montana, USA
65D3 **Chester** Pennsylvania, USA
67B2 **Chester** S Carolina, USA
68D1 **Chester** Vermont, USA
68B3 **Chester** *R* USA
7D3 **Chesterfield** England
33E2 **Chesterfield, Îles** Nouvelle Calédonie
55J3 **Chesterfield Inlet** Canada
68B3 **Chestertown** USA
65F1 **Chesuncook L** USA
70D3 **Chetumal** Mexico
35B2 **Cheviot** New Zealand
10C2 **Cheviots** *Hills* England/Scotland
60C2 **Cheyenne** USA
60C2 **Cheyenne** *R* USA
60C3 **Cheyenne Wells** USA
43E3 **Chhapra** India
43G3 **Chhātak** Bangladesh
42D4 **Chhatarpur** India
42D4 **Chhindwāra** India
43F3 **Chhukha** Bhutan
51B5 **Chiange** Angola
30C2 **Chiang Kham** Thailand
30B2 **Chiang Mai** Thailand
31E5 **Chiayi** Taiwan
29E3 **Chiba** Japan
51B5 **Chibia** Angola
55L4 **Chibougamau** Canada
28B3 **Chiburi-jima** *I* Japan
47E1 **Chibuto** Mozambique
57E2 **Chicago** USA
64B2 **Chicago Heights** USA
54E4 **Chichagof I** USA
7D4 **Chichester** England
29C3 **Chichibu** Japan
26H4 **Chichi-jima** *I* Japan
57E3 **Chickamauga L** USA
63E2 **Chickasawhay** *R* USA
56D3 **Chickasha** USA
54D3 **Chicken** USA
72B5 **Chiclayo** Peru
56A3 **Chico** USA
74C6 **Chico** *R* Argentina
51D5 **Chicoa** Mozambique
65E2 **Chicopee** USA
55L5 **Chicoutimi** Canada
51D6 **Chicualacuala** Mozambique
44B3 **Chidambaram** India
55M3 **Chidley,C** Canada
67B3 **Chiefland** USA
48B4 **Chiehn** Liberia
51C4 **Chiengi** Zambia
13C3 **Chiers** *R* France
16C2 **Chieti** Italy
31D1 **Chifeng** China
73K7 **Chifre, Serra do** *Mts* Brazil
54C3 **Chigmit Mts** USA
47E1 **Chigubo** Mozambique
70B2 **Chihuahua** Mexico
62A3 **Chihuahua** *State* Mexico
44B3 **Chik Ballāpur** India
44B3 **Chikmagalūr** India
51D5 **Chikwawa** Malawi
30A1 **Chi-kyaw** Burma
44C2 **Chilakalūrupet** India
44B4 **Chilaw** Sri Lanka
34D1 **Childers** Australia
62B2 **Childress** USA
71C6 **Chile** *Republic* S America
51C5 **Chililabombwe** Zambia
43F5 **Chilka L** India
54F4 **Chilko L** Canada
74B5 **Chillán** Chile
61E3 **Chillicothe** Missouri, USA
64C3 **Chillicothe** Ohio, USA
43G3 **Chilmari** India
74B6 **Chiloé, Isla de** Chile
51D5 **Chilongozi** Zambia
58B2 **Chiloquin** USA
70C3 **Chilpancingo** Mexico
7D4 **Chiltern Hills** *Upland* England
64B2 **Chilton** USA
51D5 **Chilumba** Malawi
Chi-lung = Keelung
51D5 **Chilwa, L** Malawi
51D5 **Chimanimani** Zimbabwe
13C2 **Chimay** Belgium
24G5 **Chimbay** Uzbekistan
72C4 **Chimborazo** *Mt* Ecuador
72C5 **Chimbote** Peru
24H5 **Chimkent** Kazakhstan
51D5 **Chimoio** Mozambique
22F4 **China** *Republic* Asia
66D3 **China L** USA
66D3 **China Lake** USA
China, National Republic of = Taiwan
70D3 **Chinandega** Nicaragua
62B3 **Chinati Peak** *Mt* USA
72C6 **Chincha Alta** Peru
34D1 **Chinchilla** Australia
51D5 **Chinde** Mozambique
28A4 **Chindo** S Korea
43G4 **Chindwin** *R* Burma
51C5 **Chingola** Zambia
51B5 **Chinguar** Angola
48A2 **Chinguetti** Mauritius
28B3 **Chinhae** S Korea
51D5 **Chinhoyi** Zimbabwe
42C2 **Chiniot** Pakistan
28B3 **Chinju** S Korea
50C3 **Chinko** *R* Central African Republic
29C3 **Chino** Japan
51D5 **Chinsali** Zambia
16C1 **Chioggia** Italy
51D5 **Chipata** Zambia
51D6 **Chipinge** Zimbabwe
44A2 **Chiplūn** India
7C4 **Chippenham** England
64A1 **Chippewa** *R* USA
57D2 **Chippewa Falls** USA
64A1 **Chippewa,L** USA
7D4 **Chipping Norton** England
7C4 **Chipping Sodbury** England
72B4 **Chira** *R* Peru
44C2 **Chīrāla** India
51D6 **Chiredzi** Zimbabwe
50B1 **Chirfa** Niger
59E4 **Chiricahua Peak** *Mt* USA
70D4 **Chiriquí, G de** Panama
72B2 **Chiriquí, Lago de** Panama
17F2 **Chirpan** Bulgaria
72B2 **Chirripó Grande** *Mt* Costa Rica
51C5 **Chirundu** Zimbabwe
51C5 **Chisamba** Zambia
55L4 **Chisasibi** Canada

61E1 Chisholm USA
31B4 Chishui He R China
Chisimaio = Kismaayo
Chişinău = Kishinev
20H4 Chistopol Russian Federation
26E1 Chita Russian Federation
51B5 Chitado Angola
51B5 Chitembo Angola
29D2 Chitose Japan
44B3 Chitradurga India
42C1 Chitral Pakistan
72B2 Chitré Panama
43G4 Chittagong Bangladesh
42C4 Chittaurgarh India
44B3 Chittoor India
51C5 Chiume Angola
74D4 Chivilcoy Argentina
51D5 Chivu Zimbabwe
29B3 Chizu Japan
28A3 Choch'iwŏn S Korea
72D2 Chocontá Colombia
28A4 Ch'o-do I S Korea
74C5 Choele Choel Argentina
33E1 Choiseul I Solomon Islands
70B2 Choix Mexico
19D2 Chojnice Poland
29D3 Chokai-san Mt Japan
50D2 Choke Mts Ethiopia
25Q2 Chokurdakh Russian Federation
66B3 Cholame USA
66B3 Cholame Creek R USA
14B2 Cholet France
72A1 Choluteca Honduras
51C5 Choma Zambia
28A3 Chŏmch'ŏn S Korea
43F3 Chomo Yummo Mt China/India
18C2 Chomutov Czech Republic
25M3 Chona R Russian Federation
28B3 Ch'ŏnan S Korea
30C3 Chon Buri Thailand
28A2 Chonchon N Korea
72C4 Chone Ecuador
74B6 Chones, Archipiélago de las Chile
28A3 Chongdo S Korea
28B2 Ch'ŏngjin N Korea
28B3 Chŏngju N Korea
28B3 Ch'ŏngju S Korea
51B5 Chongoroi Angola
28A3 Chongpyong N Korea
31B4 Chongqing China
28A3 Chŏngsŏn S Korea
28B3 Chŏngŭp S Korea
28B3 Ch'ŏnju S Korea
43F3 Cho Oyu Mt China/Nepal
75B4 Chopim R Brazil
6C3 Chorley England
19F3 Chortkov Ukraine
28B3 Ch'ŏrwŏn S Korea
19D2 Chorzów Poland
28A2 Chosan N Korea
29E3 Chōshi Japan
18D2 Choszczno Poland
43E4 Chotanāgpur Region India
58D1 Choteau USA
48C1 Chott ech Chergui L Algeria
15C2 Chott El Hodna L Algeria
48C1 Chott Melrhir L Algeria
66B2 Chowchilla USA
25N5 Choybalsan Mongolia
7D4 Christchurch England
35B2 Christchurch New Zealand
47D2 Christiana South Africa
55M2 Christian,C Canada
55N3 Christianshåb Greenland
27D8 Christmas I Indian Ocean
24J5 Chu Kazakhstan
24J5 Chu R Kazakhstan
58D2 Chubbuck USA
74C6 Chubut R Argentina
74C6 Chubut State Argentina
20E4 Chudovo Russian Federation
54D3 Chugach Mts USA
28B3 Chūgoku-sanchi Mts Japan
60C2 Chugwater USA
74F4 Chui Uruguay
30C5 Chukai Malaysia
26G1 Chukchagirskoye, Ozero L Russian Federation
25T3 Chukotskiy Khrebet Mts Russian Federation
25U3 Chukotskiy Poluostrov Pen Russian Federation
30D2 Chu Lai Vietnam
59C4 Chula Vista USA
26F1 Chulman Russian Federation
72B5 Chulucanas Peru
72E7 Chulumani Bolivia
24K4 Chulym Russian Federation
25K4 Chulym R Russian Federation
25L4 Chuma R Russian Federation
42D2 Chumar India
25P4 Chumikan Russian Federation
30B3 Chumphon Thailand
28B3 Ch'unch'ŏn S Korea
43F4 Chunchura India
28B3 Ch'ungju S Korea
Chungking = Chongqing
28A4 Ch'ungmu S Korea
28B3 Chŭngsan N Korea
28A3 Chungwa N Korea
28C2 Chunhua China
51D4 Chunya Tanzania
25M3 Chunya R Russian Federation
28B2 Chunyang China
28A3 Ch'unyang S Korea
69L1 Chupara Pt Trinidad
74C2 Chuquicamata Chile
16B1 Chur Switzerland
43G4 Churāchāndpur India
25P3 Churapcha Russian Federation
55J4 Churchill Canada
55M4 Churchill R Labrador, Canada
55J4 Churchill R Manitoba, Canada
55J4 Churchill,C Canada
55M4 Churchill Falls Canada
54H4 Churchill L Canada
42C3 Chūru India
20K4 Chusovoy Russian Federation
20H4 Chuvash Republic Russian Federation
26D4 Chuxiong China
30D3 Chu Yang Sin Mt Vietnam
75B3 Cianorte Brazil
19E2 Ciechanów Poland
70E2 Ciego de Ávila Cuba
72D1 Ciénaga Colombia
70D2 Cienfuegos Cuba
19D3 Cieszyn Poland
15B2 Cieza Spain
40B2 Cihanbeyli Turkey
15B2 Cijara, Embalse de Res Spain
27D7 Cilacap Indonesia
62B1 Cimarron USA
62C1 Cimarron R USA
16C2 Cimone, Monte Mt Italy
17F1 Cîmpina Romania
15C1 Cinca R Spain
16D2 Cincer Mt Bosnia-Herzegovina
57E3 Cincinnati USA
17E1 Cindrelu Mt Romania
17F3 Cine R Turkey
13C2 Ciney Belgium
16B2 Cinto, Monte Mt Corsica, France
54D3 Circle Alaska, USA
60B1 Circle Montana, USA
64C3 Circleville USA
27D7 Cirebon Indonesia
7D4 Cirencester England
62C2 Cisco USA
70C3 Citlaltepetl Vol Mexico
47B3 Citrusdal South Africa
70B2 Ciudad Acuña Mexico
72F2 Ciudad Bolívar Venezuela
70B2 Ciudad Camargo Mexico
70C3 Ciudad del Carmen Mexico
15C2 Ciudadela Spain
72F2 Ciudad Guayana Venezuela
70B3 Ciudad Guzman Mexico
70B1 Ciudad Juárez Mexico
56C4 Ciudad Lerdo Mexico
70C2 Ciudad Madero Mexico
70B2 Ciudad Obregon Mexico
69C4 Ciudad Ojeda Venezuela
72F2 Ciudad Piar Venezuela
15B2 Ciudad Real Spain
15A1 Ciudad Rodrigo Spain
70C2 Ciudad Valles Mexico
70C2 Ciudad Victoria Mexico
16C2 Civitavecchia Italy
40D2 Cizre Turkey
7E4 Clacton-on-Sea England
54G4 Claire,L Canada
65D2 Clairton USA
67A2 Clanton USA
47B3 Clanwilliam South Africa
9C3 Clara Irish Republic
64C2 Clare USA
65E2 Claremont USA
63C1 Claremore USA
34D1 Clarence R Australia
35B2 Clarence R New Zealand
32C2 Clarence Str Australia
63D2 Clarendon USA
55N5 Clarenville Canada
54G4 Claresholm Canada
61D2 Clarinda USA
61E2 Clarion Iowa, USA
65D2 Clarion Pennsylvania, USA
70A3 Clarión I Mexico
65D2 Clarion R USA
37M4 Clarion Fracture Zone Pacific Ocean
57E3 Clark Hill Res USA
59C3 Clark Mt USA
64C2 Clark,Pt Canada
64C3 Clarksburg USA
57D3 Clarksdale USA
58C1 Clarkston USA
63D1 Clarksville Arkansas, USA
67A1 Clarksville Tennessee, USA
75B2 Claro R Brazil
74E5 Claromecó Argentina
61D3 Clay Center USA
8E2 Claymore Oilfield N Sea
56C3 Clayton New Mexico, USA
65D2 Clayton New York, USA
10B3 Clear, C Irish Republic
68A2 Clearfield Pennsylvania, USA
58D2 Clearfield Utah, USA
59B3 Clear L USA
61E2 Clear Lake USA
58B2 Clear Lake Res USA
60B2 Clearmont USA
57E4 Clearwater USA
58C1 Clearwater Mts USA
56D3 Cleburne USA
7D3 Cleethorpes England
6E2 Cleeton Oilfield N Sea
66B1 Clements USA
32D3 Clermont Australia
13B3 Clermont France
13C3 Clermont-en-Argonne France
14C2 Clermont-Ferrand France
13D2 Clervaux Luxembourg
63D2 Cleveland Mississippi, USA
57E2 Cleveland Ohio, USA
67B1 Cleveland Tennessee, USA
63C2 Cleveland Texas, USA
6D2 Cleveland County England
75B4 Clevelândia Brazil
58D1 Cleveland,Mt USA
10B3 Clew B Irish Republic
59E4 Clifton Arizona, USA
34D1 Clifton Australia
68C2 Clifton New Jersey, USA
34A1 Clifton Hills Australia
67B1 Clinch R USA
67B1 Clinch Mts USA
63D1 Clinton Arkansas, USA
54F4 Clinton Canada
68D2 Clinton Connecticut, USA
64A2 Clinton Iowa, USA
68E1 Clinton Massachusetts, USA
63D2 Clinton Mississippi, USA
63D1 Clinton Missouri, USA
67C2 Clinton N Carolina, USA
68C2 Clinton New Jersey, USA
62C1 Clinton Oklahoma, USA
54H3 Clinton-Colden L Canada
70B3 Clipperton I Pacific Ocean
6C3 Clitheroe England
72E7 Cliza Bolivia
9C3 Clogher Hd Pt Irish Republic
9B4 Clonakilty B Irish Republic
32D3 Cloncurry Australia
9C3 Clones Irish Republic
9C3 Clonmel Irish Republic
13E1 Cloppenburg Germany
57D2 Cloquet USA
75A4 Clorinda Argentina
60B2 Cloud Peak Mt USA
66A1 Cloverdale USA
66C2 Clovis California, USA
56C3 Clovis New Mexico, USA
21C6 Cluj Romania
17E1 Cluj-Napoca Romania
35A3 Clutha R New Zealand
7C3 Clwyd County Wales
7C3 Clwyd R Wales
55M2 Clyde Canada
35A3 Clyde New Zealand
6F1 Clyde Oilfield N Sea
68B1 Clyde USA
8C4 Clyde R Scotland
8C4 Clydebank Scotland
59C4 Coachella USA
62B3 Coahuila State Mexico
59C3 Coaldale USA
59B3 Coalinga USA
7D3 Coalville England
58D2 Coalville USA
75E1 Coaraci Brazil
72F5 Coari R Brazil
67A2 Coastal Plain USA
54E4 Coast Mts Canada
56A2 Coast Ranges Mts USA
8C4 Coatbridge Scotland
68C3 Coatesville USA
65E1 Coaticook Canada
55K3 Coats I Canada
76F1 Coats Land Region Antarctica
70C3 Coatzacoalcas Mexico
55L5 Cobalt Canada
70C3 Cobán Guatemala
32D4 Cobar Australia
34C3 Cobargo Australia
72E6 Cobija Bolivia
68C1 Cobleskill USA
55L5 Cobourg Canada
32C2 Cobourg Pen Australia
18C2 Coburg Germany
72C4 Coca Ecuador
75B1 Cocalinho Brazil
72E7 Cochabamba Bolivia
13D2 Cochem Germany
55K5 Cochrane Ontario, Canada
74B7 Cochrane, Lago Argentina/Chile
34B2 Cockburn Australia
6C2 Cockermouth England
68B3 Cockeysville USA
69H1 Cockpit Country,The Jamaica
47C3 Cockscomb Mt South Africa
70D3 Coco R Honduras/Nicaragua
67B3 Cocoa USA
48C4 Cocobeach Equatorial Guinea
44E3 Coco Channel Andaman Is/Burma
53K8 Coco, Isla del Costa Rica
75D1 Côcos Brazil
69L1 Cocos B Trinidad
27C8 Cocos Is Indian Ocean
37P4 Cocos Ridge Pacific Ocean
57F2 Cod,C USA
35A3 Codfish I New Zealand
55M4 Cod I Canada
15C1 Codi, Sierra del Mts Spain
73K4 Codó Brazil
56C2 Cody USA
27H8 Coen Australia
18B2 Coesfeld Germany
56B2 Coeur d'Alene USA
58C1 Coeur d'Alene L USA
13D1 Coevorden Netherlands
56D3 Coffeyville USA
34D2 Coff's Harbour Australia
47D3 Cofimvaba South Africa
16B2 Coghinas, Lago del Sardinia, Italy
14B2 Cognac France
68B1 Cohocton USA
68B1 Cohocton R USA
65E2 Cohoes USA
34B3 Cohuna Australia
72B2 Coiba, Isla Panama
74B7 Coihaique Chile
44B3 Coimbatore India
15A1 Coimbra Portugal
72B3 Cojimies Ecuador
58D2 Cokeville USA
32D4 Colac Australia
73K7 Colatina Brazil
76F6 Colbeck,C Antarctica
14B2 Colby USA
7E4 Colchester England
68D2 Colchester USA
8D4 Coldstream Scotland
64C2 Coldwater USA
58D1 Coleman Canada
64C2 Coleman Michigan, USA
62C2 Coleman Texas, USA
47D2 Colenso South Africa
9C2 Coleraine Northern Ireland
35B2 Coleridge,L New Zealand
47D3 Colesberg South Africa
72D7 Coles, Puerta Peru
66C1 Coleville USA
59B3 Colfax California, USA
63D2 Colfax Louisiana, USA
58C1 Colfax Washington, USA
74C7 Colhué Huapí, Lago Argentina
70B3 Colima Mexico
8B3 Coll I Scotland
34C1 Collarenebri Australia
67B2 College Park Georgia, USA
68B3 College Park Washington DC, USA
63C2 College Station USA
32A4 Collie Australia
32B2 Collier B Australia
13A2 Collines de l'Artois Hills France
13B3 Collines de la Thiérache Hills France
64C2 Collingwood Canada
35B2 Collingwood New Zealand
63E2 Collins Mississippi, USA
68A1 Collins New York, USA
54H2 Collinson Pen Canada
32D3 Collinsville Australia
64B3 Collinsville Illinois, USA
63C1 Collinsville Oklahoma, USA
14D2 Colmar France
6C3 Colne England
56B3 Colnett, Cabo C Mexico
18B2 Cologne Germany
75C3 Colômbia Brazil
65D3 Colombia USA
72D3 Colombia Republic S America
44B4 Colombo Sri Lanka
74E4 Colón Argentina
70D2 Colon Cuba
72C2 Colón Panama
Colón, Arch. de = Galapagos Islands
74E4 Colonia Uruguay
74C7 Colonia Las Heras Argentina
65D3 Colonial Heights USA
8B3 Colonsay I Scotland
69E5 Coloradito Venezuela
74D5 Colorado R Buenos Aires, Argentina
56D3 Colorado R Texas, USA
56B3 Colorado R Mexico/USA
56C3 Colorado State USA
62B2 Colorado City USA
56B3 Colorado Plat USA
56C3 Colorado Springs USA
68B3 Columbia Maryland, USA
63E2 Columbia Mississippi, USA
57D3 Columbia Missouri, USA
65D2 Columbia Pennsylvania, USA
57E3 Columbia S Carolina, USA
57E3 Columbia Tennessee, USA
56A2 Columbia R USA
58D1 Columbia Falls USA
54G4 Columbia,Mt Canada
58C1 Columbia Plat USA
47B3 Columbine,C South Africa
15C2 Columbretes, Islas Spain
57E3 Columbus Georgia, USA
64B3 Columbus Indiana, USA
57E3 Columbus Mississippi, USA
58E1 Columbus Montana, USA
56D2 Columbus Nebraska, USA
62A2 Columbus New Mexico, USA
57E2 Columbus Ohio, USA
63C3 Columbus Texas, USA
64B2 Columbus Wisconsin, USA
58C1 Colville USA
54C3 Colville R USA
35C1 Colville,C New Zealand
54F3 Colville L Canada
7C3 Colwyn Bay Wales
62C2 Comanche USA
66B1 Comanche Res USA
76G2 Comandante Ferraz Base Antarctica
70D3 Comayagua Honduras
13C4 Combeaufontaine France
9D2 Comber Northern Ireland
43G5 Combermere B Burma
9C3 Comeragh Mts Irish Republic
62C2 Comfort USA
43G4 Comilla Bangladesh
70C3 Comitán Mexico
13C3 Commercy France
55K3 Committee B Canada
16B1 Como Italy
74C7 Comodoro Rivadavia Argentina
16B1 Como, L di Italy
44B4 Comorin,C India
51E5 Comoros Is, Republic Indian Ocean
14C2 Compiègne France
75C3 Comprida, Ilha Brazil
15B2 Comunidad Valenciana Region Spain
43G3 Cona China
48A4 Conakry Guinea
14B2 Concarneau France
75E2 Conceiçao da Barra Brazil
73J5 Conceição do Araguaia Brazil
75D2 Conceiçao do Mato Dentro Brazil
74E4 Concepción Argentina
75A3 Concepción Brazil/Paraguay
74B5 Concepción Chile
74E2 Concepción Paraguay
70B2 Concepción del Oro Mexico
47A1 Conception B Namibia
56A3 Conception,Pt USA
75C3 Conchas Brazil
62B1 Conchas L USA
56C4 Conchos R Mexico
59B3 Concord California, USA
57F2 Concord New Hampshire, USA
67B1 Concord North Carolina, USA
74E4 Concordia Argentina
56D3 Concordia USA
58B1 Concrete USA

34D1 Condamine Australia
75D1 Condeuba Brazil
32D4 Condobolin Australia
58B1 Condon USA
13C2 Condroz *Mts* Belgium
67A2 Conecuh *R* USA
68B1 Conesus L USA
75A3 Confuso *R* Paraguay
7C3 Congleton England
46F8 Congo *R* W Africa
46F8 Congo *Republic* Africa
Congo,R = Zaire
64C1 Coniston Canada
64C2 Conneaut USA
65E2 Connecticut *R* USA
57F2 Connecticut *State* USA
65D2 Connellsville USA
64B3 Connersville USA
10B3 Conn, Lough *L* Irish Republic
34B2 Conoble Australia
58D1 Conrad USA
63C2 Conroe USA
75D3 Conselheiro Lafaiete Brazil
6D2 Consett England
30D4 Con Son *Is* Vietnam
21D7 Constanța Romania
16B3 Constantine Algeria
74B5 Constitución Chile
58D2 Contact USA
73K6 Contas *R* Brazil
13C3 Contrexéville France
54H3 Contwoyto L Canada
57D3 Conway Arkansas, USA
65E2 Conway New Hampshire, USA
67C2 Conway South Carolina, USA
7C3 Conwy Wales
7C3 Conwy *R* Wales
32C3 Coober Pedy Australia
67A1 Cookeville USA
54C3 Cook Inlet *B* USA
37L5 Cook Is Pacific Ocean
35B2 Cook,Mt New Zealand
9C2 Cookstown Northern Ireland
33G5 Cook Str New Zealand
32D2 Cooktown Australia
34C2 Coolabah Australia
34C1 Cooladdi Australia
34C2 Coolah Australia
34C2 Coolamon Australia
32B4 Coolgardie Australia
59D4 Coolidge USA
34C3 Cooma Australia
34C2 Coonabarabran Australia
34C2 Coonambie Australia
34B2 Coonbah Australia
44A3 Coondapoor India
34C1 Coongoola Australia
44B3 Coonoor India
34B1 Cooper Basin Australia
32C3 Cooper Creek Australia
34B1 Cooper Creek *R* Australia
67C3 Cooper's Town Bahamas
68C1 Cooperstown New York, USA
61D1 Cooperstown North Dakota, USA
34A3 Coorong,The Australia
34D1 Cooroy Australia
58B2 Coos B USA
58B2 Coos Bay USA
32D4 Cootamundra Australia
9C2 Cootehill Irish Republic
60C3 Cope USA
18C1 Copenhagen Denmark
74B3 Copiapó Chile
54D3 Copper Center USA
64C1 Copper Cliff Canada
64B1 Copper Harbor USA
54G3 Coppermine Canada
54G3 Coppermine *R* Canada
64C1 Coppermine Pt Canada
Coquilhatville = Mbandaka
74B3 Coquimbo Chile
17E2 Corabia Romania
67B3 Coral Gables USA
55K3 Coral Harbour Canada
32E2 Coral S Australia/Papua New Guinea
36J5 Coral Sea Basin Pacific Ocean
32E2 Coral Sea Island Territories Australia
34B3 Corangamite,L Australia
73G3 Corantijn *R* Guyana/Surinam
13B3 Corbeil-Essonnes France
64C3 Corbin USA
6D2 Corbridge England
7D3 Corby England
66C2 Corcoran USA
74B6 Corcovado, Golfo *G* Chile
15A1 Corcubíon Spain
57E3 Cordele USA
15A1 Cordillera Cantabrica *Mts* Spain
69C3 Cordillera Central *Mts* Dominican Republic/Haiti
75A4 Cordillera de Caaguazú Paraguay
70D3 Cordillera Isabelia *Mts* Nicaragua
72C2 Cordillera Occidental *Mts* Colombia
72C3 Cordillera Oriental *Mts* Colombia
34B1 Cordillo Downs Australia
74D4 Córdoba Argentina
70C3 Córdoba Mexico
15B2 Córdoba Spain
74D4 Córdoba *State* Argentina
54D3 Cordova USA
17D3 Corfu Greece
17D3 Corfu *I* Greece
75D1 Coribe Brazil
34D2 Coricudgy,Mt Australia
16D3 Corigliano Calabro Italy
32E2 Coringa Is Australia
17E3 Corinth Greece
57E3 Corinth Mississippi, USA
68D1 Corinth New York, USA
17E3 Corinth, Gulf of Greece
73K7 Corinto Brazil
10B3 Cork Irish Republic
40A1 Çorlu Turkey
73K7 Cornel Fabriciano Brazil
75B3 Cornélio Procópio Brazil
55N5 Corner Brook Canada
34C3 Corner Inlet *B* Australia
13D4 Cornimont France
65D2 Corning USA
16C2 Corno, Monte *Mt* Italy
55L5 Cornwall Canada
7B4 Cornwall *County* England
7B4 Cornwall,C England
54H2 Cornwall I Canada
55J2 Cornwallis I Canada
72E1 Coro Venezuela
73K4 Coroatá Brazil
72E7 Coroico Bolivia
75C2 Coromandel Brazil
44C3 Coromandel Coast India
35C1 Coromandel Pen New Zealand
35C1 Coromandel Range *Mts* New Zealand
66D4 Corona California, USA
62A2 Corona New Mexico, USA
72B2 Coronado, B. de Costa Rica
54G3 Coronation G Canada
74B5 Coronel Chile
75D2 Coronel Fabriciano Brazil
74E3 Coronel Oviedo Paraguay
74D5 Coronel Pringles Argentina
72D7 Coropuna *Mt* Peru
34C3 Corowa Australia
14D3 Corps France
56D4 Corpus Christi USA
63C3 Corpus Christi,L USA
9B3 Corraun Pen Irish Republic
27F5 Corregidor *I* Philippines
75D1 Corrente *R* Bahia, Brazil
75C1 Corrente *R* Goias, Brazil
75B2 Corrente *R* Mato Grosso, Brazil
75D1 Correntina Brazil
10B3 Corrib, Lough *L* Irish Republic
74E3 Corrientes Argentina
74E3 Corrientes *State* Argentina
72C2 Corrientes, Cabo *C* Colombia
70B2 Corrientes, Cabo *C* Mexico
63D2 Corrigan USA
32A4 Corrigin Australia
34C3 Corryong Australia
Corse = Corsica
8C4 Corsewall Pt Scotland
16B2 Corsica *I* Medit Sea
56D3 Corsicana USA
55O3 Cort Adelaer, Kap *C* Greenland
16B2 Corte Corsica, France
56C3 Cortez USA
16C1 Cortina d'Ampezzo Italy
65D2 Cortland USA
21G7 Çoruh *R* Turkey
21F7 Çorum Turkey
73G7 Corumbá Brazil
75C2 Corumbá *R* Brazil
75C2 Corumbaiba Brazil
58B2 Corvallis USA
48A1 Corvo *I* Azores
7C3 Corwen Wales
16D3 Cosenza Italy
51E5 Cosmoledo Is Seychelles
66D2 Coso Junction USA
15B2 Costa Blanca *Region* Spain
15C1 Costa Brava *Region* Spain
15B2 Costa Calída *Region* Spain
15B2 Costa de Almería *Region* Spain
15A2 Costa de la Luz *Region* Spain
15B2 Costa del Sol *Region* Spain
15C1 Costa Dorada *Region* Spain
66D4 Costa Mesa USA
70D3 Costa Rica *Republic* Central America
27F6 Cotabato Philippines
72E8 Cotagaita Bolivia
14D3 Côte d'Azur *Region* France
Côte D'Ivoire = Ivory Coast
13C4 Côte-d'Or *Department* France
13C3 Côtes de Meuse *Mts* France
7B4 Cothi *R* Wales
48C4 Cotonou Benin
72C4 Cotopaxi *Mt* Ecuador
7C4 Cotswold Hills *Upland* England
58B2 Cottage Grove USA
18C2 Cottbus Germany
59D4 Cottonwood USA
62C3 Cotulla USA
68A2 Coudersport USA
13B3 Coulommiers France
65D1 Coulonge *R* Canada
66B2 Coulterville USA
54B3 Council USA
56D2 Council Bluffs USA
8D3 Coupar Angus Scotland
19E1 Courland Lagoon *Lg* Lithuania/Russian Federation
Courtrai = Kortrijk
14B2 Coutances France
7D3 Coventry England
15A1 Covilhã Portugal
67B2 Covington Georgia, USA
64C3 Covington Kentucky, USA
63D2 Covington Louisiana, USA
65D3 Covington Virginia, USA
34C2 Cowal,L Australia
34B3 Cowangie Australia
65E1 Cowansville Canada
8D3 Cowdenbeath Scotland
34C3 Cowes Australia
7D4 Cowes England
58B1 Cowichan L Canada
58B1 Cowlitz *R* USA
34C2 Cowra Australia
73H7 Coxim Brazil
75B2 Coxim *R* Brazil
68D1 Coxsackie USA
43G4 Cox's Bazar Bangladesh
66B2 Coyote USA
60D2 Cozad USA
70D2 Cozumel, Isla de Mexico
34D1 Cracow Australia
19D2 Cracow Poland
47D3 Cradock South Africa
56C2 Craig USA
9C2 Craigavon Northern Ireland
18C3 Crailsheim Germany
17E2 Craiova Romania
65E2 Cranberry L USA
54G5 Cranbrook Canada
58C2 Crane Oregon, USA
62B2 Crane Texas, USA
68E2 Cranston USA
58B2 Crater L USA
58B2 Crater Lake Nat Pk USA
73K5 Crateús Brazil
73L5 Crato Brazil
60C2 Crawford USA
64B2 Crawfordsville USA
67B2 Crawfordville USA
7D4 Crawley England
58D1 Crazy Mts USA
7C4 Crediton England
54H4 Cree L Canada
13B3 Creil France
16C1 Cremona Italy
13B3 Crépy-en-Valois France
16C2 Cres *I* Croatia
58B2 Crescent USA
56A2 Crescent City USA
61E2 Cresco USA
61E2 Creston USA
67A2 Crestview USA
34B3 Creswick Australia
61D2 Crete USA
17E3 Crete *I* Greece
17E3 Crete,S of Greece
15C1 Creus, Cabo de *C* Spain
14C2 Creuse *R* France
7C3 Crewe England
8C3 Crianlarich Scotland
7B3 Criccieth Wales
74G3 Criciuma Brazil
8D3 Crieff Scotland
21E6 Crimea *Pen* Ukraine
75C2 Cristalina Brazil
75B1 Cristalina *R* Brazil
75C1 Crixás Brazil
75C1 Crixás Acu *R* Brazil
75B1 Crixás Mirim *R* Brazil
16D1 Croatia *Republic* Europe
63C2 Crockett USA
61D2 Crofton USA
32C2 Croker I Australia
8D3 Cromarty Scotland
7E3 Cromer England
35A3 Cromwell New Zealand
6D2 Crook England
57F4 Crooked *I* The Bahamas
56D2 Crookston USA
34C2 Crookwell Australia
34D1 Croppa Creek Australia
7C3 Crosby England
61E1 Crosby USA
47A1 Cross,C Namibia
57D3 Crossett USA
54E4 Cross Sd USA
67A1 Crossville USA
16D3 Crotone Italy
63D2 Crowley USA
66C2 Crowley,L USA
69K1 Crown Pt Tobago
34D1 Crows Nest Australia
32D2 Croydon Australia
7D4 Croydon England
36E6 Crozet Basin Indian Ocean
36D7 Crozet, Îles *Is* Indian Ocean
54F2 Crozier Chan Canada
74F3 Cruz Alta Brazil
69B3 Cruz, Cabo *C* Cuba
74D4 Cruz del Eje Argentina
75D3 Cruzeiro Brazil
72D5 Cruzeiro do Sul Brazil
34A2 Crystal Brook Australia
63D1 Crystal City Missouri, USA
62C3 Crystal City Texas, USA
64B1 Crystal Falls USA
51D5 Cuamba Mozambique
51C5 Cuando *R* Angola
51B5 Cuangar Angola
Cuango,R = Kwango,R
70B2 Cuauhtémoc Mexico
68A1 Cuba USA
70D2 Cuba *Republic* Caribbean Sea
51B5 Cubango *R* Angola
51B5 Cuchi Angola
51B5 Cuchi *R* Angola
7D4 Cuckfield England
72E3 Cucuí Brazil
72D2 Cúcuta Colombia
44B3 Cuddalore India
44B3 Cuddapah India
66D3 Cuddeback L USA
32A3 Cue Australia
72C4 Cuenca Ecuador
15B1 Cuenca Spain
70C3 Cuernavaca Mexico
63C3 Cuero USA
73G7 Cuiabá Brazil
75A1 Cuiabá *R* Brazil
75D2 Cuieté *R* Brazil
8B3 Cuillin Hills Scotland
51B4 Cuilo *R* Angola/Zaïre
51B5 Cuito *R* Angola
51B5 Cuito Cuanavale Angola
30D3 Cu Lao Hon *I* Vietnam
60C1 Culbertson Montana, USA
60C2 Culbertson Nebraska, USA
34C3 Culcairn Australia
34C1 Culgoa *R* Australia
70B2 Culiacán Mexico
67A2 Cullman USA
65D3 Culpeper USA
75B1 Culuene *R* Brazil
35B2 Culverden New Zealand
72F1 Cumaná Venezuela
57F3 Cumberland Maryland, USA
64A1 Cumberland Wisconsin, USA
57E3 Cumberland *R* USA
55M3 Cumberland Pen Canada
64C3 Cumberland Plat USA
55M3 Cumberland Sd Canada
8C4 Cumbernauld Scotland
6C2 Cumbria *County* England
59B3 Cummings USA
8C4 Cumnock Scotland
51B5 Cunene *R* Angola/Namibia
16B2 Cuneo Italy
32D3 Cunnamulla Australia
8D3 Cupar Scotland
17E2 Čuprija Serbia, Yugoslavia
69D4 Curaçao *I* Caribbean Sea
74B4 Curicó Chile
75B1 Curisevo *R* Brazil
74G3 Curitiba Brazil
34A2 Curnamona Australia
51B5 Curoca *R* Angola
73K7 Curvelo Brazil
68A2 Curwensville USA
63C1 Cushing USA
58E1 Custer Montana, USA
60C2 Custer S Dakota, USA
58D1 Cut Bank USA
67B2 Cuthbert USA
67B3 Cutler Ridge USA
43F4 Cuttack India
51B5 Cuvelai Angola
18B2 Cuxhaven Germany
64C2 Cuyahoga Falls USA
66C3 Cuyama *R* USA
72D6 Cuzco Peru
7C4 Cwmbran Wales
50C4 Cyangugu Zaïre
17E3 Cyclades *Is* Greece
40B3 Cyprus *Republic* Medit Sea
55M3 Cyrus Field B Canada
19C3 Czech Republic Europe
19D2 Częstochowa Poland

D

30C1 Da *R* Vietnam
26F2 Da'an China
45D3 Dab'a Jordan
45C3 Dabab, Jebel ed *Mt* Jordan
69C4 Dabajuro Venezuela
48B4 Dabakala Ivory Coast
50E3 Dabaro Somalia
31B3 Daba Shan *Mts* China
50D2 Dabat Ethiopia
42C4 Dabhoi India
31C3 Dabie Shan *U* China
48A3 Dabola Guinea
48B4 Dabou Ivory Coast
19D2 Dabrowa Górn Poland
Dacca = Dhākā
18C3 Dachau Germany
16C1 Dachstein *Mt* Austria
31A3 Dada He *R* China
67B3 Dade City USA
42B3 Dadhar Pakistan
42B3 Dadu Pakistan
26D3 Dadu He *R* China
27F5 Daet Philippines
31B4 Dafang China
30B2 Daga *R* Burma
48A3 Dagana Senegal
21H7 Daghestan Republic Russian Federation
27F5 Dagupan Philippines
43G3 Dagzê China
40B4 Dahab Egypt
25O5 Da Hinggan Ling *Mts* China
67B2 Dahlonega USA
42C4 Dāhod India
28A2 Dahongqi China
15C2 Dahra *Region* Algeria
21G8 Dahuk Iraq
28A2 Dahushan China
43E3 Dailekh Nepal
Dairen = Lüda
40B4 Dairût Egypt
26G4 Daitō Is Pacific Ocean
32C3 Dajarra Australia
48A3 Dakar Senegal
48A2 Dakhla Morocco
49E2 Dakhla Oasis Egypt
48C3 Dakoro Niger
61D2 Dakota City USA
17E2 Dakovica Serbia, Yugoslavia
17D1 Dakovo Croatia
20B3 Dal *R* Sweden
51C5 Dala Angola
48A3 Dalaba Guinea
31D1 Dalai Nur *L* China
26D2 Dalandzadgad Mongolia
30D3 Da Lat Vietnam
31A1 Dalay Mongolia
8D4 Dalbeattie Scotland
32E3 Dalby Australia
67A1 Dale Hollow L USA
12F7 Dalen Norway
6C2 Dales,The *Upland* England
67A2 Daleville USA
56C3 Dalhart USA
65F1 Dalhousie Canada
54E2 Dalhousie,C Canada
26D4 Dali China
31E2 Dalian China
8D4 Dalkeith Scotland
56D3 Dallas USA
58B1 Dalles,The USA
54E4 Dall I USA
43E4 Dalli Rajhara India
48C3 Dallol *Watercourse* Niger
8C3 Dalmally Scotland
16D2 Dalmatia *Region* Croatia
8C4 Dalmellington Scotland
26G2 Dal'nerechensk Russian Federation
48B4 Daloa Ivory Coast
31B4 Dalou Shan *Mts* China
8C4 Dalry Scotland
43E4 Dāltenganj India
6C2 Dalton England
67B2 Dalton Georgia, USA
68D1 Dalton Massachusetts, USA
55Q3 Dalton, Kap *C* Greenland

32C2 **Daly** *R* Australia
59B3 **Daly City** USA
32C2 **Daly Waters** Australia
42C4 **Damān** India
40B3 **Damanhûr** Egypt
32B1 **Damar** *I* Indonesia
50B3 **Damara** Central African Republic
32B1 **Damar, Kepulauan** *Is* Indonesia
40C3 **Damascus** Syria
68B3 **Damascus** USA
48D3 **Damaturu** Nigeria
41F2 **Damavand** Iran
51B4 **Damba** Angola
44C4 **Dambulla** Sri Lanka
41F2 **Damghan** Iran
Damietta = Dumyât
42D4 **Damoh** India
50E3 **Damot** Ethiopia
45C2 **Damour** Lebanon
32A3 **Dampier** Australia
45C3 **Danā** Jordan
66C2 **Dana,Mt** USA
48B4 **Danané** Liberia
30D2 **Da Nang** Vietnam
27C6 **Danau Toba** *L* Indonesia
27F7 **Danau Towuti** *L* Indonesia
31A3 **Danba** China
65E2 **Danbury** USA
68D1 **Danby** USA
43E3 **Dandeldhura** Nepal
44A2 **Dandeli** India
34C3 **Dandenong** Australia
28A2 **Dandong** China
47B3 **Danger Pt** *C* South Africa
50D2 **Dangila** Ethiopia
58D2 **Daniel** USA
55N4 **Daniel's Harbour** Canada
47C2 **Danielskuil** South Africa
55P3 **Dannebrogs Øy** *I* Greenland
35C2 **Dannevirke** New Zealand
68B1 **Dansville** USA
44C2 **Dantewāra** India
17F2 **Danube** *R* E Europe
57E2 **Danville** Illinois, USA
57E3 **Danville** Kentucky, USA
68B2 **Danville** Pennsylvania, USA
57F3 **Danville** Virginia, USA
Danzig = Gdańsk
31C4 **Dao Xian** China
31B4 **Daozhen** China
43H3 **Dapha Bum** *Mt* India
45B3 **Daphnae** *Hist Site* Egypt
26C3 **Da Qaidam** China
26F2 **Daqing** China
45D2 **Dar'a** Syria
40C3 **Dar'ā** Syria
41F4 **Dārāb** Iran
49D1 **Daraj** Libya
41F3 **Dārān** Iran
43F3 **Darbhanga** India
66C1 **Dardanelle** USA
63D1 **Dardanelle,L** USA
Dar-el-Beida = Casablanca
51D4 **Dar es Salaam** Tanzania
35B1 **Dargaville** New Zealand
67B2 **Darien** USA
69B5 **Darién, G of** Colombia/Panama
Darjeeling = Dārjiling
43F3 **Dārjiling** India
32D4 **Darling** *R* Australia
34C1 **Darling Downs** Australia
55L1 **Darling Pen** Canada
34B2 **Darlington** Australia
6D2 **Darlington** England
67C2 **Darlington** USA
18B3 **Darmstadt** Germany
49E1 **Darnah** Libya
34B2 **Darnick** Australia
54F3 **Darnley B** Canada
76G10 **Darnley,C** Antarctica
15B1 **Daroca** Spain
50C3 **Dar Rounga** *Region* Central African Republic
7C4 **Dart** *R* England
7C4 **Dartmoor** England
55M5 **Dartmouth** Canada
7C4 **Dartmouth** England
32D1 **Daru** Papua New Guinea
16D1 **Daruvar** Croatia
6C3 **Darwen** England
32C2 **Darwin** Australia
41F4 **Daryācheh-ye Bakhtegan** *L* Iran
41F4 **Daryācheh-ye Mahārlū** *L* Iran
41F3 **Daryācheh-ye Namak** *Salt Flat* Iran
21H8 **Daryācheh-ye Orūmīyeh** *L* Iran
41F4 **Daryācheh-ye Tashk** *L* Iran
41G4 **Dārzīn** Iran
41F4 **Dās** *I* UAE
31C3 **Dashennongjia** *Mt* China
41G2 **Dasht** Iran
41F3 **Dasht-e-Kavir** *Salt Desert* Iran
41G3 **Dasht-e Lut** *Salt Desert* Iran
29D2 **Date** Japan
42D3 **Datia** India
31A2 **Datong** China
31C1 **Datong** China
31A2 **Datong He** *R* China
27D6 **Datuk, Tanjung** *C* Indonesia
19E1 **Daugava** *R* Latvia
20D4 **Daugavpils** Latvia
55M1 **Dauguard Jensen Land** *Region* Canada
42A1 **Daulatabad** Afghanistan
42B2 **Daulat Yar** Afghanistan
42D3 **Daulpur** India
13D2 **Daun** Germany
44A2 **Daund** India
54H4 **Dauphin** Canada
68B2 **Dauphin** USA
14D3 **Dauphiné** *Region* France
63E2 **Dauphin I** USA
48C3 **Daura** Nigeria
42D3 **Dausa** India
44B3 **Dāvangere** India
27F6 **Davao** Philippines
27F6 **Davao G** Philippines
66A2 **Davenport** California, USA
57D2 **Davenport** Iowa, USA
7D3 **Daventry** England
72B2 **David** Panama
54D3 **Davidson Mts** USA
59B3 **Davis** USA
76G10 **Davis** *Base* Antarctica
55M4 **Davis Inlet** Canada
55N3 **Davis Str** Canada/Greenland
20K5 **Davlekanovo** Russian Federation
28A2 **Dawa** China
50E3 **Dawa** *R* Ethiopia
31A4 **Dawan** China
41F4 **Dawḩat Salwah** *B* Qatar/Saudi Arabia
30B2 **Dawna Range** *Mts* Burma/Thailand
54E3 **Dawson** Canada
67B2 **Dawson** Georgia, USA
60D1 **Dawson** N Dakota, USA
32D3 **Dawson** *R* Australia
54F4 **Dawson Creek** Canada
31A3 **Dawu** China
31C3 **Dawu** China
14B3 **Dax** France
31B3 **Daxian** China
31B5 **Daxin** China
31A3 **Daxue Shan** *Mts* China
31C4 **Dayong** China
45D2 **Dayr 'Alī** Syria
45D1 **Dayr 'Aṭīyah** Syria
40D2 **Dayr az Zawr** Syria
45D1 **Dayr Shumayyil** Syria
57E2 **Dayton** Ohio, USA
67A1 **Dayton** Tennessee, USA
63D3 **Dayton** Texas, USA
58C1 **Dayton** Washington, USA
57E4 **Daytona Beach** USA
31C4 **Dayu** China
31D2 **Da Yunhe** *R* China
58C2 **Dayville** USA
31B3 **Dazhu** China
47C3 **De Aar** South Africa
69C2 **Deadman's Cay** The Bahamas
40C3 **Dead S** Israel/Jordan
60C2 **Deadwood** USA
7E4 **Deal** England
47D2 **Dealesville** South Africa
64C2 **Dearborn** USA
54F3 **Dease Arm** *B* Canada
54E4 **Dease Lake** Canada
56B3 **Death V** USA
66D2 **Death Valley Nat Mon** USA
14C2 **Deauville** France
69L1 **Débé** Trinidad
19E2 **Dębica** Poland
19E2 **Dęblin** Poland
48B3 **Débo,L** Mali
50D3 **Debre Birhan** Ethiopia
19E3 **Debrecen** Hungary
50D2 **Debre Mark'os** Ethiopia
50D2 **Debre Tabor** Ethiopia
57E3 **Decatur** Alabama, USA
67B2 **Decatur** Georgia, USA
57E3 **Decatur** Illinois, USA
64C2 **Decatur** Indiana, USA
14C3 **Decazeville** France
65D1 **Decelles, Réservoir** Canada
47C1 **Deception** *R* Botswana
31A4 **Dechang** China
61E2 **Decorah** USA
48B3 **Dedougou** Burkina
51D5 **Dedza** Malawi
8C4 **Dee** *R* Dumfries and Galloway, Scotland
7C3 **Dee** *R* England/Wales
8D3 **Dee** *R* Grampian, Scotland
65D1 **Deep River** Canada
68D2 **Deep River** USA
66D2 **Deep Springs** USA
34D1 **Deepwater** Australia
55N5 **Deer Lake** Canada
56B2 **Deer Lodge** USA
58C2 **Deeth** USA
67A2 **De Funiak Springs** USA
26C3 **Dêgê** China
50E3 **Degeh Bur** Ethiopia
32A3 **De Grey** *R* Australia
50E2 **Dehalak Arch** *Is* Eritrea
41F3 **Deh Bīd** Iran
42B1 **Dehi** Afghanistan
48D1 **Dehibat** Tunisia
44B4 **Dehiwala-Mt Lavinia** Sri Lanka
41E3 **Dehlorān** Iran
42D2 **Dehra Dūn** India
43E4 **Dehri** India
50C3 **Deim Zubeir** Sudan
45C2 **Deir Abu Sa'īd** Jordan
45D1 **Deir el Ahmar** Lebanon
21C6 **Dej** Romania
64B2 **De Kalb** Illinois, USA
63D2 **De Kalb** Texas, USA
25Q4 **De Kastri** Russian Federation
50C4 **Dekese** Zaïre
50B3 **Dekoa** Central African Republic
56B3 **Delano** USA
59D3 **Delano Peak** *Mt* USA
47D2 **Delareyville** South Africa
64C2 **Delaware** USA
65D2 **Delaware** *R* USA
57F3 **Delaware** *State* USA
57F3 **Delaware B** USA
34C3 **Delegate** Australia
13C1 **Delft** Netherlands
13D1 **Delfzijl** Netherlands
51E5 **Delgado, C** Mozambique
62B1 **Delhi** Colorado, USA
42D3 **Delhi** India
65E2 **Delhi** New York, USA
40B1 **Delice** Turkey
70B2 **Delicias** Mexico
41F3 **Delījān** Iran
61D2 **Dell Rapids** USA
15C2 **Dellys** Algeria
66D4 **Del Mar** USA
12F8 **Delmenhorst** Germany
25R2 **De-Longa, Ostrova** *Is* Russian Federation
54B3 **De Long Mts** USA
34C4 **Deloraine** Australia
54H5 **Deloraine** Canada
67B3 **Delray Beach** USA
56C4 **Del Rio** USA
56B3 **Delta** USA
68C1 **Delta Res** USA
50D3 **Dembī Dolo** Ethiopia
13C2 **Demer** *R* Belgium
19G1 **Demidov** Russian Federation
62A2 **Deming** USA
17F2 **Demirköy** Turkey
63E2 **Demopolis** USA
24H4 **Dem'yanskoye** Russian Federation
14C1 **Denain** France
39E2 **Denau** Uzbekistan
7C3 **Denbigh** Wales
13C2 **Dendermond** Belgium
50D3 **Dendi** *Mt* Ethiopia
13B2 **Dèndre** *R* Belgium
31B1 **Dengkou** China
31C3 **Deng Xian** China
Den Haag = The Hague
69H1 **Denham,Mt** Jamaica
18A2 **Den Helder** Netherlands
15C2 **Denia** Spain
32D4 **Deniliquin** Australia
58C2 **Denio** USA
61D2 **Denison** Iowa, USA
56D3 **Denison** Texas, USA
21D8 **Denizli** Turkey
12F7 **Denmark** *Kingdom* Europe
76C1 **Denmark Str** Greenland/Iceland
69P2 **Dennery** St Lucia
8D2 **Dennis Head** *Pt* Scotland
27E7 **Denpasar** Indonesia
68C3 **Denton** Maryland, USA
56D3 **Denton** Texas, USA
32E1 **D'Entrecasteaux Is** Papua New Guinea
56C3 **Denver** USA
50B3 **Déo** *R* Cameroon
48D4 **Déo** *R* Cameroon/Nigeria
43F4 **Deoghar** India
42C5 **Deolāli** India
43M2 **Deoria** *District* India
42D1 **Deosai Plain** India
68A1 **Depew** USA
68C1 **Deposit** USA
25P3 **Deputatskiy** Russian Federation
63D2 **De Queen** USA
42B3 **Dera Bugti** Pakistan
42C3 **Dera Ghazi Khan** Pakistan
42C2 **Dera Ismail Khan** Pakistan
21H7 **Derbent** Russian Federation
32B2 **Derby** Australia
68D2 **Derby** Connecticut, USA
7D3 **Derby** England
63C1 **Derby** Kansas, USA
7D3 **Derby** *County* England
21F5 **Dergachi** Ukraine
10B3 **Derg, Lough** *L* Irish Republic
63D2 **De Ridder** USA
Derna = Darnah
9C3 **Derravaragh, L** Irish Republic
50E3 **Derri** Somalia
68E1 **Derry** USA
50D2 **Derudeb** Sudan
47C3 **De Rust** South Africa
68C1 **De Ruyter** USA
6D3 **Derwent** *R* England
34C4 **Derwent Bridge** Australia
72E7 **Desaguadero** *R* Bolivia
59C4 **Descanso** Mexico
58B2 **Deschutes** *R* USA
50D2 **Desē** Ethiopia
74C7 **Deseado** Argentina
74C7 **Deseado** *R* Argentina
48A1 **Deserta Grande** *I* Madeira
59C4 **Desert Center** USA
59D2 **Desert Peak** *Mt* USA
63D1 **Desloge** USA
57D2 **Des Moines** Iowa, USA
62B1 **Des Moines** New Mexico, USA
61E2 **Des Moines** *R* USA
21E5 **Desna** *R* Russian Federation
74B8 **Desolación** *I* Chile
64B2 **Des Plaines** USA
18C2 **Dessau** Germany
54E3 **Destruction Bay** Canada
17E1 **Deta** Romania
51C5 **Dete** Zimbabwe
13E2 **Detmold** Germany
57E2 **Detroit** USA
61D1 **Detroit Lakes** USA
30D3 **Det Udom** Thailand
17E1 **Deva** Romania
18B2 **Deventer** Netherlands
8D3 **Deveron** *R* Scotland
42C3 **Devikot** India
66C2 **Devil Postpile Nat Mon** USA
66C3 **Devils Den** USA
66C1 **Devils Gate** *P* USA
6E1 **Devil's Hole** *Region* N Sea
Devil's Island = Diable, Isla du
60D1 **Devils L** N Dakota, USA
62B3 **Devils L** Texas, USA
56D2 **Devils Lake** USA
7D4 **Devizes** England
42D3 **Devli** India
17E2 **Devoll** *R* Albania
7B4 **Devon** *County* England
55J2 **Devon I** Canada
32D5 **Devonport** Australia
43G3 **Dewangiri** Bhutan
42D4 **Dewās** India
47D2 **Dewetsdorp** South Africa
57E3 **Dewey Res** USA
63D2 **De Witt** USA
6D3 **Dewsbury** England
63E1 **Dexter** Missouri, USA
62B2 **Dexter** New Mexico, USA
31A3 **Deyang** China
41G3 **Deyhuk** Iran
41E3 **Dezfūl** Iran
31D2 **Dezhou** China
41E2 **Dezh Shāhpūr** Iran
45D3 **Dhab'i, Wadi edh** Jordan
41F4 **Dhahran** Saudi Arabia
43G4 **Dhākā** Bangladesh
45B1 **Dhali** Cyprus
44B3 **Dhamavaram** India
43E4 **Dhamtari** India
43F4 **Dhanbād** India
43E3 **Dhangarhi** Nepal
43M1 **Dhang Range** *Mts* Nepal
43F3 **Dhankuta** Nepal
42D4 **Dhār** India
44B3 **Dharmapuri** India
42D2 **Dharmsāla** India
48B3 **Dhar Oualata** *Desert Region* Mauritius
43E3 **Dhaulagiri** *Mt* Nepal
43F4 **Dhenkānāl** India
45C3 **Dhībān** Jordan
17F3 **Dhíkti Óri** *Mt* Greece
Dhodhekánisos = Dodecanese
17E3 **Dhomokós** Greece
44B2 **Dhone** India
42C4 **Dhoraji** India
42C4 **Dhrāngadhra** India
43F3 **Dhuburi** India
42C4 **Dhule** India
73H2 **Diable, Isle du** French Guiana
66B2 **Diablo,Mt** USA
59B3 **Diablo Range** *Mts* USA
73K7 **Diamantina** Brazil
32D3 **Diamantina** *R* Australia
75A1 **Diamantino** Brazil
43F4 **Diamond Harbour** India
66B1 **Diamond Springs** USA
58D2 **Diamondville** USA
41G4 **Dibā** UAE
51C4 **Dibaya** Zaïre
43G3 **Dibrugarh** India
62B2 **Dickens** USA
56C2 **Dickinson** USA
67A1 **Dickson** USA
65D2 **Dickson City** USA
21G8 **Dicle** *R* Turkey
42C3 **Dīdwāna** India
47E2 **Die Berg** *Mt* South Africa
48B3 **Diébougou** Burkina
13E3 **Dieburg** Germany
74C9 **Diego Ramírez, Islas** Chile
Diégo Suarez = Antsirañana
13D3 **Diekirch** Luxembourg
48B3 **Diéma** Mali
30C1 **Dien Bien Phu** Vietnam
18B2 **Diepholz** Germany
14C2 **Dieppe** France
13C2 **Diest** Belgium
13D3 **Dieuze** France
48D3 **Diffa** Niger
43H3 **Digboi** India
55M5 **Digby** Canada
14D3 **Digne-les-B.** France
14C2 **Digoin** France
27F6 **Digos** Philippines
32C1 **Digul** *R* Indonesia
43G3 **Dihang** *R* China/India
Dijlah = Tigris
14C2 **Dijon** France
50B3 **Dik** Chad
50E2 **Dikhil** Djibouti
45A3 **Dikirnis** Egypt
13B2 **Diksmuide** Belgium
24K2 **Dikson** Russian Federation
38E2 **Dilaram** Afghanistan
27F7 **Dili** Indonesia
30D3 **Di Linh** Vietnam
13E2 **Dillenburg** Germany
62C3 **Dilley** USA
50C2 **Dilling** Sudan
54C4 **Dillingham** USA
56B2 **Dillon** USA
68B2 **Dillsburg** USA
51C5 **Dilolo** Zaïre
43G3 **Dimāpur** India
Dimashq = Damascus
50C4 **Dimbelenge** Zaïre
48B4 **Dimbokro** Ivory Coast
17F2 **Dimitrovgrad** Bulgaria
20H5 **Dimitrovgrad** Russian Federation
45C3 **Dīmona** Israel
27F5 **Dinaget** *I* Philippines
43F3 **Dinajpur** India
14B2 **Dinan** France
13C2 **Dinant** Belgium
40B2 **Dinar** Turkey
50D2 **Dinder** *R* Sudan
44B3 **Dindigul** India
31B2 **Dingbian** China
43F3 **Dinggyê** China
10A3 **Dingle** Irish Republic
10A3 **Dingle B** Irish Republic
48A3 **Dinguiraye** Guinea
8C3 **Dingwall** Scotland
31A2 **Dingxi** China
31D2 **Ding Xian** China
30D1 **Dinh Lap** Vietnam
60B2 **Dinosaur** USA
66C2 **Dinuba** USA
48A3 **Diouloulou** Senegal
43G3 **Diphu** India
50E3 **Dirē Dawa** Ethiopia
32A3 **Dirk Hartog** *I* Australia
50B2 **Dirkou** Niger
34C1 **Dirranbandi** Australia
74J8 **Disappointment,C** South Georgia
58B1 **Disappointment,C** USA
32B3 **Disappointment,L** Australia
34B3 **Discovery B** Australia
27E5 **Discovery Reef** S China Sea
52J7 **Discovery Tablemount** Atlantic Ocean
40B4 **Dishna** Egypt
55N3 **Disko** *I* Greenland
55N3 **Disko Bugt** *B* Greenland
55N3 **Diskofjord** Greenland
65D3 **Dismal Swamp** USA
19F1 **Disna** *R* Belarus
67B3 **Disney World** USA
75C2 **Distrito Federal** Brazil
42C4 **Diu** India
73K8 **Divinópolis** Brazil
21G6 **Divnoye** Russian Federation
40C2 **Divriği** Turkey
66B1 **Dixon** California, USA
64B2 **Dixon** Illinois, USA
58D1 **Dixon** Montana, USA
54E4 **Dixon Entrance** *Sd* Canada/USA
41E3 **Diyālā** *R* Iraq

21G8 **Diyarbakır** Turkey
41E3 **Diz** *R* Iran
50B3 **Dja** *R* Cameroon
50B1 **Djado,Plat du** Niger
50B4 **Djambala** Congo
48C2 **Djanet** Algeria
48C1 **Djedi** *Watercourse* Algeria
48C1 **Djelfa** Algeria
50C3 **Djéma** Central African Republic
48B3 **Djenné** Mali
48B3 **Djibo** Burkina
50E2 **Djibouti** Djibouti
50E2 **Djibouti** *Republic* E Africa
50C3 **Djolu** Zaïre
48C4 **Djougou** Benin
50B2 **Djourab, Erg du** *Desert Region* Chad
50D3 **Djugu** Zaïre
12C2 **Djúpivogur** Iceland
15C2 **Djurdjura** *Mts* Algeria
25P2 **Dmitriya Lapteva, Proliv** *Str* Russian Federation
20F4 **Dmitrov** Russian Federation
Dnepr *R* Ukraine = **Dnieper**
21E6 **Dneprodzerzhinsk** Ukraine
21F6 **Dnepropetrovsk** Ukraine
20D5 **Dneprovskaya Nizmennost'** *Region* Belarus
21C6 **Dnestr** *R* Ukraine = **Dniester**
21E6 **Dnieper** *R* Ukraine
21C6 **Dniester** *R* Ukraine
20E4 **Dno** Russian Federation
50B3 **Doba** Chad
19E1 **Dobele** Latvia
32C1 **Dobo** Indonesia
17D2 **Doboj** Bosnia-Herzegovina
17F2 **Dobrich** Bulgaria
21E5 **Dobrush** Belarus
73K7 **Doce** *R* Brazil
74D2 **Doctor P P Peña** Paraguay
44B3 **Dod** India
44B3 **Doda Betta** *Mt* India
17F3 **Dodecanese** *Is* Greece
56C3 **Dodge City** USA
64A2 **Dodgeville** USA
50D4 **Dodoma** Tanzania
64B1 **Dog L** Canada
64C1 **Dog L** Canada
29B3 **Dōgo** *I* Japan
48C3 **Dogondoutchi** Niger
41D2 **Doğubayazit** Turkey
41F4 **Doha** Qatar
43G3 **Doilungdêqên** China
13D1 **Dokkum** Netherlands
29F2 **Dokuchayevo, Mys** *C* Russian Federation
32C1 **Dolak** *I* Indonesia
61D2 **Doland** USA
55L5 **Dolbeau** Canada
14D2 **Dole** France
7C3 **Dolgellau** Wales
68C1 **Dolgeville** USA
20K2 **Dolgiy, Ostrov** *I* Russian Federation
50E3 **Dolo Odo** Ethiopia
74E5 **Dolores** Argentina
60B3 **Dolores** *R* USA
54G3 **Dolphin and Union Str** Canada
74E8 **Dolphin,C** Falkland Islands
27G7 **Dom** *Mt* Indonesia
21K5 **Dombarovskiy** Russian Federation
12F6 **Dombås** Norway
13D3 **Dombasle-sur-Meurthe** France
17D1 **Dombóvár** Hungary
14B2 **Domfront** France
69E3 **Dominica** *I* Caribbean Sea
69C3 **Dominican Republic** Caribbean Sea
55L3 **Dominion,C** Canada
55N4 **Domino** Canada
26E1 **Domna** Russian Federation
16B1 **Domodossola** Italy
74B5 **Domuyo, Vol** Argentina
34D1 **Domville,Mt** Australia
8D3 **Don** *R* Scotland
21G6 **Don** *R* Russian Federation
9C2 **Donaghadee** Northern Ireland
Donau *R* Bulgaria = **Danube**
Donau *R* Austria/Germany = **Danube**
13E4 **Donaueschingen** Germany
18C3 **Donauwörth** Germany
15A2 **Don Benito** Spain
7D3 **Doncaster** England
51B4 **Dondo** Angola
51D5 **Dondo** Mozambique
44C4 **Dondra Head** *C* Sri Lanka
10B3 **Donegal** Irish Republic
9C2 **Donegal** *County* Irish Republic
10B3 **Donegal B** Irish Republic
9C2 **Donegal Mts** Irish Republic
9B3 **Donegal Pt** Irish Republic
21F6 **Donetsk** Ukraine
31C4 **Dong'an** China
32A3 **Dongara** Australia
31A4 **Dongchuan** China
30D2 **Dongfang** China
28B2 **Dongfeng** China
32A1 **Donggala** Indonesia
26C3 **Donggi Cona** *L* China
28A3 **Donggou** China
31C5 **Donghai Dao** *I* China
31A1 **Dong He** *R* China
30D2 **Dong Hoi** Vietnam
31C5 **Dong Jiang** *R* China
28A2 **Dongliao He** *R* China
28C2 **Dongning** China
50D2 **Dongola** Sudan
31D5 **Dongshan** China
26E4 **Dongsha Qundao** *I* China
31C2 **Dongsheng** China
31E3 **Dongtai** China
31C4 **Dongting Hu** *L* China
31B5 **Dongxing** China
31D3 **Dongzhi** China
63D1 **Doniphan** USA
16D2 **Donji Vakuf** Bosnia-Herzegovina
12G5 **Dönna** *I* Norway
59B3 **Donner P** USA
13D3 **Donnersberg** *Mt* Germany
47D2 **Donnybrook** South Africa
Donostia = San Sebatián
66B2 **Don Pedro Res** USA
8C4 **Doon, Loch** *L* Scotland
31A3 **Do Qu** *R* China
14D2 **Dorbirn** Austria
7C4 **Dorchester** England
55L3 **Dorchester,C** Canada
14C2 **Dordogne** *R* France
18A2 **Dordrecht** Netherlands
47D3 **Dordrecht** South Africa
68D1 **Dorest Peak** *Mt* USA
48B3 **Dori** Burkina
47B3 **Doring** *R* South Africa
7D4 **Dorking** England
13B3 **Dormans** France
18B3 **Dornbirn** Austria
8C3 **Dornoch** Scotland
8D3 **Dornoch Firth** *Estuary* Scotland
12H6 **Dorotea** Sweden
34D2 **Dorrigo** Australia
58B2 **Dorris** USA
7C4 **Dorset** *County* England
55L3 **Dorset, Cape** Canada
13D2 **Dorsten** Germany
18B2 **Dortmund** Germany
50C3 **Doruma** Zaïre
25N4 **Dosatuy** Russian Federation
42B1 **Doshi** Afghanistan
66B2 **Dos Palos** USA
48C3 **Dosso** Niger
24G5 **Dossor** Kazakhstan
57E3 **Dothan** USA
14C1 **Douai** France
50A3 **Douala** Cameroon
34D1 **Double Island Pt** Australia
62B2 **Double Mountain Fork** *R* USA
66C3 **Double Mt** USA
14D2 **Doubs** *R* France
35A3 **Doubtful Sd** New Zealand
48B3 **Douentza** Mali
56C3 **Douglas** Arizona, USA
67B2 **Douglas** Georgia, USA
6B2 **Douglas** Isle of Man, British Islands
47C2 **Douglas** South Africa
56C2 **Douglas** Wyoming, USA
67B1 **Douglas L** USA
13C2 **Doulevant-le-Château** France
13B2 **Doullens** France
75B2 **Dourada, Serra** *Mts* Brazil
75C1 **Dourada, Serra** *Mts* Brazil
73H8 **Dourados** Brazil
75B3 **Dourados** *R* Brazil
75B3 **Dourados, Serra dos** *Mts* Brazil
13B3 **Dourdan** France
15A1 **Douro** *R* Portugal
7D3 **Dove** *R* England
62A1 **Dove Creek** USA
65D3 **Dover** Delaware, USA
7E4 **Dover** England
65E2 **Dover** New Hampshire, USA
68C2 **Dover** New Jersey, USA
64C2 **Dover** Ohio, USA
7E4 **Dover,Str of** England/France
19G2 **Dovsk** Belarus
9C2 **Down** *County* Northern Ireland
68C3 **Downingtown** USA
9D2 **Downpatrick** Northern Ireland
68C1 **Downsville** USA
68C2 **Doylestown** USA
28B3 **Dōzen** *I* Japan
65D1 **Dozois, Réservoir** Canada
48A2 **Dr'aa** *Watercourse* Morocco
75B3 **Dracena** Brazil
13D1 **Drachten** Netherlands
68E1 **Dracut** USA
14D3 **Draguignan** France
60C1 **Drake** USA
51D6 **Drakensberg** *Mts* South Africa
47D2 **Drakensberg** *Mt* South Africa
52E7 **Drake Passage** Atlantic O/Pacific Ocean
17E2 **Dráma** Greece
12G7 **Drammen** Norway
12A1 **Drangajökull** *Ice cap* Iceland
16D1 **Drava** *R* Slovenia
13D1 **Drenthe** *Province* Netherlands
18C2 **Dresden** Germany
14C2 **Dreux** France
58C2 **Drewsey** USA
68A2 **Driftwood** USA
17E2 **Drin** *R* Albania
17D2 **Drina** *R* Bosnia-Herzegovina/Serbia, Yugoslavia
19F1 **Drissa** *R* Belarus
9C3 **Drogheda** Irish Republic
19E3 **Drogobych** Ukraine
9C3 **Droihead Nua** Irish Republic
7C3 **Droitwich** England
9C2 **Dromore** Northern Ireland
76F12 **Dronning Maud Land** *Region* Antarctica
54G4 **Drumheller** Canada
58D1 **Drummond** USA
64C1 **Drummond I** USA
65E1 **Drummondville** Canada
8C3 **Drumochter Pass** Scotland
19E2 **Druskininkai** Lithuania
25Q3 **Druzhina** Russian Federation
61E1 **Dryberry L** Canada
55J5 **Dryden** Canada
68B1 **Dryden** USA
69H1 **Dry Harbour Mts** Jamaica
30B3 **Duang** *I* Burma
40C4 **Dubā** Saudi Arabia
41G4 **Dubai** UAE
54H3 **Dubawnt** *R* Canada
54H3 **Dubawnt L** Canada
32D4 **Dubbo** Australia
9C3 **Dublin** Irish Republic
67B2 **Dublin** USA
9C3 **Dublin** *County* Irish Republic
20F4 **Dubna** Russian Federation
21D5 **Dubno** Ukraine
58D2 **Dubois** Idaho, USA
65D2 **Du Bois** USA
58E2 **Dubois** Wyoming, USA
19F3 **Dubossary** Moldavia
19F2 **Dubrovica** Ukraine
17D2 **Dubrovnik** Croatia
57D2 **Dubuque** USA
59D2 **Duchesne** USA
67A1 **Duck** *R* USA
66C3 **Ducor** USA
13D3 **Dudelange** Luxembourg
24K3 **Dudinka** Russian Federation
7C3 **Dudley** England
25L2 **Dudypta** *R* Russian Federation
48B4 **Duekoué** Ivory Coast
15B1 **Duero** *R* Spain
33F1 **Duff Is** Solomon Islands
8D3 **Dufftown** Scotland
16C2 **Dugi Otok** *I* Croatia
18B2 **Duisburg** Germany
47E1 **Duiwelskloof** South Africa
41E3 **Dūkan** Iraq
50D3 **Duk Faiwil** Sudan
41F4 **Dukhān** Qatar
31A4 **Dukou** China
26C3 **Dulan** China
70D4 **Dulce, Golfo** Costa Rica
43G4 **Dullabchara** India
13D2 **Dülmen** Germany
57D2 **Duluth** USA
7C4 **Dulverton** England
45D2 **Dūmā** Syria
27D6 **Dumai** Indonesia
56C3 **Dumas** USA
45D2 **Ḑumayr** Syria
8C4 **Dumbarton** Scotland
48B1 **Dumer Rbia** Morocco
8D4 **Dumfries** Scotland
8C4 **Dumfries and Galloway** *Region* Scotland
43F4 **Dumka** India
65D1 **Dumoine,L** Canada
76G8 **Dumont d'Urville** *Base* Antarctica
49F1 **Dumyat** Egypt
Dunărea *R* Romania = **Danube**
9C3 **Dunary Head** *Pt* Irish Republic
Dunav *R* Bulgaria = **Danube**
Dunav *R* Croatia/Serbia = **Danube**
28C2 **Dunay** Russian Federation
19F3 **Dunayevtsy** Ukraine
8D4 **Dunbar** Scotland
63C2 **Duncan** USA
68B2 **Duncannon** USA
44E3 **Duncan Pass** *Chan* Andaman Islands
8D2 **Duncansby Head** *Pt* Scotland
9C2 **Dundalk** Irish Republic
68B3 **Dundalk** USA
9C3 **Dundalk B** Irish Republic
55M2 **Dundas** Greenland
54G2 **Dundas Pen** Canada
27G8 **Dundas Str** Australia
47E2 **Dundee** South Africa
8D3 **Dundee** Scotland
68B1 **Dundee** USA
34B1 **Dundoo** Australia
9D2 **Dundrum B** Northern Ireland
43M2 **Dundwa Range** *Mts* Nepal
33G5 **Dunedin** New Zealand
67B3 **Dunedin** USA
34C2 **Dunedoo** Australia
8D3 **Dunfermline** Scotland
9C2 **Dungannon** Northern Ireland
42C4 **Dūngarpur** India
9C3 **Dungarvan** Irish Republic
7E4 **Dungeness** *Pen* England
34D2 **Dungog** Australia
50C3 **Dungu** Zaïre
50D1 **Dungunab** Sudan
28B2 **Dunhua** China
26C2 **Dunhuang** China
8D3 **Dunkeld** Scotland
Dunkerque = Dunkirk
13B2 **Dunkirk** France
57F2 **Dunkirk** USA
50D2 **Dunkur** Ethiopia
48B4 **Dunkwa** Ghana
10B3 **Dun Laoghaire** Irish Republic
9B4 **Dunmanus** Irish Republic
68C2 **Dunmore** USA
69B1 **Dunmore Town** The Bahamas
67C1 **Dunn** USA
8D2 **Dunnet Head** *Pt* Scotland
60C2 **Dunning** USA
8C4 **Dunoon** Scotland
8D4 **Duns** Scotland
60C1 **Dunseith** USA
58B2 **Dunsmuir** USA
35A2 **Dunstan Mts** New Zealand
13C3 **Dun-sur-Meuse** France
31D1 **Duolun** China
60C1 **Dupree** USA
64B3 **Du Quoin** USA
45C3 **Dura** Israel
14D3 **Durance** *R* France
64A2 **Durand** USA
70B2 **Durango** Mexico
15B1 **Durango** Spain
56C3 **Durango** USA
56D3 **Durant** USA
45D1 **Duraykīsh** Syria
74E4 **Durazno** Uruguay
47E2 **Durban** South Africa
13D2 **Duren** Germany
43E4 **Durg** India
43F4 **Durgapur** India
6D2 **Durham** England
57F3 **Durham** N Carolina, USA
68E1 **Durham** New Hampshire, USA
6D2 **Durham** *County* England
34B1 **Durham Downs** Australia
17D2 **Durmitor** *Mt* Montenegro, Yugoslavia
8C2 **Durness** Scotland
17D2 **Durrës** Albania
34B1 **Durrie** Australia
17F3 **Dursunbey** Turkey
35B2 **D'Urville I** New Zealand
41H2 **Dushak** Turkmenistan
31B4 **Dushan** China
39E2 **Dushanbe** Tajikistan
68B2 **Dushore** USA
35A3 **Dusky Sd** New Zealand
18B2 **Düsseldorf** Germany
59D3 **Dutton,Mt** USA
31B4 **Duyun** China
40B1 **Düzce** Turkey
20F2 **Dvinskaya Guba** *B* Russian Federation
42B4 **Dwārka** India
58C1 **Dworshak Res** USA
57E3 **Dyersburg** USA
7B3 **Dyfed** *County* Wales
21G7 **Dykh Tau** *Mt* Russian Federation
34B1 **Dynevor Downs** Australia
26C2 **Dzag** Mongolia
26E2 **Dzamīn Üüd** Mongolia
51E5 **Dzaoudzi** Mayotte, Indian Ocean
26C2 **Dzavhan Gol** *R* Mongolia
20G4 **Dzerzhinsk** Russian Federation
25O4 **Dzhalinda** Russian Federation
24J5 **Dzhambul** Kazakhstan
21E6 **Dzhankoy** Ukraine
24H5 **Dzhezkazgan** Kazakhstan
42B1 **Dzhilikul'** Tajikistan
25P4 **Dzhugdzhur, Khrebet** *Mts* Russian Federation
24J5 **Dzhungarskiy Alatau** *Mts* Kazakhstan
18D2 **Dzierzoniów** Poland
39G1 **Dzungaria Basin** China
25L5 **Dzüyl** Mongolia

E

55K4 **Eabamet L** Canada
60B3 **Eagle** Colorado, USA
60C1 **Eagle Butte** USA
58B2 **Eagle L** California, USA
65F1 **Eagle L** Maine, USA
65F1 **Eagle Lake** USA
63C2 **Eagle Mountain L** USA
56C4 **Eagle Pass** USA
62A2 **Eagle Peak** *Mt* USA
54E3 **Eagle Plain** Canada
59C3 **Earlimart** USA
8D3 **Earn** *R* Scotland
8C3 **Earn, Loch** *L* Scotland
59D4 **Earp** USA
62B2 **Earth** USA
6D2 **Easingwold** England
67B2 **Easley** USA
65D2 **East Aurora** USA
63E2 **East B** USA
7E4 **Eastbourne** England
68C1 **East Branch Delaware** *R* USA
33G4 **East C** New Zealand
64B2 **East Chicago** USA
26F3 **East China Sea** China/Japan
7E3 **East Dereham** England
37O6 **Easter I** Pacific Ocean
51C7 **Eastern Cape** *Province* South Africa
43E5 **Eastern Ghats** *Mts* India
51C6 **Eastern Transvaal** *Province* South Africa
74E8 **East Falkland** *Is* Falkland Islands
59C3 **Eastgate** USA
61D1 **East Grand Forks** USA
7D4 **East Grinstead** England
68D1 **Easthampton** USA
68D2 **East Hampton** USA
8C4 **East Kilbride** Scotland
64B2 **East Lake** USA
7D4 **Eastleigh** England
64C2 **East Liverpool** USA
47D3 **East London** South Africa
55L4 **Eastmain** Canada
55L4 **Eastmain** *R* Canada
67B2 **Eastman** USA
64A2 **East Moline** USA
65D3 **Easton** Maryland, USA
65D2 **Easton** Pennsylvania, USA
68C2 **East Orange** USA
37O5 **East Pacific Ridge** Pacific Ocean
37O4 **East Pacific Rise** Pacific Ocean
67B2 **East Point** USA
65F2 **Eastport** USA
7D3 **East Retford** England
67A1 **East Ridge** USA
57D3 **East St Louis** USA
25R2 **East Siberian S** Russian Federation
7E4 **East Sussex** *County* England
65D3 **Eastville** USA
66C1 **East Walker** *R* USA
67B2 **Eatonton** USA
61E2 **Eau Claire** USA
27H6 **Eauripik** *I* Pacific Ocean
7C4 **Ebbw Vale** Wales
50B3 **Ebebiyin** Equatorial Guinea
68A2 **Ebensburg** USA
13E3 **Eberbach** Germany
18C2 **Eberswalde** Germany
29D2 **Ebetsu** Japan
31A4 **Ebian** China
24K5 **Ebinur** *L* China

16D2 **Eboli** Italy
50B3 **Ebolowa** Cameroon
15B1 **Ebro** *R* Spain
40A1 **Eceabat** Turkey
15C2 **Ech Cheliff** Algeria
31D2 **Eching** China
58C1 **Echo** USA
54G3 **Echo Bay** Canada
13D3 **Echternach** Luxembourg
34B3 **Echuca** Australia
15A2 **Ecija** Spain
55K2 **Eclipse Sd** Canada
72C4 **Ecuador** *Republic* S America
50E2 **Ēd** Eritrea
8D2 **Eday** *I* Scotland
50C2 **Ed Da'ein** Sudan
50D2 **Ed Damer** Sudan
50D2 **Ed Debba** Sudan
8C2 **Eddrachillis B** Scotland
50D2 **Ed Dueim** Sudan
34C4 **Eddystone Pt** Australia
13C1 **Ede** Netherlands
50A3 **Edea** Cameroon
34C3 **Eden** Australia
62C2 **Eden** Texas, USA
58E2 **Eden** Wyoming, USA
6C2 **Eden** *R* England
47D2 **Edenburg** South Africa
35A3 **Edendale** New Zealand
9C3 **Edenderry** Irish Republic
13D3 **Edenkoben** Germany
13E2 **Eder** *R* Germany
60D1 **Edgeley** USA
55M3 **Edgell I** Canada
60C2 **Edgemont** USA
24D2 **Edgeøya** *I* Svalbard, Norway
68B3 **Edgewood** USA
45C3 **Edh Dhahiriya** Israel
17E2 **Edhessa** Greece
62C3 **Edinburg** USA
8D3 **Edinburgh** Scotland
21D7 **Edirne** Turkey
66C3 **Edison** USA
67B2 **Edisto** *R* USA
58B1 **Edmonds** USA
54G4 **Edmonton** Canada
60D1 **Edmore** USA
55M5 **Edmundston** Canada
63C3 **Edna** USA
16C1 **Edolo** Italy
45C3 **Edom** *Region* Jordan
21D8 **Edremit** Turkey
17F3 **Edremit Körfezi** *B* Turkey
26C2 **Edrengiyn Nuruu** *Mts* Mongolia
54G4 **Edson** Canada
34B3 **Edward** *R* Australia
50C4 **Edward,L** Uganda/Zaïre
66D3 **Edwards** USA
56C3 **Edwards Plat** USA
64B3 **Edwardsville** USA
13B2 **Eeklo** Belgium
33F2 **Efate** *I* Vanuatu
57E3 **Effingham** USA
16C3 **Egadi,I** Sicily, Italy
59D3 **Egan Range** *Mts* USA
55N3 **Egedesminde** Greenland
54C4 **Egegik** USA
19E3 **Eger** Hungary
12F7 **Egersund** Norway
13E2 **Eggegebirge** *Mts* Germany
68C3 **Egg Harbor City** USA
54G2 **Eglinton I** Canada
35B1 **Egmont,C** New Zealand
35B1 **Egmont,Mt** New Zealand
6C2 **Egremont** England
40B2 **Eğridir Gölü** *L* Turkey
6D2 **Egton** England
75C1 **Eguas** *R* Brazil
25U3 **Egvekinot** Russian Federation
49E2 **Egypt** *Republic* Africa
15B1 **Eibar** Spain
34D1 **Eidsvold** Australia
13D2 **Eifel** *Region* Germany
8B3 **Eigg** *I* Scotland
39F5 **Eight Degree Chan** Indian Ocean
32B2 **Eighty Mile Beach** Australia
34C3 **Eildon,L** Australia
18B2 **Eindhoven** Netherlands
45C3 **Ein Yahav** Israel
18C2 **Eisenach** Germany
18C3 **Eisenerz** Austria
13D2 **Eitorf** Germany
31A1 **Ejin qi** China
60C1 **Ekalaka** USA
35C2 **Eketahuna** New Zealand
24J4 **Ekibastuz** Kazakhstan
25P4 **Ekimchan** Russian Federation
12H7 **Eksjö** Sweden
57E1 **Ekwan** *R* Canada
45A3 **El Abbâsa** Egypt
40A3 **El'Alamein** Egypt
47D2 **Elands** *R* South Africa
47C3 **Elands Berg** *Mt* South Africa
40B3 **El'Arîsh** Egypt
40B4 **Elat** Israel
50C2 **El' Atrun Oasis** Sudan
21F8 **Elazığ** Turkey
40C3 **El Azraq** Jordan
16C2 **Elba** *I* Italy
49F2 **El Balyana** Egypt
72D2 **El Banco** Colombia
17E2 **Elbasan** Albania
69D5 **El Baúl** Venezuela
18C2 **Elbe** *R* Germany
45D1 **El Beqa'a** *R* Lebanon
64B2 **Elberta** USA
56C3 **Elbert,Mt** USA
67B2 **Elberton** USA
14C2 **Elbeuf** France
40C2 **Elbistan** Turkey
19D2 **Elblag** Poland
74B6 **El Bolsón** Argentina
61D1 **Elbow Lake** USA
21G7 **Elbrus** *Mt* Russian Federation
Elburz Mts = Reshteh-ye Alborz
59C4 **El Cajon** USA
63C3 **El Campo** USA
59C4 **El Centro** USA
15B2 **Elche** Spain
74C5 **El Chocón, Embalse** *Res* Argentina
15B2 **Elda** Spain
25P3 **El'dikan** Russian Federation
72C3 **El Diviso** Colombia
48B2 **El Djouf** *Desert Region* Mauritius
63D1 **Eldon** USA
75B4 **Eldorado** Argentina
57D3 **El Dorado** Arkansas, USA
75C3 **Eldorado** Brazil
56D3 **El Dorado** Kansas, USA
70B2 **El Dorado** Mexico
62B2 **Eldorado** Texas, USA
72F2 **El Dorado** Venezuela
50D3 **Eldoret** Kenya
68A2 **Eldred** USA
45C1 **Elea, C** Cyprus
66C1 **Eleanor,L** USA
58D2 **Electric Peak** *Mt* USA
48B2 **El Eglab** *Region* Algeria
62A2 **Elephant Butte Res** USA
40D2 **Eleşkirt** Turkey
16B3 **El Eulma** Algeria
57F4 **Eleuthera** *I* The Bahamas
40B4 **El Faiyûm** Egypt
48B2 **El Farsia** *Well* Morocco
50C2 **El Fasher** Sudan
40B4 **El Fashn** Egypt
15A1 **El Ferrol** Spain
45B3 **El Firdân** Egypt
50C2 **El Fula** Sudan
48C1 **El Gassi** Algeria
50D2 **El Geteina** Sudan
50D2 **El Gezīra** *Region* Sudan
45C3 **El Ghor** *V* Israel/Jordan
57E2 **Elgin** Illinois, USA
60C1 **Elgin** N Dakota, USA
8D3 **Elgin** Scotland
40B3 **El Gîza** Egypt
48C1 **El Golea** Algeria
59D4 **El Golfo de Santa Clara** Mexico
50D3 **Elgon,Mt** Kenya/Uganda
50E3 **El Goran** Ethiopia
48B2 **El Guettara** *Well* Mali
48B2 **El Hank** *Region* Mauritius
48B2 **El Haricha** *Desert Region* Mali
40A4 **El Harra** Egypt
15C2 **El Harrach** Algeria
50D2 **El Hawata** Sudan
40B4 **El'Igma** *Desert Region* Egypt
Elisabethville = Lubumbashi
12K6 **Elisenvaara** Russian Federation
El Iskandarîya = Alexandria
21G6 **Elista** Russian Federation
32C4 **Elizabeth** Australia
65E2 **Elizabeth** USA
47B2 **Elizabeth B** Namibia
57F3 **Elizabeth City** USA
68E2 **Elizabeth Is** USA
67B1 **Elizabethton** Tennessee, USA
64B3 **Elizabethtown** Kentucky, USA
67C2 **Elizabethtown** N Carolina, USA
68B2 **Elizabethtown** Pennsylvania, USA
48B1 **El Jadida** Morocco
40C3 **El Jafr** Jordan
45D3 **El Jafr** *L* Jordan
50D2 **El Jebelein** Sudan
48D1 **El Jem** Tunisia
19E2 **Ełk** Poland
68C3 **Elk** *R* Maryland/Penn, USA
64C3 **Elk** *R* W Virginia, USA
61E2 **Elkader** USA
16B3 **El Kala** Algeria
50D2 **El Kamlin** Sudan
48C1 **El Kef** Tunisia
66B1 **Elk Grove** USA
El Khalil = Hebron Israel
45A3 **El Khânka** Egypt
40B4 **El Khârga** Egypt
40B4 **El-Khârga Oasis** Egypt
64B2 **Elkhart** USA
48B2 **El Khenachich** *Desert Region* Mali
61D2 **Elkhorn** *R* USA
17F2 **Elkhovo** Bulgaria
65D3 **Elkins** USA
68B2 **Elkland** USA
60B2 **Elk Mt** USA
58C1 **Elko** Canada
56B2 **Elko** USA
16B3 **El Kroub** Algeria
68C3 **Elkton** USA
45B3 **El Kûbri** Egypt
40B3 **El Kuntilla** Egypt
50C2 **El Lagowa** Sudan
54H2 **Ellef Ringnes I** Canada
60D1 **Ellendale** USA
59D3 **Ellen,Mt** USA
56A2 **Ellensburg** USA
68C2 **Ellenville** USA
55K2 **Ellesmere I** Canada
35B2 **Ellesmere,L** New Zealand
7C3 **Ellesmere Port** England
68B3 **Ellicott City** USA
47D3 **Elliot** South Africa
55K5 **Elliot Lake** Canada
58D2 **Ellis** USA
45C3 **El Lisān** *Pen* Jordan
47D1 **Ellisras** South Africa
65F2 **Ellsworth** USA
76F3 **Ellsworth Land** *Region* Antarctica
45A4 **El Ma'âdi** Egypt
49E1 **El Maghra** *L* Egypt
40B3 **El Mahalla el Kubra** Egypt
40B3 **El Mansûra** Egypt
45A3 **El Manzala** Egypt
45B3 **El Matarîya** Egypt
68C3 **Elmer** USA
48B3 **El Merejé** *Desert Region* Mali/Mauritius
16B3 **El Milia** Algeria
45C1 **El Mīna** Lebanon
40B4 **El Minya** Egypt
66B1 **Elmira** California, USA
57F2 **Elmira** New York, USA
59D4 **El Mirage** USA
62B3 **El Moral** Mexico
48B2 **El Mreiti** *Well* Mauritius
18B2 **Elmshorn** Germany
50C2 **El Muglad** Sudan
48B2 **El Mzereb** *Well* Mali
50D2 **El Obeid** Sudan
48C1 **El Oued** Algeria
59D4 **Eloy** USA
56C3 **El Paso** USA
59B3 **El Portal** USA
62A2 **El Porvenir** Mexico
15A2 **El Puerto del Sta Maria** Spain
El Qâhira = Cairo
45B3 **El Qantara** Egypt
El Quds = Jerusalem
45C3 **El Quseima** Egypt
45C4 **El Quwetra** Jordan
56D3 **El Reno** USA
54E3 **Elsa** Canada
45A4 **El Saff** Egypt
45B3 **El Sâlhîya** Egypt
70D3 **El Salvador** *Republic* Central America
59C4 **El Sauzal** Mexico
45B3 **El Shallûfa** Egypt
45B4 **El Shatt** Egypt
45A3 **El Simbillâwein** Egypt
66D4 **Elsinore L** USA
18C2 **Elsterwerde** Germany
62A3 **El Sueco** Mexico
El Suweis = Suez
45A4 **El Tabbin** Egypt
15A1 **El Teleno** *Mt* Spain
35B1 **Eltham** New Zealand
45C4 **El Thamad** Egypt
72F2 **El Tigre** Venezuela
40B4 **El Tîh** *Desert Region* Egypt
45B3 **El Tîna** Egypt
58C1 **Eltopia** USA
40B4 **El Tûr** Egypt
44C2 **Elūru** India
15A2 **Elvas** Portugal
72D5 **Elvira** Brazil
54H2 **Elvira,C** Canada
64B2 **Elwood** USA
7E3 **Ely** England
57D2 **Ely** Minnesota, USA
56B3 **Ely** Nevada, USA
64C2 **Elyria** USA
45A3 **El Zarqa** Egypt
41G2 **Emāmrūd** Iran
42B1 **Emām Sāheb** Afghanistan
18D1 **Eman** *R* Sweden
21K6 **Emba** Kazakhstan
21K6 **Emba** *R* Kazakhstan
Embalse de Ricobayo = Esla, Embalse
74D2 **Embarcación** Argentina
54G4 **Embarras Portage** Canada
50D4 **Embu** Kenya
18B2 **Emden** Germany
31A4 **Emei** China
32D3 **Emerald** Australia
54J5 **Emerson** Canada
58C2 **Emigrant P** USA
50B1 **Emi Koussi** *Mt* Chad
40B2 **Emirdağ** Turkey
68C2 **Emmaus** USA
18B2 **Emmen** Netherlands
13D3 **Emmendingen** Germany
13D2 **Emmerich** Germany
58C2 **Emmett** USA
68B3 **Emmitsburg** USA
56C4 **Emory Peak** *Mt* USA
70A2 **Empalme** Mexico
47E2 **Empangeni** South Africa
74E3 **Empedrado** Argentina
37K2 **Emperor Seamount Chain** Pacific Ocean
63C1 **Emporia** Kansas, USA
65D3 **Emporia** Virginia, USA
68A2 **Emporium** USA
18B2 **Ems** *R* Germany
28B2 **Emu** China
8C2 **Enard B** Scotland
74E3 **Encarnación** Paraguay
48B4 **Enchi** Ghana
62C3 **Encinal** USA
66D4 **Encinitas** USA
75D2 **Encruzilhada** Brazil
32B1 **Endeh** Indonesia
76G11 **Enderby Land** *Region* Antarctica
61D1 **Enderlin** USA
65D2 **Endicott** USA
54C3 **Endicott Mts** USA
16C3 **Enfida** Tunisia
67C1 **Enfield** USA
27F5 **Engaño, C** Philippines
29D2 **Engaru** Japan
45C3 **En Gedi** Israel
21H5 **Engel's** Russian Federation
27D7 **Enggano** *I* Indonesia
10C3 **England** UK
55N4 **Englee** Canada
67C1 **Englehard** USA
65D1 **Englehart** Canada
60C3 **Englewood** USA
10C3 **English Channel** England/France
63C1 **Enid** USA
29D2 **Eniwa** Japan
48B3 **Enji** *Well* Mauritius
13C1 **Enkhuizen** Netherlands
12H7 **Enköping** Sweden
16C3 **Enna** Sicily, Italy
50C2 **En Nahud** Sudan
50C2 **Ennedi** *Desert Region* Chad
9C3 **Ennell, L** Irish Republic
34C1 **Enngonia** Australia
60C2 **Enning** USA
10B3 **Ennis** Irish Republic
58D1 **Ennis** Montana, USA
63C2 **Ennis** Texas, USA
9C3 **Enniscorthy** Irish Republic
9C2 **Enniskillen** Northern Ireland
45C2 **Enn Nâqoûra** Lebanon
18C3 **Enns** *R* Austria
12F8 **Enschede** Netherlands
70A1 **Ensenada** Mexico
31B3 **Enshi** China
13D4 **Ensisheim** France
50D4 **Entebbe** Uganda
67A2 **Enterprise** Alabama, USA
58C1 **Enterprise** Oregon, USA
74E4 **Entre Ríos** *State* Argentina
48C4 **Enugu** Nigeria
13E3 **Enz** *R* Germany
29C3 **Enzan** Japan
14C2 **Epernay** France
40A2 **Ephesus** Turkey
59D3 **Ephraim** USA
68B2 **Ephrata** Pennsylvania, USA
58C1 **Ephrata** Washington, USA
33F2 **Epi** *I* Vanuatu
14D2 **Épinal** France
45B1 **Episkopi** Cyprus
45B1 **Episkopi B** Cyprus
7E4 **Epping** England
13E3 **Eppingen** Germany
7D4 **Epsom** England
47B1 **Epukiro** Namibia
41F3 **Eqlīd** Iran
46D7 **Equator**
48C4 **Equatorial Guinea** *Republic* W Africa
68D1 **Equinox Mt** USA
68C2 **Equinunk** USA
13E3 **Erbach** Germany
13D3 **Erbeskopf** *Mt* Germany
41D2 **Erciş** Turkey
21F8 **Erciyas Dağları** *Mt* Turkey
28B2 **Erdaobaihe** China
28B2 **Erdao Jiang** *R* China
31C1 **Erdene** Mongolia
26D2 **Erdenet** Mongolia
50C2 **Erdi** *Desert Region* Chad
74F3 **Erechim** Brazil
40B1 **Ereğli** Turkey
40B2 **Ereğli** Turkey
26E2 **Erenhot** China
15B1 **Eresma** *R* Spain
13D2 **Erft** *R* Germany
18C2 **Erfurt** Germany
40C2 **Ergani** Turkey
48B2 **Erg Chech** *Desert Region* Algeria/Mali
48D3 **Erg du Ténéré** *Desert Region* Niger
40A1 **Ergene** *R* Turkey
48B2 **Erg Iguidi** *Region* Algeria/Mauritania
19F1 **Ērgli** Latvia
50B2 **Erguig** *R* Chad
25N4 **Ergun'** *R* China/Russian Federation
26E1 **Ergun** *R* China/Russian Federation
25O4 **Ergun Zuoqi** China
50D2 **Eriba** Sudan
8C2 **Eriboll, Loch** *Inlet* Scotland
8C3 **Ericht, Loch** *L* Scotland
57F2 **Erie** USA
57E2 **Erie,L** Canada/USA
29D2 **Erimo-misaki** *C* Japan
8B3 **Eriskay** *I* Scotland
50D2 **Eritrea** *Republic* Africa
13D2 **Erkelenz** Germany
18C3 **Erlangen** Germany
63D2 **Erling,L** USA
47D2 **Ermelo** South Africa
44B4 **Ernākulam** India
9C2 **Erne, L** Northern Ireland
44B3 **Erode** India
34B1 **Eromanga** Australia
47B1 **Erongoberg** *Mt* Namibia
48B1 **Er Rachidia** Morocco
50D2 **Er Rahad** Sudan
51D5 **Errego** Mozambique
10B2 **Errigal** *Mt* Irish Republic
10A3 **Erris Head** *Pt* Irish Republic
33F2 **Erromanga** *I* Vanuatu
50D2 **Er Roseires** Sudan
45C2 **Er Rummān** Jordan
61D1 **Erskine** USA
13D3 **Erstein** France
18C2 **Erzgebirge** *Upland* Germany
21F8 **Erzincan** Turkey
21G8 **Erzurum** Turkey
29D2 **Esan-misaki** *C* Japan
29D2 **Esashi** Japan
18B1 **Esbjerg** Denmark
59D3 **Escalante** USA
56C4 **Escalón** Mexico
57E2 **Escanaba** USA
70C3 **Escárcega** Mexico
13C3 **Esch** Luxembourg
59C4 **Escondido** USA
70B2 **Escuinapa** Mexico
70C3 **Escuintla** Guatemala
50B3 **Eséka** Cameroon
13D1 **Esens** Germany
14C3 **Esera** *R* Spain
15C1 **Esera** *R* Spain
41F3 **Eşfahān** Iran
47E2 **Eshowe** South Africa
45C3 **Esh Sharā** *Upland* Jordan
8D4 **Esk** *R* Scotland
35C1 **Eskdale** New Zealand
12C1 **Eskifjörður** Iceland
12H7 **Eskilstuna** Sweden
54E3 **Eskimo Lakes** Canada
55J3 **Eskimo Point** Canada
21E8 **Eskişehir** Turkey
15A1 **Esla** *R* Spain
15A1 **Esla, Embalse del** *Res* Spain
69B2 **Esmeralda** Cuba
74A7 **Esmeralda** *I* Chile
72C3 **Esmeraldas** Ecuador
14C3 **Espalion** France
64C1 **Espanola** Canada
62A1 **Espanola** USA
32B4 **Esperance** Australia
76G2 **Esperanza** *Base* Antarctica
15A2 **Espichel, Cabo** *C* Portugal
75D2 **Espinhaço, Serra do** *Mts* Brazil
75D2 **Espírito Santo** *State* Brazil
33F2 **Espiritu Santo** *I* Vanuatu
51D6 **Espungabera** Mozambique
74B6 **Esquel** Argentina
58B1 **Esquimalt** Canada
45D2 **Es Samrā** Jordan
48B1 **Essaouira** Morocco
18B2 **Essen** Germany
73G3 **Essequibo** *R* Guyana
7E4 **Essex** *County* England

64C2 **Essexville** USA
18B3 **Esslingen** Germany
13B3 **Essonne** *Department* France
13C3 **Essoyes** France
74D8 **Estados, Isla de los** Argentina
73L6 **Estância** Brazil
47D2 **Estcourt** South Africa
72A1 **Esteí** Nicaragua
13B3 **Esternay** France
66B3 **Estero B** USA
74D2 **Esteros** Paraguay
60B2 **Estes Park** USA
54H5 **Estevan** Canada
61E2 **Estherville** USA
67B2 **Estill** USA
13B3 **Estissac** France
20C4 **Estonia** *Republic* Europe
66B3 **Estrella** *R* USA
15A2 **Estremoz** Portugal
19D3 **Esztergom** Hungary
34A1 **Etadunna** Australia
55L2 **Etah** Canada
43K2 **Etah** India
13C3 **Etam** France
14C2 **Étampes** France
34A1 **Etamunbanie,L** Australia
42D3 **Etāwah** India
50D3 **Ethiopia** *Republic* Africa
8C3 **Etive, Loch** *Inlet* Scotland
16C3 **Etna** *Vol* Sicily, Italy
51B5 **Etosha Nat Pk** Namibia
51B5 **Etosha Pan** *Salt L* Namibia
67B2 **Etowah** *R* USA
13C3 **Ettelbruck** Luxembourg
33H3 **Eua** *I* Tonga
34C2 **Euabalong** Australia
17E3 **Euboea** *I* Greece
64C2 **Euclid** USA
34C3 **Eucumbene,L** Australia
34A2 **Eudunda** Australia
63C1 **Eufala L** USA
67A2 **Eufaula** USA
56A2 **Eugene** USA
70A2 **Eugenia, Punta** *Pt* Mexico
34C1 **Eulo** Australia
63D2 **Eunice** Louisiana, USA
62B2 **Eunice** New Mexico, USA
13D2 **Eupen** Germany
40D3 **Euphrates** *R* Iraq/Syria
63E2 **Eupora** USA
14C2 **Eure** *R* France
58B2 **Eureka** California, USA
55K1 **Eureka** Canada
58C1 **Eureka** Montana, USA
56B3 **Eureka** Nevada, USA
60D1 **Eureka** S Dakota, USA
59D3 **Eureka** Utah, USA
55K2 **Eureka Sd** Canada
66D2 **Eureka V** USA
34C3 **Euroa** Australia
34C1 **Eurombah** *R* Australia
51E6 **Europa** *I* Mozambique Channel
13C2 **Europoort** Netherlands
18B2 **Euskirchen** Germany
63E2 **Eutaw** USA
55K1 **Evans,C** Canada
55L4 **Evans,L** Canada
60B3 **Evans,Mt** Colorado, USA
58D1 **Evans,Mt** Montana, USA
55K3 **Evans Str** Canada
64B2 **Evanston** Illinois, USA
56B2 **Evanston** Wyoming, USA
57E3 **Evansville** Indiana, USA
60B2 **Evansville** Wyoming, USA
47D2 **Evaton** South Africa
32C4 **Everard,L** Australia
39G3 **Everest,Mt** China/Nepal
68A2 **Everett** Pennsylvania, USA
56A2 **Everett** Washington, USA
68D1 **Everett,Mt** USA
57E4 **Everglades,The** *Swamp* USA
67A2 **Evergreen** USA
7D3 **Evesham** England
50B3 **Evinayong** Equatorial Guinea
12F7 **Evje** Norway
15A2 **Évora** Portugal
14C2 **Évreux** France
Évvoia = Euboea
8C3 **Ewe, Loch** *Inlet* Scotland
50B4 **Ewo** Congo
66C1 **Excelsior Mt** USA
66C1 **Excelsior Mts** USA
61E3 **Excelsior Springs** USA
7C4 **Exe** *R* England
59C3 **Exeter** California, USA
7C4 **Exeter** England
65E2 **Exeter** New Hampshire, USA
7C4 **Exmoor** England
7C4 **Exmouth** England
15A2 **Extremadura** *Region* Spain
70E2 **Exuma Sd** The Bahamas
50D4 **Eyasi, L** Tanzania
8D4 **Eyemouth** Scotland
50E3 **Eyl** Somalia
32B4 **Eyre** Australia
32C3 **Eyre Creek** *R* Australia
32C3 **Eyre,L** Australia
32C4 **Eyre Pen** Australia
17F3 **Ezine** Turkey

F

54G3 **Faber L** Canada
12F7 **Fåborg** Denmark
16C2 **Fabriano** Italy
50B2 **Fachi** Niger
50C2 **Fada** Chad
48C3 **Fada N'Gourma** Burkina
25Q2 **Faddeyevskiy, Ostrov** *I* Russian Federation
16C2 **Faenza** Italy
55N3 **Færingehavn** Greenland
12D3 **Faeroes** *Is* N Atlantic Oc
50B3 **Fafa** *R* Central African Republic
50E3 **Fafan** *R* Ethiopia
17E1 **Făgăraş** Romania
13C2 **Fagnes** *Region* Belgium
48B3 **Faguibine,L** Mali
41G5 **Fahūd** Oman
48A1 **Faiol** *I* Azores
62A2 **Fairacres** USA
54D3 **Fairbanks** USA
64C3 **Fairborn** USA
56D2 **Fairbury** USA
68B3 **Fairfax** USA
59B3 **Fairfield** California, USA
68D2 **Fairfield** Connecticut, USA
58D2 **Fairfield** Idaho, USA
58D1 **Fairfield** Montana, USA
64C3 **Fairfield** Ohio, USA
9C2 **Fair Head** *Pt* Northern Ireland
10C2 **Fair Isle** *I* Scotland
35B2 **Fairlie** New Zealand
61E2 **Fairmont** Minnesota, USA
64C3 **Fairmont** W Virginia, USA
68B1 **Fairport** USA
62C1 **Fairview** USA
54E4 **Fairweather,Mt** USA
27H6 **Fais** *I* Pacific Ocean
42C2 **Faisalabad** Pakistan
60C1 **Faith** USA
8E1 **Faither,The** *Pen* Scotland
33H1 **Fakaofo** *I* Tokelau Islands
7E3 **Fakenham** England
32C1 **Fakfak** Indonesia
28A2 **Faku** China
43G4 **Falam** Burma
70C2 **Falcon Res** Mexico/USA
48A3 **Falémé** *R* Mali/Senegal/ Guinea
62C3 **Falfurrias** USA
12G7 **Falkenberg** Sweden
8D4 **Falkirk** Scotland
74D8 **Falkland Is** *Dependency* S Atlantic
74E8 **Falkland Sd** Falkland Islands
12G7 **Falköping** Sweden
66D4 **Fallbrook** USA
56B3 **Fallon** USA
65E2 **Fall River** USA
60B2 **Fall River P** USA
61D2 **Falls City** USA
7B4 **Falmouth** England
69H1 **Falmouth** Jamaica
65E2 **Falmouth** Maine, USA
68E2 **Falmouth** Massachusetts, USA
7B4 **Falmouth Bay** England
47B3 **False B** South Africa
70A2 **Falso,C** Mexico
18C2 **Falster** *I* Denmark
17F1 **Fălticeni** Romania
12H6 **Falun** Sweden
40B2 **Famagusta** Cyprus
45B1 **Famagusta B** Cyprus
13C2 **Famenne** *Region* Belgium
66C3 **Famoso** USA
30B2 **Fang** Thailand
50D3 **Fangak** Sudan
31E5 **Fangliao** Taiwan
8C3 **Fannich, L** Scotland
16C2 **Fano** Italy
45A3 **Fâqûs** Egypt
76G3 **Faraday** *Base* Antarctica
50C3 **Faradje** Zaïre
51E6 **Farafangana** Madagascar
49E2 **Farafra Oasis** Egypt
38E2 **Farah** Afghanistan
27H5 **Farallon de Medinilla** *I* Pacific Ocean
26H4 **Farallon de Pajaros** *I* Marianas
48A3 **Faranah** Guinea
50E2 **Farasan Is** Saudi Arabia
27H6 **Faraulep** *I* Pacific Ocean
55J5 **Farbault** USA
7D4 **Fareham** England
55O4 **Farewell,C** Greenland
33G5 **Farewell,C** New Zealand
35B2 **Farewell Spit** *Pt* New Zealand
56D2 **Fargo** USA
45C2 **Fari'a** *R* Israel
57D2 **Faribault** USA
43F4 **Faridpur** Bangladesh
41G2 **Farīmān** Iran
45A3 **Fâriskûr** Egypt
65E2 **Farmington** Maine, USA
63D1 **Farmington** Missouri, USA
68E1 **Farmington** New Hampshire, USA
56C3 **Farmington** New Mexico, USA
58D2 **Farmington** Utah, USA
66B2 **Farmington Res** USA
6D2 **Farne Deep** N Sea
15A2 **Faro** Portugal
12H7 **Fårö** *I* Sweden
46K9 **Farquhar Is** Indian Ocean
8C3 **Farrar** *R* Scotland
64C2 **Farrell** USA
43K2 **Farrukhabad** *District* India
17E3 **Fársala** Greece
75B4 **Fartura, Serra de** *Mts* Brazil
62B2 **Farwell** USA
41F4 **Fasā** Iran
21D5 **Fastov** Ukraine
43K2 **Fatehgarh** India
43E3 **Fatehpur** India
73H7 **Fatima du Sul** Brazil
58C1 **Fauquier** Canada
47D2 **Fauresmith** South Africa
12H5 **Fauske** Norway
7E4 **Faversham** England
55K4 **Fawn** *R* Canada
12H6 **Fax** *R* Sweden
12A2 **Faxaflói** *B* Iceland
50B2 **Faya** Chad
63E2 **Fayette** USA
57D3 **Fayetteville** Arkansas, USA
57F3 **Fayetteville** N Carolina, USA
67A1 **Fayetteville** Tennessee, USA
45B3 **Fâyid** Egypt
41E4 **Faylakah** *I* Kuwait
42C2 **Fāzilka** India
48A2 **Fdérik** Mauritius
57F3 **Fear,C** USA
66B1 **Feather** *R* USA
59B3 **Feather Middle Fork** *R* USA
14C2 **Fécamp** France
18C2 **Fehmarn** *I* Germany
75D3 **Feia, Lagoa** Brazil
72D5 **Feijó** Brazil
31C5 **Feilai Xai Bei Jiang** *R* China
35C2 **Feilding** New Zealand
51D5 **Feira** Zambia
73L6 **Feira de Santan** Brazil
40C2 **Feke** Turkey
13D4 **Feldberg** *Mt* Germany
18B3 **Feldkirch** Austria
10D3 **Felixstowe** England
12G6 **Femund** *L* Norway
28A2 **Fengcheng** China
31B4 **Fengdu** China
31B3 **Fengjie** China
31D1 **Fengning** China
31B3 **Feng Xian** China
31C1 **Fengzhen** China
31C2 **Fen He** *R* China
51E5 **Fenoarivo Atsinanana** Madagascar
21F7 **Feodosiya** Ukraine
41G3 **Ferdow** Iran
13B3 **Fère-Champenoise** France
39F1 **Fergana** Uzbekistan
61D1 **Fergus Falls** USA
48B4 **Ferkessedougou** Ivory Coast
9C2 **Fermanagh** *County* Northern Ireland
67B2 **Fernandina Beach** USA
73M4 **Fernando de Noronha, Isla** Brazil
75B3 **Fernandópolis** Brazil
Fernando Poo *I* **=Bioko**
58B1 **Ferndale** USA
58C1 **Fernie** Canada
59C3 **Fernley** USA
16C2 **Ferrara** Italy
15B2 **Ferrat, Cap** *C* Algeria
72C5 **Ferreñafe** Peru
63D2 **Ferriday** USA
13B3 **Ferrières** France
48B1 **Fès** Morocco
63D1 **Festus** USA
17F2 **Feteşti** Romania
9C3 **Fethard** Irish Republic
40A2 **Fethiye** Turkey
21J7 **Fetisovo** Kazakhstan
8E1 **Fetlar** *I* Scotland
55L4 **Feuilles, Rivière aux** *R* Canada
24J6 **Feyzabad** Afghanistan
7C3 **Ffestiniog** Wales
51E6 **Fianarantsoa** Madagascar
50D3 **Fichē** Ethiopia
47D2 **Ficksburg** South Africa
45C3 **Fidan, Wadi** Jordan
17D2 **Fier** Albania
8D3 **Fife** *Region* Scotland
8D3 **Fife Ness** *Pen* Scotland
14C3 **Figeac** France
15A1 **Figueira da Foz** Portugal
Figueres = Figueras
15C1 **Figueras** Spain
48B1 **Figuig** Morocco
33G2 **Fiji** *Is* Pacific Ocean
15B2 **Filabres, Sierra de los** *Mts* Spain
73G8 **Filadelfia** Paraguay
6D2 **Filey** England
17E2 **Filiaşi** Romania
17E3 **Filiatrá** Greece
16C3 **Filicudi** *I* Italy
59C4 **Fillmore** California, USA
59D3 **Fillmore** Utah, USA
8C3 **Findhorn** *R* Scotland
57E2 **Findlay** USA
65D2 **Finger Lakes** USA
51D5 **Fingoè** Mozambique
21E8 **Finike** Turkey
15A1 **Finisterre, Cabo** *C* Spain
32C3 **Finke** *R* Australia
20C3 **Finland** *Republic* N Europe
12J7 **Finland,G of** N Europe
54F4 **Finlay** *R* Canada
54F4 **Finlay Forks** Canada
34C3 **Finley** Australia
9C2 **Finn** *R* Irish Republic
12H5 **Finnsnes** Norway
27H7 **Finschhafen** Papua New Guinea
12H7 **Finspång** Sweden
18C2 **Finsterwalde** Germany
9C2 **Fintona** Northern Ireland
35A3 **Fiordland Nat Pk** New Zealand
45C2 **Fiq** Syria
21F8 **Firat** *R* Turkey
66B2 **Firebaugh** USA
Firenze = Florence
42D3 **Firozābād** India
42C2 **Firozpur** India
8C4 **Firth of Clyde** *Estuary* Scotland
8D3 **Firth of Forth** *Estuary* Scotland
8B3 **Firth of Lorn** *Estuary* Scotland
10C2 **Firth of Tay** *Estuary* Scotland
41F4 **Firūzābād** Iran
47B2 **Fish** *R* Namibia
47C3 **Fish** *R* South Africa
66C2 **Fish Camp** USA
68D2 **Fishers I** USA
55K3 **Fisher Str** Canada
7B4 **Fishguard** Wales
55N3 **Fiskenæsset** Greenland
13B3 **Fismes** France
65E2 **Fitchburg** USA
8E2 **Fitful Head** *Pt* Scotland
67B2 **Fitzgerald** USA
32B2 **Fitzroy** *R* Australia
32B2 **Fitzroy Crossing** Australia
64C1 **Fitzwilliam I** Canada
Fiume = Rijeka
50C4 **Fizi** Zaïre
47D3 **Flagstaff** South Africa
56B3 **Flagstaff** USA
65E1 **Flagstaff L** USA
6D2 **Flamborough Head** *C* England
56C2 **Flaming Gorge Res** USA
27G7 **Flamingo, Teluk** *B* Indonesia
13B2 **Flandres, Plaine des** Belgium/France
8B2 **Flannan Isles** Scotland
56B2 **Flathead L** USA
63D1 **Flat River** USA
27H8 **Flattery,C** Australia
56A2 **Flattery,C** USA
6C3 **Fleetwood** England
12F7 **Flekkefjord** Norway
26H4 **Fleming Deep** Pacific Ocean
68C2 **Flemington** USA
18B2 **Flensburg** Germany
32C4 **Flinders** *I* Australia
32D5 **Flinders** *I* Australia
32D2 **Flinders** *R* Australia
32C4 **Flinders Range** *Mts* Australia
54H4 **Flin Flon** Canada
57E2 **Flint** USA
7C3 **Flint** Wales
57E3 **Flint** *R* USA
13B2 **Flixecourt** France
64A1 **Floodwood** USA
67A2 **Florala** USA
57E3 **Florence** Alabama, USA
59D4 **Florence** Arizona, USA
60B3 **Florence** Colorado, USA
16C2 **Florence** Italy
63C1 **Florence** Kansas, USA
58B2 **Florence** Oregon, USA
57F3 **Florence** S Carolina, USA
66C2 **Florence L** USA
72C3 **Florencia** Colombia
74C6 **Florentine Ameghino, Embalse** *Res* Argentina
13C3 **Florenville** Belgium
70D3 **Flores** Guatemala
48A1 **Flores** *I* Azores
32B1 **Flores** *I* Indonesia
27E7 **Flores S** Indonesia
73K5 **Floriano** Brazil
74G3 **Florianópolis** Brazil
74E4 **Florida** Uruguay
70D2 **Florida** *State* USA
67B3 **Florida B** USA
67B3 **Florida City** USA
33E1 **Florida Is** Solomon Islands
57E4 **Florida Keys** *Is* USA
57E4 **Florida,Strs of** USA
17E2 **Flórina** Greece
12F6 **Florø** Norway
62B2 **Floydada** USA
32D1 **Fly** *R* Papua New Guinea
17F1 **Focşani** Romania
16D2 **Foggia** Italy
48A4 **Fogo** *I* Cape Verde
14C3 **Foix** France
64C1 **Foleyet** Canada
55L3 **Foley I** Canada
16C2 **Foligno** Italy
7E4 **Folkestone** England
67B2 **Folkston** USA
16C2 **Follonica** Italy
66B1 **Folsom** USA
68C1 **Fonda** USA
54H4 **Fond-du-Lac** Canada
57E2 **Fond du Lac** USA
70D3 **Fonseca, G de** Honduras
14C2 **Fontainbleau** France
14B2 **Fontenay-le-Comte** France
17D1 **Fonyód** Hungary
Foochow = Fuzhou
54C3 **Foraker, Mt** USA
13D3 **Forbach** France
34C2 **Forbes** Australia
48C4 **Forcados** Nigeria
66C3 **Ford City** USA
12F6 **Førde** Norway
7D4 **Fordingbridge** England
34C1 **Fords Bridge** Australia
63D2 **Fordyce** USA
48A4 **Forécariah** Guinea
55P3 **Forel,Mt** Greenland
58D1 **Foremost** Canada
64C2 **Forest** Canada
63E2 **Forest** USA
61E2 **Forest City** Iowa, USA
68C2 **Forest City** Pennsylvania, USA
7C4 **Forest of Dean** England
67B2 **Forest Park** USA
66A1 **Forestville** USA
13B3 **Forêt d'Othe** France
8D3 **Forfar** Scotland
62B1 **Forgan** USA
58B1 **Forks** USA
16C2 **Forlì** Italy
7C3 **Formby** England
15C2 **Formentera** *I* Spain
15C1 **Formentor, Cabo** *C* Spain
16C2 **Formia** Italy
48A1 **Formigas** *I* Azores
Formosa = Taiwan
74E3 **Formosa** Argentina
73J7 **Formosa** Brazil
74D2 **Formosa** *State* Argentina
Formosa Channel = Taiwan Str
73G6 **Formosa, Serra** *Mts* Brazil
75C1 **Formoso** Brazil
75C1 **Formoso** *R* Brazil
8D3 **Forres** Scotland
32B4 **Forrest** Australia
57D3 **Forrest City** USA
32D2 **Forsayth** Australia
12J6 **Forssa** Finland
34D2 **Forster** Australia
63D1 **Forsyth** Missouri, USA
60B1 **Forsyth** Montana, USA
42C3 **Fort Abbas** Pakistan
55K4 **Fort Albany** Canada
73L4 **Fortaleza** Brazil
8C3 **Fort Augustus** Scotland
47D3 **Fort Beaufort** South Africa
58D1 **Fort Benton** USA
59B3 **Fort Bragg** USA
62C1 **Fort Cobb Res** USA
56C2 **Fort Collins** USA
65D1 **Fort Coulonge** Canada
62B2 **Fort Davis** USA
69E4 **Fort-de-France** Martinique
67A2 **Fort Deposit** USA

Fort Dodge

Gennargentu, Monti del

57D2 **Fort Dodge** USA
32A3 **Fortescue** *R* Australia
57D2 **Fort Frances** Canada
54F3 **Fort Franklin** Canada
54F3 **Fort Good Hope** Canada
34B1 **Fort Grey** Australia
8C3 **Forth** *R* Scotland
62A2 **Fort Hancock** USA
55K4 **Fort Hope** Canada
8F3 **Forties** *Oilfield* N Sea
65F1 **Fort Kent** USA
48C1 **Fort Lallemand** Algeria
Fort Lamy = Ndjamena
60C2 **Fort Laramie** USA
57E4 **Fort Lauderdale** USA
54F3 **Fort Liard** Canada
54G4 **Fort Mackay** Canada
54G5 **Fort Macleod** Canada
54G4 **Fort McMurray** Canada
54E3 **Fort McPherson** Canada
64A2 **Fort Madison** USA
56C2 **Fort Morgan** USA
57E4 **Fort Myers** USA
54F4 **Fort Nelson** Canada
54F3 **Fort Norman** Canada
67A2 **Fort Payne** USA
60B1 **Fort Peck** USA
56C2 **Fort Peck Res** USA
57E4 **Fort Pierce** USA
60C2 **Fort Pierre** USA
68C1 **Fort Plain** USA
54G3 **Fort Providence** Canada
54G3 **Fort Resolution** Canada
50B4 **Fort Rousset** Congo
54F4 **Fort St James** Canada
54F4 **Fort St John** Canada
63D1 **Fort Scott** USA
54E3 **Fort Selkirk** Canada
55K4 **Fort Severn** Canada
21J7 **Fort Shevchenko** Kazakhstan
54F3 **Fort Simpson** Canada
54G3 **Fort Smith** Canada
57D3 **Fort Smith** USA
54F3 **Fort Smith** *Region* Canada
56C3 **Fort Stockton** USA
62B2 **Fort Sumner** USA
62C1 **Fort Supply** USA
58B2 **Fortuna** California, USA
60C1 **Fortuna** N Dakota, USA
54G4 **Fort Vermilion** Canada
67A2 **Fort Walton Beach** USA
57E2 **Fort Wayne** USA
8C3 **Fort William** Scotland
62A1 **Fort Wingate** USA
56D3 **Fort Worth** USA
54D3 **Fort Yukon** USA
31C5 **Foshan** China
55K2 **Fosheim Pen** Canada
61D1 **Fosston** USA
50B4 **Fougamou** Gabon
14B2 **Fougères** France
8D1 **Foula** *I* Scotland
7E4 **Foulness I** England
35B2 **Foulwind,C** New Zealand
50B3 **Foumban** Cameroon
48B2 **Foum el Alba** *Region* Mali
14C1 **Fourmies** France
17F3 **Foúrnoi** *I* Greece
48A3 **Fouta Djallon** *Mts* Guinea
33F5 **Foveaux Str** New Zealand
7B4 **Fowey** England
62B1 **Fowler** USA
64B2 **Fox** *R* USA
55K3 **Foxe Basin** *G* Canada
55K3 **Foxe Chan** Canada
55L3 **Foxe Pen** Canada
60B2 **Foxpark** USA
35C2 **Foxton** New Zealand
10B2 **Foyle, Lough** *Estuary* Irish Republic/Northern Ireland
51B5 **Foz do Cuene** Angola
74F3 **Foz do Iguaçu** Brazil
68B2 **Frackville** USA
15C1 **Fraga** Spain
68E1 **Framingham** USA
73J8 **Franca** Brazil
14C2 **France** *Republic* Europe
14D2 **Franche Comté** *Region* France
47D1 **Francistown** Botswana
58E2 **Francs Peak** *Mt* USA
13E2 **Frankenberg** Germany
64B2 **Frankfort** Indiana, USA
57E3 **Frankfort** Kentucky, USA
68C1 **Frankfort** New York, USA
47D2 **Frankfort** South Africa
18B2 **Frankfurt am Main** Germany
18C2 **Frankfurt an-der-Oder** Germany
18C3 **Fränkischer Alb** *Upland* Germany
58D2 **Franklin** Idaho, USA
64B3 **Franklin** Indiana, USA
63D3 **Franklin** Louisiana, USA
68E1 **Franklin** Massachusetts, USA
67B1 **Franklin** N Carolina, USA
68E1 **Franklin** New Hampshire, USA
68C2 **Franklin** New Jersey, USA
65D2 **Franklin** Pennsylvania, USA
67A1 **Franklin** Tennessee, USA
65D3 **Franklin** Virginia, USA
54F2 **Franklin B** Canada
58C1 **Franklin D Roosevelt** *L* USA
54F3 **Franklin Mts** Canada
54J2 **Franklin Str** Canada
68A1 **Franklinville** USA
35B2 **Franz Josef Glacier** New Zealand
Franz-Josef-Land = Zemlya Frantsa Josifa
54F5 **Fraser** *R* Canada
47C3 **Fraserburg** South Africa
8D3 **Fraserburgh** Scotland
34D1 **Fraser I** Australia
68C3 **Frederica** USA
18B1 **Fredericia** Denmark
65D3 **Frederick** Maryland, USA
62C2 **Frederick** Oklahoma, USA
62C2 **Fredericksburg** Texas, USA
65D3 **Fredericksburg** Virginia, USA
64A3 **Fredericktown** USA
55M5 **Fredericton** Canada
55N3 **Frederikshåp** Greenland
12G7 **Frederikshavn** Denmark
65D2 **Fredonia** USA
12G7 **Fredrikstad** Norway
68C2 **Freehold** USA
66C1 **Freel Peak** *Mt* USA
61D2 **Freeman** USA
64B2 **Freeport** Illinois, USA
63C3 **Freeport** Texas, USA
69B1 **Freeport** The Bahamas
62C3 **Freer** USA
48A4 **Freetown** Sierra Leone
18B3 **Freiburg** Germany
13D3 **Freiburg im Breisgau** Germany
18C3 **Freistadt** Austria
32A4 **Fremantle** Australia
66B2 **Fremont** California, USA
61D2 **Fremont** Nebraska, USA
64C2 **Fremont** Ohio, USA
73H3 **French Guiana** *Dependency* S America
60B1 **Frenchman** *R* USA
34C4 **Frenchmans Cap** *Mt* Australia
37M5 **French Polynesia** *Is* Pacific Ocean
15C2 **Frenda** Algeria
70B2 **Fresnillo** Mexico
56B3 **Fresno** USA
66C2 **Fresno** *R* USA
58D1 **Fresno Res** USA
13E3 **Freudenstadt** Germany
13B2 **Frévent** France
34C4 **Freycinet Pen** Australia
48A3 **Fria** Guinea
66C2 **Friant** USA
66C2 **Friant Dam** USA
16B1 **Fribourg** Switzerland
13E2 **Friedberg** Germany
18B3 **Friedrichshafen** Germany
13C1 **Friesland** *Province* Netherlands
62C3 **Frio** *R* USA
75D3 **Frio, Cabo** *C* Brazil
62B2 **Friona** USA
55M3 **Frobisher B** Canada
55M3 **Frobisher Bay** Canada
54H4 **Frobisher L** Canada
21G6 **Frolovo** Russian Federation
7C4 **Frome** England
7C4 **Frome** *R* England
32C4 **Frome,L** Australia
63D1 **Frontenac** USA
70C3 **Frontera** Mexico
65D3 **Front Royal** USA
16C2 **Frosinone** Italy
60B3 **Fruita** USA
31C5 **Fuchuan** China
31E4 **Fuding** China
70B2 **Fuerte** *R* Mexico
75A3 **Fuerte Olimpo** Brazil
74E2 **Fuerte Olimpo** Paraguay
48A2 **Fuerteventura** *I* Canary Islands
31C2 **Fugu** China
26B2 **Fuhai** China
41G4 **Fujairah** UAE
29C3 **Fuji** Japan
31D4 **Fujian** *Province* China
26G2 **Fujin** China
29C3 **Fujinomiya** Japan
29D3 **Fuji-san** *Mt* Japan
29C3 **Fujisawa** Japan
29C3 **Fuji-Yoshida** Japan
29D2 **Fukagawa** Japan
24K5 **Fukang** China
29D3 **Fukuchiyama** Japan
28A4 **Fukue** Japan
28A4 **Fukue** *I* Japan
29D3 **Fukui** Japan
28C4 **Fukuoka** Japan
29E3 **Fukushima** Japan
29C4 **Fukuyama** Japan
61D2 **Fulda** USA
18B2 **Fulda** Germany
18B2 **Fulda** *R* Germany
31B4 **Fuling** China
69L1 **Fullarton** Trinidad
66D4 **Fullerton** USA
6F1 **Fulmar** *Oilfield* N Sea
64A2 **Fulton** Illinois, USA
64B3 **Fulton** Kentucky, USA
65D2 **Fulton** New York, USA
13C2 **Fumay** France
29D3 **Funabashi** Japan
33G1 **Funafuti** *I* Tuvalu
48A1 **Funchal** Madeira
75D2 **Fundão** Brazil
55M5 **Fundy,B of** Canada
51D6 **Funhalouro** Mozambique
31B5 **Funing** China
31D3 **Funing** China
48C3 **Funtua** Nigeria
31D4 **Fuqing** China
51D5 **Furancungo** Mozambique
29D2 **Furano** Japan
41G4 **Fūrg** Iran
75B2 **Furnas, Serra das** *Mts* Brazil
32D5 **Furneaux Group** *Is* Australia
13D1 **Furstenau** Germany
18C2 **Fürstenwalde** Germany
18C3 **Fürth** Germany
29D2 **Furubira** Japan
29E3 **Furukawa** Japan
55K3 **Fury and Hecla Str** Canada
28A2 **Fushun** China
31A4 **Fushun** Sichuan, China
28B2 **Fusong** China
18C3 **Füssen** Germany
31E2 **Fu Xian** China
31E1 **Fuxin** China
31D3 **Fuyang** China
31E1 **Fuyuan** Liaoning, China
31A4 **Fuyuan** Yunnan, China
26B2 **Fuyun** China
31D4 **Fuzhou** China
28A3 **Fuzhoucheng** China
18C1 **Fyn** *I* Denmark
8C3 **Fyne, Loch** *Inlet* Scotland

G

50E3 **Gaalkacyo** Somalia
59C3 **Gabbs** USA
66C1 **Gabbs Valley Range** *Mts* USA
51B5 **Gabela** Angola
48D1 **Gabès, G de** Tunisia
66B2 **Gabilan Range** *Mts* USA
50B4 **Gabon** *Republic* Africa
47D1 **Gaborone** Botswana
15A1 **Gabriel y Galán, Embalse** *Res* Spain
17F2 **Gabrovo** Bulgaria
41F3 **Gach Sārān** Iran
44B2 **Gadag** India
67A2 **Gadsden** Alabama, USA
59D4 **Gadsden** Arizona, USA
16C2 **Gaeta** Italy
27H6 **Gaferut** *I* Pacific Ocean
67B1 **Gaffney** USA
45A3 **Gafra, Wadi el** Egypt
48C1 **Gafsa** Tunisia
20E4 **Gagarin** Russian Federation
55M4 **Gagnon** Canada
21G7 **Gagra** Georgia
43F3 **Gaibanda** Bangladesh
74C6 **Gaimán** Argentina
67B3 **Gainesville** Florida, USA
67B2 **Gainesville** Georgia, USA
63C2 **Gainesville** Texas, USA
7D3 **Gainsborough** England
32C4 **Gairdner, L** Australia
8C3 **Gairloch** Scotland
68B3 **Gaithersburg** USA
28A2 **Gai Xian** China
44B2 **Gajendragarh** India
31D4 **Ga Jiang** *R* China
47C2 **Gakarosa** *Mt* South Africa
50D4 **Galana** *R* Kenya
72N **Galapagos Is** Pacific Ocean
Gálápagos, Islas = Galapagos Islands
8D4 **Galashiels** Scotland
17F1 **Galați** Romania
64C3 **Galax** USA
62A2 **Galeana** Mexico
54C3 **Galena** Alaska, USA
64A2 **Galena** Illinois, USA
63D1 **Galena** Kansas, USA
69L1 **Galeota Pt** Trinidad
69L1 **Galera Pt** Trinidad
64A2 **Galesburg** USA
68B2 **Galeton** USA
20G4 **Galich** Russian Federation
15A1 **Galicia** *Region* Spain
Galilee,S of = Tiberias,L
69J1 **Galina Pt** Jamaica
50D2 **Gallabat** Sudan
67A1 **Gallatin** USA
58D1 **Gallatin** *R* USA
44C4 **Galle** Sri Lanka
62A3 **Gallego** Mexico
15B1 **Gállego** *R* Spain
72D1 **Gallinas, Puerta** Colombia
Gallipolï = Gelibolu
17D2 **Gallipoli** Italy
20C2 **Gällivare** Sweden
8C4 **Galloway** *District* Scotland
8C4 **Galloway,Mull of** *C* Scotland
62A1 **Gallup** USA
66B1 **Galt** USA
9B3 **Galty Mts** Irish Republic
70C2 **Galveston** USA
57D4 **Galveston B** USA
10B3 **Galway** Irish Republic
10B3 **Galway B** Irish Republic
43F3 **Gamba** China
48B3 **Gambaga** Ghana
54A3 **Gambell** USA
48A3 **Gambia** *R* Senegal/The Gambia
48A3 **Gambia,The** *Republic* Africa
37N6 **Gambier, Îles** Pacific Ocean
50B4 **Gamboma** Congo
51B5 **Gambos** Angola
44C4 **Gampola** Sri Lanka
59E3 **Ganado** USA
50E3 **Ganale Dorya** *R* Ethiopia
65D2 **Gananoque** Canada
Gand = Gent
51B5 **Ganda** Angola
51C4 **Gandajika** Zaïre
43N2 **Gandak** *R* India/Nepal
43M2 **Gandak Dam** Nepal
42B3 **Gandava** Pakistan
55N5 **Gander** Canada
42B4 **Gāndhīdhām** India
42C4 **Gāndhīnagar** India
42D4 **Gāndhi Sāgar** *L* India
15B2 **Gandia** Spain
75E1 **Gandu** Brazil
Ganga *R* **=Ganges**
42C3 **Gangānagar** India
43G4 **Gangaw** Burma
31A2 **Gangca** China
39G2 **Gangdise Shan** *Mts* China
22F4 **Ganges** *R* India
43F4 **Ganges, Mouths of the** Bangladesh/India
28B2 **Gangou** China
43F3 **Gangtok** India
31B3 **Gangu** China
58E2 **Gannett Peak** *Mt* USA
31B2 **Ganquan** China
12K8 **Gantsevichi** Belarus
31D4 **Ganzhou** China
48C3 **Gao** Mali
31A2 **Gaolan** China
31C2 **Gaoping** China
48B3 **Gaoua** Burkina
48A3 **Gaoual** Guinea
31D3 **Gaoyou Hu** *L* China
31C5 **Gaozhou** China
14D3 **Gap** France
42D2 **Gar** China
9C3 **Gara,L** Irish Republic
34C1 **Garah** Australia
73L5 **Garanhuns** Brazil
59B2 **Garberville** USA
75C3 **Garça** Brazil
15A2 **Garcia de Sola, Embalse de** *Res* Spain
75B3 **Garcias** Brazil
16C1 **Garda, L di** Italy
62B1 **Garden City** USA
64B1 **Garden Pen** USA
42B2 **Gardez** Afghanistan
58D1 **Gardiner** USA
68D2 **Gardiners I** USA
68E1 **Gardner** USA
33H1 **Gardner** *I* Phoenix Islands
66C1 **Gardnerville** USA
16D2 **Gargano, Monte** *Mt* Italy
16D2 **Gargano, Prom. del** Italy
42D4 **Garhākota** India
43K1 **Garhmuktesar** India
20L4 **Gari** Russian Federation
47B3 **Garies** South Africa
50D4 **Garissa** Kenya
63C2 **Garland** USA
18C3 **Garmisch-Partenkirchen** Germany
41F2 **Garmsar** Iran
63C1 **Garnett** USA
56B2 **Garnett Peak** *Mt* USA
14C3 **Garonne** *R* France
49D4 **Garoua** Cameroon
49D4 **Garoua Boulai** Cameroon
60C1 **Garrison** USA
9D2 **Garron** *Pt* Northern Ireland
8C3 **Garry** *R* Scotland
54H3 **Garry L** Canada
43E4 **Garwa** India
64B2 **Gary** USA
39G2 **Garyarsa** China
63C2 **Garza-Little Elm** *Res* USA
41F2 **Gasan Kuli** Turkmenistan
14B3 **Gascogne** *Region* France
63D1 **Gasconade** *R* USA
32A3 **Gascoyne** *R* Australia
50B3 **Gashaka** Nigeria
48D3 **Gashua** Nigeria
57G2 **Gaspé** Canada
57G2 **Gaspé,C de** Canada
57G2 **Gaspé, Peninsule de** Canada
67B1 **Gastonia** USA
67C1 **Gaston,L** USA
45B1 **Gata, C** Cyprus
15B2 **Gata, Cabo de** *C* Spain
20D4 **Gatchina** Russian Federation
8C4 **Gatehouse of Fleet** Scotland
6D2 **Gateshead** England
63C2 **Gatesville** USA
13B3 **Gâtinais** *Region* France
65D1 **Gatineau** Canada
65D1 **Gatineau** *R* Canada
67B1 **Gatlinburg** USA
34D1 **Gatton** Australia
33F2 **Gaua** *I* Vanuatu
43G3 **Gauhāti** India
19E1 **Gauja** *R* Latvia
43E3 **Gauri Phanta** India
17E4 **Gávdhos** *I* Greece
75D1 **Gavião** *R* Brazil
66B3 **Gaviota** USA
12H6 **Gävle** Sweden
32C4 **Gawler Ranges** *Mts* Australia
31A1 **Gaxun Nur** *L* China
43E4 **Gaya** India
48C3 **Gaya** Niger
48C3 **Gaya** Nigeria
28B2 **Gaya He** *R* China
64C1 **Gaylord** USA
34D1 **Gayndah** Australia
20J3 **Gayny** Russian Federation
19F3 **Gaysin** Ukraine
40B3 **Gaza** Israel
40C2 **Gaziantep** Turkey
48B4 **Gbaringa** Liberia
48D1 **Gbbès** Tunisia
19D2 **Gdańsk** Poland
19D2 **Gdańsk,G of** Poland
12K7 **Gdov** Russian Federation
19D2 **Gdynia** Poland
45A4 **Gebel el Galâla el Baharîya** *Desert* Egypt
50D2 **Gedaref** Sudan
17F3 **Gediz** *R* Turkey
18C2 **Gedser** Denmark
13C2 **Geel** Belgium
34B3 **Geelong** Australia
34C4 **Geeveston** Australia
48D3 **Geidam** Nigeria
13D2 **Geilenkirchen** Germany
50D4 **Geita** Tanzania
31A5 **Gejiu** China
16C3 **Gela** Italy
50E3 **Geladī** Ethiopia
13D2 **Geldern** Germany
17F2 **Gelibolu** Turkey
40B2 **Gelidonya Burun** Turkey
13E2 **Gelnhausen** Germany
13D2 **Gelsenkirchen** Germany
12F8 **Gelting** Germany
30C5 **Gemas** Malaysia
13C2 **Gembloux** Belgium
50B3 **Gemena** Zaïre
40C2 **Gemerek** Turkey
40A1 **Gemlik** Turkey
16C1 **Gemona** Italy
47C2 **Gemsbok Nat Pk** Botswana
50C2 **Geneina** Sudan
74C5 **General Alvear** Argentina
76F2 **General Belgrano** *Base* Antarctica
76G2 **General Bernardo O'Higgins** *Base* Antarctica
74B7 **General Carrera, Lago** Chile
74D2 **General Eugenio A Garay** Paraguay
66C2 **General Grant Grove Section** *Region* USA
74C3 **General Manuel Belgrano** *Mt* Argentina
74D5 **General Pico** Argentina
74C5 **General Roca** Argentina
27F6 **General Santos** Philippines
65D2 **Genesee** *R* USA
65D2 **Geneseo** USA
61D2 **Geneva** Nebraska, USA
68B1 **Geneva** New York, USA
16B1 **Geneva** Switzerland
Geneva,L of = Léman, L
Genève = Geneva
15B2 **Genil** *R* Spain
16B2 **Gennargentu, Monti del** *Mt* Sardinia, Italy

34C3 **Genoa** Australia
16B2 **Genoa** Italy
Genova = Genoa
16B2 **Genova, G di** Italy
13B2 **Gent** Belgium
27D7 **Genteng** Indonesia
18C2 **Genthin** Germany
21H7 **Geokchay** Azerbaijan
47C3 **George** South Africa
55M4 **George** *R* Canada
34C2 **George,L** Australia
67B3 **George,L** Florida, USA
65E2 **George,L** New York, USA
35A2 **George Sd** New Zealand
34C4 **George Town** Australia
66B1 **Georgetown** California, USA
65D3 **Georgetown** Delaware, USA
73G2 **Georgetown** Guyana
64C3 **Georgetown** Kentucky, USA
30C4 **George Town** Malaysia
69N2 **Georgetown** St Vincent
67C2 **Georgetown** S Carolina, USA
63C2 **Georgetown** Texas, USA
48A3 **Georgetown** The Gambia
76G8 **George V Land** *Region* Antarctica
62C3 **George West** USA
21G7 **Georgia** *Republic* Europe
76F12 **Georg Forster** *Base* Antarctica
67B2 **Georgia** *State* USA
64C1 **Georgian B** Canada
54F5 **Georgia, Str of** Canada
32C3 **Georgina** *R* Australia
21F5 **Georgiu-Dezh** Russian Federation
21G7 **Georgiyevsk** Russian Federation
76F1 **Georg von Neumayer** *Base* Antarctica
18C2 **Gera** Germany
13B2 **Geraardsbergen** Belgium
75C1 **Geral de Goiás, Serra** *Mts* Brazil
35B2 **Geraldine** New Zealand
75C2 **Geral do Paraná, Serra** *Mts* Brazil
32A3 **Geraldton** Australia
57E2 **Geraldton** Canada
75D2 **Geral, Serra** *Mts* Bahia, Brazil
75B4 **Geral, Serra** *Mts* Paraná, Brazil
45C3 **Gerar** *R* Israel
13D3 **Gérardmer** France
54C3 **Gerdine,Mt** USA
30C4 **Gerik** Malaysia
60C2 **Gering** USA
21C6 **Gerlachovsky** *Mt* Poland
47D2 **Germiston** South Africa
13D2 **Gerolstein** Germany
15C1 **Gerona** Spain
13E2 **Geseke** Germany
50E3 **Gestro** *R* Ethiopia
15B1 **Getafe** Spain
68B3 **Gettysburg** Pennsylvania, USA
60D1 **Gettysburg** S Dakota, USA
41D2 **Gevaş** Turkey
17E2 **Gevgeliija** Macedonia, Yugoslavia
45D2 **Ghabāghib** Syria
45D3 **Ghadaf, Wadi el** Jordan
48C1 **Ghadamis** Libya
41F2 **Ghaem Shahr** Iran
43E3 **Ghāghara** *R* India
48B4 **Ghana** *Republic* Africa
47C1 **Ghanzi** Botswana
48C1 **Ghardaïa** Algeria
49D1 **Gharyān** Libya
49D2 **Ghāt** Libya
15B2 **Ghazaouet** Algeria
42D3 **Ghāziābād** India
42B2 **Ghazni** Afghanistan
17F1 **Gheorgheni** Romania
40D3 **Ghudāf, Wadi al** *Watercourse* Iraq
16D3 **Giarre** Sicily, Italy
60D2 **Gibbon** USA
47B2 **Gibeon** Namibia
15A2 **Gibraltar** *Colony* SW Europe
7E7 **Gibraltar** *Pt* England
15A2 **Gibraltar,Str of** Africa/Spain
32B3 **Gibson Desert** Australia
58B1 **Gibsons** Canada
44B2 **Giddalūr** India
45B3 **Giddi, Gebel el** *Mt* Egypt
45B3 **Giddi Pass** Egypt
50D3 **Gīdolē** Ethiopia
13B4 **Gien** France
18B2 **Giessen** Germany
8D4 **Gifford** Scotland
67B3 **Gifford** USA
29D3 **Gifu** Japan
8C4 **Gigha** *I* Scotland
16C2 **Giglio** *I* Italy
15A1 **Gijón** Spain
59D4 **Gila** *R* USA
59D4 **Gila Bend** USA
59D4 **Gila Bend Mts** USA
32D2 **Gilbert** *R* Australia
33G1 **Gilbert Is** Pacific Ocean
58D1 **Gildford** USA
51D5 **Gilé** Mozambique
45C2 **Gilead** *Region* Jordan
49E2 **Gilf Kebir Plat** Egypt
34C2 **Gilgandra** Australia
42C1 **Gilgit** Pakistan
42C1 **Gilgit** *R* Pakistan
34C2 **Gilgunnia** Australia
55J4 **Gillam** Canada
60B2 **Gillette** USA
7E4 **Gillingham** England
64B1 **Gills Rock** USA
64B2 **Gilman** USA
66B2 **Gilroy** USA
69P2 **Gimie, Mont** St Lucia
45B3 **Gineifa** Egypt
47E2 **Gingindlovu** South Africa
50E3 **Gīnīr** Ethiopia
17E3 **Gióna** *Mt* Greece
34C3 **Gippsland** *Mts* Australia
64C2 **Girard** USA
72D3 **Girardot** Colombia
8D3 **Girdle Ness** *Pen* Scotland
40C1 **Gıresun** Turkey
40B4 **Girga** Egypt
42C4 **Gīr Hills** India
50B3 **Giri** *R* Zaïre
43F4 **Girīdīh** India
42A2 **Girishk** Afghanistan
13D4 **Giromagny** France
Girona = Gerona
14B2 **Gironde** *R* France
8C4 **Girvan** Scotland
35C1 **Gisborne** New Zealand
50C4 **Gitega** Burundi
Giuba,R = Juba,R
17F2 **Giurgiu** Romania
13C2 **Givet** France
25S3 **Gizhiga** Russian Federation
19E2 **Gizycko** Poland
17E2 **Gjirokastër** Albania
54J3 **Gjoatlaven** Canada
12G6 **Gjøvik** Norway
55M5 **Glace Bay** Canada
58B1 **Glacier Peak** *Mt* USA
55K2 **Glacier Str** Canada
32E3 **Gladstone** Queensland, Australia
34A2 **Gladstone** S Aust, Australia
34C4 **Gladstone** Tasmania, Australia
64B1 **Gladstone** USA
12A1 **Gláma** *Mt* Iceland
12G6 **Glåma** *R* Norway
13D3 **Glan** *R* Germany
61D3 **Glasco** USA
64B3 **Glasgow** Kentucky, USA
60B1 **Glasgow** Montana, USA
8C4 **Glasgow** Scotland
68C3 **Glassboro** USA
66C2 **Glass Mt** USA
7C4 **Glastonbury** England
20J4 **Glazov** Russian Federation
18D3 **Gleisdorf** Austria
35C1 **Glen Afton** New Zealand
9D2 **Glenarm** Northern Ireland
68B3 **Glen Burnie** USA
47E2 **Glencoe** South Africa
59D4 **Glendale** Arizona, USA
66C3 **Glendale** California, USA
60C1 **Glendive** USA
60C2 **Glendo Res** USA
9C2 **Glengad Hd** *Pt* Irish Republic
34D1 **Glen Innes** Australia
8C4 **Glenluce** Scotland
34C1 **Glenmorgan** Australia
34D2 **Glenreagh** Australia
68B3 **Glen Rock** USA
63C2 **Glen Rose** USA
8D3 **Glenrothes** Scotland
68D1 **Glens Falls** USA
63D2 **Glenwood** Arkansas, USA
61D1 **Glenwood** Minnesota, USA
62A2 **Glenwood** New Mexico, USA
60B3 **Glenwood Springs** USA
64A1 **Glidden** USA
12F6 **Glittertind** *Mt* Norway
19D2 **Gliwice** Poland
59D4 **Globe** USA
18D2 **Głogów** Poland
12G5 **Glomfjord** Norway
51E5 **Glorieuses, Isles** Madagascar
7C3 **Glossop** England
34D2 **Gloucester** Australia
7C4 **Gloucester** England
68E1 **Gloucester** USA
7C4 **Gloucester** *County* England
68C1 **Gloversville** USA
19F1 **Glubokoye** Belarus
13E1 **Glückstadt** Germany
21E5 **Glukhov** Ukraine
18D3 **Gmünd** Austria
18C3 **Gmunden** Austria
19D2 **Gniezno** Poland
44A2 **Goa, Daman and Diu** *Union Territory* India
47B2 **Goageb** Namibia
43G3 **Goālpāra** India
50D3 **Goba** Ethiopia
47B1 **Gobabis** Namibia
31B1 **Gobi** *Desert* China/Mongolia
29C4 **Gobo** Japan
19G1 **Gobza** *R* Russian Federation
47B1 **Gochas** Namibia
7D4 **Godalming** England
44C2 **Godāvari** *R* India
66C2 **Goddard,Mt** USA
64C2 **Goderich** Canada
55N3 **Godhavn** Greenland
42C4 **Godhra** India
57D1 **Gods L** Canada
55N3 **Godthåb** Greenland
Godwin Austen *Mt* **=K2**
68E1 **Goffstown** USA
64C1 **Gogama** Canada
13E1 **Gohfeld** Germany
75C2 **Goiandira** Brazil
75C2 **Goianésia** Brazil
75C2 **Goiânia** Brazil
75B2 **Goiás** Brazil
73J6 **Goiás** *State* Brazil
75B3 **Goio-Erê** Brazil
50D3 **Gojab** *R* Ethiopia
17F2 **Gökçeada** *I* Turkey
17F3 **Gökova Körfezi** *B* Turkey
21F8 **Goksu** *R* Turkey
40C2 **Göksun** Turkey
43G3 **Golāghāt** India
9B2 **Gola, I** Irish Republic
40C2 **Gölbaşı** Turkey
24K2 **Gol'chikha** Russian Federation
58C2 **Golconda** USA
68B2 **Gold** USA
58B2 **Gold Beach** USA
34D1 **Gold Coast** Australia
35B2 **Golden B** New Zealand
58B1 **Goldendale** USA
66A2 **Golden Gate** *Chan* USA
63D3 **Golden Meadow** USA
59C3 **Goldfield** USA
66D2 **Gold Point** USA
67C1 **Goldsboro** USA
62C3 **Goldthwaite** USA
18C2 **Goleniów** Poland
66C3 **Goleta** USA
26C3 **Golmud** China
50E3 **Gololcha** Ethiopia
29F2 **Golovnino** Russian Federation
50C4 **Goma** Zaïre
43L2 **Gomati** India
48D3 **Gombe** Nigeria
19G2 **Gomel** Belarus
48A2 **Gomera** *I* Canary Islands
70B2 **Gómez Palacio** Mexico
25O4 **Gonam** *R* Russian Federation
69C3 **Gonâve, Isla de la** Cuba
41G2 **Gonbad-e Kāvūs** Iran
43E3 **Gonda** India
42C4 **Gondal** India
50D2 **Gonder** Ethiopia
43E4 **Gondia** India
40A1 **Gönen** Turkey
17F3 **Gonen** *R* Turkey
31A4 **Gongga Shan** *Mt* China
31A2 **Gonghe** China
75D1 **Gongogi** *R* Brazil
48D3 **Gongola** *R* Nigeria
66B2 **Gonzales** California, USA
63C3 **Gonzales** Texas, USA
47B3 **Good Hope,C of** South Africa
58D2 **Gooding** USA
60C3 **Goodland** USA
34C1 **Goodooga** *R* Australia
7D3 **Goole** England
34C2 **Goolgowi** Australia
34A3 **Goolwa** Australia
32A4 **Goomalling** Australia
34C2 **Goombalie** Australia
34D1 **Goomeri** Australia
34D1 **Goondiwindi** Australia
55N4 **Goose Bay** Canada
67C2 **Goose Creek** USA
58B2 **Goose L** USA
44B2 **Gooty** India
32D1 **Goraka** Papua New Guinea
43E3 **Gorakhpur** India
20K3 **Gora Koyp** *Mt* Russian Federation
25M4 **Gora Munku Sardyk** *Mt* Mongolia/Russian Federation
20K3 **Gora Narodnaya** *Mt* Russian Federation
20L2 **Gora Pay-Yer** *Mt* Russian Federation
20K3 **Gora Telpos-Iz** *Mt*
17D2 **Goražde** Bosnia-Herzegovina
54D2 **Gordon** USA
65D3 **Gordonsville** USA
50B3 **Goré** Chad
50D3 **Gorē** Ethiopia
35A3 **Gore** New Zealand
25P4 **Gore Topko** *Mt* Russian Federation
9C3 **Gorey** Irish Republic
41F2 **Gorgān** Iran
13C2 **Gorinchem** Netherlands
41E2 **Goris** Armenia
16C1 **Gorizia** Italy
19G2 **Gorki** Belarus
20M2 **Gorki** Russian Federation
Gorki = Novgorod
20G4 **Gor'kovskoye Vodokhranilishche** *Res* Russian Federation
7E3 **Gorleston** England
18C2 **Görlitz** Germany
21F6 **Gorlovka** Ukraine
66C3 **Gorman** USA
17F2 **Gorna Orjahovica** Bulgaria
26B1 **Gorno-Altaysk** Russian Federation
26H2 **Gornozavodsk** Russian Federation
20K3 **Goro Denezhkin Kamen'** *Mt* Russian Federation
20G4 **Gorodets** Russian Federation
19G2 **Gorodnya** Ukraine
19F1 **Gorodok** Belarus
19E3 **Gorodok** Ukraine
19F3 **Gorodok** Ukraine
27H7 **Goroka** Papua New Guinea
51D5 **Gorongosa** Mozambique
27F6 **Gorontalo** Indonesia
20L4 **Goro Yurma** *Mt* Russian Federation
75D2 **Gorutuba** *R* Brazil
25M4 **Goryachinsk** Russian Federation
21J7 **Gory Akkyr** *Upland* Turkmenistan
25L2 **Gory Byrranga** *Mts* Russian Federation
19F3 **Goryn'** *R* Ukraine
25L3 **Gory Putorana** *Mts* Russian Federation
19E2 **Góry Świętokrzyskie** *Upland* Poland
12H8 **Gorzów Wielkopolski** Poland
66C2 **Goshen** USA
29E2 **Goshogawara** Japan
16D2 **Gospić** Croatia
7D4 **Gosport** England
17E2 **Gostivar** Macedonia, Yugoslavia
19D2 **Gostynin** Poland
12G7 **Göteborg** Sweden
50B3 **Gotel Mts** Nigeria
60C2 **Gothenburg** USA
12H7 **Gotland** *I* Sweden
28B4 **Gotō-rettō** *Is* Japan
12H7 **Gotska Sandön** *I* Sweden
28C4 **Gōtsu** Japan
18B2 **Göttingen** Germany
28A2 **Goubangzi** China
13C2 **Gouda** Netherlands
50B2 **Goudoumaria** Niger
52H7 **Gough I** Atlantic Ocean
55L5 **Gouin, Réservoire** Canada
34C2 **Goulburn** Australia
48B3 **Goumbou** Mali
48B3 **Goundam** Mali
50B2 **Gouré** Niger
48B3 **Gourma Rharous** Mali
50B2 **Gouro** Chad
58E1 **Govenlock** Canada
27G8 **Gove Pen** Australia
21C6 **Goverla** *Mt* Ukraine
75D2 **Governador Valadares** Brazil
43E4 **Govind Ballabh Paht Sāgar** *L* India
42B3 **Gowārān** Afghanistan
7B4 **Gower** Wales
74E3 **Goya** Argentina
50C2 **Goz-Beïda** Chad
16C3 **Gozo** *I* Malta
50D2 **Goz Regeb** Sudan
47C3 **Graaff-Reinet** South Africa
65D1 **Gracefield** Canada
69A4 **Gracias à Dios, Cabo** Honduras
34D1 **Grafton** Australia
61D1 **Grafton** N Dakota, USA
64C3 **Grafton** W Virginia, USA
54E4 **Graham I** Canada
59E4 **Graham,Mt** USA
47D3 **Grahamstown** South Africa
73J5 **Grajaú** Brazil
19E2 **Grajewo** Poland
17E2 **Grámmos** *Mt* Albania/Greece
8C3 **Grampian** *Mts* Scotland
8D3 **Grampian** *Region* Scotland
72D3 **Granada** Colombia
72A1 **Granada** Nicaragua
15B2 **Granada** Spain
65E1 **Granby** Canada
60B2 **Granby** USA
48A2 **Gran Canaria** *I* Canary Islands
74D3 **Gran Chaco** *Region* Argentina
64B2 **Grand** *R* Michigan, USA
61E2 **Grand** *R* Missouri, USA
69Q2 **Grand B** Dominica
57F4 **Grand Bahama** *I* The Bahamas
13D4 **Grand Ballon** *Mt* France
55N5 **Grand Bank** Canada
52F2 **Grand Banks** Atlantic Ocean
48B4 **Grand Bassam** Ivory Coast
59D3 **Grand Canyon** USA
59D3 **Grand Canyon Nat Pk** USA
69A3 **Grand Cayman** *I* Cayman Is, Caribbean Sea
58C1 **Grand Coulee** USA
73K6 **Grande** *R* Bahia, Brazil
75C2 **Grande** *R* Minas Gerais/São Paulo, Brazil
55L4 **Grande 2, Rēservoir de la** Canada
55L4 **Grande 3, Rēservoir de la** Canada
55L4 **Grande 4, Rēservoir de la** Canada
74C8 **Grande, Bahía** *B* Argentina
51E5 **Grande Comore** *I* Comoros
75D3 **Grande, Ilha** Brazil
63C2 **Grande Prairie** USA
50B2 **Grand Erg de Bilma** *Desert Region* Niger
48C1 **Grand Erg Occidental** *Desert* Algeria
48C2 **Grand Erg Oriental** *Desert* Algeria
55L4 **Grande Rivière de la Baleine** *R* Canada
58C1 **Grande Ronde** *R* USA
59D4 **Gran Desierto** USA
55M5 **Grand Falls** New Brunswick, Canada
55N5 **Grand Falls** Newfoundland, Canada
58C1 **Grand Forks** Canada
61D1 **Grand Forks** USA
68C1 **Grand Gorge** USA
64B2 **Grand Haven** USA
60D2 **Grand Island** USA
63E2 **Grand Isle** USA
60B3 **Grand Junction** USA
63D3 **Grand L** USA
64A1 **Grand Marais** USA
65E1 **Grand Mère** Canada
15A2 **Grândola** Portugal
54G4 **Grand Prairie** Canada
54J4 **Grand Rapids** Canada
64B2 **Grand Rapids** Michigan, USA
64A1 **Grand Rapids** Minnesota, USA
16B1 **Grand St Bernard, Col du** *P* Italy/Switzerland
56B2 **Grand Teton** *Mt* USA
58D2 **Grand Teton Nat Pk** USA
60B3 **Grand Valley** USA
58C1 **Grangeville** USA
58E1 **Granite Peak** *Mt* Montana, USA
59D2 **Granite Peak** *Mt* Utah, USA
15C1 **Granollérs** Spain
16B1 **Gran Paradiso** *Mt* Italy
7D3 **Grantham** England
66C1 **Grant,Mt** USA
8D3 **Grantown-on-Spey** Scotland
62A1 **Grants** USA
58B2 **Grants Pass** USA
14B2 **Granville** France
68D1 **Granville** USA
54H4 **Granville L** Canada
75D2 **Grão Mogol** Brazil
66C3 **Grapevine** USA
66D2 **Grapevine Mts** USA
47E1 **Graskop** South Africa
54G3 **Gras, Lac de** Canada
14D3 **Grasse** France
6D2 **Grassington** England
58E1 **Grassrange** USA
59B3 **Grass Valley** USA
74F4 **Gravatai** Brazil
54H5 **Gravelbourg** Canada

13B2 **Gravelines** France
51D6 **Gravelotte** South Africa
65D2 **Gravenhurst** Canada
58D1 **Grave Peak** *Mt* USA
34D1 **Gravesend** Australia
7E4 **Gravesend** England
58B1 **Grays Harbour** *B* USA
58D2 **Grays L** USA
64C3 **Grayson** USA
64B3 **Grayville** USA
18D3 **Graz** Austria
69H1 **Great** *R* Jamaica
57F4 **Great Abaco** *I* The Bahamas
32B4 **Great Australian Bight** *G* Australia
68E1 **Great B** New Hampshire, USA
68C3 **Great B** New Jersey, USA
70E2 **Great Bahama Bank** The Bahamas
35C1 **Great Barrier I** New Zealand
32D2 **Great Barrier Reef** *Is* Australia
68D1 **Great Barrington** USA
59C2 **Great Basin** USA
54F3 **Great Bear L** Canada
62C1 **Great Bend** USA
45B3 **Great Bitter L** Egypt
68A3 **Great Cacapon** USA
44E3 **Great Coco I** Burma
32D3 **Great Dividing Range** *Mts* Australia
6D2 **Great Driffield** England
68C3 **Great Egg Harbor** *B* USA
76F10 **Greater Antarctica** *Region* Antarctica
69B2 **Greater Antilles** *Is* Caribbean Sea
7D4 **Greater London** *Metropolitan County* England
7C3 **Greater Manchester** *Metropolitan County* England
70E2 **Great Exuma** *I* The Bahamas
58D1 **Great Falls** USA
47D3 **Great Fish** *R* South Africa
8C3 **Great Glen** *V* Scotland
43F3 **Great Himalayan Range** *Mts* Asia
57F4 **Great Inagua** *I* The Bahamas
47C3 **Great Karoo** *Mts* South Africa
47D3 **Great Kei** *R* South Africa
34C4 **Great L** Australia
7C3 **Great Malvern** England
51B6 **Great Namaland** *Region* Namibia
44E4 **Great Nicobar** *I* Indian Ocean
7C3 **Great Ormes Head** *C* Wales
68E2 **Great Pt** USA
57F4 **Great Ragged** *I* The Bahamas
51D4 **Great Ruaha** *R* Tanzania
65E2 **Great Sacandaga L** USA
58D2 **Great Salt L** USA
58D2 **Great Salt Lake Desert** USA
49E2 **Great Sand Sea** Egypt/ Libya
32B3 **Great Sandy Desert** Australia
56A2 **Great Sandy Desert** USA
Great Sandy I = Fraser I
54G3 **Great Slave L** Canada
67B1 **Great Smoky Mts** USA
67B1 **Great Smoky Mts Nat Pk** USA
68D2 **Great South B** USA
47C3 **Great Tafelberg** *Mt* South Africa
32B3 **Great Victoria Desert** Australia
31B2 **Great Wall** China
7E3 **Great Yarmouth** England
48C2 **Gréboun, Mont** Niger
45C1 **Greco, C** Cyprus
15A1 **Gredos, Sierra de** *Mts* Spain
65D2 **Greece** USA
17E3 **Greece** *Republic* Europe
60C2 **Greeley** USA
55K1 **Greely Fjord** Canada
24H1 **Greem Bell, Ostrov** *I* Russian Federation
64B3 **Green** *R* Kentucky, USA
59D3 **Green** *R* Utah, USA
64B1 **Green B** USA
64B2 **Green Bay** USA
64B3 **Greencastle** Indiana, USA
68B3 **Greencastle** Pennsylvania, USA
68C1 **Greene** USA
67B1 **Greeneville** USA
66B2 **Greenfield** California, USA
66C3 **Greenfield** California, USA
68D1 **Greenfield** Massachusetts, USA
64B2 **Greenfield** Wisconsin, USA
55O2 **Greenland** *Dependency* N Atlantic Ocean
52F1 **Greenland** *I* Atlantic Ocean
52H1 **Greenland Basin** Greenland Sea
76B1 **Greenland Sea** Greenland
8D4 **Greenlaw** Scotland
8C4 **Greenock** Scotland
68D2 **Greenport** USA
59D3 **Green River** Utah, USA
58E2 **Green River** Wyoming, USA
68C3 **Greensboro** Maryland, USA
67C1 **Greensboro** N Carolina, USA
62C1 **Greensburg** Kansas, USA
64B3 **Greensburg** Kentucky, USA
65D2 **Greensburg** Pennsylvania, USA
8C3 **Greenstone Pt** Scotland
64B3 **Greenup** USA
59D4 **Green Valley** USA
67A2 **Greenville** Alabama, USA
48B4 **Greenville** Liberia
63D2 **Greenville** Mississippi, USA
67C1 **Greenville** N Carolina, USA
68E1 **Greenville** N Hampshire, USA
64C2 **Greenville** Ohio, USA
67B2 **Greenville** S Carolina, USA
63C2 **Greenville** Texas, USA
67B2 **Greenville** Florida, USA
27H8 **Greenville,C** Australia
7E4 **Greenwich** England
68D2 **Greenwich** USA
68C3 **Greenwood** Delaware, USA
63D2 **Greenwood** Mississippi, USA
67B2 **Greenwood** S Carolina, USA
63D1 **Greers Ferry L** USA
60D2 **Gregory** USA
34A1 **Gregory,L** Australia
32D2 **Gregory Range** *Mts* Australia
18C2 **Greifswald** Germany
20F2 **Gremikha** Russian Federation
18C1 **Grenå** Denmark
63E2 **Grenada** USA
69E4 **Grenada** *I* Caribbean Sea
69E4 **Grenadines,The** *Is* Caribbean Sea
34C2 **Grenfell** Australia
14D2 **Grenoble** France
69M2 **Grenville** Grenada
32D2 **Grenville,C** Australia
58B1 **Gresham** USA
63D3 **Gretna** USA
35B2 **Grey** *R* New Zealand
58E2 **Greybull** USA
55N4 **Grey Is** Canada
68D1 **Greylock,Mt** USA
35B2 **Greymouth** New Zealand
32D3 **Grey Range** *Mts* Australia
9C3 **Greystones** Irish Republic
47E2 **Greytown** South Africa
67B2 **Griffin** USA
34C2 **Griffith** Australia
32D5 **Grim,C** Australia
65D2 **Grimsby** Canada
7D3 **Grimsby** England
12B1 **Grimsey** *I* Iceland
12F7 **Grimstad** Norway
61E2 **Grinnell** USA
55J2 **Grinnell Pen** Canada
55K2 **Grise Fjord** Canada
20J3 **Griva** Russian Federation
12J7 **Grobina** Latvia
47D2 **Groblersdal** South Africa
19E2 **Grodno** Belarus
43E3 **Gromati** *R* India
13D1 **Gronan** Germany
18B2 **Groningen** Netherlands
13D1 **Groningen** *Province* Netherlands
62B1 **Groom** USA
47C3 **Groot** *R* South Africa
32C2 **Groote Eylandt** *I* Australia
51B5 **Grootfontein** Namibia
47B2 **Groot-Karasberge** *Mts* Namibia
47C1 **Groot Laagte** *R* Botswana/Namibia
47C2 **Groot Vloer** *Salt L* South Africa
69P2 **Gros Islet** St Lucia
13E2 **Grosser Feldberg** *Mt* Germany
16C2 **Grosseto** Italy
13E3 **Gross-Gerau** Germany
18C3 **Grossglockner** *Mt* Austria
58D2 **Gros Ventre Range** *Mts* USA
61D1 **Groton** USA
64C1 **Groundhog** *R* Canada
63E2 **Grove Hill** USA
66B2 **Groveland** USA
66B3 **Grover City** USA
65E2 **Groveton** USA
21H7 **Groznyy** Russian Federation
19D2 **Grudziądz** Poland
47B2 **Grünau** Namibia
8E2 **Grutness** Scotland
21G5 **Gryazi** Russian Federation
20G4 **Gryazovets** Russian Federation
74J8 **Grytviken** South Georgia
69B2 **Guacanayabo, G de** Cuba
75D3 **Guaçuí** Brazil
70B2 **Guadalajara** Mexico
15B1 **Guadalajara** Spain
33E1 **Guadalcanal** *I* Solomon Islands
15B2 **Guadalimar** *R* Spain
15B1 **Guadalope** *R* Spain
15B2 **Guadalqivir** *R* Spain
70B2 **Guadalupe** Mexico
66B3 **Guadalupe** USA
53G6 **Guadalupe** *I* Mexico
62C3 **Guadalupe** *R* USA
62B2 **Guadalupe Mtns Nat Pk** USA
62B2 **Guadalupe Peak** *Mt* USA
15A2 **Guadalupe, Sierra de** *Mts* Spain
15B1 **Guadarrama, Sierra de** *Mts* Spain
69E3 **Guadeloupe** *I* Caribbean Sea
15B2 **Guadian** *R* Spain
15A2 **Guadiana** *R* Portugal
15B2 **Guadiana** *R* Spain
15B2 **Guadix** Spain
75B3 **Guaíra** Brazil
72E6 **Guajará Mirim** Brazil
72D1 **Guajira,Pen de** Colombia
69C4 **Guajiri, Península de la** Colombia
72C4 **Gualaceo** Ecuador
27H5 **Guam** *I* Pacific Ocean
74D5 **Guaminí** Argentina
30C5 **Gua Musang** Malaysia
69A2 **Guanabacoa** Cuba
75D1 **Guanambi** Brazil
72E2 **Guanare** Venezuela
28B2 **Guandi** China
70D2 **Guane** Cuba
31C5 **Guangdong** *Province* China
31A3 **Guanghan** China
31C3 **Guanghua** China
31A4 **Guangmao Shan** *Mt* China
31A5 **Guangnan** China
31B5 **Guangxi** *Province* China
31B3 **Guangyuan** China
31D4 **Guangze** China
31C5 **Guangzhou** China
75D2 **Guanhães** Brazil
72E3 **Guania** *R* Colombia/ Venezuela
69E5 **Guanipa** *R* Venezuela
69B2 **Guantánamo** Cuba
31D1 **Guanting Shuiku** *Res* China
31A3 **Guan Xian** China
72C2 **Guapá** Colombia
72F6 **Guaporé** *R* Bolivia/Brazil
72E7 **Guaquí** Bolivia
75D1 **Guará** *R* Brazil
72C4 **Guaranda** Ecuador
75B4 **Guarapuava** Brazil
75C4 **Guaraqueçaba** Brazil
15B1 **Guara, Sierra de** *Mts* Spain
75C3 **Guaratinguetá** Brazil
75C4 **Guaratuba, B** Brazil
15A1 **Guarda** Portugal
75C2 **Guarda Mor** Brazil
56C4 **Guasave** Mexico
70C3 **Guatemala** Guatemala
70C3 **Guatemala** *Republic* Central America
72D3 **Guaviare** *R* Colombia
75C3 **Guaxupé** Brazil
69L1 **Guayaguayare** Trinidad
72B4 **Guayaquil** Ecuador
72B4 **Guayaquil, Golfo de** Ecuador
70A2 **Guaymas** Mexico
51C5 **Guba** Zaïre
25P2 **Guba Buorkhaya** *B* Russian Federation
50E3 **Guban** *Region* Somalia
18C2 **Gubin** Poland
15B1 **Gudar, Sierra de** *Mts* Spain
44B3 **Gūdūr** India
13D4 **Guebwiller** France
16B3 **Guelma** Algeria
64C2 **Guelph** Canada
48A2 **Guelta Zemmur** Morocco
50C2 **Guéréda** Chad
14C2 **Guéret** France
60C2 **Guernsey** USA
14B2 **Guernsey** *I* Channel Islands
50D3 **Gughe** *Mt* Ethiopia
25O4 **Gugigu** China
27H5 **Guguan** *I* Pacific Ocean
49D4 **Guider** Cameroon
31C4 **Guidong** China
48B4 **Guiglo** Ivory Coast
47E1 **Guijá** Mozambique
31C5 **Gui Jiang** *R* China
7D4 **Guildford** England
31C4 **Guilin** China
31A2 **Guinan** China
66A1 **Guinda** USA
48A3 **Guinea** *Republic* Africa
52H4 **Guinea Basin** Atlantic Ocean
48A3 **Guinea-Bissau** *Republic* Africa
48C4 **Guinea,G of** W Africa
69A2 **Güines** Cuba
48B3 **Guir** *Well* Mali
75B2 **Guiratinga** Brazil
72F1 **Güiria** Venezuela
6D2 **Guisborough** England
13B3 **Guise** France
27F5 **Guiuan** Philippines
31B5 **Gui Xian** China
31B4 **Guiyang** China
31B4 **Guizhou** *Province* China
42C4 **Gujarāt** *State* India
42C2 **Gujranwala** Pakistan
42C2 **Gujrat** Pakistan
34C2 **Gulargambone** Australia
44B2 **Gulbarga** India
19F1 **Gulbene** Latvia
44B2 **Guledagudda** India
63E2 **Gulfport** USA
Gulf,The = Persian Gulf
34C2 **Gulgong** Australia
31B4 **Gulin** China
17F3 **Güllük Körfezi** *B* Turkey
50D3 **Gulu** Uganda
34C1 **Guluguba** Australia
48C3 **Gumel** Nigeria
43E4 **Gumla** India
13D2 **Gummersbach** Germany
40C1 **Gümüşhane** Turkey
42D4 **Guna** India
50D2 **Guna** *Mt* Ethiopia
34C3 **Gundagai** Australia
50B4 **Gungu** Zaïre
55Q3 **Gunnbjørn Fjeld** *Mt* Greenland
34D2 **Gunnedah** Australia
60B3 **Gunnison** USA
60B3 **Gunnison** *R* USA
44B2 **Guntakal** India
67A2 **Guntersville** USA
67A2 **Guntersville L** USA
44C2 **Guntūr** India
30C5 **Gunung Batu Puteh** *Mt* Malaysia
30C5 **Gunung Tahan** *Mt* Malaysia
51B5 **Gunza** Angola
31D3 **Guoyang** China
42D2 **Gurdāspur** India
42D3 **Gurgaon** India
72F2 **Guri, Embalse de** *Res* Venezuela
43E3 **Gurkha** Nepal
40C2 **Gürün** Turkey
73J4 **Gurupi** *R* Brazil
51D5 **Guruve** Zimbabwe
31A1 **Gurvan Sayhan Uul** *Upland* Mongolia
21J6 **Gur'yev** Kazakhstan
48C3 **Gusau** Nigeria
19E2 **Gusev** Russian Federation
28A3 **Gushan** China
20G4 **Gus' Khrustalnyy** Russian Federation
55P3 **Gustav Holm, Kap** *C* Greenland
54E4 **Gustavus** USA
66B2 **Gustine** USA
57E3 **Guston** USA
18B2 **Gütersloh** Germany
64B3 **Guthrie** Kentucky, USA
63C1 **Guthrie** Oklahoma, USA
62B2 **Guthrie** Texas, USA
61E2 **Guttenberg** USA
73G3 **Guyana** *Republic* S America
52F4 **Guyana Basin** Atlantic Ocean
31C1 **Guyang** China
14B3 **Guyenne** *Region* France
62B1 **Guymon** USA
34D2 **Guyra** Australia
31B2 **Guyuan** China
62A2 **Guzmán, Laguna** *L* Mexico
43G5 **Gwa** Burma
34C2 **Gwabegar** Australia
38E3 **Gwadar** Pakistan
42D3 **Gwalior** India
47D1 **Gwanda** Zimbabwe
50C3 **Gwane** Zaïre
7C4 **Gwent** *County* Wales
51C5 **Gweru** Zimbabwe
34C1 **Gwydir** *R* Australia
7C3 **Gwynedd** Wales
21H7 **Gyandzha** Azerbaijan
43F3 **Gyangzê** China
26C3 **Gyaring Hu** *L* China
24J2 **Gydanskiy Poluostrov** *Pen* Russian Federation
43F3 **Gyirong** China
55O3 **Gyldenløves Fjord** Greenland
34D1 **Gympie** Australia
19D3 **Gyöngyös** Hungary
19D3 **Györ** Hungary

H

33H2 **Ha'apai Group** *Is* Tonga
12K6 **Haapajärvi** Finland
20C4 **Haapsalu** Estonia
18A2 **Haarlem** Netherlands
13D2 **Haarstrang** *Region* Germany
Habana, La = Havana
43G4 **Habiganj** Bangladesh
29D4 **Hachijō-jima** *I* Japan
29C3 **Hachiman** Japan
29E2 **Hachinohe** Japan
29C3 **Hachioji** Japan
68C2 **Hackettstown** USA
34A2 **Hack** *Mt* Australia
8D4 **Haddington** Scotland
34B1 **Haddon Corner** Australia
34B1 **Haddon Downs** Australia
48D3 **Hadejia** Nigeria
48C3 **Hadejia** *R* Nigeria
45C2 **Hadera** Israel
18B1 **Haderslev** Denmark
38D4 **Hadībоh** Socotra
54H2 **Hadley B** Canada
28A3 **Hadong** S Korea
31B5 **Hadong** Vietnam
38C4 **Ḩaḑramawt** *Region* Yemen
18C1 **Hadsund** Denmark
28B3 **Haeju** N Korea
28A3 **Haeju-man** *B* N Korea
28A4 **Haenam** S Korea
41E4 **Hafar al Bātin** Saudi Arabia
55M2 **Haffners Bjerg** *Mt* Greenland
42C2 **Hafizabad** Pakistan
43G3 **Hāflong** India
12A2 **Hafnarfjörður** Iceland
18B2 **Hagen** Germany
68B3 **Hagerstown** USA
28B4 **Hagi** Japan
31A5 **Ha Giang** Vietnam
13D3 **Hagondange** France
13D3 **Haguenan** France
48A2 **Hagunia** *Well* Morocco
26H4 **Haha-jima** *I* Japan
26C3 **Hah Xil Hu** *L* China
28A2 **Haicheng** China
30D1 **Hai Duong** Vietnam
45C2 **Haifa** Israel
45C2 **Haifa,B of** Israel
31D2 **Hai He** *R* China
31C5 **Haikang** China
30E1 **Haikou** China
40D4 **Hā'il** Saudi Arabia
43G4 **Hailākāndi** India
25N5 **Hailar** China
28B2 **Hailong** China
26F2 **Hailun** China
12J5 **Hailuoto** *I* Finland
30D2 **Hainan** *I* China
54E4 **Haines** USA
54E3 **Haines Junction** Canada
18D3 **Hainfeld** Austria
31B5 **Haiphong** Vietnam
28A2 **Haisgai** China
69C3 **Haiti** *Republic* Caribbean Sea
66D2 **Haiwee Res** USA
50D2 **Haiya** Sudan
31A2 **Haiyan** China
31B2 **Haiyuan** China
19E3 **Hajdúböszörmény** Hungary
29C3 **Hajiki-saki** *Pt* Japan
43G4 **Haka** Burma
66E5 **Hakalau** Hawaiian Islands
41D2 **Hakkâri** Turkey
29E2 **Hakodate** Japan
29C3 **Hakui** Japan
29C3 **Haku-san** *Mt* Japan
Ḩalab = Aleppo
41E2 **Halabja** Iraq
50D1 **Halaib** Egypt
45B3 **Halâl, Gebel** *Mt* Egypt
45D1 **Halba** Lebanon
26C2 **Halban** Mongolia
18C2 **Halberstadt** Germany
12G7 **Halden** Norway
43F4 **Haldia** India
42D3 **Haldwāni** India

55M5 **Halifax** Canada
6D3 **Halifax** England
65D3 **Halifax** USA
45D1 **Halīmah, Jabal** *Mt* Lebanon/Syria
8D2 **Halkirk** Scotland
28A4 **Halla-san** *Mt* S Korea
55M1 **Hall Basin** *Sd* Canada/ Greenland
55K3 **Hall Beach** Canada
13C2 **Halle** Belgium
18C2 **Halle** Germany
76F1 **Halley** *Base* Antarctica
65D1 **Halleybury** Canada
60C1 **Halliday** USA
12F6 **Hallingdal** *R* Norway
61D1 **Hallock** USA
55M3 **Hall Pen** Canada
32B2 **Hall's Creek** Australia
68C2 **Hallstead** USA
27F6 **Halmahera** *Is* Indonesia
12G7 **Halmstad** Sweden
16C3 **Halq el Qued** Tunisia
18B2 **Haltern** Germany
20C2 **Halti** *Mt* Finland/Norway
8D4 **Haltwhistle** England
41F4 **Halul** *I* Qatar
45C3 **Haluza** *Hist Site* Israel
28B4 **Hamada** Japan
48C2 **Hamada de Tinrhert** *Desert Region* Algeria
48B2 **Hamada du Dra** *Upland* Algeria
41E3 **Hamadān** Iran
48B2 **Hamada Tounassine** *Region* Algeria
21F8 **Ḩamāh** Syria
29C4 **Hamamatsu** Japan
12G6 **Hamar** Norway
40C5 **Hamâta, Gebel** *Mt* Egypt
29D1 **Hama-Tombetsu** Japan
44C4 **Hambantota** Sri Lanka
63D2 **Hamburg** Arkansas, USA
61D2 **Hamburg** Iowa, USA
68A1 **Hamburg** New York, USA
68C2 **Hamburg** Pennsylvania, USA
18B2 **Hamburg** Germany
68D2 **Hamden** USA
12J6 **Hämeenlinna** Finland
13E1 **Hameln** Germany
32A3 **Hamersley Range** *Mts* Australia
28B2 **Hamgyong Sanmaek** *Mts* N Korea
28B3 **Hamhŭng** N Korea
26C2 **Hami** China
45C1 **Ḩamīdīyah** Syria
63E2 **Hamilton** Alabama, USA
34B3 **Hamilton** Australia
65D2 **Hamilton** Canada
58D1 **Hamilton** Montana, USA
68C1 **Hamilton** New York, USA
35C1 **Hamilton** New Zealand
64C3 **Hamilton** Ohio, USA
8C4 **Hamilton** Scotland
66B2 **Hamilton,Mt** USA
12K6 **Hamina** Finland
43E3 **Hamīrpur** India
28A3 **Hamju** N Korea
18B2 **Hamm** Germany
49D2 **Hammādāh al Hamrā** *Upland* Libya
16C3 **Hammamet** Tunisia
16C3 **Hammamet, Golfe de** Tunisia
12H6 **Hammerdal** Sweden
12J4 **Hammerfest** Norway
64B2 **Hammond** Illinois, USA
63D2 **Hammond** Louisiana, USA
60C1 **Hammond** Montana, USA
68C3 **Hammonton** USA
35B3 **Hampden** New Zealand
7D4 **Hampshire** *County* England
63D2 **Hampton** Arkansas, USA
61E2 **Hampton** Iowa, USA
68E1 **Hampton** New Hampshire, USA
65D3 **Hampton** Virginia, USA
38D3 **Hāmūn-e-Jāz-Mūriān** *L* Iran
42B3 **Hamun-i-Lora** *Salt L* Pakistan
28A3 **Han** *R* S Korea
66E5 **Hana** Hawaiian Islands
66E5 **Hanalei** Hawaiian Islands
29E3 **Hanamaki** Japan
13E2 **Hanau** Germany
31C2 **Hancheng** China
31C3 **Hanchuan** China
65D3 **Hancock** Maryland, USA
64B1 **Hancock** Michigan, USA
68C2 **Hancock** New York, USA
29C4 **Handa** Japan
8C2 **Handa, I** Scotland
31C2 **Handan** China
50D4 **Handeni** Tanzania
66C2 **Hanford** USA
31B2 **Hanggin Qi** China
12J7 **Hangö** Finland
31E3 **Hangzhou** China
31E3 **Hangzhou Wan** *B* China
61D1 **Hankinson** USA
59D3 **Hanksville** USA
35B2 **Hanmer Springs** New Zealand
54G4 **Hanna** Canada
61E3 **Hannibal** USA
18B2 **Hannover** Germany
12G7 **Hanöbukten** *B* Sweden
30D1 **Hanoi** Vietnam
47C3 **Hanover** South Africa
68B3 **Hanover** USA
74B8 **Hanover** *I* Chile
31C3 **Han Shui** *R* China
42D3 **Hānsi** India
26D2 **Hantay** Mongolia
31B3 **Hanzhong** China
43F4 **Hāora** India
12J5 **Haparanda** Sweden
28A3 **Hapch'on** S Korea
43G3 **Hāpoli** India
43J1 **Hapur** India
40C4 **Ḩaql** Saudi Arabia
41E5 **Ḩaradh** Saudi Arabia
45C4 **Harad, Jebel el** *Mt* Jordan
50E3 **Hara Fanna** Ethiopia
29D3 **Haramachi** Japan
51D5 **Harare** Zimbabwe
50C2 **Harazé** Chad
26F2 **Harbin** China
64C2 **Harbor Beach** USA
42D4 **Harda** India
12F6 **Hardangerfjord** *Inlet* Norway
13D1 **Härdenberg** Netherlands
13C1 **Harderwijk** Netherlands
60B1 **Hardin** USA
43L2 **Hardoi** India
13D3 **Hardt** *Region* Germany
63D1 **Hardy** USA
45C3 **Hareidin, Wadi** Egypt
50E3 **Harēr** Ethiopia
50E3 **Hargeysa** Somalia
45C3 **Har Hakippa** *Mt* Israel
26C3 **Harhu** *L* China
27D7 **Hari** *R* Indonesia
29B4 **Harima-nada** *B* Japan
64C3 **Harlan** USA
7B3 **Harlech** Wales
58E1 **Harlem** USA
7E3 **Harleston** England
18B2 **Harlingen** Netherlands
63C3 **Harlingen** USA
7E4 **Harlow** England
58E1 **Harlowtown** USA
45C2 **Har Meron** *Mt* Israel
58C2 **Harney Basin** USA
58C2 **Harney L** USA
12H6 **Härnösand** Sweden
48B4 **Harper** Liberia
66D3 **Harper L** USA
65D3 **Harpers Ferry** USA
13E1 **Harpstedt** Germany
45C3 **Har Ramon** *Mt* Israel
40C4 **Harrāt al 'Uwayrid** *Region* Saudi Arabia
40D5 **Ḩarrāt Kishb** *Region* Saudi Arabia
55L4 **Harricanaw** *R* Canada
67B1 **Harriman** USA
68D1 **Harriman Res** USA
68C3 **Harrington** USA
55N4 **Harrington Harbour** Canada
8B3 **Harris** *District* Scotland
64B3 **Harrisburg** Illinois, USA
68B2 **Harrisburg** Pennsylvania, USA
47D2 **Harrismith** South Africa
63D1 **Harrison** USA
65D3 **Harrisonburg** USA
55N4 **Harrison,C** Canada
61E3 **Harrisonville** USA
8B3 **Harris,Sound of** *Chan* Scotland
64C2 **Harrisville** USA
6D2 **Harrogate** England
45C3 **Har Saggi** *Mt* Israel
45D2 **Ḩarsīr, Wadi al** Syria
12H5 **Harstad** Norway
28A2 **Hartao** China
47C2 **Hartbees** *R* South Africa
12F6 **Hårteigen** *Mt* Norway
68D2 **Hartford** Connecticut, USA
64B2 **Hartford** Michigan, USA
61D2 **Hartford** S Dakota, USA
12G6 **Hartkjølen** *Mt* Norway
65F1 **Hartland** Canada
7B4 **Hartland** England
7B4 **Hartland Pt** England
6D2 **Hartlepool** England
62B1 **Hartley** USA
67A2 **Hartselle** USA
63C2 **Hartshorne** USA
67B2 **Hartwell Res** USA
47C2 **Hartz** *R* South Africa
45C3 **Hārūn, Jebel** *Mt* Jordan
25L5 **Har Us Nuur** *L* Mongolia
38E2 **Harut** *R* Afghanistan
60B3 **Harvard,Mt** USA
60C1 **Harvey** USA
7E4 **Harwich** England
42D3 **Haryāna** *State* India
45C3 **Hāsā** Jordan
45B3 **Hasana, Wadi** Egypt
45C3 **Hāsā, Wadi el** Jordan
45C2 **Hāsbaiya** Lebanon
13E1 **Hase** *R* Germany
13D1 **Haselünne** Germany
29C4 **Hashimoto** Japan
41E2 **Hashtpar** Iran
41E2 **Hashtrūd** Iran
62C2 **Haskell** USA
7D4 **Haslemere** England
44B3 **Hassan** India
18B2 **Hasselt** Belgium
48C2 **Hassi Inifel** Algeria
48B2 **Hassi Mdakane** *Well* Algeria
48C1 **Hassi Messaoud** Algeria
12G7 **Hässleholm** Sweden
34C3 **Hastings** Australia
7E4 **Hastings** England
61E2 **Hastings** Minnesota, USA
56D2 **Hastings** Nebraska, USA
35C1 **Hastings** New Zealand
63E1 **Hatchie** *R* USA
34B2 **Hatfield** Australia
42D3 **Hāthras** India
30D2 **Ha Tinh** Vietnam
34B2 **Hattah** Australia
57F3 **Hatteras,C** USA
63E2 **Hattiesburg** USA
19D3 **Hatvan** Hungary
30D3 **Hau Bon** Vietnam
50E3 **Haud** *Region* Ethiopia
12F7 **Haugesund** Norway
35C1 **Hauhungaroa Range** *Mts* New Zealand
35B1 **Hauraki G** New Zealand
35A3 **Hauroko,L** New Zealand
48B1 **Haut Atlas** *Mts* Morocco
50C3 **Haute Kotto** *Region* Central African Republic
13C3 **Haute-Marne** *Department* France
13D4 **Haute-Saône** *Department* France
13C2 **Hautes Fagnes** *Mts* Belgium/Germany
65F2 **Haut, Isle au** USA
13C2 **Hautmont** France
13D4 **Haut-Rhin** *Department* France
42A2 **Hauz Qala** Afghanistan
70D2 **Havana** Cuba
64A2 **Havana** USA
44B4 **Havankulam** Sri Lanka
59D4 **Havasu L** USA
67C2 **Havelock** USA
35C1 **Havelock North** New Zealand
7E3 **Haverhill** England
68E1 **Haverhill** USA
44B3 **Hāveri** India
68D2 **Haverstraw** USA
18D3 **Havlíčkův Brod** Czech Republic
58E1 **Havre** USA
68B3 **Havre de Grace** USA
55M4 **Havre-St-Pierre** Canada
17F2 **Havsa** Turkey
66E5 **Hawaii** *Is, State* Pacific Ocean
66E5 **Hawaii Volcanoes Nat Pk** Hawaiian Islands
35A2 **Hawea,L** New Zealand
35B1 **Hawera** New Zealand
66E5 **Hawi** Hawaiian Islands
8D4 **Hawick** Scotland
35A2 **Hawkdun Range** *Mts* New Zealand
35C1 **Hawke B** New Zealand
34D2 **Hawke,C** Australia
34A2 **Hawker** Australia
68C2 **Hawley** USA
30B1 **Hawng Luk** Burma
41D3 **Hawr al Habbaniyah** *L* Iraq
41E3 **Hawr al Hammár** *L* Iraq
40D3 **Ḩawrān, Wadi** *R* Iraq
66C1 **Hawthorne** USA
34B2 **Hay** Australia
7C3 **Hay** England
54G3 **Hay** *R* Canada
13C3 **Hayange** France
54B3 **Haycock** USA
59D4 **Hayden** Arizona, USA
60B2 **Hayden** Colorado, USA
55J4 **Hayes** *R* Canada
55M2 **Hayes Halvø** *Region* Greenland
54D3 **Hayes, Mt** USA
7B4 **Hayle** England
7D4 **Hayling** *I* England
68B3 **Haymarket** USA
54G3 **Hay River** Canada
60D3 **Hays** USA
63C1 **Haysville** USA
66A2 **Hayward** California, USA
64A1 **Hayward** Wisconsin, USA
7D4 **Haywards Heath** England
42A2 **Hazarajat** *Region* Afghanistan
64C3 **Hazard** USA
43F4 **Hazārībāg** India
13B2 **Hazebrouck** France
63D2 **Hazelhurst** USA
54F4 **Hazelton** Canada
54B3 **Hazen B** USA
55L1 **Hazen L** Canada
54G2 **Hazen Str** Canada
45C3 **Hazeva** Israel
68C2 **Hazleton** USA
66A1 **Healdsburg** USA
34C3 **Healesville** Australia
36E7 **Heard I** Indian Ocean
63C2 **Hearne** USA
57E2 **Hearst** Canada
60C1 **Heart** *R* USA
62C3 **Hebbronville** USA
31D2 **Hebei** *Province* China
34C1 **Hebel** Australia
58D2 **Heber City** USA
58D2 **Hebgen L** USA
31C2 **Hebi** China
31C2 **Hebian** China
55M4 **Hebron** Canada
45C3 **Hebron** Israel
60C1 **Hebron** N Dakota, USA
61D2 **Hebron** Nebraska, USA
54E4 **Hecate Str** Canada
31B5 **Hechi** China
13E3 **Hechingen** Germany
54G2 **Hecla and Griper B** Canada
35C2 **Hector,Mt** New Zealand
12G6 **Hede** Sweden
12H6 **Hedemora** Sweden
58C1 **He Devil Mt** USA
18B2 **Heerenveen** Netherlands
13C2 **Heerlen** Netherlands
Hefa = Haifa
31D3 **Hefei** China
31B4 **Hefeng** China
26G2 **Hegang** China
29C3 **Hegura-jima** *I* Japan
30B1 **Heho** Burma
45C3 **Heidan** *R* Jordan
18B2 **Heide** Germany
47C3 **Heidelberg** Cape Province, South Africa
47D2 **Heidelberg** Transvaal, South Africa
18B3 **Heidelberg** Germany
18C3 **Heidenheim** Germany
25O4 **Heihe** China
47D2 **Heilbron** South Africa
18B3 **Heilbronn** Germany
18C2 **Heiligenstadt** Germany
12K6 **Heinola** Finland
28A2 **Heishan** China
31B4 **Hejiang** China
55R3 **Hekla** *Mt* Iceland
30C1 **Hekou** Vietnam
31A5 **Hekou Yaozou Zizhixian** China
31B2 **Helan** China
31B2 **Helan Shan** *Mt* China
63D2 **Helena** Arkansas, USA
58D1 **Helena** Montana, USA
66D3 **Helendale** USA
27G6 **Helen Reef** Pacific Ocean
8C3 **Helensburgh** Scotland
45A3 **Heliopolis** Egypt
41F4 **Helleh** *R* Iran
15B2 **Hellín** Spain
58C1 **Hells Canyon** *R* USA
13D2 **Hellweg** *Region* Germany
66B2 **Helm** USA
38E2 **Helmand** *R* Afghanistan/ Iran
47B2 **Helmeringhausen** Namibia
13C2 **Helmond** Netherlands
8D2 **Helmsdale** Scotland
51F5 **Helodrano Antongila** *B* Madagascar
28B2 **Helong** China
12G7 **Helsingborg** Sweden
Helsingfors = Helsinki
18C1 **Helsingør** Denmark
12J6 **Helsinki** Finland
7B4 **Helston** England
9C3 **Helvick Hd** *Pt* Irish Republic
40B4 **Helwân** Egypt
7D4 **Hemel Hempstead** England
63C2 **Hempstead** USA
12H7 **Hemse** Sweden
31A3 **Henan** China
31C3 **Henan** *Province* China
35B1 **Hen and Chickens Is** New Zealand
29C2 **Henashi-zaki** *C* Japan
64B3 **Henderson** Kentucky, USA
67C1 **Henderson** N Carolina, USA
59D3 **Henderson** Nevada, USA
63D2 **Henderson** Texas, USA
67B1 **Hendersonville** N Carolina, USA
67A1 **Hendersonville** Tennessee, USA
47D3 **Hendrik Verwoerd Dam** South Africa
31E5 **Hengchun** Taiwan
26C4 **Hengduan Shan** *Mts* China
18B2 **Hengelo** Netherlands
31B2 **Hengshan** China
31D2 **Hengshui** China
30D1 **Heng Xian** China
31C4 **Hengyang** China
30A4 **Henhoaha** Nicobar Is, India
7D4 **Henley-on-Thames** England
68C3 **Henlopen,C** USA
68E1 **Henniker** USA
62C2 **Henrietta** USA
55K4 **Henrietta Maria,C** Canada
59D3 **Henrieville** USA
63C1 **Henryetta** USA
55M3 **Henry Kater Pen** Canada
47A1 **Henties Bay** Namibia
26D2 **Hentiyn Nuruu** *Mts* Mongolia
30B2 **Henzada** Burma
31B5 **Hepu** China
38E2 **Herat** Afghanistan
54H4 **Herbert** Canada
35C2 **Herbertville** New Zealand
13E2 **Herborn** Germany
69A4 **Heredia** Costa Rica
7C3 **Hereford** England
62B2 **Hereford** USA
7C3 **Hereford & Worcester** *County* England
13C2 **Herentals** Belgium
13E1 **Herford** Germany
61D3 **Herington** USA
35A3 **Heriot** New Zealand
68C1 **Herkimer** USA
8E1 **Herma Ness** *Pen* Scotland
47B3 **Hermanus** South Africa
34C2 **Hermidale** Australia
35B2 **Hermitage** New Zealand
32D1 **Hermit Is** Papua New Guinea
45C2 **Hermon, Mt** Lebanon/ Syria
70A2 **Hermosillo** Mexico
75B4 **Hernandarias** Paraguay
68B2 **Herndon** USA
66C2 **Herndon** USA
13D2 **Herne** Germany
7E4 **Herne Bay** England
18B1 **Herning** Denmark
41E2 **Herowābad** Iran
75A4 **Herradura** Argentina
15B2 **Herrera del Duque** Spain
68B2 **Hershey** USA
7D4 **Hertford** England
7D4 **Hertford** *County* England
45C2 **Herzliyya** Israel
13C2 **Hesbaye** Region, Belgium
13A2 **Hesdin** France
31B2 **Heshui** China
66D3 **Hesperia** USA
18B2 **Hessen** *State* Germany
66C2 **Hetch Hetchy Res** USA
60C1 **Hettinger** USA
48B1 **Heuts Plateaux** Algeria/ Morocco
7E3 **Hewett** *Oilfield* N Sea
6C2 **Hexham** England
31C5 **He Xian** China
6C2 **Heysham** England
47D2 **Heystekrand** South Africa
31C5 **Heyuan** China
34B3 **Heywood** Australia
31D2 **Heze** China
67B3 **Hialeah** USA
61E1 **Hibbing** USA
67B1 **Hickory** USA
35C1 **Hicks Bay** New Zealand
34C3 **Hicks,Pt** Australia
63C2 **Hico** USA
29D2 **Hidaka-sammyaku** *Mts* Japan
70B2 **Hidalgo del Parral** Mexico
75C2 **Hidrolândia** Brazil
48A2 **Hierro** *I* Canary Islands
29D3 **Higashine** Japan
28B4 **Higashi-suidō** *Str* Japan
45B3 **Higâyib, Wadi el** Egypt
58B2 **High Desert** USA
63D3 **High Island** USA
66D3 **Highland** USA
8C3 **Highland** *Region* Scotland
8E2 **Highlander** *Oilfield* N Sea
66C1 **Highland Peak** *Mt* USA
68C2 **Highland Falls** USA
67B1 **High Point** USA
54G4 **High Prairie** Canada
54G4 **High River** Canada
67B3 **High Springs** USA
68C2 **Hightstown** USA
7D4 **High Wycombe** England
12J7 **Hiiumaa** *I* Estonia
40C4 **Hijaz** *Region* Saudi Arabia

29C4 **Hikigawa** Japan
59C3 **Hiko** USA
29C3 **Hikone** Japan
35B1 **Hikurangi** New Zealand
56C4 **Hildago del Parral** Mexico
18B2 **Hildesheim** Germany
69R2 **Hillaby,Mt** Barbados
60D3 **Hill City** USA
18C1 **Hillerød** Denmark
61D1 **Hillsboro** N Dakota, USA
68E1 **Hillsboro** New Hampshire, USA
62A2 **Hillsboro** New Mexico, USA
64C3 **Hillsboro** Ohio, USA
58B1 **Hillsboro** Oregon, USA
63C2 **Hillsboro** Texas, USA
34C2 **Hillston** Australia
64C3 **Hillsville** USA
8E1 **Hillswick** Scotland
66E5 **Hilo** Hawaiian Islands
6C2 **Hilpsford** *Pt* England
68B1 **Hilton** USA
40C2 **Hilvan** Turkey
18B2 **Hilversum** Netherlands
42D2 **Himāchal Pradesh** *State* India
Himalaya = Great Himalayan Range
39G3 **Himalaya** *Mts* Asia
43N1 **Himalchuli** *Mt* Nepal
42C4 **Himatnagar** India
29C4 **Himeji** Japan
29D3 **Himi** Japan
45D1 **Ḩimş** Syria
7D3 **Hinckley** England
61E1 **Hinckley** Minnesota, USA
68C1 **Hinckley Res** USA
42D3 **Hindaun** India
42B1 **Hindu Kush** *Mts* Afghanistan
44B3 **Hindupur** India
54G4 **Hines Creek** Canada
42D4 **Hinganghāt** India
42B3 **Hingol** *R* Pakistan
42D5 **Hingoli** India
66D3 **Hinkley** USA
12H5 **Hinnøya** *I* Norway
68D1 **Hinsdale** USA
62C1 **Hinton** USA
28A4 **Hirado** Japan
28A4 **Hirado-shima** *I* Japan
43E4 **Hirakud Res** India
40B2 **Hirfanli Baraji** *Res* Turkey
44B3 **Hirihar** India
29D2 **Hiroo** Japan
29E2 **Hirosaki** Japan
28C4 **Hiroshima** Japan
13C3 **Hirson** France
17F2 **Hîrşova** Romania
18B1 **Hirtshals** Denmark
42D3 **Hisār** India
69C3 **Hispaniola** *I* Caribbean Sea
45D1 **Ḩisyah** Syria
40D3 **Hīt** Iraq
29E3 **Hitachi** Japan
29D3 **Hitachi-Ota** Japan
7D4 **Hitchin** England
28C4 **Hitoyoshi** Japan
12F6 **Hitra** *I* Norway
29B4 **Hiuchi-nada** *B* Japan
29B4 **Hiwasa** Japan
45C3 **Hiyon** *R* Israel
18B1 **Hjørring** Denmark
30B1 **Hka** *R* Burma
48C4 **Ho** Ghana
30D1 **Hoa Binh** Vietnam
30D3 **Hoa Da** Vietnam
34C4 **Hobart** Australia
62C2 **Hobart** USA
62B2 **Hobbs** USA
18B1 **Hobro** Denmark
50E3 **Hobyo** Somalia
30D3 **Ho Chi Minh City** Vietnam
18C3 **Hochkonig** *Mt* Austria
28A2 **Hochon** N Korea
13E3 **Hockenheim** Germany
Hodeida = Al Ḩudaydah
17E1 **Hódmezö'hely** Hungary
15C2 **Hodna, Monts du** Algeria
18D3 **Hodonin** Czech Republic
13C2 **Hoek van Holland** Netherlands
28A3 **Hoengsŏng** S Korea
28B2 **Hoeryŏng** N Korea
28A3 **Hoeyang** N Korea
18C2 **Hof** Germany
55R3 **Höfn** Iceland
12B2 **Hofsjökull** *Mts* Iceland
28C4 **Hōfu** Japan
48C2 **Hoggar** *Upland* Algeria
13D2 **Hohe Acht** *Mt* Germany
13E2 **Hohes Gras** *Mts* Germany
31C1 **Hohhot** China
26C3 **Hoh Sai Hu** *L* China
39G2 **Hoh Xil Shan** *Mts* China
50D3 **Hoima** Uganda
43G3 **Hojāi** India
28B4 **Hojo** Japan
35B1 **Hokianga Harbour** *B* New Zealand
35B2 **Hokitika** New Zealand
26H2 **Hokkaidō** *I* Japan
41G2 **Hokmābād** Iran
29D3 **Hokota** Japan
7E3 **Holbeach** England
34C3 **Holbrook** Australia
59D4 **Holbrook** USA
59D3 **Holden** USA
63C1 **Holdenville** USA
60D2 **Holdrege** USA
44B3 **Hole Narsipur** India
69Q2 **Holetown** Barbados
69B2 **Holguín** Cuba
18D3 **Hollabrunn** Austria
64B2 **Holland** USA
68A2 **Hollidaysburg** USA
62C2 **Hollis** USA
66B2 **Hollister** USA
63E2 **Holly Springs** USA
66C3 **Hollywood** California, USA
67B3 **Hollywood** Florida, USA
54G2 **Holman Island** Canada
12J6 **Holmsund** Sweden
45C2 **Holon** Israel
18B1 **Holstebro** Denmark
61D2 **Holstein** USA
55N3 **Holsteinsborg** Greenland
67B1 **Holston** *R* USA
64C2 **Holt** USA
61D3 **Holton** USA
54C3 **Holy Cross** USA
7B3 **Holyhead** Wales
6D3 **Holy I** England
7B3 **Holy I** Wales
60C2 **Holyoke** Colorado, USA
68D1 **Holyoke** Massachusetts, USA
9D2 **Holywood** Northern Ireland
13E2 **Holzminden** Germany
43G4 **Homalin** Burma
13E2 **Homburg** Germany
55M3 **Home B** Canada
63D2 **Homer** Louisiana, USA
54C4 **Homer** USA
35A2 **Homer Tunnel** New Zealand
67B2 **Homerville** USA
67B3 **Homestead** USA
67A2 **Homewood** USA
44B2 **Homnābād** India
51D6 **Homoine** Mozambique
Homs = Al Khums
Homs = Ḩimş
47B3 **Hondeklip B** South Africa
62A2 **Hondo** New Mexico, USA
62C3 **Hondo** Texas, USA
70D3 **Hondo** *R* Mexico
70D3 **Honduras** *Republic* Central America
70D3 **Honduras,G of** Honduras
12G6 **Hønefoss** Norway
68C2 **Honesdale** USA
59B2 **Honey L** USA
Hong *R* **= Nui Con Voi**
30C1 **Hong** *R* Vietnam
30D1 **Hon Gai** Vietnam
28A3 **Hongchŏn** S Korea
31A4 **Hongguo** China
31C4 **Hong Hu** *L* China
31B2 **Honghui** China
31C4 **Hongjiang** China
31C5 **Hong Kong** *Colony* SE Asia
26E2 **Hongor** Mongolia
31B5 **Hongshui He** *R* China
28A3 **Hongsong** S Korea
28A3 **Hongwon** N Korea
31A3 **Hongyuan** China
31D3 **Hongze Hu** *L* China
33E1 **Honiara** Solomon Islands
7C4 **Honiton** England
29D3 **Honjō** Japan
30C4 **Hon Khoai** *I* Cambodia
30D3 **Hon Lan** *I* Vietnam
12K4 **Honningsvåg** Norway
20D1 **Honningsvåg** Norway
66E5 **Honokaa** Hawaiian Islands
66E5 **Honolulu** Hawaiian Islands
30C4 **Hon Panjang** *I* Vietnam
26G3 **Honshū** *I* Japan
58B1 **Hood,Mt** USA
58B1 **Hood River** USA
13D1 **Hoogeveen** Netherlands
62B1 **Hooker** USA
9C3 **Hook Head** *C* Irish Republic
54E4 **Hoonah** USA
54B3 **Hooper Bay** USA
47D2 **Hoopstad** South Africa
18A2 **Hoorn** Netherlands
68D1 **Hoosick Falls** USA
56B3 **Hoover Dam** USA
63D2 **Hope** Arkansas, USA
55M4 **Hopedale** Canada
24D2 **Hopen** *I* Svalbard
55M3 **Hopes Advance,C** Canada
34B3 **Hopetoun** Australia
47C2 **Hopetown** South Africa
68A2 **Hopewell** Pennsylvania, USA
65D3 **Hopewell** Virginia, USA
64B3 **Hopkinsville** USA
58B1 **Hoquiam** USA
40D2 **Horasan** Turkey
13E3 **Horb** Germany
50E2 **Hordiyo** Somalia
31B1 **Hörh Uul** *Mt* Mongolia
37L6 **Horizon Depth** Pacific Ocean
41G4 **Hormuz,Str of** Oman/Iran
18D3 **Horn** Austria
55Q3 **Horn** *C* Iceland
12H5 **Hornavan** *L* Sweden
63D2 **Hornbeck** USA
58B2 **Hornbrook** USA
35B2 **Hornby** New Zealand
7D3 **Horncastle** England
68B1 **Hornell** USA
55K5 **Hornepayne** Canada
63E2 **Horn I** USA
33H2 **Horn, Îles de** Pacific Ocean
54F3 **Horn Mts** Canada
74C9 **Hornos, Cabo de** *C* Chile
6D3 **Hornsea** England
28A2 **Horqin Zuoyi Houqi** China
74E2 **Horqueta** Paraguay
68B1 **Horseheads** USA
18C1 **Horsens** Denmark
58B1 **Horseshoe Bay** Canada
58C2 **Horseshoe Bend** USA
34B3 **Horsham** Australia
7D4 **Horsham** England
12G7 **Horten** Norway
54F3 **Horton** *R* Canada
27E6 **Hose Mts** Borneo
42D4 **Hoshangābād** India
42D2 **Hoshiārpur** India
62C1 **Hosington** USA
44B2 **Hospet** India
74C9 **Hoste** *I* Chile
39F2 **Hotan** China
47C2 **Hotazel** South Africa
63D2 **Hot Springs** Arkansas, USA
60C2 **Hot Springs** S Dakota, USA
54G3 **Hottah L** Canada
69C3 **Hotte, Massif de la** *Mts* Haiti
47A2 **Hottentot Pt** Namibia
64B1 **Houghton** USA
65F1 **Houlton** USA
31C2 **Houma** China
63D3 **Houma** USA
8C3 **Hourn, Loch** *Inlet* Scotland
68D2 **Housatonic** *R* USA
63E2 **Houston** Mississippi, USA
63C3 **Houston** Texas, USA
32A3 **Houtman** *Is* Australia
68A2 **Houtzdale** USA
26C2 **Hovd** Mongolia
26D1 **Hövsgol Nuur** *L* Mongolia
34D1 **Howard** Australia
64B2 **Howard City** USA
50C2 **Howa, Wadi** *Watercourse* Chad/Sudan
34C3 **Howe,C** Australia
58B1 **Howe Sd** Canada
47E2 **Howick** South Africa
65F1 **Howland** USA
9C3 **Howth** Irish Republic
13E2 **Höxter** Germany
8D2 **Hoy** *I* Scotland
12F6 **Høyanger** Norway
61E1 **Hoyt Lakes** USA
18D2 **Hradec-Králové** Czech Republic
19D3 **Hranice** Czech Republic
19D3 **Hron** *R* Slovakia
31E5 **Hsinchu** Taiwan
30B1 **Hsipaw** Burma
31E5 **Hsüeh Shan** *Mt* Taiwan
47A1 **Huab** *R* Namibia
31B2 **Huachi** China
72C6 **Huacho** Peru
31C1 **Huade** China
28B2 **Huadian** China
31D3 **Huaibei** China
31D3 **Huaibin** China
28A2 **Huaide** China
28A2 **Huaidezhen** China
31D3 **Huai He** *R* China
31C4 **Huaihua** China
31C5 **Huaiji** China
31D3 **Huainan** China
59D3 **Hualapai Peak** *Mt* USA
26F4 **Hualien** Taiwan
72C5 **Huallaga** *R* Peru
72C5 **Huallanca** Peru
72C5 **Huamachuco** Peru
51B5 **Huambo** Angola
72E7 **Huanay** Bolivia
72C5 **Huancabamba** Peru
72C6 **Huancavelica** Peru
72C6 **Huancayo** Peru
31D3 **Huangchuan** China
Huang Hai = Yellow Sea
31D2 **Huang He** *R* China
31B2 **Huangling** China
30D2 **Huangliu** China
28B2 **Huangnihe** China
31C3 **Huangpi** China
31D3 **Huangshi** China
31D4 **Huangshan** China
31E4 **Huangyan** China
28B2 **Huanren** China
72C5 **Huānuco** Peru
74C1 **Huanuni** Bolivia
31B2 **Huan Xian** China
72C5 **Huaráz** Peru
72C6 **Huarmey** Peru
72C5 **Huascarán** *Mt* Peru
74B3 **Huasco** Chile
31C2 **Hua Xian** China
70B2 **Huayapan** *R* Mexico
31C3 **Hubei** *Province* China
44B2 **Hubli** India
28B2 **Huch'ang** N Korea
7D3 **Hucknell Torkard** England
7D3 **Huddersfield** England
13E1 **Hude** Germany
12H6 **Hudiksvall** Sweden
67B3 **Hudson** Florida, USA
64C2 **Hudson** Michigan, USA
68D1 **Hudson** New York, USA
68D1 **Hudson** *R* USA
55K4 **Hudson B** Canada
54H4 **Hudson Bay** Canada
68D1 **Hudson Falls** USA
55L3 **Hudson Str** Canada
30D2 **Hue** Vietnam
15A2 **Huelva** Spain
15B2 **Húercal Overa** Spain
15B1 **Huesca** Spain
32D3 **Hughenden** Australia
54C3 **Hughes** USA
43F4 **Hugli** *R* India
63C2 **Hugo** USA
62B1 **Hugoton** USA
31D4 **Hui'an** China
35C1 **Huiarau Range** *Mts* New Zealand
47B2 **Huib Hochplato** *Plat* Namibia
28B2 **Hüich'ŏn** N Korea
72C3 **Huila** *Mt* Colombia
31D5 **Huilai** China
31A4 **Huili** China
28B2 **Huinan** China
70C3 **Huixtla** Mexico
31A4 **Huize** China
31C5 **Huizhou** China
40D4 **Ḩulayfah** Saudi Arabia
26G2 **Hulin** China
65D1 **Hull** Canada
6D3 **Hull** England
33H1 **Hull** *I* Phoenix Islands
18D1 **Hultsfred** Sweden
25N5 **Hulun Nur** *L* China
72F5 **Humaitá** Brazil
47C3 **Humansdorp** South Africa
7D3 **Humber** *R* England
6D3 **Humberside** *County* England
54H4 **Humboldt** Canada
61E2 **Humboldt** Iowa, USA
63E1 **Humboldt** Tennessee, USA
58C2 **Humboldt** *R* USA
58B2 **Humboldt B** USA
55M2 **Humboldt Gletscher** *Gl* Greenland
59C3 **Humboldt L** USA
34C1 **Humeburn** Australia
34C3 **Hume,L** Australia
13D1 **Hümmling** *Hill* Germany
51B5 **Humpata** Angola
66C2 **Humphreys** USA
66C2 **Humphreys,Mt** California, USA
59D3 **Humphreys Peak** *Mt* Arizona, USA
12A1 **Húnaflóri** *B* Iceland
31C4 **Hunan** *Province* China
28C2 **Hunchun** China
17E1 **Hunedoara** Romania
19D3 **Hungary** *Republic* Europe
34B1 **Hungerford** Australia
28B3 **Hüngnam** N Korea
58D1 **Hungry Horse Res** USA
28B2 **Hunjiang** China
47B2 **Hunsberge** *Mts* Namibia
13D3 **Hunsrück** *Mts* Germany
7E3 **Hunstanton** England
13E1 **Hunte** *R* Germany
34D2 **Hunter** *R* Australia
34C4 **Hunter Is** Australia
64B3 **Huntingburg** USA
7D3 **Huntingdon** England
64B2 **Huntingdon** Indiana, USA
68A2 **Huntingdon** Pennsylvania, USA
64C3 **Huntington** USA
66C4 **Huntington Beach** USA
66C2 **Huntington L** USA
35C1 **Huntly** New Zealand
8D3 **Huntly** Scotland
54F3 **Hunt, Mt** Canada
67A2 **Huntsville** Alabama, USA
65D1 **Huntsville** Canada
63C2 **Huntsville** Texas, USA
30D2 **Huong Khe** Vietnam
27H7 **Huon Peninsula** Papua New Guinea
34C4 **Huonville** Australia
64C1 **Hurd,C** Canada
28A2 **Hure Qi** China
40B4 **Hurghada** Egypt
64A1 **Hurley** USA
66B2 **Huron** California, USA
61D2 **Huron** S Dakota, USA
64C1 **Huron,L** Canada/USA
35B2 **Hurunui** *R* New Zealand
12B1 **Húsavík** Iceland
17F1 **Huşi** Romania
12G7 **Huskvarna** Sweden
45C2 **Husn** Jordan
18B2 **Husum** Germany
56D3 **Hutchinson** USA
63C1 **Hutchinson** USA
34C1 **Hutton,Mt** Australia
31D2 **Hutuo He** *R* China
13C2 **Huy** Belgium
31A2 **Huzhu** China
16D2 **Hvar** *I* Croatia
28A2 **Hwadae** N Korea
51C5 **Hwange** Zimbabwe
51C5 **Hwange Nat Pk** Zimbabwe
28A2 **Hwapyong** N Korea
68E2 **Hyannis** Massachusetts, USA
60C2 **Hyannis** Nebraska, USA
26C2 **Hyargas Nuur** *L* Mongolia
54E4 **Hydaburg** USA
68D2 **Hyde Park** USA
44B2 **Hyderābād** India
42B3 **Hyderabad** Pakistan
14D3 **Hyères** France
14D3 **Hyères, Iles d'** *Is* France
28B2 **Hyesan** N Korea
68A3 **Hyndman** USA
56B2 **Hyndman Peak** *Mt* USA
20D3 **Hyrynsalmi** Finland
7E4 **Hythe** England
12J6 **Hyvinkää** Finland

I

73K6 **Iaçu** Brazil
17F2 **Ialomiţa** *R* Romania
17F1 **Iaşi** Romania
48C4 **Ibadan** Nigeria
72C3 **Ibagué** Colombia
17E2 **Ibar** *R* Montenegro/ Serbia, Yugoslavia
72C3 **Ibarra** Ecuador
13D1 **Ibbenbüren** Germany
75C2 **Ibiá** Brazil
75E1 **Ibicaraí** Brazil
74E3 **Ibicuí** *R* Brazil
74E4 **Ibicuy** Argentina
15C2 **Ibiza** Spain
15C2 **Ibiza** *I* Spain
51E5 **Ibo** Mozambique
73K6 **Ibotirama** Brazil
50C2 **Ibra, Wadi** *Watercourse* Sudan
41G5 **'Ibrī** Oman
72C6 **Ica** Peru
72E4 **Içá** *R* Brazil
72E3 **Içana** Brazil
12A1 **Iceland** *Republic* N Atlantic Ocean
25R4 **Icha** Russian Federation
44A2 **Ichalkaranji** India
29C3 **Ichinomiya** Japan
29E3 **Ichinosek** Japan
54B2 **Icy C** USA
63D2 **Idabell** USA
61D2 **Ida Grove** USA
58D2 **Idaho** State, USA
58C2 **Idaho City** USA
58D2 **Idaho Falls** USA
60B3 **Idaho Springs** USA
45B1 **Idalion** *Hist Site* Cyprus
58B2 **Idanha** USA
13D3 **Idar Oberstein** Germany
49D2 **Idehan Marzūg** *Desert* Libya
49D2 **Idehan Ubari** *Desert* Libya
48C2 **Idelès** Algeria
26C2 **Ideriym Gol** *R* Mongolia
40B5 **Idfu** Egypt
17E3 **Ídhi Óros** *Mt* Greece
17E3 **Ídhra** *I* Greece
50B4 **Idiofa** Zaïre
40C2 **Idlib** Syria
12K7 **Idritsa** Russian Federation
47D3 **Idutywa** South Africa
13B2 **Ieper** Belgium
17F3 **Ierápetra** Greece
25N4 **Iet Oktyob'ya** Russian Federation
51D4 **Ifakara** Tanzania
27H6 **Ifalik** *I* Pacific Ocean
51E6 **Ifanadiana** Madagascar
48C4 **Ife** Nigeria
48C3 **Iférouane** Niger
27E6 **Igan** Malaysia
75C3 **Igarapava** Brazil

24K3 **Igarka** Russian Federation
75A3 **Igatimi** Paraguay
41E2 **Igdir** Iran
12H6 **Iggesund** Sweden
16B3 **Iglesias** Sardinia, Italy
55K3 **Igloolik** Canada
57D2 **Ignace** Canada
40A1 **Iğneada Burun** *Pt* Turkey
48C1 **Ignil-Izane** Algeria
44E3 **Ignoitijala** Andaman Islands
17E3 **Igoumenítsa** Greece
20J4 **Igra** Russian Federation
20L3 **Igrim** Russian Federation
74F3 **Iguaçu, Quedas do** *Falls* Argentina/Brazil
70C3 **Iguala** Mexico
74G2 **Iguape** Brazil
75C3 **Iguatama** Brazil
75B3 **Iguatemi** Brazil
75A3 **Iguatemi** *R* Brazil
73L5 **Iguatu** Brazil
50A4 **Iguéla** Gabon
51E6 **Ihosy** Madagascar
29D3 **Iida** Japan
29C3 **Iide-san** *Mt* Japan
12K6 **Iisalmi** Finland
28B4 **Iisuka** Japan
48C4 **Ijebu** Nigeria
13C1 **Ijmuiden** Netherlands
13C1 **Ijssel** *R* Netherlands
18B2 **Ijsselmeer** *S* Netherlands
17F3 **Ikaría** *I* Greece
29E2 **Ikeda** Japan
50C4 **Ikela** Zaïre
17E2 **Ikhtiman** Bulgaria
28A4 **Iki** *I* Japan
51E5 **Ikopa** *R* Madagascar
27F5 **Ilagan** Philippines
41E3 **Ilām** Iran
26C1 **Ilanskiy** Russian Federation
50C4 **Ilebo** Zaïre
13B3 **Île De France** *Region* France
65E1 **Ile d'Orleans** Canada
21K5 **Ilek** *R* Russian Federation
7B4 **Ilfracombe** England
40B1 **Ilgaz Dağları** *Mts* Turkey
73H6 **Ilha do Bananal** *Region* Brazil
75D3 **Ilha Grande, B de** Brazil
73H8 **Ilha Grande, Reprêsa** Brazil/Paraguay
75B3 **Ilha Solteira Dam** Brazil
73L6 **Ilhéus** Brazil
54C4 **Iliamna L** USA
25M4 **Ilim** *R* Russian Fed
25M4 **Ilimsk** Russian Federation
25M4 **Ilin** *R* Russian Federation
26H2 **Il'inskiy** Russian Federation
17E3 **Iliodhrómia** *I* Greece
68C1 **Ilion** USA
6D3 **Ilkley** England
74B4 **Illapel** Chile
48C3 **Illéla** Niger
64A3 **Illinois** *R* USA
64B2 **Illinois** *State* USA
48C2 **Illizi** Algeria
20E4 **Il'men, Ozero** *L* Russian Federation
72D7 **Ilo** Peru
27F5 **Iloilo** Philippines
12L6 **Ilomantsi** Finland
48C4 **Ilorin** Nigeria
19G1 **Il'yino** Russian Federation
28B4 **Imabari** Japan
29C3 **Imaichi** Japan
12L5 **Imandra, Ozero** *L* Russian Federation
28A4 **Imari** Japan
20D3 **Imatra** Finland
74G3 **Imbituba** Brazil
75B4 **Imbituva** Brazil
50E3 **Imi** Ethiopia
28A3 **Imjin** *R* N Korea
58C2 **Imlay** USA
16C2 **Imola** Italy
73J5 **Imperatriz** Brazil
16B2 **Imperia** Italy
60C2 **Imperial** USA
59C4 **Imperial V** USA
50B3 **Impfondo** Congo
43G4 **Imphāl** India
29C3 **Ina** Japan
48C2 **In Afaleleh** *Well* Algeria
29C4 **Inamba-jima** *I* Japan
48C2 **In Amenas** Algeria
12K5 **Inari** Finland
12K5 **Inarijärvi** *L* Finland
29D3 **Inawashiro-ko** *L* Japan
48C2 **In Belbel** Algeria
21F7 **Ince Burun** *Pt* Turkey
40B2 **Incekum Burun** *Pt* Turkey
8C2 **Inchnadamph** Scotland
28B3 **Inch'on** S Korea
8B4 **Indaal, Loch** *Inlet* Scotland
48B2 **In Dagouber** *Well* Mali
75C2 **Indaiá** *R* Brazil
12H6 **Indals** *R* Sweden
66C2 **Independence** California, USA
61E2 **Independence** Iowa, USA
63C1 **Independence** Kansas, USA
61E3 **Independence** Missouri, USA
58C2 **Independence Mts** USA
21J6 **Inderborskiy** Kazakhstan
39F3 **India** *Federal Republic* Asia
65D2 **Indiana** USA
64B2 **Indiana** *State* USA
36F7 **Indian-Antarctic Basin** Indian Ocean
36F7 **Indian-Antarctic Ridge** Indian Ocean
64B3 **Indianapolis** USA
Indian Desert = Thar Desert
55N4 **Indian Harbour** Canada
36E5 **Indian O**
61E2 **Indianola** Iowa, USA
63D2 **Indianola** Mississippi, USA
75C2 **Indianópolis** Brazil
59C3 **Indian Springs** USA
20H2 **Indiga** Russian Federation
25Q3 **Indigirka** *R* Russian Federation
30D2 **Indo-China** *Region* SE Asia
27F7 **Indonesia** *Republic* SE Asia
42D4 **Indore** India
14C2 **Indre** *R* France
42B3 **Indus** *R* Pakistan
42B4 **Indus, Mouths of the** Pakistan
48C2 **In Ebeggi** *Well* Algeria
21E7 **Inebolu** Turkey
48C2 **In Ecker** Algeria
40A1 **Inegöl** Turkey
48D2 **In Ezzane** Algeria
47C3 **Infantta, C** South Africa
70B3 **Infiernillo, Pico del** *Mt* Mexico
48C3 **Ingal** Niger
64C2 **Ingersoll** Canada
32D2 **Ingham** Australia
55M2 **Inglefield Land** *Region* Greenland
35B1 **Inglewood** New Zealand
34D1 **Inglewood** Queensland, Australia
66C4 **Inglewood** USA
34B3 **Inglewood** Victoria, Australia
12B2 **Ingólfshöfdi** *I* Iceland
18C3 **Ingolstadt** Germany
43F4 **Ingrāj Bāzār** India
48C3 **In Guezzam** *Well* Algeria
47E2 **Inhaca** *I* Mozambique
47E2 **Inhaca Pen** Mozambique
51D6 **Inhambane** Mozambique
51D6 **Inharrime** Mozambique
75C2 **Inhumas** Brazil
72E3 **Inirida** *R* Colombia
9C2 **Inishowen** *District* Irish Republic
9C2 **Inishtrahull Sd** Irish Republic
34C1 **Injune** Australia
34B1 **Innamincka** Australia
8D4 **Innerleithen** Scotland
31B1 **Inner Mongolia Aut. Region** China
32D2 **Innisfail** Australia
18C3 **Innsbruck** Austria
50B4 **Inongo** Zaïre
19D2 **Inowrocław** Poland
48C2 **In Salah** Algeria
28A3 **Insil** S Korea
20L2 **Inta** Russian Federation
16B1 **Interlaken** Switzerland
33H3 **International Date Line**
61E1 **International Falls** USA
29D3 **Inubo-saki** *C* Japan
55L4 **Inukjuak** Canada
54E3 **Inuvik** Canada
54E3 **Inuvik** *Region* Canada
8C3 **Inveraray** Scotland
8D3 **Inverbervie** Scotland
35A3 **Invercargill** New Zealand
34D1 **Inverell** Australia
8C3 **Invergordon** Scotland
8C3 **Inverness** Scotland
8D3 **Inverurie** Scotland
32C4 **Investigator Str** Australia
26B1 **Inya** Russian Federation
25Q3 **Inya** *R* Russian Federation
51D5 **Inyanga** Zimbabwe
66D3 **Inyokern** USA
66C2 **Inyo Mts** USA
50B4 **Inzia** *R* Zaïre
17E3 **Ioánnina** Greece
63C1 **Iola** USA
8B3 **Iona** *I* Scotland
51B5 **Iôna Nat Pk** Angola
58C1 **Ione** USA
17E3 **Ionian Is** Greece
17D3 **Ionian S** Greece/Italy
Iónioi Nísoi *Is* **= Ionian Islands**
17F3 **Íos** *I* Greece
20J3 **Iosser** Russian Federation
61E2 **Iowa** *R* USA
61E2 **Iowa** *State* USA
64A2 **Iowa City** USA
61E2 **Iowa Falls** USA
75C2 **Ipameri** Brazil
75D2 **Ipanema** Brazil
21G6 **Ipatovo** Russian Federation
72C3 **Ipiales** Colombia
75E1 **Ipiaú** Brazil
75B4 **Ipiranga** Brazil
30C5 **Ipoh** Malaysia
73H7 **Iporá** Brazil
17F2 **Ipsala** Turkey
34D1 **Ipswich** Australia
7E3 **Ipswich** England
68E1 **Ipswich** USA
19G2 **Iput** *R* Russian Federation
75C3 **Iquape** Brazil
74B2 **Iquique** Chile
72D4 **Iquitos** Peru
17F3 **Iráklion** Greece
38D2 **Iran** *Republic* SW Asia
70B2 **Irapuato** Mexico
40D3 **Iraq** *Republic* SW Asia
75B4 **Irati** Brazil
49D2 **Irāwan** *Watercourse* Libya
45C2 **Irbid** Jordan
20L4 **Irbit** Russian Federation
10B3 **Ireland, Republic of** NW Europe
73G3 **Ireng** *R* Guyana
28B3 **Iri** S Korea
27G7 **Irian Jaya** *Province* Indonesia
50C2 **Iriba** Chad
51D4 **Iringa** Tanzania
26F4 **Iriomote** *I* Ryukyu Is, Japan
69A3 **Iriona** Honduras
73H5 **Iriri** *R* Brazil
10B3 **Irish S** England/Ire
25M4 **Irkutsk** Russian Federation
32C4 **Iron Knob** Australia
64B1 **Iron Mountain** USA
32D2 **Iron Range** Australia
64B1 **Iron River** USA
64C3 **Irontown** USA
64A1 **Ironwood** USA
57E2 **Iroquois Falls** Canada
29C4 **Iro-zaki** *C* Japan
30B2 **Irrawaddy** *R* Burma
30A2 **Irrawaddy,Mouths of the** Burma
24H4 **Irtysh** *R* Russian Federation
15B1 **Irún** Spain
8C4 **Irvine** Scotland
8C4 **Irvine** *R* Scotland
63C2 **Irving** USA
66C3 **Isabella Res** USA
54H2 **Isachsen** Canada
54H2 **Isachsen,C** Canada
55Q3 **Ísafjörður** Iceland
28C4 **Isahaya** Japan
50C3 **Isangi** Zaïre
8E1 **Isbister** Scotland
16C2 **Ischia** *I* Italy
29C4 **Ise** Japan
13D2 **Iserlohn** Germany
16C2 **Isernia** Italy
29C4 **Ise-wan** *B* Japan
Isfahan = Esfahan
26F4 **Ishigaki** *I* Ryukyu Is, Japan
29E2 **Ishikari** *R* Japan
29E2 **Ishikari-wan** *B* Japan
24H4 **Ishim** Russian Federation
24H4 **Ishim** *R* Kazakhstan
29E3 **Ishinomaki** Japan
29D3 **Ishioka** Japan
42C1 **Ishkashim** Afghanistan
64B1 **Ishpeming** USA
24J4 **Isil'kul'** Russian Federation
50D3 **Isiolo** Kenya
50C3 **Isiro** Zaïre
40C2 **Iskenderun** Turkey
40C2 **Iskenderun Körfezi** *B* Turkey
40B1 **İskilip** Turkey
24K4 **Iskitim** Russian Federation
17E2 **Iskur** *R* Bulgaria
42C2 **Islamabad** Pakistan
67B4 **Islamorada** USA
57D1 **Island L** Canada
9D2 **Island Magee** Northern Ireland
58D2 **Island Park** USA
35B1 **Islands,B of** New Zealand
Islas Baleares = Balearic Islands
Islas Malvinas = Falkland Islands
8B4 **Islay** *I* Scotland
14C2 **Isle** *R* France
Isle, Island, Isola etc : see also individual island names
7D4 **Isle of Wight** *County* England
64B1 **Isle Royale Nat Pk** USA
7A5 **Isles of Scilly** England
66B1 **Isleton** USA
40B3 **Ismâ'ilîya** Egypt
40B4 **Isna** Egypt
51E6 **Isoanala** Madagascar
51D5 **Isoka** Zambia
16D3 **Isola de Correnti, C** Sicily, Italy
29C3 **Isosaki** Japan
40B2 **Isparta** Turkey
45C2 **Israel** *Republic* SW Asia
15C2 **Isser** *R* Algeria
14C2 **Issoire** France
14C2 **Issoudun** France
39F1 **Issyk Kul', Ozero** *L* Kirgizia
40A1 **İstanbul** Turkey
17E3 **Istiáia** Greece
67B3 **Istokpoga,L** USA
16C1 **Istra** *Pen* Croatia
75C2 **Itaberai** Brazil
75D2 **Itabira** Brazil
75D3 **Itabirito** Brazil
75E1 **Itabuna** Brazil
75E1 **Itacaré** Brazil
73G4 **Itacoatiara** Brazil
75A3 **Itacurubí del Rosario** Paraguay
75C1 **Itaguari** *R* Brazil
72C2 **Itagui** Colombia
75B4 **Itaipu, Reprêsa** *Res* Brazil/Paraguay
73G4 **Itaituba** Brazil
74G3 **Itajaí** Brazil
75C3 **Itajuba** Brazil
16C2 **Italy** *Republic* Europe
75E2 **Itamaraju** Brazil
75D2 **Itamarandiba** Brazil
75D2 **Itambacuri** Brazil
75D2 **Itambé** Brazil
75D2 **Itambé** *Mt* Brazil
43G3 **Itānagar** India
75C3 **Itanhaém** Brazil
75D2 **Itanhém** Brazil
75D2 **Itanhém** *R* Brazil
75D2 **Itaobím** Brazil
75C1 **Itapaci** Brazil
75C3 **Itapecerica** Brazil
75D3 **Itaperuna** Brazil
73K7 **Itapetinga** Brazil
75C3 **Itapetininga** Brazil
75C3 **Itapeva** Brazil
73L4 **Itapipoca** Brazil
75C2 **Itapuranga** Brazil
74E3 **Itaqui** Brazil
75D2 **Itarantim** Brazil
75C3 **Itararé** Brazil
75C3 **Itararé** *R* Brazil
75D3 **Itaúna** Brazil
72F6 **Iténez** *R* Bolivia/Brazil
65D2 **Ithaca** USA
45D3 **Ithrīyat, Jebel** *Mt* Jordan
50C3 **Itimbiri** *R* Zaïre
75D2 **Itinga** Brazil
75A2 **Itiquira** *R* Brazil
55N3 **Itivdleq** Greenland
29C4 **Ito** Japan
29D3 **Itoigawa** Japan
72F6 **Itonomas** *R* Bolivia
75C3 **Itu** Brazil
75E1 **Ituberá** Brazil
75C2 **Ituiutaba** Brazil
75C2 **Itumbiara** Brazil
75B2 **Iturama** Brazil
74C2 **Iturbe** Argentina
26H2 **Iturup** *I* Russian Federation
18B2 **Itzehoe** Germany
25U3 **Iul'tin** Russian Federation
19F2 **Ivacevichi** Belarus
75B3 **Ivai** *R* Brazil
12K5 **Ivalo** Finland
17D2 **Ivangrad** Montenegro, Yugoslavia
34B2 **Ivanhoe** Australia
19E3 **Ivano-Frankovsk** Ukraine
20G4 **Ivanovo** Russian Federation
20L3 **Ivdel'** Russian Federation
50B3 **Ivindo** *R* Gabon
75B3 **Ivinhema** Brazil
75B3 **Ivinhema** *R* Brazil
51E6 **Ivohibe** Madagascar
51E5 **Ivongo Soanierana** Madagascar
48B4 **Ivory Coast** *Republic* Africa
16B1 **Ivrea** Italy
55L3 **Ivujivik** Canada
29E3 **Iwaki** Japan
29D2 **Iwaki** *R* Japan
29D2 **Iwaki-san** *Mt* Japan
28C4 **Iwakuni** Japan
29D2 **Iwamizawa** Japan
29E2 **Iwanai** Japan
48C4 **Iwo** Nigeria
26H4 **Iwo Jima** *I* Japan
70C3 **Ixtepec** Mexico
28B4 **Iyo** Japan
28B4 **Iyo-nada** *B* Japan
24G4 **Izhevsk** Russian Federation
20J2 **Izhma** Russian Federation
20J2 **Izhma** *R* Russian Federation
41G5 **Izkī** Oman
19F3 **Izmail** Ukraine
40A2 **İzmir** Turkey
17F3 **İzmir Körfezi** *B* Turkey
40A1 **İzmit** Turkey
40A1 **İznik** Turkey
17F2 **Iznik Golü** *L* Turkey
45D2 **Izra'** Syria
28A4 **Izuhara** Japan
29C4 **Izumi-sano** Japan
28B3 **Izumo** Japan

J

41F5 **Jabal az Zannah** UAE
43E4 **Jabalpur** India
40D4 **Jabal Shammar** *Region* Saudi Arabia
45C1 **Jablah** Syria
18D2 **Jablonec nad Nisou** Czech Republic
73L5 **Jaboatão** Brazil
75C3 **Jaboticabal** Brazil
15B1 **Jaca** Spain
73G5 **Jacareacanga** Brazil
73H8 **Jacarezinho** Brazil
75C3 **Jacarie** Brazil
74C4 **Jáchal** Argentina
75B2 **Jaciara** Brazil
75D2 **Jacinto** Brazil
65E1 **Jackman Station** USA
62C2 **Jacksboro** USA
68B2 **Jacks Mt** USA
67A2 **Jackson** Alabama, USA
34C1 **Jackson** Australia
66B1 **Jackson** California, USA
64C2 **Jackson** Michigan, USA
61E2 **Jackson** Minnesota, USA
63D2 **Jackson** Mississippi, USA
64B3 **Jackson** Missouri, USA
64C3 **Jackson** Ohio, USA
63E2 **Jackson** Tennessee, USA
58D2 **Jackson** Wyoming, USA
35B2 **Jackson,C** New Zealand
35A2 **Jackson Head** *Pt* New Zealand
58D2 **Jackson L** USA
63D2 **Jacksonville** Arkansas, USA
67B2 **Jacksonville** Florida, USA
64A3 **Jacksonville** Illinois, USA
67C2 **Jacksonville** N Carolina, USA
63C2 **Jacksonville** Texas, USA
67B2 **Jacksonville Beach** USA
69C3 **Jacmel** Haiti
42B3 **Jacobabad** Pakistan
73K6 **Jacobina** Brazil
Jadotville = Likasi
72C5 **Jaén** Peru
15B2 **Jaén** Spain
Jaffa = Tel Aviv-Yafo
34A3 **Jaffa,C** Australia
44B4 **Jaffna** Sri Lanka
68D1 **Jaffrey** USA
43F4 **Jagannathganj Ghat** Bangladesh
44C2 **Jagdalpur** India
41G4 **Jagin** *R* Iran
44B2 **Jagtial** India
75E1 **Jaguaquara** Brazil
74F4 **Jaguarão** *R* Brazil/Uruguay
75C3 **Jaguariaiva** Brazil
21H8 **Jahan Dāgh** *Mt* Iran
41F4 **Jahrom** Iran
31A2 **Jainca** China
42D3 **Jaipur** India
42C3 **Jaisalmer** India
41G2 **Jajarm** Iran
16D2 **Jajce** Bosnia-Herzegovina
27D7 **Jakarta** Indonesia
55N3 **Jakobshavn** Greenland
12J6 **Jakobstad** Finland
62B2 **Jal** USA
42C2 **Jalalabad** Afghanistan
70C3 **Jalapa** Mexico
75B3 **Jales** Brazil
43F3 **Jaleswar** Nepal
42D4 **Jalgaon** India
48D4 **Jalingo** Nigeria
42D5 **Jālna** India
15B1 **Jalón** *R* Spain
49E2 **Jalo Oasis** Libya
42C3 **Jālor** India
43F3 **Jalpāiguri** India
49E2 **Jālū Oasis** Libya
72B4 **Jama** Ecuador
50E3 **Jamaame** Somalia
69B3 **Jamaica** *I* Caribbean Sea
69B3 **Jamaica Chan** Haiti/Jamaica
43F4 **Jamalpur** Bangladesh
27D7 **Jambi** Indonesia

42C4 Jambusar India
60D1 James R N Dakota, USA
65D3 James R Virginia, USA
55K4 James B Canada
34A2 Jamestown Australia
60D1 Jamestown N Dakota, USA
65D2 Jamestown New York, USA
68E2 Jamestown Rhode Island, USA
47D3 Jamestown South Africa
54J5 Jamestown USA
44B2 Jamkhandi India
42C2 Jammu India
42D2 Jammu and Kashmīr State India
42B4 Jāmnagar India
42C3 Jampur Pakistan
20C3 Jämsä Finland
43F4 Jamshedpur India
45D3 Janab, Wadi el Jordan
43F3 Janakpur Nepal
75D2 Janaúba Brazil
41F3 Jandaq Iran
34D1 Jandowae Australia
64B2 Janesville USA
76B1 Jan Mayen I Norwegian Sea
75D2 Januária Brazil
42D4 Jaora India
26G3 Japan, S of Japan
36J3 Japan Trench Pacific Ocean
72E4 Japurá R Brazil
40C2 Jarābulus Syria
75C2 Jaraguá Brazil
75B3 Jaraguari Brazil
15B1 Jarama R Spain
45C2 Jarash Jordan
75A3 Jardim Brazil
69B2 Jardines de la Reina Is Cuba
Jargalant = Hovd
73H3 Jari R Brazil
43G3 Jaria Jhānjail Bangladesh
13C3 Jarny France
18D2 Jarocin Poland
19E2 Jarosław Poland
12G6 Järpen Sweden
31B2 Jartai China
42C4 Jasdan India
48C4 Jasikan Ghana
41G4 Jāsk Iran
19E3 Jasło Poland
74D8 Jason Is Falkland Islands
63E2 Jasper Alabama, USA
63D1 Jasper Arkansas, USA
54G4 Jasper Canada
67B2 Jasper Florida, USA
64B3 Jasper Indiana, USA
63D2 Jasper Texas, USA
18D2 Jastrowie Poland
75B2 Jataí Brazil
15B2 Játiva Spain
75C3 Jau Brazil
72C6 Jauja Peru
43E3 Jaunpur India
44B3 Javadi Hills India
27D7 Java,I Indonesia
Javari R = Yavari
27D7 Java S Indonesia
32A2 Java Trench Indonesia
Jawa = Java
27G7 Jaya, Pk Indonesia
27H7 Jayapura Indonesia
45D2 Jayrūd Syria
63D3 Jeanerette USA
48C4 Jebba Nigeria
50C2 Jebel Abyad Desert Region Sudan
Jebel esh Sheikh = Hermon, Mt
8D4 Jedburgh Scotland
Jedda = Jiddah
19E2 Jędrzejów Poland
61E2 Jefferson Iowa, USA
63D2 Jefferson Texas, USA
58D1 Jefferson R USA
57D3 Jefferson City USA
56B3 Jefferson,Mt USA
64B3 Jeffersonville USA
45C3 Jeib, Wadi el Israel/Jordan
75A3 Jejui-Guazú R Paraguay
20D4 Jekabpils Latvia
18D2 Jelena Góra Poland
20C4 Jelgava Latvia
27E7 Jember Indonesia
62A1 Jemez Pueblo USA
18C2 Jena Germany
16B3 Jendouba Tunisia
45C2 Jenin Israel
63D2 Jennings USA
55O3 Jensen Nunatakker Mt Greenland
55K3 Jens Munk I Canada
34B3 Jeparit Australia
73L6 Jequié Brazil
75D2 Jequitai R Brazil
75D2 Jequitinhonha Brazil
73K7 Jequitinhonha R Brazil
48D1 Jerba, I de Tunisia
15A2 Jerez de la Frontera Spain
15A2 Jerez de los Caballeros Spain
45C3 Jericho Israel
34C3 Jerilderie Australia
58D2 Jerome USA
14B2 Jersey I Channel Islands
57F2 Jersey City USA
65D2 Jersey Shore USA
64A3 Jerseyville USA
40C3 Jerusalem Israel
34D3 Jervis B Australia
16C1 Jesenice Slovenia
18D2 Jeseniky Upland Czech Republic
43F4 Jessore Bangladesh
57E3 Jesup USA
62C1 Jetmore USA
13D1 Jever Germany
68E2 Jewett City USA
44C2 Jeypore India
17D2 Jezerce Mt Albania
19E2 Jezioro Mamry L Poland
19E2 Jezioro Śniardwy L Poland
45C2 Jezzine Lebanon
42C4 Jhābua India
42D4 Jhālāwār India
42C2 Jhang Maghiana Pakistan
42D3 Jhānsi India
43E4 Jhārsuguda India
42C2 Jhelum Pakistan
42C2 Jhelum R Pakistan
42D3 Jhunjhunūn India
31B3 Jialing Jiang R China
26G2 Jiamusi China
28B2 Ji'an China
31C4 Ji'an Jiangxi, China
31D4 Jiande China
31B4 Jiang'an China
31D4 Jiangbiancun China
31A5 Jiangcheng China
31C5 Jiangmen China
31D3 Jiangsu Province China
31C4 Jiangxi Province China
31A3 Jiangyou China
31D1 Jianping China
31A5 Jianshui China
31D4 Jian Xi R China
31D4 Jianyang China
28B2 Jiaohe China
31E2 Jiaonan China
31E2 Jiao Xian China
31E2 Jiaozhou Wan B China
31C2 Jiaozuo China
31E3 Jiaxiang China
26C3 Jiayuguan China
75C2 Jibão, Serra do Mts Brazil
50D1 Jiddah Saudi Arabia
31D3 Jieshou China
31C2 Jiexiu China
31A3 Jigzhi China
18D3 Jihlava Czech Republic
16B3 Jijel Algeria
50E3 Jilib Somalia
28B2 Jilin China
28B2 Jilin Province China
15B1 Jiloca R Spain
50D3 Jima Ethiopia
62B3 Jiménez Coahuila, Mexico
31D2 Jinan China
42D3 Jind India
31B2 Jingbian China
31D4 Jingdezhen China
30C1 Jinghong China
31C3 Jingmen China
31B2 Jingning China
31B4 Jing Xian China
28B2 Jingyu China
31D4 Jinhua China
31C1 Jining Inner Mongolia, China
31D2 Jining Shandong, China
50D3 Jinja Uganda
30C1 Jinping China
31A4 Jinsha Jiang R China
31C4 Jinshi China
31E1 Jinxi China
28A2 Jin Xian China
31E1 Jinzhou China
72F5 Jiparaná R Brazil
72B4 Jipijapa Ecuador
41G4 Jīroft Iran
50E3 Jirriiban Somalia
31B4 Jishou China
40C2 Jisr ash Shughūr Syria
17E2 Jiu R Romania
31D4 Jiujiang China
31C4 Jiuling Shan Hills China
31A4 Jiulong China
31D4 Jiulong Jiang R China
26G2 Jixi China
45C3 Jiza Jordan
50E2 Jīzān Saudi Arabia
48A3 Joal Senegal
75D2 João Monlevade Brazil
73M5 João Pessoa Brazil
73J7 João Pinheiro Brazil
42C3 Jodhpur India
12K6 Joensuu Finland
13C3 Joeuf France
43F3 Jogbani India
44A3 Jog Falls India
47D2 Johannesburg South Africa
59C3 Johannesburg USA
55L2 Johan Pen Canada
58C2 John Day USA
58B1 John Day R USA
57F3 John H Kerr L USA
65D3 John H. Kerr Res USA
62B1 John Martin Res USA
8D2 John o'Groats Scotland
63C1 John Redmond Res USA
68A2 Johnsonburg USA
68C1 Johnson City New York, USA
67B1 Johnson City Tennessee, USA
67B2 Johnston USA
69N2 Johnston Pt St Vincent
68C1 Johnstown New York, USA
65D2 Johnstown Pennsylvania, USA
30C5 Johor Bharu Malaysia
14C2 Joigny France
74G3 Joinville Brazil
13C3 Joinville France
20J5 Jok R Russian Federation
12H5 Jokkmokk Sweden
21H8 Jolfa Iran
57E2 Joliet USA
55L5 Joliette Canada
27F6 Jolo Philippines
27F6 Jolo I Philippines
39H2 Joma Mt China
19E1 Jonava Lithuania
31A3 Jonê China
57D3 Jonesboro Arkansas, USA
63D2 Jonesboro Louisiana, USA
55K2 Jones Sd Canada
19E1 Joniškis Lithuania
12G7 Jönköping Sweden
65E1 Jonquière Canada
57D3 Joplin USA
60B1 Jordan Montana, USA
68B1 Jordan New York, USA
40C3 Jordan Kingdom SW Asia
45C2 Jordan R Israel
58C2 Jordan Valley USA
75B4 Jordão R Brazil
43G3 Jorhāt India
20C2 Jörn Sweden
12F7 Jørpeland Norway
48C3 Jos Nigeria
32B2 Joseph Bonaparte G Australia
59D3 Joseph City USA
55M4 Joseph, Lac Canada
24B3 Jotunheimen Mt Norway
45C2 Jouai'ya Lebanon
45C2 Jounié Lebanon
43G3 Jowai India
50E3 Jowhar Somalia
54F5 Juan de Fuca,Str of Canada/USA
51E5 Juan de Nova I Mozambique Channel
72Q Juan Fernández, Islas Pacific Ocean
73K5 Juàzeiro Brazil
73L5 Juàzeiro do Norte Brazil
50D3 Juba Sudan
50E3 Juba R Somalia
45C1 Jubail Lebanon
76G2 Jubany Base Antarctica
40D4 Jubbah Saudi Arabia
15B2 Júcar R Spain
18C3 Judenburg Austria
13D1 Juist I Germany
73K8 Juiz de Fora Brazil
74C2 Jujuy State Argentina
60C2 Julesburg USA
72E7 Juli Peru
72D7 Juliaca Peru
73G3 Julianatop Mt Surinam
55O3 Julianehåb Greenland
13D2 Jülich Germany
42D2 Jullundur India
43E3 Jumla Nepal
45C3 Jum Suwwāna Mt Jordan
42C4 Jūnāgadh India
31D2 Junan China
62C2 Junction Texas, USA
59D3 Junction Utah, USA
56D3 Junction City USA
74G2 Jundiaí Brazil
54E4 Juneau USA
32D4 Junee Australia
66C2 June Lake USA
16B1 Jungfrau Mt Switzerland
68B2 Juniata R USA
74D4 Junín Argentina
66B2 Junipero Serra Peak Mt USA
31A4 Junlian China
75D2 Juparanã, Lagoa Brazil
74G2 Juquiá Brazil
50C3 Jur R Sudan
8C4 Jura I Scotland
14D2 Jura Mts France
8C3 Jura,Sound of Chan Scotland
45C3 Jurf ed Darāwīsh Jordan
24K4 Jurga Russian Federation
20C4 Jūrmala Latvia
72E4 Juruá R Brazil
73G6 Juruena R Brazil
45D1 Jūsīyah Syria
72E4 Jutaí R Brazil
70D3 Juticalpa Honduras
Jutland Pen = Jylland
69A2 Juventud, Isla de la Cuba
41G3 Jūymand Iran
18B1 Jylland Pen Denmark
12K6 Jyväskyla Finland

K

39F2 K2 Mt China/India
41G2 Kaakhka Turkmenistan
47E2 Kaapmuiden South Africa
27F7 Kabaena Indonesia
32B1 Kabaena I Indonesia
48A4 Kabala Sierra Leone
50D4 Kabale Uganda
50C4 Kabalo Zaïre
50C4 Kabambare Zaïre
50D3 Kabarole Uganda
64C1 Kabinakagami L Canada
50C4 Kabinda Zaïre
45C1 Kabīr R Syria
41E3 Kabir Kuh Mts Iran
51C5 Kabompo Zambia
51C5 Kabompo R Zambia
51C4 Kabongo Zaïre
42B2 Kabul Afghanistan
42B4 Kachchh,G of India
20K4 Kachkanar Russian Federation
25M4 Kachug Russian Federation
30B3 Kadan I Burma
42C4 Kadi India
40B2 Kadınhanı Turkey
44B3 Kadiri India
21F6 Kadiyevka Ukraine
60C2 Kadoka USA
51C5 Kadoma Zimbabwe
50C2 Kadugli Sudan
48C3 Kaduna Nigeria
48C3 Kaduna R Nigeria
44B3 Kadūr India
43H3 Kadusam Mt China
20K3 Kadzherom Russian Federation
28A3 Kaechon N Korea
48A3 Kaédi Mauritius
66E5 Kaena Pt Hawaiian Islands
28B3 Kaesŏng N Korea
48C4 Kafanchan Nigeria
48A3 Kaffrine Senegal
45D1 Kafr Behum Syria
45A3 Kafr Sa'd Egypt
45A3 Kafr Saqv Egypt
45D1 Kafrūn Bashūr Syria
51C5 Kafue Zambia
51C5 Kafue R Zambia
51C5 Kafue Nat Pk Zambia
29D3 Kaga Japan
24H6 Kagan Uzbekistan
21G7 Kağızman Turkey
19F3 Kagul Moldavia
41G2 Kāhak Iran
50D4 Kahama Tanzania
42B3 Kahan Pakistan
51B4 Kahemba Zaïre
13E2 Kahler Asten Mt Germany
41G4 Kahnūj Iran
64A2 Kahoka USA
66E5 Kahoolawe I Hawaiian Islands
40C2 Kahramanmaraş Turkey
66E5 Kahuku Pt Hawaiian Islands
66E5 Kahului Hawaiian Islands
35B2 Kaiapoi New Zealand
59D3 Kaibab Plat USA
73G2 Kaieteur Falls Guyana
31C3 Kaifeng China
27G7 Kai, Kepulauan Arch Indonesia
35B1 Kaikohe New Zealand
33G5 Kaikoura New Zealand
35B2 Kaikoura Pen New Zealand
35B2 Kaikoura Range Mts New Zealand
31B4 Kaili China
28A2 Kailu China
66E5 Kailua Hawaii
66E5 Kailua Oahu, Hawaiian Islands
27G7 Kaimana Indonesia
35C1 Kaimenawa Mts New Zealand
29C4 Kainan Japan
48C3 Kainji Res Nigeria
35B1 Kaipara Harbour B New Zealand
31C5 Kaiping China
16C3 Kairouan Tunisia
66C2 Kaiser Peak Mt USA
14D2 Kaiserslautern Germany
28B2 Kaishantun China
19E2 Kaisiadorys Lithuania
35B1 Kaitaia New Zealand
35A3 Kaitangata New Zealand
42D3 Kaithal India
66E5 Kaiwi Chan Hawaiian Islands
31B3 Kai Xian China
28A2 Kaiyuan Liaoning, China
31A5 Kaiyuan Yunnan, China
12K6 Kajaani Finland
42B2 Kajaki Afghanistan
50D4 Kajiado Kenya
42B2 Kajrān Afghanistan
50D2 Kaka Sudan
64B1 Kakabeka Falls Canada
50D3 Kakamega Kenya
28B4 Kake Japan
21E6 Kakhovskoye Vodokhranilishche Res Ukraine
41F4 Kākī Iran
44C2 Kākināda India
29B4 Kakogawa Japan
54D2 Kaktovik USA
29D3 Kakuda Japan
16B3 Kalaat Khasba Tunisia
17E3 Kalabáka Greece
51C5 Kalabo Zambia
21G5 Kalach Russian Federation
21G6 Kalach-na-Donu Russian Federation
43G4 Kaladan R Burma/India
66E5 Ka Lae C Hawaiian Islands
51C6 Kalahari Desert Botswana
47C2 Kalahari Gemsbok Nat Pk South Africa
20C3 Kalajoki Finland
25N4 Kalakan Russian Federation
27C6 Kalakepen Indonesia
42C1 Kalam Pakistan
17E3 Kalámai Greece
57E2 Kalamazoo USA
66E5 Kalapana Hawaiian Islands
19F3 Kalarash Moldavia
42B3 Kalat Pakistan
66E5 Kalaupapa Hawaiian Islands
40B1 Kalecik Turkey
50C4 Kalémié Zaïre
20E2 Kalevala Russian Federation
43G4 Kalewa Burma
32B4 Kalgoorlie Australia
43E3 Kali R India/Nepal
50C4 Kalima Zaïre
27E7 Kalimantan Terr Indonesia
17F3 Kálimnos I Greece
43F3 Kālimpang India
43K1 Kali Nadi R India
12J8 Kaliningrad Russian Federation
21D5 Kalinkovichi Belarus
19F3 Kalinovka Ukraine
56B2 Kalispell USA
19D2 Kalisz Poland
50D4 Kaliua Tanzania
12J5 Kalix R Sweden
51B6 Kalkfeld Namibia
47C1 Kalkfontein Botswana
12K6 Kallavesi L Finland
17F3 Kallonis Kólpos B Greece
12H7 Kalmar Sweden
21H6 Kalmyk Republic Russian Federation
51C5 Kalomo Zambia
64A2 Kalona USA
44A3 Kalpeni I India
42D3 Kālpi India
20F5 Kaluga Russian Federation
12G7 Kalundborg Denmark
19E3 Kalush Ukraine
44A2 Kalyān India
44B3 Kalyandurg India
20F4 Kalyazin Russian Federation
20J3 Kama R Russian Federation
29E3 Kamaishi Japan
42C2 Kamalia Pakistan
51B5 Kamanjab Namibia
25O4 Kamara China
42D2 Kamat Mt China/India
44B4 Kambam India
20J4 Kambarka Russian Federation
48A4 Kambia Sierra Leone
25S4 Kamchatka Pen Russian Federation
19F3 Kamenets Podolskiy Ukraine
20G5 Kamenka Russian Federation

24K4 **Kamen-na-Obi** Russian Federation
25S3 **Kamenskoya** Russian Federation
20L4 **Kamensk-Ural'skiy** Russian Federation
47B3 **Kamieskroon** South Africa
54H3 **Kamilukuak L** Canada
51C4 **Kamina** Zaïre
55J3 **Kaminak L** Canada
29D3 **Kaminoyama** Japan
54F4 **Kamloops** Canada
41E1 **Kamo** Armenia
29D3 **Kamogawa** Japan
50D3 **Kampala** Uganda
30C5 **Kampar** Malaysia
18B2 **Kampen** Netherlands
30B2 **Kamphaeng Phet** Thailand
30C3 **Kampot** Cambodia
20K4 **Kamskoye Vodokhranilishche** *Res* Russian Federation
42D4 **Kāmthi** India
21H5 **Kamyshin** Russian Federation
20L4 **Kamyshlov** Russian Federation
55L4 **Kanaaupscow** *R* Canada
59D3 **Kanab** USA
50C4 **Kananga** Zaïre
20H4 **Kanash** Russian Federation
29C3 **Kanayama** Japan
29D3 **Kanazawa** Japan
44B3 **Kānchipuram** India
20E2 **Kandagan** Indonesia
42B2 **Kandahar** Afghanistan
20E2 **Kandalaksha** Russian Federation
12L5 **Kandalakshskaya Guba** *B* Russian Federation
13D3 **Kandel** *Mt* Germany
48C3 **Kandi** Benin
34C2 **Kandos** Australia
44C4 **Kandy** Sri Lanka
65D2 **Kane** USA
55L1 **Kane Basin** *B* Canada
50B2 **Kanem** *Desert Region* Chad
66E5 **Kaneohe** Hawaiian Islands
20F2 **Kanevka** Russian Federation
47C1 **Kang** Botswana
48B3 **Kangaba** Mali
40C2 **Kangal** Turkey
55N3 **Kangâmiut** Greenland
41F4 **Kangān** Iran
30C4 **Kangar** Malaysia
32C4 **Kangaroo I** Australia
55N3 **Kangâtsiaq** Greenland
41E3 **Kangavar** Iran
31C1 **Kangbao** China
39G3 **Kangchenjunga** *Mt* China/Nepal
31A4 **Kangding** China
32A1 **Kangean** *Is* Indonesia
55P3 **Kangerdlugssuaq** *B* Greenland
55P3 **Kangerdlugssuatsaiq** *B* Greenland
50D3 **Kangetet** Kenya
28B2 **Kanggye** N Korea
28B3 **Kanghwa** S Korea
55M4 **Kangiqsualujjuaq** Canada
55L3 **Kangiqsujuak** Canada
55L3 **Kangirsuk** Canada
28B3 **Kangnŭng** S Korea
50B3 **Kango** Gabon
28A2 **Kangping** China
26C4 **Kangto** *Mt* China/India
31B3 **Kang Xian** China
51C4 **Kaniama** Zaïre
44B2 **Kani Giri** India
20G2 **Kanin, Poluostrov** *Pen* Russian Federation
12J6 **Kankaanpää** Finland
64B2 **Kankakee** USA
64B2 **Kankakee** *R* USA
48B3 **Kankan** Guinea
43E4 **Kānker** India
67B1 **Kannapolis** USA
44B4 **Kanniyākumari** India
48C3 **Kano** Nigeria
60C3 **Kanorado** USA
43E3 **Kānpur** India
61D3 **Kansas** *R* USA
56D3 **Kansas** *State* USA
57D3 **Kansas City** USA
31D5 **Kanshi** China
25L4 **Kansk** Russian Federation
28A3 **Kansŏng** S Korea
48C3 **Kantchari** Burkina
48C4 **Kanté** Togo
43F4 **Kanthi** India
54C3 **Kantishna** USA
9B3 **Kanturk** Irish Republic
47D1 **Kanye** Botswana
26E4 **Kaohsiung** Taiwan
51B5 **Kaoka Veld** *Plain* Namibia
48A3 **Kaolack** Senegal
51C5 **Kaoma** Zambia
66E5 **Kapaa** Hawaiian Islands
66E5 **Kapaau** Hawaiian Islands
51C4 **Kapanga** Zaïre
12H7 **Kapellskär** Sweden
Kap Farvel = Farewell, C
51C5 **Kapiri** Zambia
63D2 **Kaplan** USA
18C3 **Kaplice** Czech Republic
30B4 **Kapoe** Thailand
51C4 **Kapona** Zaïre
17D1 **Kaposvár** Hungary
55L2 **Kap Parry** *C* Greenland
28A2 **Kapsan** N Korea
27E6 **Kapuas** *R* Indonesia
34A2 **Kapunda** Australia
42D2 **Kapurthala** India
55K5 **Kapuskasing** Canada
64C1 **Kapuskasing** *R* Canada
34D2 **Kaputar** *Mt* Australia
21H8 **Kapydzhik** *Mt* Armenia
28A3 **Kapyŏng** S Korea
21G8 **Kara** *R* Turkey
40B1 **Karabük** Turkey
17F2 **Karacabey** Turkey
42B4 **Karachi** Pakistan
44A2 **Karād** India
21F7 **Kara Dağları** *Mt* Turkey
21D7 **Karadeniz Boğazi** *Str* Turkey
26E1 **Karaftit** Russian Federation
24J5 **Karaganda** Kazakhstan
24J5 **Karagayly** Kazakhstan
25S4 **Karaginskiy, Ostrov** *I* Russian Federation
44B3 **Kāraikāl** India
41F2 **Karaj** Iran
40C3 **Karak** Jordan
24G5 **Karakalpak Republic** Uzbekistan
42D1 **Karakax He** *R* China
27F6 **Karakelong** *I* Indonesia
42D1 **Karakoram** *Mts* India
42D1 **Karakoram P** China/India
48A3 **Karakoro** *Watercourse* Mali/Mauritius
24G6 **Karakumy** *Desert* Turkmenistan
45C3 **Karama** Jordan
21E8 **Karaman** Turkey
24K5 **Karamay** China
35B2 **Karamea** New Zealand
35B2 **Karamea Bight** *B* New Zealand
42D4 **Kāranja** India
21E8 **Karanlik** *R* Turkey
40B2 **Karapınar** Turkey
24J2 **Kara S** Russian Federation
47B2 **Karasburg** Namibia
12K5 **Karasjok** Norway
24J4 **Karasuk** Russian Federation
40C2 **Karataş** Turkey
24H5 **Kara Tau** *Mts* Kazakhstan
30B3 **Karathuri** Burma
28B4 **Karatsu** Japan
24K2 **Karaul** Russian Federation
45B1 **Karavostasi** Cyprus
41F4 **Karāz** Iran
41D3 **Karbalā'** Iraq
19E3 **Karcag** Hungary
17E3 **Kardhítsa** Greece
20E3 **Karelian Republic** Russian Federation
44E3 **Karen** Andaman Islands
20K3 **Karepino** Russian Federation
12J5 **Karesvando** Sweden
48B2 **Karet** *Desert Region* Mauritius
24K4 **Kargasok** Russian Federation
20F3 **Kargopol'** Russian Federation
48D3 **Kari** Nigeria
51C5 **Kariba** Zimbabwe
51C5 **Kariba Dam** Zambia/Zimbabwe
51C5 **Kariba, L** Zambia/Zimbabwe
47B1 **Karibib** Namibia
50D2 **Karima** Sudan
27D7 **Karimata** *I* Indonesia
43G4 **Karīmganj** India
44B2 **Karīmnagar** India
50E2 **Karin** Somalia
12J6 **Karis** Finland
50C4 **Karisimbe** *Mt* Zaïre
17E3 **Káristos** Greece
44A3 **Kārkal** India
27H7 **Karkar** *I* Papua New Guinea
41E3 **Karkheh** *R* Iran
21E6 **Karkinitskiy Zaliv** *B* Ukraine
25L5 **Karlik Shan** *Mt* China
18D2 **Karlino** Poland
16D2 **Karlobag** Croatia
16D1 **Karlovac** Croatia
17E2 **Karlovo** Bulgaria
18C2 **Karlovy Vary** Czech Republic
12G7 **Karlshamn** Sweden
12G7 **Karlskoga** Sweden
12H7 **Karlskrona** Sweden
18B3 **Karlsruhe** Germany
12G7 **Karlstad** Sweden
61D1 **Karlstad** USA
54C4 **Karluk** USA
43G4 **Karnafuli Res** Bangladesh
42D3 **Karnāl** India
44A2 **Karnātaka** *State* India
17F2 **Karnobat** Bulgaria
51C5 **Karoi** Zimbabwe
51D4 **Karonga** Malawi
50D2 **Karora** Sudan
17F3 **Kárpathos** *I* Greece
55N2 **Karrats Fjord** Greenland
47C3 **Karree Berge** *Mts* South Africa
21G7 **Kars** Turkey
24H5 **Karsakpay** Kazakhstan
19F1 **Kārsava** Latvia
38E2 **Karshi** Uzbekistan
24G2 **Karskiye Vorota, Proliv** *Str* Russian Federation
12J6 **Karstula** Finland
45C1 **Kartaba** Lebanon
17F2 **Kartal** Turkey
20L5 **Kartaly** Russian Federation
68A2 **Karthaus** USA
41E3 **Kārūn** *R* Iran
19D3 **Karviná** Czech Republic
43E3 **Karwa** India
44A3 **Kārwār** India
26E1 **Karymskoye** Russian Federation
50B4 **Kasai** *R* Zaïre
51C5 **Kasaji** Zaïre
51D5 **Kasama** Zambia
51D4 **Kasanga** Tanzania
44A3 **Kāsaragod** India
54H3 **Kasba L** Canada
51C5 **Kasempa** Zambia
51C5 **Kasenga** Zaïre
50D3 **Kasese** Uganda
43K2 **Kasganj** India
41F3 **Kāshān** Iran
39F2 **Kashi** China
28B4 **Kashima** Japan
42D3 **Kāshipur** India
29D3 **Kashiwazaki** Japan
41G2 **Kāshmar** Iran
22E4 **Kashmir** *State* India
20G5 **Kasimov** Russian Federation
64B3 **Kaskaskia** *R* USA
12J6 **Kaskinen** Finland
20L4 **Kasli** Russian Federation
54G5 **Kaslo** Canada
50C4 **Kasongo** Zaïre
51B4 **Kasongo-Lunda** Zaïre
17F3 **Kásos** *I* Greece
21H6 **Kaspiyskiy** Russian Federation
50D2 **Kassala** Sudan
18B2 **Kassel** Germany
48C1 **Kasserine** Tunisia
51B5 **Kassinga** Angola
40B1 **Kastamonu** Turkey
17E3 **Kastélli** Greece
40A2 **Kastellorizon** *I* Greece
17E2 **Kastoría** Greece
17F3 **Kástron** Greece
29D3 **Kasugai** Japan
29B3 **Kasumi** Japan
51D5 **Kasungu** Malawi
42C2 **Kasur** Pakistan
51C5 **Kataba** Zambia
65F1 **Katahdin,Mt** USA
50C4 **Katako-kombe** Zaïre
54D3 **Katalla** USA
25O4 **Katangli** Russian Federation
32A4 **Katanning** Australia
44E4 **Katchall** *I* Nicobar Is, Indian Ocean
17E2 **Kateríni** Greece
54E4 **Kates Needle** *Mt* Canada/USA
40B4 **Katharîna, Gebel** *Mt* Egypt
32C2 **Katherine** Australia
42C4 **Kāthiāwār** *Pen* India
45B3 **Kathib el Henu** *Hill* Egypt
43F3 **Kathmandu** Nepal
42D2 **Kathua** India
43F3 **Katihār** India
51C5 **Katima Mulilo** Namibia
48B4 **Katiola** Ivory Coast
54C4 **Katmai,Mt** USA
43E4 **Katni** India
34D2 **Katoomba** Australia
19D2 **Katowice** Poland
12H7 **Katrineholm** Sweden
8C3 **Katrine, Loch** *L* Scotland
48C3 **Katsina** Nigeria
48C4 **Katsina** *R* Cameroon/Nigeria
48C4 **Katsina Ala** Nigeria
29D3 **Katsuta** Japan
29D3 **Katsuura** Japan
29C3 **Katsuyama** Japan
24H6 **Kattakurgan** Uzbekistan
12G7 **Kattegat** *Str* Denmark/Sweden
13E3 **Katzenbuckel** *Mt* Germany
66E5 **Kauai** *I* Hawaiian Islands
66E5 **Kauai Chan** Hawaiian Islands
66E5 **Kaulakahi Chan** Hawaiian Islands
66E5 **Kaunakakai** Hawaiian Islands
20C5 **Kaunas** Lithuania
48C3 **Kaura Namoda** Nigeria
12J5 **Kautokeino** Norway
17E2 **Kavadarci** Macedonia, Yugoslavia
17D2 **Kavajë** Albania
44B3 **Kavali** India
17E2 **Kavālla** Greece
42B4 **Kāvda** India
32E1 **Kavieng** Papua New Guinea
29C3 **Kawagoe** Japan
29C3 **Kawaguchi** Japan
66E5 **Kawaihae** Hawaiian Islands
35B1 **Kawakawa** New Zealand
51C4 **Kawambwa** Zambia
43E4 **Kawardha** India
65D2 **Kawartha Lakes** Canada
29D3 **Kawasaki** Japan
66C2 **Kaweah** *R* USA
35C1 **Kawerau** New Zealand
35B1 **Kawhia** New Zealand
48B3 **Kaya** Burkina
27E6 **Kayan** *R* Indonesia
44B4 **Kāyankulam** India
60B2 **Kaycee** USA
59D3 **Kayenta** USA
48A3 **Kayes** Mali
21F8 **Kayseri** Turkey
25P2 **Kazach'ye** Russian Federation
41E1 **Kazakh** Azerbaijan
24G5 **Kazakhstan** *Republic* Asia
20H4 **Kazan'** Russian Federation
17F2 **Kazanlŭk** Bulgaria
26H4 **Kazan Retto** *Is* Japan
19F3 **Kazatin** Ukraine
21G7 **Kazbek** *Mt* Georgia
41F4 **Kāzerūn** Iran
20J3 **Kazhim** Russian Federation
41E1 **Kazi Magomed** Azerbaijan
19E3 **Kazincbarcika** Hungary
20M3 **Kazym** *R* Russian Federation
20M3 **Kazymskaya** Russian Federation
17E3 **Kéa** *I* Greece
9C2 **Keady** Northern Ireland
66E5 **Kealaikahiki Chan** Hawaiian Islands
56D2 **Kearney** USA
59D4 **Kearny** USA
40C2 **Keban Baraji** *Res* Turkey
48A3 **Kébémer** Senegal
48C1 **Kebili** Tunisia
45D1 **Kebīr** *R* Lebanon/Syria
12H5 **Kebnekaise** *Mt* Sweden
19D3 **Kecskemét** Hungary
19E1 **Kedainiai** Lithuania
65F1 **Kedgwick** Canada
27E7 **Kediri** Indonesia
48A3 **Kédougou** Senegal
20J3 **Kedva** Russian Federation
54E3 **Keele Pk** *Mt* Canada
59C3 **Keeler** USA
27C8 **Keeling Is** Indian Ocean
26F4 **Keelung** Taiwan
66C3 **Keene** California, USA
65E2 **Keene** New Hampshire, USA
47B2 **Keetmanshoop** Namibia
64B2 **Keewanee** USA
64A1 **Keewatin** USA
55J3 **Keewatin** *Region* Canada
17E3 **Kefallinía** *I* Greece
45C2 **Kefar Sava** Israel
48C4 **Keffi** Nigeria
12A2 **Keflavík** Iceland
54G4 **Keg River** Canada
30B1 **Kehsi Mansam** Burma
48C3 **Keita** Niger
34B3 **Keith** Australia
8D3 **Keith** Scotland
54F3 **Keith Arm** *B* Canada
6C3 **Keithley** England
55M3 **Kekertuk** Canada
42D3 **Kekri** India
30C5 **Kelang** Malaysia
30C4 **Kelantan** *R* Malaysia
16C3 **Kelibia** Tunisia
42B1 **Kelif** Turkmenistan
40C1 **Kelkit** *R* Turkey
50B4 **Kellé** Congo
54F2 **Kellett,C** Canada
58C1 **Kellogg** USA
24D3 **Kelloselka** Finland
33B9 **Kells** Irish Republic
8C4 **Kells Range** *Hills* Scotland
19E1 **Kelme** Lithuania
54G5 **Kelowna** Canada
54F4 **Kelsey Bay** Canada
8D4 **Kelso** Scotland
58B1 **Kelso** USA
20E3 **Kem'** Russian Federation
20E3 **Kem'** *R* Russian Federation
48B3 **Ke Macina** Mali
24K4 **Kemerovo** Russian Federation
12J5 **Kemi** Finland
12K5 **Kemi** *R* Finland
12K5 **Kemijärvi** Finland
58D2 **Kemmerer** USA
13C2 **Kempen** *Region* Belgium
62C2 **Kemp,L** USA
69B2 **Kemps Bay** The Bahamas
34D2 **Kempsey** Australia
18C3 **Kempten** Germany
65E1 **Kempt,L** Canada
54C3 **Kenai** USA
54C3 **Kenai Pen** USA
50D3 **Kenamuke Swamp** Sudan
6C2 **Kendal** England
34D2 **Kendall** Australia
32B1 **Kendari** Indonesia
27E7 **Kendawangan** Indonesia
43F4 **Kendrāpāra** India
58C1 **Kendrick** USA
63C3 **Kenedy** USA
48A4 **Kenema** Sierra Leone
50B4 **Kenge** Zaïre
30B1 **Kengtung** Burma
47C2 **Kenhardt** South Africa
48A3 **Kéniéba** Mali
48B1 **Kenitra** Morocco
60C1 **Kenmare** USA
62B2 **Kenna** USA
65F1 **Kennebec** *R* USA
68E1 **Kennebunk** USA
63D3 **Kenner** USA
63E1 **Kennett** USA
68C3 **Kennett Square** USA
58C1 **Kennewick** USA
54F4 **Kenny Dam** Canada
55J5 **Kenora** Canada
57E2 **Kenosha** USA
62B2 **Kent** Texas, USA
58B1 **Kent** Washington, USA
7E4 **Kent** *County* England
64B2 **Kentland** USA
64C2 **Kenton** USA
54H3 **Kent Pen** Canada
64C3 **Kentucky** *R* USA
57E3 **Kentucky** *State* USA
57E3 **Kentucky L** USA
63D2 **Kentwood** Louisiana, USA
64B2 **Kentwood** Michigan, USA
50D3 **Kenya** *Republic* Africa
Kenya,Mt = Kirinyaga
64A2 **Keokuk** USA
43E4 **Keonchi** India
43F4 **Keonjhargarh** India
19D2 **Kępno** Poland
44B3 **Kerala** *State* India
34B3 **Kerang** Australia
12K6 **Kerava** Finland
21F6 **Kerch'** Ukraine
20J3 **Kerchem'ya** Russian Federation
32D1 **Kerema** Papua New Guinea
58C1 **Keremeos** Canada
50D2 **Keren** Eritrea
36E7 **Kerguelen** *Is* Indian Ocean
36E7 **Kerguelen Ridge** Indian Ocean
50D4 **Kericho** Kenya
27D7 **Kerinci** *Mt* Indonesia
50D3 **Kerio** *R* Kenya
48D1 **Kerkenna, Îles** Tunisia
38E2 **Kerki** Turkmenistan
Kérkira = Corfu
33H3 **Kermadec Is** Pacific Ocean
33H4 **Kermadec Trench** Pacific Ocean
41G3 **Kermān** Iran
66B2 **Kerman** USA
41E3 **Kermānshāh** Iran
62B2 **Kermit** USA
59C3 **Kern** *R* USA
66C3 **Kernville** USA
20J3 **Keros** Russian Federation
62C2 **Kerrville** USA
9B3 **Kerry Hd** Irish Republic
67B2 **Kershaw** USA
25N5 **Kerulen** *R* Mongolia
48B2 **Kerzaz** Algeria
17F2 **Keşan** Turkey
43N2 **Kesariya** India
29E3 **Kesennuma** Japan
21G7 **Kesir Dağları** *Mt* Turkey
12L5 **Kesten'ga** Russian Federation
6C2 **Keswick** England
48C4 **Kéta** Ghana
27E7 **Ketapang** Indonesia
54E4 **Ketchikan** USA

42B4 **Keti Bandar** Pakistan
19E2 **Kętrzyn** Poland
7D3 **Kettering** England
64C3 **Kettering** USA
58C1 **Kettle** *R* Canada
66C2 **Kettleman City** USA
58C1 **Kettle River Range** *Mts* USA
55L3 **Kettlestone B** Canada
68B1 **Keuka L** USA
41G3 **Kevir-i-Namak** *Salt Flat* Iran
64B2 **Kewaunee** USA
64B1 **Keweenaw B** USA
64B1 **Keweenaw Pen** USA
64C1 **Key Harbour** Canada
67B3 **Key Largo** USA
57E4 **Key West** USA
25M4 **Kezhma** Russian Federation
45D2 **Khabab** Syria
26G2 **Khabarovsk** Russian Federation
21G8 **Khabūr, al** *R* Syria
42B3 **Khairpur** Pakistan
42B3 **Khairpur** *Division* Pakistan
47C1 **Khakhea** Botswana
45B3 **Khalig el Tîna** *B* Egypt
38D4 **Khalīj Maşīrah** *G* Oman
17F3 **Khálki** *I* Greece
17E2 **Khalkidhíki** *Pen* Greece
17E3 **Khalkís** Greece
20L2 **Khal'mer-Yu** Russian Federation
20H4 **Khalturin** Russian Federation
42C4 **Khambhāt,G of** India
42D4 **Khāmgaon** India
30C2 **Kham Keut** Laos
44C2 **Khammam** India
45B3 **Khamsa** Egypt
41E2 **Khamseh** *Mts* Iran
30C2 **Khan** *R* Laos
42B1 **Khanabad** Afghanistan
41E3 **Khānaqīn** Iraq
42D4 **Khandwa** India
42C2 **Khanewal** Pakistan
45D3 **Khan ez Zabīb** Jordan
30D4 **Khanh Hung** Vietnam
17E3 **Khaniá** Greece
26G2 **Khanka, Ozero** *L* China/Russian Federation
Khankendy = Stepanakert
42C3 **Khanpur** Pakistan
45D1 **Khān Shaykhūn** Syria
24H3 **Khanty-Mansiysk** Russian Federation
45C3 **Khan Yunis** Israel
42D1 **Khapalu** India
26E2 **Khapcheranga** Russian Federation
21H6 **Kharabali** Russian Federation
43F4 **Kharagpur** India
42B3 **Kharan** Pakistan
41G4 **Khārān** *R* Iran
41F3 **Kharānaq** Iran
41F4 **Khārg** *I* Iran
49F2 **Khârga Oasis** Egypt
42D4 **Khargon** India
45B3 **Kharîm, Gebel** *Mt* Egypt
21F6 **Khar'kov** Ukraine
20F2 **Kharlovka** Russian Federation
17F2 **Kharmanli** Bulgaria
20G4 **Kharovsk** Russian Federation
50D2 **Khartoum** Sudan
50D2 **Khartoum North** Sudan
28C2 **Khasan** Russian Federation
50D2 **Khashm el Girba** Sudan
43G3 **Khasi-Jaintīa Hills** India
17F2 **Khaskovo** Bulgaria
25M2 **Khatanga** Russian Federation
25N2 **Khatangskiy Zaliv** *Estuary* Russian Federation
25T3 **Khatyrka** Russian Federation
30B3 **Khawsa** Burma
40C4 **Khaybar** Saudi Arabia
40B5 **Khazzan an-Nasr** *L* Egypt
30C2 **Khe Bo** Vietnam
42C4 **Khed Brahma** India
15C2 **Khemis** Algeria
16B3 **Khenchela** Algeria
48B1 **Khenifra** Morocco
43L1 **Kheri** *District* India
15D2 **Kherrata** Algeria
21E6 **Kherson** Ukraine
25N4 **Khilok** Russian Federation
17F3 **Khíos** Greece
17F3 **Khíos** *I* Greece
21D6 **Khmel'nitskiy** Ukraine
19E3 **Khodorov** Ukraine
42B1 **Kholm** Afghanistan
19G1 **Kholm** Russian Federation
47B1 **Khomas Hochland** *Mts* Namibia
30D3 **Khong** Laos
41F4 **Khonj** Iran
26G2 **Khor** Russian Federation
41F5 **Khōr Duwayhin** *B* UAE
42C1 **Khorog** Tajikistan
41E3 **Khorramābad** Iran
41E3 **Khorramshahr** Iran
41G3 **Khosf** Iran
42B2 **Khost** Pakistan
21D6 **Khotin** Ukraine
21D5 **Khoyniki** Belarus
41G2 **Khrebet Kopet Dag** *Mts* Iran/Turkmenistan
20L2 **Khrebet Pay-khoy** *Mts* Russian Federation
45B1 **Khrysokhou B** Cyprus
39E1 **Khudzhand** Tajikistan
20L3 **Khulga** *R* Russian Federation
43F4 **Khulna** Bangladesh
42D1 **Khunjerāb P** China/India
41F3 **Khunsar** Iran
41E4 **Khurays** Saudi Arabia
43F4 **Khurda** India
42D3 **Khurja** India
42C2 **Khushab** Pakistan
45C2 **Khushnīyah** Syria
45D4 **Khush Shah, Wadi el** Jordan
19E3 **Khust** Ukraine
50C2 **Khuwei** Sudan
42B3 **Khuzdar** Pakistan
21H5 **Khvalynsk** Russian Federation
41G3 **Khvor** Iran
41F4 **Khvormūj** Iran
21G8 **Khvoy** Iran
42C1 **Khwaja Muhammad Ra** *Mts* Afghanistan
42C2 **Khyber P** Afghanistan/Pakistan
51C4 **Kiambi** Zaïre
63C2 **Kiamichi** *R* USA
50B4 **Kibangou** Congo
50D4 **Kibaya** Tanzania
50C4 **Kibombo** Zaïre
50D4 **Kibondo** Tanzania
50D4 **Kibungu** Rwanda
17E2 **Kicevo** Macedonia, Yugoslavia
54G4 **Kicking Horse P** Canada
48C3 **Kidal** Mali
7C3 **Kidderminster** England
48A3 **Kidira** Senegal
35C1 **Kidnappers,C** New Zealand
18C2 **Kiel** Germany
19E2 **Kielce** Poland
6C2 **Kielder Res** England
18C2 **Kieler Bucht** *B* Germany
21E5 **Kiev** Ukraine
38E2 **Kifab** Uzbekistan
48A3 **Kiffa** Mauritius
50D4 **Kigali** Rwanda
50D4 **Kigoma** Tanzania
66E5 **Kiholo** Hawaiian Islands
29C4 **Kii-sanchi** *Mts* Japan
29C4 **Kii-suidō** *Str* Japan
25R4 **Kikhchik** Russian Federation
17E1 **Kikinda** Serbia, Yugoslavia
Kikládhes = Cyclades
32D1 **Kikon** Papua New Guinea
29D2 **Kikonai** Japan
27H7 **Kikori** Papua New Guinea
50B4 **Kikwit** Zaïre
66E5 **Kilauea Crater** *Vol* Hawaiian Islands
8C4 **Kilbrannan Sd** Scotland
54C3 **Kilbuck Mts** USA
28B2 **Kilchu** N Korea
34D1 **Kilcoy** Australia
9C3 **Kildare** Irish Republic
9C3 **Kildare** *County* Irish Republic
63D2 **Kilgore** USA
50E4 **Kilifi** Kenya
50D4 **Kilimanjaro** *Mt* Tanzania
51D4 **Kilindoni** Tanzania
40C2 **Kilis** Turkey
19F3 **Kiliya** Ukraine
9D2 **Kilkeel** Northern Ireland
9C3 **Kilkenny** Irish Republic
9C3 **Kilkenny** *County* Irish Republic
17E2 **Kilkís** Greece
34D1 **Killarney** Australia
10B3 **Killarney** Irish Republic
63C2 **Killeen** USA
8C3 **Killin** Scotland
17E3 **Killíni** *Mt* Greece
9B3 **Killorglin** Irish Republic
9D2 **Killyleagh** Northern Ireland
8C4 **Kilmarnock** Scotland
20J4 **Kil'mez** Russian Federation
9C3 **Kilmichael Pt** Irish Republic
51D4 **Kilosa** Tanzania
10B3 **Kilrush** Irish Republic
8C4 **Kilsyth** Scotland
51C4 **Kilwa** Zaïre
51D4 **Kilwa Kisiwani** Tanzania
51D4 **Kilwa Kivinje** Tanzania
60C2 **Kimball** USA
54G5 **Kimberley** Canada
47C2 **Kimberley** South Africa
32B2 **Kimberley Plat** Australia
28B2 **Kimch'aek** N Korea
28B3 **Kimch'ŏn** S Korea
28A3 **Kimhae** S Korea
17E3 **Kími** Greece
28A3 **Kimje** S Korea
20F4 **Kimry** Russian Federation
28A3 **Kimwha** N Korea
27E6 **Kinabalu** *Mt* Malaysia
8D2 **Kinbrace** Scotland
64C2 **Kincardine** Canada
63D2 **Kinder** USA
48A3 **Kindia** Guinea
50C4 **Kindu** Zaïre
20J5 **Kinel'** Russian Federation
20G4 **Kineshma** Russian Federation
34D1 **Kingaroy** Australia
59B3 **King City** USA
54F4 **Kingcome Inlet** Canada
63C1 **Kingfisher** USA
76H4 **King George I** Antarctica
55L4 **King George Is** Canada
32D5 **King I** Australia
32B2 **King Leopold Range** *Mts* Australia
56B3 **Kingman** USA
50C4 **Kingombe** Zaïre
66C2 **Kingsburg** USA
59C3 **Kings Canyon Nat Pk** USA
32B2 **King Sd** Australia
64B1 **Kingsford** USA
67B2 **Kingsland** USA
7E3 **King's Lynn** England
33G1 **Kingsmill Group** *Is* Kiribati
68D2 **Kings Park** USA
56B2 **Kings Peak** *Mt* USA
67B1 **Kingsport** USA
32C4 **Kingston** Australia
55L5 **Kingston** Canada
70E3 **Kingston** Jamaica
65E2 **Kingston** New York, USA
35A3 **Kingston** New Zealand
68C2 **Kingston** Pennsylvania, USA
69N2 **Kingstown** St Vincent
56D4 **Kingsville** USA
7C3 **Kington** England
8C3 **Kingussie** Scotland
54J3 **King William I** Canada
47D3 **King William's Town** South Africa
50B4 **Kinkala** Congo
12G7 **Kinna** Sweden
8D3 **Kinnairds Head** *Pt* Scotland
29C3 **Kinomoto** Japan
8D3 **Kinross** Scotland
50B4 **Kinshasa** Zaïre
62C1 **Kinsley** USA
67C1 **Kinston** USA
27E7 **Kintap** Indonesia
8C4 **Kintyre** *Pen* Scotland
50D3 **Kinyeti** *Mt* Sudan
17E3 **Kiparissía** Greece
17E3 **Kiparissiakós Kólpos** *G* Greece
65D1 **Kipawa,L** Canada
51D4 **Kipili** Tanzania
9C3 **Kippure** *Mt* Irish Republic
51C5 **Kipushi** Zaïre
25M4 **Kirensk** Russian Federation
24J5 **Kirghizia** *Republic* Asia
39F1 **Kirgizskiy Khrebet** *Mts* Kirgizia
50B4 **Kiri** Zaïre
33G1 **Kiribati** *Is, Republic* Pacific Ocean
40B2 **Kırıkkale** Turkey
50D4 **Kirinyaga, Mt** Kenya
20E4 **Kirishi** Russian Federation
42B3 **Kirithar Range** *Mts* Pakistan
17F3 **Kirkağaç** Turkey
21H8 **Kirk Bulāg Dāgh** *Mt* Iran
6C2 **Kirkby** England
8D3 **Kirkcaldy** Scotland
8C4 **Kirkcudbright** Scotland
12K5 **Kirkenes** Norway
6C3 **Kirkham** England
55K5 **Kirkland Lake** Canada
40A1 **Kırklareli** Turkey
6C2 **Kirkoswald** England
76E7 **Kirkpatrick,Mt** Antarctica
57D2 **Kirksville** USA
41D2 **Kirkūk** Iraq
8D2 **Kirkwall** Scotland
47D3 **Kirkwood** South Africa
61E3 **Kirkwood** USA
20E5 **Kirov** Russian Federation
20H4 **Kirov** Russian Federation
41D1 **Kirovakan** Armenia
20K4 **Kirovgrad** Russian Federation
21E6 **Kirovograd** Ukraine
20E2 **Kirovsk** Russian Federation
25R4 **Kirovskiy** Kamchatka, Russian Federation
8D3 **Kirriemuir** Scotland
20J4 **Kirs** Russian Federation
40B2 **Kırşehir** Turkey
18C2 **Kiruna** Sweden
29C3 **Kiryū** Japan
50C3 **Kisangani** Zaïre
29C3 **Kisarazu** Japan
43F3 **Kishanganj** India
42C3 **Kishangarh** India
19F3 **Kishinev** Moldavia
29C4 **Kishiwada** Japan
50D4 **Kisii** Kenya
51D4 **Kisiju** Tanzania
17D1 **Kiskunfélegyháza** Hungary
19D3 **Kiskunhalas** Hungary
21G7 **Kislovodsk** Russian Federation
50E4 **Kismaayo** Somalia
29C3 **Kiso-sammyaku** *Mts* Japan
48B4 **Kissidougou** Guinea
67B3 **Kissimmee,L** USA
50D4 **Kisumu** Kenya
19E3 **Kisvárda** Hungary
48B3 **Kita** Mali
24H6 **Kitab** Uzbekistan
29D3 **Kitakami** Japan
29D3 **Kitakami** *R* Japan
29D3 **Kitakata** Japan
28C4 **Kita-Kyūshū** Japan
50D3 **Kitale** Kenya
26H4 **Kitalo** *I* Japan
29E2 **Kitami** Japan
29D2 **Kitami-Esashi** Japan
60C3 **Kit Carson** USA
55K5 **Kitchener** Canada
50D3 **Kitgum** Uganda
17E3 **Kíthira** *I* Greece
17E3 **Kíthnos** *I* Greece
45B1 **Kiti, C** Cyprus
54G2 **Kitikmeot** *Region* Canada
54F4 **Kitimat** Canada
12K5 **Kitinen** *R* Finland
28B4 **Kitsuki** Japan
65D2 **Kittanning** USA
65E2 **Kittery** USA
12J5 **Kittilä** Finland
67C1 **Kitty Hawk** USA
51D4 **Kitunda** Tanzania
51C5 **Kitwe** Zambia
18C3 **Kitzbühel** Austria
18C3 **Kitzingen** Germany
50C4 **Kiumbi** Zaïre
54B3 **Kivalina** USA
19F2 **Kivercy** Ukraine
50C4 **Kivu,L** Rwanda/Zaïre
54B3 **Kiwalik** USA
Kiyev = Kiev
19G2 **Kiyevskoye Vodokhranilishche** *Res* Ukraine
20K4 **Kizel** Russian Federation
20G3 **Kizema** Russian Federation
40C2 **Kizil** *R* Turkey
38D2 **Kizyl'-Arvat** Turkmenistan
21J8 **Kizyl-Atrek** Turkmenistan
18C2 **Kladno** Czech Republic
18C3 **Klagenfurt** Austria
20C4 **Klaipēda** Lithuania
58B2 **Klamath** *R* USA
56A2 **Klamath Falls** USA
58B2 **Klamath Mts** USA
18C3 **Klatovy** Czech Republic
45C1 **Kleiat** Lebanon
47B2 **Kleinsee** South Africa
47D2 **Klerksdorp** South Africa
19G2 **Kletnya** Russian Federation
13D2 **Kleve** Germany
19G2 **Klimovichi** Belarus
20F4 **Klin** Russian Federation
19D1 **Klintehamn** Sweden
21E5 **Klintsy** Russian Federation
47C3 **Klipplaat** South Africa
16D2 **Ključ** Bosnia-Herzegovina
18D2 **Kłodzko** Poland
54D3 **Klondike Plat** Canada/USA
18D3 **Klosterneuburg** Austria
19D2 **Kluczbork** Poland
6D2 **Knaresborough** England
7C3 **Knighton** Wales
16D2 **Knin** Croatia
32A4 **Knob,C** Australia
9B3 **Knockmealdown Mts** Irish Republic
13B2 **Knokke-Heist** Belgium
76G9 **Knox Coast** Antarctica
61E2 **Knoxville** Iowa, USA
57E3 **Knoxville** Tennessee, USA
55Q3 **Knud Rasmussens Land** *Region* Greenland
7C3 **Knutsford** England
47C3 **Knysna** South Africa
55O3 **Kobberminebugt** *B* Greenland
29D4 **Kōbe** Japan
København = Copenhagen
18B2 **Koblenz** Germany
19E2 **Kobrin** Belarus
27G7 **Kobroör** *I* Indonesia
54B3 **Kobuk** *R* USA
17E2 **Kočani** Macedonia, Yugoslavia
28B3 **Kochang** S Korea
28B3 **Koch'ang** S Korea
30C3 **Ko Chang** *I* Thailand
43F3 **Koch Bihār** India
55L3 **Koch I** Canada
44B4 **Kochi** India
29C4 **Kōchi** Japan
54C4 **Kodiak** USA
54C4 **Kodiak I** USA
44B3 **Kodikkarai** India
50D3 **Kodok** Sudan
29D2 **Kodomari-misaki** *C* Japan
19F3 **Kodyma** Ukraine
66D3 **Koehn L** USA
47B2 **Koes** Namibia
47D2 **Koffiefontein** South Africa
48B4 **Koforidua** Ghana
29D3 **Kofu** Japan
29C3 **Koga** Japan
12G7 **Køge** Denmark
42C2 **Kohat** Pakistan
42B2 **Koh-i-Baba** *Mts* Afghanistan
42B1 **Koh-i-Hisar** *Mts* Afghanistan
42B2 **Koh-i-Khurd** *Mt* Afghanistan
43G3 **Kohīma** India
42B2 **Koh-i-Mazar** *Mt* Afghanistan
42B3 **Kohlu** Pakistan
20D4 **Kohtla Järve** Estonia
28A4 **Kohung** S Korea
28A4 **Kohyon** S Korea
29C3 **Koide** Japan
30A4 **Koihoa** Nicobar Is, India
28A2 **Koin** N Korea
28B4 **Koje Dŏ** *I* S Korea
29C2 **Ko-jima** *I* Japan
24H4 **Kokchetav** Kazakhstan
12J6 **Kokemäki** *L* Finland
12J6 **Kokkola** Finland
32D1 **Kokoda** Papua New Guinea
64B2 **Kokomo** USA
27G7 **Kokonau** Indonesia
26B2 **Kokpekty** Kazakhstan
28A3 **Koksan** N Korea
55M4 **Koksoak** *R* Canada
28A3 **Koksŏng** S Korea
47D3 **Kokstad** South Africa
30C3 **Ko Kut** *I* Thailand
20E2 **Kola** Russian Federation
27F7 **Kolaka** Indonesia
30B4 **Ko Lanta** *I* Thailand
44B3 **Kolār** India
44B3 **Kolār Gold Fields** India
48A3 **Kolda** Senegal
12F7 **Kolding** Denmark
20H2 **Kolguyev, Ostrov** *I* Russian Federation
44A2 **Kolhāpur** India
18D2 **Kolín** Czech Republic
44B4 **Kollam** India
Köln = Cologne
19D2 **Koło** Poland
66E5 **Koloa** Hawaiian Islands
18D2 **Kołobrzeg** Poland
48B3 **Kolokani** Mali
20F4 **Kolomna** Russian Federation
21D6 **Kolomyya** Ukraine
25R4 **Kolpakovskiy** Russian Federation
24K4 **Kolpashevo** Russian Federation
17F3 **Kólpos Merabéllou** *B* Greece
17E2 **Kólpos Singitikós** *G* Greece
17E2 **Kólpos Strimonikós** *G* Greece
17E2 **Kólpos Toronaíos** *G* Greece
20F2 **Kol'skiy Poluostrov** *Pen* Russian Federation
20K2 **Kolva** *R* Russian Federation
12G6 **Kolvereid** Norway
51C5 **Kolwezi** Zaïre
25R3 **Kolyma** *R* Russian Federation
25R3 **Kolymskaya Nizmennost'** *Lowland* Russian Federation
25S3 **Kolymskoye Nagor'ye** *Mts* Russian Federation
17E2 **Kom** *Mt* Bulgaria/Serbia, Yugoslavia
50D3 **Koma** Ethiopia
29D3 **Koma** Japan

48D3 **Komadugu Gana** *R* Nigeria
29D2 **Komaga take** *Mt* Japan
25S4 **Komandorskiye Ostrova** *Is* Russian Federation
19D3 **Komárno** Slovakia
47E2 **Komati** *R* South Africa/Swaziland
47E2 **Komati Poort** South Africa
29D3 **Komatsu** Japan
29B4 **Komatsushima** Japan
20J3 **Komi Republic** Russian Federation
26B1 **Kommunar** Russian Federation
27E7 **Komodo** *I* Indonesia
27G7 **Komoran** *I* Indonesia
29C3 **Komoro** Japan
17F2 **Komotiní** Greece
47C3 **Kompasberg** *Mt* South Africa
30D3 **Kompong Cham** Cambodia
30C3 **Kompong Chhnang** Cambodia
30C3 **Kompong Som = Sihanoukville**
30D3 **Kompong Thom** Cambodia
30D3 **Kompong Trabek** Cambodia
19F3 **Komrat** Moldavia
47C3 **Komsberg** *Mts* South Africa
25L1 **Komsomolets, Ostrov** *I* Russian Federation
20L2 **Komsomol'skiy** Russian Federation
25P4 **Komsomol'sk na Amure** Russian Federation
24H4 **Konda** *R* Russian Federation
43E5 **Kondagaon** India
50D4 **Kondoa** Tanzania
20E3 **Kondopoga** Russian Federation
44B2 **Kondukūr** India
20F3 **Konevo** Russian Federation
55P3 **Kong Christian IX Land** *Region* Greenland
55O3 **Kong Frederik VI Kyst** *Region* Greenland
28A3 **Kongju** S Korea
24D2 **Kong Karls Land** *Is* Svalbard
50C4 **Kongolo** Zaïre
12F7 **Kongsberg** Norway
12G6 **Kongsvinger** Norway
Königsberg = Kaliningrad
19D2 **Konin** Poland
17D2 **Konjic** Bosnia-Herzegovina
20G3 **Konosha** Russian Federation
29C3 **Konosu** Japan
21E5 **Konotop** Ukraine
19E2 **Końskie** Poland
18B3 **Konstanz** Germany
48C3 **Kontagora** Nigeria
30D3 **Kontum** Vietnam
21E8 **Konya** Turkey
58C1 **Kootenay L** Canada
42C5 **Kopargaon** India
55R3 **Kópasker** Iceland
12A2 **Kópavogur** Iceland
16C1 **Koper** Slovenia
38D2 **Kopet Dag** *Mts* Iran/Turkmenistan
20L4 **Kopeysk** Russian Federation
30C4 **Ko Phangan** *I* Thailand
30B4 **Ko Phuket** *I* Thailand
12H7 **Köping** Sweden
28A3 **Kopo-ri** S Korea
44B2 **Koppal** India
16D1 **Koprivnica** Croatia
42B4 **Korangi** Pakistan
44C2 **Koraput** India
43E4 **Korba** India
18B2 **Korbach** Germany
17E2 **Korçë** Albania
16D2 **Korčula** *I* Croatia
31E2 **Korea B** China/Korea
28B2 **Korea, North** *Republic* Asia
28B3 **Korea, South** *Republic* Asia
26F3 **Korea Strait** Japan/Korea
19F2 **Korec** Ukraine
25S3 **Korf** Russian Federation
40B1 **Körğlu Tepesi** *Mt* Turkey
48B4 **Korhogo** Ivory Coast
42B4 **Kori Creek** India
Kórinthos = Corinth
29E3 **Kōriyama** Japan
20L5 **Korkino** Russian Federation
25R3 **Korkodon** Russian Federation
25R3 **Korkodon** *R* Russian Federation
40B2 **Korkuteli** Turkey
39G1 **Korla** China
45B1 **Kormakiti, C** Cyprus
16D2 **Kornat** *I* Croatia
21E7 **Köroğlu Tepesi** *Mt* Turkey
50D4 **Korogwe** Tanzania
34B3 **Koroit** Australia
27G6 **Koror** Palau, Pacific Ocean
19E3 **Körös** *R* Hungary
21D5 **Korosten** Ukraine
19F2 **Korostyshev** Ukraine
50B2 **Koro Toro** Chad
26H2 **Korsakov** Russian Federation
12G7 **Korsør** Denmark
20J3 **Kortkeros** Russian Federation
18A2 **Kortrijk** Belgium
25S3 **Koryakskoye Nagor'ye** *Mts* Russian Federation
28A3 **Koryong** S Korea
17F3 **Kós** *I* Greece
30C4 **Ko Samui** *I* Thailand
28A3 **Kosan** N Korea
19D2 **Kościerzyna** Poland
63E2 **Kosciusko** USA
32D4 **Kosciusko** *Mt* Australia
43J2 **Kosi** India
43K1 **Kosi** *R* India
19E3 **Košice** Slovakia
20J2 **Kosma** *R* Russian Federation
28B3 **Kosŏng** N Korea
17E2 **Kosovo** *Region* Serbia, Yugoslavia
17E2 **Kosovska Mitrovica** Serbia, Yugoslavia
48B4 **Kossou** *L* Ivory Coast
47D2 **Koster** South Africa
50D2 **Kosti** Sudan
19F2 **Kostopol'** Ukraine
20G4 **Kostroma** Russian Federation
18C2 **Kostrzyn** Poland
20K2 **Kos'yu** *R* Russian Federation
12H8 **Koszalin** Poland
42D3 **Kota** India
30C4 **Kota Baharu** Malaysia
42C2 **Kot Addu** Pakistan
27E6 **Kota Kinabalu** Malaysia
44C2 **Kotapad** India
20H4 **Kotel'nich** Russian Federation
21G6 **Kotel'nikovo** Russian Federation
25P2 **Kotel'nyy, Ostrov** *I* Russian Federation
12K6 **Kotka** Finland
20H3 **Kotlas** Russian Federation
54B3 **Kotlik** USA
17D2 **Kotor** Montenegro, Yugoslavia
21D6 **Kotovsk** Ukraine
42B3 **Kotri** Pakistan
44C2 **Kottagūdem** India
44B4 **Kottayam** India
50C3 **Kotto** *R* Central African Republic
44B3 **Kottūru** India
25L3 **Kotuy** *R* Russian Federation
54B3 **Kotzebue** USA
54B3 **Kotzebue Sd** USA
48C3 **Kouandé** Benin
50C3 **Kouango** Central African Republic
48B3 **Koudougou** Burkina
47C3 **Kougaberge** *Mts* South Africa
50B4 **Koulamoutou** Gabon
48B3 **Koulikoro** Mali
48B3 **Koupéla** Burkina
73H2 **Kourou** French Guiana
48B3 **Kouroussa** Guinea
50B2 **Kousséri** Cameroon
12K6 **Kouvola** Finland
12L5 **Kovdor** Russian Federation
12L5 **Kovdozero, Ozero** *L* Russian Federation
19E2 **Kovel** Ukraine
Kovno = Kaunas
20G4 **Kovrov** Russian Federation
20G5 **Kovylkino** Russian Federation
20F3 **Kovzha** *R* Russian Federation
30C4 **Ko Way** *I* Thailand
31C5 **Kowloon** Hong Kong
28A3 **Kowŏn** N Korea
42B2 **Kowt-e-Ashrow** Afghanistan
40A2 **Köyceğiz** Turkey
20G2 **Koyda** Russian Federation
44A2 **Koyna Res** India
20H3 **Koynas** Russian Federation
54C3 **Koyukuk** USA
40C2 **Kozan** Turkey
17E2 **Kozańi** Greece
44B3 **Kozhikode** India
20K2 **Kozhim** Russian Federation
20H4 **Koz'modemyansk** Russian Federation
29C4 **Kōzu-shima** *I* Japan
48C4 **Kpalimé** Togo
47D3 **Kraai** *R* South Africa
12F7 **Kragerø** Norway
17E2 **Kragujevac** Serbia, Yugoslavia
30B3 **Kra,Isthmus of** Burma/Malaysia
45D1 **Krak des Chevaliers** *Hist Site* Syria
Kraków = Cracow Poland
17E2 **Kraljevo** Serbia, Yugoslavia
21F6 **Kramatorsk** Ukraine
12H6 **Kramfors** Sweden
16C1 **Kranj** Slovenia
20H3 **Krasavino** Russian Federation
20J1 **Krasino** Russian Federation
28C2 **Kraskino** Russian Federation
19E2 **Kraśnik** Poland
21H5 **Krasnoarmeysk** Russian Federation
21F6 **Krasnodar** Russian Federation
20K4 **Krasnokamsk** Russian Federation
20L4 **Krasnotur'insk** Russian Federation
20K4 **Krasnoufimsk** Russian Federation
20K5 **Krasnousol'skiy** Russian Federation
20K3 **Krasnovishersk** Russian Federation
21J7 **Krasnovodsk** Turkmenistan
25L4 **Krasnoyarsk** Russian Federation
19E2 **Krasnystaw** Poland
21H5 **Krasnyy Kut** Russian Federation
21F6 **Krasnyy Luch** Ukraine
21H6 **Krasnyy Yar** Russian Federation
30D3 **Kratie** Cambodia
55N2 **Kraulshavn** Greenland
18B2 **Krefeld** Germany
21E6 **Kremenchug** Ukraine
21E6 **Kremenchugskoye Vodokhranilische** *Res* Ukraine
19F2 **Kremenets** Ukraine
60B2 **Kremming** USA
48C4 **Kribi** Cameroon
20E5 **Krichev** Belarus
44B2 **Krishna** *R* India
44B3 **Krishnagiri** India
43F4 **Krishnanagar** India
12F7 **Kristiansand** Norway
12G7 **Kristianstad** Sweden
24B3 **Kristiansund** Norway
12J6 **Kristiinankaupunki** Finland
12G7 **Kristinehamn** Sweden
Kríti = Crete
21E6 **Krivoy Rog** Ukraine
16C1 **Krk** *I* Croatia
47D1 **Krokodil** *R* South Africa
25S4 **Kronotskaya Sopka** *Mt* Russian Federation
25S4 **Kronotskiy, Mys** *C* Russian Federation
55P3 **Kronprins Frederik Bjerge** *Mts* Greenland
12K7 **Kronshtadt** Russian Federation
47D2 **Kroonstad** South Africa
21G6 **Kropotkin** Russian Federation
47E1 **Kruger Nat Pk** South Africa
47D2 **Krugersdorp** South Africa
17D2 **Kruje** Albania
Krung Thep = Bangkok
19F2 **Krupki** Belarus
17E2 **Kruševac** Serbia, Yugoslavia
12K7 **Krustpils** Latvia
Krym = Crimea
21F7 **Krymsk** Russian Federation
18D2 **Krzyz** Poland
15C2 **Ksar El Boukhari** Algeria
15A2 **Ksar-el-Kebir** Morocco
48C1 **Ksour, Mts des** Algeria
27C6 **Kuala** Indonesia
30C5 **Kuala Dungun** Malaysia
30C4 **Kuala Kerai** Malaysia
30C5 **Kuala Kubu Baharu** Malaysia
30C5 **Kuala Lipis** Malaysia
30C5 **Kuala Lumpur** Malaysia
30C4 **Kuala Trengganu** Malaysia
27F6 **Kuandang** Indonesia
28A2 **Kuandian** China
30C5 **Kuantan** Malaysia
21H7 **Kuba** Azerbaijan
27H7 **Kubor** *Mt* Papua New Guinea
27E6 **Kuching** Malaysia
27E6 **Kudat** Malaysia
20J4 **Kudymkar** Russian Federation
18C3 **Kufstein** Austria
41G3 **Kuh Duren** *Upland* Iran
41F3 **Kūh-e Dinar** *Mt* Iran
41G2 **Kūh-e-Hazār Masjed** *Mts* Iran
41G4 **Kūh-e Jebāl Barez** *Mts* Iran
41F3 **Kūh-e Karkas** *Mts* Iran
41G4 **Kūh-e Laleh Zar** *Mt* Iran
41E2 **Kūh-e Sahand** *Mt* Iran
38E3 **Kuh-e-Taftān** *Mt* Iran
21H9 **Kūhhaye Alvand** *Mts* Iran
21H8 **Kūhhaye Sabalan** *Mts.* Iran
41E3 **Kūhhā-ye Zāgros** *Mts* Iran
12K6 **Kuhmo** Finland
41F3 **Kūhpāyeh** Iran
41G3 **Kūhpāyeh** *Mt* Iran
41G4 **Kūh-ye Bashākerd** *Mts* Iran
41E2 **Kūh-ye Sabalan** *Mt* Iran
47B2 **Kuibis** Namibia
47B1 **Kuiseb** *R* Namibia
51B5 **Kuito** Angola
28A3 **Kujang** N Korea
29E2 **Kuji** Japan
28B4 **Kuju-san** *Mt* Japan
17E2 **Kukës** Albania
30C5 **Kukup** Malaysia
41G4 **Kūl** *R* Iran
17F3 **Kula** Turkey
21K6 **Kulakshi** Kazakhstan
50D3 **Kulal,Mt** Kenya
17E2 **Kulata** Bulgaria
20C4 **Kuldīga** Latvia
20G2 **Kulov** *R* Russian Federation
21J6 **Kul'sary** Kazakhstan
42D2 **Kulu** India
40B2 **Kulu** Turkey
24J4 **Kulunda** Russian Federation
34B2 **Kulwin** Australia
21H7 **Kuma** *R* Russian Federation
29C3 **Kumagaya** Japan
27E7 **Kumai** Indonesia
21L5 **Kumak** Russian Federation
28C4 **Kumamoto** Japan
29C4 **Kumano** Japan
17E2 **Kumanovo** Macedonia, Yugoslavia
48B4 **Kumasi** Ghana
21G7 **Kumayri** Armenia
48C4 **Kumba** Cameroon
44B3 **Kumbakonam** India
28A3 **Kŭmch'ŏn** N Korea
20K5 **Kumertau** Russian Federation
28A3 **Kumgang** N Korea
12H7 **Kumla** Sweden
28A4 **Kŭmnyŏng** S Korea
28A4 **Kŭmo-do** *I* S Korea
44A3 **Kumta** India
39G1 **Kumüx** China
28B3 **Kumwha** S Korea
42C2 **Kunar** *R* Afghanistan
29F2 **Kunashir, Ostrov** *I* Russian Federation
12K7 **Kunda** Estonia
42C4 **Kundla** India
42B1 **Kunduz** Afghanistan
Kunene *R* **= Cunene R**
12G7 **Kungsbacka** Sweden
20K4 **Kungur** Russian Federation
30B1 **Kunhing** Burma
39G2 **Kunlun Shan** *Mts* China
31A4 **Kunming** China
20M3 **Kunovat** *R* Russian Federation
28B3 **Kunsan** S Korea
12K6 **Kuopio** Finland
16D1 **Kupa** *R* Bosnia-Herzegovina/Croatia
32B2 **Kupang** Indonesia
32D2 **Kupiano** Papua New Guinea
54E4 **Kupreanof I** USA
21F6 **Kupyansk** Ukraine
39G1 **Kuqa** China
21H8 **Kura** *R* Azerbaijan
29C3 **Kurabe** Japan
29C4 **Kurashiki** Japan
29B3 **Kurayoshi** Japan
41E2 **Kurdistan** *Region* Iran
17F2 **Kŭrdzhali** Bulgaria
28C4 **Kure** Japan
20C4 **Kuressaare** Estonia
25L3 **Kureyka** *R* Russian Federation
24H4 **Kurgan** Russian Federation
12J6 **Kurikka** Finland
25Q5 **Kuril Is** Russian Federation
Kuril'skiye Ostrova *Is* **= Kuril Islands**
36J2 **Kuril Trench** Pacific Ocean
21H8 **Kurinskaya Kosa** *Sand Spit* Azerbaijan
44B2 **Kurnool** India
29D2 **Kuroishi** Japan
29D3 **Kuroiso** Japan
35B2 **Kurow** New Zealand
34D2 **Kurri Kurri** Australia
21F5 **Kursk** Russian Federation
26B2 **Kuruktag** *R* China
47C2 **Kuruman** South Africa
47C2 **Kuruman** *R* South Africa
28C4 **Kurume** Japan
44C3 **Kurunegala** Sri Lanka
24K5 **Kurunktag** *R* China
20K3 **Kur'ya** Russian Federation
20K4 **Kusa** Russian Federation
17F3 **Kuşadası Körfezi** *B* Turkey
17F2 **Kus Golü** *L* Turkey
29D4 **Kushimoto** Japan
29E2 **Kushiro** Japan
38E2 **Kushka** Afghanistan
43F4 **Kushtia** Bangladesh
21J5 **Kushum** *R* Kazakhstan
20K4 **Kushva** Russian Federation
54B3 **Kuskokwim** *R* USA
54C3 **Kuskokwim Mts** USA
43E3 **Kusma** Nepal
28B3 **Kusŏng** N Korea
24H4 **Kustanay** Kazakhstan
27E7 **Kuta** *R* Indonesia
21D8 **Kütahya** Turkey
21G7 **Kutaisi** Georgia
29D2 **Kutchan** Japan
29E2 **Kutcharo-ko** *L* Japan
18D3 **Kutná Hora** Czech Republic
19D2 **Kutno** Poland
50B4 **Kutu** Zaïre
43G4 **Kutubdia I** Bangladesh
50C2 **Kutum** Sudan
55M4 **Kuujjuaq** Canada
55L4 **Kuujjuarapik** Canada
12K5 **Kuusamo** Finland
21K5 **Kuvandyk** Russian Federation
41E4 **Kuwait** Kuwait
38C3 **Kuwait** *Sheikhdom* SW Asia
29C3 **Kuwana** Japan
24J4 **Kuybyshev** Russian Federation
Kuybyshev = Samara
20H5 **Kuybyshevskoye Vodokhranilishche** *Res* Russian Federation
20E2 **Kuyto, Ozero** *L* Russian Federation
25M4 **Kuytun** Russian Federation
21F7 **Kuzey Anadolu Dağları** *Mts* Turkey
20F2 **Kuzomen** Russian Federation
20C2 **Kvænangen** *Sd* Norway
12G5 **Kvigtind** *Mt* Norway
20B2 **Kvikkjokk** Sweden
50D4 **Kwale** Kenya
28B3 **Kwangju** S Korea
50B4 **Kwango** *R* Zaïre
28A3 **Kwangyang** S Korea
28A2 **Kwanmo-bong** *Mt* N Korea
51D6 **KwaZulu Natal** *Province* South Africa
51C5 **Kwekwe** Zimbabwe
19D2 **Kwidzyn** Poland
54B4 **Kwigillingok** USA
27G7 **Kwoka** *Mt* Indonesia
34C3 **Kyabram** Australia
30B2 **Kyaikkami** Burma
30B2 **Kyaikto** Burma
26D1 **Kyakhta** Russian Federation
30B1 **Kyaukme** Burma
30B1 **Kyauk-padaung** Burma
30A2 **Kyaukpyu** Burma
20G2 **Kychema** Russian Federation
10B2 **Kyle of Lochalsh** Scotland
13D2 **Kyll** *R* Germany
34B3 **Kyneton** Australia
50D3 **Kyoga, L** Uganda
34D1 **Kyogle** Australia
28B3 **Kyŏngju** S Korea
28A3 **Kyongsang Sanmaek** *Mts* S Korea
28A2 **Kyŏngsŏng** N Korea
29D3 **Kyōto** Japan
45B1 **Kyrenia** Cyprus
20K3 **Kyrta** Russian Federation
20L4 **Kyshtym** Russian Federation
45B1 **Kythrea** Cyprus

28B4 **Kyūshū** *I* Japan
36H4 **Kyushu-Palau Ridge** Pacific Ocean
17E2 **Kyustendil** Bulgaria
25O2 **Kyusyur** Russian Federation
26C1 **Kyzyl** Russian Federation
24H5 **Kyzylkum** *Desert* Uzbekistan
24H5 **Kzyl Orda** Kazakhstan

L

50E3 **Laascaanood** Somalia
50E2 **Laas Dawaco** Somalia
13E2 **Laasphe** Germany
50E2 **Laasqoray** Somalia
72F1 **La Asunción** Venezuela
48A2 **Laâyoune** Morocco
58D2 **La Barge** USA
48A3 **Labé** Guinea
18D2 **Labe** *R* Czech Republic
65E1 **Labelle** Canada
67B3 **La Belle** USA
21G7 **Labinsk** Russian Federation
45D1 **Laboué** Lebanon
55M4 **Labrador** *Region* Canada
55M4 **Labrador City** Canada
55N4 **Labrador S** Canada/Greenland
72F5 **Lábrea** Brazil
27E6 **Labuk B** Malaysia
30A2 **Labutta** Burma
20M2 **Labytnangi** Russian Federation
13B2 **La Capelle** France
Laccadive Is = Lakshadweep
39F4 **Laccadive Is** India
70D3 **La Ceiba** Honduras
34A3 **Lacepede B** Australia
14C2 **La Châtre** France
45C3 **Lachish** *Hist Site* Israel
32D4 **Lachlan** *R* Australia
72C2 **La Chorrera** Panama
65E1 **Lachute** Canada
65D2 **Lackawanna** USA
54G4 **Lac la Biche** Canada
55L4 **Lac L'eau Claire** Canada
65E1 **Lac Mégantic** Canada
54G4 **Lacombe** Canada
65E2 **Laconia** USA
15A1 **La Coruña** Spain
57D2 **La Crosse** USA
63D1 **La Cygne** USA
42D2 **Ladākh Range** *Mts* India
27E6 **Ladd Reef** S China Sea
42C3 **Lādnūn** India
20E3 **Ladoga, L** Russian Federation
31B5 **Ladong** China
Ladozhskoye Oz *L* = **Ladoga, L**
55K2 **Lady Ann Str** Canada
34C4 **Lady Barron** Australia
47D2 **Ladybrand** South Africa
47D2 **Ladysmith** South Africa
64A1 **Ladysmith** USA
32D1 **Lae** Papua New Guinea
30C3 **Laem Ngop** Thailand
18C1 **Laesø** *I* Denmark
60B3 **Lafayette** Colorado, USA
57E2 **Lafayette** Indiana, USA
57D3 **Lafayette** Louisiana, USA
13B3 **La Fère** France
13B3 **La-Ferté-sous-Jouarre** France
48C4 **Lafia** Nigeria
48C4 **Lafiagi** Nigeria
14B2 **La Flèche** France
16B3 **La Galite** *I* Tunisia
18C1 **Lagan** *R* Sweden
73L6 **Lagarto** Brazil
8C3 **Laggan, L** Scotland
48C1 **Laghouat** Algeria
72C4 **Lago Agrio** Ecuador
48C4 **Lagos** Nigeria
15A2 **Lagos** Portugal
70B2 **Lagos de Moreno** Mexico
56B2 **La Grande** USA
32B2 **Lagrange** Australia
57E3 **La Grange** Georgia, USA
64B3 **La Grange** Kentucky, USA
67C1 **La Grange** N Carolina, USA
63C3 **La Grange** Texas, USA
72F2 **La Gran Sabana** *Mts* Venezuela
62A2 **Laguna** USA
59C4 **Laguna Beach** USA
56C4 **Laguna Seca** Mexico
28B2 **Lagusha** N Korea
27E6 **Lahad Datu** Malaysia
41F2 **Lāhījān** Iran
13D2 **Lahn** *R* Germany
13D2 **Lahnstein** Germany
42C2 **Lahore** Pakistan
13D3 **Lahr** Germany
12K6 **Lahti** Finland
50B3 **Lai** Chad
31B5 **Laibin** China
30C1 **Lai Chau** Vietnam
13C4 **Laignes** France
12J6 **Laihia** Finland
47C3 **Laingsburg** South Africa
8C2 **Lairg** Scotland
31E2 **Laiyang** China
31D2 **Laizhou Wan** *B* China
74B5 **Laja, Lago de la** Chile
74F3 **Lajes** Brazil
66D4 **La Jolla** USA
56C3 **La Junta** USA
60D2 **Lake Andes** USA
34C2 **Lake Cargelligo** Australia
57D3 **Lake Charles** USA
67B2 **Lake City** Florida, USA
61E2 **Lake City** Minnesota, USA
67C2 **Lake City** S Carolina, USA
6C2 **Lake District** *Region* England
66D4 **Lake Elsinore** USA
32C3 **Lake Eyre Basin** Australia
65D2 **Lakefield** Canada
64B2 **Lake Geneva** USA
68D1 **Lake George** USA
55M3 **Lake Harbour** Canada
59D4 **Lake Havasu City** USA
66C3 **Lake Hughes** USA
68C2 **Lakehurst** USA
66C3 **Lake Isabella** USA
63C3 **Lake Jackson** USA
67B3 **Lakeland** USA
55J5 **Lake of the Woods** Canada
58B1 **Lake Oswego** USA
12K7 **Lake Peipus** Estonia/Russian Federation
59B3 **Lakeport** USA
63D2 **Lake Providence** USA
35B2 **Lake Pukaki** New Zealand
34C3 **Lakes Entrance** Australia
66C2 **Lakeshore** USA
34B1 **Lake Stewart** Australia
65D1 **Lake Traverse** Canada
58B2 **Lakeview** USA
58B1 **Lakeview Mt** Canada
63D2 **Lake Village** USA
67B3 **Lake Wales** USA
66C4 **Lakewood** California, USA
60B3 **Lakewood** Colorado, USA
68C2 **Lakewood** New Jersey, USA
64C2 **Lakewood** Ohio, USA
67B3 **Lake Worth** USA
43E3 **Lakhīmpur** India
42B4 **Lakhpat** India
62B1 **Lakin** USA
42C2 **Lakki** Pakistan
17E3 **Lakonikós Kólpos** *G* Greece
48B4 **Lakota** Ivory Coast
12K4 **Laksefjord** *Inlet* Norway
12K4 **Lakselv** Norway
44A3 **Lakshadweep** *Is, Union Territory* India
72B4 **La Libertad** Ecuador
15A2 **La Linea** Spain
42D4 **Lalitpur** India
54H4 **La Loche** Canada
13C2 **La Louvière** Belgium
69A4 **La Luz** Nicaragua
55L5 **La Malbaie** Canada
56C3 **Lamar** Colorado, USA
63D1 **Lamar** Missouri, USA
63C3 **La Marque** USA
50B4 **Lambaréné** Gabon
72B5 **Lambayeque** Peru
76F10 **Lambert Glacier** Antarctica
47B3 **Lamberts Bay** South Africa
68C2 **Lambertville** USA
54F2 **Lambton,C** Canada
30C2 **Lam Chi** *R* Thailand
15A1 **Lamego** Portugal
72C6 **La Merced** Peru
62B2 **Lamesa** USA
59C4 **La Mesa** USA
17E3 **Lamía** Greece
8D4 **Lammermuir Hills** Scotland
12G7 **Lammhult** Sweden
61E2 **Lamoni** USA
66C3 **Lamont** California, USA
60B2 **Lamont** Wyoming, USA
27H6 **Lamotrek** *I* Pacific Ocean
13B4 **Lamotte-Beuvron** France
60D1 **La Moure** USA
62C2 **Lampasas** USA
7B3 **Lampeter** Wales
50E4 **Lamu** Kenya
66E5 **Lanai** *I* Hawaiian Islands
66E5 **Lanai City** Hawaiian Islands
27F6 **Lanao, L** Philippines
8D4 **Lanark** Scotland
30B3 **Lanbi** *I* Burma
30C1 **Lancang** *R* China
6C3 **Lancashire** *County* England
59C4 **Lancaster** California, USA
6C2 **Lancaster** England
61E2 **Lancaster** Missouri, USA
65E2 **Lancaster** New Hampshire, USA
68A1 **Lancaster** New York, USA
64C3 **Lancaster** Ohio, USA
57F3 **Lancaster** Pennsylvania, USA
67B2 **Lancaster** S Carolina, USA
55K2 **Lancaster Sd** Canada
13E3 **Landan** Germany
18C3 **Landeck** Austria
56C2 **Lander** USA
14B3 **Landes, Les** *Region* France
67B1 **Landrum** USA
18C3 **Landsberg** Germany
54F2 **Lands End** *C* Canada
7B4 **Land's End** *Pt* England
18C3 **Landshut** Germany
12G7 **Landskrona** Sweden
67A2 **Lanett** USA
43E2 **La'nga Co** *L* China
60D1 **Langdon** USA
47C2 **Langeberg** *Mts* South Africa
18B2 **Langenhagen** Germany
13D1 **Langeoog** *I* Germany
8D4 **Langholm** Scotland
12A2 **Langjökull** *Mts* Iceland
30B4 **Langkawi** *I* Malaysia
34C1 **Langlo** *R* Australia
6B2 **Langness** *Pt* England
14B3 **Langon** France
14D2 **Langres** France
13C4 **Langres, Plateau de** France
27C6 **Langsa** Indonesia
26D2 **Lang Shan** *Mts* China
30D1 **Lang Son** Vietnam
62B3 **Langtry** USA
14C3 **Languedoc** *Region* France
74B5 **Lanin, Vol** Argentina
68C2 **Lansdale** USA
55K4 **Lansdowne House** Canada
68C2 **Lansford** USA
57E2 **Lansing** USA
48A2 **Lanzarote** *I* Canary Islands
31A2 **Lanzhou** China
27F5 **Laoag** Philippines
30C1 **Lao Cai** Vietnam
31D1 **Laoha He** *R* China
9C3 **Laois** *County* Irish Republic
28A2 **Laoling** China
13B3 **Laon** France
72C6 **La Oroya** Peru
30C2 **Laos** *Republic* SE Asia
75C4 **Lapa** Brazil
14C2 **Lapalisse** France
72C2 **La Palma** Panama
48A2 **La Palma** *I* Canary Islands
74C5 **La Pampa** *State* Argentina
66B3 **La Panza Range** *Mts* USA
72F2 **La Paragua** Venezuela
74E4 **La Paz** Argentina
72E7 **La Paz** Bolivia
70A2 **La Paz** Mexico
26H2 **La Perouse Str** Japan/Russian Federation
58B2 **La Pine** USA
45B1 **Lapithos** Cyprus
63D2 **Laplace** USA
60C1 **La Plant** USA
74E4 **La Plata** Argentina
64B2 **La Porte** USA
68B2 **Laporte** USA
12K6 **Lappeenranta** Finland
12H5 **Lappland** *Region* Finland/Sweden
62C3 **La Pryor** USA
25O2 **Laptev S** Russian Federation
12J6 **Lapua** Finland
56B4 **La Purísima** Mexico
50C1 **Laqiya Arbain** *Well* Sudan
74C2 **La Quiaca** Argentina
16C2 **L'Aquila** Italy
41F4 **Lār** Iran
15A2 **Larache** Morocco
56C2 **Laramie** USA
60B2 **Laramie Mts** USA
56C2 **Laramie Range** *Mts* USA
75B4 **Laranjeiras do Sul** Brazil
56D4 **Laredo** USA
41F4 **Larestan** *Region* Iran
Largeau = Faya
67B3 **Largo** USA
8C4 **Largs** Scotland
41E2 **Lārī** Iran
74C3 **La Rioja** Argentina
15B1 **La Rioja** *Region* Spain
74C3 **La Rioja** *State* Argentina
17E3 **Lárisa** Greece
42B3 **Larkana** Pakistan
40B3 **Larnaca** Cyprus
45B1 **Larnaca B** Cyprus
9C2 **Larne** Northern Ireland
62C1 **Larned** USA
15A1 **La Robla** Spain
13C2 **La Roche-en-Ardenne** Belgium
14B2 **La Rochelle** France
14B2 **La Roche-sur-Yon** France
15B2 **La Roda** Spain
69D3 **La Romana** Dominican Republic
54H4 **La Ronge** Canada
12F7 **Larvik** Norway
24J3 **Laryak** Russian Federation
15B2 **La Sagra** *Mt* Spain
65E1 **La Salle** Canada
64B2 **La Salle** USA
62B1 **Las Animas** USA
55L5 **La Sarre** Canada
62A2 **Las Cruces** USA
69C3 **La Selle** *Mt* Haiti
31B2 **Lasengmiao** China
74B3 **La Serena** Chile
74E5 **Las Flores** Argentina
30B1 **Lashio** Burma
16D3 **La Sila** *Mts* Italy
41F2 **Lāsjerd** Iran
42A2 **Laskar Gāh** Afghanistan
15A2 **Las Marismas** *Marshland* Spain
48A2 **Las Palmas de Gran Canaria** Canary Islands
16B2 **La Spezia** Italy
74C6 **Las Plumas** Argentina
58B2 **Lassen Peak** *Mt* USA
58B2 **Lassen Volcanic Nat Pk** USA
50B4 **Lastoursville** Gabon
16D2 **Lastovo** *I* Croatia
70B2 **Las Tres Marias** *Is* Mexico
56B3 **Las Vegas** USA
40C2 **Latakia** Syria
16C2 **Latina** Italy
69D4 **La Tortuga, I** Venezuela
34C4 **Latrobe** Australia
45C3 **Latrun** Israel
55L5 **La Tuque** Canada
44B2 **Lātūr** India
20C4 **Latvia** *Republic* Europe
8D4 **Lauder** Scotland
18B2 **Lauenburg** Germany
33H2 **Lau Group** *Is* Fiji
32D5 **Launceston** Australia
7B4 **Launceston** England
74B6 **La Unión** Chile
70D3 **La Unión** El Salvador
72C5 **La Unión** Peru
32D2 **Laura** Australia
65D3 **Laurel** Delaware, USA
68B3 **Laurel** Maryland, USA
57E3 **Laurel** Mississippi, USA
58E1 **Laurel** Montana, USA
67B2 **Laurens** USA
67C2 **Laurinburg** USA
16B1 **Lausanne** Switzerland
27E7 **Laut** *I* Indonesia
74B7 **Lautaro** Chile
13E2 **Lauterbach** Germany
13D3 **Lauterecken** Germany
65E1 **Laval** Canada
14B2 **Laval** France
66B2 **Laveaga Peak** *Mt* USA
58E1 **Lavina** USA
13C3 **La Vôge** *Region* France
73K8 **Lavras** Brazil
54A3 **Lavrentiya** Russian Federation
47E2 **Lavumisa** Swaziland
30B1 **Lawksawk** Burma
61D3 **Lawrence** Kansas, USA
65E2 **Lawrence** Massachusetts, USA
35A3 **Lawrence** New Zealand
63E1 **Lawrenceburg** USA
64B3 **Lawrenceville** Illinois, USA
68B2 **Lawrenceville** Pennsylvania, USA
56D3 **Lawton** USA
40C4 **Lawz, Jebel al** *Mt* Saudi Arabia
6B2 **Laxey** England
38C3 **Layla'** Saudi Arabia
50D3 **Laylo** Sudan
70B3 **Lázaro Cardenas** Mexico
29C2 **Lazo** Russian Federation
56C2 **Lead** USA
60B3 **Leadville** USA
63E2 **Leaf** *R* USA
62C3 **Leakey** USA
7D5 **Leamington Spa, Royal** England
61E3 **Leavenworth** USA
19D2 **Łeba** Poland
60D3 **Lebanon** Kansas, USA
63D1 **Lebanon** Missouri, USA
58B2 **Lebanon** Oregon, USA
65D2 **Lebanon** Pennsylvania, USA
64B3 **Lebanon** Tennessee, USA
40C3 **Lebanon** *Republic* SW Asia
66C3 **Lebec** USA
51D6 **Lebombo Mts** Mozambique/South Africa/Swaziland
19D2 **Lębork** Poland
74B5 **Lebu** Chile
13B2 **Le Cateau** France
17D2 **Lecce** Italy
16B1 **Lecco** Italy
13D3 **Le Champ du Feu** *Mt* France
14C2 **Le Creusot** France
7C3 **Ledbury** England
43H3 **Ledo** India
68D1 **Lee** USA
61E1 **Leech L** USA
10C3 **Leeds** England
7C3 **Leek** England
18B2 **Leer** Germany
67B3 **Leesburg** Florida, USA
68B3 **Leesburg** Virginia, USA
63D2 **Leesville** USA
34C2 **Leeton** Australia
47C3 **Leeugamka** South Africa
18B2 **Leeuwarden** Netherlands
32A4 **Leeuwin,C** Australia
66C2 **Lee Vining** USA
69E3 **Leeward Is** Caribbean Sea
45B1 **Lefka** Cyprus
45B1 **Lefkara** Cyprus
45B1 **Lefkoniko** Cyprus
27F5 **Legazpi** Philippines
18D2 **Legnica** Poland
73G2 **Leguan Island** Guyana
72D4 **Leguizamo** Peru
42D2 **Leh** India
14C2 **Le Havre** France
59D2 **Lehi** USA
68C2 **Lehigh** *R* USA
68C2 **Lehighton** USA
13D3 **Le Hohneck** *Mt* France
42C2 **Leiah** Pakistan
18D3 **Leibnitz** Austria
7D3 **Leicester** England
7D3 **Leicester** *County* England
32C2 **Leichhardt** *R* Australia
18A2 **Leiden** Netherlands
13B2 **Leie** *R* Belgium
32C4 **Leigh Creek** Australia
7E4 **Leigh on Sea** England
7D4 **Leighton Buzzard** England
18B2 **Leine** *R* Germany
9C3 **Leinster** *Region* Irish Republic
18C2 **Leipzig** Germany
15A2 **Leiria** Portugal
12F7 **Leirvik** Norway
8D4 **Leith** Scotland
31C4 **Leiyang** China
31B5 **Leizhou Bandao** *Pen* China
31C5 **Leizhou Wan** *B* China
18A2 **Lek** *R* Netherlands
16B3 **Le Kef** Tunisia
63D2 **Leland** USA
17D2 **Lelija** *Mt* Bosnia-Herzegovina
16B1 **Léman, Lac** France/Switzerland
14C2 **Le Mans** France
61D2 **Le Mars** USA
13E1 **Lemgo** Germany
58D2 **Lemhi Range** *Mts* USA
55M3 **Lemieux Is** Canada
56C2 **Lemmon** USA
59D4 **Lemmon,Mt** USA
59C3 **Lemoore** USA
14C2 **Lempdes** France
43G4 **Lemro** *R* Burma
16D2 **Le Murge** *Region* Italy
25O3 **Lena** *R* Russian Federation
20E3 **Lendery** Russian Federation
13D1 **Lengerich** Germany
31C4 **Lengshuijiang** China
Leningrad = St Petersburg
76F7 **Leningradskaya** *Base* Antarctica
20J5 **Leninogorsk** Russian Federation
26B1 **Leninogorsk** Kazakhstan
24K4 **Leninsk-Kuznetskiy** Russian Federation
26G2 **Leninskoye** Russian Federation
21H8 **Lenkoran'** Azerbaijan
13E2 **Lenne** *R* Germany
67B1 **Lenoir** USA
68D1 **Lenox** USA
13B2 **Lens** France
25N3 **Lensk** Russian Federation
16C3 **Lentini** Sicily, Italy
30B3 **Lenya** *R* Burma
16C1 **Leoben** Austria
7C3 **Leominster** England
68E1 **Leominster** USA
70B2 **León** Mexico
72A1 **León** Nicaragua
15A1 **León** Spain
47B1 **Leonardville** Namibia

45C1 **Leonarisso** Cyprus
32B3 **Leonora** Australia
75D3 **Leopoldina** Brazil
Léopoldville = Kinshasa
20D5 **Lepel** Belarus
31D4 **Leping** China
14C2 **Le Puy-en-Velay** France
50B3 **Léré** Chad
47D2 **Leribe** Lesotho
15C1 **Lérida** Spain
17F3 **Léros** *I* Greece
68B1 **Le Roy** USA
10C1 **Lerwick** Scotland
69C3 **Les Cayes** Haiti
65F1 **Les Escoumins** Canada
31A4 **Leshan** China
17E2 **Leskovac** Serbia, Yugoslavia
47D2 **Leslie** South Africa
20J4 **Lesnoy** Russian Federation
25L4 **Lesosibirsk** Russian Federation
47D2 **Lesotho** *Kingdom* South Africa
26G2 **Lesozavodsk** Russian Federation
14B2 **Les Sables-d'Olonne** France
76E4 **Lesser Antarctica** *Region* Antarctica
69E3 **Lesser Antilles** *Is* Caribbean Sea
21G7 **Lesser Caucasus** *Mts* Azerbaijan/Georgia
17F3 **Lésvos** *I* Greece
18D2 **Leszno** Poland
47E1 **Letaba** *R* South Africa
43G4 **Letha Range** *Mts* Burma
54G5 **Lethbridge** Canada
73G3 **Lethem** Guyana
19F3 **Letichev** Ukraine
72E4 **Letícia** Colombia
32B1 **Leti, Kepulauan** *I* Indonesia
47D1 **Letlhakeng** Botswana
7E4 **le Touquet-Paris-Plage** France
30B2 **Letpadan** Burma
25N4 **Let Oktyabr'ya** Russian Federation
14C1 **Le Tréport** France
9C2 **Letterkenny** Irish Republic
27C6 **Leuser** *Mt* Indonesia
18A2 **Leuven** Belgium
17E3 **Levádhia** Greece
12G6 **Levanger** Norway
62B2 **Levelland** USA
8D3 **Leven** Scotland
8D3 **Leven, Loch** *L* Scotland
27F8 **Lévèque,C** Australia
13D2 **Leverkusen** Germany
19D3 **Levice** Slovakia
35C2 **Levin** New Zealand
55L5 **Lévis** Canada
65E2 **Levittown** USA
17E3 **Lévka Óri** *Mt* Greece
17E3 **Levkás** Greece
17E3 **Levkás** *I* Greece
32B2 **Lévêque,C** Australia
17F2 **Levski** Bulgaria
7E4 **Lewes** England
62C1 **Lewis** USA
10B2 **Lewis** *I* Scotland
68B2 **Lewisburg** USA
35B2 **Lewis P** New Zealand
56B2 **Lewis Range** *Mts* USA
67A2 **Lewis Smith,L** USA
56B2 **Lewiston** Idaho, USA
57F2 **Lewiston** Maine, USA
56C2 **Lewistown** Montana, USA
65D2 **Lewistown** Pennsylvania, USA
63D2 **Lewisville** USA
57E3 **Lexington** Kentucky, USA
61E3 **Lexington** Missouri, USA
67B1 **Lexington** N Carolina, USA
60D2 **Lexington** Nebraska, USA
65D3 **Lexington** Virginia, USA
65D3 **Lexington Park** USA
62B2 **Leyburn** England
27F5 **Leyte** *I* Philippines
17D2 **Lezhe** Albania
39H3 **Lhasa** China
43F3 **Lhazê** China
27C6 **Lhokseumawe** Indonesia
43G3 **Lhozhag** China
26C4 **Lhunze** China
Liancourt Rocks = Tok-do
28B2 **Liangbingtai** China
31B3 **Liangdang** China
31C5 **Lianjiang** China
31C5 **Lianping** China
31C5 **Lian Xian** China
31D3 **Lianyungang** China
31E1 **Liaodong Bandao** *Pen* China
31E1 **Liaodong Wan** *B* China
31E1 **Liao He** *R* China
28A2 **Liaoning** *Province* China
31E1 **Liaoyang** China
28A2 **Liaoyangwopu** China
31E1 **Liaoyuan** China
28A2 **Liaozhong** China
54F3 **Liard** *R* Canada
54F4 **Liard River** Canada
13C3 **Liart** France
45C2 **Liban, Jebel** *Mts* Lebanon
58C1 **Libby** USA
50B3 **Libenge** Zaïre
56C3 **Liberal** USA
18C2 **Liberec** Czech Republic
48A4 **Liberia** *Republic* Africa
61E3 **Liberty** Missouri, USA
65E2 **Liberty** New York, USA
68B2 **Liberty** Pennsylvania, USA
63D2 **Liberty** Texas, USA
45B3 **Libni, Gebel** *Mt* Egypt
14B3 **Libourne** France
48C4 **Libreville** Equatorial Guinea
49D2 **Libya** *Republic* Africa
49E2 **Libyan Desert** Egypt/Libya/Sudan
49E1 **Libyan Plat** Egypt
16C3 **Licata** Sicily, Italy
7D3 **Lichfield** England
51D5 **Lichinga** Mozambique
47D2 **Lichtenburg** South Africa
64C3 **Licking** *R* USA
66B2 **Lick Observatory** USA
16C2 **Licosa, Punta** *Pt* Italy
66D2 **Lida** USA
20D5 **Lida** Belarus
12G7 **Lidköping** Sweden
16C2 **Lido di Ostia** Italy
16B1 **Liechtenstein** *Principality* Europe
18B2 **Liège** Belgium
19E1 **Lielupe** *R* Latvia
50C3 **Lienart** Zaïre
18C3 **Lienz** Austria
12J7 **Liepāja** Latvia
13C2 **Lier** Belgium
65E1 **Lièvre** *R* Canada
18C3 **Liezen** Austria
9C3 **Liffey** *R* Irish Republic
9C2 **Lifford** Irish Republic
33F3 **Lifu** *I* Nouvelle Calédonie
34C1 **Lightning Ridge** Australia
13C3 **Ligny-en-Barrois** France
51D5 **Ligonha** *R* Mozambique
16B2 **Ligurian S** Italy
33E1 **Lihir Group** *Is* Papua New Guinea
66E5 **Lihue** Hawaiian Islands
51C5 **Likasi** Zaïre
14C1 **Lille** France
12G6 **Lillehammer** Norway
13B2 **Lillers** France
12G7 **Lillestrøm** Norway
51D5 **Lilongwe** Malawi
17D2 **Lim** *R* Montenegro/Serbia, Yugoslavia
72C6 **Lima** Peru
57E2 **Lima** USA
15A1 **Lima** *R* Portugal
58D2 **Lima Res** USA
40B3 **Limassol** Cyprus
9C2 **Limavady** Northern Ireland
48C4 **Limbe** Cameroon
51D5 **Limbe** Malawi
18B2 **Limburg** Germany
73J8 **Limeira** Brazil
10B3 **Limerick** Irish Republic
18B1 **Limfjorden** *L* Denmark
32C2 **Limmen Bight** *B* Australia
17F3 **Límnos** *I* Greece
73L5 **Limoeiro** Brazil
14C2 **Limoges** France
70D4 **Limón** Costa Rica
56C3 **Limon** USA
14C2 **Limousin** *Region* France
14C2 **Limousin, Plateaux de** France
47E1 **Limpopo** *R* Mozambique
74B5 **Linares** Chile
56D4 **Linares** Mexico
15B2 **Linares** Spain
26C4 **Lincang** China
74D4 **Lincoln** Argentina
7D3 **Lincoln** England
64B2 **Lincoln** Illinois, USA
65F1 **Lincoln** Maine, USA
56D2 **Lincoln** Nebraska, USA
65E2 **Lincoln** New Hampshire, USA
35B2 **Lincoln** New Zealand
7D3 **Lincoln** *County* England
58B2 **Lincoln City** USA
64C2 **Lincoln Park** USA
76A2 **Lincoln Sea** Greenland
16B2 **L'Incudine** *Mt* Corsica, France
18B3 **Lindau** Germany
73G2 **Linden** Guyana
12F7 **Lindesnes** *C* Norway
51D4 **Lindi** Tanzania
50C3 **Lindi** *R* Zaïre
47D2 **Lindley** South Africa
17F3 **Lindos** Greece
66C2 **Lindsay** California, USA
65D2 **Lindsay** Canada
60B1 **Lindsay** Montana, USA
37M4 **Line Is** Pacific Ocean
31C2 **Linfen** China
30D2 **Lingao** China
27F5 **Lingayen** Philippines
18B2 **Lingen** Germany
27D7 **Lingga** *I* Indonesia
60C2 **Lingle** USA
31C4 **Lingling** China
31B5 **Lingshan** China
31C2 **Lingshi** China
48A3 **Linguère** Senegal
31E4 **Linhai** Zhejiang, China
73L7 **Linhares** Brazil
31B1 **Linhe** China
28B2 **Linjiang** China
28A2 **Linjiatai** China
12H7 **Linköping** Sweden
8C3 **Linnhe, Loch** *Inlet* Scotland
31D2 **Linqing** China
75C3 **Lins** Brazil
31A2 **Lintao** China
60C1 **Linton** USA
26E2 **Linxi** China
31A2 **Linxia** China
18C3 **Linz** Austria
14C3 **Lion, Golfe du** *G* France
16C3 **Lipari** *I* Italy
16C3 **Lipari, Isole** *Is* Italy
21F5 **Lipetsk** Russian Federation
17E1 **Lipova** Romania
18B2 **Lippe** *R* Germany
13E2 **Lippstadt** Germany
50D3 **Lira** Uganda
50B4 **Liranga** Congo
50C3 **Lisala** Zaïre
Lisboa = Lisbon
15A2 **Lisbon** Portugal
61D1 **Lisbon** USA
9C2 **Lisburn** Northern Ireland
31D4 **Lishui** China
31C4 **Li Shui** *R* China
21F6 **Lisichansk** Ukraine
14C2 **Lisieux** France
21F5 **Liski** Russian Federation
13B3 **L'Isle-Adam** France
33E3 **Lismore** Australia
9C3 **Lismore** Irish Republic
31B5 **Litang** China
45C2 **Lītāni** *R* Lebanon
73H3 **Litani** *R* Surinam
64B3 **Litchfield** Illinois, USA
61E1 **Litchfield** Minnesota, USA
32E4 **Lithgow** Australia
20C4 **Lithuania** *Republic* Europe
68B2 **Lititz** USA
26G2 **Litovko** Russian Federation
63C2 **Little** *R* USA
57F4 **Little Abaco** *I* The Bahamas
44E3 **Little Andaman** *I* Andaman Islands
67C3 **Little Bahama Bank** Bahamas
35C1 **Little Barrier I** New Zealand
58D1 **Little Belt Mts** USA
45B3 **Little Bitter L** Egypt
70D3 **Little Cayman** *I* Cayman Is, Caribbean Sea
68C3 **Little Egg Harbor** *B* USA
61E1 **Little Falls** Minnesota, USA
68C1 **Little Falls** New York, USA
62B2 **Littlefield** USA
61E1 **Littlefork** USA
61E1 **Little Fork** *R* USA
8E2 **Little Halibut Bank** *Sand-bank* Scotland
7D4 **Littlehampton** England
69C2 **Little Inagua** *I* The Bahamas
47C3 **Little Karoo** *Mts* South Africa
66D3 **Little Lake** USA
60C1 **Little Missouri** *R* USA
30A4 **Little Nicobar** *I* Nicobar Is, India
57D3 **Little Rock** USA
66D3 **Littlerock** USA
68B3 **Littlestown** USA
60B3 **Littleton** Colorado, USA
65E2 **Littleton** New Hampshire, USA
28B2 **Liuhe** China
31B2 **Liupan Shan** *Upland* China
31B5 **Liuzhou** China
17E3 **Livanátais** Greece
19F1 **Līvāni** Latvia
67B2 **Live Oak** USA
59B3 **Livermore** USA
62B2 **Livermore,Mt** USA
55M5 **Liverpool** Canada
7C3 **Liverpool** England
54E2 **Liverpool B** Canada
7C3 **Liverpool B** England
55L2 **Liverpool,C** Canada
34D2 **Liverpool Range** *Mts* Australia
56B2 **Livingston** Montana, USA
67A1 **Livingston** Tennessee, USA
63D2 **Livingston** Texas, USA
8D4 **Livingstone** Scotland
51C5 **Livingstone** Zambia
63C2 **Livingston,L** USA
16D2 **Livno** Bosnia-Herzegovina
21F5 **Livny** Russian Federation
64C2 **Livonia** USA
16C2 **Livorno** Italy
75D1 **Livramento do Brumado** Brazil
51D4 **Liwale** Tanzania
7B5 **Lizard Pt** England
16C1 **Ljubljana** Slovenia
12G6 **Ljungan** *R* Sweden
12G7 **Ljungby** Sweden
12H6 **Ljusdal** Sweden
20B3 **Ljusnan** *R* Sweden
7C4 **Llandeilo** Wales
7C4 **Llandovery** Wales
7C3 **Llandrindod Wells** Wales
7C3 **Llandudno** Wales
7D4 **Llanelli** Wales
7C3 **Llangollen** Wales
62C2 **Llano** USA
62C2 **Llano** *R* USA
56C3 **Llano Estacado** *Plat* USA
72D2 **Llanos** *Region* Colombia/Venezuela
72F7 **Llanos de Chiquitos** *Region* Bolivia
7C4 **Llantrisant** Wales
7C3 **Llanwrst** Wales
Lleida = Lérida
15A2 **Llerena** Spain
7B3 **Lleyn** *Pen* Wales
54F4 **Lloyd George,Mt** Canada
54H4 **Lloydminster** Canada
74C2 **Llullaillaco** *Mt* Argentina/Chile
74C2 **Loa** *R* Chile
50B4 **Loange** *R* Zaïre
47D2 **Lobatse** Botswana
50B3 **Lobaye** *R* Central African Republic
51B5 **Lobito** Angola
8B3 **Lochboisdale** Scotland
8C3 **Lochearnhead** Scotland
14C2 **Loches** France
8C3 **Lochgoilhead** Scotland
8C2 **Lochinver** Scotland
8D4 **Lochmaben** Scotland
8B3 **Lochmaddy** Scotland
8D3 **Lochnagar** *Mt* Scotland
8C3 **Loch Ness** Scotland
58C1 **Lochsa** *R* USA
8C3 **Lochy, Loch** *L* Scotland
8D4 **Lockerbie** Scotland
65D2 **Lock Haven** USA
65D2 **Lockport** USA
30D3 **Loc Ninh** Vietnam
16D3 **Locri** Italy
45C3 **Lod** Israel
34B3 **Loddon** *R* Australia
20E3 **Lodeynoye Pole** Russian Federation
58E1 **Lodge Grass** USA
42C3 **Lodhran** Pakistan
16B1 **Lodi** Italy
59B3 **Lodi** USA
50C4 **Lodja** Zaïre
50D3 **Lodwar** Kenya
19D2 **Łódź** Poland
47B3 **Loeriesfontein** South Africa
12G5 **Lofoten** *Is* Norway
6D2 **Loftus** England
62B1 **Logan** New Mexico, USA
56B2 **Logan** Utah, USA
54D3 **Logan,Mt** Canada
64B2 **Logansport** Indiana, USA
15D3 **Logansport** Louisiana, USA
68B2 **Loganton** USA
50B2 **Logone** *R* Cameroon/Chad
15B1 **Logroño** Spain
43E4 **Lohārdaga** India
12J6 **Lohja** Finland
30B2 **Loikaw** Burma
12J6 **Loimaa** Finland
13B3 **Loing** *R* France
14C2 **Loir** *R* France
14C2 **Loire** *R* France
13B4 **Loiret** *Department* France
72C4 **Loja** Ecuador
15B2 **Loja** Spain
12K5 **Lokan Tekojärvi** *Res* Finland
13B2 **Lokeren** Belgium
27F7 **Lokialaki, G** *Mt* Indonesia
50D3 **Lokitaung** Kenya
19F1 **Loknya** Russian Federation
50C4 **Lokolo** *R* Zaïre
50C4 **Lokoro** *R* Zaïre
55M3 **Loks Land** *I* Canada
18C2 **Lolland** *I* Denmark
58D1 **Lolo P** USA
17E2 **Lom** Bulgaria
51C4 **Lomami** *R* Zaïre
48A4 **Loma Mts** Guinea/Sierra Leone
27F7 **Lomblen** *I* Indonesia
27E7 **Lombok** *I* Indonesia
48C4 **Lomé** Togo
50C4 **Lomela** Zaïre
50C4 **Lomela** *R* Zaïre
8C3 **Lomond, Loch** *L* Scotland
20D4 **Lomonosov** Russian Federation
59B4 **Lompoc** USA
19E2 **Łomza** Poland
44A2 **Lonāvale** India
74B5 **Loncoche** Chile
55K5 **London** Canada
7D4 **London** England
64C3 **London** USA
9C2 **Londonderry** Northern Ireland
9C2 **Londonderry** *County* Northern Ireland
74B9 **Londonderry** *I* Chile
32B2 **Londonderry,C** Australia
74C3 **Londres** Argentina
74F2 **Londrina** Brazil
66D1 **Lone Mt** USA
66C2 **Lone Pine** USA
27H7 **Long** *I* Papua New Guinea
57F4 **Long** *I* The Bahamas
25T2 **Longa, Proliv** *Str* Russian Federation
69H2 **Long B** Jamaica
67C2 **Long B** USA
56B3 **Long Beach** California, USA
65E2 **Long Beach** New York, USA
65E2 **Long Branch** USA
31D5 **Longchuan** China
58C2 **Long Creek** USA
7D3 **Long Eaton** England
34C4 **Longford** Australia
9C3 **Longford** Irish Republic
9C3 **Longford** *County* Irish Republic
8E3 **Long Forties** *Region* N Sea
28B2 **Longgang Shan** *Mts* China
31D1 **Longhua** China
57F4 **Long I** Bahamas
55L4 **Long I** Canada
32D1 **Long I** Papua New Guinea
57F2 **Long I** USA
68D2 **Long Island Sd** USA
28B2 **Longjing** China
64B1 **Long L** Canada
60C1 **Long L** USA
55K4 **Longlac** Canada
31B5 **Longlin** China
8C3 **Long, Loch** *Inlet* Scotland
7E3 **Long Melford** England
56C2 **Longmont** USA
13C3 **Longny** France
61E1 **Long Prairie** USA
32D3 **Longreach** Australia
31A2 **Longshou Shan** *Upland* China
60B2 **Longs Peak** *Mt* USA
7E3 **Long Sutton** England
6C2 **Longtown** England
65E1 **Longueuil** Canada
13C3 **Longuyon** France
57D3 **Longview** Texas, USA
56A2 **Longview** Washington, USA
14D2 **Longwy** France
31A3 **Longxi** China
30D3 **Long Xuyen** Vietnam
31D4 **Longyan** China
31B5 **Longzhou** China
13D1 **Löningen** Germany
74B5 **Lonquimay** Chile
14D2 **Lons-le-Saunier** France
7B4 **Looe** England
57F3 **Lookout,C** USA
50D4 **Loolmalasin** *Mt* Tanzania
25R4 **Lopatka, Mys** *C* Russian Federation
30C3 **Lop Buri** Thailand
26C2 **Lop Nur** *L* China
15A2 **Lora del Rio** Spain
57E2 **Lorain** USA
42B2 **Loralai** Pakistan
15B2 **Lorca** Spain
41F3 **Lordegān** Iran
33E4 **Lord Howe** *I* Australia
37K6 **Lord Howe Rise** Pacific Ocean
55J3 **Lord Mayor B** Canada
56C3 **Lordsburg** USA
75C3 **Lorena** Brazil
14B2 **Lorient** France

34B3 **Lorne** Australia
18B3 **Lörrach** Germany
13C3 **Lorraine** *Region* France
56C3 **Los Alamos** USA
66B3 **Los Alamos** USA
74B5 **Los Angeles** Chile
56B3 **Los Angeles** USA
66C3 **Los Angeles Aqueduct** USA
59B3 **Los Banos** USA
59B3 **Los Gatos** USA
16C2 **Lošinj** *I* Croatia
74B5 **Los Lagos** Chile
62A2 **Los Lunas** USA
70B2 **Los Mochis** Mexico
66B3 **Los Olivos** USA
72E1 **Los Roques, Islas** Venezuela
8D3 **Lossie** *R* Scotland
8D3 **Lossiemouth** Scotland
69E4 **Los Testigos** *Is* Venezuela
66C3 **Lost Hills** USA
58D1 **Lost Trail P** USA
74B4 **Los Vilos** Chile
14C3 **Lot** *R* France
8D4 **Lothian** *Region* Scotland
50D3 **Lotikipi Plain** Kenya/Sudan
50C4 **Loto** Zaïre
47D1 **Lotsane** *R* Botswana
12K5 **Lotta** *R* Finland/Russian Federation
14B2 **Loudéac** France
48A3 **Louga** Senegal
7D3 **Loughborough** England
54H2 **Lougheed I** Canada
64C3 **Louisa** USA
27E6 **Louisa Reef** S China Sea
33E2 **Louisiade Arch** Papua New Guinea
57D3 **Louisiana** *State* USA
47D1 **Louis Trichardt** South Africa
67B2 **Louisville** Georgia, USA
57E3 **Louisville** Kentucky, USA
63E2 **Louisville** Mississippi, USA
20E2 **Loukhi** Russian Federation
61D2 **Loup** *R* USA
14B3 **Lourdes** France
Lourenço Marques = Maputo
34C2 **Louth** Australia
7D3 **Louth** England
9C3 **Louth** *County* Irish Republic
Louvain = Leuven
14C2 **Louviers** France
20E4 **Lovat** *R* Russian Federation
17E2 **Lovech** Bulgaria
60B2 **Loveland** USA
60B3 **Loveland P** USA
58E2 **Lovell** USA
59C2 **Lovelock** USA
16C1 **Lóvere** Italy
62B2 **Lovington** USA
20F2 **Lovozero** Russian Federation
55K3 **Low,C** Canada
57F2 **Lowell** Massachusetts, USA
58B2 **Lowell** Oregon, USA
68E1 **Lowell** USA
58C1 **Lower Arrow L** Canada
35B2 **Lower Hutt** New Zealand
66A1 **Lower Lake** USA
61D1 **Lower Red L** USA
7E3 **Lowestoft** England
19D2 **Łowicz** Poland
34B2 **Loxton** Australia
47C3 **Loxton** South Africa
68B2 **Loyalsock Creek** *R* USA
33F3 **Loyalty Is** New Caledonia
17D2 **Loznica** Serbia, Yugoslavia
24H3 **Lozva** *R* Russian Federation
51C5 **Luacano** Angola
51C4 **Luachimo** Angola
50C4 **Lualaba** *R* Zaïre
51C5 **Luampa** Zambia
51C5 **Luân** Angola
31D3 **Lu'an** China
51B4 **Luanda** Angola
51B5 **Luando** *R* Angola
51C5 **Luanginga** *R* Angola
30C1 **Luang Namtha** Laos
30C2 **Luang Prabang** Laos
51B4 **Luangue** *R* Angola
51D5 **Luangwa** *R* Zambia
31D1 **Luan He** *R* China
31D1 **Luanping** China
51C5 **Luanshya** Zambia
51C5 **Luapula** *R* Zaïre
15A1 **Luarca** Spain
51B4 **Lubalo** Angola
19F2 **L'uban** Belarus
51B5 **Lubango** Angola
56C3 **Lubbock** USA
18C2 **Lübeck** Germany
50C4 **Lubefu** Zaïre
50C4 **Lubefu** *R* Zaïre
50C3 **Lubero** Zaïre
51C4 **Lubilash** *R* Zaïre
19E2 **Lublin** Poland
21E5 **Lubny** Ukraine
51C4 **Lubudi** Zaïre
51C4 **Lubudi** *R* Zaïre
27D7 **Lubuklinggau** Indonesia
51C5 **Lubumbashi** Zaïre
50C4 **Lubutu** Zaïre
75A1 **Lucas** Brazil
67C3 **Lucaya** Bahamas
16C2 **Lucca** Italy
8C4 **Luce B** Scotland
63E2 **Lucedale** USA
19D3 **Lucenec** Slovakia
Lucerne = Luzern
62A2 **Lucero** Mexico
31C5 **Luchuan** China
66B2 **Lucia** USA
18C2 **Luckenwalde** Germany
47C2 **Luckhoff** South Africa
43E3 **Lucknow** India
51C5 **Lucusse** Angola
13D2 **Lüdenscheid** Germany
47B2 **Lüderitz** Namibia
42D2 **Ludhiana** India
64B2 **Ludington** USA
59C4 **Ludlow** California, USA
7C3 **Ludlow** England
68D1 **Ludlow** Vermont, USA
17F2 **Ludogorie** *Upland* Bulgaria
67B2 **Ludowici** USA
17E1 **Luduş** Romania
12H6 **Ludvika** Sweden
18B3 **Ludwigsburg** Germany
18B3 **Ludwigshafen** Germany
18C2 **Ludwigslust** Germany
50C4 **Luebo** Zaïre
50C4 **Luema** *R* Zaïre
51C4 **Luembe** *R* Angola
51B5 **Luena** Angola
51C5 **Luene** *R* Angola
31B3 **Lüeyang** China
31D5 **Lufeng** China
57D3 **Lufkin** USA
20D4 **Luga** Russian Federation
20D4 **Luga** *R* Russian Federation
16B1 **Lugano** Switzerland
51D5 **Lugela** Mozambique
51D5 **Lugenda** *R* Mozambique
9C3 **Lugnaquillia,Mt** Irish Republic
15A1 **Lugo** Spain
17E1 **Lugoj** Romania
45D2 **Luhfi, Wadi** Jordan
31A3 **Luhuo** China
51B4 **Lui** *R* Angola
51C5 **Luiana** Angola
51C5 **Luiana** *R* Angola
Luichow Peninsula = Leizhou Bandao
20D2 **Luiro** *R* Finland
51C5 **Luishia** Zaïre
26C4 **Luixi** China
51C4 **Luiza** Zaïre
31D3 **Lujiang** China
50B4 **Lukenie** *R* Zaïre
59D4 **Lukeville** USA
50B4 **Lukolela** Zaïre
19E2 **Łuków** Poland
50C4 **Lukuga** *R* Zaïre
51C5 **Lukulu** Zambia
20C2 **Lule** *R* Sweden
12J5 **Luleå** Sweden
17F2 **Lüleburgaz** Turkey
31C2 **Lüliang Shan** *Mts* China
63C3 **Luling** USA
50C3 **Lulonga** *R* Zaïre
Luluabourg = Kananga
51C5 **Lumbala Kaquengue** Angola
57F3 **Lumberton** USA
20G2 **Lumbovka** Russian Federation
43G3 **Lumding** India
51C5 **Lumeje** Angola
35A3 **Lumsden** New Zealand
12G7 **Lund** Sweden
51D5 **Lundazi** Zambia
51D6 **Lundi** *R* Zimbabwe
7B4 **Lundy** *I* England
18C2 **Lüneburg** Germany
13D3 **Lunéville** France
51C5 **Lunga** *R* Zambia
43G4 **Lunglei** India
51B5 **Lungue Bungo** *R* Angola
19F2 **Luninec** Belarus
66C1 **Luning** USA
50B4 **Luobomo** Congo
31B5 **Luocheng** China
31C5 **Luoding** China
31C3 **Luohe** China
31C3 **Luo He** *R* Henan, China
31B2 **Luo He** *R* Shaanxi, China
31C4 **Luoxiao Shan** *Hills* China
31C3 **Luoyang** China
50B4 **Luozi** Zaïre
51C5 **Lupane** Zimbabwe
51D5 **Lupilichi** Mozambique
Lu Qu *R* **= Tao He**
74E3 **Luque** Paraguay
13D4 **Lure** France
9C2 **Lurgan** Northern Ireland
51D5 **Lurio** *R* Mozambique
41E3 **Luristan** *Region* Iran
51C5 **Lusaka** Zambia
50C4 **Lusambo** Zaïre
17D2 **Lushnjë** Albania
50D4 **Lushoto** Tanzania
26C4 **Lushui** China
31E2 **Lüshun** China
60C2 **Lusk** USA
7D4 **Luton** England
21D5 **Lutsk** Ukraine
50E3 **Luuq** Somalia
61D2 **Luverne** USA
51C4 **Luvua** *R* Zaïre
51D4 **Luwegu** *R* Tanzania
51D5 **Luwingu** Zambia
27F7 **Luwuk** Indonesia
14D2 **Luxembourg** Luxembourg
13D3 **Luxembourg** *Grand Duchy* NW Europe
13D4 **Luxeuil-les-Bains** France
31A5 **Luxi** China
49F2 **Luxor** Egypt
20H3 **Luza** Russian Federation
20H3 **Luza** *R* Russian Federation
16B1 **Luzern** Switzerland
68D1 **Luzerne** USA
31B5 **Luzhai** China
31B4 **Luzhi** China
31B4 **Luzhou** China
75C2 **Luziânia** Brazil
27F5 **Luzon** *I* Philippines
27F5 **Luzon Str** Philippines
19E3 **L'vov** Ukraine
8D2 **Lybster** Scotland
12H6 **Lycksele** Sweden
7E4 **Lydd** England
51C6 **Lydenburg** South Africa
56B3 **Lyell,Mt** USA
68B2 **Lykens** USA
58D2 **Lyman** USA
7C4 **Lyme B** England
7C4 **Lyme Regis** England
7D4 **Lymington** England
57F3 **Lynchburg** USA
34A2 **Lyndhurst** Australia
65E2 **Lynn** USA
67A2 **Lynn Haven** USA
54H4 **Lynn Lake** Canada
7C4 **Lynton** England
54H3 **Lynx L** Canada
14C2 **Lyon** France
67B2 **Lyons** Georgia, USA
68B1 **Lyons** New York, USA
32A3 **Lyons** *R* Australia
20K4 **Lys'va** Russian Federation
6C3 **Lytham St Anne's** England
35B2 **Lyttelton** New Zealand
66A1 **Lytton** USA
19F2 **Lyubeshov** Ukraine
20F4 **Lyublino** Russian Federation

M

30C1 **Ma** *R* Laos/Vietnam
45C2 **Ma'agan** Jordan
45C2 **Ma'alot Tarshīhā** Israel
40C3 **Ma'ān** Jordan
31D3 **Ma'anshan** China
45D1 **Ma'arrat an Nu'mān** Syria
13C2 **Maas** *R* Netherlands
13C2 **Maaseik** Belgium
18B2 **Maastricht** Netherlands
47E1 **Mabalane** Mozambique
73G2 **Mabaruma** Guyana
7E3 **Mablethorpe** England
51D6 **Mabote** Mozambique
19E2 **Mabrita** Belarus
75D3 **Macaé** Brazil
56D3 **McAlester** USA
56D4 **McAllen** USA
51D5 **Macaloge** Mozambique
73H3 **Macapá** Brazil
75D2 **Macarani** Brazil
72C4 **Macas** Ecuador
73L5 **Macaú** Brazil
31C5 **Macau** *Dependency* SE Asia
75D1 **Macaúbas** Brazil
50C3 **M'Bari** *R* Central African Republic
58C2 **McCall** USA
62B2 **McCamey** USA
58D2 **McCammon** USA
7C3 **Macclesfield** England
55K1 **McClintock B** Canada
54H2 **McClintock Chan** Canada
68B2 **McClure** USA
66B2 **McClure,L** USA
54G2 **McClure Str** Canada
63D2 **McComb** USA
60C2 **McConaughy,L** USA
68B3 **McConnellsburg** USA
56C2 **McCook** USA
55L2 **Macculloch,C** Canada
54F4 **McDame** Canada
58C2 **McDermitt** USA
58D1 **McDonald Peak** *Mt* USA
32C3 **Macdonnell Ranges** *Mts* Australia
8D3 **MacDuff** Scotland
15A1 **Macedo de Cavaleiros** Portugal
17E2 **Macedonia** *Republic* Europe
73L5 **Maceió** Brazil
48B4 **Macenta** Guinea
16C2 **Macerata** Italy
63D2 **McGehee** USA
59D3 **McGill** USA
54C3 **McGrath** USA
58D1 **McGuire,Mt** USA
75C3 **Machado** Brazil
51D6 **Machaíla** Mozambique
50D4 **Machakos** Kenya
72C4 **Machala** Ecuador
51D6 **Machaze** Mozambique
44B2 **Mācherla** India
45C2 **Machgharab** Lebanon
65F2 **Machias** USA
44C2 **Machilīpatnam** India
72D1 **Machiques** Venezuela
72D6 **Machu-Picchu** *Hist Site* Peru
7C3 **Machynlleth** Wales
51D6 **Macia** Mozambique
Macias Nguema *I* **= Bioko**
60C1 **McIntosh** USA
34C1 **MacIntyre** *R* Australia
60B3 **Mack** USA
32D3 **Mackay** Australia
58D2 **Mackay** USA
32B3 **Mackay,L** Australia
33H1 **McKean** *I* Phoenix Islands
65D2 **McKeesport** USA
54F3 **Mackenzie** *R* Canada
54E3 **Mackenzie B** Canada
54G2 **Mackenzie King I** Canada
54E3 **Mackenzie Mts** Canada
64C1 **Mackinac,Str of** USA
64C1 **Mackinaw City** USA
54C3 **McKinley, Mt** USA
63C2 **McKinney** USA
55L2 **Mackinson Inlet** *B* Canada
66C3 **McKittrick** USA
34D2 **Macksville** Australia
60C1 **McLaughlin** USA
34D1 **Maclean** Australia
47D3 **Maclear** South Africa
54G4 **McLennan** Canada
54G3 **McLeod B** Canada
32A3 **McLeod,L** Australia
58B2 **McLoughlin,Mt** USA
54E3 **Macmillan** *R* Canada
62B2 **McMillan,L** USA
58B1 **McMinnville** Oregon, USA
67A1 **McMinnville** Tennessee, USA
76F7 **McMurdo** *Base* Antarctica
59E4 **McNary** USA
64A2 **Macomb** USA
16B2 **Macomer** Sardinia, Italy
51D5 **Macomia** Mozambique
14C2 **Mâcon** France
57E3 **Macon** Georgia, USA
61E3 **Macon** Missouri, USA
51C5 **Macondo** Angola
63C1 **McPherson** USA
34C2 **Macquarie** *R* Australia
34C4 **Macquarie Harbour** *B* Australia
36J7 **Macquarie Is** Australia
34D2 **Macquarie,L** Australia
67B2 **McRae** USA
76F11 **Mac Robertson Land** *Region* Antarctica
54G3 **McTavish Arm** *B* Canada
54F3 **McVicar Arm** *B* Canada
45C3 **Mādabā** Jordan
50C2 **Madadi** *Well* Chad
46J9 **Madagascar** *I* Indian Ocean
36D6 **Madagascar Basin** Indian Ocean
50B1 **Madama** Niger
32D1 **Madang** Papua New Guinea
48C3 **Madaoua** Niger
43G4 **Madaripur** Bangladesh
41F2 **Madau** Turkmenistan
65D1 **Madawaska** *R* Canada
48A1 **Madeira** *I* Atlantic Ocean
72F5 **Madeira** *R* Brazil
19F2 **M'adel** Belarus
55M5 **Madeleine Îles de la** Canada
61E2 **Madelia** USA
70B2 **Madera** Mexico
59B3 **Madera** USA
44A2 **Madgaon** India
43F3 **Madhubani** India
43E4 **Madhya Pradesh** *State* India
44B3 **Madikeri** India
50B4 **Madimba** Zaïre
50B4 **Madingo Kayes** Congo
50B4 **Madingou** Congo
57E3 **Madison** Indiana, USA
61D1 **Madison** Minnesota, USA
61D2 **Madison** Nebraska, USA
61D2 **Madison** S Dakota, USA
57E2 **Madison** Wisconsin, USA
58D1 **Madison** *R* USA
64B3 **Madisonville** Kentucky, USA
63C2 **Madisonville** Texas, USA
50D3 **Mado Gashi** Kenya
44C3 **Madras** India
58B2 **Madras** USA
74A8 **Madre de Dios** *I* Chile
72E6 **Madre de Dios** *R* Bolivia
70C2 **Madre, Laguna** Mexico
63C3 **Madre, Laguna** USA
15B1 **Madrid** Spain
15B2 **Madridejos** Spain
27E7 **Madura** *I* Indonesia
44B4 **Madurai** India
29C3 **Maebashi** Japan
30B3 **Mae Khlong** *R* Thailand
30B4 **Mae Luang** *R* Thailand
30C2 **Mae Nam Mun** *R* Thailand
30B2 **Mae Nam Ping** *R* Thailand
28A3 **Maengsan** N Korea
51E5 **Maevatanana** Madagascar
33F2 **Maewo** *I* Vanuatu
47D2 **Mafeteng** Lesotho
34C3 **Maffra** Australia
51D4 **Mafia I** Tanzania
47D2 **Mafikeng** South Africa
74G3 **Mafra** Brazil
40C3 **Mafraq** Jordan
25R4 **Magadan** Russian Federation
74B8 **Magallanes, Estrecho de** *Str* Chile
72D2 **Magangué** Colombia
56B3 **Magdalena** Mexico
62A2 **Magdalena** USA
72D2 **Magdalena** *R* Colombia
70A2 **Magdalena, Bahía** Mexico
70A2 **Magdalena, Isla** Mexico
18C2 **Magdeburg** Germany
73K8 **Magé** Brazil
16B1 **Maggiore, L** Italy
40B4 **Maghâgha** Egypt
45B3 **Maghâra, Gebel** *Mt* Egypt
9C2 **Maghera** Northern Ireland
9C2 **Magherafelt** Northern Ireland
17D2 **Maglie** Italy
20K5 **Magnitogorsk** Russian Federation
63D2 **Magnolia** USA
51D5 **Magoé** Mozambique
65E1 **Magog** Canada
66D2 **Magruder Mt** USA
73J4 **Maguarinho, Cabo** *C* Brazil
47E2 **Magude** Mozambique
55J3 **Maguse River** Canada
Magway = Magwe
30B1 **Magwe** Burma
21H8 **Mahābād** Iran
43F3 **Mahabharat Range** *Mts* Nepal
44A2 **Mahād** India
42D4 **Mahadeo Hills** India
68A2 **Mahaffey** USA
51E5 **Mahajamba, Baie de** *B* Madagascar
51E5 **Mahajanga** Madagascar
47D1 **Mahalapye** Botswana
43E4 **Mahānadi** *R* India
51E5 **Mahanoro** Madagascar
68B2 **Mahanoy City** USA
44A2 **Mahārāshtra** *State* India
43E4 **Māhāsamund** India
30C2 **Maha Sarakham** Thailand
51E5 **Mahavavy** *R* Madagascar
44B2 **Mahbūbnagar** India
48D1 **Mahdia** Tunisia
44B3 **Mahe** India
51D4 **Mahenge** Tanzania
42C4 **Mahesāna** India
35C1 **Mahia Pen** New Zealand
61D1 **Mahnomen** USA
42D3 **Mahoba** India
15C2 **Mahón** Spain
48D1 **Mahrès** Tunisia
42C4 **Mahuva** India
72D1 **Maicao** Colombia
7D4 **Maidenhead** England
7E4 **Maidstone** England
50B2 **Maiduguri** Nigeria
43E4 **Maihar** India
43G4 **Maijdi** Bangladesh
43E4 **Maikala Range** *Mts* India
42A1 **Maimana** Afghanistan
64C1 **Main Chan** Canada
50B4 **Mai-Ndombe, L** Zaïre
57G2 **Maine** State, USA
8D2 **Mainland** *I* Scotland
42D3 **Mainpuri** India

51E5 **Maintirano** Madagascar
18B2 **Mainz** Germany
48A4 **Maio** I Cape Verde
74C4 **Maipó, Vol** Argentina/Chile
72E1 **Maiquetía** Venezuela
43G3 **Mairābāri** India
43G4 **Maiskhal I** Bangladesh
32E4 **Maitland** New South Wales, Australia
76F12 **Maitri** Base Antarctica
70D3 **Maíz, Isla del** Caribbean Sea
29D3 **Maizuru** Japan
32A1 **Majene** Indonesia
72D7 **Majes** R Peru
50D3 **Maji** Ethiopia
31D2 **Majia He** R China
15C2 **Majorca** I Balearic Is, Spain
Majunga = Mahajanga
27E7 **Makale** Indonesia
43F3 **Makalu** Mt China/Nepal
50B3 **Makanza** Zaïre
20K2 **Makarikha** Russian Federation
16D2 **Makarska** Croatia
20G4 **Makaryev** Russian Federation
Makassar = Ujung Pandang
27E7 **Makassar Str** Indonesia
21J6 **Makat** Kazakhstan
48A4 **Makeni** Sierra Leone
13C1 **Makerwaard** Polder Netherlands
21F6 **Makeyevka** Ukraine
51C6 **Makgadikgadi** Salt Pan Botswana
21H7 **Makhachkala** Russian Federation
50D4 **Makindu** Kenya
Makkah = Mecca Saudi Arabia
55N4 **Makkovik** Canada
19E3 **Makó** Hungary
50B3 **Makokou** Gabon
35C1 **Makorako,Mt** New Zealand
50B3 **Makoua** Congo
42C3 **Makrāna** India
42A3 **Makran Coast Range** Mts Pakistan
16B3 **Makthar** Tunisia
21G8 **Mākū** Iran
50C4 **Makumbi** Zaïre
48C4 **Makurdi** Nigeria
44B3 **Malabar Coast** India
48C4 **Malabo** Equatorial Guinea
Malacca = Melaka
30C5 **Malacca,Str of** SE Asia
58D2 **Malad City** USA
72D2 **Málaga** Colombia
15B2 **Málaga** Spain
62B2 **Malaga** USA
51E6 **Malaimbandy** Madagascar
33F1 **Malaita** I Solomon Islands
50D3 **Malakal** Sudan
42C2 **Malakand** Pakistan
27F6 **Malanbang** Philippines
27E7 **Malang** Indonesia
51B4 **Malanje** Angola
48C3 **Malanville** Benin
25S3 **Mal Anyuy** R Russian Federation
12H7 **Mälaren** L Sweden
65D1 **Malartic** Canada
21F8 **Malatya** Turkey
51D5 **Malawi** Republic Africa
Malawi,L = Nyasa,L
41E3 **Malāyer** Iran
27D6 **Malaysia** Federation SE Asia
40D2 **Malazgirt** Turkey
19D2 **Malbork** Poland
18C2 **Malchin** Germany
63E1 **Malden** USA
39F5 **Maldives** Is Indian Ocean
36E4 **Maldives Ridge** Indian Ocean
7E4 **Maldon** England
74F4 **Maldonado** Uruguay
42C4 **Malegaon** India
18D3 **Malé Karpaty** Upland Slovakia
33F2 **Malekula** I Vanuatu
51D5 **Malema** Mozambique
20F3 **Malen'ga** Russian Federation
13B3 **Malesherbes** France
42B2 **Mālestān** Afghanistan
12H5 **Malgomaj** L Sweden
20B3 **Malgomaj** R Sweden
50C2 **Malha** Well Sudan
58C2 **Malheur L** USA
48B3 **Mali** Republic Africa
30B3 **Mali Kyun** I Burma
19F2 **Malin** Ukraine
27E6 **Malinau** Indonesia
50E4 **Malindi** Kenya
Malines = Mechelen
10B2 **Malin Head** Pt Irish Republic
42D4 **Malkāpur** India
17F2 **Malkara** Turkey
17F2 **Malko Tŭrnovo** Bulgaria
8C3 **Mallaig** Scotland
49F2 **Mallawi** Egypt
Mallorca I **= Majorca**
12G6 **Malm** Norway
12J5 **Malmberget** Sweden
13D2 **Malmédy** Germany
7C4 **Malmesbury** England
47B3 **Malmesbury** South Africa
12G7 **Malmö** Sweden
20J4 **Malmyzh** Russian Federation
65E2 **Malone** USA
47D2 **Maloti Mts** Lesotho
12F6 **Måloy** Norway
20J2 **Malozemel'skaya Tundra** Plain Russian Federation
71B3 **Malpelo** I Colombia
42D3 **Mālpura** India
58D2 **Malta** Idaho, USA
56C2 **Malta** Montana, USA
16C3 **Malta** I and Republic Medit Sea
16C3 **Malta Chan** Italy/Malta
47B1 **Maltahöhe** Namibia
6D2 **Malton** England
45D2 **Ma'lūlā, Jabal** Mt Syria
12G6 **Malung** Sweden
44A2 **Mālvan** India
63D2 **Malvern** USA
47E1 **Malvérnia** Mozambique
Malvinas, Islas = Falkland Islands
42D4 **Malwa Plat** India
25Q2 **Malyy Lyakhovskiy, Ostrov** I Russian Federation
25M2 **Malyy Taymyr, Ostrov** I Russian Federation
21H6 **Malyy Uzen'** R Kazakhstan
25N4 **Mama** Russian Federation
20J4 **Mamadysh** Russian Federation
50C3 **Mambasa** Zaïre
32C1 **Mamberamo** R Australia
27G7 **Mamberamo** R Indonesia
50B3 **Mambéré** R Central African Republic
48C4 **Mamfé** Cameroon
59D4 **Mammoth** USA
64B3 **Mammoth Cave Nat Pk** USA
66C2 **Mammoth Pool Res** USA
72E6 **Mamoré** R Bolivia/Brazil
48A3 **Mamou** Guinea
51E5 **Mampikony** Madagascar
48B4 **Mampong** Ghana
45C3 **Mamshit** Hist Site Israel
27E7 **Mamuju** Indonesia
47C1 **Mamuno** Botswana
48B4 **Man** Ivory Coast
66E5 **Mana** Hawaiian Islands
51E6 **Manabo** Madagascar
72F4 **Manacapuru** Brazil
15C2 **Manacor** Spain
27F6 **Manado** Indonesia
72A1 **Managua** Nicaragua
70D3 **Managua, L de** Nicaragua
51E6 **Manakara** Madagascar
32D1 **Manam** I Papua New Guinea
51E5 **Mananara** Madagascar
51E6 **Mananjary** Madagascar
35A3 **Manapouri** New Zealand
35A3 **Manapouri,L** New Zealand
39G1 **Manas** China
43G3 **Manas** R Bhutan
24K5 **Manas Hu** L China
43E3 **Manaslu** Mt Nepal
68C2 **Manasquan** USA
73G4 **Manaus** Brazil
21E8 **Manavgat** Turkey
40C2 **Manbij** Syria
6B2 **Man,Calf of** I Isle of Man, British Islands
64B2 **Mancelona** USA
44B2 **Mancherāl** India
65E2 **Manchester** Connecticut, USA
7C3 **Manchester** England
64C3 **Manchester** Kentucky, USA
57F2 **Manchester** New Hampshire, USA
68B2 **Manchester** Pennsylvania, USA
67A1 **Manchester** Tennessee, USA
68D1 **Manchester** Vermont, USA
26F2 **Manchuria** Division China
41F4 **Mand** R Iran
51D5 **Manda** Tanzania
75B3 **Mandaguari** Brazil
12F7 **Mandal** Norway
27G7 **Mandala, Peak** Mt Indonesia
30B1 **Mandalay** Burma
26D2 **Mandalgovĭ** Mongolia
56C2 **Mandan** USA
50E3 **Mandera** Ethiopia
69H1 **Mandeville** Jamaica
42D2 **Mandi** India
51D5 **Mandimba** Mozambique
75A2 **Mandiore, Lagoa** Brazil
43E4 **Mandla** India
51E5 **Mandritsara** Madagascar
42D4 **Mandsaur** India
17D2 **Manduria** Italy
42B4 **Māndvi** India
44B3 **Mandya** India
43E4 **Manendragarh** India
19F2 **Manevichi** Ukraine
40B4 **Manfalût** Egypt
16D2 **Manfredonia** Italy
75D1 **Manga** Brazil
50B2 **Manga** Desert Region Niger
35C1 **Mangakino** New Zealand
17F2 **Mangalia** Romania
50C2 **Mangalmé** Chad
44A3 **Mangalore** India
43H4 **Mangin Range** Mts Burma
26C3 **Mangnai** China
48C3 **Mango** Togo
51D5 **Mangoche** Malawi
51E6 **Mangoky** R Madagascar
27F7 **Mangole** I Indonesia
42B4 **Māngral** India
75B4 **Mangueirinha** Brazil
25O4 **Mangui** China
62C2 **Mangum** USA
21J7 **Mangyshiak, Poluostrov** Pen Kazakhstan
56D3 **Manhattan** USA
47E2 **Manhica** Mozambique
73K8 **Manhuacu** Brazil
51E5 **Mania** R Madagascar
51D5 **Manica** Mozambique
55M5 **Manicouagan** R Canada
55M5 **Manicouagan, Réservoir** Canada
41E4 **Manifah** Saudi Arabia
27F5 **Manila** Philippines
58E2 **Manila** USA
34D2 **Manilla** Australia
48B3 **Maninian** Ivory Coast
43G4 **Manipur** R Burma/India
43G4 **Manipur** State India
21D8 **Manisa** Turkey
10C3 **Man,Isle of** Irish Sea
64B2 **Manistee** USA
64B2 **Manistee** R USA
64B1 **Manistique** USA
54J4 **Manitoba** Province Canada
54J4 **Manitoba,L** Canada
60D1 **Manitou** Canada
64B1 **Manitou Is** USA
55K5 **Manitoulin** I Canada
60C3 **Manitou Springs** USA
64C1 **Manitowik L** Canada
64B2 **Manitowoc** USA
65D1 **Maniwaki** Canada
72C2 **Manizales** Colombia
51E6 **Manja** Madagascar
32A4 **Manjimup** Australia
44B2 **Mānjra** R India
57D2 **Mankato** USA
48B4 **Mankono** Ivory Coast
35B1 **Manly** New Zealand
42C4 **Manmād** India
34A2 **Mannahill** Australia
44B4 **Mannar** Sri Lanka
44B4 **Mannār,G of** India
44B3 **Mannārgudi** India
18B3 **Mannheim** Germany
67B2 **Manning** USA
34A2 **Mannum** Australia
48A4 **Mano** Sierra Leone
32C1 **Manokwari** Indonesia
51C4 **Manono** Zaïre
30B3 **Manoron** Burma
55L4 **Manouane, Lac** Canada
29C3 **Mano-wan** B Japan
28B2 **Manp'o** N Korea
42D2 **Mānsa** India
51C5 **Mansa** Zambia
55K3 **Mansel I** Canada
63D1 **Mansfield** Arkansas, USA
34C3 **Mansfield** Australia
7D3 **Mansfield** England
63D2 **Mansfield** Louisiana, USA
68E1 **Mansfield** Massachusetts, USA
57E2 **Mansfield** Ohio, USA
65D2 **Mansfield** Pennsylvania, USA
75B2 **Manso** R Brazil
27H5 **Mansyu Deep** Pacific Ocean
72B4 **Manta** Ecuador
28A2 **Mantap-san** Mt N Korea
72C6 **Mantaro** R Peru
66B2 **Manteca** USA
67C1 **Manteo** USA
14C2 **Mantes** France
59D3 **Manti** USA
75C3 **Mantiqueira, Serra da** Mts Brazil
16C1 **Mantova** Italy
12J6 **Mäntta** Finland
Mantua = Mantova
20G4 **Manturovo** Russian Federation
62B3 **Manuel Benavides** Mexico
75B3 **Manuel Ribas** Brazil
27F6 **Manukan** Philippines
33G4 **Manukau** New Zealand
27H7 **Manus** I Pacific Ocean
15B2 **Manzanares** Spain
70E2 **Manzanillo** Cuba
70B3 **Manzanillo** Mexico
25N5 **Manzhouli** China
45D3 **Manzil** Jordan
51D6 **Manzini** Swaziland
50B2 **Mao** Chad
27G7 **Maoke, Pegunungan** Mts Indonesia
31A2 **Maomao Shan** Mt China
31C5 **Maoming** China
51D6 **Mapai** Mozambique
43E2 **Mapam Yumco** L China
27G6 **Mapia** Is Pacific Ocean
27E6 **Mapin** I Philippines
54H5 **Maple Creek** Canada
47E1 **Mapulanguene** Mozambique
47E2 **Maputo** Mozambique
47E2 **Maputo** R Mozambique
47E2 **Maputo, Baia de** B Mozambique
Ma Qu = Huang He
31A3 **Maqu** China
43F3 **Maquan He** R China
50B4 **Maquela do Zombo** Angola
74C6 **Maquinchao** Argentina
73J5 **Marabá** Brazil
72D1 **Maracaibo** Venezuela
72D2 **Maracaibo, Lago de** Venezuela
73H3 **Maracá, Ilha de** I Brazil
75A3 **Maracaju** Brazil
75A3 **Maracaju, Serra de** Mts Brazil
75D1 **Máracás** Brazil
72E1 **Maracay** Venezuela
49D2 **Marādah** Libya
48C3 **Maradi** Niger
21H8 **Marāgheh** Iran
73J4 **Marajó, Baia de** B Brazil
73H4 **Marajó, Ilha de** I Brazil
28E5 **Marakech** Morocco
50D3 **Maralal** Kenya
33F1 **Maramasike** I Solomon Islands
Maramba = Livingstone
59D4 **Marana** USA
21H8 **Marand** Iran
75C1 **Maranhão** R Brazil
73J4 **Maranhão** State Brazil
34C1 **Maranoa** R Australia
72C4 **Marañón** R Peru
21F8 **Maras** Turkey
55K5 **Marathon** Canada
67B4 **Marathon** Florida, USA
68B1 **Marathon** New York, USA
62B2 **Marathon** Texas, USA
75E1 **Maraú** Brazil
27F6 **Marawi** Philippines
15B2 **Marbella** Spain
32A3 **Marble Bar** Australia
59D3 **Marble Canyon** USA
47D2 **Marble Hall** South Africa
68E1 **Marblehead** USA
18B2 **Marburg** Germany
Mar Cantabrico = Biscay, B of
51B5 **Marca, Punta da** Pt Angola
18B2 **Marche** Belgium
13C2 **Marche-en-Famenne** Belgium
15A2 **Marchena** Spain
74D4 **Mar Chiquita, Lagoa** L Argentina
67B3 **Marco** USA
65E2 **Marcy,Mt** USA
42C2 **Mardan** Pakistan
74E5 **Mar del Plata** Argentina
21G8 **Mardin** Turkey
33F3 **Maré** I New Caledonia
50D2 **Mareb** R Eritrea/Ethiopia
27H8 **Mareeba** Australia
8C3 **Maree, Loch** L Scotland
50E3 **Mareeq** Somalia
62B2 **Marfa** USA
68C1 **Margaretville** USA
69E4 **Margarita, Isla** Venezuela
72F1 **Margarita, Islas de** Venezuela
29C2 **Margaritovo** Russian Federation
7E4 **Margate** England
17E1 **Marghita** Romania
34C4 **Maria I** Australia
27H5 **Marianas** Is Pacific Ocean
36J4 **Mariana Trench** Pacific Ocean
43G3 **Mariāni** India
63D2 **Marianna** Arkansas, USA
67A2 **Marianna** Florida, USA
72B2 **Mariato, Puerta** Panama
57G4 **Maria Van Diemen,C** New Zealand
18D3 **Mariazell** Austria
16D1 **Maribor** Slovenia
47D1 **Marico** R Botswana/South Africa
66C3 **Maricopa** USA
50C3 **Maridi** Sudan
76F5 **Marie Byrd Land** Region Antarctica
69E3 **Marie Galante** I Caribbean Sea
12H6 **Mariehamn** Finland
13C2 **Mariembourg** Belgium
73H2 **Marienburg** Surinam
47B1 **Mariental** Namibia
12G7 **Mariestad** Sweden
67B2 **Marietta** Georgia, USA
64C3 **Marietta** Ohio, USA
63C2 **Marietta** Oklahoma, USA
69Q2 **Marigot** Dominica
74G2 **Marília** Brazil
20C5 **Marijampole** Lithuania
51B4 **Marimba** Angola
57E2 **Marinette** USA
74F2 **Maringá** Brazil
50C3 **Maringa** R Zaïre
63D1 **Marion** Arkansas, USA
64B3 **Marion** Illinois, USA
57E2 **Marion** Indiana, USA
57E2 **Marion** Ohio, USA
67C2 **Marion** S Carolina, USA
57E3 **Marion,L** USA
33E2 **Marion Reef** Australia
59C3 **Mariposa** USA
66B2 **Mariposa** R USA
66B2 **Mariposa Res** USA
20H4 **Mari Republic** Russian Federation
21D7 **Marista** R Bulgaria
21F6 **Mariupol'** Ukraine
45C2 **Marjayoun** Lebanon
19F2 **Marjina Gorki** Belarus
45C3 **Marka** Jordan
50E3 **Marka** Somalia
18C1 **Markaryd** Sweden
7C3 **Market Drayton** England
7D3 **Market Harborough** England
6D3 **Market Weighton** England
76E7 **Markham,Mt** Antarctica
66C1 **Markleeville** USA
25T3 **Markovo** Russian Federation
68E1 **Marlboro** Massachusetts, USA
68D1 **Marlboro** New Hampshire, USA
32D3 **Marlborough** Australia
7D4 **Marlborough** England
13B3 **Marle** France
63C2 **Marlin** USA
68D1 **Marlow** USA
14C3 **Marmande** France
17F2 **Marmara Adasi** I Turkey
40A1 **Marmara,S of** Turkey
17F3 **Marmaris** Turkey
60C1 **Marmarth** USA
64C3 **Marmet** USA
61E1 **Marmion L** Canada
16C1 **Marmolada** Mt Italy
13C3 **Marne** Department France
13B3 **Marne** R France
50B3 **Maro** Chad
51E5 **Maroantsetra** Madagascar
51D5 **Marondera** Zimbabwe
73H3 **Maroni** R French Guiana
34D1 **Maroochydore** Australia
50B2 **Maroua** Cameroon
51E5 **Marovoay** Madagascar
57E4 **Marquesas Keys** Is USA
57E2 **Marquette** USA
37N5 **Marquises, Îles** Pacific Ocean
34C2 **Marra** R Australia
47E2 **Marracuene** Mozambique
50C2 **Marra, Jebel** Mt Sudan
48B1 **Marrakech** Morocco
32C3 **Marree** Australia
63D3 **Marrero** USA
51D5 **Marromeu** Mozambique
51D5 **Marrupa** Mozambique
40B4 **Marsa Alam** Egypt
50D3 **Marsabit** Kenya
16C3 **Marsala** Sicily, Italy
13E2 **Marsberg** Germany
14D3 **Marseilles** France
75D3 **Mar, Serra do** Mts Brazil
64B3 **Marshall** Illinois, USA
64C2 **Marshall** Michigan, USA
61D2 **Marshall** Minnesota, USA
61E3 **Marshall** Missouri, USA

57D3 **Marshall** Texas, USA
68B3 **Marshall** Virginia, USA
37K4 **Marshall Is** Pacific Ocean
61E2 **Marshalltown** USA
63D1 **Marshfield** Missouri, USA
64A2 **Marshfield** Wisconsin, USA
69B1 **Marsh Harbour** The Bahamas
63D3 **Marsh I** USA
30B2 **Martaban,G of** Burma
65E2 **Martha's Vineyard** *I* USA
14D2 **Martigny** Switzerland
14D3 **Martigues** France
19D3 **Martin** Slovakia
60C2 **Martin** S Dakota, USA
63E1 **Martin** Tennessee, USA
35C2 **Martinborough** New Zealand
69E4 **Martinique** *I* Caribbean Sea
67A2 **Martin,L** USA
65D3 **Martinsburg** USA
64C2 **Martins Ferry** USA
65D3 **Martinsville** USA
52G6 **Martin Vaz** *I* Atlantic Ocean
35C2 **Marton** New Zealand
15B2 **Martos** Spain
54G3 **Martre, Lac la** Canada
42B2 **Maruf** Afghanistan
29B4 **Marugame** Japan
59D3 **Marvine,Mt** USA
42C3 **Mārwār** India
24H6 **Mary** Turkmenistan
33E3 **Maryborough** Queensland, Australia
34B3 **Maryborough** Victoria, Australia
54F4 **Mary Henry,Mt** Canada
57F3 **Maryland** *State* USA
6C2 **Maryport** England
59B3 **Marysville** California, USA
61D3 **Marysville** Kansas, USA
58B1 **Marysville** Washington, USA
57D2 **Maryville** Iowa, USA
61D2 **Maryville** Missouri, USA
67B1 **Maryville** Tennessee, USA
49D2 **Marzuq** Libya
45A3 **Masabb Dumyât** *C* Egypt
Masada = Mezada
45C2 **Mas'adah** Syria
50D4 **Masai Steppe** *Upland* Tanzania
50D4 **Masaka** Uganda
41E2 **Masally** Azerbaijan
28B3 **Masan** S Korea
51D5 **Masasi** Tanzania
70D5 **Masaya** Nicaragua
27F5 **Masbate** Philippines
27F5 **Masbate** *I* Philippines
15C2 **Mascara** Algeria
36D5 **Mascarene Ridge** Indian Ocean
75E2 **Mascote** Brazil
51D5 **Maseru** Lesotho
42B2 **Mashaki** Afghanistan
41G2 **Mashhad** Iran
50B4 **Masi-Manimba** Zaïre
50D3 **Masindi** Uganda
38D3 **Maṣīrah** *I* Oman
50C4 **Masisi** Zaïre
41E3 **Masjed Soleyman** Iran
51F5 **Masoala, C** Madagascar
66C1 **Mason** Nevada, USA
62C2 **Mason** Texas, USA
57D2 **Mason City** USA
Masqat = Muscat
16C2 **Massa** Italy
57F2 **Massachusetts** *State* USA
65E2 **Massachusetts B** USA
50B2 **Massakori** Chad
51D6 **Massangena** Mozambique
50D2 **Massawa** Eritrea
65E2 **Massena** USA
50B2 **Massénya** Chad
64C1 **Massey** Canada
14C2 **Massif Central** *Mts* France
51E6 **Massif de l'Isalo** *Upland* Madagascar
51E5 **Massif du Tsaratanana** *Mts* Madagascar
64C2 **Massillon** USA
48B3 **Massina** *Region* Mali
51D6 **Massinga** Mozambique
47E1 **Massingir** Mozambique
21J6 **Masteksay** Kazakhstan
33G5 **Masterton** New Zealand
28C4 **Masuda** Japan
50B4 **Masuku** Gabon
40C2 **Maṣyāf** Syria
64C1 **Matachewan** Canada
62A3 **Matachie** Mexico
50B4 **Matadi** Zaïre
72A1 **Matagalpa** Nicaragua
55L5 **Matagami** Canada
56D4 **Matagorda B** USA
63C3 **Matagorda I** USA
35C1 **Matakana I** New Zealand
51B5 **Matala** Angola
44C4 **Matale** Sri Lanka
48A3 **Matam** Senegal
48C3 **Matameye** Niger
70C2 **Matamoros** Mexico
49E2 **Ma'tan as Sarra** *Well* Libya
55M5 **Matane** Canada
70D2 **Matanzas** Cuba
65F1 **Matapedia** *R* Canada
44C4 **Matara** Sri Lanka
32A1 **Mataram** Indonesia
72D7 **Matarani** Peru
75E1 **Mataripe** Brazil
15C1 **Mataró** Spain
47D3 **Matatiele** South Africa
35A3 **Mataura** New Zealand
70B2 **Matehuala** Mexico
69L1 **Matelot** Trinidad
16D2 **Matera** Italy
19E3 **Mátészalka** Hungary
16B3 **Mateur** Tunisia
66C2 **Mather** USA
64C1 **Matheson** Canada
63C3 **Mathis** USA
42D3 **Mathura** India
7D3 **Matlock** England
73G6 **Mato Grosso** *State* Brazil
73G7 **Mato Grosso do Sul** *State* Brazil
47E2 **Matola** Mozambique
49E1 **Matrûh** Egypt
28C3 **Matsue** Japan
29E2 **Matsumae** Japan
29D3 **Matsumoto** Japan
29D4 **Matsusaka** Japan
28C4 **Matsuyama** Japan
55K5 **Mattagami** *R* Canada
65D1 **Mattawa** Canada
16B1 **Matterhorn** *Mt* Italy/Switzerland
58C2 **Matterhorn** *Mt* USA
69C2 **Matthew Town** The Bahamas
68D2 **Mattituck** USA
64B3 **Mattoon** USA
42B2 **Matun** Afghanistan
69L1 **Matura B** Trinidad
72F2 **Maturín** Venezuela
43E3 **Mau** India
51D5 **Maúa** Mozambique
14C1 **Maubeuge** France
34B2 **Maude** Australia
52J8 **Maud Seamount** Atlantic Ocean
26H4 **Maug Is** Marianas
66E5 **Maui** *I* Hawaiian Islands
64C2 **Maumee** USA
64C2 **Maumee** *R* USA
51C5 **Maun** Botswana
66E5 **Mauna Kea** *Vol* Hawaiian Islands
66E5 **Mauna Loa** *Vol* Hawaiian Islands
54F3 **Maunoir,L** Canada
14C2 **Mauriac** France
48A2 **Mauritania** *Republic* Africa
46K10 **Mauritius** *I* Indian Ocean
64A2 **Mauston** USA
51C5 **Mavinga** Angola
47E1 **Mavue** Mozambique
43G4 **Mawlaik** Burma
Mawlamyine = Moulmein
76G10 **Mawson** *Base* Antarctica
60C1 **Max** USA
47E1 **Maxaila** Mozambique
27D7 **Maya** *I* Indonesia
25P4 **Maya** *R* Russian Federation
40D2 **Mayādīn** Syria
57F4 **Mayaguana** *I* The Bahamas
69D3 **Mayagüez** Puerto Rico
48C3 **Mayahi** Niger
50B4 **Mayama** Congo
41G2 **Mayamey** Iran
8C4 **Maybole** Scotland
57F3 **May,C** USA
34C4 **Maydena** Australia
13D2 **Mayen** Germany
14B2 **Mayenne** France
59D4 **Mayer** USA
64B3 **Mayfield** USA
62A2 **Mayhill** USA
21G7 **Maykop** Russian Federation
30B1 **Maymyo** Burma
54E3 **Mayo** Canada
68B3 **Mayo** USA
15C2 **Mayor** *Mt* Spain
35C1 **Mayor I** New Zealand
74D1 **Mayor P Lagerenza** Paraguay
51E5 **Mayotte** *I* Indian Ocean
69H2 **May Pen** Jamaica
68C3 **May Point,C** USA
68C3 **Mays Landing** USA
64C3 **Maysville** USA
50B4 **Mayumba** Gabon
61D1 **Mayville** USA
60C2 **Maywood** USA
51C5 **Mazabuka** Zambia
42D1 **Mazar** China
45C3 **Mazār** Jordan
16C3 **Mazara del Vallo** Sicily, Italy
42B1 **Mazar-i-Sharif** Afghanistan
15B2 **Mazarrón, Golfo de** *G* Spain
70B2 **Mazatlán** Mexico
20C4 **Mazeikiai** Lithuania
45C3 **Mazra** Jordan
51D6 **Mbabane** Swaziland
50B3 **Mbaïki** Central African Republic
51D4 **Mbala** Zambia
51C6 **Mbalabala** Zimbabwe
50D3 **Mbale** Uganda
50B3 **Mbalmayo** Cameroon
50B3 **Mbam** *R* Cameroon
51D5 **Mbamba Bay** Tanzania
50B3 **Mbandaka** Zaïre
50B4 **Mbanza Congo** Angola
50B4 **Mbanza-Ngungu** Zaïre
50D4 **Mbarara** Uganda
50C3 **M'Bari,R** Central African Republic
50B3 **Mbèndza** Congo
50B3 **Mbére** *R* Cameroon/Central African Republic/Chad
51D4 **Mbeya** Tanzania
50B4 **Mbinda** Congo
48A3 **Mbout** Mauritius
50C4 **Mbuji-Mayi** Zaïre
50D4 **Mbulu** Tanzania
48B2 **Mcherrah** *Region* Algeria
51D5 **Mchinji** Malawi
30D3 **Mdrak** Vietnam
62B1 **Meade** USA
56B3 **Mead,L** USA
54H4 **Meadow Lake** Canada
64C2 **Meadville** USA
29D2 **Me-akan dake** *Mt* Japan
55N4 **Mealy Mts** Canada
34C1 **Meandarra** Australia
54G4 **Meander River** Canada
9C3 **Meath** Irish Republic
14C2 **Meaux** France
50E1 **Mecca** Saudi Arabia
59C4 **Mecca** USA
68D1 **Mechanicville** USA
24G2 **Mechdusharskiy, O** *I* Russian Federation
18A2 **Mechelen** Belgium
48B1 **Mecheria** Algeria
18C2 **Meckenburg-Vorpommern** *State* Germany
18C2 **Mecklenburger Bucht** *B* Germany
51D5 **Meconta** Mozambique
51D5 **Mecuburi** Mozambique
51E5 **Mecufi** Mozambique
51D5 **Mecula** Mozambique
27C6 **Medan** Indonesia
74C7 **Médanosa, Puerta** *Pt* Argentina
15C2 **Médéa** Algeria
72C2 **Medellín** Colombia
13C1 **Medemblik** Netherlands
48D1 **Medenine** Tunisia
56A2 **Medford** USA
17F2 **Medgidia** Romania
17E1 **Mediaş** Romania
58C1 **Medical Lake** USA
60B2 **Medicine Bow** USA
60B2 **Medicine Bow Mts** USA
60B2 **Medicine Bow Peak** *Mt* USA
54G5 **Medicine Hat** Canada
62C1 **Medicine Lodge** USA
75D2 **Medina** Brazil
60D1 **Medina** N Dakota, USA
68A1 **Medina** New York, USA
40C5 **Medina** Saudi Arabia
15B1 **Medinaceli** Spain
15A1 **Medina del Campo** Spain
15A1 **Medina de Rioseco** Spain
62C3 **Medina L** USA
43F4 **Medinīpur** India
46E4 **Mediterranean S** Europe
16B3 **Medjerda** *R* Algeria/Tunisia
16B3 **Medjerda, Mts de la** Algeria/Tunisia
21K5 **Mednogorsk** Russian Federation
25S4 **Mednyy, Ostrov** *I* Russian Federation
43H3 **Mêdog** China
50B3 **Medouneu** Gabon
21G5 **Medvedista** *R* Russian Federation
25S2 **Medvezh'i Ova** *Is* Russian Federation
20E3 **Medvezh'yegorsk** Russian Federation
32A3 **Meekatharra** Australia
60B2 **Meeker** USA
42D3 **Meerut** India
58E2 **Meeteetse** USA
50D3 **Mēga** Ethiopia
17E3 **Megalópolis** Greece
17E3 **Mégara** Greece
43G3 **Meghālaya** *State* India
43G4 **Meghna** *R* Bangladesh
45C2 **Megiddo** *Hist Site* Israel
42D4 **Mehekar** India
43M2 **Mehndawal** India
41F4 **Mehrān** *R* Iran
41F3 **Mehriz** Iran
75C2 **Meia Ponte** *R* Brazil
50B3 **Meiganga** Cameroon
30B1 **Meiktila** Burma
31A4 **Meishan** China
18C2 **Meissen** Germany
31D5 **Mei Xian** China
31D5 **Meizhou** China
72D8 **Mejillones** Chile
50B3 **Mekambo** Gabon
50D2 **Mek'elē** Ethiopia
48B1 **Meknès** Morocco
30D3 **Mekong** *R* Cambodia
30D4 **Mekong, Mouths of the** Vietnam
48C3 **Mekrou** *R* Benin
30C5 **Melaka** Malaysia
36J5 **Melanesia** *Region* Pacific Ocean
32D4 **Melbourne** Australia
57E4 **Melbourne** USA
56C4 **Melchor Muźguiz** Mexico
20K5 **Meleuz** Russian Federation
50B2 **Melfi** Chad
54H4 **Melfort** Canada
15B2 **Melilla** NW Africa
74B6 **Melimoyu** *Mt* Chile
60C1 **Melita** Canada
21F6 **Melitopol'** Ukraine
50D3 **Melka Guba** Ethiopia
13E1 **Melle** Germany
16B3 **Mellégue** *R* Algeria/Tunisia
47E2 **Melmoth** South Africa
74F4 **Melo** Uruguay
75A3 **Melo** *R* Brazil
66B2 **Melones Res** USA
8D4 **Melrose** Scotland
61E1 **Melrose** USA
7D3 **Melton Mowbray** England
14C2 **Melun** France
54H4 **Melville** Canada
55M2 **Melville Bugt** *B* Greenland
69Q2 **Melville,C** Dominica
54F3 **Melville Hills** Canada
32C2 **Melville I** Australia
54G2 **Melville I** Canada
55N4 **Melville,L** Canada
55K3 **Melville Pen** Canada
51E5 **Memba** Mozambique
32A1 **Memboro** Indonesia
18C3 **Memmingen** Germany
57E3 **Memphis** Tennessee, USA
62B2 **Memphis** Texas, USA
63D2 **Mena** USA
19G2 **Mena** Ukraine
7B3 **Menai Str** Wales
48C3 **Ménaka** Mali
64B2 **Menasha** USA
27E7 **Mendawai** *R* Indonesia
14C3 **Mende** France
50D3 **Mendebo Mts** Ethiopia
32D1 **Mendi** Papua New Guinea
7C4 **Mendip Hills** *Upland* England
58B2 **Mendocino,C** USA
37M3 **Mendocino Seascarp** Pacific Ocean
66B2 **Mendota** California, USA
64B2 **Mendota** Illinois, USA
74C4 **Mendoza** Argentina
74C5 **Mendoza** *State* Argentina
17F3 **Menemen** Turkey
13B2 **Menen** Belgium
31D3 **Mengcheng** China
30B1 **Menghai** China
31A5 **Mengla** China
30B1 **Menglian** China
31A5 **Mengzi** China
32D4 **Menindee** Australia
34B2 **Menindee L** Australia
34A3 **Meningie** Australia
64B1 **Menominee** USA
64B2 **Menomonee Falls** USA
64A2 **Menomonie** USA
51B5 **Menongue** Angola
Menorca *I* **= Minorca**
27C7 **Mentawi, Kepulauan** *Is* Indonesia
62A1 **Mentmore** USA
27D7 **Mentok** Indonesia
64C2 **Mentor** USA
27E6 **Menyapa** *Mt* Indonesia
31A2 **Menyuan** China
16B3 **Menzel** Tunisia
20J4 **Menzelinsk** Russian Federation
13D1 **Meppel** Netherlands
18B2 **Meppen** Germany
15B1 **Mequinenza, Embalse de** *Res* Spain
63D1 **Meramec** *R* USA
16C1 **Merano** Italy
27E7 **Meratus, Pegunungan** *Mts* Indonesia
32D1 **Merauke** Indonesia
56A3 **Merced** USA
66B2 **Merced** *R* USA
74B4 **Mercedario** *Mt* Argentina
74E4 **Mercedes** Buenos Aires, Argentina
74E3 **Mercedes** Corrientes, Argentina
74C4 **Mercedes** San Luis, Argentina
74E4 **Mercedes** Uruguay
35C1 **Mercury B** New Zealand
35C1 **Mercury Is** New Zealand
54F2 **Mercy B** Canada
55M3 **Mercy,C** Canada
62B1 **Meredith,L** USA
30B3 **Mergui** Burma
30B3 **Mergui Arch** Burma
70D2 **Mérida** Mexico
15A2 **Mérida** Spain
72D2 **Mérida** Venezuela
72D2 **Mérida, Cordillera de** Venezuela
57E3 **Meridian** USA
34C3 **Merimbula** Australia
34B2 **Meringur** Australia
27G6 **Merir** *I* Pacific Ocean
62B2 **Merkel** USA
50D2 **Merowe** Sudan
32A4 **Merredin** Australia
8C4 **Merrick** *Mt* Scotland
64B1 **Merrill** USA
64B2 **Merrillville** USA
68E1 **Merrimack** *R* USA
60C2 **Merriman** USA
67B3 **Merritt Island** USA
34D2 **Merriwa** Australia
50E3 **Mersa Fatma** Eritrea
7E4 **Mersea** *I* England
15B2 **Mers el Kebir** Algeria
7C3 **Mersey** *R* England
7C3 **Merseyside** *Metropolitan County* England
21E8 **Mersin** Turkey
30C5 **Mersing** Malaysia
42C3 **Merta** India
7C4 **Merthyr Tydfil** Wales
15A2 **Mertola** Portugal
13B3 **Méru** France
50D4 **Meru** *Mt* Tanzania
21F7 **Merzifon** Turkey
13D3 **Merzig** Germany
56B3 **Mesa** USA
62A1 **Mesa Verde Nat Pk** USA
13E2 **Meschede** Germany
40D1 **Mescit Dağ** *Mt* Turkey
50C3 **Meshra'er Req** Sudan
17E3 **Mesolóngion** Greece
59D3 **Mesquite** Nevada, USA
63C2 **Mesquite** Texas, USA
51D5 **Messalo** *R* Mozambique
47D1 **Messina** South Africa
16D3 **Messina** Sicily, Italy
16D3 **Messina, Stretto de** *Str* Italy/Sicily
17E3 **Messíni** Greece
17E3 **Messiniakós Kólpos** *G* Greece
Mesta *R* **= Néstos**
17E2 **Mesta** *R* Bulgaria
16C1 **Mestre** Italy
72D3 **Meta** *R* Colombia/Venezuela
20E4 **Meta** *R* Russian Federation
55M3 **Meta Incognita Pen** Canada
63D3 **Metairie** USA
58C1 **Metaline Falls** USA
74D3 **Metán** Argentina
51D5 **Metangula** Mozambique
16D2 **Metaponto** Italy
8D3 **Methil** Scotland
68E1 **Methuen** USA
35B2 **Methven** New Zealand
54E4 **Metlakatla** USA
64B3 **Metropolis** USA
44B3 **Mettūr** India
14D2 **Metz** France
27C6 **Meulaboh** Indonesia
13D3 **Meurthe** *R* France
13D3 **Meurthe-et-Moselle** *Department* France
13C3 **Meuse** *Department* France
13C2 **Meuse** *R* Belgium
14D2 **Meuse** *R* France
7D3 **Mexborough** England
63C2 **Mexia** USA
70A1 **Mexicali** Mexico
59E3 **Mexican Hat** USA
70C3 **México** Mexico
61E3 **Mexico** USA
70B2 **Mexico** *Federal Republic* Central America
70C2 **Mexico,G of** Central America
24H6 **Meymaneh** Afghanistan
45C3 **Mezada** *Hist Site* Israel

20G2 **Mezen'** Russian Federation
20H3 **Mezen'** *R* Russian Federation
14C3 **Mézenc, Mount** France
19G1 **Mezha** *R* Russian Federation
20J1 **Mezhdusharskiy, Ostrov** *I* Russian Federation
42D4 **Mhow** India
59D4 **Miami** Arizona, USA
57E4 **Miami** Florida, USA
63D1 **Miami** Oklahoma, USA
57E4 **Miami Beach** USA
21H8 **Miandowāb** Iran
51E5 **Miandrivazo** Madagascar
21H8 **Mīāneh** Iran
42C2 **Mianwali** Pakistan
31A3 **Mianyang** China
31C3 **Mianyang** China
31A3 **Mianzhu** China
31E2 **Miaodao Qundao** *Arch* China
31B4 **Miao Ling** *Upland* China
20L5 **Miass** Russian Federation
19E3 **Michalovce** Slovakia
58D1 **Michel** Canada
69D3 **Miches** Dominican Republic
57E2 **Michigan** *State* USA
64B2 **Michigan City** USA
57E2 **Michigan,L** USA
64C1 **Michipicoten** Canada
55K5 **Michipicoten I** Canada
17F2 **Michurin** Bulgaria
21G5 **Michurinsk** Russian Federation
36J4 **Micronesia, Fed. States of** *Is* Pacific Ocean
36J4 **Micronesia** *Region* Pacific Ocean
52F4 **Mid Atlantic Ridge** Atlantic Ocean
47C3 **Middelburg** Cape Province, South Africa
13B2 **Middelburg** Netherlands
47D2 **Middelburg** Transvaal, South Africa
58B2 **Middle Alkali L** USA
37O4 **Middle America Trench** Pacific Ocean
44E3 **Middle Andaman** *I* Indian Ocean
68E2 **Middleboro** USA
68B2 **Middleburg** Pennsylvania, USA
68B3 **Middleburg** Virginia, USA
68C1 **Middleburgh** USA
65E2 **Middlebury** USA
57E3 **Middlesboro** USA
6D2 **Middlesbrough** England
68D2 **Middletown** Connecticut, USA
68C3 **Middletown** Delaware, USA
65E2 **Middletown** New York, USA
64C3 **Middletown** Ohio, USA
68B2 **Middletown** Pennsylvania, USA
68C1 **Middleville** USA
7C3 **Middlewich** England
48B1 **Midelt** Morocco
7C4 **Mid Glamorgan** *County* Wales
50E2 **Mīdī** Yemen
36E5 **Mid Indian Basin** Indian Ocean
36E5 **Mid Indian Ridge** Indian Ocean
55L5 **Midland** Canada
64C2 **Midland** Michigan, USA
56C3 **Midland** Texas, USA
9B4 **Midleton** Irish Republic
51E6 **Midongy Atsimo** Madagascar
37K4 **Mid Pacific Mts** Pacific Ocean
58C2 **Midvale** USA
37L3 **Midway Is** Pacific Ocean
60B2 **Midwest** USA
63C1 **Midwest City** USA
40D2 **Midyat** Turkey
17E2 **Midžor** *Mt* Serbia, Yugoslavia
19E2 **Mielec** Poland
17F1 **Miercurea-Ciuc** Romania
15A1 **Mieres** Spain
68B2 **Mifflintown** USA
13B4 **Migennes** France
28B4 **Mihara** Japan
17E2 **Mikhaylovgrad** Bulgaria
21G5 **Mikhaylovka** Russian Federation
28C2 **Mikhaylovka** Russian Federation
24J4 **Mikhaylovskiy** Russian Federation
45C4 **Mikhrot Timna** Israel
12K6 **Mikkeli** Finland
17F3 **Mikonos** *I* Greece
18D3 **Mikulov** Czech Republic
51D4 **Mikumi** Tanzania
20J3 **Mikun** Russian Federation
29D3 **Mikuni-sammyaku** *Mts* Japan
29C4 **Mikura-jima** *I* Japan
61E1 **Milaca** USA
72C4 **Milagro** Ecuador
16B1 **Milan** Italy
63E1 **Milan** USA
51D5 **Milange** Mozambique
Milano = Milan
21D8 **Milas** Turkey
61D1 **Milbank** USA
32D4 **Mildura** Australia
31A5 **Mile** China
41D3 **Mileh Tharthār** *L* Iraq
32E3 **Miles** Australia
56C2 **Miles City** USA
16C2 **Miletto, Monte** *Mt* Italy
62D2 **Milford** Connecticut, USA
65D3 **Milford** Delaware, USA
61D2 **Milford** Nebraska, USA
68E1 **Milford** New Hampshire, USA
68C2 **Milford** Pennsylvania, USA
59D3 **Milford** Utah, USA
7B4 **Milford Haven** Wales
7B4 **Milford Haven** *Sd* Wales
61D3 **Milford L** USA
35A2 **Milford Sd** New Zealand
15C2 **Miliana** Algeria
54G4 **Milk** *R* Canada/USA
60B1 **Milk** *R* USA
25R4 **Mil'kovo** Russian Federation
50C2 **Milk, Wadi el** *Watercourse* Sudan
14C3 **Millau** France
68D2 **Millbrook** USA
67B2 **Milledgeville** USA
61E1 **Mille Lacs L** USA
61E1 **Mille Lacs, Lac des** Canada
60D2 **Miller** USA
21G6 **Millerovo** Russian Federation
68B2 **Millersburg** USA
68D1 **Millers Falls** USA
68D2 **Millerton** USA
66C2 **Millerton L** USA
65E2 **Millford** Massachusetts, USA
34B3 **Millicent** Australia
63E1 **Millington** USA
65F1 **Millinocket** USA
34D1 **Millmerran** Australia
6C2 **Millom** England
8C4 **Millport** Scotland
9B3 **Millstreet** Irish Republic
65F1 **Milltown** Canada
58D1 **Milltown** USA
66A2 **Mill Valley** USA
65E3 **Millville** USA
55Q2 **Milne Land** *I* Greenland
66E5 **Milolii** Hawaiian Islands
17E3 **Mílos** *I* Greece
32D3 **Milparinka** Australia
68B2 **Milroy** USA
67A2 **Milton** Florida, USA
35A3 **Milton** New Zealand
68B2 **Milton** Pennsylvania, USA
7D3 **Milton Keynes** England
57E2 **Milwaukee** USA
29D2 **Mimmaya** Japan
66C1 **Mina** USA
15C2 **Mina** *R* Algeria
41E4 **Mīnā' al Aḩmadī** Kuwait
41G4 **Mīnāb** Iran
74E4 **Minas** Uruguay
73J7 **Minas Gerais** *State* Brazil
75D2 **Minas Novas** Brazil
70C3 **Minatitlán** Mexico
30A1 **Minbu** Burma
30A1 **Minbya** Burma
8B3 **Minch,Little** *Sd* Scotland
8B2 **Minch,North** *Sd* Scotland
10B2 **Minch,The** *Sd* Scotland
27F6 **Mindanao** *I* Philippines
63D2 **Minden** Louisiana, USA
66C1 **Minden** Nevada, USA
18B2 **Minden** Germany
34B2 **Mindona L** Australia
27F5 **Mindoro** *I* Philippines
27F5 **Mindoro Str** Philippines
7C4 **Minehead** England
73H7 **Mineiros** Brazil
63C2 **Mineola** USA
62C2 **Mineral Wells** USA
68B2 **Minersville** USA
34B2 **Mingary** Australia
21H7 **Mingechaurskoye Vodokhranilische** *Res* Azerbaijan
8B3 **Mingulay, I** Scotland
31A2 **Minhe** China
44A4 **Minicoy** *I* India
31D4 **Min Jiang** *R* Fujian, China
31A4 **Min Jiang** *R* Sichuan, China
66C2 **Minkler** USA
34A2 **Minlaton** Australia
31A2 **Minle** China
48C4 **Minna** Nigeria
57D2 **Minneapolis** USA
54J4 **Minnedosa** Canada
61D2 **Minnesota** *R* USA
57D2 **Minnesota** *State* USA
15A1 **Miño** *R* Spain
15C1 **Minorca** *I* Spain
56C2 **Minot** USA
31A2 **Minqin** China
31A3 **Min Shan** *Upland* China
20D5 **Minsk** Belarus
19E2 **Mińsk Mazowiecki** Poland
54G2 **Minto Inlet** *B* Canada
55L4 **Minto,L** Canada
60B3 **Minturn** USA
26C1 **Minusinsk** Russian Federation
31A3 **Min Xian** China
45A3 **Minya el Qamn** Egypt
55N5 **Miquelon** *I* France
66D3 **Mirage L** USA
40D3 **Mīrah, Wadi al** *Watercourse* Iraq/Saudi Arabia
44A2 **Miraj** India
74E5 **Miramar** Argentina
42B2 **Miram Shah** Pakistan
75A3 **Miranda** Brazil
75A2 **Miranda** *R* Brazil
15B1 **Miranda de Ebro** Spain
75B3 **Mirante, Serra do** *Mts* Brazil
42B2 **Mīr Bachchen Kūt** Afghanistan
13C3 **Mirecourt** France
27E6 **Miri** Malaysia
48A3 **Mirik,C** Mauritius
74F4 **Mirim, Lagoa** *L* Brazil/Uruguay
25K3 **Mirnoye** Russian Federation
25N3 **Mirnyy** Russian Federation
76G9 **Mirnyy** *Base* Antarctica
19G3 **Mironovka** Ukraine
42C2 **Mirpur** Pakistan
42B3 **Mirpur Khas** Pakistan
17E3 **Mirtoan S** Greece
28B3 **Miryang** S Korea
43E3 **Mirzāpur** India
42C1 **Misgar** Pakistan
64B2 **Mishawaka** USA
28B4 **Mi-shima** *I* Japan
43H3 **Mishmi Hills** India
33E2 **Misima** *I* Papua New Guinea
74F3 **Misiones** *State* Argentina
19E3 **Miskolc** Hungary
45D2 **Mismīyah** Syria
27G7 **Misoöl** *I* Indonesia
49D1 **Misrātah** Libya
55K5 **Missinaibi** *R* Canada
64C1 **Missinaibi L** Canada
60C2 **Mission** S Dakota, USA
62C3 **Mission** Texas, USA
58B1 **Mission City** Canada
65D2 **Mississauga** Canada
57D3 **Mississippi** *R* USA
57D3 **Mississippi** *State* USA
63E3 **Mississippi Delta** USA
56B2 **Missoula** USA
48B1 **Missour** Morocco
57D3 **Missouri** *R* USA
57D3 **Missouri** *State* USA
61D2 **Missouri Valley** USA
57F1 **Mistassini,Lac** Canada
72D7 **Misti** *Mt* Peru
34C1 **Mitchell** Australia
56D2 **Mitchell** USA
32D2 **Mitchell** *R* Australia
57E3 **Mitchell,Mt** USA
27H8 **Mitchell River** Australia
45A3 **Mīt el Nasâra** Egypt
45A3 **Mīt Ghamr** Egypt
42C3 **Mithankot** Pakistan
17F3 **Mitilíni** Greece
45B3 **Mitla Pass** Egypt
29E3 **Mito** Japan
33G2 **Mitre** *I* Solomon Islands
Mits'iwa = Massawa
13D1 **Mittel Land Kanal** Germany
72D3 **Mitú** Colombia
51C4 **Mitumba, Chaine des** *Mts* Zaïre
50C4 **Mitumbar Mts** Zaïre
51C4 **Mitwaba** Zaïre
50B3 **Mitzic** Gabon
29C3 **Miura** Japan
31C3 **Mi Xian** China
26G3 **Miyake** *I* Japan
29C4 **Miyake-jima** *I* Japan
29E3 **Miyako** Japan
26F4 **Miyako** *I* Ryukyu Is, Japan
29C3 **Miyazu** Japan
28C4 **Miyoshi** Japan
31D1 **Miyun** China
31D1 **Miyun Shuiku** *Res* China
29D2 **Mi-zaki** *Pt* Japan
50D3 **Mīzan Teferī** Ethiopia
49D1 **Mizdah** Libya
17F1 **Mizil** Romania
43G4 **Mizo Hills** India
43G4 **Mizoram** *Union Territory* India
45C3 **Mizpe Ramon** Israel
29E3 **Mizusawa** Japan
12H7 **Mjölby** Sweden
51C5 **Mkushi** Zambia
47E2 **Mkuzi** South Africa
18C2 **Mladá Boleslav** Czech Republic
19E2 **Mława** Poland
17D2 **Mljet** *I* Croatia
47D2 **Mmabatho** South Africa
48A4 **Moa** *R* Sierra Leone
56C3 **Moab** USA
45C3 **Moab** *Region* Jordan
47E2 **Moamba** Mozambique
50B4 **Moanda** Congo
50B4 **Moanda** Gabon
9C3 **Moate** Irish Republic
51C4 **Moba** Zaïre
29D3 **Mobara** Japan
50C3 **Mobaye** Central African Republic
50C3 **Mobayi** Zaïre
57D3 **Moberly** USA
57E3 **Mobile** USA
57E3 **Mobile B** USA
63E2 **Mobile Pt** USA
56C2 **Mobridge** USA
51E5 **Moçambique** Mozambique
Moçâmedes = Namibe
30C1 **Moc Chau** Vietnam
Mocha = Al Mukhā
47D1 **Mochudi** Botswana
51E5 **Mocimboa da Praia** Mozambique
72C3 **Mocoa** Colombia
75C3 **Mococa** Brazil
51D5 **Mocuba** Mozambique
47D2 **Modder** *R* South Africa
16C2 **Modena** Italy
13D3 **Moder** *R* France
56A3 **Modesto** USA
66B2 **Modesto Res** USA
16C3 **Modica** Sicily,
18D3 **Mödling** Austria
8D4 **Moffat** Scotland
42D2 **Moga** India
50E3 **Mogadishu** Somalia
75C3 **Mogi das Cruzes** Brazil
19G2 **Mogilev** Belarus
21D6 **Mogilev Podol'skiy** Ukraine
75C3 **Mogi-Mirim** Brazil
51E5 **Mogincual** Mozambique
26E1 **Mogocha** Russian Federation
24K4 **Mogochin** Russian Federation
47D1 **Mogol** *R* South Africa
15A2 **Moguer** Spain
35C1 **Mohaka** *R* New Zealand
47D3 **Mohale's Hoek** Lesotho
60C1 **Mohall** USA
15C2 **Mohammadia** Algeria
43G4 **Mohanganj** Bangladesh
59D3 **Mohave,L** USA
68C1 **Mohawk** USA
65E2 **Mohawk** *R* USA
51E5 **Mohéli** *I* Comoros
51D4 **Mohoro** Tanzania
24J5 **Mointy** Kazakhstan
12G5 **Mo i Rana** Norway
14C3 **Moissac** France
59C3 **Mojave** USA
66D3 **Mojave** *R* USA
56B3 **Mojave Desert** USA
43F3 **Mokama** India
35B1 **Mokau** *R* New Zealand
66B1 **Mokelumne** *R* USA
66B1 **Mokelumne Aqueduct** USA
66B1 **Mokelumne Hill** USA
47D2 **Mokhotlong** Lesotho
16C3 **Moknine** Tunisia
43G3 **Mokokchūng** India
50B2 **Mokolo** Cameroon
28B4 **Mokp'o** S Korea
20G5 **Moksha** *R* Russian Federation
17E3 **Moláoi** Greece
7C3 **Mold** Wales
Moldavia = Moldova
12F6 **Molde** Norway
21D6 **Moldova** *Republic* Europe
17E1 **Moldoveanu** *Mt* Romania
47D1 **Molepolole** Botswana
13D3 **Molesheim** France
16D2 **Molfetta** Italy
72D7 **Mollendo** Peru
20D5 **Molodechno** Belarus
76G11 **Molodezhnaya** *Base* Antarctica
66E5 **Molokai** *I* Hawaiian Islands
20H4 **Moloma** *R* Russian Federation
34C2 **Molong** Australia
47C2 **Molopo** *R* Botswana/South Africa
50B3 **Molounddu** Cameroon
56D1 **Molson L** Canada
32B1 **Molucca S** Indonesia
27F7 **Moluccas** *Is* Indonesia
51D5 **Moma** Mozambique
73K5 **Mombaça** Brazil
50D4 **Mombasa** Kenya
29D2 **Mombetsu** Japan
75B2 **Mombuca, Serra da** *Mts* Brazil
50C3 **Mompono** Zaïre
18C2 **Mon** *I* Denmark
8B3 **Monach Is** Scotland
14D3 **Monaco** *Principality* Europe
8C3 **Monadhliath Mts** Scotland
9C2 **Monaghan** Irish Republic
9C2 **Monaghan** *County* Irish Republic
62B2 **Monahans** USA
69D3 **Mona Pass** Caribbean Sea
60B3 **Monarch P** USA
54G4 **Monashee Mts** Canada
10B3 **Monastereven** Irish Republic
16C3 **Monastir** Tunisia
29D2 **Monbetsu** Japan
73J4 **Monção** Brazil
12L5 **Monchegorsk** Russian Federation
18B2 **Mönchen-gladbach** Germany
70B2 **Monclova** Mexico
55M5 **Moncton** Canada
15A1 **Mondego** *R* Portugal
16B2 **Mondovi** Italy
69H1 **Moneague** Jamaica
65D2 **Monessen** USA
63D1 **Monett** USA
16C1 **Monfalcone** Italy
15A1 **Monforte de Lemos** Spain
50C3 **Monga** Zaïre
50C3 **Mongala** *R* Zaïre
50D3 **Mongalla** Sudan
30D1 **Mong Cai** Vietnam
50B2 **Mongo** Chad
26C2 **Mongolia** *Republic* Asia
51C5 **Mongu** Zambia
8D4 **Moniaive** Scotland
59C3 **Monitor Range** *Mts* USA
50C4 **Monkoto** Zaïre
64A2 **Monmouth** USA
7C4 **Monmouth** Wales
48C4 **Mono** *R* Benin/Togo
59C3 **Mono L** USA
17D2 **Monopoli** Italy
15B1 **Monreal del Campo** Spain
63D2 **Monroe** Louisiana, USA
64C2 **Monroe** Michigan, USA
67B2 **Monroe** N Carolina, USA
58B1 **Monroe** Washington, USA
64B2 **Monroe** Wisconsin, USA
61E3 **Monroe City** USA
48A4 **Monrovia** Liberia
66D3 **Monrovia** USA
18A2 **Mons** Belgium
68D1 **Monson** USA
18D1 **Mönsterås** Sweden
47C3 **Montagu** South Africa
54D4 **Montague I** USA
14B2 **Montaigu** France
16D3 **Montallo** *Mt* Italy
56B2 **Montana** *State* USA
15A1 **Montañas de León** *Mts* Spain
14C2 **Montargis** France
14C3 **Montauban** France
65E2 **Montauk** USA
65E2 **Montauk Pt** USA
13C4 **Montbard** France
14D2 **Montbéliard** France
Montblanc = Montblanch
16B1 **Mont Blanc** France/Italy
15C1 **Montblanch** Spain
14C2 **Montceau-les-Mines** France
16B1 **Mont Cenis, Col du** *P* France/Italy
15C1 **Montceny** *Mt* Spain
13C3 **Montcornet** France
14B3 **Mont-de-Marsan** France
14C2 **Montdidier** France
72F7 **Monteagudo** Bolivia
73H4 **Monte Alegre** Brazil
75D2 **Monte Azul** Brazil
65D1 **Montebello** Canada
32A3 **Monte Bello Is** Australia
14D3 **Monte Carlo** Monaco
75C2 **Monte Carmelo** Brazil
69C3 **Montecristi** Dominican Republic
16C2 **Montecristo** *I* Italy
69H1 **Montego Bay** Jamaica
14C3 **Montélimar** France
75A3 **Montelindo** *R* Paraguay
70C2 **Montemorelos** Mexico
15A2 **Montemor-o-Novo** Portugal

17D2 **Montenegro** *Republic* Yugoslavia
51D5 **Montepuez** Mozambique
13B3 **Montereau-Faut-Yonne** France
56A3 **Monterey** California, USA
65D3 **Monterey** Virginia, USA
56A3 **Monterey B** USA
72C2 **Montería** Colombia
72F7 **Montero** Bolivia
70B2 **Monterrey** Mexico
73K7 **Montes Claros** Brazil
15B2 **Montes de Toledo** *Mts* Spain
74E4 **Montevideo** Uruguay
61D2 **Montevideo** USA
62A1 **Monte Vista** USA
62B1 **Montezuma** USA
66D2 **Montezuma Peak** *Mt* USA
57E3 **Montgomery** Alabama, USA
68B2 **Montgomery** Pennsylvania, USA
7C3 **Montgomery** Wales
66C2 **Montgomery P** USA
13C3 **Monthermé** France
63D2 **Monticello** Arkansas, USA
64A2 **Monticello** Iowa, USA
61E1 **Monticello** Minnesota, USA
68C2 **Monticello** New York, USA
56C3 **Monticello** Utah, USA
13C3 **Montier-en-Der** France
55L5 **Mont-Laurier** Canada
14C2 **Montluçon** France
55L5 **Montmagny** Canada
13C3 **Montmédy** France
13B3 **Montmirail** France
Mont, Monte : see also individual mt. names
65E1 **Montmorency** Canada
15B2 **Montoro** Spain
68B2 **Montoursville** USA
58D2 **Montpelier** Idaho, USA
64C2 **Montpelier** Ohio, USA
57F2 **Montpelier** Vermont, USA
14C3 **Montpellier** France
55L5 **Montréal** Canada
14C1 **Montreuil** France
16B1 **Montreux** Switzerland
56C3 **Montrose** Colorado, USA
68C2 **Montrose** Pennsylvania, USA
10C2 **Montrose** Scotland
8F3 **Montrose** *Oilfield* N Sea
14B2 **Mont-St-Michel** France
69E3 **Montserrat** *I* Caribbean Sea
57F1 **Monts Otish** Canada
56B3 **Monument V** USA
50C3 **Monveda** Zaïre
30B1 **Monywa** Burma
16B1 **Monza** Italy
51C5 **Monze** Zambia
47E2 **Mooi** *R* South Africa
47D2 **Mooi River** South Africa
34B1 **Moomba** Australia
34D2 **Moonbi Range** *Mts* Australia
34B1 **Moonda L** Australia
34D1 **Moonie** Australia
34C1 **Moonie** *R* Australia
34A2 **Moonta** Australia
32A4 **Moora** Australia
34B1 **Mooraberree** Australia
60C2 **Moorcroft** USA
32A3 **Moore,L** Australia
48D4 **Moorfoot Hills** Scotland
56D2 **Moorhead** USA
66C3 **Moorpark** USA
47B3 **Moorreesburg** South Africa
55K4 **Moose** *R* Canada
65F1 **Moosehead L** USA
54H4 **Moose Jaw** Canada
61E1 **Moose Lake** USA
54H4 **Moosomin** Canada
55K4 **Moosonee** Canada
68E2 **Moosup** USA
51D5 **Mopeia** Mozambique
48B3 **Mopti** Mali
72D7 **Moquegua** Peru
12G6 **Mora** Sweden
61E1 **Mora** USA
42D3 **Morādābād** India
73L5 **Morada Nova** Brazil
75C2 **Morada Nova de Minas** Brazil
51E5 **Morafenobe** Madagascar
51E5 **Moramanga** Madagascar
58D2 **Moran** USA
69J2 **Morant Bay** Jamaica
69J2 **Morant Pt** Jamaica
8C3 **Morar, Loch** *L* Scotland
44B4 **Moratuwa** Sri Lanka
18D3 **Morava** *R* Austria/ Czechoslovakia
17E2 **Morava** *R* Serbia, Yugoslavia
41G2 **Moraveh Tappeh** Iran
10C2 **Moray Firth** *Estuary* Scotland
42C4 **Morbi** India
41D2 **Mor Dağ** *Mt* Turkey
54J5 **Morden** Canada
20G5 **Mordovian Republic** Russian Federation
60C1 **Moreau** *R* USA
7C2 **Morecambe** England
7C2 **Morecambe B** England
32D3 **Moree** Australia
64C3 **Morehead** USA
67C2 **Morehead City** USA
70B3 **Morelia** Mexico
42D3 **Morena** India
15A2 **Morena, Sierra** *Mts* Spain
54E4 **Moresby I** Canada
34D1 **Moreton I** Australia
13B3 **Moreuil** France
63D3 **Morgan City** USA
66B2 **Morgan Hill** USA
66C2 **Morgan,Mt** USA
67B1 **Morganton** USA
65D3 **Morgantown** USA
47D2 **Morgenzon** South Africa
13D3 **Morhange** France
29E2 **Mori** Japan
69K1 **Moriah** Tobago
62A2 **Moriarty** USA
29E3 **Morioka** Japan
34D2 **Morisset** Australia
25N3 **Morkoka** *R* Russian Federation
14B2 **Morlaix** France
69Q2 **Morne Diablotin** *Mt* Dominica
34B1 **Morney** Australia
32C2 **Mornington** *I* Australia
42B3 **Moro** Pakistan
32D1 **Morobe** Papua New Guinea
48B1 **Morocco** *Kingdom* Africa
27F6 **Moro G** Philippines
51D4 **Morogoro** Tanzania
51E6 **Morombe** Madagascar
69B2 **Morón** Cuba
51E6 **Morondava** Madagascar
15A2 **Moron de la Frontera** Spain
51E5 **Moroni** Comoros
27F6 **Morotai** *I* Indonesia
50D3 **Moroto** Uganda
21G6 **Morozovsk** Russian Federation
6D2 **Morpeth** England
45B1 **Morphou** Cyprus
45B1 **Morphou B** Cyprus
60C2 **Morrill** USA
63D1 **Morrilton** USA
75C2 **Morrinhos** Brazil
35C1 **Morrinsville** New Zealand
61D1 **Morris** Canada
61D1 **Morris** USA
68C2 **Morristown** New Jersey, USA
65D2 **Morristown** New York, USA
67B1 **Morristown** Tennessee, USA
68C1 **Morrisville** New York, USA
68C2 **Morrisville** Pennsylvania, USA
66B3 **Morro Bay** USA
51D5 **Morrumbala** Mozambique
51D6 **Morrumbene** Mozambique
20G5 **Morshansk** Russian Federation
Mortes *R* **= Manso**
73H6 **Mortes** *R* Mato Grosso, Brazil
75D3 **Mortes** *R* Minas Gerais, Brazil
34B3 **Mortlake** Australia
62B2 **Morton** USA
69L1 **Moruga** Trinidad
34D3 **Moruya** Australia
34C1 **Morven** Australia
8C3 **Morvern** *Pen* Scotland
34C3 **Morwell** Australia
13E3 **Mosbach** Germany
30B3 **Moscos Is** Burma
58C1 **Moscow** Idaho, USA
68C2 **Moscow** Pennsylvania, USA
42F4 **Moscow** Russian Federation
18B2 **Mosel** *R* Germany
47C2 **Moselebe** *R* Botswana
13D3 **Moselle** *Department* France
13D3 **Moselle** *R* France
58C1 **Moses Lake** USA
35B3 **Mosgiel** New Zealand
50D4 **Moshi** Tanzania
64B2 **Mosinee** USA
12G5 **Mosjøen** Norway
25Q4 **Moskal'vo** Russian Federation
Moskva = Moscow
62B1 **Mosquero** USA
75D2 **Mosquito** *R* Brazil
72B2 **Mosquitos, Golfo de los** Panama
12G7 **Moss** Norway
50B4 **Mossaka** Congo
Mossâmedes = Namibe
47C3 **Mossel Bay** South Africa
50B4 **Mossendjo** Congo
34B2 **Mossgiel** Australia
73L5 **Mossoró** Brazil
18C2 **Most** Czech Republic
15C2 **Mostaganem** Algeria
17D2 **Mostar** Bosnia-Herzegovina
19E2 **Mosty** Belarus
41D2 **Mosul** Iraq
12H7 **Motala** Sweden
8D4 **Motherwell** Scotland
43E3 **Motihāri** India
15B2 **Motilla del Palancar** Spain
47D1 **Motloutse** *R* Botswana
15B2 **Motril** Spain
60C1 **Mott** USA
35B2 **Motueka** New Zealand
35B2 **Motueka** *R* New Zealand
50B4 **Mouila** Gabon
34B2 **Moulamein** Australia
54G2 **Mould Bay** Canada
69P2 **Moule à Chique, Cap** St Lucia
14C2 **Moulins** France
30B2 **Moulmein** Burma
48B1 **Moulouya** *R* Morocco
67B2 **Moultrie** USA
67C2 **Moultrie,L** USA
64B3 **Mound City** Illinois, USA
61D2 **Mound City** Missouri, USA
50B3 **Moundou** Chad
64C3 **Moundsville** USA
67A2 **Mountain Brook** USA
63D1 **Mountain Grove** USA
63D1 **Mountain Home** Arkansas, USA
58C2 **Mountain Home** Idaho, USA
66A2 **Mountain View** USA
54B3 **Mountain Village** USA
68B3 **Mount Airy** Maryland, USA
67B1 **Mount Airy** N Carolina, USA
47D3 **Mount Ayliff** South Africa
68B2 **Mount Carmel** USA
65F2 **Mount Desert I** USA
47D3 **Mount Fletcher** South Africa
34B3 **Mount Gambier** Australia
32D1 **Mount Hagen** Papua New Guinea
68C3 **Mount Holly** USA
68B2 **Mount Holly Springs** USA
32C3 **Mount Isa** Australia
68A3 **Mount Jackson** USA
68A2 **Mount Jewett** USA
34A2 **Mount Lofty Range** *Mts* Australia
32A3 **Mount Magnet** Australia
34B2 **Mount Manara** Australia
9C3 **Mountmellick** Irish Republic
32E3 **Mount Morgan** Australia
68B1 **Mount Morris** USA
34D1 **Mount Perry** Australia
63D2 **Mount Pleasant** Texas, USA
59D3 **Mount Pleasant** Utah, USA
68C2 **Mount Pocono** USA
58B1 **Mount Rainier Nat Pk** USA
7B4 **Mounts B** England
58B2 **Mount Shasta** USA
68B2 **Mount Union** USA
63E2 **Mount Vernon** Alabama, USA
64B3 **Mount Vernon** Illinois, USA
63D1 **Mount Vernon** Missouri, USA
58B1 **Mount Vernon** Washington, USA
50C2 **Mourdi, Dépression du** *Desert Region* Chad
9C2 **Mourne Mts** Northern Ireland
50B2 **Moussoro** Chad
48C2 **Mouydir, Mts du** Algeria
50B4 **Mouyondzi** Congo
13C3 **Mouzon** France
18D3 **M'óvár** Hungary
9C2 **Moville** Irish Republic
9B2 **Moy** *R* Irish Republic
50D3 **Moyale** Kenya
48A4 **Moyamba** Sierra Leone
48B1 **Moyen Atlas** *Mts* Morocco
47D3 **Moyeni** Lesotho
25M3 **Moyero** *R* Russian Federation
50D3 **Moyo** Uganda
72C5 **Moyobamba** Peru
42D1 **Moyu** China
51D6 **Mozambique** *Republic* Africa
51D6 **Mozambique Chan** Madagascar/ Mozambique
20J4 **Mozhga** Russian Federation
12K8 **Mozyr'** Belarus
50D4 **Mpanda** Tanzania
51D5 **Mpika** Zambia
51D4 **Mporokosa** Zambia
51C5 **Mposhi** Zambia
48B4 **Mpraeso** Ghana
51D4 **Mpulungu** Zambia
50D4 **Mpwapwa** Tanzania
16C3 **M'saken** Tunisia
15C2 **M'Sila** Algeria
19G2 **Mstislavl'** Belarus
20F5 **Mtsensk** Russian Federation
47E2 **Mtubatuba** South Africa
51E5 **Mtwara** Tanzania
30C2 **Muang Chainat** Thailand
30C2 **Muang Chiang Rai** Thailand
30C2 **Muang Kalasin** Thailand
30C2 **Muang Khon Kaen** Thailand
30B2 **Muang Lampang** Thailand
30B2 **Muang Lamphun** Thailand
30C2 **Muang Loei** Thailand
30C2 **Muang Lom Sak** Thailand
30C2 **Muang Nakhon Phanom** Thailand
30B2 **Muang Nakhon Sawan** Thailand
30C2 **Muang Nan** Thailand
30C2 **Muang Phayao** Thailand
30C2 **Muang Phetchabun** Thailand
30C2 **Muang Phichit** Thailand
30C2 **Muang Phitsanulok** Thailand
30C2 **Muang Phrae** Thailand
30C2 **Muang Roi Et** Thailand
30C2 **Muang Sakon Nakhon** Thailand
30C3 **Muang Samut Prakan** Thailand
30C2 **Muang Uthai Thani** Thailand
30C2 **Muang Yasothon** Thailand
30C5 **Muar** Malaysia
27D7 **Muara** Indonesia
30A2 **Muaungmya** Burma
50D3 **Mubende** Uganda
49D3 **Mubi** Nigeria
45C3 **Mubrak, Jebel** *Mt* Jordan
51D5 **Muchinga Mts** Zambia
7C3 **Much Wenlock** England
8B3 **Muck** *I* Scotland
34C1 **Muckadilla** Australia
9B2 **Muckros Hd,** *Pt* Irish Republic
51C5 **Muconda** Angola
75E2 **Mucuri** Brazil
75D2 **Mucuri** *R* Brazil
51C5 **Mucusso** Angola
26F2 **Mudanjiang** China
60B2 **Muddy Gap P** USA
45D3 **Mudeisisat, Jebel** *Mt* Jordan
34C2 **Mudgee** Australia
66D2 **Mud L** USA
30B2 **Mudon** Burma
20F3 **Mud'yuga** Russian Federation
51D5 **Mueda** Mozambique
33F3 **Mueo** New Caledonia (Nouvelle Calédonie)
51C5 **Mufulira** Zambia
31C4 **Mufu Shan** *Hills* China
40C4 **Mughayra** Saudi Arabia
40A2 **Muğla** Turkey
21K5 **Mugodzhary** *Mts* Kazakhstan
43E3 **Mugu** Nepal
31A3 **Muguaping** China
40D3 **Muhaywir** Iraq
13E3 **Mühlacker** Germany
18C3 **Mühldorf** Germany
18C2 **Mühlhausen** Germany
12K6 **Muhos** Finland
30C4 **Mui Bai Bung** *C* Cambodia
9C3 **Muine Bheag** Irish Republic
45C3 **Mujib, Wadi** Jordan
51C5 **Mujimbeji** Zambia
19E3 **Mukachevo** Ukraine
27E6 **Mukah** Malaysia
29D2 **Mukawa** Japan
26H4 **Muko-jima** *I* Japan
43E3 **Muktinath** Nepal
42B2 **Mukur** Afghanistan
63D1 **Mulberry** USA
18C2 **Mulde** *R* Germany
60C2 **Mule Creek** USA
62B2 **Muleshoe** USA
27H8 **Mulgrave I** Australia
15B2 **Mulhacén** *Mt* Spain
13D2 **Mülheim** Germany
13D4 **Mulhouse** France
31A4 **Muli** China
8C3 **Mull** *I* Scotland
44C4 **Mullaittvu** Sri Lanka
34C2 **Mullaley** Australia
27E6 **Muller, Pegunungan** *Mts* Indonesia
9A2 **Mullet, The** *Pt* Irish Republic
32A3 **Mullewa** Australia
13D4 **Müllheim** Germany
68C3 **Mullica** *R* USA
9C3 **Mullingar** Irish Republic
8C4 **Mull of Kintyre** *Pt* Scotland
8B4 **Mull of Oa** *C* Scotland
34D1 **Mullumbimby** Australia
51C5 **Mulobezi** Zambia
42C2 **Multan** Pakistan
51C5 **Mumbwa** Zambia
21H6 **Mumra** Russian Federation
27F7 **Muna** Indonesia
München = Munich
28A3 **Munchŏn** N Korea
64B2 **Muncie** USA
34A1 **Muncoonie,L** Australia
68B2 **Muncy** USA
18B2 **Münden** Germany
34D1 **Mundubbera** Australia
34C1 **Mungallala** Australia
34C1 **Mungallala** *R* Australia
50C3 **Mungbere** Zaïre
43E4 **Mungeli** India
43F3 **Munger** India
34C1 **Mungindi** Australia
18C3 **Munich** Germany
64B1 **Munising** USA
74B8 **Muñoz Gamero,Pen** Chile
28A3 **Munsan** S Korea
13D3 **Munster** France
18B2 **Münster** Germany
13D2 **Münsterland** *Region* Germany
17E1 **Munţii Apuseni** *Mts* Romania
17E1 **Munţii Călimani** *Mts* Romania
17E1 **Munţii Carpaţii Meridionali** *Mts* Romania
17E1 **Munţii Rodnei** *Mts* Romania
17E1 **Munţii Zarandului** *Mts* Romania
40C2 **Munzur Silsilesi** *Mts* Turkey
30C1 **Muong Khoua** Laos
30D3 **Muong Man** Vietnam
30D2 **Muong Nong** Laos
30C1 **Muong Ou Neua** Laos
30C1 **Muong Sai** Laos
30C2 **Muong Sen** Vietnam
30C1 **Muong Sing** Laos
30C1 **Muong Son** Laos
12J5 **Muonio** Finland
12J5 **Muonio** *R* Finland/ Sweden
28A3 **Muping** China
Muqdisho = Mogadishu
16C1 **Mur** *R* Austria
29D3 **Murakami** Japan
74B7 **Murallón** *Mt* Argentina/ Chile
20H4 **Murashi** Russian Federation
40D2 **Murat** *R* Turkey
16B3 **Muravera** Sardinia, Italy
29D3 **Murayama** Japan
41F3 **Murcheh Khvort** Iran
35B2 **Murchison** New Zealand
32A3 **Murchison** *R* Australia
15B2 **Murcia** Spain
15B2 **Murcia** *Region* Spain
60C2 **Murdo** USA
17E1 **Mureş** *R* Romania
67C1 **Murfreesboro** N Carolina, USA
67A1 **Murfreesboro** Tennessee, USA
13E3 **Murg** *R* Germany
24H6 **Murgab** *R* Turkmenistan
42A1 **Murghab** *R* Afghanistan
42B2 **Murgha Kibzai** Pakistan
34D1 **Murgon** Australia
43F4 **Muri** India
75D3 **Muriaé** Brazil
51C4 **Muriege** Angola
20E2 **Murmansk** Russian Federation
20G4 **Murom** Russian Federation
29E2 **Muroran** Japan
15A1 **Muros** Spain
29C4 **Muroto** Japan
29B4 **Muroto-zaki** *C* Japan
58C2 **Murphy** Idaho, USA
67B1 **Murphy** N Carolina, USA
66B1 **Murphys** USA
64B3 **Murray** Kentucky, USA
58D2 **Murray** Utah, USA

34B2 **Murray** *R* Australia
34A3 **Murray Bridge** Australia
27H7 **Murray,L** Papua New Guinea
67B2 **Murray,L** USA
47C3 **Murraysburg** South Africa
37M3 **Murray Seacarp** Pacific Ocean
34B2 **Murrumbidgee** *R* Australia
34C2 **Murrumburrah** Australia
34D2 **Murrurundi** Australia
34B3 **Murtoa** Australia
28A2 **Muruin Sum** *R* China
35C1 **Murupara** New Zealand
43E4 **Murwāra** India
34D1 **Murwillimbah** Australia
27E7 **Muryo** *Mt* Indonesia
40D2 **Muş** Turkey
17E2 **Musala** *Mt* Bulgaria
28B2 **Musan** N Korea
41G4 **Musandam Pen** Oman
38D3 **Muscat** Oman
61E2 **Muscatine** USA
32C3 **Musgrave Range** *Mts* Australia
50B4 **Mushie** Zaïre
68E2 **Muskeget Chan** USA
64B2 **Muskegon** USA
64B2 **Muskegon** *R* USA
63C1 **Muskogee** USA
65D2 **Muskoka,L** Canada
50D2 **Musmar** Sudan
50D4 **Musoma** Tanzania
32D1 **Mussau** *I* Papua New Guinea
58E1 **Musselshell** *R* USA
51B5 **Mussende** Angola
14C3 **Mussidan** France
17F2 **Mustafa-Kemalpasa** Turkey
43E3 **Mustang** Nepal
74C7 **Musters, Lago** Argentina
28A2 **Musu-dan** *C* N Korea
34D2 **Muswellbrook** Australia
49E2 **Mut** Egypt
75E1 **Mutá, Ponta do** *Pt* Brazil
51D5 **Mutarara** Mozambique
51D5 **Mutare** Zimbabwe
20K2 **Mutnyy Materik** Russian Federation
51D5 **Mutoko** Zimbabwe
51E5 **Mutsamudu** Comoros
51C5 **Mutshatsha** Zaïre
29E2 **Mutsu** Japan
29E2 **Mutsu-wan** *B* Japan
75C1 **Mutunópolis** Brazil
31B2 **Mu Us Shamo** *Desert* China
51B4 **Muxima** Angola
25N4 **Muya** Russian Federation
20E3 **Muyezerskiy** Russian Federation
50D4 **Muyinga** Burundi
51C4 **Muyumba** Zaïre
39E1 **Muyun Kum** *Desert* Kazakhstan
42C2 **Muzaffarābad** Pakistan
42C2 **Muzaffargarh** Pakistan
42D3 **Muzaffarnagar** India
43F3 **Muzaffarpur** India
24H3 **Muzhi** Russian Federation
39G2 **Muzlag** *Mt* China
39F2 **Muztagala** *Mt* China
51D5 **Mvuma** Zimbabwe
50D4 **Mwanza** Tanzania
51C4 **Mwanza** Zaïre
50C4 **Mweka** Zaïre
51C4 **Mwene Ditu** Zaïre
51D6 **Mwenezi** Zimbabwe
47E1 **Mwenezi** *R* Zimbabwe
50C4 **Mwenga** Zaïre
51C4 **Mweru, L** Zaïre/Zambia
51C5 **Mwinilunga** Zambia
30B2 **Myanaung** Burma
Myanmar = Burma
18D3 **M'yaróvár** Hungary
30B1 **Myingyan** Burma
30B3 **Myinmoletkat** *Mt* Burma
30B3 **Myitta** Burma
43G4 **Mymensingh** Bangladesh
7C3 **Mynydd Eppynt** Wales
26G3 **Myojin** *I* Japan
28A2 **Myongchon** N Korea
28A2 **Myonggan** N Korea
12F6 **Myrdal** Norway
12B2 **Myrdalsjökull** *Mts* Iceland
67C2 **Myrtle Beach** USA
58B2 **Myrtle Creek** USA
12G7 **Mysen** Norway
20G2 **Mys Kanin Nos** *C* Russian Federation
19D3 **Myślenice** Poland
18C2 **Myśliborz** Poland
44B3 **Mysore** India
21E7 **Mys Sarych** *C* Ukraine
25U3 **Mys Shmidta** Russian Federation
20F2 **Mys Svyatoy Nos** *C* Russian Federation
68E2 **Mystic** USA
21J7 **Mys Tyub-Karagan** *Pt* Kazakhstan
24H2 **Mys Zhelaniya** *C* Russian Federation
30D3 **My Tho** Vietnam
58B2 **Mytle Point** USA
51D5 **Mzimba** Malawi
51D5 **Mzuzú** Malawi

N

66E5 **Naalehu** Hawaiian Islands
12J6 **Naantali** Finland
9C3 **Naas** Irish Republic
29C4 **Nabari** Japan
20J4 **Naberezhnyye Chelny** Russian Federation
16C3 **Nabeul** Tunisia
75A3 **Nabileque** *R* Brazil
45C2 **Nablus** Israel
51E5 **Nacala** Mozambique
58B1 **Naches** USA
51D5 **Nachingwea** Tanzania
66B3 **Nacimiento** *R* USA
66B3 **Nacimiento Res** USA
63D2 **Nacogdoches** USA
70B1 **Nacozari** Mexico
13E2 **Nadel** *Mt* Germany
42C4 **Nadiād** India
15B2 **Nador** Morocco
41F3 **Nadūshan** Iran
20E3 **Nadvoitsy** Russian Federation
19E3 **Nadvornaya** Ukraine
18C1 **Naestved** Denmark
49E2 **Nafoora** Libya
27F5 **Naga** Philippines
28B4 **Nagahama** Japan
43H3 **Naga Hills** India
29C3 **Nagai** Japan
43G3 **Nāgāland** *State* India
29D3 **Nagano** Japan
29D3 **Nagaoka** Japan
44B3 **Nāgappattinam** India
42C4 **Nagar Parkar** Pakistan
28B4 **Nagasaki** Japan
29C4 **Nagashima** Japan
28B4 **Nagato** Japan
42C3 **Nāgaur** India
44B4 **Nāgercoil** India
42B3 **Nagha Kalat** Pakistan
42D3 **Nagīna** India
13E3 **Nagold** Germany
29D3 **Nagoya** Japan
42D4 **Nāgpur** India
39H2 **Nagqu** China
18D3 **Nagykanizsa** Hungary
19D3 **Nagykörös** Hungary
26F4 **Naha** Okinawa, Japan
42D2 **Nāhan** India
54F3 **Nahanni Butte** Canada
45C2 **Nahariya** Israel
41E3 **Nahāvand** Iran
13D3 **Nahe** *R* Germany
31D2 **Nahpu** China
74B6 **Nahuel Haupí, Lago** Argentina
31E1 **Naimen Qi** China
55M4 **Nain** Canada
41F3 **Nā'īn** Iran
42D3 **Naini Tal** India
43E4 **Nainpur** India
8D3 **Nairn** Scotland
50D4 **Nairobi** Kenya
41F3 **Najafābād** Iran
40C4 **Najd** *Region* Saudi Arabia
28C2 **Najin** N Korea
50E2 **Najrān** Saudi Arabia
28A3 **Naju** S Korea
28A4 **Nakadori-jima** Japan
28B4 **Nakama** Japan
29E3 **Nakaminato** Japan
28B4 **Nakamura** Japan
29C3 **Nakano** Japan
29B3 **Nakano-shima** *I* Japan
28C4 **Nakatsu** Japan
29C3 **Nakatsu-gawa** Japan
50D2 **Nak'fa** Eritrea
21H8 **Nakhichevan** Azerbaijan
45B4 **Nakhl** Egypt
28C2 **Nakhodka** Russian Federation
30C3 **Nakhon Pathom** Thailand
30C3 **Nakhon Ratchasima** Thailand
30C4 **Nakhon Si Thammarat** Thailand
55K4 **Nakina** Ontario, Canada
54C4 **Naknek** USA
12G8 **Nakskov** Denmark
28A3 **Naktong** *R* S Korea
50D4 **Nakuru** Kenya
21G7 **Nal'chik** Russian Federation
44B2 **Nalgonda** India
44B2 **Nallamala Range** *Mts* India
49D1 **Nālūt** Libya
47E2 **Namaacha** Mozambique
24G6 **Namak** *L* Iran
41G3 **Namakzar-e Shadad** *Salt Flat* Iran
24J5 **Namangan** Uzbekistan
51D5 **Namapa** Mozambique
51B7 **Namaqualand** *Region* South Africa
34D1 **Nambour** Australia
34D2 **Nambucca Heads** Australia
30D4 **Nam Can** Vietnam
39H2 **Nam Co** *L* China
30D1 **Nam Dinh** Vietnam
51D5 **Nametil** Mozambique
47A1 **Namib Desert** Namibia
51B5 **Namibe** Angola
51B6 **Namibia** *Republic* Africa
27F7 **Namlea** Indonesia
43F3 **Namling** China
34C2 **Namoi** *R* Australia
58C2 **Nampa** USA
48B3 **Nampala** Mali
30C2 **Nam Phong** Thailand
28B3 **Namp'o** N Korea
51D5 **Nampula** Mozambique
12G6 **Namsos** Norway
30B1 **Namton** Burma
25O3 **Namtsy** Russian Federation
51D5 **Namuno** Mozambique
13C2 **Namur** Belgium
51B5 **Namutoni** Namibia
56A2 **Nanaimo** Canada
28B2 **Nanam** N Korea
34D1 **Nanango** Australia
29D3 **Nanao** Japan
29C3 **Nanatsu-jima** *I* Japan
31B3 **Nanbu** China
31D4 **Nanchang** China
31B3 **Nanchong** China
44E4 **Nancowry** *I* Nicobar Is, Indian Ocean
14D2 **Nancy** France
43E2 **Nanda Devi** *Mt* India
44B2 **Nānded** India
34D2 **Nandewar Range** *Mts* Australia
42C4 **Nandurbār** India
44B2 **Nandyāl** India
50B3 **Nanga Eboko** Cameroon
42C1 **Nanga Parbat** *Mt* Pakistan
27E7 **Nangapinon** Indonesia
13B3 **Nangis** France
28A2 **Nangnim** N Korea
28B2 **Nangnim Sanmaek** *Mts* N Korea
43G3 **Nang Xian** China
44B3 **Nanjangūd** India
31D3 **Nanjing** China
Nanking = Nanjing
29B4 **Nankoku** Japan
31C4 **Nan Ling** *Region* China
30D1 **Nanliu** *R* China
31B5 **Nanning** China
55O3 **Nanortalik** Greenland
31A5 **Nanpan Jiang** *R* China
43E3 **Nānpāra** India
31D4 **Nanping** China
28B2 **Nanping** China
55J1 **Nansen Sd** Canada
27E5 **Nanshan** *I* S China Sea
50D4 **Nansio** Tanzania
14B2 **Nantes** France
68C2 **Nanticoke** USA
31E3 **Nantong** China
68E2 **Nantucket** USA
68E2 **Nantucket I** USA
68E2 **Nantucket Sd** USA
7C3 **Nantwich** England
33G1 **Nanumanga** *I* Tuvalu
33G1 **Nanumea** *I* Tuvalu
75D2 **Nanuque** Brazil
31C3 **Nanyang** China
31D2 **Nanyang Hu** *L* China
50D3 **Nanyuki** Kenya
28A2 **Nanzamu** China
15C2 **Nao, Cabo de la** *C* Spain
29D3 **Naoetsu** Japan
42B4 **Naokot** Pakistan
66A1 **Napa** USA
65D2 **Napanee** Canada
24K4 **Napas** Russian Federation
55N3 **Napassoq** Greenland
30D2 **Nape** Laos
35C1 **Napier** New Zealand
67B3 **Naples** Florida, USA
16C2 **Naples** Italy
68B1 **Naples** New York, USA
63D2 **Naples** Texas, USA
31B5 **Napo** China
72D4 **Napo** *R* Ecuador/Peru
60D1 **Napoleon** USA
Napoli = Naples
41E2 **Naqadeh** Iran
45C3 **Naqb Ishtar** Jordan
29C4 **Nara** Japan
48B3 **Nara** Mali
32D4 **Naracoorte** Australia
44B2 **Narasarāopet** India
30C4 **Narathiwat** Thailand
43G4 **Narayanganj** Bangladesh
44B2 **Nārāyenpet** India
14C3 **Narbonne** France
30A3 **Narcondam** *I* Indian Ocean
42D2 **Narendranagar** India
55L2 **Nares Str** Canada
19E2 **Narew** *R* Poland
28B2 **Narhong** China
29D3 **Narita** Japan
42C4 **Narmada** *R* India
42D3 **Nārnaul** India
20F4 **Naro Fominsk** Russian Federation
50D4 **Narok** Kenya
19F2 **Narovl'a** Belarus
42C2 **Narowal** Pakistan
32D4 **Narrabri** Australia
34C1 **Narran** *R* Australia
34C2 **Narrandera** Australia
34C1 **Narran L** Australia
32A4 **Narrogin** Australia
34C2 **Narromine** Australia
64C3 **Narrows** USA
68C2 **Narrowsburg** USA
42D4 **Narsimhapur** India
44C2 **Narsīpatnam** India
55O3 **Narssalik** Greenland
55O3 **Narssaq** Greenland
55O3 **Narssarssuaq** Greenland
47B2 **Narubis** Namibia
29D3 **Narugo** Japan
29B4 **Naruto** Japan
20D4 **Narva** Russian Federation
12H5 **Narvik** Norway
42D3 **Narwāna** India
20J2 **Nar'yan Mar** Russian Federation
34B1 **Narylico** Australia
24J5 **Naryn** Kirgizia
48C4 **Nasarawa** Nigeria
52D6 **Nasca Ridge** Pacific Ocean
68E1 **Nashua** USA
63D2 **Nashville** Arkansas, USA
67A1 **Nashville** Tennessee, USA
17D1 **Našice** Croatia
42C4 **Nāsik** India
50D3 **Nasir** Sudan
69B1 **Nassau** The Bahamas
68D1 **Nassau** USA
49F2 **Nasser,L** Egypt
12G7 **Nässjö** Sweden
55L4 **Nastapoka Is** Canada
51C6 **Nata** Botswana
73L5 **Natal** Brazil
27C6 **Natal** Indonesia
36C6 **Natal Basin** Indian Ocean
41F3 **Natanz** Iran
55M4 **Natashquan** Canada
55M4 **Natashquan** *R* Canada
63D2 **Natchez** USA
63D2 **Natchitoches** USA
34C3 **Nathalia** Australia
55Q2 **Nathorsts Land** *Region* Greenland
59C4 **National City** USA
29D3 **Natori** Japan
50D4 **Natron, L** Tanzania
40A3 **Natrun, Wadi el** *Watercourse* Egypt
32A4 **Naturaliste,C** Australia
18C2 **Nauen** Germany
68D2 **Naugatuck** USA
18C2 **Naumburg** Germany
45C3 **Naur** Jordan
33F1 **Nauru** *I, Republic* Pacific Ocean
25M4 **Naushki** Russian Federation
47B2 **Naute Dam** *Res* Namibia
56C3 **Navajo Res** USA
15A2 **Navalmoral de la Mata** Spain
25T3 **Navarin, Mys** *C* Russian Federation
74C9 **Navarino** *I* Chile
15B1 **Navarra** *Province* Spain
63C2 **Navasota** USA
63C2 **Navasota** *R* USA
8C2 **Naver, L** Scotland
15A1 **Navia** *R* Spain
42C4 **Navlakhi** India
21E5 **Navlya** Russian Federation
70B2 **Navojoa** Mexico
17E3 **Návpaktos** Greece
17E3 **Návplion** Greece
42C4 **Navsāri** India
45D2 **Nawá** Syria
42B3 **Nawabshah** Pakistan
43F4 **Nawāda** India
42B2 **Nawah** Afghanistan
31B4 **Naxi** China
17F3 **Náxos** *I* Greece
41F4 **Nāy Band** Iran
41G3 **Nāy Band** Iran
29E2 **Nayoro** Japan
75E1 **Nazaré** Brazil
45C2 **Nazareth** Israel
72D6 **Nazca** Peru
40A2 **Nazilli** Turkey
25L4 **Nazimovo** Russian Federation
50D3 **Nazrēt** Ethiopia
41G5 **Nazwa'** Oman
24J4 **Nazyvayevsk** Russian Federation
51B4 **Ndalatando** Angola
50C3 **Ndélé** Central African Republic
50B4 **Ndendé** Gabon
33F2 **Ndende** *I* Solomon Islands
50B2 **Ndjamena** Chad
50B4 **Ndjolé** Gabon
51C5 **Ndola** Zambia
34C1 **Neabul** Australia
10B3 **Neagh, Lough** *L* Northern Ireland
17E3 **Neápolis** Greece
7C4 **Neath** Wales
34C1 **Nebine** *R* Australia
24G6 **Nebit Dag** Turkmenistan
56C2 **Nebraska** *State* USA
61D2 **Nebraska City** USA
16C3 **Nebrodi, Monti** *Mts* Sicily, Italy
63C2 **Neches** *R* USA
74E5 **Necochea** Argentina
43G3 **Nêdong** China
7E3 **Needham Market** England
59D4 **Needles** USA
7D4 **Needles** *Pt* England
64B2 **Neenah** USA
54J4 **Neepawa** Canada
13C2 **Neerpelt** Belgium
25M4 **Neftelensk** Russian Federation
50D3 **Negelē** Ethiopia
45C3 **Negev** *Desert* Israel
75A3 **Negla** *R* Paraguay
21C6 **Negolu** *Mt* Romania
44B4 **Negombo** Sri Lanka
30A2 **Negrais,C** Burma
72B4 **Negritos** Peru
72F4 **Negro** *R* Amazonas, Brazil
74D5 **Negro** *R* Argentina
74F4 **Negro** *R* Brazil/Uruguay
75A2 **Negro** *R* Mato Grosso do Sul, Brazil
75A3 **Negro** *R* Paraguay
15A2 **Negro, Cap** *C* Morocco
27F6 **Negros** *I* Philippines
17F2 **Negru Vodă** Romania
31B4 **Neijiang** China
64A2 **Neillsville** USA
Nei Monggol Zizhiqu = Inner Mongolia Aut. Region
72C3 **Neiva** Colombia
50D3 **Nejo** Ethiopia
50D3 **Nek'emte** Ethiopia
20E4 **Nelidovo** Russian Federation
61D2 **Neligh** USA
44B3 **Nellore** India
26G2 **Nel'ma** Russian Federation
54G5 **Nelson** Canada
6C3 **Nelson** England
35B2 **Nelson** New Zealand
34B3 **Nelson,C** Australia
47E2 **Nelspruit** South Africa
48B3 **Néma** Mauritius
31A1 **Nemagt Uul** *Mt* Mongolia
16B3 **Nementcha, Mts Des** Algeria
17F1 **Nemira** *Mt* Romania
13B3 **Nemours** France
19E1 **Nemunas** *R* Lithuania
29F2 **Nemuro** Japan
29F2 **Nemuro-kaikyō** *Str* Japan/Russian Federation
25O5 **Nen** *R* China
10B3 **Nenagh** Irish Republic
54D3 **Nenana** USA
7D3 **Nene** *R* England
26F2 **Nenjiang** China
63C1 **Neodesha** USA
63D1 **Neosho** USA
25M4 **Nepa** Russian Federation
39G3 **Nepal** *Kingdom* Asia
43E3 **Nepalganj** Nepal
59D3 **Nephi** USA
45C3 **Neqarot** *R* Israel
26E1 **Nerchinsk** Russian Federation
17D2 **Neretva** *R* Bosnia-Herzegovina/Croatia
27H5 **Nero Deep** Pacific Ocean
20G2 **Nes'** Russian Federation
12C1 **Neskaupstaður** Iceland
13B3 **Nesle** France
62C1 **Ness City** USA
8C3 **Ness, Loch** *L* Scotland
17E2 **Néstos** *R* Greece
45C2 **Netanya** Israel
68C2 **Netcong** USA
18B2 **Netherlands** *Kingdom* Europe
53M7 **Netherlands Antilles** *Is* Caribbean Sea
43G4 **Netrakona** Bangladesh
55L3 **Nettilling L** Canada
18C2 **Neubrandenburg** Germany
16B1 **Neuchâtel** Switzerland
13C3 **Neufchâteau** Belgium

13C3 **Neufchâteau** France
14C2 **Neufchâtel** France
18B2 **Neumünster** Germany
16D1 **Neunkirchen** Austria
13D3 **Neunkirchen** Germany
74C5 **Neuquén** Argentina
74C5 **Neuquén** *R* Argentina
74B5 **Neuquén** *State* Argentina
18C2 **Neuruppin** Germany
67C1 **Neuse** *R* USA
13D2 **Neuss** Germany
18C2 **Neustadt** Germany
13E3 **Neustadt an der Weinstrasse** Germany
13E1 **Neustadt a R** Germany
13E4 **Neustadt im Schwarzwald** Germany
18C2 **Neustrelitz** Germany
13E1 **Neuwerk** *I* Germany
13D2 **Neuwied** Germany
63D1 **Nevada** USA
56B3 **Nevada** *State* USA
15B2 **Nevada, Sierra** *Mts* Spain
45C3 **Nevatim** Israel
20D4 **Nevel'** Russian Federation
14C2 **Nevers** France
34C2 **Nevertire** Australia
Nevis = St Kitts-Nevis
40B2 **Nevşehir** Turkey
20L4 **Nev'yansk** Russian Federation
64C3 **New** *R* USA
51D5 **Newala** Tanzania
64B3 **New Albany** Indiana, USA
63E2 **New Albany** Mississippi, USA
73G2 **New Amsterdam** Guyana
34C1 **New Angledool** Australia
65D3 **Newark** Delaware, USA
57F2 **Newark** New Jersey, USA
68B1 **Newark** New York, USA
64C2 **Newark** Ohio, USA
7D3 **Newark-upon-Trent** England
65E2 **New Bedford** USA
58B1 **Newberg** USA
67C1 **New Bern** USA
67B2 **Newberry** USA
47C3 **New Bethesda** South Africa
69B2 **New Bight** The Bahamas
64C3 **New Boston** USA
62C3 **New Braunfels** USA
68D2 **New Britain** USA
32E1 **New Britain** *I* Papua New Guinea
32E1 **New Britain Trench** Papua New Guinea
68C2 **New Brunswick** USA
55M5 **New Brunswick** *Province* Canada
68C2 **Newburgh** USA
7D4 **Newbury** England
68E1 **Newburyport** USA
33F3 **New Caledonia** *I* SW Pacific Ocean
68D2 **New Canaan** USA
34D2 **Newcastle** Australia
64B3 **New Castle** Indiana, USA
9D2 **Newcastle** Northern Ireland
64C2 **New Castle** Pennsylvania, USA
47D2 **Newcastle** South Africa
60C2 **Newcastle** Wyoming, USA
8D4 **New Castleton** Scotland
7C3 **Newcastle under Lyme** England
6D2 **Newcastle upon Tyne** England
32C2 **Newcastle Waters** Australia
66C3 **New Cuyama** USA
42D3 **New Delhi** India
34D2 **New England Range** *Mts* Australia
68A1 **Newfane** USA
7D4 **New Forest,The** England
55N5 **Newfoundland** *I* Canada
55M4 **Newfoundland** *Province* Canada
52F2 **Newfoundland Basin** Atlantic Ocean
61E3 **New Franklin** USA
8C4 **New Galloway** Scotland
33E1 **New Georgia** *I* Solomon Islands
55M5 **New Glasgow** Canada
32D1 **New Guinea** *I* SE Asia
66C3 **Newhall** USA
57F2 **New Hampshire** *State* USA
61E2 **New Hampton** USA
47E2 **New Hanover** South Africa
32E1 **New Hanover** *I* Papua New Guinea
7E4 **Newhaven** England
65E2 **New Haven** USA
33F3 **New Hebrides Trench** Pacific Ocean
63D2 **New Iberia** USA
32E1 **New Ireland** *I* Papua New Guinea
57F2 **New Jersey** *State* USA
62B2 **Newkirk** USA
55L5 **New Liskeard** Canada
68D2 **New London** USA
32A3 **Newman** Australia
66B2 **Newman** USA
7E3 **Newmarket** England
65D3 **New Market** USA
58C2 **New Meadows** USA
56C3 **New Mexico** *State* USA
68D2 **New Milford** Connecticut, USA
68C2 **New Milford** Pennsylvania, USA
67B2 **Newnan** USA
34C4 **New Norfolk** Australia
57D3 **New Orleans** USA
68C2 **New Paltz** USA
64C2 **New Philadelphia** USA
35B1 **New Plymouth** New Zealand
63D1 **Newport** Arkansas, USA
7D4 **Newport** England
64C3 **Newport** Kentucky, USA
68D1 **Newport** New Hampshire, USA
58B2 **Newport** Oregon, USA
68B2 **Newport** Pennsylvania, USA
65E2 **Newport** Rhode Island, USA
65E2 **Newport** Vermont, USA
7C4 **Newport** Wales
58C1 **Newport** Washington, USA
66D4 **Newport Beach** USA
57F3 **Newport News** USA
69B1 **New Providence** *I* The Bahamas
7B4 **Newquay** England
7B3 **New Quay** Wales
55L3 **New Quebec Crater** Canada
7C3 **New Radnor** Wales
7E4 **New Romney** England
9C3 **New Ross** Irish Republic
9C2 **Newry** Northern Ireland
New Siberian Is = Novosibirskye Ostrova
67B3 **New Smyrna Beach** USA
32D4 **New South Wales** *State* Australia
61E2 **Newton** Iowa, USA
63C1 **Newton** Kansas, USA
68E1 **Newton** Massachusetts, USA
63E2 **Newton** Mississippi, USA
68C2 **Newton** New Jersey, USA
9D2 **Newtonabbey** Northern Ireland
7C4 **Newton Abbot** England
9C2 **Newton Stewart** Northern Ireland
8C4 **Newton Stewart** Scotland
60C1 **New Town** USA
7C3 **Newtown** Wales
9D2 **Newtownards** Northern Ireland
61E2 **New Ulm** USA
68B2 **Newville** USA
54F5 **New Westminster** Canada
57F2 **New York** USA
57F2 **New York** *State* USA
33G5 **New Zealand** *Dominion* SW Pacific Ocean
37K7 **New Zealand Plat** Pacific Ocean
20G4 **Neya** Russian Federation
41F4 **Neyrīz** Iran
41G2 **Neyshābūr** Iran
21E5 **Nezhin** Ukraine
50B4 **Ngabé** Congo
51C6 **Ngami, L** Botswana
49D4 **Ngaoundéré** Cameroon
30A1 **Ngape** Burma
35C1 **Ngaruawahia** New Zealand
35C1 **Ngaruroro** *R* New Zealand
35C1 **Ngauruhoe,Mt** New Zealand
50B4 **Ngo** Congo
30D2 **Ngoc Linh** *Mt* Vietnam
50B3 **Ngoko** *R* Cameroon/Central African Republic/Congo
26C3 **Ngoring Hu** *L* China
50D4 **Ngorongoro Crater** Tanzania
50B4 **N'Gounié** *R* Gabon
50B2 **Nguigmi** Niger
27G6 **Ngulu** *I* Pacific Ocean
48D3 **Nguru** Nigeria
30D3 **Nha Trang** Vietnam
75A2 **Nhecolândia** Brazil
34B3 **Nhill** Australia
47E2 **Nhlangano** Swaziland
30D2 **Nhommarath** Laos
32C2 **Nhulunbuy** Australia
48B3 **Niafounké** Mali
64B1 **Niagara** USA
65D2 **Niagara Falls** Canada
65D2 **Niagara Falls** USA
27E6 **Niah** Malaysia
48B4 **Niakaramandougou** Ivory Coast
48C3 **Niamey** Niger
50C3 **Niangara** Zaïre
50C3 **Nia Nia** Zaïre
27E6 **Niapa** *Mt* Indonesia
27C6 **Nias** *I* Indonesia
70D3 **Nicaragua** *Republic* Central America
70D3 **Nicaragua, L de** Nicaragua
16D3 **Nicastro** Italy
14D3 **Nice** France
69B1 **Nicholl's Town** The Bahamas
68C2 **Nicholson** USA
39H5 **Nicobar Is** India
45B1 **Nicosia** Cyprus
72A2 **Nicoya, Golfo de** Costa Rica
70D3 **Nicoya,Pen de** Costa Rica
6D2 **Nidd** *R* England
13E2 **Nidda** *R* Germany
19E2 **Nidzica** Poland
13D3 **Niederbronn** France
18B2 **Niedersachsen** *State* Germany
50C4 **Niemba** Zaïre
18B2 **Nienburg** Germany
13D2 **Niers** *R* Germany
48B4 **Niete,Mt** Liberia
73G2 **Nieuw Amsterdam** Surinam
73G2 **Nieuw Nickerie** Surinam
47B3 **Nieuwoudtville** South Africa
13B2 **Nieuwpoort** Belgium
40B2 **Niğde** Turkey
48B3 **Niger** *R* W Africa
48C3 **Niger** *Republic* Africa
48C4 **Nigeria** *Federal Republic* Africa
48C4 **Niger, Mouths of the** Nigeria
43L1 **Nighasan** India
64C1 **Nighthawk L** Canada
17E2 **Nigríta** Greece
29D3 **Nihommatsu** Japan
29D3 **Niigata** Japan
29C4 **Niihama** Japan
29C4 **Nii-jima** *I* Japan
29B4 **Niimi** Japan
29D3 **Niitsu** Japan
45C3 **Nijil** Jordan
18B2 **Nijmegen** Netherlands
20E2 **Nikel'** Russian Federation
48C4 **Nikki** Benin
29D3 **Nikko** Japan
21E6 **Nikolayev** Ukraine
21H6 **Nikolayevsk** Russian Federation
25Q4 **Nikolayevsk-na-Amure** Russian Federation
20H5 **Nikol'sk** Penza, Russian Federation
20H4 **Nikol'sk** Russian Federation
21E6 **Nikopol** Ukraine
40C1 **Niksar** Turkey
17D2 **Nikšić** Montenegro, Yugoslavia
33G1 **Nikunau** *I* Kiribati
27F7 **Nila** *I* Indonesia
38B3 **Nile** *R* NE Africa
64B2 **Niles** USA
44B3 **Nilgiri Hills** India
42C4 **Nimach** India
14C3 **Nîmes** France
34C3 **Nimmitabel** Australia
50D3 **Nimule** Sudan
39F5 **Nine Degree Chan** Indian Ocean
36F5 **Ninety-East Ridge** Indian Ocean
34C3 **Ninety Mile Beach** Australia
31D4 **Ningde** China
31D4 **Ningdu** China
26C3 **Ningjing Shan** *Mts* China
30D1 **Ningming** China
31A4 **Ningnan** China
31B2 **Ningxia** *Province* China
31B2 **Ning Xian** China
31B5 **Ninh Binh** Vietnam
32D1 **Ninigo Is** Papua New Guinea
75A3 **Nioaque** Brazil
60C2 **Niobrara** *R* USA
50B4 **Nioki** Zaïre
48B3 **Nioro du Sahel** Mali
14B2 **Niort** France
54H4 **Nipawin** Canada
55K5 **Nipigon** Canada
64B1 **Nipigon B** Canada
55K5 **Nipigon,L** Canada
64C1 **Nipissing,L** Canada
66B3 **Nipomo** USA
59C3 **Nipton** USA
75C1 **Niquelândia** Brazil
44B2 **Nirmal** India
43F3 **Nirmāli** India
17E2 **Niš** Serbia, Yugoslavia
38C4 **Nişāb** Yemen
26H4 **Nishino-shima** *I* Japan
28C3 **Nishino-shima** *I* Japan
28A4 **Nishi-suidō** *Str* S Korea
29B4 **Nishiwaki** Japan
33E1 **Nissan Is** Papua New Guinea
55L4 **Nitchequon** Canada
73K8 **Niterói** Brazil
8D4 **Nith** *R* Scotland
19D3 **Nitra** Slovakia
64C3 **Nitro** USA
33J2 **Niue** *I* Pacific Ocean
33G2 **Niulakita** *I* Tuvalu
27E6 **Niut** *Mt* Indonesia
33G1 **Niutao** *I* Tuvalu
28A2 **Niuzhuang** China
13C2 **Nivelles** Belgium
14C2 **Nivernais** *Region* France
12L5 **Nivskiy** Russian Federation
44B2 **Nizāmābād** India
45C3 **Nizana** *Hist Site* Israel
26C1 **Nizhneudinsk** Russian Federation
20K4 **Nizhniye Sergi** Russian Federation
20G5 **Nizhniy Lomov** Russian Federation
20G4 **Nizhiny Novgorod** Russian Federation
20J3 **Nizhniy Odes** Russian Federation
20K4 **Nizhniy Tagil** Russian Federation
25L3 **Nizhnyaya Tunguska** *R* Russian Federation
20G2 **Nizhnyaya Zolotitsa** Russian Federation
40C2 **Nizip** Turkey
12C1 **Njarðvik** Iceland
51C5 **Njoko** *R* Zambia
51D4 **Njombe** Tanzania
50B3 **Nkambé** Cameroon
51D5 **Nkhata Bay** Malawi
50B3 **Nkongsamba** Cameroon
48C3 **N'Konni** Niger
43G4 **Noakhali** Bangladesh
54B3 **Noatak** USA
54B3 **Noatak** *R* USA
28C4 **Nobeoka** Japan
29D2 **Noboribetsu** Japan
75A1 **Nobres** Brazil
63C2 **Nocona** USA
70A1 **Nogales** Sonora, Mexico
59D4 **Nogales** USA
28B4 **Nogata** Japan
13C3 **Nogent-en-Bassigny** France
13B3 **Nogent-sur-Seine** France
20F4 **Noginsk** Russian Federation
42C3 **Nohar** India
29D2 **Noheji** Japan
14B2 **Noirmoutier, Ile de** *I* France
47C1 **Nojane** Botswana
29C4 **Nojima-zaki** *C* Japan
50B3 **Nola** Central African Republic
20H4 **Nolinsk** Russian Federation
68E2 **Nomans Land** *I* USA
54B3 **Nome** USA
13D3 **Nomeny** France
31B1 **Nomgon** Mongolia
28A4 **Nomo-saki** *Pt* Japan
54H3 **Nonacho L** Canada
30C2 **Nong Khai** Thailand
47E2 **Nongoma** South Africa
33G1 **Nonouti** *I* Kiribati
28A3 **Nonsan** S Korea
13C1 **Noord Holland** *Province* Netherlands
47B2 **Noordoewer** Namibia
13C1 **Noordoost Polder** Netherlands
13C1 **Noordzeekanal** Netherlands
54B3 **Noorvik** USA
50B4 **Noqui** Angola
55L5 **Noranda** Canada
13B2 **Nord** *Department* France
24D2 **Nordaustlandet** *I* Svalbard
13D1 **Norden** Germany
13E1 **Nordenham** Germany
13D1 **Norderney** *I* Germany
12F6 **Nordfjord** *Inlet* Norway
12F8 **Nordfriesische** *Is* Germany
18C2 **Nordhausen** Germany
13D1 **Nordhorn** Germany
18B2 **Nordrhein Westfalen** *State* Germany
12J4 **Nordkapp** *C* Norway
55N3 **Nordre Strømfyord** *Fyord* Greenland
12G5 **Nord Storfjället** *Mt* Sweden
25N2 **Nordvik** Russian Federation
9C3 **Nore** *R* Irish Republic
61D2 **Norfolk** Nebraska, USA
65D3 **Norfolk** Virginia, USA
7E3 **Norfolk** *County* England
33F3 **Norfolk I** Pacific Ocean
37K6 **Norfolk I Ridge** Pacific Ocean
63D1 **Norfolk L** USA
25K3 **Noril'sk** Russian Federation
64B2 **Normal** USA
63C1 **Norman** USA
14B2 **Normandie** *Region* France
67B1 **Norman,L** USA
32D2 **Normanton** Australia
54F3 **Norman Wells** Canada
20B2 **Norra Storfjället** *Mt* Sweden
67B1 **Norris L** USA
65D2 **Norristown** USA
12H7 **Norrköping** Sweden
12H6 **Norrsundet** Sweden
12H7 **Norrtälje** Sweden
32B4 **Norseman** Australia
26F1 **Norsk** Russian Federation
75A1 **Nortelândia** Brazil
6D2 **Northallerton** England
32A4 **Northam** Australia
47D2 **Northam** South Africa
52E3 **North American Basin** Atlantic Ocean
32A3 **Northampton** Australia
7D3 **Northampton** England
65E2 **Northampton** USA
7D3 **Northampton** *County* England
44E3 **North Andaman** *I* Indian Ocean
54G3 **North Arm** *B* Canada
67B2 **North Augusta** USA
55M4 **North Aulatsivik** *I* Canada
54H4 **North Battleford** Canada
55L5 **North Bay** Canada
58B2 **North Bend** USA
8D3 **North Berwick** Scotland
68E1 **North Berwick** USA
55M5 **North,C** Canada
62B1 **North Canadian** *R* USA
57E3 **North Carolina** *State* USA
58B1 **North Cascades Nat Pk** USA
64C1 **North Chan** Canada
6B2 **North Chan** Ire/Scotland
56C2 **North Dakota** *State* USA
7E4 **North Downs** England
65D2 **North East** USA
52H2 **North East Atlantic Basin** Atlantic Ocean
54B3 **Northeast C** USA
51C6 **Northern Cape** *Province* South Africa
10B3 **Northern Ireland** UK
61E1 **Northern Light L** Canada/USA
27H5 **Northern Mariana Is** Pacific Ocean
69L1 **Northern Range** *Mts* Trinidad
32C2 **Northern Territory** Australia
51C6 **Northern Transvaal** *Province* South Africa
8D3 **North Esk** *R* Scotland
68D1 **Northfield** Massachusetts, USA
61E2 **Northfield** Minnesota, USA
7E4 **North Foreland** England
35B1 **North I** New Zealand
28B3 **North Korea** *Republic* SE Asia
North Land = Severnaya Zemlya
63D2 **North Little Rock** USA
60C2 **North Loup** *R* USA
76B4 **North Magnetic Pole** Canada
67B3 **North Miami** USA
67B3 **North Miami Beach** USA
66C2 **North Palisade** *Mt* USA
60C2 **North Platte** USA
56C2 **North Platte** *R* USA
76A **North Pole** Arctic
69R3 **North Pt** Barbados
64C1 **North Pt** USA
61E2 **North Raccoon** *R* USA
10B2 **North Rona** *I* Scotland
8D2 **North Ronaldsay** *I* Scotland
52F7 **North Scotia Ridge** Atlantic Ocean
10D2 **North Sea** NW Europe
44E3 **North Sentinel** *I* Andaman Islands
54D3 **North Slope** *Region* USA

34D1 **North Stradbroke I** Australia
68B1 **North Syracuse** USA
35B1 **North Taranaki Bight** *B* New Zealand
68A1 **North Tonawanda** USA
56C3 **North Truchas Peak** *Mt* USA
8B3 **North Uist** *I* Scotland
6C2 **Northumberland** *County* England
32E3 **Northumberland Is** Australia
55M5 **Northumberland Str** Canada
58B1 **North Vancouver** Canada
68C1 **Northville** USA
7E3 **North Walsham** England
54D3 **Northway** USA
51C6 **North West** *Province* South Africa
32A3 **North West C** Australia
42C2 **North West Frontier Province** Pakistan
55M4 **North West River** Canada
54G3 **North West Territories** Canada
61D1 **Northwood** USA
6D2 **North York Moors** England
6D2 **North Yorkshire** *County* England
60D3 **Norton** *R* USA
54B3 **Norton Sd** USA
76F1 **Norvegia,C** Antarctica
68D2 **Norwalk** Connecticut, USA
64C2 **Norwalk** Ohio, USA
12F6 **Norway** *Kingdom* Europe
54J4 **Norway House** Canada
55J2 **Norwegian B** Canada
52H1 **Norwegian Basin** Norwegian Sea
24B3 **Norwegian S** NW Europe
68D2 **Norwich** Connecticut, USA
7E3 **Norwich** England
68C1 **Norwich** New York, USA
68E1 **Norwood** Massachusetts, USA
64C3 **Norwood** Ohio, USA
17F2 **Nos Emine** *C* Bulgaria
29E2 **Noshiro** Japan
17F2 **Nos Kaliakra** *C* Bulgaria
47B1 **Nosob** *R* Namibia
20J2 **Nosovaya** Russian Federation
19G2 **Nosovka** Ukraine
8E1 **Noss** *I* Scotland
8D2 **Noss Head, Pt** Scotland
51E5 **Nosy Barren** *I* Madagascar
51E5 **Nosy Bé** *I* Madagascar
51F5 **Nosy Boraha** *I* Madagascar
51E6 **Nosy Varika** Madagascar
18D2 **Notéc** *R* Poland
54G4 **Notikewin** Canada
16D3 **Noto** Italy
12F7 **Notodden** Norway
29C3 **Noto-hantō** *Pen* Japan
55N5 **Notre Dame B** Canada
48C4 **Notsé** Togo
7D3 **Nottingham** England
7D3 **Nottingham** *County* England
55L3 **Nottingham** Canada
55L3 **Nottingham Island** Canada
48A2 **Nouadhibou** Mauritius
48A3 **Nouakchott** Mauritius
33F3 **Nouméa** New Caledonia
48B3 **Nouna** Burkina
8D2 **Noup Head, Pt** Scotland
47C3 **Noupoort** South Africa
55L3 **Nouvelle-France, Cap de** *C* Canada
75C2 **Nova América** Brazil
51B4 **Nova Caipemba** Angola
75B3 **Nova Esparança** Brazil
75D3 **Nova Friburgo** Brazil
51B5 **Nova Gaia** Angola
75C3 **Nova Granada** Brazil
75C3 **Nova Horizonte** Brazil
75D3 **Nova Lima** Brazil
Nova Lisboa = Huambo
75B3 **Nova Londrina** Brazil
51D6 **Nova Mambone** Mozambique
16B1 **Novara** Italy
75C1 **Nova Roma** Brazil
73K4 **Nova Russas** Brazil
55M5 **Nova Scotia** *Province* Canada
66A1 **Novato** USA
75D2 **Nova Venécia** Brazil
21E6 **Novaya Kakhovka** Ukraine
25R2 **Novaya Sibir, Ostrov** *I* Russian Federation
24G2 **Novaya Zemlya** *I* Russian Federation
17F2 **Nova Zagora** Bulgaria
19D3 **Nové Zámky** Slovakia
20E4 **Novgorod** Russian Federation
16B2 **Novi Ligure** Italy
17F2 **Novi Pazar** Bulgaria
17E2 **Novi Pazar** Serbia, Yugoslavia
17D1 **Novi Sad** Serbia, Yugoslavia
21K5 **Novoalekseyevka** Kazakhstan
21G5 **Novoanninskiy** Russian Federation
21F6 **Novocherkassk** Russian Federation
20G3 **Novodvinsk** Russian Federation
21D5 **Novograd Volynskiy** Ukraine
19F2 **Novogrudok** Belarus
74F3 **Novo Hamburgo** Brazil
24H5 **Novokazalinsk** Kazakhstan
24K4 **Novokuznetsk** Russian Federation
76F12 **Novolazarevskaya** *Base* Antarctica
16D1 **Novo Mesto** Slovenia
19G3 **Novomirgorod** Ukraine
20F5 **Novomoskovsk** Russian Federation
Novo Redondo = Sumbe
21F7 **Novorossiysk** Russian Federation
25M2 **Novorybnoye** Russian Federation
24K4 **Novosibirsk** Russian Federation
25P2 **Novosibirskye Ostrova** *Is* Russian Federation
21K5 **Novotroitsk** Russian Federation
21H5 **Novo Uzensk** Russian Federation
19E2 **Novovolynsk** Ukraine
20H4 **Novo Vyatsk** Russian Federation
21E5 **Novozybkov** Russian Federation
24J3 **Novvy Port** Russian Federation
19E2 **Novy Dwór Mazowiecki** Poland
20L4 **Novyy Lyalya** Russian Federation
20N2 **Novyy Port** Russian Federation
21J7 **Novyy Uzen** Kazakhstan
18D2 **Nowa Sól** Poland
63C1 **Nowata** USA
43G3 **Nowgong** India
34D2 **Nowra** Australia
41F2 **Now Shahr** Iran
42C2 **Nowshera** Pakistan
19E3 **Nowy Sącz** Poland
13B3 **Noyon** France
14B2 **Nozay** France
48B4 **Nsawam** Ghana
47E1 **Nuanetsi** Zimbabwe
50D2 **Nuba Mts** Sudan
50D1 **Nubian Desert** Sudan
56D4 **Nueces** *R* USA
54J3 **Nueltin L** Canada
28A2 **Nü'erhe** China
70B1 **Nueva Casas Grandes** Mexico
75A3 **Nueva Germania** Paraguay
69A2 **Nueva Gerona** Cuba
70B2 **Nueva Rosita** Mexico
69B2 **Nuevitas** Cuba
70B1 **Nuevo Casas Grandes** Mexico
70C2 **Nuevo Laredo** Mexico
50E3 **Nugaal** *Region* Somalia
55N2 **Nûgâtsiaq** Greenland
55N2 **Nûgussuaq** *I* Greenland
55N2 **Nûgussuaq** *Pen* Greenland
33G1 **Nui** *I* Tuvalu
31A5 **Nui Con Voi** *R* Vietnam
13C4 **Nuits** France
40D3 **Nukhayb** Iraq
33G1 **Nukufetau** *I* Tuvalu
33G1 **Nukulaelae** *I* Tuvalu
33H1 **Nukunon** *I* Tokelau Islands
24G5 **Nukus** Uzbekistan
54C3 **Nulato** USA
32B4 **Nullarbor Plain** Australia
48D4 **Numan** Nigeria
29C3 **Numata** Japan
50C3 **Numatinna** *R* Sudan
29D3 **Numazu** Japan
27G7 **Numfoor** *I* Indonesia
34C3 **Numurkah** Australia
68A1 **Nunda** USA
7D3 **Nuneaton** England
42D2 **Nunkun** *Mt* India
16B2 **Nuoro** Sicily, Italy
41F3 **Nurābād** Iran
34A2 **Nuriootpa** Australia
42C1 **Nuristan** *Region* Afghanistan
20J5 **Nurlat** Russian Federation
12K6 **Nurmes** Finland
18C3 **Nürnberg** Germany
34C2 **Nurri,Mt** Australia
40D2 **Nusaybin** Turkey
45D1 **Nuşayrīyah, Jabalan** *Mts* Syria
42B3 **Nushki** Pakistan
55M4 **Nutak** Canada
Nuuk = Godthåb
43E3 **Nuwakot** Nepal
44C4 **Nuwara-Eliya** Sri Lanka
47C3 **Nuweveldreeks** *Mts* South Africa
55L3 **Nuyukjuak** Canada
54C3 **Nyac** USA
68D2 **Nyack** USA
50D3 **Nyahururu Falls** Kenya
34B3 **Nyah West** Australia
26C3 **Nyainqentanglha Shan** *Mts* Tibet, China
50D4 **Nyakabindi** Tanzania
20L3 **Nyaksimvol'** Russian Federation
50C2 **Nyala** Sudan
43F3 **Nyalam** China
50C3 **Nyamlell** Sudan
51D6 **Nyanda** Zimbabwe
20G3 **Nyandoma** Russian Federation
50B4 **Nyanga** *R* Gabon
51D5 **Nyasa, L** Malawi/Mozambique
30B2 **Nyaunglebin** Burma
20K4 **Nyazepetrovsk** Russian Federation
12G7 **Nyborg** Denmark
12H7 **Nybro** Sweden
24J3 **Nyda** Russian Federation
55M1 **Nyeboes Land** *Region* Canada
50D4 **Nyeri** Kenya
51D5 **Nyimba** Zambia
39H2 **Nyingchi** China
19E3 **Nyíregyháza** Hungary
50D3 **Nyiru,Mt** Kenya
12J6 **Nykarleby** Finland
12F7 **Nykøbing** Denmark
12G8 **Nykøbing** Denmark
12H7 **Nyköping** Sweden
47D1 **Nyl** *R* South Africa
47D1 **Nylstroom** South Africa
34C2 **Nymagee** Australia
12H7 **Nynäshamn** Sweden
34C2 **Nyngan** Australia
50B3 **Nyong** *R* Cameroon
28A3 **Nyongwol** S Korea
28A3 **Nyongwon** N Korea
14D3 **Nyons** France
18D2 **Nysa** Poland
58C2 **Nyssa** USA
20H3 **Nyukhcha** Russian Federation
26F1 **Nyukzha** *R* Russian Federation
25N3 **Nyurba** Russian Federation
50D4 **Nzega** Tanzania
48B4 **Nzérékoré** Guinea
51B4 **N'zeto** Angola

O

60D2 **Oacoma** USA
60C2 **Oahe,L** *Res* USA
66E5 **Oahu** *I* Hawaiian Islands
34B2 **Oakbank** Australia
66B2 **Oakdale** USA
61D1 **Oakes** USA
34D1 **Oakey** Australia
59B3 **Oakland** California, USA
61D2 **Oakland** Nebraska, USA
58B2 **Oakland** Oregon, USA
64B3 **Oakland City** USA
64B2 **Oak Lawn** USA
66B2 **Oakley** California, USA
60C3 **Oakley** Kansas, USA
67B1 **Oak Ridge** USA
58B2 **Oakridge** USA
65D2 **Oakville** Canada
35B3 **Oamaru** New Zealand
66D2 **Oasis** California, USA
58D2 **Oasis** Nevada, USA
76F7 **Oates Land** *Region* Antarctica
34C4 **Oatlands** Australia
70C3 **Oaxaca** Mexico
24H3 **Ob'** *R* Russian Federation
29C3 **Obama** Japan
35A3 **Oban** New Zealand
8C3 **Oban** Scotland
29D3 **Obanazawa** Japan
13D2 **Oberhausen** Germany
60C3 **Oberlin** USA
13E3 **Obernburg** Germany
27F7 **Obi** *I* Indonesia
73G4 **Obidos** Brazil
29E2 **Obihiro** Japan
26G2 **Obluch'ye** Russian Federation
50C3 **Obo** Central African Republic
50E2 **Obock** Djibouti
18D2 **Oborniki** Poland
21F5 **Oboyan'** Russian Federation
58B2 **O'Brien** USA
21J5 **Obshchiy Syrt** *Mts* Russian Federation
24J3 **Obskaya Guba** *B* Russian Federation
48B4 **Obuasi** Ghana
67B3 **Ocala** USA
72D2 **Ocaña** Colombia
15B2 **Ocaña** Spain
65D3 **Ocean City** Maryland, USA
68C3 **Ocean City** New Jersey, USA
54F4 **Ocean Falls** Canada
Ocean I = Banaba
66B3 **Oceano** USA
66D4 **Oceanside** USA
63E2 **Ocean Springs** USA
20J4 **Ocher** Russian Federation
8D3 **Ochil Hills** Scotland
67B2 **Ochlockonee** *R* USA
69H1 **Ocho Rios** Jamaica
67B2 **Ocmulgee** *R* USA
67B2 **Oconee** *R* USA
64B2 **Oconto** USA
70B2 **Ocotlán** Mexico
48B4 **Oda** Ghana
28B3 **Oda** Japan
12B2 **Ódáðahraun** *Region* Iceland
28A2 **Ŏdaejin** N Korea
50D1 **Oda, Jebel** *Mt* Sudan
29E2 **Odate** Japan
29D3 **Odawara** Japan
12F6 **Odda** Norway
48C4 **Ode** Nigeria
63C3 **Odem** USA
15A2 **Odemira** Portugal
17F3 **Ödemiş** Turkey
47D2 **Odendaalsrus** South Africa
12G7 **Odense** Denmark
18C2 **Oder** *R* Germany/Poland
62B2 **Odessa** Texas, USA
21E6 **Odessa** Ukraine
58C1 **Odessa** Washington, USA
48B4 **Odienné** Ivory Coast
Odra = Oder
19D2 **Odra** *R* Poland
73K5 **Oeiras** Brazil
60C2 **Oelrichs** USA
61E2 **Oelwein** USA
16D2 **Ofanto** *R* Italy
45C3 **Ofaqim** Israel
9C3 **Offaly** *County* Irish Republic
13E2 **Offenbach** Germany
13D3 **Offenburg** Germany
29D3 **Ofunato** Japan
29D3 **Oga** Japan
50E3 **Ogaden** *Region* Ethiopia
29D3 **Ōgaki** Japan
60C2 **Ogallala** USA
26H4 **Ogasawara Gunto** *Is* Japan
48C4 **Ogbomosho** Nigeria
61E2 **Ogden** Iowa, USA
58D2 **Ogden** Utah, USA
65D2 **Ogdensburg** USA
67B2 **Ogeechee** *R* USA
54E3 **Ogilvie Mts** Canada
67B2 **Oglethorpe,Mt** USA
48C4 **Ogoja** Nigeria
19E1 **Ogre** Latvia
48B2 **Oguilet Khenachich** *Well* Mali
16D1 **Ogulin** Croatia
68E1 **Ogunquit** USA
21J8 **Ogurchinskiy, Ostrov** *I* Turkmenistan
35A3 **Ohai** New Zealand
35C1 **Ohakune** New Zealand
48C2 **Ohanet** Algeria
29D2 **Ōhata** Japan
35A2 **Ohau,L** New Zealand
74B7 **O'Higgins, Lago** Chile
64B3 **Ohio** *R* USA
57E2 **Ohio** *State* USA
13E2 **Ohm** *R* Germany
51B5 **Ohopoho** Namibia
18C2 **Ohre** *R* Czech Republic
17E2 **Ohrid** Macedonia, Yugoslavia
17E2 **Ohridsko Jezero** *L* Albania/Macedonia, Yugoslavia
35B1 **Ohura** New Zealand
73H3 **Oiapoque** French Guiana
65D2 **Oil City** USA
66C3 **Oildale** USA
13B3 **Oise** *Department* France
14C2 **Oise** *R* France
28C4 **Ōita** Japan
66C3 **Ojai** USA
70B2 **Ojinaga** Mexico
29C3 **Ojiya** Japan
74C3 **Ojos del Salado** *Mt* Argentina
20F5 **Oka** *R* Russian Federation
47B1 **Okahandja** Namibia
58C1 **Okanagan Falls** Canada
58C1 **Okanogan** USA
58C1 **Okanogan** *R* USA
58B1 **Okanogan Range** *Mts* Canada/USA
42C2 **Okara** Pakistan
47B1 **Okasise** Namibia
51B5 **Okavango** *R* Angola/Namibia
51C5 **Okavango Delta** *Marsh* Botswana
29D3 **Okaya** Japan
29C4 **Okayama** Japan
29C4 **Okazaki** Japan
67B3 **Okeechobee** USA
67B3 **Okeechobee,L** USA
67B2 **Okefenokee Swamp** USA
48C4 **Okene** Nigeria
42B4 **Okha** India
43F3 **Okhaldunga** Nepal
25Q4 **Okhotsk** Russian Federation
25Q4 **Okhotsk, S of** Russian Federation
26F4 **Okinawa** *I* Japan
26F4 **Okinawa gunto** *Arch* Japan
28C3 **Oki-shotō** *Is* Japan
28A2 **Okkang-dong** N Korea
56D3 **Oklahoma** *State* USA
63C1 **Oklahoma City** USA
63C1 **Okmulgee** USA
48C4 **Okoja** Nigeria
47B1 **Okombahe** Namibia
50B4 **Okondja** Gabon
29D2 **Okoppe** Japan
50B4 **Okoyo** Congo
48C4 **Okpara** *R* Benin/Nigeria
20A2 **Okstindan** *Mt* Norway
21K6 **Oktyabr'sk** Kazakhstan
20J5 **Oktyabr'skiy** Bashkirskaya, Russian Federation
26J1 **Oktyabr'skiy** Kamchatka, Russian Federation
20M3 **Oktyabr'skoye** Russian Federation
25L2 **Oktyabrskoy Revolyutsii, Ostrov** *I* Russian Federation
29D2 **Okushiri-tō** Japan
47C1 **Okwa** *R* Botswana
12B1 **Olafsjorðr** Iceland
66D2 **Olancha** USA
66C2 **Olancha Peak** *Mt* USA
12H7 **Öland** *I* Sweden
34B2 **Olary** Australia
61E3 **Olathe** USA
74D5 **Olavarría** Argentina
16B2 **Olbia** Sicily, Italy
68A1 **Olcott** USA
54E3 **Old Crow** Canada
18B2 **Oldenburg** Niedersachsen, Germany
18C2 **Oldenburg** Schleswig-Holstein, Germany
68C2 **Old Forge** USA
7C3 **Oldham** England
10B3 **Old Head of Kinsale** *C* Irish Republic
68D2 **Old Lyme** USA
8D3 **Oldmeldrum** Scotland
54G4 **Olds** Canada
65F2 **Old Town** USA
31B1 **Öldziyt**
68A1 **Olean** USA
25O4 **Olekma** *R* Russian Federation
25O3 **Olekminsk** Russian Federation
20E2 **Olenegorsk** Russian Federation
25N3 **Olenek** Russian Federation
25O2 **Olenek** *R* Russian Federation
19F2 **Olevsk** Ukraine
29D2 **Ol'ga** Russian Federation
47C3 **Olifants** *R* Cape Province, South Africa
47B1 **Olifants** *R* Namibia
47E1 **Olifants** *R* Transvaal, South Africa
47C2 **Olifantshoek** South Africa
17E2 **Ólimbos** *Mt* Greece
75C3 **Olímpia** Brazil
73M5 **Olinda** Brazil
74C4 **Olivares** *Mt* Argentina/Chile
75D3 **Oliveira** Brazil
61E2 **Olivia** USA
74C2 **Ollagüe** Chile
74C2 **Ollagüe, Vol** Bolivia
7D3 **Ollerton** England
64B3 **Olney** Illinois, USA
62C2 **Olney** Texas, USA

26E1 **Olochi** Russian Federation
12G7 **Olofström** Sweden
50B4 **Olombo** Congo
18D3 **Olomouc** Czech Republic
20E3 **Olonets** Russian Federation
14B3 **Oloron-Ste-Marie** France
26E1 **Olovyannaya** Russian Federation
13D2 **Olpe** Germany
19E2 **Olsztyn** Poland
16B1 **Olten** Switzerland
17E2 **Olt** *R* Romania
58B1 **Olympia** USA
58B1 **Olympic Nat Pk** USA
Olympus *Mt* = **Ólimbos**
45B1 **Olympus,Mt** Cyprus
58B1 **Olympus,Mt** USA
25T4 **Olyutorskiy, Mys** *C* Russian Federation
29C3 **Omachi** Japan
29C4 **Omae-zaki** *C* Japan
9C2 **Omagh** Northern Ireland
61D2 **Omaha** USA
58C1 **Omak** USA
38D4 **Oman** *Sultanate* Arabian Pen
38D3 **Oman,G of** UAE
47B1 **Omaruru** Namibia
47A1 **Omaruru** *R* Namibia
29D2 **Ōma-saki** *C* Japan
50A4 **Omboué** Gabon
50D2 **Omdurman** Sudan
50D2 **Om Häjer** Eritrea
29D2 **Ōminato** Japan
54F4 **Omineca Mts** Canada
29C3 **Omiya** Japan
54H2 **Ommanney B** Canada
50D3 **Omo** *R* Ethiopia
16B2 **Omodeo, L** Sardinia, Italy
25R3 **Omolon** *R* Russian Federation
25P3 **Omoloy** *R* Russian Federation
29D3 **Omono** *R* Japan
24J4 **Omsk** Russian Federation
29D2 **Ōmu** Japan
28C4 **Omura** Japan
47C1 **Omuramba Eiseb** *R* Botswana
28C4 **Ōmuta** Japan
20J4 **Omutninsk** Russian Federation
64A2 **Onalaska** USA
65D3 **Onancock** USA
43K1 **Onandausi** India
64C1 **Onaping L** Canada
61D2 **Onawa** USA
51B5 **Oncócua** Angola
51B5 **Ondangua** Namibia
19E3 **Ondava** *R* Slovakia
48C4 **Ondo** Nigeria
26E2 **Öndörhaan** Mongolia
39F5 **One and Half Degree Chan** Indian Ocean
42F3 **Onega** Russian Federation
20F3 **Onega** *R* Russian Federation
20F3 **Onega, L** Russian Federation
68C1 **Oneida** USA
68B1 **Oneida L** USA
60D2 **O'Neill** USA
26J2 **Onekotan** *I* Kuril Is, Russian Federation
50C4 **Onema** Zaïre
68C1 **Oneonta** USA
17F1 **Oneşti** Romania
20F3 **Onezhskaya Guba** *B* Russian Federation
Onezhskoye, Oz *L* = **Onega, L**
47C3 **Ongers** *R* South Africa
51B5 **Ongiva** Angola
28B3 **Ongjin** N Korea
31D1 **Ongniud Qi** China
44C2 **Ongole** India
51E6 **Onilahy** *R* Madagascar
48C4 **Onitsha** Nigeria
26D2 **Onjüül** Mongolia
29C3 **Ōno** Japan
29C4 **Ōnohara-jima** *I* Japan
29C4 **Onomichi** Japan
33G1 **Onotoa** *I* Kiribati
32A3 **Onslow** Australia
67C2 **Onslow B** USA
29C3 **Ontake-san** *Mt* Japan
66D3 **Ontario** California, USA
58C2 **Ontario** Oregon, USA
55J4 **Ontario** *Province* Canada
65D2 **Ontario,L** Canada/USA
15B2 **Onteniente** Spain
33E1 **Ontong Java Atoll** Solomon Islands
28A3 **Onyang** S Korea
66C3 **Onyx** USA
32C3 **Oodnadatta** Australia
32C4 **Ooldea** Australia
63C1 **Oologah L** USA
13C1 **Oostelijk Flevoland** *Polder* Netherlands
13B2 **Oostende** Belgium
13B2 **Oosterschelde** *Estuary* Netherlands
44B3 **Ootacamund** India
25R4 **Opala** Russian Federation
50C4 **Opala** Zaïre
44C4 **Opanake** Sri Lanka
20H4 **Oparino** Russian Federation
19D3 **Opava** Czech Republic
67A2 **Opelika** USA
63D2 **Opelousas** USA
60B1 **Opheim** USA
19F1 **Opochka** Russian Federation
19D2 **Opole** Poland
15A1 **Oporto** Portugal
35C1 **Opotiki** New Zealand
67A2 **Opp** USA
12F6 **Oppdal** Norway
35B1 **Opunake** New Zealand
17E1 **Oradea** Romania
12B2 **Öræfajökull** *Mts* Iceland
42D3 **Orai** India
15B2 **Oran** Algeria
72F8 **Orán** Argentina
28A2 **Orang** N Korea
34C2 **Orange** Australia
66D4 **Orange** California, USA
14C3 **Orange** France
63D2 **Orange** Texas, USA
47B2 **Orange** *R* South Africa
67B2 **Orangeburg** USA
73H3 **Orange, Cabo** *C* Brazil
61D2 **Orange City** USA
47D2 **Orange Free State** *Province* South Africa
67B2 **Orange Park** USA
64C2 **Orangeville** Canada
18C2 **Oranienburg** Germany
47B2 **Oranjemund** Namibia
47D1 **Orapa** Botswana
27F5 **Oras** Philippines
17E1 **Orăştie** Romania
17E1 **Oraviţa** Romania
16C2 **Orbetello** Italy
68B2 **Orbisonia** USA
34C3 **Orbost** Australia
13B2 **Orchies** France
66B3 **Orcutt** USA
60D2 **Ord** USA
32B2 **Ord** *R* Australia
59D3 **Orderville** USA
32B2 **Ord,Mt** Australia
25M6 **Ordos** *Desert* China
40C1 **Ordu** Turkey
62B1 **Ordway** USA
12H7 **Örebro** Sweden
64C2 **Oregon** USA
56A2 **Oregon** *State* USA
58B1 **Oregon City** USA
12H6 **Öregrund** Sweden
20F4 **Orekhovo Zuyevo** Russian Federation
21F5 **Orel** Russian Federation
59D2 **Orem** USA
21J5 **Orenburg** Russian Federation
15A1 **Orense** Spain
18C1 **Oresund** *Str* Denmark/Sweden
35A3 **Oreti** *R* New Zealand
19F3 **Orgeyev** Moldavia
17F3 **Orhaneli** *R* Turkey
26D2 **Orhon Gol** *R* Mongolia
34B1 **Orientos** Australia
15B2 **Orihuela** Spain
65D2 **Orillia** Canada
72F2 **Orinoco** *R* Venezuela
68C1 **Oriskany Falls** USA
43E4 **Orissa** *State* India
16B3 **Oristano** Sicily, Italy
16B3 **Oristano, G. di** Sardinia, Italy
12K6 **Orivesi** *L* Finland
73G4 **Oriximiná** Brazil
70C3 **Orizaba** Mexico
75C2 **Orizona** Brazil
8D2 **Orkney** *Is, Region* Scotland
75C3 **Orlândia** Brazil
67B3 **Orlando** USA
14C2 **Orléanais** *Region* France
14C2 **Orléans** France
68E2 **Orleans** USA
25L4 **Orlik** Russian Federation
67B3 **Ormond Beach** USA
7C3 **Ormskirk** England
13C3 **Ornain** *R* France
14B2 **Orne** *R* France
12H6 **Örnsköldsvik** Sweden
28A2 **Oro** N Korea
72D3 **Orocué** Colombia
58C1 **Orofino** USA
45C3 **Oron** Israel
8B3 **Oronsay, I** Scotland
Orontes = **Asi**
19E3 **Orosháza** Hungary
25R3 **Orotukan** Russian Federation
59B3 **Oroville** California, USA
58C1 **Oroville** Washington, USA
19G2 **Orsha** Belarus
21K5 **Orsk** Russian Federation
12F6 **Ørsta** Norway
14B3 **Orthez** France
15A1 **Ortigueira** Spain
14E2 **Ortles** *Mt* Italy
69L1 **Ortoire** *R* Trinidad
61D1 **Ortonville** USA
25O3 **Orulgan, Khrebet** *Mts* Russian Federation
72E7 **Oruro** Bolivia
7E3 **Orwell** *R* England
20K4 **Osa** Russian Federation
61E2 **Osage** Iowa, USA
60C2 **Osage** Wyoming, USA
63D1 **Osage** *R* USA
29D4 **Ōsaka** Japan
70D4 **Osa,Pen de** Costa Rica
63E1 **Osceola** Arkansas, USA
61E2 **Osceola** Iowa, USA
58C2 **Osgood Mts** USA
29D2 **Oshamambe** Japan
65D2 **Oshawa** Canada
29D4 **Ō-shima** *I* Japan
60C2 **Oshkosh** Nebraska, USA
55K5 **Oshkosh** USA
64B2 **Oshkosh** Wisconsin, USA
21H8 **Oshnovīyeh** Iran
48C4 **Oshogbo** Nigeria
50B4 **Oshwe** Zaïre
17D1 **Osijek** Croatia
24K4 **Osinniki** Russian Federation
19F2 **Osipovichi** Belarus
61E2 **Oskaloosa** USA
20B4 **Oskarshamn** Sweden
12G6 **Oslo** Norway
40C2 **Osmaniye** Turkey
18B2 **Osnabrück** Germany
74B6 **Osorno** Chile
15B1 **Osorno** Spain
58C1 **Osoyoos** Canada
32D5 **Ossa,Mt** Australia
64A2 **Osseo** USA
68D2 **Ossining** USA
25S4 **Ossora** Russian Federation
20E4 **Ostashkov** Russian Federation
13E1 **Oste** *R* Germany
Ostend = Oostende
12G6 **Østerdalen** *V* Norway
13E1 **Osterholz-Scharmbeck** Germany
12G6 **Östersund** Sweden
13D1 **Ostfriesland** *Region* Germany
12H6 **Östhammär** Sweden
16C2 **Ostia** Italy
19D3 **Ostrava** Czech Republic
19D2 **Ostróda** Poland
19E2 **Ostrołęka** Poland
20D4 **Ostrov** Russian Federation
19D2 **Ostrów Wlkp** Poland
19E2 **Ostrowiec** Poland
19E2 **Ostrów Mazowiecka** Poland
15A2 **Osuna** Spain
65D2 **Oswego** USA
68B1 **Oswego** *R* USA
7C3 **Oswestry** England
19D3 **Oświęcim** Poland
29C3 **Ota** Japan
35B3 **Otago Pen** New Zealand
35C2 **Otaki** New Zealand
29E2 **Otaru** Japan
72C3 **Otavalo** Ecuador
51B5 **Otavi** Namibia
29D3 **Otawara** Japan
68C1 **Otego** USA
58C1 **Othello** USA
17E3 **Óthris** *Mt* Greece
60C2 **Otis** Colorado, USA
68D1 **Otis** Massachusetts, USA
68C2 **Otisville** USA
47B1 **Otjimbingwe** Namibia
51B6 **Otjiwarongo** Namibia
6D3 **Otley** England
31B2 **Otog Qi** China
29D2 **Otoineppu** Japan
35C1 **Otorohanga** New Zealand
12F7 **Otra** *R* Norway
17D2 **Otranto** Italy
17D2 **Otranto,Str of** *Chan* Albania/Italy
64B2 **Otsego** USA
68C1 **Otsego L** USA
29C3 **Ōtsu** Japan
12F6 **Otta** Norway
65D1 **Ottawa** Canada
64B2 **Ottawa** Illinois, USA
63C1 **Ottawa** Kansas, USA
65D1 **Ottawa** *R* Canada
55K4 **Ottawa Is** Canada
13E1 **Otterndorf** Germany
55K4 **Otter Rapids** Canada
55K1 **Otto Fjord** Canada
47D2 **Ottosdal** South Africa
64A2 **Ottumwa** USA
13D3 **Ottweiler** Germany
48C4 **Oturkpo** Nigeria
72C5 **Otusco** Peru
34B3 **Otway,C** Australia
19E2 **Otwock** Poland
30C1 **Ou** *R* Laos
63D2 **Ouachita** *R* USA
63D2 **Ouachita,L** USA
63D2 **Ouachita Mts** USA
48A2 **Ouadane** Mauritius
50C3 **Ouadda** Central African Republic
50C2 **Ouaddai** *Desert Region* Chad
48B3 **Ouagadougou** Burkina
48B3 **Ouahigouya** Burkina
50C3 **Ouaka** *R* Central African Republic
48C3 **Oualam** Niger
48C2 **Ouallen** Algeria
50C3 **Ouanda Djallé** Central African Republic
13B4 **Ouanne** *R* France
48A2 **Ouarane** *Region* Mauritius
48C1 **Ouargla** Algeria
48B2 **Ouarkziz, Jbel** *Mts* Morocco
50C3 **Ouarra** *R* Central African Republic
15C2 **Ouarsenis, Massif de l'** *Mts* Algeria
48B1 **Ouarzazate** Morocco
15C2 **Ouassel** *R* Algeria
50B3 **Oubangui** *R* Central African Republic/Congo/Zaïre
13B2 **Oudenaarde** Belgium
47C3 **Oudtshoorn** South Africa
15B2 **Oued Tlĕlat** Algeria
48B1 **Oued Zem** Morocco
40B4 **Ouena, Wadi** *Watercourse* Egypt
14A2 **Ouessant, Ile d'** *I* France
50B3 **Ouesso** Congo
48B1 **Ouezzane** Morocco
9C2 **Oughter, L** Irish Republic
50B3 **Ouham** *R* Chad
48C4 **Ouidah** Benin
48B1 **Oujda** Morocco
12J6 **Oulainen** Finland
15C3 **Ouled Nail, Monts des** Algeria
12K5 **Oulu** Finland
12K6 **Oulu** *R* Finland
12K6 **Oulujärvi** *L* Finland
50C2 **Oum Chalouba** Chad
16B3 **Oumel Bouaghi** Algeria
50B2 **Oum Hadjer** Chad
50C2 **Oum Haouach** *Watercourse* Chad
12K5 **Ounas** *R* Finland
20C2 **Ounastunturi** *Mt* Finland
50C2 **Ounianga Kebir** Chad
13D2 **Our** *R* Germany
62A1 **Ouray** USA
13C3 **Ource** *R* France
13B3 **Ourcq** *R* France
Ourense = Orense
73K5 **Ouricurí** Brazil
75C3 **Ourinhos** Brazil
75D3 **Ouro Prêto** Brazil
13C2 **Ourthe** *R* Belgium
7E3 **Ouse** *R* Norfolk, England
6D2 **Ouse** *R* N Yorks, England
10B2 **Outer Hebrides** *Is* Scotland
66C4 **Outer Santa Barbara** *Chan* USA
51B6 **Outjo** Namibia
12K6 **Outokumpu** Finland
34B3 **Ouyen** Australia
16B2 **Ovada** Italy
74B4 **Ovalle** Chile
51B5 **Ovamboland** *Region* Namibia
13D1 **Overijssel** *Province* Netherlands
59D3 **Overton** USA
12J5 **Övertorneå** Sweden
60C2 **Ovid** Colorado, USA
68B1 **Ovid** New York, USA
15A1 **Oviedo** Spain
12F6 **Øvre** Norway
21D5 **Ovruch** Ukraine
25O4 **Ovsyanka** Russian Federation
35A3 **Owaka** New Zealand
68B1 **Owasco L** USA
29C4 **Owase** Japan
61E2 **Owatonna** USA
68B1 **Owego** USA
66C2 **Owens** *R* USA
64B3 **Owensboro** USA
66D2 **Owens L** USA
64C2 **Owen Sound** Canada
32D1 **Owen Stanley Range** *Mts* Papua New Guinea
48C4 **Owerri** Nigeria
58E2 **Owl Creek Mts** USA
48C4 **Owo** Nigeria
64C2 **Owosso** USA
58C2 **Owyhee** USA
58C2 **Owyhee** *R* USA
58C2 **Owyhee Mts** USA
72C6 **Oxapampa** Peru
12H7 **Oxelösund** Sweden
7D3 **Oxford** England
68E1 **Oxford** Massachusetts, USA
63E2 **Oxford** Mississippi, USA
68C1 **Oxford** New York, USA
7D4 **Oxford** *County* England
66C3 **Oxnard** USA
29D3 **Oyama** Japan
50B3 **Oyen** Gabon
8C3 **Oykel** *R* Scotland
25Q3 **Oymyakon** Russian Federation
34C4 **Oyster B** Australia
27F6 **Ozamiz** Philippines
19F2 **Ozarichi** Belarus
67A2 **Ozark** USA
63D1 **Ozark Plat** USA
63D1 **Ozarks,L of the** USA
19E3 **Ózd** Hungary
62B2 **Ozona** USA
40D1 **Ozurgety** Georgia

P

47B3 **Paarl** South Africa
8B3 **Pabbay** *I* Scotland
19D2 **Pabianice** Poland
43F4 **Pabna** Bangladesh
19F1 **Pabrade** Lithuania
72F3 **Pacaraima, Serra** *Mts* Brazil/Venezuela
72C5 **Pacasmayo** Peru
70C2 **Pachuca** Mexico
66B1 **Pacific** USA
37N7 **Pacific-Antarctic Ridge** Pacific Ocean
66B2 **Pacific Grove** USA
37L4 **Pacific O**
75D2 **Pacuí** *R* Brazil
27D7 **Padang** Indonesia
20E3 **Padany** Russian Federation
18B2 **Paderborn** Germany
54J3 **Padlei** Canada
43G4 **Padma** *R* Bangladesh
16C1 **Padova** Italy
50B4 **Padrão, Ponta do** *Pt* Angola
56D4 **Padre I** USA
7B4 **Padstow** England
34B3 **Padthaway** Australia
Padua = Padova
64B3 **Paducah** Kentucky, USA
62B2 **Paducah** Texas, USA
12L5 **Padunskoye More** *L* Russian Federation
28A2 **Paegam** N Korea
35C1 **Paeroa** New Zealand
47E1 **Pafuri** Mozambique
16C2 **Pag** *I* Croatia
27D7 **Pagai Selatan** *I* Indonesia
27C7 **Pagai Utara** *I* Indonesia
27H5 **Pagan** *I* Pacific Ocean
59D3 **Page** USA
27F8 **Pago Mission** Australia
17F3 **Pagondhas** Greece
62A1 **Pagosa Springs** USA
66E5 **Pahala** Hawaiian Islands
35C2 **Pahiatua** New Zealand
66E5 **Pahoa** Hawaiian Islands
67B3 **Pahokee** USA
12K6 **Päijänne** *L* Finland
66E5 **Pailola Chan** Hawaiian Islands
64C2 **Painesville** USA
59D3 **Painted Desert** USA
64C3 **Paintsville** USA
8C4 **Paisley** Scotland
15B1 **País Vasco** *Region* Spain
72B5 **Paita** Peru
12J5 **Pajala** Sweden
38E3 **Pakistan** *Republic* Asia
30C2 **Pak Lay** Laos
43H4 **Pakokku** Burma
16D1 **Pakrac** Croatia
17D1 **Paks** Hungary
30C2 **Pak Sane** Laos
30D2 **Pakse** Laos
50D3 **Pakwach** Uganda
50B3 **Pala** Chad
16D2 **Palagruža** *I* Croatia
13B3 **Palaiseau** France
47D1 **Palala** *R* South Africa
44E3 **Palalankwe** Andaman Islands
25S4 **Palana** Russian Federation
27E7 **Palangkaraya** Indonesia
44B3 **Palani** India
42C4 **Pālanpur** India
47D1 **Palapye** Botswana
67B3 **Palatka** USA
36H4 **Palau** *USA Dependency* Pacific Ocean
30B3 **Palaw** Burma
27E6 **Palawan** *I* Philippines
44B4 **Palayankottai** India
12J7 **Paldiski** Estonia
27D7 **Palembang** Indonesia
15B1 **Palencia** Spain
45B1 **Paleokhorio** Cyprus
16C3 **Palermo** Sicily, Italy
63C2 **Palestine** USA

43G4 **Paletwa** Burma
44B3 **Pālghāt** India
42C3 **Pāli** India
60B3 **Palisade** USA
42C4 **Pālitāna** India
44B4 **Palk Str** India/Sri Lanka
21H5 **Pallasovka** Russian Federation
12J5 **Pallastunturi** *Mt* Finland
35B2 **Palliser B** New Zealand
35C2 **Palliser,C** New Zealand
51E5 **Palma** Mozambique
15C2 **Palma de Mallorca** Spain
73L5 **Palmares** Brazil
69A5 **Palmar Sur** Costa Rica
75B4 **Palmas** Brazil
48B4 **Palmas,C** Liberia
75D1 **Palmas de Monte Alto** Brazil
69B2 **Palma Soriano** Cuba
67B3 **Palm Bay** USA
67B3 **Palm Beach** USA
66C3 **Palmdale** USA
59C4 **Palm Desert** California, USA
75C4 **Palmeira** Brazil
73L5 **Palmeira dos Indos** Brazil
54D3 **Palmer** USA
76G3 **Palmer** *Base* Antarctica
76G3 **Palmer Arch** Antarctica
76F3 **Palmer Land** *Region* Antarctica
35B3 **Palmerston** New Zealand
35C2 **Palmerston North** New Zealand
68C2 **Palmerton** USA
67B3 **Palmetto** USA
16D3 **Palmi** Italy
72C3 **Palmira** Colombia
32D2 **Palm Is** Australia
59C4 **Palm Springs** USA
64A3 **Palmyra** Missouri, USA
68B1 **Palmyra** New York, USA
68B2 **Palmyra** Pennsylvania, USA
43F4 **Palmyras Pt** India
66A2 **Palo Alto** USA
27D6 **Paloh** Indonesia
50D2 **Paloích** Sudan
59C4 **Palomar Mt** USA
27F7 **Palopo** Indonesia
15B2 **Palos, Cabo de** *C* Spain
27E7 **Palu** Indonesia
40C2 **Palu** Turkey
42D3 **Palwal** India
48C3 **Pama** Burkina
27E7 **Pamekasan** Indonesia
14C3 **Pamiers** France
39F2 **Pamir** *Mts* Tajikistan
67C1 **Pamlico** *R* USA
67C1 **Pamlico Sd** USA
62B1 **Pampa** USA
74C4 **Pampa de la Salinas** *Plain* Argentina
74D5 **Pampas** *Plains* Argentina
72D2 **Pamplona** Colombia
15B1 **Pamplona** Spain
64B3 **Pana** USA
59D3 **Panaca** USA
17E2 **Panagyurishte** Bulgaria
44A2 **Panaji** India
72C2 **Panamá** Panama
72B2 **Panama** *Republic* Central America
69B5 **Panama Canal** Panama
67A2 **Panama City** USA
70E4 **Panamá, G de** Panama
59C3 **Panamint Range** *Mts* USA
66D2 **Panamint V** USA
27F5 **Panay** *I* Philippines
17E2 **Pancevo** Serbia, Yugoslavia
27F5 **Pandan** Philippines
44B2 **Pandharpur** India
34A1 **Pandie Pandie** Australia
19E1 **Panevežys** Lithuania
24K5 **Panfilov** Kazakhstan
30B1 **Pang** *R* Burma
50D4 **Pangani** Tanzania
50D4 **Pangani** *R* Tanzania
50C4 **Pangi** Zaïre
27D7 **Pangkalpinang** Indonesia
55M3 **Pangnirtung** Canada
30B1 **Pangtara** Burma
59D3 **Panguitch** USA
62B1 **Panhandle** USA
42D3 **Pānīpat** India
42B2 **Panjao** Afghanistan
28B3 **P'anmunjom** S Korea
43E4 **Panna** India
75B3 **Panorama** Brazil
28A2 **Panshan** China
28B2 **Panshi** China
75A2 **Pantanal de São Lourenço** *Swamp* Brazil
75A2 **Pantanal do Rio Negro** *Swamp* Brazil
75A2 **Pantanal do Taquari** *Swamp* Brazil
16C3 **Pantelleria** *I* Italy
31A4 **Pan Xian** China
16D3 **Paola** Italy
63D1 **Paola** USA
64B3 **Paoli** USA
18D3 **Pápa** Hungary
72A1 **Papagaya, Golfo del** Nicaragua
70D3 **Papagayo, G de** Costa Rica
66E5 **Papaikou** Hawaiian Islands
35B1 **Papakura** New Zealand
70C2 **Papantla** Mexico
8E1 **Papa Stour** *I* Scotland
35B1 **Papatoetoe** New Zealand
8D2 **Papa Westray** *I* Scotland
13D1 **Papenburg** Germany
45B1 **Paphos** Cyprus
8B4 **Paps of Jura** Scotland
32D1 **Papua,G of** Papua New Guinea
32D1 **Papua New Guinea** *Republic* SE Asia
30B2 **Papun** Burma
73J4 **Pará** *R* Brazil
73H4 **Pará** *State* Brazil
32A3 **Paraburdoo** Australia
72C6 **Paracas,Pen de** Peru
75C2 **Paracatu** Brazil
75C2 **Paracatu** *R* Brazil
30E2 **Paracel Is** SE Asia
34A2 **Parachilna** Australia
42C2 **Parachinar** Pakistan
17E2 **Paracin** Serbia, Yugoslavia
75D2 **Pará de Minas** Brazil
59B3 **Paradise** California, USA
59D3 **Paradise** Nevada, USA
66D1 **Paradise Peak** *Mt* USA
63D1 **Paragould** USA
72F6 **Paraguá** *R* Bolivia
72F2 **Paragua** *R* Venezuela
75D1 **Paraguaçu** *R* Brazil
73G7 **Paraguai** *R* Brazil
75A4 **Paraguarí** Paraguay
74E2 **Paraguay** *R* Paraguay
74E2 **Paraguay** *Republic* S America
75C3 **Paraíba** *R* Brazil
73L5 **Paraíba** *State* Brazil
75D3 **Paraíba do Sul** *R* Brazil
48C4 **Parakou** Benin
44B4 **Paramakkudi** India
73G2 **Paramaribo** Surinam
75D1 **Paramirim** Brazil
26J1 **Paramushir** *I* Russian Federation
74D4 **Paraná** Argentina
74E4 **Paraná** *R* Argentina
75B3 **Paraná** *R* Brazil
73J6 **Paranã** *R* Brazil
74F2 **Paraná** *State* Brazil
75C4 **Paranaguá** Brazil
75B2 **Paranaíba** Brazil
75B2 **Paranaíba** *R* Brazil
75B3 **Paranapanema** *R* Brazil
75C3 **Paranapiacaba, Serra do** *Mts* Brazil
75B3 **Paranavaí** Brazil
75D2 **Paraope** *R* Brazil
35B2 **Paraparaumu** New Zealand
75D1 **Paratinga** Brazil
44B2 **Parbhani** India
45C2 **Pardes Hanna** Israel
75E2 **Pardo** *R* Bahia, Brazil
75B3 **Pardo** *R* Mato Grosso do Sul, Brazil
75C2 **Pardo** *R* Minas Gerais, Brazil
75C3 **Pardo** *R* São Paulo, Brazil
18D2 **Pardubice** Czech Republic
26G4 **Parece Vela** *Reef* Pacific Ocean
75A1 **Parecis** Brazil
72F6 **Parecis, Serra dos** *Mts* Brazil
57F2 **Parent** Canada
65D1 **Parent,L** Canada
32A1 **Parepare** Indonesia
69E4 **Paria, G de** Trinidad/Venezuela
27D7 **Pariaman** Indonesia
69E4 **Paria, Península de** Venezuela
72F3 **Parima, Serra** *Mts* Brazil
14C2 **Paris** France
64C3 **Paris** Kentucky, USA
63E1 **Paris** Tennessee, USA
63C2 **Paris** Texas, USA
59D4 **Parker** USA
64C3 **Parkersburg** USA
34C2 **Parkes** Australia
68C3 **Parkesburg** USA
64A1 **Park Falls** USA
66B3 **Parkfield** USA
64B2 **Park Forest** USA
61D1 **Park Rapids** USA
61D2 **Parkston** USA
58B1 **Parksville** Canada
58D2 **Park Valley** USA
44C2 **Parlākimidi** India
44B2 **Parli** India
16C2 **Parma** Italy
64C2 **Parma** USA
73K4 **Parnaiba** Brazil
73K4 **Parnaiba** *R* Brazil
17E3 **Párnon Óros** *Mts* Greece
20C4 **Pärnu** Estonia
43F3 **Paro** Bhutan
34B1 **Paroo** *R* Australia
34B2 **Paroo Channel** *R* Australia
17F3 **Páros** *I* Greece
59D3 **Parowan** USA
34D2 **Parramatta** Australia
56C4 **Parras** Mexico
55K3 **Parry B** Canada
54G2 **Parry Is** Canada
55L2 **Parry, Kap** *C* Canada
55L5 **Parry Sound** Canada
18C3 **Parsberg** Germany
54F4 **Parsnip** *R* Canada
63C1 **Parsons** Kansas, USA
65D3 **Parsons** West Virginia, USA
14B2 **Parthenay** France
16C3 **Partinico** Italy
28C2 **Partizansk** Russian Federation
9B3 **Partry** *Mts* Irish Republic
73H4 **Paru** *R* Brazil
44C2 **Parvatipuram** India
47D2 **Parys** South Africa
63C3 **Pasadena** Texas, USA
66C3 **Pasadena** USA
30B2 **Pasawing** Burma
63E2 **Pascagoula** USA
17F1 **Paşcani** Romania
58C1 **Pasco** USA
75E2 **Pascoal, Monte** Brazil
Pascua, Isla de = Easter I
13B2 **Pas-de-Calais** *Department* France
12G8 **Pasewalk** Germany
41G4 **Pashū'īyeh** Iran
32B4 **Pasley,C** Australia
74E3 **Paso de los Libres** Argentina
74E4 **Paso de los Toros** Uruguay
74B6 **Paso Limay** Argentina
66B3 **Paso Robles** USA
68C2 **Passaic** USA
18C3 **Passau** Germany
74F3 **Passo Fundo** Brazil
75C3 **Passos** Brazil
72C4 **Pastaza** *R* Peru
72C3 **Pasto** Colombia
19E1 **Pasvalys** Lithuania
74B8 **Patagonia** *Region* Argentina
42C4 **Pātan** India
43F3 **Patan** Nepal
43J1 **Patandi** India
34B3 **Patchewollock** Australia
35B1 **Patea** New Zealand
35B2 **Patea** *R* New Zealand
6D2 **Pateley Bridge** England
16C3 **Paterno** Sicily, Italy
68C2 **Paterson** USA
35A3 **Paterson Inlet** *B* New Zealand
42D2 **Pathankot** India
60B2 **Pathfinder Res** USA
42D2 **Patiāla** India
72C6 **Pativilca** Peru
17F3 **Pátmos** *I* Greece
43F3 **Patna** India
40D2 **Patnos** Turkey
25N4 **Patomskoye Nagor'ye** *Upland* Russian Federation
73L5 **Patos** Brazil
75C2 **Patos de Minas** Brazil
74F4 **Patos, Lagoa dos** *Lg* Brazil
17E3 **Pátrai** Greece
20L3 **Patrasuy** Russian Federation
75C2 **Patrocínio** Brazil
50E4 **Patta I** Kenya
30C4 **Pattani** Thailand
30C3 **Pattaya** Thailand
66B2 **Patterson** California, USA
63D3 **Patterson** Louisiana, USA
66C2 **Patterson Mt** USA
68A2 **Patton** USA
73L5 **Patu** Brazil
43G4 **Patuakhali** Bangladesh
70D3 **Patuca** *R* Honduras
14B3 **Pau** France
54F3 **Paulatuk** Canada
73K5 **Paulistana** Brazil
47E2 **Paulpietersburg** South Africa
63C2 **Pauls Valley** USA
30B2 **Paungde** Burma
42D2 **Pauri** India
75D2 **Pavão** Brazil
16B1 **Pavia** Italy
24J4 **Pavlodar** Kazakhstan
20K4 **Pavlovka** Russian Federation
20G4 **Pavlovo** Russian Federation
21G5 **Pavlovsk** Russian Federation
63C1 **Pawhuska** USA
68A3 **Paw Paw** USA
68E2 **Pawtucket** USA
60C2 **Paxton** USA
58C2 **Payette** USA
55L4 **Payne,L** Canada
61E1 **Paynesville** USA
74E4 **Paysandú** Uruguay
17E2 **Pazardzhik** Bulgaria
54G4 **Peace** *R* Canada
67B3 **Peace** *R* USA
54G4 **Peace River** Canada
59D3 **Peach Springs** USA
7D3 **Peak District Nat Pk** England
65F1 **Peaked Mt** USA
34C2 **Peak Hill** Australia
7D3 **Peak,The** *Mt* England
59E3 **Peale,Mt** USA
63D2 **Pearl** *R* USA
66E5 **Pearl City** Hawaiian Islands
66E5 **Pearl Harbor** Hawaiian Islands
62C3 **Pearsall** USA
47D3 **Pearston** South Africa
54H2 **Peary Chan** Canada
51D5 **Pebane** Mozambique
17E2 **Peć** Serbia, Yugoslavia
75D2 **Peçanha** Brazil
63D3 **Pecan Island** USA
12L5 **Pechenga** Russian Federation
20K2 **Pechora** Russian Federation
20J2 **Pechora** *R* Russian Federation
20J2 **Pechorskaya Guba** *G* Russian Federation
20J2 **Pechorskoye More** *S* Russian Federation
16D3 **Pecoraro** *Mt* Italy
62B2 **Pecos** USA
62B2 **Pecos** *R* USA
19D3 **Pécs** Hungary
45B1 **Pedhoulas** Cyprus
75D2 **Pedra Azul** Brazil
75C3 **Pedregulho** Brazil
69B3 **Pedro Cays** *Is* Caribbean Sea
74C2 **Pedro de Valdivia** Chile
75B2 **Pedro Gomes** Brazil
75A3 **Pedro Juan Caballero** Paraguay
44C4 **Pedro,Pt** Sri Lanka
34B2 **Peebinga** Australia
8D4 **Peebles** Scotland
67C2 **Pee Dee** *R* USA
68D2 **Peekskill** USA
6B2 **Peel** Isle of Man, British Islands
54E3 **Peel** *R* Canada
54J2 **Peel Sd** Canada
Pefos = Paphos
27G7 **Peg Arfak** *Mt* Indonesia
35B2 **Pegasus B** New Zealand
30B2 **Pegu** Burma
32C1 **Pegunungan Maoke** *Mts* Indonesia
30B2 **Pegu Yoma** *Mts* Burma
74D5 **Pehuajó** Argentina
Peipsi Järv = Lake Peipus
75B1 **Peixe** *R* Mato Grosso, Brazil
75B3 **Peixe** *R* São Paulo, Brazil
31D3 **Pei Xian** China
30C5 **Pekan** Malaysia
27D6 **Pekanbaru** Indonesia
64B2 **Pekin** USA
Peking = Beijing
30C5 **Pelabohan Kelang** Malaysia
14D3 **Pelat, Mont** France
17E1 **Peleaga** *Mt* Romania
25N4 **Peleduy** Russian Federation
64C2 **Pelee I** Canada
32B1 **Peleng** *I* Indonesia
61E1 **Pelican L** USA
47A1 **Pelican Pt** South Africa
17D2 **Pelješac** *Pen* Croatia
12J5 **Pello** Finland
55K3 **Pelly Bay** Canada
54E3 **Pelly Mts** Canada
74F4 **Pelotas** Brazil
74F3 **Pelotas** *R* Brazil
45B3 **Pelusium** *Hist Site* Egypt
14D2 **Pelvoux, Massif du** *Mts* France
20L3 **Pelym** *R* Russian Federation
51E5 **Pemba** Mozambique
51E5 **Pemba, Baiá de** *B* Mozambique
50D4 **Pemba I** Tanzania
61D1 **Pembina** USA
65D1 **Pembroke** Canada
67B2 **Pembroke** USA
7B4 **Pembroke** Wales
68E1 **Penacook** USA
75B3 **Penápolis** Brazil
15A2 **Peñarroya** Spain
15B1 **Peñarroya** *Mt* Spain
7C4 **Penarth** Wales
15A1 **Peñas, Cabo de** *C* Spain
74B7 **Penas, Golfo de** *G* Chile
15A1 **Peña Trevinca** *Mt* Spain
50B3 **Pende** *R* Central African Republic/Chad
58C1 **Pendleton** USA
58C1 **Pend Oreille** *R* USA
73L6 **Penedo** Brazil
42D5 **Penganga** *R* India
31D5 **Pengho Lieh Tao** *Is* Taiwan
31E2 **Penglai** China
31B4 **Pengshui** China
8D4 **Penicuik** Scotland
30C5 **Peninsular Malaysia** Malaysia
7D3 **Penistone** England
44B3 **Penner** *R* India
6C2 **Pennine Chain** *Mts* England
68C3 **Penns Grove** USA
57F2 **Pennsylvania** *State* USA
68B1 **Penn Yan** USA
55M3 **Penny Highlands** *Mts* Canada
65F1 **Penobscot** *R* USA
65F2 **Penobscot B** USA
34B3 **Penola** Australia
32C4 **Penong** Australia
69A5 **Penonomé** Panama
6C2 **Penrith** England
63E2 **Pensacola** USA
76E2 **Pensacola Mts** Antarctica
33F2 **Pentecost** *I* Vanuatu
54G5 **Penticton** Canada
8D2 **Pentland Firth** *Chan* Scotland
8D4 **Pentland Hills** Scotland
6C2 **Pen-y-ghent** *Mt* England
20H5 **Penza** Russian Federation
7B4 **Penzance** England
25S3 **Penzhina** *R* Russian Federation
25S3 **Penzhinskaya Guba** *B* Russian Federation
64B2 **Peoria** USA
30C5 **Perak** *R* Malaysia
75A3 **Perdido** *R* Brazil
72C3 **Pereira** Colombia
75B3 **Pereira Barreto** Brazil
21G6 **Perelazovskiy** Russian Federation
19G2 **Pereyaslav** Ukraine
74D4 **Pergamino** Argentina
40B2 **Perge** Turkey
55L4 **Péribonca** *R* Canada
14C2 **Périgueux** France
72C2 **Perlas, Archipiélago de las** Panama
69A4 **Perlas, Laguna de** Nicaragua
20K4 **Perm'** Russian Federation
Pernambuco = Recife
73L5 **Pernambuco** *State* Brazil
17E2 **Pernik** Bulgaria
13B3 **Péronne** France
14C3 **Perpignan** France
66D4 **Perris** USA
67B2 **Perry** Florida, USA
67B2 **Perry** Georgia, USA
68A1 **Perry** New York, USA
63C1 **Perry** Oklahoma, USA
54H3 **Perry River** Canada
64C2 **Perrysburg** USA
62B1 **Perryton** USA
63E1 **Perryville** Missouri, USA
Persia = Iran
38D3 **Persian Gulf** SW Asia
32A4 **Perth** Australia
65D2 **Perth** Canada
8D3 **Perth** Scotland
68C2 **Perth Amboy** USA
64B2 **Peru** USA
72D6 **Peru** *Republic* S America
37P5 **Peru Basin** Pacific Ocean
52E6 **Peru-Chile Trench** Pacific Ocean
16C2 **Perugia** Italy
16D2 **Perušic** Croatia
40D2 **Pervari** Turkey
20G5 **Pervomaysk** Russian Federation
21E6 **Pervomaysk** Ukraine
20K4 **Pervoural'sk** Russian Federation
16C2 **Pesaro** Italy
66A2 **Pescadero** USA
Pescadores = Pengho Lieh Tao
16C2 **Pescara** Italy
42C2 **Peshawar** Pakistan
17E2 **Peshkopi** Albania
64B1 **Peshtigo** USA
20F4 **Pestovo** Russian Federation
70B3 **Petacalco, B de** Mexico
45C2 **Petah Tiqwa** Israel
59B3 **Petaluma** USA
13C3 **Pétange** Luxembourg

51D5 **Petauke** Zambia
64B2 **Petenwell L** USA
34A2 **Peterborough** Australia
65D2 **Peterborough** Canada
7D3 **Peterborough** England
68E1 **Peterborough** USA
8E3 **Peterhead** Scotland
55M1 **Petermann Gletscher** *Gl* Greenland
32B3 **Petermann Range** *Mts* Australia
74B5 **Peteroa, Vol** Argentina/ Chile
76G4 **Peter 1 Øy** *I* Antarctica
54E4 **Petersburg** USA
65D3 **Petersburg** Virginia, USA
7D4 **Petersfield** England
16B3 **Petite Kabylie** *Hills* Algeria
55M4 **Petit Mècatina, Rivière du** *R* Canada
42C4 **Petlād** India
70D2 **Peto** Mexico
64C1 **Petoskey** USA
45C3 **Petra** *Hist Site* Jordan
25N2 **Petra, Ostrova** *Is* Russian Federation
28C2 **Petra Velikogo, Zaliv** *B* Russian Federation
59E3 **Petrified Forest Nat Pk** USA
73K5 **Petrolina** Brazil
24H4 **Petropavlovsk** Kazakhstan
26J1 **Petropavlovsk-Kamchatskiy** Russian Federation
75D3 **Petrópolis** Brazil
21H5 **Petrovsk** Russian Federation
25M4 **Petrovsk Zabaykal'skiy** Russian Federation
20E3 **Petrozavodsk** Russian Federation
47D2 **Petrusburg** South Africa
47D2 **Petrus Steyn** South Africa
47C3 **Petrusville** South Africa
25T3 **Pevek** Russian Federation
20H2 **Peza** *R* Russian Federation
13E2 **Pfälzer Wald** *Region* Germany
18B3 **Pforzheim** Germany
42D2 **Phagwara** India
47E1 **Phalaborwa** South Africa
42C3 **Phalodī** India
13D3 **Phalsbourg** France
44A2 **Phaltan** India
30B4 **Phangnga** Thailand
30C3 **Phanom Dang** *Mts* Cambodia/Thailand
30D3 **Phan Rang** Vietnam
30D3 **Phan Thiet** Vietnam
62C3 **Pharr** USA
67C1 **Phelps L** USA
67A2 **Phenix City** USA
30B3 **Phet Buri** Thailand
30D3 **Phiafay** Laos
63E2 **Philadelphia** Mississippi, USA
68C2 **Philadelphia** Pennsylvania, USA
60C2 **Philip** USA
Philippeville = Skikda
13C2 **Philippeville** Belgium
27F5 **Philippine S** Pacific Ocean
27F5 **Philippines** *Republic* SE Asia
36H4 **Philippine Trench** Pacific Ocean
47D3 **Philippolis** South Africa
58D1 **Philipsburg** Montana, USA
65D2 **Philipsburg** Pennsylvania, USA
54D3 **Philip Smith Mts** USA
47C3 **Philipstown** South Africa
55K1 **Phillips B** Canada
60D3 **Phillipsburg** Kansas, USA
68C2 **Phillipsburg** New Jersey, USA
55K2 **Philpots Pen** Canada
30C3 **Phnom Penh** Cambodia
59D4 **Phoenix** Arizona, USA
68B1 **Phoenix** New York, USA
33H1 **Phoenix Is** Pacific Ocean
68C2 **Phoenixville** USA
30C1 **Phong Saly** Laos
30C3 **Phra Nakhon** Thailand
30C2 **Phu Bia** *Mt* Laos
30D3 **Phu Cuong** Vietnam
30B4 **Phuket** Thailand
43E4 **Phulbāni** India
30C2 **Phu Miang** *Mt* Thailand
30D2 **Phu Set** *Mt* Laos
30D1 **Phu Tho** Vietnam
30D4 **Phu Vinh** Vietnam
16B1 **Piacenza** Italy
34D1 **Pialba** Australia
34C2 **Pian** *R* Australia
16C2 **Pianosa** *I* Italy
16D2 **Pianosa** *I* Italy
19E2 **Piaseczno** Poland
75D1 **Piatã** Brazil
17F1 **Piatra-Neamţ** Romania
73K5 **Piauí** *State* Brazil
16C1 **Piave** *R* Italy
50D3 **Pibor** *R* Sudan
50D3 **Pibor Post** Sudan
13B3 **Picardie** *Region* France
63E2 **Picayune** USA
74B4 **Pichilemu** Chile
6D2 **Pickering** England
55J4 **Pickle Lake** Canada
48A1 **Pico** *I* Azores
69C5 **Pico Bolivar** *Mt* Venezuela
15A1 **Pico de Almanzor** *Mt* Spain
15C1 **Pico de Aneto** *Mt* Spain
69C3 **Pico Duarte** *Mt* Dominican Republic
73K5 **Picos** Brazil
15B1 **Picos de Europa** *Mt* Spain
34D2 **Picton** Australia
35B2 **Picton** New Zealand
50B1 **Pic Toussidé** *Mt* Chad
75C3 **Piedade** Brazil
66C2 **Piedra** USA
66B3 **Piedras Blancas,Pt** USA
70B2 **Piedras Negras** Mexico
64B1 **Pie I** Canada
12K6 **Pieksämäki** Finland
12K6 **Pielinen** *L* Finland
47D2 **Pienaar's River** South Africa
60C2 **Pierre** USA
19D3 **Piešťany** Slovakia
47E2 **Pietermaritzburg** South Africa
47D1 **Pietersburg** South Africa
47E2 **Piet Retief** South Africa
17F1 **Pietrosul** *Mt* Romania
27H6 **Pigailoe** *I* Pacific Ocean
63D1 **Piggott** USA
28A3 **Pihyŏn** N Korea
55J4 **Pikangikum L** Canada
60B3 **Pikes Peak** USA
47B3 **Piketberg** South Africa
64C3 **Pikeville** USA
55O3 **Pikiutaleq** Greenland
39F2 **Pik Kommunizma** *Mt* Tajikistan
50B3 **Pikounda** Congo
39G1 **Pik Pobedy** *Mt* China/ Kirgizia
18D2 **Piła** Poland
74E3 **Pilar** Paraguay
74D2 **Pilcomayo** *R* Argentina/ Bolivia/Paraguay
47E1 **Pilgrim's Rest** South Africa
42D3 **Pīlībhīt** India
19D2 **Pilica** *R* Poland
34C4 **Pillar,C** Australia
75C2 **Pilões, Serra dos** *Mts* Brazil
17E3 **Pílos** Greece
58C1 **Pilot Knob** *Mt* USA
66D1 **Pilot Peak** *Mt* USA
63E3 **Pilottown** USA
73G4 **Pimenta** Brazil
30C4 **Pinang** *I* Malaysia
69A2 **Pinar del Rio** Cuba
13C2 **Pinche** Belgium
73J4 **Pindaré** *R* Brazil
17E3 **Píndhos** *Mts* Greece
63D2 **Pine Bluff** USA
60C2 **Pine Bluffs** USA
61E1 **Pine City** USA
32C2 **Pine Creek** Australia
68B2 **Pine Creek** *R* USA
66C1 **Pinecrest** USA
66C2 **Pinedale** California, USA
58E2 **Pinedale** Wyoming, USA
66C2 **Pine Flat Res** USA
20G3 **Pinega** Russian Federation
20H3 **Pinega** *R* Russian Federation
68B2 **Pine Grove** USA
67B3 **Pine Hills** USA
67C1 **Pinehurst** USA
67B3 **Pine I** USA
63D2 **Pineland** USA
67B3 **Pinellas Park** USA
66B3 **Pine Mt** USA
54G3 **Pine Point** Canada
60C2 **Pine Ridge** USA
63D2 **Pines,L. o'the** USA
63D2 **Pineville** USA
31C3 **Pingdingshan** China
31B5 **Pingguo** China
31B2 **Pingliang** China
31B2 **Pingluo** China
31D4 **Pingtan Dao** *I* China
31E5 **Pingtung** Taiwan
31A3 **Pingwu** China
31B5 **Pingxiang** Guangxi, China
31C4 **Pingxiang** Jiangxi, China
73J4 **Pinheiro** Brazil
27C6 **Pini** *I* Indonesia
17E3 **Piniós** *R* Greece
32A4 **Pinjarra** Australia
66B2 **Pinnacles Nat. Mon.** USA
34B3 **Pinnaroo** Australia
Pinos,I de = Juventud, Isla de la
66C3 **Pinos,Mt** USA
59B3 **Pinos,Pt** USA
27E7 **Pinrang** Indonesia
33F3 **Pins, Île des** New Caledonia
21D5 **Pinsk** Belarus
20H3 **Pinyug** Russian Federation
59D3 **Pioche** USA
16C2 **Piombino** Italy
58D1 **Pioneer Mts** USA
25K2 **Pioner, Ostrov** *I* Russian Federation
20L3 **Pionerskiy** Russian Federation
19D2 **Piotrków Trybunalski** Poland
8F2 **Piper** *Oilfield* N Sea
66D2 **Piper Peak** *Mt* USA
61D2 **Pipestone** USA
57F2 **Pipmuacan, Rés** *Res* Canada
64C2 **Piqua** USA
75B4 **Piquiri** *R* Brazil
75C2 **Piracanjuba** Brazil
75C3 **Piracicaba** Brazil
75C3 **Piraçununga** Brazil
75C3 **Piraí do Sul** Brazil
17E3 **Piraiévs** Greece
75C3 **Pirajuí** Brazil
75B2 **Piranhas** Brazil
75D2 **Pirapora** Brazil
75C2 **Pirenópolis** Brazil
75C2 **Pires do Rio** Brazil
17E3 **Pírgos** Greece
14B3 **Pirineos** *Mts* France/ Spain
73K4 **Piripiri** Brazil
13D3 **Pirmasens** Germany
17E2 **Pirot** Serbia, Yugoslavia
42C2 **Pīr Panjāl Range** *Mts* Pakistan
27F7 **Piru** Indonesia
66C3 **Piru Creek** *R* USA
16C2 **Pisa** Italy
72C6 **Pisco** Peru
68C1 **Piseco** USA
18C3 **Písek** Czech Republic
42B2 **Pishin** Pakistan
66B3 **Pismo Beach** USA
74C3 **Pissis** *Mt* Argentina
16C2 **Pistoia** Italy
15B1 **Pisuerga** *R* Spain
58B2 **Pit** *R* USA
72C3 **Pitalito** Colombia
37N6 **Pitcairn** *I* Pacific Ocean
12H5 **Pite** *R* Sweden
12J5 **Piteå** Sweden
17E2 **Piteşti** Romania
25L4 **Pit Gorodok** Russian Federation
13B3 **Pithiviers** France
20E3 **Pitkyaranta** Russian Federation
8D3 **Pitlochry** Scotland
20M2 **Pitlyar** Russian Federation
33H5 **Pitt** *I* New Zealand
54F4 **Pitt I** Canada
66B1 **Pittsburg** California, USA
63D1 **Pittsburg** Kansas, USA
65D2 **Pittsburgh** USA
64A3 **Pittsfield** Illinois, USA
68D1 **Pittsfield** Massachusetts, USA
68C2 **Pittston** USA
34D1 **Pittsworth** Australia
72B5 **Piura** Peru
66C3 **Piute Peak** *Mt* USA
43E3 **Piuthan** Nepal
66C3 **Pixley** USA
12B2 **Pjórsá** *R* Iceland
55N5 **Placentia B** Canada
66B1 **Placerville** USA
13C3 **Plaine Lorraine** *Region* France
62B1 **Plains** USA
61D2 **Plainview** Nebraska, USA
62B2 **Plainview** Texas, USA
66B2 **Planada** USA
73H7 **Planalto de Mato Grosso** *Plat* Brazil
73L5 **Planalto do Borborema** *Plat* Brazil
33E1 **Planet Deep** Papua New Guinea
60D2 **Plankinton** USA
63C2 **Plano** USA
67B3 **Plantation** USA
67B3 **Plant City** USA
15A1 **Plasencia** Spain
20L5 **Plast** Russian Federation
26G2 **Plastun** Russian Federation
74E5 **Plata, Río de la** Argentina/ Uruguay
13D2 **Plateau Lorrain** France
69C5 **Plato** Colombia
45B1 **Platres** Cyprus
60D2 **Platte** USA
60C2 **Platte** *R* USA
64A2 **Platteville** USA
65E2 **Plattsburgh** USA
61D2 **Plattsmouth** USA
18C2 **Plauen** Germany
20F5 **Plavsk** Russian Federation
72B4 **Playas** Ecuador
66B2 **Pleasanton** California, USA
62C3 **Pleasanton** Texas, USA
68C3 **Pleasantville** USA
64B3 **Pleasure Ridge Park** USA
30D3 **Pleiku** Vietnam
35C1 **Plenty,B of** New Zealand
60C1 **Plentywood** USA
20G3 **Plesetsk** Russian Federation
19D2 **Pleszew** Poland
55L4 **Pletipi,L** Canada
17E2 **Pleven** Bulgaria
17D2 **Pljevlja** Montenegro, Yugoslavia
17D2 **Ploče** Bosnia-Herzegovina
19D2 **Płock** Poland
14B2 **Ploërmel** France
17F2 **Ploieşti** Romania
13D4 **Plombières-les-Bains** France
20C5 **Płońsk** Poland
17E2 **Plovdiv** Bulgaria
58C1 **Plummer** USA
51C6 **Plumtree** Zimbabwe
66B1 **Plymouth** California, USA
7B4 **Plymouth** England
64B2 **Plymouth** Indiana, USA
68E2 **Plymouth** Massachusetts, USA
68C2 **Plymouth** Pennsylvania, USA
68E2 **Plymouth B** USA
7B4 **Plymouth Sd** England
7C3 **Plynlimon** *Mt* Wales
18C3 **Plzeň** Czech Republic
18D2 **Pniewy** Poland
48B3 **Po** Burkina
16C2 **Po** *R* Italy
48C4 **Pobé** Benin
26H2 **Pobedino** Russian Federation
58D2 **Pocatello** USA
19G2 **Pochinok** Russian Federation
75D1 **Poções** Brazil
65D3 **Pocomoke City** USA
75A2 **Poconé** Brazil
75C3 **Poços de Caldas** Brazil
17D2 **Podgorica** Montenegro, Yugoslavia
25L3 **Podkamennaya Tunguska** *R* Russian Federation
20F4 **Podol'sk** Russian Federation
19F3 **Podol'skaya Vozvyshennost'** *Upland* Ukraine
20E3 **Podporozh'ye** Russian Federation
20G3 **Podyuga** Russian Federation
47B2 **Pofadder** South Africa
42A2 **Poghdar** Afghanistan
28B3 **P'ohang** S Korea
76G9 **Poinsett,C** Antarctica
34C2 **Point** Australia
69E3 **Pointe-à-Pitre** Guadeloupe
50B4 **Pointe Noire** Congo
34B3 **Point Fairy** Australia
69L1 **Point Fortin** Trinidad
54B3 **Point Hope** USA
54G3 **Point L** Canada
54B3 **Point Lay** USA
68C2 **Point Pleasant** New Jersey, USA
64C3 **Point Pleasant** W Virginia, USA
14C2 **Poitiers** France
14B2 **Poitou** *Region* France
13A3 **Poix** France
42C3 **Pokaran** India
34C1 **Pokataroo** Australia
43E3 **Pokhara** Nepal
25O3 **Pokrovsk** Russian Federation
59D3 **Polacca** USA
68C1 **Poland** USA
19D2 **Poland** *Republic* Europe
40B2 **Polatlı** Turkey
49D4 **Poli** Cameroon
16D3 **Policastro, G di** Italy
27F5 **Polillo Is** Philippines
25P4 **Poliny Osipenko** Russian Federation
45B1 **Polis** Cyprus
17E2 **Políyiros** Greece
44B3 **Pollāchi** India
16D3 **Pollino, Monte** *Mt* Italy
19F2 **Polonnye** Ukraine
19F1 **Polotsk** Belarus
58D1 **Polson** USA
21E6 **Poltava** Ukraine
16D1 **Pölten** Austria
20L3 **Polunochoye** Russian Federation
12L5 **Poluostrov Rybachiy** *Pen* Russian Federation
62A2 **Polvadera** USA
20E2 **Polyarnyy** Murmansk, Russian Federation
25Q2 **Polyarnyy** Yakutskaya, Russian Federation
20L2 **Polyarnyy Ural** *Mts* Russian Federation
37L4 **Polynesia** *Region* Pacific Ocean
72C5 **Pomabamba** Peru
75D3 **Pomba** *R* Brazil
9C2 **Pomeroy** Northern Ireland
66D3 **Pomona** USA
61D3 **Pomona Res** USA
67B3 **Pompano Beach** USA
68C2 **Pompton Lakes** USA
63C1 **Ponca City** USA
69D3 **Ponce** Puerto Rico
67B3 **Ponce de Leon B** USA
44B3 **Pondicherry** India
55L2 **Pond Inlet** Canada
15A1 **Ponferrada** Spain
48C4 **Pongara, Pte** Equatorial Guinea
50C3 **Pongo** *R* Sudan
47E2 **Pongola** *R* South Africa
44B3 **Ponnāni** India
43G4 **Ponnyadoung Range** *Mts* Burma
24F3 **Ponoy** Russian Federation
20G2 **Ponoy** *R* Russian Federation
14B2 **Pons** France
48A1 **Ponta Delgada** Azores
75B4 **Ponta Grossa** Brazil
75C3 **Pontal** Brazil
13C3 **Pont-à-Mousson** France
75A3 **Ponta Pora** Brazil
14D2 **Pontarlier** France
63D2 **Pontchartrain,L** USA
75A1 **Ponte de Pedra** Brazil
16C2 **Pontedera** Italy
7D3 **Pontefract** England
16B2 **Ponte Leccia** Corsica, France
15A1 **Pontevedra** Spain
64B2 **Pontiac** Illinois, USA
64C2 **Pontiac** Michigan, USA
27D7 **Pontianak** Indonesia
14B2 **Pontivy** France
13B3 **Pontoise** France
63E2 **Pontotoc** USA
13B3 **Pont-sur-Yonne** France
7C4 **Pontypool** Wales
7C4 **Pontypridd** Wales
16C2 **Ponziane, I** Italy
7D4 **Poole** England
Poona = Pune
34B2 **Pooncarie** Australia
34B2 **Poopelloe,L** Australia
72E7 **Poopó, Lago** Bolivia
54C3 **Poorman** USA
72C3 **Popayán** Colombia
13B2 **Poperinge** Belgium
34B2 **Popilta L** Australia
60B1 **Poplar** USA
63D1 **Poplar Bluff** USA
63E2 **Poplarville** USA
70C3 **Popocatepetl** *Vol* Mexico
50B4 **Popokabaka** Zaïre
27H7 **Popondetta** Papua New Guinea
17F2 **Popovo** Bulgaria
75C1 **Porangatu** Brazil
42B4 **Porbandar** India
75C1 **Porcos** *R* Brazil
54D3 **Porcupine** *R* Canada/ USA
16C1 **Poreč** Croatia
75B3 **Porecatu** Brazil
12J6 **Pori** Finland
35B2 **Porirua** New Zealand
12H5 **Porjus** Sweden
69E4 **Porlamar** Venezuela
26H2 **Poronaysk** Russian Federation
20E3 **Porosozero** Russian Federation
12K4 **Porsangen** *Inlet* Norway
12F7 **Porsgrunn** Norway
9C2 **Portadown** Northern Ireland
9D2 **Portaferry** Northern Ireland
64B2 **Portage** USA
60C1 **Portal** USA
54F5 **Port Alberni** Canada
15A2 **Portalegre** Portugal
62B2 **Portales** USA
47D3 **Port Alfred** South Africa
54F4 **Port Alice** Canada
68A2 **Port Allegany** USA
63D2 **Port Allen** USA
58B1 **Port Angeles** USA
69B3 **Port Antonio** Jamaica
9C3 **Portarlington** Irish Republic
63D3 **Port Arthur** USA
8B4 **Port Askaig** Scotland
32C4 **Port Augusta** Australia
69C3 **Port-au-Prince** Haiti

64C2 **Port Austin** USA
44E3 **Port Blair** Andaman Islands
34B3 **Port Campbell** Australia
43F4 **Port Canning** India
55M5 **Port Cartier** Canada
35B3 **Port Chalmers** New Zealand
67B3 **Port Charlotte** USA
68D2 **Port Chester** USA
64C2 **Port Clinton** USA
65D2 **Port Colborne** Canada
34C4 **Port Davey** *B* Australia
69C3 **Port-de-Paix** Haiti
30C5 **Port Dickson** Malaysia
47E3 **Port Edward** South Africa
75D2 **Porteirinha** Brazil
64C2 **Port Elgin** Canada
47D3 **Port Elizabeth** South Africa
8B4 **Port Ellen** Scotland
6B2 **Port Erin** Isle of Man, British Islands
69N2 **Porter Pt** St Vincent
66C2 **Porterville** USA
32D4 **Port Fairy** Australia
50A4 **Port Gentil** Gabon
63D2 **Port Gibson** USA
58B1 **Port Hammond** Canada
48C4 **Port Harcourt** Nigeria
54F4 **Port Hardy** Canada
55M5 **Port Hawkesbury** Canada
7C4 **Porthcawl** Wales
32A3 **Port Hedland** Australia
7B3 **Porthmadog** Wales
55N4 **Port Hope Simpson** Canada
66C3 **Port Hueneme** USA
64C2 **Port Huron** USA
15A2 **Portimão** Portugal
34D2 **Port Jackson** *B* Australia
68D2 **Port Jefferson** USA
68C2 **Port Jervis** USA
34D2 **Port Kembla** Australia
7C4 **Portland** England
64C2 **Portland** Indiana, USA
65E2 **Portland** Maine, USA
34C2 **Portland** New South Wales, Australia
58B1 **Portland** Oregon, USA
34B3 **Portland** Victoria, Australia
69H2 **Portland Bight** *B* Jamaica
7C4 **Portland Bill** *Pt* England
34C4 **Portland,C** Australia
35C1 **Portland I** New Zealand
69H2 **Portland Pt** Jamaica
9C3 **Port Laoise** Irish Republic
63C3 **Port Lavaca** USA
32C4 **Port Lincoln** Australia
48A4 **Port Loko** Sierra Leone
51F6 **Port Louis** Mauritius
34B3 **Port MacDonnell** Australia
34D2 **Port Macquarie** Australia
68A2 **Port Matilda** USA
32D1 **Port Moresby** Papua New Guinea
47B2 **Port Nolloth** South Africa
68C3 **Port Norris** USA
Porto = Oporto
74F4 **Pôrto Alegre** Brazil
Porto Alexandre = Tombua
69A5 **Porto Armuelles** Panama
75A1 **Pôrto Artur** Brazil
75B3 **Pôrto 15 de Novembro** Brazil
75B1 **Pôrto dos Meinacos** Brazil
74F2 **Pôrto E Cunha** Brazil
75A2 **Pôrto Esperança** Brazil
16C2 **Portoferraio** Italy
69L1 **Port of Spain** Trinidad
75A2 **Pôrto Jofre** Brazil
75B3 **Pôrto Mendez** Brazil
75A3 **Pôrto Murtinho** Brazil
48C4 **Porto Novo** Benin
75B3 **Pôrto Primavera, Represa** *Res* Brazil
58B1 **Port Orchard** USA
58B2 **Port Orford** USA
75B3 **Pôrto Santa Helena** Brazil
48A1 **Porto Santo** *I* Madeira
75B3 **Pôrto São José** Brazil
73L7 **Pôrto Seguro** Brazil
16B2 **Porto Torres** Sardinia, Italy
75B4 **Pôrto União** Brazil
16B2 **Porto Vecchio** Corsica, France
72F5 **Pôrto Velho** Brazil
8C4 **Portpatrick** Scotland
35A3 **Port Pegasus** *B* New Zealand
34B3 **Port Phillip B** Australia
34A2 **Port Pirie** Australia
8B3 **Portree** Scotland
58B1 **Port Renfrew** Canada
69J2 **Port Royal** Jamaica
67B2 **Port Royal Sd** USA
9C2 **Portrush** Northern Ireland
45B3 **Port Said** Egypt
67A3 **Port St Joe** USA
47D3 **Port St Johns** South Africa
55N4 **Port Saunders** Canada
47E3 **Port Shepstone** South Africa
69Q2 **Portsmouth** Dominica
7D4 **Portsmouth** England
68E1 **Portsmouth** New Hampshire, USA
64C3 **Portsmouth** Ohio, USA
65D3 **Portsmouth** Virginia, USA
34D2 **Port Stephens** *B* Australia
9C2 **Portstewart** Northern Ireland
50D2 **Port Sudan** Sudan
63E3 **Port Sulphur** USA
12K5 **Porttipahdan Tekojärvi** *Res* Finland
15A2 **Portugal** *Republic* Europe
9B3 **Portumna** Irish Republic
68A1 **Portville** USA
64B2 **Port Washington** USA
30C5 **Port Weld** Malaysia
72E6 **Porvenir** Bolivia
12K6 **Porvoo** Finland
74E3 **Posadas** Argentina
15A2 **Posadas** Spain
41G3 **Posht-e Badam** Iran
27F7 **Poso** Indonesia
28A4 **Posŏng** S Korea
20M2 **Pos Poluy** Russian Federation
75C1 **Posse** Brazil
62B2 **Post** USA
19F1 **Postavy** Belarus
47C2 **Postmasburg** South Africa
16C1 **Postojna** Slovenia
28C2 **Pos'yet** Russian Federation
47D2 **Potchefstroom** South Africa
63D1 **Poteau** USA
16D2 **Potenza** Italy
47D1 **Potgietersrus** South Africa
62C3 **Poth** USA
21G7 **Poti** Georgia
48D3 **Potiskum** Nigeria
58C1 **Potlatch** USA
47C3 **Potloer** *Mt* South Africa
58C1 **Pot Mt** USA
65D3 **Potomac** *R* USA
72E7 **Potosí** Bolivia
74C3 **Potrerillos** Chile
18C2 **Potsdam** Germany
60C2 **Potter** USA
68C2 **Pottstown** USA
68B2 **Pottsville** USA
68D2 **Poughkeepsie** USA
75C3 **Pouso Alegre** Brazil
35C1 **Poverty B** New Zealand
20F3 **Povonets** Russian Federation
21G5 **Povorino** Russian Federation
55L4 **Povungnituk** Canada
60B1 **Powder** *R* USA
60B2 **Powder River** USA
58E2 **Powell** USA
32C2 **Powell Creek** Australia
59D3 **Powell,L** USA
54F5 **Powell River** Canada
7C3 **Powys** *County* Wales
75B2 **Poxoréo** Brazil
31D4 **Poyang Hu** *L* China
40C2 **Pozantı** Turkey
70C2 **Poza Rica** Mexico
18D2 **Poznań** Poland
74E2 **Pozo Colorado** Paraguay
16C2 **Pozzuoli** Italy
48B4 **Pra** *R* Ghana
30C3 **Prachin Buri** Thailand
30B3 **Prachuap Khiri Khan** Thailand
18D2 **Praděd** *Mt* Czech Republic
14C3 **Pradelles** France
75E2 **Prado** Brazil
18C2 **Prague** Czech Republic
Praha = Prague
48A4 **Praia** Cape Verde
75A1 **Praia Rica** Brazil
72F5 **Prainha** Brazil
62B2 **Prairie Dog Town Fork** *R* USA
64A2 **Prairie du Chien** USA
61E3 **Prairie Village** USA
30C3 **Prakhon Chai** Thailand
75C2 **Prata** Brazil
75C2 **Prata** *R* Brazil
Prates *I* **= Dongsha Qundao**
16C2 **Prato** Italy
68C1 **Prattsville** USA
67A2 **Prattville** USA
14B1 **Prawle Pt** England
25L4 **Predivinsk** Russian Federation
25O3 **Predporozhnyy** Russian Federation
19E2 **Pregolyu** *R* Russian Federation
30D3 **Prek Kak** Cambodia
64A1 **Prentice** USA
18C2 **Prenzlau** Germany
44E3 **Preparis I** Burma
18D3 **Přerov** Czech Republic
59D4 **Prescott** Arizona, USA
63D2 **Prescott** Arkansas, USA
65D2 **Prescott** Canada
60C2 **Presho** USA
74D3 **Presidencia Roque Sáenz Peña** Argentina
75B3 **Presidente Epitácio** Brazil
75B2 **Presidente Murtinho** Brazil
75B3 **Presidente Prudente** Brazil
75B3 **Presidente Venceslau** Brazil
62B3 **Presidio** USA
19E3 **Prešov** Slovakia
65F1 **Presque Isle** USA
6C3 **Preston** England
56B2 **Preston** Idaho, USA
61E2 **Preston** Minnesota, USA
63D1 **Preston** Missouri, USA
8C4 **Prestwick** Scotland
73J8 **Prêto** Brazil
75C2 **Prêto** *R* Brazil
47D2 **Pretoria** South Africa
17E3 **Préveza** Greece
30D3 **Prey Veng** Cambodia
59D3 **Price** USA
63E2 **Prichard** USA
21E6 **Prichernomorskaya Nizmennost'** *Lowland* Ukraine
69M2 **Prickly Pt** Grenada
19F3 **Pridneprovskaya Vozvyshennost'** *Upland* Ukraine
19E1 **Priekule** Lithuania
47C2 **Prieska** South Africa
58C1 **Priest L** USA
58C1 **Priest River** USA
17E2 **Prilep** Albania/Macedonia, Yugoslavia/Greece
21E5 **Priluki** Ukraine
76G3 **Primavera** *Base* Antarctica
12K6 **Primorsk** Russian Federation
21F6 **Primorsko-Akhtarsk** Russian Federation
54H4 **Prince Albert** Canada
47C3 **Prince Albert** South Africa
54F2 **Prince Albert,C** Canada
54G2 **Prince Albert Pen** Canada
54G2 **Prince Albert Sd** Canada
55L3 **Prince Charles I** Canada
76F10 **Prince Charles Mts** Antarctica
55M5 **Prince Edward I** *Province* Canada
36C7 **Prince Edward Is** Indian Ocean
54F4 **Prince George** Canada
54H2 **Prince Gustaf Adolf Sea** Canada
27H8 **Prince of Wales I** Australia
54H2 **Prince of Wales I** Canada
54E4 **Prince of Wales I** USA
54G2 **Prince of Wales Str** Canada
54G2 **Prince Patrick I** Canada
55J2 **Prince Regent Inlet** *Str* Canada
54E4 **Prince Rupert** Canada
32D2 **Princess Charlotte B** Australia
69L1 **Princes Town** Trinidad
54F5 **Princeton** Canada
64B2 **Princeton** Illinois, USA
64B3 **Princeton** Kentucky, USA
61E2 **Princeton** Missouri, USA
68C2 **Princeton** New Jersey, USA
64C3 **Princeton** W Virginia, USA
54D3 **Prince William Sd** USA
48C4 **Príncipe** *I* Sao Tome & Principe
58B2 **Prineville** USA
55O3 **Prins Christian Sund** Greenland
76F12 **Prinsesse Astrid Kyst** *Region* Antarctica
76F12 **Prinsesse Ragnhild Kyst** *Region* Antarctica
24C2 **Prins Karls Forland** *I* Svalbard, Norway
70D3 **Prinzapolca** Nicaragua
20E3 **Priozersk** Russian Federation
19F2 **Pripet** *R* Belarus
Pripyat' *R* Belarus **= Pripet**
17E2 **Prispansko Jezero** *L* Albania/Macedonia, Yugoslavia/Greece
17E2 **Priština** Serbia, Yugoslavia
18C2 **Pritzwalk** Germany
20G5 **Privolzhskaya Vozvyshennost'** *Upland* Russian Federation
17E2 **Prizren** Serbia, Yugoslavia
27E7 **Probolinggo** Indonesia
61E1 **Proctor** USA
44B3 **Proddatūr** India
70D2 **Progreso** Mexico
58B2 **Project City** USA
21G7 **Prokhladnyy** Russian Federation
24K4 **Prokop'yevsk** Russian Federation
21G6 **Proletarskaya** Russian Federation
Prome = Pyè
75A2 **Promissão** Brazil
19G2 **Pronya** *R* Belarus
73L6 **Propriá** Brazil
32D3 **Proserpine** Australia
68C1 **Prospect** New York, USA
58B2 **Prospect** Oregon, USA
18D3 **Prostějov** Czech Republic
55N2 **Prøven** Greenland
14D3 **Provence** *Region* France
68E2 **Providence** USA
69A4 **Providencia, Isla de** Caribbean Sea
25U3 **Provideniya** Russian Federation
68E1 **Provincetown** USA
13B3 **Provins** France
59D2 **Provo** USA
54G4 **Provost** Canada
75B4 **Prudentópolis** Brazil
54D2 **Prudhoe Bay** USA
55M2 **Prudhoe Land** *Region* Greenland
19E2 **Pruszkow** Poland
19F3 **Prut** *R* Moldavia/Romania
21D6 **Prutul** *R* Romania
19E2 **Pruzhany** Belarus
63C1 **Pryor** USA
19E3 **Przemyśl** Poland
17F3 **Psará** *I* Greece
20D4 **Pskov** Russian Federation
19F2 **Ptich** *R* Belarus
17E2 **Ptolemaïs** Greece
28A3 **Puan** S Korea
72D5 **Pucallpa** Peru
31D4 **Pucheng** China
12K5 **Pudasjärvi** Finland
20F3 **Pudozh** Russian Federation
44B3 **Pudukkottai** India
70C3 **Puebla** Mexico
15A1 **Puebla de Sanabria** Spain
15A1 **Puebla de Trives** Spain
62B1 **Pueblo** USA
73L5 **Puerta do Calcanhar** *Pt* Brazil
47E2 **Puerta do Oro** *Pt* South Africa
75B3 **Puerto Adela** Brazil
74B7 **Puerto Aisén** Chile
70D4 **Puerto Armuelles** Panama
73G6 **Puerto Artur** Brazil
72C3 **Puerto Asis** Colombia
72E2 **Puerto Ayacucho** Venezuela
70D3 **Puerto Barrios** Guatemala
72D2 **Puerto Berrio** Colombia
72E1 **Puerto Cabello** Venezuela
70D3 **Puerto Cabezas** Nicaragua
72E2 **Puerto Carreńo** Colombia
75A3 **Puerto Casado** Brazil
75A3 **Puerto Cooper** Brazil
70D4 **Puerto Cortés** Costa Rica
70D3 **Puerto Cortés** Honduras
48A2 **Puerto del Rosario** Canary Islands
73H8 **Puerto E. Cunha** Brazil
72D1 **Puerto Fijo** Venezuela
73J5 **Puerto Franco** Brazil
75A3 **Puerto Guaraní** Brazil
72E6 **Puerto Heath** Bolivia
70D2 **Puerto Juárez** Mexico
72F1 **Puerto la Cruz** Venezuela
15B2 **Puertollano** Spain
69C4 **Puerto López** Colombia
74D6 **Puerto Madryn** Argentina
72E6 **Puerto Maldonado** Peru
74B6 **Puerto Montt** Chile
73G8 **Puerto Murtinho** Brazil
74B8 **Puerto Natales** Chile
70A1 **Puerto Peñasco** Mexico
75A3 **Puerto Pinasco** Brazil
74D6 **Puerto Pirámides** Argentina
69C3 **Puerto Plata** Dominican Republic
74F3 **Puerto Presidente Stroessner** Brazil
27E6 **Puerto Princesa** Philippines
72C3 **Puerto Rico** Colombia
69D3 **Puerto Rico** *I* Caribbean Sea
69D3 **Puerto Rico Trench** Caribbean Sea
73H4 **Puerto Santana** Brazil
75A3 **Puerto Sastre** Brazil
74E1 **Puerto Suárez** Bolivia
70B2 **Puerto Vallarta** Mexico
74B6 **Puerto Varas** Chile
72F7 **Puerto Villarroel** Bolivia
21H5 **Pugachev** Russian Federation
42C3 **Pūgal** India
15C1 **Puigcerdá** Spain
28A2 **Pujŏn** N Korea
28A2 **Pujŏn Res** N Korea
35B2 **Pukaki,L** *L* New Zealand
28A2 **Pukchin** N Korea
28B2 **Pukch'ŏng** N Korea
35B1 **Pukekohe** New Zealand
35B2 **Puketeraki Range** *Mts* New Zealand
20G3 **Puksoozero** Russian Federation
16C2 **Pula** Croatia
65D2 **Pulaski** New York, USA
67A1 **Pulaski** Tennessee, USA
64C3 **Pulaski** Virginia, USA
27G7 **Pulau Kolepom** *I* Indonesia
27C7 **Pulau Pulau Batu** *Is* Indonesia
Pulau Pulau Macan - Kepulauan = Takabonerate
19E2 **Puławy** Poland
44C3 **Pulicat L** India
42B1 **Pul-i-Khumri** Afghanistan
44B4 **Puliyangudi** India
58C1 **Pullman** USA
27G6 **Pulo Anna** *I* Pacific Ocean
12L5 **Pulozero** Russian Federation
19E2 **Pułtusk** Poland
74C3 **Puna de Atacama** Argentina
72B4 **Puná, Isla** Ecuador
43F3 **Punakha** Bhutan
42C2 **Pūnch** Pakistan
47E1 **Punda Milia** South Africa
44A2 **Pune** India
28A2 **Pungsan** N Korea
28A2 **Pungso** N Korea
50C4 **Punia** Zaïre
74B4 **Punitaqui** Chile
42C2 **Punjab** *Province* Pakistan
42D2 **Punjab** *State* India
72D7 **Puno** Peru
74D5 **Punta Alta** Argentina
74B8 **Punta Arenas** Chile
59C4 **Punta Banda, Cabo** *C* Mexico
74F4 **Punta del Este** Uruguay
70D3 **Punta Gorda** Belize
67B3 **Punta Gorda** USA
72B1 **Puntarenas** Costa Rica
31C4 **Puqi** China
24J3 **Pur** *R* Russian Federation
72C3 **Purace, Vol** Colombia
63C1 **Purcell** USA
62B1 **Purgatoire** *R* USA
43F5 **Puri** India
44B2 **Pūrna** India
43F3 **Pūrnia** India
30C3 **Pursat** Cambodia
72F4 **Purus** *R* Brazil
63E2 **Purvis** USA
27D7 **Purwokerto** Indonesia
28B2 **Puryŏng** N Korea
42D5 **Pusad** India
28B3 **Pusan** S Korea
20E4 **Pushkin** Russian Federation
20F3 **Pushlakhta** Russian Federation
19F1 **Pustoshka** Russian Federation
43H3 **Putao** Burma
35C1 **Putaruru** New Zealand
31D4 **Putian** China
27E7 **Puting, Tanjung** *C* Indonesia
68E2 **Putnam** USA
68D1 **Putney** USA
44B4 **Puttalam** Sri Lanka
18C2 **Puttgarden** Germany
72C4 **Putumayo** *R* Colombia/Ecuador/Peru
27E6 **Putussiban** Indonesia
12K6 **Puulavesi** *L* Finland
58B1 **Puyallup** USA
35A3 **Puysegur Pt** New Zealand
51C4 **Pweto** Zaïre
7B3 **Pwllheli** Wales
51C6 **PWV** *Province* South Africa
20F3 **Pyal'ma** Russian Federation
20E2 **Pyaozero, Ozero** *L* Russian Federation
30B2 **Pyapon** Burma
25K2 **Pyasina** *R* Russian Federation

21G7 **Pyatigorsk** Russian Federation
43H5 **Pyè** Burma
12K6 **Pyhäselkä** *L* Finland
30B2 **Pyinmana** Burma
28A2 **Pyŏktong** N Korea
28A3 **Pyonggang** N Korea
28A3 **Pyŏnggok-dong** S Korea
28A3 **P'yŏngsan** N Korea
28A3 **P'yŏngt'aek** S Korea
28B3 **P'yŏngyang** N Korea
34B3 **Pyramid Hill** Australia
59C2 **Pyramid L** USA
35A2 **Pyramid,Mt** New Zealand
14B3 **Pyrénées** *Mts* France/Spain
19F1 **Pytalovo** Russian Federation
30B2 **Pyu** Burma

Q

45D4 **Qa'ash Shubyk, Wadi** Jordan
45C2 **Qabatiya** Israel
45D3 **Qā'el Hafīra** *Mud Flats* Jordan
45D3 **Qa'el Jinz** *Mud Flats* Jordan
55O3 **Qagssimiut** Greenland
26C3 **Qaidam Pendi** *Salt Flat* China
45D2 **Qa Khanna** *Salt Marsh* Jordan
50D2 **Qala'en Nahl** Sudan
42B2 **Qalat** Afghanistan
45D1 **Qal'at al Ḥiṣn** Syria
45C1 **Qal'at al Marqab** *Hist Site* Syria
50E2 **Qal'at Bīshah** Saudi Arabia
41E3 **Qal'at Sālih** Iraq
26C3 **Qamdo** Tibet, China
Qaqortoq = Julianehåb
50E2 **Qandala** Somalia
49E2 **Qara** Egypt
50E3 **Qardho** Somalia
21H8 **Qareh Dāgh** *Mts* Iran
41E4 **Qaryat al Ulyā** Saudi Arabia
45C3 **Qasr ed Deir, Jebel** *Mt* Jordan
45D3 **Qasr el Kharana** Jordan
41E3 **Qāṣr e Shīrīn** Iran
49E2 **Qasr Farâfra** Egypt
45D2 **Qaṭanā** Syria
41F4 **Qatar** *Emirate* Arabian Pen
45C4 **Qatim, Jebel** *Mt* Jordan
45D3 **Qatrāna** Jordan
49E2 **Qattâra Depression** Egypt
41G3 **Qāyen** Iran
41F2 **Qazvīn** Iran
40B4 **Qena** Egypt
Qeqertarsuaq = Julianehåb
41E2 **Qeydār** Iran
41F4 **Qeys** *I* Iran
21H8 **Qezel Owzan** *R* Iran
45C3 **Qeziot** Israel
31B5 **Qian Jiang** *R* China
31E1 **Qian Shan** *Upland* China
31E3 **Qidong** China
31B4 **Qijiang** China
26C2 **Qijiaojing** China
42B2 **Qila Saifullah** Pakistan
31A2 **Qilian** China
26C3 **Qilian Shan** China
25L6 **Qilian Shan** *Mts* China
31B3 **Qin'an** China
31E2 **Qingdao** China
28A3 **Qingduizi** China
31A2 **Qinghai** *Province* China
26C3 **Qinghai Hu** *L* China
31D3 **Qingjiang** Jiangsu, China
31D4 **Qingjiang** Jiangxi, China
31B3 **Qing Jiang** *R* China
31C2 **Qingshuihe** China
31B2 **Qingshui He** *R* China
31B2 **Qingtongxia** China
31B2 **Qingyang** China
28A2 **Qingyuan** China
31D4 **Qingyuan** Zhejiang, China
39G2 **Qing Zang** *Upland* China
31B5 **Qingzhou** China
31D2 **Qinhuangdao** China
31B3 **Qin Ling** *Mts* China
30D1 **Qinzhou** China
30E2 **Qionghai** China
31A3 **Qionglai Shan** *Upland* China
30D1 **Qiongzhou Haixia** *Str* China
26F2 **Qiqihar** China
45C3 **Qīraīya, Wadi** Egypt
45C2 **Qiryat Ata** Israel
45C3 **Qiryat Gat** Israel
45C2 **Qiryat Shemona** Israel
45C2 **Qiryat Yam** Israel
45C2 **Qishon** *R* Israel
25K5 **Qitai** China
31C4 **Qiyang** China
31B1 **Qog Qi** China
41F2 **Qolleh-ye Damavand** *Mt* Iran
41F3 **Qom** Iran
41F3 **Qomisheh** Iran
Qomolangma Feng *Mt* **= Everest,Mt**
45D1 **Qornet es Saouda** *Mt* Lebanon
55N3 **Qôrnoq** Greenland
41E2 **Qorveh** Iran
41G4 **Qotbābad** Iran
21H8 **Qotur** *R* Iran
68D1 **Quabbin Res** USA
47C2 **Quaggablat** South Africa
13D1 **Quakenbrück** Germany
68C2 **Quakertown** USA
30C3 **Quam Phu Quoc** *I* Vietnam
62C2 **Quanah** USA
30D2 **Quang Ngai** Vietnam
30D2 **Quang Tri** Vietnam
30D4 **Quan Long** Vietnam
31D5 **Quanzhou** Fujian, China
31C4 **Quanzhou** Guangxi, China
54H4 **Qu' Appelle** *R* Canada
59D4 **Quartzsite** USA
41G2 **Quchan** Iran
34C3 **Queanbeyan** Australia
65E1 **Québec** Canada
55L4 **Quebec** *Province* Canada
75C2 **Quebra-Anzol** *R* Brazil
74F3 **Quedas do Iguaçu** *Falls* Argentina/Brazil
68C3 **Queen Anne** USA
54E4 **Queen Charlotte Is** Canada
54F4 **Queen Charlotte Sd** Canada
54F4 **Queen Charlotte Str** Canada
54H1 **Queen Elizabeth Is** Canada
76F9 **Queen Mary Land** *Region* Antarctica
54H3 **Queen Maud G** Canada
76E6 **Queen Maud Mts** Antarctica
68D2 **Queens** *Borough* New York, USA
27F8 **Queen's Ch** Australia
34B3 **Queenscliff** Australia
32D3 **Queensland** *State* Australia
34C4 **Queenstown** Australia
35A3 **Queenstown** New Zealand
47D3 **Queenstown** South Africa
68B3 **Queenstown** USA
51B4 **Quela** Angola
51D5 **Quelimane** Mozambique
62A2 **Quemado** USA
70B2 **Querétaro** Mexico
42B2 **Quetta** Pakistan
70C3 **Quezaltenango** Guatemala
27F5 **Quezon City** Philippines
51B5 **Quibala** Angola
51B4 **Quibaxe** Angola
72C2 **Quibdó** Colombia
14B2 **Quiberon** France
51B4 **Quicama Nat Pk** Angola
75A4 **Quiindy** Paraguay
72D6 **Quillabamba** Peru
72E7 **Quillacollo** Bolivia
14C3 **Quillan** France
54H4 **Quill Lakes** Canada
74B4 **Quillota** Chile
34B1 **Quilpie** Australia
51B4 **Quimbele** Angola
14B2 **Quimper** France
14B2 **Quimperlé** France
59B3 **Quincy** California, USA
64A3 **Quincy** Illinois, USA
68E1 **Quincy** Massachusetts, USA
30D3 **Qui Nhon** Vietnam
15B2 **Quintanar de la Orden** Spain
51B5 **Quirima** Angola
34D2 **Quirindi** Australia
51E5 **Quissanga** Mozambique
51D6 **Quissico** Mozambique
72C4 **Quito** Ecuador
73L4 **Quixadá** Brazil
31A4 **Qujing** China
47D3 **Qumbu** South Africa
32C4 **Quorn** Australia
40B4 **Qus** Egypt
40B4 **Quseir** Egypt
55N3 **Qutdligssat** Greenland
Quthing = Moyeni
31B3 **Qu Xian** Sichuan, China
31D4 **Qu Xian** Zhejiang, China
30D2 **Quynh Luu** Vietnam
31C2 **Quzhou** China
43G3 **Qüzü** China

R

12J6 **Raahe** Finland
8B3 **Raasay** *I* Scotland
8B3 **Raasay,Sound of** *Chan* Scotland
50F2 **Raas Caseyr** Somalia
16C2 **Rab** *I* Croatia
27E7 **Raba** Indonesia
18D3 **Rába** *R* Hungary
48B1 **Rabat** Morocco
32E1 **Rabaul** Papua New Guinea
45C3 **Rabba** Jordan
40C5 **Rābigh** Saudi Arabia
55N5 **Race,C** Canada
68E1 **Race Pt** USA
45C2 **Rachaya** Lebanon
18C3 **Rachel** *Mt* Germany
30D3 **Rach Gia** Vietnam
64B2 **Racine** USA
19F3 **Rădăuţi** Romania
64B3 **Radcliff** USA
64C3 **Radford** USA
42C4 **Radhanpur** India
69L1 **Radix,Pt** Trinidad
19E2 **Radom** Poland
19D2 **Radomsko** Poland
19F2 **Radomyshl'** Ukraine
18C3 **Radstad** Austria
19E1 **Radviliškis** Lithuania
54G3 **Rae** Canada
43E3 **Rāe Bareli** India
55K3 **Rae Isthmus** Canada
54G3 **Rae L** Canada
35C1 **Raetihi** New Zealand
74D4 **Rafaela** Argentina
45C3 **Rafah** Egypt
50C3 **Rafai** Central African Republic
41D3 **Rafhā** Saudi Arabia
41G3 **Rafsanjān** Iran
50C3 **Raga** Sudan
69Q2 **Ragged Pt** Barbados
16C3 **Ragusa** Sicily, Italy
50D2 **Rahad** *R* Sudan
42C3 **Rahimyar Khan** Pakistan
41F3 **Rāhjerd** Iran
44B2 **Rāichur** India
43E4 **Raigarh** India
34B3 **Rainbow** Australia
67A2 **Rainbow City** USA
58B1 **Rainier** USA
58B1 **Rainier,Mt** USA
61E1 **Rainy** *R* Canada/USA
55J5 **Rainy L** Canada
61E1 **Rainy L** Canada/USA
61E1 **Rainy River** Canada
43E4 **Raipur** India
44C2 **Rājahmundry** India
27E6 **Rajang** *R* Malaysia
42C3 **Rajanpur** Pakistan
44B4 **Rājapālaiyam** India
42C3 **Rājasthān** *State* India
42D4 **Rājgarh** Madhya Pradesh, India
42D3 **Rājgarh** Rājasthān, India
42C4 **Rājkot** India
43F4 **Rājmahāl Hills** India
43E4 **Raj Nāndgaon** India
42C4 **Rājpīpla** India
43F4 **Rajshahi** Bangladesh
42D4 **Rājur** India
35B2 **Rakaia** *R* New Zealand
39G3 **Raka Zangbo** *R* China
19E3 **Rakhov** Ukraine
42A3 **Rakhshan** *R* Pakistan
47C1 **Rakops** Botswana
19F2 **Rakov** Belarus
67C1 **Raleigh** USA
45C4 **Ram** Jordan
45C2 **Rama** Israel
75D1 **Ramalho, Serra do** *Mts* Brazil
45C3 **Ramallah** Israel
44B4 **Rāmanāthapuram** India
26H3 **Ramapo Deep** Pacific Ocean
45C2 **Ramat Gan** Israel
13D3 **Rambervillers** France
14C2 **Rambouillet** France
43F4 **Rāmgarh** Bihār, India
42C3 **Rāmgarh** Rājasthān, India
41E3 **Rāmhormoz** Iran
45C4 **Ram, Jebel** *Mt* Jordan
45C3 **Ramla** Israel
59C4 **Ramona** USA
42D3 **Rāmpur** India
42D4 **Rāmpura** India
43G5 **Ramree I** Burma
21J8 **Rāmsar** Iran
6B2 **Ramsey** Isle of Man, British Islands
68C2 **Ramsey** USA
7B4 **Ramsey I** Wales
7E4 **Ramsgate** England
45D2 **Ramtha** Jordan
32D1 **Ramu** *R* Papua New Guinea
27E6 **Ranau** Malaysia
74B4 **Rancagua** Chile
60B2 **Ranchester** USA
43F4 **Rānchi** India
43E4 **Rānchi Plat** India
74B6 **Ranco, Lago** Chile
47D2 **Randburg** South Africa
12F7 **Randers** Denmark
47D2 **Randfontein** South Africa
65E2 **Randolph** Vermont, USA
66D3 **Randsburg** USA
35B3 **Ranfurly** New Zealand
43G4 **Rangamati** Bangladesh
60B2 **Rangely** USA
35B2 **Rangiora** New Zealand
35C1 **Rangitaiki** *R* New Zealand
35B2 **Rangitata** *R* New Zealand
35C1 **Rangitikei** *R* New Zealand
30B2 **Rangoon** Burma
43F3 **Rangpur** Bangladesh
44B3 **Rānībennur** India
43F4 **Rānīganj** India
55J3 **Rankin Inlet** Canada
34C2 **Rankins Springs** Australia
8C3 **Rannoch, Loch** *L* Scotland
42B4 **Rann of Kachchh** *Flood Area* India
30B4 **Ranong** Thailand
27C6 **Rantauparapat** Indonesia
27F7 **Rantekombola, G** *Mt* Indonesia
64B2 **Rantoul** USA
75B1 **Ranuro** *R* Brazil
13D3 **Raon-l'Etape** France
33H3 **Raoul** *I* Pacific Ocean
16B2 **Rapallo** Italy
55M3 **Raper,C** Canada
60C2 **Rapid City** USA
64B1 **Rapid River** USA
65D3 **Rappahannock** *R* USA
43M2 **Rapti** *R* India
68C2 **Raritan B** USA
40C5 **Ras Abû Dâra** *C* Egypt
40C5 **Ra's Abu Madd** *C* Saudi Arabia
50D1 **Ras Abu Shagara** *C* Sudan
40D2 **Ra's al 'Ayn** Syria
41G4 **Ras al Khaimah** UAE
38D4 **Ra's al Madrakah** *C* Oman
50E2 **Ras Andadda** *C* Eritrea
41E4 **Ra's az Zawr** *C* Saudi Arabia
40C5 **Râs Banâs** *C* Egypt
45B3 **Ras Burûn** *C* Egypt
50D2 **Ras Dashan** *Mt* Ethiopia
41E3 **Ra's-e Barkan** *Pt* Iran
45A3 **Râs el Barr** *C* Egypt
16B3 **Ras El Hadid** Algeria
40A3 **Râs el Kenâyis** *Pt* Egypt
45C4 **Râs el Nafas** *Mt* Egypt
45B4 **Râs el Sudr** *C* Egypt
45C4 **Ras en Naqb** *Upland* Jordan
38D4 **Ra's Fartak** *C* Yemen
40B4 **Râs Ghârib** Egypt
50D2 **Rashad** Sudan
45C3 **Rashādīya** Jordan
40B3 **Rashîd** Egypt
41E2 **Rasht** Iran
45C1 **Ra's ibn Hāni'** *C* Syria
50E2 **Ras Khanzira** *C* Somalia
42B3 **Ras Koh** *Mt* Pakistan
45B4 **Râs Matarma** *C* Egypt
40B4 **Râs Muhammad** *C* Egypt
48A2 **Ras Nouadhibou** *C* Mauritius/Morocco
26J2 **Rasshua** *I* Kuril Is, Russian Federation
21G5 **Rasskazovo** Russian Federation
41E4 **Ra's Tanāqib** *C* Saudi Arabia
41F4 **Ra's Tannūrah** Saudi Arabia
18B3 **Rastatt** Germany
Ras Uarc = Tres Forcas, Cabo
45C4 **Ras Um Seisabān** *Mt* Jordan
50E2 **Ras Xaafuun** *C* Somalia
42C3 **Ratangarh** India
30B3 **Rat Buri** Thailand
42D3 **Rāth** India
18C2 **Rathenow** Germany
9C2 **Rathfriland** Northern Ireland
9C2 **Rathlin I** Northern Ireland
9C2 **Rathmelton** Irish Republic
45D4 **Ratiyah, Wadi** Jordan
42C4 **Ratlām** India
44A2 **Ratnāgiri** India
44C4 **Ratnapura** Sri Lanka
19E2 **Ratno** Ukraine
62B1 **Raton** USA
12H6 **Rättvik** Sweden
35C1 **Raukumara Range** *Mts* New Zealand
75D3 **Raul Soares** Brazil
12J6 **Rauma** Finland
43E4 **Raurkela** India
41E3 **Ravānsar** Iran
41G3 **Rāvar** Iran
19E2 **Rava Russkaya** Ukraine
68D1 **Ravena** USA
16C2 **Ravenna** Italy
18B3 **Ravensburg** Germany
32D2 **Ravenshoe** Australia
6E2 **Ravenspurn** *Oilfield* N Sea
42C2 **Ravi** *R* Pakistan
55Q3 **Ravn Kap** *C* Greenland
42C2 **Rawalpindi** Pakistan
41D2 **Rawāndiz** Iraq
18D2 **Rawicz** Poland
32B4 **Rawlinna** Australia
56C2 **Rawlins** USA
74D6 **Rawson** Argentina
6C3 **Rawtenstall** England
44B3 **Rāyadurg** India
44C2 **Rāyagada** India
45D2 **Rayak** Lebanon
55N5 **Ray,C** Canada
41G4 **Rāyen** Iran
66C2 **Raymond** California, USA
58D1 **Raymond** Canada
68E1 **Raymond** New Hampshire, USA
58B1 **Raymond** Washington, USA
34D2 **Raymond Terrace** Australia
63C3 **Raymondville** USA
41E2 **Razan** Iran
19G3 **Razdel'naya** Ukraine
28C2 **Razdol'noye** Russian Federation
17F2 **Razgrad** Bulgaria
17F2 **Razim** *L* Romania
7D4 **Reading** England
68C2 **Reading** USA
54G3 **Read Island** Canada
68D1 **Readsboro** USA
49E2 **Rebiana** *Well* Libya
49E2 **Rebiana Sand Sea** Libya
12L6 **Reboly** Russian Federation
29E1 **Rebun-tō** *I* Japan
32B4 **Recherche,Arch of the** *Is* Australia
19G2 **Rechitsa** Belarus
73M5 **Recife** Brazil
47D3 **Recife,C** South Africa
75E2 **Recifes da Pedra Grande** *Arch* Brazil
33F2 **Récifs d'Entrecasteaux** New Caledonia
13D2 **Recklinghausen** Germany
74E3 **Reconquista** Argentina
61D1 **Red** *R* Canada/USA
63D2 **Red** *R* USA
30C4 **Redang** *I* Malaysia
68C2 **Red Bank** New Jersey, USA
67A1 **Red Bank** Tennessee, USA
59B2 **Red Bluff** USA
62B2 **Red Bluff L** USA
6D2 **Redcar** England
34D1 **Redcliffe** Australia
34B2 **Red Cliffs** Australia
60D2 **Red Cloud** USA
54G4 **Red Deer** Canada
54G4 **Red Deer** *R* Canada
58B2 **Redding** USA
7D3 **Redditch** England
60D2 **Redfield** USA
7D4 **Redhill** England
62C1 **Red Hills** USA
57D2 **Red L** USA
55J4 **Red Lake** Canada
61D1 **Red Lake** *R* USA
66D3 **Redlands** USA
68B3 **Red Lion** USA
58E1 **Red Lodge** USA
58B2 **Redmond** USA
66D3 **Red Mountain** USA
61D2 **Red Oak** USA
14B2 **Redon** France
66C4 **Redondo Beach** USA
31B5 **Red River Delta** Vietnam
7B4 **Redruth** England
38B3 **Red Sea** Africa/Arabian Pen
54G4 **Redwater** Canada
61E2 **Red Wing** USA
66A2 **Redwood City** USA
61D2 **Redwood Falls** USA
64B2 **Reed City** USA
66C2 **Reedley** USA
58B2 **Reedsport** USA
65D3 **Reedville** USA
35B2 **Reefton** New Zealand
10B3 **Ree, Lough** *L* Irish Republic
6D2 **Reeth** England
40C2 **Refahiye** Turkey
63C3 **Refugio** USA
75E2 **Regência** Brazil
18C3 **Regensburg** Germany
48C2 **Reggane** Algeria
16D3 **Reggio di Calabria** Italy
16C2 **Reggio nell'Emilia** Italy
17E1 **Reghin** Romania
54H4 **Regina** Canada
42A2 **Registan** *Region* Afghanistan
47B1 **Rehoboth** Namibia
65D3 **Rehoboth Beach** USA
45C3 **Rehovot** Israel

67C1 **Reidsville** USA
7D4 **Reigate** England
14B2 **Ré, Ile de** *I* France
13B3 **Reims** France
74B8 **Reina Adelaida, Archipiélago de la** Chile
61E2 **Reinbeck** USA
54H4 **Reindeer L** Canada
15B1 **Reinosa** Spain
68B3 **Reisterstown** USA
47D2 **Reitz** South Africa
54H3 **Reliance** Canada
58E2 **Reliance** USA
15C2 **Relizane** Algeria
34A2 **Remarkable,Mt** Australia
27E7 **Rembang** Indonesia
13D3 **Remiremont** France
13D2 **Remscheid** Germany
68C1 **Remsen** USA
12G6 **Rena** Norway
64B3 **Rend L** USA
18B2 **Rendsburg** Germany
65D1 **Renfrew** Canada
8C4 **Renfrew** Scotland
27D7 **Rengat** Indonesia
19F3 **Reni** Ukraine
50D2 **Renk** Sudan
55Q2 **Renland** *Pen* Greenland
34B2 **Renmark** Australia
33F2 **Rennell** *I* Solomon Islands
14B2 **Rennes** France
59C3 **Reno** USA
16C2 **Reno** *R* Italy
68B2 **Renovo** USA
68D1 **Rensselaer** USA
58B1 **Renton** USA
27F7 **Reo** Indonesia
19G2 **Repki** Ukraine
75C3 **Represa de Furnas** *Dam* Brazil
75C2 **Represa Três Marias** *Dam* Brazil
58C1 **Republic** USA
60D2 **Republican** *R* USA
55K3 **Repulse Bay** Canada
41F2 **Reshteh-ye Alborz** *Mts* Iran
31A2 **Reshui** China
74E3 **Resistencia** Argentina
17E1 **Reşiţa** Romania
55J2 **Resolute** Canada
35A3 **Resolution I** New Zealand
55M3 **Resolution Island** Canada
47E2 **Ressano Garcia** Mozambique
13C3 **Rethel** France
17E3 **Réthimnon** Greece
36D6 **Réunion** *I* Indian Ocean
15C1 **Reus** Spain
18B3 **Reutlingen** Germany
20K4 **Revda** Russian Federation
54G4 **Revelstoke** Canada
13C3 **Revigny-sur-Ornain** France
70A3 **Revillagigedo** *Is* Mexico
37O4 **Revilla Gigedo, Islas** Pacific Ocean
13C3 **Revin** France
45C3 **Revivim** Israel
43E4 **Rewa** India
42D3 **Rewāri** India
58D2 **Rexburg** USA
12A2 **Reykjavik** Iceland
70C2 **Reynosa** Mexico
14B2 **Rezé** France
19F1 **Rezekne** Latvia
20L4 **Rezh** Russian Federation
7C3 **Rhayader** Wales
45C1 **Rhazīr** Lebanon
13E2 **Rheda Wiedenbrück** Germany
18B2 **Rhein** *R* W Europe
18B2 **Rheine** Germany
14D2 **Rheinland Pfalz** *Region* Germany
Rhine *R* **= Rhein**
68D2 **Rhinebeck** USA
64B1 **Rhinelander** USA
65E2 **Rhode Island** *State* USA
68E2 **Rhode Island Sd** USA
17F3 **Rhodes** Greece
17F3 **Rhodes** *I* Greece
47D1 **Rhodes Drift** *Ford* Botswana/South Africa
58D1 **Rhodes Peak** *Mt* USA
7C4 **Rhondda** Wales
14C3 **Rhône** *R* France
7C3 **Rhyl** Wales
73L6 **Riachão do Jacuipe** Brazil
75D1 **Riacho de Santana** Brazil
15A1 **Ria de Arosa** *B* Spain
15A1 **Ria de Betanzos** *B* Spain
15A1 **Ria de Corcubion** *B* Spain
15A1 **Ria de Lage** *B* Spain
15A1 **Ria de Sta Marta** *B* Spain
15A1 **Ria de Vigo** *B* Spain
42C2 **Riāsi** Pakistan
27D6 **Riau, Kepulauan** *Is* Indonesia
15A1 **Ribadeo** Spain
75B3 **Ribas do Rio Pardo** Brazil
51D5 **Ribauè** Mozambique
6C3 **Ribble** *R* England
75C3 **Ribeira** Brazil
75C3 **Ribeirão Prêto** Brazil
72E6 **Riberalta** Bolivia
65D2 **Rice L** Canada
64A1 **Rice Lake** USA
47E2 **Richard's Bay** South Africa
63C2 **Richardson** USA
54E3 **Richardson Mts** Canada
59D3 **Richfield** USA
68C1 **Richfield Springs** USA
66C3 **Richgrove** USA
58C1 **Richland** USA
64C3 **Richlands** USA
66A2 **Richmond** California, USA
47C3 **Richmond** Cape Province, South Africa
6D2 **Richmond** England
64C3 **Richmond** Kentucky, USA
47E2 **Richmond** Natal, South Africa
34D2 **Richmond** New South Wales, Australia
35B2 **Richmond** New Zealand
32D3 **Richmond** Queensland, Australia
65D3 **Richmond** Virginia, USA
35B2 **Richmond Range** *Mts* New Zealand
68C1 **Richmondville** USA
7D4 **Rickmansworth** England
65D2 **Rideau Lakes** Canada
67B2 **Ridgeland** USA
68A2 **Ridgway** USA
69D4 **Riecito** Venezuela
18C2 **Riesa** Germany
74B8 **Riesco** *I* Chile
47C2 **Riet** *R* South Africa
16C2 **Rieti** Italy
15B2 **Rif** *Mts* Morocco
48B1 **Rif** *R* Morocco
60B3 **Rifle** USA
19E1 **Riga** Latvia
11H2 **Riga,G of** Estonia/Latvia
Rīgas Jūrās Līcis = Gulf of Riga
58D2 **Rigby** USA
58C1 **Riggins** USA
55N4 **Rigolet** Canada
Riia Laht = Gulf of Riga
12J6 **Riihimaki** Finland
16C1 **Rijeka** Croatia
29D3 **Rikuzen-Tanaka** Japan
12H7 **Rimbo** Sweden
16C2 **Rimini** Italy
17F1 **Rîmnicu Sărat** Romania
17E1 **Rîmnicu Vîlcea** Romania
57G2 **Rimouski** Canada
12F7 **Ringkøbing** Denmark
27E7 **Rinjani** *Mt* Indonesia
8B4 **Rinns Point** Scotland
13E1 **Rinteln** Germany
72C4 **Riobamba** Ecuador
48C4 **Rio Benito** Equatorial Guinea
72E5 **Rio Branco** Brazil
75C4 **Rio Branco do Sul** Brazil
62C3 **Rio Bravo** Mexico
70B1 **Rio Bravo del Norte** *R* Mexico/USA
75B3 **Rio Brilhante** Brazil
75C3 **Rio Claro** Brazil
69L1 **Rio Claro** Trinidad
74D4 **Ríocuarto** Argentina
75D3 **Rio de Janeiro** Brazil
75D3 **Rio de Janeiro** *State* Brazil
48A2 **Rio de Oro, Bahia de** *B* Morocco
74C8 **Río Gallegos** Argentina
74C8 **Río Grande** Argentina
74F4 **Rio Grande** Brazil
69A4 **Río Grande** Nicaragua
70B2 **Rio Grande** *R* Mexico/USA
70D3 **Rio Grande** *R* Nicaragua
62C3 **Rio Grande City** USA
70B2 **Rio Grande de Santiago** *R* Mexico
73L5 **Rio Grande do Norte** *State* Brazil
74F3 **Rio Grande Do Sul** *State* Brazil
52G6 **Rio Grande Rise** Atlantic Ocean
69C4 **Ríohacha** Colombia
14C2 **Riom** France
72E7 **Rio Mulatos** Bolivia
75C4 **Rio Negro** Brazil
74C5 **Río Negro** *State* Argentina
74E4 **Río Negro, Embalse de** *Res* Uruguay
74F3 **Rio Pardo** Brazil
74B8 **Río Turbio** Argentina
75B2 **Rio Verde** Brazil
75B2 **Rio Verde de Mato Grosso** Brazil
7D3 **Ripley** England
64C3 **Ripley** Ohio, USA
63E1 **Ripley** Tennessee, USA
64C3 **Ripley** West Virginia, USA
6D2 **Ripon** England
66B2 **Ripon** USA
29E1 **Rishiri-tō** *I* Japan
45C3 **Rishon le Zion** Israel
68B3 **Rising Sun** USA
12F7 **Risør** Norway
44E3 **Ritchie's Arch** *Is* Andaman Islands
55N2 **Ritenbenk** Greenland
66C2 **Ritter,Mt** USA
58C1 **Ritzville** USA
74B3 **Rivadavia** Chile
72A1 **Rivas** Nicaragua
74E4 **Rivera** Uruguay
66B2 **Riverbank** USA
48B4 **River Cess** Liberia
66C2 **Riverdale** USA
68D2 **Riverhead** USA
34B3 **Riverina** *Region* Australia
35A3 **Riversdale** New Zealand
47C3 **Riversdale** South Africa
66D4 **Riverside** USA
35A3 **Riverton** New Zealand
58E2 **Riverton** USA
67B3 **Riviera Beach** USA
65F1 **Rivière-du-Loup** Canada
28A2 **Riwon** N Korea
41E5 **Riyadh** Saudi Arabia
40D1 **Rize** Turkey
31D2 **Rizhao** China
45C1 **Rizokaipaso** Cyprus
16D3 **Rizzuto, C** Italy
12F7 **Rjukan** Norway
8B2 **Roag, Loch** *Inlet* Scotland
55K2 **Roanes Pen** Canada
14C2 **Roanne** France
67A2 **Roanoke** Alabama, USA
65D3 **Roanoke** Virginia, USA
65D3 **Roanoke** *R* USA
67C1 **Roanoke Rapids** USA
59D3 **Roan Plat** USA
58D2 **Roberts** USA
59C3 **Roberts Creek Mt** USA
12J6 **Robertsfors** Sweden
63D1 **Robert S Kerr Res** USA
47B3 **Robertson** South Africa
48A4 **Robertsport** Liberia
55L5 **Roberval** Canada
6D2 **Robin Hood's Bay** England
34B2 **Robinvale** Australia
63C3 **Robstown** USA
15A2 **Roca, Cabo de** *C* Portugal
70A3 **Roca Partida** *I* Mexico
73M4 **Rocas** *I* Brazil
74F4 **Rocha** Uruguay
7C3 **Rochdale** England
75B2 **Rochedo** Brazil
14B2 **Rochefort** France
64B2 **Rochelle** USA
54G3 **Rocher River** Canada
34B3 **Rochester** Australia
55L5 **Rochester** Canada
7E4 **Rochester** England
61E2 **Rochester** Minnesota, USA
68E1 **Rochester** New Hampshire, USA
68B1 **Rochester** New York, USA
64B2 **Rock** *R* USA
52H2 **Rockall** *I* UK
64B2 **Rockford** USA
67B2 **Rock Hill** USA
67C2 **Rockingham** USA
64A2 **Rock Island** USA
64B1 **Rockland** Michigan, USA
34B3 **Rocklands Res** Australia
67B3 **Rockledge** USA
63C3 **Rockport** USA
61D2 **Rock Rapids** USA
60B2 **Rock River** USA
60B1 **Rock Springs** Montana, USA
62B2 **Rocksprings** Texas, USA
58E2 **Rock Springs** Wyoming, USA
35B2 **Rocks Pt** New Zealand
34C3 **Rock,The** Australia
68D2 **Rockville** Connecticut, USA
64B3 **Rockville** Indiana, USA
68B3 **Rockville** Maryland, USA
65F1 **Rockwood** USA
62B1 **Rocky Ford** USA
64C1 **Rocky Island L** Canada
67C1 **Rocky Mount** USA
60B2 **Rocky Mountain Nat Pk** USA
56B1 **Rocky Mts** Canada/USA
18C2 **Rødbyhavn** Denmark
14C3 **Rodez** France
Ródhos = Rhodes
16D2 **Rodi Garganico** Italy
17E2 **Rodopi Planina** *Mts* Bulgaria
32A3 **Roebourne** Australia
47D1 **Roedtan** South Africa
13D2 **Roer** *R* Netherlands
13C2 **Roermond** Netherlands
13B2 **Roeselare** Belgium
55K3 **Roes Welcome Sd** Canada
19F2 **Rogachev** Belarus
72E6 **Rogaguado, Lago** Bolivia
63D1 **Rogers** USA
64C1 **Rogers City** USA
66D3 **Rogers L** USA
64C3 **Rogers,Mt** USA
58D2 **Rogerson** USA
47B3 **Roggeveldberge** *Mts* South Africa
58B2 **Rogue** *R* USA
42B3 **Rohri** Pakistan
42D3 **Rohtak** India
19E1 **Roja** Latvia
70C2 **Rojo, Cabo** *C* Mexico
75B3 **Rolândia** Brazil
63D1 **Rolla** USA
58D1 **Rollins** USA
Roma = Rome
34C1 **Roma** Australia
67C2 **Romain,C** USA
17F1 **Roman** Romania
52H5 **Romanche Gap** Atlantic Ocean
27F7 **Romang** *I* Indonesia
21C6 **Romania** *Republic* E Europe
67B3 **Romano,C** USA
14D2 **Romans-sur-Isère** France
27F5 **Romblon** Philippines
67A2 **Rome** Georgia, USA
16C2 **Rome** Italy
68C1 **Rome** New York, USA
65D2 **Rome** USA
14C2 **Romilly-sur-Seine** France
65D3 **Romney** USA
21E5 **Romny** Ukraine
18B1 **Rømø** *I* Denmark
14C2 **Romorantin** France
8C3 **Rona, I** Scotland
8B3 **Ronay, I** Scotland
75B1 **Roncador, Serra do** *Mts* Brazil
15A2 **Ronda** Spain
15A2 **Ronda, Sierra de** *Mts* Spain
72F6 **Rondônia** Brazil
72F6 **Rondônia** *State* Brazil
75B2 **Rondonópolis** Brazil
31B4 **Rong'an** China
31B4 **Rongchang** China
31E2 **Rongcheng** China
54H4 **Ronge, Lac la** Canada
31B4 **Rongjiang** China
31B4 **Rong Jiang** *R* China
30A1 **Rongklang Range** *Mts* Burma
12G7 **Rønne** Denmark
12H7 **Ronneby** Sweden
76F2 **Ronne Ice Shelf** Antarctica
13B2 **Ronse** Belgium
13D1 **Roodeschool** Netherlands
56C3 **Roof Butte** *Mt* USA
42D3 **Roorkee** India
13C2 **Roosendaal** Netherlands
59D2 **Roosevelt** USA
76E6 **Roosevelt I** Antarctica
61E2 **Root** *R* USA
32C2 **Roper** *R* Australia
8D2 **Rora Head** *Pt* Scotland
72F2 **Roraima** *Mt* Brazil/Guyana/Venezuela
72F3 **Roraima** *State* Brazil
12G6 **Røros** Norway
12G6 **Rorvik** Norway
19G3 **Ros'** *R* Ukraine
69Q2 **Rosalie** Dominica
66C3 **Rosamond** USA
66C3 **Rosamond L** USA
74D4 **Rosario** Argentina
73K4 **Rosário** Brazil
75A3 **Rosario** Paraguay
75A1 **Rosario Oeste** Brazil
68C2 **Roscoe** USA
14B2 **Roscoff** France
10B3 **Roscommon** Irish Republic
9C3 **Roscrea** Irish Republic
69Q2 **Roseau** Dominica
34C4 **Rosebery** Australia
60B1 **Rosebud** USA
58B2 **Roseburg** USA
63C3 **Rosenberg** USA
18C3 **Rosenheim** Germany
54H4 **Rosetown** Canada
66B1 **Roseville** USA
12G7 **Roskilde** Denmark
20E5 **Roslavl'** Russian Federation
20G4 **Roslyatino** Russian Federation
17E2 **Roşorii de Vede** Romania
35B2 **Ross** New Zealand
16D3 **Rossano** Italy
10B3 **Rossan Pt** Irish Republic
63E2 **Ross Barnett Res** USA
65D1 **Rosseau L** Canada
33E2 **Rossel** *I* Papua New Guinea
76E6 **Ross Ice Shelf** Antarctica
58B1 **Ross L** USA
9C3 **Rosslare** Irish Republic
35C2 **Ross,Mt** New Zealand
48A3 **Rosso** Mauritius
16B2 **Rosso, C** Corsica, France
7C4 **Ross-on-Wye** England
21F5 **Rossosh** Russian Federation
54E3 **Ross River** Canada
76F6 **Ross S** Antarctica
41F4 **Rostāq** Iran
18C2 **Rostock** Germany
20F4 **Rostov** Russian Federation
21F6 **Rostov-na-Donu** Russian Federation
67B2 **Roswell** Georgia, USA
62B2 **Roswell** New Mexico, USA
27H5 **Rota** *I* Pacific Ocean
27F8 **Rote** *I* Indonesia
18B2 **Rotenburg** Niedersachsen, Germany
13E2 **Rothaar-Geb** *Region* Germany
6D2 **Rothbury** England
76G3 **Rothera** *Base* Antarctica
7D3 **Rotherham** England
8C4 **Rothesay** Scotland
8D3 **Rothes-on-Spey** Scotland
34C2 **Roto** Australia
35B2 **Rotoiti,L** New Zealand
35B2 **Rotoroa,L** New Zealand
35C1 **Rotorua** New Zealand
35C1 **Rotorua,L** New Zealand
13E3 **Rottenburg** Germany
18A2 **Rotterdam** Netherlands
13E3 **Rottweil** Germany
33G2 **Rotuma** *I* Fiji
13B2 **Roubaix** France
14C2 **Rouen** France
6E3 **Rough** *Oilfield* N Sea
Roulers = Roeselare
51F6 **Round I** Mauritius
66D1 **Round Mountain** USA
34D2 **Round Mt** Australia
58E1 **Roundup** USA
8D2 **Rousay** *I* Scotland
14C3 **Roussillon** *Region* France
47D3 **Rouxville** South Africa
65D1 **Rouyn** Canada
12K5 **Rovaniemi** Finland
16C1 **Rovereto** Italy
16C1 **Rovigo** Italy
16C1 **Rovinj** Croatia
19F2 **Rovno** Ukraine
41E2 **Row'ān** Iran
34C1 **Rowena** Australia
55L3 **Rowley I** Canada
32A2 **Rowley Shoals** Australia
27F5 **Roxas** Philippines
67C1 **Roxboro** USA
35A3 **Roxburgh** New Zealand
58E1 **Roy** USA
9C3 **Royal Canal** Irish Republic
64B1 **Royale, Isle** USA
7D3 **Royal Leamington Spa** England
64C2 **Royal Oak** USA
7E4 **Royal Tunbridge Wells** England
14B2 **Royan** France
13B3 **Roye** France
7D3 **Royston** England
19E3 **Rožňava** Slovakia
13B3 **Rozoy** France
21G5 **Rtishchevo** Russian Federation
7C3 **Ruabon** Wales
51D4 **Ruaha Nat Pk** Tanzania
35C1 **Ruahine Range** *Mts* New Zealand
35C1 **Ruapehu,Mt** New Zealand
38C4 **Rub' al Khālī** *Desert* Saudi Arabia
8B3 **Rubha Hunish** *C* Scotland
8C3 **Rubha Réidh** *Pt* Scotland
75B3 **Rubinéia** Brazil
24K4 **Rubtsovsk** Russian Federation
54C3 **Ruby** USA
59C2 **Ruby Mts** USA
41G4 **Rudan** Iran
43L2 **Rudanli** India
41E2 **Rūdbār** Iran
29F2 **Rudnaya** Russian Federation
26G2 **Rudnaya Pristan'** Russian Federation
19G2 **Rudnya** Russian Federation
17E2 **Rudoka Planina** *Mt* Macedonia, Yugoslavia
24G1 **Rudol'fa, Ostrov** *I* Russian Federation
31E3 **Rudong** China
64C1 **Rudyard** USA
14C2 **Ruffec** France
51D4 **Rufiji** *R* Tanzania
74D4 **Rufino** Argentina
48A3 **Rufisque** Senegal
51C5 **Rufunsa** Zambia

7D3 **Rugby** England
60C1 **Rugby** USA
12G8 **Rügen** *I* Germany
13D2 **Ruhr** *R* Germany
31D4 **Ruijin** China
17E2 **Rujen** *Mt* Bulgaria/ Macedonia, Yugoslavia
51D4 **Rukwa, L** Tanzania
8B3 **Rum** *I* Scotland
17D1 **Ruma** Serbia, Yugoslavia
41E4 **Rumāh** Saudi Arabia
50C3 **Rumbek** Sudan
69C2 **Rum Cay** *I* The Bahamas
65E2 **Rumford** USA
32C2 **Rum Jungle** Australia
29D2 **Rumoi** Japan
51D5 **Rumphi** Malawi
35B2 **Runanga** New Zealand
35C1 **Runaway,C** New Zealand
7C3 **Runcorn** England
51B5 **Rundu** Namibia
51D4 **Rungwa** Tanzania
51D4 **Rungwa** *R* Tanzania
51D4 **Rungwe** *Mt* Tanzania
39G2 **Ruoqiang** China
26D2 **Ruo Shui** *R* China
17F1 **Rupea** Romania
58D2 **Rupert** USA
55L4 **Rupert** *R* Canada
13D2 **Rur** *R* Germany
72E6 **Rurrenabaque** Bolivia
51D5 **Rusape** Zimbabwe
17F2 **Ruse** Bulgaria
64A2 **Rushville** Illinois, USA
60C2 **Rushville** Nebraska, USA
34B3 **Rushworth** Australia
63C2 **Rusk** USA
67B3 **Ruskin** USA
35B1 **Russell** New Zealand
60D3 **Russell** USA
63E2 **Russellville** Alabama, USA
63D1 **Russellville** Arkansas, USA
64B3 **Russellville** Kentucky, USA
59B3 **Russian** *R* USA
20F4 **Russian Federation** *Republic* Asia/Europe
25L2 **Russkiy, Ostrov** *I* Russian Federation
41E1 **Rustavi** Georgia
47D2 **Rustenburg** South Africa
63D2 **Ruston** USA
50C4 **Rutana** Burundi
27F7 **Ruteng** Indonesia
47E1 **Rutenga** Zimbabwe
59C3 **Ruth** USA
13E2 **Rüthen** Germany
65E2 **Rutland** USA
44E3 **Rutland** *I* Andaman Islands
42D2 **Rutog** China
Ruvu = Pangani
51E5 **Ruvuma** *R* Mozambique/ Tanzania
45D4 **Ruweila, Wadi** Jordan
50D3 **Ruwenzori Range** *Mts* Uganda/Zaïre
51D5 **Ruya** *R* Zimbabwe
19D3 **Ružomberok** Slovakia
50C4 **Rwanda** *Republic* Africa
8C4 **Ryan, L** Scotland
20F5 **Ryazan'** Russian Federation
20G5 **Ryazhsk** Russian Federation
20F4 **Rybinsk** Russian Federation
20F4 **Rybinskoye Vodokhranilishche** *Res* Russian Federation
19F3 **Rybnitsa** Moldavia
7D4 **Ryde** England
7E4 **Rye** England
58C2 **Rye Patch Res** USA
21E5 **Ryl'sk** Russian Federation
21H6 **Ryn Peski** *Desert* Kazakhstan
28A3 **Ryoju** S Korea
29D3 **Ryōtsu** Japan
19F3 **Ryskany** Moldavia
26F4 **Ryūkyū Is** Japan
19E2 **Rzeszów** Poland
20E4 **Rzhev** Russian Federation

S

41F3 **Sa'ādatābād** Iran
40B5 **Saad el Aali** *Dam* Egypt
18C2 **Saale** *R* Germany
13D3 **Saar** *R* Germany
13D3 **Saarbrücken** Germany
13D3 **Saarburg** Germany
12J7 **Saaremaa** *I* Estonia
13D3 **Saarland** *State* Germany
13D3 **Saarlouis** Germany
45B3 **Saba'a** Egypt
17D2 **Šabac** Serbia, Yugoslavia
15C1 **Sabadell** Spain
29C3 **Sabae** Japan
27E6 **Sabah** *State* Malaysia
69C4 **Sabanalarga** Colombia
27C6 **Sabang** Indonesia
44C2 **Sabari** *R* India
45C2 **Sabastiya** Israel
72E7 **Sabaya** Bolivia
40C3 **Sab'Bi'ār** Syria
45D2 **Sabhā** Jordan
49D2 **Sabhā** Libya
51D6 **Sabi** *R* Zimbabwe
47E2 **Sabie** *R* South Africa
70B2 **Sabinas** Mexico
70B2 **Sabinas Hidalgo** Mexico
63C2 **Sabine** *R* USA
63D3 **Sabine L** USA
41F5 **Sabkhat Maṭṭī** *Salt Marsh* UAE
45B3 **Sabkhet el Bardawîl** *Lg* Egypt
55M5 **Sable,C** Canada
67B3 **Sable,C** USA
55M5 **Sable I** Canada
50E2 **Ṣabyā** Saudi Arabia
41G2 **Sabzevār** Iran
58C1 **Sacajawea Peak** USA
68C1 **Sacandaga Res** USA
61E2 **Sac City** USA
57D1 **Sachigo** *R* Canada
28A3 **Sach'on** S Korea
18C2 **Sachsen** *State* Germany
18C2 **Sachsen-Anhalt** *State* Germany
54F2 **Sachs Harbour** Canada
65E2 **Saco** Maine, USA
60B1 **Saco** Montana, USA
66B1 **Sacramento** USA
66B1 **Sacramento** *R* USA
59B2 **Sacramento V** USA
62A2 **Sacramento Mts** USA
50E2 **Ṣa'dah** Yemen
17E2 **Sadanski** Bulgaria
43H3 **Sadiya** India
15A2 **Sado** *R* Portugal
29D3 **Sado-shima** *I* Japan
42C3 **Sādri** India
Safad = Zefat
42A2 **Safed Koh** *Mts* Afghanistan
12G7 **Säffle** Sweden
59E4 **Safford** USA
7E3 **Saffron Walden** England
40C3 **Safi** Jordan
48B1 **Safi** Morocco
45D1 **Ṣāfītā** Syria
19G1 **Safonovo** Russian Federation
20H2 **Safonovo** Russian Federation
41E3 **Safwān** Iraq
43F3 **Saga** China
28B4 **Saga** Japan
30B1 **Sagaing** Burma
29C4 **Sagami-nada** *B* Japan
42D4 **Sāgar** India
68D2 **Sag Harbor** USA
64C2 **Saginaw** USA
64C2 **Saginaw B** USA
55M4 **Saglek B** Canada
28A3 **Sagŏ-ri** S Korea
62A1 **Saguache** USA
69B2 **Sagua de Tánamo** Cuba
69B2 **Sagua la Grande** Cuba
57F2 **Saguenay** *R* Canada
48A2 **Saguia el Hamra** *Watercourse* Morocco
15B2 **Sagunto** Spain
45D3 **Sahāb** Jordan
15A1 **Sahagún** Spain
48C2 **Sahara** *Desert* N Africa
42D3 **Sahāranpur** India
43K1 **Sahaswan** India
45B4 **Saheira, Wadi el** Egypt
42C2 **Sahiwal** Pakistan
41D3 **Ṣaḥrā al Hijārah** *Desert Region* Iraq
40B4 **Sahra esh Sharqiya** *Desert Region* Egypt
70B2 **Sahuayo** Mexico
45D1 **Sahyūn** *Hist Site* Syria
32D1 **Saibai I** Australia
Saïda = Sidon
41G4 **Sa'īdābad** Iran
15B2 **Saïdia** Morocco
43F3 **Saidpur** Bangladesh
42C2 **Saidu** Pakistan
29B3 **Saigō** Japan
Saigon = Ho Chi Minh City
43G4 **Saiha** India
26E2 **Saihan Tal** China
29B4 **Saijo** Japan
28C4 **Saiki** Japan
12K6 **Saimaa** *L* Finland
8D4 **St Abb's Head** *Pt* Scotland
7D4 **St Albans** England
65E2 **St Albans** Vermont, USA
64C3 **St Albans** West Virginia, USA
7C4 **St Albans Head** *C* England
13B2 **St Amand-les-Eaux** France
14C2 **St Amand-Mont Rond** France
67A3 **St Andrew B** USA
8D3 **St Andrews** Scotland
67B2 **St Andrew Sd** USA
61D1 **Ste Anne** Canada
65E1 **Ste Anne de Beaupré** Canada
69H1 **St Ann's Bay** Jamaica
55N4 **St Anthony** Canada
58D2 **St Anthony** USA
34B3 **St Arnaud** Australia
51E6 **St Augustin, Baie de** *B* Madagascar
67B3 **St Augustine** USA
7B4 **St Austell** England
7B4 **St Austell Bay** England
13D3 **St-Avold** France
6C2 **St Bees Head** *Pt* England
7B4 **St Brides B** Wales
14B2 **St-Brieuc** France
65D2 **St Catharines** Canada
69M2 **St Catherine,Mt** Grenada
67B2 **St Catherines I** USA
7D4 **St Catherines Pt** England
14C2 **St-Chamond** France
58D2 **St Charles** Idaho, USA
61E3 **St Charles** Missouri, USA
64C2 **St Clair** USA
64C2 **St Clair,L** Canada/USA
64C2 **St Clair Shores** USA
14D2 **St Claude** France
61E1 **St Cloud** USA
69E3 **St Croix** *I* Caribbean Sea
65F1 **St Croix** *R* Canada/USA
64A1 **St Croix** *R* USA
64A1 **St Croix Falls** USA
7B4 **St Davids Head** *Pt* Wales
13B3 **St Denis** France
51F6 **St Denis** Réunion
13D3 **St-Dié** France
13C3 **St-Dizier** France
54D3 **St Elias, Mt** USA
54E3 **St Elias Mts** Canada
14B2 **Saintes** France
14C2 **St-Étienne** France
65E1 **St-Félicien** Canada
16B2 **St Florent, G de** Corsica, France
13B3 **St-Florentin** France
60C3 **St Francis** USA
63D1 **St Francis** *R* USA
47C3 **St Francis B** South Africa
47C3 **St Francis,C** South Africa
16B1 **St Gallen** Switzerland
14C3 **St-Gaudens** France
34C1 **St George** Australia
67B2 **St George** South Carolina, USA
59D3 **St George** Utah, USA
67B3 **St George I** Florida, USA
13E3 **St Georgen im Schwarzwald** Germany
58B2 **St George,Pt** USA
65E1 **St-Georges** Canada
69M2 **St George's** Grenada
7A4 **St George's Chan** Irish Republic/Wales
33E1 **St George's Chan** Papua New Guinea
16B1 **St Gotthard** *Pass* Switzerland
7B4 **St Govans Head** *Pt* Wales
66A1 **St Helena** USA
52H5 **St Helena** *I* Atlantic Ocean
47B3 **St Helena B** South Africa
67B2 **St Helena Sd** USA
34C4 **St Helens** Australia
7C3 **St Helens** England
58B1 **St Helens** USA
58B1 **St Helens,Mt** USA
14B2 **St Helier** Jersey, Channel Islands
13C2 **St-Hubert** Belgium
55L5 **St-Hyacinthe** Canada
64C1 **St Ignace** USA
64B1 **St Ignace I** Canada
7D3 **St Ives** Cambs, England
7B4 **St Ives** Cornwall, England
61E2 **St James** Minnesota, USA
63D1 **St James** Missouri, USA
54E4 **St James, C** Canada
65E1 **St-Jean** Canada
14B2 **St Jean-d'Angely** France
65E1 **St-Jean,L** Canada
65E1 **St-Jérôme** Canada
58C1 **St Joe** *R* USA
55M5 **Saint John** Canada
65F1 **St John** *R* Canada/USA
59E4 **St Johns** Arizona, USA
55N5 **St John's** Canada
64C2 **St Johns** Michigan, USA
67B3 **St Johns** *R* USA
65E2 **St Johnsbury** USA
6C2 **St John's Chapel** England
9D2 **St John's** *Pt* Northern Ireland
68C1 **St Johnsville** USA
65E1 **St-Joseph** Canada
63D2 **St Joseph** Louisiana, USA
64B2 **St Joseph** Michigan, USA
61E3 **St Joseph** Missouri, USA
69L1 **St Joseph** Trinidad
64C2 **St Joseph** *R* USA
64C1 **St Joseph I** Canada
63C3 **St Joseph I** USA
55J4 **St Joseph,L** Canada
14C2 **St-Junien** France
13B3 **St-Just-en-Chaussée** France
8A3 **St Kilda** *I* Scotland
69E3 **St Kitts-Nevis** *Is* Caribbean Sea
55M5 **St Lawrence** *R* Canada
55M5 **St Lawrence,G of** Canada
54B3 **St Lawrence I** USA
65D2 **St Lawrence Seaway** Canada/USA
65F1 **St Leonard** Canada
7E4 **St Leonards** England
14B2 **St-Lô** France
48A3 **St-Louis** Senegal
64A3 **St Louis** USA
13D4 **St-Loup-sur-Semouse** France
69E4 **St Lucia** *I* Caribbean Sea
47E2 **St Lucia,L** South Africa
8E1 **St Magnus B** Scotland
14B2 **St-Malo** France
14B2 **St-Malo, Golfe de** *B* France
13D3 **Ste-Marie-aux-Mines** France
58C1 **St Maries** USA
69E3 **St Martin** *I* Caribbean Sea
32D1 **St Mary,Mt** Papua New Guinea
34A2 **St Mary Peak** *Mt* Australia
34C4 **St Marys** Australia
65D2 **St Marys** USA
7A5 **St Marys** *I* England
67B2 **St Marys** *R* USA
32E1 **Saint Mathias Group** *Is* Papua New Guinea
65E1 **St Maurice** *R* Canada
13C3 **Ste-Menehould** France
54B3 **St Michael** USA
68B3 **St Michaels** USA
13C3 **St-Mihiel** France
16B1 **St Moritz** Switzerland
14B2 **St-Nazaire** France
7D3 **St Neots** England
13C2 **St-Niklaas** Belgium
13B2 **St-Omer** France
65F1 **St-Pascal** Canada
54G4 **St Paul** Canada
61E2 **St Paul** Minnesota, USA
60D2 **St Paul** Nebraska, USA
36E6 **St Paul** *I* Indian Ocean
48A4 **St Paul** *R* Liberia
61E2 **St Peter** USA
20E4 **St Petersburg** Russian Federation
67B3 **St Petersburg** USA
55N5 **St Pierre** *I* France
65E1 **St Pierre,L** Canada
13B2 **St-Pol-sur-Ternoise** France
18D3 **St Pölten** Austria
13B3 **St-Quentin** France
14D3 **St Raphaël** France
65F1 **St-Siméon** Canada
67B2 **St Simons I** USA
67B2 **St Stephen** USA
64C2 **St Thomas** Canada
14D3 **St Tropez** France
13C2 **St Truiden** Belgium
61D1 **St Vincent** USA
69E4 **St Vincent and The Grenadines** *Is* Caribbean Sea
34A2 **St Vincent,G** Australia
13D2 **St-Vith** Germany
13D3 **St Wendel** Germany
27H5 **Saipan** *I* Pacific Ocean
42B2 **Saiydabad** Afghanistan
72E7 **Sajama** *Mt* Bolivia
47C3 **Sak** *R* South Africa
29D4 **Sakai** Japan
29B4 **Sakaidi** Japan
28B3 **Sakaiminato** Japan
40D4 **Sakākah** Saudi Arabia
60C1 **Sakakawea,L** USA
57F1 **Sakami,L** Canada
51C5 **Sakania** Zaïre
51E6 **Sakaraha** Madagascar
21E7 **Sakarya** *R* Turkey
19E1 **Sakasleja** Latvia
29D3 **Sakata** Japan
48C4 **Sakété** Benin
26H1 **Sakhalin** *I* Russian Federation
26F4 **Sakishima guntō** *Is* Japan
47C3 **Sakrivier** South Africa
48A4 **Sal** *I* Cape Verde
21G6 **Sal** *R* Russian Federation
12H7 **Sala** Sweden
59C4 **Salada, Laguna** *L* Mexico
74D3 **Salado** *R* Sante Fe, Argentina
48B4 **Salaga** Ghana
30C3 **Sala Hintoun** Cambodia
50B2 **Salal** Chad
38D4 **Ṣalālah** Oman
15A1 **Salamanca** Spain
68A1 **Salamanca** USA
50B3 **Salamat** *R* Chad
27H7 **Salamaua** Papua New Guinea
45B1 **Salamis** *Hist Site* Cyprus
12H5 **Salangen** Norway
74C2 **Salar de Arizaro** *Salt Pan* Argentina
74C2 **Salar de Atacama** *Salt Pan* Chile
72E7 **Salar de Coipasa** *Salt Pan* Bolivia
72E8 **Salar de Uyuni** *Salt Pan* Bolivia
20K5 **Salavat** Russian Federation
32C1 **Salawati** *I* Indonesia
37O6 **Sala y Gómez** *I* Pacific Ocean
14C2 **Salbris** France
47B3 **Saldanha** South Africa
19E1 **Saldus** Latvia
34C3 **Sale** Australia
20M2 **Salekhard** Russian Federation
64B3 **Salem** Illinois, USA
44B3 **Salem** India
68E1 **Salem** Massachusetts, USA
68C3 **Salem** New Jersey, USA
68D1 **Salem** New York, USA
58B2 **Salem** Oregon, USA
64C3 **Salem** Virginia, USA
12G6 **Sälen** Sweden
16C2 **Salerno** Italy
7C3 **Salford** England
17D1 **Salgót** Hungary
19D3 **Salgótarján** Hungary
73L5 **Salgueiro** Brazil
60B3 **Salida** USA
17F3 **Salihli** Turkey
51D5 **Salima** Malawi
61D3 **Salina** Kansas, USA
59D3 **Salina** Utah, USA
16C3 **Salina** *I* Italy
70C3 **Salina Cruz** Mexico
75D2 **Salinas** Brazil
66B2 **Salinas** USA
66B2 **Salinas** *R* USA
15C2 **Salinas, Cabo de** *C* Spain
74D3 **Salinas Grandes** *Salt Pans* Argentina
62A2 **Salinas Peak** *Mt* USA
63D2 **Saline** *R* Arkansas, USA
60C3 **Saline** *R* Kansas, USA
69M2 **Salines,Pt** Grenada
66D2 **Saline V** USA
73J4 **Salinópolis** Brazil
Salisbury = Harare
7D4 **Salisbury** England
65D3 **Salisbury** Maryland, USA
67B1 **Salisbury** North Carolina, USA
55L3 **Salisbury I** Canada
7D4 **Salisbury Plain** England
45D2 **Ṣalkhad** Syria
12K5 **Salla** Finland
63D1 **Sallisaw** USA
55L3 **Salluit** Canada
43E3 **Sallyana** Nepal
41D2 **Salmas** Iran
12L6 **Salmi** Russian Federation
58C1 **Salmo** Canada
58D1 **Salmon** USA
58C1 **Salmon** *R* USA
54G4 **Salmon Arm** Canada
58C1 **Salmon River Mts** USA
12J6 **Salo** Finland
14D3 **Salon-de-Provence** France
Salonica = Thessaloníki
17E1 **Salonta** Romania
12K6 **Salpausselkä** *Region* Finland
21G6 **Sal'sk** Russian Federation
45C2 **Salt** Jordan
47C3 **Salt** *R* South Africa
59D4 **Salt** *R* USA
74C2 **Salta** Argentina
74C2 **Salta** *State* Argentina
7B4 **Saltash** England
9C3 **Saltee, I** Irish Republic
70B2 **Saltillo** Mexico
58D2 **Salt Lake City** USA
72D3 **Salto Angostura** *Waterfall* Colombia
75E2 **Salto da Divisa** Brazil
75B3 **Salto das Sete Quedas** Brazil
72F2 **Salto del Angel** *Waterfall* Venezuela
74E2 **Salto del Guaíra** *Waterfall* Brazil
72D4 **Salto Grande** *Waterfall* Colombia
59C4 **Salton S** USA
75B4 **Saltos do Iguaçu** *Waterfall* Argentina
74E4 **Salto Tacuarembó** Uruguay
42C2 **Salt Range** *Mts* Pakistan
69H2 **Salt River** Jamaica
67B2 **Saluda** USA

44C2 **Sālūr** India
73L6 **Salvador** Brazil
63D3 **Salvador,L** USA
41F5 **Salwah** Qatar
30B1 **Salween** *R* Burma
21H8 **Sal'yany** Azerbaijan
64C3 **Salyersville** USA
18C3 **Salzburg** Austria
18C2 **Salzgitter** Germany
18C2 **Salzwedel** Germany
26C1 **Samagaltay** Russian Federation
69D3 **Samaná** Dominican Republic
40C2 **Samandağı** Turkey
42B1 **Samangan** Afghanistan
29D2 **Samani** Japan
45A3 **Samannûd** Egypt
27F5 **Samar** *I* Philippines
20J5 **Samara** Russian Federation
32E2 **Samarai** Papua New Guinea
27E7 **Samarinda** Indonesia
38E2 **Samarkand** Uzbekistan
41D3 **Sāmarrā'** Iraq
43E4 **Sambalpur** India
27D6 **Sambas** Indonesia
51F5 **Sambava** Madagascar
42D3 **Sambhal** India
19E3 **Sambor** Ukraine
13B2 **Sambre** *R* France
28B3 **Samch'ŏk** S Korea
28A4 **Samch'ŏnp'o** S Korea
28A3 **Samdŭng** N Korea
50D4 **Same** Tanzania
51C5 **Samfya** Zambia
30B1 **Samka** Burma
30C1 **Sam Neua** Laos
33H2 **Samoan Is** Pacific Ocean
17F3 **Sámos** *I* Greece
17F2 **Samothráki** *I* Greece
27E7 **Sampit** Indonesia
63D2 **Sam Rayburn Res** USA
30C3 **Samrong** Cambodia
18C1 **Samsø** *I* Denmark
28A2 **Samsu** N Korea
40C1 **Samsun** Turkey
48B3 **San** Mali
30D3 **San** *R* Cambodia
19E2 **San** *R* Poland
50E2 **San'ā** Yemen
50B3 **Sanaga** *R* Cameroon
74C4 **San Agustín** Argentina
52D6 **San Ambrosia, Isla** Pacific Ocean
41E2 **Sanandaj** Iran
66B1 **San Andreas** USA
69A4 **San Andres, Isla de** Caribbean Sea
62A2 **San Andres Mts** USA
70C3 **San Andrés Tuxtla** Mexico
62B2 **San Angelo** USA
16B3 **San Antioco** Sardinia, Italy
16B3 **San Antioco** *I* Sardinia, Italy
56B4 **San Antonia, Pt** Mexico
74B4 **San Antonio** Chile
62A2 **San Antonio** New Mexico, USA
62C3 **San Antonio** Texas, USA
66B2 **San Antonio** *R* California, USA
63C3 **San Antonio** *R* Texas, USA
15C2 **San Antonio Abad** Spain
69A2 **San Antonio, Cabo** *C* Cuba
62B2 **San Antonio de Bravo** Mexico
69A2 **San Antonio de los Banos** Cuba
66D3 **San Antonio,Mt** USA
74D6 **San Antonio Oeste** Argentina
66B3 **San Antonio Res** USA
66B2 **San Ardo** USA
42D4 **Sanāwad** India
70A3 **San Benedicto** *I* Mexico
63C3 **San Benito** USA
66B2 **San Benito** *R* USA
66B2 **San Benito Mt** USA
66D3 **San Bernardino** USA
74B4 **San Bernardo** Chile
59C4 **San Bernardo Mts** USA
67A3 **San Blas,C** USA
70E4 **San Blas, Puerta** *Pt* Panama
74E3 **San Borja** Brazil
74B5 **San Carlos** Chile
72B1 **San Carlos** Nicaragua
59D4 **San Carlos** USA
74B6 **San Carlos de Bariloche** Argentina
20H4 **Sanchursk** Russian Federation
66D4 **San Clemente** USA
59C4 **San Clemente I** USA
70C3 **San Cristóbal** Mexico
72D2 **San Cristóbal** Venezuela
33F2 **San Cristobal** *I* Solomon Islands
70E2 **Sancti Spíritus** Cuba
14C2 **Sancy, Puy de** *Mt* France
47D1 **Sand** *R* South Africa
8C4 **Sanda, I** Scotland
27E6 **Sandakan** Malaysia
8D2 **Sanday** *I* Scotland
62B2 **Sanderson** USA
7E4 **Sandgate** England
59C4 **San Diego** USA
74C8 **San Diego, Cabo** Argentina
40B2 **Sandıklı** Turkey
43E3 **Sandīla** India
12F7 **Sandnes** Norway
12G5 **Sandnessjøen** Norway
51C4 **Sandoa** Zaïre
19E2 **Sandomierz** Poland
43G5 **Sandoway** Burma
7D4 **Sandown** England
12D3 **Sandoy** *I* Faeroes
58C1 **Sandpoint** USA
63C1 **Sand Springs** USA
32A3 **Sandstone** Australia
61E1 **Sandstone** USA
31C4 **Sandu** China
64C2 **Sandusky** USA
12H6 **Sandviken** Sweden
68E2 **Sandwich** USA
55J4 **Sandy L** Canada
75A3 **San Estanislao** Paraguay
56B3 **San Felipe** Baja Cal, Mexico
74B4 **San Felipe** Chile
69D4 **San Felipe** Venezuela
15C1 **San Felíu de Guixols** Spain
52D6 **San Felix, Isla** Pacific Ocean
74B4 **San Fernando** Chile
27F5 **San Fernando** Philippines
15A2 **San Fernando** Spain
69L2 **San Fernando** Trinidad
66C3 **San Fernando** USA
72E2 **San Fernando** Venezuela
67B3 **Sanford** Florida, USA
65E2 **Sanford** Maine, USA
67C1 **Sanford** N Carolina, USA
57E4 **Sanford** USA
54D3 **Sanford, Mt** USA
74D4 **San Francisco** Argentina
69C3 **San Francisco** Dominican Republic
66A2 **San Francisco** USA
66A2 **San Francisco B** USA
70B2 **San Francisco del Oro** Mexico
66D3 **San Gabriel Mts** USA
42C5 **Sangamner** India
64B3 **Sangamon** *R* USA
25O3 **Sangar** Russian Federation
44B2 **Sangāreddi** India
66C2 **Sanger** USA
31C2 **Sanggan He** *R* China
27E6 **Sanggau** Indonesia
50B3 **Sangha** *R* Congo
42B3 **Sanghar** Pakistan
27F6 **Sangir** *I* Indonesia
27F6 **Sangir, Kepulauan** *Is* Indonesia
30B3 **Sangkhla Buri** Thailand
27E6 **Sangkulirang** Indonesia
44A2 **Sāngli** India
50B3 **Sangmélima** Cameroon
56B3 **San Gorgonio Mt** USA
62A1 **Sangre de Cristo Mts** USA
66A2 **San Gregorio** USA
42D2 **Sangrūr** India
47E1 **Sangutane** *R* Mozambique
74E3 **San Ignacio** Argentina
72D2 **San Jacinto** Colombia
59C4 **San Jacinto Peak** *Mt* USA
28A2 **Sanjiangkou** China
29D3 **Sanjō** Japan
74H2 **San João del Rei** Brazil
66B2 **San Joaquin** *R* USA
66B2 **San Joaquin Valley** USA
62B1 **San Jon** USA
74C7 **San Jorge, Golfo** *G* Argentina
15C1 **San Jorge, Golfo de** *G* Spain
72B1 **San José** Costa Rica
70C3 **San José** Guatemala
66B2 **San Jose** USA
56B4 **San José** *I* Mexico
72F7 **San José de Chiquitos** Bolivia
56C4 **San José del Cabo** Mexico
74G2 **San José do Rio Prêto** Brazil
70B2 **San Joseé del Cabo** Mexico
28A3 **Sanju** S Korea
74C4 **San Juan** Argentina
69D3 **San Juan** Puerto Rico
69L1 **San Juan** Trinidad
72E2 **San Juan** Venezuela
69B2 **San Juan** *Mt* Cuba
66B3 **San Juan** *R* California, USA
70D3 **San Juan** *R* Costa Rica/ Nicaragua
59D3 **San Juan** *R* Utah, USA
74C4 **San Juan** *State* Argentina
74E3 **San Juan Bautista** Paraguay
66B2 **San Juan Bautista** USA
70D3 **San Juan del Norte** Nicaragua
69D4 **San Juan de los Cayos** Venezuela
70D3 **San Juan del Sur** Nicaragua
58B1 **San Juan Is** USA
62A1 **San Juan Mts** USA
74C7 **San Julián** Argentina
50C4 **Sankuru** *R* Zaïre
66A2 **San Leandro** USA
40C2 **Sanliurfa** Turkey
72C3 **San Lorenzo** Colombia
72B4 **San Lorenzo, Cabo** *C* Ecuador
15B1 **San Lorenzo de Escorial** Spain
66B2 **San Lucas** USA
74C4 **San Luis** Argentina
59D4 **San Luis** USA
74C4 **San Luis** *State* Argentina
66B2 **San Luis Canal** USA
66B3 **San Luis Obispo** USA
66B3 **San Luis Obispo B** USA
70B2 **San Luis Potosí** Mexico
66B2 **San Luis Res** USA
16B3 **Sanluri** Sardinia, Italy
72E2 **San Maigualida** *Mts* Venezuela
63C3 **San Marcos** USA
76G3 **San Martin** *Base* Antarctica
74B7 **San Martin, Lago** Argentina/Chile
66A2 **San Mateo** USA
73G7 **San Matías** Bolivia
74D6 **San Matías, Golfo** *G* Argentina
31C3 **Sanmenxia** China
70D3 **San Miguel** El Salvador
66B3 **San Miguel** USA
66B3 **San Miguel** *I* USA
74C3 **San Miguel de Tucumán** Argentina
74F3 **San Miguel d'Oeste** Brazil
31D4 **Sanming** China
74D4 **San Nicolas** Argentina
56B3 **San Nicolas** *I* USA
47D2 **Sannieshof** South Africa
48B4 **Sanniquellie** Liberia
19E3 **Sanok** Poland
69B5 **San Onofore** Colombia
66D4 **San Onofre** USA
27F5 **San Pablo** Philippines
66A1 **San Pablo B** USA
48B4 **San Pédro** Ivory Coast
74D2 **San Pedro** Jujuy, Argentina
74E2 **San Pedro** Paraguay
59D4 **San Pedro** *R* USA
66C4 **San Pedro Chan** USA
56C4 **San Pedro de los Colonias** Mexico
70D3 **San Pedro Sula** Honduras
16B3 **San Pietro** *I* Sardinia, Italy
8D4 **Sanquar** Scotland
70A1 **San Quintin** Mexico
74C4 **San Rafael** Argentina
66A2 **San Rafael** USA
66C3 **San Rafael Mts** USA
16B2 **San Remo** Italy
62C2 **San Saba** *R* USA
71B2 **San Salvador** El Salvador
69C2 **San Salvador** *I* The Bahamas
74C2 **San Salvador de Jujuy** Argentina
15B1 **San Sebastián** Spain
16D2 **San Severo** Italy
66B3 **San Simeon** USA
72E7 **Santa Ana** Bolivia
70C3 **Santa Ana** Guatemala
66D4 **Santa Ana** USA
66D4 **Santa Ana Mts** USA
62C2 **Santa Anna** USA
70B2 **Santa Barbara** Mexico
66C3 **Santa Barbara** USA
66C4 **Santa Barbara** *I* USA
66B3 **Santa Barbara Chan** USA
66C3 **Santa Barbara Res** USA
66C4 **Santa Catalina** *I* USA
66C4 **Santa Catalina,G of** USA
74F3 **Santa Catarina** *State* Brazil
74G3 **Santa Catarina, Isla de** Brazil
69B2 **Santa Clara** Cuba
66B2 **Santa Clara** USA
66C3 **Santa Clara** *R* USA
74C8 **Santa Cruz** Argentina
72F7 **Santa Cruz** Bolivia
27F5 **Santa Cruz** Philippines
66A2 **Santa Cruz** USA
66C4 **Santa Cruz** *I* USA
59D4 **Santa Cruz** *R* USA
74B7 **Santa Cruz** *State* Argentina
75E2 **Santa Cruz Cabrália** Brazil
66C3 **Santa Cruz Chan** USA
48A2 **Santa Cruz de la Palma** Canary Islands
69B2 **Santa Cruz del Sur** Cuba
48A2 **Santa Cruz de Tenerife** Canary Islands
51C5 **Santa Cruz do Cuando** Angola
75C3 **Santa Cruz do Rio Pardo** Brazil
33F2 **Santa Cruz Is** Solomon Islands
66A2 **Santa Cruz Mts** USA
72F3 **Santa Elena** Venezuela
74D4 **Santa Fe** Argentina
62A1 **Santa Fe** USA
74D3 **Santa Fe** *State* Argentina
75B2 **Santa Helena de Goiás** Brazil
31B3 **Santai** China
74B8 **Santa Inés** *I* Chile
33E1 **Santa Isabel** *I* Solomon Islands
66B2 **Santa Lucia Range** *Mts* USA
48A4 **Santa Luzia** *I* Cape Verde
66B3 **Santa Margarita** USA
66D4 **Santa Margarita** *R* USA
70A2 **Santa Margarita, Isla** Mexico
74F3 **Santa Maria** Brazil
66B3 **Santa Maria** USA
48A1 **Santa Maria** *I* Azores
62A2 **Santa María** *R* Chihuahua, Mexico
47E2 **Santa Maria, Cabo de** *C* Mozambique
75D1 **Santa Maria da Vitória** Brazil
17D3 **Santa Maria di Leuca, Capo** *C* Italy
62A2 **Santa María Laguna de** *L* Mexico
69C4 **Santa Marta** Colombia
72D1 **Santa Marta, Sierra Nevada de** *Mts* Colombia
66C3 **Santa Monica** USA
66C4 **Santa Monica B** USA
75D1 **Santana** Brazil
74E4 **Santana do Livramento** Brazil
72C3 **Santander** Colombia
15B1 **Santander** Spain
15C2 **Santañy** Spain
66C3 **Santa Paula** USA
73K4 **Santa Quitéria** Brazil
73H4 **Santarém** Brazil
15A2 **Santarém** Portugal
75B2 **Santa Rita do Araguaia** Brazil
74D5 **Santa Rosa** Argentina
66A1 **Santa Rosa** California, USA
70D3 **Santa Rosa** Honduras
62B2 **Santa Rosa** New Mexico, USA
66B3 **Santa Rosa** *I* USA
70A2 **Santa Rosalía** Mexico
58C2 **Santa Rosa Range** *Mts* USA
73L5 **Santa Talhada** Brazil
75D2 **Santa Teresa** Brazil
16B2 **Santa Teresa di Gallura** Sardinia, Italy
66B3 **Santa Ynez** *R* USA
66B3 **Santa Ynez Mts** USA
67C2 **Santee** *R* USA
74B4 **Santiago** Chile
69C3 **Santiago** Dominican Republic
72B2 **Santiago** Panama
72C4 **Santiago** *R* Peru
15A1 **Santiago de Compostela** Spain
69B2 **Santiago de Cuba** Cuba
74D3 **Santiago del Estero** Argentina
74D3 **Santiago del Estero** *State* Argentina
66D4 **Santiago Peak** *Mt* USA
33F2 **Santo** Vanuatu
75C3 **Santo Amaro, Ilha** Brazil
75B3 **Santo Anastatácio** Brazil
74F3 **Santo Angelo** Brazil
48A4 **Santo Antão** *I* Cape Verde
75B3 **Santo Antônio da Platina** Brazil
75E1 **Santo Antônio de Jesus** Brazil
75A2 **Santo Antônio do Leverger** Brazil
69D3 **Santo Domingo** Dominican Republic
75C3 **Santos** Brazil
75D3 **Santos Dumont** Brazil
59C4 **Santo Tomas** Mexico
74E3 **Santo Tomé** Argentina
74B7 **San Valentin** *Mt* Chile
16C3 **San Vito, C** Sicily, Italy
28B2 **Sanyuanpu** China
51B4 **Sanza Pomba** Angola
75C3 **São Carlos** Brazil
75C1 **São Domingos** Brazil
73H5 **São Félix** Mato Grosso, Brazil
75D3 **São Fidélis** Brazil
75D2 **São Francisco** Brazil
73L5 **São Francisco** *R* Brazil
74G3 **São Francisco do Sul** Brazil
75C4 **São Francisco, Ilha de** Brazil
75C2 **São Gotardo** Brazil
51D4 **Sao Hill** Tanzania
75A2 **São Jerônimo, Serra de** *Mts* Brazil
75D3 **São João da Barra** Brazil
75C3 **São João da Boa Vista** Brazil
75C1 **São João d'Aliança** Brazil
75D2 **São João da Ponte** Brazil
75D3 **São João del Rei** Brazil
75D2 **São João do Paraíso** Brazil
75C3 **São Joaquim da Barra** Brazil
48A1 **São Jorge** *I* Azores
75C3 **São José do Rio Prêto** Brazil
75C3 **São José dos Campos** Brazil
75C4 **São José dos Pinhais** Brazil
75A2 **São Lourenço** *R* Brazil
73K4 **São Luís** Brazil
75C2 **São Marcos** *R* Brazil
73K4 **São Marcos, Baia de** *B* Brazil
75D2 **São Maria do Suaçuí** Brazil
75E2 **São Mateus** Brazil
75D2 **São Mateus** *R* Brazil
48A1 **São Miguel** *I* Azores
75B1 **São Miguel de Araguaia** Brazil
14C2 **Saône** *R* France
48A4 **São Nicolau** *I* Cape Verde
75D1 **São Onofre** *R* Brazil
75C3 **São Paulo** Brazil
75B3 **São Paulo** *State* Brazil
71H3 **São Pedro e São Paulo** *Is* Atlantic Ocean
73K5 **São Raimundo Nonato** Brazil
75C2 **São Romão** Brazil
75C3 **São Sebastia do Paraíso** Brazil
75C3 **São Sebastião, Ilha de** Brazil
75B2 **São Simão,Barragem de** Brazil
75B2 **São Simão** Goias, Brazil
75C3 **São Simão** São Paulo, Brazil
48A4 **São Tiago** *I* Cape Verde
48C4 **São Tomé** *I* W Africa
48C4 **Sao Tome and Principe** *Republic* W Africa
75D3 **São Tomé, Cabo de** *C* Brazil
48B2 **Saoura** *Watercourse* Algeria
75A1 **Saouriuiná** *R* Brazil
75C3 **São Vicente** Brazil
15A2 **São Vicente, Cabo de** *C* Portugal
48A4 **São Vincente** *I* Cape Verde
17F2 **Sápai** Greece
48C4 **Sapele** Nigeria
29E2 **Sapporo** Japan
16D2 **Sapri** Italy
63C1 **Sapulpa** USA
41E2 **Saqqez** Iran
21H8 **Sarāb** Iran
17D2 **Sarajevo** Bosnia-Herzegovina
21K5 **Saraktash** Russian Federation
25K4 **Sarala** Russian Federation
65E2 **Saranac Lake** USA
17E3 **Sarandë** Albania
20L3 **Saranpaul'** Russian Federation
20H5 **Saransk** Russian Federation
20J4 **Sarapul** Russian Federation
67B3 **Sarasota** USA
17F1 **Sărat** Romania
19F3 **Sarata** Ukraine
60B2 **Saratoga** USA
68D1 **Saratoga Springs** USA

21H5 **Saratov** Russian Federation
21H5 **Saratovskoye Vodokhranilishche** *Res* Russian Federation
30D2 **Saravane** Laos
27E6 **Sarawak** *State* Malaysia
40A2 **Saraykoy** Turkey
49D2 **Sardalas** Libya
41E2 **Sar Dasht** Iran
Sardegna = Sardinia
16B2 **Sardinia** *I* Medit Sea
12H5 **Sarektjåkkå** *Mt* Sweden
42C2 **Sargodha** Pakistan
50B3 **Sarh** Chad
48B1 **Sarhro, Jbel** *Mt* Morocco
41F2 **Sārī** Iran
45C2 **Sarida** *R* Israel
27H5 **Sarigan** *I* Pacific Ocean
40D1 **Sarıkamış** Turkey
32D3 **Sarina** Australia
42B1 **Sar-i-Pul** Afghanistan
49E2 **Sarīr** Libya
49D2 **Sarir Tibesti** *Desert* Libya
28B3 **Sariwŏn** N Korea
14B2 **Sark** *I* Channel Islands
40C2 **Şarkışla** Turkey
27G7 **Sarmi** Indonesia
74C7 **Sarmiento** Argentina
12G6 **Särna** Sweden
64C2 **Sarnia** Canada
19F2 **Sarny** Ukraine
42B2 **Sarobi** Afghanistan
17E3 **Saronikós Kólpos** *G* Greece
17F2 **Saros Körfezi** *B* Turkey
20M2 **Saroto** Russian Federation
12G7 **Sarpsborg** Norway
55N2 **Sarqaq** Greenland
13D3 **Sarralbe** France
13D3 **Sarrebourg** France
13D3 **Sarreguemines** France
13D3 **Sarre-Union** France
15B1 **Sarrion** Spain
42B3 **Sartanahu** Pakistan
16B2 **Sartène** Corsica, France
14B2 **Sarthe** *R* France
45D1 **Sārūt** *R* Syria
21J6 **Sarykamys** Kazakhstan
24H5 **Sarysu** *R* Kazakhstan
43E4 **Sasarām** India
28B4 **Sasebo** Japan
54H4 **Saskatchewan** *Province* Canada
54H4 **Saskatchewan** *R* Canada
54H4 **Saskatoon** Canada
25N2 **Saskylakh** Russian Federation
47D2 **Sasolburg** South Africa
20G5 **Sasovo** Russian Federation
48B4 **Sassandra** Ivory Coast
48B4 **Sassandra** *R* Ivory Coast
16B2 **Sassari** Sardinia, Italy
18C2 **Sassnitz** Germany
28A4 **Sasuna** Japan
44A2 **Sātāra** India
54G2 **Satellite B** Canada
12H6 **Säter** Sweden
67B2 **Satilla** *R* USA
20K4 **Satka** Russian Federation
42D2 **Satluj** *R* India
43E4 **Satna** India
42C4 **Sātpura Range** *Mts* India
17E1 **Satu Mare** Romania
12B1 **Sauðárkrókur** Iceland
12F7 **Sauda** Norway
38C3 **Saudi Arabia** *Kingdom* Arabian Pen
13D3 **Sauer** *R* Germany/ Luxembourg
13D2 **Sauerland** *Region* Germany
64B2 **Saugatuck** USA
68D1 **Saugerties** USA
61E1 **Sauk Center** USA
64B2 **Sauk City** USA
64C1 **Sault Ste Marie** Canada
64C1 **Sault Ste Marie** USA
27G7 **Saumlaki** Indonesia
14B2 **Saumur** France
51C4 **Saurimo** Angola
69M2 **Sauteurs** Grenada
17D2 **Sava** *R* Serbia, Yugoslavia
33H2 **Savai'i** *I* Western Samoa
48C4 **Savalou** Benin
67B2 **Savannah** Georgia, USA
63E1 **Savannah** Tennessee, USA
67B2 **Savannah** *R* USA
30C2 **Savannakhet** Laos
69G1 **Savanna la Mar** Jamaica
55J4 **Savant Lake** Canada
48C4 **Savé** Benin
51D6 **Save** *R* Mozambique
41F3 **Sāveh** Iran
13D3 **Saverne** France
13B3 **Savigny** France
20G3 **Savinskiy** Russian Federation
14D2 **Savoie** *Region* France
16B2 **Savona** Italy
12K6 **Savonlinna** Finland
54A3 **Savoonga** USA
32B2 **Savu** *I* Indonesia
12K5 **Savukoski** Finland
27F7 **Savu S** Indonesia
30A1 **Saw** Burma
42D3 **Sawai Mādhopur** India
30C2 **Sawankhalok** Thailand
29D3 **Sawara** Japan
60B3 **Sawatch Mts** USA
49D2 **Sawdā', Jabal as** *Mts* Libya
58C2 **Sawtooth Range** *Mts* USA
27F8 **Sawu** *I* Indonesia
7E3 **Saxmundham** England
68A2 **Saxton** USA
48C3 **Say** Niger
42B1 **Sayghan** Afghanistan
38D4 **Sayḥūt** Yemen
21H6 **Saykhin** Kazakhstan
26D2 **Saynshand** Mongolia
62C1 **Sayre** Oklahoma, USA
68B2 **Sayre** Pennsylvania, USA
21J7 **Say-Utes** Kazakhstan
68D2 **Sayville** USA
18C3 **Sázava** *R* Czech Republic
15C2 **Sbisseb** *R* Algeria
6C2 **Scafell Pike** *Mt* England
8E1 **Scalloway** Scotland
8C3 **Scalpay, I** Scotland
8D2 **Scapa Flow** *Sd* Scotland
65D2 **Scarborough** Canada
6D2 **Scarborough** England
69K1 **Scarborough** Tobago
8B2 **Scarp** *I* Scotland
16B1 **Schaffhausen** Switzerland
18C3 **Schärding** Austria
13E1 **Scharhörn** *I* Germany
13D2 **Scharteberg** *Mt* Germany
55M4 **Schefferville** Canada
13B2 **Schelde** *R* Belgium
59D3 **Schell Creek Range** *Mts* USA
68D1 **Schenectady** USA
62C3 **Schertz** USA
13C2 **Schiedam** Netherlands
13D1 **Schiermonnikoog** *I* Netherlands
13D2 **Schleiden** Germany
18B2 **Schleswig** Germany
18B2 **Schleswig Holstein** *State* Germany
68C1 **Schoharie** USA
32D1 **Schouten Is** Papua New Guinea
13E3 **Schramberg** Germany
55K5 **Schreiber** Canada
9B4 **Schull** Irish Republic
59C3 **Schurz** USA
68C2 **Schuylkill** *R* USA
68B2 **Schuylkill Haven** USA
18B3 **Schwabische Alb** *Upland* Germany
27E7 **Schwaner, Pegunungan** *Mts* Indonesia
47B2 **Schwarzrand** *Mts* Namibia
13E3 **Schwarzwald** *Mts* Germany
18C2 **Schweinfurt** Germany
47D2 **Schweizer Reneke** South Africa
18C2 **Schwerin** Germany
16B1 **Schwyz** Switzerland
16C3 **Sciacca** Italy
7A5 **Scilly, Isles of** England
64C3 **Scioto** *R* USA
60B1 **Scobey** USA
34D2 **Scone** Australia
55Q2 **Scoresby Sd** Greenland
52F7 **Scotia Sea** Atlantic Ocean
8C3 **Scotland** U K
76F7 **Scott** *Base* Antarctica
47E3 **Scottburgh** South Africa
62B1 **Scott City** USA
76G6 **Scott I** Antarctica
55L2 **Scott Inlet** *B* Canada
58B2 **Scott,Mt** USA
32B2 **Scott Reef** Timor Sea
60C2 **Scottsbluff** USA
67A2 **Scottsboro** USA
34C4 **Scottsdale** Australia
59D4 **Scottsdale** USA
68C2 **Scranton** USA
61D2 **Scribner** USA
7D3 **Scunthorpe** England
Scutari = Shkodër
47C3 **Seacow** *R* South Africa
7E4 **Seaford** England
54J4 **Seal** *R* Canada
34B3 **Sea Lake** Australia
59D3 **Searchlight** USA
63D1 **Searcy** USA
66D3 **Searles** USA
66B2 **Seaside** California, USA
58B1 **Seaside** Oregon, USA
68C3 **Seaside Park** USA
58B1 **Seattle** USA
65E2 **Sebago L** USA
70A2 **Sebastian Vizcaino, B** Mexico
66A1 **Sebastopol** USA
50D2 **Sebderat** Eritrea
19F1 **Sebez** Russian Federation
65F1 **Seboomook L** USA
67B3 **Sebring** USA
35A3 **Secretary I** New Zealand
61E3 **Sedalia** USA
13C3 **Sedan** France
6C2 **Sedbergh** England
35B2 **Seddonville** New Zealand
45C3 **Sede Boqer** Israel
45C3 **Sederot** Israel
48A3 **Sédhiou** Senegal
45C3 **Sedom** Israel
59D4 **Sedona** USA
47B2 **Seeheim** Namibia
76E4 **Seelig,Mt** Antarctica
35B2 **Sefton,Mt** New Zealand
30C5 **Segamat** Malaysia
20E3 **Segezha** Russian Federation
15B2 **Segorbe** Spain
48B3 **Ségou** Mali
Segovia = Coco
15B1 **Segovia** Spain
15C1 **Segre** *R* Spain
48B4 **Séguéla** Ivory Coast
63C3 **Seguin** USA
15B2 **Segura** *R* Spain
15B2 **Segura, Sierra de** *Mts* Spain
42B3 **Sehwan** Pakistan
62C1 **Seiling** USA
13D3 **Seille** *R* France
12J6 **Seinäjoki** Finland
61E1 **Seine** *R* Canada
14C2 **Seine** *R* France
13B3 **Seine-et-Marne** *Department* France
50D4 **Sekenke** Tanzania
48B4 **Sekondi** Ghana
50D2 **Sek'ot'a** Ethiopia
58B1 **Selah** USA
27G7 **Selaru** *I* Indonesia
27D6 **Selatan** *I* Indonesia
27G7 **Selat Dampier** *Str* Indonesia
27E7 **Selat Lombok** *Chan* Indonesia
27D7 **Selat Sunda** *Str* Indonesia
27F7 **Selat Wetar** *Chan* Indonesia
54C3 **Selawik** USA
32B1 **Selayar** *I* Indonesia
6D3 **Selby** England
60C1 **Selby** USA
17F3 **Selçuk** Turkey
47D1 **Selebi Pikwe** Botswana
25Q3 **Selennyakh** *R* Russian Federation
13D3 **Selestat** France
55Q3 **Selfoss** Iceland
60C1 **Selfridge** USA
50C1 **Selima Oasis** Sudan
19G1 **Selizharovo** Russian Federation
54J4 **Selkirk** Canada
8D4 **Selkirk** Scotland
54G4 **Selkirk Mts** Canada/USA
67A2 **Selma** Alabama, USA
66C2 **Selma** California, USA
63E1 **Selmer** USA
15B2 **Selouane** Morocco
72D5 **Selvas** *Region* Brazil
48A2 **Selvegens, Ilhas** *Is* Atlantic Ocean
58C1 **Selway** *R* USA
32D3 **Selwyn** Australia
54E3 **Selwyn Mts** Canada
27E7 **Semarang** Indonesia
20G4 **Semenov** Russian Federation
21F5 **Semiluki** Russian Federation
60B2 **Seminoe Res** USA
63C1 **Seminole** Oklahoma, USA
62B2 **Seminole** Texas, USA
67B2 **Seminole,L** USA
24K4 **Semipalatinsk** Kazakhstan
41F3 **Semirom** Iran
41F2 **Semnān** Iran
13C3 **Semois** *R* Belgium
72E5 **Sena Madureira** Brazil
51C5 **Senanga** Zambia
63E2 **Senatobia** USA
29E3 **Sendai** Japan
42D4 **Sendwha** India
68B1 **Seneca Falls** USA
68B1 **Seneca L** USA
62A2 **Senecu** Mexico
48A3 **Sénégal** *R* Mauritius/ Senegal
48A3 **Senegal** *Republic* Africa
47D2 **Senekal** South Africa
73L6 **Senhor do Bonfim** Brazil
16C2 **Senigallia** Italy
16D2 **Senj** Croatia
26F4 **Senkaku Gunto** *Is* Japan
13B3 **Senlis** France
50D2 **Sennar** Sudan
55L5 **Senneterre** Canada
13D3 **Senones** France
13B3 **Sens** France
17D1 **Senta** Serbia, Yugoslavia
50C4 **Sentery** Zaïre
42D4 **Seoni** India
28B3 **Seoul** S Korea
35B2 **Separation Pt** New Zealand
75D3 **Sepetiba, B de** Brazil
27H7 **Sepik** *R* Papua New Guinea
28A3 **Sep'o** N Korea
30D2 **Sepone** Laos
75A2 **Sepotuba** *R* Brazil
55M4 **Sept-Iles** Canada
50B1 **Séquédine** Niger
66C2 **Sequoia Nat Pk** USA
45C1 **Serai** Syria
27F7 **Seram** *I* Indonesia
27F7 **Seram Sea** Indonesia
17D2 **Serbia** *Republic* Yugoslavia
21G5 **Serdobsk** Russian Federation
13B4 **Serein** *R* France
30C5 **Seremban** Malaysia
50D4 **Serengeti Nat Pk** Tanzania
51D5 **Serenje** Zambia
19F3 **Seret** *R* Ukraine
20H4 **Sergach** Russian Federation
28C2 **Sergeyevka** Russian Federation
24H3 **Sergino** Russian Federation
73L6 **Sergipe** *State* Brazil
20F4 **Segiyev Posad** Georgia
27E6 **Seria** Brunei
27E6 **Serian** Malaysia
17E3 **Sérifos** *I* Greece
49E2 **Serir Calanscio** *Desert* Libya
13C3 **Sermaize-les-Bains** France
32B1 **Sermata** *I* Indonesia
55P3 **Sermilik** *Fjord* Greenland
20J5 **Sernovodsk** Russian Federation
20L4 **Serov** Russian Federation
47D1 **Serowe** Botswana
15A2 **Serpa** Portugal
20F5 **Serpukhov** Russian Federation
15A1 **Serra da Estrela** *Mts* Portugal
73H3 **Serra do Navio** Brazil
17E2 **Sérrai** Greece
70D3 **Serrana Bank** *Is* Caribbean Sea
15B1 **Serraná de Cuenca** *Mts* Spain
75B2 **Serranópolis** Brazil
16B3 **Serrat, C** Tunisia
13B3 **Serre** *R* France
73L6 **Serrinha** Brazil
75D2 **Serro** Brazil
15C2 **Sersou, Plateau du** Algeria
75B3 **Sertanópolis** Brazil
31A3 **Sêrtar** China
47D1 **Serule** Botswana
51B5 **Sesfontein** Namibia
51C5 **Sesheke** Zambia
29D2 **Setana** Japan
14C3 **Sète** France
75D2 **Sete Lagoas** Brazil
15C2 **Sétif** Algeria
29C3 **Seto** Japan
28B4 **Seto Naikai** *S* Japan
48B1 **Settat** Morocco
6C2 **Settle** England
15A2 **Setúbal** Portugal
55J4 **Seul, Lac** Canada
21H7 **Sevan, Ozero** *L* Armenia
21E7 **Sevastopol'** Ukraine
7E4 **Sevenoaks** England
55K4 **Severn** *R* Canada
7C3 **Severn** *R* England
20G3 **Severnaya Dvina** *R* Russian Federation
25L1 **Severnaya Zemlya** *I* Russian Federation
20L3 **Severnyy Sos'va** *R* Russian Federation
20K3 **Severnyy Ural** *Mts* Russian Federation
25M4 **Severo Baykal'skoye Nagor'ye** *Mts* Russian Federation
21F6 **Severo Donets** *R* Ukraine
20F3 **Severodvinsk** Russian Federation
24H3 **Severo Sos'va** *R* Russian Federation
20L3 **Severoural'sk** Russian Federation
59D3 **Sevier** *R* USA
59D3 **Sevier Desert** USA
59D3 **Sevier L** USA
Sevilla = Seville
15A2 **Seville** Spain
17F2 **Sevlievo** Bulgaria
48A4 **Sewa** *R* Sierra Leone
61D2 **Seward** Nebraska, USA
54D3 **Seward** USA
54B3 **Seward Pen** USA
46K8 **Seychelles** *Is, Republic* Indian Ocean
40C2 **Seyhan** *R* Turkey
12C1 **Seyðisfjörður** Iceland
21F5 **Seym** *R* Russian Federation
25R3 **Seymchan** Russian Federation
34C3 **Seymour** Australia
68D2 **Seymour** Connecticut, USA
64B3 **Seymour** Indiana, USA
62C2 **Seymour** Texas, USA
13B3 **Sézanne** France
48D1 **Sfax** Tunisia
17F1 **Sfînto Gheorghe** Romania
's-Gravenhage = The Hague
8C3 **Sgúrr na Lapaich,** *Mt* Scotland
31B3 **Shaanxi** *Province* China
50E3 **Shabeelle** *R* Ethiopia/ Somalia
50C4 **Shabunda** Zaïre
39F2 **Shache** China
76G9 **Shackleton Ice Shelf** Antarctica
42B3 **Shadadkot** Pakistan
41F3 **Shādhām** *R* Iran
66C3 **Shafter** USA
7C4 **Shaftesbury** England
28A2 **Shagang** China
74J8 **Shag Rocks** *Is* South Georgia
44B2 **Shāhābād** India
41E3 **Shāhābād** Iran
45D2 **Shahbā** Syria
41G3 **Shahdāb** Iran
43E4 **Shahdol** India
41E2 **Shāhīn Dezh** Iran
41G3 **Shāh Kūh** *Mt* Iran
41G3 **Shahr-e Bābak** Iran
Shahresa = Qomisheh
41F3 **Shahr Kord** Iran
21J8 **Shahsavār** Iran
20L3 **Shaim** Russian Federation
45C4 **Sha'īra, Gebel** *Mt* Egypt
40B5 **Sha'it, Wadi** *Watercourse* Egypt
42D3 **Shājahānpur** India
42D4 **Shājāpur** India
21G6 **Shakhty** Russian Federation
20H4 **Shakhun'ya** Russian Federation
48C4 **Shaki** Nigeria
61E2 **Shakopee** USA
29D2 **Shakotan-misaki** *C* Japan
20K4 **Shamary** Russian Federation
50D3 **Shambe** Sudan
68B2 **Shamokin** USA
62B1 **Shamrock** USA
68C1 **Shandaken** USA
66B3 **Shandon** USA
31D2 **Shandong** *Province* China
31C5 **Shangchuan Dao** *I* China
31C1 **Shangdu** China
31E3 **Shanghai** China
31C3 **Shangnan** China
51C5 **Shangombo** Zambia
31D3 **Shangqiu** China
31D4 **Shangrao** China
31B5 **Shangsi** China
31C3 **Shang Xian** China
7D4 **Shanklin** England
9B3 **Shannon** *R* Irish Republic
28B2 **Shansonggang** China
26G1 **Shantarskiye Ostrova** *I* Russian Federation
31D5 **Shantou** China
31C2 **Shanxi** *Province* China
31D3 **Shan Xian** China
31C5 **Shaoguan** China
31E4 **Shaoxing** China
31C4 **Shaoyang** China
8D2 **Shapinsay** *I* Scotland
45D2 **Shaqqā** Syria
41E4 **Shaqra'** Saudi Arabia
31A1 **Sharhulsan** Mongolia
29D2 **Shari** Japan
41G2 **Sharifābād** Iran
41G4 **Sharjah** UAE
32A3 **Shark B** Australia
41G2 **Sharlauk** Turkmenistan
45C2 **Sharon,Plain of** Israel
68B3 **Sharpsburg** USA
40C3 **Sharqi, Jebel esh** *Mts* Lebanon/Syria
20H4 **Sharya** Russian Federation
50D3 **Shashamenē** Ethiopia
47D1 **Shashani** *R* Zimbabwe
47D1 **Shashe** *R* Botswana

31C3 **Shashi** China
58B2 **Shasta L** USA
58B2 **Shasta,Mt** USA
45D1 **Shaṯḥah at Taḥtā** Syria
41E3 **Shaṭṭ al Gharraf** *R* Iraq
45C3 **Shaubak** Jordan
66C2 **Shaver L** USA
68C2 **Shawangunk Mt** USA
64B2 **Shawano** USA
65E1 **Shawinigan** Canada
63C1 **Shawnee** Oklahoma, USA
60B2 **Shawnee** Wyoming, USA
31D4 **Sha Xian** China
32B3 **Shay Gap** Australia
45D2 **Shaykh Miskīn** Syria
50E2 **Shaykh 'Uthmān** Yemen
21F5 **Shchigry** Russian Federation
21E5 **Shchors** Ukraine
24J4 **Shchuchinsk** Kazakhstan
50E3 **Shebele** *R* Ethiopia
64B2 **Sheboygan** USA
50B3 **Shebshi Mts** Nigeia
9C3 **Sheelin, L** Irish Republic
9C2 **Sheep Haven** *Estuary* Irish Republic
7E4 **Sheerness** England
45C2 **Shefar'am** Israel
63E2 **Sheffield** Alabama, USA
7D3 **Sheffield** England
62B2 **Sheffield** Texas, USA
8C3 **Sheil, Loch** *L* Scotland
42C2 **Shekhupura** Pakistan
25T2 **Shelagskiy, Mys** *C* Russian Federation
68D1 **Shelburne Falls** USA
64B2 **Shelby** Michigan, USA
58D1 **Shelby** Montana, USA
67B1 **Shelby** N Carolina, USA
64B3 **Shelbyville** Indiana, USA
67A1 **Shelbyville** Tennessee, USA
61D2 **Sheldon** USA
54C4 **Shelikof Str** USA
58D2 **Shelley** USA
34D2 **Shellharbour** Australia
35A3 **Shelter Pt** New Zealand
58B1 **Shelton** USA
41E1 **Shemakha** Azerbaijan
61D2 **Shenandoah** USA
65D3 **Shenandoah** *R* USA
65D3 **Shenandoah Nat Pk** USA
48C4 **Shendam** Nigeria
50D2 **Shendi** Sudan
20G3 **Shenkursk** Russian Federation
31C2 **Shenmu** China
31E1 **Shenyang** China
31C5 **Shenzhen** China
42D3 **Sheopur** India
19F2 **Shepetovka** Ukraine
68B3 **Shepherdstown** USA
34C3 **Shepparton** Australia
7E4 **Sheppey** *I* England
55K2 **Sherard,C** Canada
7C4 **Sherborne** England
48A4 **Sherbro I** Sierra Leone
65E1 **Sherbrooke** Canada
68C1 **Sherburne** USA
42C3 **Shergarh** India
63D2 **Sheridan** Arkansas, USA
60B2 **Sheridan** Wyoming, USA
7E3 **Sheringham** England
63C2 **Sherman** USA
18B2 **'s-Hertogenbosch** Netherlands
10C1 **Shetland** *Is* Scotland
21J7 **Shevchenko** Kazakhstan
60D1 **Sheyenne** USA
60D1 **Sheyenne** *R* USA
41F4 **Sheyk Sho'eyb** *I* Iran
8B3 **Shiant, Sd of** Scotland
26J2 **Shiashkotan** *I* Kuril Is, Russian Federation
42B1 **Shibarghan** Afghanistan
29D3 **Shibata** Japan
29D2 **Shibetsu** Japan
49F1 **Shibîn el Kom** Egypt
45A3 **Shibîn el Qanâtir** Egypt
29C3 **Shibukawa** Japan
68B2 **Shickshinny** USA
28A3 **Shidao** China
31C2 **Shijiazhuang** China
42B3 **Shikarpur** Pakistan
26G3 **Shikoku** *I* Japan
29B4 **Shikoku-sanchi** *Mts* Japan
26H2 **Shikotan** *I* Russian Federation
29D2 **Shikotsu-ko** *L* Japan
20G3 **Shilega** Russian Federation
43F3 **Shiliguri** India
26E1 **Shilka** Russian Federation
26E1 **Shilka** *R* Russian Federation
68C2 **Shillington** USA
43G3 **Shillong** India
20G5 **Shilovo** Russian Federation
28B4 **Shimabara** Japan
29C4 **Shimada** Japan
26F1 **Shimanovsk** Russian Federation
29D3 **Shimizu** Japan
29C4 **Shimoda** Japan
44B3 **Shimoga** India
28C4 **Shimonoseki** Japan
29C3 **Shinano** *R* Japan
41G5 **Shināṣ** Oman
38E2 **Shindand** Afghanistan
68A2 **Shinglehouse** USA
29D4 **Shingū** Japan
29D3 **Shinjō** Japan
8C2 **Shin, Loch** *L* Scotland
29D3 **Shinminato** Japan
45D1 **Shinshār** Syria
50D4 **Shinyanga** Tanzania
29E3 **Shiogama** Japan
29C4 **Shiono-misaki** *C* Japan
31A5 **Shiping** China
68B2 **Shippensburg** USA
62A1 **Shiprock** USA
31B3 **Shiquan** China
29D3 **Shirakawa** Japan
29C3 **Shirane-san** *Mt* Japan
41F4 **Shīraz** Iran
45A3 **Shirbîn** Egypt
29F2 **Shiretoko-misaki** *C* Japan
29D2 **Shiriya-saki** *C* Japan
41F3 **Shīr Kūh** *Mt* Iran
29C3 **Shirotori** Japan
41G2 **Shirvān** Iran
54B3 **Shishmaref** USA
31B2 **Shitanjing** China
64B3 **Shively** USA
42D3 **Shivpuri** India
45C3 **Shivta** *Hist Site* Israel
59D3 **Shivwits Plat** USA
51D5 **Shiwa Ngandu** Zambia
31C3 **Shiyan** China
31B2 **Shizuishan** China
29C3 **Shizuoka** Japan
17D2 **Shkodër** Albania
19G2 **Shkov** Belarus
25L1 **Shmidta, Ostrov** *I* Russian Federation
34D2 **Shoalhaven** *R* Australia
28B4 **Shobara** Japan
44B3 **Shoranūr** India
44B2 **Shorāpur** India
59C3 **Shoshone** California, USA
58D2 **Shoshone** Idaho, USA
58E2 **Shoshone** *R* USA
58D2 **Shoshone L** USA
59C3 **Shoshone Mts** USA
58E2 **Shoshoni** USA
21E5 **Shostka** Ukraine
59D4 **Show Low** USA
63D2 **Shreveport** USA
7C3 **Shrewsbury** England
7C3 **Shropshire** *County* England
31E1 **Shuangliao** China
28B2 **Shuangyang** China
26G2 **Shuangyashan** China
21K6 **Shubar-Kuduk** Kazakhstan
20N2 **Shuga** Russian Federation
31D2 **Shu He** *R* China
31A4 **Shuicheng** China
42C3 **Shujaabad** Pakistan
42D4 **Shujālpur** India
26C2 **Shule He** *R* China
17F2 **Shumen** Bulgaria
20H4 **Shumerlya** Russian Federation
31D4 **Shuncheng** China
54C3 **Shungnak** USA
31C2 **Shuo Xian** China
38D3 **Shūr Gaz** Iran
51C5 **Shurugwi** Zimbabwe
20G4 **Shuya** Russian Federation
30B1 **Shwebo** Burma
30B2 **Shwegyin** Burma
42A2 **Siah Koh** *Mts* Afghanistan
42C2 **Sialkot** Pakistan
Sian = Xi'an
27F6 **Siargao** *I* Philippines
27F6 **Siaton** Philippines
19E1 **Šiauliai** Lithuania
20K5 **Sibay** Russian Federation
47E2 **Sibayi L** South Africa
16D2 **Šibenik** Croatia
25L5 **Siberia** Russian Federation
27C7 **Siberut** *I* Indonesia
42B3 **Sibi** Pakistan
50B4 **Sibiti** Congo
50D4 **Sibiti** *R* Tanzania
17E1 **Sibiu** Romania
61D2 **Sibley** USA
27C6 **Sibolga** Indonesia
43G3 **Sibsāgar** India
27E6 **Sibu** Malaysia
50B3 **Sibut** Central African Republic
31A3 **Sichuan** *Province* China
Sicilia = Sicily
16C3 **Sicilian Chan** Italy/Tunisia
16C3 **Sicily** *I* Medit Sea
72D6 **Sicuani** Peru
42C4 **Siddhapur** India
44B2 **Siddipet** India
43E4 **Sidhi** India
49E1 **Sidi Barrani** Egypt
15B2 **Sidi-bel-Abbès** Algeria
48B1 **Sidi Kacem** Morocco
8D3 **Sidlaw Hills** Scotland
76F5 **Sidley,Mt** Antarctica
7C4 **Sidmouth** England
58B1 **Sidney** Canada
60C1 **Sidney** Montana, USA
60C2 **Sidney** Nebraska, USA
68C1 **Sidney** New York, USA
64C2 **Sidney** Ohio, USA
67B2 **Sidney Lanier,L** USA
45C2 **Sidon** Lebanon
75B3 **Sidrolândia** Brazil
19E2 **Siedlce** Poland
13D2 **Sieg** *R* Germany
13D2 **Siegburg** Germany
13D2 **Siegen** Germany
30C3 **Siem Reap** Cambodia
16C2 **Siena** Italy
19D2 **Sierpc** Poland
62A2 **Sierra Blanca** USA
70B2 **Sierra de los Alamitos** *Mts* Mexico
48A4 **Sierra Leone** *Republic* Africa
48A4 **Sierra Leone,C** Sierra Leone
70B3 **Sierra Madre del Sur** Mexico
66B3 **Sierra Madre Mts** USA
70B2 **Sierra Madre Occidental** *Mts* Mexico
70B2 **Sierra Madre Oriental** *Mts* Mexico
56C4 **Sierra Mojada** Mexico
59B3 **Sierra Nevada** *Mts* USA
59D4 **Sierra Vista** USA
75A3 **Siete Puntas** *R* Paraguay
17E3 **Sífnos** *I* Greece
15B2 **Sig** Algeria
20E2 **Sig** Russian Federation
19E3 **Sighetu Marmaţiei** Romania
17E1 **Sighişoara** Romania
12B1 **Siglufjörður** Iceland
72A1 **Siguatepeque** Honduras
15B1 **Sigüenza** Spain
48B3 **Siguiri** Guinea
30C3 **Sihanoukville** Cambodia
42D4 **Sihora** India
40D2 **Siirt** Turkey
43J1 **Sikandarabad** India
42D3 **Sīkar** India
42B2 **Sikaram** *Mt* Afghanistan
48B3 **Sikasso** Mali
63E1 **Sikeston** USA
26G2 **Sikhote-Alin'** *Mts* Russian Federation
17F3 **Síkinos** *I* Greece
17E3 **Sikionía** Greece
43F3 **Sikkim** *State* India
25O3 **Siktyakh** Russian Federation
15A1 **Sil** *R* Spain
43G4 **Silchar** India
48C2 **Silet** Algeria
43E3 **Silgarhi** Nepal
40B2 **Silifke** Turkey
45D1 **Şilinfah** Syria
39G2 **Siling Co** *L* China
17F2 **Silistra** Bulgaria
20A3 **Siljan** *L* Sweden
12F7 **Silkeborg** Denmark
6C2 **Silloth** England
63D1 **Siloam Springs** USA
63D2 **Silsbee** USA
50B2 **Siltou** *Well* Chad
19E1 **Šilute** Lithuania
40D2 **Silvan** Turkey
75C2 **Silvania** Brazil
42C4 **Silvassa** India
61E1 **Silver Bay** USA
59C3 **Silver City** Nevada, USA
62A2 **Silver City** New Mexico, USA
58B2 **Silver Lake** USA
66D2 **Silver Peak Range** *Mts* USA
68B3 **Silver Spring** USA
34B2 **Silverton** Australia
62A1 **Silverton** USA
27E6 **Simanggang** Malaysia
30C1 **Simao** China
65D1 **Simard,L** Canada
41E3 **Simareh** *R* Iran
17F3 **Simav** Turkey
17F3 **Simav** *R* Turkey
65D2 **Simcoe,L** Canada
27C6 **Simeulue** *I* Indonesia
21E7 **Simferopol'** Ukraine
17F3 **Sími** *I* Greece
43E3 **Simikot** Nepal
42D2 **Simla** India
60C3 **Simla** USA
13D2 **Simmern** Germany
66C3 **Simmler** USA
47B3 **Simonstown** South Africa
14D2 **Simplon** *Mt* Switzerland
16B1 **Simplon** *Pass* Italy/ Switzerland
54C2 **Simpson,C** USA
32C3 **Simpson Desert** Australia
55K3 **Simpson Pen** Canada
12G7 **Simrishamn** Sweden
26J2 **Simushir** *I* Kuril Is, Russian Federation
50E3 **Sina Dhaga** Somalia
40B4 **Sinai** *Pen* Egypt
72C2 **Sincelejo** Colombia
67B2 **Sinclair,L** USA
75D1 **Sincora, Serra do** *Mts* Brazil
42D3 **Sind** *R* India
42B3 **Sindh** *Province* Pakistan
17F3 **Sindirği** Turkey
43F4 **Sindri** India
15A2 **Sines** Portugal
15A2 **Sines, Cabo de** *C* Portugal
50D2 **Singa** Sudan
30C5 **Singapore** *Republic* SE Asia
30C5 **Singapore,Str of** SE Asia
27E7 **Singaraja** Indonesia
13E4 **Singen** Germany
50D4 **Singida** Tanzania
43H3 **Singkaling Hkamti** Burma
27D6 **Singkawang** Indonesia
27D7 **Singkep** *I* Indonesia
34D2 **Singleton** Australia
30B1 **Singu** Burma
47E1 **Singuédeze** *R* Mozambique
28A3 **Sin'gye** N Korea
28A2 **Sinhŭng** N Korea
16B2 **Siniscola** Sardinia, Italy
40D2 **Sinjár** Iraq
42B2 **Sinkai Hills** *Mts* Afghanistan
50D2 **Sinkat** Sudan
39G1 **Sinkiang** *Autonomous Region* China
43K2 **Sinkobabad** India
73H2 **Sinnamary** French Guiana
45B4 **Sinn Bishr, Gebel** *Mt* Egypt
28A3 **Sinnyong** S Korea
40C1 **Sinop** Turkey
28A2 **Sinpa** N Korea
28A2 **Sinp'o** N Korea
28A3 **Sinp'yong** N Korea
17E1 **Sîntana** Romania
27E6 **Sintang** Indonesia
63C3 **Sinton** USA
15A2 **Sintra** Portugal
72C2 **Sinú** *R* Colombia
28A2 **Sinŭiju** N Korea
19D3 **Siófok** Hungary
16B1 **Sion** Switzerland
61D2 **Sioux City** USA
61D2 **Sioux Falls** USA
69L1 **Siparia** Trinidad
28A2 **Siping** China
76F3 **Siple** *Base* Antarctica
76F5 **Siple I** Antarctica
27C7 **Sipora** *I* Indonesia
63E2 **Sipsey** *R* USA
45B4 **Sîq, Wadi el** Egypt
44B3 **Sira** India
Siracusa = Syracuse
43F4 **Sirajganj** Bangladesh
41F5 **Şir Banī Yās** *I* UAE
32C2 **Sir Edward Pellew Group** *Is* Australia
17F1 **Siret** *R* Romania
40C3 **Sirhān, Wādi as** *V* Jordan/Saudi Arabia
40D2 **Şirnak** Turkey
42C4 **Sirohi** India
44C2 **Sironcha** India
42D4 **Sironj** India
17E3 **Síros** *I* Greece
66C3 **Sirretta Peak** *Mt* USA
41F4 **Sīrrī** *I* Iran
42C3 **Sirsa** India
44A3 **Sirsi** India
49D1 **Sirt** Libya
49D1 **Sirte Desert** Libya
49D1 **Sirte,G of** Libya
21H9 **Sirvan** *R* Iran
16D1 **Sisak** Croatia
30C2 **Sisaket** Thailand
30C3 **Sisophon** Cambodia
66B3 **Sisquoc** USA
66C3 **Sisquoc** *R* USA
61D1 **Sisseton** USA
13B3 **Sissonne** France
14D3 **Sisteron** France
25L4 **Sistig Khem** Russian Federation
43E3 **Sītāpur** India
17F3 **Sitía** Greece
75C1 **Sitio d'Abadia** Brazil
54E4 **Sitka** USA
30B2 **Sittang** *R* Burma
13C2 **Sittard** Netherlands
43G4 **Sittwe** Burma
40C2 **Sivas** Turkey
40C2 **Siverek** Turkey
40B2 **Sivrihisar** Turkey
25S4 **Sivuchiy, Mys** *C* Russian Federation
49E2 **Siwa** Egypt
42D2 **Siwalik Range** *Mts* India
43E3 **Siwalik Range** *Mts* Nepal
20G3 **Siya** Russian Federation
31D3 **Siyang** China
18C1 **Sjaelland** *I* Denmark
12G7 **Skagen** Denmark
12F7 **Skagerrak** *Str* Denmark/ Norway
58B1 **Skagit** *R* USA
58B1 **Skagit Mt** Canada
54E4 **Skagway** USA
68B1 **Skaneateles** USA
68B1 **Skaneateles L** USA
12G7 **Skara** Sweden
19E2 **Skarzysko-Kamienna** Poland
54F4 **Skeena** *R* Canada
54F4 **Skeene Mts** Canada
54D3 **Skeenjek** *R* USA
7E3 **Skegness** England
20B2 **Skellefte** *R* Sweden
12J6 **Skellefteå** Sweden
9C3 **Skerries** Irish Republic
17E3 **Skíathos** *I* Greece
54E4 **Skidegate** Canada
19E2 **Skiemiewice** Poland
12F7 **Skien** Norway
16B3 **Skikda** Algeria
6D3 **Skipton** England
17E3 **Skíros** *I* Greece
12F7 **Skive** Denmark
18B1 **Skjern** Denmark
55O3 **Skjoldungen** Greenland
64B2 **Skokie** USA
17E3 **Skópelos** *I* Greece
17E2 **Skopje** Macedonia, Yugoslavia
12G7 **Skövde** Sweden
25O4 **Skovorodino** Russian Federation
65F2 **Skowhegan** USA
47E1 **Skukuza** South Africa
54C3 **Skwentna** USA
18D2 **Skwierzyna** Poland
10B2 **Skye** *I* Scotland
12G7 **Slagelse** Denmark
27D7 **Slamet** *Mt* Indonesia
9C3 **Slaney** *R* Irish Republic
17E2 **Slatina** Romania
54G3 **Slave** *R* Canada
19G2 **Slavgorod** Belarus
24J4 **Slavgorod** Russian Federation
19F2 **Slavuta** Ukraine
21F6 **Slavyansk** Ukraine
18D2 **Sławno** Poland
7D3 **Sleaford** England
8C3 **Sleat,Sound of** *Chan* Scotland
54C3 **Sleetmute** USA
63E2 **Slidell** USA
68C2 **Slide Mt** USA
9B3 **Slieve Aughty Mts** Irish Republic
9C3 **Slieve Bloom** *Mts* Irish Republic
10B3 **Sligo** Irish Republic
10B3 **Sligo B** Irish Republic
17F2 **Sliven** Bulgaria
59C3 **Sloan** USA
17F2 **Slobozia** Romania
19F2 **Slonim** Belarus
7D4 **Slough** England
66B2 **Slough** *R* USA
19D3 **Slovakia** *Republic* Europe
16C1 **Slovenia** *Republic* Europe
18C2 **Słubice** Poland
19F2 **Sluch'** *R* Ukraine
18D2 **Słupsk** Poland
19F2 **Slutsk** Belarus
19F2 **Slutsk** *R* Belarus
10A3 **Slyne Head** *Pt* Irish Republic
25M4 **Slyudyanka** Russian Federation
55M4 **Smallwood Res** Canada
48A2 **Smara** Morocco
17E2 **Smederevo** Serbia, Yugoslavia
17E2 **Smederevska Palanka** Serbia, Yugoslavia
21E6 **Smela** Ukraine
68A2 **Smethport** USA
66C1 **Smith** USA
54F3 **Smith Arm** *B* Canada
54F4 **Smithers** Canada
67C1 **Smithfield** N Carolina, USA
47D3 **Smithfield** South Africa
58D2 **Smithfield** Utah, USA
55L3 **Smith I** Canada
65D2 **Smiths Falls** Canada
34C4 **Smithton** Australia
60C3 **Smoky** *R* USA
34D2 **Smoky C** Australia
60D3 **Smoky Hills** USA
58D2 **Smoky Mts** USA
12F6 **Smøla** *I* Norway
20E5 **Smolensk** Russian Federation
17E2 **Smólikas** *Mt* Greece
17E2 **Smolyan** Bulgaria

19F2 **Smorgon'** Belarus
Smyrna = Izmir
68C3 **Smyrna** Delaware, USA
67B2 **Smyrna** Georgia, USA
12B2 **Snæfell** *Mt* Iceland
6B2 **Snaefell** *Mt* Isle of Man, British Islands
58C1 **Snake** *R* USA
56B2 **Snake River Canyon** USA
58D2 **Snake River Plain** USA
33F5 **Snares Is** New Zealand
18B2 **Sneek** Netherlands
66B2 **Snelling** USA
18D2 **Sněžka** *Mt* Czech Republic/Poland
8B3 **Snizort, Loch** *Inlet* Scotland
12F6 **Snøhetta** *Mt* Norway
58B1 **Snohomish** USA
58B1 **Snoqualmie P** USA
30D3 **Snoul** Cambodia
7B3 **Snowdon** *Mt* Wales
7B3 **Snowdonia Nat Pk** Wales
54G3 **Snowdrift** Canada
59D4 **Snowflake** USA
54H4 **Snow Lake** Canada
68B2 **Snow Shoe** USA
34A2 **Snowtown** Australia
58D2 **Snowville** USA
34C3 **Snowy Mts** Australia
62B2 **Snyder** USA
28B4 **Soan Kundo** *Is* S Korea
8B3 **Soay, I** Scotland
28A3 **Sobaek Sanmaek** *Mts* S Korea
50D3 **Sobat** *R* Sudan
73K4 **Sobral** Brazil
19E2 **Sochaczew** Poland
21F7 **Sochi** Russian Federation
28A3 **Sŏch'on** S Korea
37M5 **Société, Îles de la** Pacific Ocean
49D2 **Socna** Libya
62A2 **Socorro** USA
70A3 **Socorro** *I* Mexico
38D4 **Socotra** *I* Yemen
66C3 **Soda L** USA
12K5 **Sodankylä** Finland
58D2 **Soda Springs** USA
50D3 **Soddo** Ethiopia
12H6 **Söderhamn** Sweden
12H7 **Södertälje** Sweden
50C2 **Sodiri** Sudan
50D3 **Sodo** Ethiopia
68B1 **Sodus Point** USA
13E2 **Soest** Germany
51D5 **Sofala** Mozambique
17E2 **Sofia** Bulgaria
Sofiya = Sofia
20E2 **Sofporog** Russian Federation
26H4 **Sofu Gan** *I* Japan
72D2 **Sogamoso** Colombia
12F6 **Sognefjorden** *Inlet* Norway
28A4 **Sŏgwi-ri** S Korea
39H2 **Sog Xian** China
40B4 **Sohâg** Egypt
33E1 **Sohano** Papua New Guinea
13B2 **Soignies** Belgium
13B3 **Soissons** France
42C3 **Sojat** India
28A3 **Sokcho** S Korea
40A2 **Söke** Turkey
19E2 **Sokołka** Poland
48C4 **Sokodé** Togo
20G4 **Sokol** Russian Federation
48B3 **Sokolo** Mali
55Q3 **Søkongens Øy** *I* Greenland
48C3 **Sokoto** Nigeria
48C3 **Sokoto** *R* Nigeria
35A3 **Solander I** New Zealand
44B2 **Solāpur** India
69C4 **Soledad** Colombia
66B2 **Soledad** USA
7D4 **Solent** *Sd* England
13B2 **Solesmes** France
19F2 **Soligorsk** Belarus
20K4 **Solikamsk** Russian Federation
21J5 **Sol'Iletsk** Russian Federation
72D4 **Solimões** Peru
13D2 **Solingen** Germany
47B1 **Solitaire** Namibia
12H6 **Sollefteå** Sweden
27D7 **Solok** Indonesia
33E1 **Solomon Is** Pacific Ocean
64A1 **Solon Springs** USA
20F2 **Solovetskiye, Ostrova** *I* Russian Federation
12F8 **Soltau** Germany
66B3 **Solvang** USA
68B1 **Solvay** USA
8D4 **Solway Firth** *Estuary* England/Scotland
51C5 **Solwezi** Zambia
29D3 **Sōma** Japan
17F3 **Soma** Turkey
38C5 **Somalia** *Republic* E Africa
36D4 **Somali Basin** Indian Ocean
17D1 **Sombor** Serbia, Yugoslavia
44E4 **Sombrero Chan** Nicobar Is, Indian Ocean
32D2 **Somerset** Australia
64C3 **Somerset** Kentucky, USA
68E2 **Somerset** Massachusetts, USA
65D2 **Somerset** Pennsylvania, USA
7C4 **Somerset** *County* England
47D3 **Somerset East** South Africa
55J2 **Somerset I** Canada
68D1 **Somerset Res** USA
68C3 **Somers Point** USA
68E1 **Somersworth** USA
68C2 **Somerville** USA
63C2 **Somerville Res** USA
17E1 **Someş** *R* Romania
13B3 **Somme** *Department* France
13B3 **Somme** *R* France
13C3 **Sommesous** France
72A1 **Somoto** Nicaragua
43E4 **Son** *R* India
28A3 **Sŏnch'ŏn** N Korea
47D3 **Sondags** *R* South Africa
12F8 **Sønderborg** Denmark
55N3 **Søndre Strømfjord** Greenland
55N2 **Søndre Upernavik** Greenland
14D2 **Sondrio** Italy
30D3 **Song Ba** *R* Vietnam
30D3 **Song Cau** Vietnam
28A3 **Sŏngch'on** N Korea
51D5 **Songea** Tanzania
28A2 **Songgan** N Korea
26F2 **Songhua** *R* China
31E3 **Songjiang** China
28A3 **Songjŏng** S Korea
30C4 **Songkhla** Thailand
30C5 **Sông Pahang** *R* Malaysia
31A3 **Songpan** China
28A4 **Sŏngsan-ni** S Korea
31C1 **Sonid Youqi** China
42D3 **Sonīpat** India
30C1 **Son La** Vietnam
42B3 **Sonmiani** Pakistan
42B3 **Sonmiani Bay** Pakistan
59D4 **Sonoita** Mexico
66A1 **Sonoma** USA
66B2 **Sonora** California, USA
62B2 **Sonora** Texas, USA
70A2 **Sonora** *R* Mexico
59D4 **Sonora** *State* Mexico
56B3 **Sonoran Desert** USA
66C1 **Sonora P** USA
70D3 **Sonsonate** El Salvador
27G6 **Sonsorol** *I* Pacific Ocean
57E2 **Soo Canals** Canada/USA
19D2 **Sopot** Poland
18D3 **Sopron** Hungary
66B2 **Soquel** USA
16C2 **Sora** Italy
45C3 **Sored** *R* Israel
65E1 **Sorel** Canada
34C4 **Sorell** Australia
40C2 **Sorgun** Turkey
15B1 **Soria** Spain
24C2 **Sørkapp** *I* Barents Sea
12J5 **Sørkjosen** Norway
21J6 **Sor Mertvyy Kultuk** *Plain* Kazakhstan
75C3 **Sorocaba** Brazil
20J5 **Sorochinsk** Moldavia
19F3 **Soroki** Russian Federation
27H6 **Sorol** *I* Pacific Ocean
29D2 **Soroma-ko** *L* Japan
27G7 **Sorong** Indonesia
50D3 **Soroti** Uganda
12J4 **Sørøya** *I* Norway
16C2 **Sorrento** Italy
12K5 **Sorsatunturi** *Mt* Finland
12H5 **Sorsele** Sweden
20E3 **Sortavala** Russian Federation
28B3 **Sŏsan** S Korea
19D2 **Sosnowiec** Poland
20L4 **Sos'va** Russian Federation
50B3 **Souanké** Congo
48B4 **Soubré** Ivory Coast
68C2 **Souderton** USA
69P2 **Soufrière** St Lucia
69N2 **Soufrière** *Mt* St Vincent
14C3 **Souillac** France
16B3 **Souk Ahras** Algeria
Sŏul = Seoul
15C2 **Soummam** *R* Algeria
Sour = Tyre
47D2 **Sources,Mt aux** Lesotho
60C1 **Souris** Manitoba, Canada
60C1 **Souris** *R* Canada/USA
73L5 **Sousa** Brazil
16C3 **Sousse** Tunisia
51C7 **South Africa** *Republic* Africa
68C2 **S Amboy** USA
64C2 **Southampton** Canada
7D4 **Southampton** England
68D2 **Southampton** USA
55K3 **Southampton I** Canada
44E3 **South Andaman** *I* Indian Ocean
55M4 **South Aulatsivik I** Canada
32C3 **South Australia** *State* Australia
36H6 **South Australian Basin** Indian Ocean
63E2 **Southaven** USA
62A2 **South Baldy** *Mt* USA
67B3 **South Bay** USA
64C1 **South Baymouth** Canada
64B2 **South Bend** Indiana, USA
58B1 **South Bend** Washington, USA
65D3 **South Boston** USA
68E1 **Southbridge** USA
South Cape = Ka Lae
57E3 **South Carolina** *State* USA
27E5 **South China S** SE Asia
56C2 **South Dakota** *State* USA
68D1 **South Deerfield** USA
7D4 **South Downs** England
34C4 **South East C** Australia
37O7 **South East Pacific Basin** Pacific Ocean
54H4 **Southend** Canada
7E4 **Southend-on-Sea** England
35A2 **Southern Alps** *Mts* New Zealand
32A4 **Southern Cross** Australia
54J4 **Southern Indian L** Canada
67C1 **Southern Pines** USA
69H2 **Southfield** Jamaica
37K6 **South Fiji Basin** Pacific Ocean
7E4 **South Foreland** *Pt* England
62A1 **South Fork** USA
66B1 **South Fork** *R* California, USA
66B1 **South Fork American** *R* USA
66C3 **South Fork Kern** *R* USA
71G9 **South Georgia** *I* S Atlantic Ocean
7C4 **South Glamorgan** *County* Wales
64B2 **South Haven** USA
54J3 **South Henik L** Canada
65D3 **South Hill** USA
36J3 **South Honshu Ridge** Pacific Ocean
35A2 **South I** New Zealand
68D2 **Southington** USA
28B3 **South Korea** *Republic* S Korea
59B3 **South Lake Tahoe** USA
36D6 **South Madagascar Ridge** Indian Ocean
76G8 **South Magnetic Pole** Antarctica
67B3 **South Miami** USA
68B3 **South Mt** USA
54F3 **South Nahanni** *R* Canada
69G1 **South Negril Pt** Jamaica
52F8 **South Orkney Is** Atlantic Ocean
71B5 **South Pacific O**
60C2 **South Platte** *R* USA
76E **South Pole** Antarctica
64C1 **South Porcupine** Canada
7C3 **Southport** England
69Q2 **South Pt** Barbados
68C2 **South River** USA
8D2 **South Ronaldsay** *I* Scotland
52G7 **South Sandwich Trench** Atlantic Ocean
66A2 **South San Francisco** USA
54H4 **South Saskatchewan** *R* Canada
6D2 **South Shields** England
35B1 **South Taranaki Bight** *B* New Zealand
8B3 **South Uist** *I* Scotland
South West Africa = Namibia
32D5 **South West C** Australia
36D6 **South West Indian Ridge** Indian Ocean
37M6 **South West Pacific Basin** Pacific Ocean
52D5 **South West Peru Ridge** Pacific Ocean
7E3 **Southwold** England
7D3 **South Yorkshire** *County* England
47D1 **Soutpansberg** *Mts* South Africa
19E1 **Sovetsk** Russian Federation
20H4 **Sovetsk** Russian Federation
26G2 **Sovetskaya Gavan'** Russian Federation
20L3 **Sovetskiy** Russian Federation
47D2 **Soweto** South Africa
29D1 **Sōya-misaki** *C* Japan
51B4 **Soyo Congo** Angola
19G2 **Sozh** *R* Belarus
13C2 **Spa** Belgium
15 **Spain** *Kingdom* SW Europe
Spalato = Split
7D3 **Spalding** England
64C1 **Spanish** *R* Canada
59D2 **Spanish Fork** USA
69J1 **Spanish Town** Jamaica
59C3 **Sparks** USA
64A2 **Sparta** USA
67B2 **Spartanburg** USA
17E3 **Spartí** Greece
16D3 **Spartivento, C** Italy
26G2 **Spassk Dal'niy** Russian Federation
60C2 **Spearfish** USA
62B1 **Spearman** USA
69R2 **Speightstown** Barbados
54D3 **Spenard** USA
55J3 **Spence Bay** Canada
64B3 **Spencer** Indiana, USA
61D2 **Spencer** Iowa, USA
32C4 **Spencer G** Australia
55L3 **Spencer Is** Canada
35B2 **Spenser Mts** New Zealand
9C2 **Sperrin Mts** Northern Ireland
8D3 **Spey** *R* Scotland
18B3 **Speyer** Germany
69K1 **Speyside** Tobago
58C1 **Spirit Lake** USA
54G4 **Spirit River** Canada
24C2 **Spitsbergen** *I* Svalbard, Norway
Spitsbergen *Is* **= Svalbard**
18C3 **Spittal** Austria
13D1 **Spjekeroog** *I* Germany
12F6 **Spjelkavik** Norway
16D2 **Split** Croatia
58C1 **Spokane** USA
64A1 **Spooner** USA
Sporádhes *Is* **= Dodecanese**
27E6 **Spratly** *I* S China Sea
27E6 **Spratly Is** S China Sea
58C2 **Spray** USA
18C2 **Spree** *R* Germany
47B2 **Springbok** South Africa
63D1 **Springdale** USA
62B1 **Springer** USA
59E4 **Springerville** USA
62B1 **Springfield** Colorado, USA
64B3 **Springfield** Illinois, USA
68D1 **Springfield** Massachusetts, USA
61E2 **Springfield** Minnesota, USA
63D1 **Springfield** Missouri, USA
64C3 **Springfield** Ohio, USA
58B2 **Springfield** Oregon, USA
67A1 **Springfield** Tennessee, USA
65E2 **Springfield** Vermont, USA
47D3 **Springfontein** South Africa
59C3 **Spring Mts** USA
47D2 **Springs** South Africa
68A1 **Springville** New York, USA
59D2 **Springville** Utah, USA
68B1 **Springwater** USA
58D2 **Spruce Mt** USA
7E3 **Spurn Head** *C* England
58B1 **Spuzzum** Canada
16D3 **Squillace, G di** Italy
25S4 **Sredninnyy Khrebet** *Mts* Russian Federation
25R3 **Srednekolymsk** Russian Federation
20F5 **Sredne-Russkaya Vozvyshennost'** *Upland* Russian Federation
25M3 **Sredne Sibirskoye Ploskogorye** *Tableland* Russian Federation
20K4 **Sredniy Ural** *Mts* Russian Federation
30D3 **Srepok** *R* Cambodia
26E1 **Sretensk** Russian Federation
30C3 **Sre Umbell** Cambodia
44C2 **Srīkākulam** India
44B3 **Sri Kālahasti** India
39G5 **Sri Lanka** *Republic* S Asia
42C2 **Srīnagar** Pakistan
44A2 **Srīvardhan** India
18D2 **Środa Wlk.** Poland
8C2 **Stack Skerry** *I* Scotland
13E1 **Stade** Germany
13E1 **Stadthagen** Germany
8B3 **Staffa** *I* Scotland
7C3 **Stafford** England
7C3 **Stafford** *County* England
68D2 **Stafford Springs** USA
Stalingrad = Volgograd
47B3 **Stallberg** *Mt* South Africa
55J1 **Stallworthy,C** Canada
19E2 **Stalowa Wola** Poland
68D2 **Stamford** Connecticut, USA
7D3 **Stamford** England
68C1 **Stamford** New York, USA
62C2 **Stamford** Texas, USA
47B1 **Stampriet** Namibia
47D2 **Standerton** South Africa
64C2 **Standish** USA
58D1 **Stanford** USA
47E2 **Stanger** South Africa
6C2 **Stanhope** England
66B2 **Stanislaus** *R* USA
17E2 **Stanke Dimitrov** Bulgaria
34C4 **Stanley** Australia
74E8 **Stanley** Falkland Islands
58D2 **Stanley** Idaho, USA
60C1 **Stanley** N Dakota, USA
44B3 **Stanley Res** India
Stanleyville = Kisangani
70D3 **Stann Creek** Belize
26F1 **Stanovoy Khrebet** *Mts* Russian Federation
34D1 **Stanthorpe** Australia
8A3 **Stanton Banks** *Sand-bank* Scotland
60C2 **Stapleton** USA
19E2 **Starachowice** Poland
17E2 **Stara Planiná** *Mts* Bulgaria
20E4 **Staraya Russa** Russian Federation
17F2 **Stara Zagora** Bulgaria
18D2 **Stargard Szczecinski** Poland
63E2 **Starkville** USA
18C3 **Starnberg** Germany
19D2 **Starogard Gdański** Poland
19F3 **Starokonstantinov** Ukraine
7C4 **Start Pt** England
21F5 **Staryy Oskol** Russian Federation
68B2 **State College** USA
68C2 **Staten I** USA
67B2 **Statesboro** USA
67B1 **Statesville** USA
65D3 **Staunton** USA
12F7 **Stavanger** Norway
13C2 **Stavelot** Belgium
13C1 **Stavoren** Netherlands
21G6 **Stavropol'** Russian Federation
34B3 **Stawell** Australia
58B2 **Stayton** USA
60B2 **Steamboat Springs** USA
68B2 **Steelton** USA
58C2 **Steens Mt** USA
55N2 **Steenstrups Gletscher** *Gl* Greenland
13D1 **Steenwijk** Netherlands
54H2 **Stefansson I** Canada
47E2 **Stegi** Swaziland
61D1 **Steinbach** Canada
12G6 **Steinkjer** Norway
47B2 **Steinkopf** South Africa
47C2 **Stella** South Africa
47B3 **Stellenbosch** South Africa
13C3 **Stenay** France
18C2 **Stendal** Germany
21H8 **Stepanakert** Azerbaijan
61D1 **Stephen** USA
35B2 **Stephens,C** New Zealand
34B2 **Stephens Creek** Australia
64B1 **Stephenson** USA
55N5 **Stephenville** Canada
62C2 **Stephenville** USA
47D3 **Sterkstroom** South Africa
60C2 **Sterling** Colorado, USA
64B2 **Sterling** Illinois, USA
62C1 **Sterling** Kansas, USA
60C1 **Sterling** N Dakota, USA
62B2 **Sterling City** USA
64C2 **Sterling Heights** USA
20K5 **Sterlitamak** Russian Federation
54G4 **Stettler** Canada
64C2 **Steubenville** USA
7D4 **Stevenage** England
64B2 **Stevens Point** USA
54D3 **Stevens Village** USA
54F4 **Stewart** Canada
59C3 **Stewart** USA
54E3 **Stewart** *R* Canada
35A3 **Stewart I** New Zealand
33F1 **Stewart Is** Solomon Islands
8C4 **Stewarton** Scotland
54E3 **Stewart River** Canada
68B3 **Stewartstown** USA
61E2 **Stewartville** USA
47D3 **Steynsburg** South Africa
18C3 **Steyr** Austria
47C3 **Steytlerville** South Africa

54F4 **Stikine** *R* Canada
61E1 **Stillwater** Minnesota, USA
63C1 **Stillwater** Oklahoma, USA
59C3 **Stillwater Range** *Mts* USA
62B1 **Stinnett** USA
34A2 **Stirling** Australia
8D3 **Stirling** Scotland
12G6 **Stjørdal** Norway
13E4 **Stockach** Germany
68D1 **Stockbridge** USA
18D3 **Stockerau** Austria
12H7 **Stockholm** Sweden
7C3 **Stockport** England
66B2 **Stockton** California, USA
6D2 **Stockton** England
62D3 **Stockton** Kansas, USA
63D1 **Stockton L** USA
7C3 **Stoke-on-Trent** England
12G5 **Stokmarknes** Norway
25P2 **Stolbovoy, Ostrov** *I* Russian Federation
12K8 **Stolbtsy** Russian Federation
19F2 **Stolin** Belarus
7C3 **Stone** England
68C3 **Stone Harbor** USA
8D3 **Stonehaven** Scotland
63C2 **Stonewall** USA
7D3 **Stony Stratford** England
12H5 **Storavan** *L* Sweden
12G6 **Støren** Norway
34C4 **Storm B** Australia
61D2 **Storm Lake** USA
8B2 **Stornoway** Scotland
19F3 **Storozhinets** Ukraine
68D2 **Storrs** USA
12G6 **Storsjön** *L* Sweden
12H5 **Storuman** Sweden
60B2 **Story** USA
68E1 **Stoughton** USA
7E4 **Stour** *R* England
7C3 **Stourbridge** England
7C3 **Stourport** England
7E3 **Stowmarket** England
9C2 **Strabane** Northern Ireland
34C4 **Strahan** Australia
18C2 **Stralsund** Germany
47B3 **Strand** South Africa
12F6 **Stranda** Norway
9D2 **Strangford Lough** *L* Irish Republic
12H7 **Strängnäs** Sweden
8C4 **Stranraer** Scotland
14D2 **Strasbourg** France
65D3 **Strasburg** USA
66C2 **Stratford** California, USA
64C2 **Stratford** Canada
68D2 **Stratford** Connecticut, USA
35B1 **Stratford** New Zealand
62B1 **Stratford** Texas, USA
7D3 **Stratford-on-Avon** England
34A3 **Strathalbyn** Australia
8C4 **Strathclyde** *Region* Scotland
65E1 **Stratton** USA
64B2 **Streator** USA
8D2 **Stroma, I** Scotland
16D3 **Stromboli** *I* Italy
8D2 **Stromness** Scotland
61D2 **Stromsburg** USA
12H6 **Strömsund** Sweden
12G6 **Ströms Vattudal** *L* Sweden
8D2 **Stronsay** *I* Scotland
7C4 **Stroud** England
68C2 **Stroudsburg** USA
17E2 **Struma** *R* Bulgaria
7B3 **Strumble Head** *Pt* Wales
17E2 **Strumica** Macedonia, Yugoslavia
19E3 **Stryy** Ukraine
19E3 **Stryy** *R* Ukraine
34B1 **Strzelecki Creek** *R* Australia
67B3 **Stuart** Florida, USA
60D2 **Stuart** Nebraska, USA
54F4 **Stuart L** Canada
12G8 **Stubice** Poland
30D3 **Stung Sen** *R* Cambodia
30D3 **Stung Treng** Cambodia
16B2 **Stura** *R* Italy
76G7 **Sturge I** Antarctica
64B2 **Sturgeon Bay** USA
65D1 **Sturgeon Falls** Canada
64B3 **Sturgis** Kentucky, USA
64B2 **Sturgis** Michigan, USA
60C2 **Sturgis** S Dakota, USA
32B2 **Sturt Creek** *R* Australia
34B1 **Sturt Desert** Australia
47D3 **Stutterheim** South Africa
63D2 **Stuttgart** USA
18B3 **Stuttgart** Germany
12A1 **Stykkishólmur** Iceland
19F2 **Styr'** *R* Ukraine
75D2 **Suaçuí Grande** *R* Brazil
50D2 **Suakin** Sudan
28A3 **Suan** N Korea
31E5 **Suao** Taiwan
17D1 **Subotica** Serbia, Yugoslavia
21D6 **Suceava** Romania
72E7 **Sucre** Bolivia
75B2 **Sucuriú** *R* Brazil
50C2 **Sudan** *Republic* Africa
64C1 **Sudbury** Canada
7E3 **Sudbury** England
50C3 **Sudd** *Swamp* Sudan
73G2 **Suddie** Guyana
45B4 **Sudr** Egypt
50C3 **Sue** *R* Sudan
40B4 **Suez** Egypt
40B3 **Suez Canal** Egypt
40B4 **Suez,G of** Egypt
68C2 **Suffern** USA
65D3 **Suffolk** USA
7E3 **Suffolk** *County* England
65E2 **Sugarloaf Mt** USA
34D2 **Sugarloaf Pt** Australia
25R3 **Sugoy** *R* Russian Federation
41G5 **Suhār** Oman
26D1 **Sühbaatar** Mongolia
42B3 **Sui** Pakistan
31C2 **Suide** China
28C2 **Suifen He** *R* China
26F2 **Suihua** China
31B3 **Suining** China
13C3 **Suippes** France
10B3 **Suir** *R* Irish Republic
31C3 **Sui Xian** China
31E1 **Suizhong** China
42C3 **Sujāngarh** India
27D7 **Sukadana** Indonesia
29E3 **Sukagawa** Japan
26C3 **Sukai Hu** *L* China
28B3 **Sukch'ŏn** N Korea
20F5 **Sukhinichi** Russian Federation
20G4 **Sukhona** *R* Russian Federation
21G7 **Sukhumi** Georgia
55N3 **Sukkertoppen** Greenland
55N3 **Sukkertoppen Isflade** *Ice field* Greenland
12L6 **Sukkozero** Russian Federation
42B3 **Sukkur** Pakistan
44C2 **Sukma** India
51B6 **Sukses** Namibia
28B4 **Sukumo** Japan
21F5 **Sula** *R* Russian Federation
42B3 **Sulaiman Range** *Mts* Pakistan
32B1 **Sula, Kepulauan** *I* Indonesia
8B2 **Sula Sgeir** *I* Scotland
27E7 **Sulawesi** *Is* Indonesia
41E2 **Sulaymānīyah** Iraq
8C2 **Sule Skerry** *I* Scotland
17F1 **Sulina** Romania
13E1 **Sulingen** Germany
12H5 **Sulitjelma** Norway
72B4 **Sullana** Peru
63D1 **Sullivan** USA
13B4 **Sully-sur-Loire** France
16C2 **Sulmona** Italy
63D2 **Sulphur** Louisiana, USA
63C2 **Sulphur** Oklahoma, USA
63C2 **Sulphur Springs** USA
21E8 **Sultan Dağları** *Mts* Turkey
43E3 **Sultānpur** India
27F6 **Sulu Arch** *Is* Philippines
27E6 **Sulu S** Philippines
13E3 **Sulz** Germany
74D3 **Sumampa** Argentina
27C6 **Sumatera** *I* Indonesia
27E8 **Sumba** *I* Indonesia
27E7 **Sumbawa** *I* Indonesia
27E7 **Sumbawa Besar** Indonesia
51D4 **Sumbawanga** Tanzania
51B5 **Sumbe** Angola
8E2 **Sumburgh Head** *Pt* Scotland
43N2 **Sumesar Ra** *Mts* Nepal
21H7 **Sumgait** Azerbaijan
26H3 **Sumisu** *I* Japan
54F4 **Summit Lake** Canada
59C3 **Summit Mt** USA
35B2 **Sumner,L** New Zealand
29B4 **Sumoto** Japan
67B2 **Sumter** USA
21E5 **Sumy** Ukraine
58D1 **Sun** *R* USA
29D2 **Sunagawa** Japan
28A3 **Sunan** N Korea
8C3 **Sunart, Loch** *Inlet* Scotland
68B2 **Sunbury** USA
28B3 **Sunch'ŏn** N Korea
28B4 **Sunch'ŏn** S Korea
60C2 **Sundance** USA
43E4 **Sundargarh** India
43F4 **Sunderbans** *Swamp* Bangladesh/India
6D2 **Sunderland** England
65D1 **Sundridge** Canada
12H6 **Sundsvall** Sweden
58C1 **Sunnyside** USA
59B3 **Sunnyvale** USA
64B2 **Sun Prairie** USA
25N3 **Suntar** Russian Federation
58D2 **Sun Valley** USA
48B4 **Sunyani** Ghana
20E3 **Suojarvi** Russian Federation
28B4 **Suō-nada** *B* Japan
12K6 **Suonenjoki** Finland
43F3 **Supaul** India
59D4 **Superior** Arizona, USA
61D2 **Superior** Nebraska, USA
64A1 **Superior** Wisconsin, USA
64B1 **Superior,L** Canada/USA
30C3 **Suphan Buri** Thailand
40D2 **Süphan Dağ** *Mt* Turkey
27G7 **Supiori** *I* Indonesia
41E3 **Sūq ash Suyūkh** Iraq
45D1 **Şuqaylibīyah** Syria
31D3 **Suqian** China
Suqutra = Socotra
38D3 **Sūr** Oman
20H5 **Sura** *R* Russian Federation
27E7 **Surabaya** Indonesia
29C4 **Suraga-wan** *B* Japan
27E7 **Surakarta** Indonesia
45D1 **Şūrān** Syria
34C1 **Surat** Australia
42C4 **Sūrat** India
42C3 **Sūratgarh** India
30B4 **Surat Thani** Thailand
42C4 **Surendranagar** India
68C3 **Surf City** USA
24J3 **Surgut** Russian Federation
44B2 **Suriāpet** India
27F6 **Surigao** Philippines
30C3 **Surin** Thailand
73G3 **Surinam** *Republic* S America
66B2 **Sur,Pt** USA
7D4 **Surrey** *County* England
49D1 **Surt** Libya
12A2 **Surtsey** *I* Iceland
16B1 **Susa** Italy
28B4 **Susa** Japan
29B4 **Susaki** Japan
59B2 **Susanville** USA
68C2 **Susquehanna** USA
68B3 **Susquehanna** *R* USA
68C2 **Sussex** USA
7D4 **Sussex West** England
47C3 **Sutherland** South Africa
60C2 **Sutherland** USA
42C2 **Sutlej** *R* Pakistan
59B3 **Sutter Creek** USA
64C3 **Sutton** USA
29D2 **Suttsu** Japan
29D3 **Suwa** Japan
19E2 **Suwałki** Poland
67B3 **Suwannee** *R* USA
45C2 **Suweilih** Jordan
28B3 **Suwŏn** S Korea
31D3 **Su Xian** China
29C3 **Suzaka** Japan
31E3 **Suzhou** China
29D3 **Suzu** Japan
29C4 **Suzuka** Japan
29C3 **Suzu-misaki** *C* Japan
24C2 **Svalbard** *Is* Barents Sea
19E3 **Svalyava** Ukraine
55N2 **Svartenhuk Halvø** *Region* Greenland
12G5 **Svartisen** *Mt* Norway
30D3 **Svay Rieng** Cambodia
12G6 **Sveg** Sweden
12G7 **Svendborg** Denmark
Sverdlovsk = Yekaterinburg
55J1 **Sverdrup Chan** Canada
54H2 **Sverdrup Is** Canada
26G2 **Svetlaya** Russian Federation
19E2 **Svetlogorsk** Russian Federation
12K6 **Svetogorsk** Russian Federation
17E2 **Svetozarevo** Serbia, Yugoslavia
17F2 **Svilengrad** Bulgaria
19F2 **Svir'** Belarus
20E3 **Svir'** *R* Russian Federation
18D3 **Svitavy** Czech Republic
26F1 **Svobodnyy** Russian Federation
12G5 **Svolvær** Norway
7E3 **Swaffam** England
33E3 **Swain Reefs** Australia
67B2 **Swainsboro** USA
33H2 **Swains I** American Samoa
47B1 **Swakop** *R* Namibia
47A1 **Swakopmund** Namibia
6D2 **Swale** *R* England
27E6 **Swallow Reef** S China Sea
44B3 **Swāmihalli** India
70D3 **Swan** *I* Honduras
7D4 **Swanage** England
34B3 **Swan Hill** Australia
69A3 **Swan I** Caribbean Sea
54H4 **Swan River** Canada
7C4 **Swansea** Wales
7C4 **Swansea B** Wales
47C3 **Swartberge** *Mts* South Africa
47D2 **Swartruggens** South Africa
Swatow = Shantou
47E2 **Swaziland** *Kingdom* South Africa
12G7 **Sweden** *Kingdom* N Europe
58B2 **Sweet Home** USA
62B2 **Sweetwater** USA
60B2 **Sweetwater** *R* USA
47C3 **Swellendam** South Africa
18D2 **Świdnica** Poland
18D2 **Świdwin** Poland
18D2 **Świebodzin** Poland
19D2 **Świecie** Poland
54H4 **Swift Current** Canada
9C2 **Swilly, Lough** *Estuary* Irish Republic
7D4 **Swindon** England
18C2 **Świnoujście** Poland
14D2 **Switzerland** Europe
9C3 **Swords** Irish Republic
43M1 **Syang** Nepal
9A3 **Sybil Pt** Irish Republic
34D2 **Sydney** Australia
20H3 **Syktyvkar** Russian Federation
67A2 **Sylacauga** USA
12G6 **Sylarna** *Mt* Sweden
43G4 **Sylhet** Bangladesh
18B1 **Sylt** *I* Germany
64C2 **Sylvania** USA
76G11 **Syowa** *Base* Antarctica
16D3 **Syracuse** Italy
62B1 **Syracuse** Kansas, USA
68B1 **Syracuse** New York, USA
65D2 **Syracuse** USA
24H5 **Syr Darya** *R* Kazakhstan
40C2 **Syria** *Republic* SW Asia
20L4 **Sysert'** Russian Federation
20H5 **Syzran'** Russian Federation
18C2 **Szczecin** Poland
18D2 **Szczecinek** Poland
19E2 **Szczytno** Poland
19E3 **Szeged** Hungary
19D3 **Székesfehérvar** Hungary
19D3 **Szekszárd** Hungary
19D3 **Szolnok** Hungary
18D3 **Szombathely** Hungary
18D2 **Szprotawa** Poland

T

47D3 **Tabankulu** South Africa
32E1 **Tabar Is** Papua New Guinea
16B3 **Tabarka** Tunisia
41G3 **Tabas** Iran
72E4 **Tabatinga** Brazil
48B2 **Tabelbala** Algeria
30C3 **Tabeng** Cambodia
54G5 **Taber** Canada
47B3 **Table Mt** South Africa
63D1 **Table Rock Res** USA
18C3 **Tábor** Czech Republic
50D4 **Tabora** Tanzania
20L4 **Tabory** Russian Federation
48B4 **Tabou** Ivory Coast
41E2 **Tabrīz** Iran
40C4 **Tabūk** Saudi Arabia
39G1 **Tacheng** China
27F5 **Tacloban** Philippines
72D7 **Tacna** Peru
59D4 **Tacna** USA
56A2 **Tacoma** USA
68D1 **Taconic Range** USA
75A3 **Tacuatí** Paraguay
48C2 **Tademait, Plateau du** Algeria
50E2 **Tadjoura** Djibouti
65F1 **Tadoussac** Canada
44B3 **Tādpatri** India
28B3 **Taebaek Sanmaek** *Mts* N Korea/S Korea
28B3 **T'aech'ŏn** N Korea
28A3 **Taech'on** S Korea
28A3 **Taedasa-Do** N Korea
28A3 **Taedong** *R* N Korea
28A3 **Taegang-got** *Pen* N Korea
28B3 **Taegu** S Korea
28A2 **Taehung** N Korea
28B3 **Taejŏn** S Korea
15B1 **Tafalla** Spain
48C2 **Tafasaset** *Watercourse* Algeria
7C4 **Taff** *R* Wales
45C3 **Tafila** Jordan
66C3 **Taft** USA
21F6 **Taganrog** Russian Federation
48A3 **Tagant** *Region* Mauritius
48B2 **Taguenout Hagguerete** *Well* Mali
33E2 **Tagula** *I* Papua New Guinea
Tagus = Tejo
48C2 **Tahat** *Mt* Algeria
37M5 **Tahiti** *I* Pacific Ocean
63C1 **Tahlequah** USA
59B3 **Tahoe City** USA
59B3 **Tahoe,L** USA
62B2 **Tahoka** USA
48C3 **Tahoua** Niger
40B4 **Tahta** Egypt
27F6 **Tahuna** Indonesia
31D2 **Tai'an** China
28A2 **Tai'an** China
31B3 **Taibai Shan** *Mt* China
31D1 **Taibus Qi** China
31E5 **Taichung** Taiwan
35B3 **Taieri** *R* New Zealand
31C2 **Taihang Shan** *Upland* China
35C1 **Taihape** New Zealand
31E3 **Tai Hu** *L* China
29D2 **Taiki** Japan
34A3 **Tailem Bend** Australia
8C3 **Tain** Scotland
31E5 **Tainan** Taiwan
75D2 **Taiobeiras** Brazil
31E5 **Taipei** Taiwan
30C5 **Taiping** Malaysia
29D3 **Taira** Japan
28B3 **Taisha** Japan
74B7 **Taitao,Pen de** Chile
31E5 **Taitung** Taiwan
12K5 **Taivalkoski** Finland
26F4 **Taiwan** *Republic* China
31D5 **Taiwan Str** China/Taiwan
45C3 **Taiyiba** Jordan
31C2 **Taiyuan** China
31D3 **Taizhou** China
50E2 **Ta'izz** Yemen
39E2 **Tajikistan** *Republic* Asia
15B1 **Tajo** *R* Spain
30B2 **Tak** Thailand
32B1 **Takabonerate, Kepulauan** *Is* Indonesia
29D3 **Takada** Japan
29B4 **Takahashi** Japan
35B2 **Takaka** New Zealand
29C4 **Takamatsu** Japan
29D3 **Takaoka** Japan
35B1 **Takapuna** New Zealand
29D3 **Takasaki** Japan
29C3 **Takayama** Japan
29D3 **Takefu** Japan
27C6 **Takengon** Indonesia
30C3 **Takeo** Cambodia
28B4 **Takeo** Japan
Take-shima = Tok-do
41E2 **Takestān** Iran
28B4 **Taketa** Japan
29D2 **Takikawa** Japan
29D2 **Takinoue** Japan
54G3 **Takiyvak L** Canada
50D2 **Takkaze** *R* Eritrea/Ethiopia
48B4 **Takoradi** Ghana
42C2 **Talagang** Pakistan
44B4 **Talaimannar** Sri Lanka
48C3 **Talak** *Desert Region* Niger
72B4 **Talara** Peru
32E1 **Talasea** Papua New Guinea
45B3 **Talata** Egypt
27F6 **Talaud, Kepulauan** *Is* Indonesia
15B2 **Talavera de la Reina** Spain
74B5 **Talca** Chile
74B5 **Talcahuano** Chile
43F4 **Tālcher** India
39F1 **Taldy Kurgan** Kazakhstan
27F7 **Taliabu** *I* Indonesia
42B1 **Taligan** Afghanistan
50D3 **Tali Post** Sudan
27E7 **Taliwang** Indonesia
54D3 **Talkeetna** USA
45A3 **Talkha** Egypt
67A2 **Talladega** USA
40D2 **Tall 'Afar** Iraq
67B2 **Tallahassee** USA
45D1 **Tall Bīsah** Syria
20C4 **Tallinn** Estonia
40C3 **Tall Kalakh** Syria
63D2 **Tallulah** USA
26B1 **Tal'menka** Russian Federation
21E6 **Tal'noye** Ukraine
19E2 **Talpaki** Russian Federation
74B3 **Taltal** Chile
34C1 **Talwood** Australia
61E2 **Tama** USA
27E6 **Tamabo Ra** *Mts* Borneo
48B4 **Tamale** Ghana
29C4 **Tamano** Japan
48C2 **Tamanrasset** Algeria
48C2 **Tamanrasset** *Watercourse* Algeria
68C2 **Tamaqua** USA
7B4 **Tamar** *R* England
Tamatave = Toamasina
48A3 **Tambacounda** Senegal

21G5 **Tambov** Russian Federation
15A1 **Tambre** *R* Spain
50C3 **Tambura** Sudan
48A3 **Tamchaket** Mauritius
15A1 **Tamega** *R* Portugal
70C2 **Tamiahua, L de** *Lg* Mexico
44B3 **Tamil Nādu** *State* India
17E1 **Tamiş** *R* Romania
30D2 **Tam Ky** Vietnam
67B3 **Tampa** USA
67B3 **Tampa B** USA
12J6 **Tampere** Finland
70C2 **Tampico** Mexico
26E2 **Tamsagbulag** Mongolia
31E4 **Tamsui** Taiwan
43G4 **Tamu** Burma
34D2 **Tamworth** Australia
7D3 **Tamworth** England
20D1 **Tana** Norway
12K5 **Tana** *R* Finland/Norway
50E4 **Tana** *R* Kenya
29C4 **Tanabe** Japan
12K4 **Tanafjord** *Inlet* Norway
27E7 **Tanahgrogot** Indonesia
27G7 **Tanahmerah** Indonesia
50D2 **Tana, L** Ethiopia
54C3 **Tanana** USA
54C3 **Tanana** *R* USA
Tananarive = Antananarivo
28B2 **Tanch'ŏn** N Korea
74E5 **Tandil** Argentina
27G7 **Tandjung d'Urville** *C* Indonesia
27G7 **Tandjung Vals** *C* Indonesia
42B3 **Tando Adam** Pakistan
42B3 **Tando Muhammad Khan** Pakistan
34B2 **Tandou L** Australia
44B2 **Tāndūr** India
35C1 **Taneatua** New Zealand
30B2 **Tanen Range** *Mts* Burma/Thailand
48B2 **Tanezrouft** *Desert Region* Algeria
50D4 **Tanga** Tanzania
33E1 **Tanga Is** Papua New Guinea
50C4 **Tanganyika,L** Tanzania/Zaïre
Tanger = Tangiers
39H2 **Tanggula Shan** *Mts* China
15A2 **Tangiers** Morocco
28A3 **Tangjin** S Korea
39G2 **Tangra Yumco** *L* China
31D2 **Tangshan** China
26D1 **Tanguy** Russian Federation
27G7 **Tanimbar, Kepulauan** *Arch* Indonesia
51E6 **Tanjona Ankaboa** *C* Madagascar
51E5 **Tanjona Anorontany** *C* Madagascar
51E5 **Tanjona Bobaomby** *C* Madagascar
51E5 **Tanjona Vilanandro** *C* Madagascar
51E6 **Tanjona Vohimena** *C* Madagascar
27C6 **Tanjungbalai** Indonesia
27D7 **Tanjungpandan** Indonesia
27D7 **Tanjung Priok** Indonesia
27E6 **Tanjungredeb** Indonesia
32A1 **Tanjung Selatan** *Pt* Indonesia
27E6 **Tanjungselor** Indonesia
32C1 **Tanjung Vals** *Pt* Indonesia
42C2 **Tank** Pakistan
33F2 **Tanna** *I* Vanuatu
26C1 **Tannu Ola** *Mts* Russian Federation
48B4 **Tano** *R* Ghana
48C3 **Tanout** Niger
43E3 **Tansing** Nepal
49F1 **Tanta** Egypt
48A2 **Tan-Tan** Morocco
54B3 **Tanunak** USA
28A3 **Tanyang** S Korea
50D4 **Tanzania** *Republic* Africa
31A3 **Tao He** *R* China
31B2 **Taole** China
62A1 **Taos** USA
48B1 **Taourirt** Morocco
20D4 **Tapa** Estonia
70C3 **Tapachula** Mexico
73G4 **Tapajós** *R* Brazil
27D7 **Tapan** Indonesia
35A3 **Tapanui** New Zealand
72E5 **Tapauá** *R* Brazil
42D4 **Tāpi** *R* India
43F3 **Taplejung** Nepal
65D3 **Tappahannock** USA
35B2 **Tapuaenuku** *Mt* New Zealand
75C3 **Tapuaritinga** Brazil
72F4 **Tapurucuara** Brazil
75B2 **Taquaral, Serra do** *Mts* Brazil
75B2 **Taquari** *R* Brazil
34D1 **Tara** Australia
24J4 **Tara** Russian Federation
24J4 **Tara** *R* Russian Federation
17D2 **Tara** *R* Bosnia-Herzegovina
48D4 **Taraba** *R* Nigeria
72F7 **Tarabuco** Bolivia
Tarābulus = Tripoli (Libya)
35C1 **Taradale** New Zealand
27E6 **Tarakan** Indonesia
Taranaki, Mt = Egmont, Mt
15B1 **Tarancón** Spain
8B3 **Taransay** *I* Scotland
16D2 **Taranto** Italy
16D2 **Taranto, G di** Italy
72C5 **Tarapoto** Peru
14C2 **Tarare** France
35C2 **Tararua Range** *Mts* New Zealand
20H2 **Tarasovo** Russian Federation
48C2 **Tarat** Algeria
35C1 **Tarawera** New Zealand
15B1 **Tarazona** Spain
39G1 **Tarbagatay, Khrebet** *Mts* Russian Federation
8D3 **Tarbat Ness** *Pen* Scotland
42C2 **Tarbela Res** Pakistan
8C4 **Tarbert** Strathclyde, Scotland
8B3 **Tarbert** Western Isles, Scotland
14B3 **Tarbes** France
67C1 **Tarboro** USA
32C4 **Tarcoola** Australia
34C2 **Tarcoon** Australia
34D2 **Taree** Australia
48A2 **Tarfaya** Morocco
58D2 **Targhee P** USA
49D1 **Tarhūnah** Libya
41F5 **Tarīf** UAE
72F8 **Tarija** Bolivia
44B3 **Tarikere** India
38C4 **Tarīm** Yemen
50D4 **Tarime** Tanzania
39G1 **Tarim He** *R* China
39G2 **Tarim Pendi** *Basin* China
42B2 **Tarin Kut** Afghanistan
47D3 **Tarkastad** South Africa
61D2 **Tarkio** USA
27F5 **Tarlac** Philippines
72C6 **Tarma** Peru
14C3 **Tarn** *R* France
19E2 **Tarnobrzeg** Poland
19E3 **Tarnów** Poland
16B2 **Taro** *R* Italy
32D3 **Taroom** Australia
48B1 **Taroudannt** Morocco
15C1 **Tarragona** Spain
34C4 **Tarraleah** Australia
15C1 **Tarrasa** Spain
68D2 **Tarrytown** USA
40B2 **Tarsus** Turkey
8E2 **Tartan** *Oilfield* N Sea
26H2 **Tartarskiy Proliv** *Str* Russian Federation
20D4 **Tartu** Estonia
40C3 **Tartūs** Syria
75D2 **Tarumirim** Brazil
27C6 **Tarutung** Indonesia
16C1 **Tarvisio** Italy
65D1 **Taschereau** Canada
38D1 **Tashauz** Turkmenistan
43G3 **Tashigang** Bhutan
39E1 **Tashkent** Uzbekistan
24K4 **Tashtagol** Russian Federation
25K4 **Tashtyp** Russian Federation
45C2 **Tasīl** Syria
55N2 **Tasiussaq** Greenland
50B2 **Tasker** *Well* Niger
35B2 **Tasman B** New Zealand
32D5 **Tasmania** *I* Australia
35B2 **Tasman Mts** New Zealand
34C4 **Tasman Pen** Australia
33E4 **Tasman S** Australia/New Zealand
40C1 **Taşova** Turkey
48C2 **Tassili du Hoggar** *Desert Region* Algeria
48C2 **Tassili N'jjer** *Desert Region* Algeria
48B2 **Tata** Morocco
19D3 **Tatabánya** Hungary
48D1 **Tataouine** Tunisia
24J4 **Tatarsk** Russian Federation
20J4 **Tatarstan** *Republic* Russian Federation
29C3 **Tateyama** Japan
54G3 **Tathlina L** Canada
55J4 **Tatnam, Cape** Canada
19D3 **Tatry** *Mts* Poland/Slovakia
29B4 **Tatsuno** Japan
42B4 **Tatta** Pakistan
75C3 **Tatuí** Brazil
62B2 **Tatum** USA
40D2 **Tatvan** Turkey
33H2 **Ta'u** *I* American Samoa
73K5 **Tauá** Brazil
75C3 **Taubaté** Brazil
13E2 **Taufstein** *Mt* Germany
35C1 **Taumarunui** New Zealand
47C2 **Taung** South Africa
30B2 **Taungdwingyi** Burma
30B1 **Taung-gyi** Burma
30A2 **Taungup** Burma
42C2 **Taunsa** Pakistan
7C4 **Taunton** England
68E2 **Taunton** USA
40B2 **Taunus** *Mts* Turkey
13E2 **Taunus** *Region* Germany
35C1 **Taupo** New Zealand
35C1 **Taupo,L** New Zealand
19E1 **Taurage** Lithuania
35C1 **Tauranga** New Zealand
35C1 **Tauranga Harbour** *B* New Zealand
35B1 **Tauroa Pt** New Zealand
40B2 **Taurus Mts** Turkey
55J3 **Tavani** Canada
24H4 **Tavda** Russian Federation
24H4 **Tavda** *R* Russian Federation
33H2 **Taveuni** *I* Fiji
15A2 **Tavira** Portugal
7B4 **Tavistock** England
30B3 **Tavoy** Burma
30B3 **Tavoy Pt** Burma
40A2 **Tavşanli** Turkey
7C4 **Taw** *R* England
35B2 **Tawa** New Zealand
63C2 **Tawakoni,L** USA
64C2 **Tawas City** USA
27E6 **Tawau** Malaysia
50C2 **Taweisha** Sudan
27F6 **Tawitawi** *I* Philippines
70C3 **Taxco** Mexico
8D3 **Tay** *R* Scotland
27E7 **Tayan** Indonesia
50E3 **Tayeeglow** Somalia
8C3 **Tay, Loch** *L* Scotland
64C2 **Taylor** Michigan, USA
63C2 **Taylor** Texas, USA
54B3 **Taylor** USA
62A1 **Taylor,Mt** USA
64B3 **Taylorville** USA
40C4 **Taymā'** Saudi Arabia
25L3 **Taymura** *R* Russian Federation
25M2 **Taymyr, Ozero** *L* Russian Federation
25L2 **Taymyr, Poluostrov** *Pen* Russian Federation
30D3 **Tay Ninh** Vietnam
25L4 **Tayshet** Russian Federation
26C2 **Tayshir** Mongolia
8D3 **Tayside** *Region* Scotland
27E5 **Taytay** Philippines
48B1 **Taza** Morocco
29D3 **Tazawako** Japan
29D3 **Tazawa-ko** *L* Japan
49E2 **Tāzirbū** Libya
24J3 **Tazovskiy** Russian Federation
21G7 **Tbilisi** Georgia
50B4 **Tchibanga** Gabon
50B1 **Tchigai,Plat du** Niger
48C3 **Tchin Tabaradene** Niger
50B3 **Tcholliré** Cameroon
19D2 **Tczew** Poland
35A3 **Te Anau** New Zealand
35A3 **Te Anua,L** New Zealand
35C1 **Te Aroha** New Zealand
35C1 **Te Awamutu** New Zealand
16B3 **Tébessa** Algeria
16B3 **Tébessa, Mts De** Algeria/Tunisia
16B3 **Téboursouk** Tunisia
59C4 **Tecate** Mexico
20L4 **Techa** *R* Russian Federation
70B3 **Tecomán** Mexico
70B3 **Tecpan** Mexico
17F1 **Tecuci** Romania
61D2 **Tecumseh** USA
24H6 **Tedzhen** Turkmenistan
24H6 **Tedzhen** *R* Turkmenistan
6D2 **Tees** *R* England
72F4 **Tefé** Brazil
70D3 **Tegucigalpa** Honduras
66C3 **Tehachapi** USA
66C3 **Tehachapi Mts** USA
59C3 **Tehachapi P** USA
54J3 **Tehek L** Canada
41F2 **Tehrān** Iran
70C3 **Tehuacán** Mexico
70C3 **Tehuantepec** Mexico
70C3 **Tehuantepec, G de** Mexico
70C3 **Tehuantepec, Istmo de** *isthmus* Mexico
7B3 **Teifi** *R* Wales
7C4 **Teignmouth** England
15A2 **Tejo** *R* Portugal
66C3 **Tejon P** USA
61D2 **Tekamah** USA
35B2 **Tekapo,L** New Zealand
39F1 **Tekeli** Kazakhstan
40A1 **Tekirdağ** Turkey
17F2 **Tekir Dağları** *Mts* Turkey
43G4 **Teknaf** Bangladesh
35C1 **Te Kuiti** New Zealand
70D3 **Tela** Honduras
21H7 **Telavi** Georgia
45C2 **Tel Aviv Yafo** Israel
54E4 **Telegraph Creek** Canada
74C5 **Telén** Argentina
59C3 **Telescope Peak** *Mt* USA
73G5 **Teles Pires** *R* Brazil
7C3 **Telford** England
25K4 **Teli** Russian Federation
45C3 **Tell el Meise** *Mt* Jordan
54B3 **Teller** USA
44B3 **Tellicherry** India
30C5 **Telok Anson** Malaysia
20K3 **Tel'pos-iz, Gory** *Mt* Russian Federation
19E1 **Telšiai** Lithuania
27D7 **Telukbetung** Indonesia
27F7 **Teluk Bone** *B* Indonesia
27G7 **Teluk Cendrawasih** *B* Indonesia
27E6 **Teluk Darvel** *B* Malaysia
27F7 **Teluk Tolo** *B* Indonesia
27F6 **Teluk Tomini** *B* Indonesia
27F6 **Teluk Weda** *B* Indonesia
64C1 **Temagami,L** Canada
69E5 **Temblador** Venezuela
66B3 **Temblor Range** *Mts* USA
7C3 **Teme** *R* England
30C5 **Temerloh** Malaysia
24G5 **Temir** Kazakhstan
24J4 **Temirtau** Kazakhstan
65D1 **Temiscaming** Canada
65F1 **Témiscouata,L** Canada
34C2 **Temora** Australia
59D4 **Tempe** USA
63C2 **Temple** USA
9C3 **Templemore** Irish Republic
66B3 **Templeton** USA
74B5 **Temuco** Chile
35B2 **Temuka** New Zealand
72C4 **Tena** Ecuador
44C2 **Tenāli** India
30B3 **Tenasserim** Burma
7B4 **Tenby** Wales
50E3 **Tendaho** Ethiopia
16B2 **Tende, Colle de** *P* France/Italy
44E4 **Ten Degree Chan** Indian Ocean
29E3 **Tendo** Japan
50B2 **Ténéré, Erg du** *Desert Region* Niger
48A2 **Tenerife** *I* Canary Islands
15C2 **Ténés** Algeria
30B1 **Teng** *R* Burma
31A2 **Tengger Shamo** *Desert* China
24H4 **Tengiz, Ozero** *L* Kazakhstan
76G2 **Teniente Rodolfo Marsh** *Base* Antarctica
44B4 **Tenkāsi** India
51C5 **Tenke** Zaïre
48B3 **Tenkodogo** Burkina
32C2 **Tennant Creek** Australia
63E1 **Tennessee** *R* USA
57E3 **Tennessee** *State* USA
60B3 **Tennessee P** USA
27E6 **Tenom** Malaysia
70C3 **Tenosique** Mexico
34D1 **Tenterfield** Australia
67B3 **Ten Thousand Is** USA
75D2 **Teófilo Otôni** Brazil
70B2 **Tepehuanes** Mexico
70B2 **Tepic** Mexico
18C2 **Teplice** Czech Republic
35C1 **Te Puke** New Zealand
15C1 **Ter** *R* Spain
48C3 **Téra** Niger
29C3 **Teradomari** Japan
16C2 **Teramo** Italy
48A1 **Terceira** *I* Azores
19F3 **Terebovlya** Ukraine
75B3 **Terenos** Brazil
73K5 **Teresina** Brazil
75D3 **Teresópolis** Brazil
44E4 **Teressa** *I* Nicobar Is, Indian Ocean
40C1 **Terme** Turkey
38E2 **Termez** Uzbekistan
70C3 **Términos, L de** *Lg* Mexico
16C2 **Termoli** Italy
27F6 **Ternate** Indonesia
16C2 **Terni** Italy
19F3 **Ternopol** Ukraine
26H2 **Terpeniya, Zaliv** *B* Russian Federation
66C3 **Terra Bella** USA
64B1 **Terrace Bay** Canada
16C2 **Terracina** Italy
51C6 **Terrafirma** South Africa
76G8 **Terre Adélie** *Region* Antarctica
63D3 **Terre Bonne B** USA
64B3 **Terre Haute** USA
63C2 **Terrell** USA
60B1 **Terry** USA
18B2 **Terschelling** *I* Netherlands
15B1 **Teruel** Spain
54C2 **Teshekpuk Lake** USA
29D2 **Teshikaga** Japan
29E2 **Teshio** *R* Japan
29D2 **Teshio dake** *Mt* Japan
25L5 **Tesiyn Gol** *R* Mongolia
54E3 **Teslin** Canada
75B2 **Tesouro** Brazil
48C2 **Tessalit** Mali
48C3 **Tessaoua** Niger
7D4 **Test** *R* England
51D5 **Tete** Mozambique
19F2 **Teterev** *R* Ukraine
58D1 **Teton** *R* USA
58D2 **Teton Range** *Mts* USA
48B1 **Tetouan** Morocco
20H5 **Tetyushi** Russian Federation
72F8 **Teuco** *R* Argentina
74D2 **Teuco** *R* Paraguay
16B3 **Teulada, C** Sardinia, Italy
27F7 **Teun** *I* Indonesia
29D2 **Teuri-tō** *I* Japan
13E1 **Teutoburger Wald** *Hills* Germany
16C2 **Tevere** *R* Italy
8D4 **Teviot** *R* Scotland
24J4 **Tevriz** Russian Federation
35A3 **Te Waewae B** New Zealand
34D1 **Tewantin** Australia
7C3 **Tewkesbury** England
31A3 **Tēwo** China
63D2 **Texarkana** USA
63D2 **Texarkana,L** USA
34D1 **Texas** Australia
56C3 **Texas** *State* USA
63D3 **Texas City** USA
18A2 **Texel** *I* Netherlands
62B1 **Texhoma** USA
63C2 **Texoma,L** USA
47D2 **Teyateyaneng** Lesotho
42A2 **Teyvareh** Afghanistan
43G3 **Tezpur** India
30C1 **Tha** *R* Laos
47D2 **Thabana Ntlenyana** *Mt* Lesotho
47D2 **Thaba Putsoa** *Mt* Lesotho
47D1 **Thabazimbi** South Africa
30B3 **Thagyettaw** Burma
30D1 **Thai Binh** Vietnam
30C2 **Thailand** *Kingdom* SE Asia
30C3 **Thailand,G of** Thailand
30D1 **Thai Nguyen** Vietnam
30D2 **Thakhek** Laos
42C2 **Thal** Pakistan
30C4 **Thale Luang** *L* Thailand
34C1 **Thallon** Australia
35C1 **Thames** New Zealand
7E4 **Thames** *R* England
21G8 **Thamhar, Wadi ath** *R* Iraq
44A2 **Thāne** India
30D2 **Thanh Hoa** Vietnam
44B3 **Thanjāvūr** India
13D4 **Thann** France
42C3 **Thar Desert** India
34B1 **Thargomindah** Australia
17E2 **Thásos** *I* Greece
30B2 **Thaton** Burma
30A2 **Thayetmyo** Burma
7E3 **The Broads** England
54F5 **The Dalles** USA
60C2 **Thedford** USA
48A3 **The Gambia** *Republic* W Africa
41F4 **The Gulf** SW Asia
18A2 **The Hague** Netherlands
54H3 **Thelon** *R* Canada
7E4 **The Naze** *Pt* England
32E3 **Theodore** Australia
59D4 **Theodore Roosevelt L** USA
72F6 **Theodore Roosevelt, R** Brazil
54H4 **The Pas** Canada
17E2 **Thermaïkós Kólpos** *G* Greece
58E2 **Thermopolis** USA
54F2 **Thesiger B** Canada
64C1 **Thessalon** Canada
17E2 **Thessaloníki** Greece
7E3 **Thetford** England
65E1 **Thetford Mines** Canada
47D2 **Theunissen** South Africa
63D3 **Thibodaux** USA
54J4 **Thicket Portage** Canada
61D1 **Thief River Falls** USA
58B2 **Thielsen,Mt** USA
14C2 **Thiers** France
48A3 **Thiès** Senegal
50D4 **Thika** Kenya
43F3 **Thimphu** Bhutan
14D2 **Thionville** France
17F3 **Thíra** *I* Greece

6D2 **Thirsk** England
44B4 **Thiruvananthapuram** India
12F7 **Thisted** Denmark
27E5 **Thitu** S China Sea
17E3 **Thívai** Greece
14C2 **Thiviers** France
66C2 **Thomas A Edison,L** USA
67B2 **Thomaston** Georgia, USA
65F2 **Thomaston** Maine, USA
9C3 **Thomastown** Irish Republic
63E2 **Thomasville** Alabama, USA
67B2 **Thomasville** Georgia, USA
67C1 **Thomasville** N Carolina, USA
55J2 **Thom Bay** Canada
54J4 **Thompson** Canada
61E2 **Thompson** *R* USA
58C1 **Thompson Falls** USA
54G3 **Thompson Landing** Canada
68D2 **Thompsonville** USA
67B2 **Thomson** USA
32D3 **Thomson** *R* Australia
30C3 **Thon Buri** Thailand
30B2 **Thongwa** Burma
62A1 **Thoreau** USA
6D2 **Thornaby** England
7D3 **Thorne** England
8D4 **Thornhill** Scotland
14B2 **Thouars** France
65D2 **Thousand Is** Canada/USA
58D1 **Three Forks** USA
64B1 **Three Lakes** USA
30B2 **Three Pagodas P** Thailand
48B4 **Three Points, C** Ghana
66C2 **Three Rivers** California, USA
64B2 **Three Rivers** Michigan, USA
62C3 **Three Rivers** Texas, USA
58B2 **Three Sisters** *Mt* USA
55M2 **Thule** Greenland
16B1 **Thun** Switzerland
64B1 **Thunder Bay** Canada
30B4 **Thung Song** Thailand
18C2 **Thüringen** *State* Germany
18C2 **Thüringer Wald** *Upland* Germany
9C3 **Thurles** Irish Republic
8D2 **Thurso** Scotland
76F4 **Thurston I** Antarctica
34B1 **Thylungra** Australia
31B5 **Tiandong** China
31B5 **Tian'e** China
31D2 **Tianjin** China
31B5 **Tianlin** China
28B2 **Tianqiaoling** China
24J5 **Tian Shan** *Mts* China/ Kirgizia
31B3 **Tianshui** China
31A2 **Tianzhu** China
15C2 **Tiaret** Algeria
75B3 **Tibagi** *R* Brazil
48D4 **Tibati** Cameroon
45C2 **Tiberias** Israel
45C2 **Tiberias,L** Israel
Tiber,R = Tevere,R
58D1 **Tiber Res** USA
50B1 **Tibesti** *Mountain Region* Chad
39G2 **Tibet** *Autonomous Region* China
34B1 **Tibooburra** Australia
43E3 **Tibrikot** Nepal
70A2 **Tiburón** *I* Mexico
48B3 **Tichitt** Mauritius
48A2 **Tichla** Morocco
65E2 **Ticonderoga** USA
70D2 **Ticul** Mexico
48C2 **Tidikelt, Plaine du** *Desert Region* Algeria
48A3 **Tidjikja** Mauritius
48A3 **Tidra, Isla** Mauritius
13C2 **Tiel** Netherlands
28A2 **Tieling** China
13B2 **Tielt** Belgium
13C2 **Tienen** Belgium
13E4 **Tiengen** Germany
Tientsin = Tianjin
12H6 **Tierp** Sweden
62A1 **Tierra Amarilla** USA
70C3 **Tierra Blanca** Mexico
71C9 **Tierra del Fuego** *I* Argentina/Chile
74C8 **Tierra del Fuego** *Territory* Argentina
74C8 **Tierra del Fuego, Isla Grande de** Argentina/ Chile
75C3 **Tietê** Brazil
75B3 **Tiete** *R* Brazil
64C2 **Tiffin** USA
67B2 **Tifton** USA
25R4 **Tigil** Russian Federation
72C4 **Tigre** *R* Peru
72F2 **Tigre** *R* Venezuela
50D2 **Tigre** *Region* Ethiopia
41E3 **Tigris** *R* Iraq
45B4 **Tīh, Gebel el** *Upland* Egypt
59C4 **Tijuana** Mexico
42D4 **Tikamgarh** India
21G6 **Tikhoretsk** Russian Federation
20E4 **Tikhvin** Russian Federation
33F2 **Tikopia** *I* Solomon Islands
41D3 **Tikrīt** Iraq
25O2 **Tiksi** Russian Federation
13C2 **Tilburg** Netherlands
7E4 **Tilbury** England
74C2 **Tilcara** Argentina
34B1 **Tilcha** Australia
48C3 **Tilemis, Vallée du** Mali
43K2 **Tilhar** India
30A1 **Tilin** Burma
48C3 **Tillabéri** Niger
58B1 **Tillamook** USA
44E4 **Tillanchong** *I* Nicobar Is, Indian Ocean
48C3 **Tillia** Niger
6D2 **Till, R** England
17F3 **Tílos** *I* Greece
34B2 **Tilpa** Australia
8D3 **Tilt** *R* Scotland
20H2 **Timanskiy Kryazh** *Mts* Russian Federation
35B2 **Timaru** New Zealand
21F6 **Timashevsk** Russian Federation
17E3 **Timbákion** Greece
63D3 **Timbalier B** USA
48B3 **Timbédra** Mauritius
Timbuktu = Tombouctou
48B3 **Timétrine Monts** *Mts* Mali
48C3 **Timia** Niger
17E1 **Timiș** *R* Romania
48C2 **Timimoun** Algeria
17E1 **Timișoara** Romania
64C1 **Timmins** Canada
32B1 **Timor** *I* Indonesia
32B2 **Timor S** Australia/ Indonesia
45B3 **Timsâh,L** Egypt
67A1 **Tims Ford L** USA
27F6 **Tinaca Pt** Philippines
69D5 **Tinaco** Venezuela
44B3 **Tindivanam** India
48B2 **Tindouf** Algeria
66C2 **Tinemaha Res** USA
48B2 **Tinfouchy** Algeria
48C2 **Tin Fouye** Algeria
55O3 **Tingmiarmiut** Greenland
72C5 **Tingo María** Peru
48B3 **Tingrela** Ivory Coast
43F3 **Tingri** China
75E1 **Tinharé, Ilha de** Brazil
27H5 **Tinian** Pacific Ocean
74C3 **Tinogasta** Argentina
17F3 **Tínos** *I* Greece
43H3 **Tinsukia** India
7B4 **Tintagel Head** *Pt* England
48C2 **Tin Tarabine** *Watercourse* Algeria
34B3 **Tintinara** Australia
48C2 **Tin Zaouaten** Algeria
60C1 **Tioga** USA
68B2 **Tioga** *R* USA
66C2 **Tioga P** USA
30C5 **Tioman** *I* Malaysia
68B1 **Tioughnioga** *R* USA
10B3 **Tipperary** Irish Republic
9C3 **Tipperary** *County* Irish Republic
66C2 **Tipton** California, USA
61E3 **Tipton** Missouri, USA
44B3 **Tiptūr** India
17D2 **Tiranë** Albania
19F3 **Tiraspol** Moldavia
45A3 **Tir'at el Ismâilîya** *Canal* Egypt
17F3 **Tire** Turkey
40C1 **Tirebolu** Turkey
8B3 **Tiree** *I* Scotland
17F2 **Tîrgoviște** Romania
17E1 **Tîrgu Jiu** Romania
17E1 **Tîrgu Mureș** Romania
42C1 **Tirich Mir** *Mt* Pakistan
48A2 **Tiris** *Region* Morocco
20K5 **Tirlyanskiy** Russian Federation
17E1 **Tîrnăveni** Romania
17E3 **Tírnavos** Greece
42D4 **Tirodi** India
16B2 **Tirso** *R* Sardinia, Italy
44B4 **Tiruchchendūr** India
44B3 **Tiruchchirāppalli** India
44B4 **Tirunelveli** India
44B3 **Tirupati** India
44B3 **Tiruppattūr** India
44B3 **Tiruppur** India
44B3 **Tiruvannāmalai** India
63C2 **Tishomingo** USA
45D2 **Tisīyah** Syria
19E3 **Tisza** *R* Hungary
72E7 **Titicaca, Lago** Bolivia/ Peru
43E4 **Titlagarh** India
17E2 **Titov Veles** Macedonia, Yugoslavia
50C3 **Titule** Zaïre
67B3 **Titusville** USA
8B2 **Tiumpan Head** *Pt* Scotland
7C4 **Tiverton** England
16C2 **Tivoli** Italy
70D2 **Tizimín** Mexico
15C2 **Tizi Ouzou** Algeria
48B2 **Tiznit** Morocco
48B1 **Tlemcen** Algeria
51E5 **Toamasina** Madagascar
29C4 **Toba** Japan
42B2 **Toba and Kakar Ranges** *Mts* Pakistan
69E4 **Tobago** *I* Caribbean Sea
27F6 **Tobelo** Indonesia
64C1 **Tobermory** Canada
8B3 **Tobermory** Scotland
27G6 **Tobi** *I* Pacific Ocean
59C2 **Tobin,Mt** USA
29C3 **Tobi-shima** *I* Japan
27D7 **Toboah** Indonesia
24H4 **Tobol** *R* Russian Federation
27F7 **Toboli** Indonesia
24H4 **Tobol'sk** Russian Federation
Tobruk = Tubruq
20J2 **Tobseda** Russian Federation
73J4 **Tocantins** *R* Brazil
73J6 **Tocantins** *State* Brazil
67B2 **Toccoa** USA
74B2 **Tocopilla** Chile
74C2 **Tocorpuri** Bolivia/Chile
72E1 **Tocuyo** *R* Venezuela
42D3 **Toda** India
28B3 **Todong** S Korea
73L6 **Todos os Santos, Baia de** *B* Brazil
56B4 **Todos Santos** Mexico
59C4 **Todos Santos,B de** Mexico
33H2 **Tofua** *I* Tonga
32B1 **Togian, Kepulauan** *I* Indonesia
48C4 **Togo** *Republic* W Africa
31C1 **Togtoh** China
62A1 **Tohatchi** USA
29E2 **Tokachi** *R* Japan
29C3 **Tokamachi** Japan
50D2 **Tokar** Sudan
26F4 **Tokara Retto** *Arch* Japan
40C1 **Tokat** Turkey
28B3 **Tok-do** *I* S Korea
33H1 **Tokelau Is** Pacific Ocean
39F1 **Tokmak** Kirgizia
35C1 **Tokomaru Bay** New Zealand
26F4 **Tokuno** *I* Ryukyu Is, Japan
29C4 **Tokushima** Japan
28B4 **Tokuyama** Japan
29D3 **Tōkyō** Japan
35C1 **Tolaga Bay** New Zealand
51E6 **Tôlañaro** Madagascar
73H8 **Toledo** Brazil
15B2 **Toledo** Spain
64C2 **Toledo** USA
63D2 **Toledo Bend Res** USA
51E6 **Toliara** Madagascar
72C2 **Tolina** *Mt* Colombia
19F2 **Tolochin** Belarus
15B1 **Tolosa** Spain
28A4 **Tolsan-do** *I* S Korea
74B5 **Toltén** Chile
70C3 **Toluca** Mexico
20H5 **Tol'yatti** Russian Federation
64A2 **Tomah** USA
64B1 **Tomahawk** USA
29E2 **Tomakomai** Japan
15A2 **Tomar** Portugal
19E2 **Tomaszów Mazowiecka** Poland
63E2 **Tombigbee** *R* USA
51B4 **Tomboco** Angola
75D3 **Tombos** Brazil
48B3 **Tombouctou** Mali
59E4 **Tombstone** USA
51B5 **Tombua** Angola
47D1 **Tomburke** South Africa
74B5 **Tomé** Chile
15B2 **Tomelloso** Spain
28A4 **Tomie** Japan
8D3 **Tomintoul** Scotland
32B3 **Tomkinson Range** *Mts* Australia
25O4 **Tommot** Russian Federation
17E2 **Tomorrit** *Mt* Albania
24K4 **Tomsk** Russian Federation
68C3 **Toms River** USA
70C3 **Tonalá** Mexico
58C1 **Tonasket** USA
7E4 **Tonbridge** England
33H3 **Tonga** *Is, Kingdom* Pacific Ocean
47E2 **Tongaat** South Africa
33H3 **Tongatapu** *I* Tonga
33H3 **Tongatapu Group** *Is* Tonga
33H3 **Tonga Trench** Pacific Ocean
28A2 **Tongchang** N Korea
31D3 **Tongcheng** China
31B2 **Tongchuan** China
31A2 **Tongde** China
13C2 **Tongeren** Belgium
30E2 **Tonggu Jiao** *I* China
31A5 **Tonghai** China
28B2 **Tonghua** China
28B3 **Tongjosŏn-Man** *S* N Korea
30D1 **Tongkin,G of** China/ Vietnam
31E1 **Tongliao** China
31D3 **Tongling** China
28A3 **Tongnae** S Korea
34B2 **Tongo** Australia
31B4 **Tongren** Guizhou, China
31A2 **Tongren** Qinghai, China
43G3 **Tongsa** Bhutan
30B1 **Tongta** Burma
26C3 **Tongtian He** *R* China
8C2 **Tongue** Scotland
60B1 **Tongue** *R* USA
31D2 **Tong Xian** China
31B2 **Tongxin** China
28A2 **Tongyuanpu** China
31B4 **Tongzi** China
25L5 **Tonhil** Mongolia
56C4 **Tónichi** Mexico
50C3 **Tonj** Sudan
42D3 **Tonk** India
63C1 **Tonkawa** USA
30C3 **Tonle Sap** *L* Cambodia
13C4 **Tonnerre** France
29D3 **Tono** Japan
59C3 **Tonopah** USA
58D2 **Tooele** USA
34D1 **Toogoolawah** Australia
34B1 **Toompine** Australia
34D1 **Toowoomba** Australia
66C1 **Topaz L** USA
61D3 **Topeka** USA
59D4 **Topock** USA
56C4 **Topolobampo** Mexico
20E2 **Topozero, Ozero** *L* Russian Federation
58B1 **Toppenish** USA
68E1 **Topsfield** USA
50D3 **Tor** Ethiopia
17F3 **Torbalı** Turkey
41G2 **Torbat-e-Heydarīyeh** Iran
15A1 **Tordesillas** Spain
18C2 **Torgau** Germany
13B2 **Torhout** Belgium
26H3 **Tori** *I* Japan
Torino = Turin
50D3 **Torit** Sudan
75B2 **Torixoreu** Brazil
15A1 **Tormes** *R* Spain
12J5 **Torne** *R* Sweden
12H5 **Torneträsk** *L* Sweden
55M4 **Torngat** *Mts* Canada
12J5 **Tornio** Finland
74C3 **Toro, Cerro del** *Mt* Argentina/Chile
65D2 **Toronto** Canada
20E4 **Toropets** Russian Federation
50D3 **Tororo** Uganda
Toros, Dağlari = Taurus Mts
7C4 **Torquay** England
66C4 **Torrance** USA
15A2 **Torrão** Portugal
15C1 **Torreblanca** Spain
16C2 **Torre del Greco** Italy
15B1 **Torrelavega** Spain
15B2 **Torremolinos** Spain
32C4 **Torrens, L** Australia
56C4 **Torreón** Mexico
33F2 **Torres Is** Vanuatu
32D2 **Torres Str** Australia
15A2 **Torres Vedras** Portugal
7B4 **Torridge** *R* England
8C3 **Torridon, Loch** *Inlet* Scotland
68D2 **Torrington** Connecticut, USA
60C2 **Torrington** Wyoming, USA
12D3 **Tórshavn** Faeroes
15C1 **Tortosa** Spain
15C1 **Tortosa, Cabo de** *C* Spain
72C3 **Tortugas, Golfo de** Colombia
41G2 **Torūd** Iran
19D2 **Toruń** Poland
10B2 **Tory I** Irish Republic
9B2 **Tory Sol** Irish Republic
20E4 **Torzhok** Russian Federation
29B4 **Tosa** Japan
28C4 **Tosashimizu** Japan
29C4 **Tosa-Wan** *B* Japan
29C4 **To-shima** *I* Japan
12L7 **Tosno** Russian Federation
28B4 **Tosu** Japan
40B1 **Tosya** Turkey
15B2 **Totana** Spain
20G4 **Tot'ma** Russian Federation
7C4 **Totnes** England
73G2 **Totness** Surinam
34C2 **Tottenham** Australia
29C3 **Tottori** Japan
48B4 **Touba** Ivory Coast
48A3 **Touba** Senegal
48B1 **Toubkal** *Mt* Morocco
13B4 **Toucy** France
48B3 **Tougan** Burkina
48C1 **Touggourt** Algeria
48A3 **Tougué** Guinea
13C3 **Toul** France
14D3 **Toulon** France
14C3 **Toulouse** France
48B4 **Toumodi** Ivory Coast
30B2 **Toungoo** Burma
13B2 **Tourcoing** France
48A2 **Tourine** Mauritius
13B2 **Tournai** Belgium
14C2 **Tours** France
47C3 **Touws River** South Africa
29E2 **Towada** Japan
29E2 **Towada-ko** *L* Japan
68B2 **Towanda** USA
66D2 **Towne P** USA
60C1 **Towner** USA
58D1 **Townsend** USA
32D2 **Townsville** Australia
68B3 **Towson** USA
7C4 **Towy** *R* Wales
62B2 **Toyah** USA
29D2 **Toya-ko** *L* Japan
29D3 **Toyama** Japan
29C3 **Toyama-wan** *B* Japan
29C4 **Toyohashi** Japan
29C4 **Toyonaka** Japan
29B3 **Toyooka** Japan
29D3 **Toyota** Japan
48C1 **Tozeur** Tunisia
13D3 **Traben-Trarbach** Germany
Trâblous = Tripoli
40C1 **Trabzon** Turkey
61D2 **Tracy** Minnesota, USA
66B2 **Tracy** USA
15A2 **Trafalgar, Cabo** *C* Spain
54G5 **Trail** Canada
10B3 **Tralee** Irish Republic
9C3 **Tramore** Irish Republic
12G7 **Tranås** Sweden
30B4 **Trang** Thailand
27G7 **Trangan** *I* Indonesia
34C2 **Trangie** Australia
76E3 **Transantarctic Mts** Antarctica
Transylvanian Alps *Mts* **= Munții Carpații Meridionali**
16C3 **Trapani** Italy
34C3 **Traralgon** Australia
48A3 **Trarza** *Region* Mauritius
30C3 **Trat** Thailand
34B2 **Traveller's L** Australia
18C2 **Travemünde** Germany
64B2 **Traverse City** USA
35B2 **Travers,Mt** New Zealand
62C2 **Travis,L** USA
18D3 **Třebíč** Czech Republic
17D2 **Trebinje** Bosnia-Herzegovina
18C3 **Trebon** Czech Republic
74F4 **Treinta y Tres** Uruguay
74C6 **Trelew** Argentina
12G7 **Trelleborg** Sweden
7B3 **Tremadog B** Wales
65E1 **Tremblant,Mt** Canada
16D2 **Tremiti, Is** Italy
68B2 **Tremont** USA
58D2 **Tremonton** USA
19D3 **Trenčín** Slovakia
74D5 **Trenque Lauquén** Argentina
7D3 **Trent** *R* England
16C1 **Trento** Italy
65D2 **Trenton** Canada
61E2 **Trenton** Missouri, USA
68C2 **Trenton** New Jersey, USA
55N5 **Trepassey** Canada
74D5 **Tres Arroyos** Argentina
75C3 **Três Corações** Brazil
15B2 **Tres Forcas, Cabo** *C* Morocco
75B2 **Três Irmãos, Reprêsa** *Res* Brazil
74F2 **Três Lagoas** Brazil
66B2 **Tres Pinos** USA
74C7 **Tres Puntas, Cabo** Argentina
75D3 **Três Rios** Brazil
16C1 **Treviso** Italy
7B4 **Trevose Hd** *Pt* England
13E2 **Treysa** Germany
62B1 **Tribune** USA
44B3 **Trichūr** India
34C2 **Trida** Australia
13D3 **Trier** Germany
16C1 **Trieste** Italy

45B1 Trikomo Cyprus
9C3 Trim Irish Republic
44C4 Trincomalee Sri Lanka
52G6 Trindade *I* Atlantic Ocean
72F6 Trinidad Bolivia
74E4 Trinidad Uruguay
62B1 Trinidad USA
69E4 Trinidad *I* Caribbean Sea
69E4 Trinidad & Tobago *Is Republic* Caribbean Sea
63C2 Trinity USA
56D3 Trinity *R* USA
55N5 Trinity B Canada
67A2 Trion USA
45C1 Tripoli Lebanon
49D1 Tripoli Libya
17E3 Trípolis Greece
43G4 Tripura *State* India
52H6 Tristan da Cunha *Is* Atlantic Ocean
19D3 Trnava Slovakia
32E1 Trobriand Is Papua New Guinea
65F1 Trois Pistoles Canada
65E1 Trois-Riviéres Canada
20L5 Troitsk Russian Federation
20K3 Troitsko Pechorsk Russian Federation
12G7 Trollhättan Sweden
12F6 Trollheimen *Mt* Norway
46K9 Tromelin *I* Indian Ocean
47D3 Trompsburg South Africa
12H5 Tromsø Norway
66D3 Trona USA
12G6 Trondheim Norway
12G6 Trondheimfjord *Inlet* Norway
45B1 Troödos Range *Mts* Cyprus
8C4 Troon Scotland
52J3 Tropic of Cancer
52K6 Tropic of Capricorn
48B2 Troudenni Mali
55J4 Trout L Ontario, Canada
58E2 Trout Peak *Mt* USA
68B2 Trout Run USA
7C4 Trowbridge England
67A2 Troy Alabama, USA
58C1 Troy Montana, USA
68D1 Troy New York, USA
64C2 Troy Ohio, USA
68B2 Troy Pennsylvania, USA
17E2 Troyan Bulgaria
13C3 Troyes France
59C3 Troy Peak *Mt* USA
41F5 Trucial Coast *Region* UAE
59B3 Truckee *R* USA
70D3 Trujillo Honduras
72C5 Trujillo Peru
15A2 Trujillo Spain
72D2 Trujillo Venezuela
59D3 Trumbull,Mt USA
34C2 Trundle Australia
55M5 Truro Canada
7B4 Truro England
62A2 Truth or Consequences USA
26C2 Tsagaan Nuur *L* Mongolia
26C1 Tsagan-Tologoy Russian Federation
51E5 Tsaratanana Madagascar
51C6 Tsau Botswana
50D4 Tsavo Kenya
50D4 Tsavo Nat Pk Kenya
60C1 Tschida,L USA
24J4 Tselinograd Kazakhstan
47B2 Tses Namibia
26D2 Tsetserleg Mongolia
48C4 Tsévié Togo
47C2 Tshabong Botswana
47C1 Tshane Botswana
21F6 Tshchikskoye Vdkhr *Res* Russian Federation
50B4 Tshela Zaïre
51C4 Tshibala Zaïre
50C4 Tshikapa Zaïre
50C4 Tshuapa *R* Zaïre
21G6 Tsimlyanskoye Vodokhranilishche *Res* Russian Federation
Tsinan = Jinan
Tsingtao = Qingdao
51E6 Tsiombe Madagascar
51E5 Tsiroanomandidy Madagascar
19F2 Tsna *R* Belarus
31B1 Tsogt Ovoo Mongolia
47D3 Tsomo South Africa
26D2 Tsomog Mongolia
29C4 Tsu Japan
29C3 Tsubata Japan
29E3 Tsuchiura Japan
29E2 Tsugarū-kaikyō *Str* Japan
51B5 Tsumeb Namibia
51B6 Tsumis Namibia
29D3 Tsuruga Japan
29C3 Tsurugi Japan
29D3 Tsuruoka Japan
29C3 Tsushima Japan
28B4 Tsushima *Is* Japan
Tsushima-Kaikyō = Korea Str
29C3 Tsuyama Japan
15A1 Tua *R* Portugal
37M5 Tuamotu, Îles Pacific Ocean
21F7 Tuapse Russian Federation
35A3 Tuatapere New Zealand
59D3 Tuba City USA
37M6 Tubai, Îles Pacific Ocean
74G3 Tubarão Brazil
45C2 Tubas Israel
18B3 Tübingen Germany
49E1 Tubruq Libya
68C3 Tuckerton USA
59D4 Tucson USA
74C3 Tucumán *State* Argentina
62B1 Tucumcari USA
72F2 Tucupita Venezuela
15B1 Tudela Spain
40C3 Tudmur Syria
47E2 Tugela *R* South Africa
34D2 Tuggerah L Australia
27F5 Tuguegarao Philippines
25P4 Tugur Russian Federation
31D2 Tuhai He *R* China
27F7 Tukangbesi, Kepulauan *Is* Indonesia
54E3 Tuktoyaktuk Canada
19E1 Tukums Latvia
25O4 Tukuringra, Khrebet *Mts* Russian Federation
51D4 Tukuyu Tanzania
42B1 Tukzar Afghanistan
20F5 Tula Russian Federation
66C2 Tulare USA
66C2 Tulare Lake Bed USA
62A2 Tularosa USA
72C3 Tulcán Ecuador
21D6 Tulcea Romania
19F3 Tul'chin Ukraine
66C2 Tule *R* USA
51C6 Tuli Zimbabwe
47D1 Tuli *R* Zimbabwe
62B2 Tulia USA
45C2 Tulkarm Israel
67A1 Tullahoma USA
9C3 Tullarnore Irish Republic
14C2 Tulle France
63D2 Tullos USA
9C3 Tullow Irish Republic
68B1 Tully USA
63C1 Tulsa USA
72C3 Tuluá Colombia
40C3 Tulūl ash Shāmīyah *Desert Region* Iran/Syria
25M4 Tulun Russian Federation
72C3 Tumaco Colombia
25R3 Tumany Russian Federation
34C3 Tumbarumba Australia
72B4 Tumbes Ecuador
28B2 Tumen China
28B2 Tumen R China/N Korea
44B3 Tumkūr India
30C4 Tumpat Malaysia
42D4 Tumsar India
48B3 Tumu Ghana
73H3 Tumucumaque, Serra *Mts* Brazil
34C3 Tumut Australia
34C3 Tumut *R* Australia
69L1 Tunapuna Trinidad
7E4 Tunbridge Wells, Royal England
40C2 Tunceli Turkey
51D4 Tunduma Zambia
51D5 Tunduru Tanzania
17F2 Tundzha *R* Bulgaria
44B2 Tungabhadra *R* India
26E4 Tungkang Taiwan
12B2 Tungnafellsjökull *Mts* Iceland
25M3 Tunguska *R* Russian Federation
44C2 Tuni India
16C3 Tunis Tunisia
16C3 Tunis, G de Tunisia
48C1 Tunisia *Republic* N Africa
72D2 Tunja Colombia
68C2 Tunkhannock USA
Tunxi = Huangshan
66C2 Tuolumne Meadows USA
75B3 Tupã Brazil
75C2 Tupaciguara Brazil
63E2 Tupelo USA
19G1 Tupik Russian Federation
72E8 Tupiza Bolivia
66C3 Tupman USA
65E2 Tupper Lake USA
74C4 Tupungato *Mt* Argentina
43L3 Tura India
25L3 Tura Russian Federation
20L4 Tura *R* Russian Federation
41G2 Turān Iran
25L4 Turan Russian Federation
40C3 Turayf Saudi Arabia
38E3 Turbat Pakistan
72C2 Turbo Colombia
17E1 Turda Romania
24K5 Turfan Depression China
24H5 Turgay Kazakhstan
25L5 Turgen Uul *Mt* Mongolia
40A2 Turgutlu Turkey
40C1 Turhal Turkey
12K7 Türi Estonia
15B2 Turia *R* Spain
16B1 Turin Italy
20L4 Turinsk Russian Federation
26G2 Turiy Rog Russian Federation
50D3 Turkana, L Ethiopia/Kenya
38E1 Turkestan *Region* C Asia
40C2 Turkey *Republic* W Asia
38D1 Turkmenistan *Republic* Asia
41F2 Turkmenskiy Zaliv *B* Turkmenistan
69C2 Turks Is Caribbean Sea
12J6 Turku Finland
50D3 Turkwel *R* Kenya
66B2 Turlock USA
66B2 Turlock L USA
35C2 Turnagain,C New Zealand
70D3 Turneffe I Belize
68D1 Turners Falls USA
13C2 Turnhout Belgium
17E2 Turnu Măgurele Romania
17E2 Turnu-Severin Romania
25K5 Turpan China
69B2 Turquino *Mt* Cuba
8D3 Turriff Scotland
38E1 Turtkul' Uzbekistan
61D3 Turtle Creek Res USA
25K3 Turukhansk Russian Federation
26D1 Turuntayevo Russian Federation
75B2 Turvo *R* Goias, Brazil
75C3 Turvo *R* São Paulo, Brazil
19E2 Tur'ya *R* Ukraine
63E2 Tuscaloosa USA
68B2 Tuscarora Mt USA
64B3 Tuscola Illinois, USA
62C2 Tuscola Texas, USA
63E2 Tuscumbia USA
41G3 Tusharīk Iran
68A2 Tussey Mt USA
Tutera = Tudela
44B4 Tuticorin India
17F2 Tutrakan Bulgaria
18B3 Tuttlingen Germany
33H2 Tutuila *I* American Samoa
26D2 Tuul Gol *R* Mongolia
25L4 Tuva Republic Russian Federation
33G1 Tuvalu *Is* Pacific Ocean
45C4 Tuwayīlel Hāj *Mt* Jordan
70B2 Tuxpan Mexico
70C2 Tuxpan Mexico
70C3 Tuxtla Gutiérrez Mexico
15A1 Túy Spain
30D3 Tuy Hoa Vietnam
40B2 Tuz Gölü *Salt L* Turkey
41D3 Tuz Khurmātū Iraq
17D2 Tuzla Bosnia-Herzegovina
20F4 Tver' Russian Federation
8D4 Tweed *R* England/Scotland
34D1 Tweed Heads Australia
8D4 Tweedsmuir Hills Scotland
59C4 Twentynine Palms USA
55N5 Twillingate Canada
58D1 Twin Bridges USA
62B2 Twin Buttes Res USA
58D2 Twin Falls USA
35B2 Twins,The *Mt* New Zealand
66B3 Twitchell Res USA
64A1 Two Harbors USA
58D1 Two Medicine *R* USA
64B2 Two Rivers USA
25O4 Tygda Russian Federation
63C2 Tyler USA
26H1 Tymovskoye Russian Federation
26F1 Tynda Russian Federation
6D2 Tyne *R* England
6D2 Tyne and Wear *Metropolitan County* England
6D2 Tynemouth England
12G6 Tynset Norway
Tyr = Tyre
45C2 Tyre Lebanon
62A2 Tyrone New Mexico, USA
68A2 Tyrone Pennsylvania, USA
9C2 Tyrone *County* Northern Ireland
34B3 Tyrrell,L Australia
16C2 Tyrrhenian S Italy
21J7 Tyuleni, Ova *Is* Kazakhstan
24H4 Tyumen' Russian Federation
25O3 Tyung *R* Russian Federation
7B3 Tywyn Wales
47E1 Tzaneen South Africa
17E3 Tzoumérka *Mt* Greece

U

75D3 Ubá Brazil
75D2 Ubaí Brazil
75E1 Ubaitaba Brazil
50B3 Ubangi *R* Central African Republic/Congo/Zaïre
40D3 Ubayyid, Wadi al *Watercourse* Iraq
28B4 Ube Japan
15B2 Ubeda Spain
55N2 Ubekendt Ejland *I* Greenland
75C2 Uberaba Brazil
75A2 Uberaba, Lagoa Brazil
75C2 Uberlândia Brazil
30D2 Ubon Ratchathani Thailand
19F2 Ubort *R* Belarus
50C4 Ubundu Zaïre
72D5 Ucayali *R* Peru
42C3 Uch Pakistan
25P4 Uchar *R* Russian Federation
29E2 Uchiura-wan *B* Japan
13E1 Uchte Germany
58A1 Ucluelet Canada
25L4 Uda *R* Russian Federation
42C4 Udaipur India
43F3 Udaipur Garhi Nepal
12G7 Uddevalla Sweden
12H5 Uddjaur *L* Sweden
44B2 Udgir India
42D2 Udhampur India
16C1 Udine Italy
20J4 Udmurt Republic Russian Federation
30C2 Udon Thani Thailand
25P4 Udskaya Guba *B* Russian Federation
44A3 Udupi India
25N2 Udzha Russian Federation
29C3 Ueda Japan
50C3 Uele *R* Zaïre
25U3 Uelen Russian Federation
18C2 Uelzen Germany
50C3 Uere *R* Zaïre
20K5 Ufa Russian Federation
20K4 Ufa *R* Russian Federation
51B6 Ugab *R* Namibia
50D4 Ugaila *R* Tanzania
50D3 Uganda *Republic* Africa
45C3 'Ugeiqa, Wadi Jordan
26H2 Uglegorsk Russian Federation
20F4 Uglich Russian Federation
28C2 Uglovoye Russian Federation
20F5 Ugra *R* Russian Federation
8B3 Uig Scotland
51B4 Uige Angola
28A3 Ŭijŏngbu S Korea
21J6 Uil Kazakhstan
58D2 Uinta Mts USA
28A3 Ŭiryŏng S Korea
28A3 Uisŏng S Korea
47D3 Uitenhage South Africa
19E3 Újfehértó Hungary
29C4 Uji Japan
50C4 Ujiji Tanzania
74C2 Ujina Chile
42D4 Ujjain India
32A1 Ujung Pandang Indonesia
50D4 Ukerewe I Tanzania
43G3 Ukhrul India
20J3 Ukhta Russian Federation
59B3 Ukiah California, USA
58C1 Ukiah Oregon, USA
56A3 Ukiah USA
19E1 Ukmerge Lithuania
21D6 Ukraine *Republic* Europe
28A4 Uku-jima *I* Japan
26D2 Ulaanbaatar Mongolia
26C2 Ulaangom Mongolia
31C1 Ulaan Uul Mongolia
Ulan Bator = Ulaanbaatar
39G1 Ulangar Hu *L* China
26F2 Ulanhot China
26D1 Ulan Ude Russian Federation
26C3 Ulan Ul Hu *L* China
25Q3 Ul'beya *R* Russian Federation
28B3 Ulchin S Korea
17D2 Ulcinj Montenegro, Yugoslavia
26E2 Uldz Mongolia
26C2 Uliastay Mongolia
27G5 Ulithi *I* Pacific Ocean
19F1 Ulla Belarus
34D3 Ulladulla Australia
8C3 Ullapool Scotland
12H5 Ullsfjorden *Inlet* Norway
6C2 Ullswater *L* England
28C3 Ullung-do *I* Japan
18C3 Ulm Germany
34A1 Uloowaranie,L Australia
28B3 Ulsan S Korea
9C2 Ulster *Region* Northern Ireland
24K5 Ulungur He *R* China
24K5 Ulungur Hu *L* China
8B3 Ulva *I* Scotland
6C2 Ulverston England
34C4 Ulverstone Australia
25Q4 Ulya *R* Russian Federation
19G3 Ulyanovka Ukraine
20H5 Ul'yanovsk Russian Federation
62B1 Ulysses USA
21E6 Uman' Ukraine
55N2 Umanak Greenland
43E4 Umaria India
42B3 Umarkot Pakistan
58C1 Umatilla USA
20E2 Umba Russian Federation
50D4 Umba *R* Kenya/Tanzania
32D1 Umboi I Papua New Guinea
12H6 Ume *R* Sweden
12J6 Umea Sweden
45C2 Um ed Daraj, Jebel *Mt* Jordan
45C4 Um el Hashīm, Jebel *Mt* Jordan
47E2 Umfolozi *R* South Africa
54C3 Umiat USA
45C4 Um Ishrīn, Jebel *Mt* Jordan
47E3 Umkomaas *R* South Africa
41G4 Umm al Qaiwain UAE
50C2 Umm Bell Sudan
50C2 Umm Keddada Sudan
40C4 Umm Lajj Saudi Arabia
50D2 Umm Ruwaba Sudan
41F5 Umm Sa'id Qatar
51C5 Umniaiti *R* Zimbabwe
58B2 Umpqua *R* USA
42D4 Umred India
Umtali = Mutare
47D3 Umtata South Africa
75B3 Umuarama Brazil
47D3 Umzimkulu South Africa
47E3 Umzimkulu *R* South Africa
47D3 Umzimvubu *R* South Africa
47D1 Umzingwane *R* Zimbabwe
75E2 Una Brazil
16D1 Una *R* Bosnia-Herzegovina/Croatia
68C1 Unadilla USA
68C1 Unadilla *R* USA
75C2 Unaí Brazil
54B3 Unalakleet USA
41D4 Unayzah Saudi Arabia
68D2 Uncasville USA
60B3 Uncompahgre Plat USA
47D2 Underberg South Africa
60C1 Underwood USA
20E5 Unecha Russian Federation
45C3 Uneisa Jordan
55M4 Ungava B Canada
28C2 Unggi N Korea
74F3 União de Vitória Brazil
63D1 Union Missouri, USA
67B2 Union S Carolina, USA
65D2 Union City Pennsylvania, USA
63E1 Union City Tennessee, USA
47C3 Uniondale South Africa
67A2 Union Springs USA
65D3 Uniontown USA
41F5 United Arab Emirates Arabian Pen
4E3 United Kingdom of Gt Britain & N Ireland NW Europe
53H4 United States of America
55K1 United States Range *Mts* Canada
58C2 Unity USA
62A2 University Park USA
13D2 Unna Germany
43E3 Unnāo India
28A2 Unsan N Korea
8E1 Unst *I* Scotland
40C1 Ünye Turkey
20G4 Unzha *R* Russian Federation
72F2 Upata Venezuela
51C4 Upemba Nat Pk Zaïre
55N2 Upernavik Greenland
47C2 Upington South Africa
66D3 Upland USA
33H2 Upolu *I* Western Samoa
35C2 Upper Hutt New Zealand
58B2 Upper Klamath L USA
58B2 Upper L USA
9C2 Upper Lough Erne *L* Northern Ireland

69L1 **Upper Manzanilla** Trinidad
61E1 **Upper Red L** USA
68B3 **Upperville** USA
12H7 **Uppsala** Sweden
61E1 **Upsala** Canada
60C2 **Upton** USA
40D4 **'Uqlat as Suqūr** Saudi Arabia
72C2 **Uraba, Golfo de** Colombia
31B1 **Urad Qianqi** China
41E4 **Urairah** Saudi Arabia
29D2 **Urakawa** Japan
21J5 **Ural** *R* Kazakhstan
34D2 **Uralla** Australia
20M4 **Ural Mts** Russian Federation
21J5 **Ural'sk** Kazakhstan
24G4 **Ural'skiy Khrebet** *Mts* Russian Federation
75D1 **Urandi** Brazil
54H4 **Uranium City** Canada
27G8 **Urapunga** Australia
60B3 **Uravan** USA
29C3 **Urawa** Japan
20L3 **Uray** Russian Federation
64B2 **Urbana** Illinois, USA
64C2 **Urbana** Ohio, USA
16C2 **Urbino** Italy
15B1 **Urbion, Sierra de** *Mt* Spain
6C2 **Ure** *R* England
20H4 **Uren'** Russian Federation
38E1 **Urgench** Uzbekistan
24J3 **Urengoy** Russian Federation
42B2 **Urgun** Afghanistan
17F3 **Urla** Turkey
17E2 **Uroševac** Serbia, Yugoslavia
75C1 **Uruaçu** Brazil
70B3 **Uruapan** Mexico
75C2 **Urucuia** *R* Brazil
74E3 **Uruguaiana** Brazil
74E4 **Uruguay** *R* Argentina/Uruguay
74E4 **Uruguay** *Republic* S America
41E2 **Urumīyeh** Iran
39G1 **Ürümqi** China
26J2 **Urup** *I* Kuril Is, Russian Federation
24J1 **Urup, Ostrov** *I* Russian Federation
42B2 **Uruzgan** Afghanistan
29D2 **Uryū-ko** *L* Japan
21G5 **Uryupinsk** Russian Federation
20J4 **Urzhum** Russian Federation
17F2 **Urziceni** Romania
39G1 **Usa** China
28B4 **Usa** Japan
20L2 **Usa** *R* Russian Federation
40A2 **Uşak** Turkey
47B1 **Usakos** Namibia
24J1 **Ushakova, Ostrov** *I* Russian Federation
50D4 **Ushashi** Tanzania
24J5 **Ush Tobe** Kazakhstan
74C8 **Ushuaia** Argentina
25O4 **Ushumun** Russian Federation
7C4 **Usk** *R* Wales
40A1 **Üsküdar** Turkey
20H3 **Usogorsk** Russian Federation
25M4 **Usolye Sibirskoye** Russian Federation
26G2 **Ussuri** *R* China/Russian Federation
28C2 **Ussuriysk** Russian Federation
25T3 **Ust'-Belaya** Russian Federation
25R4 **Ust'Bol'sheretsk** Russian Federation
16C3 **Ustica** *I* Sicily, Italy
18C2 **Ústi-nad-Laben** Czech Republic
24J4 **Ust'Ishim** Russian Federation
18D2 **Ustka** Poland
25S4 **Ust'Kamchatsk** Russian Federation
24K5 **Ust'-Kamenogorsk** Kazakhstan
20L2 **Ust' Kara** Russian Federation
25L4 **Ust Karabula** Russian Federation
20K5 **Ust' Katav** Russian Federation
25M4 **Ust'-Kut** Russian Federation
21F6 **Ust Labinsk** Russian Federation
25P3 **Ust'Maya** Russian Federation
20K3 **Ust' Nem** Russian Federation
25Q3 **Ust'Nera** Russian Federation
25O4 **Ust'Nyukzha** Russian Federation
25M4 **Ust'Ordynskiy** Russian Federation
20J2 **Ust' Tsil'ma** Russian Federation
25P4 **Ust-'Umal'tu** Russian Federation
20G3 **Ust'ya** *R* Russian Federation
20M2 **Ust' Yuribey** Russian Federation
21J7 **Ustyurt Plateau** *Plat* Kazakhstan
28B4 **Usuki** Japan
70C3 **Usumacinta** *R* Guatemala/Mexico
47E2 **Usutu** *R* Swaziland
28A4 **Usuyŏng** S Korea
19G1 **Usvyaty** Russian Federation
56B3 **Utah** *State* USA
59D2 **Utah L** USA
19F1 **Utena** Lithuania
42B3 **Uthal** Pakistan
68C1 **Utica** USA
15B2 **Utiel** Spain
18B2 **Utrecht** Netherlands
47E2 **Utrecht** South Africa
15A2 **Utrera** Spain
12K5 **Utsjoki** Finland
29D3 **Utsonomiya** Japan
30C2 **Uttaradit** Thailand
43E3 **Uttar Pradesh** *State* India
7D3 **Uttoxeter** England
12J6 **Uusikaupunki** Finland
62C3 **Uvalde** USA
24H4 **Uvat** Russian Federation
33F3 **Uvéa** *I* New Caledonia
50D4 **Uvinza** Tanzania
50C4 **Uvira** Zaïre
55N2 **Uvkusigssat** Greenland
26C1 **Uvs Nuur** *L* Mongolia
28C4 **Uwajima** Japan
50C1 **Uweinat, Jebel** *Mt* Sudan
31B2 **Uxin Qi** China
25Q3 **Uyandina** *R* Russian Federation
25L4 **Uyar** Russian Federation
72E8 **Uyuni** Bolivia
45B4 **Uyûn Mûsa** *Well* Egypt
38E1 **Uzbekistan** *Republic* Asia
14C2 **Uzerche** France
19F2 **Uzh** *R* Ukraine
17D2 **Užice** Serbia, Yugoslavia
19E3 **Uzhgorod** Ukraine
20F5 **Uzlovaya** Russian Federation
40A1 **Uzunköprü** Turkey

V

47C2 **Vaal** *R* South Africa
47D2 **Vaal Dam** *Res* South Africa
47D1 **Vaalwater** South Africa
12J6 **Vaasa** Finland
19D3 **Vác** Hungary
74F3 **Vacaria** Brazil
75B3 **Vacaria** *R* Mato Grosso do, Brazil
75D2 **Vacaria** *R* Minas Gerais, Brazil
59B3 **Vacaville** USA
42C4 **Vadodara** India
12K4 **Vadsø** Norway
16B1 **Vaduz** Liechtenstein
20G3 **Vaga** *R* Russian Federation
19D3 **Váh** *R* Slovakia
45C3 **Vahel** Israel
44B3 **Vaigai** *R* India
8E1 **Vaila, I** Scotland
33G1 **Vaitupu** *I* Tuvalu
74C6 **Valcheta** Argentina
20E4 **Valday** Russian Federation
20E4 **Valdayskaya Vozvyshennost'** *Upland* Russian Federation
72E2 **Val de la Pascua** Venezuela
15B2 **Valdepeñas** Spain
54D3 **Valdez** USA
74B5 **Valdivia** Chile
13B3 **Val d'Oise** *Department* France
65D1 **Val-d'Or** Canada
67B2 **Valdosta** USA
58C2 **Vale** USA
75E1 **Valença** Bahia, Brazil
75D3 **Valença** Rio de Janeiro, Brazil
14C3 **Valence** France
15B2 **Valencia** Spain
72E1 **Valencia** Venezuela
Valencia *Region* = **Comunidad Valenciana**
15A2 **Valencia de Alcantara** Spain
15C2 **Valencia, Golfo de** *G* Spain
13B2 **Valenciennes** France
60C2 **Valentine** Nebraska, USA
62B2 **Valentine** Texas, USA
6D2 **Vale of Pickering** England
6D2 **Vale of York** England
72D2 **Valera** Venezuela
12K7 **Valga** Russian Federation
7E3 **Valiant** *Oilfield* N Sea
17D2 **Valjevo** Serbia, Yugoslavia
12J6 **Valkeakoski** Finland
70D2 **Valladolid** Mexico
15B1 **Valladolid** Spain
69D5 **Valle de la Pascua** Venezuela
72D1 **Valledupar** Colombia
72F7 **Valle Grande** Bolivia
66A1 **Vallejo** USA
74B3 **Vallenar** Chile
75D1 **Valle Pequeno** Brazil
61D1 **Valley City** USA
58B2 **Valley Falls** USA
65E1 **Valleyfield** Canada
15C1 **Valls** Spain
19F1 **Valmiera** Latvia
14B2 **Valognes** France
75B3 **Valparaíso** Brazil
74B4 **Valparaíso** Chile
67A2 **Valparaiso** USA
47D2 **Vals** *R* South Africa
42C4 **Valsād** India
21F5 **Valuyki** Russian Federation
15A2 **Valverde del Camino** Spain
12J6 **Vammala** Finland
41D2 **Van** Turkey
25M3 **Vanavara** Russian Federation
63D1 **Van Buren** Arkansas, USA
65F1 **Van Buren** Maine, USA
13C3 **Vancouleurs** France
54F5 **Vancouver** Canada
58B1 **Vancouver** USA
54F5 **Vancouver I** Canada
64B3 **Vandalia** Illinois, USA
64C3 **Vandalia** Ohio, USA
54F4 **Vanderhoof** Canada
27G8 **Van Diemen,C** Australia
32C2 **Van Diemen G** Australia
12G7 **Vänern** *L* Sweden
12G7 **Vänersborg** Sweden
68B1 **Van Etten** USA
51E6 **Vangaindrano** Madagascar
40D2 **Van Gölü** *Salt L* Turkey
29C2 **Vangou** Russian Federation
30C2 **Vang Vieng** Laos
62B2 **Van Horn** USA
65D1 **Vanier** Canada
33F2 **Vanikoro** *I* Solomon Islands
26G2 **Vanino** Russian Federation
25U3 **Vankarem** Russian Federation
12H6 **Vännäs** Sweden
14B2 **Vannes** France
47B3 **Vanrhynsdorp** South Africa
55K3 **Vansittart I** Canada
33F2 **Vanua Lava** *I* Vanuatu
33G2 **Vanua Levu** *I* Fiji
37K5 **Vanuatu** *Is, Republic* Pacific Ocean
64C2 **Van Wert** USA
47C3 **Vanwyksvlei** South Africa
14D3 **Var** *R* France
41F2 **Varāmīn** Iran
43E3 **Vārānasi** India
20K2 **Varandey** Russian Federation
12K4 **Varangerfjord** *Inlet* Norway
12L4 **Varangerhalvøya** *Pen* Norway
16D1 **Varazdin** Croatia
12G7 **Varberg** Sweden
12F7 **Varde** Denmark
12L4 **Vardø** Norway
13E1 **Varel** Germany
19E2 **Varéna** Lithuania
16B1 **Varese** Italy
75C3 **Varginha** Brazil
12K6 **Varkaus** Finland
17F2 **Varna** Bulgaria
12G7 **Värnamo** Sweden
20K2 **Varnek** Russian Federation
67B2 **Varnville** USA
75D2 **Várzea da Palma** Brazil
20H3 **Vashka** *R* Russian Federation
21E5 **Vasil'kov** Ukraine
64C2 **Vassar** USA
12H7 **Västerås** Sweden
12H7 **Västervik** Sweden
16C2 **Vasto** Italy
16C2 **Vaticano, Citta del** Italy
12B2 **Vatnajökull** *Mts* Iceland
17F1 **Vatra Dornei** Romania
12G7 **Vättern** *L* Sweden
62A2 **Vaughn** USA
72D3 **Vaupés** *R* Colombia
33H2 **Vava'u Group** *Is* Tonga
44C4 **Vavuniya** Sri Lanka
12G7 **Växjö** Sweden
20K1 **Vaygach, Ostrov** *I* Russian Federation
13D1 **Vecht** *R* Germany/Netherlands
13E1 **Vechta** Germany
13D1 **Veendam** Netherlands
62B1 **Vega** USA
12G5 **Vega** *I* Norway
15A2 **Vejer de la Frontera** Spain
12F7 **Vejle** Denmark
47B3 **Velddrif** South Africa
16D2 **Velebit** *Mts* Croatia
16D1 **Velenje** Slovenia
75D2 **Velhas** *R* Brazil
25T3 **Velikaya** *R* Russian Federation
19F1 **Velikaya** *R* Russian Federation
12K7 **Velikaya** *R* Russian Federation
20E4 **Velikiye Luki** Russian Federation
20H3 **Velikiy Ustyug** Russian Federation
17F2 **Veliko Tŭrnovo** Bulgaria
48A3 **Vélingara** Senegal
19G1 **Velizh** Russian Federation
33E1 **Vella Lavella** *I* Solomon Islands
44B3 **Vellore** India
13E2 **Velmerstat** *Mt* Germany
20G3 **Vel'sk** Russian Federation
13C1 **Veluwe** *Region* Netherlands
60C1 **Velva** USA
44B4 **Vembanad L** India
74D4 **Venado Tuerto** Argentina
75C3 **Vençeslau Braz** Brazil
13C3 **Vendeuvre-sur-Barse** France
14C2 **Vendôme** France
Venezia = Venice
16C1 **Venezia, G di** Italy
72E2 **Venezuela** *Republic* S America
69C4 **Venezuela,G de** Venezuela
44A2 **Vengurla** India
16C1 **Venice** Italy
44B3 **Venkatagiri** India
18B2 **Venlo** Netherlands
19E1 **Venta** *R* Latvia
47D2 **Ventersburg** South Africa
7D4 **Ventnor** England
19E1 **Ventspils** Latvia
72E3 **Ventuarí** *R* Venezuela
66C3 **Ventura** USA
20E3 **Vepsovskaya Vozvyshennost'** *Upland* Russian Federation
74D3 **Vera** Argentina
15B2 **Vera** Spain
70C3 **Veracruz** Mexico
75A4 **Verá, L** Paraguay
42C4 **Verāval** India
16B1 **Vercelli** Italy
75A1 **Vérde** *R* Brazil
75B2 **Verde** *R* Goias, Brazil
75B2 **Verde** *R* Mato Grosso do Sul, Brazil
59D4 **Verde** *R* USA
Verde,C = Cap Vert
75D2 **Verde Grande** *R* Brazil
13E1 **Verden** Germany
14D3 **Verdon** *R* France
13C3 **Verdun** France
47D2 **Vereeniging** South Africa
20J4 **Vereshchagino** Russian Federation
48A3 **Verga,C** Guinea
15A1 **Verin** Spain
25N4 **Verkh Angara** *R* Russian Federation
20K5 **Verkhneural'sk** Russian Federation
25O3 **Verkhnevilyuysk** Russian Federation
20H3 **Verkhnyaya Toyma** Russian Federation
25P3 **Verkhoyansk** Russian Federation
25O3 **Verkhoyanskiy Khrebet** *Mts* Russian Federation
25K3 **Verkneimbatskoye** Russian Federation
20H3 **Verkola** Russian Federation
75B2 **Vermelho** *R* Brazil
13B4 **Vermenton** France
54G4 **Vermilion** Canada
61E1 **Vermilion L** USA
61D2 **Vermillion** USA
57F2 **Vermont** *State* USA
58E2 **Vernal** USA
66B2 **Vernalis** USA
47C3 **Verneuk Pan** *Salt L* South Africa
54G4 **Vernon** Canada
62C2 **Vernon** USA
67B3 **Vero Beach** USA
17E2 **Véroia** Greece
16C1 **Verona** Italy
13B3 **Versailles** France
48A3 **Vert, Cap** *C* Senegal
47E2 **Verulam** South Africa
13C2 **Verviers** Belgium
13B3 **Vervins** France
19G3 **Veselinovo** Ukraine
13C3 **Vesle** *R* France
14D2 **Vesoul** France
12G5 **Vesterålen** *Is* Norway
12G5 **Vestfjorden** *Inlet* Norway
12A2 **Vestmannaeyjar** Iceland
16C2 **Vesuvio** *Vol* Italy
19D3 **Veszprém** Hungary
12H7 **Vetlanda** Sweden
20G4 **Vetluga** *R* Russian Federation
13B2 **Veurne** Belgium
16B1 **Vevey** Switzerland
13C3 **Vézelise** France
Viangchan = Vientiane
15A1 **Viana do Castelo** Portugal
16C2 **Viareggio** Italy
12F7 **Viborg** Denmark
16D3 **Vibo Valentia** Italy
Vic = Vich
76G2 **Vice-commodoro Marambio** *Base* Antarctica
16C1 **Vicenza** Italy
15C1 **Vich** Spain
72E3 **Vichada** *R* Colombia/Venezuela
20G4 **Vichuga** Russian Federation
14C2 **Vichy** France
63D2 **Vicksburg** USA
75D3 **Vicosa** Brazil
32C4 **Victor Harbor** Australia
63C3 **Victoria** USA
32C2 **Victoria** *R* Australia
34B3 **Victoria** *State* Australia
69B2 **Victoria de las Tunas** Cuba
51C5 **Victoria Falls** Zambia/Zimbabwe
54G2 **Victoria I** Canada
34B2 **Victoria,L** Australia
50D4 **Victoria,L** C Africa
76F7 **Victoria Land** *Region* Antarctica
43G4 **Victoria,Mt** Burma
27H7 **Victoria,Mt** Papua New Guinea
50D3 **Victoria Nile** *R* Uganda
35B2 **Victoria Range** *Mts* New Zealand
32C2 **Victoria River Downs** Australia
54H3 **Victoria Str** Canada
65E1 **Victoriaville** Canada
47C3 **Victoria West** South Africa
59C4 **Victorville** USA
67B2 **Vidalia** USA
17F2 **Videle** Romania
17E2 **Vidin** Bulgaria
42D4 **Vidisha** India
19F1 **Vidzy** Belarus
74D6 **Viedma** Argentina
74B7 **Viedma, Lago** Argentina
69A4 **Viejo** Costa Rica
Vielha = Viella
15C1 **Viella** Spain
18D3 **Vienna** Austria
64B3 **Vienna** Illinois, USA
64C3 **Vienna** W Virginia, USA
14C2 **Vienne** France
14C2 **Vienne** *R* France
30C2 **Vientiane** Laos
14C2 **Vierzon** France
16D2 **Vieste** Italy
27D5 **Vietnam** *Republic* SE Asia
30D1 **Vietri** Vietnam
69P2 **Vieux Fort** St Lucia
27F5 **Vigan** Philippines
14B3 **Vignemale** *Mt* France/Spain
15A1 **Vigo** Spain
44C2 **Vijayawāda** India
17D2 **Vijosë** *R* Albania
17E2 **Vikhren** *Mt* Bulgaria
12G6 **Vikna** *I* Norway
51D5 **Vila da Maganja** Mozambique
51D5 **Vila Machado** Mozambique
51D6 **Vilanculos** Mozambique
Vilanova i la Geltrú = Villanueva-y-Geltrú
15A1 **Vila Real** Portugal
51D5 **Vila Vasco da Gama** Mozambique
75D3 **Vila Velha** Brazil

19F2 **Vileyka** Belarus
12H6 **Vilhelmina** Sweden
73G6 **Vilhena** Brazil
19F2 **Viliya** Belarus
20D4 **Viljandi** Estonia
47D2 **Viljoenskroon** South Africa
25L2 **Vilkitskogo, Proliv** *Str* Russian Federation
19F3 **Vilkovo** Ukraine
62A2 **Villa Ahumada** Mexico
15A1 **Villaba** Spain
16C1 **Villach** Austria
74C4 **Villa Dolores** Argentina
74E5 **Villa Gesell** Argentina
75A4 **Villa Hayes** Paraguay
70C3 **Villahermosa** Mexico
74D4 **Villa Huidobro** Argentina
74D4 **Villa María** Argentina
72F8 **Villa Montes** Bolivia
15A1 **Villa Nova de Gaia** Portugal
15A2 **Villanueva de la Serena** Spain
15C1 **Villanueva-y-Geltrú** Spain
15B2 **Villarreal** Spain
74E3 **Villarrica** Paraguay
15B2 **Villarrobledo** Spain
62B3 **Villa Unión** Coahuila, Mexico
72D3 **Villavicencio** Colombia
14C2 **Villefranche** France
55L5 **Ville-Marie** Canada
15B2 **Villena** Spain
13B3 **Villeneuve-St-Georges** France
14C3 **Villeneuve-sur-Lot** France
13B3 **Villeneuve-sur-Yonne** France
63D2 **Ville Platte** USA
13B3 **Villers-Cotterêts** France
14C2 **Villeurbanne** France
47D2 **Villiers** South Africa
13E3 **Villingen-Schwenningen** Germany
44B3 **Villupuram** India
19F2 **Vilnius** Lithuania
25N3 **Vilyuy** *R* Russian Federation
25O3 **Vilyuysk** Russian Federation
15C1 **Vinaroz** Spain
64B3 **Vincennes** USA
12H5 **Vindel** *R* Sweden
42D4 **Vindhya Range** *Mts* India
68C3 **Vineland** USA
68E2 **Vineyard Haven** USA
30D2 **Vinh** Vietnam
30D3 **Vinh Cam Ranh** *B* Vietnam
30D4 **Vinh Loi** Vietnam
30D3 **Vinh Long** Vietnam
63C1 **Vinita** USA
17D1 **Vinkovci** Croatia
19F3 **Vinnitsa** Ukraine
76F3 **Vinson Massif** *Upland* Antarctica
61E2 **Vinton** USA
74B4 **Viõna del Mar** Chile
51B5 **Virei** Angola
75D2 **Virgem da Lapa** Brazil
59D3 **Virgin** *R* USA
47D2 **Virginia** South Africa
61E1 **Virginia** USA
57F3 **Virginia** *State* USA
65D3 **Virginia Beach** USA
59C3 **Virginia City** USA
69E3 **Virgin Is** Caribbean Sea
64A2 **Viroqua** USA
16D1 **Virovitica** Croatia
13C3 **Virton** Belgium
44B4 **Virudunagar** India
16D2 **Vis** *I* Croatia
66C2 **Visalia** USA
12H7 **Visby** Sweden
54H2 **Viscount Melville Sd** Canada
17D2 **Višegrad** Bosnia-Herzegovina
15A1 **Viseu** Portugal
44C2 **Vishākhapatnam** India
20K3 **Vishera** *R* Russian Federation
16B2 **Viso, Monte** *Mt* Italy
59C4 **Vista** USA
Vistula *R* = **Wisła**
44A2 **Vite** India
19G1 **Vitebsk** Belarus
16C2 **Viterbo** Italy
15A1 **Vitigudino** Spain
25N4 **Vitim** *R* Russian Federation
73K8 **Vitória** Brazil
15B1 **Vitoria** Spain
73K6 **Vitória da Conquista** Brazil
14B2 **Vitré** France
13C3 **Vitry-le-François** France
12J5 **Vittangi** Sweden
13C3 **Vittel** France
16C3 **Vittoria** Sicily, Italy
26J2 **Vityaz Depth** Pacific Ocean
Viviero = Vivero
15A1 **Vivero** Spain
25L3 **Vivi** *R* Russian Federation
15B1 **Vizcaya, Golfo de** Spain
25M4 **Vizhne-Angarsk** Russian Federation
44C2 **Vizianagaram** India
20J3 **Vizinga** Russian Federation
17E1 **Vlădeasa** *Mt* Romania
21G7 **Vladikavkaz** Russian Federation
20G4 **Vladimir** Russian Federation
19E2 **Vladimir Volynskiy** Ukraine
28C2 **Vladivostok** Russian Federation
18A2 **Vlieland** *I* Netherlands
13B2 **Vlissingen** Netherlands
47B2 **Vloosdrift** South Africa
17D2 **Vlorë** Albania
18C3 **Vltara** *R* Czech Republic
18C3 **Vöcklabruck** Austria
30D3 **Voeune Sai** Cambodia
13E2 **Vogelsberg** *Region* Germany
Vohemar = Vohimarina
Vohibinany = Ampasimanolotra
51F5 **Vohimarina** Madagascar
50D4 **Voi** Kenya
48B4 **Voinjama** Liberia
14D2 **Voiron** France
17D1 **Vojvodina** *Region* Serbia, Yugoslavia
60B1 **Volborg** USA
69A5 **Volcán Barú** *Mt* Panama
Volcano Is = Kazan Retto
20K4 **Volchansk** Russian Federation
21H6 **Volga** *R* Russian Federation
21G6 **Volgodonsk** Russian Federation
21G6 **Volgograd** Russian Federation
21H5 **Volgogradskoye Vodokhranilishche** *Res* Russian Federation
20E4 **Volkhov** Russian Federation
20E4 **Volkhov** *R* Russian Federation
19E2 **Volkovysk** Belarus
47D2 **Volksrust** South Africa
25L2 **Volochanka** Russian Federation
20G4 **Vologda** Russian Federation
17E3 **Vólos** Greece
21H5 **Vol'sk** Russian Federation
66B2 **Volta** USA
48B3 **Volta Blanche** *R* Burkina/Ghana
48B4 **Volta, L** Ghana
48B3 **Volta Noire** *R* W Africa
75D3 **Volta Redonda** Brazil
48B3 **Volta Rouge** *R* Burkina/Ghana
21G6 **Volzhskiy** Russian Federation
20F3 **Vonguda** Russian Federation
55R3 **Vopnafjörður** Iceland
18C1 **Vordingborg** Denmark
21C8 **Voriái** *I* Greece
20L2 **Vorkuta** Russian Federation
12G6 **Vorma** *R* Norway
21F5 **Voronezh** Russian Federation
12M5 **Voron'ya** *R* Russian Federation
21F6 **Voroshilovgrad** Ukraine
12K7 **Võru** Estonia
13D3 **Vosges** *Department* France
14D2 **Vosges** *Mts* France
12F6 **Voss** Norway
25L4 **Vostochnyy Sayan** *Mts* Russian Federation
76F9 **Vostok** *Base* Antarctica
20J4 **Votkinsk** Russian Federation
13C3 **Vouziers** France
61E1 **Voyageurs Nat Pk** USA
20K3 **Voy Vozh** Russian Federation
21E6 **Voznesensk** Ukraine
17E2 **Vranje** Serbia, Yugoslavia
17E2 **Vratsa** Bulgaria
17D1 **Vrbas** Serbia, Yugoslavia
16D2 **Vrbas** *R* Bosnia-Herzegovina
16C1 **Vrbovsko** Croatia
47D2 **Vrede** South Africa
47B3 **Vredendal** South Africa
73G2 **Vreed en Hoop** Guyana
44B3 **Vriddhāchalam** India
17E1 **Vršac** Serbia, Yugoslavia
16D2 **Vrtoče** Bosnia-Herzegovina
47C2 **Vryburg** South Africa
47E2 **Vryheid** South Africa
17D1 **Vukovar** Croatia
20K3 **Vuktyl'** Russian Federation
7F3 **Vulcan** *Oilfield* N Sea
16C3 **Vulcano** *I* Italy
30D3 **Vung Tau** Vietnam
12J5 **Vuollerim** Sweden
20E3 **Vyartsilya** Russian Federation
20J4 **Vyatka** *R* Russian Federation
26G2 **Vyazemskiy** Russian Federation
20E4 **Vyaz'ma** Russian Federation
20G4 **Vyazniki** Russian Federation
20D3 **Vyborg** Russian Federation
20F3 **Vygozero, Ozero** *L* Russian Federation
20J3 **Vym** *R* Russian Federation
7C3 **Vyrnwy** *R* Wales
20E4 **Vyshniy-Volochek** Russian Federation
18D3 **Vyškov** Czech Republic
20F3 **Vytegra** Russian Federation

W

48B3 **Wa** Ghana
13C2 **Waal** *R* Netherlands
54G4 **Wabasca** *R* Canada
64B2 **Wabash** USA
64B3 **Wabash** *R* USA
64C1 **Wabatongushi L** Canada
54J4 **Wabowden** Canada
55M4 **Wabush** Canada
67B3 **Waccasassa B** USA
68E1 **Wachusett Res** USA
63C2 **Waco** USA
42B3 **Wad** Pakistan
49D2 **Waddān** Libya
13C1 **Waddenzee** *S* Netherlands
54F4 **Waddington,Mt** Canada
7B4 **Wadebridge** England
61D1 **Wadena** USA
45C3 **Wadi es Sir** Jordan
50D1 **Wadi Halfa** Sudan
45C3 **Wādi Mūsā** Jordan
50D2 **Wad Medani** Sudan
28A3 **Waegwan** S Korea
28A2 **Wafang** China
41E4 **Wafra** Kuwait
13C2 **Wageningen** Netherlands
55K3 **Wager B** Canada
55J3 **Wager Bay** Canada
34C3 **Wagga Wagga** Australia
32A4 **Wagin** Australia
61D2 **Wagner** USA
66E5 **Wahiawa** Hawaiian Islands
61D2 **Wahoo** USA
61D1 **Wahpeton** USA
44A2 **Wai** India
66E5 **Waialua** Hawaiian Islands
35B2 **Waiau** New Zealand
35B2 **Waiau** *R* New Zealand
27G6 **Waigeo** *I* Indonesia
35C1 **Waihi** New Zealand
35C1 **Waikaremoana,L** New Zealand
35C1 **Waikato** *R* New Zealand
34A2 **Waikerie** Australia
35B3 **Waikouaiti** New Zealand
66E5 **Wailuku** Hawaiian Islands
35B2 **Waimakariri** *R* New Zealand
35B2 **Waimate** New Zealand
66E5 **Waimea** Hawaiian Islands
32B1 **Waingapu** Indonesia
54G4 **Wainwright** Canada
54B2 **Wainwright** USA
35C1 **Waioura** New Zealand
35B2 **Waipara** New Zealand
35C2 **Waipukurau** New Zealand
35C2 **Wairarapa,L** New Zealand
35B2 **Wairau** *R* New Zealand
35C1 **Wairoa** New Zealand
35C1 **Wairoa** *R* New Zealand
35B2 **Waitaki** *R* New Zealand
35B1 **Waitara** New Zealand
35C1 **Waitomo** New Zealand
35B1 **Waiuku** New Zealand
29C3 **Wajima** Japan
50E3 **Wajir** Kenya
29C3 **Wakasa-wan** *B* Japan
35A3 **Wakatipu,L** New Zealand
29D4 **Wakayama** Japan
60D3 **Wa Keeney** USA
7D3 **Wakefield** England
69H1 **Wakefield** Jamaica
64B1 **Wakefield** Michigan, USA
68E2 **Wakefield** Rhode Island, USA
30B2 **Wakema** Burma
29E1 **Wakkanai** Japan
34B3 **Wakool** *R* Australia
18D2 **Wałbrzych** Poland
34D2 **Walcha** Australia
18D2 **Wałcz** Poland
13D2 **Waldbröl** Germany
68C2 **Walden** USA
13E4 **Waldshut** Germany
54B3 **Wales** USA
7C3 **Wales** *Principality* U K
55K3 **Wales I** Canada
34C2 **Walgett** Australia
76F4 **Walgreen Coast** *Region* Antarctica
50C4 **Walikale** Zaïre
61E1 **Walker** USA
66C1 **Walker L** USA
66C3 **Walker Pass** USA
64C2 **Walkerton** Canada
60C2 **Wall** USA
58C1 **Wallace** USA
32C4 **Wallaroo** Australia
34C3 **Walla Walla** Australia
58C1 **Walla Walla** USA
68D2 **Wallingford** USA
37K5 **Wallis and Futuna** *Is* Pacific Ocean
33H2 **Wallis, Îles** Pacific Ocean
58C1 **Wallowa** USA
58C1 **Wallowa Mts** USA
34C1 **Wallumbilla** Australia
6C2 **Walney** *I* England
63D1 **Walnut Ridge** USA
68D1 **Walpole** USA
7D3 **Walsall** England
62B1 **Walsenburg** USA
67B2 **Walterboro** USA
67A2 **Walter F George Res** USA
62C2 **Walters** USA
68E1 **Waltham** USA
68C1 **Walton** USA
7E4 **Walton-on-the Naze** England
47A1 **Walvis Bay** Namibia
52J6 **Walvis Ridge** Atlantic Ocean
48C4 **Wamba** Nigeria
50B4 **Wamba** *R* Zaïre
61D3 **Wamego** USA
58E2 **Wamsutter** USA
42B2 **Wana** Pakistan
34B1 **Wanaaring** Australia
35A2 **Wanaka** New Zealand
35A2 **Wanaka,L** New Zealand
64C1 **Wanapitei L** Canada
28A4 **Wando** S Korea
34C1 **Wandoan** Australia
34B3 **Wanganella** Australia
35B1 **Wanganui** New Zealand
35C1 **Wanganui** *R* New Zealand
34C3 **Wangaratta** Australia
13D1 **Wangerooge** *I* Germany
28B2 **Wangqing** China
28A3 **Wanjialing** China
Wankie = Hwange
50E3 **Wanleweyne** Somalia
30E2 **Wanning** China
44B2 **Wanparti** India
6D2 **Wansbeck, R** England
7D4 **Wantage** England
31B3 **Wanxian** China
31B3 **Wanyuan** China
63D1 **Wappapello,L** USA
68D2 **Wappingers Falls** USA
61E2 **Wapsipinicon** *R* USA
44B2 **Warangal** India
34C4 **Waratah** Australia
34C3 **Waratah B** Australia
13E2 **Warburg** Germany
34C3 **Warburton** Australia
34C1 **Ward** *R* Australia
47D2 **Warden** South Africa
42D4 **Wardha** India
35A3 **Ward,Mt** New Zealand
54F4 **Ware** Canada
68D1 **Ware** USA
7C4 **Wareham** England
68E2 **Wareham** USA
13D2 **Warendorf** Germany
34D1 **Warialda** Australia
30D2 **Warin Chamrap** Thailand
47B2 **Warmbad** Namibia
51C6 **Warmbad** South Africa
7C4 **Warminster** England
68C2 **Warminster** USA
59C3 **Warm Springs** USA
18C2 **Warnemünde** Germany
58B2 **Warner Mts** USA
67B2 **Warner Robins** USA
34B3 **Warracknabeal** Australia
32D3 **Warrego** *R* Australia
63D2 **Warren** Arkansas, USA
34C2 **Warren** Australia
61D1 **Warren** Minnesota, USA
64C2 **Warren** Ohio, USA
65D2 **Warren** Pennsylvania, USA
68E2 **Warren** Rhode Island, USA
9C2 **Warrenpoint** Northern Ireland
61E3 **Warrensburg** USA
47C2 **Warrenton** South Africa
65D3 **Warrenton** USA
48C4 **Warri** Nigeria
7C3 **Warrington** England
63E2 **Warrington** USA
34B3 **Warrnambool** Australia
61D1 **Warroad** USA
19E2 **Warsaw** Poland
68A1 **Warsaw** USA
50E3 **Warshiikh** Somalia
Warszawa = Warsaw
19D2 **Warta** *R* Poland
34D1 **Warwick** Australia
7D3 **Warwick** England
68C2 **Warwick** New York, USA
68E2 **Warwick** Rhode Island, USA
7D3 **Warwick** *County* England
59D3 **Wasatch Range** *Mts* USA
47E2 **Wasbank** South Africa
66C3 **Wasco** USA
61E2 **Waseca** USA
64A1 **Washburn** USA
54H2 **Washburn L** Canada
58D2 **Washburn,Mt** USA
42D4 **Wāshīm** India
57F3 **Washington** District of Columbia, USA
67B2 **Washington** Georgia, USA
64B3 **Washington** Indiana, USA
61E2 **Washington** Iowa, USA
61E3 **Washington** Missouri, USA
67C1 **Washington** N Carolina, USA
68C2 **Washington** New Jersey, USA
64C2 **Washington** Pennsylvania, USA
59D3 **Washington** Utah, USA
56A2 **Washington** *State* USA
64C3 **Washington Court House** USA
55M1 **Washington Land** *Region* Canada
65E2 **Washington,Mt** USA
62C1 **Washita** *R* USA
7E3 **Wash,The** *B* England
42A3 **Washuk** Pakistan
51L4 **Waskaganish** Canada
69A4 **Waspán** Nicaragua
66C1 **Wassuk Range** *Mts* USA
13C3 **Wassy** France
27F7 **Watampone** Indonesia
47D3 **Waterberge** *Mts* South Africa
68D2 **Waterbury** USA
10B3 **Waterford** Irish Republic
9C3 **Waterford** *County* Irish Republic
9C3 **Waterford Harbour** Irish Republic
13C2 **Waterloo** Belgium
61E2 **Waterloo** USA
64B1 **Watersmeet** USA
58D1 **Waterton-Glacier International Peace Park** USA
65D2 **Watertown** New York, USA
61D2 **Watertown** S Dakota, USA
64B2 **Watertown** Wisconsin, USA
47E2 **Waterval-Boven** South Africa
65F2 **Waterville** Maine, USA
68C1 **Waterville** New York, USA
68D1 **Watervliet** USA
54G4 **Waterways** Canada
7D4 **Watford** England
60C1 **Watford City** USA
68B1 **Watkins Glen** USA
62C1 **Watonga** USA
56C1 **Watrous** Canada
62B1 **Watrous** USA
50C3 **Watsa** Zaïre
54F3 **Watson Lake** Canada
66B2 **Watsonville** USA
27H7 **Wau** Papua New Guinea
50C3 **Wau** Sudan
34D2 **Wauchope** Australia
67B3 **Wauchula** USA
64B2 **Waukegan** USA
64B2 **Waukesha** USA
64B2 **Waupaca** USA
64B2 **Waupun** USA
63C2 **Waurika** USA
64B2 **Wausau** USA
64B2 **Wauwatosa** USA
32C2 **Wave Hill** Australia
7E3 **Waveney** *R* England
60E2 **Waverly** Iowa, USA
68B1 **Waverly** New York, USA
64C3 **Waverly** Ohio, USA
13C2 **Wavre** Belgium
64C1 **Wawa** Canada
49D2 **Wāw Al Kabīr** Libya
49D2 **Wāw an Nāmūs** *Well* Libya

66C2 **Wawona** USA
63C2 **Waxahachie** USA
67B2 **Waycross** USA
61D2 **Wayne** USA
67B2 **Waynesboro** Georgia, USA
63E2 **Waynesboro** Mississippi, USA
68B3 **Waynesboro** Pennsylvania, USA
65D3 **Waynesboro** Virginia, USA
63D1 **Waynesville** Missouri, USA
67B1 **Waynesville** N Carolina, USA
42B2 **Wazi Khwa** Afghanistan
8E1 **W Burra** *I* Scotland
7E4 **Weald,The** *Upland* England
6C2 **Wear** *R* England
62C1 **Weatherford** Oklahoma, USA
63C2 **Weatherford** Texas, USA
58B2 **Weaverville** USA
64C1 **Webbwood** Canada
68B1 **Webster** New York, USA
61D1 **Webster** S Dakota, USA
68E1 **Webster** USA
61E2 **Webster City** Massachusetts, USA
64A3 **Webster Groves** USA
74D8 **Weddell** *I* Falkland Islands
76G2 **Weddell Sea** Antarctica
58B2 **Weed** USA
68A2 **Weedville** USA
47E2 **Weenen** South Africa
34C2 **Wee Waa** Australia
31D1 **Weichang** China
18C3 **Weiden** Germany
31D2 **Weifang** China
31E2 **Weihai** China
31C3 **Wei He** *R* Henan, China
31C2 **Wei He** *R* Shaanxi, China
34C1 **Weilmoringle** Australia
13E3 **Weinheim** Germany
31A4 **Weining** China
32D2 **Weipa** Australia
64C2 **Weirton** USA
58C2 **Weiser** USA
31D3 **Weishan Hu** *L* China
18C2 **Weissenfels** Germany
67A2 **Weiss L** USA
64C3 **Welch** USA
50E2 **Weldiya** Ethiopia
66C3 **Weldon** USA
47D2 **Welkom** South Africa
65D2 **Welland** Canada
7D3 **Welland** *R* England
32C2 **Wellesley Is** Australia
68E2 **Wellfleet** USA
7D3 **Wellingborough** England
34C2 **Wellington** Australia
60C2 **Wellington** Colorado, USA
7C4 **Wellington** England
63C1 **Wellington** Kansas, USA
66C1 **Wellington** Nevada, USA
35B2 **Wellington** New Zealand
47B3 **Wellington** South Africa
62B2 **Wellington** Texas, USA
55J2 **Wellington Chan** Canada
74B7 **Wellington, Isla** Chile
7C4 **Wells** England
58D2 **Wells** Nevada, USA
68C1 **Wells** New York, USA
68B2 **Wellsboro** USA
35B1 **Wellsford** New Zealand
32B3 **Wells,L** Australia
7E3 **Wells-next-the-Sea** England
68B1 **Wellsville** USA
18C3 **Wels** Austria
7C3 **Welshpool** Wales
7D4 **Welwyn Garden City** England
55L4 **Wemindji** Canada
58B1 **Wenatchee** USA
58C1 **Wenatchee** *R* USA
48B4 **Wenchi** Ghana
31E2 **Wendeng** China
58D2 **Wendover** USA
31E4 **Wenling** China
31A5 **Wenshan** China
6D2 **Wensleydale** England
7E3 **Wensum** *R* England
34B2 **Wentworth** Australia
31A3 **Wen Xian** China
31E4 **Wenzhou** China
31C4 **Wenzhu** China
47D2 **Wepener** South Africa
47C2 **Werda** Botswana
50E3 **Werder** Ethiopia
18C2 **Werra** *R* Germany
34D2 **Werris Creek** Australia
13D2 **Wesel** Germany
18B2 **Weser** *R* Germany
60C3 **Weskan** USA
63C3 **Weslaco** USA
55N5 **Wesleyville** Canada
32C2 **Wessel Is** Australia
60D2 **Wessington Springs** USA
64B2 **West Allis** USA
36F5 **West Australian Basin** Indian Ocean
36F6 **West Australian Ridge** Indian Ocean
63E3 **West B** USA
43F4 **West Bengal** *State* India
68C1 **West Branch Delaware** *R* USA
68A2 **West Branch Susquehanna** *R* USA
7D3 **West Bromwich** England
65E2 **Westbrook** USA
64A2 **Westby** USA
68C3 **West Chester** USA
67C3 **West End** Bahamas
66D3 **Westend** USA
13D2 **Westerburg** Germany
18B2 **Westerland** Germany
68E2 **Westerly** USA
32B3 **Western Australia** *State* Australia
51B7 **Western Cape** *Province* South Africa
44A2 **Western Ghats** *Mts* India
8B3 **Western Isles** *Region* Scotland
48A2 **Western Sahara** *Region* Morocco
33H2 **Western Samoa** *Is* Pacific Ocean
13B2 **Westerschelde** *Estuary* Netherlands
13D1 **Westerstede** Germany
13D2 **Westerwald** *Region* Germany
14D1 **Westfalen** *Region* Germany
74D8 **West Falkland** *Is* Falkland Islands
68D1 **Westfield** Massachusetts, USA
65D2 **Westfield** New York, USA
68B2 **Westfield** Pennsylvania, USA
64B3 **West Frankfort** USA
34C1 **Westgate** Australia
7C4 **West Glamorgan** *County* Wales
65F1 **West Grand L** USA
52E3 **West Indies** *Is* Caribbean Sea
64C3 **West Liberty** USA
64C2 **West Lorne** Canada
9C3 **Westmeath** *County* Irish Republic
63D1 **West Memphis** USA
7D3 **West Midlands** *County* England
7D4 **Westminster** England
68B3 **Westminster** Maryland, USA
67B2 **Westminster** S Carolina, USA
47D1 **West Nicholson** Zimbabwe
27E6 **Weston** Malaysia
64C3 **Weston** USA
7C4 **Weston-super-Mare** England
67B3 **West Palm Beach** USA
63D1 **West Plains** USA
66B1 **West Point** California, USA
63E2 **West Point** Mississippi, USA
61D2 **West Point** Nebraska, USA
68D2 **West Point** New York, USA
35B2 **Westport** New Zealand
10C2 **Westray** *I* Scotland
6E3 **West Sole** *Oilfield* N Sea
57E3 **West Virginia** *State* USA
66C1 **West Walker** *R* USA
34C2 **West Wyalong** Australia
58D2 **West Yellowstone** USA
7D3 **West Yorkshire** *County* England
27F7 **Wetar** *I* Indonesia
54G4 **Wetaskiwin** Canada
50D4 **Wete** Tanzania
13E2 **Wetter** *R* Germany
13E2 **Wetzlar** Germany
Wevok = Lisburne, Cape
32D1 **Wewak** Papua New Guinea
63C1 **Wewoka** USA
9C3 **Wexford** Irish Republic
9C3 **Wexford** *County* Irish Republic
7D4 **Weybridge** England
54H5 **Weyburn** Canada
7C4 **Weymouth** England
68E1 **Weymouth** USA
35C1 **Whakatane** New Zealand
35C1 **Whakatane** *R* New Zealand
8E1 **Whalsay** *I* Scotland
35B1 **Whangarei** New Zealand
6D3 **Wharfe** *R* England
63C3 **Wharton** USA
60B2 **Wheatland** USA
68B3 **Wheaton** Maryland, USA
61D1 **Wheaton** Minnesota, USA
59D3 **Wheeler Peak** *Mt* Nevada, USA
62A1 **Wheeler Peak** *Mt* New Mexico, USA
66C3 **Wheeler Ridge** USA
64C2 **Wheeling** USA
65D2 **Whitby** Canada
6D2 **Whitby** England
7C3 **Whitchurch** England
63D1 **White** *R* Arkansas, USA
60B2 **White** *R* Colorado, USA
64B3 **White** *R* Indiana, USA
60C2 **White** *R* S Dakota, USA
55N4 **White B** Canada
60C1 **White Butte** *Mt* USA
34B2 **White Cliffs** Australia
10C2 **White Coomb** *Mt* Scotland
58D1 **Whitefish** USA
64B1 **Whitefish Pt** USA
55M4 **Whitegull L** Canada
65E2 **Whitehall** New York, USA
68C2 **Whitehall** Pennsylvania, USA
64A2 **Whitehall** Wisconsin, USA
6C2 **Whitehaven** England
54E3 **Whitehorse** Canada
35C1 **White I** New Zealand
63D3 **White L** USA
34C4 **Whitemark** Australia
59C3 **White Mountain Peak** *Mt* USA
66C2 **White Mts** California, USA
65E2 **White Mts** New Hampshire, USA
50D2 **White Nile** *R* Sudan
68D2 **White Plains** USA
55K5 **White River** Canada
60C2 **White River** USA
65E2 **White River Junction** USA
White Russia = Belarus
58B1 **White Salmon** USA
20F2 **White Sea** Russian Federation
58D1 **White Sulphur Springs** USA
67C2 **Whiteville** USA
48B4 **White Volta** W Africa
64B2 **Whitewater** USA
8C4 **Whithorn** Scotland
67B2 **Whitmire** USA
66C2 **Whitney,Mt** USA
66C4 **Whittier** California, USA
7D3 **Whittlesey** England
54H3 **Wholdaia** Canada
32C4 **Whyalla** Australia
64C2 **Wiarton** Canada
8B3 **Wiay, I** Scotland
60C1 **Wibaux** USA
63C1 **Wichita** USA
62C2 **Wichita** *R* USA
62C2 **Wichita Falls** USA
62C2 **Wichita Mts** USA
8D2 **Wick** Scotland
59D4 **Wickenburg** USA
9C3 **Wicklow** Irish Republic
9C3 **Wicklow** *County* Irish Republic
9C3 **Wicklow Hd** *Pt* Irish Republic
9C3 **Wicklow Mts** Irish Republic
34C1 **Widgeegoara** *R* Australia
7C3 **Widnes** England
13D2 **Wied** *R* Germany
19D2 **Wielun** Poland
Wien = Vienna
18D3 **Wiener Neustadt** Austria
19E2 **Wieprz** *R* Poland
13E2 **Wiesbaden** Germany
13D4 **Wiese** *R* Germany
7C3 **Wigan** England
63E2 **Wiggins** USA
7D4 **Wight, I of** *County* England
6C2 **Wigton** England
8C4 **Wigtown** Scotland
8C4 **Wigtown B** Scotland
58C1 **Wilbur** USA
34B2 **Wilcannia** Australia
59C3 **Wildcat Peak** *Mt* USA
13E1 **Wildeshausen** Germany
16C1 **Wildspitze** *Mt* Austria
67B3 **Wildwood** Florida, USA
68C3 **Wildwood** New Jersey, USA
62B1 **Wiley** USA
47D2 **Wilge** *R* South Africa
32D1 **Wilhelm,Mt** Papua New Guinea
18B2 **Wilhelmshaven** Germany
68C2 **Wilkes-Barre** USA
76F8 **Wilkes Land** *Region* Antarctica
58B2 **Willamette** *R* USA
34B2 **Willandra** *R* Australia
58B1 **Willapa B** USA
59E4 **Willcox** USA
69D4 **Willemstad** Curaçao
34B3 **William,Mt** Australia
59D3 **Williams** Arizona, USA
59B3 **Williams** California, USA
65D3 **Williamsburg** USA
54F4 **Williams Lake** Canada
64C3 **Williamson** USA
68B2 **Williamsport** USA
67C1 **Williamston** USA
68D1 **Williamstown** Massachusetts, USA
64C3 **Williamstown** W Virginia, USA
68D2 **Willimantic** USA
68C2 **Willingboro** USA
32E2 **Willis Group** *Is* Australia
67B3 **Williston** Florida, USA
60C1 **Williston** N Dakota, USA
47C3 **Williston** South Africa
61D1 **Willmar** USA
34A3 **Willoughby,C** Australia
60B1 **Willow Bunch** Canada
47C3 **Willowmore** South Africa
58B2 **Willow Ranch** USA
59B3 **Willows** USA
63D1 **Willow Springs** USA
34A2 **Wilmington** Australia
68C3 **Wilmington** Delaware, USA
67C2 **Wilmington** N Carolina, USA
68D1 **Wilmington** Vermont, USA
60D3 **Wilson** Kansas, USA
67C1 **Wilson** N Carolina, USA
68A1 **Wilson** New York, USA
57F3 **Wilson** USA
34B1 **Wilson** *R* Australia
55K3 **Wilson,C** Canada
60D3 **Wilson L** USA
66C3 **Wilson,Mt** California, USA
62A1 **Wilson,Mt** Colorado, USA
58B1 **Wilson,Mt** Oregon, USA
34C3 **Wilson's Promontory** *Pen* Australia
13E1 **Wilstedt** Germany
7D4 **Wiltshire** *County* England
13C3 **Wiltz** Luxembourg
32B3 **Wiluna** Australia
64B2 **Winamac** USA
47D2 **Winburg** South Africa
7C4 **Wincanton** England
68D1 **Winchendon** USA
65D1 **Winchester** Canada
7D4 **Winchester** England
64C3 **Winchester** Kentucky, USA
68D1 **Winchester** New Hampshire, USA
65D3 **Winchester** Virginia, USA
58E2 **Wind** *R* USA
60C2 **Wind Cave Nat Pk** USA
6C2 **Windermere** England
6C2 **Windermere** *L* England
47B1 **Windhoek** Namibia
61D2 **Windom** USA
32D3 **Windorah** Australia
58E2 **Wind River Range** *Mts* USA
34D2 **Windsor** Australia
68D2 **Windsor** Connecticut, USA
7D4 **Windsor** England
67C1 **Windsor** N Carolina, USA
55M5 **Windsor** Nova Scotia, Canada
64C2 **Windsor** Ontario, Canada
65E1 **Windsor** Quebec, Canada
67B2 **Windsor Forest** USA
68D2 **Windsor Locks** USA
69E4 **Windward Is** Caribbean Sea
69C3 **Windward Pass** Caribbean Sea
63E2 **Winfield** Alabama, USA
63C1 **Winfield** Kansas, USA
34D2 **Wingham** Australia
55K4 **Winisk** *R* Canada
55K4 **Winisk L** Canada
30B2 **Winkana** Burma
58B1 **Winlock** USA
48B4 **Winneba** Ghana
61E2 **Winnebago** USA
64B2 **Winnebago,L** USA
58C2 **Winnemucca** USA
60D2 **Winner** USA
63D2 **Winnfield** USA
61E1 **Winnibigoshish L** USA
54J4 **Winnipeg** Canada
54J4 **Winnipeg,L** Canada
54J4 **Winnipegosis** Canada
65E2 **Winnipesaukee,L** USA
61E2 **Winona** Minnesota, USA
63E2 **Winona** Mississippi, USA
55J5 **Winona** USA
65E2 **Winooski** USA
13D1 **Winschoten** Netherlands
59D4 **Winslow** USA
68D2 **Winsted** USA
67B1 **Winston-Salem** USA
13E2 **Winterberg** Germany
67B3 **Winter Garden** USA
67B3 **Winter Park** USA
66B1 **Winters** USA
13D2 **Winterswijk** Netherlands
16B1 **Winterthur** Switzerland
61E2 **Winthrop** USA
32D3 **Winton** Australia
35A3 **Winton** New Zealand
7E3 **Wisbech** England
64A2 **Wisconsin** *R* USA
57E2 **Wisconsin** *State* USA
64B2 **Wisconsin Dells** USA
55K5 **Wisconsin Rapids** USA
54C3 **Wiseman** USA
19D2 **Wisła** *R* Poland
18C2 **Wismar** Germany
13D3 **Wissembourg** France
73G2 **Witagron** Surinam
47D2 **Witbank** South Africa
56D3 **Witchita Falls** USA
7E3 **Witham** England
7D3 **Witham** *R* England
6E3 **Withernsea** England
7D4 **Witney** England
13D2 **Witten** Germany
18C2 **Wittenberg** Germany
16B1 **Wittenberg** France/Italy
18C2 **Wittenberge** Germany
32A3 **Wittenoom** Australia
13D2 **Wittlich** Germany
47B1 **Witvlei** Namibia
19D2 **Władysławowo** Poland
19D2 **Włocławek** Poland
19E2 **Włodawa** Poland
34C3 **Wodonga** Australia
27G7 **Wokam** *I* Indonesia
7D4 **Woking** England
68B1 **Wolcott** USA
27H6 **Woleai** *I* Pacific Ocean
64B1 **Wolf** *R* USA
13E3 **Wolfach** Germany
58B2 **Wolf Creek** USA
62A1 **Wolf Creek P** USA
60B1 **Wolf Point** USA
18C3 **Wolfsberg** Austria
18C2 **Wolfsburg** Germany
74C9 **Wollaston, Islas** Chile
54H4 **Wollaston L** Canada
54H4 **Wollaston Lake** Canada
54G3 **Wollaston Pen** Canada
34D2 **Wollongong** Australia
47D2 **Wolmaransstad** South Africa
18D2 **Wołow** Poland
34B3 **Wolseley** Australia
7C3 **Wolverhampton** England
7D3 **Wolverton** England
68B2 **Womelsdorf** USA
34D1 **Wondai** Australia
28B3 **Wŏnju** S Korea
28B3 **Wŏnsan** N Korea
34C3 **Wonthaggi** Australia
68C3 **Woodbine** USA
7E3 **Woodbridge** England
65D3 **Woodbridge** USA
54G4 **Wood Buffalo Nat. Pk** Canada
34D1 **Woodburn** Australia
58B1 **Woodburn** USA
68C3 **Woodbury** USA
54D3 **Woodchopper** USA
66C1 **Woodfords** USA
66C2 **Woodlake** USA
59B3 **Woodland** California, USA
66B1 **Woodland** USA
58B1 **Woodland** Washington, USA
33E1 **Woodlark** *I* Papua New Guinea
32C3 **Woodroffe,Mt** Australia
61E1 **Woods,L of the** Canada/USA
64B2 **Woodstock** Illinois, USA
65F1 **Woodstock** New Brunswick, Canada
64C2 **Woodstock** Ontario, Canada
68A3 **Woodstock** Virginia, USA
68C3 **Woodstown** USA
35C2 **Woodville** New Zealand
63D2 **Woodville** USA
62C1 **Woodward** USA
6D2 **Wooler** England
32C4 **Woomera** Australia
65E2 **Woonsocket** USA
64C2 **Wooster** USA
7D4 **Wootton Bassett** England
7C3 **Worcester** England
47B3 **Worcester** South Africa
68E1 **Worcester** USA
6C2 **Workington** England
7D3 **Worksop** England
58E2 **Worland** USA
13E3 **Worms** Germany
7B4 **Worms Head** *Pt* Wales
7D4 **Worthing** England
61D2 **Worthington** USA
64C2 **Worthington** USA
60C2 **Wounded Knee** USA
27F7 **Wowoni** Indonesia
25T2 **Wrangel I** Russian Federation
54E4 **Wrangell** USA
54D3 **Wrangell Mts** USA

10B2 **Wrath,C** Scotland
60C2 **Wray** USA
7C3 **Wrexham** Wales
59D4 **Wrightson, Mt** USA
67B2 **Wrightsville** USA
66D3 **Wrightwood** USA
54F3 **Wrigley** Canada
18D2 **Wrocław** Poland
19D2 **Września** Poland
26F2 **Wuchang** China
30E1 **Wuchuan** China
31E2 **Wuda** China
31C2 **Wuding He** *R* China
31A3 **Wudu** China
31C4 **Wugang** China
31B2 **Wuhai** China
31C3 **Wuhan** China
31D3 **Wuhu** China
31D5 **Wuhua** China
42D2 **Wūjang** China
31B1 **Wujia He** *R* China
31B4 **Wu Jiang** *R* China
48C4 **Wukari** Nigeria
31B4 **Wuling Shan** *Mts* China
31A4 **Wumeng Shan** *Upland* China
13E1 **Wümme** *R* Germany
13E1 **Wunstorf** Germany
43H4 **Wuntho** Burma
13D2 **Wuppertal** Germany
31B2 **Wuqi** China
31D2 **Wuqing** China
18B3 **Würzburg** Germany
18C2 **Wurzen** Germany
31C2 **Wutai Shan** *Mt* China
27H7 **Wuvulu** *I* Pacific Ocean
31A2 **Wuwei** China
31E3 **Wuxi** China
31E3 **Wuxing** China
31C2 **Wuyang** China
31D4 **Wuyi Shan** *Mts* China
31B1 **Wuyuan** China
30D2 **Wuzhi Shan** *Mts* China
31B2 **Wuzhong** China
31C5 **Wuzhou** China
64C2 **Wyandotte** USA
34C1 **Wyandra** Australia
7C4 **Wye** *R* England
7C4 **Wylye** *R* England
7E3 **Wymondham** England
32B2 **Wyndham** Australia
63D1 **Wynne** USA
54G2 **Wynniatt B** Canada
34C4 **Wynyard** Australia
64B2 **Wyoming** USA
56C2 **Wyoming** *State* USA
58D2 **Wyoming Peak** *Mt* USA
58D2 **Wyoming Range** *Mts* USA
34D2 **Wyong** Australia
64C3 **Wytheville** USA

X

42D1 **Xaidulla** China
47E2 **Xai Xai** Mozambique
51B5 **Xangongo** Angola
13D2 **Xanten** Germany
17E2 **Xánthi** Greece
31D1 **Xar Moron He** *R* China
47C1 **Xau,L** Botswana
64C3 **Xenia** USA
Xiaguan = Dali
31A2 **Xiahe** China
31D5 **Xiamen** China
31B3 **Xi'an** China
31B4 **Xianfeng** China
31C3 **Xiangfan** China
31C4 **Xiang Jiang** *R* China
31C4 **Xiangtan** China
31C4 **Xianning** China
31B3 **Xianyang** China
26F2 **Xiao Hinggan Ling** *Region* China
31C4 **Xiao Shui** *R* China
31D4 **Xiapu** China
31A4 **Xichang** China
30C2 **Xieng Khouang** Laos
31B4 **Xifeng** China
28A2 **Xifeng** China
43F3 **Xigazê** China
31A1 **Xi He** *R* China
28A2 **Xi He** *R* China
31B2 **Xiji** China
31C5 **Xi Jiang** *R* China
31E1 **Xiliao He** *R* China
31B5 **Xilin** China
28A2 **Xinbin** China
28A2 **Xinchengzi** China
31D4 **Xinfeng** China
31C1 **Xinghe** China
31D5 **Xingning** China
31B4 **Xingren** China
31C2 **Xingtai** China
73H4 **Xingu** *R* Brazil
26C2 **Xingxingxia** China
31A4 **Xingyi** China
31A2 **Xining** China
31E2 **Xinjin** Liaoning, China
31A3 **Xinjin** Sichuan, China
28A2 **Xinlitun** China
28A2 **Xinmin** China
31D2 **Xinwen** China
31C2 **Xin Xian** China
31C2 **Xinxiang** China
31C3 **Xinyang** China
31C5 **Xinyi** Guangdong, China
31D3 **Xinyi** Jiangsu, China
28B2 **Xinzhan** China
28A2 **Xiongyuecheng** China
31D1 **Xi Ujimqin Qi** China
28A2 **Xiuyan** China
31D3 **Xuancheng** China
31B3 **Xuanhan** China
31D1 **Xuanhua** China
31A4 **Xuanwei** China
31C3 **Xuchang** China
50E3 **Xuddur** Somalia
28A2 **Xujiatun** China
31A2 **Xunhua** China
31C5 **Xun Jiang** *R* China
26F2 **Xunke** China
31D5 **Xunwu** China
31C4 **Xupu** China
43N1 **Xurgru** China
30E1 **Xuwen** China
31B4 **Xuyong** China
31D3 **Xuzhou** China

Y

31A4 **Ya'an** China
34B3 **Yaapeet** Australia
50B3 **Yabassi** Cameroon
26D1 **Yablonovyy Khrebet** *Mts* Russian Federation
45D2 **Yabrūd** Syria
58B2 **Yachats** USA
72F8 **Yacuiba** Bolivia
44B2 **Yādgīr** India
49D1 **Yafran** Libya
29D2 **Yagishiri-tō** *I* Japan
19G2 **Yagotin** Ukraine
50C3 **Yahuma** Zaïre
29C3 **Yaita** Japan
29C4 **Yaizu** Japan
31A4 **Yajiang** China
54D3 **Yakataga** USA
58B1 **Yakima** USA
58B1 **Yakima** *R* USA
48B3 **Yako** Burkina
50C3 **Yakoma** Zaïre
29E2 **Yakumo** Japan
25O3 **Yakut Republic** Russian Federation
54E4 **Yakutat** USA
54E4 **Yakutat B** USA
25O3 **Yakutsk** Russian Federation
30C4 **Yala** Thailand
58B1 **Yale** Canada
50C3 **Yalinga** Central African Republic
34C3 **Yallourn** Australia
26C3 **Yalong** *R* China
31A4 **Yalong Jiang** *R* China
17F2 **Yalova** Turkey
21E7 **Yalta** Ukraine
28B2 **Yalu Jiang** *R* China/N Korea
29D3 **Yamada** Japan
29E3 **Yamagata** Japan
28C4 **Yamaguchi** Japan
24J2 **Yamal, Poluostrov** *Pen* Russian Federation
26E1 **Yamarovka** Russian Federation
34D1 **Yamba** New S Wales, Australia
34B2 **Yamba** S Australia, Australia
50C3 **Yambio** Sudan
17F2 **Yambol** Bulgaria
27G7 **Yamdena** *I* Indonesia
30B1 **Yamethin** Burma
Yam Kinneret = Tiberias,L
34B1 **Yamma Yamma,L** Australia
48B4 **Yamoussoukro** Ivory Coast
60B2 **Yampa** *R* USA
25R4 **Yamsk** Russian Federation
42D3 **Yamuna** *R* India
43G3 **Yamzho Yumco** *L* China
25P3 **Yana** *R* Russian Federation
34B3 **Yanac** Australia
28B4 **Yanagawa** Japan
44C2 **Yanam** India
31B2 **Yan'an** China
40C5 **Yanbu'al Baḩr** Saudi Arabia
34B2 **Yancannia** Australia
31E3 **Yancheng** China
31B2 **Yanchi** China
34B1 **Yandama** *R* Australia
50C3 **Yangambi** Zaïre
28A3 **Yanggu** S Korea
31C1 **Yang He** *R* China
31C5 **Yangjiang** China
Yangon = Rangoon
31C2 **Yangquan** China
28A3 **Yangsan** S Korea
31C5 **Yangshan** China
31C3 **Yangtze Gorges** China
31E3 **Yangtze,Mouths of the** China
28A3 **Yangyang** S Korea
31D3 **Yangzhou** China
31B4 **Yanhe** China
28B2 **Yanji** China
34C3 **Yanko** Australia
61D2 **Yankton** USA
26B2 **Yanqqi** China
39G1 **Yanqqi** China
31D1 **Yan Shan** *Hills*
25P2 **Yanskiy Zaliv** *B* Russian Federation
34B1 **Yantabulla** Australia
31E2 **Yantai** China
28B2 **Yantongshan** China
31D2 **Yanzhou** China
50B3 **Yaoundé** Cameroon
27G6 **Yap** *I* Pacific Ocean
27G7 **Yapen** *I* Indonesia
70B2 **Yaqui** *R* Mexico
20H4 **Yaransk** Russian Federation
7E3 **Yare** *R* England
20H3 **Yarenga** Russian Federation
20H3 **Yarensk** Russian Federation
72D3 **Yari** *R* Colombia
29D3 **Yariga-take** *Mt* Japan
39F2 **Yarkant He** *R* China
43G3 **Yarlung Zangbo Jiang** *R* China
55M5 **Yarmouth** Canada
45C2 **Yarmūk** *R* Jordan/Syria
20F4 **Yaroslavl'** Russian Federation
45C2 **Yarqon** *R* Israel
34C3 **Yarram** Australia
34D1 **Yarraman** Australia
34C3 **Yarrawonga** Australia
20N2 **Yar Sale** Russian Federation
20E4 **Yartsevo** Russian Federation
25L3 **Yartsevo** Russian Federation
72C2 **Yarumal** Colombia
48C3 **Yashi** Nigeria
48C4 **Yashikera** Nigeria
21G6 **Yashkul'** Russian Federation
42C1 **Yasin** Pakistan
19E3 **Yasinya** Ukraine
34C2 **Yass** Australia
34C2 **Yass** *R* Australia
28B3 **Yasugi** Japan
63C1 **Yates Center** USA
54J3 **Yathkyed L** Canada
50C3 **Yatolema** Zaïre
45C3 **Yatta** Israel
72D4 **Yavari** Peru
42D4 **Yavatmāl** India
28C4 **Yawatahama** Japan
30D2 **Ya Xian** China
41F3 **Yazd** Iran
41F3 **Yazd-e Khvāst** Iran
63D2 **Yazoo** *R* USA
63D2 **Yazoo City** USA
30B2 **Ye** Burma
19F3 **Yedintsy** Moldavia
20F5 **Yefremov** Russian Federation
21G6 **Yegorlyk** *R* Russian Federation
50D3 **Yei** Sudan
20L4 **Yekaterinburg** Russian Federation
21F5 **Yelets** Russian Federation
25Q4 **Yelizavety, Mys** *C* Russian Federation
10C1 **Yell** *I* Scotland
44C2 **Yellandu** India
56B1 **Yellowhead P** Canada
54G3 **Yellowknife** Canada
34C2 **Yellow Mt** Australia
Yellow R = Huang He
26F3 **Yellow Sea** China Korea
56C2 **Yellowstone** *R* USA
58D2 **Yellowstone L** USA
58D2 **Yellowstone Nat Pk** USA
8E1 **Yell Sd** Scotland
19G2 **Yel'nya** Russian Federation
19F2 **Yel'sk** Belarus
55K1 **Yelverton B** Canada
48C3 **Yelwa** Nigeria
38C4 **Yemen** *Republic* Arabian Pen
30C1 **Yen Bai** Vietnam
48B4 **Yendi** Ghana
30B1 **Yengan** Burma
24K3 **Yenisey** *R* Russian Federation
25L4 **Yeniseysk** Russian Federation
25L3 **Yeniseyskiy Kryazh** *Ridge* Russian Federation
24J2 **Yeniseyskiy Zaliv** *B* Russian Federation
7C4 **Yeo** *R* England
34C2 **Yeoval** Australia
7C4 **Yeovil** England
25M3 **Yerbogachen** Russian Federation
21G7 **Yerevan** Armenia
59C3 **Yerington** USA
20J2 **Yermitsa** Russian Federation
59C4 **Yermo** USA
25O4 **Yerofey-Pavlovich** Russian Federation
45C3 **Yeroham** Israel
25S3 **Yeropol** Russian Federation
21H5 **Yershov** Russian Federation
Yerushalayim = Jerusalem
40C1 **Yeşil** *R* Turkey
25M3 **Yessey** Russian Federation
45C2 **Yesud Hama'ala** Israel
34D1 **Yetman** Australia
48B2 **Yetti** Mauritius
43H4 **Yeu** Burma
14B2 **Yeu, Ile d'** *I* France
21H7 **Yevlakh** Azerbaijan
21E6 **Yevpatoriya** Ukraine
31E2 **Ye Xian** China
21F6 **Yeysk** Russian Federation
45B3 **Yi'allaq, Gebel** *Mt* Egypt
45C1 **Yialousa** Cyprus
17E2 **Yiannitsá** Greece
31A4 **Yibin** China
31C3 **Yichang** China
26F2 **Yichun** China
31B2 **Yijun** China
17F2 **Yıldız Dağları** *Upland* Turkey
40C2 **Yıldızeli** Turkey
31A5 **Yiliang** China
31B2 **Yinchuan** China
31D3 **Ying He** *R* China
28A2 **Yingkou** China
31D3 **Yingshan** Hubei, China
31B3 **Yingshan** Sichuan, China
31D4 **Yingtan** China
39G1 **Yining** China
31B1 **Yin Shan** *Upland* China
50D3 **Yirga' Alem** Ethiopia
50D3 **Yirol** Sudan
25N5 **Yirshi** China
31B5 **Yishan** China
31D2 **Yishui** China
17E3 **Yíthion** Greece
28B2 **Yitong** China
28A2 **Yi Xian** China
31C4 **Yiyang** China
20D2 **Yli-Kitka** *L* Finland
12J5 **Ylitornio** Sweden
12J6 **Ylivieska** Finland
63C3 **Yoakum** USA
27E7 **Yogyakarta** Indonesia
50B3 **Yokadouma** Cameroon
29C4 **Yokkaichi** Japan
29D3 **Yokobori** Japan
29C3 **Yokohama** Japan
29C3 **Yokosuka** Japan
29D3 **Yokote** Japan
48D4 **Yola** Nigeria
29C3 **Yonago** Japan
28A3 **Yŏnan** N Korea
29E3 **Yonezawa** Japan
28A4 **Yongam** S Korea
31D4 **Yong'an** China
31A2 **Yongchang** China
28B3 **Yŏngch'ŏn** S Korea
31B4 **Yongchuan** China
31A2 **Yongdeng** China
31D5 **Yongding** China
31D2 **Yongding He** *R* China
28B3 **Yŏngdŏk** S Korea
28A3 **Yŏnggwang** S Korea
28B3 **Yŏnghŭng** N Korea
28A3 **Yŏnghŭng-man** *I* N Korea
28A3 **Yŏngil-man** *B* S Korea
28B2 **Yongji** China
28B3 **Yongju** S Korea
31B2 **Yongning** China
28A3 **Yŏngsanp'o** S Korea
28A3 **Yŏngyang** S Korea
68D2 **Yonkers** USA
13B4 **Yonne** *Department* France
14C2 **Yonne** *R* France
6D3 **York** England
61D2 **York** Nebraska, USA
68B3 **York** Pennsylvania, USA
32D2 **York,C** Australia
55J4 **York Factory** Canada
55M2 **York, Kap** *C* Greenland
27F8 **York Sd** Australia
6C4 **Yorkshire Dales Nat Pk** England
10C3 **Yorkshire Moors** England
7D2 **Yorkshire Wolds** *Upland* England
56C1 **Yorkton** Canada
65D3 **Yorktown** USA
68E1 **York Village** USA
66B2 **Yosemite L** USA
66C1 **Yosemite Nat Pk** USA
29B3 **Yoshii** *R* Japan
29B4 **Yoshino** *R* Japan
20H4 **Yoshkar Ola** Russian Federation
28B4 **Yŏsu** S Korea
45C4 **Yotvata** Israel
10B3 **Youghal** Irish Republic
31B5 **You Jiang** *R* China
34C2 **Young** Australia
35A2 **Young Range** *Mts* New Zealand
68A1 **Youngstown** New York, USA
64C2 **Youngstown** Ohio, USA
66A1 **Yountville** USA
31B4 **Youyang** China
40B2 **Yozgat** Turkey
75A3 **Ypané** *R* Paraguay
58B2 **Yreka** USA
12G7 **Ystad** Sweden
7C3 **Ystwyth** *R* Wales
8D3 **Ythan** *R* Scotland
31C4 **Yuan Jiang** *R* Hunan, China
31A5 **Yuan Jiang** *R* Yunnan, China
31A4 **Yuanmu** China
31C2 **Yuanping** China
59B3 **Yuba City** USA
29E2 **Yūbari** Japan
48A2 **Yubi,C** Morocco
70D3 **Yucatan** *Pen* Mexico
70D2 **Yucatan Chan** Cuba/Mexico
59D4 **Yucca** USA
31C2 **Yuci** China
25P4 **Yudoma** *R* Russian Federation
31D4 **Yudu** China
31A4 **Yuexi** China
31C4 **Yueyang** China
20L2 **Yugorskiy Poluostrov** *Pen* Russian Federation
17D2 **Yugoslavia** *Federal Republic* Europe
31B5 **Yu Jiang** *R* China
54D3 **Yukon** *R* Canada/USA
54E3 **Yukon Territory** Canada
30E1 **Yulin** Guangdong, China
31C5 **Yulin** Guangxi, China
31B2 **Yulin** Shaanxi, China
59D4 **Yuma** USA
26C3 **Yumen** China
31C5 **Yunkai Dashan** *Hills* China
34A2 **Yunta** Australia
31C3 **Yunxi** China
31C3 **Yun Xian** China
31B3 **Yunyang** China
72C5 **Yurimaguas** Peru
31E5 **Yu Shan** *Mt* Taiwan
20E3 **Yushkozero** Russian Federation
39H2 **Yushu** Tibet, China
31D2 **Yutian** China
75A4 **Yuty** Paraguay
31A5 **Yuxi** China
29D3 **Yuzawa** Japan
19F3 **Yuzhnyy Bug** *R* Ukraine
26H2 **Yuzhno-Sakhalinsk** Russian Federation
20K5 **Yuzh Ural** *Mts* Russian Federation

Z

13C1 **Zaandam** Netherlands
18A2 **Zaanstad** Netherlands
21G8 **Zab al Asfal** *R* Iraq
41D2 **Zāb al Babīr** *R* Iraq
41D2 **Zāb aş Şaghīr** *R* Iraq
26E2 **Zabaykal'sk** Russian Federation
18D3 **Zabreh** Czech Republic
19D2 **Zabrze** Poland
70B2 **Zacatecas** Mexico
16D2 **Zadar** Croatia
30B4 **Zadetkyi** *I* Burma
15A2 **Zafra** Spain
49F1 **Zagazig** Egypt
16C3 **Zaghouan, Dj** *Mt* Tunisia
48B1 **Zagora** Morocco
16D1 **Zagreb** Croatia
Zagros Mts = Kūhhā-ye Zāgros
38E3 **Zāhedān** Iran
45C2 **Zahle** Lebanon
15C2 **Zahrez Chergui** *Marshland* Algeria
20J4 **Zainsk** Russian Federation
50B4 **Zaïre** *R* Congo/Zaïre
50C4 **Zaïre** *Republic* Africa
17E2 **Zaječar** Serbia, Yugoslavia
26D1 **Zakamensk** Russian Federation
21H7 **Zakataly** Azerbaijan
40D2 **Zakho** Iraq
17E3 **Zákinthos** *I* Greece
19D3 **Zakopane** Poland
18D3 **Zalaegerszeg** Hungary
17E1 **Zalău** Romania
18C2 **Zalew Szczeciński** *Lg* Poland
40D5 **Zalim** Saudi Arabia
50C2 **Zalingei** Sudan

25P4 **Zaliv Akademii** *B* Russian Federation
25M2 **Zaliv Faddeya** *B* Russian Federation
21J7 **Zaliv Kara-Bogaz-Gol** *B* Turkmenistan
25R3 **Zaliv Shelikhova** *B* Russian Federation
49D2 **Zaltan** Libya
51C5 **Zambezi** Zambia
51C5 **Zambezi** *R* Africa
51C5 **Zambia** *Republic* Africa
27F6 **Zamboanga** Philippines
19E2 **Zambrów** Poland
72C4 **Zamora** Ecuador
70B2 **Zamora** Mexico
15A1 **Zamora** Spain
66B1 **Zamora** USA
19E2 **Zamość** Poland
31A3 **Zamtang** China
50B4 **Zanaga** Congo
15B2 **Záncara** *R* Spain
42D2 **Zanda** China
64C3 **Zanesville** USA
42D2 **Zangla** India
41E2 **Zanjān** Iran
Zante = Zákinthos
50D4 **Zanzibar** Tanzania
50D4 **Zanzibar** *I* Tanzania
48C2 **Zaouatallaz** Algeria
31D3 **Zaozhuang** China
41D2 **Zap** *R* Turkey
19G1 **Zapadnaya Dvina** Russian Federation
20L3 **Zapadno-Sibirskaya Nizmennost'** Lowland, Russian Federation
25L4 **Zapadnyy Sayan** *Mts* Russian Federation
74C5 **Zapala** Argentina
62C3 **Zapata** USA
20E2 **Zapolyarnyy** Russian Federation
21F6 **Zaporozh'ye** Ukraine
40C2 **Zara** Turkey
15B1 **Zaragoza** Spain
41F2 **Zarand** Iran
41G3 **Zarand** Iran
38E2 **Zaranj** Afghanistan
72E2 **Zarara** Venezuela
19F1 **Zarasai** Lithuania
41E3 **Zard Kuh** *Mt* Iran
42B2 **Zarghun Shahr** Afghanistan
42B2 **Zargun** *Mt* Pakistan
48C3 **Zaria** Nigeria
40C3 **Zarqa** Jordan
45C2 **Zarqa** *R* Jordan
72C4 **Zaruma** Ecuador
18D2 **Zary** Poland
48D1 **Zarzis** Tunisia
42D2 **Zāskār** *R* India
42D2 **Zāskār Mts** India
47D3 **Zastron** South Africa
45D2 **Zatara** *R* Jordan
Zatoka Gdańska = Gdańsk,G of
26F1 **Zavitinsk** Russian Federation
19D2 **Zawiercie** Poland
45D1 **Zāwīyah, Jabal az** *Upland* Syria
25M4 **Zayarsk** Russian Federation
45D2 **Zaydī, Wadi az** Syria
24K5 **Zaysan** Kazakhstan
24K5 **Zaysan, Ozero** Kazakhstan
43H3 **Zayü** China
26C4 **Zayü** China
19D2 **Zduńska Wola** Poland
13B2 **Zeebrugge** Belgium
45C3 **Zeelim** Israel
47D2 **Zeerust** South Africa
45C2 **Zefat** Israel
48C3 **Zegueren** *Watercourse* Mali
50E2 **Zeila** Somalia
18C2 **Zeitz** Germany
31A2 **Zêkog** China
20E2 **Zelenoborskiy** Russian Federation
20H4 **Zelenodol'sk** Russian Federation
12K6 **Zelenogorsk** Russian Federation
50C3 **Zemio** Central African Republic
24F1 **Zemlya Aleksandry** *I* Russian Federation
24F2 **Zemlya Frantsa Iosifa** *Is* Russian Federation
24F1 **Zemlya Georga** *I* Russian Federation
24H1 **Zemlya Vil'cheka** *I* Russian Federation
17D2 **Zenica** Bosnia-Herzegovina
45C3 **Zenifim** *R* Israel
31B4 **Zenning** China
21G7 **Zestafoni** Georgia
13E1 **Zeven** Germany
45B1 **Zevgari, C** Cyprus
25O4 **Zeya** Russian Federation
25O4 **Zeya Res** Russian Federation
15A1 **Zêzere** *R* Portugal
45C1 **Zghorta** Lebanon
19D2 **Zgierz** Poland
31D1 **Zhangjiakou** China
31D4 **Zhangping** China
31D2 **Zhangwei He** *R* China
31E1 **Zhangwu** China
31A2 **Zhangye** China
31D5 **Zhangzhou** China
31C5 **Zhanjiang** China
31A4 **Zhanyi** China
31C5 **Zhaoqing** China
31A4 **Zhaotong** China
31D2 **Zhaoyang Hu** *L* China
21K6 **Zharkamys** Kazakhstan
19G1 **Zharkovskiy** Russian Federation
19G3 **Zhashkov** Ukraine
25O3 **Zhatay** Russian Federation
31D4 **Zhejiang** *Province* China
20J3 **Zheleznodorozhnyy** Russian Federation
31C3 **Zhengzhou** China
31D3 **Zhenjiang** China
31A4 **Zhenxiong** China
31B4 **Zhenyuan** China
21G5 **Zherdevka** Russian Federation
31C3 **Zhicheng** China
26D1 **Zhigalovo** Russian Federation
25O3 **Zhigansk** Russian Federation
31B4 **Zhijin** China
19F2 **Zhitkovichi** Belarus
19F2 **Zhitomir** Ukraine
19F2 **Zhlobin** Belarus
19F3 **Zhmerinka** Ukraine
42B2 **Zhob** Pakistan
19F2 **Zhodino** Belarus
43E3 **Zhongba** China
31B2 **Zhongning** China
31C5 **Zhongshan** China
76F10 **Zhongshan** *Base* Antarctica
31B2 **Zhongwei** China
26C4 **Zhougdian** China
31E3 **Zhoushan Qundao** *Arch* China
19G3 **Zhovten'** Ukraine
31E2 **Zhuanghe** China
31A3 **Zhugqu** China
31C3 **Zhushan** China
31C4 **Zhuzhou** China
31D2 **Zibo** China
32C3 **Ziel,Mt** Australia
18D2 **Zielona Góra** Poland
45A3 **Zifta** Egypt
30A1 **Zigaing** Burma
31A4 **Zigong** China
48A3 **Ziguinchor** Senegal
45C2 **Zikhron Ya'aqov** Israel
19D3 **Žilina** Slovakia
19F1 **Zilupe** Latvia
25M4 **Zima** Russian Federation
47D1 **Zimbabwe** *Republic* Africa
45C3 **Zin** *R* Israel
48C3 **Zinder** Niger
59D3 **Zion Nat Pk** USA
31C4 **Zi Shui** *R* China
18C2 **Zittau** Germany
31D2 **Ziya He** *R* China
31A3 **Ziyang** China
20K4 **Zlatoust** Russian Federation
19D3 **Zlin** Czech Republic
24K4 **Zmeinogorsk** Russian Federation
19D2 **Znin** Poland
18D3 **Znojmo** Czech Republic
47D1 **Zoekmekaar** South Africa
31A3 **Zoigê** China
19E3 **Zolochev** Ukraine
19G3 **Zolotonosha** Ukraine
51D5 **Zomba** Malawi
50B3 **Zongo** Zaïre
40B1 **Zonguldak** Turkey
48B4 **Zorzor** Liberia
48A2 **Zouerate** Mauritius
13D1 **Zoutkamp** Netherlands
17E1 **Zrenjanin** Serbia, Yugoslavia
16B1 **Zug** Switzerland
21G7 **Zugdidi** Georgia
13C1 **Zuidelijk Flevoland** *Polder* Netherlands
15A2 **Zújar** *R* Spain
51D5 **Zumbo** Mozambique
61E2 **Zumbrota** USA
48C4 **Zungeru** Nigeria
62A1 **Zuni** USA
62A1 **Zuni Mts** USA
31B4 **Zunyi** China
30D1 **Zuo** *R* China
31B5 **Zuo Jiang** *R* China
14D2 **Zürich** Switzerland
13D1 **Zutphen** Netherlands
49D1 **Zuwārah** Libya
49D2 **Zuwaylah** Libya
20J4 **Zuyevka** Russian Federation
19G3 **Zvenigorodka** Ukraine
51C6 **Zvishavane** Zimbabwe
19D3 **Zvolen** Slovakia
17D2 **Zvornik** Bosnia-Herzegovina
26G1 **Zvoron, Ozero** *L* Russian Federation
13D3 **Zweibrücken** Germany
18C2 **Zwickau** Germany
18B2 **Zwolle** Netherlands
19E2 **Zyrardów** Poland
25R3 **Zyryanka** Russian Federation
24K5 **Zyryanovsk** Kazakhstan
19D3 **Żywiec** Poland
45B1 **Zyyi** Cyprus

ACKNOWLEDGEMENTS

PICTURE CREDITS

The sources for the photographs and illustrations appearing in the atlas are listed below.

page	
48-61	Physical maps by Duncan Mackay, copyright © Times Books., London
62	*Mercury* NSSDC/NASA *Venus* NASA/Science Photo Library *Mars* NASA/Science Photo Library *Neptune* NASA/Science Photo Library *Uranus* Jet Propulsion Laboratory/NASA *Saturn* NASA
63	*Rock and Hydrological Cycles* Encyclopaedia Universalis Editeur, Paris
90	*Manhattan* Adapted from map by Nicholson Publications Ltd.
94-99	Robert Harding Picture Library Ltd.
Rear Endpaper	G.L. Fitzpatrick and M.J. Modlin: *Direct Line Distances. International Edition Metuchen* N.J. and London, 1986

			5167	3260	14244	4975	5142	5972	4637	2003	10735	5158	13534	2367	3471	7498	11688	4845	2317	4903	4892	6071	13865	2987	2043	5478	13481
	ABU DHABI			2164	18728	9185	1237	7841	577	6864	5575	174	11424	3282	7620	9647	6628	623	6368	690	367	9300	11676	2213	3350	359	8963
		AMSTERDAM			16775	7933	1822	7633	1803	5179	7639	2092	11677	1120	6325	7979	8765	2136	5019	1710	2026	8560	13439	562	1256	2394	11118
			ATHENS			9566	19204	10388	17743	12294	14478	18279	10372	16573	11176	11796	13181	17525	12482	18609	17813	9121	7052	17042	16287	18330	10479
3211				AUCKLAND			9692	3291	8613	3010	13733	9263	16885	7279	1610	10144	13789	8628	2917	9249	8824	1723	10634	7477	6895	9544	13319
2026	1345				BANGKOK			8822	1500	7044	5881	1063	10447	2897	8084	8502	7101	1760	6782	624	1473	10087	12766	2238	3122	1138	9677
8851	11637	10424				BARCELONA			7375	4760	10860	7983	19265	7557	3271	12947	10626	7218	3788	8223	7492	1972	8171	7072	7135	8160	10082
3091	5707	4930	5944				BEIJING			6298	6098	654	11890	2891	7045	9588	7103	355	5791	876	255	8770	11782	1739	2903	934	9332
3195	769	1132	11933	6023				BERLIN			12275	6891	14937	4363	1664	8216	12976	6430	1156	6725	6544	4311	12928	4818	4017	7205	14021
3711	4872	4743	6455	2045	5482				BOMBAY			5598	8619	8737	12517	12411	1369	5904	11504	5929	5843	12831	8191	7783	8884	5280	4179
2881	358	1120	11025	5352	932	4583				BOSTON			11282	3212	7689	9490	6679	769	6427	533	491	9416	11825	2185	3302	320	9055
1245	4265	3218	7639	1870	4377	2958	3914				BRUSSELS			11811	16535	6891	8978	12046	15800	11045	11773	18463	12160	12235	12236	11105	9828
6671	3464	4747	8996	8534	3654	6748	3789	7628				BUENOS AIRES			5708	7208	9881	3206	4436	2816	3125	8158	14239	1234	426	3513	12223
3205	108	1300	11358	5756	661	4961	406	4282	3479				CAIRO			9684	12861	7083	1307	7651	7264	2654	11357	5867	5314	7978	13141
8410	7099	7256	6445	10492	6492	11971	7388	9282	5356	7011				CALCUTTA			13658	9942	9284	8958	9725	11867	18562	8367	7481	9635	16054
1471	2039	696	10298	4523	1800	4696	1796	2711	5429	1996	7339				CAPE TOWN			6860	12047	7069	6850	12560	6849	8834	9978	6371	2810
2157	4735	3930	6945	1000	5023	2033	4378	1034	7778	4778	10275	3547				CHICAGO			5857	1145	289	8688	11428	2021	3191	958	9026
4659	5995	4958	7330	6303	5283	8045	5958	5105	7712	5897	4282	4479	6018				COPENHAGEN			6363	6020	3770	11930	4560	4032	6724	12882
7263	4119	5447	8191	8568	4413	6603	4414	8063	851	4150	5579	6140	7992	8487				DELHI			862	9544	12358	1921	2959	748	9519
3011	387	1327	10890	5361	1094	4485	221	3996	3669	478	7485	1992	4401	6178	4263				GENEVA			8934	11629	1988	3150	723	9098
1440	3957	3119	7756	1813	4214	2354	3599	718	7148	3994	9818	2757	812	5769	7486	3640				HAMBURG			8945	8034	7740	9646	11674
3047	429	1063	11563	5747	388	5110	544	4179	3684	331	6863	1750	4754	5566	4393	712	3954				HONG KONG			13068	13969	11653	4125
3040	228	1259	11069	5483	915	4655	159	4066	3631	305	7291	1942	4514	6043	4257	180	3741	536				HONOLULU			1170	2504	11043
3772	5779	5319	5668	1071	6268	1225	5450	2679	7973	5851	11473	5069	1649	7374	7805	5399	2343	5931	5552				ISTANBUL			3615	12210
8616	7255	8351	4382	6608	7933	5077	7321	8033	5090	7348	7556	8848	7057	11534	4256	7101	7413	7679	7226	5558				JERUSALEM			8778
1856	1375	349	10590	4646	1391	4394	1081	2994	4836	1358	7603	767	3646	5199	5489	1256	2834	1194	1235	4992	8120				LONDON		
1270	2082	781	10121	4285	1940	4434	1804	2496	5520	2052	7603	265	3302	4649	6200	1983	2505	1839	1957	4810	8680	727				LOS ANGELES	
3404	223	1488	11390	5931	707	5071	580	4477	3281	199	6901	2183	4957	5987	3959	595	4178	465	449	5994	7241	1556	2246				
8377	5570	6909	6512	8276	6013	6265	5799	8713	2597	5627	6107	7595	8166	9976	1746	5609	8005	5915	5653	7254	2563	6862	7587	5455			
3500	921	1475	12174	6336	314	5744	1163	4688	3410	818	6229	2085	5337	5304	4191	1289	4529	637	1111	6562	7874	1705	2238	785	5833		
7263	10280	9289	1634	4573	10458	5650	9924	6096	10521	10325	7226	8678	5547	6424	9673	9930	6333	10271	10057	4593	5507	9090	8521	10503	7930		
8932	5739	7024	6802	9739	5909	7754	6056	9739	2279	5757	4577	7700	9504	8515	1691	5921	9121	5962	5898	8796	3789	7114	7800	5560	1549		
2893	514	910	11482	5614	452	5031	523	4029	3838	434	6943	1599	4619	5493	4542	720	3816	155	560	5823	7764	1041	1685	597	6051		
6616	3428	4737	8935	8337	3677	6518	3740	7522	251	3451	5593	5427	7615	7919	744	3606	7013	3677	3581	7744	4918	4803	5502	3256	2469		
2321	1337	1386	10063	4393	1873	3610	1002	3129	4498	1404	8365	1801	3443	6277	4984	971	2702	1504	1109	4672	7048	1091	1660	1557	6085		
2126	4133	2828	8678	4485	3652	5727	3948	2816	7190	4066	6472	2186	3839	2542	8010	4155	3373	3764	4080	5449	10741	2952	2276	4229	9664		
6860	3654	4937	8816	8668	3842	6843	3979	7808	191	3669	5276	5618	7936	7799	713	3857	7319	3874	3820	8068	4969	5026	5711	3471	2451		
4808	5742	5797	5532	2615	6421	1110	5494	3956	6871	5840	9786	5796	2955	8906	6500	5363	3415	6036	5541	1549	4104	5448	5535	5919	5724		
6692	3512	4825	8835	8353	3772	6509	3820	7582	313	3536	5612	5516	7649	8010	645	3682	7061	3766	3661	7734	4819	4887	5588	3342	2366		
3260	266	1306	11521	5877	517	5118	547	4365	3446	163	6853	1998	4892	5783	4143	639	4102	257	464	5996	7449	1405	2075	212	5658		
5614	8779	7628	3312	3301	8788	4944	8427	4514	11621	8793	7839	6992	4163	5416	10979	8499	4877	8660	8579	3728	6777	7467	6850	8989	9337		
7310	5937	6033	7636	9993	5294	10766	6207	8338	4829	5844	1223	6141	9372	3775	5284	6321	8749	5673	6147	11005	8291	6380	6405	5750	6294		
2674	804	655	11433	5494	534	5061	735	3845	4102	729	6919	1327	4495	5230	4821	951	3684	433	813	5779	8038	857	1435	891	6346		
8145	5468	6792	6517	7930	5963	5918	567	8405	2699	5532	6453	7466	7828	10245	1859	5474	7693	5833	5533	6910	4261	672	7436	5369	347		
9097	7452	7797	6021	10968	6923	11842	7772	9984	5217	7375	705	7954	10961	4946	5294	7835	10518	7274	7677	11607	6861	8136	2005	7240	5578		
7527	6077	6221	7483	10196	5452	10933	6356	8558	4795	5985	1044	6345	9592	3949	5209	6462	8967	5826	6290	11221	8090	6567	6610	5885	6149		
4299	5332	5305	5963	2312	5982	595	5064	3488	6815	5425	12073	5284	2514	8519	6546	4948	2920	5601	5123	1303	4549	4956	5023	5519	5968		
4068	5530	5318	5815	1784	6119	669	5233	3131	7314	5616	12190	5199	2113	8053	7081	5143	2640	5753	5310	755	4955	4973	4934	5731	6507		
3669	6526	5629	5227	887	6767	2775	6169	2428	9410	6566	9873	5139	1794	6009	9375	6195	2574	6525	6306	1600	6726	5376	4924	6748	8784		
2978	701	1497	10565	5143	1417	4179	505	3878	3753	799	7793	2115	4204	6421	4286	325	3467	1032	505	5122	6872	1352	2064	892	5531		
6085	2875	9523	1343	4675	10677	5545	9998	6305	10092	10404	7345	8957	5668	6856	9242	9963	6472	10422	10111	4566	5065	9286	8778	10557	7497		
5018	5788	5922	5475	2865	6487	1307	5556	4195	6718	5888	11412	5957	3200	9157	6311	5415	3640	6101	5594	1798	3858	5574	5699	5956	5486		
6905	3728	5044	8624	8480	3989	6594	4035	7777	431	3754	5545	5734	7810	8134	437	3896	7243	3985	3877	7815	4659	5103	5806	3560	2176		
2635	582	797	11094	5251	1026	4647	326	3721	4045	570	7328	1480	4262	5653	4698	541	3465	500	462	5437	7634	794	1504	769	6116		
7063	3858	5141	8621	8806	4044	6941	4181	8002	395	3873	5194	5822	8102	7892	595	4058	7501	4075	4023	8163	4838	5231	5915	3676	2300		

MILES